"Something fascinating on every page….The details are so rich and complex as to make the book an event in the life of every reader."
The New York Times Book Review

"I am prepared to argue that Helen Keller was the most sensuous woman who ever lived….Drawing on a wealth of previously unused sources, [Joseph Lash] moves skillfully through the trials and triumphs and vivid feelings of the legendary story. Several times I was moved to tears…. Her life has enlarged the meaning of the word 'love' for us."
Roger Shattuck in *New York* magazine

"Joseph P. Lash understands that the story of Helen Keller and Anne Sullivan Macy is the story of a marriage and he has written it accordingly. His sensitivity to the yearnings of his two subjects is acute."

Jonathan Yardley in *The Washington Star*

"Distinguished in every way . . . immensely human. Lash is a practiced storyteller . . . *Helen and Teacher* is a luminous book. It's the real stuff. Chalk up one for the human spirit."
Newsday

"A grand story. It may be better than *Eleanor and Franklin*."
Susan Brownmiller

"We learn from Lash that Helen Keller was a more interesting, more complicated woman than we knew."
Newsweek

"Doubly remarkable, because even though it reveals some startling and even unpleasant truths about the two women, it does not demean or diminish their accomplishments."
Henry Kisor in the *Chicago Sun-Times*

RADCLIFFE BIOGRAPHY SERIES

RADCLIFFE BIOGRAPHY SERIES

On behalf of Radcliffe College, I am pleased to present this volume in the Radcliffe Biography Series.

The series is an expression of the value we see in documenting and understanding the varied lives of women. Exploring the choices and circumstances of these extraordinary women—both famous and unsung—is not merely of interest to the historian, but is central to anyone grappling with what it means to be a woman. The biographies of these women teach us not only about their lives and their worlds, but about ours as well. When women strive to forge their identities, as they do at many points throughout the lifespan, it is crucial to have models to look toward. These women provide such models. We are inspired through their example and are taught by their words.

Radcliffe College's sponsorship of the Radcliffe Biography Series was sparked by the publication in 1972 of *Notable American Women,* a scholarly encyclopedia sponsored by Radcliffe's Schlesinger Library. We became convinced of the importance of expanding the public's awareness of the many significant contributions made by women to America, continuing the commitment to educating people about the lives and work of women that is reflected in much of Radcliffe's work. In addition to commissioning new biographies, we decided to add reprints of distinguished books already published, with introductions written for this series.

It is with great pride and excitement that I present this latest volume.

Linda Wilson, President
Radcliffe College
Cambridge, Massachusetts

RADCLIFFE BIOGRAPHY SERIES

HELEN and TEACHER

The Story of
Helen Keller and Anne Sullivan Macy

JOSEPH P. LASH

A Merloyd Lawrence Book

Addison-Wesley Publishing Company, Inc.

Reading, Massachusetts   Menlo Park, California   New York
Don Mills, Ontario   Harlow, England   Amsterdam   Bonn
Sydney   Singapore   Tokyo   Madrid   San Juan
Paris   Seoul   Milan   Mexico City   Taipei

ACKNOWLEDGMENTS

Photograph of Anne Sullivan Macy and Nella Braddy copyright 1974 by Keith
Henney.
Excerpts from *THE BLIND IN SCHOOL AND SOCIETY* by Thomas
Cutsforth, expanded edition, (American Foundation for the Blind, 1951). Used
by permission.
MY RELIGION by Helen Keller: Reprinted with permission of the Swedenborg
Foundation, Inc., New York. Copyright 1960 by the Swedenborg Foundation,
Inc. All rights reserved.
THE WORLD OF THE BLIND by Pierre Villey-Desmeserets, translated by Alys
Hillard. Used by permission of Gerald Duckworth & Co. Ltd.

Originally published as a Merloyd Lawrence Book by Delacorte Press/Seymour Lawrence.

Cover design by Suzanne Heiser
Text design by MaryJane DiMassi

1   2   3   4   5   6   7   8   9—MA—0100999897
First printing, March 1997

ISBN 0-201-69468-9 (paperback)

To Elissa, Matthew and Emily

Here is some advice that is worth remembering,
from Edward Everett Hale, Helen Keller's friend—

> I am only one,
> But still I am one.
> I cannot do everything,
> But still I can do something;
> And because I cannot do everything.
> I will not refuse to do the something
>   that I can do.

Acknowledgments

When Dr. Matina Horner, the president of Radcliffe College, inquired as to my availability to write a biography of Helen Keller, Radcliffe '04, my first impulse was to decline, as I was at work on a successor volume to *Roosevelt and Churchill* for which I had completed most of the research. "Have the grace," my wife advised me, "in saying no to show your appreciation that a woman's college asked you, a man, to write a biography of a woman." Her admonition caused me to hesitate. The invitation was a singular honor in this feminist era. Did I wish to say no out of hand? Moreover, it would be good for me to get away for a time from those power-oriented men, Roosevelt, Churchill and Stalin. A trip to the Edgartown Library to reread Helen Keller's classic *The Story of My Life* undecided me even more. It was difficult to resist the enchantment of that book.

So I wrote Dr. Horner that if the Helen Keller archives at the American Foundation for the Blind were such as to enable me to write a fresh portrait of her, I would undertake the book. Those archives had never been used before by anyone outside of Helen Keller and a circle of intimates with a commitment to the Helen Keller canon. A sampling of the letters, diaries, clippings that were assembled for me by the Foundation's archivist Marguerite Levine and by Patricia Smith, who was then the director of the Foundation's Public Information Department and a biography buff on the side, quickly persuaded me that there was indeed a book to be written. The Foundation, through its director Gene Apple, offered me its cooperation without any restrictions on what I could write.

So with the reluctant forbearance of my regular publisher, W.W. Norton, I undertook to write this book for Seymour and Merloyd Lawrence. The latter served as my editor. She is a woman of tact and sympathy whose comments have immeasurably improved the text.

There are three main collections of Helen Keller material. First and foremost there is the archive of the American Foundation for the Blind, presided over by Mrs. Levine, a cultivated Frenchwoman, who catalogued the archive's materials and knows them in formidable detail. She and Pat

Smith made many suggestions and kept me from many errors. An archive of almost equal value is to be found at the Perkins Institution in Watertown, Massachusetts. Many of Anne Sullivan Macy's papers are deposited there, as well as the priceless journals and other papers of Nella Braddy Henney, Mrs. Macy's biographer. Kenneth Stuckey, the energetic curator of the Samuel P. Hayes Library at Perkins, was always helpful and steered me to some crucial documents I might otherwise have overlooked. He also called my attention to the news clipping about a cache of some Anne Sullivan Macy letters that had just come to light at the American Antiquarian Society in Worcester, Massachusetts, and that added a fascinating new dimension to the Helen Keller story. A third major archive is at the Alexander Graham Bell Association for the Deaf (the Volta Bureau) in Washington, D.C. It contains important correspondence between Helen and Annie and Dr. Bell and his "picturesque secretary" John Hitz. I am grateful to the Volta Bureau's archivist, Lawrence Miller, for his help and cooperation.

Other archival materials came from the Schlesinger Library at Radcliffe, the Houghton Library at Harvard, the New York Public Library, the Hadley School for the Blind in Illinois, the Alabama Department of Archives and History in Montgomery, the Henry Wallace Collection at the University of Iowa, the Francis Bacon Library in southern California, the Lawrence Hutton Collection at Princeton University, the Mark Twain papers at Berkeley, the Marietta College Library in Ohio and the Roosevelt Library at Hyde Park. Many individuals helped with their recollections. I spent a profitable day at Helen Keller's birthplace, Ivy Green in Tuscumbia, and am grateful to Helen Keller's nieces, Katherine Tyson in Montgomery and Mrs. William Johnson in Tuscumbia, for their help. I owe special thanks to Susan Macy, grandniece of John Macy, for sharing her own researches with me, as well as some letters from Mrs. Macy and Helen Keller that she found in her family's attic.

In the interests of readability and keeping down the book's costs I decided to omit detailed footnotes. Scholars who wish to consult the letters, diaries, and the like that are cited in the text will find annotated copies of the book on deposit at the American Foundation for the Blind, the Perkins Institution, the Alexander Graham Bell Association and the Schlesinger Library.

As usual my manuscript was read by various members of my family, beginning with my wife, our son Jonathan and his wife Eleanor, and my sister and brother-in-law the Joseph Deliberts. All helped improve the book. The first half-dozen chapters on Anne Sullivan and Helen were greatly benefited by the comments of Dr. Belinda Straight, a child psychiatrist.

The manuscript was expertly and expeditiously typed by Mrs. Freda Weiner.

I cannot end these acknowledgments without a word of thanks to Evan Thomas and George Brockway for their patience and understanding.

JOSEPH P. LASH

contents

Photo sections follow pages 268 and 556

CHRONOLOGY

part one
ANNIE

I

The Making of Annie Sullivan

"A fire of hatred blazed up in me which burned for many years."

In 1955, in her seventy-fifth year, Helen Keller, a woman heaped with honors, still resolute in the service of the blind, esteemed by all and loved by those close to her, at long last finished her book about her teacher Anne Sullivan Macy. Although she lived another thirteen years, it was her last book. She subtitled it *A Tribute of the Foster-Child of Her Mind*. "To this day," she wrote—and it was nineteen years since the death of the woman she always called Teacher—"I cannot 'command the uses of my soul' or stir my mind to action without the memory of the quasi-electric touch of Teacher's fingers upon my palm." Nella Braddy Henney, whom Helen Keller described as "beloved friend and literary counselor" and who had written the definitive biography of Teacher, noted in her introduction to Helen's memoir that "as long as Annie Sullivan lived, and she died in 1936, a question remained as to how much of what was called Helen Keller was in reality Annie Sullivan. The answer is not simple. During the creative years neither could have done without the other." It is impossible to write a book about Helen Keller that is not also a book about Annie Sullivan, and the story therefore begins with her.

In 1880, when Annie Sullivan, aged fourteen, was permitted to enroll in the Perkins Institution for the Blind in South Boston and begin her schooling, she discovered that history for her schoolmates was the Civil War. For Annie there was only one event in history, the Great Famine in

Ireland of 1847 that had subsequently driven her impoverished young parents, like thousands of others, to the United States. "I knew very little about my parents," she said later. "There was no Bible record of births and deaths in my family. A few facts have been dug out of church and municipal records. I know that Limerick, Ireland was their birthplace. I presume, without knowing the facts, that they were victims of the 'hungry forties.' . . . They left all that was dear to them and came to a strange land, perhaps with Tom Hood's cry upon their lips,

> 'O God, that bread should be so dear,
> And flesh and blood so cheap!' "

Annie was born in April 1866 in Feeding Hills, a village outside of Springfield, Massachusetts, in circumstances of poverty that were not uncommon among Irish immigrants. But the destitution of the Sullivans was starker and more desolate than even that of their compatriots. Annie's father, red-haired Thomas Sullivan, was not only illiterate and unskilled but a drinker and a brawler, and shiftless. Her gentle mother, born Alice Cloesy (spelled Cloahassy on Annie's baptismal certificate), was tubercular, and after a fall when Annie was three or four, was unable to walk again except on crutches. She bore five children. Annie, christened Johanna, was the oldest. The fifth, John, died before he was three months old. A sister, Nellie, had died before that. Her little brother Jimmie was born with a tubercular hip. Only Mary, next to the youngest, did not ail. Annie, although physically robust, contracted trachoma when she was about five. Untreated, this was gradually destroying her vision. One of her earliest memories was of a neighbor saying, "She would be so pretty if it were not for her eyes." A woman urged her mother to wash them in geranium water, and Annie remembers thin hands dabbing her "bad" eyes.

Half-blind, hot-tempered like her father, Annie responded to the miseries within and about her by lashing out, childishly, throwing things, going into tantrums. "What a terrible child," the neighbors said. "You little devil," her father often shouted, and tried to control her by beatings so severe that, to save her, Annie's mother would try to hide her little daughter. Horror followed horror. Her mother, "gentle Alice Cloesy," as her neighbors from Limerick called her, died. This was Annie's memory of that dreadful event as she told it fifty years later to Nella Braddy, with a vividness of detail and dramatic sweep that testified to her narrative power:

I am being dragged out of bed. I had a feeling that something very unusual had happened, and I must let them do with me as they liked. I was taken into a room where people were moving about. Soon Jimmy and Mary were there too. They were crying, and other children came and looked at us. Then a blank space. The next thing I remember, I was back in my mother's room. The men were taking the slats out of the trundle-bed and putting them on carpenters' horses. I was intensely interested, and watched them quietly. They put three or four slats together. When their work was finished, and they went away, two women laid on the slats the mattress that was on the trundle-bed, then they went over to my mother's bed. I wondered what they were going to do, and I was afraid. I must have made a noise for I was jerked out of the room. When I went into it again, I saw my mother on the improvised bed. I was astonished to see her in a brown habit which the priests had brought. Her hair was very smooth, and she looked so still! Her hands were crossed. There were white bands around her neck and her sleeves, and there was something on her breast which I knew was a word in white. Many years afterwards, when I read 'Jesu' in print, I realized in a flash that was the word I had seen on the death robe. There was also a green ribbon round her neck with a little cross which I had never seen, and which almost touched her hands. I saw Mary and Jimmie sobbing, and Mary was sitting on my father's knee. I didn't cry or move. Somehow they didn't seem to belong to me, or I to them. They seemed more like other people who were sitting around—strangers. I don't remember anyone speaking to me, or anything that happened afterwards, until my father, Jimmie, Mary and I were together in a big, black carriage. And I was furious with Jimmie because he wouldn't give me his place by the window so that I could watch the horses. He began to cry, saying I hurt him, and my father struck me sharply on the side of my head. A fire of hatred blazed up in me which burned for many years.

There was no money for the funeral, and the town helped to defray the expenses. She was buried in Potter's Field, a kinswoman told Annie years later. She remembered her father saying after the funeral, "God put a curse on me for leaving Ireland and the old folks." Then he would rage wildly against "the landlords" and weep.

Although the other Sullivans had lost patience with Thomas, an uncle took in Mary and Jimmie, while eight-year-old Annie undertook to keep house for her father in a dilapidated little cabin on her uncle's farm. Her memories of this brief period were not punctuated with hostility and rage. She did not go to school and no one ever read stories to her, but her imagination and mind were fired by the Irish folklore with which her father regaled her in his heavy brogue.

"My colleen bawn, you can't hear the little people in this new land," my father would say, "but in Ireland the brake is full of voices, lowlike, and many are the times I heard them meself. When it's still-like, and night is coming on like a black rook spreading its wings —it's then you hear them talking of the sheep that went astray on the shepherd, and how the wheezing sould of old Patrick Munn passed on the wind of last night, and how Mrs. Shea's new baby had cut its teeth before ever it was born. As swately as mating doves they whisper. But if any man or woman meddles with them, they'll nurse a grudge till the end of time. There was Michael Doane who kicked a stone in a cairn. 'Let them move it as can,' he says, and turns his back. The next night the stone was moved to his door-step! Mike never knew a peaceful night until they put him under six feet of Irish soil."

To her father, the River Shannon that flowed through Limerick was holy water. Once he took her to a Westfield oculist, and when that visit did nothing for her eyes, he sought to comfort her by saying that a drop from the River Shannon would cure them. How, she wanted to know. "I've told ye more times that ye's got fingers and toes that the Shannon begins in the eyes of the Lord hisself. He looking down from the high place and seeing the beautiful green land of Ireland He had created, not minding what He was doing, tears gushed out of His eyes, like the springs out of the hills, and there in the great plain afore Limerick, the Shannon began. Galway and Killslee have mountains, I hear say; but Limerick has the river Shannon for her glory."

He also filled his daughter with hate for landlords. In his father's house there had been four windows, he told her, but three of them were boarded up. Why? asked Annie. "Because openings are taxed in Ireland. You pay the landlord for air and light. Everything belongs to the landlord. He owns the farm you till. He grows fat on the harvest you reap. You handle the spade, follow the plough, plant, sow, and he is always before you or behind you like your own shadow. He orders you about, 'This must be done today, that must be begun tomorrow.' With difficulty you keep from splitting his head wide-open with the spade, but you only curse the devil under your breath." Irish hatred of landlords and the British, he told her, "smoulders on and on like turf-fire."

Even the run-down shack on her uncle's place was too much for her father to maintain. He gave it up, and she too went to live in the house of her uncle and aunt who had taken in Jimmie and Mary. Her uncle was doing well as a tobacco farmer; but, unable to get any help from her father toward the children's support, he appealed to the town. Mary was taken in by another aunt. On February 22, 1876, Annie and Jimmie, who was on a crutch because of his diseased hip, were delivered in a Black Maria to the state poorhouse in Tewksbury. It was an isolated, forbidding huddle of grimy structures. The attendant who received them proposed to separate them, sending Annie to the women's ward and Jimmie to the men's; but Annie, whose whole childhood had been one abandonment after another, protested with such passionate sobs that the attendant relented and sent them both to a women's ward. No matter that it was unpainted, overcrowded, peopled with misshapen, diseased, often manic women; they were together.

Somehow it all seemed "very homelike" to Annie. The children's cots were next to each other. They had the "dead house" where corpses were prepared for burial to play in, and old issues of the *Godey's Lady's Book* and the *Police Gazette* to cut up. It seemed homelike to Annie, too, because most of the women were Irish, the Catholic priest was always about—and she was no stranger to filth and disease.

In the years that Annie was at Tewksbury the poorhouse cared for an average of 940 men, women and children. The mortality rate was very high, particularly among the children. In the summer there were no screens to keep out the mosquitos and flies, and in the winter the heating often broke down because of rusty pipes. The superintendent repeatedly begged the state for a separate building in which to house the dangerous inmates, especially those with delirium tremens and offensive diseases. Men and women were inadequately separated. Some women arrived pregnant, others were made pregnant at Tewksbury. Every day at the blast of a whistle the women rushed to the narrow windows crying, "The Horribles! The Horribles!" to watch the procession of the men to the dining hall. Deformed, legless, some with faces distorted by cancer or goiters, they pushed like animals to get to their food, often using canes and crutches as prods if someone slowed down or got in their way. For almost all of six years this constituted Annie's whole world.

Death was a common occurrence, and all her life Annie remembered the clatter of the cots being wheeled over the wooden floor in the dead house. Then the dead house claimed Jimmie. She awoke suddenly in the middle of the night and, sensing the empty space next to her, knew immediately what had happened. She began to tremble. She crept to the dead room and, feeling his cold body under the sheets, began to scream, wakening everyone. As the women dragged her away, she clung to the lifeless body and kicked and screamed. Only when it was light was she permitted to go into the dead room again and sit on a chair beside the bed. Then the sheet was lifted for her and again she flung herself on the little body "and kissed and kissed and kissed his face—the dearest thing in the world—the only thing I had ever loved." Later the matron allowed her to go outside to pick an armful of flowers. These she placed on the little body. She begged to be allowed to follow the coffin to the burial ground. No priest was there as it was lowered into the bare, sandy spot. "When I got back, I saw that they had put Jimmie's bed back in its place. I sat down between my bed and his empty bed, and I hoped desperately to die. I believe very few children have ever been so completely left alone as I was."

Although the Catholic Church was a constant and comforting presence in the almshouse, the priest because of illness had not come to Jimmie's funeral. Fifty years later, in 1927, after she revisited Tewksbury together with Nella, she tried to put Jimmie's death into unrhymed verse:

> The women told each other how they liked to look at him
> Cutting out pictures.
> "His hair was curly, you mind,
> You'd think it was done on curl-papers,
> And his eyes were like the sky at night
> With stars shining in them.
> They shouldn't bury the dead little boy Jimmie
> Before the priest comes,
> Heathens that they are!
> If God heard the prayers of the poor,
> He'd strike them dead for their hard hearts.
> The sister will miss the dead little boy, I say,
> It's crazed with grief she is—any one can see that.
> She was never hard with him,
> And her having a bad temper

The pair of them was like two turtle-doves together.
That'll make her trouble, I'm telling you.
It's a time they had getting him out,
And her holding fast to the pine box!
Holy Mother! it would melt the hardest heart to hear
How the girl is grieving,
But they have stones for hearts.
God's curse be on them that have stones for hearts!
What's that you said, woman?"
I said, God pity the little dead boy's sister.
It's a fair prayer that—
And God be merciful to the poor wherever they are,
And God rest the soul of the little dead boy Jimmie.

Not long after Jimmie's death, an estrangement from the Church began. Someone gave her an Agnus Dei to wear around her neck. Curious to see whether it really held the body of the Lord as she had been told, she broke open the silken covers. When the priest learned what she had done, he scolded her. "You have wounded the body of the Lord." That outraged her, and she told him she was through with confession. He imposed penances—fasting and telling her beads—but that only made her more defiant. After a time he was transferred and another priest—Father Barbara, a Jesuit—replaced him, and her attitude toward the Church shifted again. Father Barbara, a big man, was warm and protective. He befriended the young girl, and she responded to his concern. One day he announced, "This is no place for you, little woman; I am going to take you away." So in February 1877, almost a year after she arrived, she went to the Hospital of Les Soeurs de la Charité in Lowell, Massachusetts. There she underwent another operation. Two had been performed at Tewksbury, but they had not helped her vision. This one, too, while providing some relief from pain and the shooting lights in her eyes, left her vision so blurred that she continued to be listed on the public records as blind.

Father Barbara now was a frequent companion, in the church next door where he took her around the Stations of the Cross, along the banks of the Merrimac where they strolled hand in hand, and in the hospital ward in the evening when he read her the lives of the saints and told her how Protestants had persecuted the Catholics. He was kind and fatherly and liked to play with her hair. But this idyll came to an end. Father Barbara took her to Boston to some friends for whom she was to do light kitchen-work. But her eyes troubled her, and she was sent to the city infirmary for two more operations. She came out of the hospital to discover that the Boston family did not want her back and that Father Barbara had been sent to another part of the country. So it was back to Tewksbury despite her screams of rage and protest. This time she was placed in a ward of younger women, many of them unwed and pregnant. Although some in the ward were diseased, crippled and perverted, it was a relief to her to be with younger women.

"Very much of what I remember about Tewksbury is indecent, cruel, melancholy," she told Nella Braddy Henney fifty years later, "gruesome in the light of grown-up experience; but nothing corresponding with my present understanding of these ideas entered my child mind. Everything interested me. I was not shocked, pained, grieved, or troubled by what happened. Such things happened. People behaved like that—that was all that there was to it. It was all the life I knew. Things impressed themselves upon me because I had a receptive mind. Curiosity kept me alert and keen to know everything."

The inmates in the section across the hall from Annie's were some twenty-five young women in all stages of pregnancy. As soon as one was removed to the lying-in ward, another came to take her place. They fascinated Annie. The matron of her ward, Maggie Hogan, tried unsuccessfully to keep her from visiting the fallen ladies. Their talk was coarse, but Annie did not mind. "They blasphemed against every respectability," she later wrote. They talked of the romances that had brought them to Tewksbury. "Then it happened," one would say, or "I couldn't help myself." What happened or what the connection was with the baby that was about to be born did not remain a mystery to Annie for long. There were girls there from bawdy houses, girls who had been seduced, girls who had been set up in "secret brothels connived at by the guardians of law and order, which brought forth mocking laughter from bedridden creatures who seemed to rejoice in human corruptibility." She heard of "trysting in courtyards, love-making in closets, drunkenness, amours of people that frequented sinister alleys like cats, and children begotten and abandoned on door-steps, or otherwise disposed of. There was nothing I did not hear broadly discussed in gutter-language."

Men were dangerous; they also fascinated her. Two men who crossed her life personally at the almshouse did not enhance her trust of the breed. One was "Beefy," whose name did him justice. He supervised the dining room and constantly touched and fondled the more attractive women.

They did not mind this as much as they did the rancid food. When the women complained, he called them "beggars, thieves, whores." Few dared answer him back. He tried to kiss Annie, but she pushed him away.

Then there was Jimmy Burns, an insane boy, always talking about his "Jennie." He was considered safe enough to run errands for the asylum. One day while Annie was out walking with another woman from the ward, he came by with a hamper of bread, stopped and, with a bow to Annie, said, "Fair maiden, I have sought thee far." Annie knew he was insane; still she found his masculine voice sweetly attractive. Her companion ordered him to get along with his bread, but he refused. She fled, but Annie, who had a flirtatious nature, stood her ground "to hear more flattery." He touched her cheek and begged her to fly away with him. A little frightened now, she put him off with a promise. "I'll meet you tomorrow and we'll go off together." "Kiss me, Jennie, and I will know that you mean it," he came back. There seemed to be no escape. She put her face up for the kiss. He grasped her tightly for what seemed to her years and finally let her go. Annie thought he would not remember her promise. Back in the ward everyone knew what had happened. The women teased her, and Maggie Hogan warned her to keep out of the way "of that lunatic. There's no telling what he might do if you annoyed him."

She made up her mind never to meet Jimmy again. Her resolve lasted one day. "How silly to be afraid. . . . I am going to meet Jimmy once, just once more." When he spotted her, he ran toward her, shouting, "Jennie, Jennie, Jennie, I am here, I'm coming." Now she wished she had not come, for there was something in Jimmy's voice that made her tremble. Jimmy proposed to leave his bread hamper in the middle of the path where he had put it down. Annie reminded him that there were hungry people waiting for him. "Let us both take the bread to the poor people who are waiting for it," she suggested. "You are trying to fool me again," he cried, grabbing her around the waist. When he thought she would take flight, he snatched from under his coat a long bread knife that he had stolen from the bakery.

She shrieked in terror. Someone knocked Jimmy down from behind. The knife fell out of his hands. "Pick it up and run," the man's voice commanded. He pinioned Jimmy's arms, and while Jimmy struggled to free himself, Annie ran back to the ward. "Serves you right," mumbled one of the women. "He should have cut your heart out, that crazy boy you run after."

Maggie Hogan, the quiet little woman in charge of her ward who had tried to save her from her recklessness, took a special interest in her. She introduced Annie to Tewksbury's small library and persuaded a mildly deranged girl, Tilly, to read to Annie books that she selected, mostly by Irish authors. Later Annie selected the books herself. Those that she remembered and listed for her biographer were: *Caste, The Octoroon, The Lamplighter, Ten Nights in a Barroom, The Breadwinner, Cast up by the Sea, Winiford, Stepping Heavenward, Darkness and Daylight, Tempest and Sunshine,* a life of St. Theresa and "the story of some saint who gave Jesus her rosary and He turned it into jewels."

Annie's overriding ambition was to get out of the almshouse and to go to school. The women in the ward accused her of putting on airs when she spoke of it, which was often. "She'll be walking out of here some day on the arm of the Emperor of Penzance," they scoffed. A sense that she was different, that she wanted something more from life than these women, was always with her. Even in the first months at Tewksbury she had talked of wanting to go to school when she heard from a blind inmate that there were schools for the blind. One of the women had made light of her ambition, saying that "education doesn't make any difference, if the Lord wills otherwise; Our life is the Lord's and death's." She had retorted hotly, "I don't see what the Lord has to do with it. And all the same, I'm going to school when I grow up."

Her chance to escape from Tewksbury came when she heard that an investigating commission headed by Frank B. Sanborn, chairman of the State Board of Charities, had arrived to inspect the institution. Gruesome stories about Tewksbury were rife in the state, even rumors of skins being sold from dead bodies to make shoes. She followed the group from ward to ward, trying to screw up her courage to approach it directly. Finally, as the men stood at the gate, she acted. Without knowing which figure was the exalted Mr. Sanborn, she flung herself into the group, crying, "Mr. Sanborn, Mr. Sanborn, I want to go to school!" "What is the matter with you?" a voice asked. "I can't see very well." "How long have you been here?" She was unable to tell him. The men left, but soon afterwards a woman came and told her she was to leave Tewksbury and go to school.

Two calico dresses were found for her. The red one she wore; the blue one, along with a coarse-grained chemise and two pairs of black cotton stockings, was tied up in a newspaper bundle. The women in the ward crowded around her shouting advice as she walked to the Black Maria. "Don't tell anyone you came from the poorhouse." "Keep your head up, you're as good as any of them." "Be a good girl and mind your teachers." When Tim, the driver, handed her over to a state charity official, he added his own bit of advice: "Don't ever come back to this place. Do you hear? Forget this and you will be all right."

In Boston, the charity worker handed her over to another official. When he told her Annie came from Tewksbury, she patted the girl on the head. "Poor child," she said pityingly. Annie's face burned. She had thought the calico dress pretty, but the woman's pity suddenly aroused in her a sense of how poorly dressed she must be. "The essence of poverty," she told Nella Braddy, "is shame. Shame to have been overwhelmed by ugliness, shame to be a hole in the perfect pattern of the universe."

That day—October 7, 1880—she entered the Perkins Institution for the Blind. Her humiliations were only beginning.

"I often wonder," she wrote in one note for her biographer, "how I escaped contamination in that slum—that 'rookery,' (as it was spoken of during the investigation at the State House). Helen, Polly, Nella might say it was a terrible school in which to learn about life." And so it was. "Yet I was not corrupted by it." Birth, death and sin "do not always besmirch the spirit," she went on, in explanation of what she meant by *corruption.* "They leave their impression on the tender mind, but they do not impart knowledge. One cannot learn such things vicariously. There are nascent in the child-mind countless pure immunities that prevent it from being harmed."

On the level of knowledge, perhaps; but as William Faulkner wrote in *Light in August,* "memory knows even when knowing would no longer remember." In later days, when she least expected it, memory would suddenly reach up and sweep her being with vague terrors, absurd insecurities, violent rages. Elsewhere, in one of the "scribblings" that Helen preserved, she wrote differently of the Tewksbury experience: It had left her with "the conviction that life is primarily cruel and bitter. . . . I doubt if life or for that matter eternity is long enough to erase the terrors and ugly blots scored upon my mind during those dismal years from 8 to 14."

II

Boston, Perkins and Samuel Gridley Howe

"... Can nothing be done to disinter this human soul?"

Boston in the nineteenth century was America's Olympus. Even in the twilight of its greatness, the cobblestoned streets still echoed to the measured footsteps of its deities. They were minor on the scale of the world's great thinkers and poets, but major within the context of a young nation still seeking to define its national character. The Bostonian influence was a distinctive and guiding presence in America—here beat the nation's philanthropic heart. "There is a city in our world upon which the light of the sun of righteousness has risen," wrote Bronson Alcott in 1828. "It is Boston. The morality of Boston is more pure than that of any other city in America." And a decade later, a thoughtful English observer, Harriet Martineau, wrote after her travels in America, "I know no large city where there is so much mutual helpfulness, so little neglect and ignorance of the concerns of other classes." Helen Howe, the daughter of the city's chronicler, Mark deWolfe Howe, called her engaging memoir of the Boston of her parents *The Gentle Americans;* and Helen Keller, describing Boston at the turn of the century when she arrived there from Tuscumbia, Alabama, saw it as "The City of Kind Hearts, a city of friends and lovers of liberty."

No one better exemplified Boston's philanthropic impulse than Dr. Samuel Gridley Howe. No institution better embodied the city's compassion than the Perkins Institution for the Blind, which under his leadership came to be a synonym throughout the United States for the nascent sense of social responsibility that was just beginning to influence public policy. Although Annie arrived at Perkins four years after Dr. Howe's death, his influence was still pervasive. His successor, Michael Anagnos, was married to his eldest daughter; and Perkins continued to be a second home to the Howes, especially Dr. Howe's widow, Julia Ward Howe, a vivid and forceful woman, author of "The Battle Hymn of the Republic," suffragette, American aristocrat—and in time the focus of all of Annie's hatred for the well-born, the powerful, the people who lived in ease and splendor.

The Howes were a dominating influence on Annie during her stay at Perkins. Dr. Howe's work with Laura Bridgman shaped her own approach to Helen Keller, while her detestation of Julia Ward Howe fanned a rebelliousness and independence that carried her beyond Dr. Howe and made her one of the greatest teachers in American history.

Many Bostonians considered Samuel Gridley Howe one of the handsomest men in their city. Black-bearded like an Assyrian, he was as tempestuous in his aspirations for the human race as he was gentle in his dealings with its individual members. Immediately upon finishing his medical studies, he set sail for Europe to join Lord Byron in helping the Greek revolution against the Turks. There, he spent seven years and on his way home was at the side of Lafayette in Paris during the 1830 July revolution. "Reserve yourself for the service of America, young friend," Lafayette advised him. "This is our fight, not yours." Although the essayist John Jay Chapman felt there was always a touch of the buccaneer about Howe, Lafayette's words struck home. When, therefore, on the streets of Boston a fellow doctor accosted him with words that suggested another form of work for humankind, he listened. "Just the man," cried Dr. Fisher while riding with him in 1832. "Howe, while you have been away freeing the Greeks from the unspeakable Turks and reconstructing the Cretans, we here have incorporated a school for the blind and now need someone to organize and run it; you are the very man to do it."

Howe accepted within a week and set off again for Europe to procure books and teachers and to study how it handled the blind, especially the pioneering school in Paris established by Valentin Haüy. Inevitably there was a detour, this time to aid the Polish revolutionaries, an undertaking that landed him in a Prussian jail for five weeks. He returned to Boston in the summer of 1832, bringing with him two teachers of the blind, one from Haüy's school, the other from a school in Edinburgh.

They had to go into the countryside to find their first blind children. The school was launched, but the "Lafayette of Boston," as he was called, was not to be contained by one cause. He was an abolitionist and a friend of the downtrodden and impoverished Irish who were beginning to arrive in considerable numbers. He was among the Boston aristocrats who sought to defend the Irish ghetto in 1837 against a Boston mob intent on plunder and assault. During the "Broad Street Riot," as it was called, he came to the aid of a fellow Bostonian who had been knocked down. It was Charles Sumner, a rising young politician and abolitionist.

They became staunch friends; and a few weeks later Howe, in the company of Sumner and some of his intimate friends—the poet Longfellow, the eminent lawyer Rufus Choate, a young collegian, Samuel Eliot, and George Hillard, who was to address the learned societies at Dartmouth College—journeyed to Hanover, New Hampshire. It was there that Dr. Howe heard of Laura Bridgman, who, stricken with scarlet fever at the age of two, had become deaf, blind and mute, her senses of taste and smell impaired. He persuaded her parents to send her to Perkins. Howe was a scientist with a flair for generalization and principle. The principles that he established for Perkins were that the blind should be educated to become self-reliant and to regard themselves as "active" citizens of the Commonwealth. They were to be trained manually for some occupation, and they were to exercise daily in order to strengthen their bodies. Books were to be printed in raised type so that they could learn to read by themselves.

Some of these principles he had laid down at the school's inception. Some he developed in the course of his intensive work with Laura Bridgman. She presented a special and seemingly intractable problem: how to reach a mind that was sealed from the outside world by the destruction of all the channels that led into it except for the sense of touch. Language, Howe decided, was the key to her development, and his first step was to show Laura that words—arbitrary signs—were the means of communicating her thoughts and feelings. He began with a spoon and a key, upon which he pasted in raised print the words *key* and *spoon.* She was encouraged to stroke the labels with her fingers and sense that they differed. Next, similar labels on detached pieces of paper were given to her, and after a time she grasped that they matched the labels on the key and the spoon. She next attached the appropriate label to the right object. Many familiar objects were la-

beled in the same way. Words were then scrambled into their separate
letters, and she learned to arrange them in the correct order. "Day
after day, week after week" this laborious process went on, until at
last, wrote Dr. Howe, "the truth began to flash upon her. Her intellect began to work. She perceived that there was a way by which she
could herself make a sign of anything that was in the mind, and show
it to another mind, and at once her countenance lighted up with a
human expression; it was no longer a dog or a parrot—it was an immortal spirit seizing upon a new link of union with other spirits."

Dr. Howe devised a slate with type on which Laura could set up
any word she wished to use, but shortly afterwards the manual alphabet was introduced. This alphabet consists of simple movements of the
fingers of one person's hand upon the palm of another person's. It was
invented by a group of Spanish monks who had taken a vow of silence
and used it to communicate without breaking the vow.

By 1839 Perkins had outgrown its original quarters on Pearl Street,
which had been given to it by Colonel Thomas H. Perkins, and moved
to South Boston, where, said Dr. Howe, there was "space, fresh air, a
commanding situation." Horace Mann, himself a great educational in-
novator, said of Perkins in 1841: "I would rather have built up the Blind
Asylum than have written *Hamlet*, and one day everybody will think so."
Howe's work with Laura Bridgman brought world fame, and Perkins
became an obligatory stop for European dignitaries. On January 29, 1842,
one of the most notable visitors, Charles Dickens, escorted by Charles
Sumner and Boston's Mayor Jonathan Chapman, went there by sleigh
from Tremont House in South Boston, then a little way outside the town.
(Dr. Howe was away in the South.) "I went to see this place one very fine
winter morning," he wrote in *American Notes*, "an Italian sky above, and
the air so clear and bright, that even my eyes, which are none the best,
could follow the minute lines and scraps of tracery in distant buildings."
He visited other institutions in South Boston, the Insane Asylum, the
House of Correction, as well as Perkins. Of all the places he visited and
persons he talked with, Perkins and Laura Bridgman most strongly engaged his interest:

> Good order, cleanliness, and comfort, pervaded every corner of the
> building. The various classes, who were gathered around their teach-
> ers, answered the questions put to them with readiness and intelli-
> gence, and in a spirit of cheerful contest for precedence which pleased

me very much. Those who were at play were as gleesome and noisy as other children.

Of Laura Bridgman he wrote:

> . . . a fair young creature with every human faculty and hope and power of goodness and affection enclosed within her delicate frame, and but one outward sense—the sense of touch. There she was before me, built up, as it were, in a marble cell, impervious to any ray of light or particle of sound; with her poor white hand peeping through a chink in the wall, beckoning to some good man for help, that an immortal soul might be awakened.

> Long before I looked upon her, the help had come. Her face was radiant with intelligence and pleasure. Her hair, braided by her own hands, was bound about a head, whose intellectual capacity and development were beautifully expressed in its graceful outline, and its broad open brow; her dress, arranged by herself, was a pattern of neatness and simplicity; the work she had knitted lay beside her, her writing book was on the desk she leaned upon. From the mournful ruin of such bereavement there had slowly risen up this gentle, tender, guileless, grateful-hearted being.

Laura's teacher-companion wrote in the diary that Dr. Howe had her keep, "Today Laura had the honor of a call from Charles Dickens. His great interest in her caused him to remain for several hours. She was animated in conversation and I think he received a very correct impression."

Howe was world famous even before he married Julia Ward of New York—heiress, poetess, free spirit—in 1843. "The great Doctor Howe whose figure towers over little Boston," wrote Chapman. When he went abroad with his wife on their honeymoon, it was no longer as the "Lafayette of Boston" that he was received everywhere, but as the "liberator" of Laura Bridgman's sense-imprisoned soul. Boston's poets sang his glories. In *The Autocrat of the Breakfast-Table,* Oliver Wendell Holmes wrote:

> He asked not whence the fountains roll
> No traveler's foot has found,

But mapped the desert of the soul
Untouched by sight or sound.

And Whittier in "The Hero," after detailing his subject's prowess in the cause of the oppressed, ended with Howe's work for the blind:

Woulds't know him now? Behold him,
The Cadmus of the blind,
Giving the dumb lip language
The idiot clay a mind.

A letter from Charles Sumner to Lord Morpeth announced the visit to Europe of "my dear friend Howe, and his newly married wife. I cannot write too warmly of Howe. He is shy, reserved, modest, but full of worth, intelligence, and virtue. Perhaps you will remember his wife."

Julia Howe, the daughter of the banker Sam Ward and the toast of Knickerbocker society, wrote of her marriage and removal to Boston: "The change had already been great, from my position as a family idol and 'the superior young lady' of an admiring circle to that of a wife overshadowed for a time by the splendor of her husband's reputation." She had been reared in conditions of great affluence—"As the Irishman said, I had everything a pig could want." She had achieved considerable notice by some essays that she later thought "were probably more remarked at the time of their publication than their merit would have warranted. But women writers were by no means as numerous sixty years ago as they are today. Neither was it possible for a girl student in those days to find the help and guidance towards a literary career which may be easily commanded today."

On their weddng trip abroad the Howes called on Carlyle and Wordsworth. Most of the talk with Wordsworth turned on the losses of a kinsman in American securities. To Julia, the aged poet's only interesting comment was on the Irish question: "The misfortune of Ireland is that it was only a partially conquered country." Dr. Howe as usual made the rounds of the institutions dealing with the handicapped and afflicted. A visit to a blind deaf-mute woman caused him to write:

And here the question will recur to you (for I doubt not that it has occurred a dozen times already), can nothing be done to disinter this human soul? It is late, but perhaps not too late. The whole neighborhood would rush to save this woman if she were buried alive by the caving in of a pit, and labour with zeal until she were dug out. Now if there were one who had as much patience as zeal, and who, having observed carefully how a little child learns language, would attempt to lead her gently through the same course, he might possibly awaken her to a consciousness of her immortal nature. The chance is small indeed; but with a smaller chance they would have dug desperately for her in the pit; and is the life of the soul of less import than that of the body?

On his return to America Howe plunged into work not only for the blind but for the feeble-minded. Elected to the state legislature, he obtained the appointment of a legislative commission to ascertain the number of idiots and imbeciles, as they were called at that time. He wrote the commission's report afterward on the need for and usefulness of teaching feeble-minded children and obtained the first state appropriation for the purpose, $2,500. "There is one thing I want much to do," he wrote Horace Mann in 1852, "and with your active aid could do (that is, if I get the Idiot School fairly established and in public favour)—viz. establish a school for teaching the deaf-mute to articulate." As a result of his prodding and inspiration, two schools to teach the deaf articulate speech were established, the Clarke School in Northampton and the Horace Mann School in Boston. "There floats not upon the stream of life," he believed, "any wreck of humanity so utterly shattered and crippled that the signals of distress should not challenge attention and command assistance." It was said of Howe at this time that "he was driving all of the charities and reform of the state abreast." He brought about the establishment of the State Board of Charities "on such fundamental principles," wrote the director of the Perkins Institution in 1932, "that they are still the guiding posts to those charged with the administration of charity."

In later years, when asked how Dr. Howe was, Julia Ward Howe would answer, half in complaint and half in pride, "I really can't tell you, because as I'm neither *deaf, dumb,* nor *blind,* an idiot or a nigger, I really see very little of my husband, dear Dr. Howe."

As the Civil War approached, Howe became increasingly involved in abolitionist activities. He went so far as to help John Brown with funds, although after John Brown's raid, he thought it prudent to publish a notice disclaiming knowledge and complicity in the affair. But his wife wrote "The Battle Hymn of the Republic," which became the North's semireligious anthem in that sanguinary conflict.

Howe died in 1876. "He belongs rather to that class of reappearing reputations which die through successive resurrections," wrote Chapman, "and distribute their message to humanity through many undulations of loss and rediscovery."

One of Howe's final actions as chairman of the Board of State Charities had been to urge an investigation of the Tewksbury almshouse. It was one of the investigatory visits resulting from this plea that had brought Frank B. Sanborn of Concord—friend of Emerson, Hawthorne and Thoreau, champion of John Brown, and regarded by Boston conservatives as a "subversive thinker"—to Tewksbury on the occasion when Annie Sullivan commanded his attention with the cry "I want to go to school."

When Annie arrived there, Perkins was led by Howe's successor, his son-in-law, an enthusiastic, ardent and affectionate Greek, Michael Anagnos. He would have a great influence on Annie and later on Helen, and was an important figure in the Helen Keller story. Subsequently, relations between them were ruptured; and Annie and Helen seem never to have forgiven him, going out of their way to deprecate his influence.

Michael Anagnostopoulos was born in 1837 in a small village in Epirus, then under Turkish rule. His father was a baker, and Michael was educated in a local school in Janina. He managed to qualify for admission to the University of Athens, then astir with ideas of liberty and progress, only to abandon his studies to become a revolutionary and journalist. In 1866 Crete revolted against Turkish rule. Anagnos favored its annexation by Greece and resigned from his paper when he was outvoted by his fellow editors, who favored independence. In the United States Dr. Howe, on fire again with his youthful enthusiasm for Cretan freedom, was raising money to aid the Cretan cause. He arrived in Athens in 1867 carrying funds for the relief of Cretan refugees, of whom there were thousands in Athens and the Piraeus. He needed someone to serve as administrator and interpreter while he traveled about Europe to study new developments in the treatment of the handicapped. He selected Anagnos as his secretary.

When the time came to return to the United States, he asked the young Greek how much he should pay him. An indignant Anagnos would not hear of being paid. Dr. Howe had not worked for pay. Why should Anagnos, when it was his compatriots whom the doctor had aided? But he would like to return with Howe to the United States. He did, and first supported himself by serving as a tutor to Howe's daughters. Then he taught Latin and Greek at Perkins. He married Howe's eldest daughter, Julia, and became Howe's assistant in the management of Perkins. He had a flair for finance, economy of management and administrative detail—

"by no means," noted Sanborn, who knew them both well, "Dr. Howe's forte"—and in 1875 when Howe fell ill, he managed the Institution so well that at Howe's death he was the logical candidate to succeed him. But the trustees hesitated to entrust "Boston's darling charity" to a foreigner. They felt they must elect one of their own and chose Dr. John Homans, a young Boston physician. But Anagnos informed them that he would "not stay there and play second fiddle to any man." He carried the day and remained in charge as director until his death in 1906.

He expanded and improved the Perkins plant. He introduced Swedish gymnastics and emphasized corrective work with the children who needed it. He selected his teachers with great care. He understood the need to manufacture books and appliances to assist the blind and established the Howe Memorial Press. He started a kindergarten for the blind, "the first school for little blind children in the world," and raised a million dollars to house the kindergarten in a splendid set of buildings at Jamaica Plain.

But there was a marked difference between his father-in-law and himself. Dr. Howe, when he first began his work with the blind, went around for a week with bandaged eyes in order to understand better how to reach them. Anagnos never quite mastered the manual alphabet. One was a scientist, the other a promoter when it came to educational innovation. Sanborn brought out the difference at a memorial meeting for Anagnos in 1906. "Dr. Howe was a genius, capable, as the epigram says, of 'generalizing from a single instance.' " In the Laura Bridgman case "he did what nobody had done before. . . . His success made the way easy for all others, and no one as yet has improved on Dr. Howe's method of instruction in such cases."

But having done it, "he turned to other and harder tasks. At this point Anagnos took up the work and proceeded to apply Howe's methods to many cases, and with greater success in some than poor Laura's conditions afforded. Among these successes, one in particular has attracted notice and calls for mention today." And Sanborn closed his address by telling the story of Annie Sullivan.

III

The Taming of "Miss Spitfire"

"When a superior intellect and psychopathic temperament coalesce . . . in the same individual we have the best possible condition for the kind of effective genius that gets into the biographical dictionaries. . . ."—William James

Charles Dickens speaks of the "secret agony" of his soul when at eleven he was hired out to the "blacking house"; and though his bondage there was of comparatively short duration, he came away from it with such a deep sense of neglect, hopelessness and shame, his whole nature "so penetrated with the grief and humiliation . . . that even now, famous and caressed and happy, I often forget in my dreams that I have a dear wife and children; even that I am a man; and wander desolately back to that time of my life."

Fourteen-year-old Annie arrived at Perkins seeking to put Tewksbury and its grotesque horrors out of her mind. For almost two years at Perkins she never let the other girls know that she had come from the state poorhouse. She never wanted to see anyone from Tewksbury again; but while she might command her conscious being, her whole nature—like Dickens's—was in the grip of the Tewksbury experience. Almost all her recollections of six years at Perkins, as she told them fifty years later to her biographer, Nella Braddy Henney, were incidents of inner shame, humiliation, mortification, which her strong, combative personality transmuted into public defiance, hostility, impudence and discontent.

Her admission record read:

No. 985. Born in Agawam, Mass. July 4, 1863, entered October 7, 1880. [Her real birth date was April 14, 1866.] Partial blindness at the age of eleven years is attributed to inflammation. Her father, a healthy but intemperate Irishman, does not contribute to Annie's support, and [though] her uncles are said to be prosperous farmers she enters from the Tewksbury almshouse a state charge. Her mother died of pthisis at the age of twenty-eight years.

Diagnosis is by Dr. H.W. Williams, November 22, 1881. Says she has had sore eyes for twelve years. Lids still rough, and cartilages somewhat incurvated from trachomytous degeneration. Diffused haziness of cornea in both eyes with slight prominence of the same. Cloudiness seems to be confined to the epithelial layer and probably susceptible of considerable improvement.

On her first day at the school she was sent to a sewing class of nine-year-olds, although she was in reality fourteen. She did not know how to hold a needle. "How old are you?" the surprised teacher asked. "I do not know," she replied. The girls dissolved in laughter and her face crimsoned. "Where did you come from?" was the next question, and again Annie replied, this time because she was ashamed to admit it, "I don't know," and again the class, including the teacher, laughed. As the class broke up, the teacher advised her to "find out something about yourself before you come to class tomorrow." "I will if I want to, and I won't if I don't," she flared back.

A girl who had volunteered to show her to the cottage where she was to live admonished her not to talk that way to the teacher. "I won't if she minds her own business," answered Annie, inwardly in agony because she sensed she was making a bad start of her life at Perkins. "No one will like you if you are rude," the girl went on, "and you will be punished." "Who said so?" demanded Annie belligerently.

It remained her attitude for a long time. "Because I was ignorant, and felt inferior, I pretended that I was scornful and contemptuous of everybody. As a matter of fact, I was extremely unhappy. My mind was a question mark, my heart a frustration." Tewksbury had unfitted her for "living a normal life." She had the most powerful mind in the school, both because of her native abilities and because of the knowledge of the world's ways that she had acquired at the poorhouse. But on the level of reading, writing, arithmetic, manners and diction, she was less developed than the youngest child in the school.

"I quickly became aware that I was different from the people about me. I learned quickly and thought myself superior to the other girls." The new competencies and ideas that she acquired "sown in the deep, dark soil of my Tewksbury experiences" quickly "overshadowed the puny thoughts of my schoolmates which were more delicately nourished." The rudiments of education were acquired at great psychic cost. "When 'big Annie' failed to spell the simplest words correctly, the class laughed uproariously. Stung to the quick by their glee, yet outwardly brazen and impudent, I plodded on." These moments of mortification remained "scars" on her memory that fifty years had not healed. "No doubt they intensified my perception and spurred me to stronger effort. I advanced rapidly in my studies, leaving behind me most of the scoffers. I became puffed up with pride, and inwardly I criticised even my teachers. I thought, 'They don't know so very much after all. In a little while I shall know all they know, and more too.' "

There were other humiliations. She had never slept in a nightgown and had to borrow one from a girl in her cottage. She did not own a comb for her hair. She overheard the matrons speaking indignantly of how neglected she had been.

The Perkins day consisted of classes from eight to three, with a break at noon for dinner. At the end of the school day the students spent an hour walking. She was not one for walks or gymnastics. She felt ungainly and envied the girls with slender bodies and agile movements. "I preferred to sit and meditate." The hour outdoors was followed by classes in singing and in sewing. After supper the teachers read to them from the *Boston Transcript,* omitting, however, the items they considered unfit for feminine ears, the stories of scandal, crime and violence—precisely the items on which the women in the Tewksbury wards had fed. The *Transcript* bored Annie, and the reading of Macaulay's *Life and Letters,* to which the newspaper gave way, bored her even more.

Some teachers she hated—those who sought to discipline her by humiliation and command. "When is your brain awake?" her exasperated teacher in mathematics flung out at her one day. "When I leave your class," she replied tartly as her classmates gasped. She found geometry tedious. "What is the use of it?" she asked her teacher. Unable to restrain a tone of superiority, the teacher answered, "It trains the mind, teaches self-control—a virtue which some of us need to cultivate."

"How long have you been teaching it?" the saucy Annie wanted to know.

"Several years," the guileless woman replied, "but why do you ask?"

"Because I don't see that it has trained your mind." And while her teacher was getting back her breath, Annie plunged on, "I wish there was a study that would teach everyone how stupid they are."

"If there were such a science," the thoroughly aroused teacher replied, "you would do well to devote your whole life to it."

Annie asked many questions that disconcerted her teachers, and when she sensed their discomfort she quickly followed up her advantage. Often she was sent out of the classroom. There were a few teachers, however, who refused to be provoked by this Irish hellion. They sought to understand and to help her in ways she would accept.

In 1882 General Benjamin Butler, populist and demagogue, was making his fifth try for governor, this time on the Democratic ticket. Respectable Boston was alarmed and up in arms to prevent the election of "Beast Butler," as they called him. He was an advocate of votes for women and a ten-hour day for workingmen. He had the support of Boston's Irish. Annie had heard of him from the women at Tewksbury, who adored him, and he became her hero when he made conditions at Tewksbury a major point in his campaign against the respectable establishment that controlled Massachusetts politics. "I believe everyone in the Institution hated him," she later recalled. "Therefore I made him the idol of my imagination." The *Boston Transcript* was filled with denunciatory editorials which were regularly read to the girls after supper. The general theme of the editorials was that Butler's election would disgrace Massachusetts, the most enlightened commonwealth in the nation, a state whose institutions were a model for the country—"Massachusetts, the cradle of liberty," one such editorial ended.

"The cradle where liberty was rocked to sleep," an exasperated Annie suddenly heard herself saying before the assembled group. "You do nothing but abuse General Butler because he wants to help the poor people at Tewksbury." Miss Cora Newton, the history teacher, was one of two teachers in the school whom Annie secretly admired. She turned to Annie and said calmly, "Explain what you mean by that remark, Annie." The dark-haired heckler was dumbfounded. She had expected a reprimand, not a request to speak up and explain herself. "I really had not the faintest idea of what I meant by the exclamation. The words had been rushed to my lips by the seething protest within me." She hesitated, but the giggles of the girls at her apparent discomfiture spurred her on. "Read history and you will find out." "What history shall I read?" Miss Newton asked evenly. Again Annie was stumped. The only histories she knew were Bancroft's *History of the United States* and Dickens's *Child's History of England,* which in raised print she was reading in her history class with her fingers. "I don't know," she confessed, as her eyes began to brim with tears.

Then, however, goaded by the jeers of the girls, she attacked, "I don't know the names of the histories that tell the truth yet, but I do know nobody here knows the truth about Tewksbury. You don't know General Butler. It isn't he that is a disgrace to Massachusetts; it's the state itself because it knows that Tewksbury is a terrible place, and it pretends that it is a nice institution. I have lived there," she blurted out as a clincher to her argument. Her face reddened as she realized what she had just admitted, but on she went with a courage born of desperation. "I know all about it, and every word General Butler says about it is true. People like to hear lies better than the truth. They would rather be ignorant about Tewksbury and all the poor people who stay there than have Massachusetts blamed. That's why I said liberty is asleep."

She sat down, her whole body quivering. Miss Newton did not speak for a time. Then she said, "You have spoken out of an angry heart, Annie, and anger is seldom wise; but I understand now why you think as you do about many things. Will you stay after Reading, and let us have a good talk? I do really want to know the truth."

But Annie feared that her teacher's superior knowledge would lead to further humiliation. "I went instead to my bedroom and coddled my wrath." She comforted herself with the thought that Miss Newton's knowledge was secondhand, what she had obtained from newspapers and books and *The Nation,* at that time a magazine of conservative opinion. "It's stupid the way she reads that *Nation* every Saturday morning. We ought to be allowed to have our Saturdays free. She seems to think that God speaks out of that paper. When I tell her something that was in *The Pilot* * she talks as if the devil wrote the articles in it! Well! I like what the Devil says. If God thinks the way they do, they can have Him."

In history class Annie had objected violently to the account of the Inquisition. Everyone knew, she had argued, that Protestants persecuted Catholics, not the other way around. She had shocked Miss Newton with the announcement that Thomas Jefferson was a hypocrite. "Why do you

---

*The Boston Catholic weekly, edited by the ebullient John Boyle O'Reilly, who in fact, according to Van Wyck Brooks, more than anyone, helped reconcile Boston's Catholics and Protestants.

say such a thing?" the teacher had asked. "Because he wrote the Declaration of Independence and kept slaves."

Grievance, prejudice, rebelliousness, chased through her mettlesome heart, each feeding upon the other. "They think having a lot of dead ancestors makes them fine folk. They feel important when they talk about their grandfathers. They seem to forget that everybody must have had a dead grandfather. I guess all those queer people in Tewksbury had an ancestor too, only, nobody remembered their names, or what they did when they were alive. Who knows? Perhaps the noble dead they lecture about were like the board of overseers that visited the almshouse. Perhaps they were liars too, dressed up in fine clothes. Perhaps they sold slaves to other rich folk like themselves. Perhaps they deceived poor girls about marrying them. Perhaps they were wicked landlords, and robbed the people until there was famine in Ireland."

Fiery echoes of O'Connell, Parnell, of John Boyle O'Reilly, words she had heard from her father and from the women in Tewksbury, rang in her thoughts. "My precious *Pilot* was right. The men 'nice people' admired rose on the backs of bleeding slaves, black and white, to power and wealth and education."

The ferocity of her feelings surprised her. "I could not but remember how I had despised the inmates of Tewksbury when I was one of them. I cannot recall that their misfortunes and afflictions and wrongs awakened in me any emotion either of pity or indignation. It seems to me that I accepted life as it presented itself there as a matter of course. When the idea of going away to school took possession of my thoughts, I realized that everything about the place was horrid, and I knew I should be glad to leave it forever. No regret at parting with any of my associates troubled me." So Annie, fifty years later, recalled bits and pieces of her stream of consciousness in the hours and days after the Butler episode.

Miss Newton, one of the few who sought to probe the roots of Annie's angers and resentments, wrote of her, " . . . a wholesome, vigorously active, impulsive, self-assertive, generally happy girl, inclined to be impatient and combative towards criticism or any opinion not in agreement with her own. She evidenced much executive ability and initiative. She was almost passionately fond of pretty clothes. . . ." The more conventional view of Annie was expressed by a classmate in 1927: "As Miss Sullivan was a homeless girl, it was no discredit to her that she came to our school from a charitable institution unkempt and badly clothed. Nor is it strange that, from such surroundings, she came with strong prejudices and a narrow point of view. . . . Politically Annie was always a radical Democrat with which point of view I had no sympathy."

Another teacher who liked her was Miss Mary C. Moore, a Canadian who taught literature. Miss Moore had gained Annie's favor in her first year at Perkins when she had provided her with the carfare to go into downtown Boston to attend a performance of *The Mikado*. It was her first opera, and she sat in one of the seats that the theaters of Boston reserved for the pupils of Perkins. "I thought I could listen to it forever." She loved "Koko and the three little maids and the flowers that bloom in the spring-time, which brought encore after encore. . . .

"Miss Moore exerted a salutary influence over me. I respected her mind, and I fancied she did not think I was quite such a dyed-in-the-wool black sheep as the others did. When I was deliberately rude, or expressed opinions which betrayed the meagreness of my information, she often pretended not to notice it. She changed the subject so adroitly that I was not sure she had really noticed it. Sometimes I had the uncomfortable feeling that she was getting me under her thumb, which made me uneasy and suspicious. The mind was willing and docile, but the spirit carried a chip on its shoulder. I now wonder at her good-will towards me. It might easily have collapsed before a student so intractable as I was. Little by little she disciplined my unorderly mind."

Miss Moore understood the bifurcation of Annie's mind, one side as undeveloped as a child's, the other astonishingly mature. When Annie brought her a composition, she did not seize upon its inadequacies. "This composition has many faults," she commented. "It is ungrammatical, the spelling is fearlessly unconventional, but it is interesting." Annie went away resolved to master the mysteries of grammar and the intricacies of orthography. "If I could only learn to spell," she had wailed. "I shall never catch up with the people who had a fair start."

"Oh, yes, you will, Annie, if you put such thoughts out of your mind, and have faith in yourself."

Fifty years later Annie was unable to pinpoint when such counsel began "to gain on my wilfulness. But I know that gradually I began to accept things as they were, and rebel less and less. The realization came to me that I could not alter anything but myself. I must accept the conventional order of society if I were to succeed in anything. I must bend to the inevitable, and govern my life by experience, not by might-have-beens."

It was fortunate that Annie had some partisans. Her hairtrigger temper and headstrong ways brought her several times to the point of expulsion, saved only by the intervention of teachers like Miss Newton and Miss Moore. She could even infuriate the school's director, Michael Anagnos. He sensed that there was something remarkable about this young woman, but in the face of repeated instances of insubordination he felt sometimes that she would have to leave if he were to hold the school together. One such instance was the hearings on Tewksbury at the State House. Denied permission to attend, Annie went to the hearings on the pretext of a visit to the Eye and Ear Infirmary, taking along a classmate. Only the pleas of Miss Moore and others kept him from expelling her when he learned what she had done.

Improvement in her sight made reconciliation with her surroundings easier. Annie's summer plans always constituted a problem for the Institution. The first summer when the school scattered for vacation she had gone to a classmate's family farm in New Hampshire, a not wholly happy experience because of the farmer's queer ways. The second summer the school's music teacher, Mr. Kilbourne, found her a place doing light housework at Miss Dudley's boardinghouse in Boston. One of the boarders insisted that she go to the Carney Catholic Hospital to have her eyes examined. A young doctor became interested and performed two operations. By the time she left the hospital she was able to thread a needle* and read with her eyes. Previously she had read with her fingers books in embossed type, books such as *Silas Marner, The Vicar of Wakefield, The Scarlet Letter, Quentin Durward, The Last Days of Pompeii* and Dickens's *The Old Curiosity Shop,* which Dickens had put in raised type at his own expense. Now she was able to read more widely, including the stories in the newspaper that were not read aloud, as well as such periodicals as *St. Nicholas* and *The Youth's Companion, The Living Age, The Atlantic* and *Scribner's,* even *The Nation.*

She took Miss Moore's class in Shakespeare. "As I look back, it seems as if those hours contained all that was stimulating and fine in my school days. I used to leave the classroom in a trance." Miss Moore read beautifully, and together the class read *The Tempest, King Lear, As You Like It, Macbeth.* "For the first time I felt the magic of great poetry."

Another mellowing influence was the new house mother in her cottage, Mrs. Hopkins. She was the widow of a sea captain, who after the death

---

*She never managed to do so without the use of her tongue, but Helen Keller did, and Laura Bridgman, reports Nella Braddy Henney, was able to thread a needle fine enough to carry 120 thread.

of her daughter chanced to see some Perkins children vacationing at the Cape, where she lived in Brewster, and decided to offer her services. She seemed stiff and reserved, was straitlaced and church-going, but she had a heart full of mother love with no one to lavish it upon. She took Annie under her wing, and henceforth her home in Brewster became Annie's in the summer.

Religion also created difficulties for Annie. On Sunday Perkins pupils attended the church of their faith. The handful of Catholic girls went to the nearby Gate of Heaven Church. She did not intend to go to Sunday school, Annie promptly informed its priest, and at confession she declared she had nothing to confess. Although she continued to accompany the Catholic girls to morning Mass and evening vespers for about two years, her alienation from the Church was not concealed and the Church authorities blamed it on Perkins's teachers. Anagnos was appealed to, but he pointed out that there was no statute that obliged Annie to attend. "To avoid unnecessary complications, Mr. Anagnos asked me to remain in the Church until the end of the school year. I swallowed my impetuosity, and continued to exchange meaningless amenities with the Roman Church three months after I had renounced it."

With Michael Anagnos, the director of the school, Annie had a love-hate relationship. He personified authority and discipline, to which she never accommodated herself easily. But he also used his authority on behalf of liberty and tolerance, and that she thought admirable. Besides, he was a man, and Annie was responsive to that, wishing at times that all her teachers were men; nor was Anagnos, then in his late forties—a tall, slender man with straggly, mandarin-type whiskers—indifferent to the appeal of this saucy Irish lass.

Anagnos's handling of a theft within the school strengthened him in her esteem; indeed, she idolized him—"at least for two weeks," she quickly qualified. Some articles had been stolen from a locker, and the head teacher, whom she hated anyway, organized what Annie called a "Star Chamber" investigation. The teachers sat at a long table in the exhibition hall. Each girl was called in separately, questioned solemnly and dismissed with the order not to repeat what had been said to her. The girls, in fact, were directed not to speak to each other on any subject until the court adjourned. Annie considered it an outrageous procedure and told the girls waiting to be summoned that they reminded her of a nest of blind mice. One of the girls tattled, and she was promptly brought before the tribunal. The teachers had no right to treat them as thieves without any evidence, she argued when asked to explain her remark. Asked direct questions about the theft, she stood silent. Anagnos was summoned, but he sided with Annie, disapproved of the trial and the court broke up.

On the way out Anagnos seized her arm and said sternly, "Come with me, I'm going to search you. I suspect you of being the thief." Before Annie's rush of anger could explode, he laughed "in his loud way" and said, "What would you have done, Miss Spitfire, if I had searched you?"

"Scratch your eyes out," Annie said determinedly.

"You know what happens to undesirable cats," he cautioned, "putting his arm around my shoulder caressingly. I decided then and there that I liked men better than women, and I have never changed my mind since."

But a few weeks later her wrath was turned against her protector. Thursday was Exhibition Day at the school, when the public was admitted to the Institution and special exercises were held illustrative of the school's work. Annie's responsibility was to make the Exhibition Hall as attractive as possible. She hauled plants from the cottages, and on this particular occasion lodged stuffed birds from one of the classes on branches of the rubber plants. Then she hurried to her cottage to get dressed and, since Mrs. Hopkins was in the city, sat down at her dressing table, dabbed her cheeks with rouge, added a generous dusting with the powder puff and rushed back to the Exhibition Hall. At the entrance she met Mr. Anagnos and a group of visitors.

"What is the matter with your face?" he demanded sternly. Annie tried to push by him to her seat, but he caught her arm and ordered, "Go to the sink and wash it off." "I ran seething with rage to my room. I did not return to the hall, nor did I go to the sink." On such occasions the Tewksbury mood took possession of her being. Shame, a subconscious sense of injury that was always there, were followed by self-assertion and self-justification, black rage and hopelessness.

Miss Moore would try to pull her out of such bouts of desperation. "Healthy-minded people, especially young people, are not pessimistic," she would counsel Annie. "If you look about you, Annie, you cannot help seeing that a lot of things in the world are fine. A lot of people are kind and generous. The sun shines most of the time. The air we breathe is plentiful. Some of the books we read are delightful. Make up your mind to see the pleasant side of life and you will be happier."

The philosophy of "God's in His Heaven, all's right with the world" exasperated Annie. Miss Moore was too patient, too ready to accept things as they were. "She seemed on a high hill where I could not reach her hand, could not see her face, could not hear above me what she was saying to me. Her words had a quaint sound in my ears like the Beatitudes."

Irritated as Anagnos was from time to time, he also valued "Miss Spitfire." His overriding passion during Annie's years at Perkins was to create a kindergarten for blind children. Always the showman and promoter, although he considered himself scholar and educator, he knew that proper Bostonians upon whom he depended for funds would be offended by the sight of a pupil with rouged and powdered cheeks; but his own angers, like Annie's were quick to cool. He delegated her and another girl to call on all the Boston papers, ask for their editors, and then appeal to them to print an announcement of a fair for the kindergarten. The combination of femininity, Annie's liveliness and her companion's blindness, he shrewdly estimated, would get him some free space.

The editor of the *Transcript* did at first take refuge behind the excuse that a newspaper was a business enterprise and that he doubted his readers would tolerate advertisments disguised as news stories. "Our teachers," said Annie pertly, "say there is nothing in the paper." The editor chuckled and called in his associates to hear what the girls had to say about the paper. The editor of the *Globe* assented immediately. "What else is a paper for," he remarked, "but to please the ladies?" At the *Pilot,* Annie's "precious" Irish newspaper, the handsome John Boyle O'Reilly asked whether they knew that a paper was run for money. "How do you think I'm going to get paid?" Annie did not know. "I'd like to print the announcement, but I must get paid," he said, leading up to his price—which turned out to be a kiss. Annie paid with pleasure, and they left.

There was another defect in Mr. Anagnos, in Annie's eyes—the fact that Julia Ward Howe was his mother-in-law. Almost from the moment of Annie's arrival at Perkins she developed a dislike for Mrs. Howe, who personified a Brahmin class that seemed wholly beyond her reach. She was a grande dame. Mark de Wolfe Howe, who was not related to her, used the word "convoy" when he volunteered to escort her to dinner. Annie did not like women who radiated authority and elegance and who expected homage, even if it was merited. And it was. The cause of abolition had marched to her battle hymn. Julia Ward Howe was a poetess and a musician who played the piano well. She was a leader of the woman suffrage movement, and a tireless pulpiteer who also made peace her theme. She was a witty hostess to whose table the most distinguished foreign visitors felt privileged to receive an invitation, often to find themselves commanded—even the aesthete Oscar Wilde—to join her in a visit to the blind children at Perkins. But "neither she nor her circle ever forgot that there were laurels on her brow," wrote John Jay Chapman, who also remarked, "I cannot feel sure that her own hopes and illusions as to greatness were not a part of her charm."

Although she fought valiantly for the rights of blacks and of women, she served these causes while retaining a fastidious disdain for the lower classes. "The old-time American servants were no longer to be obtained," she wrote in her *Reminiscences*. "The Irish girls who supplied their places were for the most part ignorant and untrained, their performance calling for discipline and instruction which I never having received, was quite unable to give them." It was one thing to be for abolition as a cause, but to her the freed blacks were "niggers."

She had a barbed tongue which she curbed for no one; and even General Butler, when he introduced her at a fair in 1882, thought it prudent to warn, "Mrs. Howe may say some things which we might not want to hear, but it is my office to present her to this audience." She was in great demand as a public speaker and delighted to give public readings —of her own essays and the classics. Although she spent her summers at Newport, she avoided the teas and the balls, and amused herself instead with such projects as reading Plato's *Phaedo* in the original Greek.

Annie first encountered her when she came to the school, as she did frequently, to read aloud the *Oedipus Rex* of Sophocles in preparation for a presentation of the play by the Harvard Dramatic Society. Annie refused to listen to the great woman and pretended to herself she was more interested in the forthcoming race between the yachts *Mayflower* and *Galatea*. Once, when all had gathered in Mr. Anagnos's drawing room after a talk Mrs. Howe gave the girls in defense of women preachers, Annie volunteered that she intended to become an evangelist after she left school. Mrs. Howe looked her up and down and said after a pause:

"I am afraid you sacrifice modesty to your ambition, young woman." Angered, Annie flashed back, "Self-effacement is not your brightest virtue, is it, Madam Howe?" The members of the Howe cult standing about were dumbfounded at her audacity. Annie retired to the corner trembling with rage. A memo of Mrs. Howe that Annie wrote for Nella Braddy showed that resentment of the woman was still alive in her fifty years later. "Mrs. Julia Ward Howe had the air of one who confers a favor by acknowledging one's existence," she began. "She liked to create an impression by appearing to fall asleep while one was speaking to her. If the great suffragist had not taken these moments of repose in the presence of her inferiors, the women of America might never have gained the ballot."

Mrs. Howe's prominence in the suffrage movement may have been the reason Annie never worked up any enthusiasm for it, even later when Helen Keller and her mother became ardent converts. She considered class discrimination more insufferable than sexual discrimination; and Nella Braddy conveyed Annie's attitude by citing a statement of Mother Jones, the militant leader of the mine workers, "You don't need a vote to raise hell! You need convictions and a voice!"

"I wanted to get back at the great lady somehow," continued Annie's memoir of Mrs. Howe, "and at last I had my chance." The older girls were commanded to attend a Saturday afternoon reading of the *Iliad.* They bitterly resented having their only free afternoon thus preempted. "The *Iliad* seemed so remote and 'high brow' that, instead of feeling grateful to her, we regarded her kindness as an imposition." They decided to put on a demonstrative display of boredom. "We agreed that when Susie S. dropped her thimble (we were invited to bring our sewing and knitting) we would all yawn." The thimble fell, but the others lost their courage. Annie did not. "I let out a monstrous yawn." Silence and then giggles. Mrs. Howe expressed surprise that the young ladies had no better manners, but she continued. By the end of an hour all the girls' heads were drooping. "I thought it time to let out another yawn."

"I do not wish to seem annoyed at your unladylike conduct, but, in spite of my sincere desire to entertain you, I shall discontinue the reading," Mrs. Howe, her voice somewhat edgy, said, closing the book. The girls were embarrassed by their victory and began to trail out of the room. "They did not know," the vignette ended, "that Mrs. Howe had already departed."

Somehow Annie survived the Howes, the teachers she despised, the darker promptings of her nature. She was learning—even, it seems, from Mrs. Howe. As a teacher of younger students (which Anagnos, sensing her talents, encouraged her to do) she made Greek history come alive by having each ten-year-old personify a Greek character—Pericles, Lydia, Aristedes.

She came to know Laura Bridgman well. A frail, wispy woman, Laura was then in her fifties. Although able to communicate with the outside world, she had never learned to cope with it, and Dr. Howe had raised a fund to enable her to stay permanently at Perkins. She moved from cottage to cottage, and Annie learned the manual alphabet in order to spell into her hand the gossip of the girls.

Annie was twenty as the years at Perkins drew to a close. Despite the rebellions and withdrawals, the rages and depressions, she had, as she wrote, "a mind capable of growth and discrimination. . . . Many of the false ideas I had hugged to my heart fell away like dead leaves, and truer ones came to take their place. The light of knowledge spread slowly, putting darkness to flight. Little by little abstract notions grew into concrete things. Love, understanding and sympathy began to take the place of bitterness and ignorance." She was chosen valedictorian of her class of eight. Anagnos made much of the commencement exercises. The ceremonies were held at Tremont Temple, and the entire school was involved in drills and plays and musical performances designed to gain the sympathy and approval of the city. Mrs. Howe carried sufficient weight to make the ceremony a considerable public event. The governor and other Massachusetts notables would be there.

But even commencement was attended with a flash of irreverence. Anagnos had remarked that Annie looked very much like Frances Folsom, President Grover Cleveland's beautiful young ward, whom he had just married in a White House ceremony that had been the amused talk of the country. So Mrs. Hopkins and Annie decided to model Annie's hairstyle on the bride's and her dress on Mrs. Cleveland's college graduation dress. Mrs. Hopkins piled Annie's dark hair on top of her head, pompadour style, and with her curling iron made little ringlets at her temple, like Mrs. Cleveland's. Her dress was of white muslin with elbow-length sleeves and ruffles edged with lace. Mrs. Hopkins also managed to find a pair of white slippers for her. She dug out the pink sash that her daughter had worn at her high-school graduation and tied it around Annie's waist. "I gazed at my reflection speechless with delight. It was true! I did look like the bride of the White House."

As the graduates mounted the steps of the platform in Tremont Temple, Miss Moore pinned a bunch of roses the color of her sash at Annie's belt. "Mr. Anagnos took my hand and led me to my seat, speaking kind words all the time which I did not hear." Through a haze she heard the other speakers—Leverett Saltonstall, Dr. Samuel Eliot, the president of the corporation, and Governor Robinson. A fellow graduate played Handel's Fifth Concerto on the organ. The school's brass band, with clarinets, gave a rousing performance of the Bridal Chorus from *Lohengrin.* Another graduate spoke briefly of the "Laws of Mechanics," which she illustrated by the sewing machine before her. A double male quartet sang a haunting chorus from a manuscript opera, whose libretto was described as one of the last literary works of Julia R. Anagnos, "the gifted and lamented wife of the director of the Institution." There were exercises in geography for Annie to sit through, dumbbell exercises, a march-through and manual of arms display under a student "colonel." It all seemed to Annie dreamlike.

"Then my turn came, I heard the Governor speak my name, I rose trembling in every limb." Would she make it to the center of the platform? she wondered. Would she remember the words of her speech? The throng before her was huge—twenty-five hundred, the papers said. She hesitated, and the governor spoke her name again. She stepped forward to face the great throng. The governor began to clap, and everyone followed suit. "Ladies and gentlemen," she began, and from then on it was easy. *The Christian Register* wrote of her valedictory: "It was in an altogether earnest, sincere, thoughtful spirit, full of wise suggestions, and spoken in tones that vibrated with true feeling and with genuine refinement; a fit prelude to the touching wise remarks of Dr. Eliot before presenting diplomas to the eight graduates of the day." Even Anagnos was startled by the maturity of the speech's sentiments. It is worth quoting in full.

Today we are standing face to face with the great problem of life.

We have spent years in the endeavor to acquire the moral and intellectual discipline, by which we are enabled to distinguish truth from falsehood, receive higher and broader views of duty, and apply general principles to the diversified details of life. And now we are going out into the busy world, to take our share in life's burdens, and do our little to make that world better, wiser and happier.

We shall be most likely to succeed in this, if we obey the great law of our being. God has placed us here to grow, to expand, to progress. To a certain extent our growth is unconscious. We receive impressions and arrive at conclusions without any effort on our part; but we also have the power of controlling the course of our lives. We can educate ourselves; we can, by thought and perseverance, develop all the powers and capacities entrusted to us, and build for ourselves true and noble characters. Because we can, we must. It is a duty we owe to ourselves, to our country and to God.

All the wondrous physical, intellectual and moral endowments, with which man is blessed, will, by inevitable law, become useless, unless he uses and improves them. The muscles must be used, or they become unserviceable. The memory, understanding and judgment must be used, or they become feeble and inactive. If a love for truth and beauty and goodness is not cultivated, the mind loses the strength which comes from truth, the refinement which comes from beauty, and the happiness which comes from goodness.

Self-culture is a benefit, not only to the individual, but also to mankind. Every man who improves himself is adding to the progress of society, and every one who stands still, holds it back. The advancement of society always has its commencement in the individual soul. It is by battling with the circumstances, temptations and failures of the world, that the individual reaches his highest possibilities.

The search for knowledge, begun in school, must be continued through life in order to give symmetrical self-culture.

For the abundant opportunities which have been afforded to us for broad self-improvement we are deeply grateful.

Annie ended with graceful tributes to the governor and the legislature, and improvised what was referred to as the speaker's "tender references to the late Mrs. Anagnos" that moved many to tears. The valedictory, wrote the *Boston Home Journal,* was "worthy of special mention for its felicity of thought and grace of expression. It was emphatically a beautifully original production."

With the applause and kind wishes of the throng still ringing in her ears, Annie returned to her little room. "I must shed my white splendor before the supper bell rang. Reluctantly I unfastened the sash and smoothed it out on the bed. I wondered if I should ever wear it again." She did not. Mrs. Hopkins stowed it away with the other things that had belonged to her daughter. "The dress was my own. I knew I should wear it again. I fingered the little white buttons as if they had been real pearls. It took a lot of will power to remove the white slippers. I had never worn white slippers before. I brushed them with my face towel, and put them back in the box they had come in, wrapped up in tissue paper. . . . The girls were calling me, but I pretended not to hear. The hour was mine and nothing should interfere with my enjoyment." Tears welled up as she thought of Mrs. Hopkins's kindness. "How good she was! How lovely the things were! They must have cost a lot! The thought of money brought me back to reality."

Another chain of thought started. How would she earn a living? Where would she go? "The thought that I might have to return to Tewksbury after all stabbed my heart. From the peak of happiness I had climbed to that day I tumbled headlong into the Valley of Despond." She had to go to supper. She put Miss Moore's bouquet in a tumbler of water and braced herself for the teasing and chatter that faced her in the dining room. Slowly she left her room, "resolved that nobody should guess that I wasn't the happiest girl in the world, just for one evening."

In the days that followed commencement the uncertainties of her future pressed in upon her. She had not fitted herself for a definite occupation. Miss Moore wanted her to enroll in normal school and prepare herself to be a teacher, and Mr. Anagnos promised to raise the necessary funds so that she should receive instruction in "pedagogy," as he put it.

What he now thought of Annie he put in a later Perkins report, the fifty-sixth, after her success with Helen Keller:

> When she was admitted to this institution, her stock of information was painfully meagre. . . . Hence she was obliged to begin her education from the lowest and most elementary point, but she showed from the very start that she had in herself the force and capacity which ensures success. The furnace of hardships through which she passed was not without beneficent results. . . . An iron will was hammered out on the anvil of misfortune.

She thought she did not want to teach. She had watched the teachers at Perkins toil day after day to teach an uninteresting subject matter with painfully meager results. She was too restless, too eager to experience life in all its richness, to shut herself up in a classroom as a schoolmistress. The music teacher Frank Kilbourne thought he might persuade a Boston lady of his acquaintance to take her on as a governess for her two children. That, too, did not appeal to her. "Well, Miss High and Mighty," Mr. Kilbourne teased her good-naturedly, "perhaps you would prefer to wash dishes in Mrs. D's kitchen." "I would rather wash dishes than be a nursery maid," she insisted.

In anticipation of graduation she had written a letter to Frank B. Sanborn, the head of the State Board of Charities. She wanted him to know that the girl he had plucked from Tewksbury was now about to graduate and that she thanked him for having given her the chance. There was no reply.

Her mind in turmoil, her future unsettled, she put off a decision and went as usual with Mrs. Hopkins to Cape Cod, never imagining that before another year she would have become the private instructor of a blind, deaf and mute child. "Life certainly plays queer tricks on us," she later said of this unexpected turn of events.

part two
TEACHER _and_ HELEN

IV

The Key Is Turned

"The education of this child will be the distinguishing event of my life."

"Something very unpleasant happened to me once, but most of it was very dull in my memory. Perhaps I was sick. I think I was lying in somebody's lap, and suddenly I was raised into a bright light. I felt a great pain which made me scream violently." So Annie wrote about Helen's earliest recollections in the fragment of a report that recently turned up at the Hadley School for the Blind.

> The aunt [Ev, Captain Keller's sister] says she remembers distinctly that a few days after Helen was taken sick, James [her half-brother] went into the sitting room where she was lying on her sofa with her face in the pillow and took her in his arms. As soon as she was raised in the light she "screamed violently."
>
> She seems unable to put into words any of her impressions relative to her illness. She says, "I cannot remember how I felt when the light went out of my eyes. I suppose I thought it was always night and perhaps I wondered why day did not come."

There has never been a definitive diagnosis of the disease that ravaged nineteen-month-old Helen Keller. The family doctor, according to Helen, called it "acute congestion of the stomach and brain." The high fever that had accompanied it subsided "as mysteriously and suddenly as it had come," and then the young mother discovered that her firstborn could no longer see or hear. "Congestion"—like another much overworked medical term at the time, "the flux"—could mean anything.

After Helen's fever abated, her blindness was not total, for she wrote of "the once-loved light, which came to me dim and yet more dim each day." Not even the supposedly curative waters of Eureka Springs, Arkansas, to which her mother and Aunt Ev took her for six weeks, were of any help. Before her illness she had seemed an unusually bright child, walking when she was one year old in pursuit of a sunbeam, delighting the grown-ups with her mimicry of words that her acute ears picked up. "How 'd'ye" and "tea, tea, tea." Even after her illness, she said, she remembered one of the words "I had learned in those early months. It was the word 'water,' and I continued to make some sound for that word after all other speech was lost. I ceased making the sound 'wah-wah' only when I learned to spell the word." Although the world was suddenly sealed off, she had in those first nineteen months seen blue skies and green fields, tall trees and dancing blossoms "which the darkness that followed could not wholly blot out. If we have once seen, 'the day is ours and what the day has shown.'" Recent psychological studies of infancy have confirmed Helen Keller's insight. There is a growing consensus among investigators from diverse fields, Dr. Selma Fraiberg has written, "that the human capacities for love and learning [are] rooted in the first two years of life, the embryonic period of personality development." Her own studies of blind children (*Insights from the Blind*) confirm this observation, for they indicate that children blinded postnatally—as Helen Keller was—are less likely to show "abnormalities in development and behavior" than children blinded at birth.

Helen Keller was born June 27, 1880. Her father, Captain Arthur H. Keller, fought with the Confederate army at the siege of Vicksburg. He was descended of Swiss stock on his father's side. His mother was the great-granddaughter of Alexander Spotswood, the first colonial governor of Virginia. He was an agreeable companion, fond of fishing and hunting, a good shot and a great storyteller. Until 1885 he had been editor and proprietor of the *North Alabamian,* a country weekly that he had turned into a Democratic newspaper. With the election of Grover Cleveland he was appointed U.S. marshal for the Northern District of Alabama, and unable to sell his weekly, he leased it.

Until his appointment as marshal he was always short of ready cash and had engaged in such business ventures as "receiving and forwarding," printing, the sale of lumber and of cows bred by a prize bull. His straitened circumstances were characteristic of much of the Southern upper middle class. His nomination as U.S. marshal was endorsed by the entire Alabama delegation in Congress, and the *Memphis Avalanche* wrote that "Arthur is not only a simon pure Democrat but he is a simon pure man also. He is brave, honest, respected by his fellow citizens and competent." His view of the Civil War was that the South had been the innocent martyr, the North, the mercenary aggressor. He was kind to Negroes, providing they kept their place, were deferential and polite. "We never think of them as human beings," he told a shocked Northern visitor.

Helen's mother was twenty years younger than her husband. She was his second wife; and Arthur Keller already had two sons, James in his early twenties and Simpson, who was thirteen, at the time of their marriage. The new Mrs. Keller was tall and shapely, fair complexioned, with finely molded features and blue eyes. She was a Memphis belle. Her father, Charles W. Adams, a lawyer, had been a brigadier general in the Confederate army. He had come originally from New England and was related to *the* Adams family. Her mother was an Everett and a Sherman, but that was no longer mentioned in the postbellum South. She also had New England connections, and Edward Everett Hale, the famous New England preacher, would later claim kinship with Helen. Mrs. Keller had a lively intelligence, was widely read and had an excellent memory. She was witty and rather high voiced. While the Kellers raised almost everything they needed on their farm, they were not wealthy. There were black servants, but Mrs. Keller toiled from dawn until dinner time, after which she sat down and played a game of euchre with her husband and friends. She did all the sewing for the children and was a wonderful cook. In Memphis she had led the life of a pampered belle; now it was the more rugged life of a frontierswoman. Her husband considered himself "a gentleman farmer who loved to direct rather than work." Kate Adams had, in fact, married Captain Keller in a pique and by the time of Helen's birth realized she had made a mistake. Sometimes she went for days without speaking to her husband. A friend of Helen's later said that Kate Keller "had the most sensitive mouth she had ever seen, that every line of all that she had suffered was there." She was an early convert to woman suffrage.

Tuscumbia was more nearly a village than a town, with but one very broad street through it. This was lined with large houses enveloped in magnolia trees. There were shops, too, on the street; and away from it, out of sight, the Negroes—more than half Tuscumbia's population—lived in dilapidated shacks. Nearby flowed the Tennessee River, its water colored by the red soil through which it ran. The Kellers lived in a large house at the end of a dirt lane. Mrs. Keller's flair for gardening, the magnolias and the large mulberry tree in front had turned it into a place of scented loveliness.

Mrs. Keller was an aloof person, very private, fastidious, whom an error of taste offended more than a real fault. She did not like to acknowledge, scarcely to publish, the difficulties she had in her household, or the dreadful troubles they had with little Helen after she was stricken and before Annie Sullivan took her in hand. Helen's younger sister, Mildred, shared this aversion to talking of unpleasant things. "Teacher insists that two of the more unpleasant letters be destroyed," Helen wrote Mildred in 1933 after the latter had protested the wrong and disagreeable impression of the Keller family circumstances that Helen and others were responsible for spreading about the country. The letters that Mrs. Macy wanted to destroy were two that had been written by Helen's mother, "in which she denied that I was 'a wild, uncouth little creature' before Teacher came to me. . . . There are letters from Cousin Leila, Aunt Ev, Cousin Sally Newsum, Johnny Pope, Mrs. Grace—and I do not know how many more, in which they said just what Teacher says, and what I know from my own actual memories, that I was 'a wild, destructive little animal.' They told how I broke dishes and lamps, how I put my hands into everybody's plates, how I came into the parlor in my red flannel underwear and pinched Grandma Adams, chasing her from the room, which I remember perfectly. There is also a letter in which Uncle Fred told Mother never to bring me to Grandma's house again in Memphis."

In Helen Keller's book *Teacher* she underscored the "grueling" task that Teacher undertook by the portrait of herself as she really was after her illness. She spoke of herself in the third person. "With appalling suddenness she [Helen] moved from light to darkness and became a phantom." She had been the most lively of babies, gay and affectionate. Now there was a desolating "unresponsiveness of tone and look in place of the smile that used to gladden everyone. . . . Helplessly the family witnessed the baffled intelligence as Phantom's hands stretched out to feel the shapes which she could reach but which meant nothing to her. . . . Nothing was part of anything, and there blazed up in her frequent fierce anger which I remember not by the emotion but by a factual memory of the kicks or blows that she dealt to the object of that anger. In the same way I remember tears rolling down her cheeks but not the grief. There were no words for that emotion or any other, and consequently they did not register."

This was not the whole picture of Helen before Annie arrived in Tuscumbia. She had a natural tendency to gesture and with great native intelligence had contrived signs for many things—in fact, they numbered sixty. If she wanted bread and butter, she imitated the motions of cutting bread and spreading butter. A desire for ice cream was shown by the motion of turning the freezer and a little shiver. Putting on glasses meant her father. Knotting hair on the back of her head symbolized her mother. An aunt was represented by tying bonnet strings under the chin, and her baby sister by sucking her fingers. She learned the use of a key and locked her mother in the pantry. She learned to fold and put away clothes after they were ironed. She seemed to have a sixth-sense awareness of what was going on around her. She was fascinated that others used their lips. Her father had his favorite armchair in which he read his newspaper. When he put it down, little Helen clambered into the chair and held the paper before her eyes, in imitation of her father, even putting on his spectacles.

She raged and stormed, but she was also a loving and lovable child. Mrs. Keller was a cultivated Southern woman with a Southern woman's characteristic grace of movement and courtesy of manner. These qualities, too, had lodged somewhere in Helen's mind before she was stricken. There were members of the family, particularly Mrs. Keller's brother, who considered the child mentally defective and urged that she be put away. But Aunt Ev (Miss Eveline Keller), Captain Keller's sister, vigorously disagreed. "This child has more sense than all the Kellers," she insisted, "if there is any way to reach her mind." Aunt Ev adored her. Whatever Helen wanted, she did. Once in the middle of the night Helen awoke and, not knowing the difference between night and day, demanded that she be allowed to get up, dress and have her breakfast. Aunt Ev complied and began her own day at midnight. Aunt Ev came one day to take her for a drive in the surrey, but when Helen's bonnet was tied on Helen pulled it off and threw it to the ground. She did this several times. Then she groped for her nurse and pulled at the bandanna on her head. Light dawned on the grown-ups. Aunt Ev found a handkerchief, tied knots in it like those in the bandanna and put it on Helen. That satisfied her, and she went for the ride and wore the bandanna the rest of the summer.

Kate Keller had read Charles Dickens's account in his *American Notes* of Dr. Howe's success with Laura Bridgman, and although Dr. Howe was dead and Boston very distant, she began to press her husband that perhaps something might be done for Helen. And as Helen grew older and her thwarted passion to communicate produced increasingly violent tantrums, they turned for advice to Dr. Alexander Graham Bell of Washington, inventor of the telephone, whose wife was deaf and who was deeply concerned with teaching the deaf. A letter in the summer of 1886 from Bell to Thomas Gallaudet, himself a figure in American history because of his work with the deaf, announced the visit of Captain Keller and Helen.

> Mr. A.H. Keller of Alabama will dine with me this evening and bring with him his little daughter (age about 6-1/2) who is deaf and blind and has been so from nearly infancy.

> He is in search of light regarding methods of education. The little girl is evidently an intelligent child and altogether this is such an interesting case that I thought you would like to know about it. I am now residing at 1739 Rhode Island Avenue and hope you may be able to look in in the course of the evening.

Dr. Bell urged Captain Keller to write to Anagnos to ask whether he might not have someone able to work with Helen. He did so, and the Perkins director replied immediately and in some excitement: ". . . The case of your little daughter is of exceeding interest to me. Your brief description of her mental activity reminds me possibly of Laura Bridgman, and I would certainly go and see her if the distance which separates us were not so great." He will try to find a competent person. Can Captain Keller let him know what compensation he is prepared to offer?

Anagnos wrote to Annie, who was at Brewster with Mrs. Hopkins, to ask whether she was interested in the position of "governess," and enclosed Captain Keller's letter. "[If] you decide to be a candidate for the position, it is an easy matter to write and ask for further particulars." In Anagnos's annual report for 1887, in which he devoted 38 of its 107 pages to "Helen Keller—A Second Laura Bridgman," he said that his thoughts on reading Captain Keller's letter "were almost instinctively turned towards Miss Annie M. Sullivan. She had just graduated from our school, where she had stood at the head of her class, and her valedictory address —a beautiful original production, teeming with felicitous thoughts clothed in a graceful style—was a revelation even to those who were acquainted with her uncommon powers."

Annie was interested but unsure she could do the job. She returned to Boston and to Perkins to prepare herself, but Anagnos delayed a reply to Captain Keller until he and she were satisfied with her competence. "She studied Laura Bridgman's case in all its phases," he later wrote, "perused voluminous books on mental development, read the reports of Dr. Howe with assiduous care, mastered his methods and processes in their minutest details. . . ." By January 1887 Anagnos was ready to recommend Annie. "She is exceedingly intelligent, strictly honest, industrious, ladylike in her manner and very [word undecipherable]. Her moral character is all that can be desired. The valedictory address which she composed and delivered at the commencement exercises of the institution last June, and which you will find on the 125th page of our annual report, will give you some idea of her literary ability. She is familiar with Laura Bridgman's case and with the methods of teaching deaf, mute and blind children, and I assure you she will make an excellent instructress and most reliable guide for your little daughter."

Captain Keller, on the letterhead of the "Office of U.S. Marshal for Northern Alabama," replied that he was about to go to Washington with "my little daughter to consult an eminent oculist and aurist there. As soon as I shall have done this I will be enabled to determine definitely as to employing a teacher for her, and think it more than probable that I will do so. I would be willing to give Miss Sullivan her board, washing, etc., and twenty-five dollars per month and we would treat her as one of our immediate family." Annie was ready to accept his terms, Anagnos replied. "I have sufficient reason to believe that Miss Sullivan will make an efficient teacher and most excellent companion for your little daughter."

All of Perkins was astir with Annie's forthcoming adventure. The little girls gave her a doll for Helen. Laura Bridgman, with whom Annie spent many hours, made a dress for it and sent a note "to my sister in Christ." Anagnos, Mrs. Hopkins and Miss Fanny Marrett, the teacher who had replaced Miss Moore and to whom Annie had taken immediately, went to the depot to see her off. Anagnos lent her the money for her fare and in a rush of affection gave her a garnet ring.

Annie's ticket was made out incompetently, with many unnecessary changes of train. It was a dreadful journey that took many days. Her eyes bothered her from a recent operation for mild cross-eye.

"Here I am," wrote Annie a year later about her thoughts on arrival at Tuscumbia, "more than a thousand miles from any human being I ever saw before! But somehow I was not sorry I had come. I felt that the future held something good for me. And the loneliness in my heart was an old acquaintance. Anyway, I had been lonely all my life. My surroundings only were to be different."

In Tuscumbia on March 3, the day Annie was expected to arrive, the tension was as great as it had been at Perkins over her departure. The Kellers had been meeting every train for two days. From all the bustle in the household Helen knew something special was about to happen. She went out to the sun-warmed porch, fragrant with honeysuckle, and waited. When the train pulled in, Mrs. Keller was in the carriage to meet it. Annie was surprised by her youth; she seemed no older than Annie herself. "When she spoke, a great weight rolled off my heart, there was such sweetness and refinement in her voice." The fruit trees were in bloom as they drove through Tuscumbia. There was an earthy smell of ploughed fields. "This is a good time and a pleasant place to begin my life's work," she said to herself. They came to a narrow lane. At its end stood Ivy Green, the Keller home. "I became so excited and eager to see my little pupil that I could hardly sit still in my seat. I felt like getting out and pushing the horse faster. I wondered that Mrs. Keller could endure such a slow beast. I have discovered since that all things move slowly in the South."

"I felt approaching footsteps," Helen wrote in *The Story of My Life.* "I stretched out my hand as I supposed to my mother. Someone took it, and I was caught up and held close in the arms of her who had come to reveal all things to me, and more than all things else, to love me." Annie's account, even a year later, was saltier. She ran up the porch steps when she saw Helen standing by the porch door with one hand stretched out as if she expected someone. "Her little face wore an eager expression, and I noticed that her body was well formed and sturdy. For this I was most thankful. I did not mind the tumbled hair, the soiled pinafore, the shoes tied with white strings—all that could be remedied in time, but if she had been deformed, or had acquired any of those nervous habits that so often accompany blindness . . . how much harder it would have been for me! I remember how disappointed I was when the untamed little creature stubbornly refused to kiss me, and struggled to free herself from my embrace. I remember, too, how her eager, impetuous fingers felt my face and dress and my bag which she insisted on opening at once, showing by signs that she expected to find something good to eat in it." Helen later always celebrated March 3 as her "soul's birthday."

When Mrs. Keller took the bag from Helen her

face grew red to the roots of her hair and she began to clutch at her mother's dress and kick violently. I took her hand and put it on my little watch and showed her that by pressing the spring she could open it. She was interested instantly and the tempest was over. Then she followed me upstairs to my room, and she helped me to remove my hat, which she put on her own head, tilting it from side to side, in imitation, I learned afterwards, of her Aunt Ev. When the hat was put away, we opened my bag, and Helen was much disappointed to find nothing but toilet articles and clothing. She put her hand to her mouth and shook her head with ever greater emphasis as she neared the bottom of the bag. There was a trunk in the hall, and I led Helen to it and by using her signs tried to tell her that I had a trunk like it, and in it there was something very good to eat. She understood; for she put both her hands to her mouth and went through the motion of eating something she liked extremely, then pointed to the trunk and me, nodding emphatically, which meant, I suppose, 'I understand you have some candy in your trunk,' and she ran downstairs to her mother, telling her by the same signs what she had discovered. This was my introduction to that bit of my life. . . .

This letter was written a year after her arrival. In the first letter she wrote to Mrs. Hopkins at the time, she said of those first few days, "The greatest problem I shall have to solve is how to discipline and control her without breaking her spirit. I shall go rather slowly at first and try to win her love. I shall not attempt to conquer her by force alone; but I shall insist on reasonable obedience from the start." Even on that first afternoon, when she took out the doll from the Perkins children, she began to spell into Helen's hand D-O-L-L; and later, when she sought to divert Helen from the doll, she spelled out C-A-K-E. Although Helen quickly imitated the hand signs, she made no connection between them and the objects they symbolized, and after an exhausting struggle Annie let her have both. Another grueling contest came at the breakfast table. Annie did not allow her to put her hand into her (Annie's) plate and take what she wanted, as she had been accustomed to do with her family. It became a test of wills —hand thrust into the plate, hand firmly put aside. The family, much upset, left the dining room. Annie locked the door and proceeded to eat her breakfast while Helen lay on the floor kicking and screaming, pushing and pulling at Annie's chair. After half an hour she arose to see what Annie was doing; and when she sensed that Annie was eating, she tried again to put her hand into the plate. Annie still did not allow it, so Helen pinched her. Annie slapped her. This too went on for a time. Helen then went aound the table looking for her family. She discovered no one else was there, and that bewildered her. Finally, she sat down and began to eat her breakfast, but with her hands. Annie gave her a spoon. Down to the floor it clattered, and the contest of wills began anew. Breakfast at last finished, it took another hour to get her to fold her napkin. She let Helen out into the sunshine, and she herself went up to her room and fell onto the bed exhausted. "I had a good cry and felt better."

The family found these battles difficult to witness. "To get her to do the simplest thing, such as combing her hair or washing her hands or button-ing her boots, it was necessary to use force, and of course, a distressing scene followed. The family naturally felt inclined to interfere, especially her father, who cannot bear to see her cry." So Annie persuaded the Kellers to allow them to live by themselves in a little garden house a quarter of a mile away from Ivy Green.

It took enormous courage for Annie, newly arrived in Tuscumbia, to remove Helen from the main house—and persuasiveness; or perhaps it was a measure of Mrs. Keller's forbearance and understanding that she permitted Annie to take the child away from her. "I saw clearly," wrote Annie, "that it was useless to try to teach her language or anything else until she learned to obey me. I have thought about it a great deal, and the more I think, the more certain I am that obedience is the gateway through which knowledge, yes, and love, too, enter the mind of a child." But she could not report progress. "Helen knows several words now, but she has no idea how to use them, or that anything has a name. I think, however, she will learn quickly enough by and by. As I have said before, she is wonderfully bright and active and quick as lightning in her movements."

Her first letters had been to Mrs. Hopkins. On March 13 she wrote Anagnos. The Kellers were very kind people. "Helen, my little pupil, is all that her father described her. It is really wonderful the knowledge the little thing has acquired by the sense of touch and I may add the sense of smell for that sense is very quick. I have not yet been able to tell about her taste. . . . Helen loves dearly to play in the open air and laughs and frolics with the little negroes as if she had all her senses. I find considerable trouble in controlling her. She has always done just as her fancy inclined and it is next to impossible to make her obey. . . . She can spell hat, doll and mug but does not understand the object in making the words yet." Annie told Anagnos that he should come South and visit them while nature was in all its spring finery.

Anagnos was in bed with "fever and general weakness," but he replied immediately. "Helen is truly a remarkable child," he said in a letter that suggested the germination of hopes that here indeed might be a second Laura Bridgman—one in whose liberation he, too, might have a part. "Strive by every means to conquer and control her. When you achieve this, you will have no difficulty with her. I learned through Mrs. Hopkins that you and Helen keep house by yourselves. That is a movement in the right direction, and it will help you more than anything else to overcome all difficulties."

Having moved into the little house, Annie's worst ordeal was ahead. Its furnishings had been rearranged so that Helen did not know where she was, and her father had taken her for a walk in the woods and led her to it by a strange path to ensure that she did not recognize the place. "Her father stopped by every morning on his way to town to look at them through the windows," Cousin Leila later recalled, "but never to let Helen know that he was near. One morning he saw Helen on the floor —the picture of despair—still in her nightgown—her breakfast untasted over on the little table. She was in a bad humor when she waked up or maybe Miss Annie did not understand what the trouble was. When she gave Helen her shoes and clothes to put on she threw them away and would not dress—so could not have breakfast until in a good humor and dressed.

"Uncle Arthur," Leila's recollection continued, "a splendid man, large and fine looking and a genuine Christian came to my room with his eyes filled with tears. He said, 'Leila I have a great mind to send that Yankee girl back to Boston. It is ten o'clock and poor little Helen has not been allowed to have breakfast. She is still in her gown looking so miserable and Miss Annie will not let her have breakfast until she dresses.' His sister, Ev Keller, was present, she always had the faith that Helen would come into her own. . . . She said, 'No, Arthur—you must not feel that way. Miss Annie is going to be Helen's salvation. We must be patient—she knows best. Helen must learn obedience and feel her dependence upon her. . . .' "

A week after they moved into the small house—the same day, in fact, on which Anagnos had written that she should "conquer her"—the deed was done. "My heart is singing with joy this morning," she wrote Mrs. Hopkins. "A miracle has happened! The light of understanding has shown upon my little pupil's mind, and behold, all things are changed!

"The wild little creature of two weeks ago has been transformed into a gentle child. . . . She lets me kiss her now, and when she is in a particularly gentle mood, she will sit in my lap for a minute or two; but she does not return my caresses. The great step—the step that counts—has been taken. The little savage has learned her first lesson in obedience, and finds the yoke easy. It now remains my pleasant task to direct and mould the beautiful intelligence that is beginning to stir in the child-soul. Already people remark the change in Helen. . . ."

We long to know more about this remarkable conversion. Helen does not talk of it; for her the great event was the key that was soon to turn in her mind and unlock the mystery of language. What combination of natural disposition on the part of the little pupil and brilliant insight into the proper mixture of affection and firmness on the part of the teacher transformed violent anger and raging willfulness into obedience and self-control? What combination of fear and love shaped the will to useful purposes rather than broke it?

The Kellers were unhappy over the separation from Helen, and within the month Annie and Helen were moved out of their "bower" back to Ivy Green. Sensing that her power over Helen gave her power over the parents, Annie made them promise in return not to interfere in any way. That first evening at dinner, the pledge was forgotten. Helen, thinking to test her return to the family dining table, refused to use her napkin. Annie started to take her out of the room, but Captain Keller "objected and said that no child of his should be deprived of food on any account."

Annie taught her to sew and crochet. At eleven o'clock they did gymnastics. Twelve to one, they learned new words. "But you mustn't think this is the only time I spell to Helen; for I spell in her hand everything we do all day long, although she has no idea yet what the spelling means." Here was the germ of an important difference between Annie's way of teaching Helen and Dr. Howe's methods with Laura. The latter worked tirelessly to teach Laura how to communicate, but he was not the child's daylong companion. He had many other concerns. Dr. Howe was a scientist and teacher, Annie a substitute mother, the child's alter ego. Helen now slept in her bed. Mrs. Keller had wanted to get a nurse, but Annie decided she would be the nurse. "I like to have Helen depend on me for everything and I find it much easier to teach her things at odd moments than at set times."

Helen took her "second great step" in her education two weeks after she had learned to obey. They had been wrestling with the words *M-U-G* and *W-A-T-E-R*, recorded Helen, and she persisted in confusing the two.

Later they went for a walk by the well-house. Someone was pumping water. Annie placed Helen's hand under the spout and "as the cool stream gushed over one hand, she [Annie] spelled into the other the word water, first slowly, then rapidly. I stood still, my whole attention fixed upon the motions of her fingers. Suddenly I felt a misty consciousness as of something forgotten—a thrill of returning thought; and somehow the mystery of language was revealed to me. I knew then that W-A-T-E-R meant the wonderful cool something that was flowing over my hand. . . . I left the well-house eager to learn. Everything had a name, and each name gave birth to a new thought. As we returned to the house every object which I touched seemed to quiver with life."

In Annie's letter to Mrs. Hopkins about the "miracle," she wrote: "She has learned that everything has a name and that the manual alphabet is the key to everything she wants to know. . . . Helen got up this morning like a radiant fairy. She has flitted from object to object, asking the name of everything and kissing me for very gladness. Last night when I got into bed, she stole into my arms of her own accord and kissed me for the first time, and I thought my heart would burst, so full was it of joy."

With her first month's salary, Annie repaid Anagnos the money he had lent her for her fare South. He wanted none of it. She should wait until she had a bank account, and if she needed any more money he would be happy to send it. "I need scarcely say that I am deeply interested in your little pupil. She certainly is a remarkable child. I have asked Mrs. Hopkins to write to you, that it will be well to obtain a blank book and keep an exact account of what she learns and does every day. . . . I have no doubt that ere long she will be able to talk, and then you will be a Caesar or Bonaparte. A biographical sketch of Helen should also be written and preserved." He was not above a little flirting. He was confident of her final success, "provided the citadel of your heart resists the bombardment of some physician, for which profession you seem to have an incurable weakness." Annie had written that the Keller family doctor was giving her lessons in horsemanship.

Helen now pressed forward eagerly, exultantly, to learn the names of everything she encountered. Her face daily grew more expressive as she acquired new words. Annie shifted her focus in teaching her, and in this, too, she moved beyond Dr. Howe: "It occurred to me the other day that it is absurd to require a child to come to a certain place at a certain time and recite certain lessons when he has not yet acquired a working vocabulary. I sent Helen away and sat down to think. I asked myself, 'How does a normal child learn language?' The answer was simple. 'By imitation.' The child comes into the world with the ability to learn, and he learns of himself, provided he is supplied with sufficient outward stimulus. He sees people do things, and he tries to do them. But long before he utters his first word, he understands what is said to him. . . ." Henceforth she intended to talk into Helen's hand "as we talk into the baby's ear. I shall assume that she has the normal child's capacity of assimilation and imitation. I shall use complete sentences in talking to her, and fill out the meaning with gestures and her descriptive signs when necessity requires it; but I shall not try to keep her mind fixed on any one thing. I shall do all I can to interest and stimulate it, and wait for results."

"Helen is a truly wonderful child," she wrote to Anagnos. "She knows almost three hundred words and is learning five or six a day. Their length does not seem to make any difference to her. . . . I suppose Laura's teachers did not teach her titles, because they thought she would not perceive the difference between the name and the title, but I have made Helen pause after Mr., Mrs., or Uncle, as the case may be, and when she is a little farther advanced I can very easily explain this to her. . . . Whenever I give her a new word, especially a word expressing action, like *hop* or *jump,* or any of those already mentioned, she throws her arms around me and kisses me."

Annie had become suspicious of the special systems of education that she had read about during her preparatory period at Perkins. "They seem to be built up on the supposition that every child is a kind of idiot who must be taught to think. Whereas, if the child is left to himself, he will think more and better, if less showily. Let him go and come freely, let him touch real things and combine his impressions for himself, instead of sitting indoors at a little round table, while a sweet-voiced teacher suggests that he build a stone wall with his wooden blocks or make a rainbow out of strips of colored paper, or plant straw trees in bead flower-pots. Such teaching fills the mind with artificial associations that must be got rid of, before the child can develop independent ideas out of actual experiences."

She reports another success to Anagnos and also trouble with the Kellers. "She is becoming attached to me and I can see that she obeys more from love than because she thinks she must. She is naturally so imitative and so easily controlled when away from her parents that I feel sure if she could only be away long enough she would become a lovely and lovable woman. She inherits a quick temper and a good deal of obstinacy, but I think she is learning to control her temper and if her obstinacy can be turned in the right direction, it may serve her well." But the family was a trial. "They do not pay the slightest attention to my request that I should be the only one to give her words." Captain Keller had told her the word *gone,* whose meaning she did not know. "You can see what a bad effect this is going to have on her development."

She sensed her growing indispensability to Helen; she sensed, too, that it gave her a hold over the Kellers, especially Helen's mother. But she used that power cautiously, especially with the Captain. She warned Anagnos that she saw breakers ahead in her relations with Captain Keller. He sent for Helen "whenever he pleases, and of course this interference is very annoying to me and harmful to Helen." He had sent for her in the middle of a lesson, and although Helen did not want to leave her work, "I was obliged to make her go. She was not willing to come back and Captain Keller would not insist upon it, so we have both had a vacation."

The letter to Anagnos was warmly affectionate. There was no one "whose admiration more highly or whose good opinion I shall strive harder to deserve than yours." She congratulated him on the opening of the kindergarten and praised his perseverance in the face of difficulties. She hoped that now he would give his "poor brain the rest it must be needing," and assured him in a postscript that "the citadel is not in the least danger of being captured" by the doctor.

She also assured Anagnos that she was not overworking Helen. Whenever the child became restless, they went outdoors or she let Helen out to play. They took long walks after breakfast through the strawberry-scented countryside to Keller's Landing on the Tennessee, about two miles from Ivy Green. "I feel as if I had never seen anything until now, Helen finds so much to ask about along the way." They catch a butterfly and it becomes a sacrificial victim to a lesson in botany. "Her mind grows through its ceaseless activity." When they return home, Helen eagerly reports to her mother, who has learned the manual language, all they have seen. "This desire to repeat what has been told her shows a marked advance in the development of her intellect, and it is an invaluable stimulus to the acquisition of language. I ask all her friends to encourage her to tell them of her doings, and to manifest as much curiosity and pleasure in her little adventures as they possibly can."

Annie was alive to the wonders of a child "so spontaneous and eager to learn. . . . It is a rare privilege to watch the birth, growth and first feeble struggles of a living mind; this privilege is mine; and moreover, it is given me to raise and guide this bright intelligence." She felt the inadequacy of her preparation. "[M]y mind is undisciplined and full of slips and jumps. . . . How I long to put it in order. Oh, if only there were someone to help me! I need a teacher quite as much as Helen. I know that the education of this child will be the distinguishing event of my life, if I have the brains and perseverance to accomplish it. I have made up my mind about one thing: Helen must learn to use books—indeed, we must both learn to use them, and that reminds me—will you please ask Mr. Anagnos to get Perez's and Sully's Psychologies? I think I shall find them useful."

She needed better teaching materials and turned to Anagnos: "My little pupil can now read every word she can spell. When she reaches a word she knows her face grows radiant and if by any chance she finds part of a sentence that conveys any meaning to her mind her joy is unbounded." But to have to feel through whole books to find a few familiar words seems too bad. "She became very angry a few days ago, because I could not find Helen or Simpson [her brother's name] in her book, and all I could do would not make her touch the book the remainder of the afternoon." Would Anagnos, if she sent him a list of common words any child might use, have them printed in blocks? Captain Keller was willing to pay.

By June the strenuous exertions of pupil and teacher were beginning to tell on both of them. Annie complained of headaches and an inability to sleep. "Sometimes I get so nervous that I cannot stay in bed." The rumor that another Laura Bridgman miracle was in the making was getting about. Anagnos asked her to have a photograph taken to send to him. She was invited to write a paper for the *Alumnae,* a Perkins publication. "Of course, I declined. Here I have the care of this child for seven to eight hours a day besides at the table. She [the editor] must think I have lots of time to write papers, allowing I had the ability." Her eyes bothered her. "I have stopped reading Byron because I thought it was hurting my eyes."

Helen had become so nervous and excitable they had to call in the doctor. "She is restless at night and has no appetite." The doctor said her mind was too active, "but how are we to keep her from thinking? She begins to spell the minute she wakes up in the morning and continues all day long. If I refuse to talk to her, she spells into her own hand, and apparently carries on the liveliest conversations with herself." The people who worried that Annie was overtaxing Helen's brain exasperated her.

They were the same people who a few months earlier had asserted that she had no mind at all. "But so far nobody seems to have thought of chloroforming her, which is, I think, the only effective way of stopping the natural exercise of her faculties."

The two were out of doors most of the time, and work was really a form of play. Annie would describe a vine as a "creeper." The idea that plants moved amused Helen. Did they also, as she did, run, hop, skip, bend, fall and climb? She was a "walk-plant," she announced to her teacher. To Helen the most earnest study "seemed more like play." She wrote later that her teacher had an intuitive understanding of her pleasures and desires. "Whenever anything delighted or interested me she talked it over with me as if she were a little girl herself." Everything out-of-doors contained a lesson, which Annie spelled into her hand vividly and with an uncanny flair for the right detail. "Indeed, everything that could hum, or buzz, or sing, or bloom, had a part in my education. . . ."

On June 19 Annie sent Anagnos a detailed report on Helen's progress, one that he would include verbatim in his annual report for 1887:

> If it is not too late will you please have these words added to the list I sent and when you send them please put in two or three square hand alphabets and a writing board. I have written to Miss Bennet for a few things in the kindergarten and which you may include in the bill.
>
> My little pupil continues to manifest the same eagerness to learn as at first. Every waking moment is spent in the endeavor to satisfy her innate desire for knowledge and her mind works so incessantly that we have feared for her health. But her appetite which left her a few weeks ago has returned and her sleep seems quiet and natural. She will be seven years old the 27th of this month. Her height is four feet one inch and her head measures twenty inches in circumference, the line drawn around the head and passing over the prominences of the parietal and frontal bones. Above this line the head rises one inch and one fourth. The two other measurements that Dr. Howe made of Laura's head, I do not know how to take.
>
> There is seldom a cloud seen upon her face and we observe that it grows brighter every day. She is always ready to share whatever she has with those around, often keeping but very little for herself. She is very fond of dress and all kinds of finery and is very unhappy when

she finds a hole in any thing she has on. She will insist on having her hair put in curl papers when she is so sleepy she can scarcely stand. She discovered a hole in her boot the other morning and after breakfast she went to her father and spelled "Helen new boot Simpson (her brother) buggy store man." One can easily see her meaning. During our walk she keeps up a continual spelling and delights to accompany the spelling with actions as skip, hop, jump, run, walk fast, walk slow and the like.

When she drops stitches she says, "Helen wrong, teacher will cry." If she wants water she says, "Give Helen drink water." She knows four hundred words, not counting the numerous proper nouns. In one lesson I taught her these words, bedstead, mattress, sheet, blanket, comforter, spread, pillow. I found the next day that she remembered all but spread. The same day she learned at different times these words, house, weed, dust, raspberry, swing, molasses, fast, slow, maple sugar, counter. She had not forgotten one of these last.

This will give you an idea of what a retentive memory she possesses. She can count up to thirty very quickly and can write seven of the square hand letters and the words which can be made with them. She seems to understand about writing letters and is impatient to "write Frank letter." She enjoys punching holes with the stiletto. I supposed it was because she could feel the result of her work, but we watched her some time ago and I was much surprised to find that she imagined herself writing a letter. She would spell Eva (a cousin of whom she is very fond) with one hand, then make believe write it, then spell "sick in bed" and write that. She kept this up for nearly one hour. She was or imagined she was putting on paper the things which had interested her. When she had finished she brought it to her mother and spelled "Frank letter" and gave it to her brother to take to the office. She has been with me to take letters to [the] Post Office. She recognizes instantly a person she has ever met and spells the name. Unlike Laura, she is fond of gentlemen. We notice that she makes friends with a gentleman sooner than with a lady. When a gentleman is about to leave Helen always kisses him, but will seldom kiss a lady. In fact, I think her mother and myself are the only ladies she will allow to caress her. This is owing, I think to the fact that she sees more gentlemen than ladies and they always make much of her.

I have tried to give you some idea of my little charge as she appears after four months of instruction. I need scarcely say that her progress is gratifying to me as I am sure it is to you. If I succeed in laying a good foundation on which more accomplished teachers may build the superstructure, I shall feel that my first effort was not a failure and that I accomplished something by coming South.

I shall be grateful for any suggestions you may offer from your store of experience as to what and how she should be taught. I feel that from this time on everything connected with Helen's education is extremely important to her and I often feel myself very incompetent to do the work which seems to have fallen to me. I trust the good she will realize will be proportionate to the pleasure I receive from teaching her.

But to her real confidante, Mrs. Hopkins, she wrote with greater self-assurance. "I am glad Mr. Anagnos thinks so highly of me as a teacher. But 'genius' and 'originality' are words that we should not use lightly. If, indeed, they apply to me even remotely, I do not see that I deserve any laudation on that account."

Yet deep down a different voice spoke within her. She sensed her powers as a teacher. "And right here I want to say something which is for your ears alone," her letter to Mrs. Hopkins went on.

Something within me tells me that I shall succeed beyond my dreams. Were it not for some circumstances that make such an idea highly improbable, even absurd, I should think Helen's education would surpass in interest and wonder Dr. Howe's achievement. I know that she has remarkable powers, and I believe that I shall be able to develop and mould them. I cannot tell how I know these things. I had no idea a short time ago how to go to work; I was feeling about in the dark; but somehow I know now, and I know that I know. I cannot explain it; but when difficulties arise, I am not perplexed or doubtful. I know how to meet them; I seem to divine Helen's peculiar needs. It is wonderful.

Already people are taking a deep interest in Helen. No one can see her without being impressed. She is no ordinary child, and people's interest in her education will be no ordinary interest. Therefore let us be exceedingly careful what we say and write about her. I shall write freely to you and tell you everything, on one condition: It is this: you must promise never to show my letters to any one. My beautiful Helen shall not be transformed into a prodigy if I can help it.

The woman who wrote this letter was twenty-one years old.

V

No Room for a Lover

"I have found a real friend—one who will never get away from me."

During a summer visit to Huntsville, Alabama, with her father, Helen wrote her first letter. It was to her mother. It was in pencil on paper fitted over a grooved writing board. Helen formed the letters in the grooves, guiding the pencil with the forefinger of her left hand, in a script called "square-hand." When Annie showed Mrs. Keller a letter she had received from Laura Bridgman, Mrs. Keller exclaimed, "Why, Miss Annie, Helen writes almost as well as that now!" And Annie commented to Mrs. Hopkins, "It is true."

Anagnos was unable to contain his pride and pleasure. He printed the letter verbatim in his annual report, as Dr. Howe had done with Laura Bridgman's letter forty-eight years earlier. Helen Keller's knowledge acquired in four months exceeds that of Laura Bridgman in two years, he commented. Her letter to her mother was "superior in every respect" to the letter that Laura had written at ten years of age. Helen's letter read:

Helen will write mother letter papa did give helen medicine mildred will sit in swing mildred will kiss helen teacher did give helen peach george is sick in bed george arm is hurt anna did give helen lemonade dog did stand up conductor did punch ticket papa did give helen drink of water in car carlotta did give helen flowers anna will buy helen pretty new hat helen will hug and kiss mother helen will come home and mother does love helen

good-by

On Helen's return from Huntsville she told her mother what she had seen, especially during the drive to the top of a nearby mountain. "She remembers all that I told her about it," wrote Annie, "and in telling her mother repeated the very words and phrases I had used in describing it to her." She did so with one significant difference. She asked her mother whether she too would not like to see the "very high mountain and beautiful *cloud caps.*" Annie had not used that expression. She had said, "The clouds touch the mountain softly, like beautiful flowers." Helen had never seen a mountain, "and I don't see how anyone is ever to know," Annie went on, "what impression she did receive, or the cause of her pleasure in what was told her about it. All that we do know certainly is that she has a good memory and imagination and the faculty of association."

A new educational challenge arose for Annie when Cousin Leila had a baby. This inevitably produced a torrent of questions such as "Where do new babies come from?" "From the beginning I have made it a practice

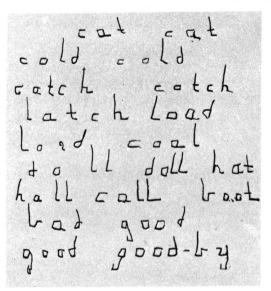

A sample of Helen's writing, June 20, 1887. Courtesy American Foundation for the Blind

Helen will write mother
letter papa did give hel-
en medicine mildred
will sit in swing
mildred will kiss
helen teacher did give
helen peach
... george is sick in
bed george arm is hurt.
anna did give helen
lemonade dog did
stand up.
conductor did punch
ticket papa did give
helen drink of water
in can
carlotta did give helen
flowers ann will buy
helen pretty new hat
helen will hug and kiss
mother helen will come
home grandmother does
love helen

good-by

to answer all Helen's questions to the best of my ability in a way intelligible to her, and at the same time, truthfully." She had no reason to treat the processes of reproduction differently, she decided, except that she herself was deplorably ignorant of biology, "of the great facts that underlie our physical existence." So she and Helen retired to the tree up whose branches they had often climbed to read, taking with them this time Annie's botany textbook on *How Plants Grow.* "I told her in simple words the story of plant-life," proceeding to animal life, "but the function of sex I passed over as lightly as possible.* I did, however, try to give her the idea that love is the great continuer of life." Helen's quickness of compre-

*By contemporary standards of child development and education, Annie's replies to Helen's questions left her almost wholly ignorant of human reproduction.

hension confirmed Annie in the view that "the child has dormant within him when he comes into the world, all the experiences of the race. These experiences are like photographic negatives, until language develops them and brings out the memory-images."

The summer heat was oppressive, not conducive to the writing of letters. Finally, however, Annie got around to thanking Anagnos for sending her the words in block letters that she had requested. "If you could have seen Helen's joy as her fingers discovered each familiar name or object you would have been made very happy." She enclosed a letter Helen had just written her cousin George in Huntsville. It would give Anagnos a better idea of her command of language than anything Annie herself might write. It was in this letter that she told Anagnos about the beautiful letter Helen had written her mother, "but Mrs. Keller will not part with it."

Annie's satisfaction and pleasure in Helen's development rang in every sentence. "Never did a teacher have more reason to be proud of a pupil. A sweeter or brighter child it will be impossible to find. . . . I feel I have accomplished something worth while in the world. I am prouder of having made a gentle, lovable child of her than I should be of teaching her Greek and Latin.

"I have trials here," her letter went on, "but they are of a nature I will not try to describe in a letter. I will tell you my troubles when I have the pleasure of conversing with you." Without trials, she went on philosophically, "there would be no victories. I have been contented most of the time, and I have tried to do my best for my pupil all the time." Helen now knew 575 words and had mastered "the multiplication tables as high as five and has learned the Braille system." Then Annie let out her secret hope: "If her parents would only consent to her going to Boston I should be so glad. There I would have an opportunity to improve. I know so little about the kindergarten system and cannot get the materials to work with her." Would Anagnos please send her two writing boards and two or three square-hand and Braille alphabets?

Anagnos replied quickly. He sensed Annie's restlessness, and from experience had learned that when such a mood was upon her she would be readier to let fire with her trigger-quick anger at family members who might challenge her methods. He had read her letter with "profound interest," he replied. Helen's progress was remarkable, and the letter to her Cousin George that Annie had enclosed was indeed "the best and most convincing proof of the marvellous work, which has been accom-

plished during the past six months." Then the letter continued with a
pause and renewed salutation to underscore the importance of what he
was about to say.

> Dear Annie, I am aware of the many difficulties of your position and
> of the thorns which are scattered in your pathway: but take as little
> notice of them as possible. Remember always the following words of
> Horace,—*Tu ne cede malis, sed contra audiator ito,* which may be inter-
> preted in your case—'Yield not to trials, but on the contrary, meet
> them with fortitude.' Do not allow yourself to be troubled by petty
> annoyances, or to remember them and harbor ill feelings even tempo-
> rarily against anyone, however ignorant or indiscreet he or she may
> be. Look steadily at the polar star of your work, and I have not the
> slightest doubt but that you will weather all storms and reach the port
> of success. Perseverance, patience, tact, and charity will help you
> conquer the most formidable difficulties. Then the crown will be
> yours as the prize of victory. Your strenuous efforts have been so far
> richly rewarded, and you have good reasons to be proud of your
> achievements.

Some of Annie's trials, as she called them, during those first months in
Tuscumbia arose from the mores and emotions of a South that, unrecon-
ciled to the abolition of slavery, had simply replaced it with the doctrine
and practice of white supremacy. Annie underwent no greater cultural
shock in the shift from Tewskbury to Perkins than she did in the move
from Boston to Tuscumbia. Among her most vivid memories at Perkins
was the day her teachers had taken all the pupils to the State House in
Boston, "to touch the tattered flags and trophies preserved there, and
listen to their [the teachers'] account of the sufferings of our soldiers who
were taken prisoner in the South. I was seldom so sincerely in accord with
their views as I was on that day when Miss Newton, I think it was, said
that the bullet-riddled flag was the most sacred symbol in the world to all
Americans."

Annie's friends in Boston had cautioned her against her saucy tongue
and quick temper, especially in talking about the Civil War. They warned
her to steer clear of it as well as the racial issue. On the anniversary of of
her arrival in Tuscumbia she wrote to Mrs. Hopkins that indeed "I have
lived peaceably with all men, except Uncle Frank, and all women too.
There have been murder and arson in my heart; but they haven't got out.

. . . The arrogance of these Southern people is most exasperating to a Northerner. To hear them talk, you would think they had won every battle in the Civil War, and the Yankees were little better than targets for them to shoot at!''

Mrs. Keller was an enlightened woman with a saving sense of wit, whose poise and delicacy of manner Annie so much admired that she tried to imitate them, but on the subject of the Civil War she would say simply that "the Southern side was so right that it was distressing to think about it." Kate Keller appreciated, however, that Annie had feelings on the subject, too, and as an employee might be dismissed but was not to be abused. But her brother-in-law, Uncle Frank of Knoxville, on his visits to Tuscumbia, seemed to go out of his way to flaunt his unrepentant Confederate views before her. He was bitter, argumentative and vindictive and never lost a chance at meals to bait her with slurring remarks about Sumner, Grant, even Lincoln. Finally Annie's restraint yielded to outrage:

"You take advantage of my position in this family to get even with the North for winning the war and taking your slaves from you," she flung at him. "The things you say to injure my feelings, and the bucketfuls of abuse you pour upon the heads of our army is part of the spirit that created Anderson Prison."

Captain Keller came to the defense of his brother. Annie was outrageous, he said, ignoring the provocation that had given rise to her retort. She was prejudiced and ignorant. Captain Keller's joining forces against her was more than she would take. She rose from the table, moved to the door, stopping only for a parting gibe: "Don't talk to me of Southern courtesy. I have had enough of it," and out she went to pack her bags.

The angry words appalled Mrs. Keller. She followed Annie upstairs where she found her preparing to leave Tuscumbia forever. She acknowledged that Annie had good reason to get angry, but Uncle Frank's bitterness, she went on kindly, was not unnatural, since he had lost his sons and many friends in the war. Annie softened. "Helen helped me unpack my things, and I was soon so interested in teaching her new words that I forgot about Uncle Frank."

There were other occasions on which she started to pack her bags because of "unendurable rudeness" relating to the Civil War. Each time she decided that "despite the loneliness and the insults to my patriotism and pride which I had to endure, my work interested me." The Southern attitude toward the Negro bewildered her. White Southerners treated him as a subhuman, and "to behave towards them as equals" was a cardinal offense. "Always there was a pain in my heart when I thought about the colored people," but she decided there was nothing she could do about it. "The Negroes themselves made it rather easy to acquiesce in white folks' belief in their superiority."

It is doubtful that Helen was aware at the time of these clashes. She was accustomed to playing with black children; and one in particular, Martha Washington, the daughter of their cook, was her constant companion. She understood Helen's signs. "It pleased me to domineer over her and she generally submitted to my tyranny rather than risk a hand-to-hand encounter." Helen was six and Martha two or three years older. A few months before Annie's arrival, she and Martha were sitting on the porch steps cutting out paper dolls. They wearied of this, and Helen began to cut off the "little bunches of fuzzy hair tied with shoestrings sticking out all over her head like corkscrews," and Martha in turn began to cut off Helen's curls "and would have cut them all off but for my mother's timely interference." Although this vignette has the appeal of a childhood memory, the way it was told by Helen later in life suggests, that despite her blindness and deafness, the germs of racism may have taken root early.

Scarcely less distressing to Annie than the code of white supremacy were the rituals of male superiority. She encountered them in their crudest form at a visit to Mrs. Keller's brother, Fred Adams of Memphis. She was prejudiced against him anyway, because he was the kinsman who had said to Mrs. Keller, "You ought to really put that child away, Kate, she is mentally defective and it is not very pleasant to see her about." Now he was amazed by the improvement in Helen. He could not get over it. He further annoyed Annie by ignoring her. "He rarely deigned to acknowledge my existence. He talked about Helen's improvement as if I were not present." He held strong views about the role and status of women. "I would rather see Helen and Louise [his daughters] die right now than to have them work. I can't imagine a daughter of mine having to work, to take orders from an employer."

Southern men in general, noted Annie, "spoke disparagingly of girls who were ambitious, and wanted to make their own way in the world." Their concept of femininity required that women be shielded from the world of work (except in the home, where the alternative was for the men to work themselves) and from corrupting ideas. Captain Keller came into the living room to find his wife and Annie absorbed in reading Thomas Hardy. He took the book and threw it into the fireplace.

Tradition, and nostalgia for the antebellum South, kept Captain Keller from acting on his more generous impulses. He became fascinated with Tolstoy's *What Is Religion?* This is real religion, he informed his wife and Annie, real religion, that we should turn the other cheek. At that moment some Negroes came down the road, a little drunk and boisterous. Captain Keller went outside, yelled at them, and shot his pistol into the air. Why did he not put some of that religion into practice? asked Kate Keller when he came back into the room. He flung Tolstoy on a shelf and never looked at the book again. "He would face forward," recalled Annie, "take two or three encouraging steps, then rightaboutface, and he would run backward as far as he had progressed."

As cynical as Annie became of Southern males, she developed a deep admiration for Southern women. "It seemed to me that the burdens of life were carried by them. I had many opportunities of observing the selfishness of the men. The much talked-of chivalry was a very thin veneer. If a servant left the 'lot,' it was the woman who looked after the animals. If a hod of coal was needed, it was the woman who got it while three or four men sat around talking politics or playing cards. Never in those early days did I see a white man who did any little job round the house or farm."

Captain Keller was neighborly and genial and considered "everything Southern desirable, noble and eternal," but despite Annie's partiality for men, it was Kate Keller whom she really admired. She made her own butter, lard, bacon and ham. She was celebrated for her preserves and dried fruits. "Hers was a hard life. From dawn she was at it—too tired when night came to protest against the hunting-dogs' occupation of the hearth." Her life was shadowed by Helen's affliction. "Fate," she said to Annie when they got to know one another better, "ambushed the joy in my heart when I was twenty-four, and left it dead." But she found time to read and tend her flowers and to raise the most beautiful roses Annie had ever seen outside of a hothouse.

She had also given birth to a second child: "Wednesday was Mildred's birthday," Annie reported to Mrs. Hopkins. "She was one year old, and Mrs. Keller gave a dinner by way of celebrating the event. We obeyed the Scriptural injunction to eat, drink and be merry, but we didn't die, although we ate a turkey, a roast pig, and an unheard quantity of other good things." Southern women were fine cooks, she went on. "The frugal North never tasted such delicious viands as are concocted here. I'd rather be a good cook than the Czar of Russia—a good dinner is a great achievement. I particularly like the smell of a roast pig, and a broiled partridge fills my soul with delight!"

Over the years Annie and Kate Keller would develop a deep and understanding relationship. Cousin Leila and Ev also took to this Yankee from the North. "I don't know just what we Kellers thought of her at first," recalled Cousin Leila, "but it was not long before we had the greatest respect and affection for her." She remembered Annie as a woman of dignity and cordiality with a voice that was soft and sweet. "One of the first things we had to do after she came was to see that there was always bakers' bread for her as she did not care for our Southern hot breads. We Kellers detested bought bread and never ate it if there was anything else to be had. After a few days she was persuaded to just try a hot cornmeal muffin and from that time on I don't believe she ever looked at a slice of cold light bread."

Aunt Ev, Helen's champion, was struck at her first meeting by Annie's "poise, affability and cheer in manner and speech and especially in her attitude towards Helen, which was assumed 'as a companion.' . . . The amiable, tender attitude towards Helen's nervousness and anxiety to be in with the talk of others and immediate communication with Helen on the subject attracted my attention and interest." Miss Sullivan gained a great deal, but "the greatest beneficiary was Helen."

Then this discerning woman went on to say, "No one can judge how much Helen owes to her originality and suggestion of ideals. Certain it is the great mind of Miss Sullivan absorbed, digested and fed Helen's mind and heart until she was independent, and that independence was greatly due to Miss Sullivan's determination to make her so, even to the choice of language and manner." Even if we make allowances for the fact that these remarks were recorded long after Helen and her Teacher had become world famous, they suggest that Annie and her Southern hosts—certainly the women—got along better than Annie's inner pressures, the constant need to strike back at those she considered luckier and less burdened than she, allowed her to admit.

She herself acknowledged (in her interviews with Nella Braddy Henney) that although she remained quite conflicted about the South, "in less than a year a remarkable change came over me. My mind opened to a different understanding of history from that taught at Perkins. My outlook on life became more liberal. . . . As the days passed, and I understood the South better, my cocksureness and complacency suffered many a rude shock. In less than six months I had sheathed my flaming sword of righteousness, and quelled the nonchalance of the crusader spirit I brought with me from Boston."

In his letter urging patience, perseverance, tact and charity, Anagnos had earnestly petitioned her to prepare for inclusion in his forthcoming report "a brief account of Helen's history and education, giving her age, the cause of her blindness and deafness, her temperament, her natural aptitudes, the steps taken and the methods employed in her training, and what has already been accomplished." She should do this for her own sake and for the credit of her alma mater, "and after saying 'oh dear! oh dear!' as many times as you please, pray go right to work and write a little every day until the paper is finished."

"I do not wonder you were surprised to hear that I was going to write something for the report," she wrote Mrs. Hopkins. "I do not know myself how it happened except that I got tired of saying 'no' and Captain Keller urged me to do it. He agreed with Mr. Anagnos that it was my duty to give others the benefit of my experience. Besides, they said Helen's wonderful deliverance might be a boon to other afflicted children." She would take his advice, she wrote Anagnos at the same time, "and notice as little as possible the unpleasant things connected with my position. There are pleasant ones enough to occupy my spare moments and if my royal turn of mind is to be gratified by wearing the *crown,* all will be well." She had worked on the report but was not getting very far. "I wish you had asked me for the facts and put them together yourself." She thanked him for the writing boards and alphabets. "When I told Helen that Man had sent them to her, she said, 'Man is good. Helen does love Man.'"

Although she complained to Mrs. Hopkins that her thoughts froze when she sat down to write, and when she did get something on paper "they look like wooden soldiers all in a row, and if a live one happens along, I put him in a strait-jacket," within two weeks the report—approximately 3,100 words—was finished. It gainsaid her sense of insecurity as a writer. In publishing it verbatim as part of his report, Anagnos said that it told "concisely, but with force and clearness, the simple facts relating to the education of one of the most remarkable children in existence. . . ." He was sure that scholars, men of science, indeed, all thinking persons, would find it "of profound interest."

Delicately, subtly, Annie was setting her nets and bait to catch the prize that she most wanted, but scarcely hoped for—a trip to Boston. "My most persistent foe," she wrote Mrs. Hopkins, "is that feeling of restlessness that takes possession of me sometimes. It overflows my soul like a tide, and there is no escape from it. It is more torturing than any physical pain I have ever experienced. I pray constantly that my love for this dear child

may grow so large and satisfying that there will be no room in my heart
for uneasiness and discontent." Helen became her co-conspirator in promoting the trip to Boston. Annie told her how the little blind girls at
Perkins had just returned from their vacations; and Helen, needing little
encouragement, decided to write them a letter:

> Helen will write little blind girls a letter Helen and teacher will come
> to see little blind girls Helen and teacher will go in steam car to
> boston Helen and blind girls will have fun blind girls can talk on
> fingers Helen will see Mr. Anagnos Mr Anagnos will love and kiss
> Helen Helen will go to school with blind girls Helen can read and
> count and spell and write like blind girls Mildred will not go to
> boston Mildred does cry prince and jumbo will go to boston papa
> does shoot ducks with gun and ducks do fall in water and jumbo and
> mamie do swim in water and bring ducks out in mouth to papa Helen
> does play with dogs Helen does ride on horseback with teacher
> Helen does give hardee grass in hand teacher does whip hardee to
> go fast Helen is tired Helen will put letter in envelope for blind girls
>
> good-by
> Helen Keller

The child's letter captivated Anagnos. He had to include it in his report
because it is "as charming as [it] is indicative of the wonderful progress
which she has made in so short a time under your care and tuition."

The children at Perkins were equally excited, and for days they busied
themselves putting together a reply to Helen. The latter was already
turning into an indefatigable letter writer, and on October 24 she wrote
again:

> dear little blind girls
> I will write you a letter I thank you for pretty desk I did write to
> mother in memphis on it mother and mildred came home wednesday
> mother brought me a pretty new dress and hat papa did go to hunts-
> ville he brought me apples and candy I and teacher will come to
> boston and see you nancy is my doll she does cry I do rock nancy to
> sleep mildred is sick doctor will give her medicine to make her well
> I and teacher did go to church sunday mr lane did read in book and
> talk lady did play on organ I did give man money in basket. I will be

good girl and teacher will curl my hair lovely. I will hug and kiss little blind girls mr. anagnos will come to see me.

good-by

Helen Keller

"I am aware that the progress she has made between the two letters must seem incredidable [sic]. Her passion for letter writing and putting her thoughts upon paper grows more intense. . . ." wrote Annie. Anagnos made clear in his report how thoroughly impressed he was: "That the little witch could, in the course of twenty-five days, make such strides in the acquisition of language, and the enlargement of her vocabulary, as are indicated by this letter, seems almost incredible. Yet the evidence before us is so clear and conclusive that it leaves no room for the slightest doubt. Pronouns are undoubtedly the most difficult part of speech for children

Courtesy American Foundation for the Blind

to learn and use correctly, and Helen's employment of them is one of the most noticeable features of her last composition."

The speed of Helen's progress in the acquisition and use of words does seem remarkable. It was as if Annie's turning of the key to her mind had released the word-hunger that is a characteristic of children of Helen's age in whom impressions outrace vocabulary. For five years the process of matching words to impressions had been dammed up, and now she was furiously fitting labels to experiences that were stored up somewhere in her memory, as well as the new ones that crowded in upon her. "The rapidity with which Helen absorbed language and formed concepts of her surroundings," Teacher told Nella Braddy, "suggests the waking from a dream. It actually seemed to me as if she were rubbing her mental eyes and saying to herself, 'Oh yes, I saw that a long time ago!'"

In her commentary on Helen's progress, Annie referred with pathos to Helen's discovery that she was unlike other children and disclosed also how desolating her own blindness had been. "The other day she asked, 'What do my eyes do?' I told her that I could see things with my eyes and she could see them with her fingers. After thinking a moment she said, 'My eyes are bad,' then changed it to 'My eyes are sick.' What a blessing it is that she will never realize fully her great loss. If I thought she would ever suffer from a knowledge of her deprivation, as I have suffered from mine my courage would fail me."

Helen completed her conquest of Mr. Anagnos by sending him a letter for his birthday, which he "could not resist the temptation to publish":

dear mr anagnos I will write you a letter. I and teacher did have picture, teacher will send it to you. photographer does make pictures. carpenter does build new houses. gardener does dig and hoe ground and plant vegetables. my doll nancy is sleeping. she is sick. mildred is well uncle frank has gone hunting deer. we will have venison for breakfast when he comes home. I did ride in wheel barrow and teacher did push it. simpson did give me popcorn and walnuts. cousin rosa has gone to see her mother. people do go to church sunday. I did read in my book about fox and box. fox can sit in the box. I do like to read in my book. you do love me. I do love you.

good by
Helen Keller

Anagnos replied immediately, as we learn from Annie. "Helen is de-lighted with your letter," she informed him. "It is surprising to see the pleasure which a letter affords her. She seems to value a letter more than any sweetmeat or plaything and she will have it read to her until she knows every word it contains." Then, in language more cordial and generous than she had ever before used, she went on:

> My dear Mr. Anagnos how shall I ever thank you for the trouble and expense you are taking to make my pupil's progress known. I feel deeply indebted to you for the many kindnesses I have received at your hand. I cannot tell what a help your sympathy and interest have been to me during the months that have just passed. If I had not been certain of both I doubt if November would have found me at my post. The thought that you were pleased with my efforts has given me courage and patience and sometimes I have need[ed] both. But I will not try to express the love and gratitude which I feel.

But to Mrs. Hopkins she wrote more cautiously, irritated by Anagnos's tendency to overstate her accomplishments. "Have you seen the paper I wrote for the 'Report'? Mr. A was delighted with it. He says Helen's progress has been 'a triumphal march from the beginning,' and had many flattering things to say about her teacher. I think he is inclined to exagger-ate somewhat. At all events, his language is too glowing, and simple facts are set forth in such a fashion that they bewilder one. Doubtless the work of the past five months does seem like a triumphal march to him; but then people seldom see the halting and practical steps by which the most insignificant success is achieved."

Annie's false modesty was sometimes accompanied by a touch of malice, as can be seen in her comments about a classmate who had been assigned by Anagnos to help a little deaf-blind child. "I had a letter from Lillie last week. She said, Edith is a bright, active child but had the temper of a little 'tygeress.' She added that it was very hard to control Edith because Mr. Anagnos 'posatively' refused to have her punished. So far she has learned only a 'fiew' nouns, but she 'entends' to give her verbs very soon. Poor Lillie—or should I rather not say, poor Edith! I didn't suppose that a more incompetent girl could be found to undertake the education of an unfortu-nate child than myself; but I think Lillie has me beaten by a head at least."

She recognized that there was a streak of maliciousness in her. In her memoir of life in Tuscumbia, when she spoke of Uncle Frank's having been "argumentative, aggressive, and vindictive," she added, "as I was." And in this softening of Annie Sullivan, Helen—who met the world with a disarming and open affection—played her part. Helen had turned the whole Christmas season into an event of radiance and love. "Helen's delight with her gifts, and the interest other children took in her were very touching," she wrote Anagnos. "We had many proofs of the sweetness and the goodness of her disposition during the week. At one of the Christmas trees she discovered a child who had not received a present. She seemed very much troubled for a few moments then her face became radiant and she spelled to me. 'I will give Nellie mug.' The mug was one of the presents which afforded her great pleasure. She had chosen her prettiest gift and the one which had pleased her most to give to a little stranger. Such an instance of self-denial so simply and so naturally done, is most gratifying in a world so full of selfishness."

The Kellers were deeply moved at the difference that Helen's enjoyment of this Christmas had made in their own ability to enjoy the festivities. When Annie came down on Christmas morning, Mrs. Keller met her with tears in her eyes. "Miss Annie, I thank God every day in my life for sending you to us; but I never realized until this morning what a blessing you have been to us." Captain Keller took her hand, but was unable to speak. "But his silence was more eloquent than words."

"You may tell Mr. Anagnos," another letter to Mrs. Hopkins said, "that he need not fear I shall fall in love with the Good Doctor [the local physician]. I have something better to do. My work occupies my mind, heart and body, and there is no room in them for a lover. I feel in every heart beat that I belong to Helen, and it awes me when I think of it—this giving of one's self that another may live. God help me make the gift worth-while! It is a privilege to love and minister to such a rare spirit. It is not in the nature of man to love so entirely and dependently as Helen. She does not merely absorb what I give, she returns my love with interest, so that every touch and act seem a caress."

And Helen concluded the chapters in her story that dealt with the months from her teacher's arrival in Tuscumbia to Christmas, 1887, in almost the same words: "My teacher is so near to me that I scarcely think of myself apart from her. How much of my delight in all beautiful things is innate, and how much is due to her influence, I can never tell. I feel that her being is inseparable from my own, and that the footsteps of my life are in hers. All the best of me belongs to her—there is not a talent, or an aspiration or a joy in me that has not been awakened by her loving touch."

The key to Helen's conquest of her teacher was in Annie's remark that it was not in the nature of men "to love so entirely and dependently as Helen." Until Annie's arrival at Perkins, everyone whom she had really loved—her mother, Jimmie—had been taken from her. Helen not only had an extraordinarily affectionate nature, but Annie could feel secure that her love would continue. In late May when Mrs. Hopkins had confessed to her own loneliness since Annie's departure, she wrote back, "Indeed, I can understand your yearning to be loved. Have I not all my life been lonely? Until I knew you, I never loved anyone, except my little brother, and I have always felt that the one thing needful to happiness is love. To have a friend is to have one of the sweetest gifts that life can bring, and my heart sings for joy now; for I have found a real friend—one who will never get away from me, or try to, or want to."

VI

The Conquest of Boston

"Child of the spotless brow."

Eighteen hundred and eighty-eight was a year of triumph for Annie and Helen. On New Year's Day Annie wrote Mrs. Hopkins that Mrs. Keller's two brothers from Memphis had come to Tuscumbia for Christmas turkey:

> I made Helen as pretty as possible. I tied her curls with red ribbons and put on a red sailor-suit trimmed with silver braid, which is very becoming, and gave her minute directions as to her behavior. When the dinner-bell rang, I waited until all were seated, so that our entrance might be all the more impressive. It would have done your heart good to see the way they stared! When I introduced Helen to her uncles, she kissed them demurely and quietly went to her own place. She did look pretty, and carried out my instructions to the letter. . . . Mr. Adams exclaimed, 'Is it possible, Kate, that this is Helen?' After dinner Helen displayed her accomplishments for the benefit of her uncles. Her father gave her problems in arithmetic, and she wrote their names and her own for them.

A few days later Anagnos sent her a copy of the report that would make both Helen and her teacher famous. "Of all the blind and deaf-mute children," his report began, "Helen Keller of Tuscumbia, Alabama, is undoubtedly the most remarkable. It is no hyperbole to say that she is a phenomenon. History presents no case like hers. In many respects, such as intellectual alertness, keenness of observation, eagerness for information, and in brightness and vivacity of temperament she is unquestionably equal to Laura Bridgman; while in quickness of perception, grasp of ideas, breadth of comprehension, insatiate thirst for solid knowledge, self-reliance and sweetness of disposition she certainly exceeds her prototype." Anagnos buttressed his claims with quotations from Annie's letters and with Helen's own letters in facsimile. Those letters, he said, "presented in chronological order, are sufficient in themselves without comment or explanation to show that their tiny author is a most extraordinary little individual. . . . In view of all the circumstances her achievements are little short of a miracle."

He went on to praise the miracle worker, placing her on a level with Dr. Howe. "Miss Sullivan's talents are of the highest order. In breadth of intellect, in opulence of mental power, in fertility of resource, in originality of device and in practical sagacity she stands in the first rank." Then, in a paragraph that he came to regret when he and Annie fell out, he said: "She undertook the task with becoming modesty and diffidence, and accomplished it alone, quietly and unostentatiously. She had no coadjutors in it, and there will therefore be no plausible opportunity for any one to claim a share in the origin of the architectural design of the magnificent structure because he or she was employed as helper to participate in the execution of the plan."

"The report came last night," Annie wrote Mrs. Hopkins. "I appreciate the kind things Mr. Anagnos has said about Helen and me; but his extravagant way of saying them rubs me the wrong way. The simple facts would be so much more convincing! Why, for instance, does he take the trouble to ascribe motives to me that I never dreamed of? You know, and he knows, and I know, that my motive in coming here was not in any sense philanthropic. How ridiculous it is to say I had drunk so copiously of the noble spirit of Dr. Howe that I was fired with the desire to rescue from darkness and obscurity the little Alabamian! I came here simply because circumstances made it necessary for me to earn my living, and I seized upon the first opportunity that offered itself, although I did not suspect, nor did he, that I had any special fitness for the work."

Anagnos was given to hyperbole. He was the classic schoolmaster, and his rococo paragraphs were studded with quotations from the poets and the ancients. Annie was right in that regard, but she was wrong in saying that Anagnos had not discerned in her a gifted woman. Perhaps the key to her irritation with Anagnos was his failure to give her enough credit by his reference to the debt she owed Dr. Howe. She already resented suggestions that she, "the miracle worker," had had some help. To Anagnos she wrote in a more kindly vein than to Mrs. Hopkins: "I have read the report with great pleasure, especially the pages devoted to myself. I hardly know how to describe the satisfaction I felt at being thus spoken of by you. . . . But my dear Mr. Anagnos, you could not say anything that would give me half the happiness your friendship does. I value it highly, how highly you must judge by the efforts I make to prove worthy of it. . . . I look back over the year which is past with more satisfaction that I remember ever to have felt before."

She was unhappy with Mrs. Keller. Helen's mother had learned the manual language in order to be able to communicate with her child, but "instead of making Helen describe things in her own language, thereby learning to express herself freely and naturally," Mrs. Keller, eager to be helpful, rushed in with descriptions of her own. "It is easier to tell than to make the child tell," Annie lamented to Anagnos. Was this just pedagogical dissatisfaction with an interfering parent, or was it part of Annie's unconscious drive to displace Mrs. Keller? Aware as Mrs. Keller was of Annie's indispensability to Helen, Teacher's gradual assumption of a mother's prerogatives must have caused Mrs. Keller considerable agony. Annie had many reasons for wanting to go to Boston, but not least among them was the sense that at Perkins she would have Helen to herself. "If you would only find it in your heart," her letter to Anagnos continues, "to give your poor head a rest and come here and see if you could not induce her family to let Helen spend a few months in Boston each year, you would be doing *yourself* and *Helen* an invaluable service and affording *me* great pleasure."

Annie wanted Helen not only to acquire a large vocabulary and to spell the words correctly, but to be able to use them freely and accurately. That was why from the time Helen had grasped that all objects have names that can be communicated through certain movements of the fingers, she had talked to her exactly as she should have done had Helen been able to hear. Helen's tendency was to use shortcuts. "She would say, 'Helen milk.' I would get the milk to show her that she had used the correct word, but I would not allow her to drink it, until she had, with my assistance, made a complete sentence, as 'give Helen some milk to drink.' " She accustomed her, too, to the use of different forms of expression for conveying the same idea. "If she were eating some candy, I would say, 'will Helen please give teacher some candy?' or 'teacher would like to eat some of Helen's candy,'—emphasizing the 's." New experiences generated a search for new expressions, and as she learned "more of the world about her, her judgment acquires accuracy, her reasoning powers grow stronger, more active and subtle, and the language by which she expresses this intellectual activity gains in fluency and logic."

A journal Helen began to keep at about this time shows how her daily experiences were translated into enlargement of her vocabulary.

Jan. 9, 1888   Apples have no edges and no angles. Apples grow on trees. They grow in orchards. When they are ripe they fall on the ground. . . .

March 1, 1888   Oranges look like golden apples hanging on the trees. They have a thick skin, and inside is the sweet juicy pulp and seeds. All boys and girls like oranges to eat. Bananas have a thick, smooth skin, and hang on trees in long branches.

I learned what view means. People can see view trees and flowers and grass and hills and sky is view. Worms squirm. After supper I talked to teacher and played with Mildred and went to bed.

Experience was translated into words, and words were communicated by writing and by manual language. "It has become so natural for her to use the finger language as a vehicle for the expression of her thought, that each idea, as it flashes through her busy brain, suggests the words which they should embody. Indeed, she seems always to think in words. Even while she sleeps, her fingers are spelling the confused and rambling dream-thoughts."

Annie's warm thank-you letter of January 13 hoping to prove worthy of his friendship set Anagnos aglow with love and pride. Busy as he was with trying to raise funds for the kindergarten, he wanted her to know "I use no formal phrase in saying that I am deeply interested both in you and your work and that I love you and take as much pride in you as if you were my daughter." The part of his report that related to Helen, he informed her, was being printed as a pamphlet, "as well as in Mr. [Edward Everett]

Hale's monthly magazine 'Lend a Hand.' "* He signed himself "with much love," and in a postscript added a few lines "to dear little Helen, which please give to her with my love. Please do not fail to forward to me whatever she writes to me regardless of its quality."

Anagnos's report let loose a hurricane of publicity. The skeptical and credulous, theologian and scientist, poet and philosopher, all were fascinated by his account of this phenomenal child. As in the case of Laura Bridgman, religious leaders in particular saw in Annie's report as well as in Anagnos's paeans a vindication of the soul's existence—that, contrary to Darwin and the materialists, the soul was indeed a reality, touched by the divine spark. In December the celebration of Laura Bridgman's completion of fifty years at Perkins had verged on a religious service.

But Laura was a frail, wispy woman, fifty-eight years old, with a trite mind and stereotyped religious views, who had been sermonized about so lengthily that the public had become a little jaded. "Poor staid Laura Bridgman," Dr. Hale himself later wrote, "who had been brought up in all the conventionalities of the most rigid New England propriety, used to say that Helen was crazy. It was the craziness of sweet natural love." Chestnut-haired Helen, with her radiant, loving personality, ceaseless mental activity and originality of expression provided proof anew that man was touched by the divine. Dr. Hale on reading Anagnos's report not only asked to reprint it, but wrote Captain Keller "boldly," as he put it, claiming kinship with little Helen since they were both Everetts. Helen acknowledged Dr. Hale's letter, and it was the beginning of a cordial and intimate relationship. "I am happy to write you a letter this morning. Teacher told me about kind gentleman. I shall be glad to read pretty story I do read stories in my book about tigers and lions and sheep. I am coming to Boston in June to see little blind girls and I will come to see you. . . ." There was a letter, too, from Dr. Bell. He wrote, according to Annie, that "Helen's progress is without parallel in the education of the deaf, or something like, and he says many nice things about her teacher." "Dear Dr. Bell," Helen—not Annie or Captain Keller—wrote him in reply:

---

*Hale was one of the great New England divines and social reformers. He had formed his Lend a Hand Society in 1871, and it now constituted a national network of clubs, whose motto, composed by Hale, stated:

> Look up and not down:
> Look forward and not back;
> Look out and not in—
> Lend a Hand!

I am glad to write you a letter. Father will send you a picture. I and Father and aunt did go to see you in Washington. I did play with your watch. I do love you. I saw doctor in Washington. He looked at my eyes. I can read stories in my book. I can write and spell and count. good girl. My sister can walk and run. We do have fun with Jumbo. Prince is not good dog. He can not get birds. Rad did kill baby pigeons. I am sorry. Rad does not know wrong. I and mother and teacher will go to Boston in June. I will see little girls. Nancy will go with me. She is a good doll. Father will buy me lovely new watch. Cousin Anna gave me a pretty doll. Her name is Allie.

Good-by, Helen Keller.

In addition to Anagnos, another culprit in spreading the news of the Tuscumbia "miracle"—if "culprits" they should be considered—was Dr. Bell, who in 1888 furnished a New York newspaper with a picture of Helen and one of her letters to him. But Bell could do no wrong in Annie's eyes. And in fact she enjoyed the praise and comment, even if she was not willing to admit it in regard to some persons or on some occasions. "I was gratified to read what the *Nation* had to say about Helen last week," she wrote Mrs. Hopkins. On a visit to Memphis along with Captain Keller, they were besieged. "I believe half the white population of Memphis called on us. Helen was petted and caressed enough to spoil an angel; but I do not think it possible to spoil her, she is too unconscious of herself, and too loving." But when she tried to get Helen to write her Uncle Frank, she objected to writing in pencil. She would write in Braille, she said. But he cannot read Braille, Annie pointed out. When she finally persuaded her to write a few lines in pencil, she broke the point six times. "You are a naughty girl," Annie said. "No," she replied, "pencil is very weak." Annie thought she objected to pencil writing because "she had been asked to write so many specimens for friends and strangers. You know how the children at the Institution detest it." But did Helen? Or was her teacher projecting onto the child her own feelings?

"Indeed, I am heartily glad that I don't know all that is being said and written about Helen and myself," she confided to Mrs. Hopkins. "I assure you I know quite enough. Nearly every mail brings some absurd statement, printed or written. The truth is not wonderful enough to suit the newspapers; so they enlarge upon it and invent ridiculous embellishments." Although Tuscumbia was difficult to reach, reporters were seeking them out. One knocked on the door after all were in bed. He wanted to interview Miss Sullivan, he informed Captain Keller, who had gone to the door. The Captain sent him away.

The great events that both she and Helen were looking forward to were Anagnos's visit and, even more, their own impending trip to Boston. "Our plan is to reach Boston in time for the closing exercises."

Helen's journal for March was full of entries relating to Mr. Anagnos. As he set out on a trip to the South that brought him to Tuscumbia, he sent Helen a geographical reader: "It tells about the world and countries, and people and strong forces and water. . . ." "Teacher had a letter from Mr. Anagnos," she noted on March 7. "He is in Florida. He will climb trees on ladder and pull sweet oranges. . . . Mr. Anagnos will go to Tuscumbia to see us. He will tell me about Macon and Florida. I will hug and kiss him. . . ." March 22: "Mr. Anagnos came to see me Thursday. I was glad to hug and kiss him. He takes care of sixty little blind girls and seventy little blind boys. I do love them. Little blind girls sent me a pretty workbasket. . . . I will write little blind girls a letter to thank them. . . . Mr. Anagnos went to Louisville Monday to see little blind children. . . . I did learn about calm. . . . It means quiet and happy. . . ." March 26: "I had a letter from Mr. Anagnos. He does love me. He saw thirty-four little blind girls and forty-one little blind boys in Nashville, Tennessee. There are thirty girls and forty boys in school for blind children in Louisville Kentucky. Mr. Anagnos sent me four hugs and five kisses. Today I did learn to write examples on the type slate and I learned many new words. Flock does mean many birds near together. Brood means six little chickens. . . . Observe means to look at everything very carefully. I observed teacher's hair was coiled this morning."

Anagnos's letter to Annie showed a significant deepening in their relationship. "I state a simple fact when I say that I take as much interest in you and in the success of your work as if you were my own daughter. In fact I consider you as such, and I am proud of what you have already accomplished. . . . Believe me, my dear Annie, with much love and paternal greetings." And from Cincinnati the next day he wrote even more affectionately, "Dearest child, I can hardly tell you how glad I was to receive your very kind letter in Louisville. . . . Pray write to me when you can. Take good care of yourself and do not hesitate to let me know if you have any trouble."

Anagnos was in his early fifties, a widower and childless. Into this pool of loneliness, twenty-two-year-old Annie cast her next note. ". . . I am going to ask a favor of you—something to please me very much. Will you do it? When you have plenty of time and feel like writing to me, will you do so freely? I would like so very much to be a grown-up 'daughter' to you. Will you let me?''

Annie was trying to rewrite in a simple style, presumably in Braille, a few stories for Helen. "I'm obliged to be extremely careful, and get them just as I want them, at first, because the little witch has such a wonderfully retentative [sic] memory that she can remember the thread of a tale after it has been read to her once, and she does not like for me to change it in the slightest particular. I will send you by today's mail, several numbers of her diary, also a story which she wrote in Braille after having read it once. Of course it is considerably changed, especially in the forms of expression, and in the construction of sentences. But she has not omitted a single essential idea. . . . If one of the Magazines would like to publish a facsimile it might help your cause." Annie was impatient to start homewards, "but Captain Keller has his heart set upon our stopping over in Washington to see the President and Mrs. Cleveland. So I suppose we must. . . . Helen sends you six kisses and ten hugs. . . .''

Annie was an original, a young woman of great strength; she was also a flirt. She knew the arts and wiles of pleasing men, particularly older ones. Anagnos replied instantly to her offer to be a "grown-up daughter" to him. "I think of you and of your noble work and of your little but wonderful pupil so constantly, that I must give expression to my thoughts now and then." Her letter had been handed to him that morning just as he was setting off for a quarterly meeting of the Perkins trustees, "but I read it more than twice. . . . I consider you as my daughter and I take great pride in your achievements. If you were my own child, I could hardly love you any more or be more proud of you than I am now. You will not therefore be surprised if I tell you that I feel considerable anxiety about your overworking yourself, and I beg of you most earnestly, yes, I command you not to do more than is absolutely necessary between now and the first of June. Let the stories and tales alone." Morrison Heady, a deaf and blind poet who lived in Kentucky, had begun a correspondence with Helen, and Anagnos was glad that "Uncle Morrie," as Helen called him, was going to prepare some stories in Braille for Helen. "Remember that, if you break down, you cannot be of service either to Helen or to yourself. We want you to come to us well and sound. Now, pray give heed to this earnest, paternal admonition, for it comes directly from my heart. . . . To dearly beloved Helen I send a bundle of kisses and hugs. Tell her I love her little blind children, but she is my darling."

Four days later he again wrote her:

> After writing to you last week I received the portions of Helen's diary and the little story in pencil which you were so very good to send me. I have just finished reading them carefully, and I find that the progress she is making in fluency of expression, in breadth of ideas, in variety of conceptions and coherency of thought, is as great as ever, but judging by the entries in the diary, I am inclined to think that you deem it necessary to teach the child as much as possible. This is contrary to my poor advice. As I have already told you, Helen needs no regular lessons *at present.* She must play and be in the woods and in the open air most of [the] time. She must romp in the fields, gather wild flowers, chase Mildred, caress the dogs, examine the hens and chickens, make mud pies and do all sorts of things of a similar kind. The health of the child is of greater importance than her rapid development, and I trust that you will pay more attention to the former than to the latter. Forgive me, dearest friend, for this little lecture, which was suggested to me by Helen's writings.

He enclosed a note to "My darling Helen." "I thank you very much for the little story which you wrote in pencil and which teacher sent me. It was a very great pleasure to me to read it as well as the parts of your diary which I received with it. Our blind girls have just returned from their homes after a week's vacation, and I will tell them tomorrow morning all about my visit to Florida and Tuscumbia." It was cold in Boston, but by June "it will be very pleasant" and "many, very many friends in Boston will be glad to see you all, and I will be delighted to have you here."

Alas, the price of parenthood, even of the foster variety, is to refrain from admonitions, not to mention commands. Beneath the affectionate tone of Annie's response, steely signals glinted. "I did not mind the 'little lecture' the least bit. This does not mean that I shall not endeavor to do as you advised in all things in regards to my dear little pupil. I like very much to have you make suggestions, and it gives me great pleasure to do as you wish. And, will you please remember that 'commands' are quite unnecessary. I dislike them from those I love; but I will gladly do anything you wish me to."

She did take his advice about Helen's education. "Owing to the nervousness of Helen's temperament, all attempts to confine her to a regular and systematic course of instruction have been abandoned, and every precaution has been taken to avoid unduly exciting her already very active brain . . . [but] she continues to manifest the same eagerness to learn as at first. She seems never to tire of gathering new facts and ideas. From the time when she rises in the morning until she retires at night, she never rests, and any little scrap of knowledge, which comes within her reach, she seizes with avidity. It is never necessary to urge her to study. Indeed, I am often obliged to coax her to leave an example or a composition."

Anagnos recorded the same. Regular instruction had ceased as of "March last. . . . Nevertheless, it is utterly impossible to prevent her studying. . . . Her hunger for knowledge is insatiate. She is always on the *qui vive* for something new which seems beyond her reach. No sooner does one begin to converse with her, than the interrogatives, 'why,' 'how many,' 'who,' 'what,' 'when,' and 'where,' fly from her fingers in rapid succession."

The trip to Boston was much on their minds. The directors of the Sheffield Sand Company and the Alabama Presbytery held meetings in the vicinity of Tuscumbia. "Both the speculators in land and religion wished to see the wonderful little girl of whom they had heard so much." They bored Annie, but Helen delighted in their attention, and portrayed in pantomime what she intended to do up North, especially on Cape Cod during the summer, and "at last with a natural grace all her own [she] dropped upon the floor and showed them how she would swim." One of the ministers had Annie ask Helen, "What do ministers do?" She said, "They read and talk loud to people to be good."

Boston created anxieties for Annie. "Do you think the Bostonians will be disappointed in Helen?" she wrote Anagnos. "I am afraid they will, because they are expecting so much of the dear child. If her parents will not allow her to stay at the Institution a few months, do you know what I am going to do? I shall write to the Duke of Norfolk and ask him if he does not want me to teach his son?" She commiserated with Anagnos over his money-raising difficulties. "It does seem strange to me that the Boston people do not open their moneybags and give you the hundred thousand."

The principal of the Normal School in Florence, Alabama, had invited Annie to talk to the teachers-in-training on the education of the blind. The invitation pricked an insecurity, and her response was irritation. There was nothing "ridiculous" in the invitation, Anagnos replied reassuringly. It seemed to him natural and reasonable, and he wished she could accept it. As to her anxiety about Helen's reception by Boston, "Many Bostonians will be delighted to see Helen, and I do not think there is a living person endowed with average intelligence who can be disappointed in her." As for the letters that were arriving as a result of the publicity, she should answer those that seemed to merit a reply. "Use your judgment and exercise as much charity towards your fellow men and women as you possibly can." He proposed to write Captain Keller and renew his offer to have Helen and Annie spend several months at Perkins in the autumn free of expense. "I think he will consent to it. But whether he will do so or not, your work, my dear child, is with Helen and not with the sons of dukes and princes. Stick to it under all circumstances, face all its sides bravely, and let the future take care of itself. This is the deliberate advice of one who believes in you implicitly, who loves you as his own daughter and who will always be ready and glad to be of service to you and to help you in all your efforts."

"Mother is making me pretty new dresses to wear in Boston and I will look lovely to see little girls and boys and you," Helen wrote him at the beginning of May. Before she left for Boston, her uncle took her to a medical convention in Cincinnati on the slight hope that some specialists there might be able to help her sight or hearing. They were not, but she was made much of by the hundreds of physicians and their families. Six months later when Annie asked her whom she had seen in Cincinnati, "she unhesitatingly spelled more than a hundred names; and she also remembered the states and cities in which many of these gentlemen resided." Her memory was extraordinary.

True to his promise, Anagnos in mid-May did urge Captain Keller to permit Helen and her teacher to remain at Perkins in the autumn. "The child must not be confined to a mere routine of instruction. She must have all the advantages which she can derive from the equipment of a school, from the best appliances for the illustration and from the association with other children. Moreover, her teacher must be posted in the simplest and most approved methods of instruction."

Helen, Annie and Mrs. Keller left for Boston via Washington, where Dr. Bell came to visit them. The "Professor," as Annie called him, had annoyed the Kellers because he had turned over Helen's letter to him to Professor Joseph Jastrow, who had published a facsimile in *Science Monthly* along with pictures of Annie and Helen. "The family were considerably displeased that such a use had been made of what was meant for Mr. Bell's private pleasure." But the Kellers also knew how obligated they were to Dr. Bell for having directed them in the first place to Perkins and Anagnos. Besides, he was a great man. The visit was a success. Dr. Bell rejoiced in Helen's progress, talked with her and later sent her a toy elephant. "Mr. Bell came to see us," Helen wrote about the visit. "He talked very fast with his fingers about lions and tigers and elephants. He was very kind to send me a fine elephant." She then went into an item-by-item description of the characteristics of "real elephant," which ended, "When wild animals hunt the elephant he is very angry and he strikes them with his tusks."

Helen, Annie and Mrs. Keller also were received by President Cleveland. "We went to see Mr. Cleveland," Helen narrated. "He lives in a very large and beautiful white house, and there are lovely flowers and many trees and much fresh and green grass around. And broad smooth paths to walk on. . . . Mr. Cleveland was very glad to see me." But Annie was disappointed. Mrs. Cleveland, whose coiffure and dress she had copied at commencement, did not appear.

They arrived in Boston on May 26 and went directly to Perkins. "On finding that almost every one whom she [Helen] met understood her language, she was overjoyed." Helen entered with delight into the occupations of the blind children, modeling in clay, learning beadwork and knitting. She carefully examined the school apparatus, embossed maps, typewriters built specially for the blind and physiological models.

And Anagnos also pressed her into service. Commencement exercises were scheduled for June 6, as usual in Tremont Temple, but there were two drawbacks this year: There were no graduates, and the little children from the kindergarten, which had just finished its first year, were unable to take part because there had been an outbreak of scarlet fever among them. But these deficiencies "were perhaps more than counterbalanced," wrote Anagnos, "by the unexpected contribution to the interest of the occasion made by little Helen Keller." There was an overflow crowd in the Temple as usual. The pupils' brass band performed. Ten little boys were examined in mental arithmetic. Then Helen appeared. There were three tables. At one a girl read fluently by touch. At the second table another girl read a pretty poem about flowers. At the third table Helen stood with Annie. As the moment approached for her to perform, her face glowed, her frame quivered. With the fingers of her left hand she read in embossed type a little poem telling what the birds do, at the same time translating with her right hand into Annie's palm what she was reading with the left, which Annie gave orally to the audience, "and so rapid were the movements of her little fingers, that the three processes of reception, transmission and expression of ideas became simultaneous." The whole story, noted Anagnos, was acted out with such "an electric play of gestures and of features, an unconscious eloquence of the whole body, that she seemed inspired." Then she skipped gracefully back to her seat, her face radiant. The great audience, which had been gripped by sympathy for this lovely child, ended up enthralled.

They stayed with Anagnos until Perkins closed for the summer. They visited the William Endicotts at Beverly Farms. With Annie, her mother and Mrs. Hopkins, Helen inspected the Bunker Hill monument at Charlestown, and she was told about the battle that had been fought there. As she climbed the steps to the top of the monument (stating afterward that there were 292), she wondered whether the soldiers, too, had climbed the stairway and shot at the enemy below. They took a boat to visit Plymouth, and on the way Annie told her the story of the Pilgrims.

Anagnos provided an interesting sidelight on this trip to Plymouth. "For six weeks I have had the rare pleasure of sitting by her side at the table, and of walking, playing, romping and travelling with her constantly, and only once during this period did I see her exhibit a spirit of impatience. This occurred during a visit to Pilgrim Hall at Plymouth, where, after examining various articles, such as a model of the 'Mayflower,' a spinning wheel, Peregrine White's cradle, and several ancient chairs, tables and utensils, she was very much disappointed because everything was not explained to her minutely, and because she was not allowed to lay her hands on the contents of the cabinets, and on all the precious relics that are treasured in that sacred shrine." Beneath the sweetness there was a streak of stubbornness, even willfulness.

In mid-July Annie and Helen went to Cape Cod to spend the rest of the summer with Mrs. Hopkins. They left a lonely Anagnos: "It is very quiet here and I miss you, dearest child, more than I can tell you. My desk is as crowded and disorderly as of old, and its condition reminds me constantly of the good care which you bestowed upon it during your visit. . . . Pray give my kindest regards to Mrs. Hopkins, and six kisses and as many hugs to dear Helen, and believe me, with much love for yourself. . . ." Annie's letters to Anagnos during the stay at Brewster on the Cape have not survived, but the nature of her letter of the fourteenth may be surmised by Anagnos's prompt reply: "I am exceedingly sorry, that Miss C. failed to introduce you to the ladies as she ought to have done;

but you must remember that she is inclined to be absent-minded, and I doubt not that her omission was the result of thoughtlessness rather than of premeditated intention. She is a good woman, and would not hurt anyone's feelings intentionally." This became a recurrent problem for Annie as Helen and she became world celebrities. She was easily hurt, and later complained to Nella Braddy of the hostesses who lionized Helen and treated her as hired help.

"It is not as lonesome in the house now as it was last week," Anagnos's letter went on, "but I miss you constantly, dearest child." He wanted her to begin at once to write her account of Helen's progress since the last Perkins report "and to make it very interesting. Please make Helen to write in pencil a brief account of her experiences in Boston, and to continue her diary. Has she written to the Endicotts? Don't be impatient or cross on account of my requests. Remember, that I have solely in view the child's and your own good and nothing, absolutely nothing else."

Helen made her first acquaintance with the surf. Taken to the beach, she ran toward the water, tripping, dancing, fearless. Her foot struck a stone and she went under; she came out, her mouth full, terrified. "The waves seemed to be playing a game with me," but at last the breakers threw her back upon the shore "and in another instant I was clasped in my teacher's arms." When her panic had abated sufficiently so that she could spell again into Annie's hand, her first question was: "Who put salt in water?" It took several days before she ventured into the water again, but gradually she recovered her boldness and soon was wading in up to her ears, enjoying most of all the waves that swept her back. At the end of the summer she wrote Annie's friend Miss Moore, "We splashed and jumped and waded in the deep water. I am not afraid to float now."

He had been pleasantly surprised, Anagnos wrote Annie, that "instead of a brief postal card" he had received a fat letter "full of spirit and true representation of yourself in your better moods." Annie had told him about a discussion among Perkins girls who were vacationing in the neighborhood, about marriage among blind persons. He was very firm in his disapproval.

> In regard to the question which the girls have under discussion I do not think that you or any sensible person ought to hesitate to express a clear, definite and most decided opinion. Say to them emphatically, that, all things being considered, blind persons ought to exercise a certain degree of self-denial and to abstain from matrimony; that it

is very wrong for persons whose loss of sight is due to some organic disorder to marry any one; and that it is a terrible and unpardonable sin to encourage the union of two such persons. The offspring of those who suffer by inheritance will be almost invariably defective. . . . If a man or woman is so utterly destitute of conscience or so criminally selfish as to seek his personal convenience or the gratification of his desires regardless of the distressing effects of the monstrous consequences of his deliberate action, pray in what respect does he or she differ from the lowest and meanest species of the brute creation? The community,—or to be more correct,—society has a perfect right to expect, that all educated blind persons should have proper respect for the eternal laws of nature and should use their influence to enlighten others and to diminish instead of increasing the number of defective children.

Just before leaving Boston, Helen had heard a high school youngster say something about a course in Latin. What was "Latin"? she immediately wanted to know. Told by Annie it was a language spoken long ago, and that the word *mensa,* for example, meant table, she asked in rapid sequence, " 'What is girl? boy? father? mother?' and in a few minutes she had learned seven or eight Latin words. The next morning, she asked, 'Where is my *pater?*' When we went out for a walk, and I told her about a little boy whom I saw, she remarked, 'I would like to see little *puer.' "* Even earlier, when she had chanced to put her hand on a copy of Bach's chorales, edited for the use of the blind, that was lying on Anagnos's desk, she asked the meanings of *wie, schon,* and *leuchtet* in the title of the first hymn. During the summer she informed Anagnos that she was studying French with her teacher and included some short sentences that contained a single mistake, *ma chère* instead of *mon cher monsieur.* "I will learn to talk Latin, too," she announced, "and some day you will teach me Greek. I do want to learn much about everything."

Helen's French surprised Anagnos. "What a burning thirst for knowledge has the precious pet? Give her to drink, but in very moderate drafts." A little dubious, evidently, about Annie's own proficiency, he turned schoolteacher. "Teach her to use the possessive pronouns and adjectives correctly. Both are changed in form in their agreement with the natural or grammatical gender of the nouns." He complained of rheumatism and was likely to be confined to his rooms for the whole month. "The house seems more lonesome and gloomy than ever before; but we must bear

trials patiently, pursue our work persistently, and make the best of everything."

Annie mutinied against writing a new installment on Helen's development for his fifty-seventh annual report, but he pleaded earnestly with her
to do so: "I assure you, dearest, that nothing would give me greater
pleasure than to relieve you from any extra work; but I deem it absolutely
necessary, as a matter of propriety and justice to yourself, that you should
take up the thread where you left it last year and give an account of what
you have accomplished during the past twelve months. It is an easy matter
to employ some one to put the facts together; but what is needed is a
continuation of the authentic statement which you began to write a year
ago and which will serve as the basis of all future biographies of the
wonderful child, and no one else can or ought to prepare it." He was, of
course, absolutely right, and it is a little sad, as we shall see, that Annie
in later years was unable to acknowledge his contribution to her development.

As the summer at the Cape ended, she wrote him a letter filled with
youthful *Weltschmerz,* and he quickly wrote back:

> That you are discontented and disposed to take a gloomy view of your
> ability to reach the heights of absolute bliss, I am exceedingly sorry.
> Fairies and their magical wands are inventions or fabulous creations
> of the imagination which will never be of practical use to any human
> being. It is knowledge of the realities of life that will help us to do
> our work well and be satisfied with our environment. Happiness is
> like sleep. It is not to be obtained by direct effort. . . . We shall never
> find lasting pleasure by seeking it for ourselves. The path to it lies
> through the good of others, which is precisely the way indicated by
> conscience. We are a part of the universe, and have its law, which is
> the good of all, written upon our hearts. . . . But I must stop here.
> Although I am writing on Sunday morning, I must not indulge in
> preaching sermons.

They returned to Boston to spend September and October at Perkins
before returning to Tuscumbia. Helen continuously pressed Anagnos to
teach her the Greek equivalents of many familiar expressions. Six weeks
later she astounded him with a letter from Roxbury, where the kindergarten was located, that was studded with her gleanings of French and Greek.
"That the little witch should have stored in the capacious treasury of her
memory every scrap of knowledge which she had picked up in her irregu-

lar linguistic excursions, and that she should be able to use it correctly whenever she pleases, seems inconceivable," he wrote in his annual report as an introduction to the facsimile of the letter.

"Mon cher Monsieur Anagnos," the letter began correctly. Helen described the kindergarten in her clipped, staccato phrases, expressed the hope that he would visit her and her sister in Alabama, and announced her intention to travel abroad. "I shall visit Lord Fauntleroy in England and he will be glad to show me his grand and very ancient castle. . . . When I get to France I will talk French. A little French boy will say, *Parlez-vous français?* and I will say, *Oui, monsieur, vous avez un joli chapeau. Donnez-moi un baiser.* I hope you will go with me to Athens to see the maid of Athens. She is a very lovely lady and I will talk Greek to her. I will say *se agapo* and *pos eeseh* and I think she will say, *kala,* and then I will say *chaere.* Will you please come to see me soon and take me to the theater? When you come I will say, *kalemera,* and when you go home I will say, *kale nykta.* Now I am too tired to write more, *je vous aime. Au revoir.* From your darling little friend Helen A. Keller."*

Annie and Helen left Perkins in early November. They had benefited, as had Perkins and Anagnos. Just as Laura Bridgman had once made Perkins the cynosure of the philanthropic world, so now did Helen. There were resentments and jealousies. At the celebration in December 1887 of the fiftieth anniversary of Laura's arrival at Perkins, Julia Ward Howe had been the dominating presence; at the June 1888 commencement that had featured Helen, Mrs. Howe had not been in evidence. Anagnos was unable to conceal his belief that Helen was a greater "miracle" than Laura, at any rate a more attractive personality. There was another deaf, mute and blind child at Perkins, Edith Thomas, who was working under the supervision of the "Lillie" of whom Annie had written so scornfully to Mrs. Hopkins. Anagnos printed facsimiles of letters that Helen and Edith, who was a year older, had exchanged, and noted Helen's superiority in the use of language—"having a natural gift in that direction"—ending his comparison as follows:

> Helen, the child of the South, with her sweet, clinging, affectionate disposition, is unfolding as rapidly as a tropical plant and winning all hearts by her loving ways and by her brilliant success in

*The Greek phrases in order mean in English—I love you, how do you do, well, good-bye, good morning and good night.

the acquirement of language; while Edith,—sturdy, self-reliant, independent,—in her tardier advancement in one direction, in which Helen excels, shows, nevertheless, indications of a deep moral nature and a strength of character, which, if wisely guided in their development, give promise of a noble womanhood.

It was difficult to resist Helen. Her passion for doing good, her sympathy for all living creatures, the unbreakable conviction that was mirrored in her very mobile and expressive little body that everyone was as good and loving as she was, made sophisticated men and women believe she was a direct emanation of the Lord.

One of the teachers in the girls' department at Perkins, Miss Fanny S. Marrett, placed a tadpole—one of eleven that were in a glass globe—in Helen's hand. She explored it eagerly, tenderly, gently, as if instinctively she had realized the delicacy of the organism. When Miss Marrett explained why it had to be returned to the water, Helen did so, and from then on would not have any tadpole taken out of its natural element. One day on their daily inspection of the tadpoles, which Helen insisted upon, Miss Marrett found that one had leapt out of the dish and was on the floor. She placed it in Helen's hands. "Suddenly the tail moved, and at the first sign of life Helen gave a quick and joyous spring, and signified her wish that the tadpole at once be put in water. She then named it 'the sick tadpole.' For some days afterwards, the first question she asked upon entering the schoolroom was, 'How is tadpole?' "

She was fond of all living things, wrote Annie, and would not have them treated unkindly. Riding in the carriage, she did not allow the driver to use the whip because "poor horses will cry." When her father wrote that the birds and bees were eating all his grapes, she was at first indignant with the little creatures, but when Annie explained that birds and bees also were subject to hunger, and did not know that it was selfish, she wrote:

> I am very sorry that bumble-bees and hornets and birds and large flies and worms are eating all of my father's delicious grapes. They like juicy fruit to eat as well as people and they are hungry. They are not very wrong to eat too many grapes because they do not know much.

She was already showing a tendency to modify the facts about—even to block out—the violent, the disgusting and the distasteful. Perhaps she had to do this. Life was difficult enough for her as it was. Almost instinctively she was learning that to make the best of everything strengthened her ability to survive.

A visit was always an occasion for hugs and kisses. They went to visit the Freemans, close friends of Edward Everett Hale, a family with many children, living just outside of Boston. "I was delighted to see my dear little friends and I hugged and kissed them," she wrote her mother. "Clifton did not kiss me because he doesn't like to kiss little girls. He is shy. I am very glad that Frank and Clarence and Robbie and Eddie and Charles and George were not very shy." "She is naturally a very sweet, affectionate and generous child," wrote Annie in the masterly account of Helen's development that she turned in to Anagnos despite all her rebelliousness over having to do it, "and a very slight appeal to her sensitive little heart will invariably bring tears to her eyes."

"I am aware," the same report said, "that my description of Helen may seem to those, who do not know her, extravagant in its praise; but her numerous friends will bear testimony most gladly to the sweetness, unselfishness and beauty of her disposition. Every day of her life she is teaching us gratitude and contentment; and she teaches those great lessons with such truth, patience and joyousness, that we never tire of her radiant presence."

Anagnos, after having watched and studied her closely for more than three months, said the same:

It is no hyperbole to say that she is a personification of goodness and happiness. She never repines, and is always so contented and gay, so bright and lively that

While we converse with her, we mark
No want of day, nor think it dark.

Of sin and evil, of malice and wickedness, of meanness and perverseness, she is absolutely ignorant. She is as pure as the lily of the valley, and as innocent and joyous as the birds of the air or the lambs in the field.No germ of depravity can be detected in the soul of her moral constitution, even by means of the most powerful microscope. . . . To her envy and jealousy are utterly unknown. . . . By her benevolence and good will towards all, she teaches us how to seek the highest goal,

To earn the true success;
To live, to love, to bless.

As Helen recalled the visit North when later she wrote *The Story of My Life,* "I am filled with wonder at the richness and variety of experiences that cluster about it. It seems to have been the beginning of everything." But in Tuscumbia, in the world of the adults, life had turned worrisome: "The greatest excitement has existed here since election day," Annie wrote Anangos. "Everyone is anxious about the result and some show considerable temper when possibility of a Republican victory is suggested. The Captain keeps his temper, however, and it can hardly be guessed from his manner that he has anything at stake. . . . If Cleveland is not elected, he will have to go back to the newspaper."

Her reaction to the news that Cleveland indeed had not been reelected was acutely feminine. Now Mrs. Cleveland will have the President "all to herself and can make him miserable at her convenience." One consequence of Cleveland's defeat, as Annie foresaw, was Captain Keller's replacement as marshal of North Alabama with a Republican, and that meant straitened circumstances for the household.

Although Anagnos, who now constantly reported ailments of one sort or another, still struggled to put together his section of the annual report, he wholly approved of Annie's seven-thousand-word contribution, which despite her reluctance she had turned in before returning to Tuscumbia. "Your style of writing has improved wonderfully. This is not my opinion alone, others think so, too." Helen should not forget, he went on, "that she has many friends in Boston who love her dearly. You can hardly imagine, dearest child, how often I think of you and of sweet little Helen and how much I miss you both. I feel lonesome without you." He began to talk of himself as their "grandfather," perhaps because of the illnesses that were sweeping his body. For Christmas he sent her a box of presents from her friends at Perkins, including a handbag and package of sweets from himself. The report would make a volume of about 280 pages, he said, "one-fourth of which [is] wholly devoted to Helen's case." He was going over a final proof of Annie's contribution, and an experienced proofreader paid her "a very high compliment by saying that your narrative is fascinating."

Annie worried over his persistent illness. He was carrying too much of the burden at Perkins, she advised him. "If you think the cause of the blind of sufficient importance to die for it, pray why do you not use a little philosophy and more common sense and decide to live for 'the cause'?" She was discontented with Tuscumbia and slipping into one of her dangerous restless moods. Every day was like another in Tuscumbia. "It seems to me that of all existences, a life in which nothing happens is most unbearable." Helen, however, continued to enchant her. "The other day she asked me, 'why do people do wrong things?' " She pressed Annie continuously to be allowed to write to her friends in Boston, but Annie, admonished on all sides not to allow the child to overwork, kept her out-of-doors more than in the past. Told by Annie one morning that today she could write letters, she hugged Annie for joy and "by dinner time she had written five letters and no two alike."

An invitation to a Christmas party became a minor cause célèbre because Annie sensed some slight in the way it was worded. Had she done right? she asked Anagnos. He was not able to tell on the basis of the information she had provided, he replied, "but why did you not lay the whole matter before Mrs. Keller and ask her advice about it? Why do you not tell me the whole story, so that I may advise you intelligently and tell you what to do?" She was in a truculent mood, and a worried Anagnos's letters were filled with paternal admonitions against impulsive decisions.

> I doubt not, that you have reasons to be discontented and to feel uncomfortable; but I beg of you, darling, to make the best of everything that is unpleasant and to be generous in your dealings with everyone. Keep your rebellious heart under strict control. Do not allow yourself either to show temper or to say a sharp word. You have a glorious work before you. Do it in your usual way. Be kind and accommodating to all regardless of the treatment you receive from them, and the victory is yours. What do you care about society or about people's ridiculous notions and silly distinctions? Go on with your holy mission, and the time will come when you will be tired of social attentions. You know, dearest how anxious I am to see your work crowned with entire success and how happy I shall be to see you triumphant over all difficulties. Helen's education is your polar star. Look at it steadily, and take no notice of what is going on around you.

Their letters were full of their respective ailments. The trustees gave Anagnos a three-month leave of absence. Annie's eyes were beginning to bother her again, and she had to stay in her room. But Helen's fame marched on. "I enclose a poem to Helen, written by Mr. Edmund Clarence Stedman of New York. As you know, he is one of the leading literary men in this country and I am exceedingly glad that Helen's case has attracted his attention." The poem shows the impact Helen was having on sensitive and thoughtful people everywhere:

> Mute, sightless visitant,
> From what uncharted world
> Hast voyaged into Life's rude sea
> With guidance scant;
> As if some bark mysteriously
> Should hither glide, with spars aslant
> and sails all furled!
>
> In what perpetual dawn,
> Child of the spotless brow,
> Hast kept thy spirit far withdrawn. . . .
> Pity thy unconfined
> Clear spirit, whose enfranchised eyes
> Use not their grosser sense?
> Ah, no! Thy bright intelligence
> Hath its own Paradise,
> A realm where to hear and see
> Things hidden from our kind.
> Not thou, not thou—'tis we
> Are deaf, are dumb, are blind!

The "child of the spotless brow," as Stedman called her, was at the moment giving Annie problems. "This afternoon she seemed a little fretful," Annie wrote Anagnos, "and I said to her what shall I do with a naughty girl? She replied 'make me not to be naughty.' I asked her how was I to keep her from being naughty? Quick in thought she answered, 'love me and kiss me and hug me very much and I will not be naughty!' She is very anxious that her father should buy a fine house in Boston and take us all there to live. Last night she was discussing the matter with him, and he told her he was too poor to live in Boston. Helen settled the matter by saying, 'you *must work very hard* and *get a great deal of money.'* "

At the end of January, the fifty-seventh Perkins annual report, described earlier, arrived in Tuscumbia. Since one fourth of it dealt with the account of Helen's development, much of it has been covered in this chapter. Anagnos, who had the benefit of Annie's work, had closely modeled his own observations on those of his pupil's. The insights and originality were clearly hers. He added a few embellishments. What Annie said plainly, directly and with the force and feeling that arose from the drama and tension of the events she was describing, he translated into a florid, purple prose. But he paid Annie high tribute. "No one interferes with Miss Sullivan's plans or shares in her tasks. . . . Only those, who are familiar with the particulars of the grand achievements, know that the credit is largely due to the intelligence, wisdom, sagacity, unremitting perseverance and unbending will of the instructress. . . ." Yet none of this impressed Annie, and her irate reaction perplexed Anagnos. Anagnos's statement that she need not have worried on her arrival at Tuscumbia that she might fail angered her. He had written, "She had no uncertain problems to solve, no untried experiments to make, no new processes to invent, and no trackless forest to traverse. Her course was clearly and definitely indicated by the finger of the illustrious liberator of Laura Bridgman. His glorious achievement stood before her like a peerless beacon. . . . Following the simplest and most direct methods of Dr. Howe, Miss Sullivan sought anxiously to find some aperture in the rocky walls. . . . The stupendous feat was accomplished instantaneously, as by the touch of a magic wand."

She was grateful to him, her sharp letter began:

> . . . and your evident delight in my poor efforts to do something worthy of a woman made the obstacles in my path seem less formidable, and helped me to be patient and persevering. Still, I cannot help wishing that there had been less publicity about the matter of Helen's education. There is very little good to come of it all and notoriety is invariably accompanied by various annoyances. If a knowledge of the methods used in leading my precious little charge into the light of knowledge and freedom could be of the slightest use to the busy educators of our day I would gladly give whatever information on the subject I may possess and I would hail with joy accounts of Helen's progress from the pens of others but you say in your report that there are no uncertain problems to solve, no untried experiments to make, no new processes to invent, and no trackless forest to traverse.

And here she reached the hub of her grievance and fury:

> If these statements are correct is it not the height of presumption to ask teachers and philosophers to read seventy pages of matter on a subject which was exhausted some forty years ago by the illustrious liberator of Laura Bridgman? For, surely it is these people we wish

to interest and not the ignorant masses. I would rather be shot than to gratify the idle curiosity of a news loving public. And dear friend, I think you will understand me when I say, that it puzzles me to know why I deserve especial congratulations for following a course which was clearly and definitely indicated by another. Do you not think it would be better and juster to let Dr. Howe's glorious achievements to stand as the goals, which it is not possible for his successors to attain? Pray, forgive me if I have failed to catch the true meaning of your words, and forgive me also when I tell you, that if you do believe what your words seem to indicate that I do not share your opinions. . . .

Anagnos had just finished writing her a most affectionate letter, saying that both he and Mrs. Hopkins were concerned that they had not heard from her in so long, and deploring her sarcastic reaction to the prepublication praise of her contribution that he had reported, when her angry missive arrived. "This letter was sealed last evening," he added in a postscript, "and opened to add a few words. It is evident to me, that you misunderstand or misinterpret the spirit and the direct meaning of my remarks. Need I say that my words neither belittle your work nor detract anything from its real value. I am deeply grieved that you should think so."

A few weeks later he felt duty bound to explain his position in detail.

By reading them [his words] carefully, you will find that they relate *exclusively* to the means and methods employed in penetrating the double wall of deafness and blindness and bringing the incarcerated mind in direct communication with the outer world. They have no reference whatever to the *education* [Anagnos's emphases] of persons deprived of the sense of hearing and sight. Now, is there the slightest doubt, that Dr. Howe, and he alone, established this royal road and that all his successors follow in his path step by step? Has any one thought of using a way or process differing from his in order to reach an entombed soul? Has it ever occurred to you to convey information to Helen's mind through her toes or the back of her head or her nose? You may say that Dr. Howe did not invent the manual alphabet or the raised letters, nor did he construct any unknown or uncommon conveyance for reaching Laura's mind. No, certainly, he did not. Neither did Christopher Columbus form the Atlantic Ocean or invent the sails of the ships which were fitted out for his perilous voyage in search of a vast continent. . . . No one thought that all educational problems were solved by him [Howe] in Laura's case, and that he left nothing for others to do. Nor is there any doubt or dispute as to the fact that it is impossible to apply the same educational methods and processes to children of different temperaments and mental constitutions.

In regard to the character of the publicity of Helen's case, of which you have spoken repeatedly with a certain degree of severity, I beg to differ from you. True, there are persons, who prompted by curiosity, ask all sorts of questions in a thoughtless manner; but these, I am glad to say, are few as compared with the vast army of intelligent, thoughtful, considerate and well-educated men and women, who are seeking information for higher and better purposes than the gratification of a morbid desire for novelty and excitement. When a man of deep learning and unusual common sense tells me that if he were rich, he would have one hundred thousand copies of Helen's education printed at his expense for free distribution, so that each teacher in the land might have one and study it, the objectionable portions of the publicity vanish in view of the good which may be derived from it. I am aware that your annoyance increases in proportion to the spread of the knowledge of the uncommon talents of your pupil; but you and everyone else have to follow the example of sweet patience set by the little heroine herself and to make the best of the inconvenience. Considering the latter in its true light, the eagerness of the public to learn something of Helen's success is perfectly natural. . . . The admiration and earnestness with which people follow Helen's progress is creditable to their intelligence and do honor to our civilization. The tendency to exclusiveness and to satisfaction and the enjoyment of comforts and luxuries within the narrow circle of the family is altogether too strong in our days, and we cannot be thankful enough when we see signs in the opposite direction.

The pupil had outgrown the teacher. That was clear from their respective contributions about Helen. But the points he made were sound: Annie's achievement was not in establishing a new route of communication to the world of the deaf and the blind, but in the methods of education that she employed once communication had been established. She was a great educator and within a few years would be recognized as such. His point about the usefulness of the publicity he had given to Helen's case was also sound. Ironically, the greatest beneficiaries would be Helen and herself, as Captain Keller ran out of funds and the two were thrown upon the resources of the new friends they had made in Boston.

A week after his letter of sharp disagreement, Anagnos wrote Annie again that he had to tell her "in a few words, that the little discussion we have had was one of those passing events which leave no unfortunate traces behind them. I want you to forget it entirely and to believe, that it did not have the slightest effect on my love and feelings towards you."

But for Annie, although she, too, resumed her letters to him as if nothing had happened, it was a peal of thunder that heralded the storm.

VII

Helen Finds a Vocation; Annie Almost Loses Hers

". . . Her marvellous inner nature [is] a greater glory to humanity than her learning."

Although Helen and Annie were in Tuscumbia, their thoughts and hopes turned constantly to Boston, Perkins, and Anagnos. "It made me feel very sad to leave Boston," Helen wrote Dr. Hale, "and I missed all of my friends greatly, but of course I was glad to get back to my lovely home once more."

"Do you have to write so many letters?" Annie asked her pupil in wonderment and some exasperation. "It makes me very tired," Helen replied, "but it would be very unkind not to write to my friends." "But most of these letters are written to strangers and not to your friends," protested Annie. "You are mistaken," Helen came back firmly. "They are my friends because they think of me and write to me." Annie quoted this to Anagnos in a letter that signified a truce in their argument over Dr. Howe. "Sometimes I look at the child and wonder how she can be so patient and sweet-tempered when I am ready to devour my best friend," she added.

One approached the world with a chip on her shoulder and assumed everyone was ready to knock it off; the other reached out to the world with a heart filled with love and kindness and assumed the world would reciprocate. It was the difference between the manners of Tewksbury and Tuscumbia, between being brought up amid the cruelties of the almshouse and the affectionate warmth of an upper-middle-class Southern home, between an Irish cultural heritage of black pessimism and hot hatred of patronizing rulers and the genial, self-confident outlook of a class that despite the Civil War was still master. There were also genetic forces at work, producing a basic difference in temperaments, so that one always viewed the world "through a glass darkly" while the other, though sightless, surrounded it with sunshine and gaiety.

Helen's goodness of heart never ceased to amaze Annie. "Speaking of animals the other day, she said, 'they cannot think and know much with their heads, but they can feel with their hearts, and they know when people are cruel and hurt them, and they are very happy when I love them.' " Annie took Helen to visit some little friends in the vicinity. One of the boys, Lee, had a pony and wanted to take Helen for a ride. Helen pleaded and Annie finally agreed. Sam, the pony, moved off with the two children on his back, but he was too much for the little boy to handle, and both he and Helen rolled off, Helen banging her head on a rock on the ground. The bruise was not serious but it hurt. "I must not cry," she said to her teacher, scarcely able to hold back her tears, "because he will feel sad." Annie must tell him, she spelled into her hand, "You did not mean to let me fall. I am afraid Sam was too large for a small boy to hold up."

Her teacher sought to shield her from premature contact with persons and ideas that might coarsen her nature. Affectionate parents would do the same, yet Annie's decision in this regard contradicted her claim at other times that she wanted Helen to become sturdily self-reliant. In June 1888 when they saw Dr. Bell in Washington, he had shown Helen how to use a "glove" that he had devised that would enable her to converse with anyone. "The letters [of the alphabet] are written on a glove," she explained. "By touching these letters as one would the keys of a piano, words may be spelled, and after a little practise this method of communication can be very rapidly used." But Annie discouraged Helen's use of the "glove." "I must say, that I shrink from this easy mode of communication. I cannot bring myself to the mental state, where I can feel contented to allow irresponsible and unreasoning persons to have easy access to my darling's pure and loving little heart. I am sure that while I stay with her, she will never have occasion to feel the solitude of her life, and when I go, the glove, I doubt not, will add greatly to her enjoyment. But until then, I am determined to keep my beautiful treasure pure and unspotted from the world. Perhaps, too, by that time her nature, now so fresh and tender, shall have acquired a firmness and consistency, which will enable her to resist whatever evil may appear in her environment."

But what if Annie had been suddenly removed because of illness or accident? What about other members of her family who did not know the manual alphabet, such as her father, who would have enjoyed talking with his child? And could Annie have been sure of the purity of her own motives—was it the protection of her charge, or was it not also a guarantee of her control over her?

A few days later, in fact, Annie requested a leave of absence in order to go to Boston to have her eyes treated. "I am coming home next June to stay several months," she wrote Anagnos, "and see if I can get rested and have some things done for my eyes. I have spoken to Capt. and Mrs. Keller and while they do not like the idea of my leaving them for so long a time, still they think it will be the best thing I can do to go away from my sweet little charge for a time. I propose to return to Tuscumbia next October, that is, if I do not change my mind and do something quite different. To tell you the truth, I have a strong notion of joining a circus or a menagerie. I think the circus would suit me admirably because it's always on the move."

She knew Helen would be very lonely. Mrs. Keller had very little time, and that which she had was given to Helen's little sister, Mildred. "The poor woman actually cried when I talked to her about going away." Annie proposed that a Perkins classmate, Eva Ramsdell, somewhat older than Helen, come down and serve as a companion to her. "Her only care would be to amuse the sweetest and loveliest little girl in the world." Anagnos disliked Annie's leaving Helen, "even for a few months, but it cannot be helped." He approved the suggestion of Eva Ramsdell and so wrote Captain Keller. He was scarcely in a position to deny Annie's plea that her eyes needed attention. He was himself in a constant torment because of some "internal" disorder, and "in order to get rid of it, I must have absolute rest and the best medical advice. I have therefore decided to go abroad this summer and stay in Europe until I am thoroughly cured."

"My precious darling," Anagnos wrote Helen as the time neared for his departure (May 13, 1889). He thought of her constantly, and he would have come to Tuscumbia to visit her, as she had proposed, if it had been possible; but he looked forward to seeing her in Boston on his return. "It will be one of the greatest delights of my life to have you near me, because I love you with all my heart and soul, and I think of you more than of any other child."

"I am very sorry that you are going so far away," Helen's farewell note said. "We shall miss you very, very much. I would love to visit many beautiful cities with you. . . . I hope you will please write to me from all the cities you visit. When you go to Holland please give my love to the lovely princess Wilhelmina. She is a dear little girl and when she is old enough she will be the queen of Holland. If you go to Roumania please ask the good Queen Elizabeth about her little invalid brother, and tell her that I am very sorry that her darling little girl died. I should like to send a kiss to Vittorio, the little prince of Naples, but teacher says she is afraid you will not remember so many messages. When I am thirteen years old I shall visit them all myself." She thanked him for sending her the beautiful story about Lord Fauntleroy and expressed the wish that when he came home he would be "all well."

She informed Mr. Dwight*, a trustee of Perkins who had written her, that Mr. Anagnos had promised to write to her from each of the cities he visited—which, indeed, he would do. She also reported that "my little friend Eva has come to stay with me while my dear teacher goes home to rest. I shall miss her greatly, but I must not cry for that would make teacher unhappy. I should like very much to go to Boston with her, but I cannot. So I will write her every day." Not until Annie's trunk was packed had she fully taken in that her teacher was going off. "Her distress was very great, but when the time for saying farewell arrived she was calm, and fully resolved not to grieve teacher by crying. . . ."

For over two years Annie and Helen had been together day and night. They were now separated for three and a half months. Only twice in the remainder of Annie's life (and she died in 1936) would they be apart for more than a few days. During the summer of 1889 Annie received many letters from Helen and presumably wrote some in return. Except for Helen's letter of August 7, 1889, none, unfortunately, have survived. It is a particular pity in the case of Helen, for they would have provided the clearest picture of Helen unmediated, uncoached, unedited by her teacher. This, as we shall see, was to become of some importance.

"Dearest Teacher," she wrote on August 7, "I am very glad to write to you this evening, for I have been thinking much about you all day." She reported on her dolls—"perhaps the mocking bird is singing them to sleep"—and on the flowers that were in bloom—"the air is sweet with the perfume of jasmine, heliotrope and roses." Cousin Leila's little boy Arthur "is growing very fast," and her sister Mildred is dear and sweet and "very roguish, too." Her father had been out

---

*John S. Dwight (1813–1893) Brook-Farmer; his biography was said to be the history of music in Boston; a Perkins trustee for eighteen years.

hunting and shot thirty-eight birds, and her half-brother Simpson "shot a pretty crane. The crane is a large and strong bird. His wings are as long as my arms, and his bill is as long as my foot. He eats little fishes, and other small animals. Father says he can fly nearly all day without stopping." She had gone to church. "I love to go to church, because I like to see my friends."

Only once did she refer to her companion for the summer. "Eva has been telling me a story about a lovely little girl named Heidi. Will you please send it to me? I shall be delighted to have a typewriter." A query: "What was the name of the little boy who fell in love with the beautiful star? . . . I read in my books every day. I love them very, very, very much. I do want you to come to me soon. I miss you so very, very much. I cannot know about many things when my dear teacher is not here. I send you five thousand kisses, and more love than I can tell. I send Mrs. H[opkins] much love and a kiss."

On Annie's return in September she and the Kellers decided it would be best if Helen could attend Perkins. The ten-year-old child's insatiable curiosity, her rapid-fire questions, her passion to learn, indicated that she was ready for systematic instruction of a kind that Annie, despite her superb insights into a child's mind, was unable to provide. So Annie wrote to the acting director of Perkins, John A. Bennett. But there were no vacancies, and "even if there were accommodations for [the] two, I think in the absence of Mr. Anagnos I should desire a vote of the trustees before she were admitted without expense." Evidently Bennett was unhappy with his own reply, for two days later he informed Captain Keller on behalf of the trustees, whom he had canvassed individually, that they would be happy to have Helen and Miss Sullivan as "permanent guests of the Perkins Institution."

"Mon cher Monsieur Anagnos," Helen wrote the absent director, who had gone from Paris to Vienna to Athens.

> Today is your birthday, and how I wish I could put my two arms around your neck and give you many sweet kisses. . . . Now, I am going to tell you something which will surprise you very much. I came to Boston three weeks ago to study with my dear teacher. . . . I enjoy being at the Institution very, very much, I learn a great many new and interesting things every day. When you come home I shall be happy to tell you all about them. You must be sure not to forget how to spell with your fingers. . . .

Teacher says she thinks you would like to know what I do every day. At eight I study arithmetic, and I enjoy it greatly. I can do some very difficult examples. At nine I go to the gymnasium with the little girls, and we play pretty games. . . . At ten I study geography. Yesterday I found Athens on the map and I thought about you. At eleven I have lessons in form, and at twelve, I have zoology. The other day I recited in exhibition about the kangaroos. At two I usually sew, and at three I have a walk. At four and five I read, write and talk. I have just been reading about a beautiful fountain that rippled and sparkled in the bright sunshine and made sweet music all the day long. The pretty birds and tiny ferns and the soft mosses loved the beautiful fountain.

About one course of instruction, French, she said nothing to Anagnos, perhaps because she wanted to surprise him, as she did a few months later, with a letter in that language. " 'Will you teach me French?' Those were the words which Helen's fingers rapidly spelled to me one day, as we sat at the dinner table," reported Miss Fanny Marrett, one of the teachers in the girls' department. Helen gave up a free afternoon hour in order to do so, "and five o'clock always found her ready for the French lessons." She quickly learned the French equivalent of several short, everyday expressions. "Her first perplexity was caused by the varying forms of the definite and indefinite article; yet when her questions regarding them had been answered, and she understood that memory must be the chief aid in the correct use of these words, she fitted them to the various nouns in her vocabulary, with an earnestness which was a certain prophecy of a future accuracy, and in all her later work a mistake in their use was rarely made. Indeed accuracy is one of Helen's prominent characteristics."

Miss Marrett also remarked on her memory. "Helen was most distressed by a failure to remember anything which she had ever known, and it was seldom that she suffered this pain. It became evident, during our second lesson, that she would not need reviews. The sentences of the first lesson comprised so many new words, that I thought it best to have them repeated before more were learned. When I asked questions to suggest the sentences of the previous lesson, Helen said, in an emphatic, surprised way: 'I know them! Please teach me something new!' I was, however, assured of her knowledge by a perfect recitation, and a review was never again requested." The French course lasted through May 1890. She was soon reading simple French stories that Miss Marrett wrote out for her in Braille and by February wrote letters in French, including one to a delighted Mr. Anagnos in Athens, which Miss Marrett assured him had been written without any assistance from her. "Paris was often before her mind, as the place to which the French lessons were surely leading her," Miss Marrett's account continued, "and she would frequently give imaginary dialogues between herself and little French children." Miss Marrett was pleased with Helen's swift grasp of the language, but it was Helen's character that made the strongest impression. "I shall always be grateful for the question which, with its answer brought me for a few weeks so near to Helen's wonderful mind and heart, and revealed to me all the most precious characteristics of her rich nature."

Another growing passion was poetry. Its rhythms and imagery enchanted her. "Teacher's lithe fingers were part of the charm," she wrote at the end of her life, "wantoning as it were in the flowering musical rhythms, now and then clasping Helen's with the utmost sense of joy or pain that touch can embody." One poet she and Teacher read together was John Greenleaf Whittier. He was a favorite of Annie's, who when a student at Perkins loved to recite his great abolitionist poem, "Massachusetts to Virginia." "Dear Poet," Helen wrote him on November 27, 1889,

I think you will be surprised to receive a letter from a little girl whom you do not know, but I thought you would be glad to hear that your beautiful poems make me very happy. Yesterday I read "In School Days" and "My Playmate," and I enjoyed them greatly. I was very sorry that the poor little girl with the browns [brown eyes] and the "tangled golden curls" died. It is very pleasant to live here in our beautiful world. I cannot see the lovely things with my eyes, but my mind can see them all, and so I am joyful all the day long.

When I walk out in my garden I cannot see the beautiful flowers but I know that they are all around me; for is not the air sweet with their fragrance? I know too that the tiny lily-bells are whispering pretty secrets to their companions else they would not look so happy. I love you very dearly, because you have taught me so many lovely things about flowers, and birds, and people. Now I must say good-bye. I hope [you] will enjoy the Thanksgiving very much.

From your loving little friend,
Helen A. Keller.

"I had a lovely letter from the poet Whittier," she wrote her mother. "He loves me."

Another of the last surviving great New England writers also became a friend. Shortly after she wrote to Whittier she visited Dr. Oliver Wendell Holmes. She described her visit in the popular young people's magazine *St. Nicholas.* She wondered whether the boys and girls who read *St. Nicholas* had read the sad story about "Little Jakey," blind and poor, her letter began. Jakey's explanation of his blindness was "Venn Gott make my eyes, my moder say he not put ze light in zem."

"I used to think," Helen's letter to *St. Nicholas* continued, "when I was a very small child, before I had learned to read—that everybody was always happy, and at first I was grieved to know about pain and great sorrows; but now I understand that if it were not for these things people would never learn to be brave and patient and loving." She then described her visit to the Autocrat of the Breakfast Table.

> One bright Sunday, a little while ago, I went to see a very kind and gentle poet. I will tell you the name of one of his beautiful poems, and you will then be able to guess his name. The 'Opening of the Piano' is the poem. I know it and several others by heart; and I had learned to love the sweet poet long before I ever thought I should put my arms around his neck, and tell him how much pleasure he had given me, and all of the little blind children,—for we have his poems in raised letters. The poet was sitting in his library, by a cheerful fire, with his much-loved books all about him. I sat in his great easy chair, and examined the pretty things, and asked Dr. Holmes questions about people in his poems. Teacher told me about the beautiful river that flows beneath the library window. I think our gentle poet is very happy when he writes in this room, with so many wise friends near him.
>
> Please give my love to all of your little readers.

Whittier and Holmes, the last survivors of New England's Golden Age, found Helen's guileless avowals of love irresistible. They answered her letters. They encouraged her visits. Holmes did her bidding. "I am sorry that you have no little children to play with sometimes," she wrote him after her visit, "but I think you are very happy with your books, and your many, many friends. On Washington's birthday a great many people came here to see the little blind children, and I read for them from your poems, and showed them some beautiful shells which came from a little island near Palos*. . . . I am studying about insects in Zoology, and I have learned many things about butterflies. . . . If my little sister comes to Boston next June, will you let me bring her to see you?" Holmes printed her letter in the column that he regularly contributed to *The Atlantic Monthly,* called, as was the book that collected the columns, "Over the Teacups." The reading of Helen's letter, he wrote, "made many eyes glisten, and a dead silence hushed the whole circle. All at once Delilah, our pretty table-maid, forgot her place,—what business had she to be listening to our conversation and reading?—and she began sobbing, just as if she had been a lady. She couldn't help it, she explained afterwards, —she had a blind sister at the asylum, who had told her about Helen's reading to the children."

Annie reported Helen's progress to Anagnos. "Her mind continues to grow and expand with astonishing rapidity. Difficulties in Geography, Zoology and other studies vanish almost before I realize they are difficulties. . . . She reads everything she can get her hands on. . . . Miss Lane, I think, has told about her love of writing stories. She has written three little stories, perfect in every way, to change a word would ruin them. But her brilliant intellect is of small account compared with her lovely disposition. She is like a ray of sunshine in this cloudy world and wherever she is, in the street, in the car [tram], or in the bosom of our family, there is an atmosphere of love and tender sympathy. I do not believe that a selfish or unkind thought has ever entered her head."

There were skeptics. The principal of the Hartford Institution for Deaf Mutes, Dr. John H. Williams, considered the reports about Helen "grossly exaggerated." He asked to see Helen and to be allowed to talk with her alone. He came to Boston and talked with Helen in manual language for more than an hour. He confessed to Annie afterwards that he had been prepared to find Helen "an unusually bright child, but she is more than that, she is a miracle."

Another aspect of the miracle now began to unfold. One of Laura Bridgman's teachers, Mary Swift Lamson, returned from Norway, where she had interviewed Ragnhild Kaata, a blind deaf-mute who was being taught to speak with remarkable results. On her arrival in Boston, Mrs. Lamson immediately sought out Annie and Helen and told them the story

*They had been sent to her by Dr. Edward Everett Hale.

of the Norwegian girl. Helen's excitement mounted as Mrs. Lamson related the story, and she scarcely was finished when Helen announced, " 'I shall learn to speak, too!'. . . . I would not rest satisfied until my teacher took me for advice and assistance to Miss Sarah Fuller, principal of the Horace Mann School." They had visited the school in June 1888, and at that time Miss Fuller suggested that Helen be taught to speak; but Annie had discouraged the notion, fearful, she later claimed, that it might interfere with Helen's mastery of the manual language as her chief means of communication. A very different account of this episode is given by Sarah Fuller in an undated memorandum deposited in the Helen Keller files of the Volta Bureau in Washington:

> Her quickness of thought and her correct use of English impelled me to say as we were going from room to room, 'I believe she could learn to speak.' Miss Sullivan immediately said, 'I do not want her to speak, the voices of deaf children are not agreeable to me.' I said no more at the time, but when about a week later, I took the teachers of the Horace Mann School by permission of Mr. Anagnos and Mrs. Keller, to call upon Helen, I again expressed my belief in her ability to learn to speak, Miss Sullivan repeated her previous remark expressing her dislike of the voices of deaf children, Mrs. Keller agreeing as before. I could say nothing further and it was not until the twenty-sixth day of March 1890 that I learned that Helen was to be permitted to learn to speak.

The account is enlightening. It showed Annie's resistance to Helen's mastering methods of communication that might make her less dependent on her. It showed, too, how she dominated Helen's mother. It confirms, too, Helen's account that it was she, although not yet ten years of age, who prodded Anne Sullivan into taking her to Miss Fuller. The hunger to speak was so strong within her that by the time they came to Miss Fuller she had learned to say *papa, mama, baby* and *sister* clearly enough for Annie to understand her. To Miss Fuller, when Annie urged Helen to say *mama, papa,* the words sounded like *mum mum, pup pup;* but Helen's vehement desire to speak impressed her, and when Helen spelled out "I must speak," Miss Fuller agreed to take her on and started her first lesson then and there.

Placing Helen's hand lightly on the lower part of her face and the fingers of her other hand in her mouth so that she could sense the position of the tongue, she made the sound of *i* in *it.* By the end of that first of the eleven lessons that Miss Fuller gave her, Helen pronounced distinctly *M, P, A, S, T* and *I.* In between the lessons Helen practiced doggedly with Annie. "She was an ideal pupil," wrote Miss Fuller, "for she followed every direction with the utmost care, and seemed never to forget anything told her." By the time of her seventh lesson, the three lunched with a friend of Miss Fuller's. The latter encouraged Helen to talk and she did, telling of her home, her studies, her family and of her visit to Dr. Holmes. Her success elated her and on the way home she announced to Annie, "I am not dumb now." Annie was equally triumphant. "Within the past six weeks," she wrote Anagnos, "Helen has learned to speak. Yes, I tell the truth. She can express her thoughts and joys in distinct and not unpleasant speech. . . . How often we have wished that you were here to watch each step of this new development. . . . Her voice and pronunciation improve every day. . . . Think of it! She has achieved in less than two months what it takes the people of the schools for the deaf several years to accomplish, and then they do not speak as plainly as she does."

The celebration was premature. Annie and Miss Fuller alone were able to understand Helen. And, indeed, despite Miss Fuller's accomplishments, it would later be realized that her method of teaching the deaf to speak had its priorities wrong. "[T]he tragic fact is," Helen wrote in *Teacher,* "that she [Annie] and Miss Fuller blundered at the beginning by not developing my vocal organs first and then going on to articulation. . . . It was not until Mr. Charles White, a distinguished teacher of singing at the Boston Conservatory of Music, gave me speech lessons during three summers, out of the goodness of his heart, that Teacher and I realized our initial mistake—we had tried to build up speech without sound production!"

Annie's letter to Anagnos about Helen's achievement in articulation also included a summary of Helen's eight months at Perkins. "This year at the Institution has been invaluable to her. It has done more to enrich and broaden her life than many years of study at home would have done."

But their stay at Perkins ended unhappily. How much Helen knew of the episode is unclear. As always, it was Annie's caustic tongue that got them into trouble. Teacher oscillated between sudden seizures of self-importance and equally precipitate spasms of self-abasement. It took only a slight, imagined or real, to trigger either mood. Often Anagnos or Mrs. Hopkins was able to save her from herself. This time they were not. Her letter to Anagnos had spoken of what Helen had gained "through contact with the best people in Boston," but the "best people" were those who caused offense. Once on a party in the country she was infuriated because she felt the hosts treated her like a servant. She grabbed Helen and took the train back to Boston—only to discover she lacked the money with which to pay the fare. A kindly conductor did not put them off. When an invitation to Helen from a powerful Boston Brahmin did not include her, she refused to go, which meant that Helen, too, had to decline.

There were problems with Julia Ward Howe. "One day when an admiring group were saying complimentary things about my success in teaching Helen, I turned to Mrs. Howe who had not joined in the conversation, and said, 'Can it be possible, Madam, that the almshouse has trained a teacher?'

" 'I would say,' she answered coldly, 'it has nurtured the vanity of an ill-mannered person.' "

"It was not easy," commented Teacher to Nella Braddy, "for a young woman of my humble origin and limited education to defend herself against people like the Howes. They are offended if one tries to be friendly with them, and they are still more deeply offended if one dislikes them. If they wanted me to take Helen to one of their children's parties, and I did not comply with their haughtily expressed command, they were convinced I was a vulgar upstart. They seemed to think . . . their invitation is like God's which no one can refuse. . . . As a matter of fact, I was always uncomfortable, and consequently painfully aggressive when I was with them."

The Howes did not make things easy for Teacher. There was resentment and jealousy. Until Teacher's success with Helen, Dr. Howe's work with Laura Bridgman had represented the "great deliverance"; now Teacher was the "miracle worker" and Helen the "miracle." In Maud Howe Elliott's Diary for 1890 there is the revealing entry:

April 20th. The reception at the Kindergarten for the Blind. A lovely day, a great crowd of people. Helen Keller the main attraction, as in the old days at the Perkins Institution, Laura Bridgman. She is a most extraordinary child. I think Anagnos has made a mistake in choosing Miss Sullivan for her teacher. Miss S. is well prepared in one way, having herself been educated at the Perkins Institution, and having known Laura Bridgman, and become familiar with Papa's methods, but she has not the right feeling, remembering the beautiful modesty of Laura's behavior, compared to the hoydenish ways of this child. Helen recited some verses of Mr. Holmes'. Her voice, Mr. Dwight said, was like that of a Pythoness. It was to me the loneliest sound I have ever heard, like waves breaking on the coast of some lonely desert island.

Annie betrayed her hostility to the Brahmin philanthropic establishment in a column-length interview that she gave the *Boston Daily Journal* (May 17, 1890). One paragraph in particular offended many Perkins trustees and friends. "Helen is not a regular pupil at the Perkins Institution being under the care of a private teacher there," she was quoted as saying. "She is there simply to obtain the advantages of the apparatus which the Institution contains, and for those other advantages desirable for a child in her condition in the possession of which the city of Boston excels all others. I have the whole charge of her and my salary is paid by her father; so you can see that she is not a pupil of the Institution. Her father went North for a teacher and I went South and taught her in her own home for two years." Trustees and friends were further mystified when Helen did not appear at the June commencement exercises.

One of the Perkins trustees, Mr. William Endicott, Jr., a direct descendant of one of the Pilgrim fathers, at whose home in Beverly Teacher and Helen had often stayed, inquired of the acting director what had occasioned the interview and why had Helen not appeared at the commencement.* Bennett replied that some time in the winter of 1889–1890 Miss Sullivan had run afoul of the school's medical director, Dr. Homans—the man, it will be remembered, whom the trustees had wanted to put in over Anagnos as successor to Dr. Howe because he belonged more to Boston. Helen had developed warts on her hand, which Annie had treated with muriatic acid obtained from the teacher of chemistry. Despite the efforts of the local doctor the acid was eating into one of Helen's joints. Dr. Homans heard of it and he reprimanded Annie. "[S]he lost her temper," Bennett's account went on, "and told him it was none of his business. He told her he should report her for her insolence and was informed that he could do as he pleased; that neither he nor the Institution had any control over her or Helen but that they were here as guests."

Dr. Homans went to Dr. Samuel Eliot, the president of the trustees, a

*Letter of F. B. Sanborn to Board of Trustees of the Perkins Institution, October 10, 1906, after the death of Michael Anagnos, which described this episode.

formidable figure, closely connected by blood and marriage with the inner circles of Boston society. After graduating first in his class at Harvard, he had started as a teacher by giving free instruction to the children of workingmen. He had taught history at Trinity College and then became its president before returning to Boston to become a "quasi professional trustee and chairman of boards."

When Eliot heard Dr. Homans, he sent immediately for the acting director. That unhappy, insecure man said that Miss Sullivan had been correct, that she and Helen had come as "guests and had not been subject to directions from anyone." Dr. Eliot reacted strongly. He thought it highly unwise to have in the school persons entirely independent of it, and if Miss Sullivan and Helen wished to remain, they would have to consider themselves subject to the school's regulations. If Miss Sullivan dissented, Mr. Bennett should send her to him. "She went to see him," Mr. Bennett said in his account to Mr. Endicott, "and I suppose he talked over her status with her."

There is no record of what was said; but shortly afterwards, when Mr. Bennett asked Dr. Eliot for suggestions about commencement, he replied he had only two—the program should not be too long and that no one not a pupil should take part. The latter could only apply to Helen, whom Mr. Bennett had hoped to include in the exercises. That was his quandary when the *Journal* interview appeared. "I immediately took it to Miss Sullivan, and asked if the reporter had done her justice. She said that he had and that she had corrected the proof. I criticized her taste in making such a public disclaimer of this eminent Institution, when they were here as invited guests, and she said that she was 'sick and tired' to death of having people speak of Helen as belonging to this Institution and that she wanted to put a stop to it. The conversation became spirited and she lost her temper and was quite insolent. I told her that I would not tolerate that from any inmate, whether guest or not, and that so long as she remained, she would have to be at least outwardly civil." Bennett also informed her that with her attitude she and Helen could not take part in the commencement exercises.

Annie evidently realized that she had blundered, or perhaps Mrs. Hopkins told her she had. Annie's friends moved in to the rescue, as they had so often done when, as a student at Perkins, she had been threatened with expulsion. The next morning Bennett received a letter (the identity of the writer is not known) that denied the genuineness of the interview and intimated that "if it were necessary a copy of the letter might be placed before the Trustees and Captain Keller." Later an unidentified friend of Annie's requested that Helen be allowed to go on the platform "and pronounce a few sentences for which she was being drilled." Bennett thought that would be in bad taste and dishonest, "for our school had nothing to do with articulation, and it would be endeavoring to get credit which belonged elsewhere." "I was told," continued Bennett, "that Miss Sullivan had declared that Helen should go on, anyway, whether I consented or not," but Bennett had not troubled to verify that.

The exercises were held. Helen did not appear. Annie knew she was in trouble. Whether the Kellers knew anything of all this is unclear. But Annie was well aware that in the eyes of Helen's mother and father, her authority rested on what they assumed to be her relationship to Anagnos and Perkins. "Next to our own," Captain Keller wrote to Anagnos two years later, "we recognize no claims upon our dear child to be as strong as yours and it will always be our purpose to consult and advise with you on all that concerns her welfare."

Annie went to see Dr. Eliot again to do a little fence mending. What that austere figure said to her is unrecorded, but Mr. Sanborn, Dr. Howe's friend and the chronicler of these events, reported that it was intimated to Miss Sullivan that "Alabama was a more fitting place than South Boston for her peculiar manifestations of gratitude." The upshot was a handsomely contrite letter from Annie to Dr. Eliot for the board of trustees:

> I cannot leave Boston without expressing to you the deep sorrow I feel for the wrong impression of my own and Helen Keller's relations to the Institution, given in an interview reported in the Boston *Journal.* I consider myself wholly at fault for having seen a reporter at all. But the report does not represent me truly. There it would appear that to me alone is due all the credit of Helen's education; whereas the truth is that the advantages she had at the Institution during the past year have done more to develop and broaden her mind than any training that I could possibly have given her in years, alone.
>
> And much as Helen is indebted to the Institution I am much more so, for as you know, I was educated there and since Helen had been my charge I have been constantly encouraged by its Director, Mr. Anagnos. . . .

It was farthest from my mind to speak lightly of my great obligation to my school and I beg that though you blame me for indiscretion, you will not blame me for ingratitude.

She sent a copy to Anagnos: "I am sending it to you in the faint hope that it will help you to judge me kindly, or at least fairly, in this matter. At any rate it will prove to you that I did all that I could to correct the false impression given in the miserable interview." She was worried about his reaction. Two weeks later she wrote him again, from Tuscumbia, but not about the newspaper interview—she was too politic to do that; she wrote instead about Helen's learning to speak. He deserved the pleasure of hearing the news from Helen herself. "She said many times 'how delighted Mr. Anagnos will be when he hears my beautiful secret.' "

Anagnos was equally diplomatic. He had already seen the offending article, but he referred only to its account of Helen's success in articulation. "Good Mrs. Lane had the kindness to send me a copy of the Boston *Journal* and I was truly delighted to learn through it, that Miss Fuller had taught you how to articulate and that you already have learned to speak distinctly," he wrote to Helen, not Annie, from Rome. "This is certainly one of your greatest achievements, and I earnestly hope that you will continue to practice with your accustomed eagerness. . . ." He did not refer to the lack of gratitude that had exercised Dr. Eliot and Mr. Bennett. He would not have done so in a letter to Helen, and perhaps he did not write to Annie because he thought it best to keep his views to himself. He understood her moodiness, her emotional tantrums, and was a large enough man to perceive also Annie's more-than-offsetting talents. Nor would he have lent himself to any move that might keep Helen and Annie from returning to Perkins in the autumn, when he would again be home.

His tour of Europe, while not quite the triumphal march that Dr. Howe's had been, nevertheless, because of Helen's fame, had opened many doors to him. In his first letter from England, a year earlier, he had reported to Helen that wherever he went he was asked about her. And especially in Athens, "where I spent the best years of my youth," the leading intellectuals, organized in the Parnassus Club, and the royal family, were fascinated by his account of the wonder child. He read one of Helen's letters to the queen and she wept. He had promised Helen to send her a detailed description of every city he visited, and the letters during his fifteen-month absence had turned into a veritable Baedeker. He was sorry to have been away from Boston during her stay there, he wrote

Helen as his search for health and rest drew to an end, but it would not be very long before he had the pleasure of welcoming her back to Boston. "Yes, darling, to me it will be one of the greatest pleasures of my life to take you in my lap and hear you speak."

But he did not write Annie, and his failure to do so troubled her, judging from the letter he finally wrote her from Dresden on August 5. "Illness and constant travelling from place to place must be my excuse for not having written to you sooner. Your account of Helen's wonderful achievement in learning to speak is truly excellent, and I thank you for it. But why do you deem it necessary to urge me to make the accomplishments of the dear child known to the world by writing or giving lectures? Do you think that my deep interest in her is becoming lukewarm and needs a little stirring up? If you do, allow me to assure you that you are wholly mistaken. Helen is permanently enthroned in my heart. I love her as dearly as I ever did." He was already planning his annual report. It would be the first in two years dealing with Helen, and "in order to prepare something worth reading you must go to work at once and write a full authentic account" upon which he will base his own observations, giving Annie "all the credit," and reserving for himself only the role of "humble . . . chronicler" in order to make its contents known "to scientific and thinking men and women."

Annie's burst of zeal to have Anagnos publicize Helen's achievements contrasts ironically with the aversion that she professed at other times to publicity. She was a volatile young woman, full of contradictory impulses, often high-handed and impetuous. Her unwillingness to contribute to Anagnos's report herself and provide accurate information about Helen's development lent itself to the very exaggerations that taxed her patience and tolerance. All of which, of course, it must constantly be borne in mind, was overshadowed by the service and love that she rendered Helen, a service that despite her own rebellious and angry nature brought out Helen's extraordinary qualities of tenderness, compassion and sympathy.

She resisted Anagnos's appeal because anger still flared when she thought of the way she had been humiliated by the Boston Establishment at the end of the previous term. She should put aside her reluctance, Anagnos wrote from Boston, "and undertake the task with as much grace as you can gather in the inner chambers of your feelings. So far as I am personally concerned, I shrink from no labor which my sense of duty would impose upon me, or my warm love for the angelic child would indicate to me as necessary or desirable to be performed; but it will be almost presumptuous on my part, or that of anyone else, to write with any degree of authority on a subject in which we are outsiders. . . . I beg of you not to postpone the commencement of your work any longer, nor to allow any misunderstandings to interfere with your earnestness in doing it in the best possible manner. I must assure you in the most positive manner, that I continue to value your services as much as ever, and that your notion to the contrary is wholly groundless."

Annie was adamant, but she took refuge behind the claim that her eyes again troubled her. Anagnos retreated. "The preservation of your sight is of greater importance and of a higher consideration than anything else." Her eyes were always needing treatment, "but I must confess," she told Nella Braddy, "that I sometimes used them as an excuse for getting out of things I didn't want to do." The result was that Anagnos's report for the year ending September 30, 1890, simply notified its readers that a full report on Helen would be issued later—as it turned out, a year later.

Captain Keller was in straitened financial circumstances, and there was question about Helen's return to Perkins; but finally, on October 29, Anagnos received an exuberant letter from Helen. "I have some very good news for you. . . . I am coming to Boston next week! Is it not a beautiful surprise. . . . Shall you and Mrs. Hopkins be at the station to meet us? Teacher says you will not know me. I am so tall. . . ." It was a long letter, authentic, spontaneous, radiant and affectionate. The thought of leaving her family, her faithful dog and her donkey made her sad, but when she thought of being with her friends and playmates again she was glad. "Is it not queer for a child to feel like laughing and crying all at once?" Her heart had been stirred. She had written a sad story about a newsboy. "Does it not make your heart mournful to think how many little boys and girls are poor and friendless? . . . Mr. Brown [a minister] wrote me about a little boy in Pittsburgh [Tommy Stringer] who is blind and deaf, and his family are too poor to pay a teacher for educating him. He is only five years old. Will you please ask his parents to send him to your Institution, and teacher and I will teach him. You must help me to make my little strange friend happy. Everybody is good to me, and my dear heavenly Father wants me to be more helpful for others."

An equally affectionate and excited letter reported her arrival at Perkins to her mother. Their train had been much delayed and as a result she had been "much disappointed because we did not arrive on Mr. Anagnos's birthday." She missed her family; she missed Neddy, her donkey, and Lioness, her bull mastiff. Both animals had been gifts of William Wade, a Pennsylvania philanthropist deeply interested in the deaf and the blind, with whom they had spent a week the previous June. An equally important announcement: "There are many new books in the library. What a nice time I shall have reading them."

They planned to spend Christmas at Perkins. "We are going to have a Christmas tree in the parlor just as we did last year. I can hardly wait for the fun to begin." Mr. Anagnos often came to see her. "He loves your little girl very much, and she loves him dearly," she wrote her father. The letter ends on an astonishing note. "Teacher would send her love if she were here. You must not call her a fraud and a humbug. She is my own precious teacher, you know." Fraud and humbug? The words leap out at one. Why did Captain Keller call her that? There is no explanation. But the characterization must be noted, for in the next twenty years others would say the same.

It was Helen's Christmas party. The tree was hers and the guests were hers. The brightly decorated hemlock was loaded with gifts. The angel that topped it was a present of one of Julia Ward Howe's grandchildren, Rosalind (Rosy) Richards of Gardiner, Maine, a girl her own age with whom she had often played. At the last moment Helen learned that Mrs. Howe herself would be one of the guests, and she "hastily procured a pretty lily pen-wiper and wrote a little note to accompany it, which was full of love and kind wishes for the 'dear lady.' " She appointed herself "messenger of Santa Claus" and proceeded to carry out her mission when the guests were all assembled. "Skipping gracefully to and fro, and pronouncing the name of each recipient, she enhanced the value of the previous tokens by her keen and vivid delight in their presentation." Her work done as Santa's deputy, she sought out her own presents. They included a book of poems in embossed print, *Stray Chords,* by the late Julia Anagnos, "and at once the child was wholly absorbed in its contents. She read aloud with an intense earnestness of expression and a happy look on her sweet face, which surprised and charmed her audience,—especially the 'dear lady,' to whom evidently it recalled the past, —the great work which her noble husband accomplished for Laura Bridgman, and which thus opened the pathway to this joyous Christmas for Helen Keller."

Whatever Annie's private thoughts were of the Howe women, she did not force them upon Helen. When Helen read Florence Howe Hall's account of her father's work in *Wide Awake,* Dr. Hale's magazine, she wrote Mrs. Hall that all children must have been greatly interested in her story, "but they cannot love Dr. Howe as we little blind children do. Teacher says she would not have known how to teach me if your father had not taught Laura Bridgman first, and that is why I feel so grateful to him."

"She has no memory for injuries, and no inclination for revenge," observed Anagnos in the mammoth report on Helen that he wrote for the three-year period that ended September 30, 1891. "She knows absolutely nothing of the unkindness, hostility, narrow-mindedness, hatefulness and wickedness of the world around her. . . . Helen has implicit trust and confidence in the good intent of everyone." William Wade, who had observed her carefully during her visits to his home, concurred with this judgment: "The child herself is a greater wonder than her progress," he reported to Anagnos, "her marvellous inner nature a greater glory to humanity than her learning. A mightier power than any ever known to schools of learning was needed to fill that little heart with the most over-flowing sympathy, the most complete unselfishness and the rarest delicacy and beauty of thought and expression." People doubted that "the loving, unselfish disposition portrayed in *Little Lord Fauntleroy*" could be that of a real human being, Wade went on, yet anyone who has watched Helen knows that she is "superior even to the creation of Mrs. Burnett's pen."

When she had arrived at Wade's estate in Hulton, Pennsylvania, tired as she was, she had been eager to ride Neddy, the donkey Wade had promised her, and gloried in the ride; but as soon as Annie said "Teacher is tired," she slipped off Neddy's back, "merely delaying to get permission to take Neddy to the stable and feed him." The next day Mr. Wade's groom, Michael, an Irishman, took her and Neddy for a ride. They paused in the shade to get cool. When he asked her whether she was ready to go again, her reply was, "Is Michael rested?" Mr. Wade's son was late for supper. Someone said, "Isn't Archer a naughty boy to be away from supper?" As soon as the first three letters of *naughty* had been spelled out, Helen shook her head. "No. Something has kept him. Perhaps he didn't hear the bell." When Archer did come in and explained that he had been after the donkeys, which had broken out of the pasture, she was "in a state of triumphant delight, and would not be satisfied until Archer came to be kissed." She recoiled in horror when a club was handed to her with the suggestion that she use it to make Neddy go. " 'Oh, no; this is better!' she insisted, *this* being a twig that might have tickled one of the donkey's ears but would not have stimulated him out of the slowest of walks." Michael, the groom, caught a foal for her to examine, but on learning that the mother was pushing toward the colt, she cried, "Oh, let it go. Its mother will be worried about it."

A visiting clergyman, Mr. Brown, the same who wrote her about Tommy Stringer, asked what she knew of prayer. Annie explained that the child's knowledge was rudimentary, but turning to Helen asked her, Did she pray? "Low in those exquisitely muffled tones of hers, came the answer:

> 'I pray the prayer of Plato old,
> God make me beautiful within,
> And make mine eyes the good behold
> In everything save sin.' "

Even Annie had been surprised. "Why, baby, where did you learn that?" It was from Mr. Whittier, she said. "I like it." "Many must have been the triumphs of Mr. Whittier," commented Wade, "yet I am sure that none can have given him the pleasure that it will give him to learn of this quotation from his poems. What nobler shrine could the poet's work have than the lovely, innocent heart of this little child?"

"If the Perkins Institution," concluded Wade, "had done nothing more than develop the system by which such a wonderful mind and heart as Helen's has been rescued from darkness, it would have done, in that alone, a greater work for the world than has been accomplished by many philosophers."

Helen's compassionate heart already was shaping her life's mission. When Mr. Brown, the Pittsburgh minister, heard of Tommy Stringer, the motherless deaf-mute child whose father was unable to care for him, he had thought of Annie Sullivan and wrote to her in Tuscumbia, asking for advice and help. The hapless five-year-old had been sent to the Allegheny General Hospital because there was no other place that could care for him, and he was destined for the almshouse. As Anagnos later commented sarcastically, "There was no other place for him in the great and wealthy state of Pennsylvania." Helen joined in the correspondence with Mr. Brown. The latter now wrote that a school for the blind was opening in Pittsburgh, but without a tutor Tommy could not be admitted. "I ask my dear heavenly Father every day to bless the new school," Helen wrote, "and to send the dear little deaf blind child a teacher like mine. I wish he lived near me so that I could teach him myself."

Tommy's plight preoccupied her. Why could he not be brought to

Boston, she asked Anagnos, almost upon her arrival at Perkins. It will take a great deal of money, he replied. "We will raise it," she answered firmly, and began at once to solicit contributions from friends and to save money herself by forgoing her daily sweet. Petitions began to arrive from Pittsburgh and Philadelphia urging the admission of Tommy; and Dr. Bell, approached for his views, advised the child's friends to send him to Perkins if it could be managed. Anagnos called the case to the attention of some of his trustees, and Mr. Endicott told him, "Do not hesitate to have the little fellow brought to the kindergarten. There will be no difficulty in raising a sufficient sum to pay his expenses. I shall be glad to contribute some of it myself." Why did Anagnos not arrange to care for all such children? Endicott suggested. "Contrast these sentiments," Anagnos said, "with the proposal of one of the managers of the Allegheny General Hospital,—to send poor Tommy to the almshouse; or with the contemptible suggestion made by a member of the Pittsburgh society for the prevention of cruelty to animals at one of its meetings,—that a part of the money given by the lovers of little dogs for the little boy's benefit should be paid to the hospital for the mischief which he did during his stay there,—and then you will feel it a privilege to belong to Boston and breath[e] in the atmosphere of benevolence."

The reference to the dogs arose from Tommy's having become a beneficiary of the death of Helen's beloved Lioness. The mastiff, off her leash, had wandered into the public square in Sheffield, Alabama, and a policeman had shot and killed her. Helen wept when she heard the news, but her reaction was characteristically generous: "I am sure they never could have done it, if they had only known what a dear good dog Lioness was." Mr. Wade's heart was deeply stirred, and he published Helen's letter in *Forest and Stream.* Offers poured in from all over the United States, from Canada and from England to provide Helen with another dog. But Tommy Stringer was on her mind, and her letters of thanks all brought up his case. "I tell all of my friends about the dear little fellow, because I am sure they will want to bring light and music into his sad life." The dog lovers took the hint, and soon a subscription list was opened in her name to help Tommy. "And now I want to tell you what the dog lovers in America are going to do," she wrote a gentleman in London who had offered to buy her a mastiff. "They are going to send me some money for a poor little deaf and dumb and blind child." The Londoner started a subscription list in England.

On April 6 Tommy was brought to the kindergarten, and Helen and her teacher went there to take care of him until a special tutor could be found. "Dear little Tommy has come," she wrote her Canadian correspondent, Mr. Goodhue. "He is very small and helpless, just like an infant. He has had no loving mother to teach him how to do like other children, and that is why he cannot walk and eat as other little boys do. But teacher will be very gentle and patient with him, and soon his mind will escape from the dark prison and be filled with light and music,—that is what education will do for baby Tom."

A week later she wrote Mr. Wade, "We have taught him to walk a little by himself, and to take some food, and soon we hope to give him his first word." A contribution came in from the English painter John Millais. "You will be glad to hear," she wrote him in acknowledgement, "that Tommy has a kind lady to teach him, and that he is a pretty active fellow. He loves to climb much better than to spell, but that is because he does not know yet what a wonderful thing language is." She passed up no chance to raise money. She visited Abbot Academy, a girl's school in Andover, in company with teacher and Miss Marrett. It was, wrote the reporter for *The Transcript,* a "memorable" week because of the way Helen immediately entered into the school's life. She was particularly interested in meeting some teachers from nearby Phillips Academy, because it had been attended by Dr. Holmes. They told her about his poem "The School-Boy," and she responded by reciting some Holmes poems she had read, but the incident that won all hearts was an impromptu speech she made after Miss Marrett had told the assembled girls about the work at Perkins. "I would like to speak to my friends," she said, advancing to the front of the platform: "Dear friends of Andover, I thank you for the pleasure I have had here, and for the gift I have to take to Tommy from you. . . . It seems to me that the world is full of goodness, beauty, and love, and how grateful we must be to our heavenly Father who has given us so much to enjoy. His love and care are written all over the walls of nature. I hope you will all come to South Boston some day to see what little blind children can do. . . ."

The effect of the little speech, wrote the reporter, was overpowering. "The eyes of all others were nearly blind with tears," a witness of the moving scene wrote Anagnos.

The ladies' visiting committee of Perkins held a reception at the kindergarten to raise money for Tommy. It drew a large number of people, wrote Anagnos, "representing the intelligence, the benevolence and the wealth of Boston." The venerable Boston sage, Dr. Holmes, came as a result of Helen's special invitation: "I want you to see baby Tom, the little blind and deaf and dumb child who has just come to our pretty garden. . . . If you do come, you will want to ask the kind people of Boston to help brighten Tommy's whole life." He did come, but begged off making the appeal for funds; so she prevailed upon the Reverend Phillips Brooks, who had just been made a bishop, to do so. "I do not understand very well what a bishop's work is," she wrote in a note of congratulation, "but I am sure it must be good and helpful, and I am glad that my dear friend is brave, and wise, and loving enough to do it. It is very beautiful to think that you can tell so many people of the heavenly Father's tender love for all His children even when they are not gentle and noble as He wishes them to be."

The bishop made the fund-raising appeal, acting, he said, only as Helen's interpreter, and ending his speech, "Helen is asking her friends to help her in this work, and surely the appeal of one such child on behalf of another cannot go unanswered." It did not, and a substantial sum was raised—but not enough, so Helen turned to the newspapers. She published appeals for Tommy in all of Boston's papers and acknowledged even the smallest contribution in her own hand. When the contributions had reached six hundred dollars, it was suggested to her that publication of the list of contributors would lead to additional contributions. She promptly sat down with pencil and grooved writing board to send brief notes to the editors. "Will you please publish, in your paper, the enclosed list of the friends who have sent us money to help our poor little Tommy?" Each note was different. The *Boston Globe* published her letter in facsimile. "Here is a letter from Helen Keller, who is deaf, dumb and blind," commented the *Globe,* "yet the editor of the *Globe* has never received a letter better than hers in diction or spirit." The total sum raised was $1,636.21, sufficient to cover Tommy's expenses for two years.

"I am glad that you read about our reception in the papers," she wrote her mother. "Dr. Holmes and many other good and wise people came to see the little blind children in their happy home. Baby Tom was there and he looked very cunning in his new sailor suit. Edith [Thomas] and pretty little Willie Robin [two other deaf-blind children] were there too. Tommy climbed into everybody's arms, and the ladies and gentlemen were so kind to him that he must have thought that the world was full of loving friends. Bishop Brooks told Tommy's sad story, and asked the people to see that Tommy was educated." From the letter one could not have learned how instrumental she had been in the whole affair.

Second only to her works of goodness was her passion for books. Whenever Anagnos saw her, her first questions were about Tommy; then there were questions about subjects that had come up in her reading— who Memnon was, and Sappho and Tantalus, and Orpheus, Phidion and Amphion. "I am sitting in a sunny corner of the library," she wrote a friend, "with many curious and interesting companions." She referred to the shells, stuffed animals and models as well as books. "The books please me most because they have so much to tell me about everything. They are very wise." Why did she spend so much time with books? Annie asked her; and her reply, full of pathos, was a measure of how dependent she was, despite all her inner glow of spirit, on the people around her. "Because they tell me so much that is interesting about things I cannot see, and they are never tired or troubled like people. They tell me over and over what I want to know."

She read quickly, running the forefinger of her right hand over the printed page, taking in the main points, turning over the pages with energetic rapidity. "[S]he seems to live in a sort of double life," wrote Annie, "in which the scenes and characters she has read of are as real to her as the everyday occurrences and the people in the house. Yesterday I read to her the story of Macbeth, as told by Charles and Mary Lamb. She was very greatly excited by it, and said, 'It is terrible! It makes me tremble!' After thinking a little while, she added: 'I think Shakespeare made it very terrible, so the people would see how fearful it is to do wrong.' " One day when they left the library Teacher asked her why she seemed so serious. "I am thinking how much wiser we always are when we leave here than we are when we come," she replied.

She preferred the library to the sewing room and the other manual pursuits in which she engaged. "She is as eager and as enthusiastic in her pursuit of knowledge as she was three years ago," wrote Annie in the account of Helen's development that she prepared in bits and pieces for Anagnos's forthcoming report. "She has an advantage over ordinary children, that nothing from without distracts her attention from her studies; so that each new thought makes upon her mind a distinct impression which is rarely forgotten." But her concentration carried a price. There was always the danger of "unduly severe mental application. Her mind is so constituted that she is in a state of feverish unrest while conscious that there is something she does not comprehend." Several times Annie, in consultation with others—usually Anagnos—had to direct that systematic instruction be halted. The intensive work with Miss Fuller on articulation had produced a period of nervous exhaustion, and during the following summer she had had a fainting spell. Annie dictated absolute rest, but Helen had not fully recovered in October when she returned to Perkins. She was "far from well," recorded Anagnos—nervous, excitable, restless. She neither ate nor slept as well as she had formerly. The school insisted on a light schedule, and by the spring of 1891 she had fully recovered. And Anagnos in his report could state that she had grown "amazingly fast in body and mind alike. . . . She is now 5'2" in height and of symmetrical figure, and weighs 122 pounds. Her physique is magnificent. . . . Her head is finely formed, and decked with beautiful brown hair falling in luxuriant curls over her pretty shoulders."

As the 1891 school year drew to a close, a very successful year for her, she gave thought to her two favorite poets. On Memorial Day she and Annie visited Whittier. "He was very kind to me, because he loves children, and likes to make them happy. . . . He was very kind to show me all the things in his study, to entertain me. Then we had some nice cake, and we thanked the kind gentleman and came away." On the way back they crossed the Merrimac River. "I shall always call the Merrimac, Whittier's River because he lives near it and loves it, and I like to call the Charles, Holmes' Gentle River, because it is very dear to him."

"Dear Gentle Poet," she wrote to Holmes almost the same day, "I cannot begin to tell you how delighted I was when Mr. Anagnos told me that you had sent him some money to help educate 'Baby Tom'. . . . He is the same restless creature he was when you saw him. . . . I have been to Andover since I saw you. . . . I tried to imagine my gentle poet when he was a school-boy and I wondered if it was in Andover he learned the songs of the birds and the secrets of the shy little woodland children. I am sure his heart was always full of music, and in God's beautiful world he must have heard love's sweet replying. When I came home teacher read to me 'The School-boy,' for it is not in our print.

"Did you know that the blind children are going to have their commencement exercises in Tremont Temple, next Tuesday afternoon? I enclose a ticket hoping that you will come. We shall all be proud and happy to welcome our poet friend. I shall recite about the beautiful cities of sunny Italy."

This commencement she was again the star. Dr. Samuel Eliot, who had vetoed her participation in 1890, introduced her. She played a little piece on the piano, "The Echoes," for which she had been rehearsed by Miss M.E. Riley, who had taught her to read Braille musical notation and apply it to the piano. She demonstrated an exercise in geography, with Teacher interpreting as she made a tour of Italy. "The fingers of the child moved with the rapidity of lightning," commented a proud Anagnos, "and the words flowed from them at the rate of about eighty per minute." She wrote her mother that she had recited "about Italy and the beautiful Italian cities. I saw many dear friends there—Dr. Brooks, Mrs. Howe, Dr. Eliot, Mr. Peabody, Mr. Dwight and many others."

After visits to Gardiner, Maine, with Rosy Richards, and to Hulton, Pennsylvania, with William Wade, she and Teacher returned to Tuscumbia. Helen's world seemed to be complete. She had her reading, her correspondence (especially about Tommy Stringer), her pets—the donkey Neddy, "fat and lazy," and a high-spirited pony, "Black Beauty," that Mr. Wade had given her. There were her sister, Mildred, and a newly arrived baby brother, Phillips Brooks Keller. Teacher worked on her contribution to Anagnos's forthcoming report, but she had other duties, as Helen lamented to Mr. Anagnos. "Teacher is downstairs helping mother prepare plums, and nurse little Phillips, for his nurse would not stay and poor mother is not very strong, I fear. I do not know what I should do without teacher. When she is helping mother, the hours seem very very long to me; but I will not fret. As soon as she can she will come to me, and we will be happy, oh, so happy together! Mother says I have a great deal to thank you for and I do thank you."

"My account of Helen will be as voluminous as yours," Anagnos wrote Annie. "I cannot cut it down. The subject is immense."

The more than two hundred-page account began with a flourish of trumpets. Helen's story "continues to be as fascinating as a fairy tale. . . . Helen is a phenomenal child. She is in every sense a very remarkable person. . . . Her mind is as clear as her brain is fertile, while her heart flames with earnestness and glows with charity."

VIII

Expulsion from Eden

"I think if this sorrow had come to me when I was older, it would have broken my spirit beyond repairing."

Shortly before Anagnos sent his book-length annual report, most of it devoted to Helen, to the printer, he received from Annie in Tuscumbia a copy of a story Helen had written for him: "The Frost King." "I think you will be pleased with this little story Helen wrote for your birthday. We thought it pretty and original. She was greatly disappointed because she could not get it bound. She wanted 'pretty covers with autumn leaves scattered all over them,' but nothing of the kind could be obtained here."

"The Frost King" was a delightful little invention that told how King Frost first came to paint the trees in their autumn hues and thus "comfort us for the flight of summer." The king possessed a large treasure of precious stones, some of which he decided to send to his neighbor Santa Claus, "to buy presents of food and clothing for the poor, that they might not suffer so much when King Winter went near their homes." He had his merry little fairies fill jars and vases with the stones and take them to the palace of Santa Claus. But on the way the fairies were diverted, and while they loitered and played, the jars and vases that they had hidden in the trees were searched out by Mr. Sun, who melted the rubies and other gems, thus coloring the leaves of the oaks and maples with gold, crimson and emerald. When King Frost learned what had happened he was very angry; but when he saw the majestic colors of the trees, his anger disappeared, for he had been taught a new way of doing good. "From that time, I suppose, it has been part of Jack Frost's work to paint the trees with the glowing colors we see in the autumn; and if they are *not* covered with gold and precious stones, I do not know how he makes them so bright, do you?"

Helen had worked on the story, according to Annie, most of October, writing a bit each day. When she had read it to the family, all were astonished by "the beautiful imagery used, and we could not understand how Helen could describe such pictures without the aid of sight." Where had she read the story? her family wanted to know. "I did not read it; it is my story for Mr. Anagnos's birthday," she replied. "And while I was surprised that she could write like this," Annie wrote a few months later, "I was not more astonished than I had been many times before at the unexpected achievements of my little pupil, especially as we had exchanged many beautiful thoughts on the subject of the ripening foliage during the autumn of this year."

Anagnos was as impressed as Helen's family with the story. It was a "precious gift," he wrote Helen. He had shown it to teachers and trustees and inserted it in his report with the comment, "If there be a pupil in any of the private or public grammar schools of New England who can write an original story like this, without assistance from any one, he or she certainly is a rare phenomenon." Since the report was not scheduled to appear until late winter, he turned the story over to *The Mentor,* the magazine of the alumni association, to publish immediately. It was promptly picked up by *The Goodson Gazette,* a weekly published at the Virginia Institution for the Education of the Deaf and Dumb and of the Blind, which ran the story verbatim with the comment that "we believe it to be without parallel in the history of literature." A week later, alas, the *Gazette* was obliged to report that a friend of one of the Institution's teachers had brought in a copy of a child's book, *Birdie and his Fairy Friends* by Margaret T. Canby, which had been given her in early 1874. One of the stories in the book was "The Frost Fairies," and the *Gazette* ran in parallel columns phrases, paragraphs and similes that word for word were the same in Helen's and Miss Canby's stories.

"Comment is unnecessary," the editor wrote, but a week later he did comment. *"The Goodson Gazette* does not blame little Helen Keller for the attempt at fraud, far from it. She is not to blame. She has merely done what she was told to do. The blame for the fraud rests not upon her, but upon whoever knowingly attempted to palm off the Frost King as her composition and there the blame will lie."*

The *Gazette*'s discovery jolted Perkins. A note in Helen's diary, January 30, 1892, reported how Teacher "told me some very sad news which made me unhappy all day. Someone wrote Mr. Anagnos that the story which I sent him as a birthday gift, and which I wrote myself, was not my story at all, but that a lady had written it a long time ago. The person said her story was called 'Frost Fairies.' I am sure I never heard it. It made us feel so bad to think that people thought we had been untrue and wicked. My heart was full of tears, for I love the beautiful truth with my whole heart and mind." Mr. Anagnos, she went on, is "much troubled. It grieves me to think that I have been the cause of his unhappiness, but of course I did not mean to do it."

She went on to explain the origin of the story:

> I thought about my story in the autumn, because teacher told me about the autumn leaves while we walked in the woods at Fern Quarry. I thought fairies must have painted them because they are so wonderful, and I thought, too, that King Frost must have jars and vases containing precious treasures because I knew that other kings long ago had, and because teacher told me that the leaves were painted ruby, emerald, gold, crimson and brown; so I thought the paint must be melted stones. I knew that they must make children happy because they are so lovely, and it makes me very happy to think that the leaves were so beautiful and that the trees glowed so, although I could not see them.

> I thought everybody had the same thought about the leaves, but I do not know now. I thought very much about the sad news when teacher went to the doctor's; she was not here at dinner and I missed her.

---

*Quoted in "Miss Sullivan's Methods," pp. 125–31. This is a 171-page typescript, bound in leather, that has sat on the shelves of the Perkins Institution Library since it was written. No author is listed on the title page. It is largely a lawyerlike analysis of *The Story of My Life* by Helen Keller and was probably written in 1906 after the death of Anagnos. The latter's friends, and the Howe clan particularly, were incensed by some hostile comments that reflected Annie's ingratitude towards Anagnos. A letter from Frank B. Sanborn to the acting director of Perkins, A.O. Caswell, dated September 16, 1906, states that "I have perused and made notes from the long analysis by Mr. Hall, as Mrs. Howe and Mrs. Hall know." This would suggest that the analysis was done by David Prescott Hall, Mrs. Howe's son-in-law and a lawyer. Sanborn, in preparation of his address on Anagnos at the memorial service, visited Perkins "to look over some of your records," because he wished to emphasize how much Anagnos had done for Annie Sullivan.

Helen's family learned from Teacher about the plagiarism, and Captain Keller hastened to assure Anagnos that Helen "could not have received any idea of the story from any of her relatives or friends here, none of whom can communicate with her readily enough to impress her with the details of a story of that character. When Miss Annie first read it to us I questioned her closely about it and told her I did not think the dear child could have written it without suggestions from some older person, when she assured me that it was original as she now claims."

Anagnos was unwilling to believe that Annie and Helen, whom he loved and who had repeatedly assured him of their love for him, had made him the victim of deception. But his own credibility was at stake. He instituted a "careful inquiry," as he phrased it in the note of apology that he managed to insert in the report before it appeared, "of her parents, her teachers and those who are accustomed to converse with her."

The apology incorporated in briefer form the explanation that Teacher wrote to John Hitz for publication in the new edition of the Helen Keller *Souvenir* that Dr. Bell's Volta Bureau proposed to publish:

As I myself never read this story ('Frost Fairies'), or even heard of the book *(Birdie and His Fairy Friends)*, I inquired of Helen if she knew anything of the matter, and found that she did not. She was utterly unable to recall either the name of the story or of the book. Careful examination was made of the books in raised print in the library of the Perkins Institution, to learn if any extracts from this volume could be found there; but nothing was discovered. I then concluded that the story must have been read to her a long time ago, as her memory usually retains with great distinctness facts and impressions which have been committed to its keeping.

After making careful inquiry, I succeeded in obtaining the information that our friend Mrs. S.C. Hopkins had a copy of the book in 1888, which was presented to her little daughter in 1873 or 1874. Helen and myself spent the summer of 1888 with Mrs. Hopkins at her home in Brewster, Mass., where she kindly relieved me, a part of the time, of the care of my little charge. She amused and entertained Helen by reading to her from a collection of juvenile publications among which was the copy of *Birdie and His Fairy Friends;* and while Mrs. Hopkins does not remember the story of "Frost Fairies," she is confident that she read to Helen extracts, if not entire stories, from this volume. But as she was not able to find her copy, and applications for the volume at bookstores in Boston, Albany, New York, Philadelphia, and other places resulted only in failure, search was instituted for the author herself. . . .

This explanation was accepted by Anagnos. Although "deeply troubled," as Helen wrote, he was "unusually tender and kind," and to please him Helen "tried not to be unhappy, and to make myself as pretty as possible for the celebration of Washington's birthday. . . . I was to be Ceres in a kind of masque given by the blind girls." But the night before, one of the teachers, Helen's account continued, had asked her a question connected with "The Frost King," and Helen told her that Teacher had talked to her about "Jack Frost and his wonderful works. Something I said made her think she detected in my words a confession I did remember Miss Canby's story of 'The Frost Fairies,' and she laid her conclusion before Mr. Anagnos, although I had told her most emphatically that she was mistaken."

Here is the teacher's report (she is not further identified) to Anagnos. It is a startling document:

On the afternoon of February 22nd I had a conversation with Helen Keller a part of which I feel it is my duty to record for future reference. Mr. Munsell* and his mother dined with us that day, so after dinner we adjourned to the front parlor where there was some general conversation for several moments, Helen and her pictures forming the principal topics. Soon Helen of her own accord, at least from no persuasion of mine, seated herself beside me on the sofa, and we entered into a little playful conversation. Shortly afterward our guests took their departure, but still we continued to chat pleasantly. At length Helen said to me 'Did you ever write a story out of your own head?' I replied I might have done so in composition class. Helen said 'I do not mean that. I mean did you ever write a story out of your own head?' I then tried to tell her that there were different ways of composing; that it could be in the form of a story or a poem or a letter. I then asked 'Did you ever write a story out of your own head?' She said 'Once I wrote a story King Frost from Frost King,

---

*Albert H. Munsell was a young and promising artist whose studio in Boston Helen had visited in the company of Teacher and Anagnos. She had so enchanted Munsell with her "lively and winning ways" that he had begged to paint her portrait, which he was in the course of doing.

but it was not exactly that.' I said 'Some one read it to you?' She said 'Yes.' I asked 'Who?' Her answer came promptly, 'Teacher.' I spelled with my fingers, 'Teacher,' for I could not believe my ears. She said 'Yes.' I then asked 'Last summer?' She said 'No, last fall.' I said 'In the mountains?' She said 'No, in my own home.' I said 'Was it from a little book called 'Birdie and his friends,—fairy friends?' She said 'I think so—it was something about birdie.' I said 'I thought it was Mrs. Hopkins who read it to you.' She said: 'Yes?—No.' I said 'It was teacher herself who read it to you?' She replied 'Yes' and added what I understood to be this: 'Teacher says I must not get mixed up, that Mrs. Hopkins read it to me when I was little.' We then talked about *Quentin Durward* which she was reading for herself. I did not like to leave the previous theme of conversation without asking why she did not tell Miss Marrett that Teacher read her the story, and so ventured to renew the subject although I felt sure Miss Sullivan must have seen or heard enough to make her conscious and concerned about our conversation. I said 'You did not remember Miss Marrett asked you about the story?' She began to reply that 'it was a wrong story,' when she was interrupted by her teacher who silently took her upstairs.

After tea, when I went into the parlor to sit upon the sofa, as is my custom, I was surprised and pleased to find Helen there and evidently expecting me, for she received me cordially and chatted about gymnastics and how strong she was and how high she could climb. Presently she said 'Do you remember what we were talking about this afternoon?' I began spelling the question whereupon she repeated it to me. I said 'Yes.' She said 'Did you think I told you that teacher read me that story?' I said emphatically, 'Yes, Helen, you did.' She said 'I did not mean to tell you that. I meant to tell you that she read me frost stories.' I repeated my reply more earnestly 'Yes, Helen, you did tell me so,' and I drew my hand gently away. She immediately arose and went to her teacher who sat opposite, talking busily with Miss Marrett and apparently not heeding our conversation. Helen's manner was unmistakably troubled and hesitating and my heart went out toward the child in painful sympathy. I felt there was some struggle going on within her mind that she could not express. I then felt I ought to tell Mr. Anagnos the circumstances and what Helen had told me. He received the tiding calmly, but, as he said, it was more painful than anything which had come to him since 1886 [the year of his wife's death]. He thanked me and said it was my duty to tell him. During the time of the after-dinner conversation with Helen, Miss Sullivan and Miss Marrett were sitting by the front window engaged in conversation, and I felt that they would certainly hear what Helen said, but as they did not appear to be paying any attention to us my first impulse on receiving Helen's startling announcement was to speak right out and express the astonishment and grief it caused me, but I checked myself because it did not seem best under the circumstances to make an open declaration of such a statement. I had never exchanged one word with Miss Sullivan on the subject, but I knew her repeated and positive denial of any knowledge of the story; therefore I deemed it wise to acquaint Mr. Anagnos with the simple facts as they came to me and let him sift out the truth.*

Anagnos now felt compelled to institute a more searching inquiry. He sent a formal questionnaire to Miss Marrett, the teacher who was second only to Annie in Helen's affections, and who at his request had talked with Helen about the Frost King story. He directed a similar questionnaire to Teacher. And he instituted a court of investigation composed of teachers and officers of Perkins, four blind and four sighted. This elaborate apparatus of investigation directed at a girl not yet twelve years of age seems a little absurd. Anagnos knew Helen. He knew her gifts. These were and would remain realities, whatever the truth about "The Frost King"; the same was true about Annie Sullivan. But his professional reputation was at stake. He knew that some of his colleagues thought that he had exaggerated the achievements of the two. Moreover, his image of himself as the foster-father and guide of Helen and Annie began to crumble. He felt he had to get at the truth.

"In compliance with your request," Fanny Marrett wrote him on March 6, "I send you my answers to the questions which you asked concerning Helen Keller and the story of 'The Frost King.'

1.   'What does Helen say about the story? Does she claim that it was original with her?' These are Helen's words. 'It is my own story. I wrote it myself for Mr. Anagnos's birthday.'

---

*The document is quoted in "Miss Sullivan's Methods." The original is not in the Perkins files. Nor are there any records or minutes of the proceedings of this extraordinary "court of investigation."

2. 'Does she have a clear idea of the difference between original composition and reproduction?' I think so as she has spoken of 'making up stories out of her own head' as contrasted with telling stories which had been written or told by other people.

3. 'Does she know what plagiarism means?' Until the recent sad revelations concerning the story 'The Frost King' Helen had no knowledge of the meaning of the word plagiarism.

4. 'Has she always been truthful?' Yes, truth has ever seemed to me the strongest element of her character.

5. 'Has she made any reference to the story or parts of it in conversation since the summer of 1888?' No, not to my knowledge.

6. 'How did she feel when she was told the story was an adaptation of somebody else's words?' She was very much surprised and grieved. She could not keep back the tears and the chief cause of her pain seemed to be the fear that people should think her untrue. She said with great intensity of feeling—'I love the beautiful truth.''

Teacher did not take kindly to Anagnos's questionnaire. His three questions were directed at finding out whether Helen knew what plagiarism meant. No one seems to have thought to ask Annie whether *she* had known the meaning of plagiarism before the unfolding of the Frost King episode. Or perhaps, remembering Annie's defiance of a similar court at Perkins when she was a student there, no one dared. "I know of no good reason why I should answer the questions," she wrote him from Brewster, "but I shall do so in accordance with your urgent request."

1st: I cannot say positively whether Helen has, or has not a clear idea of the difference between original composition and reproduction. I do not know certainly that she has ever had an original idea. If she has not, of course, she can not have a clear conception of what is meant by original composition. But, supposing that she has been conscious of the birth of ideas in her own brain, it is not probable, I think that she makes any wise discriminations between such ideas and others which she has unconsciously absorbed in the course of her reading.

2nd: The meaning of plagiarism was explained to Helen last evening on the receipt of your letter.

3rd: Helen's diary for January 30th will give you a better idea of her feelings, when told that King Frost was not her own story, than I can at this late day. I should be very happy to furnish you with a copy of the diary when I return to Boston. I do not remember the exact words used by Helen in our conversation, but I do remember that she denied most emphatically any knowledge of *Frost Fairies.* I did not then explain to her the difference between original and adaptation or reproduction. Should you have immediate use for that portion of Helen's diary which relates to the story, Mrs. Pratt can furnish you with a copy. I shall be in Boston on the 12th. Please have it plainly understood by all seekers for further information regarding Helen's story that this is the last statement which I shall make in relation to it, and believe me Very truly yours, Anne M. Sullivan.

Of Helen's appearance before the court of inquiry, we have to rely chiefly on her account. It evidently took place before she and Teacher went to Brewster.

. . . Miss Sullivan was asked to leave me. Then I was questioned and cross-questioned with what seemed to me a determination on the part of my judges to force me to acknowledge that I remembered having had 'The Frost Fairies' read to me. I felt in every question the doubt and suspicion that was in their minds, and I felt, too, that a loved friend [Anagnos] was looking at me reproachfully, although I could not have put all this into words. The blood pressed about my thumping heart, and I could scarcely speak except in monosyllables. Even the consciousness that it was only a dreadful mistake did not lessen my sufferings; and when at last I was allowed to leave the room, I was dazed and did not notice my teacher's caresses, or the tender words of my friends who said I was a brave little girl and they were proud of me. As I lay in my bed that night, I wept as I hope few children have wept. I felt so cold, I imagined I should die before morning, and the thought comforted me. I think if this sorrow had come to me when I was older, it would have broken my spirit beyond repairing. But the angel of forgetfulness has gathered up and carried away much of the misery and all the bitterness of those sad days.

The jealousy of the other teachers was a big factor in the way the court of inquiry was run, Lydia Hayes told Nella Braddy. She had been a student at Perkins when Teacher was there and later became commissioner of the blind in New Jersey. She was very fond of Anagnos and worked with him after she was graduated from the Institution and felt toward him "as a daughter might." The women teachers at Perkins were "spinsters," she said, "institutionalized, catty, with no vision, many of them religious." Anagnos in time was infected by them. "Besides he had to keep peace among them." "The mischief about the investigation," William Wade once said, "was in the beastly, brutal way in which Xenophon [Anagnos] permitted the 'Mentor' gang, Smith and Miss Riley (I reckon) to put Helen in the dock as if a criminal." Smith, a teacher at Perkins since 1863, was known as an Anagnos loyalist. "Miss Sullivan used to boast of her power over Michael Anagnos," he wrote in 1898, "and she did so not without reason until the conditions changed and the spell was broken."

Anagnos, at the time, considered Helen and Annie innocent of the intent to deceive. The court divided; four believed Helen knew the Canby story had been read to her, four voted in Helen's favor. In a letter to the *American Annals of the Deaf* dated March 11, 1892, Anagnos declared that "a most rigid examination of the child of about two hours duration, at which eight persons were present and asked all sorts of questions with perfect freedom, failed to elicit in the least any testimony convicting either her teacher or any one else of the intention or the attempt to practice deception." He accepted Annie's explanation that the story had been read to Helen in 1888, that it had been superseded in her conscious memory by *Little Lord Fauntleroy,* which she had read shortly afterwards, only to reappear three years later in the guise of the Frost King when she was told of Jack Frost. "This theory is shared by many persons who are perfectly well acquainted with the child and who are able to rise above the clouds of a narrow prejudice," Anagnos concluded his communication.

"For two years he [Anagnos] seems to have held the belief that Miss Sullivan and I were innocent," Helen wrote in her autobiography. "Then he evidently retracted his favorable judgment, why I do not know."

Some clue to the doubts that may have persisted in Anagnos's mind even though he voted as he did is given in a letter that Margaret Canby, at last located, wrote to Annie Sullivan and which the latter used in her account in *Souvenir* of the "Frost King" episode. Miss Canby wrote her how impressed she was by what she had learned about Helen. Would Miss Sullivan send her some of the documents relating to the controversy? "I find traces, in the Report which you so kindly sent me, of little Helen having heard other stories than that of the Frost Fairies," she wrote Teacher on March 9.

> On Page 132, in a letter, there is a passage which must have been suggested by my story called 'The Rose Fairies,' and on pages 93 and 94 of the Report the description of a thunderstorm is very much like Birdies' idea of the same in the 'Dew Fairies' on pages 59 and 60 of my book. What a wonderfully active and retentive mind that gifted child must have! If she had remembered and written down, accurately, a short story, and that soon after hearing it, it would have been a marvel; but to have heard the story once, three years ago, and in such a way that neither her parents nor teacher could ever allude to it or refresh her memory about it, and then to have been able to reproduce it so vividly, even adding some touches of her own in perfect keeping with the rest, which really improve the original, is something that very few girls of riper years, and with every advantage of sight, hearing, and even great talents for composition, could have done as well, if at all. Under the circumstances, I do not see how any one can be so unkind as to call it a plagiarism; it is a wonderful feat of memory, and stands *alone,* as doubtless much of her work will in the future, if her mental powers grow and develop with her years as greatly as in the few years past.

We turn now to the anonymous document that has been resting on the shelves of the Perkins Library. Did the sponsors or the writer of that harsh indictment wish to have it sit there, did they wish to send it as a letter to posterity in order to shatter Anne Sullivan's reputation and vindicate Anagnos?* What "Miss Sullivan's Methods" does is to examine line by line, phrase by phrase, letters and stories of Helen Keller for the period 1888–1891, as published in the Perkins reports, for evidence of plagiarism from Margaret Canby's book. It found duplications and similes from

---

*Sanborn left a sheaf of letters, most of them by Anne Sullivan to Anagnos, to the American Antiquarian Society in Worcester, Massachusetts, where they remained unnoticed until 1978. Perhaps this friend of the New England Transcendentalists felt he was thus fulfilling his obligations as a gentleman, to Helen and Anne Sullivan, and as a thinker, to the truth.

five of the eight stories in the Canby volume. Echoes and themes from those stories began to crop up in Helen's writing as early as the autumn of 1889. They become particularly numerous in 1890. Helen's account of a dream which she sent to Anagnos, then in Athens, in February 1890— and which that gentleman, impressed with its "exquisite imagery," read to the Queen, who wept as she listened—was an "adaptation" or "assimilation" of Canby's story "The Rose Fairies" (our anonymous analyst borrows these extenuative words from Annie Sullivan but uses them ironically).

Some of these borrowings were noted by Helen and Annie themselves, especially in *The Story of My Life;* others were not. In Annie's explanation of the "Frost King" episode, she asserted that in 1891 they had stayed later than usual at Fern Quarry and that her descriptions of the autumn foliage had reawakened a dormant memory in Helen of the story that had been read to her in 1888 by Mrs. Hopkins. Fern Quarry was a cottage on a mountain near Tuscumbia that belonged to the Kellers. Helen and Teacher loved it. In 1890 they had tarried there until early fall, but in 1891, our analyst notes, they had left Fern Quarry by September 13, judging by a letter from Teacher to Anagnos that was so dated. "Now prior to September 13th the leaves would not have more than begun to change upon the trees."

The anonymous writer then quotes from a letter that Helen wrote to Anagnos September 29, 1891, from Tuscumbia: "If you read my letter to Miss Lane you know what we did while we were in the mountains. Oh, how I enjoyed the books teacher read to me! [Our analyst underlined this sentence, for he was persuaded the Canby book was one of them.] Reading new books is like making new friends. The days were bright and cool on the mountain, and I enjoyed the walks and rides through the woods with dear teacher. We were especially happy when the trees began to put on their autumn robes. Oh yes! I could imagine how beautiful the trees were all aglow, and rustling in the sunlight. *We thought the leaves as pretty as flowers, and carried great bunches home to mother. The golden leaves I called buttercups and the red ones roses. One day teacher said, 'Yes, they are beautiful enough to comfort us for the flight of summer.'* " The underlined sentences all appear in Margaret Canby's "Frost Fairies." Far from being unaware of the Canby book, our investigator concluded, Miss Sullivan was constantly feeding Helen similes and fancies from it.

Anagnos left no record of why his views altered, as Helen subsequently asserted that they did. There is some question whether he had in fact changed his position. According to Frank Sanborn's October 10, 1906 letter to the Perkins trustees, when Anagnos had voted in favor of Helen and Teacher, he simply was voting the

> Scotch verdict of 'not proven.' Mr. Anagnos, whatever his impressions might be in regard to other matters, not entering into the special enquiry, felt justified (and in the opinion of all who understood what the word gentleman implies) he was justified in casting [his] vote for 'not proven.' He was not willing to blight the reputation of two persons whom he had originally benefitted by pronouncing the opinion that perhaps an indifferent person would have uttered. He followed a more illustrious example, 'Neither do I condemn thee; go sin no more' was the effect of his vote; he did not in fact pronounce upon the main question. He had nobly fulfilled an obligation towards two unfortunate children; it was not for him to injure his own work by forbidding the benefit of a doubt to the person investigated. [Sanborn meant Teacher.]
>
> The subsequent course of that person may have turned that doubt into conviction as had happened with other persons who have learned the actual facts. It is an assumption quite unwarranted to say that he might at that time have established 'our' integrity [as Helen was asserting and which Sanborn construed to mean Miss Sullivan's integrity] by a word. He was not the sole repository of facts, which mere words could not annul. His silence under persistent misrepresentations and perverse ingratitude was more useful to the inculpated than any publication of the exact truth could have been. But he probably was not at liberty to deny his own belief when questioned by those who had a right to know it. And we have reason to think that his final opinion was not founded on words but on facts and events better known to him than any other.

The writer of this biography believes that Miss Sullivan did know the Canby book and made frequent use of it in talks with Helen, especially in describing what she saw. This does not diminish her remarkable insights and achievements as a teacher. She was flawed, which is only to say that she was human. She was deeply conscious of the gaps in her own education. The best of tutors frequently stay but one lesson ahead of their charges. It is quite conceivable that Annie Sullivan boned up on fairy tales, children's histories and poems in order to enrich her communications to Helen and stimulate the child's imagination. Nella Braddy, in a note about a conversation with Teacher, recorded, "She had to get Helen's lessons out of the material at hand—they worked together—she asked Helen to write what she saw. Then Annie would give touches like color, then they would read stories in "Youth's Library" and notice what these had described that they hadn't. Then they would add those details to make it more interesting." Back in April 1888 Annie had written Anagnos that she had to be extremely careful in rewriting stories for Helen "because the little witch has such a wonderfully retentative [sic] memory that she can remember the thread of a tale after it has been read to her once, and she does not like for me to change it in the slightest particular." As for Helen, the ways of the mind are unpredictable, mysterious and infinite, particularly when one is endowed, as Helen was, with an extraordinary memory. It is doubtful, in view of her denials and her almost holy feeling about telling the truth and despite the anonymous teacher's report of her conversation with Helen, that she had read any of the Canby stories, and if they were read to her by her teacher, that she was made aware that Margaret Canby was their author.

Teacher's explanation in the letter to Hitz that was published in *Souvenir* placed heavy stress on the unpredictably absorptive qualities of Helen's mind:

> . . . While I have always known that Helen made great use of such descriptions and comparisons as appeal to her imagination and fine poetic nature, yet recent developments in her writings convince me of the fact that I have not in the past been fully aware to what extent she absorbs the language of her favorite authors. In the early part of her education I had full knowledge of all the books she read, and of nearly all the stories which were read to her, and could without difficulty trace the authority of any adaptations noted in her writing or conversation; and I have always been much pleased to observe how appropriately she applies the expressions of a favorite author in her own compositions. . . .

> The pages of the books she reads become to her like paintings, to which her imaginative powers give life and color. She is at once transported into the midst of the events portrayed in the story she reads or is told, and the characters and descriptions become real to

her; she rejoices when justice wins, and is sad when virtue goes unrewarded. The pictures the language paints on her memory appear to make an indelible impression; and many times when an experience comes to her similar in character, the language starts forth with wonderful accuracy, like the reflection from a mirror.

Helen's mind is so gifted by nature that she seems able to understand, with only the faintest touch of explanation, every possible variety of external relations. One day in Alabama, as we were gathering wildflowers near the springs on the hillsides, she seemed to understand for the first time that the springs were surrounded by mountains, and she exclaimed, 'The mountains are crowding around the springs, to look at their own beautiful reflections!' I am not able to state where she obtained this language, yet it is evident that it must have come to her from without, as it would hardly be possible for a person deprived of the visual sense to originate such a description. In mentioning a visit to Lexington, Mass., she writes: 'As we rode along we could see the forest monarchs bend their proud forms to listen to the little children of the woodlands whispering their secrets. The anemone, the wild violet, the hepatica, and the funny little curled-up ferns all peeped out at us from beneath the brown leaves.' She closes this letter with 'I must go to bed, for Morpheus has touched my eyelids with his golden wand.' Here again I am unable to state where she acquired these expressions.

The "Frost King" episode is significant because of what it says about the protagonists, not because of the significance of the event itself. Mark Twain, when he read about it in Helen's *Story of My Life,* sent her some pithy comments on the absurdity of the "court" and the subject of plagiarism:

Oh, dear me, how unspeakably funny and owlishly idiotic and grotesque was that 'plagiarism' farce! As if there was much of anything in any human utterance, oral or written, *except* plagiarism! The kernel, the soul—let us go further and say the substance, the bulk, the actual and valuable material of *all* human utterances—is plagiarism. For substantially all ideas are secondhand, consciously and unconsciously drawn from a million outside sources, and daily used by the garnerer with a pride and satisfaction born of the superstition that he originated them: whereas there is not a rag of originality about them anywhere except the little discoloration they get from his mental and moral calibre and his temperament, which is revealed in characteristics of phrasing. . . . It takes a thousand men to invent a telegraph, or a steam engine, or a phonograph, or a photograph, or a telephone, or any other important thing—and the last man gets the credit and we forget the others. He added his little *mite*—that is all he did. These object lessons should teach us that ninety-nine parts of all things that proceed from the intellect are plagiarism, pure and simple; and the lesson ought to make us modest. But nothing can do that. Then why don't we unwittingly reproduce the *phrasing* of a story, as well as the story itself? It can hardly happen —to the extent of fifty words—except in the case of a child; its memory tablet is not lumbered with impressions, and the natural language can have graving room there and preserve the language a year or two, but a grown person's memory tablet is a palimpsest, with hardly a bare space upon which to engrave a phrase. It must be a very rare thing that a whole page gets so sharply printed on a man's mind, by a single reading that it will stay long enough to turn up some time or other to be mistaken by him for his own. No doubt we are constantly littering our literature with *disconnected* sentences borrowed from books at some unremembered time and now imagined to be our own, but that is about the most we can do. In 1886 I read Dr. Holmes's poems in the Sandwich Islands. A year and a half later I stole his dedication, without knowing it, and used it to dedicate my *Innocents Abroad* with. Ten years afterward I was talking with Dr. Holmes about it. He was not an ignorant ass—no, not he; he was not a collection of decayed human turnips, like your 'Plagiarism Court,' and so when I said, 'I know where I stole it, but who did *you* steal it from?' he said, 'I don't remember; I only know I stole it from somebody, because I have never originated anything altogether myself, nor met anybody who had.'

To think of these solemn donkeys breaking a little child's heart with their ignorant damned rubbish about plagiarism! I couldn't sleep for blaspheming about it last night. Why, their whole histories, their whole lives, all their learning, all their thoughts, all their opinions were one solid rock of plagiarism, and they didn't know it and never suspected it. A gang of dull and hoary pirates piously setting

themselves the task of disciplining and purifying a kitten that they
think they've caught filching a chop! Oh, dam—

But you finish it dear, I am running short of vocabulary today.

Dr. Bell—not as personally involved with Helen and her teacher as
were Anagnos and others at Perkins, more a man of the world, sure that
Helen and Teacher were extraordinary creatures and enormous assets in
helping the blind and the deaf—moved swiftly to their help when he
heard about the "Frost King" plagiarism. He was not totally disinterested. "The public has already become interested in Helen Keller," he
had written in 1891, "and through her may perhaps be led to take an
interest in the more general subject of the Education of the Deaf." He
sent John Hitz, the superintendent of the Volta Bureau, to make an
independent inquiry. Hitz was an elderly gentleman who, in his cape
and long white beard—a beard longer than that of Anagnos—caused
many, including Anagnos, to call him "picturesque." He had been born
in Switzerland and was an ardent Swedenborgian, a faith in which he
tried to interest Annie and to which he did convert Helen. By the end
of his investigation, he was calling Annie "daughter" and she was addressing him as *"mon père."* The outcome of his inquiries was the second
edition of the Helen Keller *Souvenir*. This, with the authority of Dr. Bell
behind it, effectively silenced the doubters. Hitz printed Helen's "Frost
King" and Margaret Canby's "Frost Fairies" side by side and followed
them with Annie Sullivan's long letter in explanation of Helen's "adap-
tations" of the one from the other. Annie included in her letter Margaret Canby's generous words of unfeigned pleasure in the use Helen had
made of her book as well as a poem, "A Silent Singer," that Miss Canby
had "lovingly dedicated to Helen A. Keller, after reading some of her
beautiful letters." It began:

> Sweet Helen, when I think of thee,
>   With sightless eye and sealed ear,
> Yet pining not in misery,
>   But with a spirit full of cheer,
> Seeing with inward vision clear
>   The loveliness of earth and sky,
>   I blush that mortals blest as I,
> So little see,—so little hear!

The poem consisted of five stanzas and ended with a verse that referred to Helen's mission:

> But e'en on earth thy tuneful soul,
>   Replete with love of all things fair,
> May find a voice in written scroll
>   To smooth the brow of grief and care;
> To bid all burdened spirits bear,
>   Bravely as thine, their daily cross,
>   Till, purified by pain and loss,
> In heaven the angels' song they share.

"Please give her my warm love," Miss Canby wrote Teacher, "and tell her not to feel troubled about it any more. No one shall be allowed to think it was anything wrong; and some day she will write a great beautiful story or poem that will make many people happy. Tell her there are a few bitter drops in every one's cup, and the only way is, to take the bitter patiently, and the sweet thankfully. I shall love to hear of her reception of the book, and how she likes the stories which are new to her."

Dr. Bell and Mr. Hitz also published in the *Annals,* the monthly journal of the American Association to Promote the Teaching of Speech to the Deaf, an article on "Is Helen Keller A Fraud?" written by Mr. J. Williams, the principal of the institution for deaf-mutes at Hartford, Connecticut, who had himself been among skeptics until two long personal interviews with Helen had turned him into a believer:

> It will not do to write down Helen Keller as 'a fraud,' 'a humbug,' 'a back number,' however much we may feel annoyed by the 'Frost King' composition. She has been in the full blaze of public curiosity too long, and been tested by too many scientific men and educational experts, to be a successful deceiver. Every facility has been given for such tests, and I have never known of a failure.

> Great verbal memory, though a rare gift, is present whenever the language facility exists in a high degree. . . . It is said of Macaulay, who had a marvellously wide range of information and was an omnivorous reader, that he could quote almost any fact which he wished to use in the exact words of the author from whom he obtained it.

With all men language is largely a matter of memory. . . .

Taking this child all in all, and making allowances for every possible aid that has been given her and for all unconscious exaggeration due to friendly admiration, there yet remains so much that is marvellous as to place her beyond comparison with any other child of whom we have ever heard. The whole history of literature reveals nothing equal to her language productions from one of her years, even among those possessed of all their faculties. She is a genius, a prodigy, a phenomenon.

Nowhere, not even in Helen's last book, *Teacher,* written when she no longer needed to concern herself with public opinion, is there the slightest hint that any explanation except that which she and Teacher gave in 1892 and subsequently reaffirmed in *The Story of My Life* in 1902 was the true one. In her autobiography she wrote of her feelings when she finally understood that "Frost King" and "Frost Fairies" were so much alike that hers could only have been copied from Miss Canby and that "Frost Fairies" had been read to her by Mrs. Hopkins. "It was difficult to make me understand this, but when I did understand it I was astonished and grieved. No child ever drank deeper of the cup of bitterness than I did. I had disgraced myself. I had brought suspicion upon those I loved best."

Here perhaps is the clue to Helen's behavior at the time. She had brought suspicion on Annie Sullivan, her liberator, her creator, her link to the world. The writer of this book does not know what exchanges took place between Teacher and Helen during those painful days, but he is persuaded Helen would have done anything Teacher asked of her. He also believes Annie did not understand the meaning of plagiarism, and that is why she allowed Helen to send the story to Anagnos and to present it as her own, and then, taking fright because of the uproar, denied she had read the *Birdie* stories.

IX

The Break with Anagnos

". . . I wish to be near you because I love you and I am happier near you
than anywhere else in the world." —Annie to Anagnos

The reaction of the major actors in the "Frost King" affair—
Helen, Annie and Anagnos—took time to crystallize. To Boston, perhaps
even to themselves, things seemed to be the same as they had been. In
April the ladies' visiting committee gave its annual reception on Froebel's
birthday at the kindergarten. Helen had her own list of personal friends
to whom she sent special invitations—Bishop Brooks, Dr. Holmes, Dr.
Hale, Reverend Minot J. Savage, Mr. John S. Spaulding, Dr. Bell, Mr.
Hitz, Mr. F. B. Sanborn and others.

"Dear Kind Poet," she wrote Holmes, "my heart sings for joy these
lovely April days! . . . I feel the glad awakened spirit of life in everything;
and long to show the dear friend, who has made me feel the beauty and
melody filling all this great world of ours, how deeply grateful I am for
his beautiful poems. . . . I would like very much to see you before I go
home. It would give everyone great pleasure if you could come to the
reception at the Kindergarten next Thursday. I shall be there to welcome
you with a loving kiss." Who would resist such an invitation? "My dear
sweet Helen," Holmes replied, "it is delightful to find what a world you
have made for yourself. You must have eyes and ears in your soul, spiritual
organs of sense, which do for you what our outward organs do for us poor
seeing and hearing mortals. . . . You meet and will always meet with love
and tender regard everywhere. There is no human heart that does not

warm with affection to the dear little sister who finds light in the darkness which envelops her, and music in the silence in which she moves and has her being. I think God has granted you a cheerful temperament, one of the very greatest blessings granted us mortals. . . ."

Because of illness, Holmes was unable to come, so Helen prevailed on Dr. Hale, his junior by some dozen years, although weary from the festivities that attended his seventieth birthday, to come and make the collection speech. "Ladies and Gentlemen," he began, "I am here as Helen's retained counsel. She came to see me last week, dear child, and said, as she could not speak, she wanted me to speak for her. I asked her what I should say. . . ." And if any still kept their hands on their wallets, they, too, capitulated when Helen stepped forward at the end of Dr. Hale's appeal and asked Dr. Eliot's permission to say a few words: "I want to say something to you myself. I cannot speak very well yet, but my heart is full of thoughts and I must express some of them. Kindness is like rain in April, it makes everything grow. Your kindness will make the little plantlets here grow and blossom. Think how happy we shall all be when Tommy's mind bursts beautiful and bright from behind the clouds that hide it now. . . ."

"It is hardly possible," commented Anagnos in his annual report, "to describe adequately the tremendous effect of Helen's appeal. It was as though some wizard of olden time had cast his spell over the assembly."

Encouraged by her success at the reception, she decided on an even bolder venture. Talking one day with her friends Rosalind "Rosy" Richards and Caroline Derby about the money that could be raised for charitable purposes at "teas and fairs," she felt a challenge and temptation. "Why can I not give a 'tea' in aid of the kindergarten?" she asked the two. "Money is needed for a new building, and we must help Mr. Anagnos to raise it." The two agreed and said they would help. "I tried to persuade her to give it up at first," Annie wrote John Hitz after the event, "knowing that such an affair would make a great deal of very hard work for both of us, but when I found that the dear child's heart was set upon carrying out her plan I felt that it would not be right to discourage so beautiful a manifestation of her heart."

Although exhausting to the main movers, the tea proved to be, wrote Annie, "a great success socially and financially. The net proceeds amounted to eleven hundred and thirty-five dollars and you will see from the newspaper clippings that the best people of Boston came to pay their respects to the little hostess and wish her a pleasant summer and an early return to Boston. Think of it! A little girl not yet twelve years of age receiving with grace and unaffected simplicity the love and admiration of such men as Dr. Holmes, Bishop Brooks, Dr. Hale and women like Mrs. Howe, Louise Chandler Moulton, Lucy Larcan and Mrs. Deland!''

This was the view not only of Annie, whose partiality for Helen might be discounted; the Boston *Evening Transcript* wrote: "All Boston was at Helen Keller's feet yesterday afternoon. 'I did not know you had so many friends, Helen,' a gentleman said to her, after waiting a long time in the crush for his turn to greet her. 'All the people in Boston are my friends,' she answered, smiling not confidently, but gratefully, in her seraphic way. Only a moment before the room had rung with laughter when Dr. Holmes (who, by the way, did not look any older nor step any older than he did ten years ago) was chatting with Helen. But it really was no laughing matter when she assured him that really she had not been deceiving him all the while and that she does *not* possess eyes to see and ears to hear!''

"Such a happy, rapturous face!" wrote the correspondent for the *Salem Gazette.* "No sign of deprivation, darkness or suspicion, but life, light and love. 'I love everybody,' she said, kissing the little children, taking them in her arms, and passing her hand lightly over their faces and hair."

After the severe strain of the "Frost King" affair, Annie had thought they should return immediately to Tuscumbia because of Helen's need for quiet. "So far as I am personally concerned," she wrote Hitz early in April, having to stay until June "would not be unpleasant as there is no place in the world so dear to me as Boston, but my first thought must always be for Helen and her welfare;—and it is on her account that I longed for the quiet of her Southern home." Either Annie misjudged her charge's resilience or she was projecting onto her her own feelings. They did not start homeward until the end of May, foregoing only the June commencement exercises. Anagnos wanted them to stay, and while Captain Keller pressed them to return, the decision really was up to Annie. In deciding to leave, she may have sensed that another public appearance by Helen would be anticlimactic and cause the public to weary of her.

She and Helen had seen a good deal of Dr. Bell and Mr. Hitz during the spring. Dr. Bell was in Boston defending his telephone patents in the Boston courts. The two men were captivated by Helen and Annie, but they also had designs on them. Helen was deaf as well as blind, but up to now she had been used, brilliantly, by Anagnos to promote the cause of the blind. Bell and Hitz wanted to use her to help the deaf. When Dr.

Bell was in Boston in March, he had given Helen a lesson in articulation, and Helen was eager for another, Annie wrote Hitz.

Hitz was sixty-four years old, with a grown daughter. He was a lonely man, a deeply religious Swedenborgian, cultivated and sensitive. He was much drawn to Annie. He stopped in Boston on his way to the Clarke School for the Deaf in Northampton. "What you say of the results in articulation which have been obtained there," Annie wrote him afterwards, "has forced me to the conclusion that much may be accomplished for Helen. I confess I have not been especially pleased with the articulation of the few persons (graduates of the Northampton School) who I have met . . . but you have convinced me of the good work that is being done at the Clarke Institution." Not only had Hitz praised the Institution, but —innocent, unworldly man that he was—he had extolled a Miss Yale, who was a teacher there. "I must confess that I was a wee bit jealous of her when I read your last letter, and realized how much there was to love and admire in the lady. I am sure that she deserved every word of the praise which you gave her and I have driven every ungenerous thought of her out of my heart, and rejoice with you that the Clarke Institution possesses such a treasure." But Teacher never pursued further the question of Helen's attendance at Clarke. She was, as she acknowledged, quite resistant to Helen's spending her energies on articulation—and as we have noted earlier, she may not have wished to make it easier for Helen to communicate with others.

But a plan that Dr. Bell designed to teach Helen articulation was not to be dismissed offhandedly. Annie suggested that he send it to Captain Keller. Helen's enunciation could be perfected, he advised her father, but Miss Sullivan was not qualified to do so because she was unfamiliar with the mechanisms of speech and the ways of teaching articulation. He proposed that she should visit some of the outstanding schools for the deaf and observe their methods of instruction. He also wanted Teacher and Helen to attend the forthcoming meeting of the American Association to Promote the Teaching of Speech to the Deaf. It was to take place at Lake George at the end of June, and the expenses of both would be paid by the Association. Teacher would speak of the methods and principles she had followed with Helen, and Helen's presence would inspire the teachers of the deaf and send them "back to their schools with the conviction and belief that if such results could be obtained in the case of a child who had been blind as well as deaf from infancy, they can surely do more for their own pupils than they have yet accomplished."

In sending Dr. Bell to Captain Keller, Annie may have surmised what his reply would be. In March when the Captain had turned aside Anagnos's request that she and Helen be permitted to stay on in Boston, he had explained that he wanted them back in Tuscumbia sooner rather than later. "My wife's life in the absence of Helen and Miss Annie is quite a lonely one, as I am absent from home a great deal." In turning down Dr. Bell, Captain Keller stressed Helen's health. The previous year Helen on her arrival at Tuscumbia had shown symptoms "of nervous prostration, resulting in a fainting spell which alarmed us very much." The family physician blamed it on the oppressive heat of the train. He did not want her to travel in the heat again. His reply would have reassured Annie had she known of it, but by that time she and Helen were at the Wades in Hulton. "Have you seen Mr. Bell?" she wrote Anagnos. "If so did he tell you whether he expects Helen at the summer meeting. . . . I cannot and I must not go to Lake George, and you must try to help me out like a good father."

Whatever Anagnos's suspicions of Annie in regard to the "Frost King," he relished the role of protector. He had dined with Dr. and Mrs. Bell, he advised Annie, and it was a "very pleasant" evening. He had arrived early at the hotel, "but as both of them were out, the picturesque secretary [Mr. Hitz] urged me to stay until their return. I did so, and he availed himself of the opportunity to ask me a number of questions indicative of his profound interest in Helen and you; or properly speaking in you via Helen. I answered them to the best of my ability. When Mr. Bell came in he expressed much pleasure at seeing me. Evidently he was disappointed at Captain Keller's negative reply to his request. He told me that he has written to you to leave Helen at home and go to Lake George. Without assuming the authority with which the good Mrs. Hopkins is prone to clothe herself on such occasions, I explained to him how difficult it will be for Mrs. Keller to take care of Helen and her ailing baby, and how tired you were when you reached Hulton."

Anagnos was off to Canada for a convention of teachers of the blind. He knew Helen's fascination with foreign places and he sent her a voluminous letter, just as he had done during his trip to Europe, describing the Canadian cities that he visited. At the convention he talked with the director of the Florida Institution (for the deaf and the blind) who had come to Canada by way of Dr. Bell's meeting at Lake George. "He says that about 150 persons are in attendance, and that Mr. Bell and his picturesque secretary do everything in their power to amuse and instruct them." They could well have used the assistance of Teacher and Helen.

Annie replied to Anagnos only six weeks later. It was indicative of her love-hate relationship with Anagnos, and perhaps also of her desperation at being immured in Tuscumbia, that she should blurt out, "I only wish I were near you, dear. Why? A woman is constantly getting warned against following the impulses of her heart. Why, I never could imagine, for all the blunders I am conscious of having committed have resulted from having neglected the impulses of my heart to follow the insight of my understanding, or, worse still, the understanding of others. And so I am now arrived at this. I have flung my understanding to the dogs, and think, do, say, and feel just exactly as nature prompts me. Very bad you will say. Nevertheless, it is true and I wish to be near you because I love you and I am happier near you than anywhere else in the world."

Of her two "fathers," she was grateful to Hitz but passionately involved with Anagnos. She had sensed how disappointed Hitz would be not only because of her unwillingness to go to Lake George, but because of her decision to return to Tuscumbia by way of Hulton and a stay with Mr. Wade, rather than via Washington and a visit with him. The decision had not come easily, she wrote him, "but I rejoice to say that finally duty triumphed over inclination. Mr. Wade has been exceedingly kind to Helen. Indeed I think she has not a better friend in the world than this noble-hearted man; and surely it would not be right to disappoint him for my own pleasure. I am confident that the kind friend who does me the honor to call me his daughter, will understand my feelings in forming this decision, because he more than any other appreciates my great love for Helen, and understands that my first thought must always be for her best good. She is a part of my life—all of my life that is worth living and her happiness constitutes my happiness."

Her letter did wound him, he replied, and he did not know how long the scar would last, "but you can rest assured that the hand that gave it is loved nonetheless." He did not understand her reasons, but he had "implicit faith" in her "and loving you as I do more than I do myself your and Helen's happiness precedes my own." If Annie appears somewhat manipulative in her relations with men, especially Hitz, she was behaving little differently than attractive young women generally do caught in the dilemma of hurting an older, sensitive man by brutal candor or by permitting him to believe his feelings are being reciprocated. And when the man had much to offer, not only to her but to Helen, in the way of guidance and support, her use of feminine wiles was almost inevitable. A woman of formidable intellectual powers, she was nevertheless no bluestocking. Hitz, like Anagnos, represented deliverance from Tuscumbia.

The trip home from the Wades' had been a horror. "Of course no sane person would plan a pleasure trip to Alabama in June," Annie wrote Wade afterwards. "From Cincinnati to Chattanooga we travelled in that abomination known as the 'Manor Car' with the thermometer at 97."

Misery awaited them in the Keller household on their arrival at the end of June (close to Helen's twelfth birthday). The baby, Phillips Brooks, had the whooping cough, and Captain Keller's eldest son, Helen's half brother James, was down with what the family thought was typhoid fever. Mrs. Keller was busy with caring for the sick, and she shifted most of the household duties onto "poor inexperienced me," Annie complained to Hitz. Then she sounded a graver note. Helen was "not at all well though much better than she was when we first got home. I knew all the time that in the nature of things, the reaction from all the excitement and nervous strain of last winter would come when she got home and it has."

The humid heat finally broke, only to be succeeded by days that were "cold, dark and dreary," as Helen wrote to Anagnos. "We had intended going to the mountain before this, but the rain and little Phillips' illness have kept us here. Teacher says if she had known how much sickness there was here we would not have come home until autumn." Helen, however, was happy to be home. "Mildred is a dear little sister, and we have happy times together. She is anxious to go to school and she is making all her plans to go to Boston next winter." Her books had arrived. "I have been reading the history of your own dear, beautiful country since my return. . . . I can easily believe that of all ancient peoples the Greeks were the greatest." Moving Helen's books was a substantial operation. In Braille or embossed print, they were bulky volumes five to ten times the size of the original books.

They went to Fern Quarry as soon as James was able to be shifted. But that, too, turned into a nightmare. Money was scarce. "I loaned Cap. Keller thirty-five dollars and this with Helen's thirty-five has, I believe, constituted the family income for the past two months. Mrs. Keller told me a short time ago when I asked her where they got the money to live during the winter that everything they had in the world was mortgaged. Besides Captain Keller was heavily in debt." As a consequence, they found themselves at Fern Quarry without a cook or a nurse. Every drop of water had to be carted a quarter of a mile, and milk for the baby meant a mile's hike along the railroad tracks. Captain Keller claimed business in

Tuscumbia "and left us—two lone women here in the woods without a protector save Eumer [Helen's new mastiff given her by Mr. Wade]. Did you ever hear of a greater outrage? We lived this way for nearly two weeks until the election was over and the head of its family found time to bestow a thought upon his beloved family." They were now comfortable, had an efficient girl in the kitchen and little Phillips was better. "But it will not be difficult for you to understand that Mrs. Keller and her better half are not in a honeymoon state of mind as regards each other."

Her "letter of desperation" to Anagnos turned even darker. "Indeed our family life is far from pleasant. Captain Keller's visits are not frequent and when he does come the rest of us find the woods pleasanter than the house. Poor little Helen, my heart aches for her! While I am near her I can shield her from the knowledge of much that would distress her; but I cannot go on living this way a great while longer."

But Annie knew what she wanted and why she stayed. "Love for Helen," she went on, "and pride in her achievements have kept me here when I should have been happier elsewhere. If they would only give me Helen, I am sure I can find a way of making her life brighter than it will ever be here. . . . Helen can never be happy here. Already the shadow of trouble has fallen on her sensitive heart. She continues to write in her diary [it has not survived] and the record which she has made of her thoughts and impressions since she came home would distress you inexpressibly. She does not seem to feel inclined to write letters and I have not the heart to urge her to do so. She was greatly interested in your letter describing your trip and also in Mr. Munsell's first letter from Venice. Miss Derby writes to her once a week and she has had letters from several other friends.

"No, dearest, I have not been busy with my distinguished correspondents. Mr. Hitz continues to write but I do not trouble about writing to him. I hear from Dr. Bell occasionally and have written to him once. Next to you I have not had a truer and gentler friend than Mr. Bell."

Having unburdened her heart of its woes and secrets, she made the avowal of love and the need to be near him already cited, but to this anguished cry for rescue there was no response, even though previous to the arrival of this letter Anagnos had reproached her for having forgotten the "art of writing." It fell to Helen two months later to take the initiative. "I begin to fear you are not going to write to me any more," her letter began. "It has been such a long time since we heard from you." Little Mildred wanted "to go to Boston to live with you," and baby Phillips was "plump and rosy." She spoke about the deaths of Whittier and Tennyson. The thought that they "will never more make music upon earth fills my heart with sorrow." She chided Anagnos for not having sent her *The Last Days of Pompeii,* as he had promised to do, and reported almost casually, "You will be very sorry to hear that I cannot come to Boston this winter."

It had not been a happy summer for her, and though she thought of him often, "I must confess I did not feel much like writing letters. I was not quite as well as usual, and I suppose that is why I sometimes felt unhappy."

Anagnos still loved Helen, however he felt about Annie. He had not forgotten her, he hastened to reply, but he had learned, he explained— probably from Mrs. Hopkins, who always reported the news from Tuscumbia to him—"that you were tired out and in great need of rest." But he loved her letter. "You appeared in it just like your dear self," and he had read and reread it. "I think of you day and night. I miss you more than I can tell you. You are nearer to my heart than any living person." He would send her a supply of books through Mrs. Hopkins, including *Black Beauty,* if she did not have it. But he had no comment on her casually conveyed message that they were not returning to Boston, perhaps because he thought it best for Helen to remain in the quiet surroundings of Tuscumbia.

With Anagnos silent and withdrawn, Annie turned to Hitz, to whom she had not written since early July. It was not forgetfulness, she now wrote; "it would be strange indeed if I could forget you. I have had few friends in my life so deserving of my grateful remembrance." But she had "collapsed" upon reaching Fern Quarry, and Helen's condition had caused her great anxiety. She then launched into a description of Helen's lassitude and sadness. It is the only contemporary account that has survived of Helen's depression after the "Frost King" episode:

> I think I wrote you after we got home, that Helen was very complaining. The excitement of the last few weeks in Boston had overtaxed her strength; but we thought the pure mountain air and perfect quiet would soon restore her health and spirit. But the days passed and we failed to see any change in her. She remained pale and listless—taking very little interest in her surroundings. Even her books were neglected. She would sit in the same place for hours without speaking and in every way was so unlike her own bright self that a great anxiety

took possession of my heart. Her mother and I watched her help-lessly. There seemed to be nothing we could do but wait for a change, and waiting is so hard. Then there were other trials, misunderstand-ings which I cannot explain here, which made my summer peculiarly unpleasant, and my Helen's sunny smile and sweet companionship were sadly missed. Do you wonder that I had no heart for letter-writing? Had I written to you, Mon Père, my letters would have been full of trouble and vexation of spirit.

. . . Since our return to town Helen has seemed better—more in-terested and cheerful. I have endeavored to keep her as quiet and free from excitement as possible. We all feel it will be best for her not to resume her regular studies for at least a year. But you have no idea how difficult it is to keep her quiet. She becomes restless and depressed if she does not have something to do. In-deed we seem to have a difficult problem upon our hands. She has two or three lessons, irregularly, just to relieve the monotony. She has written a very few letters on her typewriter recently and they have been full of the old sweetness and joy. She says, in one of them, 'God has hidden the sad days, I know not where—I know only that he has sent these bright, beautiful autumn days in place of them.' These words filled my heart with a new, glad hope. Surely a change for the better has come.

I have tried several times to persuade her to write to Miss Canby; but without success. She seems to shrink from any reference to the sad experience with which that kind lady's name is connected. I wish I knew what I ought to do about it. It seems almost as if Helen ought to be made to write a proper acknowledgement of Miss Canby's generous treatment and yet, I do not think she would value such a letter. She would only value a spontaneous expression of the child's love. Can you advise me in this matter? . . .

I am purposely living without purpose, from hand to mouth, as it were, taking the good the gods provide me, and as much as possible shirking the evil—the only manner of existence which seems in ac-cordance with my present surroundings. I wish I could have a nice talk with you. I hate writing. I never can say what I want to say, not as I want to say it. . . .

The presidential election and the return of Grover Cleveland, a Democrat, to the White House, created a stir in Tuscumbia. Captain Keller's hopes soared, and he decided to enlist the help of Helen's friends, as well as his own, to secure reappointment as marshal for North Alabama. A letter from Caroline Derby, who had joined with Helen the previous May in organizing the tea for the kindergarten, conveyed an affectionate message to Helen from Mrs. Cleveland. Helen promptly wrote her thanks to Mrs. Cleveland—"I am glad, very glad that such a kind, beautiful lady loves me"—and Captain Keller began to plan a trip to Washington for the inaugural accompanied by Helen and Miss Annie.

Annie decided to write to Anagnos again. Although she had not really heard from him since July, she felt confident that his affection for Helen would make him responsive even if his feeling for her had shriveled—a development a pretty twenty-six-year-old woman found it difficult to admit to herself. Her letter started out bravely. She had been the laggard about writing, but she had written him mentally every day. Anyway, what was there in Tuscumbia to "interest the great and wise who dwell in the Athens of the West." And if he said "nonsense," he should be patient and charitable and read on. "I have written to Mrs. Hopkins regularly, and I suppose she has kept you informed of the state of affairs here." Cleveland's election "has brightened our prospects a little. . . ." Southerners expected business to revive; she herself was dubious. "The Democrats have never distinguished themselves as financiers and I doubt if they have improved in that direction in the passed [sic] four years. They are too much for the spoils to take a patriotic interest in the country's well-being." Then to the real point of her letter. "If Captain Keller gets the office of Marshal it will be through outside influence. Two or three of his best friends in this state have written him that they are pledged to others for that place. If you could in any way interest Governor Russell [of Massachusetts] in his behalf, it would be a great thing. It is generally believed that Gov. Russell has the president-elect's ear. The Derbys, too, are friends of the Clevelands. . . . I know you will do what you can for Helen's and my sake."

Captain Keller was writing him directly, she went on. Then came another desperate plea for rescue. "If something does not happen before long I do not see how I am to stay here, dearly as I love Helen." She reported the news about Helen. Mrs. Hopkins had neglected to send a typewriter ribbon. Helen needed her machine to type an article for *Youth's Companion*. Would he send it? A Philadelphia florist had named a new "pink" for Helen, and the florists were going to name a rose for her. She had received a considerable package of books in raised print from London through the kind offices of Mr. Wade, and also a magazine for the blind that had an account of his speech at the July convention of teachers of the blind, "and you never saw a child so delighted as Helen was when she read it. I am sure you would have laughed as I did could you have heard her declare, when she had finished reading your speech, 'I firmly believe everything he said.'"

Her letter ended on a note of pathos. "I wish you would write to me sometimes," and then a shy query that must have amused Anagnos, remembering his difficulties with Annie in the past on the subject, "Are you going to say anything about Helen in the report? Do write to me."

The ribbon came. It took Annie a day to discover how to put it on the typewriter. Helen transcribed her sketch. "It made fifteen typewritten pages—about two thousand words," and Annie sent it directly to Mr. Chamberlin of *Youth's Companion* to save time, with a request that he show it to Anagnos. Annie had a new anxiety:

> Have you seen the reports concerning Helen's health which have been going the rounds of the papers? We have had several clippings sent to us taken from papers published in the interest of the deaf and a few from newspapers. They state that Helen is a 'wreck' 'broken down mentally and physically,' 'given over to melancholy' and 'dwelling constantly on the thought of death.' What does it mean? Where do they get this news I wonder? I have not written to a soul about her condition but Mrs. Hopkins and yourself [she had, as we have seen, written to Hitz], and surely I have not given either of you to understand that she was a 'wreck' mentally or physically. If my letters have given that impression I am very sorry for it is [not] true, and certainly was not intended by me. Last summer she was, as she says herself, sad, or as I expressed it, depressed, and when she had a chill and was really ill for a few days, she did seem somewhat concerned about her life, and naturally it troubled her friends that such a thought should have come to her at all. I wrote to you about it because I always tell you everything about Helen freely and just how I feel about her, thinking that you more than anyone else, ought to know everything. But surely this explanation is not necessary and you have not misunderstood me. I believe all these reports and

exaggerations originated at the Institution. Helen's old enemies were the originators and malice was motive.

Could he not contradict these rumors and assertions in his report? Mrs. Keller and Helen wanted him to come to Tuscumbia for Christmas. "I might tell also how much I should like to have you come if I thought it would make any difference to you. Write me what you think about the sketch as soon as you see it, that is, if you are ever going to write me again."

Anagnos intended to write about Helen in his report, but not in the main section devoted to the school. For the supplementary section, however, devoted to the kindergarten, he had drafted a detailed account of Helen's part in the two money-raising parties for Tommy Stringer and the kindergarten. This was quite eloquent, detailed and vivid. But there was no reference to Annie, no report from Annie on Helen's development, no discussion of Helen's health. However, Anagnos did reply to Annie's letter: "I have not breathed a word to anyone about Helen's health or about her intention not to come to Boston. I felt that a sentence in one of your notes to Mrs. Hopkins, stating that Helen had no interest in what had been written to her about Tommy's tricks was not guarded with sufficient strictures. Permit me to give you a little advice in this connection. Love women with all your strength and soul; but do not tell them what you do not want other people to know. I enclose a copy of a letter which I wrote in reply to inquiries concerning Helen's health. I will see that the whole matter is set right."

He did not comment on the coquettish seconding she had written to the Keller invitation to come to Tuscumbia for Christmas. To "dearly beloved Helen" he wrote that he was "chained" to his duties in Boston, "but my mind is constantly with you, and if I cannot take you in my physical arms and kiss you with my lips, I do so in spirit."

The report on Helen's condition that had upset Annie had been in *The Silent Worker,* and the clipping had been sent to her by Hitz. The reports were "not true at all," Helen wrote Hitz. "Sometimes I am not well; but I am not a 'wreck' and there is nothing 'distressing' about my condition." Teacher had not written him, she went on, because "her eyes have been hurting so that she could not write to anyone," and she, Helen, had been busy with her sketch. "Before I left Boston, I was asked to write a sketch of my life for *Youth's Companion.* I had intended to write the sketch during my vacation; but I was not well, and I did not feel able to write even to my friends. But when the bright, pleasant autumn days came, and I felt strong again, I began to think about the sketch. It was some time before I could plan it to suit me. You see it is not very pleasant to write all about one's self. At last, however, I got something bit by bit that Teacher thought would do, and I set about putting the scraps together, which was not an easy task; for, although I worked on it every day, I did not finish it until a week ago Saturday. I sent the sketch to the *Companion* as soon as it was finished, but I do not know that they will accept it."

Annie kept Anagnos informed of this work in progress. "I have not encouraged the undertaking. I knew that she would not find writing about herself an easy task, and I strongly advised her not to bother with the sketch, as she calls it, but she would not rest until it was begun and finished. Her object in writing has been to get money for Christmas and when she brought me her manuscript to read, I had not the heart to tell her that I did not think the *Companion* would accept it. But I am very sure it is too long, and I fear too elaborate to answer Mr. Chamberlin's idea of a simple account of her education.

"In my opinion it is the most touching and the most beautiful thing she has ever written."

Anagnos was eager to see it, and he promptly got in touch with the *Companion* and was able to report to Annie that "Helen's article was received with great pleasure at the office of *Youth's Companion*. Mr. Ford [the editor] has decided to send Helen one hundred dollars for it. This pleased good Mr. Chamberlin very much. I have not seen the article yet."

Gifts, principally for Helen, poured in at Christmas time, but Helen was unable to acknowledge them. Usually robust physically, she had, as Teacher put it, a "delicately organized" constitution. The strain of writing her autobiographical sketch seemed to make her more vulnerable physically. She ailed through the holidays and in January was in bed with a sore throat and cough, unable to write anyone. Some gifts, Teacher felt, had to be acknowledged. William Wade had sent fifty dollars, and the editor of the *Companion* had sent her a New Year's gift of fifty dollars in addition to the one hundred dollars that he paid her for the sketch. And John S. Spaulding, who had put together the Sugar Trust, sent her "fifteen more shares of the Sugar Stock."

Not only did Captain Keller write to Spaulding, but he took custody of the shares of stock and the checks that Helen received for Christmas, "even the story money," Annie lamented to Anagnos. "He says he will keep it until Helen needs it. I doubt though if he will ever be willing to spend the money as she would like to do." Helen had hoped to use the story money to start a library in Tuscumbia. "Her father assured her she would find other uses for her money in a manner that pained her deeply. You know how generous and self-forgetful Helen is. She cannot understand the indifference and selfishness of those dear to her, and her tender sensitive nature receives many painful shocks, I assure you."

Peter Putnam, the blind scholar and historian, has written that at one time or another every blind man comes to feel his kinship with every minority. Instructed by Boston, which had been an abolitionist stronghold, and guided by her own compassionate nature, Helen's attitude toward Negroes changed. "The servants, and indeed the Negroes generally," Annie went on, "are devoted to her. Several of them have learned to talk to her and it is touching to see how patient and gentle she is with them always—ever ready with an excuse in extenuation of their faults. She has two little darkey namesakes, and Christmas she wanted to give them something but was not allowed to do so. I bought two little things for her with my own money but the joy of giving was of course lessened."

Helen's father also had Annie ask Anagnos to talk with Spaulding about lending him fifteen thousand dollars. Spaulding did grant the loan, although whether Anagnos had anything to do with it is not clear.

The arrangements to attend the inaugural moved ahead. Hitz had invited them to be his guests in Washington. "For several reasons I would have preferred to have gone to a hotel," Annie confided to Anagnos, "but Captain Keller has accepted Mr. Hitz's invitation, and he could not have done otherwise without offending a very kind friend." Perhaps Anagnos could meet them in Washington. "I think Helen will receive a good deal of attention and I know nothing delights you so much as to see Helen admired and appreciated. Then, too, I think you could be of service to Captain Keller, could you not? If he does not get an appointment of some sort I do not see what is to become of us."

This letter, too, began with an apology for not having written, which in reality was another plea to reestablish their relationship on its old basis: "I dislike to be always making apologies, but for this once you will accept them. You will always accept them, I am sure. You have ever been kind and forbearing with me and I cannot believe that any force of circumstances, or inconsideration on my part will ever make any difference with you. And whenever our stars bring us together I shall always find in you the same warmhearted friend that you have ever been."

But even as this letter was on its way to Boston, another storm was brewing. It had to do with Helen's sketch for the *Companion.* "You have not told me what you thought of Helen's story," Annie wrote in her letter of the twenty-third. The silence, as so often happened with Anagnos, reflected repressed anger. Two days after the letter pouring out her heart to Anagnos, she was writing again. "I have it seems been more painfully negligent than I was aware of when I wrote to you a few days ago. I am sorry, sorrier than I can tell you in words that I have again been the cause of annoyance to you. But the truth is I forgot all about the stupid notes." She apologized, but pointed out that he had not asked for them three times, as he claimed.

> In only *one* of your letters—the last one dated December 19th, 1892, is there any mention of them. Then you simply ask 'why do you not return to me the notes which I sent you some time ago to revise and correct?' Had I supposed that the question implied that you really wanted the notes I certainly should not have forgotten to answer it. But if you have read the sketch which Helen wrote for the *Youth's Companion* I am greatly surprised that you should still care to have the notes returned to you. For in this sketch she has in her own and beautiful and impressive language given a description of the real or fancied impressions of her early childhood. She records the same incidents which I had gathered from her conversation and noted down in the notes which I sent you last year and which you returned to me for revision and correction. When I found that Helen had omitted nothing which could be of interest from her touching and beautiful story I very naturally, I think, saw no further use for my poor trash and straightway consigned it to the flames. You had always given me to understand that you considered my notes of very slight importance, and I had no way of knowing that you had changed your mind with regard to them. Whenever anything I have written has not met with your approval I have always felt a keen satisfaction in destroying it, and I must say, I was truly glad when these particular notes disappeared never to be seen again. But I am very, very sorry to have displeased you, and I humbly ask forgiveness for this and innumerable offences.

It is not clear how Anagnos had communicated with Annie about the notes—whether by a letter that has vanished or through Mrs. Hopkins. Nor is it clear what the notes contained that made him so anxious to have them and Annie so anxious to destroy them. The explanation may lie in Anagnos's failure to say anything about Helen's autobiographical sketch, which must have appeared to him as a kind of "revisionist" account of her education, for there was no reference to Perkins. She was generous to Anagnos personally, but did not identify him as the head of Perkins. She described her visit to the Horace Mann School for the Deaf in the summer of 1888 when she and Teacher had first come to Boston, but not Perkins, although they had stayed with Anagnos in his apartment at the Institution. She managed to tell the story of Tommy Stringer without mentioning that it was Perkins that had taken him in. For such omissions Anagnos would have held Annie responsible, for it had happened before—in 1890, when Annie had told the Boston *Journal* that she and not Perkins had the "whole care" of Helen, that the latter was not even a student at Perkins.

The sketch was called "My Story" and appeared in the January 4, 1894 issue of the *Companion*. "Her sketch is beautifully composed," commented *The Illustrated American*, "a distinctly fine quality of literary skill." It launched Helen on a second career, that of a writer. But it confirmed Anagnos's lack of trust in Annie.

He did not go to Washington to meet them at Cleveland's inaugural, and in fact, Helen's appearance did not attract the attention Annie and Captain Keller had expected. They were not invited to call on the Clevelands, but the Captain did enlist the assistance of Dr. Bell and Mr. Hitz in trying to get federal jobs for himself and his son. Then all three journeyed to Boston. That was a melancholy experience for Annie. "Mon cher, cher Père," she wrote Hitz the day after their arrival. She had torn up the letter she had written the night before because it was "very rebellious. Just such a letter as you would expect an excitable and vindictive character like me to write under certain circumstances, after a tiresome journey." Her wrathfulness, she explained later in the letter, was largely due to Anagnos's coldness. "Mr. Anagnos's reception of me has not been cordial. I do not mean that he has been rude or anything of that kind: but he has made me understand his displeasure in many ways. . . . I will write more particularly when I feel less rebellious, and have a more charitable feeling for some of my former admirers."

"It was after 1893," Helen wrote F.B. Sanborn in 1906 after the death of Anagnos, "after we had ceased to avail ourselves of the hospitality of the Perkins Institution that Mr. Anagnos proved untrue to the friendship between us. It was then that he began, not in written statements but by word of mouth, to impugn our integrity. . . . And after we, of our own will and contrary to Mr. Anagnos's wish, had left the Institution finally, he declared and continued to declare to one person and another his opinion that we were one or both guilty. Once at the Kindergarten for the Blind in the presence of several friends, one of whom reported the matter direct to us, he said, 'Helen Keller is a living lie.' Another friend went straight to him from us and demanded explanation. He did not deny that he had said that thing, but reported that my teacher had taught me to deceive. . . . That was the wrong Mr. Anagnos did my teacher. That was the untruth he told of me."

X

No One Can Refuse Helen

"I feel that in this child I have seen more of the Divine than has been manifest in anyone I ever met before."—Dr. Bell

The expenses of their trip to Boston were paid by John S. Spaulding, who, together with Bell, Hitz and Wade, became increasingly important in their lives as their ties with Perkins and Anagnos frayed and Captain Keller, far from being able to pay Teacher's salary and Helen's bills, borrowed money from them. Men and women alike gained pleasure from helping them—but men particularly, and the more elderly the gentleman, the greater the satisfaction.

John Spaulding became one of their major benefactors. He was a legendary figure in Boston. A bachelor, he lived on a floor of Boston's United States Hotel, which he owned and whose employees he "spoiled," as some had it, with gifts and bonuses, just as he had done with the employees of the sugar company by making over stock to them. He was famous for his benefactions—having contributed, for example, $100,000 to the seventieth birthday fund of Dr. Hale, not to mention the $30,000 in Christmas gifts that he bestowed on seven young women who worked at the hotel. A delegation of worthy ladies had called on the hotel's manager to insist that benefactions such as the latter be made through the channels of organized charity, lest the young ladies in question be corrupted.

Spaulding loved Helen. He had met her through Elsie Leslie Lyde, the most popular child actress of the day. Elsie was just a year younger than Helen and, in 1890 when they met, had been starring in Mark Twain's

The Prince and the Pauper. "My teacher has told me about you," Helen
wrote her, "and I have read Little Lord Fauntleroy [in which Elsie also
had starred] with my fingers. I thought Cedric was a lovely little boy. Will
you please let me come to see you?" Bishop Brooks, a friend of both
children, took Elsie and her mother in his carriage to Perkins to introduce
them and suggested that Annie should bring Helen to the theater. Once
the idea was proposed, Helen's heart was set upon it, and Elsie wrote in
her diary, "I don't see how anyone can refuse Helen anything." After the
matinee Helen went backstage, and Elsie introduced her to her friend and
patron, John Spaulding, whom she called "King John," for the cartoonists
of the trusts invariably showed the men who controlled them with crowns
on their heads. After the play, Helen recalled later, "Mr. Spaulding took
us all out to his country place in Dorchester for dinner, and after that, all
during Elsie's engagements, we saw Mr. Spaulding almost every day, and
when we did not see him, great boxes of roses and sweets . . . were sent
to us both."

Like many others, "King John" fell under Helen's spell—and Annie's,
too. He would come to Perkins to join them for their midday meal, or,
best of all, he collected Elsie and Helen and took them for long drives in
the country, delighted at having his "two darlings together." Helen, who
was always practicing articulation, had difficulty with "Elsie Leslie Lyde,"
but by dint of working on it for a day—and she was a very determined
little girl—she mastered it, to the great delight of Spaulding. And when
he was unable to understand her, he would hug her and say, "If I can't
understand you, I can always love you."

"Sugar Stock was one of his hobbies," said *The New York Times,* and
while Helen and Teacher were still at Perkins he had given them some
shares. "It was because of his interest in me, and in Teacher too, that Mr.
Spaulding lent Father fifteen thousand dollars," Helen wrote her sister in
1933. "But later the heirs were very suspicious of this loan" and, after
Spaulding's death in early 1896, made "insulting remarks to the effect that
Teacher's charms might have influenced their uncle to make the (un-
secured) loan to Father." Before his death, Teacher told Nella Braddy,
"Spaulding became more interested in Helen than he was in the actress
[Elsie] and gave her about $300 a month."

While Annie and Teacher were in Boston, Dr. Bell turned up. His was
a benevolent patronage. He was a happily married man with two daughters near Helen in age. The son of a deaf mother and the husband of a
deaf wife, Mabel—a woman of great loveliness and charm to whom he was

deeply attached—he was passionately determined to help the deaf to speak. Following in the footsteps of his father and grandfather, he became a teacher of elocution and made a close study of the physiology of speech and even after his success with the telephone continued to give much time and money to devising ways to impart to the deaf a knowledge of the proper use of their vocal organs in speech. He was devoted to Annie, whose greatness as a teacher he sensed, and to Helen, who he felt would leave her mark on the times. Despite the fame and wealth that were coming to him as a result of the invention of the telephone, he remained simple and unpretentious, inquisitive and reflective. "I never felt at ease with anyone until I met him," said Annie. "I was always extremely conscious of my crudeness. . . . Dr. Bell had a happy way of making people feel pleased with themselves. He had a remarkable facility of bringing out the best that was in them. . . . I learned more from him than from anyone else."

"He always assumed that anyone could understand anything," wrote Helen. He was wholly undogmatic and would look at a differing point of view "with genuine interest and enthusiasm. 'Perhaps you are right. Let us see.'" It was Dr. Bell who first spelled into her hand the name of Charles Darwin. "What did he do?" she asked. "He wrought the miracle of the nineteenth century," he replied, and went on to tell her about *The Origin of Species* and how it had "widened the horizon of human vision and understanding." He used money wisely, not permitting it to dominate his life. "One would think I had never done anything worthwhile but the telephone," he spelled into Helen's hand. "That is because it is a money-making invention. It is a pity so many people make money the criterion of success. I wish my experiences had resulted in enabling the deaf to speak with less difficulty. That would have made me truly happy."

Dr. Bell was still after Annie and Helen to go to a school that taught speech to the deaf. He spoke to Captain Keller about it on the latter's return to Tuscumbia via Washington. "Mr. Bell is extremely anxious to have her and Helen make a visit to Northampton and to the Pennsylvania Institution," he wrote Anagnos. "Says he will go up to them as soon as Miss Annie's condition will permit. I hope she will be able to go."

"Teacher, Mrs. Pratt [a Boston friend and assistant of Dr. Bell's] and I very unexpectedly decided to take a journey with dear Dr. Bell," Helen informed her mother. Together they visited the Rochester School for the Deaf headed by Zenas Westervelt. Dr. Bell thought highly of this institution, which was actively supported by Edmund Lyon, a lawyer and businessman. Lyon was an early and heavy investor in Eastman-Kodak and, like Dr. Bell, an inventor. He had mastered the finger alphabet and devised a phonetic system to aid the deaf to enunciate more clearly, an invention that endeared him to Dr. Bell, who together with his father was deeply interested in what they called "visible speech." The March 31, 1893 issue of the Rochester School's newspaper was largely devoted to Helen's visit. At supper at the School, with Dr. Bell spelling into her hand, Helen was largely preoccupied with proposing conundrums. "My first is a body of water," she spelled. "My second is an exclamation; my third is used in fishing." Since no one figured it out, she gave the answer triumphantly—B A Y O N E T. "Here is a conundrum for you, Mr. Westervelt," she continued, reaching for the superintendent's hand. "Why can I not spell *cupid?*" The superintendent gave up. Helen again gave the answer. "Because when I C U [see you] I can go no farther." A reporter from *The Herald* asked her about her political affiliations. "My father is a Democrat," she parried. "But what are you?" "I am afraid that I am a mugwump," Helen replied. "Don't you think you ought to be what your father is?" the reporter persisted. Helen's hand lovingly sought her teacher's face and "bending lovingly toward her, she settled the matter with 'Oh, but Teacher is a Republican.'"

How could she be so happy? the reporter went on. "I have lost only two of God's gifts. I still have many powers, and the greatest gift of all is mind—mind that can be cultivated, and through which I can enjoy most of God's blessings."

"I feel that in this child I have seen more of the Divine," Dr. Bell was heard to remark, "than has been manifest in anyone I ever met before." There were times in the mid-nineties when Bell's two daughters felt twinges of jealousy because the attentions of their warm, affectionate father were so centered on Helen.

Helen and Dr. Bell hatched a surprise for her teacher, a trip to Niagara Falls. As Dr. Bell was unable to go, black-bearded Edmund Lyon took them. They stayed in a hotel near the "rushing" river, and the next day stood in the presence of Niagara; she felt the water "rushing and plunging with impetuous fury at my feet. . . . We went down a hundred and twenty feet in an elevator that we might see the violent eddies and whirlpools in the deep gorge below the Falls."

On the way back to Boston they stopped at the Clarke School in Northampton. Nothing came of this visit, but in Boston Helen reported to her mother that "a kind lady whose name is Miss Hooker is endeavoring to improve my speech. Oh I do so hope and pray that I shall speak well some day!''

They tarried with Mrs. Pratt in Chelsea and with Mrs. Hopkins in South Boston, determined not to go back to Tuscumbia. To appease Captain Keller they worked on his affairs. "You will be interested to hear," Annie wrote Hitz, "that my visit to the State Department on behalf of Major Keller [why he suddenly became Major this writer does not know] was not a failure. Mr. Spaulding has seen Mr. Quincy and that gentleman says Major Keller's affairs are in very good shape." That may very well have been so, but no federal appointment followed. Hitz had bought handsome gifts for both Helen and Annie. "I wonder greatly why I of all people should be so blest," Annie, overwhelmed by his kindness, wrote him. "I am most unworthy—do not shake your head; I know myself better than you can—and it pains me that people should think me better than I am." Helen would thank him herself. At the moment she was very tired. "We have both been on a social whirl since our return to Boston. Tonight we attend a reception at the Christian Union. There will be a great crowd and the usual excitement for Helen. I shall be thankful when it is all over and we turn our faces Hultonwards. . . . I wish you were going to be here Thursday. Helen will recite Longfellow's poem "Flowers" in the Boston Theatre and I am sure you would like to be present."

They reached the Wade's estate in Hulton in mid-June, and Annie succumbed to its tranquillity and quiet after Boston's excitements. There were times when she thought she wanted to live in such bucolic surroundings the rest of her life, but at other times she knew she needed "change, excitement, variety." She was putting off until the autumn taking up her work in earnest, she assured Hitz, but then she would work, for "after all our happiness depends on courage and work, does it not, mon père." He had sent her a set of photographs of Helen. Would he send Miss Marrett two of them with the "head bent slightly downwards—St. Cecilia effect," and one, too, to Mr. Anagnos "with my compliments."

Mr. Wade was delighted to have Helen with him again. Her natural goodness was a "continual joy and light." Here was another gem, he reported to Anagnos. "I was sitting beside her yesterday, on the leeward side, reading and smoking, when she said, 'I am glad you like to smoke as it gives you pleasure.' When I then noticed that the wind had changed and she was getting my cigar smoke, I blessed her lovely heart and told her that she, as ever, was teaching me a lesson, this time in gracious ways of calling attention to a disagreeable act, and she added, 'But I do mean that I am glad you enjoy things.' "

Mrs. Wade and her son Archer were going to the 1893 World's Fair in Chicago, and they prevailed upon Annie and Helen to accompany them. Would Hitz join them? Annie wrote. Anagnos and Mrs. Hopkins would also be in Chicago. "Yesterday several of the leaders of the Western Pennsylvania Institution for the Deaf came out to see Helen. They seemed amazed at the amount of general information which she possesses, and left expressing themselves as being more than satisfied that all which has been written about Helen is perfectly true."

In the end it was Dr. Bell who escorted them to the fair. But first they visited him in Washington. He had prepared a paper on Helen's education and Annie's methods for the Literary Society, an elite group of scientists, academic people and government officials. In his lecture Dr. Bell compared Helen's letter to her mother after she had been under Miss Sullivan's care for three months with the letter that she had written the previous April after her visit to Niagara Falls, a letter that he called a "prose poem." A Washington reporter who was present was astounded. "That this poem could have been the production of a child not yet thirteen years of age seemed almost incredible; but many of those present have since had the pleasure of meeting this remarkable child at the residence of Professor Bell, and no evidence of intellectual power she may give will again by them thought to be incredible."

The evening at Dr. Bell's also received a notice in the press. "During the evening the quickness and fitness of her answers to Professor Newcomb and other scientific gentlemen surprised everybody. So did her accurate repetition of Longfellow's *Psalm of Life,* and so did her keen enjoyment of stories told to her and of the conundrums with which she puzzled the friends who were talking with her." She asked a justice of the Supreme Court, "Do you know my friend, Judge Holmes?" Holmes was then Chief Judge of the Supreme Judicial Court of Massachusetts. "No dear, he lives in Boston," the Washington justice pointed out. "Oh, I thought you knew him, because you see you are brothers-in-law," she smilingly riposted. "Washington has just had a visit from wonderful Helen Keller," wrote the Washington *Star,* "who has been the guest, much petted and loved, of Professor Graham Bell."

SEES WITH HER SOUL was the way the *Star* aptly headlined its article, and Helen's "prose poem" about Niagara, which Dr. Bell had read, was a spiritual rather than a poetical exercise. It illustrated her strengths as well as limitations as a writer:

> Oh Niagara! Thou art grand and awful beyond expectation!
> I have dreamed of thee, and in imagination
> I have pictured to myself thy glorious beauty;
> But now, when thou risest before my soul's inward vision
> I stand helpless and overwhelmed; hushed
> Into reverent silence, by unutterable thoughts.
> Thou art a messenger from God,—a symbol
> Of the life of his children upon earth.
> Thou dost represent Eternal struggle
> But what words can paint thy passionate unrest:
> The awe inspiring grandeur of thy fierce majestic tread?
> It can not be that thou art a senseless thing
> A rushing irresistible force; Thou seemest to be
> A soul hurried on to the fulfillment of a terrible fate
> By some unconquerable necessity.
> Thou springest from rock to rock in thy frenzied glee
> Heedless of the abyss a hundred fathoms deep
> Which yawns beneath thy wayward feet.
> On the brink of the precipice thou hangest
> An instant: as if seized by sudden fear.
> Thy waters spring apart, then reembrace, and
> With white outstretched arms, thou rushest on
> Hurling fearful defiance at vast death.
>
> Thy mighty struggle is ended, Oh Niagara!
> And ere long thou shalt find the rest thou seekest
>   In the bosom of the Ontario,
> Thou has taught me, Oh Niagara
> Many a lesson deep and weird,
> Thou hast been a generous giver,
> I can give thee but a rose—
> But 'twill be to thee a promise, and a hope;
> For in its heart, it bears a message from God.

The "pathetic fallacy" is defined in the dictionary as "the ascription of human traits or feelings to inanimate nature." It is often the source of arresting imagery, but here one senses it is a substitute for the images that would be crowding in upon Helen were she able to see and hear. The few concrete images—"passionate unrest," "rushing, irresistible force," waters springing apart and reembracing "with white outstretched arms"— are basically kinetic, originating in her superb sense of touch. Such observations on the poem of a thirteen-year-old deaf-blind child seem pedantic; but Helen would make a name and career for herself as a writer, and while "Niagara" is a triumph of the spirit, it is less so of the sensuous imagination.

After Washington they went to the Chicago World's Fair. This was a landmark exposition that created a fabulous "White City" that, wrote Ada Louise Huxtable in 1978, "turned American architectural taste from colorful Victorian revivals to snowy Beaux Arts classicism in the space of one summer season." The exposition housed some 150 buildings and covered 550 acres in Jackson Park facing Lake Michigan. Ninety-seven of the country's most distinguished architects took part.

Helen's presence in the "White City" attracted as much attention as its peristyle, arcades and porticos. She and Annie stayed three weeks. Dr. Bell often accompanied them "and in his delightful way described to me the objects of greatest interest." He was particularly happy to show them some of the "historic telephones" in the Electrical Building. In the Anthropological Exhibit he carefully told her about the ancient Inca and Aztec civilizations. The organizers of the exposition permitted her to run her fingers over the exhibits. This added vastly to her enjoyment, especially of "the wonderful French bronzes. . . . I think they gave me more pleasure than anything else at the Fair: they were so lifelike and beautiful to my touch." She fingered everything—Cape of Good Hope diamonds, rare works of art; "she was allowed even to climb upon the great Krupp gun," reported Teacher, "and the workings were explained to us by one of the German officers." She shrank back only when given a chance to touch the Egyptian mummies. The Third Summer Meeting of the American Association to Promote the Teaching of Speech to the Deaf took place at the World's Fair, and in addition to the Bells, Edmund Lyon of Rochester was there and a teacher at the Rochester Institution whom he later married, Carolyn Talcott. Annie entrusted the care of Helen to the latter one afternoon when she decided to do some sightseeing on her own. "Miss Talcott, is anybody watching us?" Helen asked, and when the answer came in the negative, the thirteen-year-old exclaimed with alacrity, "Then let's romp."

This went unreported in Helen's long letter to Mr. Spaulding about her visit to the World's Fair. The letter was filled with the scenes that her teacher had, as she expressed it, "so vividly" spelled into her hand.

We approached the White City the first time from the lake side, and got our first impression of the Fair from the peristyle. It was a bright, clear day; the sky and water were a perfect blue, making a most beautiful setting for the Dream City, crowned by the glistening dome of the Exposition Building. Then we moved slowly up the Court of Honor, pausing every now and then while teacher described the beautiful scene to me; the groups of noble buildings; the lagoons dotted with fast-moving boats; the stately statue of the Republic; the fluted columns of the peristyle; and, beyond, the deep, deep, blue lake. Oh, how wonderful it all was. . . . Late in the afternoon, when the day was almost done, we stepped into a gondola, and made the trip through the lagoons. The burning sun, as he sank westward in his golden car, threw a soft rosy light over the White City, making it seem more than ever like Fairyland. When it was quite dark the illuminations began, and the fountains were all lighted up. Teacher described everything to me so vividly and clearly that it seemed as if I could really see the wonderful showers of light dart up into the sky, tremble there for an instant, sink and fall, like stars into the depths of the lake.

St. Nicholas published the letter with an introductory note by Teacher in its December 1893 issue. Its editor, aware that *Youth's Companion* was scheduled to publish Helen's autobiographical story in its January 1894 issue, carefully noted that "the story of Helen's life has already been told to readers of this magazine in the notable article 'Helen Keller,' written by Mrs. Florence Howe Hall, and printed in *St. Nicholas* for September, 1889." For thirteen-year-old Helen, acceptance of her writing by the two most respected and widely-read magazines for young people nurtured a budding ambition to become a writer. Dr. Bell had noticed and encouraged this ambition during her stay with him. "Dr. Bell believes," the *Star* had quoted him, "that this girl is destined to make her mark in English literature."

They spent September in Tuscumbia and then returned to Mr. Wade's. He had arranged for Helen to be tutored by Dr. John D. Irons, a classicist as well as a Presbyterian minister. "Helen will study with a minister who has much experience, I believe, in teaching," Annie reported to Hitz, who had assumed a kind of spiritual guardianship over the two. "Anyway he knows more than I do and together we may succeed in giving Miss Helen some knowledge of Latin and the higher mathematics. It was my wish that she should go to some good school with seeing girls of her own age, but her father was unable to pay the expenses, and our good friend Mr. Wade proposed our coming here. . . . Of course a school would be better in many ways; but this arrangement is better than staying in Tuscumbia. Captain Keller's affairs are far from satisfactory. Indeed I hardly see how they are to make both ends meet this winter."

She did not consult Anagnos, and there appear to have been no letters exchanged between the two until November. It was Helen who wrote him. He was delighted to hear from her, he replied, "and to know that you have not forgotten one of your early friends who will never cease to love you dearly." He was happy to hear that she was pursuing her studies at Mr. Wade's "under the tuition of a wise and kind master. For some time past I felt that you were in need of regular and systematic teaching; and your parents cannot be grateful enough to Mr. and Mrs. Wade for making such a generous provision for your intellectual wants, as well as for your physical comfort."

To this letter Annie replied, explaining that Helen had asked her to thank him, and she wanted to add on her own account "that I also was pleased to know that you had not forgotten old friends." Helen had mentioned a poem that she had written, and Anagnos wanted to see it. "I shall feel slighted if you will fail to favor me with it."

Helen had no time to write, Annie said, so she was sending on the poem, "and at the same time avail myself of this opportunity to write you a few lines." It was one of Helen's "most beautiful" compositions, Annie went on:

> Indeed nothing which she has recently written can be compared with it unless it be a letter soon to appear in St. Nicholas describing her visit to the World's Fair. They paid Helen thirty dollars for it, and in a letter to me the assistant editor speaks very highly of the composition. The poem, a beautiful word picture of Autumn, has many fascinating touches. The 'armies' of golden rod; the little birds southward going who linger like travellers at an inn; and most unexpected of all, Autumn fleeing to the protecting arms of Winter 'as a child to her father.' I am not prepared to say that these ideas are original in the

sense that nobody has ever had similar thoughts. But it seems to me that a thought may be original, though it has been uttered a hundred times. The memory, imagination and associations of the mind through which it has passed give it their hue and individualize it by a new arrangement of its elements. But whether Helen's beautiful composition is original or not it breathes of the essence of truth and is filled with the sweetness of happier spheres. It also gives us a glimpse of the beautiful world of thought in which she dwells.

"The thought that what I wrote might not be absolutely my own tormented me," Helen wrote of the period after the "Frost King" affair, "and often when an idea flashed out in the course of a conversation I would spell softly to her [Teacher], 'I am not sure it is mine.' . . . And even now I sometimes feel the same uneasiness and disquietude." Annie also sent a copy of "Autumn" to Hitz, along with Helen's description. "It is a word picture of Autumn as I see it with the eyes of my soul." It has more color and varied imagery than "Niagara." Undoubtedly Annie had spelled many of these scenes into her hand, but it is equally evident that her imagination and mind had been at work and transformed what Annie had supplied into a composition of her own.

AUTUMN

Oh, what a beauty doth the world put on
These peerless perfect autumn days;
There is a beautiful spirit of gladness everywhere.
The wooded waysides are luminous with brightly painted leaves;
The forest trees with royal grade have donned
Their gorgeous autumn tapestries.
And even the rocks are broidered
With ferns, sumachs and brilliantly tinted ivies;
But so exquisitely blended are the lights and shades,
The golds, scarlets and purples, that no sense is wearied,
For God himself hath painted the landscape.
The hillsides gleam with golden corn;
Apple and peach-trees bend beneath their burden of golden fruit.
The golden-rods, too, are here; whole armies of them
With waving plumes, resplendent with gold;
And about the wild grapes, purple and fair and full of sunshine,

The little birds southward going
Linger like travelers at an inn,
And sip the perfumed wine.
And far away the mountains against the blue sky stand,
Calm and mysterious, like prophets of God.

A mysterious hand has stripped the trees,
And with a rustle and whirr, the leaves descend,
And like frightened birds,
Lie trembling on the ground.
Bare and sad the forest-monarchs stand
Like kings of old, all their splendor swept away.
Down from his ice-bound realm in the North
Comes Winter, with snowy locks and tear-drops frozen on his
   cheeks;
For he is the brother of Death and acquainted with sorrow.
Autumn sees him from afar
And as a child to her father runneth,
She to the protecting arms of kindly winter fleeth,
And in his mantle of snow
Tenderly he folds her lovely form;
And on his breast she falls asleep.

Although Anagnos did not comment on the poem, Helen wrote him an affectionate Christmas note—"I wish I could give you a sweet Christmas kiss"—and then in February she sent him a letter written in Latin telling him about her studies of Caesar's Commentaries. Her letter was accompanied by another olive branch from Annie:

Now, do you deserve that we should send you any letters, any sympathy, any love, anything, thou dear, provoking incomprehensible one? I think not; but if everyone had his deserts which of us should escape whipping? And besides I see not what virtues remain possible for me, unless it be the passive ones of patience and forgiveness; for which, thank Heaven, there is always some little need in this otherwise tangled world. Indeed, dear friend, I was exceedingly sad to hear a few days ago, that you had been sick. You see, I do not want you to suffer physically for those provoking ways of yours, and to know of your being confined to your room by illness gives me no wicked satisfaction, but makes me quite unhappy. I wonder how you are today, and if you will be annoyed or glad to hear from your children. The enclosed letter from Helen, is her first attempt at putting her own thoughts into Latin. Her affection for you is as sweet and tender as it has ever been, and you must pardon me if I give you pain, when I tell you that your very evident neglect of her has grieved her loving heart not a little. Of course I know that your feelings towards her have not changed. You have felt annoyed with her teacher, most reasonably, I acknowledge, and so you have found it rather difficult to write to Helen, but surely in your innermost heart, which I believe to be one of the kindest in the world, you know that it is not just to make your sweet friend unhappy [because] of my faults, many and glaring though they may be. Confess that you have been the tiniest bit wrong in this little matter and turn the sunshine of your smile upon your children, I pray you, and in the meantime believe them, Always affectionately yours . . .

Again Anagnos elected to reply to Helen and thus make more emphatic his silence toward Annie. He congratulated Helen on her epistle "written in the language of the old Romans," explained that his long silence had been "due to the unsatisfactory state of my health and to no other cause," and reaffirmed that "I love you as dearly as ever and I will not cease to do so during my life." He did send Annie a copy of his annual report for 1893. She thanked him belatedly, explaining that she had no time before this "to read so lengthy a publication." Now that she had read it, she wanted to say that she had found it his "most intensely interesting report," especially its "charming accounts of Edith, Willie and dear little Tommy," the three deaf-blind children at Perkins. "I am sure their stories so touchingly told in your report will attract much special attention." She did not need to make explicit her belief that the attention would be considerably less than that which had been evoked in the past by his accounts of Helen, concerning whom the report was silent. There was a note on Annie's letter that it had been "answered," but that answer, too, has disappeared.

Helen no longer needed publicists. She had become an international celebrity and attracted attention simply by being herself. Nor was Annie enthusiastic about press notices as such, as she explained to Hitz, who faithfully sent her newspaper clippings about the two of them:

Mon cher ami, I try to think as little as possible about what the papers say relative to Helen and myself. Of course, I am gratified when a competent person speaks favorably of my work but desire for general commendation is strongest in the heart when there is no hope of attaining it. Fame of any kind, be it little or great has the unpleasant side, in the uncomfortableness of publicity, and in the painful necessity of keeping up to the standards other people set for one, and most of all in the feeling that one really does not deserve what he gets, that quite unconsciously he is passing for more than he is worth. Then there are the numberless letters, often impertinent and rarely welcome which strangers inflict upon the helpless one who happens to get his name into print. . . . Some one has said, and truly, I think, that 'there is nothing so to be dreaded as a wish realized.'

They spent the spring in Tuscumbia. She invited Hitz to visit them there, "for I have decided never to leave Tuscumbia again until things are different—financially I mean." Mrs. Hopkins was with them. Captain Keller pressed them to stay home. "We think it best to keep Helen and Miss Annie quiet at home until next fall," he wrote Anagnos, "when if I can see my way clear to do so, I hope to send her to some good Institute to commence a regular Collegiate course. . . . Helen is sitting by me and says 'please give Dear Mr. Anagnos my love; and tell him we would dearly love to see him.' "

Staying quietly at home was not to the taste of either Helen or Annie. Helen busied herself with correspondence to raise funds and books for the Tuscumbia Library, which she had played such a large part in founding. Teacher persuaded Hitz to join them in Tuscumbia and proposed that the four of them (for Mrs. Hopkins was still there) "take a little trip down the Mississippi to New Orleans." There is no record of such a trip, but after Hitz's departure Annie wrote him, "I found all well at home and I had to tell them all about our dear little visit. . . . The Captain asks who in the world are you writing to Miss Annie? And they all laugh when I tell them, (and) say suggestively so soon?" He was spoiling her with kindness, she protested, especially in giving her the feeling she had a right to make him carry some of her burdens, including the answering of many of the letters with which she and Helen were inundated.

They went to nearby Huntsville, where Helen raised fifty dollars from those she called "my friends," and they also made what Teacher described as an "interesting and touching visit to the colored peoples' Normal School." In May they visited Helen's uncle Doctor Keller in Hot Springs, Arkansas, a trip about which Annie was less than enthusiastic, for it meant receptions and visits to institutions; but Captain Keller insisted and so she complied. But her mind was preoccupied with other business. She had finally agreed to speak to Dr. Bell's Association for the Promotion of Speech at Chautauqua in the summer, and this loomed over her. Much more important was a plan that Hitz had discussed with her to establish a group of friends to raise a fund for Helen's education. Mr. Goodhue, who had organized the Canadian fund to replace Lioness, the mastiff, was interested, as was William Wade. Dr. Bell became the prime mover and enlisted the support of Dr. Hale. It was Dr. Bell who broached the plan to Captain Keller, a proud man, whose consent was not to be taken for granted. If the proposition, "so delicately and generously made," had come from other sources, the Captain wrote Bell, "I would be reluctant to consent to it.—But after giving it careful consideration and knowing the disinterested and unselfish motives which prompted it, and with an eye to Miss Annie's future, in which I feel almost, if not quite, a father's interest, as well as Helen's, I am constrained to consent to any plan you have in view for their welfare and happiness."

The plans for the fund were temporarily overshadowed by preparations for Chautauqua. Mrs. Bell wrote Annie offering to provide her and Helen with suitable wardrobes for the trip. She had finally decided to bring Helen with her, Annie wrote back, accepting the offer. "I hesitated for a long time, fearing that the nervous strain and excitement she would be subjected to there would be too great a tax upon her strength; but the little trip to Hot Springs has benefitted her wonderfully, and now I think and so does Mrs. Keller that it will be perfectly safe for her to attend the meeting, provided too great demands are not made upon her in the way of speechmaking and handshaking. I think you will agree that there has been too much of that sort of thing in the past. Indeed had she not been a very exceptional child she could not have stood half what she has endured and it is all so unnecessary—people can see her and hear her speak and judge of her acquirements without subjecting her to these ordeals."

One standby, Hitz, was not at Chautauqua. He had sailed for Europe and a visit to Switzerland and his daughter. That was a blow to Annie, who found him more approachable than Dr. Bell and frequently used him to send messages to the Doctor. Hitz's last letter before sailing was to Annie. He also sent her a watch and some sonnets that he had transcribed for the two of them. "I wonder if I shall ever have the joy of adding to your happiness and comfort as you have added to mine ever since I have known you," she wrote him abroad. "You have one of those noble natures which delight in loving more than in being loved while my selfish heart loves to be loved." She was looking forward to Chautauqua, she claimed, but worried about Helen. "I know how anxious Dr. Bell is that she should be at the meeting; and I do believe it will be of great benefit to the cause to have her present where she can be seen by all the teachers and intellectual people outside of the Association who also meet at Chautauqua. I hope if we do go, Mr. Bell will see that the dear child is protected as much as possible."

Annie's anxiety seems excessive. Helen always prospered in society—in fact throve on its rituals, thrusting herself forward to speak and to promote her causes, assuming few would turn her down. Not even the "Frost King" affair had dampened her pleasure in social occasions. It was Annie who felt insecure, inadequate and clumsy in new social settings; and at Chautauqua she was scheduled to read a paper—the type of challenge that always created anxiety bordering on panic. She need not have worried.

Her speech on "The Instruction of Helen Keller" was a triumph, even though at the last moment nervousness overcame her and Dr. Bell had to read her paper for her. It effectively restated the principles and methods that she had followed in her work with Helen and that she had written out for Anagnos in her contributions to his reports and in her letters to Mrs. Hopkins. But it began with a caveat she had never been able to persuade Anagnos to include:

> I shall also have cause for gratification if I succeed in convincing you that Helen Keller is neither a 'phenomenal child,' 'an intellectual prodigy,' nor an 'extraordinary genius,' [phrases that had been used by Anagnos] but simply a very bright and lovely child, unmarred by self-consciousness or any taint of evil. Every thought mirrored on her beautiful face, beaming with intelligence and affection, is a fresh joy, and this workaday world seems fairer and brighter because she is in it. And while it is unsafe to predict what Helen's future will be, I know she is destined to be the instrument of great good in the world, not only by drawing forth the sympathies, and putting into exercise the kind emotions of others, but by teaching them how great things may be achieved under the worst difficulties and how pure, and sweet and joyous may be the existence under the darkest cloud.

If there was a new note in the speech, it was in Annie's strongly stated conviction that learning should be a pleasurable process for children:

> I believe every child has hidden away somewhere in its being noble qualities and capacities which may be quickened and developed if we go about it in the right way; but we shall never properly develop the higher natures of our little ones while we continue to fill their minds with the so-called rudiments. Mathematics will never make them loving, nor will the accurate knowledge of the size and shape of the world help them to appreciate its wondrous beauties. Let us lead them, then, during the first years they are intrusted to our care, to find their greatest pleasure in nature, by training them to notice everything familiar or strange in our walks with them through the fields, the woods on the hill-tops, or by the seashore. The child who loves and appreciates the wonders of the outdoor world will never have room in his heart for the mean and low. Such a child will have risen to a higher plane, and in a wise study of God's law in Nature he will ever find his highest joy.

Books had played an important part in Helen's education:

> Indeed it is claimed by some that she reads too much, that a great deal of originative force is dissipated in the enjoyment of books, that when she might see and say things for herself, she sees them only through the eyes of others and says them in their language; but I am convinced that original composition without some mental preparation in the way of conscientious reading is an impossibility.

Of one thing she was sure: "Children should be encouraged to read for the pure delight of it."

The speech opened the eyes of a wider public to a fact that Dr. Bell had acutely perceived: that here was one of the great teachers of the time. Hitz talked of her as "an American Rousseau," "a pedagogical Columbus," which she scoffed at but nonetheless found very pleasant.* Self-depreca-

---

*Not everyone thought so highly of Miss Sullivan's speech. The superintendent of the Michigan School for the Deaf, Francis D. Clarke, later wrote Arthur Gilman of the Cambridge Academy: "Miss Sullivan's cool assumption at Chautauqua that all Helen is, is the result of her superior teaching—struck me as the greatest exhibition of supreme vanity that I ever saw. She told me at Chautauqua that she was looking around for another blind-deaf

tory as she was at times, she took herself and her ideas seriously, and when
a relatively obscure institutional journal published her speech without her
permission, she was angered: "If I had the paper now I think the *Century*
would publish it with some of Helen's journals." Of more immediate
significance in terms of Helen's and Annie's future was their encounter
at Chautauqua with two young men, John D. Wright and Dr. Thomas
Humason, who were planning to open a school in New York City to teach
oral language to the deaf. They heard Helen speak and felt sure that with
new methods her voice might be normalized and her mastery of lipreading
considerably improved. She might even be taught to sing. In October the
two went to New York, their expenses underwritten by John Spaulding.
Before that, however, they visited Mrs. Hopkins on the Cape, and that
gave Annie a chance to make a sortie into Boston to see her old friends.
She sought out a meeting with Anagnos. Neither left a record of what was
said, but there was no reconciliation. The likelihood is that he was very
displeased with their decision to abandon Boston for a school in New
York. Both Annie and Helen later maintained that this was at the bottom
of Anagnos's turning against Helen as well as Annie. At the end of the
year, during a visit to Boston, Annie confided to Hitz, "Mr. Anagnos, I
hear, is preparing something about Helen for his report—an explanation
of his position with regard to her—how he was deceived, etc. etc. I am
very impatient to see it—it will be such fun to compare past reports with
the forthcoming one."

---

child, in order that she could train her, and by the experiences which she had with Helen,
make of her a greater wonder than Helen ever would be. I was so completely taken aback
that I could not say a word."

XI

The Conquest of New York

"For it took the pair of you to make a complete and perfect whole."
—Mark Twain

They found the Wright-Humason School, just west of Central Park on Seventy-sixth Street, a homelike place in a setting that still was semibucolic. "The school is very pleasant," Helen wrote Caroline Derby, her old Boston friend, "and bless you! it is quite fashionable. . . . I study Arithmetic, English Literature and United States history, as I did last winter. I also keep a diary. I enjoy my singing lessons with Dr. Humason more than I can say. I expect to take piano lessons sometimes. . . ." But five months later she was less hopeful (about learning to speak, not to mention sing!): "Dr. Humason is still trying to improve my speech. Oh, Carrie, how I should like to speak like other people! I should be willing to work night and day if it could only be accomplished. Think of what a joy it would be to all of my friends to hear me speak naturally." Her lipreading had improved, Teacher wrote Hitz, "but her speech is no better as far as I can tell."

The school became a base for forays into the city. She was reading *The New York Times,* she told a reporter for that paper, even keeping track of reform efforts to defeat Tammany. A visit to the Metropolitan Club on Fifth Avenue, which was followed two days later by a tour of some East Side slums and the Tombs, provoked an expression of social outrage: "[S]he had some pointed things to say about those who had great wealth and were content to use it for their own pleasure." Thinking to test the breadth of her interests, a reporter inquired whether she knew who John L. Sullivan was: "Yes. He is a prize-fighter. I have heard of him. I do not see how men could do such things. It seems such a pity that God's creatures should fight with each other." The entire school went on expeditions —to museums, to the dog show at Madison Square Garden, to the Statue of Liberty. Helen's description of the latter was dominated by visual imagery: "Liberty is a gigantic figure of a woman in Greek draperies, holding in her right hand a torch. . . . We climbed up to the head which will hold forty persons, and viewed the scene on which Liberty gazes day and night, and O, how wonderful it was! . . . The glorious bay lay calm and beautiful in the October sunshine, and the ships came and went like idle dreams, those seaward going slowly disappeared like clouds that change from gold to gray; those homeward coming sped more quickly like birds that seek their mother's nest. . . ."

They quickly made a social life for themselves as intense as they had known in Boston. "The reception [at the school] was quite a success," a pleased Annie wrote Hitz. "The people whom we most desired to meet came and went away enthusiastic admirers of dear Helen. Mr. Stedman and Mr. Gilder were especially charmed with her. The Rockefellers and the Parsons also expressed surprise and pleasure and we received many invitations to dine and so forth." Clarence Stedman was the poet (and banker) who had written a much-quoted poem about Helen, which he now transcribed onto parchment and sent her for Christmas. Richard Watson Gilder, poet and editor of *The Century,* sent her a volume of his verse and a few weeks later a poem about Helen whose last stanzas bespoke the effect she had on those who saw her:

> Sight brings she to the seeing,
>   New song to those that hear
> Her braver spirit sounding
>   Where mortals fail and fear.

They spent Christmas in Boston as guests of Caroline Derby. "Santa Claus was very good to Teacher and me," Helen wrote her mother. She and Carrie had stolen downstairs at five in the morning and she listed the presents she had found in her stocking. "Teacher and I had an overwhelming surprise, and even now I can scarcely believe it was really so—a gift of a thousand dollars apiece from dear, good King John." "We saw many of our Boston friends and every one was delighted to see Helen," Annie reported to Hitz. "A few, Mr. Spaulding among them, declared they saw great improvement in her speech. Mr. Anagnos did not come to see us. Miss Derby invited him to one of her afternoon receptions but he excused himself on the plea of a cold but did not so much as refer to Helen in any way. Miss Derby did not like it much and said he should hear from her some time. He is really doing himself harm and not convincing anybody that Helen and I are humbugs."

His avoidance of Annie and Helen was entirely deliberate. Bitterness was beginning to consume him. His annual report for 1894 devoted thirty-four pages to Edith Thomas, a deaf-blind girl about Helen's age. Pointedly he wrote that "the case of this interesting girl bears convincing testimony to the efficiency and fruitfulness of the system which we pursue in the training of children who are deprived of the faculties of vision and hearing." Edith's development, as shown by her letters and school exercises, was all the more striking in that she was not "a brilliant or exceptionally gifted child." He had asked Fanny Marrett, the teacher who had been closest to Annie, to write a full statement of how the child had been taught. "In preparing this account Miss Marrett adhered strictly to the facts of the case and has woven them with scrupulous care into a most interesting narrative."

Helen made one more effort at reconciliation. She wrote him on April 21, 1895, asking whether, indeed, his affection for her had ceased. "Your impression in regard to the change of my feelings towards you is entirely erroneous," he wrote back. "I love you as dearly as ever. . . . I was very glad indeed to learn of the good times which you have been having in the great metropolis of America and of the progress which you have been making in reading speech from the lips." Then a dig at Annie: "It was my earnest wish for a long time that you should be so thoroughly trained in this particular direction as to be able to dispense wholly with the use of the manual alphabet, and I can scarcely tell you how thankful I am that you are striving to reach this goal." That appears to have been the last letter between them.

The two winters at Wright-Humason were on the whole a gay time for her—of "frolics" on Friday evenings, cosy chats, games. "We were such a rambunctious bunch of scapegraces—playing when we should work, spelling secretly when we should be improving our speech, making believe we were ill when it was time to go to church, and raising old Nick behind his [Mr. Wright's] back!" Yet she was always a girl apart. The school was primarily for the deaf. She was the only one who was deaf-blind. That alone separated her from the others. A classmate, Robert Moulton, remembered how the whole school marveled when she read the words written on the blackboard by tracing the chalk marks with her fingers or at her excellence at checkers played on a specially constructed board. She tried her best to be one of the gang. "Robbie" was a special friend because he came from Tennessee, and he remembered her as a girl full of fun. They were having strawberry shortcake for dessert "half a mile long," he informed her one day. "Why, that's only a hundred yards for each of us," she laughingly rejoined. When the school put on a play, she had a part, a touch on the arm being the cue for her to speak her lines. She went bobsledding in Central Park with the rest and shared in the spills that elicited only chuckles of delight. She also persuaded Teacher to allow her to take riding lessons after Mr. Wright and Dr. Humason were prevailed upon to withdraw their objections. Every morning Dr. Humason, who was a fine horseman, Teacher and Helen set out from Durland's Academy at Columbus Circle, with either Teacher or Dr. Humason holding the leading rein, "the only requirement being that the horses trot or gallop at about the same pace."

There was another thing that, despite all her efforts to be like the other young people, set her apart: her fame. She was fourteen and fifteen during her years at Wright-Humason, years of budding womanhood when the companionship of one's peers should absorb all thoughts and emotions and young men and women seek to define and confirm who they are in the others' eyes and embraces. But that was not for Helen, who was usually in the company of Annie. At the twenty-fifth reunion of the school, a dinner in honor of "Professor" Wright at which she was the featured speaker, she referred a little sadly to her spouseless state: "I feel like the last rose of summer left blooming alone! And my blush is deeper than that of a red, red rose because I come to this banquet and bring no beau, tall and debonair! His chair is vacant—the noblest Roman of them all!"

How could this most affectionate of human beings not have been touched by serious thoughts of love, by fires of desire during these years of womanly awakening? Her autobiography in *Youth's Companion* had ended with the passionate cry, "Love is everything! And God is love!" Perhaps her adoration of Annie satisfied this side of her nature. The *Times* reporter who interviewed her early in 1895 was struck by the way Helen "stops every once in a while, and her hand finds its way to her teacher's and wanders up to her face, as she leans over, in a pretty, affectionate way, to be kissed, like a little child who needs to be encouraged." When she was separated from Annie, who had gone to Boston for a week, she wrote her mother that her teacher's departure "made a great gap in my life. You are one of the very few who can understand how precious our friendship is. Love is our very life, and Teacher seems a part of myself."

She had little time for romance, even if a boy had come along who interested her. She carried on a voluminous correspondence, using three school typewriters of different makes, with special keyboards. Then Mr. Spaulding bought her a Remington, which she thought was "the best writing machine that is made." She spent several hours a day with her brailled books—a four-volumed Latin grammar, *David Copperfield* in five volumes, Tennyson's poems in large print, *Hamlet,* and selections from Swedenborg faithfully supplied by John Hitz. She kept a journal, which was occasionally published in the school paper, *Progress.* Here is one entry that has survived. Despite a juvenile tone influenced by her Swedenborgian readings, it showed a seriousness of purpose and ability to dream large dreams that also set her apart from her classmates:

October 23, 1894. This century—the wonderful 19th century—is nearing its end, and right in front of us stands the closed gate of the new century, on which in letters of light, God has written these words, 'Here is the way to wisdom, virtue and happiness.' What do you think this means, diary? Shall I tell you what I think it means? Why, these words, written on the gate of the new century, are a prophecy. They foretell that in the beautiful sometime all wrong will be made right, and all the sorrows of life will find their fulfillment in perfect happiness. Do you not see now, diary, that the noblest dreams of the greatest and wisest of men are to be the realities of the future? So, we must trust God securely. We must not doubt Him because of the great mystery of pain, and sin, and death. Hope is our privilege and our duty. . . .

Hope makes me glad and content with my life; for I know that in God's beautiful sometime I shall have the things for which I pray now so earnestly,—fulness of life, like the sea and the sun, mind equal and beyond all fulness; greatness and goodness of soul higher than all things. Yes! I know that they will all come sometimes, perhaps in this beautiful new century.

These were the words of sibyl, not schoolgirl, and it was as a seraph that she conquered New York society, Hyperion and satyr alike. "I cannot give expression to, nor can I altogether explain to myself, the impression she made upon us," wrote Lawrence Hutton, writer, bibliophile, collector of death masks and hand casts and urbane man of means. "We felt as if we were looking into a perfectly clear fresh soul, exhibited to us by a person of more than usual intellect and intelligence, freely and without reserve. Here was a creature who absolutely knew no guile and no sorrow; from whom all that was impure and unpleasant had been kept. . . . She was a revelation and an inspiration to us. And she made us think and shudder, and think again. She had come straight from the hands of God, and for fourteen years the world and the flesh and the devil had not obtained possession of her."

He was startled by the extrasensory means of communication that appeared to bind Helen to her teacher:

> She seems to have a sixth sense. She receives and understands somehow what of course she cannot hear. The devotion she has for her teacher is beyond all words; her absolute dependence upon that teacher is inexpressibly touching; and when some one spoke of this, and wondered what would become of Helen in case of any separation, the child, hearing nothing of course, turned to the teacher, and pulling her face towards her own kissed her on the lips, as if to say she could not think of it. This to me was the most startling of all her actions—almost an evidence of psychological impression. She had perceived through some unconscious movement of the teacher's hand, which she held, the teacher's own inmost feelings at the suggestion of this idea—perhaps a new one even to her; certainly one never before entering the head of the child. Miss Sullivan told us that with no conscious movement, no intentional or perceptible 'talking with her fingers,' she could make the child follow her own thoughts, do what she wished her to do, go where she wished her to go, perform any of the acts of 'mind-reading' which the professional psychologists exhibit on the stage, or in an amateur way. The teacher, however, was not aware of anything like phenomenal thought-transference. She could not control the child except by the power of touch.

Hutton also was struck by Helen's gaiety: "She laughed at everything. She smiled with every one. Everything was pleasant to her. Everybody was good. God grant that she may never find out the innate cussedness of things and of men!" It was at the Huttons that Helen and Annie met the two greatest writers of the "Gilded Age," as one of them, Mark Twain, had himself characterized the post–Civil War period. There were about fifteen men and women whom the Huttons had assembled for Sunday lunch. The Standard Oil executive Henry H. Rogers and Mark Twain came together and stood with the other guests awaiting the arrival of Helen and Annie. "The wonderful child arrived now, with her almost equally wonderful teacher, Miss Sullivan," Mark Twain recalled a decade later. "The girl began to deliver happy ejaculations, in her broken speech. Without touching anything, of course, and without hearing anything, she seemed quite well to recognize the character of her surroundings. She said, 'Oh, the books, the books, so many, many books. How lovely!' " All the distinguished guests, including William Dean Howells, were presented to her. "Mr. Howells seated himself by Helen on the sofa and she put her fingers on his lips and he told her a story of considerable length and you could see each detail of it pass into her mind and strike fire there and throw the flash of it into her face. Then I told her a long story, which she interrupted all along and in the right places, with cackles, chuckles, and care-free bursts of laughter. Then Miss Sullivan put one of Helen's hands against her lips and spoke against it the question, 'What is Mr. Clemens distinguished for?' Helen answered, in her crippled speech, 'For his humor.' I spoke up modestly and said, 'And for his wisdom.' Helen said the same words instantly—'and for his wisdom.' I suppose it was mental telegraphy for there was no way for her to know what I had said."

Mark Twain was as famous for his white thatch, which Helen promptly fingered, as he was for his nom de plume, Mark Twain, which he explained to Helen meant a depth of twelve feet and the sound of which carried further than "ten fathoms." It had been the pseudonym of a river pilot, and he had appropriated it when the original had gone to port— "And you made it famous," Helen interrupted. It was not inappropriate, Mark Twain went on, because he was sometimes light on the surface and —again Helen finished the thought for him—sometimes "deep." Howells, meanwhile, had drifted out of the encounter. He had been shy and embarrassed. When Helen had placed her fingers on his lips, he had protested, "But Clemens, I don't know where to begin, this is too embarrassing. Why don't *you* tell her some of your experiences?" Clemens replied, "Oh, no, that would be too much like hell."

She sensed resistance in Howells, but not in Clemens. She felt his hair and his face with her fingers and took some violets that she had been given and placed them in his buttonhole. "He was peculiarly lovely and tender with her—even for Mr. Clemens," wrote Hutton, "and she kissed him when he said goodbye." A few minutes later he came back into the room and ran his hand through her hair to see if she recognized him. She did. Mark Twain was entering the period of female acolytes, young girls whom he called "granddaughters" and "angel fish." Their attraction, for this man who himself had three daughters, was an alloy of remembrance and wish-fulfillment. And sixteen he considered "the dearest and sweetest of all ages." Elsie Leslie Lyde was a great favorite of Clemens, as she had been of Spaulding's. He and William Gillette, the actor, even embroidered a pair of slippers for Elsie. Helen never saw the slippers, but later read his description of the pattern. "Every stitch has cost us blood. I've got twice as many pores in me now as I used to have and you would never believe how many places you can stick a needle in yourself until you go into the embroidery line and devote yourself to art."

"Mr. Clemens told us many entertaining stories, and made us laugh till we cried," Helen wrote her mother. "I think he is very handsome indeed. . . . Teacher said he looked something like Paredeuski. (If that is the way to spell the name.)" And Mr. Rogers "kindly left his carriage to bring us home."

Another writer, Charles Dudley Warner, Mark Twain's collaborator on *The Gilded Age* and a distinguished editor and essayist, was so taken with Helen that he turned up a few days after the Hutton party, bringing the great naturalist John Burroughs with him. "Mr. Burroughs reminded me of dear Mr. Whittier," Helen wrote Mrs. Hutton. "He has the same calm, gentle ways, and makes one feel that he lives very near to our Father all the time."

The Huttons, in addition to introducing them to their eminent friends, also took in hand the establishment of a fund for Helen's further education. The absence of such a fund haunted Annie throughout their stay at Wright-Humason. "King John" was very generous and had promised to provide for both of them in his will, but Teacher, very wisely, did not wish to be dependent on one person. She had constantly jogged Hitz to remind Dr. Bell of his offer to help with a plan and with money:

> Dr. Bell was in town last week. I saw him only once; but we had a long talk about Helen's education, and our plans for the future. He says he intends to give the thousand dollars he promised; but he

thinks there should be some business-like arrangement,—trustees or
something of that sort. He said Mr. Spaulding's plan would deter
Helen's friends from giving, etc. I told him something must be done
if her education is to go on, and he promised he would see what could
be done when he went to Boston the last of this month. I have begun
to worry already about next year. I am utterly in the dark as to what
is the best course to pursue. I am sure Helen is improving in speech
and lip-reading; and these are the things she came to this school for.
. . . On the other hand, her Boston friends think she should be there
in school with seeing and hearing girls. . . .

She did not like New York City, but Boston had its drawbacks. "We
should be constantly at the beck and call of certain people in Boston and
there would be the unpleasantness arising from the attitude of Mr. Anagnos towards us. He was in New York several days lately, and did not even
come near us." Did the Volta Bureau have a set of Perkins reports? "Mr.
Wright wrote to Mr. Anagnos for them the other day, and he only sent
the last one. The first two, in which he spoke of my work in such glowing
terms, he did not send. . . . Naturally Mr. Anagnos wishes them out of
existence."

"Everything is about the same," she wrote dispiritedly from Tuscumbia
a month later, "a little more dilapidated if that is possible." It was a dull
summer. "I am sitting on the piazza with my back to the sun. Helen is in
the hammock reading Swedenborg and Phillips and Mildred are eating
peaches on the steps. I can see Mrs. Keller out in the garden gathering
the vegetables for dinner." She spent $125 on a horse, "simply perfect,"
but he turned out a disappointment, and riding in the humid summer heat
not at all what she had thought it would be. A bad summer, she wrote Hitz
when they were back in New York. She had been ill and Helen "very
complaining." On their way to New York, they had spent two weeks with
the Wades in Hulton and with Mrs. William Thaw in Pittsburgh. Mrs.
Thaw was the mother of Harry Thaw, who shot Stanford White. "Helen
is to have more advanced work this year. Dr. Humason is to have her in
arithmetic and Mr. Wright will teach her science and she is to have
German and French besides so we both look forward to a very busy year."

But on their return to the city they learned also that "good Mr. Spaulding is seriously—in fact dangerously ill." She had telegraphed to his
friends to find out whether they should come to Boston. "I cannot but feel
very anxious should he die without making provision for Helen. I do not

know what would become of us." They went to Boston. Spaulding had had "catarrh of the stomach for several years" and the disease had been "greatly aggravated by over-indulgence in drink." Death and dying always terrified her, and now there was added anxiety—"What would become of Helen and me if Mr. Spaulding should be taken away is the question I am constantly asking myself." She and Helen were permitted to see him for a few minutes each day, but then he weakened and they were no longer allowed in to his room. They returned to New York. "Where are the Bells?" was her anxious query to Hitz.

"King John" died at the beginning of January. His heirs not only lacked his interest in providing for Helen and Annie but pressed Captain Keller for repayment of the Spaulding loan to him. Although they said they would settle for $10,000, Captain Keller was unable to raise that amount and wrote to Annie's friend Mrs. Hopkins demanding that whatever funds had been raised for Helen's education should be turned over to him as Helen's guardian. "If this can't be done I will ask the heirs of Mr. Spaulding to extend this offer long enough to have Helen raise the money by doing what I have always opposed her doing—that is giving the public a chance to see and hear her from the platform." She should not agree to anything, Mrs. Hopkins advised Annie. It was "dreadful" that Captain Keller should propose to take Helen out of school "and show her as you would a monkey." As Helen later explained to her sister, "Mother wrote a heartbroken letter to Teacher declaring that she would die before this happened. The idea of showing me off was suggested to father by a proposal of B.F. Keith to pay me five hundred dollars a week to do his circuit."

Dr. Bell wrote to Spaulding's main heir, William Spaulding:

> As one of Helen Keller's friends, I was delighted to hear, a year or two ago, that Mr. John Spaulding had set apart a sum of $19,000 for the benefit of Helen Keller. I understood at the time that Mr. Spaulding did not wish to place this fund in the control of Helen's father, who, of course, is her natural guardian, and so, pending the formation of a proper legal trust, he had simply deposited in a bank in his own name sugar stock or bonds to the amount specified, with instructions to the bank to pay the interest to Mrs. Hopkins for the benefit of Helen Keller; and the expenses of Helen's education so far have been paid from this fund.

Can it be possible that the late Mr. Spaulding has left no written memorandum or statement concerning his intentions towards Helen? Miss Sullivan seems to be under the impression that he has not remembered Helen in his will, and that the stock or bonds which were set apart for her use, being in his own name, have gone to his legal heirs and representatives, and are no longer available for the original purpose intended.

If no provision has been made for Helen, it seems to me imperative that her friends immediately look into the matter, and by joint action create a permanent trust sufficient to provide for her education and support. Miss Sullivan tells me that you, as the heir of Mr. Spaulding, are inclined to be generous towards Helen, and would be glad to make a substantial contribution to such a fund, if I and others would join with you.

Quite a number of Helen's friends (myself among the number) are prepared to help in this matter. It only needs the proposition of a definite plan. I know that Mrs. J. Pierpont Morgan of New York and some of her friends would be glad to assist; Mrs. Lawrence Hutton of New York, would also, I have no doubt join us, and Mrs. William Thaw, of Pittsburgh, Pennsylvania.

Last night I met Mr. Dudley Warner, and he voluntarily referred to the subject, and said that he also would like to help. There can be no doubt that permanent provision for Helen could be made now by a common understanding among her friends. I should be very much obliged if you would write me freely concerning the matter. Would you meet me and other friends of Helen in New York for a conference upon this subject?

"Well, mother, our plans for the summer and next year are slowly beginning to take shape," Helen wrote home. "Dr. Bell is coming here tomorrow to meet several gentlemen and arrange with them about money for my education. . . . If you and father are willing, what do you think I'm going to do? I'm going to Cambridge to prepare for the Harvard Annex!!!"

But matters of this kind take time to arrange. "Nothing happened on Friday before last as far as Teacher knows," Helen informed her mother. "Nobody was at the meeting except Dr. Bell and dear, kind Mr. Warner.

(I saw Mr. Westervelt of Rochester at the hotel.) They talked over various plans; but of course they could not do anything without the assistance of others. Mr. Bell is coming to New York again soon, and he thinks something may be done then."

Annie Sullivan, who was a woman of action and decision, expressed herself much more forcefully. The visit was "most unsatisfactory," she wrote Hitz, "for it brought only disappointment and discouragement. Mr. Bell did a great deal of talking which was not to the point, and when it came to doing, he was not in it. Why, he would not even consent to become Helen's nominal guardian with no responsibility whatever attached to the position! Indeed, he would do nothing but contribute a thousand dollars." As for Helen's plans the coming year, "after carefully considering the advantages offered by the various schools and colleges in various places, I decided that we would make the Harvard Annex [Radcliffe] our goal, and the Cambridge School, preparatory to the Annex our haven for the next three or four years. The school is an excellent one, and the Harvard Annex is practically the same as Harvard; and of course the intellectual atmosphere of the place is all that can be desired. Besides, Helen will have the use of books and apparatus at the Perkins Institution, which will be of great help to her in her advanced work."

In July Annie went up to Boston from Brewster to see Dr. Bell. She stayed at the Parker House, as did Dr. Bell and Elsie Leslie. Helen's letter to her mother is more lighthearted than either of them felt:

> Elsie is a young lady now, and they tell me she is very handsome. She is going to make her debut in society next winter! Teacher found Mr. Bell in a most unhappy state of mind. Poor man! He was very much frightened about himself. He was quite deaf, had a toothache and a headache, and felt generally wretched. Teacher and Elsie spent all day Sunday running all over the city with him, looking up aurists and dentists who were out of town, and visiting drug stores. Late in the afternoon they found an aurist who soon restored Mr. Bell's hearing and his spirits at the same time, and a dentist who relieved him of a troublesome tooth, and he returned to the hotel a new man! In the course of the afternoon they drove to dear King John's place in Dorchester. How changed it was,—no furniture in the house, and no flowers in the greenhouse, and a great sign over the gate, saying that the place was for sale. How sad and strange it seemed! Mr. William Spaulding, King John's nephew, lunched at the Parker House with

them, and was very nice, Teacher says. He inquired for father, and
said he hoped Mr. Keller was all right on the great financial question.
[This was a reference to the gold versus silver issue that the nomination of William Jennings Bryan a week earlier had placed at the center
of the 1896 presidential election.] Teacher replied that she hoped so.
By the way, she says I must tell you that nothing definite has been
done to raise the fund she spoke of. Everybody is in Europe or away
in the country, and it is difficult to get at them. However, she feels
sure that all things will come out right in the end. But if they do not,
we know that we have a happy home awaiting us in Tuscumbia, so
we don't allow ourselves to worry abut the future.

The problem with the fund was to persuade someone to take charge.
Dr. Bell had sent Charles Dudley Warner a check payable to his order for
Helen's education. This alarmed the novelist, who wrote Mrs. Hutton: "I
have also a letter from Mrs. Hopkins asking me to take charge, and one
from Mr. Spaulding offering to send his $6,000 to me as trustee. I cannot
undertake it. I am not a business man enough to work in patents and all
that. If I send you this $400 you can put it with the rest you have for
Helen. In the Fall we can see what can be done here to it."
There were other anxieties. "[H]ave you really decided on Helen's
having a college course?" Lucy Derby Fuller wrote Annie in midsummer.
She was not sure that was the wisest course. "Helen holds the interest of
the whole world today—it seems to me the sweetest and greatest moment
in her career certainly so far. She is just sixteen, her abounding heart of
love—her spontaneous enthusiasm both draw people to her in a wonderful way—is not *now* the moment for her mind to begin to express itself
in creative work—and is not now the time for her to gather her hearers
about her—accompanying any creative work she does with study with a
tutor in some especial direction—but not giving all her time to study as
will be necessary if she takes a college course? I ask all this—I am not sure
—but Helen has wakened such deep tenderness and such a different kind
of interest from that which was awakened by Laura Bridgman."
She knew Annie's worries about returning to Boston. "I feel that you
are very wise in returning to Boston to live and to live down Mr. Anagnos's reflections. I know so well how such things cut—that I can see as you
cannot, how you must magnify it all, but right on the battlefield is the place
to be."
Anagnos's report for 1895 preserved the surface courtesies, but it was

a harsh criticism of Annie. Even though she went unnamed, those in the know understood his meaning. His denigration took the form of praise for Fanny Marrett, who again wrote the account of Edith Thomas's progress. Edith's teachers, wrote Anagnos, "instead of striving to impress upon her their own personalities . . . have endeavored to lead her to express the truth that is in her, and to enable her to observe and to compare, to reason and to judge, to resolve and to do."

> This sort of training has developed in Edith that creative and organizing force which marks the difference between the pupil who can originate and conceive new thoughts and ideas and the one who either unconsciously repeats or merely remembers, imitates and copies what he is told or what he reads on the printed page. Without the mixture of the distinctive and positive traits that constitute originality, the mind becomes only a sponge or a slate. . . . Individuality is the transfusing and transforming power. Those who are wanting in it are but mere harps played by every passing wind of circumstance and opinion, docile enough to learn from others or from books, but with small power to create, or to think and act for themselves. Edith was fortunate enough not only to be spared from such methods of teaching and such pernicious personal influences as tend to degrade the mental faculties and moral susceptibilities and render the process of learning stultifying to the whole nature but to be kept scrupulously free from all excitement which an artificial mode of life produces, and from one of the most ardent and deteriorating stimulants, the love of praise and notoriety.

This was a low blow. Anagnos did carry a great deal of responsibility for projecting Helen into the limelight, often over Annie's protests. He knew, too, how admiring he had been of Annie's methods in teaching Helen. But Anagnos was widely respected. In returning to Boston and setting as Helen's goal her admission to Radcliffe, Annie and Helen were accepting his challenge, and if they succeeded would conclusively and finally answer the whispered cry of "humbug."

But the decision to have Helen enroll in a Cambridge preparatory school did not come easily to Annie. Aside from Boston's uncomfortable associations with Anagnos, Annie, self-educated herself, had a profound distrust of formal education. "Sometimes it seems to me as if I could not endure the thought of going to another school," she had written Hitz after a year at Wright-Humason, "and at such times it seems as if I had better let another person more capable of continuing Helen's education take my place. . . . Really, mon cher père, you do not know how tired I am of this endless worry and strain, the trying to know what I do not know and to be what I am not. For myself, I have no especial attachment for this school. I am interested in the work these young men [she was herself all of thirty!] are trying to accomplish, but nothing more."

Occasionally she took a class in the absence of a regular teacher, and those experiences reinforced her antipathy to classroom instruction and may explain her cryptic comment to Hitz after she announced the decision to go to Cambridge, "You will be surprised to hear that our friends here have made no objection to our leaving the school." She was a strong-minded woman who did not easily brook opposition, and in a letter to Hitz she pungently expounded her educational theories about classroom learning:

> Thank Heaven, I didn't have to follow a curriculum when I began teaching Helen. I am convinced she wouldn't have learned language as easily as she did. It seems to me, it is made as difficult as possible in school for a child to learn anything.
>
> Helen learned language almost as unconsciously as a normal child. Here it is made a 'lesson.' The child sits indoors, and for an hour the teacher endeavors more or less skilfully to engrave words upon his brain. As I look back, it seems as if Helen were always on the jump when I was teaching her. We were generally in the open air doing something. Words were learned as they were needed. She rarely forgot a word that was given her when the action called it forth, and she learned a phrase or even a sentence as readily as a single word when it was needed to describe the action.
>
> Apparently, children learn language more quickly when they are free to move about among objects that interest them. They absorb words and knowledge simultaneously. In the class-room they cease to be actors in the drama, they sit and watch the teacher doing something with her mouth which does not excite their curiousity particularly. Passivity does not stimulate interest or mental energy. The child learns eagerly what he wants to know, and indifferently what you want him to know.

I have thought much about methods of teaching since I came here. The contrast between these children's plodding pursuit of knowledge and Helen's bounding joyousness makes me wonder. When I go into one of the classrooms and see little children sitting demurely behind their small desks, while a teacher sits in front of them, holding an object in her hand for their inspection, then slowly speaking the name of the object which they vainly try to imitate, I feel somehow as if they were chained to their seats, and forced to gaze intently at a giantess who made faces at them.

I very seldom speak what is in my mind. I do not think teachers are at all open-minded. To say that they do not welcome ideas which imply criticism of their methods is to put it mildly. I do not know if all teachers close their minds to the stupidities they practice. I have known only teachers of the blind and the deaf, and I pity them more than I blame them. When you consider the huge doses of knowledge which they are expected to pour into the brains of their small pupils, you cannot demand of them initiative or originality. The pressure upon them is so great, they find it necessary to resort to forcing methods. There follows the intensive cultivation of the memory. The little brains are crammed with knowledge to the point of indigestion. They learn a little of everything, and by a super-effort to retain it until examinations and tests are over when they straightway forget it, not having learned any use for their too vast learning.

There isn't a doubt in my mind that schools force upon the young an abnormal life. The hours are too long, too many subjects are taught, too complicated methods are employed. The teacher has no time to give to the individual needs of the children.

I wish you would let Dr. Bell read this letter. If he thinks I am right, perhaps he could use his great influence at the coming convention to impress upon the instructors of the deaf that what their pupils need is more out-of-door lessons—lessons about living things—trees and flowers and animals—things they love, and are curious about. The number of subjects taught is not so important as that the children should learn language for the joy of it. The miracle of education is achieved when this happens.

The child happily interested in his work learns quickly and without conscious effort.

All I have written may be antediluvian to Dr. Bell. If he says nothing can be done about it, I have labored enormously with pen and ink, and brought forth an inky mouse.

The fifth annual convention of Dr. Bell's Association to Promote the Teaching of Speech to the Deaf was scheduled to meet at Mt. Airy in Philadelphia in July; and Hitz quickly wrote back, "Dr. Bell is so delighted with your criticism of educational methods in the schools for the deaf that he is very desirous for you to prepare a paper (it need not be long) for the Convention on the subject. I am sure you have not kept a copy of the letter, so I am mailing a copy to you."

It was Helen, not Annie, who spoke at Mt. Airy, presumably because Annie, remembering her panic at Chautauqua, where Dr. Bell had to read her paper, declined to do so. Her own insecurities caused her to promote Helen rather than herself. "Her greatest handicap all through life has been her lack of self-confidence," Wright told Nella Braddy, "but she has the courage of her convictions, and has never been afraid to 'take a chance.' She is more apt to believe in others than (in) herself." Wright's partner made the same point a little differently. He had gotten to know Annie well. A fine musician, he had enjoyed escorting Annie to the opera, especially Wagnerian operas, often running over the score on the piano for her beforehand. "I used to wonder," he told Nella Braddy, "about her personal ambition in contrast with her ambition for Helen." Individuals with great abilities but with equally great compulsive drives that keep them from manifesting those talents often marry their fortunes to those who need their gifts and are not encumbered by their feelings of inadequacy. The relationship of Louis Howe to Eleanor and Franklin Roosevelt is a classic contemporary case. To be successful the bond must constitute a genuine mutual dependence. Helen's need of Teacher is obvious. But equally powerful was Teacher's reliance on Helen to keep her misanthropic impulses under control and to give her a sense of purpose in life. The mutual dependence released certain gifts and energies in both while it repressed others.

"Teacher and I spent nine days at Philadelphia," Helen wrote Hitz afterwards from Brewster. "We were busy all the time; we attended the meeting and talked with hundreds of people among whom were dear Dr. Bell, Mr. Banerji of Calcutta, Monsieur Magrat of Paris, with whom I conversed in French exclusively, and many other distinguished persons." "Helen Keller was the object of the greatest interest to all," the *American Annals of the Deaf* reported. "On the afternoon when she spoke on the platform, the hall where the meetings were held, was crowded to its utmost capacity. Advantage was taken of the interest thus excited to invite outsiders to join the Association as active or life members, and a considerable number availed themselves of the opportunity to do so."

She told her audience, Helen's letter to Hitz went on, "what an unspeakable blessing speech has been to me, and urging them to give every little deaf child an opportunity to learn to speak. Every one said I spoke very well and intelligibly. After my little 'speech,' we attended a reception, at which over six hundred people were present. I must confess, I do not like such large receptions; the people crowd so, and we have to do so much talking; and yet it is at receptions like the one at Philadelphia that we often meet friends who [sic] we learn to love afterwards."

Annie also wrote Hitz after they reached Brewster—a depressed letter, full of self-reproaches. She thanked him for his birthday remembrance: "It always seems very strange to me when anybody remembers my birthday because I cannot understand why anybody should be glad that I was born. To me it seems the greatest of misfortunes."

They did not return to Tuscumbia that summer. Most of the time they were with Mrs. Hopkins at Brewster, and three weeks were spent with Joseph Edgar Chamberlin, "Uncle Ed," the associate editor of *Youth's Companion* and writer of a column in the *Transcript* called "The Listener." He and his family lived in a large red house on a lake in Wrentham, just outside of Boston but a rural area still, with boating and swimming and convivial gatherings of Boston's literary lights at picnics under the trees. In Tuscumbia Captain Keller was busy with politics. Like so many Southerners whose bleak economic fortunes seemed to be at the mercy of the Eastern banks and trusts, he was a populist and supporter of William Jennings Bryan. He asked Hitz to send Mrs. Bryan a photograph of Helen with his compliments. Teacher says, Helen wrote her mother, "tell father that he must be moderate in the coming campaign. Right or wrong, gold is sure to win, and father will gain nothing by being overzealous in the cause of silver."

A few weeks later Captain Keller died. "My father is dead," a stricken Helen wrote Dr. Bell. "He died last Saturday at my home in Tuscumbia and I was not there. My own dear loving father! Oh, dear friend, how shall I bear it! . . . How strange it is! I never knew how dearly I loved my father until I realized that I had lost him. I think we do not know the depth of love in our hearts until some dreadful sorrow reveals it to us, and then we realize a little what God's love must be like."

"Dear Helen's father is dead!" Annie wrote Hitz from Brewster.

> He died Saturday morning. Poor Helen is heart broken. We had no idea that anything was wrong till Friday and the end came in a few hours. Helen was frantic with grief and her one desire was to get to her mother. There was no train from here until Monday and of course there was nothing to do but wait. Such a day! Helen cried and sobbed all day long. I telegraphed Mrs. Keller that we would leave Boston Monday evening. Sunday noon I got an answer saying Do not come, wait for letter. The letter came Wednesday. Mrs. Keller thought it would be inadvisable and far from prudent for us to go South as it was the beginning of their sickliest season. This was another blow to Helen and she is still inconsolable.

> I never dreamed there was the possibility of such great sorrow in the dear child's nature. She bears and has always borne her own terrible afflictions so patiently and uncomplainingly that I am afraid I had come to feel that her peculiar limitations had dulled her emotional nature so that she did not feel as intensely as many. But I see that I was wrong and I am sorry. I thought she would at least be spared the acute mental suffering which our griefs so often bring with them.

"She often shows uncanny insight into the springs of human action, and takes frequent advantage of this power," Mr. Wright wrote Nella Braddy years later about Teacher. That was undoubtedly true, but it is also true that Annie occasionally surprises us by what she failed to see, or misunderstood—in this case her belief that blindness and deafness had dulled Helen's emotional nature, a view that she would have considered outrageous had it been offered by someone else. Annie was Helen's deliverer and her bridge to the world; but the bridge had its weaknesses, and they added to Helen's limitations.

There is a more disturbing aspect. One can discount Anagnos's attacks on Annie for, in his view, seeking to impose her own personality, values and judgments upon Helen; but Teacher herself in her talks with Nella Braddy lent support to Anagnos's accusation. "It is not a teacher that the deaf-blind want," says Teacher. "It is another self. . . . Helen not original, not a genius—good mental equipment—perseverance—no aptitude for emotional expression—A(nnie) used to tell her to hug her mother and then she would tell her how pleased her mother was."

Perhaps those who felt that separating Helen from Annie might release new potentialities in both were not wholly mistaken. But that was not so easily done, as the episode at the Cambridge Preparatory School was to show.

XII

Another Schoolmaster Meets His Waterloo at the Hands of Annie

"All the powers on Earth cannot separate Helen and me."

Elizabeth Cary Agassiz, president emeritus of Radcliffe, had recommended to Annie the Cambridge School for Young Ladies, headed by Arthur Gilman, as the best place to prepare Helen for Radcliffe. Annie saw Gilman in June and asked him to admit Helen to the classes with hearing and seeing girls. "This proposition startled me," the Cambridge educator wrote in *The Century,* "and I thought it was impracticable. However, Miss Sullivan was, as usual, deeply in earnest, and urged me not to decide at once. She afterwards gave me the opportunity to discover Miss Keller's mental powers, and also to learn something of her educational progress. I decided it was possible to fit Helen for the examinations, and determined to make the trial."

"We visited the school at Cambridge and saw Mr. Gilman, the principal," Helen wrote Hitz in mid-July. "He is a very kind gentleman, and the school is an ideal one, I believe. . . . How splendid it will be if I can go to Radcliffe College." To another friend she wrote, "It seems sometimes as if I could never accomplish all I wish to. But I am going to think *I can;* for I know patience and perseverance always conquer in the end. You know the old adage about a faint heart and a fair lady. Well, I think it is equally true of a college degree."

Annie dreaded failure, but she knew, too, that entrance into Radcliffe and obtaining a degree without special favors or allowances for Helen's

handicaps would dispose forever of charges of humbuggery. In a letter to
St. Nicholas that accompanied Helen's on the eve of beginning her studies
at the Cambridge School, Annie wrote, borrowing phrases from Lucy
Fuller's letter:

> Now that a definite plan for Helen's future has been decided upon,
> people are more than ever interested in her. It seems to me the
> sweetest and greatest moment in Helen's life thus far. She is just
> sixteen. Certainly up to the present time her abounding heart of love
> and her spontaneous enthusiasm for all that is good have drawn
> people to her in a wonderful way, and it now remains for her to show
> the world what more may be accomplished under the greatest misfor-
> tunes.

Helen entered the Cambridge School October 1. Gilman decided to
give her a set of old Harvard entrance examinations as samples to test how
much she already knew in the subjects that she intended to be examined
on—English, German, French, and Greek and Roman history. She passed
them all. In reading Helen's papers, Gilman "was struck by the literary
style, which was original, and by the leisurely way in which the thoughts
were brought out." And to check his judgment, he showed her papers to
the people at Harvard who read the admission books, "and in every case
I was assured the grade was sufficient to pass the examination." Gilman
was no run-of-the-mill schoolmaster. It was he who had proposed, at a time
when higher education for women was still an unconventional notion, that
Harvard start an "Annex" for women. This subsequently became Radcliffe College. He was a member of its Governing Corporation, and he had
a long list of books to his credit. His testimony as to Helen's success with
the examinations impressed thoughtful people.

"They were the entrance examinations for Harvard College," Helen,
elated, wrote Mrs. Hutton, "so I feel pleased to think I could pass them.
. . . You must tell Mr. Howells when you see him, that we are living in
his house. . . ." The interest in Helen's newest venture was great, and
Gilman informed the press of Helen's success. "To our mind," commented the *Baltimore News,* "no record of bravery in war or fortitude in
exploration or adventure speaks more eloquently of the power of human
will or human courage in their struggle against adverse fate than does the
silent work of these two women, pupil and teacher."

They lived in Howells House, which was one of the Cambridge School dormitories. Annie accompanied Helen to all her classes, for this was not Perkins where many of the teachers knew the manual language. Gilman and Frau Grote, the German teacher, did learn it; but none of the other teachers did, and the girls in Howells House usually had to have Annie as intermediary if they wished to talk with Helen. She realized how hard it was on Teacher, and emphasized Teacher's dedication in letters to such friends as Mrs. Thaw and Mr. Hitz. About this time Helen began to capitalize "Teacher," a practice Annie did not discourage. She was always ready to have Helen—the miracle—take the bows, provided the world recognized that standing in the shadows was the miracle worker.

> You see, it takes me a long time to prepare my lessons because Teacher is obliged to spell every word of them into my hand. Not one of the text-books which I use in school is in raised print; so of course our work is harder than it would be if I could read my lessons over by myself. I have a great deal of German to read, and that is especially trying on her poor eyes. Sometimes I really cannot help worrying about them; but at other times I enjoy my lessons more than I can say.

One oppressive anxiety had been considerably eased—money. The capable Mrs. Hutton, when the men faltered, had taken charge of raising a fund sufficient to support Helen and Annie. "The idea is to raise fifty thousand (50,000) dollars from which to obtain an annual income of two thousand dollars for the maintenance of Helen and Miss Sullivan—the $50,000 covering and including all the sums already stored by and for Helen." So Mary Mapes Dodge, the influential editor of *St. Nicholas,* wrote Mrs. William Randolph Hearst at the end of 1896, thanking her for her pledge of five hundred dollars a year for three years. A public appeal to raise fifty thousand dollars and thus assure the "financial independence" of Helen and Miss Sullivan was issued in the names of Mrs. Hutton, Dean Howells, Charles Dudley Warner, Bishop Greer, Edwin King and Hampden Robb. Mark Twain was not a signer because he was in London in seclusion, but Mrs. Hutton appealed to him to try to interest rich Englishmen in Helen's case. "I see nobody," he wrote Mrs. Rogers, the wife of H. H. Rogers. "Nothing but the strictest hiding can enable me to write my long book in time." But he appealed to her and through her to her husband to help: "It won't do for America to allow this marvellous child to retire from her studies because of poverty. If she can go on with them she will make a name that will endure in history for centuries. . . . There is danger that she must retire from the struggle for a College degree for lack of support for herself and for Miss Sullivan, (the teacher who has been with her from the start—Mr. Rogers will remember her)." He begged her to "lay siege" to her husband to get him to interest himself and the Rockefellers in Helen's case, "get them to subscribe an annual aggregate of six or seven hundred or a thousand dollars—and agree to continue this for three or four years, until she has completed her college course. I'm not trying to limit their generosity—indeed no, they may pile that Standard Oil, Helen Keller College Fund as high as they please, they have my consent."

The Rogers contribution was for one hundred dollars a month. This together with the interest on the fund collected by Mrs. Hutton assured them of better than two thousand dollars a year. Helen later testified to how much this meant to her when she wrote, "That I have not missed my small part of usefulness in the world, I owe to Mr. Clemens and Mr. Rogers." Uncharacteristically, the Rogers gift was one she failed to acknowledge. It was a sign of how concentratedly she was working on her studies. She had to be nudged to write an appropriate letter of thanks: "Mrs. Hutton had a little talk with Mr. Rogers this afternoon," Lawrence Hutton wrote Annie, "in which it came out that Helen had not written to thank him for his great generosity to you both." He knew how absorbed Helen was in her studies, but "let her drop her mathematics and her ancient history long enough to say to her good friends that she appreciates their goodness."

Helen and Teacher decided not to take the time off at Christmas to travel down to Tuscumbia; instead Mrs. Keller came to Boston, with her children Mildred and Phillips. Helen looked forward to Christmas with her family: "What a beautiful day Christmas is. The better I understand what it means, the more I love it. When it steals silently through the brightening sky, I always seem to hear the angels singing the joyous song of old which greeted the dear Christ-child as he lay in his cradle." Everyone fell in love with her sister Mildred, and Gilman offered to let her study in his school, an offer that Mrs. Keller accepted.

Helen's studies the first year were intended to prepare her to take nine of the sixteen hours of preliminary examinations required for entrance into Radcliffe. She took courses in German, French, Latin, English and Greek and Roman history and a course in arithmetic, which gave her the most trouble of all. It is doubtful that Helen's plan was workable without Annie. Gilman testified to Annie's indispensability and dedication:

Miss Sullivan sat at Helen's side in the classes, interpreting to her with infinite patience the instruction of every teacher. In study-hours Miss Sullivan's labors were even more arduous, for she was obliged to read everything that Helen had to learn, excepting what was prepared in Braille; she searched the lexicons and encyclopaedias, and gave Helen the benefit of it all. When Helen went home Miss Sullivan went with her, and it was hers to satisfy the busy, unintermitting demands of the intensely active brain, for, though others gladly helped, there were many matters which could be treated only by the one teacher who had awakened the activity and had followed its development from the first. Now it was a German grammar which had to be read, now a French story, and then some passages from Caesar's Commentaries. It looked like drudgery, and drudgery it would certainly have been had not love shed its benign influence over all, lightening each step and turning hardship into pleasure.

If Annie's devotion impressed Gilman, Helen's consecration to study amazed him:

The avidity with which Helen read whatever was placed within her range kept her always ahead of the respective lessons. School-girls sometimes study as though it were a 'task,' as indeed our fathers called it, but Helen never. With her a new text-book was a fresh and delightful field for investigation. Difficulties were merely new heights to be scaled. The exhilaration of overcoming obstacles kept this school-girl as much interested as another might be in achieving conquest in a game of golf or tennis.

Gilman himself taught her English literature and learned the manual language in order to be better able to talk with her. "Helen is the liveliest and happiest girl in the world yet!" he wrote Richard Watson Gilder. "I am personally reading to her English & German & French & by proxy, Latin also." He liked Helen. He also was aware how much her presence added luster to his school. It was an admission card to the pages of the influential *Century,* for which he promptly wrote an article on his pupil's progress. Gilder, in addition to being a genteel poet with a considerable output, was a force in the intellectual world and a social reformer. When he visited Boston that March, he noted in his diary: "On Monday a lot of young Harvardians came in and cross-questioned me about tenements. At night I spoke to a fine audience on Tenements and Public Opinion, the first by special request. President Eliot, William James, Peabody, etc., etc. and Mrs. Palmer turned out, and it really seemed to give them a surprising amount of satisfaction. Dear Helen Keller 'heard' it! through her teacher. I went slow in some places so she could take it in. . . ." Gilman urged Gilder to spend a morning at the school, writing him, "I am watching Helen's intellectual independence with great interest. I have read *As You Like It* to her with my own hands and am now at Burke's great speech."

Gilman's reference to "intellectual independence" was a novel note —not a surprising one since he was talking about the education of a gifted sixteen-year-old, but striking, nevertheless, in view of Anagnos's stated views that Annie had prevented Helen's development as an autonomous, self-reliant individual. Was Gilman already reaching a similar conclusion? "There are reasons," his letter to Gilder said, "which I should be glad to give you when I can talk to you why I am especially anxious that Helen's friends should see her here in her school and her home."

Annie found it difficult to share authority over Helen with anyone. Conflict with Gilman was brewing. He sent her a typewritten note. Evidently he wanted it on record, for he could just as easily have spoken with her:

My dear Miss Sullivan,

It has come to me emphatically that we must have some explicit understanding in reference to the management of Helen, and I would like it if you could come to see me Monday afternoon so that we may consult about it.

I have said in public and in private that it is your wish and mine that Helen should lead the life of a normal girl of her age, and that she should not be 'exploited' in public. I cannot stultify myself by permitting things to be done which seem to have my approval or at least my consent which are contrary to my expressed statements.

I know that you approve what I write as thoroughly as I do. You can no more allow yourself to appear in a false light before the public than I can. Helen and her interests suffer if we do so appear.

In order that I may carry out the plan that I understood you to ask me to carry out, I must be placed in a position to do it. You and Mrs.

Keller are able to give me the direction that will be sufficient for the purpose. In case you do this, I am willing to carry Helen's education to any point that may be desired. The present arrangement is loose.

It has been my intention to do the work you asked me to do, and to do it in the way that you wished me to do it: nothing else has been in my mind. The interests of Helen are my only criterion, and ever shall be.

Please let me see you. Four o'clock would be a good hour, but I will meet your convenience.

The letter is not further explained. Gilman had a high regard for Annie Sullivan and for the processes by which she had educated Helen, but clearly the germs of disagreement were at work: the issue was his authority in relation to Annie's over Helen's further education. But everything now gave way to a final burst of reading and study for the examinations. On July 3 an exultant Gilman reported to Gilder:

I wish you could sit by me this afternoon as I give Helen her Harvard examination-admission papers in French and German. I am appointed special officer to give her her examinations and it is a great pleasure. Yesterday I gave her the papers in English and History. She fairly reveled in them both. You never saw a happier girl than she when the work was completed and I had told her that I felt sure that the college examiner would say that it was well done. The day previous I had given her two hours of Latin. On the 29th, I had given her a two-hour paper in Advanced German. That was the first one, and it was the most difficult that she had to take. I think that she has passed in all! What a triumph it will be for her, if my belief proves true! Well, I am as happy as she is, and as Miss Sullivan is. It was in order that Miss *S.* might be quite out of the matter and that no one could ever say that she had in the remotest way assisted Helen, (some think there is an unconscious thought transference, you know) that the entire work of these examinations was placed in my inexperienced hands, for I *am* 'inexperienced,' having read to Helen with my hands since Christmas only. Radcliffe College made me a special officer for the purpose, and as I am a member of the Corporation, and the

only member who could in any way do the work, the examination
was made as safe as could be. . . .

A week later at Gilder's request he sent him a detailed account of the
examination, an account that was incorporated into his contribution to the
new *Souvenir,* assembled and edited by Hitz and published by the Volta
Bureau in 1899: The account ended:

> She was successful in every subject and took 'honors' in English and
> German. I think I may say that no candidate in Harvard or Radcliffe
> was graded higher than Helen in English. The result is remarkable,
> especially when we consider that Helen had been studying on strictly
> college preparatory lines for one year only. She had had long and
> careful instruction, it is true, and she had had always the loving
> ministrations of Miss Sullivan, in addition to the inestimable advan-
> tage of a concentration that the rest of us never know. No man or
> woman has ever in my experience got ready for these examinations
> in so brief a time. How has it been accomplished? By a union of
> patience, determination, and affection, with the foundation of an
> uncommon brain.

Here is a sampling of the questions she was asked: "Where are the
following: Arbela, Coryere, Dacia, Lade, Rubicon, Trasimene; and with
what famous events is each connected?" Another: "Explain the following
terms: Comitia, Tributa, Delator, Deme, Pontifex, Trireme." And in
English: "Write a paragraph or two on Silas Marner. On the coming of
Eppie. On the death of Gabriel. Tell the story of the Merchant of Venice,
showing how many and what stories are interwoven in it."
They spent the summer in Wrentham with the Chamberlins at their Red
House overlooking King Phillips Pond. After a year of "fear and trembling, lest I should fail," the pressure was off, she wrote her mother. She
had passed with credit, "but what I consider my crown of success is the
happiness and pleasure that my victory has brought dear Teacher. Indeed,
the success is hers more than mine: for she is my constant inspiration." She
also had celebrated her seventeenth birthday, and "I could not help feeling a little sorry that my childhood had passed away so quickly." Now she
was immersed in *The Lady of the Lake,* and her comment reflected a
maturing social conscience: "It is simply exquisite! Its verses, as my fingers
run over them, pour out a stream of song and romance, and the easy,

graceful flow of the poet's thoughts and his beautiful descriptions of Beauty, Valor and martial Faith render it most charming. But I cannot help being glad that the poem belongs to the past and not the present: for I see through the shadowy veil, which Scott has drawn over those olden days, the ruins and desolation and sorrow that were so much a part of the wars and struggles celebrated in the poem as the heroic exploits of Roderick Dhu and his warriors."

She read history and literature with a lively sense that they dealt with real people and with issues that had a bearing on the present and called for her judgment. She already wanted to shape her own destiny and that of her times: "We took up Burke's celebrated speech on Conciliation with the Colonies, and every point made an impression," Gilman recorded. "The political bearing of the arguments, the justice or injustice of this or that, the history of the times, the character of the actors, the meaning of the work and the peculiarities of style, all came under review, whether I wished it or not, by the force of Helen's interest." To her mother she wrote, "I think it the most masterly speech I have ever read, and it seems very strange that it should have had so little effect on the members of Parliament. Speaking of Burke's speech, are you not interested in the Cretan question? Oh, mother, it makes me hold my breath to think about it. I only hope brave little Greece will triumph, and that the apparently unfeeling Powers will be silenced and put to shame. Then perhaps the cruelties of Turkey will cease, and Freedom, sweet Freedom, will be more widely spread over the Old World."*

The Dreyfus case touched with fire her passion for freedom and justice. She wrote in her diary on February 27, 1897:

> For the last three days I've been most intensely interested in the trial of Zola, the hero and martyr of France. I can't find words strong enough to express the emotions which have kept me stirred up. The outrageous proceedings of the French Government against Captain Dreyfus and Zola's heroism and self-sacrifice —I think of them all the time and my heart overflows with admiration for the martyr.

*A Greek-inspired rebellion by the Christians in Crete against Turkish rule, and terrible massacres of Moslems, had brought the intervention of the European concert of powers, which imposed a solution. Greece was forbidden to annex Crete, but the latter's inhabitants were given autonomy under the nominal suzerainty of the Sultan. Union with Greece was achieved only in 1913.

What! He too convicted and sentenced to imprisonment! Is this his reward, after his forty years of endeavor to promote the welfare of his country? And do the French people, whom he has tried to save from disgrace, consent thus to let their bravest friend suffer ignominy? No, no, I can't believe it! Surely the day will come when he shall triumph, when the French people will rise up against the government, and release the defender of the innocent and oppressed.

But how dreadful it all is now—the sufferings of a great, noble soul, the cold indifference of a nation to the demands of justice, the prolonged agony of an innocent man, doomed by his country to live and die with the shame of treason upon his name and character! I was breathless when I heard Zola's appeal for Dreyfus, and his last words ring with awful insistence in my heart.

'Dreyfus is innocent. I swear it. Before the Jury—the incarnation of my country, I swear it.'

The cry for justice and freedom penetrated to the very marrow of her being, and soon she would be asking, as she did in the case of little Tommy Stringer, "What must I do?"

Several newspapers interviewed her after her examinations. "At 17 years Helen Keller is a handsome, well-formed, graceful girl," wrote one reporter. "The waist of her dress fits loosely, and there are no suggestions of corsets or of tight bands about the young girl's waist or neck." Her hands deserved a chapter to themselves, he went on. "Their whiteness and delicacy and beauty of shape are delights to the eye, and the extraordinary sensitiveness of their finger-tips cannot be imagined by one who has only the usual sense of touch. Her chief beauty, next to her hands, is the mass of short brown curly hair that falls on her shoulders and which is confined only by a small comb.

"Looking at the face you are struck first, of course, by the pathos of the eyes that show all too plainly their affliction. Aside from these there is nothing to sadden one in Helen Keller's appearance. Her chin is beautifully formed, the mouth and teeth are good, her complexion is clear and healthy and the expression of her face wonderfully attractive in its bright alertness."

Another interviewer noted her determination to enter Radcliffe: "Her enthusiasm for Radcliffe is most inspiring. If a Radcliffe student calls upon her her expressive face lights up, and she says eagerly, 'So you study at Radcliffe.' "

"In a few years she will be at the college," the reporter went on. "There is no hurry." Gilman had made the point of no hurry in his article in *The Century*:

> Miss Sullivan and I have always before us a sense of the novelty of the work, and we feel that we cannot lay it out far in advance. We are obliged to be constantly on the alert, watching development, and prepared to do what is best at the time. While, therefore, we have the Harvard examinations before us as a goal, we are not willing to say today that Helen will take those examinations at any given time in the future, or that we shall not at another stage find that her nature demands a cultivation different from that which is planned for the average woman. We simply desire to feel free to take one step at a time.

But hurry there was—at least in Annie Sullivan's plans for Helen; and it was this that occasioned a harrowing conflict with Gilman. "It was my own wish to study hard," Helen insisted in her book about Teacher, "and Teacher was only following where I desired to go." Although Helen had passed the nine hours of examinations brilliantly, the seven hours that remained to be taken were on subjects in which she had little or no preparation—Greek, advanced Latin, mathematics, including algebra and geometry, physics and astronomy. When Gilman first discussed Helen's schedule with Annie, he had thought she should take five years. Annie demurred, and the assistant principal, according to Annie, agreed with her, saying it could be done in three. They had compromised on four, but her success in the examinations confirmed Annie and the assistant principal in the view that Helen could complete her preparatory work in another two years.

Although Annie pressed, Gilman resisted. The argument was mainly over how much work Helen's health would permit, but other motives entered. Annie's constant attendance in class at Helen's side, along with the work at home, imposed a dreadful strain upon her. The sooner Helen entered Radcliffe, the sooner this ordeal would be ended. There was a deeper motive, too. If Helen completed her work in three years, Annie's detractors would be decisively routed. Her claims about Helen's abilities would be verified, her methods vindicated. Whether placing Helen into an intellectual forcing house, which an accelerated program meant, was best for Helen, in terms of enjoying these years of study, of reflecting and making part of her usable knowledge the materials that her fine memory and power of concentration enabled her to pick up so quickly, was a question Annie did not ask. And she suspected that Gilman wanted to prolong Helen's stay because of the prestige she was bringing to the Cambridge School and to himself. He extended himself to be agreeable, even to the point of arranging to have Helen's sister, Mildred, attend the school. But Annie had her way, and Helen's autumn schedule included physics, astronomy, geometry, algebra, Latin, English and French—twenty-seven recitations in all each week.

The schedule was too heavy. Soon Gilman's teachers reported to him that Helen's work was beginning to fall off. He became alarmed. Annie blamed the decline on the nonarrival of Braille textbooks from London because of Queen Victoria's jubilee and on the delay in acquiring a special Greek typewriter and a machine for embossing algebra. "Yes, Mr. Gilman, that is true," she said in reply to his remonstration about overwork, "but as soon as she acquires facility in the use of all these new machines, she will be all right, and her work will become easier and improve." This was Annie's account in a statement she later wrote for Hitz.

On November 12 Helen had "an unusually hard time with Geometry," Annie's deposition continued. "She was not well, due to natural causes [a reference to Helen's menstrual period]. I thought it best for her to go to bed." It was Friday, and on Monday Helen returned to class "refreshed, and with her usual clear head." But Helen's illness persuaded Gilman and his staff that her program had to be lightened. "I begged of him to allow the program to remain unchanged until after Christmas, knowing well her illness was not caused by overwork. He said, he thought I was unwise, and that he would not be party to it, and would drop English." So Annie's account of the break ran.

Although Gilman and his teachers were worried that Anne Sullivan was overtaxing Helen, it was her old friend Mrs. Hopkins who brought matters to a head. She had been to Cambridge, she informed Gilman, and "found Helen in what I might term a state of collapse." She thought Gilman was responsible for Helen's heavy schedule, and one of the consequences, she said, was that Helen was now "more entirely cut off from intercourse with young people than she has ever been in her life and she is not happy. She told me that she missed the girls sadly and in a very pathetic way added, but I have teacher and sister and ought to be happy."* When Gilman informed Mrs. Hopkins that Miss Sullivan was responsible for Helen's work schedule, she replied that "Helen cannot stand this pressure and it is necessary that she should have companionship." She knew she had more influence with Annie than anyone else did, and she intended to talk with her. "My interview was stormy as I expected," she advised him afterwards.

Fortified by Mrs. Hopkins' strongly expressed advice, Gilman alerted Mrs. Keller that he was having "amiable" differences with Miss Sullivan over Helen's schedule. But two days later he felt he had to act and wrote her again, as he did also Mrs. Hutton and William Wade. He had written her, his letter to Mrs. Keller said, only after he had been warned by all his teachers of the effect upon Helen's health.

> In my brief letter I did not tell you that Dr. Bell has been here and had given Miss Sullivan the same warning, and that Mrs. Hopkins had written to me as well as to Miss Sullivan, in the strongest terms. Yesterday afternoon Mrs. Hopkins called on me and insisted that an immediate change should be made in Helen's work. Of course, I was in full sympathy with her. She then went to say the same to Miss Sullivan. . . .

> The hard work has its influence on Miss Sullivan. Mrs. Hopkins told me this, but it was not necessary, for my teachers had reported that she no longer exhibits the 'patience' that I had formerly remarked, and Miss Sullivan had told me that she was irritated by the 'stupidity' that Helen showed at times. . . .

> Mrs. Hopkins tells me that it is her ambition that leads Miss Sullivan to hurry Helen.

Gilman's letter to Mrs. Hutton brought an admonitory note to Annie:

> . . . There is no reason why she should not take her time in fitting for Radcliffe. . . . Mr. Hutton and I have felt for some time, as have others of her friends, that she was overdoing her strength. This forcing process is all wrong. Mr. Hutton says the people who succeed in life, make haste, slowly. . . . Don't be too ambitious for her. . . .

*The correspondence relating to the Gilman affair is bound in an unmarked volume that has sat, evidently unused, on the shelves of the Perkins Library.

She enclosed a copy of this letter to Gilman and in an accompanying note said, "It would be very possible for Miss Sullivan to be tired and nervous, think of this tension which she has had to carry unaided for the last eight years. . . . I do not believe in all this tremendously high standard of education for women any way; only in Helen's case it seemed to be what she really wanted, and it seemed a sin to deny her anything which she so craved. . . ."

In his letter to Wade, Gilman made the additional point that Annie's irritability was related also to a growing sense of inadequacy. She was better adapted to the training of a young girl than to that of a young lady "who has already far outstripped her. . . ." Wade's response, considering his friendship with both Helen and her teacher, astonished Gilman:

> When Helen and Miss Sullivan were with us that winter, there was that same feverish frenzy. We gently remonstrated and tried all sorts of quiet, mild efforts, and at last Mrs. Wade could stand it no longer and took Helen in hand as far as physical conditions went. . . . I found the same conditions when I met them at Chautauqua. Helen would come down in the morning with hands as cold as they should be in the winter. . . . She [Annie] made Helen re-write long papers for the merest typewritered errors, perhaps only one in five hundred words, far more accurate than I ever am, and we were all distressed about such things, but could not interfere in such strictly professional matters of education. So while you are doubtless correct that Helen has got beyond Miss Sullivan's ability to lead her in the path of learning, I hardly think that causes the irritation and impatience Miss S now shows, for it seems to be exactly the condition she was in while with us—at least during part of the time. . . .

Mrs. Hopkins, in the meantime, had written Helen's mother, saying to her much of what she had said to Gilman; and on the basis of this letter as well as Gilman's, Mrs. Keller concluded, according to her deposition to Hitz, "that Miss Sullivan's ambition for the child had warped her judgment, and at once wrote to Mr. Gilman and to Annie that Helen's program must be cut down to what she could do with safety."

Only a part of her letter to Annie of November 22nd is quoted in Nella Braddy:

> I do not need to be told that if you realized there was danger to Helen in this course that not for your right arm would you let her do it.

There is no one living who knows and appreciates the faithful love, the unwearied patience that you have shown in teaching Helen. You know how largely I have left her to you, what faith and confidence I have in you, and I hope you love and [have] enough confidence in me to believe that only the firm conviction that it is injuring Helen to be pressed in this way could make me oppose myself to your ambition. However much you might suspect interested motives in anyone else you cannot imagine that I have any save feelings of love for you. . . .

The rest of this important letter has disappeared. Armed with Mrs. Keller's authorization, Gilman after Thanksgiving cut geometry and astronomy from Helen's program and reinstituted the course in English. "I was indignant," Annie attested, "and told Mr. Gilman I would not submit to this change, and would write to her mother. After consulting with a friend, I decided to accept the situation. I went to Mr. Gilman, and told him that, although I differed with him as much as ever, yet I had made up my mind to work as he had arranged for the remainder of the term—that I would do my duty, and do it cheerfully. I supposed this ended the matter." "[H]ardest of all," Helen wrote her mother of her curtailed program, "I was to have only two lessons on several of the week-days, and not a single one after recess! Oh, the humiliation was harder than I could bear; it seemed as if I had been cheated out of my proper share in the school work."

Annie did not yield to the change of schedule as easily as she reported to Hitz. Several times she threatened to leave, sometimes with Helen, at others without her. "I understand Miss Sullivan so well," Mrs. Hopkins wrote Gilman, "that I know to be thwarted in what she had fixed her heart upon, and having had unlimited authority, it is very hard for her to bear. I suppose she feels very bitter towards me for she feels that I have stirred up the whole trouble, but I can endure that if she will only come to see the right. . . ."

Her letter had not settled the matter, Gilman advised Mrs. Keller: "Miss Sullivan has boasted frequently to me and to others that she has complete power over Helen, that she can take her from this school at any moment, transfer her to Europe or elsewhere, and, in fact, do what she pleases without your interference." Mrs. Gilman, worried about the strain the controversy was placing upon her husband, also wrote Mrs. Keller: "Perhaps you have noticed that wherever she has been she has fallen out with those who have tried to do [good] for Helen. . . . Mrs. Hopkins told her that by her present obstinacy she was digging her own grave." To Gilman Mrs. Hopkins wrote insistently that "if Miss Sullivan still remains in the stubborn state of mind . . . you will be justified in arranging matters in relation to Helen as you deem right. . . . For dear Helen's sake we should do now what is necessary to protect her. . . . [Miss Sullivan] needs to understand that Helen is not her property."

Even after Annie agreed to the reduction in Helen's schedule, she carried on a rear-guard action, confirming the school's view that she could not abide any sharing of authority over Helen. "I have been on the point of writing to you," Gilman wrote Mrs. Keller a week later, "that it will not be possible for me to continue to have Miss S. in the Howells House or in the School on account of the exceedingly unfortunate remarks that she makes in the School before teachers and pupils and in the residence before Mildred and the servants." The next day he was more emphatic. Mrs. Keller had better come to Cambridge; he will underwrite her travel expenses:

> . . . Miss Sullivan is alienating Helen and Mildred from me, and her opportunities for doing this are so complete that I fear that it may be best for you to remove both children from Cambridge. No interest of mine shall stand in your way in doing all that you think best for them. Helen takes all her views of others from Miss S. and as you have no direct communication with her yourself and cannot have unless you are here, you cannot understand the situation. If you do not come soon, you will find that matters have progressed too far for your effectual interference.

> I must have the matter settled soon, and I have decided that the influence of Miss Sullivan in the school and in the residence [is such] that I cannot permit her to remain there. What is to be done, is for you, the mother, to say. I am, as I have said, willing to assume as much of the care of Helen as you wish, but I cannot divide the responsibility with another, nor permit another whom I find unsuitable, to work under me in it.

There was no money to be raised in Boston, his letter further informed Mrs. Keller, toward Helen's educational fund. Miss Sullivan thought it was the work of Michael Anagnos, "but it is possible it comes from an opposition to her." His letter crossed one from Mrs. Keller: "I have no idea that she will remain with her [Helen] and I much prefer that she should, as she expresses it, 'leave,' than that I should have to tell her that she cannot remain with Helen. . . . Would you be willing to act as Helen's guardian?" Wade also was resigned to a separation between Helen and her teacher. So he wrote John Macy in 1903 when the latter was helping Helen with the editing of *The Story of My Life:*

> My recommendation that Miss Sullivan and Helen be separated was distinctively an alternative for Mr. Gilman, and I not only suggested, but insisted that Miss Sullivan's fatal lack of tact, leading her to criticize Mr. Gilman at the table before pupils, teachers and servants made her presence in the school fatal to it, and that either one or both must leave. I have not yet found the head of a school who disagreed from that.

On December 7 Gilman had a lengthy meeting with his teachers about Helen's work. "The unanimous opinion was that Helen's present difficulty is that her teacher is behind her in knowledge and is contantly irritated with her." The next day he received a telegram from Mrs. Keller authorizing him to act as Helen's guardian.

"Then, all of a sudden, the most dreadful sorrow burst upon us which we ever endured," wrote Helen. "On the 8th of December, I had just finished my Greek lesson, and spoke to Miss Sullivan. I touched her trembling hand and at once saw that something terrible had happened. 'What is it, Teacher?' I cried in dismay. 'Helen, I fear we are going to be separated!' 'What! Separated? What do you mean?' I said utterly bewildered. She said something about a letter she had received from some one, who expressed his opinion to my mother that Miss Sullivan and I should be separated. Mr. Gilman, whom I had trusted, had done it all."

Here is Annie's account of that frightening day. "On December 8, I learned that a movement was under consideration to separate Helen from me. In my distress I could think of nothing better to do than to take Helen and Mildred (her sister, who was also at Mr. Gilman's school, in my care), to Tuscumbia, to their mother. I sent for Mr. Gilman to tell him of my decision. He came and said, 'I cannot allow you to take the children from this house.' I said, 'What do you mean?' He replied, 'I have orders from their mother to keep them in my care,' and he showed me a telegram from Mrs. Keller, authorizing him to take charge of Helen. There was nothing for me to say, and I left the room."

"That night," wrote Helen, "my poor teacher left Howells House, and fled to our dear friend Mrs. Fuller." So Helen wrote in the deposition for Hitz at the time. In *Teacher* she disclosed that Annie left the school in such despair that as she approached the Charles River on her way to the Fullers', "an almost overmastering impulse seized her to throw herself into the water."

Annie's report to the Fullers that Gilman intended to separate her and Helen astounded them. They considered it a barbarity. It was inconceivable to them that anyone could be found who would care for Helen with the devotion and insight of Annie, whatever her shortcomings. On their advice she sent telegrams to Mrs. Keller, Dr. Bell, J.E. Chamberlin, and Mrs. Pratt, the friend of the Bells. A cry for help went from Helen to Hitz: "Oh, dear friend, they are trying to take my dear teacher from me! My heart is broken. You know what she has been to me—You know how dearly and truly we have always loved each other. Oh, dear friend, help us! Come to us if you can. Our hearts yearn for your dear presence."

The Fullers wrote to Mrs. Hutton, whose control of the fund made her support indispensable against Gilman's effort to separate Helen and Annie. "Against this action," Mrs. Hutton immediately informed Gilman, "if it can be possible that such an action is contemplated, Mr. Hutton and I must protest in the very strongest terms. Mrs. Keller must realize how peculiarly strong is the tie which binds pupil and teacher, and that the result upon Helen of any severance of this tie would be very disastrous, besides being unjustly cruel to Miss Sullivan herself." She pointed out that the fund she administered was for Miss Sullivan as well as for Helen. He was acting on Mrs. Keller's behalf, Gilman replied.

> Mrs. Keller has written to me that Captain Keller wished before he died to remove Helen from her teacher, and that she herself felt that she should never have allowed her authority to lapse. I have told her that if she wished me to be of service to her in any way, I would serve her, but that I should not perform any acts on my personal responsibility. Of course I cannot separate Helen and Miss Sullivan, nor can I have any part in such separation unless, indeed, the mother assumes her personal responsibility.

> My position is that the mother has a right to her child, and that some one ought to sustain her. My advisers tell me that on account of my own delicate health it is my duty to undertake nothing further for

Helen, and that is my personal preference, and has been since the late erratic doings of Miss S.

Your letter shall be brought to Mrs. Keller's attention on her arrival here. I asked her to come and she writes that I may expect her this afternoon.

In the meantime Helen and Mildred, with Gilman's consent, had gone to stay with the Chamberlins in Wrentham. After Annie had stormed out, Gilman had tried to persuade Helen to go to classes. "They all tried to persuade sister to go to school that morning," wrote Mildred in her statement, "but she could not, she had not slept any that night, and had not eaten anything either. We both felt so badly at having Miss Annie go away, that we couldn't keep from crying all day." Later that day, Annie returned to the school and insisted on seeing Helen. Gilman put her off: " 'Helen is much excited, and I think I should not be acting according to Mrs. Keller's wish if I permitted you to see her.' I told him I would not leave the house until I did see her, except by force." After a couple of hours Gilman relented. And a few hours later Mr. Chamberlin and Mrs. Pratt arrived. Mr. Chamberlin seeing the dangerous state Helen was in, went immediately to Mr. Gilman, and obtained his consent to take us all to his house in Wrentham." "Rightly or wrongly," Chamberlin wrote Nella Braddy in 1933, "I had become convinced that Gilman intended to use Mrs. Keller's authority to separate Helen from Annie. At Wrentham I took Helen alone in my study, and told her it might soon be incumbent on her to decide whether she would stay with Annie or go away from her with her mother. She said to me, 'Uncle Ed, if I have to decide between my mother and Teacher, I will stay with Teacher.' This decided me as to my own sympathies in the case."

Mrs. Keller, arriving in Boston, saw Gilman and Mrs. Hopkins, and learning that her children were in Wrentham, immediately went there. "I really did not realize at the moment what a cruel thing I was doing," in giving Gilman the authority to separate the two, Mrs. Keller subsequently wrote. "Very soon the injustice of it overcame me and I had already decided to come to Boston when Miss Sullivan's telegram 'we need you,' brought me on the first train. I found that Mr. Gilman had made a cruel use of the authority I had given him to distress my children and Miss Sullivan, after ten years of service. I certainly never dreamed of Miss Sullivan being forced away from Helen. I could not but feel on my arrival in Wrentham that I had been made to endure most unnecessary and uncalled for distress. Helen is in perfect physical condition and if she shows any evidence of nervous prostration or over-work, I cannot discover it."

"Not until her arrival at Wrentham," Hitz, who had been sent by the Bells to investigate, reported to them, "and conferring with Helen, Mildred and Miss Sullivan, did Mrs. Keller realize how erroneously she had been informed of the real state of affairs, alike by Mr. Gilman, and her trusted friends Mrs. Hopkins and Mr. Wade. . . . Helen, whom according to reports sent her, she expected to find in a state of collapse, proved to be enjoying unimpaired health, and indignantly resenting the idea of having been treated cruelly by Miss Sullivan."

Chamberlin reported Mrs. Keller's change of mind to the Fullers. She read his note with "a sense of profound relief," Lucy Fuller wrote Annie. "I feel sure that Mrs. Keller knows the tie between Helen and yourself so truly, that now that she has once reached you she cannot be moved." The Fullers and Chamberlin had been in touch with Edward H. Clement, the editor of *The Transcript*, for which Chamberlin did his column. "Mr. Clement is outraged," Lucy reported to Annie, "and will do anything to help you—and if it comes to the worst pass the paper will call the wrath of the world down on the heads of those who try to kill this child—but that is not to be—and the misery of a newspaper controversy is not to be —for I am sure that Helen will guide her mother's heart."

In the midst of the heartbreak over Gilman's moves, Anagnos suddenly offered an olive branch to Helen. It evidently was ignored. We learn of it through a reference in Lucy Fuller's almost daily bulletins to Annie. "Mr. Clement writes me that Miss Smith* went to South Boston to Mr. Anagnos—and so did Mrs. Hall (Mrs. Howe's daughter) on that Sunday, a week ago last Sunday. Mr. Anagnos was entirely disappointed and overcome when Helen whom Miss Smith was invited to meet, did not appear. . . . We are eager to hear what your plan will now be—Do you consider it absolutely impossible to finish the year at Cambridge after what has happened?"

"He has made the greatest blunder of his life!" Lucy wrote Annie. "I told Miss (Minna) Smith that in writing you yesterday I had asked the question whether it was absolutely impossible to return to the school—but that all the same I believed it was."

---

*Minna C. Smith, a visitor to Boston, was a well-known journalist and author, a writer of juvenile stories and a translator of some note from the Spanish and French.

Gilman, not realizing that he had been defeated, went to New York to talk to the Wright-Humason people. What they told him can be surmised from a comment of Annie's to Hitz. "Have you heard anything from the Wright-Humason wing? I really was astonished at their attitude. I thought as Mr. Bell did that they had only the friendliest feeling towards me."

Aware of Minna Smith's efforts to persuade Helen to return to his school, Gilman wrote her from New York:

> I have been here several days, and facts connected with Helen's two years here have been brought to me which cause me to wish to let you know that though I am as desirous as ever not to stop Helen's work now, but to continue it to a successful close, I shall not be able to do it with the present 'Teacher,' as Mrs. Gilman suggested.

> I have avoided seeing any of my friends here who are contributing to the increase of Mrs. Hutton's Fund, lest I might be thought to be interfering with that. However, a fund that is to bind the child for life to her Teacher would be a calamity.

To Mrs. Hutton he wrote, "You know the agreeable side of Miss Sullivan. You do not know her as those do who have worked with her. I think that no one who has studied Miss Sullivan in her work with Helen would think of her as a suitable guide for a young woman in whom he had a serious interest." He was more persuaded than ever that the two should be separated, he wrote Chamberlin. "Miss Sullivan should be rewarded for her work, of course, but any arrangement binding her to Helen for life would be a disaster for Helen. If the friends of Helen who have seen her teacher as a guest or visitor or in her agreeable social guise, only knew her as those do who have worked with her, there would be a revulsion of sentiments. No fund would be raised to bind the two together for life."

Someone at Wright-Humason kept Hitz informed, and he in turn informed Annie. She was outraged:

> Why, I wonder, does Mr. Gilman continue such an unrighteous warfare? What have I done to deserve it? God knows I have tried to do my duty to the best of my ability. I have given Helen all that I had to give—myself, my service, my love, and she has given me in return the tenderest love in the world. We are both satisfied. Why should people persecute us? What can Mr. Gilman expect to gain by it all

—Helen will never go back to his school. If he thinks she will, he is reckoning without his host. Mrs. Keller is as positive about that, as I am; but even mere suggestion of such a possibility excites and distresses her unspeakably, so what can Mr. Gilman's motive be in continuing this unhappy controversy? All the powers on Earth cannot separate Helen and me. He may succeed in making it difficult to give her an education we all wish her to have, but that is all. It is possible that he has not yet grasped fully this fact. We shall see.

Hitz concluded his six-page report to the Bells with a harsh judgment about Gilman:

To my mind, it would seem in summing up this whole affair, that Mr. Gilman had either unwittingly been led to commit a most serious blunder as to the personal relations which actually exist between Helen and Miss Sullivan, and likewise as to the estimation in which Miss Sullivan is held by Helen's more intelligent friends, and especially so by the Trustees of the Helen Keller Fund, or, in allowing of late, his ambition to get the better of his judgment, he sought, by disreputable means to displace Miss Sullivan from her well-earned and legitimate place, as dearest friend and teacher of Helen, in order that (as has been alleged) the Cambridge school might claim the exclusive credit of her higher education.

But if Helen was not to return to Gilman's school, a plan had to be agreed upon for the continuation of her education. Private tutors were interviewed, other schools were investigated. Mrs. Keller considered and rejected, because it might be considered she was living off the Helen Keller Fund, taking a house in Boston and having Annie and Helen live with her. Lucy cautioned Annie that she and Mrs. Keller had to make a decision soon: "My own experience of the great wisdom of remaining on the spot where the difficulty arises makes me incline to your own plan of Cambridge and tutors—and Helen quietly taking the Radcliffe examinations—and so shutting off all comment from the world at large. When you have found a boarding place and tutors telegraph the fact and the expenses to Mrs. Hutton. The time has come when *prompt* and firm action on your part is necessary to prove your good judgment for Helen. The uncertainty for her is most injurious and unnecessary."

Mrs. Hutton came to Boston. All their friends were on the lookout for tutors. "You will be glad to know that Dean Irwin of Radcliffe is assisting me in the selection of tutors," Annie wrote Hitz. "I had a long talk with her the other day and she agrees with me that it will be quite possible for Helen to take her finals in June of 1899." Mrs. Hutton arranged "everything," Annie's next letter to Hitz reported. "The tutor, a Mr. Keith— is to come out here (Wrentham) once a week when we will have a three hours' session. He came Saturday for the first time. I was not particularly pleased with him but perhaps I shall like him better as time goes on. I hope so at any rate. He comes to us very highly recommended by President Eliot and the Dean of Harvard, so he ought to be good. . . ."

The press had finally gotten hold of the Gilman story; and the account in the *Transcript,* Annie wrote Hitz, was pretty accurate. "Not a word has been heard from Mr. Gilman. I thought he would make some sort of a reply to the *Transcript* article but he did not so much as squeal." Perhaps the poor man (one can only feel sorry for him) had realized that to be an adversary to Helen and Annie was something like taking on motherhood and God; or perhaps he was just being a gentleman, like Anagnos, not wishing to hurt two women. In a previous letter Annie had used an interesting expression. "I think Mr. Gilman has met his Waterloo. . . ." But was it such a famous victory, and was the prize Helen? Had Annie thought in terms of what was best for Helen? She was as incapable of asking that question in relation to herself as any star-crossed lover; and perhaps the friends who had rallied to their help—the Fullers, the Chamberlins, Mrs. Hutton, the Bells, Hitz—had realized, as had Mrs. Keller on her arrival at Wrentham, that these two, for better or worse, were married for life.

part three

HELEN and TEACHER

XIII

My Teacher, My Self

"She ceased to treat me as a child."

No explanation has survived of what Gilman, Wade, Wright, Humason and others meant when they spoke of Teacher's "cruelty" to Helen. Her moods and tempers we know. Were they also vented on Helen? It would not be surprising. The abused child is more likely to become an abuser of children than the child brought up in gentleness and courtesy. The savage beatings Annie's father administered in his rages, the brutal coercions of Tewksbury, had left their imprint on her character.

She is constantly admonishing Hitz that she does not deserve his love and respect: "I would much prefer to have people despise me as they certainly would if they guessed how full of distrust and contempt my heart is towards my fellow beings. I know it grieves you to hear me speak in this way and doubtless it will hurt you still more to have me write it, but I want you to know just how detestable I am. I find people hateful and I hate them."

Annie was, indeed, a split personality. On one level she overflowed with insight and self-understanding, with love and solicitude and a desire to serve; on another level she was beset with fears and terrors, riven with resentments, hating, as she says, both herself and others. She is afraid her friends will really find her out, and at the same time she is obsessed with the desire to have them see her as she really is. Not until 1930 did she tell Helen of the horrors of her childhood in Feeding Hills and in Tewksbury. "She kept that dark secret until she was sixty-four and I was fifty," wrote Helen in *Teacher,* published in 1955. Only when Teacher at last told her the "secret" of her past did Helen understand why she had "occasionally felt alone and bewildered by some of her peculiarities . . . the strangeness was there. Something too subtle for words was lacking in our relations to each other. . . ." In the same book Helen disclosed that after Teacher had married John Macy, and all three were living together at Wrentham, Helen learned that Teacher herself was keeping a diary. One day she sniffed smoke and asked Teacher what was happening. She was burning her diary, Teacher answered, and as Helen protested, she explained, "I wouldn't have had a moment's peace if it had been read by you or John. . . . It seemed to me horrid, vindictive, one-sided." It is sad that Annie, because of fears that Helen or John might think less of her—even possibly withdraw their love—destroyed her journals. When not in the grip of her demons, she was a keen observer and a vivid, forceful writer. Indeed, as will be seen, she had aspirations as a writer, of poetry as well as prose; and the diaries would have supplied her—not to mention future biographers—with invaluable material. But her insecurity, her sense of shame over the diary's entries, outweighed her interest in using the material in her writing.

Teacher was the least read of Helen Keller's books. It is too full of "purple" passages, too protective, too lacking the clear narrative line of Nella Braddy's biography. It is nonetheless one of the most interesting of Helen's books. For within the context of her passionate devotion to her begetter and companion, she gently introduces some hints about teacher's methods and character that are quite startling and must be seen in context. The tone of the book is curiously defensive, as if Teacher still needed defending against her critics—or was it really to answer questions that Helen did not permit herself to ask consciously? It was her, not Teacher's, ambition that she should go to Radcliffe, and Teacher supported her in it. "It was my own wish to study hard, and Teacher was only following where I desired to go." Yet at other places Helen wrote, "She [Teacher] could not simplify herself or restrain her ambition (I prefer to call it love of perfection) or circumscribe her dream-nurtured plans for me." And when Helen did not live up to Teacher's hopes for her, the consequences were quite devastating.

We learn that a year or two after Annie first arrived at Tuscumbia, she wanted to break Helen of some childish habits. "[S]omething had to be done to save her from the habits that make children repulsive," Helen wrote, speaking of herself in the third person. "Helen kept biting her nails and one day there descended upon her a human whirlwind who boxed her ears and tied her hands behind her back, *thus shutting off all means of communication* [author's emphasis]." But the culprit did not suffer as much as Annie, wrote Helen, "who paced up and down the room, unable to read or interest herself in anything else."

And in telling that story Helen, in her seventies, was reminded of how she had "sinned in another way, by spelling constantly to herself with her fingers, even after she had learned to speak with her mouth." Helen asserts that it was she herself who determined to stop spelling to herself before it became "a habit I could not break, and so I asked her to tie my fingers up in paper. She did it, but she was sorrowful at the thought of my deprivation. In fact, she cried. For many hours, day and night, I ached to form the words that kept me in touch with others, but the experiment succeeded except that even now, in moments of excitement or when I wake from sleep, I occasionally catch myself spelling with my fingers."

Annie had large goals for Helen: of Helen's self-fulfillment in attaining "normality to more than a small degree"; of Helen as "an angel child"; of Helen as "a maiden fair and full of grace"; of Helen as " 'a young woman pleading the cause of the unfortunate with a natural voice'; and other images whose nonrealization makes tears start to my eyes." Nonrealization? One stares at the words with disbelief—few women of the twentieth century have achieved more. Where did Helen get this sense of nonfulfillment? In her letters written while at the Gilman school and afterwards, Helen seems to betray a profound sense of guilt toward Annie, of not realizing Annie's dreams for her, despite Annie's sacrifices, especially of her eyes.

At Teacher's urging she committed many stories and poems to memory so that she would be able, Teacher told her, to hold her listeners spellbound with the aptness of her observations and the brightness of her diction; but, lamented Helen, "I often failed to visit the Muses. Instead I read *The Last Days of Pompeii*—with a bad conscience. 'Caught, discovered, trapped!' Teacher would say coming upon me with anything but a classic in my lap, and I would beg for another chance." Or if she was just loitering among the rose bushes, breathing in their fragrance, and Teacher discovered her, she would spell out her exasperation. " 'For shame! You have those books full of choice words and interesting thoughts, and here you sit like a calf with not a spark of expression on your face!' *Then she would not have another word for me until the next day* [author's emphasis].

After that she was all smiles, saying, 'Come now, let us practice the long words you like—you say them better than short ones, and I want to find out why.' "

Teacher's conception of the "classics" of literature was limited by what she had been taught at Perkins. "It was not until we met you," Helen wrote "Uncle Ed" Chamberlin in 1934, "that our education in literature and literary ways began." Helen referred to the period during which they stayed with Chamberlin and his family at Wrentham after the break with Gilman. "Uncle Ed" introduced them to Whitman, whose poetry Teacher had resisted because of "prudery" and its lack of conventional rhymes and meters. Helen's formulation here reflects her protectiveness towards Teacher. She could not bring herself to say that in some respects Teacher was prim and conformist. She wrote instead that Teacher "had been prejudiced against Whitman by those whose prudery and unmeasured admiration of refined meters and rhymed verse prevented them from getting the true stature of that modern prophet."

For a brief time, spurred on by Albert H. Munsell, the painter who had done Helen's portrait, Teacher was persuaded that Helen had a talent for sculpture. They both took lessons, first in wax, then in clay. Helen, wishing to please Teacher, worked "until my hands were exhausted. She read me biographies of sculptors to show their tremendous determination until they succeeded in getting what they wanted, and I tried again." Teacher wanted her to do a fern, and to do it over again when the first copy lacked verisimilitude. Helen said she preferred to read. "She would not permit it, and subjected me to an ordeal of drudgery. No satisfactory results appeared, and *one morning her anger flared up and she slapped my cheek with the cold wet clay* [author's emphasis]." Soon afterwards, she was all penitence and self-reproaches. "Do forgive me Helen! I can never imagine you as deaf-blind. I love you too much for that. But I should remember that you are a human being, and I shouldn't be so ambitious as not to let you relax now and then."

The moral that Helen drew from this memory measures the extent of her gratitude and guilt. She regretted that she had not persevered at sculpting. "Later in life I have shaped heads which at least suggested to one or two artist friends hints of the spiritual ideals I was following, and if I had been free then, I might have labored intensely just for Teacher's sake and for the satisfaction of accomplishing something that the deaf-blind had not attempted. It was not Teacher, but fate or I, obstinate with the unconscious cruelty of a strong-willed child, who cast the die for my future."

Teacher often was gripped by pessimism and utter despair, and as Helen grew older "she [Teacher] let loose upon me all her varied moods." In Teacher's bouts with melancholy she "had a wretched incapacity to respond even to the kindest approaches of her intimate friends. She would fly from them to the woods, or if she were near the water, she would conceal herself for hours under a boat on the shore. But then she would come back to her friends asking forgiveness." Even in 1955 Helen Keller felt unable to tell the whole truth about Teacher's black moods. No doubt they appeared in her youth, she surmised, "and they continued to harass her every once in a while until her death: and they did not help her sight. She gallantly rallied each time, and though she often fretted, she never lost the free exercise of her mental faculties or suspended them except when she slept. . . ."

Turning to another of Teacher's characteristics, Helen stated flatly that "Teacher was not logical. . . . One had to beware of her impetuous rejoinders when she spoke too positively or enthusiastically of this or that. She was bored by the commonplace on any subject—education, politics, religion, or any other area of social intercourse. A drawn-out talk on science or philosophy was a trial to her nerves. . . ."

Annie was not logical or systematic. Her observations on the education of Helen and of children in general sparkled with brilliance. At a time when the concept was revolutionary, she emphasized the importance of permitting children to find their own gait and follow their own interests. "Words were learned as they were needed. . . . The child learns eagerly what he wants to know and indifferently what you want him to know," she had written at Wright-Humason. How does one reconcile such insights with Annie's draconian resort to cutting Helen off from communication with the world when Helen did not work as diligently as Annie thought she should or follow the paths of education that Annie had laid out for her? Full of breathtaking psychological insights about the learning process, she was incapable of coherence and discipline in their application and development.

What saved her was her ability, when those black moods during which she did dreadful things had eased, to stand off from herself and see herself realistically, to ask with sweetness and humor for forgiveness of those whom she had injured, especially Helen, and to redouble her energies on their behalf. She loved Helen and Helen loved her, and that made reconciliation the sweeter.

"She was consumed with restlessness and moderation was beyond her power to develop," Helen wrote further. "She could not submit to any fate if it meant defeat for us. . . . Every morning she would brace herself with a resolve that the day should pass happily for us both, and often as she watched the sunset, her eyes absorbing its lovely hues, her heart was filled with the sense of work well done; but sometimes a composition I wrote did not please her, or I could not solve a problem in geometry, or some other stupidity angered her—it seemed as if a thundercloud passed over me."

The stay at Red Farm with the Chamberlins after the Gilman affair was a period of convalescence for Teacher. She was deeply shaken and depressed. Not until the spring, wrote Helen, did she regain her "old spontaneity. . . . She was fired with renewed hope. The melancholy which had oppressed her slackened its hold upon her. The future was uncertain, but her doubts concerning me were lessening, and her grasp upon life was growing firmer. Her powers and executive ability were expanding, *and she ceased to treat me as a child, she did not command me any more* [author's emphasis]."

Helen did not further explain this quiet observation, which would appear an understated way of dealing with what the modern temper considers a pivotal point in a young person's development. A few entries from Helen's journals for the period 1897–1898 have survived and give us a glimpse of Helen's restiveness under Teacher's "commands":

February 21, 1897—Today I've been X plus Y equal cross with things in general without any reason. My studies have gone all right. Algebra has run pretty smoothly, and I did the last twelve examples in less than fifteen minutes. But I haven't been cheerful or patient. Almost everything has seemed like a cat flying in my face!

This morning I had no taste for breakfast, and I've had to use all my conscience (What's conscience anyway?) to keep myself at the helm of duty. Why doesn't it help me that I've done my work nicely? I simply despise the spirit in which I've gone about my work. It's so much better to rejoice and say, 'Here's a new day, let us see if we can't do something new, or overcome an old difficulty.' But I haven't thought it until this minute!

When shall I ever get out of me? I'm tired of all my failures, fruitless resolutions. I'm tired of always fearing that I shall be stupid or do something clumsy or careless. Altogether, this has been one of the most discouraging days of my life.

My character seems no good, and it will cost me a long, long effort to build it up. But I do want to be worthy of what life seems to hold in store for me—the power to help others, the love of my friends—and Teacher. Oh, when shall I ever get anywhere near accomplishing this?

Note: I feel indeed humble when I realize how short I fall of what I aspired to do then. With Thomas Hood I think I may be farther from heaven than when I was 16.*

She was always doing battle with her conscience, delighted when she was free from its commands.

[Red Farm] March 11, 1898—This has been a perfectly wonderful day! Teacher and I took a little drive this morning, and the air was so fresh, I wanted to breathe it all in, I could never have enough of it! It was full of fragrant messages of coming spring. I could feel a throb of joy in every breeze as it came dancing across the fields. Teacher said the very trees seemed to tremble with expectancy. Even old Jerry,—Uncle Ed's horse that is usually *un peu paradeux* [sic]—felt the glad influence and trotted away gaily, he would hardly wait for us to get into the carriage if we jumped out for any purpose.

Everything except algebra—my bête noire—has contributed to our happiness today. I only hope tomorrow will be as full of freshness and sunshine, and that nothing will be wrong within or without or anywhere. It's lovely when one can look back and see perfect days—days with neither a cloud in the sky nor a shadow in one's heart.

But by the next entry her sense of "God's in His Heaven" had yielded to questions why He did not do something to kill off the stirrings of Old Nick in her bosom:

*It was a childish ignorance,
  But now 'tis little joy,
To know I'm farther off from heaven
  Than when I was a boy.   (Thomas Hood, "I Remember")

[Red Farm] March 22, 1898—Tonight I'm having a hard fight with —I don't know what—myself or some bad fairy that doesn't love me. I haven't done well in Algebra, and my temper has been unmanageable. I am usually willing to persevere, but I wouldn't today because I was treated so much like—well—a naughty child. I don't know what other expression to use. Something new has come over me—I'm really trying to 'do my duty' and no one realizes what a strange thing that is for me. I've been so accustomed to neglect my studies! I've left so many things poorly done—or not done at all! Something in me resists fiercely, and I can't explain it. But I'm getting a clearer idea of the importance of character, and Swedenborg's words about 'loving the right because it is right' are helping me somehow. Still, it is mighty hard to keep from wandering away. . . .

Am I a bad girl after all? Or is it that bad fairy that seems to want to spoil all I do? Was it born with me, or did it slip in when God wasn't looking? I wonder why He doesn't kill it now? He is all love and wisdom, 'too pure to behold iniquity.' Why doesn't He pull me out of this bad fairy's power when I WANT to get away?

"Treated like a naughty child"—how many adolescent rebellions, opening the way to self-discovery and definition, have been sparked by outrage at such treatment? She was almost eighteen. That she should think of herself as "a bad girl," suggests a childlikeness and naiveté that is startling even for those Victorian times. Yet they should not obscure the reality of her adolescent protest against Teacher's too zealous protection and tutelage. If the outrage did not turn into tempestuous rebellion, that was an indication in part of Helen's total dependence on Teacher for communication with the world. Teacher made life possible for her. And the energies and aggressions that might have gone into rebellion against her surrogate mother were channeled into her studies and into a mounting interest, instinctively reformist, in political affairs, as another entry in her diary shows:

[Red Farm] March 18, 1898—Are we to have war or peace? This question presses upon me with new force and meaning each day as we read the newspapers. Are we to have war or peace?

Senator Proctor has returned from Cuba, and has given a terrible account of the situation there. We can no longer shut our eyes to the truth. Desolation and hunger reign everywhere in Cuba. Every week hundreds of women and children are dying in the towns where the Spanish soldiers have driven them, and where they can't do anything to earn their bread. Their men-folk can't help them, they must fight on. What will happen now? Surely it will be impossible for us to remain on friendly terms with a country which permits such atrocities. I'm told how ignorant the Cubans are, and that they can't govern themselves. But isn't Spain just as ignorant? And does she really 'govern herself' when she treats helpless people with such unbridled cruelty? Surely America will interfere, but I should hate to think war should be her only way to save Cuba.

The United States did intervene; and the report of Republican Senator Proctor of Vermont on what he saw in Cuba—"It is not peace, nor is it war. It is desolation and distress, misery and starvation"—played a part in reconciling the public mind to this United States venture in aid of Cuba's national liberation movement, to use the language of a later time. A joint resolution of Congress on April 20 declared the "relinquishment" of Spanish authority over Cuba the main purpose of American intervention. Two days later President McKinley ordered the blockade of Cuban ports, whereupon Spain declared war on the United States.

[Red Farm] April 27, 1898—Again war is to darken this land of peace. Again brave men are to pour out their blood for their country. How the family all talk and talk, some for war and others dead against it! I'm tossed up and down like a locust in the wind, their arguments perplex me so inexpressibly.

Oh cruel, cruel war, I hate it with perfect hatred, and nothing makes it seem right to my mind. Freedom? Yes—but—how does that really help if it brings all kinds of wicked things with it—hate, revenge, murder of thousands, plunder, and making millions of human beings miserable? I can't understand. But of course we can't leave Cuba to her fate, and I suppose America has got to fight unless Spain backs down. But what does it all lead to—war, more war and again more war?

An even more painful confrontation between competing loyalties arose a few weeks later when Teacher applied to the War Department to serve as a nurse in Cuba. Helen was devastated:

[Red Farm, no date]—Now I'm all excited, frightened and worried. My precious teacher is thinking of going to Cuba as a nurse! She says her country needs her, and I don't know what to say. America is my country too, but if I am to tell the truth, I feel I need Teacher more. I don't see why America should separate us any more than Mr. Gilman. But it would be selfish and unpatriotic in me to hold her back, and so I can only sit here alone, wondering blindly what it all means.

It's dreadful! With all that sickness out there, will she ever come back, if she goes? She has already sent her application to the War Department. She's so wonderful and has done such noble work, they will of course want her—and whatever shall I do without her?

I know everybody here loves me and tries to help me. But everybody is not Teacher. I seem always to have had her, and she's the only one who knows how to teach me life's big things, or help me with all kinds of difficulties. Just to think of her going makes me feel utterly lost and sick at heart.

What is one to make of this evidence of Teacher's capriciousness? What furies gripped her? Why did she feel a compulsion to escape, and from what? The usually conscientious Nella Braddy is silent about the affair. Nor is any light shed in the letters of Helen and Annie. Helen does mention it in *Teacher,* but in view of her journal entry her account is highly misleading; or perhaps the memory of what really happened was too painful for her to recall:

During our stay at Red Farm the United States declared war on Spain, and Teacher applied for a position as nurse in the Army. She and I were likeminded in our wish to have her serve, but she learned that it would take her as long to be trained for that work as building a ship, and she gave up the idea.

The next two entries deal with Helen's difficulty in living up to what Teacher expected of her and what she expected of herself in her studies and in matters of personal neatness. Perhaps impatience with Helen had had as much to do as patriotism with Teacher's decision to volunteer for Cuba. Perhaps it was the condition of her eyes, which had suddenly worsened, partly as a result of the work with the tutor Merton S. Keith. He came out once a week for a three-and-a-half-hour session from February on. "Miss Sullivan was sometimes well-nigh exhausted," he wrote. He did not know the manual alphabet. Teacher had to do the translating and all the reading and looking-up of words in the volumes that were not in Braille. After four months she was desperate about her eyes. Mrs. Chamberlin, "Aunt Ida," secretly wrote Hitz, "While in N.Y. Dr. Derby made a thorough examination and his verdict has frightened her almost to desperation. He said that unless her eyes were operated upon that she must lose her sight." She had given up hope and refused to see a doctor in Boston. " 'Dr. Derby stands at the head, he has told me the truth. I will not be operated upon so there is nothing but blindness ahead, and then death, for I will not live blind.' I know her so well now that I know this is no idle threat, nor could I blame her for feeling so about it." Hitz must come to Wrentham. "She is not to be commanded but you and I, I am sure are the only ones who really *love* Annie Sullivan and if we cannot *persuade,* no one else can *make* her do what she should now. . . . I dare not write for Mrs. Hutton's aid or advice in this matter, for I know she would try to use authority and that would fail in this, and perhaps injure our chances with Annie."

Nothing, alas, was done; but the failure of Annie's sight might well explain in large measure Annie's erratic conduct, for it must have added to the pressure to run away. When she abandoned the thought of going to Cuba, she decided to rent a camp for the summer on Lake Wollomonapoag, near Wrentham, and invited Helen's mother, Mildred and Phillips to join them for the summer. We return to Helen's Journal:

[Red Farm] June 28, 1898—My vacation has begun, and I'm left to myself. Now I have three long, lovely months at my disposal, and this thought spurs me to make the best use of them. I'm happy because I have some of the books required in preparation for college. It's such a comfort to be able to read them with my fingers! I can read them over and over, and give enough time to what I don't understand without taxing the strength of poor Teacher or any one else. So I can digest the knowledge I shall gain from the embossed books more easily than I could if they had to be spelled out to me.

In Greek, for instance, I've been obliged to review the irregular verbs at least twenty times the last three months, and they still slide off my mind like water off a duck's back. I have the queerest memory that ever afflicted a poor mortal. Sometimes when Teacher gives me problems in Algebra to write out in Braille, my memory leaves me right away—and I can't remember equations in which the terms are alike, only reversed! I feel about like a cat trying to walk on hot bricks at such times, and I thank my stars that no one sees the wild work I make of these problems.

But I'm going to try not to be such a goose this summer—and certainly I've resolved not to waste my vacation. I shall take each day at least two hours for study. If possible, I shall finish my *Anabasis* and Virgil and push on further in Mathematics. Thus I shall try to make next year as easy for both Teacher and myself as possible. . . .

[Red Farm] June 30, 1898—(Alas for the good resolutions of the youthful egotist!) Nothing to record, except that I again lost my temper, and it was so silly. I said I'd like to learn to keep house. 'Don't talk such nonsense,' the family said. 'You will never like it. You don't do anything neatly. You leave your bed looking as if Buff (the puppy) had dug into it. You leave your windows open when a thunderstorm is coming. You'd send all the dishes to limbo if you tried to wash them.' I was hit, and said, 'Why do you keep telling me those things all the time?' That wasn't true or fair, they were only laughing at me. I suppose mother would say I'm as cranky and touchy as a wet hen.

Helen's family had arrived to spend a few days at Red Farm before all journeyed to the camp. Helen's next entry is noteworthy because it contains a critical reference to her sister, Mildred. That was new. Usually a reference to a family member was preceded by an obligatory "dear" or "dearest" that also was characteristic of the Victorians:

[Red Farm] July 1, 1898—What a cool, breezy day it has been! And the children and I have been like kittens all day—never stopping our play a minute. This morning we rambled off to the woods. No, rather, we skipped along the road helter-skelter, as the peas do on the piazza sometimes when I don't shell them properly. We tried to push each other off the path every chance we had, and once when we were crossing a field, the children ran with me plump into a pile of hay!

Away we went rolling over and over with Buff jumping on us and barking in high glee.

When we got to the woods, we tried to make our way through a balsam fir thicket, and we were kept busy falling down and disentangling ourselves from briers and small trees. But we did come out of the tangle, all sweet with the smell of the firs we had rubbed up against, and as happy as bobolinks! I've never laughed so much as I did then. I seem to laugh more all the time here at Red Farm, and I get happier and happier. I wonder why Mildred doesn't laugh nearly so heartily as we do. She has no use for our giggles, and just walks along with a sort of scornful dignity until we calm down. Bettie [Chamberlin] notices it too, and wonders why. Perhaps Mildred has no imagination. . . .

The time at Red Farm had been one of intellectual growth. It was a gathering place for young poets and writers. "When you included us in the circle of your charming hospitality," Helen wrote Uncle Ed in 1930, "we entered the intellectual atmosphere of which Teacher had dreamed. Through you she enjoyed satisfying conversation—with persons who had seen or written or travelled or done large things. Eagerly she drank with me the fresh, sweet waters that flowed under the old linden in the yard at Red Farm. I remembered how we sat in its shade, listened to the poems of Bliss Carman, Richard Hovey, Louise Guiney, Archibald Lampman, and heard the comments of you, Edward Everett Hale, Miss Minna Smith and Mary Wilkins." Uncle Ed was a pioneer environmentalist and naturalist who filled his column in the *Transcript* with reports on the streams, woods and wildlife of New England and who that spring and summer initiated Helen "into the mysteries of trees and wild flowers, the stone walls and green pastures of New England," and who introduced her to Bradford Torrey, "whose talk about birds made their songs and habits an unfailing source of joy in my silent world." Uncle Ed challenged her to think more systematically and critically:

[Lake Wollomonapoag] August 8, 1898—But what's the matter with life? It's so different for different people who try to do something splendid. To some it brings success, and to others—failure and disappointment.

Famous men like Franklin, James Watt, Robert Fulton, Daniel Boone were poor, but they persevered, conquered many obstacles and succeeded in all their undertakings, and were happy. But Uncle Ed says there are a great many people with brains who struggle and struggle, and can't accomplish what they want to, or if they do, they wear themselves out, so that they can't enjoy their success. . . .

Another thing, Uncle Ed has told me, that there are some kinds of success not admirable. He has talked about Caesar and Napoleon. I had supposed they were benefactors because they were praised and extolled to the skies in everything I read about them. But he said they became famous by killing great numbers of their fellowmen, ruining their lands, and spreading misery and hatred everywhere. He went on to say that whatever good they accomplished was small compared with the evil they did and the suffering they caused. . . .

On their return to Wrentham, they decided to move to a boardinghouse on Newbury Street in Boston in order to be closer to Mr. Keith, Helen's tutor. It seems to have been a spur-of-the-moment decision. "We have been in such a whirl ever since we decided to come to Boston," she wrote Mrs. Hutton. "It seemed as if we should never get settled. Poor Teacher has had her hands full, attending to movers, and expressmen, and all sorts of people. I wish it were not such a bother to move, especially as we have to do it so often." The impersonality of a boardinghouse puzzled her: "It seems very odd to be where people keep coming and going, whom you do not know, and never speak to." Keith came five days a week at half past three for an hour's lesson. They worked on the *Iliad,* the *Aeneid,* Cicero, "besides doing a lot of Geometry and Algebra." They walked in the Public Gardens, which were not quite the woods and pastures of Wrentham: "Even the trees seem citified and self-conscious." She missed Red Farm, which she and Teacher would later look back on "as the richest brightest experience of our lives." But she was not unhappy, she assured Mrs. Hutton: "I have Teacher and my books, and I have the certainty that something sweet and good will come to me in this great city where human beings struggle so bravely all their lives to wring happiness from cruel circumstances. Anyway I am glad to have my share in life whether it be bright or sad."

There was one final journal entry, final in the sense of what has been preserved. It had to do with mathematics and an analogy between the "theory of limits" and the effort to understand God's perfection. Helen called it "A Young Girl's Thoughts:"

[Boston] October 31, 1898—I wonder if any one who did not know of God would divine His existence after studying Mathematics. This grand science seems to emphasize strongly the general ideas which we form of Him. It illustrates His inapproachableness and the fixedness of His laws. This thought flashed across my mind while Mr. Keith was explaining to me what is called in Geometry "the Theory of Limits." He told me to suppose that the numbers one-half, one-fourth, one-eighth, one-sixteenth approach 1 as their limit. I kept adding these fractions and getting the sum three-fourths, seven-eighths, fifteen-sixteenths. Still I could not quite make them reach 1, and I found that they never would, even if I were to add them until the end of the world.

Then, all of a sudden, my mind was filled with the thought. Even so is God the Limit of Man, inapproachable. Each one of us is a tiny part of Him. Taken all together, our good qualities and deeds are a sum that grows constantly, and approaches nearer, ever nearer to the limit of His Oneness—Perfection. But we can never in all eternity reach the Completeness of His Being!

I also have found that Mathematics is rigid. Its results never change. It will give the desired results if one does the work correctly, but NOT otherwise. Similarly, God's laws are unchanging. If we obey them and use good sense in so doing, their results will always be bigger life, beauty, love, work, joy. But we can never, never, never have these precious things any other way.

The spur that mathematics provided to religious reflection reconciled her to the difficulties of algebra and geometry. By mid-December Helen was able to report to Hitz that "I am nearly through with Plane Geometry, and shall in a few days begin review, and take up purely original work. I have almost finished Elementary Algebra too, and Mr. Keith thinks I shall be able to do good work in advanced Algebra. . . . They think I shall be ready to take my 'finals' in June." Teacher had been right, after all, in her insistence that Helen could be prepared for her finals in three years; but the cost we shall never know.

Helen had other "glad news" to comment on in her letter to Hitz—"the signing of the Peace Treaty! So, in some way or other the war is over; but alas, we shall now have to face the consequences, which, I think, will be far-reaching." Under the treaty Spain "relinquished" control of Cuba to the United States, which was to exercise a temporary trusteeship over the island. It ceded outright to the United States Puerto Rico and the Philippines for twenty million dollars. But the Filipinos were no readier to accept U.S. sovereignty than Spanish. An insurrection broke out that would take the United States three years to suppress. "Imperialism" would replace "free silver" as the paramount issue between the Republican and Democratic parties. Helen's letter to Hitz foreshadowed this cleavage: "I suppose you were taken quite by surprise when our country decided to take the Philippines, were you not? Now that we have taken them, what do you suppose we shall do with them? Almost all my friends here are bitterly opposed to the 'Expansion Policy' of the Government. I do not know what to think myself. It is possible that infinite good to all concerned may result from what seems now to many a grievous mistake. I remember the old hymn which says, 'God moves in a mysterious way his wonders to perform.' "

Among her most ardently peace-minded friends were Dr. Hale and the Fullers. Dr. Hale was the leading spirit in the Lake Mohonk conferences in New York, one of the earliest efforts to find peaceful alternatives to war for the settlement of international disputes. "We are in this beautiful place," Lucy Fuller wrote Annie, "and are attending the Peace Conference or Arbitration Conference which is held here and of which dear Dr. Hale is the leading spirit. We have known him before but now we love him—and I am writing this letter to tell you that he properly estimates you and satisfies my soul in that."

Helen was fervently pacifist and trying hard to reconcile her pacifism with her belief that the United States should aid oppressed and backward peoples. As she did with increasing frequency, she turned to her *Pflegevater*, Mr. Hitz: "What do you think of 'expansion?' Here the controversy is very sharp. It is surprising to see how many different opinions can be expressed with equal force on the same subject by different men having equally noble sentiments! One feels moved by the eloquence of each, and one hardly knows what to think. Freedom of speech reminds me of a whetstone; on it every one whets his opinion, and thus gives it a sharp edge. But, on the whole, keeping the Philippine Islands seems to me the only honorable policy we can adopt. It would be too dreadful to leave the poor natives alone, an easy prey to nations greedy of wealth and conquest, would it not?"

"You do not believe in war, then?" an interviewer asked her in June 1899, shortly before she took her examinations.

"Certainly not, unless it be a war for liberty. I am in sympathy with the Filipinos," she added with great earnestness.

"Then you are an anti-Imperialist?" queried the reporter.

"I guess so, but it is really hard to tell what we are in these days. All I know is that I do not believe in killing so many helpless savages, especially when they are fighting for liberty." The reporter then commented that "Miss Keller is very patriotic but large and liberal in her ideas which soar beyond all narrow, partisan or political prejudices. Her sympathies are with the masses, the burden-bearers, and, like all friends of the people and of universal progress, she is intensely interested in the Peace Congress." This was the Lake Mohonk conference, and in reference to it she told the interviewer, "I hope the nations will carry out the project of disarmament. I wonder which nation will be brave enough to lay down its arms first?"

"Don't you hope it will be America?"

"Yes, I hope so, but I do not think it will. We are only just beginning to fight now, and I am afraid we like it. I think it will be one of the old, experienced nations that has had enough of war."

The interview which appeared in the November issue of *Success* magazine took place in early June, just as Helen entered the final phase of preparation for her examinations. The reporter was impressed with her ease of manner and described her as a "blithesome, rosy-cheeked, light-hearted maiden of nineteen, whose smile is a benediction, and whose ringing laugh is fresh and joyous as that of a child. . . ." Her self-confidence soared as she mastered the difficulties with mathematics. In algebra Keith had approached the subject "as if she knew nothing of it," and after many tussles and much practice "she became accurate and rapid in her work" and even had come to "delight in the work for itself. . . . She has seen order and simplicity and neatness and rigid exactitude issue from confusion and complexity." There had been even greater mental obstacles in mastering geometry. Sometimes she seemed "obstinately stupid," but in each case he had discovered that "a misconception had thwarted our efforts." She had excelled in Latin and Greek; indeed, Keith felt his pupil was "capable of giving the world at some future time, in rhythmical prose, a new version of Virgil, which would possess high and peculiar merit."

As the week of the examinations neared, Helen, Annie and Keith were so confident of her readiness that the two women went out to Wrentham, where Helen rode her newly acquired tandem bicycle and paddled the Chamberlin canoe. Then, suddenly, a new hurdle and anxiety. "The college authorities objected to Miss Sullivan's reading the examination paper to me; so Mr. Eugene C. Vining, one of the instructors at the Perkins Institution for the Blind, was employed to copy the papers for me in American Braille." There were different systems of Braille notation—English, American and New York Point—and while Helen was familiar with "all literary Braille," she had used only the English notation in her work in mathematics, and its symbols were very different from the American. She tried to familiarize herself with the latter in the two days before the examination; but work as she might, both she and her tutor were "distressed and full of forebodings" as the day of the examination arrived. The geometry paper was confusing enough; "but when I took up Algebra I had a harder time still. I was terribly handicapped by my imperfect knowledge of the notation. . . . Consequently my work was painfully slow," and she exceeded the time limit. But the authorities had previously agreed that because of the mechanical difficulties with the papers in mathematics, she should be allowed a longer time for those papers; and she passed, receiving from Radcliffe College on July 4, 1899, her certificate of admission to the freshman class signed by Dean Irwin, with the added notation that "Miss Keller passed with credit in Advanced Latin."

It was an impressive achievement, a triumph, as her tutor noted, of "ambition stimulated by obstacles, persistent will and patience." But Helen was disconsolate: "I was bitterly disappointed not to have done better," she wrote Keith, "and my disappointment often throws a shadow upon the pleasure which the summer is bringing me; but, dear Mr. Keith, I did my best, and I hope that in the future I may find a far better medium through which to show you my gratitude, and appreciation of what you have done for me."

Their friends were elated by Helen's success. Dr. Bell wanted Annie to do a paper on the progress of Helen's education, and Hitz began to prepare a new Helen Keller *Souvenir,* Number 2, 1892–1899. Annie was uncooperative. Even before the examinations she had written Hitz, "But I would like to make a suggestion, and I wonder that it has not occurred to Mr. Bell, if he really is interested in what Helen has been doing the past two years. Would it not be well for you to ask Mr. Keith to prepare a brief paper to read before the Association? He is a sensible, practical teacher, with no nonsense or sentimentality about him. He has done more towards developing and stimulating her mind than all the Wright, Humason, Anagnos and Gilman clique put together, and we both like and respect him. He would be willing to write a paper along any line of thought, which you or Mr. Bell might suggest."

Keith did do a lengthy paper for *Souvenir* No. 2, as did Helen; but Teacher turned over an old paper on how Helen had learned to speak. As she wrote Hitz in May 1900 after its publication:

Nevertheless, you will forgive me, will you not, if I tell you frankly that I am not more pleased with the realization of the idea than I was with the idea itself. You know I told you last summer that I did not believe in enlightening the public further as to what we had done, were doing and intended to do. I said then, and repeat now, I do not believe our affairs concern the public, and personally I would not turn my hand to set it right on any particular point. Helen and I have suffered more than you or any one else in the world can ever understand, through the publicity that has been given to her education. I am not saying this because I blame you in any way, far from it, but simply to explain my lack of enthusiasm in something which has been done in Helen's and my best interest. I cannot think the new *Souvenir* will unravel the tangled web of truth and falsehood that overzealous friends and enemies have drawn about us. Time only can do that, and, as far as I am concerned, I am more than willing to work and wait, knowing that right and justice must triumph in the end.

But Annie's views on publicity, as we have seen, were as capricious and contradictory as her moods. The fund for Helen's education depended on public support. She permitted and abetted the interview that Helen gave, just before her examinations, to *Success.* In her previous letter to Hitz, moreover, she had asked him to help her with a book about Helen's education that had been suggested by Mary Mapes Dodge of *St. Nicholas.* "I mean to have it ready for the publishers early in the fall. I have all the Perkins Institution Reports, which will save a great deal of copying. Mrs. Hutton has a lot of material which she says I may use, and I am counting on the Volta Bureau to help me out. I suppose it will be rather difficult to get unpublished letters. It's always such a nuisance to write and ask people for things; they never understand what is wanted, and they are possessed with the idea that you are trying to get them into some sort of a trap."

Teacher wrote of the book project as if it were hers, and in the same letter speaks of having household help during the summer, which would "leave me free to work on the book when I feel in the mood for it." In Helen's letter to Hitz on the same subject, it is Helen's book. "She (Mrs. Dodge) proposes to have published a collection of my letters with an introduction by one of my friends and a brief account of my life by some one else. She thinks such a book would have a great sale, and thus furnish at least part of the money necessary for my education." In the end, they would be in this, as in almost everything else, collaborators; but Helen would occupy center stage, and the book's title would be *The Story of My Life.*

Despite the certificate of admission to the freshman class, she did not enter Radcliffe in the autumn of 1899. Her friends were divided as to what she should do. "Many think I ought not to attempt the regular course— they think I should develop along the lines of study which I like best, and get all I can out of special courses. Personally I should very much prefer to take the regular course. I should be proud and glad to win a degree, but what the final decision will be, neither my teacher nor I know at this moment." So she wrote at the end of September to a friendly newspaper reporter. Mrs. Hutton came to Cambridge to consult Dean Irwin, telling her how strongly Helen desired to take the regular course. The dean was opposed to Helen's making the attempt. Finally Helen and Annie called upon her, "and she persuaded me to take a special course, this year at any rate. She said, that I had already shown the world that I could do the college work, by passing all my examinations successfully in spite of many obstacles. She showed me how very foolish it would be for me to pursue a four years' course of study at Radcliffe simply to be like other girls, when I might better be cultivating whatever ability I had in writing. She said, she thought I had a 'gift' and that I could accomplish most by studying, and doing a great deal of translation and composition in the subjects I liked best—language and literature. Her arguments seemed so wise and practical, that I could not but yield.

"But I found it hard, very hard to give up the idea of going to Radcliffe. . . ."

Teacher suspected conspiracy, especially when Gilman sent Hitz a comparison of the grades Helen had scored on the examinations after she had attended his school with her marks after tutoring by Keith. Gilman was skeptical that the explanation was Helen's confusion over the Braille systems. "It is plain what is in Gilman's mind," Annie raged to Hitz. "He thinks a comparison of the marks convincing enough without comment. . . . How much did he influence the marks? We shall probably never know. . . .

"No word from Dean Irwin with regard to Helen's work yet!! Helen is restless and disappointed and I am utterly discouraged. How absurd the idea of a *Souvenir* such as you are getting out seems at this time. Here is the subject of it clamoring at the door of a nineteenth century university for instruction and getting splendidly snubbed for her audacity. I am so indignant I cross my ts, even. Helen did not say the American Braille was unknown to her. The exact difficulty was explained in the *World* article. The mention of the Frost King story shows that he has been consulting Mr. Anagnos, who I understand is shortly to publish another statement in regard to that episode. Things begin to look interesting, don't they?"

Although Annie suspected Gilman of having "influenced" the marks, that did not keep her from complaining to Hitz that Radcliffe's certificate of admission, which *Souvenir* reproduced, was incomplete. "Two 'honors' which Helen received in her preliminary examinations were omitted, which is a very unfortunate circumstance, as it now appears that she received 'honors' only in advanced Latin."

Helen asked Dean Irwin whether Radcliffe professors might not privately give her courses similar to those they gave in the classroom. The dean did not object and offered to consult the professors. They were unwilling to take on such a chore. "They all said they were too busy," she reported to Hitz. "But now I am going to study with Mr. Keith, and see how much I can accomplish in a quiet, simple way. My studies are to be English, English Literature, French, German and Latin." In the spring she decided to apply formally for admission to the freshman class. If Radcliffe would not have her, there were indications that Cornell or the University of Chicago might. In May she wrote formally to the chairman of the academic board of Radcliffe College to be allowed to take the regular course:

> Since receiving my certificate of admission to Radcliffe last July, I have been studying with a private tutor, Horace, Aeschylus, French, German, Rhetoric, English History, English Literature and Criticism, and English Composition.
>
> In college I should wish to continue most, if not all of these subjects. The conditions under which I work require the presence of Miss Sullivan, who has been my teacher and companion for thirteen years, as an interpreter of oral speech and as a reader of examination papers. In college she, or possibly in some subjects some one else, would of necessity be with me in the lecture-room and at recitations. I should do all my written work on a typewriter, and if a Professor could not understand my speech, I could write out my answers to his questions and hand them to him after the recitation.

A month later she still had not heard, she informed Mrs. Hutton. "My friends think it very strange that they should hesitate so long. . . . Cornell has offered to make arrangements suited to the conditions under which I work, if I should decide to go to that college, and the University of Chicago has made a similar offer; but I am afraid if I went to any other college, it would be thought that I did not pass my examinations for Radcliffe satisfactorily. . . ." Finally Radcliffe yielded. With justice the *Boston Evening Transcript* noted that in addition to her innate abilities and the expert teaching she had received, Helen Keller possessed the "all powerful" characteristic "of ambition, without which neither her natural gifts nor her teachers' exertions would have resulted so brilliantly."

If ambition spurred her on to attend Radcliffe, her heart, yearning for duties, turned her in another direction. Oppression and misery stirred it; injustice provoked it. French and international outrage obliged the French government, which had sent Captain Dreyfus to Devil's Island, to release him. Helen was overjoyed when he was freed in September 1899; "but it makes our blood boil to think they freed him with the scandal of a 'pardon,' " she wrote Hitz. "I cried out, 'What was he pardoned for? for his very innocence, one would believe!' " When the Boer War began the following spring, she was on the side of the Afrikaners. She started out strongly in favor of Great Britain, she wrote Dr. Bell and Mrs. Hutton; but the more she read, the more she sympathized with the "heroic Boers." Britain had made a "terrible mistake, and . . . from the seeds of discord and hatred which she is now sowing in her empire, she will some day reap a harvest of tares."

The project that almost derailed her from going to college was a brainchild of Aunt Ida. The latter wrote Hitz:

> . . . Helen has talked with me a good deal about what is to be her lifework. She does not seem to feel as though "Literature" that is for a vocation was the thing, because she does not feel that she is gifted. We all think differently about that I guess, but I think she wants to *do* something that will make her feel her active usefulness to her fellow-creatures. She told me one time that she would like to give her life to College Settlement work. I don't quite see how she could do much, except by use of her name and that would mean little to her as she does not value the use of a name. It is something greater that she is groping for. Now, for *my secret*.

> I want to see Helen and Annie at the head of an institution or home, for the deaf, dumb and blind children, the triply afflicted only, to be known as the *Helen Keller Home*. . . . You know Annie Sullivan has a wonderful amount of power for this work, which should not be lost to the world. Her active work for Helen is nearly over. She can no longer teach Helen, and ought not to do the reading even which she is doing now. Her eyes are very bad again. . . . If she were doing something of this kind she would be more likely to keep the sight she

now has. You can see as well as I her peculiar ability for this kind of work. She has said a good many times, that lack of force in his teachers was a potent factor working against Tommy Stringer's development.* It seems to me the *proper* thing for Helen too. She would then feel that she had a part in the world instead of just existing, which I know to be her great hope. She is very beautiful with children and could have certain duties later on in connection with them. Until that time should come her study could continue. . . . I have no 'axe to grind.' I have only a great desire to see these girls strong and useful in the world, not living on the caprice of a few wealthy ones, who, even now are showing less interest. . . . Then, too, we must admit, painful as it is, that Helen, through animosity toward Annie, has enemies. . . .

Helen enthusiastically supported the scheme. Her fear for Teacher's eyes tugged her strongly. "I really dread going to college next fall on her account," she had written Hitz. "I cannot bear the thought of the constant and terrible strain upon her poor eyes which I fear will come with our new studies."

Even after her Radcliffe classes began she still clung to the scheme. She went down to New York to consult her friends there. They were vigorously against it, Helen reported to Hitz:

. . . I quite forgot that there might be many obstacles in the way of accomplishing anything like what Aunt Ida proposed. Not until I went to New York Wednesday night did I begin to realize that a school for deaf and blind children maintained by money obtained from the public and perhaps managed more or less by committees might involve dangerous complications and unforeseen difficulties which I have not the experience or ability to deal with. Still I hoped that my friends in New York might be able to make suggestions as to how these perplexities might be averted.

On our arrival in New York we went straight to Mr. Rhoades'** and took breakfast with him. To my surprise and disappointment he em-

---

*Helen encountered Tommy Stringer at the railroad station, "a great, strong boy. . . . His progress is astonishing, they say; but it doesn't show as yet in his conversation, which is limited to 'Yes' and 'No.' "
**John Harsen Rhoades, president of the Greenwich Savings Bank and father of one of their closest friends, Miss Nina Rhoades, a blind girl.

phatically disapproved of the scheme from the first and declared that it must be stopped at once. He said that it really meant that my name was to be used as a means for raising money for the erection of a school building and for the education of children. Of course I knew that was not the real object. Neither Aunt Ida nor I were considering the advantage to me only, and I told him so; but he went on to say that if my name was used in that way, I should lose the sympathy of my friends—lose their support and find myself without the means of accomplishing anything. He pointed out the financial problems and other questions which Teacher, at the head of such an institution, would be called upon to solve, to say nothing of the tremendous expense we should incur each year.

My friends thought we might have one or two pupils in our own home, thereby securing to me the advantage of being helpful to others without any of the disadvantages of a large school. They were very kind, but I could not help feeling that they spoke more from a business than a humanitarian point of view. I am sure they did not quite understand how passionately I desire that all who are afflicted like myself shall receive their rightful inheritance of thought, knowledge and love. Still I could not shut my eyes to the force and weight of their arguments, and I saw plainly that I must abandon Aunt Ida's scheme as impracticable.

Teacher's attitude towards Aunt Ida's scheme is not wholly clear. After it had been abandoned, she wrote Hitz, "I feel sorry for Mrs. C. She has worked hard to carry out her plan, and I believe disinterestedly. Her whole heart was in it, and naturally she could not give it up without a struggle. That she should be disappointed and hurt, is not strange; for Helen gave her enthusiastic support to the plan from the beginning and withdrew only at the eleventh hour." One unanticipated result of the visit to New York was the establishment of an advisory committee to control Helen's affairs while at Radcliffe:

I considered this suggestion carefully, then I told Mr. Rhoades that I should be proud and glad to have wise friends to whom I could always turn for advice in all important matters. For this committee I chose six, my mother, Teacher because she is like a mother to me, Mrs. Hutton, Mr. Rhoades, Dr. Greer and Mr. Rogers, because it is they who have supported me all these years and made it possible for me to enter college. Mrs. Hutton has already written to mother, asking her to telegraph if she was willing for me to have other advisers beside herself and Teacher. This morning we received word that mother has given her consent to this arrangement. Now it remains for me to write to Dr. Greer and Mr. Rogers.

Dr. Bell had another suggestion. He saw them in Boston after their visit to New York. Why should not Aunt Ida and those of her friends who were interested in her scheme organize an association for the promotion of the education of the deaf and the blind? The association would appoint Teacher to train others to instruct deaf and blind children in their own homes, just as she had taught Helen. Helen meanwhile should fight her way through Radcliffe in competition with seeing and hearing girls, "while the great desire of my heart was being fulfilled. We clapped our hands and shouted; Aunt Ida went away beaming with pleasure, and Teacher and I felt more light of heart than we had for some time. Of course we can do nothing just now; but the painful anxiety about my college work and the future welfare of the deaf and blind has been lifted from our minds."

A few weeks later she was writing John D. Wright of Wright-Humason, "Radcliffe girls are always up to their ears in work. . . . I hope to obtain my degree in four years, but I'm not particular about that. There's no great hurry, and I want to get as much as possible out of my studies. Many of my friends would be well pleased if I would take two or even one course a year; but I rather object to spending the rest of my life in college. . . ."

XIV

Radcliffe: Class of 1904

". . . The wonderful feat of drawing Helen Keller out of her hopeless darkness was only accomplished by sacrificing for it another woman's whole life." —*New York Sun*

Helen entered Radcliffe in September 1900, a freshman in the class of 1904. It numbered about one hundred, the largest in Radcliffe's brief history. Higher education for women was a sturdy growth, but the women who went to college still were considered pioneers by some, eccentrics by others, and there were fears that college life would "unsex" American womanhood and unfit it for its role of raising the nation's moral tone. The handful of women's colleges leaned over backwards to be and to appear to be staid and respectable. A reputation for conservatism and old-fashionedness was welcomed. Radcliffe was not quite as prim and sober as it had been in 1879 when it was established. That was a time when Mary Lyon, the austere founder of Mount Holyoke, decreed that "fun is a word no young lady should use," and Radcliffe was described as a Harvard Annex

> . . . for select young ladies,
> Spinsters, spectacled and learned,
> With a genius for hard study,
> For plain living and hard thinking
> With a thirst for self-improvement. . . .

But under Dean Agnes Irwin, there were still too many "no's" to life rather than "yesses"; and the dean was perceived by one of Helen's classmates as "Inhibition Incarnate." Miss Irwin came from Main Line Philadelphia and had been principal of a highly regarded girls' school there. "She would not accept," wrote Agnes Repplier, her biographer, *"Innocents Abroad* over which a generation easily moved to mirth was shaking with laughter, because of the fashion in which Mark Twain had chosen to tell the story of Abelard and Heloise."

Dean Irwin conducted the college along the lines "of a large boarding school"; and her admonitions, while kindly, were firm, precise and unbudgeable. She was unpopular with the majority of students, who thought her autocratic, considering that she was a woman without a college degree. Radcliffe's chief claim on the attention "of feminine America" lay in the fact that "it provides for girls Harvard courses conducted by Harvard instructors."

Like college generations from time immemorial, the class of 1904 considered itself unique; and its particular "genius," as the class poet Helen Cartwright McCleary wrote, was in its denial of the traditional Radcliffe stereotype. The class constituted

> A most famous class of maidens
> Modern (?), up-to-date and merry,
> With a genius for athletics
> And dramatic enterprises,
> With some operatic talent,
> With a native social instinct
> And a thirst for cutting lectures.

There were four Helens in the class, including

> . . . a marvellous lass,
> HELEN KELLER! the Queen of the Four!
>   Of her fame we are proud
>   And we shout it aloud;
> While her English we mention with awe!

"Today I took luncheon with the Freshman Class of Radcliffe," Helen wrote in one of her themes for English 22. "This was my first real experience in college life, and a delightful experience it was! For the first time since my entrance into Radcliffe I had the opportunity to make friends with all my classmates, and the pleasure of knowing that they regarded me as one of themselves instead of thinking of me as living apart and taking no interest in the every day nothings of their life, as I had sometimes feared they did. I have often been surprised to hear this opinion expressed or rather implied by girls of my own age and even by people advanced in years. Once some one wrote to me that in his mind I was always 'sweet and earnest,' thinking only of what is wise, good and interesting—as if he thought I was one of those wearisome saints of which there are only too many in the world."

There was another occasion on which she met the whole class. Tradition prescribed that the juniors give the freshmen a welcoming party in the gymnasium. It was an informal afternoon dance. "Bonnie" was Helen's assigned partner. They danced, and then Bonnie had to attend to some refreshment duties. Would Helen recognize her on her return? she asked. "You replied that you should know me by the hand and that if the hand failed, you should know me by the ring and hand together." Many activities Helen was unable to join, but her affectionate disposition and eagerness to be involved made her very much a part of the class. Students brought her little gifts—posies and boxes of fudge—and she rewarded them by throwing her arms about their necks and kissing them. She was unable to join her bloomered classmates on the hockey field or basketball court, but she was a strong swimmer, needing only a little guidance to hold a straight line. She played chess and checkers with unusual concentration, and was an enthusiastic "wheelwoman" often seen on the Cambridge streets on her tandem. The Idler Club presented theatricals every two weeks and the Emmanuel Club original plays and an annual original operetta. Helen was unable to participate in these. She did join the "Cheerful Correspondence Club." It was "something like the 'Sunshine Society,' " she explained to Hitz. Members write "in a sweet, cheerful way to people who are cut off from the pleasures enjoyed by others because they are sick, crippled or blind." In December when elections for class officers were held, she was chosen vice-president and made a pretty speech of thanks.

But there were differences with the other girls. Helen dwelt on them in a speech to the Radcliffe alumnae a few months before her graduation. Speaking about her four years as an undergraduate, she began on a melancholy note. She envied the alumnae the pleasures of their reunion and the renewal of old ties.

The conditions under which I work are such that I have not been often able to attend the meetings of the clubs to which I belong or to which I have been invited. It is not indifference which has prevented me from joining in the frolics of my classmates. My separation from them is inevitable. I have had moments of loneliness when the girls have passed me on the stairs and in the lecture-rooms without a sign. I have sometimes had a depressing sense of isolation in the midst of my classmates. There are times when one wearies of books, which after all are only symbols of the spirit, and when one reaches out to the warm, living touch of a friendly hand. But I understand perfectly how the girls feel. They cannot speak to me, and they do not see the light of recognition in my face as we pass. The situation to them must be strange and discouraging.

It was not often that Helen admitted to the difficulties of being deaf-blind. But the cheerful, blithe face that she turned to the world masked a deep vein of sadness; she was not like the other girls. She had been unable to join in their pleasures, their little gossips, their escapades. "You will not misunderstand me," she went on, "if I say that much of my life in college has been tedious. Slowness was unavoidable in the manual labor of Miss Sullivan's task and mine. Most of the books I have had to read are not in raised print and I have had them spelled out in my hand word by word.* . . . Another difficulty has been that I cannot make notes in class. When I go home I jot down in Braille what I remember of the lecture. That takes extra time. Moreover, I must depend largely on my memory to retain what my fingers have gathered. So my pleasures in what we call college life are necessarily few. . . ."

She had not boarded with girls her age. Instead she and Teacher rented a little house, the first on Coolidge Avenue, then on the outskirts of Cambridge.

"At college," Helen reported to a friend, "one sees from the window almost nothing but long streets, buildings and students hurrying to and fro; out here one sees trees and fields and at a short distance the winding Charles River." Annie had much pleasure in furnishing the house, which had two bedrooms, a tiny parlor, a dining room and a study for Helen, as well as a room for Bridget, their housekeeper. Their household possessions were accumulating. There were two statues, a Venus and a Winged Victory, to which Helen was particularly responsive because her sense of

---

*For her course in nineteenth-century literature with Dr. Neilson, William Wade ordered books that filled a large case and that it took a dozen people months to transcribe. Unfortunately most instructors did not give Helen their reading lists in time for Wade to have them transcribed.

touch enabled her to enjoy them. They were gifts of Hitz, as were the many plants. Teacher hung lace curtains in the parlor and beautiful pictures. Hitz should visit them and see "how Teacher's wonderful artistic skill has transformed our little home." As for the Venus, "As often as I touch her, I have the sweet, dreamy feeling described by Heine:

> Aus alten Märchen winkt es
> Hervor mit weisser Hand,
> Da singt es und da klingt es
> Von einem Zauberland!

Living off campus was slightly unorthodox, but then the presence of a deaf-blind girl in class was unprecedented. "Radcliffe did not desire Helen Keller as a student," Dean Irwin told Agnes Repplier. "It was necessary that all instruction should reach her through Miss Sullivan, and this necessity presented difficulties. They were overcome and all went well if not easily."

Two letters in the Schlesinger Library Archives at Radcliffe clarify the reasons for Dean Irwin's coolness. "I am in a kind of despair about Miss Sullivan and Helen Keller," Chamberlin had written Miss Irwin on August 31, 1900. "Are you willing to help me out of it? Helen wishes very much to go to Radcliffe and Miss Sullivan wants to have her go. But can Miss Sullivan go with Helen there (as surely she must if Helen goes) if she is completely shut out from the chance of giving examinations, even in an emergency, to Helen? Do you not think it would be an unbearably hard position for Miss Sullivan to be in, and a poor acknowledgement and crown of her remarkable work? Is it really true that such a condition is imposed?"

Such a condition was imposed. Ella J. Spooner, who taught at Perkins and who gave Helen examinations all through the four years, wrote after Helen's death: "When the word became public that Helen was to enter Radcliffe there was much talk—'Why don't they say outright that Miss Sullivan is entering Radcliffe instead of Helen Keller, a blind, deaf and dumb girl?'

"The Dean at that time was anxious to prove in every way that Helen was the important one. She made certain rules: Miss Sullivan was to leave the building when the exams started on their way from Harvard. She, the Dean, would pay personally for two proctors, one to proctor Helen and another to proctor Helen's proctor. She had her typewriter for her work in answering the exam questions. I had my Braille typewriter to translate the questions. . . ."

Except for examinations, Teacher accompanied Helen to all her classes and recitations, spelling into Helen's hand with lightning rapidity (but with selectivity) what the lecturer was saying: from the lecturer to Annie to Helen. The hand had become as quick and sensitive as the ear to Teacher's communications, and sometimes Helen with her other hand followed in an embossed book the text to which the lecturer was referring. Classes over, they hurried home; and Helen sat down to her Braille writer to make the notes she had been unable to write in the lecture hall. Although fine points were lost and some slipped from memory, she managed to capture the gist of most of the lectures. "That concentration of mind," wrote Agnes Repplier, "which nature gives eminently to the blind, and preeminently to the blind deaf-mute, can work miracles. Our senses so distract our attention every minute of our lives that we cannot even comprehend the intensity of application which is made possible by their unhappy loss."

The notes that had to be remembered and transcribed after class, the collateral reading that had to be done, with Teacher having to read to her those assignments that were not in raised print, the homework in the form of themes for English and translations from Latin, French and German, left little time for assimilating what she was hearing or for extracurricular activities. "There are disadvantages, I find, in going to college," she wrote in one of her daily themes for Professor Copeland's English 22. Dr. Charles T. Copeland, later Boylston Professor of Rhetoric, had just begun his dazzling ascendancy over Harvard's courses in writing. "The one I feel most is lack of time. I used to have time to think, to reflect—my mind and I. . . . But in college there is no time to commune with one's thoughts. One goes to college to learn, not to think, it seems. . . ."

Helen soon ran up against an even more agonizing problem—what did she have to say that was her own rather than an echo or paraphrase of her reading? "Copey" and the other readers of the daily themes in English 22 considered her the best writer of freshman English they had encountered at either Radcliffe or Harvard, and their criticism was intended to be helpful: "We want more of you and less of what you have read" was the nub of their dissatisfaction. But their comments coincided with her depression over her inability to get her friends to back Aunt Ida Chamberlin's scheme for a school run by Teacher. It fed an ever-present fear that deprivation of sight and hearing had indeed thinned her experiences to a point of aridity. She found it difficult to produce the daily themes, and days passed without her submitting them. "There are moments when I experience a strange feeling of vacancy both in mind and heart," she began on a paper that she did not turn in. "In my heart there seems to be no feeling—only a void; [a] vacuum, waiting to be filled by a rush of fresh spiritual life. . . ." She wrote a letter to Copey the same day. He should not think that she had stopped writing because she had become discouraged or was unwilling to accept criticism.

> I am confident that I could go on writing themes like those I have written and I suppose I should get through the course with fairly good marks; but this sort of literary patch-work has lost all interest for me. I have never been satisfied with my work; but I never knew what my difficulty was until you pointed it out to me. . . .
>
> I have always accepted other people's experiences and observations as a matter of course. It never occurred to me that it might be worthwhile to make my own observations and describe the experiences peculiarly my own. Henceforth I am resolved to be myself, to live my own life and write my own thoughts when I have any. When I have written something that seems to me fresh and spontaneous and worthy of your criticism, I will bring it to you, if I may, and if you think it good, I shall be happy; but if your verdict is unfavorable, I shall try again and yet again until I have succeeded in pleasing you.

Outwardly gay, inwardly she was draining to the dregs Werther's cup of sorrows, a classic case of Goethean *Weltschmerz,* that existential late adolescent sadness that seems unbearable at the time but in later years one looks back to and writes of nostalgically—as Helen did in *Midstream,* "Youth, Oh Youth." In a post–New Year's theme that she typed out but did not submit, she laments:

> Again, tonight I feel the emptiness of heart and the utter want of something essential to self-improvement that often depress me. What is that something I lack? I repeat this question often, but in vain. Self-reproach sweeps down upon me each time I reflect on this subject; I deny none of the charges of my conscience, they are all too true. I know I am not brave, or strong or resolute; in fact I regard myself as a failure in all that is highest and noblest in a woman. Not

only have I strayed from the way of truth; but I have not performed my duties fully enough or utilized the precious opportunities that have offered themselves. Even the tender impulses that have stolen into my soul and made me weep have vanished into indifference. . . . Once this melancholy would have filled my heart with bitterness and despair; now it is a constant trouble which I forget in my enthusiasm over something beautiful or my anxiety not to disturb the people I live with and love. . . .

From total dejection to absolute joy—the ecstatic swings that in *The Sorrows of Young Werther* Goethe caught in the unforgettable phrase *himmelhoch jauchzend, zu Tode betrubt* (from sky-reaching joy to death's despair). "Tonight I am in a mood entirely different from the discouraged, morose mood in which I fretted out half an hour on paper last week. The idleness and folly of such despondency comes over me like a dash of cold water, and I am nerved anew to persevere." But the prevailing mood was melancholy and self-reproach, youth's growing pains that mark the realization of limits and the closing down of options.

Another day of sadness and loneliness again discharged itself into a lament over her writing:

> . . . I am also discouraged about writing. I suppose I ought not to give way to such feelings, especially as this is no time for weakness or relaxation; but how can I help it? No one that I know or have heard of has the same difficulty in composition as I, namely a slow, halting mind. My ideas obstinately refuse to flow when I try to write. Oh, how pleasant and interesting literary work would be for me but for this cruel, needless hindrance! As it is, I find it a burden, not a pleasure, and at times I HATE it. No one can understand or conceive the worry, suspense and irritation I endure as the process of composition drags on! If there is anything to alienate me from writing, it is this agonizing slowness, the discomfort caused by the sense of wasted time and the harrowing uncertainty of the result—feelings which fairly make me writhe in my seat as if I were in actual pain. It is this difficulty, and NO OTHER that foils my efforts and frustrates the most ardent wishes of my teacher and myself. It is this, too, which sours my temper and makes me vicious at times. Not a word of exaggeration in all this, only words that have burnt deep into my soul and wrung secret tears from a smarting heart. And yet there is no one,

no one who can understand. It really seems too much sometimes, and yet I must bear it or else plunge deeper into trouble and misunderstanding.

She is chagrined by her private sense of failure—or at best, mediocre achievement—and the public plaudits with which she was constantly beset:

> . . . Neither have my studies been marked with anything like brilliant progress. I have only managed to avoid the shame of being regarded as an utterly incapable scholar. . . . Why is it that more has been done for me than for many a brighter, more deserving person? Year after year gifts have been showered upon me, and I have had splendid opportunities to enjoy the wonderful experiences of travel and of society. Many distinguished people have spoken to me kindly, even tenderly, as if I were their young sister, instead of the simple, uninteresting, unpromising girl who stood before them, awed by their brilliancy and oppressed with her own unworthiness. More than this, one or two of them have become numbered among my dearest friends. . . . And yet I am a simple nobody, expecting no career of any sort! Oh, the terror and anxiety with which I ask why such a life should be mine! Is it all a mockery, or is it a great, unknown fate by which it is decreed that great things shall happen because I have lived? . . .

Teacher must have spoken to one of Copey's readers, suggesting that Helen needed encouragement and support. One of them, a bit conscience stricken, wrote her: "There is current among us theme readers a certain vocabulary of withered sapless words—the academic slang of the English Department—the habit of which has grown so inveterate upon us, that give us only red ink and a sheet of paper folded length-wise, and none other will write themselves upon the sheet." Whatever comments he had made upon Helen's work, "I have constantly felt that any criticism of mine must necessarily do it injustice, subjecting it (tacitly at least) to standards far beyond what it has already passed."

Although the reader had sent his note to Annie, it was Helen who answered him after her midyear examinations. "It is my ambition to write well; but I think one must have extraordinary ability in order to write at the present time. It seems as if everything one would care to say, had been said by somebody else. The fresh joyous creative spirit seems to have died out of literature. Sometimes I feel ideas beating against my brain like caged birds; but they will not sing themselves in words, at least not yet." And when they did "sing" in one of her themes written after the Easter recess contrasting rural and urban pleasures, the reader wrote "good," but added, "a little too much the rhythm of verse." Her German professor, however, said of her translation of a passage from Schiller's *Die Glocke*, "as well translated as prose can do."

Copey, famous for his readings, styled himself Harvard's "reader-in-ordinary." "Ramrod straight, about five feet four, he would march into the room, green bag in hand, carrying a tightly folded umbrella, like a scepter of his sovereignty" and in his Maine-accented, gravelly voice hold forth.*

It was Copey's course on which her aspirations centered. Copeland was not enamored of having to give English 22 at Radcliffe. Girls rather frightened him, although that did not inhibit his crustiness. "It always seemed to me that Copey could not get out of the Radcliffe Yard fast enough," wrote one Radcliffe graduate. "If he felt more than impatient toleration for his girl students, he concealed it well." But his attitude toward Helen was different. "She was a joy to Mr. Copeland in English 22, our course in English Composition," recalled one of Helen's classmates, "and, when, choosing from themes on his desk, he came upon one of Helen Keller's contributions, he brightened hopefully." The most highly praised themes, Helen discovered, were the autobiographical ones. "He read us her descriptions, now well known, of her walk across the snow, with the dazzling, blinding sun upon it; of her first sea bath, when tossed by a wave, she swallowed a large part of it, and learned that the sea is salt."

Although her hopes—and griefs—were centered on English composition, she carried a full schedule. That first year she also took courses in medieval history, Latin, French, and German. The ever-helpful Hitz obtained the French and German texts in raised print for her. "I have just read 'Das Lied von der Glocke' the favorite 'Lied' of the Germans as I hear, and Goethe's 'Hermann und Dorothea'. . . . The latter is exquisitely simple, and yet deep as life itself. . . . Next week I shall begin 'Wallenstein' and Goethe's 'Tasso.' By the way, speaking of books reminds me to ask you if you will please have the second part of 'Wallenstein' sent to me. 'Die Piccolomini' must be in raised print by this time, and as I may need

*John Herling in *The Vineyard Gazette*, August 19, 1977.

Anne Sullivan, 1881. Courtesy of the American Foundation for the
Blind. *At 15 years old, her mind was "a question mark,"
her "heart a frustration."*

Laura Bridgman threading a
needle with her tongue.
Courtesy of the
Perkins School for the Blind.

Samuel Gridley Howe, circa
1859. Courtesy of the PSB.
"The Lafayette of Boston."

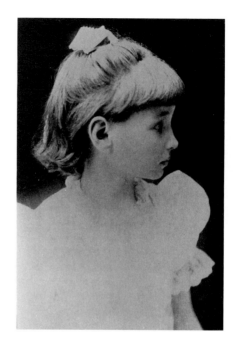

Helen, August 1, 1887.
Photograph credit: Ira F. Collins,
Huntsville, Alabama.
Courtesy of the AFB.
*"She inherits a quick temper, and
a good deal of obstinacy. . ."*
(Anne Sullivan to Mrs. Hopkins.)

Anne Sullivan, circa 1887.
Courtesy of the PSB. *A
graduate of Perkins, her
mind teemed "with
felicitous thoughts."*

Helen's mother, Kate Adams Keller.
Courtesy of the Helen Keller Property
Board, Tuscumbia, Alabama.
*A cultivated woman, she learned of the
Perkins Institution from Charles Dickens'
account of Dr. Howe's success
with Laura Bridgman.*

Helen's father, Capt. Arthur H. Keller.
Courtesy of the Helen Keller Property
Board, Tuscumbia, Alabama.
*". . .A splendid man, large and fine looking,
and a genuine Christian. . . ."*

Helen's sister, Mildred Keller.
Courtesy of the PSB.

Helen reading at Perkins School, circa 1888.
Courtesy of the PSB. *"She has learned that
everything has a name. . . ."*

Helen and Anne Sullivan,
circa 1890. Courtesy of the
AFB. *"I do not know what I
should do without Teacher."*

Helen and three
other deaf-blind
children at Perkins.
Tommy Stringer is
at lower right.
Courtesy of the PSB.

Helen and Anne Sullivan in 1893. Photograph
credit: Brown. Courtesy of the AFB.
*They had left Perkins and were staying with the
philanthropist William Wade at his rural
estate near Pittsburgh, Pennsylvania.*

Helen and Anne Sullivan circa 1894. Courtesy of the AFB.
". . . And she ceased to treat me as a child. She did not command me anymore."

(LEFT) Anne Sullivan, Helen, Edmund Lyon,
and Mrs. Pratt, a Boston genealogist,
at Niagara Falls, Spring 1893.
Courtesy of Carolyn Lyon Remington.

Helen and Anne Sullivan at Radcliffe, circa 1899.
Courtesy of the AFB.

Helen, Anne Sullivan, and Alexander Graham
Bell, July 1894. Library of Congress,
Grosvenor-Bell Collection.

Helen circa 1903. Courtesy of the AFB.
*Her "whole appearance and bearing made upon me the
immediate impression of a sweet and gentle nature,
quite unspoiled by notoriety."—a Swedish observer.*

Helen and Alexander Graham Bell, 1901.
Courtesy of the AFB.
*Anne Sullivan said of him, "He imparted
knowledge with a beautiful courtesy."*

Helen, Anne Sullivan, Mark Twain, and Lawrence Hutton, circa 1902. Photograph credit: E.C. Kopp, Princeton, N.J. Courtesy of the AFB.
"You are a wonderful creature, the most wonderful in the world," Mark Twain wrote her, *"you and your other half together—Miss Sullivan, I mean, for it took the pair of you to make a complete and perfect whole."*

Helen, Anne Sullivan Macy, and Edward Everett Hale, May 2, 1905. Courtesy of the AFB.

Helen and a sculpture given to her by John Hitz.
Courtesy of the PSB.

Helen and Anne Sullivan Macy in Wrentham, Massachusetts.
Courtesy of the AFB.

the book in class, I would like to have the missing volume as soon as possible."

She reported on her midyear examinations. "I took an examination in French on January 26th and another in History the following Tuesday. The French was provokingly difficult; but the History was easier, the only trouble being that the few questions on the paper were as comprehensive as Dr. [Archibald Cary] Coolidge's lectures. Just imagine me struggling through the bewildering maze of details in my attempt to give an account (1) of Charlemagne's reign, (2) of the first three Crusades, (3) of the chief contests between the Papacy and the German Empire, and only three hours to do it in!"

Professor Coolidge seemed to her "singularly shy." When she and Teacher approached him at the end of a lecture with a question, his impulse was to bolt. But his lectures gave history vitality and meaning, and the fear that she had not done well on her final examination mortified her. Professor Coolidge might interpret that as a lack of appreciation:

Cambridge, June 1, 1901

My dear Miss Irwin:

I am greatly troubled about my History Examination, and I feel that I ought to make one or two explanations.

In the first place, I was not told that I could omit the second question on the paper, and as I had not reviewed English History, I spent much valuable time trying to recall what I knew about Edward the First. I suppose I should have passed it over without being told, but I thought Dr. Coolidge had some good reason for putting it on the paper, and I did my best to answer it. Then I think that if you had been there, you would have allowed me a little extra time in which to answer the geographical question, which takes much longer when every word has to be spelled out, than when the places can be indicated on a map. As it was, I had still fifteen minutes when they stopped me. No doubt, in my nervousness I mistook the time.

I make these explanations, not because I expect them to affect my marks—I can bear a low mark, or even to fail; but I cannot bear to have Dr. Coolidge think that I have been unfaithful in my work. I really have studied hard, and I felt fully prepared for my examination yesterday; but things got twisted, as they will sometimes. Please do not tell Dr. Coolidge this; only to say to him, when you have an opportunity, that I have enjoyed his course in History more than any of my studies at college. He has made me realize that History is not a mere catalogue of dry facts and drier dates, but the most wonderful, the most sublime of all dramas, the underlying motive of which is the salvation of the whole world. . . .

> I am
> Sincerely yours
> Helen Keller

Helen took seventeen and a half courses all in all, and thus fulfilled the requirements for a Bachelor of Arts degree. A course consisted of three lectures or recitations a week for one year. She took two courses in French, one in German, two in English composition, a half course in Milton, one in government, one in economics, the one in history, two in Shakespeare, one in Elizabethan literature, one in English literature of the nineteenth century, one in the English Bible, and a course with Professor Josiah Royce in the history of philosophy. She took no science, no mathematics, no fine arts, music or drawing. Chiefly, this was because of the limitations imposed by her deafness and blindness, but it was also a matter of preference and aptitude.

She had a first-rate memory, a relentless will and great depth of feeling, which expressed itself in moral terms. Ever the moralist, she felt she spoke more effectively than she wrote: "A curious fatality seems to compel me to 'blurt out' in conversation and to soften in writing." Emotion, she discovered, helped her to write: "I am trying an experiment. Every one says that in the absence of everything else passion guides thought and compels it to pursue a fixed course. I find that when I am excited or angry I think and write steadily for a certain length of time."

Passion helped her to write, but its occasion was moral outrage or sympathy, not the need to produce a theme for English 22. She was a True Believer who viewed the world "as a conflict between light and darkness, God and the Devil." That was partly a matter of youth. The adolescent mind, wrote Erik H. Erikson, is essentially "an ideological mind." It was also a matter of temperament, the predominance of her "affectional" nature over her intellectual. It was also a consequence of being deaf and blind. The world is full of signals suggesting shadow, ambiguity, uncertainty, that Helen could not experience. Here she differed from Teacher, who, knowing herself, knew how bad qualities were intertwined with good.

One day Helen recited Horace's ode on the *auream mediocritatem*—the golden mean. Teacher liked that very much. "Horace is right, Helen. There are few things you can absolutely call black or white. The Stoics say that you cannot justify faults as such, but in many individuals there are faults that have a good side, as it were." So Helen described their exchange in *Teacher.* Helen rejected moral ambiguity. As she wrote in a classroom theme, "I can see no substantial good in a course that neither embraces the good with a single heart nor quite shuns evil." She was unable to find "any middle between good and evil that seemed to me a 'golden mean.' This is a contradiction of terms. I can find no middle course between love and hatred, cruelty and kindness, truth and falsehood, or any of the great, inconvertible opposites that is excellent or compatible with enlightened self-interest or the principles of a genuine civilization. A middle course is really a compromise with evil, it is the same as lukewarmness."

The attraction for Helen of Swedenborgianism, to which the gentle Hitz had introduced her, was its imaginative and dramatic presentation of morality as a clash between God and the devil. Teacher was unable to follow Hitz and Helen in their devotion to Swedenborgianism. "We do not look at life or anything through the same eyes," she wrote Hitz, "but what of that! We both have that rarer gift—true sympathy. Under all your imagination and ideality there is [a] rich vein of practical wisdom and what is better still you know how to soothe the troubled heart. I only wish it was given to me to reflect the peace and happiness which shine so clearly from you."

In a paper on Browning's religion, Helen enthusiastically concluded that "the deliberate choice of good or evil alone justifies our existence," and agreed with the poet that "there is nothing so unpardonable as to consent to a senseless, aimless, purposeless life." Better to strive to achieve a false ideal than not to try at all. "[W]e are not so deeply condemned as the lady and the duke in 'The Statue and the Bust' who never made an effort to gain that for which they longed."

She applauded love like the biblical Ruth's—a "love which can rise above conflicting creeds and deep-seated racial prejudice, is rare, like everything else that is most beautiful in this world." But she had no tolerance for those who persecuted others: "I have no charity for the rulers who organized the Spanish Inquisition, and I think that Cromwell's ruthless subjugation of Ireland was a heinous crime, which his genius and even his grand virtues as a statesman and general could never extenuate or atone."

Neither did she have charity for those who treated women as inferiors. She scourged the "male chauvinists" with gusto:

> What, a woman should be trained physically and her mind left undisciplined? Ah me! it must be the far-off rustle of bloomers heard in the future or the story of a pickle thrown in by a woman for a ballot that has excited the shriekers! Their advice is very good, very salutary, very acceptable; but they will have to begin at the very end, not at the beginning as is the usual case and carry their advice into execution at the bayonet's point. Let them regard the life of a modern woman as a knit stocking which has to be ravelled from the top to the foot before it can be trodden upon with serenity. Let them begin by compelling us to leave our seats in college, at meetings and at the theatre. Next, they must forbid our entrance into society and shut up the rebellious 'society buds.' Now only a few inches of the 'blue stocking' unravelled so far. Another essential measure is to prohibit girls of all ages from attending schools, public, private, or conventual. Of course each step must be taken slowly and the results stamped on our life and on the constitutions of all countries, not the smallest neglect allowed; for that would serve as an outlet for our exuberant spirit to burst forth and drown all creation!

Human growth and development are intimately related to sexuality, but this was not a subject that Helen and Annie discussed. Only a few psychologists knew about Freud's investigations. But one of the most noted, G. Stanley Hall, who later brought Freud to America to deliver the series of lectures at Clark University "Five Lectures on Psycho-Analysis," wrote Annie on April 1, 1901:

> My dear Madam,
>
> I am just completing a book for publication on adolescence in the preparation of which I have found so many things that suggest Miss Keller, that I am going to make bold to ask you a few questions and should be greatly obliged for the answer to any of them, with permission, if you are also willing, to quote in my book. What I am after may be stated as follows.
>
> Was the dawn of puberty at 12 or the early teens marked by any noticeable changes in

(a) Touch? Was it final, was there more propensity to shake or hold hands; love of being petted or stroked; of warm baths; or was there any modification of the dermal consciousness which you or she recall? Sometimes there is great modification of ticklishness, occasionally unwonted fears of insects or aversion to the touch of certain objects or persons; and half imagined fear of dirt. Miss Keller's experience would be particularly interesting because touch with her has had to substitute for the highest sense.

(b) Was there a change in her appetite and tastes; were there new favorites in food, drink, sweetmeats, or new aversions, or in the quantity of food and drink in digestion shown by any eruptions in any part of the body, etc.?

(c) Smell? Was this modified in any of the above ways? Was she affected in any new way by perfumes or had she new associations with the smell of incense, new mown fields, or things offensive, or a sense of personal odors?

(d) Was there any modification of her vocal utterances that could suggest a change of voice, or did the vocal utterances tend to be more or less at this period?

It would be especially interesting to know, what I have never seen, whether there has been anything that suggests spontaneous dreams of sex or any other indication of the awakening of this new consciousness?

I regret to say that I have never met Miss Keller, and I know I am making a great task upon your kindness and time, but I am not without hope that you may be disposed to help me out a little, and if so, I need not say that I shall be very grateful and be pleased to make due acknowledgements.

To this letter there evidently was no response. Not that Helen and Annie were opposed to scientific study of Helen's abilities and development. Professor Joseph Jastrow, another distinguished psychologist of the period, was invited to spend a week at Wrentham with them so that he could observe and talk with Helen. But his approach did not emphasize sexual development in relation to character formation.

Stimulated perhaps by Professor Hall's letter as well as by Professor Jastrow's interest in dreams, she wrote some themes on her dreams. The first she published in *The Story of My Life,* as the ending to that book; the second one (pp. 275–76), more significant, more disagreeable, she did not.

Ah, the pranks that the pixies of Dreamland play on us while we sleep!

Now I rarely sleep without dreaming, but before Miss Sullivan came to me, my dreams were few and far between, devoid of thought or coherency, except those of a purely physical nature. In my dreams something was always falling suddenly and heavily, and at times my nurse seemed to punish me for my unkind treatment of her in the daytime and returned at a usurer's interest my kickings and pinchings. I would wake with a start or struggle frantically to escape from my tormentor. I was very fond of bananas, and one night I dreamed that I found a long string of them in the dining-room, near the cupboard, all peeled and deliciously ripe, and all I had to do was to stand under the string and eat as long as I could eat.

After Miss Sullivan came to me, the more I learned, the oftener I dreamed; but with the making of my mind there came many dreary fancies and vague terrors which troubled my sleep for a long time. I dreaded the darkness and loved the wood-fire. Its warm touch seemed so like a human caress. I really thought it was a sentient being, capable of loving and protecting me. One cold winter night I was alone in my room. Miss Sullivan had put out the light and gone away, thinking I was sound asleep. Suddenly I felt my bed shake, and a wolf seemed to spring on me and snarl in my face. It was only a dream, but I thought it real, and my heart sank within me. I dared not scream, and I dared not stay in bed. Perhaps this was a confused recollection of the story I had heard not long before about Red Riding Hood. At all events I slipped down from the bed and nestled close to the fire which had not flickered out. The instant I felt its warmth, I was reassured, and I sat a long time watching it climb higher and higher in shining waves. At last sleep surprised me, and when Miss Sullivan returned, she found me wrapped in a blanket by the hearth.

Often when I dream, thoughts pass through my mind like cowled shadows, silent and remote, and disappear. Perhaps they are ghosts of thoughts that once inhabited the mind of an ancestor. At other times the things I have learned and the things I have been taught, drop away, as the lizard sheds its skin, and I see my soul as God sees it. There are also rare and beautiful moments when I see and hear in Dreamland. What if in my waking hours a sound should ring through the silent halls of hearing? What if a ray of light should flash through the darkened chambers of my soul? What would happen, I ask many and many a time. Would the bow-and-string tension of life snap? Would the heart overweighted with sudden joy, stop beating for very excess of happiness?

Even at the turn of the century dreams were recognized as significant, just because in sleep the mind was freed from "the watchfulness of self-observation" and the discipline of "what is possible, right or commendable." So the following dream about Teacher Helen found too distressing to publish:

When I am in Dreamland, I generally have the same thoughts, emotions and affections that I have in my waking hours. However, there are some unaccountable contradictions in my dreams. For instance, although I have the strongest, deepest affection for my teacher, yet when she appears to me in my sleep, we quarrel and fling the wildest reproaches at each other. She seizes me by the hand and drags me by main force [towards] I can never decide what—an abyss, a perilous mountain pass or a rushing torrent, whatever in my terror I may imagine. One night we stood at the foot of a stairway that seemed to rise to the very stars, and she commanded me to climb it. I refused stubbornly, declaring that my feet would stumble, and I should be hurled from the dizzying heights. At last, unable to make me yield, she struck a match and flashing it in my face tried to make me swallow it. Still I resisted and remonstrated, and at last I tore myself away from her firm grasp. I rushed blindly in an opposite direction, pursued by my teacher and was just letting myself down into a cellar by a trap-door when I awoke.

Sometimes my teacher changes her conduct strangely and smiles at me; but then she is so far away, I cannot reach her. Once I dreamed that I saw her all robed in white, standing on the brink of Niagara Falls. At first I did not recognize her; but I thought she was an angel. Suddenly she was swept out of sight, and I dashed forward; for I knew she had plunged into the whirlpool. In another instant she rose on

the crest of a huge wave, and with superhuman strength I seized her
and held her fast. In a flash I knew who she was, and my efforts to
save her were most frantic; but in vain. I could not draw her ashore,
I could only prevent her from sinking below the water's surface. It
seemed as if some unseen power were trying to wrest her away from
me, and forgetting our past quarrels I thrust my love between her and
her destruction. At last, mustering all her strength, she threw herself
on the shore; but to my surprise she vanished without appearing to
know who I was, or what danger she had been in; I really thought
she must indeed be an angel, and therefore beyond all harm. Yet I
was at a loss how to account for her ignoring me—that was worse than
all our quarrels put together.

Sir Arthur Mitchell, the distinguished British psychologist, discussed
Helen's dreams in his book *About Dreaming, Laughing and Blushing*
(London, 1905). Teacher had sent him Helen's first dream with the
comment that Helen's dreams were "literary not only in their content
but in the way they phrase themselves to her." She insisted that
Helen's dreams were "strikingly normal" and added the information
that Helen "has never been detected in a wrong act" and that she did
"not believe she has ever committed a wilful conscious wrong deed."
This was too much for Sir Arthur, who noted that "the best people on
earth do bad and wicked things in their dreams." And to him the second dream, the one that Helen had not published in her autobiography, which Teacher also sent him—about her quarrel with Teacher—
seemed more normal. He showed it to an associate of his, who observed, "I do not think that the theory of the non-existence of the
moral sense in dreams could have a more striking exemplification than
the case of the amiable Helen Keller."

Part of the meaning of Helen's unpublished dream is to be found in
some of Helen's statements about Teacher during the years at Radcliffe.
Teacher, she said, was not satisfied with anything less than the highest
honors in every subject Helen studied, yet her work was scarcely at a *cum
laude* level. "She was rent with emotion and overwrought," commented
Helen, "by my apparent lack of zeal in obtaining the *summa.*" This made
Helen feel guilty enough, but her sense of guilt was heightened by her
awareness of the price Teacher was paying in the deterioration of her eyes.
When Teacher was prevailed upon to consult Dr. Morgan, an eminent
ophthalmologist whom Mrs. Hutton had recommended, and he learned

that Annie read to Helen four and five hours daily, he exclaimed, "Oh, my God! That is sheer madness, Miss Sullivan. You must rest your eyes completely if Miss Keller is to finish her course." Helen "hated" books at that moment because of what the required readings were doing to Teacher's eyes, and when Teacher would ask her if she wanted certain passages reread, "I lied and declared that I could recall them. As a matter of fact, they had slipped from my mind." Helen was unable to admit to her conscious mind that sometimes she resented Teacher; it achieved open expression only in her dreams.

She protected Teacher in another way, she admitted in *Teacher*. Despite daily headaches she refused to consult doctors lest Teacher be accused, as she had been at the Cambridge preparatory school, of overworking her. She shook off the headaches "by starving myself for a day or two and eating little or no breakfast." The headaches vanished, only to be succeeded by "anemia and long sieges of neuralgia."

Despite what she called her "affectional" nature, young men seem to have played little part in Helen's undergraduate life. Teacher encouraged her to be with young people, Helen wrote. One of her themes described a Christmas expedition to the shut-up, ice-bound cottage at Lake Wollomonapoag in which she spoke of "the boys huddled together in the room just over the fireplace," while she and Teacher and Phiz, her bull terrier—a gift of classmates—had the "tiny room over the kitchen"; but the boys were not further identified nor their activities dwelt on, except that one of them, after a Christmas Day turkey and plum-pudding dinner prepared by Annie, sat on a tree-trunk and played his banjo.

Their old friend and counsellor Dr. Bell was worried over Helen's failure to see more of young men her age. Helen and Annie visited him at the end of Helen's freshman year at his summer retreat in Nova Scotia, Beinn Bhreagh, "beautiful mountain." The inventor's interest had shifted to aeronautics, and he was building kites in order to develop a stronger space frame for a "flying machine." Helen was given a chance to fly one of Bell's great kites and was almost lifted into the air. "He makes you feel," she said of Bell, "that if you only had a little more time, you too could be an inventor."

The visit to Beinn Bhreagh was an enchanted affair. Bell's daughters Elsie and Daisy were there, along with many other young relatives and the young men who assisted Bell. All the Bells knew the manual language. Several scientists were frequent guests at Beinn Bhreagh, among them the aviation pioneer Samuel Pierport Langley and the astronomer Simon

Newcomb. Helen and Annie tried to follow the discussion, but when the talk seemed to turn the living room into "a scientific congress," Annie, Daisy, Elsie and Helen slipped away to spend the night on the Bell houseboat, eating their supper on a sunset-bathed deck, swimming in the lake by moonlight, and awakening with the dawn.

On the last night of their stay Dr. Bell drew her aside to speak to her alone. He talked of his own youth and how fate had intervened, turning him from his heart's desire to be a musician to experiments with the telephone and now aeronautics. He had not been master of his fate, at least not in the sense of choosing his work. That brought him to Helen. "Your limitations have placed you before the world in an unusual way. You have learned to speak, and I believe you are meant to break down the barriers which separate the deaf from mankind. . . . There are unique tasks waiting for you, an unique woman." Her purpose, said Helen, after graduation, was to "retreat to the country and to write." Circumstances will decide, Bell cautioned her. She should not limit herself "to any particular kind of self-expression. Write, speak, study, do whatever you possibly can. The more you accomplish, the more you will help the deaf everywhere."

Dr. Bell was the oldest friend Helen and Annie had. From the time when he had urged Captain Keller after his visit with little Helen to seek help from Anagnos, he had been their protector, benefactor and counsellor. He was persuaded that Annie was a great teacher and that her work lay in becoming a teacher of teachers of the deaf and the blind. Sometimes in his suggestions of work that Annie might undertake there was the implication that the total dependence of these two gifted women on each other was not altogether best for either of them. His next remarks, uttered after a considerable pause, made Helen intensely uncomfortable.

"It seems to me, Helen, a day must come when love, which is more than friendship, will knock at the door of your heart and demand to be let in."

"What made you think of that?" Helen asked.

"Oh, I often think of your future. To me you are a sweet, desirable young girl, and it is natural to think about love and happiness when we are young."

"I do think of love sometimes," Helen admitted; "but it is like a beautiful flower which I may not touch, but whose fragrance makes the garden a place of delight just the same."

His fingers touched her hand. "Do not think that because you cannot see or hear, you are debarred from the supreme happiness of woman. Heredity is not involved in your case, as it is in so many others."

"Oh, but I am happy, very happy," Helen protested. "I have my teacher and my mother and you, and all kinds of interesting things to do. I really don't care a bit about being married."

"I know," Dr. Bell answered, "but life does strange things to us. You may not always have your mother, and in the nature of things Miss Sullivan may marry, and there may be a barren stretch in your life when you will be very lonely."

"I can't imagine a man wanting to marry me," Helen commented. "I should think it would seem like marrying a statue."

"You are very young," he said, patting her hand. He had long wanted to tell her how he felt about her marrying, he went on. "If a good man should desire to make you his wife, don't let anyone persuade you to forego that happiness because of your peculiar handicap."

"I was glad," Helen wrote in *Midstream,* where twenty-eight years later she reported this conversation with such exactitude, "when Mrs. Bell and Miss Sullivan joined us, and the talk became less personal."

The talk was to have a sequel. John Macy now entered their lives.

XV

Helen Writes a Classic

"Kipling's *Kim* and Helen's book are the two most important contributions to literature which 1902 [has] given us."—Dr. Hale

As a beginning freshman Helen had suffered the anxieties of a young seaman setting forth onto unknown seas. "But now that the first voyage is made, my fears have vanished, and I enter upon my second year with a heart full of joy and hope." So Helen, all of twenty-one and a sophomore, wrote encouragingly to a blind friend of Hitz's about to begin college. But her sense of contentment soon vanished. Those who have a passion for accomplishment and success have a faculty for finding new burdens. Within a few weeks of the semester's opening Helen, urged on by Teacher, had signed a contract with Curtis Bok's *Ladies' Home Journal* to do the story of her life in five installments. The first was to be delivered in time for April publication.

Ever since Mary Mapes Dodge of *St. Nicholas* had suggested that she and Teacher do an autobiographical book, the idea had been simmering. It was as a writer that she thought she might make a contribution to the world. "I have been so long nothing in the world," she wrote in *American Magazine* on the eve of entering Radcliffe, "that I have made up my mind that I must be something before I die.

"The question is what?

"I believe I should love to write. I have always had aspirations in that direction, but who knows if college life will not develop something else in me."

Perhaps it was through Copey that Curtis Bok of the *Ladies' Home Journal* learned that here was a student with a book in her. One day she was called out of her Latin class by Mr. William Alexander, an editor of the magazine, and informed that Mr. Bok wanted to publish her autobiography in monthly installments. Her first impulse was to protest: She was having a difficult time as it was managing her college work. He was ready for that. "You have already written a considerable part of it in your themes," he encouraged her. How did he know that? she exclaimed. It was an editor's business to find out such things, he replied, adding that pulling the themes together into magazine-size installments would not be much of a chore, and Mr. Bok would pay three thousand dollars. "At the moment I thought of nothing but the three thousand dollars," she wrote later. The princely sum inspired euphoria; the agony of composition came later. Copey's willingness to accept the manuscript in lieu of work for the second year's course in composition added to the temptation. She signed and was launched upon an enterprise that would overshadow her work in class and again bring her to the attention of the reading public throughout the world.

She managed at the same time to fulfill all the requirements for a degree as well as do some work for the deaf-blind. Whatever her self-doubts and reproaches, she was a most unusual undergraduate. But it is doubtful that Helen would have taken on the assignment without Teacher's pressure. The latter saw the project as a joint venture in which Helen's "autobiography" would be supplemented by her account of how she had achieved the "miracle." Lenore Smith, a good friend who had learned the manual alphabet in order to be able to speak directly to Helen and who sometimes substituted for Teacher in the classroom, said that the older woman "had a will like iron and when she felt that Helen ought to do a thing she stood by until she did it." That was the case with *The Story of My Life.* By the end of December Helen had written enough to satisfy the *Ladies' Home Journal* that it would get the articles and that they were very good. They sent her a check for one thousand dollars for the first installment. "Was it not good in them to let me have it [for] Christmas? I did not expect the money so soon, or so much of it! They also sent Teacher some money, because they were pleased that she had persuaded me to write the article."

The first article, which described how she had been stricken, her subsequent isolation, Teacher's arrival and the "miracle," was the easiest to write. But subsequent episodes, those that covered her friendships with the great and eminent, the Frost King controversy, the struggle to get into

Radcliffe, proved more difficult to structure into a moving and dramatic narrative. Here Teacher, whose mind moved by flashes and intuitions, was of little help. Lenore Smith rescued them. She and her husband, Philip, who was at the beginning of a distinguished career as a geologist, were often at Helen and Annie's apartment, for among Annie's other aptitudes she was a superb cook, a skill that she had developed in the South under Mrs. Keller's tutelage. As Helen and Annie groaned over their literary travails, Lenore thought John Macy might help. He was a young Harvard instructor, an editor of *Youth's Companion,* who boarded at the same house with them. Lenore asked him to talk to Annie. He had received his A.B. from Harvard in 1899 and his A.M. a year later, majoring in English and philosophy. Macy's undergraduate career was brilliant. He held a Bowditch scholarship for three years, which had been necessary because he came from an old but poor Nantucket whaling family. The first Macy had settled in Nantucket in 1639. As editor-in-chief of the *Harvard Advocate* and as an editor of the *Lampoon* he showed a sense of humor as well as seriousness of purpose. His own short stories dealt with the evils of industrial society, and he had rebelled against physical education classes, which he said were more appropriate to a barracks than to an academic environment. He was elected to the best clubs and was chosen class poet. He had won all sorts of prizes, for translations from the Latin and for an essay on Tolstoy's *Theory of Art,* and had been elected to Phi Beta Kappa. He wrote well and knew the writer's craft.

Both Annie and Helen took to the tall young man in his early twenties, and when they wanted something they were difficult to resist. Soon Macy had learned the manual language and went to work with them. Macy later described the relationship of writer to editor:

> When she began to work at her story, more than a year ago, she set up on the Braille machine about a hundred pages of what she called 'material,' consisting of detached episodes and notes put down as they came to her without definite order or coherent plan. Then she wrote on her typewriter two articles, the first of which is, with a very few minor changes which she made later, the opening chapter, which was published in the April number of *The Journal.*
>
> The second article, as she first wrote it, contained some material that belonged elsewhere in point of time, and lacked the account of her early training in language, which she did not write until it was almost

time for *The Journal* to go to press. Besides these articles she had remaining a pile of material still in Braille. . . .

Then came the task where one who has eyes to see must help her. Miss Sullivan and I read the disconnected passages, put them into chronological order, and counted the words to be sure the articles should be the right length. All this work we did with Miss Keller beside us, referring everything, especially matters of phrasing, to her for revision. We read to her the sentences on each side of a gap and took down the connecting sentences that she supplied.

Her memory of what she had written was astonishing. She remembered whole passages, some of which she had not seen for many weeks, and could tell, before Miss Sullivan had spelled into her hand a half-dozen words of the paragraphs under discussion, where they belonged and what sentences were necessary to make the connections clear.

Macy also served as their agent in the negotiations with the publishers for the best terms. "We are making efforts to get the right publisher for the book," Annie wrote Hitz, "and the young man who is editing it, is I think competent." Despite the enthusiasm of the publisher, Helen had mixed feelings about going on, and even more so about writing a book. "It does not seem worth writing," she wrote Hitz the same day as Annie wrote him, "and only the loving interest shown by my friends gives me courage to go on to the end. I am worried, too, about Teacher. I did not approve of her undertaking to publish the book she told you of, and now her eyes are being taxed to the utmost."

Only twenty-five, Macy negotiated the contract with the aplomb of an old hand in the publishing game. Were Charles Scribner's Sons interested? he wrote that publishing house on February 12, 1902. They were, but asked to see the manuscript, or part of it. Macy replied on the eighteenth:

Of course, if the whole book were now in manuscript, we could submit it to you and get your decision. But some of Miss Keller's work will not be done for several weeks: some of the last of her autobiography she will not put in final shape until it is quite necessary for Mr. Bok to have it. Moreover, the second part of the book, selections from journals and letters (perhaps 30,000 words) and the third part, 'As Others See Her,' in which I shall set forth all that has not been fully covered in the other two parts, will take two months to prepare and cannot be done until we come to terms with our publisher. . . .

I should be glad, therefore, if you would say what you can about the matter of royalties. As I said, Miss Sullivan will make the ultimate decision on the various offers which we are receiving from publishers. . . .

The choice narrowed down to the Century Company and Doubleday Page, both then located on Union Square in New York City. Doubleday offered a sliding scale of royalties: 10 percent on the first 2,500 copies sold; 12 1/2 percent on the second 2,500; 15 percent on the next 10,000 and 20 percent on all sold above 25,000. In addition they proposed to issue an Edition de Luxe and to arrange for publication in London and for translation rights. "As an alternative proposition," Walter Hines Page wrote Macy, "we should be willing to offer 15 percent royalty on the retail price on the trade edition from the beginning to the end; but if the book is successful, as we hope it will be, the sliding scale of royalties will be more profitable to Miss Keller." Century offered a flat 15 percent, asserting that except for popular novels, a sliding scale did not work to the advantage of authors. If Macy wanted something more, the Century people said they were willing to consider it, but Page had favorably impressed the young man, and on March 17 he told him to draw up the contract and prepare to meet with Miss Sullivan. Page was a man of affairs, and he had to put off the meeting because of Nicholas Murray Butler's inauguration as President of Columbia University and then because of a trip south as a member of the General Education Board. "But I take it that apart from the pleasure of seeing you and Miss Keller, there is no business that needs attention which cannot be attended to in Cambridge a little later," he wrote Miss Sullivan. He was enchanted with the installment in the *Journal*. "I know of nothing in the world more interesting. How charmingly and simply she writes it! . . . I congratulate you, too, on Mr. Macy's enthusiasm for it and his clear grasp and good management of the whole thing. He spent one evening with me when he was here, and his work in connection with it seemed to us all admirably laid out." On April 28 the contract was signed, Page for Doubleday on one side, Helen, Annie and Macy on the other.

The public reception of the installments in the *Journal* (they ran from April through August) was little short of lyrical. The first article made him weep, Dr. Hale wrote Helen, and at the end of the series he still was enthusiastic. The author of *The Man Without a Country* was himself a considerable stylist, and it meant a great deal to Helen to have him write, "They are very simply written, and that generally means very well written," and he would tell the *Chicago Post* at the end of the year that "Kipling's *Kim* and Helen's book are the two most important contributions to literature which 1902 [has] given us."

Annie prodded Helen, and John prodded Annie. "We are well but *busy busy busy,*" Annie advised Hitz. "Last week we got off about five thousand words to the Journal. . . ." The businesslike influence of Macy was visible. Would Hitz please make the wife of the superintendent of an institution for the deaf "understand in a polite way that Helen is receiving about fifteen cents a word for the sort of material she is asking for her Art Class"?

The *Journal* series was so universally acclaimed that Bok wanted more. He commissioned Macy to write two articles on "Helen Keller as She Really Is," which would supplement Helen's account of her education with an account of Annie's part in it. Suddenly Annie turned shy. Why is unclear. She had wanted the book written. She aspired to write. Perhaps Macy's competence, for which she was increasingly grateful, also triggered her own insecurity. She knew she had many enemies who loved Helen but would leap at a chance to tear her apart. Then there was the deep secret of the Tewksbury almshouse, which not even Helen and John knew about. She was especially reluctant to have her letters to Mrs. Hopkins published or any description of her childhood and youth before arriving in Tuscumbia. "I *know* that the public wants to know more about you than Miss Keller will tell in her articles or Mr. Macy in his," Bok wrote her on May 12, 1902. "Now I think you can feel safe in the hands of Mr. Macy and ourselves in what shall be said, and I simply want to ask your permission to this plan: That you give Mr. Macy permission to write what we desire and use his full discretion in the matter. Surely you can trust him to write tactfully and delicately about you. . . ." He would add an editor's note, Bok assured her, "that it is done even now under your protest. . . ." In its final form *The Story of My Life* included Helen's own story, a selection of Helen's letters and the supplementary account of Helen's education written by Macy that included many of the letters that Annie had written Mrs. Hopkins, cleaned up for spelling and grammar and woven together so as to make a running account. There was only the vaguest reference to Annie's beginnings in Feeding Hills and none to Tewksbury.

"Our literary work is nearly done," Helen relievedly wrote Hitz. "We have now more of John, and less of Mr. Macy, the editor. The book was sent off on the 24th of November, and we look for the proofs every day. . . . I must tell you that the letters which Teacher wrote to Mrs. Hopkins when she began to teach me, are to be published in the book. The spelling has been corrected, and the grammar fixed up, and I know you will think them as wonderful as I do. They show the inborn wisdom and courage with which Teacher went to her task. They also tell a great deal about your naughty monkey of a 'Tochter,' that I have entirely forgotten, and that made me feel, when I heard it, as if I were making the acquaintance of quite another self."

The rest of the letter was devoted to the problems they were having with getting coal because of the coal strike, their loss of a maid because the house was so cold, and her pleasure in Dr. Josiah Royce's course in philosophy. But Hitz should not worry that she might be weaned away from Swedenborgianism. "In Dr. Royce's course I am studying the 'history of human thought,' not one branch of philosophy in particular, or for the sake of being converted; so there is little danger, as you seem to think, of my being misled by the speculations of those 'wise men.' I have now come to the schools that were formed immediately after Socrates's death. I have read the 'Apology,' 'Phaedo,' and several of Plato's Socratic dialogues. They are so interesting, that I can scarcely shut the book to take up other lessons." She was also gathering material for a long thesis on Peele's *The Love of King David and Fair Bethsabe* for the course in Elizabethan literature for Dr. William A. Neilson. She was "copying the play in Braille, so that I can have it at my finger-ends while I write."

The book appeared in March 1903. Helen had a dinner party for the Cambridge group that had helped her in its preparation. They were eight in all: Helen, Annie and John; the Philip Smiths; two Harvard instructors, Dr. Arthur W. Ryder, a Sanskrit scholar, and Dr. Neilson, both of whom had read proof; and a friend of John's, C.F.C. Arensberg, a lawyer who had read and criticized the work in manuscript. At each seat there was a copy of the book with a few words of dedication in Helen's own hand. Dr. Neilson's made play with his reputation as an editor of Shakespeare. In reading proof he had borne down on the spelling and punctuation, so Helen wrote on the flyleaf of his copy: "To Dr. Neilson, who with his wise judgment and kindly eye has established the spelling in another great

English classic." Arensberg's flyleaf read "To Carl—who criticized the book in the making and so helped make it."

The book was an instant critical success, its appearance attended by long stories in the news columns and leading reviews everywhere. But it did not become the runaway best-seller that Page and the authors had anticipated. The sliding scale of royalties worked to the authors' disadvantage, since in the first two years the total sales did not reach ten thousand. An unhappy Macy badgered Page to do more for the book. The future ambassador to the Court of St. James had to use all his diplomatic skill to soothe Helen's discontented representative: "[W]hen, as I say, we are putting our whole strength on this book and have advertised it, perhaps, too much, why do you jump right down, in the face of a very favorable report, it seems to me, and complain? And the book goes well—is going —will go—is but starting in fact." The second royalty report, for the six months ending February 1, 1904, showed sales of 3,500. *"The Story of My Life* is only beginning its existence," Page consoled Macy. "It is going to keep on and on and on, and there is no book I feel prouder of." And then in a postscript he inquired, "What is the next book Miss Keller ought to do?"

Gilder reviewed the book in *The Century* belatedly, perhaps out of chagrin that the book had not gone to him; but what he wrote was generous indeed. He called the volume "unique in the world's literature" for its graphic portrayal of Helen's delivery from isolation and darkness, and since "by good fortune her teacher proved to be a writer of precision and grace . . . the double narrative constitutes an absorbing presentation of an astonishing experience." Dr. Joseph Jastrow, the psychologist, also remarked in *The Dial* on the value of Miss Sullivan's letters, which "indicate an appreciation of the psychological and educational problems involved in bringing up a bright but sightless and silent child, which one would have expected from the result, but which it is most assuring to read in print as a contemporaneous record." Nevertheless, "the book in the main is Helen Keller's book, and the interest in her is a genuine interest in her personality," and "the most sincere testimony to the inherent value of her narrative is that in reading it one is often more engrossed by the sentiment and the vigor of what is said than by the peculiar condition of the writer." Some reviewers were struck by its style—"full of force, individuality and charm," wrote the *San Francisco Chronicle.* "It seems to be the style of a practiced writer rather than that of a college girl." "[A]n instinctive stylist," wrote *The Churchman;* and a very different type of publication, *The Army and Navy Register,* observed that Helen told her story "with a surprising facility of expression." *The Congregationalist* was relieved to find an autobiography that was "wholly free from morbid self-consciousness," and *The Literary Digest* also remarked on the absence of "morbidness or self-pity."

Equally fulsome acclaim greeted publication of the book in England by Hodder and Stoughton. One review was so lavish that John in reading it to Helen suggested that she must have submitted it herself. The British press discreetly noted Queen Victoria's interest in Helen from the time that Dr. Bell had sent her a copy of the Volta Bureau's *Souvenir I;* and later, when Bishop Phillips Brooks had called upon her, she had expressed a wish to see Helen if she should visit England. The London press also noted that the Duke of Westminster had "asked Mrs. Pierpont Morgan to procure for him a picture of Miss Keller and Miss Sullivan, her teacher, and it is said the Duke of Westminster always kept the picture on his desk." The interest in Helen of queen, duke and commoner is easily understood, for as one reviewer noted, her courage and tenacity to make the best of herself "in the face of obstacles that seem overwhelming, makes one ashamed of the ordinary excuses which are offered for failure to make the best of one's opportunities."

As a good editor Macy had known that to disarm the jealous and the sceptical, the book had to deal with the "Frost King" affair. Helen and Annie not only gave their version, but Margaret Canby's story and Helen's rendition of it were printed in adjoining columns. Macy had even gone to see Anagnos in February to inform him of the proposed book and solicit his cooperation. Anagnos had been ready to do so—short, however, of turning over his personal notes. But the offer led to nothing, perhaps because Anagnos and his Perkins friends were outraged by what they read in the *Journal,* with its studied minimization of the role that the director and the Institution had played in Helen's education. In November Macy addressed a formal request to Anagnos, a letter that was "witnessed" by Arensberg, stating that it was Miss Sullivan's wish that everyone concerned with Helen's education should be given an opportunity to have their say. "I ask you therefore whether there is anything you can send to me for publication, or for my guidance in preparing my part of the book." He wrote a similar letter to Gilman. Neither replied. A week later Macy wrote Anagnos again, saying that the publishers were pressing him for the manuscript and that as its editor "I cannot be satisfied until I have made an effort to find out from everybody who has known her what at the present time his views are of the nature of her mind and the manner in which she has been educated."

The next day Anagnos did reply. He had nothing to send Macy "for addition to your account of Helen Keller's life and education. I must take this opportunity, however, of saying that Helen in her own story, makes an erroneous statement in regard to the investigation which took place in this institution." Then he gave his version, which has already been quoted in the account of the "Frost King" affair.* His letter ended with a warning: "Whether due credit will be given to the institution and its teachers for laying the foundation of Helen's education or not, it is entirely immaterial to us, but I do hope that any facts relating to her case will not be distorted and misrepresented as to make it necessary for me to make them public in their correct form at some future day."

Macy read Anagnos's letter to Helen and wrote the director again: "She has written for her book an additional statement embodying the substance of your letter. She does not believe, however, that she ever said before the investigation that Miss Canby's story or any other story like it had been read to her." Macy pressed this last point, asking nine specific questions to elicit what basis Anagnos had for asserting that Helen had admitted the Canby story had been read to her, ending, "Finally, whom, if anybody, do you hold guilty of intention to deceive, Miss Sullivan, Helen Keller, or both?" Anagnos retreated somewhat. He had not been persuaded at the time that the Canby story had been read to Helen, he wrote. That was why he had set up an investigating committee and that was why he had "felt justified in throwing the influence of my vote in Helen's favor." His sole purpose in writing now, he went on, "has been to point out that Helen's statement concerning the attitude of the majority of the members of the investigating committee toward her was incorrect. This I was desirous of doing for the sake of the truth and in justice to those of Helen's friends who stood by her during the investigation. I was very glad to learn through your letter that she has corrected her misunderstanding." As to whether he personally now thought that Helen had known that Miss Canby's story had been read to her, whether and when he had changed his opinion, and whom he held guilty of deception, "as they concern me personally, I must decline to pursue the subject further."

Three of Helen's friends—Mark Twain, Dr. Bell and Gilder—praised

*See page 132.

Annie Sullivan's contribution. They also fastened on the book's account of the "Frost King" affair to make some pungent comments on the issue of plagiarism, and who was better qualified to bear witness to the thin line between creativity and imitation? Mark Twain wrote:

> I must steal half a moment from my work to say how glad I am to have your book and how highly I value it, both for its own sake and as a remembrance of an affectionate friendship which has subsisted between us for nine years without a break and without a single act of violence that I can call to mind. I suppose there is nothing like it in heaven; and not likely to be, until we get there and show off. I often think of it with longing, and how they'll say, 'there they come—sit down in front!' I am practising with a tin halo. You do the same. I was at Henry Rogers's last night, and of course we talked of you. He is not at all well—you will not like to hear that; but like you and me, he is just as lovely as ever.
>
> I am charmed with your book—enchanted. You are a wonderful creature, the most wonderful in the world—you and your other half together—Miss Sullivan, I mean, for it took the pair of you to make a complete and perfect whole. How she stands out in her letters! her brilliancy, penetration, originality, wisdom, character, and the fine literary competencies of her pen—they are all there. . . .

Mark Twain's remarks on plagiarism have already been quoted in Chapter VIII. (See page 146.)

"We all do what Helen did," Dr. Bell wrote Annie:

> Our most original compositions are composed exclusively of expressions derived from others. The fact that the language presented to Helen was in the early days, so largely taken from books, has enabled us in many cases to trace the origin of her expressions but they are nonetheless original with Helen for all that. We do the very same thing. Our forms of expression are copied— *verbatim et literatim*—in our earlier years from the expressions of others which we have heard in childhood. It is difficult for us to trace the origin of our expressions because the language addressed to us in infancy has been given by word of mouth, and not permanently recorded in books so that investigators—being

unable to examine the printed records of the language addressed to us in childhood—are unable to charge us with plagiarism. We are all of us, however, nevertheless unconscious plagiarists, especially in childhood. As we grow older and read books the language we absorb through the eye, unconsciously affects our style. Books however do not affect our language to the same extent that they affected Helen because our habits of language, have already been formed before we come to read books. Nevertheless our style IS affected, hence the very great importance of selecting with care, the kinds of books to be read by children.

Intrigued anew as Bell was by the problems of originality and the acquisition of language, it was Annie's letters that seized hold of him and reconfirmed his sense that she was a gifted, original teacher.

Why in the world did you not tell us about those letters to Mrs. Hopkins, when we were preparing the Volta Bureau souvenirs; they are of the greatest value and importance, and contain internal evidence of the fact that you were entirely wrong when you gave us the idea that you proceeded without method in the education of Helen, and only acted on the spur of the moment, in everything you did. These letters to Mrs. Hopkins will become a standard, the principles that guided you in the early education of Helen are of the greatest importance to all teachers. . . .

Now what I want to impress upon you is this:—It is your duty to use your brilliant abilities as a teacher FOR THE BENEFIT OF OTHER TEACHERS.

I don't want to bother you with this thought too much at the present time; but as soon as Helen has finished Radcliffe College, I AM GOING FOR YOU.

You must be placed in a position to impress your ideas upon other teachers. YOU MUST TRAIN TEACHERS so that the deaf as a whole may get the benefit of your instruction. . . .

Gilder's letter to Annie, whom he congratulated on the "directness, clarity and restrained fervor" of her style, took Mark Twain's and Bell's view of plagiarism:

There is a sonnet in my own *New Day* that seems to be re-written from
Mrs. Browning. I myself came upon the resemblance. I could not
remember having read it at all; my mind had no recollection of it—
but surely I had read all the sonnets some time before. Yet for the
life of me I cannot tell now what *her* sonnet had to do with mine, if
it had anything at all to do with it! I thought of omitting it, but
resolved to retain it, after finding an old English lyric containing the
same thought; which lyric, of course, out-dated both Mrs. Browning
and myself.

Gilder considered the book one of

the most remarkable of modern times. . . . It would be less interesting
and important if it contained only Helen's part, as exquisite as that
is; —the supplementing of hers by her teacher's narrative makes a
dramatic form, like one of Browning's, —the story of a soul told by
two. . . . My dear Miss Sullivan, I cannot tell you how touched, how
moved, I was by your account, —and by nothing more deeply than
your description of your first meeting with Helen—when she
'rushed' at you with such force as almost to throw you down. I think
your two souls rushed there together. It would take a Blake to picture
that significant scene.

Gilder saw the book as a milestone in Helen's development as a writer.
Hereafter her writing should be at the same time more scientific and more
imaginative. "If she were as others, some times her writing might be called
sentimental—but it does not strike me as such—what might be sentimental
in others is in her the joy in a new world—a world of things, of ideas, of
language, of literature. . . . Helen's writings from this time forward are
likely to partake more and more of the character of literature. I can
imagine her writing an allegory supplied by the 'journey' of her own
'mind.' I can imagine her writing things about *her* world that will surpass
in beauty all she has yet done. . . . If there is any way in which I can serve
her and you I hope you will call upon me."

Despite the views of men like Mark Twain and Bell, the issue of Helen's
originality persisted. Some of Macy's friends charged that he had done
most of the book. His invariable reply was, "You are just the person who
needs to read the book." Much more serious was the review in *The Nation.*
Dr. Hale called the magazine "sulky and crusty," not like the London

Nation, which is "the organ of the philanthropic liberals." But the New York *Nation* was taken seriously, and the review was reprinted in the *New York Post.* "All her knowledge is hearsay knowledge," wrote the reviewer, "her very sensations are for the most part vicarious, and yet she writes of things beyond her powers of perception with the assurance of one who has verified every word." The book therefore lacked "literary veracity." The problem was rooted in Miss Keller's effort to be like other people. "If it could have been brought home to her that such likeness in her case could be attained only by the sacrifice of truth; if she could only realize that it is better to be one's self, however limited and afflicted, than the best imitation of somebody else that could be achieved! . . . One resents the pages of second-hand description of natural objects, when what one wants is a sincere account of the attitude, the natural attitude towards life of one whose eyes and ears are sealed."

Macy replied in a three-column letter to the *Boston Evening Transcript:* "It leaves the impression that her autobiography is borrowed knowledge and borrowed observation and so perversely misses the very lesson of the book. The one hundred and forty pages of her story are packed with individual experiences, much of which no one else in the world but Miss Keller ever possessed or ever put into words." The *Nation* critic was "guilty of a kind of arrogance of his senses. He thinks that a blind person cannot know what we know, or imagine we know, through our eyes and ears. Worse than that, this critic thinks he knows what only a deaf-blind person can know—that is, her attitude toward life." The alleged "mistake" with which the critic charged Helen, of trying to be like other people, was on the contrary "the foundation of her education as a human being. . . . Can one read her book through and not know that if she had not tried to be like other people, if her teacher had not made her try, we should never have heard of her? . . . The writer has missed Helen's life. No wonder he has missed the truth in her story of her life."

Helen's answer was to compare her dilemma upon being stricken to that of a shipwrecked sailor cast upon on a strange island

> where the inhabitants speak a language unknown to him, and their experiences are unlike anything he has known. I was one, they were many, there was no chance of compromise. I must learn to see with their eyes, to hear with their ears, to think in their language, and I bent all my energies to the task. . . . Had it occurred to me to build a little tower of Babel for myself and others shipwrecked like me, do

you think you would have scaled my castle wall or ventured to communicate with my dumb hieroglyphics? Should you have thought it worthwhile to find out what kind of ideas the silent, sightless inhabitants of that tower had originated in their isolation from the rest of mankind? . . . I suspect that if I had confined myself strictly to that which I knew of my own observation, without mingling it with derived knowledge, my critic would have understood me as little as he probably does the Chinese.

The relationship of sense impoverishment to the larger powers of the mind and imagination has been patiently and painstakingly investigated during the twentieth century.* Contemporary psychological thought at the time of the publication of Helen's book sharply disagreed with the implications of the *Nation* reviewer. Hitz in a paper in the *American Anthropologist* cited John Dewey, already an eminent psychologist associated with Chicago University. Dewey felt that "in certain phases of the imaginative faculty they [the blind-deaf] *excel* all others" and, indeed, there was a danger of "laying too much stress upon *sense* perception" in the education of a child. He had found that "the wonderful and varied imagery which these minds in silence and darkness have created for themselves stands as a perpetual challenge to those teachers who are encouraging their pupils to revel in the endless panorama of sense perception. It is not necessary to make our pupils blind-deaf, but it may be well sometimes to require them to shut their eyes and ears, if need be, and think."

A Viennese psychologist, Professor Dr. W. Jerusalem, used the cases of Helen Keller, Laura Bridgman and a European girl, Marie Heurtin, to illustrate that the sense of touch and muscular motor sensations by themselves could be "a gateway to mental conceptions. . . . We can no longer deny the fact that sense perceptions serve only as *auslösende Reize* (releasing stimulants), by means of which the center of power of our soul life is awakened." For Professor McDougall, an outstanding American psychologist, Helen's case illustrated that "in spite of continued blindness and deafness, the child grew up to be a woman of high intelligence and refined moral sensibilities, revealed in her many literary compositions. The last fact shows clearly that the higher powers of the mind can attain a high development on the basis of tactual and manipulatory abilities, and that these abilities can serve as the basis of a system of symbols of meanings

*(See Chapter XXXII, "The Dupe of Words.")

hardly, if at all, less rich than is commonly developed from the basis of visual, auditory, and articulatory abilities."

Publication of *The Story of My Life* revived another controversy relating to Annie and Helen—which one was the "genius"? Dr. Neilson, their soft-spoken Scotch friend, made the point forcefully in his review of the book: "For if genius is to be spoken of here at all, it is when we turn to the other heroine of the book, her teacher, Miss Sullivan." The week-by-week record in the letters to Mrs. Hopkins "of a great experiment, carried out almost singlehanded by a young girl with no equipment but a fair education and an intuition amounting to genius, holds one spell-bound. Nowhere does one read of a process so nearly approaching the creation of a soul."

"The lives of teacher and pupil are inseparable," Macy wrote in his first article for the *Journal* on "Helen Keller As She Really Is," and then in a passage that he would omit from *The Story of My Life* he paid his respects to Anagnos and Gilman in underscoring the uniqueness of Annie's contribution to Helen:

> Not one person in all the world, even of those who could write bigger pamphlets on the subject than Miss Sullivan could have taken her place. Strange that the two or three men who at different times have thought they could 'direct' Helen Keller's education, better than Miss Sullivan should have failed to understand—and they knew so much about the science of teaching—that the unanalyzable kinship between these two women is the foundation of Helen Keller's career.
>
> . . . Let me give an example from my own experience of what I mean by saying that Miss Sullivan is the only person who can be the best interpreter between Miss Keller and the world of people and books. I happen to know more about two or three subjects Miss Keller is studying in college than either she or Miss Sullivan. I have taught them and know how they should be presented to the ordinary student. It happens, too, that I can use the manual alphabet with fair facility, and have talked much with Miss Keller about her college work and her articles for *The Journal.* Yet if I should try to take Miss Sullivan's place during the routine of one day's studying, I should be quite useless. Miss Sullivan's skill in presenting material, some of which she does not try to retain herself, but allows to pass through her to the busy fingers of her pupil; her instinct in striking out the

inessential; her feeling, which is now a matter of long experience, for
just the turn of thought that Miss Keller needs at the moment—all
this is quite beyond me and, I believe, beyond anybody else. Miss
Sullivan has the knack of teaching. Mr. Hitz of the Volta Bureau, cuts
the Gordian knot with a very short solution. 'Miss Sullivan is a genius.'

Such claims brought William Wade, that self-educated philanthropist
from Western Pennsylvania, roaring back into the arena. He had made up
with Helen. He visited her in Cambridge and undertook to have all the
books that she needed in her college courses copied for her in Braille. The
reunion was a happy one for both. "I still feel the warm pressure of his
hand when he bade me goodbye, saying, 'Never forget me, Helen. Always write to me when I can help you.'"

But his reconciliation with Helen did not keep him from upbraiding
Macy and Neilson for suggesting that Annie's methods rather than Helen
herself were the miracle:

> It is useless to discuss with you and Dr. Neilson whether Miss Sullivan
> is a 'strikingly original and detached discoverer.' She may be to you,
> who know nothing of other teachers of the blind-deaf, or of other
> such pupils. To me, knowing more or less of all such teachers, and
> how they did their work, I know that all used the same methods as
> Miss S., and one of the ablest of them says that Miss S naturally and
> inevitably fell into those methods. As both you and Dr. Neilson dwell
> heavily on Miss S's letters and on her proceeding on the conception
> that normal children learn by imitation, I suppose this is one of your
> 'discoveries,' while I know that every teacher of the blind-deaf has
> gone on exactly that idea from Dr. Howe down. You ask 'what
> difference does it make?' Just this—you (plural) try unconsciously to
> make the education of the blind-deaf even a more miraculous feat
> than the public now believe it. I care more for the welfare of the class
> at large than I do even for Helen and Miss Sullivan, and through thick
> and thin, I will fight for the principle that any thoroughly good
> teacher can do all for an equivalent pupil that Miss Sullivan did for
> Helen. . . .

Wade saw Miss Sullivan's "noblest merit in her self-sacrifice, devotion,
etc., as those [qualities] did the work." Let discussions of her "genius,"

he added, "be hanged." Annie's "self-sacrifice" was what had impressed the reviewer for the *New York Sun,* and he put it more emphatically:

> It is perhaps worth reminding the readers that the wonderful feat of drawing Helen Keller out of her hopeless darkness was only accomplished by sacrificing for it another woman's whole life, and if ever the attempt is made in another similar case, it must be at the same cost.

Annie herself, in a haunting fragment that she dashed off in one of those moments when she thought she, too, might be a writer, later said:

> I have never known the deep joy of complete surrender to my own, I cannot say genius since I have not that immortal gift of the gods . . . but to my individual bent or powers. I have been compelled to pour myself into the spirit of another and to find satisfaction in the music of an instrument not my own and to contribute always to the mastery of that instrument by another.

The Story of My Life has, as Page predicted, become a classic. Annie's letters to Mrs. Hopkins continue to astonish educators and parents with their deep insights into children's ways of learning. "No one else," wrote Josh Greenfield, author of *A Place for Noah,* in the Book-of-the-Month Club News, "has written more clearly and concisely about the nitty-gritty of the educational processes involved in teaching and learning language." But it is Helen's story, as she told it in the first third of the book, that has had a universal appeal. For that story bears witness to what the human spirit can accomplish in the face of the most formidable obstacles. "Tell her this," Dr. Maria Montessori said to Annie in 1915, "that my children [in the House of Childhood] understand her: they know the triumph of the soul over difficulties. But the children of the future, the men of the future, will understand even better than men do now, for they will be liberated and will know how the spirit can prevail over the senses."

XVI

A Triumph Dearly Bought

"Philosophy is the history of a deaf-blind person writ large."

Publication of *The Story of My Life* had many consequences—on their finances, on their relationship to one another, on the shaping of their careers. For the first time since Spaulding's death, Helen and Annie had sufficient money to spend freely, and while they were not extravagant, they began to indulge a taste for expensive clothes, good design in house furnishings, a spacious house in the country and traveling in comfort. Teacher in particular, who had always been compelled to curb her flair for stylish living, was at last able to give it its head.

John Macy became an increasingly important part of their lives. Even before the manuscript had been sent off to the publishers he had begun to help Helen with her studies and to concern himself with Teacher's health. On his insistence they journeyed up to Wolfeboro, New Hampshire, where old Dr. Bradford, who had restored Teacher's sight during her years at Perkins, lived in retirement. He was the only ophthalmologist in whom she had any confidence: "He told her she must wear glasses, and that she should have worn them three years ago, and he urged her to use her eyes less." The trip and Teacher's overburdened eyes caused Helen to fall behind in her reading and her work on the Peele thesis. "Indeed, without John's assistance, I fear we could not have managed it. . . ." He was becoming indispensable. "I do not know what we should do without John," she wrote Hitz. "He is most kind and helpful. He helps me in

Philosophy and looks up what I want to know in other subjects; so Teacher does not have to use her eyes half as much as she did last year.''

Another health scare came at the beginning of 1903. Teacher's leg joints pained her so that she was scarcely able to walk without stumbling. John insisted that she go to a Boston foot specialist. The latter said that he had to operate at once. Teacher refused. The operation would have to wait until Helen finished college. "Miss Sullivan, your health is more important than Helen Keller's education," the doctor admonished, but agreed to wait until Helen finished her midyear examinations. He performed the operation in their apartment, for they now lived at 72 Dana Street in Cambridge, and Teacher was under ether for three hours. The postoperative pain "was something terrible at first," and almost as difficult for Helen, who despite the kindness and cheeriness of the nurse was being deprived of access to the world around her. But John was in and out, as were the Phil Smiths, and after a week Teacher was able to get up and at the end of the month to go out.

Easter they spent in Wrentham. "Lenore and Phil Smith stayed with us, and John came down for the night as often as he could." The fact was that John, although ten years younger than Annie, had fallen in love with her, and she with him. . . . Helen, a lovely figure of a woman, only twenty-two, would have seemed a more likely partner for the twenty-six-year-old John, but Annie had what the Theodore Roosevelts called "the root of the matter" in her in a way that the more sentimental Helen lacked. Annie had, said the Phil Smiths, a "fascination" for men. She was saucy, droll, determined, with a flawless eye for essentials. "She has humor, buoyancy, exhaustless nervous energy," Macy testified in his article on "Helen Keller as She Really Is." "He is really very good," Helen confided to Hitz in April 1903. "He reads to me every chance he has, especially in Shakespeare's plays, because the print is so fine it hurts Teacher's eyes. He also reads in English literature and makes very helpful suggestions. If he only remains as considerate and kind as he now is, (and I am sure he will) Teacher's happiness is safe and my longing for her peace is satisfied." He also drank a good deal, but, according to Dr. Neilson, another intimate of theirs who was very fond of "Jack," was never the worse for it, at least during those first years.

A few of Annie's love letters to John have survived. They show the strength of her passion and the same flair for vivid and intense expression that made her letters to Mrs. Hopkins such a sensation. The first letter admits to a sense of liberation from the self-effacement of a lifetime, including even the commitment to Helen. It was dated July 2, 1902, six months after Macy appeared on the scene.

Dearest Heart:

I was very sorry to say good-by to you yesterday after the pleasant hours we spent together. The sense of being at home comes to me so deeply when I am near you that I am always a little shivery when you leave me, as if the spirit of death shut his wings over me, but the next moment the thought of your love for me brings a rush of life back to my heart.

The house seemed very empty when I got home in spite of the fact that it held the dearest thing in all the world to me until a few months ago—dear, dear Helen. The evening was very beautiful and I took Mrs. Ferreri* and Helen out in the canoe. They talked and I thought. Later after every one had gone to bed I went out on the porch to say good-night to the fragrant, beautiful world lying so quietly under the pines. There was only the sound of one bird talking in his sleep to break the stillness. The lake had lost the glow that earlier in the evening had made it so alluring and looked white and peaceful in the twilight. Somehow, I felt out of sympathy with the calm loveliness of the night. My heart was hot and impatient—impatient because the repression and self-effacement of a life-time—and my life seems a century long as I look back upon it—have not stilled its passionate unrest. I sat a long time thinking of you and trying to find a reason for your love for me. How wonderful it is! And how impossible to understand! Love is the very essence of life itself. Reason has nothing to do with it! It is above all things and stronger! For one long moment I gave myself up to the supremest happiness—the certainty of a love so strong that fate had no dominion over it and in that moment all the shadows of life became beautiful realities.

Then I groped and stumbled my way back to earth again—the dreary flat earth where real things are seldom beautiful.

---

*G. Ferreri of Rome, a professor of pedagogy and psychology. In an article on Helen Keller, translated and published in *The Association Review,* Mrs. Ferreri wrote that: "It was then arranged that she should have Italian, and that I should be her teacher. Thus it came about that during the two months of July and August [1902], I had the pleasure and satisfaction of conversing every day with Helen Keller, and of giving her instruction in the Italian language."

Dearest—this is the first letter I have written to you and I am afraid I have said things in it which you will not like. You will say that we have no right to test present happiness by harping on possible sorrow. It is because your love is so dear to me beyond all dreams of dearness that I rebel against the obstacles the years have built up between us. But you will not leave off loving me will you—not for a long time at least. . . .

I kiss you my own John and I love you, I love you, I love *you*

Nan

The second letter that we have from Annie to Macy, dated February 28 (1903) shows a down-to-earth quality and spiciness that are in sharp contrast to Helen's intense spirituality and piety. In this case, Professor Lyman Kittredge, the eminent Shakespearian scholar, is the butt of her caustic wit, but it was symptomatic of her general scorn of the academic enterprise. But the letter tells us more. Her love for Macy had made her impatient with the classroom routine. Restlessness was stirring again, and she was groping for escape—not from Helen, but from a college grind that she found trivial and irrelevant. The letter's salutation was quite risky, one would have thought, for an older woman to use with a young lover. She loved John, but she already was mothering him. The disparity in their ages troubled her and was one of the reasons she hesitated to marry him:

My own dear little Johnny:

I miss you very much. I suppose I should say, in the language of lovers, I think of you oftener than I breathe; but I don't, at least not consciously, though it's inconceivable, isn't it, that one may so live in her lover that he becomes a part of the substance of her thoughts.

I'm lonely, but not utterly cast down, thanks to Carl [Arensberg] who remembers me in the days of my bereavement. Still there are many lonely hours when I move with the careless majesty of a sometime goddess amid the ruins of joys that have been.

Haven't you had enough of New York? Idling about clubs and going to the opera isn't so very much fun, is it? Aren't you longing to come back to your twelve or fifteen hours of work every day—and Me?

I'm going to college this week. Just think. I was idle nearly four weeks! So far I haven't been able to take up my work in good earnest. My eyes refuse to read, and my mind won't think. It's full of impatience to do things; but nothing comes of it. I don't know when this imbecility will cease. Perhaps it's the result of my having lost certain customary visits—and other things.

I must confess to you the cruel conviction that is growing upon me, (I know I shall never have your scholarly sympathy) that I can't much longer bear up under the Kittredge's word cannonade. They talk of victims of war, of epidemics; but alas, who remembers the battlefields of education? Three times a week I drink in desperation at every pore, until I feel—but I smell a mixed metaphor, and Shakespeare, it seems, has a 'corner' on them. I wish he had a 'corner' on the interpretation of his works. It costs one nothing to wish for much —I wish you were here! I've convinced myself deeply once and for all of one thing; but I don't think it's advisable to tell you my convictions. That's all.

Nan

Apart from Macy's collaboration with Annie and Helen, his chief enterprise at the moment was as an associate editor of *Youth's Companion* and his own writing—poetry and literary criticism. His first book, *Edgar Allan Poe,* would appear in 1907. He lived in Boston, had a large circle of friends, was already a robust drinker; but the emotional center of his life was with Annie and Helen.

The summer of 1903 was again spent at Wrentham. Helen's mother joined them. "She went everywhere with us, walking, driving and taking now and then a day's 'ride' on the electrics," Helen wrote Hitz. Her Southern courtesy and general helpfulness conquered everyone. "All my friends who met her were enthusiastic, and I loved to hear what they said about her." With the agony of the book over, they had a gay summer, entertaining eighty-one guests, according to their count, including Mrs. Hopkins, several of Helen's classmates, and Nina Rhoades, the blind daughter of the New York banker. Dr. Neilson spent a week with them. "He has always attracted me strongly," Helen wrote Hitz, "and I was glad to know the man as well as the scholar." At the end of the summer she went to Seabright, New Jersey, to visit Nina Rhoades. Lenore Smith, who was with her all September, accompanied her so that Teacher and John could have some time alone. "We reached Seabright just in time to witness a tremendous storm which lasted four days. The surf was so high, it almost flew over the top of the house, and it looked very much like a snowstorm. The roar of the sea was terrific, I could feel it everywhere in the house."

At the end of 1903 Teacher "bought the house Uncle Ed [Chamberlin] spoke of. We had long wanted a home where we could go after my graduation, and here was a fine opportunity to buy a pleasant one in beautiful Wrentham! The house is on one of the prettiest village streets, and has trees around it. Is it not lovely to look forward to living in a home of our own and doing just as we like?" It cost them $2700, and they used some shares of Spaulding's sugar stock to purchase it. The house had seventeen rooms and seven acres as well as barns and other outbuildings.

Although it was not their intent in making the purchase, the house turned out to be one of their best investments. Not all were. The first thousand dollars Helen received from the *Ladies' Home Journal,* Annie turned over to a smooth-talking speculator. As she explained to Mrs. Hutton:

> I judged from your letter to Helen that you did not quite approve of my acting without the advice of her New York friends, and I want to explain how it happened.
>
> I heard of Mr. Brown through a very dear friend of mine, who has known him practically all his life. She told me how successful he had been in developing his mining property, and suggested that if I had money, I had better invest it in the Boston Coal and Fuel Company. I went to see Mr. Brown, and liked him very much. He knew Mr. Spaulding and was greatly surprised to hear that he had not provided for Helen. He manifested the deepest interest in our affairs and said that it would give him the greatest pleasure to be of service to us. I did not, however, decide at once to put the money in his hands. I asked several good business men to inquire about Mr. Brown and his business standing; and they were so favorably impressed that they not only advised me by all means to invest, but also bought stock in the Company themselves. But in order to avoid running any risk whatever and to satisfy Helen's friends, Mr. Brown guaranteed that in case the mines were not successful, he personally would pay back the money and the six per cent interest during the time it had been in the Company. I thought it would be of no use to write to Mr. Rhoades or Mr. Rogers, because they would not know anything about Mr.

Brown or his business, and would no doubt advise me to put the money in the Savings Bank, or in trust; and this would mean only a very small interest; whereas, if our hopes are realized, the investment we have made will help considerably to relieve Helen's friends of the burden of her support. On the other hand, if the investment should by any chance prove unsuccessful, we lose nothing and are still better off than if we had put it in trust.

The mine failed to materialize and Mr. Brown did not make good the one thousand dollars. Desperate, Annie appealed to H.H. Rogers. He was distressed, he wrote back, but doubtful that he could do anything. She should have consulted him before turning their money over to Mr. Brown, he gently admonished her. But Rogers was very generous, and between his help and that of Mrs. Hutton's fund and the royalties that Helen was earning from her writings, by the end of her college career she had an income of about five thousand dollars a year, a princely sum for those times.

Her busy college years were drawing to a close. Radcliffe had done its best to protect her from the world's glare and to treat her like any other girl, but she and Annie were celebrities, and already, as Dr. Neilson observed, it was impossible to have a simple, relaxed human relationship with them. "Perhaps the postman has but none of their friends. Everybody who comes near them is sucked into the vortex." When she and Annie visited the Bells in Washington in the spring of 1902, they were invited to call at the White House and talk with President Roosevelt. "When I clasped his hand, I felt that I was in touch with one of those who 'bate not a jot in heart or hope' in their efforts to promote the welfare of the nation. He talked to me about his six children and told me a story about little Archie and a rabbit which he had caught that morning in the garden. I read his lips, and he repeated the words I did not catch until I understood."

But she was no longer a little girl to be amused with stories about rabbits. At Princeton a few days later they stayed with the Huttons and heard Mark Twain—"he is not one of those who save their bright thoughts for their books"—on Roosevelt and American policy in the Philippines. He savaged the policy in public, and in private, its author, the President. In his indignation, wrote Helen, "he would suddenly rise and stand like an eagle on Sunset Crag, his plumage all ruffled by the storm of his feelings." T.R., he told Helen, "has never grown up. He has the mental calibre of a boy of fourteen. A boy is all right in his place. . . . We say 'he'll know better when he grows up.' But a boy in the President's office is ludicrous! Roosevelt is ignorant, boastful, narrow. He has never given up the ideals and standards of the jungle. He's in the piratical stage of his development." This was too strong for Helen. Perhaps, too, she remembered that she had favored American trusteeship over the Philippines in line with shouldering "the white man's burden," which was the moral justification among men and women of good will for imperialist expansion. Sometimes it seemed to Helen that Mark Twain's denunciations were "so sweeping that they lost significance." But she agreed wholly with him a year later about "the rape of Panama," as Mark Twain called it. He wondered that John Hay, Roosevelt's secretary of state, could have given it his approval. "I'm sorry for John Hay," he said. "He did not want to do it. There was nothing mean or sordid about him. There is an explanation. He belonged to his party and his party compelled him to stand by and watch a big bully beat up a mob of confiding children. . . ." Helen chimed in, "Mr. Clemens and I agreed that we might have respected Messrs. Roosevelt and Hay if they had come out boldly and given notice to Colombia that they intended to take the Canal Zone because the U.S. needed it. Such a course might have been defended on the plea that a superior people was endeavoring to promote civilization and found itself balked by inferior peoples—the superior people found it necessary to act under the law of eminent domain."

The same "white man's burden" philosophy infected Helen's response to an appeal to help India's children, for her fame had already spread there. The Anagarika Dharmapala sought her help to establish a manual training school for the Sudra children of India. She would do what little she could while she was still in college, she replied. She hoped many in America were ready to respond to his appeal. But he should "seek and find help in England, too. . . . if the conquest of India is to be justified in the history of mankind. Great Britain must give her better schools, better government, better laws, better ideals. She must see to it that the poor are befriended and the sick tended, and the deaf and the blind are not left to die."

Helen sometimes thought Mark Twain "was obsessed by the idea of a cruel Jehovah and a deluded humanity." Perhaps he clung to Helen because she exemplified the more benign forces at work in the world that kept him from total despair. "The world is full of unseeing eyes, vacant, staring, soulless eyes," he said to her, and he and Gilder good-naturedly swapped views on what Helen, sightless, was able to see by virtue of her imaginative powers. Gilder was describing his summer home when suddenly he stopped and, turning to the company, exclaimed: "I wonder what sort of pictures my words are projecting upon Helen's mind." Mark Twain was sure that Helen's mental pictures "were far more beautiful than the reality." He had read many descriptions of the Taj Mahal. "Why," he went on, "it looked like a rat hole in comparison with what I thought it was going to be." Helen's mind was "full of the eloquence and poetry of other great minds. She has blended together your conception of the Temple of Karnak and mine," he said to Gilder. Gilder thereupon began to recite his poem on Karnak, but Mark Twain interrupted him. "Keep an open mind about Karnak, Helen, until I have read you my masterpiece." Someone ventured the view that Helen's concept of things outside the reach of her hands must lack reality. Perhaps, drawled Mark Twain, "but a well put together unreality is pretty hard to beat." Turning back to the editor of *The Century,* he said, "Now, Gilder, she probably thinks you are a handsome man. I thank God she can't see."

Helen did not allow such discussions to turn her head. Even when she was the subject, she took an impersonal, almost detached attitude, concerned more that the world should arrive at a juster view of what the deaf and the blind were capable of than with the praises that were heaped upon her personally. She returned from this visit to the Bells, the White House, the Huttons and wrote Sister Mary Joseph—a nun who had received papal dispensation to Braille books for Helen—"I really need some one to take care of. I could not be satisfied with literary work only." She felt this more strongly after the success of *The Story of My Life.* "I am planning to write a little essay on optimism. I do not want to do any literary work for its own sake. Every line I write is forced out at the point of the bayonet."

"Labor is the content of Miss Keller's genius," John Macy remarked about Helen's writing, "the secret of her advancement. Not a good paragraph which she has written, even in a private letter, has been 'dashed off.' ... She writes well not by virtue of a facile gift, but by scrupulous revision, patient thinking, and diligent attention to the criticism of her instructors, and to the advice of Miss Sullivan."

Macy negotiated the details of the contract for "Optimism." It is a 7,500-word essay on "the goodness of life" that made considerable use of what she was hearing in Professor Royce's course on philosophy, but belongs more to the category of devotional literature than to that of philosophic.

"The value of this bit of sunshine," wrote Lyman Abbott's *Outlook,* "in the light of which Miss Keller interprets life lies in the fact that it comes out of such dense darkness." "Most people," wrote Helen, "measure their happiness in terms of physical pleasures and material possessions. . . . If happiness is to be so measured I who cannot hear or see, have every reason to sit in a corner with folded hands and weep. If I am happy in spite of my deprivations; if my happiness is so deep that it is a faith; my testimony to the creed of 'optimism' is worth hearing." From what Josiah Royce was saying it seemed to her that "Philosophy is the history of a deaf-blind person writ large. . . . A deaf-blind person ought to find special meaning in Plato's Ideal World. These things which you see and hear and touch are not the reality of what is, but imperfect manifestations of the Idea, the Principle, the Spiritual; the idea is the truth, the rest is delusion." She read the history of mankind in the manner of Hegel, except that history found its final apotheosis not in the Prussian state, but in the American. "From the first hour of the new nations each century has seen a better Europe, until the development of the world demanded America." But not even America was the final goal of the questing Spirit: "Out of the fierce struggle and turmoil of contending systems and powers I see a brighter spiritual era slowly emerge—an era in which there shall be no England, no France, no Germany, no America, no this people or that, but one family, the human race; one law, peace; one need, harmony; one means, labor; one taskmaster, God."

Published by Crowell, the little essay did well, selling more than ten thousand copies in a few years and earning her a tidy little sum. Mark Twain, the pessimist, understandably had nothing to say about this book. But his great friend the actor Joseph Jefferson was so taken with it that he presented copies to his friends, including Gilder, who thanked him with a poem dedicated to the "Two Optimists," Jefferson and Helen, whom heaven had sent "this troubled world to bless." And Dr. Hale, beginning a period as chaplain of the United States Senate, wrote her that "I have had nothing for months past which gave me so much courage." He noted that Dr. Johnson had not included the word *optimism* in the early editions of his dictionary, which showed "how late the philosophy of it has been growing."

Helen herself came to think less of the book. "I agree with you that 'Optimism' lacks depth," she wrote the secretary of the Socialist Party in Ottawa in 1911. "I could not possibly write such an essay now. When I wrote it I was an inexperienced college girl. I got tired of hearing others say how hard, how sad it is to be blind. I did not know what I have learned since about the extent of moral blindness."

Helen's literary labors and keeping up with her friends and doing her work for Radcliffe did not stop her from responding to appeals to help the deaf and the blind. "How busy these days are," she wrote Hitz after an Easter holiday at Wrentham. Teacher's feet were "getting stronger every day, though it still tires her to walk long distances, and I rub them quite often." She had toiled over her senior thesis on "the Puritan and Cavalier elements in Milton's minor poems," and she was determined to make "two or three A's." But people were constantly calling on her for help. "[S]everal friends have asked me to go to New York to make a speech at the dedication of the New York Eye and Ear Infirmary. It comes very near the finals, and I can ill spare the time; but an opportunity to do a kindness is too precious to neglect, and my heart is warm in the cause of the poor sufferers who need every comfort and advantage that money and skill can secure."

The platform at the dedication was crowded with notables and friends. Bishop Potter presided. Gilder was there, as was Lucy Derby Fuller. Several spoke, but the moments of genuine feeling came with Helen's speech. Hearts went out to this lass in a dark skirt and white shirtwaist who "slowly and laboriously," as the press reported, spoke her few words. She was almost inaudible, but Annie was there to interpret, and afterwards Joseph Jefferson in his rich voice read what she had said. She began with a graceful and discerning tribute to New York City. "In spite of the harsh words that are spoken against this great city, I find here a wide human sympathy. New York receives every year thousands of starving and naked of every race, every country and every faith and more than any other city in the United States, she clothes the naked, feeds the hungry, teaches the ignorant and relieves those who suffer." She reserved her most forceful words for a plea that society train the deaf and the blind for useful work. "A human being who does not work is not a member of society and can have no standing in it. . . . It is not enough to erect handsome buildings. . . . It is cooperation in the work of mercy that makes it complete."

She was an effective advocate. Two months earlier she had spoken at a legislative hearing in Boston on a proposal to establish a commission to investigate the conditions of the adult blind. Her testimony had been "the highlight" of the hearings. Employment for the blind was the main burden of her plea. "It has long been my earnest desire that something be done to help the blind to support themselves. It is terrible to be blind and to be uneducated; but it is worse for the blind who have been educated to be idle." The blind did not need higher education. "It is not Greek and Latin, but an industrial training and some one with influence and authority to help them to [find a] place in the industrial world" that the blind needed. "The best of all the addresses at the State House this morning on behalf of the blind of Massachusetts was made by a blind girl—Helen Keller," wrote the correspondent for the *Boston Herald*.

A commission was appointed. A Massachusetts Association for Promoting the Interest of the Adult Blind was established with the energetic Charles F.F. Campbell, son of Sir Francis Campbell, founder and director of the Royal Normal College for the Blind, as its "agent." The Association held a rally in Lynn, Massachusetts, to spur the commission. Helen was the chief speaker. She made the headlines with an attack on Perkins. "I have always wondered why the Perkins Institution with its wealth and prestige, has not taken the initiative in the work that our Association is trying to do for the blind.

"Instead it has taught its pupils the nobility and necessity of work, given them high ideals of citizenship and the consciousness of inspiring books and has sent them into the world to fight their little battles as best they could."

She urged the state to establish an industrial workshop to teach the blind self-supporting skills and a state agency to help them find employment. And then she let loose another unamiable volley at Anagnos: "Nothing of consequence has been done for the adult blind since Dr. Howe's day."

With some justice, Anagnos described Helen's charges as "absolutely false and without any foundation. . . . We have the finest manual training school for the blind in the world." He enumerated the types of vocational training that had been instituted since Dr. Howe's day. "The conditions are very different from Dr. Howe's day, for now the trusts make it hard for even the seeing individual and almost impossible for the blind individual to earn a living. In Dr. Howe's day there was no machinery." He dismissed her attack on Perkins. It was intended to draw the headlines by highlighting her plea for jobs for the adult blind, he said.

In Nella Braddy's working papers for her life of Annie she noted that "for all her love for mankind she [Helen] could be harsh towards individual man or woman. In the last book she ever wrote, she said that 'the sin I cannot forgive' was the accusation made at the time of The Frost King episode that Teacher had warped her mind; the incident had happened more than 60 years ago." Nevertheless she wrote in *Teacher* of Mr. F.B. Sanborn's 'insult' to Teacher in bringing up her sordid background and her 'ingratitude' to Perkins, "To this day I cannot excuse his mean-spirited behavior. Little did he remember that, however impatient we may be with our fellow men, we are all bound together and live for and by one another." "And 'little' sometimes, [added Nella in her notes,] did Helen herself remember. Teacher's anger mellowed. Helen's festered."

Helen's departure from Radcliffe was attended by as much publicity as her entrance had been. The *Ladies' Home Journal* commissioned her to do an article on "My Future As I See It," and published it with an editorial note that what Helen intended to take up as her life work was the only point she had not covered in the story of her life. There were many jobs to be done, even by a deaf-blind woman, she began. "Our worst foes are not belligerent circumstances, but wavering spirits. As a man thinketh, so is he. The field in which I may work is narrow, but it stretches before me limitless." The first challenge that she listed sounded a feminist theme: "I am much interested in work that woman may do in the world. It is a fine thing to be an American. It is a splendid thing to be an American woman. . . . I think the degree of a nation's civilization may be measured by the degree of enlightenment of its women. So I shall study the economic questions relating to women and do my best to further her advancement, for God and His world are for everybody."

Perhaps she could teach and do for other afflicted children what Annie Sullivan had done for her. Certainly she would write, but she realized that her subject matter was limited. Her deafness and blindness meant that she might have little to say to those who see and hear. But perhaps she could do translations from the classics, and "if opportunity offers I shall certainly write on topics connected with the deaf and the blind." Editors were already suggesting subjects. Settlement work among the poor also appealed to her. "As I reflect on the enormous amount of good work that is left undone I cannot but say a word and look my disapproval when I hear that my country is spending millions upon millions of dollars for war and war engines—more I have heard, than twice as much as the entire public school system of the United States costs us."

The role of social critic had always been latent in her thought and action. In 1899 Uncle Ed Chamberlin, after Helen and Annie's long stay with him at Wrentham, wrote in the *Ladies' Home Journal* that "Helen is an unconquerable liberal in her ideas. She inclines to take the side of the people in all matters which they make their concern. She is instinctively philanthropical and benevolent. Her notions in sociological matters are pretty nearly the direct opposite of those of Miss Sullivan, who is extremely conservative."

The class yearbook for 1904 prophesied a life role for each of the seniors. Next to Helen's photograph was inscribed "H. K. missionary?" She had already by her example moved the world to a larger sympathy for the problems of the deaf and the blind, and it was as a crusader for justice that she was moving into the wider world. "And indeed for all earnest college graduates there is great work in the world," she ended her speech to the alumnae, "work that they can do in sweet unaggressive ways. There are harsh customs to be made sweet with love; hearts in which a kind, tolerant brotherly love must be awakened; time-hallowed prejudices that must be overthrown. One evil that must be checked is the ignorance of the learned who have never learned the simple, honest language of the heart, which is the most vital of all, and is more satisfying than all the Greek or Latin ever written."

"Now 'the whole boundless universe is yours,' " Dr. Hale, unable to attend her commencement, wrote her. He congratulated her on "having worked through to one who knows what she wants, or what she needs, —the necessary conditions of college life often require a great deal of sacrifice;—sacrifice of time or strength, which after this is all over you can direct for yourself."

It was a measure of John Macy's deep involvement with Helen and Annie that he wrote for *Youth's Companion* an article on "Helen Keller at Radcliffe College" that *The Association Review,* connected with the Volta Bureau, republished with the comment: "It is so complete in its details and speaks with such evident knowledge and authority that we are constrained to reprint it in full." She is not a "brilliant genius," he summarized her intellectual qualities. "She is not even scholarly in her interests. Her mind is stout and energetic, of solid endurance. Many women have keener minds and deeper capacity for scholarship. I, for one, cannot see that she has the intellect of a genius, or much creative power, or great originality. But her heart is noble; the world has yet to see a finer spirit, a loftier and more steadfast will to do the best."

If Helen was "not scholarly in her interests," that reflected in part Teacher's impatience with disciplined scholarship. Helen's potential for academic work was largely channeled by Annie. There were roads untaken—especially in science, mathematics and the fine arts; and that in some degree was due as much to Teacher's limitations and preferences as to Helen's. But this having been said, it must quickly be added that without Annie sitting beside her in the lecture hall and classroom, translating, summarizing, with an ear for the essential in what a lecturer was saying, it is doubtful that Helen could have gone through Radcliffe. Lenore Smith, who occasionally had spelled Teacher, found the tension and strain of a day's work with Helen so killing that her husband gently discouraged her impulse to substitute for Teacher on a regular basis.

She did not participate in the gaieties of commencement week. Although elected class "lawyer" and therefore responsible for the preparation of the class's last will and testament, the "junior counsel" had to take on the job because Helen "has unfortunately been prevented from assuming the duties of her office." It was said that she was ill. Perhaps she was; it was also true that she and Annie had little stomach for the commencement celebrations. Helen's grades had earned her a cum laude; only a summa would have satisfied Teacher. She was not among the graduates given a part in the graduation day exercises. But even more pertinent to Helen's sense of aloofness was her resentment that some sort of recognition was not being given to Teacher. She had sat through all the classes with Helen. She knew what Helen knew, although Dr. Neilson, who had come to know them both quite well, scoffed at the notion that Annie should have been given a degree when questioned about it later by Nella Braddy: "Teacher criticized the educational machinery at Radcliffe quite freely—her attitude kept her from getting the benefit from it she might have had. [There was] no reason why she should not have come to the end with as good an education as Helen Keller, but she didn't. She made herself the channel for Miss Helen's knowledge and it was almost as if she could see how much knowledge could pass through her without sticking —very little stuck."

But that was not the way Helen and Annie saw it. In 1932 when Temple University conferred honorary degrees on Annie as well as Helen, the latter voiced publicly the resentment that she felt in 1904 over Radcliffe's failure to recognize Annie's achievement as well as her own. "Together we went through Radcliffe College. Day after day during four years she sat beside me in the lecture halls and spelled into my hand word by word what the professors said; and nearly all the books she read to me in the same way.

"Yet when I received my degree from Radcliffe, not a word of recognition was given her! The pain caused me by that indifference or thoughtlessness is still a thorn in my memory."

The old social sensitivities, the pride quick to sense a slight, were still alive in Annie, and much of Helen's resentment undoubtedly reflected her own. Twenty-five years later she still was piqued by the failure of Alice Freeman Palmer to call upon them. She was Cambridge's reigning hostess, who had become president of Wellesley in 1881 when only twenty-six, and then left to marry Professor George Herbert Palmer. Nor did they ever see Harvard's august President Eliot. But if they had been entertained by Eliot and made a fuss over by Mrs. Palmer, said Dr. Neilson, the public would never have believed in the authenticity of Helen's degree. "Doubt always pursued her in those early days, although one conversation with her was enough to dispel such doubt."

Radcliffe's commencement exercises on June 28 were held in the Sanders Theater. Ninety-six graduates were to receive their diplomas, the largest number in Radcliffe's twenty-five-year history. The hall was crowded. A small company of musicians in the balcony above the stage played Mendelssohn's "Spring Song" as the procession, capped and gowned except for Annie Sullivan, filed into their seats. A prayer opened the exercises. Then the newly installed President LeBaron R. Briggs—Dean Irwin had been passed over—spoke a few solemn words. Radcliffe was a college "for women who are in earnest, and who are willing that their earnestness should be tested,—for these and for no others. Those who are tainted with the great evil of the age,—unwillingness to do a day's work, will find plenty of institutions which, in the name of learning, will receive them, teach them a good deal, and graduate them; but Radcliffe College is for the stronger sisters."

The "stronger sisters" rose after he had finished to be awarded their diplomas. There were ripples of applause and waves of recognition as the young women mounted the steps to the stage, bowed to the college officer who called out their names and advanced to receive their diplomas from President Briggs. As Helen—tall, erect, grave-looking—rose and moved to the platform, a hush fell over the audience. She mounted the steps gracefully, Annie's guiding hand on her arm, bowed to the college secretary, approached the president, bowed again and stretched forward her hand and with firm fingers grasped the coveted diploma. To Hitz*, who sat in the audience, the applause seemed to have turned into an ovation. In addition to cum laude her diploma carried the words (also in Latin)

*Two other luminaries of the world of the deaf and the blind attended the exercise: Dr. E.M. Gallaudet, President of Gallaudet College in Washington, D.C., and Mr. Weston Jenkins, head of the Talledega, Alabama, School for the Deaf.

"Not only approved in the whole academic course, but excellent in English letters."

But immediately after the ceremonies, reported the *Boston Globe,* Helen with Annie at her side "disappeared from the auditorium as quietly as she had entered, and those who desired to extend congratulations looked for her in vain." "A most remarkable intellectual feat," editorialized the *Transcript.* "It is greatly to the credit of both Miss Keller and her instructors that while she has studied, so to speak, in competition with other girls, there has not been the slightest difference of treatment in her favor. She was awarded her degree with high standing because she had accomplished what anyone else must do to receive such an honor."

Her classmates best caught the uniqueness of Helen's feat. In the yearbook they wrote:

> Beside her task our efforts pale,
> She never knew the word for fail;
> Beside her triumphs ours are naught,
> For hers were far more dearly bought.

Courtesy American Foundation for the Blind

In her speech to the alumnae shortly before commencement Helen spoke of what Radcliffe had given her, and the sense of purpose was bright in what she said: "College has breathed new life into my mind and given me new views of things, a perception of new truths and of new aspects of the old ones. I grow stronger in the conviction that there is nothing good or right which we cannot accomplish if we have the will to strive. The assured reality and nearness of the end of my school days fills me with bright anticipations. The doors of the bright world are flung open before me and a light shines upon me, the light kindled by the thought that there is something for me to do beyond the threshold."

part four

HELEN *and* TEACHER *and* JOHN

XVII

Extraordinary Triangle

"There is a belief in original sin, but I can't accept it after hearing
Helen Keller."—William Wade

"Our chief happiness is that we have a real home of our own,"
Helen wrote Sister Mary Joseph about their house in Wrentham, in which
they were spending their first summer. "It is old-fashioned, roomy and
cheerful. I never had a room for all my books before." She became
particularly fond of "a stonewall overgrown with fruit-trees, pines and
spruces. I can walk there alone, and I feel rich in having all this space to
myself." Usually she was unable to go out without a companion, but here
she wandered at will, gathering flowers and berries and sitting under the
branches.

Here, too, the Smiths were in and out, and John Wright of Wright-
Humason, their friend again, spent some time. "Teacher had a wonderful
home-making gift," he reported. John Macy was practically a member of
the household. "John has had a two weeks' vacation," she wrote Hitz,
"and he has done nothing but work around in play-time. He has fixed the
barn-doors and steps and many other things, and cleaned out the barn and
under it. He has also lengthened my walk in the field, so that I can go from
tree to tree, as far as the hazel-coverts. He made a nice bookcase in the
study, sawing, planing, and painting it all himself.

"So you see how full our home is of love and happiness."

At Wrentham, too, they received visitors—the curious, the sceptical,
the believing. "Half Rome believes Annie Sullivan is just a governess and

interpreter, riding to fame on Helen's genius," the often caustic John Macy observed, while "the other half of Rome" believes Helen is "only Annie's puppet, speaking and writing lines that are fed to her by Annie's genius." Her graduation from Radcliffe had answered most of the doubters in the United States, but abroad there still was disbelief. "In Berlin I found much scepticism among educators regarding the remarkable education of Helen Keller," wrote the principal of the Milwaukee Day School. "They call it 'Uebertreibung' [exaggeration] and 'Amerikanische Aufschneiderei' [braggadocio]." Rudolph Brohman, the eminent teacher of the deaf-blind, insisted that *"The Story of My Life* by Helen Keller, is mainly the work of her teacher, Miss Sullivan."

A Swedish specialist in the education of the deaf-blind, Miss Elizabeth Anrep-Nordin, described her journey to America to study how that country handled the deaf-blind and especially to see Helen Keller. She stopped at Perkins at the invitation of her old friend Michael Anagnos, and observed the progress made by the four deaf-blind children there. Perkins's success, she was told, owed itself "to the fact that each of them had a special teacher, who was in every case a bright and intelligent young lady who had gone through a college course. . . . And the remarkable thing is that these young-lady teachers have had no special training in teaching the blind-deaf."

From Perkins she went on to Wrentham. "The house, a roomy, two-story villa, is beautifully situated in a large park," she wrote afterwards, "the whole property (together with all the furniture in the house) having been bought by national subscription and presented to her along with a yearly allowance of two thousand dollars, which sum on her death shall be used for the training of blind-deaf children."

Helen and Annie prided themselves on being self-reliant, independent women, making their own way. They were alternately amused and outraged by descriptions of their home as a great estate that had been bestowed on them by a grateful nation, as the Romans did with their victorious generals. Yet the description was not too far wrong, although a farmhouse is not quite a "villa" and Mrs. Hutton's fund not quite a "national subscription." Still, the Swedish observer had missed the basic point of their way of life at Wrentham. They worked hard. They had to supplement their annual income with earnings from writing, and later, from lecturing. The two women were determined, although one was deaf-blind and the other half-blind, to run their own lives and to make it on their own.

The Swedish visitor continued her narrative with a reference to the "dread" that she felt as she entered the house in Wrentham to meet Helen. "Shall all the wonderful things I have read and heard about this girl prove to be realities, or shall I find only a fresh example of American exaggeration?" She feared, too, that she might not be given the chance to test her doubts in direct intercourse with Helen. A moment's talk with Annie, who met her at the door, dispelled this last fear. Annie fetched Helen and promptly took herself off. Helen's "whole appearance and bearing made upon me the immediate impression of a sweet and gentle nature, quite unspoiled by notoriety. The pleasant impression was deepened by her first greeting, uttered in a sweet musical voice,—'I am very glad to see you, because I know of your work among the blind-deaf.'" They talked all afternoon—about Swiss travel, the *Vierwaldstättersee,* Schiller, Goethe, Heine, Rome and its art, Sweden and its climate. "In all these subjects she displayed remarkable knowledge, and such a readiness of comprehension (and that in German, no less than in English) that she began to answer my questions when only half-spelled out. By this time my doubts were completely removed. . . ." Annie came back into the room, and tea was served while they chatted about the "wild" stories that were in circulation in Europe about Helen, including the claim that she was an accomplished pianist, which provoked guffaws from Helen. Annie explained how such stories had their origin in the writing of overeager professors and journalists. The visitor left Wrentham "overpowered by the sense of the great things human love and skill can accomplish, and with the earnest hope that this beautiful and delicate plant, after a spring bright with promise, might not forthwith fall into decay, but give forth full bloom and fragrance for many years to come."

They promised to see each other again, at the St. Louis Exposition in late October. The Exposition celebrated the one hundredth anniversary of the Louisiana Purchase. It should have opened in 1903, but it had taken longer than planned to put together. Among its events was an International Conference on the Deaf and the Dumb. Dr. Anrep-Nordin was to deliver a paper, and there was to be a "Helen Keller Day." The president of the Exposition, David Rowland Francis, later Woodrow Wilson's ambassador to Czarist Russia, invited Helen, Annie and John to attend and to stay with his sister while in St. Louis.

Any hopes that Dr. Anrep-Nordin may have had of another talk with Helen vanished amid the mob scenes that attended Helen's appearance. The Swedish woman showed her own myth-making propensities when she later wrote of the nation sending "400,000 of its representatives to do her honor," mixing up, no doubt, the total attendance at the Exposition that day with the number interested in Helen. But the crush of people was intimidating wherever Helen went. Most of the first day she spent touring the Philippine "reservation," where entire villages of Moros and Igorrotes had been re-created. When the Filipinos were told of Helen's affliction, wrote a newspaperman, "they showed her a deference that amounted almost to a superstitious reverence." Great crowds trailed after her through the exhibitions, eager to shake her hand, or to touch the hem of her garment, as if she were a healing saint, or just "to catch a glimpse of her radiantly happy face."

Helen was the magnet that drew the crowds. As usual Annie was at her side, but few paid attention to her. Helen wore a high-necked lace gown and a hat with flowers, some of which were snatched by worshipful bystanders. Annie was in black with jet trimmings at the bodice. When they entered Congress Hall, it was packed to the doors. People clambered onto chairs and into the high windows, while outside some stood on ladders straining to catch a sound of her voice. President Francis introduced her. She spoke with sufficient clarity and modulation that he was able to repeat her speech sentence by sentence without the intervention of Annie. "I have been asked to come here today and lend my voice to what is being done in the world for the uplifting of those who struggle in unequal and untoward circumstances," she began. "Many have been invited here because of learning, skill or achievement," she went on. "I am here, not for what I have done, but what has been done for me—to raise me to the level of those that see and hear. . . . My evidence is of able men and women who have done what they could to unstop ears, open eyes, give speech to the lips of the dumb and light to darkened minds." But she wanted to convey a broader message than the need to help the deaf, the blind and the mute. "This exposition symbolizes the will of the American people that there shall be an open way to education for all, no matter how humble their circumstances or how limited their capacity. . . . Enlightened public opinion will not permit a child of God to perish from neglect. This exposition tells us that the world is on our side. . . . God bless the nation that provides education and opportunity for all her children."

After Helen spoke, the blind Van Zant twins from the Kansas School for the Blind played the violin—not well, but this did not bother the audience. In the reception that followed, when three thousand filed by to greet Helen, few were allowed to shake hands with her; but when the twins filed past, she insisted on kissing them, and when "a little old man" came by, Helen recognized the touch, and as the crowd whispered "her father," she threw both arms around the neck of her friend and benefactor William Wade. Afterwards Wade told the press: "She is the embodiment of purity. There is a belief in original sin, but I can't accept it after hearing Helen Keller."

Helen, Annie and John returned from St. Louis with John better aware than before that in wanting to marry Annie, he was hitching himself to a cyclone, and Annie aware that she had to make up her mind about his desire to marry her. He had been proposing for over a year. She was held back not only by her concern for Helen and by the disparity in their ages, but by fear of her volcanolike moods, her restlessness and even by her Catholic upbringing, for John was a Protestant, and although she was a freethinker who long ago had turned her back on the Church, marriage was a sacrament, and it made her uneasy to marry outside of it. An unexplained note from Dr. Hale, to whom they often turned for counsel, suggests she may even have consulted Church authorities on whether they would permit it. "You are quite right as you are apt to be," Dr. Hale wrote her. "Let them wriggle out of their red tape as they can. I do not believe it any fault of the Bishop himself,—but it is that of the people. . . . who surround him."

She changed her mind continually about marrying John. Helen in her book *Teacher* talks (though elusively) about the troubled courtship. She speaks of a meeting for the blind in Boston where John, not Annie, acted as her interpreter. Afterwards Helen sat in Annie's room, and Annie told her "how pretty and graceful I had looked standing before the audience, and announced that she would never marry. 'Oh, Teacher,' I exclaimed, 'if you love John, and let him go, I shall feel like a hideous accident!' " Why did Helen's prettiness on the stage activate Annie's insecurities to the point of deciding she would never marry John? The Boston newspapers were beginning to speculate about a romance between Helen and John. Did Annie fear that marriage to a man ten years younger would seem hilariously incongruous? Had she suddenly realized anew that she could never love John with the force with which she loved Helen?

Macy came from an old Nantucket family and was a dyed-in-the-wool Yankee who later became convinced that Massachusetts was going to the dogs because the Puritans were being pushed aside by the Irish—a view that he must have kept to himself, if he held it then, in the days of his courtship of Annie. It is part of Macy family lore that he really married

Annie in order to stay close to Helen. He had wanted to marry the latter; but Helen's mother, so the story goes, fearing he was a publicity seeker, and Helen herself, because she felt she would be an "unnatural burden" to any husband, turned him down. It was the reverse, said his nephew Arthur Macy, "of petting the calf to get to the cow."

This writer has been unable to find any independent substantiation of this story. John was one of five children. As a literary critic he was already beginning an effective assault on the genteel tradition in American literature. He got his unorthodoxy and vigor of views from his mother. She was only five feet in height, but very determined, very strong willed, a Unitarian and a suffragist. Her children were devoted to her. In 1928, long after John had separated from Annie, he wrote to Harvard classmate, Walter Arensberg, after the death of Myla, a deaf-mute sculptress, very beautiful, with whom he had lived in the twenties:

> My extraordinary mother, who trots about New York like a young flapper attending Unitarian conferences and women's alliances and is to others a most beloved person, is nearer to me than ever. When she first came to see me after the disaster, in my dingy hole in the wall, her saying of the right thing was exquisite, incredibly wise, no damned palaver. She knew, she has been in Hell herself. Only some people who have been in the valley of the shadows emerge without any enlargement of heart and mind. When I see her, I bring the toe of my right boot against the back cords of the left ankle and say, 'You damned fool, with that midget of courage for mother, you don't dare fail.' Pitts calls her Dresden China, which is pretty and the way she looks, but superficial.

"Annie never wholly acquiesced in the fact of her marriage," Helen wrote in *Teacher*. The reason, she thought, was that she, Helen, alone was able "to keep her quiet and reasonable" when her darker moods came upon her. "John was marvellous in counseling me about my literary work, reading aloud to her a wealth of books delightful or witty . . . and driving away her spells of melancholy." But Teacher was temperamental, edgy and restless, "and even the wise did not always chart the currents of her nature rightly," wrote Helen. Helen alone was able to handle her. John had seen this clearly in the early months of their relationship. He had written in the *Ladies' Home Journal*, "The two are naturally responsive, they stimulate each other. Yet when one is in an unhappy mood, the better mood of the other prevails. I have seen Miss Sullivan, who is intense and excitable, become a little fretful when the work was not going well. Miss Keller's touch, I thought, stilled her."

Although friends like Dr. Bell worried that Teacher's marriage to John meant inevitably that Helen would have less of her, Teacher arranged her marriage to John so that it became a kind of insurance for Helen in the event of her own death. She made him promise that should she die before him, which was likely, he would be a brother to Helen, look after her happiness and take charge of her affairs.

Helen went south to spend the Christmas holidays with her sister, Mildred, and her mother, who now lived in Florence, Alabama. She went alone. "My teacher does not feel she can go, her days are so filled with household affairs," she wrote Sister Mary Joseph. Someone must have escorted her, but she does not say who. "I went to receptions and parties and danced and had great fun," she wrote on her return to Wrentham in February. "It all rested me very much after the constant work of the past eight years. But I was happy to get back to my teacher, I had never been so homesick."

The engagement was announced on January 16, 1905. But it must have been settled before Helen went to Alabama. A newspaper story that could only have come from Annie and John gives some of the details. It was a friendly story, and its point was to reassure Helen's friends that the marriage had her approval and that she would not be left alone because of it. "Helen Keller ALMOST Married!" the headline read. When the "bridegroom elect" had first proposed marriage, the story began, a surprised Miss Sullivan had answered, "I cannot marry anyone."

"Why not?" asked the wooer.

"Because—Helen."

"But you need not be separated from Helen. Our home will be hers. You may go on teaching her all your life." The two tussled and argued until Annie finally said, "If you will ask Helen and if she is willing, I will think about it."

So John went into Helen's study and putting his hands on hers spelled out his proposal of marriage. What had her teacher said?

"She said—she spoke of you." Did he love her? John answered with a press of his hand. "Does she love you?" Another press of the hand. "Then, marry, of course, and I hope you will be very, very happy."

"We want you to be with us always. You will be as dear and as necessary to Miss Sullivan as you have always been. We would not marry unless your life and hers were to go on just as before." Helen thanked him, her eyes misting, and sent him off to tell Annie "that I will be very unhappy unless she marries you."

She then rushed in to congratulate Annie. "It is almost as wonderful as though I were going to be a bride myself. I would have been miserable if you had not accepted him." What was the name for a third person in a marriage? she asked Annie.

"She—she may be the bridesmaid."

"And after that?"

"Then she may be the companion, the very dear friend, the house-mate."

"And after that," Helen volunteered, "the friend and teacher and godmother of the children?"

"Perhaps we ought not to talk about that now," protested Annie.

The story went on to say that it was Helen who, alleging homesickness for Alabama, discreetly took herself off for Christmas. What gives the account a badge of authenticity is the letter from Helen to Annie from Alabama that is included in the reporter's account:

> . . . My family are so proud of me because I can dance and keep time rhythmically without hearing the music. That and everything else I owe to you. I say to them as I have so many times said, 'My teacher is so near to me that I can scarcely think of myself apart from her. How much of my delight in all beautiful things is innate and how much due to her influence I can never tell. All the best of me belongs to her, there is not a talent, or an aspiration, or a joy in me that has not been awakened by her touch.' Think of my happiness! I am to have two teachers instead of one.

The story concluded with a reference to the rumors about John and Helen. "Persons who saw his indefatigable attentions to the twain believed that they saw the budding of a romance for the blind girl. And it is her romance, a happier romance than that of Nydia, the blind girl in *The Last Days of Pompeii*. It is not given to any one else to be so important a third, to be as nearly engaged and married as Helen Keller." When Helen wrote Sister Mary Joseph the news, the latter misread the letter as an announcement that Helen was to be married. "I laughed until I nearly cried," Helen wrote back, "when I read what you said about thinking I was to be married."

Dr. Neilson, who had taken himself off to Columbia because at Harvard the formidable figure of Kittredge had barred his way to teaching the subject in which he was most interested, Shakespeare, wrote Annie and John that he had hoped for such news: "I know you both pretty well, don't I? and I feel that if I had been Providence I would have arranged this as it has turned out. It is not merely that I did not see how either of you could get along without the other: it is also that I believe you will make each other very happy. My only regret is that I cannot sit in a hammock with Teacher any more." He was sure Helen "is very glad, too. If I understand her at all, she will give you a quite extraordinary sympathy, and will share your joy as few third persons could."

"This brings you still nearer to our wonderful & well-loved Helen," Gilder wrote Macy. "I hesitate to say all I feel about Miss Sullivan. She is one of the women of our times, her fate and her happiness are matters of interest to many. She, too, should be a writer—for she has shown great force of direct, sincere, discerning narrative. I am glad that she is to have the life that every woman should. Whether you are good enough to hook her life to yours is a matter that she should be able to judge. The presumption is in your favor—owing to her choice!"

The Fullers were in Paris and heard the news from the Bradfords (the friends of Spaulding). "I suspected it!" Lucy wrote. She wished them both much happiness. "With Mr. Macy's devotion to Helen and interest in her it seems as if this step might add to her joy and not cause any sense of loss. I feel sure her generous impulse is one of great satisfaction in your rejoicing and in his."

"Yes, Yes. Yes—a hundred times: even if I had to walk," Dr. Hale acknowledged Annie's letter urging his attendance at the wedding. "I can now confide to you what I have taken care never to say to you—that life really begins when you are married—and not until then.

"I have always liked Mr. Macy and since you have put on him the seal of your approbation, I like him more than [ever].

"Give my love to my dear Cousin. She is fortunate in having such a new Brother."

How Annie's "cher Père," John Hitz, almost deaf, was told the news, and his reaction to it, we do not know. Helen and Annie journeyed down to Washington to see Dr. Bell and assuredly would have talked with Hitz at the same time. Dr. Bell reminded Helen that he had warned her this might happen when he had urged her to consider marriage. "I told you, Helen, she would marry. Are you going to take my advice and build your own nest?"

Helen still answered no. "I feel less inclined than ever to embark upon the great adventure. I have fully made up my mind that a man and a woman must be equally equipped to weather successfully the vicissitudes of life. It would be a severe handicap to any man to saddle upon him the dead weight of my infirmities. I know I have nothing to give a man that would make up for such an unnatural burden." She recited Elizabeth Barrett Browning's sonnet "What can I give thee back, O liberal and princely giver . . . ?"

Dr. Bell was not persuaded. " 'You will change your mind some day, young woman, if the right man comes a-wooing.' And I almost did—but that is another story," Helen reported in *Midstream.*

Annie sent an important letter to Mrs. Hutton, trying to unscramble her and Helen's finances:

> This is to be a business letter. I have left Helen the pleasure of telling you the news, and judging from the clicking of her typewriter she has a good budget this time.
>
> We are to be married a good deal sooner than we expected when we announced our engagement. Mr. Macy's affairs are such that we can be married in May. As the time draws near for me to enter new legal relations, I feel that I ought to make a statement of Helen's and my affairs and suggest a plan for the management of her income in the future. If there is any point that you do not approve, will you kindly tell me how I ought to change it? And will you also kindly let Mr. Rogers see my letter?
>
> If I had always been a good business woman, I should now be able to make a more satisfactory accounting of my stewardship. Had I kept all the accounts I ought to have kept, and written all the letters I ought to have written, I should at this moment feel very good and very happy; but I much doubt if I should have accomplished anything else. I have shirked business affairs as much as possible. I hate the very thought of addition and subtraction, and whenever I try to fathom the mysteries of my accounts, I am convinced of the necessity of sending all my daughters to a business college where they shall learn cooking and bookkeeping, and how to keep a servant good-natured, and I do not care if they know nothing else. In the absence of intelligible records, it seems to me that our friends must be content with what I have to show in the way of accomplishment, and believe that the

details have been fairly well attended to, since the results are not altogether unsatisfactory. Clearly, this letter is not the place for sentiment. I have said it is to be a business letter; but as I go over in my mind all that the past eighteen years have brought Helen and me of kindness, of generous aid and disinterested service, I feel that we have fallen upon good days, and among God's people.

Our house and furnishings and seven acres of land represent what Helen and I together have earned and saved of what has been given us. I have made a will, leaving the house to Helen and she intends to make a similar will in my favor. In consideration of her part ownership of the house and furnishings, she shall always have her home here, and the expenses of her living Mr. Macy and I shall bear.

There remains two sources of income to be accounted for. The first is the money from the Fund which is now in trust in New York, and which yields us eight hundred and forty dollars a year. All this I wish to go to Helen, and I shall now open a separate bank account for her. The second source of income is the book contracts now active, and the money likely to come from magazine articles and further book contracts.

Of course you know that whatever Helen writes represents my labor as well as hers. The genius is hers, but much of the drudgery is mine. The conditions are such that she could not prepare a paper for publication without my help. The difficulties under which she works are insurmountable. Some one must always be at her side to read to her, to keep her typewriter in order, to read over her manuscript, make corrections and look up words for her, and to do the many things which she would do for herself if she had her sight. I make this statement because Helen's friends have not always understood what the relations between her and me really are. They have thought her earning capacity independent of me, and one person at least has hinted that financially she might be better off without me. Helen feels very differently and when the book contracts were made, she insisted that they should revert to me on her death. It is also her wish to divide equally with me, during her life, all the money that comes to her as our joint earnings. I am willing to accept one third. Does this seem a just arrangement?

Helen will have something more than a thousand dollars a year. With no living expenses she hopes to have Mildred with her. I hope this can be arranged; for it would make for Helen's happiness, giving her a congenial young companion and making it possible for her to go about and see her friends oftener. This means Mildred would have to depend on Helen for her support.* She is now teaching in Alabama and in part supporting her mother. Mr. Macy and I shall be very glad to make a home for them both.

I am afraid I have forgotten more than I have remembered of business. But one thing is certain, my marriage shall make no difference in my love and care for Helen, and as far as possible I shall share every happiness with her.

I have said nothing about that unfortunate investment in a coal mine, because there is nothing to say that I have not said before. I have suffered sharply for that piece of folly, and I hardly need add that I shall not again venture upon the troubled waters of the stock market. I believe the mine is to be sold next month. It is vastly irritating to think how many pleasures and nice things went down with that coalship.

The marriage took place on May 2. John and Annie asked Dr. Hale to perform the ceremony. "Yes. Certainly," he wrote John. "It is always good to marry and be married when the right people meet. And the sooner the better." The wedding invitations went out. John threatened to print "subject to change without notice," at the bottom. Their friends, when they were not worrying how the impending marriage was really affecting Helen, were importuning her about wedding gifts. Bell sent a note with a covering letter "A Secret for Helen Keller—I don't want Miss Sullivan or Mr. Macey [sic] to read this note. Let some one else read it to Helen." Could she keep a secret from teacher and Mr. Macy? he began. He had just received an unexpected $194, and the thought came to him "why not spend this on a wedding present for Miss Sullivan. The trouble is I don't know what to get her that would please her and I want someone to help me. Why not you?"

To Hitz, *"mein liebster Pflegevater,"* she wrote on April 17, "I think she would like something for her nice new bureau. We are all looking forward

*Mildred not long afterwards married and settled in Montgomery, Alabama.

to seeing you again. I am sure you will find Teacher lovelier than ever, and our home real cosy and pretty." They were hurrying to finish the housecleaning before her mother arrived. "She has made a suggestion which has led me to change my summer plans. I am going home with her after the wedding, and shall spend a month or so down there. . . . My going home will give Teacher and John a good chance to be happy alone. Just think, all this time they have had to share their society and their happiness with others!"

They were married in the early afternoon in the flower-heaped living room, in front of a large window. Dr. Hale, almost eighty-five—still the "shaggy prophet," still the seer with reverberating, sacral voice—led them through the marriage vows, while Helen with her hand on his arm stood by his side with Lenore translating into the palm of her hand the words that united her two dearest friends. Twenty guests were present. Hitz, "the picturesque secretary" with the flowing white beard, now close to eighty, Helen's mother, John's family, the Phil Smiths, Mrs. Hopkins, Mrs. Polly Pratt. Helen described the simple ceremony to Sister Mary Joseph:

> I did not think you would care for the little details of my teacher's wedding; but you shall have them. She wore a dark blue travelling dress and a white silk waist. I wore a moss green dress, and I stood up with the bride. My friend Mrs. Smith sat near enough to tell me what was going on without interrupting the ceremony. Mr. Macy wore a gray frock-coat which was most becoming.
>
> We had luncheon immediately after the ceremony, quite without formality. My teacher made the wedding cake herself, and for that matter she prepared the salad and the punch. They had many beautiful flowers, and each of the guests carried away a bunch of carnations as a souvenir of the occasion. There were about twenty persons invited.
>
> The wedding presents were very handsome—a fine French clock with candelabra from Dr. Bell, a large punch bowl with glasses from Mr. Wade, spoons enough to stir tea for the village, a splendid box of silver, containing one hundred and twenty-five pieces from Mr. and Mrs. H.H. Rogers, a silver bureau set and many other gifts I cannot remember. [The newspapers reported English spoons from the Hut-

tons, an immense silver loving cup from some of John Macy's class-mates, a handsome brooch from Mrs. J.P. Morgan.] For weeks I was crammed with secrets, my friends told me what their gifts were going to be, and I had great fun trying to keep them, and if a girl ever kept a secret with difficulty, it was I.

At four thirty Annie and John bade good-bye to Helen and their other guests, took the train for Boston to catch a boat to New Orleans. Dr. Hale back at his home in Roxbury thought of Helen separated from her Teacher and wrote her a tender, understanding letter:

I could not talk to you yesterday nearly as much as I wanted to, but I do want to congratulate you with all my heart and soul and strength as to the possibilities for you which I see in the new marriage, and I long to say that you have gained a brother and not lost a sister.

The tie between you and our dear Annie is as close as any tie can possibly be. I dare say plenty of people have told you that there is nothing like it in history or literature. You do not care anything about that. You know just how much she loves you and how much you love her. Now, bear in mind that love is not something to be measured out in pints or pecks. It is infinite in all its relations. And never permit yourself for an instant to think that Annie loves you less than she ever did, or that the tie to her husband can tempt her to love you less. She will love you more.

I suppose that God put us into the world for this, that from week to week we might love more, that we might be more, and do more and enjoy more. That we might be grown up children of his instead of being babies of his. Now as life enlarges this power of love increases. Take my case: with every new subject that I have studied, for instance, with every new language which I have learned my life has been enlarged. My life enlarged when I went to Europe; my life enlarged when I learned about the Roentgen ray. And under exactly this law my life has enlarged with every true friend who I have ever really known and really trusted. Dear Helen, your life may be enlarged and will, with your intercourse with your new brother.

I hope your mother will read you this note. I am sure she will say that it is all true. And I shall be very glad if she says that there is no use in writing it to you.

Mrs. Keller had worried for Helen. "It would have been too cruel if you had not loved Helen!" she wrote to John. Some worried for John. Helen Howe, the daughter of the Boston chronicler Mark A. DeWolfe Howe, a fellow editor of John's at *Youth's Companion,* wrote cryptically in her book *The Gentle Americans* of "John Macy, that unsung optimist who, married at the time to the great Anne Sullivan Macy, was hoping to pursue a marriage contained within the most extraordinary prefabricated triangle in history."

But that was not the way Teacher's friends saw it. They worried about Teacher, said Villa Curren, who was one of the wedding party. The Phil Smiths put it more bluntly: "They said that Teacher had nothing to do with her marrying John. It was all his fault, and as for his saying afterwards that he had married an institution, he knew that in the beginning, Helen came first. He was willing to have it so."

XVIII

A Successful Book—More Doubts

"The sum of it is that you're a blessing." —William James

Helen and her mother tarried at Wrentham, tidying up the house, answering mail, writing, her mother said, "a fine letter" to Dr. Hale and "a tactful one" to Mrs. Thaw. Hitz stayed on also, as did Mrs. Hopkins. After Helen and her mother left for Alabama, Mrs. Hopkins would look after Wrentham, sleeping with the newlyweds' silver until they should return from their wedding trip. Hitz went for his constitutional every morning before breakfast. Twice Helen accompanied him, as much out of worry for the old gentleman as for the pleasure of his company. He was beginning to fail. On their second walk he stopped and leaned against the stone wall, unable to go forward. "I am not quite awake," he apologized.

All this Helen wrote in a note that the Macys would find upon their return to Wrentham. "I leave my love here to greet you when you come back, as I trust you will from the happiest of trips. I have thought of you daily, hourly since you were married, and such has my happiness in yours been that I am not homesick yet." Her thoughts were for Annie and John; and if she had any misgivings that marriage might mean less of Teacher —and inevitably, therefore, less of the world—she concealed them well. Change there was bound to be, certainly for the next few months, when she made the second of her rare visits to her family in Alabama. She loved them dearly, but Florence was parochial. Alabama's treatment of the blacks distressed her. And though her mother knew the manual language, her reports on the world about them did not have the pith and sparkle of Teacher's. Her mother, moreover, had to attend to the household, and there were long spans of time when Helen was left to her own devices, to grope about in her silent, black world as best she could.

An episode at Wrentham before they left, though she described it whimsically, had shown anew how cut off from the world she really was when Teacher was not there, and also how vulnerable to its lurking perils:

> I must tell you something awful. I was as black Wednesday morning as I had been fair to look upon the day before. I was in the bathroom complacently combing my hair. I had just washed my face VERY clean, as I supposed. Suddenly Aunt Sophia burst in with 'Oh, oh, come out quick, come quick, it is terrible, terrible.' She seemed in hysterics, and I thought someone must have been murdered, or your silver stolen. But I discovered that the lamp had been left lighted until midnight when the bathroom smoked like a furnace! Of course I was one color with the towels, the marble, the tub and shelves.

Oddly, for someone who loved to write and to receive letters, she did not take her typewriter with her, "because I knew I could not get any rest if I did." It was another way of saying that her real life was at Wrentham with Teacher and now John. Those two, debarking in New Orleans, went directly to Florence to spend some time with Helen before proceeding north to Wrentham. Annie's letter to her "cher Père" had interpolations by John and showed the high spirits and good humor that bound them all together: "I am much the same person that I was (I agree to that, both as to the good and as to the naughty—J.A.M.)—just as perverse, just as unreasonable, just as full of love for my friends, just as adverse to writing them. Yet when I realize what has happened to me it seems as if the great happiness which is mine should make me better and wiser in every way and a good deal more of a Swedenborgian (who ever heard of an Irish Swedenborgian? J.A.M.)." She and John had spent a fortnight in Florence with Helen, "rambling in the woods, visiting the Quarry, and studying the Negro question within smelling distance of the subject. (It is full of the fragrance of a deep and stagnant pit.)" They had reached Wrentham at the end of May. "It is the sweetest, loveliest, happiest home in the world."

Helen followed afterwards. She had been happy to return to Wrentham, she wrote Minna Smith, who had invited her to Bermuda. "I was even happier than usual because of the new joy that had come to fill my teacher's life." She was very fond of John, almost as happy as Teacher was with him, and she had Teacher to thank that "he will always be near me. Three months have now passed, and with this new affection our home life has enlarged and become more beautiful, more complete!" If Annie's marriage presented difficulties to her, she was one of the rare persons who are able to convert troubles into new strengths. "The great enduring realities are love and service," she wrote in *Youth's Companion* in a message addressed "To Girls Who Are Going to College." She lived by that creed.

Except when Michael Anagnos crossed her path—even, sad to report, in death. The final years of his life had been darkened by the separation from Annie and Helen. Their banishment from his life, even though it had been of his doing, had been a bereavement as personal as the loss of a beloved member of his family. He might tell visitors that any college-educated woman could do what Annie had done for Helen, but he had felt her force and wit, and Helen's enchanting ways, and he had never ceased loving them, as he must have realized when pride and bitterness permitted it.

In 1906, an ailing man, he was off again to his beloved Greece. In July news of his death reached Boston. Frank Sanborn, now seventy-five, who had been the associate of Dr. Howe in his antislavery work as well as in his efforts for the blind, and who as his successor as the head of the State Board of Charities had been instrumental in rescuing Annie from Tewksbury, wrote the memorial tribute in *The Transcript.* He covered Anagnos's beginnings as a young revolutionary in Greece, his thirty years at Perkins, and ended with a claim for Anagnos that Helen considered a provocation when it was read to her: "The wonderful success of Dr. Howe in training Laura Bridgman has been outdone by Anagnos in the education of Helen Keller and Elizabeth Robbin, not to mention others; and it is to be hoped that none of the blind and the deaf who have shared the instruction of Anagnos and benefited by his generosity will fail to imitate the truly touching gratitude which Laura Bridgman showed towards him who had brought her from solitude to the companionship of her kind."

In a rare outburst of anger Helen replied the next day by letter to *The Transcript:* "This statement is misleading and contrary to fact. Mr. Anagnos did not educate me. . . . He did not attempt to give me instruction in any subject, for he was never able to use the manual language fluently." She was surprised that Mr. Sanborn, "an intimate of the great and wise," should have made such an error. She was grateful to Dr. Howe, to Perkins and to Anagnos, who threw open the doors of Perkins to her, "a stranger from a far State. . . . These tender memories fill my heart so completely that they exclude any unpleasant feeling about the wrong which Mr. Anagnos afterwards did my teacher and me, and with his death have died all but the kindest thoughts of him."

He had no need to search for the truth, Sanborn a few days later replied from his home in Concord, "since it was I who procured the admission of Miss Sullivan to the school of Mr. Anagnos about the time, I believe, that Miss Keller was born, and have naturally kept myself acquainted with the facts of the case, in the quarter of a century since." With a trace of irony, Sanborn, remembering Helen's attacks on Perkins in her speeches about what Massachusetts should do for its blind, said he was glad to learn that Miss Keller did not "underestimate her obligation to Mr. Anagnos." He would be equally pleased to hear "a similar acknowledgement from her who was Miss Sullivan when I knew her, and who, at the end of six years of instruction under Mr. Anagnos, expressed to me her sense of obligation for the slight official action I had taken in the matter."

Anagnos had many friends in Boston, where there was a considerable community of Greek-Americans. The Howe clan still was one of the most respected and potent. A small conspiracy developed to settle scores with Teacher, who Sanborn and the Howes thought was the instigator of Helen's letter. Sanborn journeyed to Newport to spend several days with Julia Ward Howe. The temporary director of Perkins, Mr. Caswell, joined them. "From several sources I am getting facts about Annie Sullivan," Sanborn informed Laura Richards, one of Mrs. Howe's daughters, "and I rather think she and her friends will be startled when they come forward in October, if they do, to maintain their accusation of 'wrong' done to her by Anagnos. It seems that Anagnos was warned at the time that Helen could not have written The Frost King story, but refused to distrust Anne Sullivan. When the truth appeared he was proportionately mortified."

Sanborn carefully went over the papers that were placed at his disposal by the executors of Anagnos's will. Someone—probably David Hall, Mrs. Howe's son-in-law, a lawyer—took the letters and other materials and in the lengthy lawyer's brief called "Miss Sullivan's Methods" referred to in Chapter VIII, compared the account of Helen's education given in *The Story of My Life* with her letters to Anagnos at the time to show how deliberately the role of the Perkins Institution in Helen's education had been minimized and concealed.*

Since Anagnos had been known as a man more likely "to suffer a wrong than to commit one," Sanborn wrote Helen on September 26, he was obliged to ask her to state specifically what the wrong was that Anagnos had done Miss Sullivan, as he intended to lay the whole matter before the corporation of the Perkins Institution. He ended this letter to Helen with words that must have appeared to Annie as a threat: "This is the first letter I have ever written you,—not because I was lacking in the interest which we all found in your education, but because I seemed to perceive that your teacher, Miss Sullivan, did not want to be reminded of the circumstances (by no means discreditable to her) in which we first met; and it therefore seemed to be improper for me to bring them to her recollection, by seeking your acquaintance or correspondence."

Two days later Helen responded with a five-page typewritten document. The letters between Anagnos and themselves, she began, for the period between 1886 and 1893 indeed showed "no evidence of wrong, but only evidence of affection and gratitude." It was only after 1893, "after we had ceased to avail ourselves of the hospitality of the Perkins Institution that Mr. Anagnos proved untrue to the friendship between us" and began by "word of mouth to impugn our integrity." Although at the "trial" he had expressed belief in "our innocence," he had subsequently told several people that he believed one or both guilty, and even had said to one of their friends that "Helen Keller is a living lie," and when an explanation was demanded insisted that Helen's teacher had taught her to deceive. "That was the wrong Mr. Anagnos did my teacher. That was the untruth he told of me." And when in 1902 John Macy had asked him to attest in writing to their integrity, he had refused. He did not dare to make his accusations publicly. "He pursued us insidiously with the subtle breath of words that are spoken and exist no more for one to seize and bring to him for explanation. . . . I know that he entangled the path we trod." But she did not complain, since she had profited by the need to prove her authenticity every step of the way.

Her Teacher bade her to say, Helen's letter ended, "that she has always been glad to be reminded of the circumstances in which she first met you. . . . She asked me to say that your suggestion that you seemed to perceive

*The unsigned document, handsomely bound, will be found on the shelves of the Perkins Library.

in her an unwillingness to be reminded of the services you rendered her is a misreading of her character, for all her friends and even newspaper editors know her story." Helen, too, ended with a threat that she explained neither then nor since: "If it is necessary to account for Mr. Anagnos's turning against us, I can explain his motives very clearly, but I hope for the sake of his memory that will not be required of me."

He would submit her letter to the corporation at its annual meeting, Sanborn informed her. And on October 10 he did present to the meeting a record of "the main facts" concerning Annie's and Helen's relations with Perkins. He included Helen's letter, with the comment: "Assuming all these statements have a real foundation, and were not imposed by an interested person upon the mind of a person singularly cut off by a sad infirmity from receiving those impressions which sight and hearing furnish, what do they imply? First, that a tale-bearer had undertaken to report conversations which carried from one to another may naturally have been misquoted as in the case of tale bearers is almost sure to happen. Second that they misconstrue that verdict of Mr. Anagnos in the so-called court of inquiry. His was the casting vote and it was for 'the Scotch verdict of not proven.' " The heading on Sanborn's exposition of "the facts" states that he moved its adoption by a vote of the corporation. The document was never published.

At the memorial services for Anagnos at Tremont Temple two weeks later, to which Julia Ward Howe contributed a poem and which was addressed by the governor and the mayor, Sanborn delivered the major address. It ended with an account of how he had procured the admission of Anne Sullivan, "a poor child," to Perkins, Anagnos's selection of her to go to Tuscumbia, the connections between the two women and Perkins from 1887 to 1894 and the gratitude to Perkins that Annie had expressed at the time. He made no reference to Tewksbury, yet in her book *Teacher* Helen upbraids him for not honoring "her reticence concerning Tewksbury"; instead "he brought up her humble origin against her and dwelt on her 'ingratitude' to the institution which had accepted 'a state charge' as a pupil. Teacher never said a word to me about the affair, but, contrary to her wishes, I poured out my indignation in a letter to Mr. Sanborn. To this day I cannot excuse his mean-spirited behavior." The account is puzzling. Helen's letter to Sanborn showed clearly that Teacher knew of her letter. Moreover, she accuses Sanborn of bringing up Teacher's origins not in connection with Anagnos's memorial service, but because of his anger over her criticisms of Perkins at the hearings before the legislature. Her statement in *Teacher* is additionally mystifying because Annie's disclosure, even to Helen, of her years in Tewksbury came only in the late 1920s. Helen's hostility to Sanborn, long since dead, when *Teacher* was published, testifies again to the strength of her devotion to Teacher.

At the time (1906) neither side wanted to continue the feud. The members of the corporation showed their attitude in the selection of a successor to Anagnos. Among those present at the Tremont memorial service was Dr. Edward E. Allen, superintendent of the Pennsylvania School for the Blind and an instructor at Perkins during some of the time that Helen spent there. A Harvard graduate, he had spent three years in England working for Francis J. Campbell at the Royal Normal College for the Blind. He was "young, handsome, and unmarried and very English in dress and speech" when he arrived at Perkins in 1888, Annie recalled, adding, "then everybody was talking about the new master." The Perkins trustees were sure of one thing, said Dr. Allen: They did not want another member of the Howe clan; nor did they want anyone connected with the Annie Sullivan faction, for among the applicants for the job was John Macy. "She and Teacher had pushed him into that," Helen told Nella Braddy in 1954. The trustees chose Dr. Allen.

Did Macy really want to become superintendent of the Perkins Institution? His real interest was literature. His poems were beginning to appear in various monthlies. His monograph on Poe was about to be published. But under the influence of Annie and Helen he was making himself knowledgeable in the problems of the deaf and the blind and wrote several articles—"Teaching the Deaf," "Our Blind Citizens"—all of them pleas for work opportunities for the handicapped. Or would he, if chosen, have continued with his literary work, while Annie directed Perkins?

All three—Annie, John and Helen—were subject to the competing pulls of writing and of work for the blind and afflicted. Unsuccessful at getting an article from Helen on the St. Louis Exposition, Gilder had suggested that she do an essay on the hand. "Cannot I hope to have some of Helen's writing for the Century?" he inquired of Annie just after Helen's graduation from Radcliffe. "How about the article on *recognition* —and how about some travel articles?—Europe?" John answered him, saying someone had already "spoken" for an article. "Lord love you!" Gilder exploded. "I have been 'speaking' too." They agreed on an article "on the hand—and her methods of recognition—of *not less* than 3,000 words for which we will pay $500." And Gilder wanted pictures.

Helen finished the article by November. Gilder liked it. "Perhaps it has your best and firmest and most mature writing. . . . I wonder if you have ever read Diderot on blindness? . . . It seems that one blind man said he would rather have long arms than sight. He would rather, as I understand, feel the moon than see it. How do you feel about that?" Perhaps she could still incorporate it in her article?

The additions were not made, but Gilder was asked whether he might not be interested in a book by Helen about her ways of knowing her world. He thought that a book about The World I Live In was a splendid idea, and then was astonished to discover that John was shopping around to see where he could get the best contract. "There seems to be some complication about the Keller Hand article written at my suggestion!" he wrote Macy reproachfully. "I am very sorry, I don't like to 'compete' with Doubleday and Page on this matter—and I didn't know we were doing so. You see our publishers thought that if we were to pay such heavy prices we ought to have a book, especially as it was our suggestion. What think you?"

Gilder also wrote directly to Helen: "My suggestions as to an article on the hand has worked so well that I am inclined to make some further suggestions, somewhat in the same direction, hoping that a little book may grow out of it—a book which would not only have literary value but a great psychological value; showing, in fact, *the world in which you live.*" Century paid a thousand dollars for the next two essays, with the option of first refusal of any book that might result from them. Helen not only completed the essay to Gilder's satisfaction but submitted as a phase of the world in which she lived a poem, "The Chant of Darkness." "I think you are very truly to be congratulated on the poem and the later essay," Gilder informed her. "It fulfills what I hoped you would do. . . . The poem is very moving and fine, and the rhythm of your prose is remarkable. . . . All this writing of yours illustrates the finest thing in art, i.e. emotion under artistic control." The Century Company was ready to make a book out of her essays, but was not pressing her: "You have a wise, experienced and disinterested adviser in Mr. Macy and all will be done for your best interests."

Evidently the terms in which Gilder praised John caused problems at Wrentham, for Gilder wrote him a week later, "I never heard the suspicion that you were Helen's 'agent' in any way except that of firm friendship." A Dutch visitor had told him he would like to ask Helen about her dreams. Had Helen said all she can on the subject? "The book would be an appropriate place to tell about 'the world she dreams of!' " She had already written on the subject for Professor Jastrow, Macy said. Well, could she not amplify that for the magazine as "The World I Dream Of"? —"Oh my! why can't we have that?"

Two chapters on dreams went into the book. Century offered generous terms, "a royalty of 20 per cent which is the very highest royalty paid by us, and that to only a few authors, Kipling and men of that sort!"

"The Chant of Darkness," with which the book was to end, suddenly caused an embarrassing difficulty. "Here is a state of affairs," a subeditor at *The Century* advised Gilder. In preparing the "Chant" for the press, "I met many old friends"—in particular many lines that "word for word are given in Job. . . . The spirit of the whole is the spirit of Job, though the latter part has a more personal note. It is a curious case." The publishers were more embarrassed than Helen and her friends. "I hope you will not be too much disturbed over Job in Miss Keller's poem," wrote William Ellsworth for the publishing house. "I am glad that it was discovered and I am sure that everything can be fixed." The best solution, advised Gilder's assistant, might be to omit the first two pages. When John objected to that, the magazine proposed to precede the "Chant" with an editorial note that it was "a blending of the author's remarkable imagination with cited passages from the book of Job and, to a lesser extent, from some of the modern poets. The quotations from Job are, so to speak, the text and origin of Miss Keller's own work and add impressiveness to the point of view of the author, who has constructed the poem with a definite biographical interest." Such an editorial note was needed for Helen's "protection," and the only "ethical question" was that the poem should be presented for what it was.

The issue of Helen's borrowings arose again when a minister who had planned to base his sermon on a passage from Dr. James Martineau wrote *The Century* saying that Helen had taken that passage literally from Martineau, without ascription. Gilder sent the letter to Helen. She would gladly have put in the author's name, Helen replied, "for it would have given added distinction to the idea," but she had not remembered the source until the reader sent in his letter. Then she had recalled that an old magazine sent to her by Dr. Hale had contained an essay by Martineau, "God in Nature." One of the dilemmas of a blind person who wishes to write, she went on, was that

interesting fragments are often read to me in a promiscuous manner by my friends. They give me, as they read, paragraphs that strike

them, and I do not always know the name of the book or the author.
. . . I wish I could always indicate the exact source of my ideas. This
is possible when those sources are in books I can read myself. But it
is not easy to trace fugitive sentences and paragraphs as they are
spelled into my hand.

Many cases similar to this one have arisen and I have been troubled
by them. Sometimes I think I ought to stop writing altogether, since
I cannot tell surely which of my ideas are borrowed feathers, except
for those which I gather from books in raised print. . . .

Gilder proposed to print Helen's letter as an editorial with comment by
himself. He was being "overanxious," John said. Why did he not handle
it by quoting Mark Twain's letter on plagiarism?* "I don't think Mr.
Clemens's letter has any appropriateness to this situation," Gilder remonstrated. "Helen is not a 'child' now and we are not 'breaking her heart.'
Moreover, I don't agree with him about plagiarism, but think it, when
intentional, one of the meanest forms of stealing ever devised."
The book was a critical success. "You have eloquently, graciously vindicated your right to speak in terms of light and color and form and
sound," Professor Copeland of Harvard wrote her. He had already read
most of the chapters, "not a few of them to my classes in Radcliffe.
. . . Fate narrowed the world you live in, but you have burst the bonds
of Fate and contrived to make us—if we have any sense—think better of
the world." None of the reviews questioned its originality, and when
Helen a few months later sent Gilder "A Chant of the Stone Wall" with
the cautionary note, "I commit the folly of sending you another poem
when I am not poet," the delighted Gilder immediately offered to pay
three hundred dollars for the magazine rights to the six-hundred-line
poem.
The World I Live In explained how Helen made the senses of touch,
smell and taste compensate for her two missing senses. One reviewer
called the essays "psychological classics," the work of "a genius," which
no one else could have written. Imagination was the key to the world that
she had constructed with the use of only three senses. "Without imagination what a poor thing my world would be," she wrote. "With imagination," commented one reviewer, "Miss Keller knows more of the world

*See page 146.

around her and enjoys it more vividly than most persons who have all their senses but no imagination."

Taste was not much use to her in the acquisition of knowledge, she wrote, and smell was an atrophying sense among civilized people. She called it "the fallen angel," but it served her well for pleasure, a means of recognition and the judgment of character.

Her reliance on smell was brought out on another occasion by Ernest Gruening, then a beginning reporter for the *Boston Herald.* He interviewed her at Wrentham after she had spoken to an International Congress of Otologists at Harvard Medical School. "Had she known there was a crowd when she had spoken at the Medical School?" he asked her.

"I should say I did," Miss Keller replied. "I could feel them and smell them."

"How did you feel them?"

"By any number of vibrations through the air, and through the floor, from the moving of feet or the scraping of chairs and by the warmth when there are people around."

"How could you tell by your sense of smell?"

"There was a doctor's odor."

"Do you mean to say that doctors have a special odor which you can recognize?"

"A very decided odor," Miss Keller said. "It's partly the smell of ether and partly the smell that lingers from the sick rooms in which they have been. But I can tell many professions from their odor."

"Which ones?" I asked.

"Doctors, painters, sculptors, masons, carpenters, druggists, and cooks."

"What does the carpenter smell like, and the druggist?"

"The carpenter is always accompanied by the odor of wood. The druggist is saturated with various drugs. There is a painter who comes here often and I can always tell the minute he comes anywhere near me."

"Could you tell my work in that way?" I asked. "Do you smell any ink?"

"No, a typewriter, I think," Miss Keller answered quickly, laughing.

"Could you really tell that?"

Miss Keller's rippling laugh continued. "I'm afraid that was a guess," she admitted.

It was touch, she pointed out in her book, that gave her the firmest hold on the world around her. "If I had to make a man, I should certainly have put the brain and the soul in his fingertips." Reviewers noted her educated powers of touch by citing passages such as the following:

> The delicate tremble of a butterfly's wings in my hand, the soft petals of violets curling in the cool folds of their leaves or lifting sweetly out of the meadow grass, the clear, firm outline of face and limb, the smooth arch of a horse's neck and the velvety touch of his nose—all these, and a thousand resultant combinations, which take shape in my mind, constitute my world.

The reviewer who had called the essays "psychological classics" was seconded by the most respected figure in American psychology and philosophy, William James. His comments strikingly echoed the last chord of the blind Milton's lines:

> So much the rather thou, Celestial Light
> Shine inward, and the mind through all her powers
> Irradiate.

She had occasionally met James in Cambridge but had not had the opportunity to take a class with him. "Dear Miss Keller," he wrote her in longhand,

> I cannot forbear sending you a word of thanks for having written 'the world I live in,' and of praise for the success with which you have told so much truth about human nature which nobody had suspected. Evidently sensations as such form the relatively smaller part of the world we mentally live in, *relations* being the things of most interest there, and the whole spread & extent and interest consisting of material suggested and treated analogically, and being practically quite as vast in one person as in another, and similar in effects of contrast etc., and in aesthetic and moral appeal in us all. I have found the book extraordinarily instructive.
>
> I won't praise your power over language, or your clearness of discrimination or your genius for psychological insight, for I don't want to add to the *spoiling* process to which you have been subjected so

long!!! The sum of it is that you're a *blessing* & I'll kill any one who says you're not!

He had one reservation. "I think your love of writing has let your pen run away with you the least bit in Chaps XIV & XV ["Dreams and Reality" and "A Waking Dream"], but I admire the Whitmanesque poem, and I think that the optimism that streams from this book is a splendid moral inspiration to the reader."

It flattered Helen to be praised by the great William James. She agreed with him that "my fancy ran away with me in chapters 14 and 15. I was trying to describe some impressions I have of our dream-experiences. I had too much fun with the waking dreams to be precise." She would welcome a chance to study psychology. "I do not think I truly remember emotions which I experienced before I was taught. I knew I had them because I have a tactual memory of shedding tears, screaming, kicking, and other acts which indicate feeling. Yet in no case can I recall the emotions as such. I used to hunt for good things to eat, and when I failed to find them, I cried. But, to save my life, I can't remember the disappoint-ment which caused the tears. I am astonished that there should be such distinct images of different acts in my mind side by side with such a vacuum of emotional memory." James replied a few days later:

I have no explanation of the lack of emotional memory you speak of, and in general I am quite disconcerted, professionally speaking, by your account of yourself before your 'consciousness' was awakened by instruction. But whatever you were or are, you're a blessing!

It is no paradox that you live in a world so indistinguishable from ours. The great world of the *background,* in all of us is the world of our *beliefs:* That is the world of the permanencies and the immensities, and our relations with it are mostly verbal. We think of its history and structure in verbal terms exclusively—the sensations we have of the remote and the hidden being the merest incipiencies and hints which, as you so well show, we extend by imagination or add to by analogy.

But it makes no difference in what shape the content of our verbal material may come. In some it is more optical, in others more motor in nature. In you it is motor and tactile, but its functions are the same as ours, the relations meant by the words symbolizing the relations existing between the things.

James understandably was "disconcerted" by her account of her "consciousness"—or rather lack of it—before Teacher's arrival in Tuscumbia. Her description of herself in "Before the Soul Dawn" is of an autistic child:

> Before my teacher came to me, I did not know that I am. I lived in a world that was a no-world. I cannot hope to describe adequately that unconscious, yet conscious time of nothingness. I did not know that I knew aught, or that I lived or acted or desired. I had neither will nor intellect. I was carried along to objects and acts by a certain blind natural impetus. I had a mind which caused me to feel anger, satisfaction, desire. . . .

Her mother did not like that passage and wanted her to omit it, lest it confirm those of their kin who before Teacher's arrival had implied that she was an idiot. It took much tactful argument by Teacher to persuade her mother that "dormancy" was not the same as "feeble-mindedness," and the passage went in as Helen wrote it. This was a victory not so much over her mother as over herself. She had come to believe that the account she had given in *The Story of My Life* had been too bland, too much a reflection of her desire to appear like other young people. It pleased Teacher "to have me assert personal freedom by thinking for myself," she later wrote.

But Helen's recollection of events, what she chose to emphasize and what to omit, was influenced by her immediate purpose in writing. When she came to write *Teacher,* she brought out the autistic aspects of her "consciousness" in order to underscore more strongly the extraordinary difficulties of the task that confronted Teacher on her arrival in Tuscumbia.

Yet this was not the whole story. Helen lost her sight and hearing when she was eighteen months old. She had already learned to toddle, to acquire language, feeding and toilet habits, to love and to be loved by her parents. "We know, of course," writes Selma Fraiberg, "that in the absence of a human partner the baby cannot acquire a sense of self and other, of 'me' and 'you.'" But Helen at the age of one and a half had such partners in a family who adored their firstborn child. Although the loss of sight and hearing in a considerable sense "robbed" her of these partners "and of a large measure of the sensory experience that linked her to the world outside" (I borrow these expressions from Fraiberg's splendid book *Insights from the Blind),* she had learned enough to run to her mother for comfort in the rages and despairs that now beset her, and to cling to her as she went about her household duties. She had also learned to make signs —considerably over fifty, she once calculated—for her various wants and feelings. There are "givens" in personality that unfold silently in a biologically ordained sequence; and while their development (as Selma Fraiberg so patiently elucidated) can be slowed or even arrested by the absence of vision and hearing, that was not the case with Helen. The vital, energetic child who rushed at Teacher on her arrival at Tuscumbia was clearly not autistic.

Teacher herself told Nella Braddy in the late twenties:

> I have always thought I was fortunate in having a wild, wilful and destructive child for a pupil because she was more interesting than a mild, orderly child would have been. Energy is one of nature's choicest gifts to the child. There is always a battle between the vigorous, wilful child and the grown-up who demands submission from him, and many of these splendidly equipped children are destroyed in the process of educating them. They turn to wickedness because of the unnatural restraints and repressions they suffer.
>
> In a few days I became Helen's playmate, and shared her life completely.

XIX

A Winsome Woman and
Some Benefactors

"He [Mark Twain] treated me not as a freak but as a
handicapped woman. . . ."

"I do not remember writing anything in such a happy mood as
The World I Live In." Part of her delight arose from John's collaboration.
"His hands were seldom still, and even when he was not speaking to me
I could tell by his gestures whether he was arguing or joking or simply
carrying on an ordinary conversation.

"I cannot enumerate the helpful kindnesses with which he smoothed my
rugged paths of endeavor. Once, when my typewriter was out of order,
and I was tired of the manual labor of copying, he sat up all night and
typed forty pages of my manuscript so that they might reach the press in
time. . . . He kept me faithfully in touch with the chief happenings of the
day, the discoveries of science, and the new trends in literature. If he was
particularly pleased with a book, he would have Mr. John Hitz put it into
Braille for me, or he would read it to me himself when he had time."

She needed collaborators. At Wrentham there were John and Teacher,
with John the more helpful in her literary labors. Teacher always minimized her own part in Helen's writing—except, as we have seen, in her
letter to Mrs. Hutton.* "It has been suggested that I helped Helen with
her writing," she said in the early thirties. "This is a deep injustice. I have
no such talent as hers. Almost feverishly she has written every line herself.

*See page 328.

The only help I have given her is in the process of selection after they were completed. For she has much to say, and she enjoys the saying of it to such a degree, that the pages run away from her, defying the limitations of her publishers."

So happily busy was she with her literary work that she cut down on meetings, as she informed Hitz. John usually spent his days in Boston at the *Youth's Companion* where he was still an editor, and working on his own writing, often staying the night at the St. Botolph's Club, while Helen contentedly worked away on her typewriter, eager to have new pages to show him on his return.

One drawback to living in Wrentham was holding on to household help. "Such absurd predicaments as we get into with every servant who comes along!" she wrote Hitz, after their latest treasure decamped because she was unable "to wake up in time for her early work." So things were as usual, her letter continued. "And the usual thing is for us to be in the kitchen"—which meant that, however much Helen tried to help with the household chores, it was Annie who did the work, unless Helen's mother was with them. Annie chafed under the burden. She loathed household duties. She felt that she had important things to say to the world herself. Often in the grip of rebellious rage, she rode off on her horse, for she was a superb horsewoman. Once she was badly thrown by a horse that she had been warned was unsafe. Helen lost patience and told her what she thought of such "mad escapades." "Is that the sympathy I get when I am in trouble?" Teacher replied bitterly and stalked out of the room. A few hours later she was all contrition: "I am sorry, Helen. I was trying to run away from the kitchen and everything that makes one old. Kiss me, and I will turn over a new leaf."

Teacher had considerable creative power, and John spurred her on to write; but the public was interested only in Helen. John's poems were appearing in many magazines, but Helen's commanded high prices. *The Century* had paid five hundred dollars for the two hundred-odd lines of "The Chant of Darkness," with which she had ended *The World I Live In.*

Their farm gave her the idea for another poem. "Our farm looks fine now," she wrote Hitz. "We have about 600 feet of stone wall and quite a wide sweep of land. They say our field looks like a park already." They were rebuilding and lengthening the old stone wall. "As we laid one stone upon another, I kept fingering the various shapes, textures and sizes, and I became aware of a beauty in them that I had not sensed before." John brought her a book on geology, and with her marvelous tactual responsiveness she soon was weaving cosmogonical fantasies around the boulders. "Oh, Teacher," she said finally, "here's a poem to write in these stone walls, if there is enough of the poet in me for such a task." Teacher encouraged her, and "sat right down then and there, looked closely at the wall" and began to describe the play of light and shadow, of flower and bush. "There was a Celtic tinge in some of her words as I wove them in afterwards with mine," wrote Helen:

> The walls are astir. . . .
> Soft whispers of showers and flowers
> Are mingled in the spring song of the walls. . . .
>
> The walls sing the song of wild bird, the hoofbeat of deer,
> The murmur of pine and cedar, the ripple of many streams. . . .

As the poem began to take shape, Helen decided to link the stone walls with the story of the Puritan settlers who first subdued New England's stony fields. John took them to an old cemetery, where Helen touched the ancient tombstones and read the inscriptions. She immersed herself in New England chronicles and ballads. As the lines emerged, she read Teacher what she wrote "and asked her to say my lines over and let me read her lips so that I might ascertain whether there was anything worth while in my rude verse."

In July 1909, less than a year after she had finished *The World I Live In,* John sent the poem to Gilder and asked five hundred dollars for it. Gilder objected: "That price was all right for her articles published last year, and for the Chant, her first poem and very unusual one. But this material does not seem to us to be quite in that class,—that is, for magazine purposes." They settled on a price of three hundred dollars, with royalties of 15 percent on the first five thousand and 20 percent thereafter. "Of course, you will realize," the publisher wrote, "that at this price (75 cents for the book) the amount we will receive will be about 50¢ net. After deducting the cost of the plates, pictures and manufacture of the book, there would not be a great deal of profit for either of us,—but we want to do the book, and we certainly ought not to differ widely as to the division of the profits whatever they may be."

"O beautiful blind stones," the sightless bard chanted, beginning a statement of the vitalistic faith that grayer, more philosophic heads have endorsed:

O beautiful blind stones, inarticulate and dumb!
In the deep gloom of their hearts there is a gleam
Of the primeval sun whick looked upon them
When they were begotten.
So in the heart of man shines forever
A beam from the everlasting sun of God.
Unresponsive, rude are the stones;
Yet in them divine things lie concealed.
I hear their imprisoned chant:
'We are fragments of the universe. . . .'

From the wall as a symbol of cosmic beginnings she turned to the wall as a "tapestry" on which was written the story of the Pilgrims, of the *Mayflower:*

O, tiny craft, bearing a nation's seed!
Frail shallop, quick with unborn states!

On a visit to a New England graveyard, the headstones remind her of the "steadfast, angular beliefs" of the region's Puritan forbears, while

Close by the wall a peristyle of pines
Sings requiems to all the dead that sleep.

The return of spring to the flinty fields becomes an ode to love:

I see a young girl—the spirit of spring she seems,
Sister of the winds that run through the rippling daisies.
Sweet and clear her voice calls father and brother,
And one whose name her shy lips will not utter.

With delicate brushstrokes she names the flowers and blossoming trees that whisper the name of the lover she is too shy to speak

All Nature's eyes and tongues conspire
In the unfolding of the tale
That Adam and Eve beneath the blossoming rose-tree
Told each other in the Garden of Eden.

The wall speaks also of the grimmer side of the Puritans—the witchcraft trials, the groans of women, the woman put to death "for her God was the Lord Jehovah," and the monster cloud of slavery, a "nation's shame" that it took the blood spilled at Gettysburg to wash away. She ends her chant on a note of hope, beseeching the stones to tell her of "the greater things to be," of the time

> When love and wisdom are the only creed,
> And law and right are one.

"By what mystery of education," asked the reviewer for the London *Times,* "has the world that most of us know by sight and hearing been made so real to one who cannot see nor hear? And whence comes this power over sound?" That Helen was able to see so much with the "inward eye" seemed to another reviewer "a spiritual triumph," a rebuke to the "blatant positivism of the age."

It is intriguing to speculate on the lyric of the young girl in love with one whose name she would not tell. Was she perhaps in love with John? Young Helen in the ripeness of womanly beauty not having had the experience of love is a melancholy thought, although it seems that she sublimated her sexual drives in good works. In 1930, two decades after he had left Annie, John wrote his last book, *About Women.* It was a confused exercise. "This essay is not an attack on women, except on certain kinds of women, egregiously assertive feminists," it begins; and to underline his goodwill toward the ladies he includes a chapter on "Some Noble Dames." Macy numbers Heloise among these and tells the story of Heloise and Abelard. The latter was one of the "kings of thought," while Heloise, twenty years younger, was "pretty, intelligent and well-educated, knowing not only Latin but something of Greek and Hebrew. Abelard falls in love with her and there is no reason to doubt the genuiness of his love, whether or not he abused it and took unfair advantage of youth and innocence or simply lost control of himself and followed his passion to its ultimate delight and disaster. He deliberately sought and won her love and made himself a welcome inmate in the house of Fulbert, who was flattered to have so distinguished a man as his guest—a paying guest. Abelard became the tutor of the intellectual and lovely girl; the courtship was a meeting of minds and hearts. He says that under the pretext of study they gave themselves up to love."

Macy goes on to describe how Heloise emerged as the strong partner in the affair, refusing to marry Abelard because marriage and family life would interfere with his studies, holding to her position "with a boldness and intelligence and independent direction worthy of the best feminist thought of to-day." It amazed Macy that a convent-bred girl in the twelfth century could write, "How often I have protested that it was infinitely preferable to me to live with Abelard as his mistress than with any other as Empress of the World." Abelard is castrated by Fulbert's servants; Heloise withdraws to a convent, from where she tries to rally Abelard from his despair, writing reproachfully at one point, "What a shame it is that a philosopher cannot accept what might befall any man."

Perhaps Macy told the story because of its inherent interest and to demonstrate that he admired certain kinds of strength in women. Perhaps the story does have some autobiographic overtones. Obviously the author of this book thinks it does, and so he has reported it. Or was it just a case of mild philandering on John's part and an equally mild flirtation on Helen's? None of Macy's letters to Helen, or for that matter to Annie, have survived; and in all of Helen's letters, as well as in Annie's, John and Helen consider their relationship to be that of sister and brother.

The Song of the Stone Wall was dedicated to Dr. Hale, "a great Puritan." He had been alive while it was being written but was dead by the time it appeared. She had loved him "ever since he called me his little cousin more than twenty years ago."

Another old standby had died in 1908—Helen's *Pflegevater,* the everhelpful Hitz, who, like Hale, had stood by them in their many crises. With Lenore Smith, whose husband was then working for the Geological Survey in Washington, Hitz had gone to Union Station to meet Helen and her mother. "He put his arm around Helen," her mother later wrote, "and stooped and kissed her and spelled in German in her hand some affectionate words of greeting . . . his usual custom upon meeting her." They walked a short distance toward the exits when he halted and leaned against a post. His breathing became very labored. Mrs. Keller appealed to some nearby men for help. They procured a wheelchair. An ambulance was summoned, but by the time it reached the hospital he was dead. Helen, who had followed behind in a carriage with her mother and Lenore, said upon arrival at the hospital that she must see him. Hospital attendants took her to where the body was lying. "She passed her hands over his face and head and kissed him, and then they led her out."

"How shall I write of his kindness to me, whom he called 'meine innigst geliebte Tochter?' " she memorialized him in *The Association Review.* * "Every day he had a plan for giving me pleasure." At the age of seventy

---

*Published by the American Association to Promote the Teaching of Speech to the Deaf.

he had learned Braille "so that I could read his letters myself. Every morning he worked an hour before breakfast, transcribing whatever he thought I should enjoy reading." Not the least of his virtues was his attitude toward women. "To women he brought a special message for he was in sympathy with all sane work for their advancement." He tried ceaselessly "to foster in us a larger activity. He exhorted us to think, that we might develop a greater capacity for usefulness. He disapproved our shrinking from independent, fearless thought and reflection."

Not long after Hitz and Hale, another old benefactor, H.H. Rogers, died. Helen, Annie and John had visited him at his summer home in Fairhaven in September 1908. "I cannot tell you how much we enjoyed our visit at Fairhaven—your home, the beautiful yacht, the dear grandchildren and the buildings with which you have enabled the town to live up to its name." But the pleasantest aspect of the visit, Helen's thank-you letter continued, had been the opportunity to get to know him better. Rogers enjoyed their company and on the spur of the moment had motored down to Hyannis with them. The oil magnate was at the time not in a happy frame of mind. It was the heyday of the muckrakers, and as one of the masters of Standard Oil he was a favorite target of attack.

Helen dedicated *The World I Live In* to him, "My dear Friend of Many Years." He was very pleased, Mrs. Rogers wrote her. "He has much unpleasant criticism to disturb him and your loving dedication is a balm to his wounds."

Doubtless Helen did such things out of genuine affection. But there was also an element of calculation. For it was followed soon afterwards by a bid for additional financial help, not directly, but through an intermediary who approached Rogers on a matter of a "confidential" nature. The Wrentham trio were again beset by financial difficulties, John unable to pay even his dues to the St. Botolph's Club. His distress was so great that "Teacher was made ill by his anxiety, she told Miss Rogers about it. Miss Rogers paid the dues to relieve us of the strain." Annette P. Rogers, an old Bostonian not related to H. H. Rogers, was an old friend of Annie's and one of the stalwarts of the social welfare movement in Massachusetts. She gave Annie two thousand dollars with which to pay off the debts that had accumulated since her marriage.

Annie may have been emboldened to make a new approach to Rogers because he had cut his annuity to Helen in half at the time of Teacher's marriage, from one hundred dollars monthly to fifty, the principal at Helen's death to go to the Unitarian Association. He had rebuffed a plea from Annie at the time that the entire sum should go to Helen: "I have just made provision for Helen so that she will have a monthly income for the rest of her life; therefore I do not feel like doing anything in the line suggested in your communication."

The intermediary to Rogers was John Wright of the Wright-Humason days. What did Wright want? Rogers inquired of Annie. "I do not know the gentleman sufficiently to receive a confidential communication, unless I am sure there is nothing of an embarrassing nature. I write because I know your good judgment in all matters." Annie replied at length, a little disingenuously:

> Although you did not enclose the copy of Mr. Wright's letter, I think the business he wishes to consult you about concerns Helen, and I am sorry that you should be troubled with it. Mr. Wright is an old friend. Helen was in his school during the winter when we met you. The other day he was here and we were telling him that we thought we should have to leave this house and go into Maine where we should be freer and where we might feel the burden of living less than we do here. It is a rather complicated and difficult position, for the more widely Helen becomes known, the greater grow the demands upon us. Mr. Wright thought that our difficulties were a question of money and asked if you knew the circumstances. I told him there was every reason why we should not trouble you with our affairs. I assume that he must have written to you about Helen, since you have written to me, and that his purpose has something to do with what we told him. Whatever his errand, Mr. Wright is a trustworthy man and a true friend, and I imagine he would not approach you on any subject except our welfare, a subject which, as I know, has been near to your heart for a long time. In case he does present our difficulty to you, I do not see what you can do to get us out of it. Because you are a rich man and Helen's friend should not subject your shoulders to the weight of our burdens or your ears to a recital of our perplexities. I certainly should not bother you with them though I am in part responsible if the zeal of Mr. Wright's friendship has led him to approach you in our behalf.
>
> One thing you can do for us, and that is, instruct your gardener to send us some of the prize melon seeds. The little trees came and are 'heeled in' for the winter. If we go to Maine, they go too.

Two weeks ago we went to spend a few days with Mr. Clemens. He was kind and delightful and he seemed to be happy in his new house. We spoke of you and of your last visit to Bermuda. Mr. Clemens is beautiful with Helen. He read aloud the whole of *Eve's Diary* and I could spell her every word of it. Miss Lyon took some pictures of Helen and Mr. Clemens in which he said he had 'worked off' three old expressions and invented a new one.

We, too, think often of our visit to Fairhaven and look forward to the time when we may come again.

Rogers's response to this letter was generous and sympathetic: "I know the struggle of life, and so I am going to take the liberty of just speaking plainly and say what is in my mind. When I made the little endowment for Helen a few years ago, I knew that it was but a small affair; but just handed it in for the little good it might do. I am of the opinion that now you need a little help, and so I am going to take the liberty of telling Miss Harrison, my Secretary, that she is to send you $50 a month for the year 1909. . . . The melon seeds you shall have in due time." Four months later he was dead. "How good and thoughtful he was," Helen wrote his widow. "[H]ad he never done anything for us, I should have loved and admired him as I have." She wrote his daughter, who had also been at Fairhaven that weekend: "How lovable he was in quiet, unnoticed ways! I remember that the last day we were at Fairhaven he sent some beautiful roses up to us, saying they were his 'Good-morning,' and he was always doing a kindness without any thought of return or thanks."

The last approach to Rogers for help may well have been encouraged by Mark Twain during their visit to Stormfield in early January 1909. Rogers had helped him recoup his fortune. He might well be hurt, Mark Twain would have advised, if Helen and Annie, of whom Rogers was genuinely fond, did not turn to him for help. Like Holmes and Hale and Hitz, Mark Twain was usually ready to do Helen's bidding. In 1906 when Helen fell ill a few days before a meeting in New York City to launch an association to improve the condition of the blind, he read Helen's letter to the meeting, which was chaired by the eminent lawyer Joseph Choate, the U.S. ambassador to Britain. "Mr. Clemens," as Helen addressed him in her letter, introduced her words by describing his own relationship with Helen, who he said "is fellow to Caesar, Alexander, Napoleon, Homer,

Shakespeare and the rest of the immortals. She will be as famous a thousand years from now as she is today."

But when Helen tried to get him for another meeting, he demurred, on the reasonable ground that such meetings did not bring in money:

> You say, 'As a reformer, you know that ideas must be driven home again and again.'
>
> Yes, I know it; and by old experience I know that speeches and documents, and public meetings are a pretty poor and lame way of accomplishing it. . . .
>
> Give me a battalion of 200 winsome young girls and matrons, and let me tell them what to do and how to do it, and I will be responsible for showing results. If I could mass them on the stage in front of the audience, and instruct them there, I could make a public meeting take hold of itself, and do something really valuable for once. . . .
>
> But it isn't going to happen—the good old way will be stuck to; there'll be a public meeting: with music and prayer, and a wearying report, and a verbal *description* of the marvels the blind do, and seventeen speeches—then the call, upon all present who are still alive, to contribute. This hoary program was invented in the idiot asylum and will never be changed. Its function is to breed hostility to good causes.
>
> Some day somebody will recruit my 200—my dear beguilesome Knights of the Golden Fleece—and you will see them make good their ominous name.
>
> Mind, we must meet! not in the grim and ghastly air of the platform, may-hap, but by the friendly fire—here at 21.

Their last meeting with Clemens was at Stormfield—his new Italian villa-like home in the Connecticut hills near Redding. Helen had sent him a copy of *The World I Live In,* and a note came back, "I command you all three to come and spend a few days with me in Stormfield." The trees were hoary with icicles, but Mark Twain was standing on the verandah in his white linen suit to greet them on their arrival. Isabel Lyons, one of his "angel fish," served as hostess. They had tea and toured the house, and when they reached the billiard room with its billiard table that had been given him by H.H. Rogers, Mark Twain told Helen he would teach her to play. "Oh, Mr. Clemens, it takes sight to play billiards," Helen protested. Not the kind of billiards that Rogers played, he answered. "The blind couldn't play worse."

They inspected his bedroom and his large bed with its carved bedposts and the far-stretching view over the snowcovered hills that he tried to picture to Helen. Dinner was a considerable event in the Clemens household, and he relieved guests of the anxiety of finding something to say by telling them it was a house rule that he do all the talking in his own house. At the end of the evening he took Helen to her room himself and told her where to find cigars and a thermos of bourbon. He would not be down before lunchtime because he spent the morning in bed writing; but if Helen felt like coming to see him at ten thirty, he would be delighted—"there were some things he would like to say to me when my Guardian Angel was not present." He was in a lavish dressing gown when she appeared, dictating notes to a secretary. If his way of working appealed to her, he teased, she could have half the bed, provided she did not talk. Helen replied that the price was prohibitive. "I could never yield woman's only prerogative, great as the temptation was." Helen did not report what Clemens wanted to say to her out of Annie's presence.

Later they rambled through the hills, Clemens in a fur-lined greatcoat and a fur cap, his pocket lined with cigars. They were away so long that Miss Lyons sent out a search party, and when she finally found them and tearfully reproached the aging Clemens, he murmured, "It has happened again—the woman has tempted me."

The final evening was the most heady. Clemens offered to read from his new book, *Eve's Diary,* and Helen persuaded him to do so in the scarlet robe he had acquired when he had received an honorary degree from Oxford. Standing there in the firelight he seemed to Helen the "embodiment of gracious majesty"; and responding to her affection Mark Twain drew her toward him and kissed her on the brow as a cardinal "might have kissed a little child." Then, with Helen seated on a low chair so that her hand could reach to his lips, he began to read. Forgetting himself as he read, he began to gesture with his pipe, sprinkling ashes around, so they had to rearrange themselves with Annie spelling the words into Helen's hand. Helen wept when the tale ended and Adam standing at Eve's grave lamented, "Wherever she was, there was Eden."

In Mark Twain's portrait of Eve there were echoes of Helen and the way she had learned the names of things. In the guest book Helen wrote for the three of them: "I have been in Eden three days and I saw a King. I knew he was a King the minute I touched him though I had never touched a King before. A daughter of Eve, Helen Keller, Jan. 11." And beneath Helen's words, Clemens added: "The point of what Helen says above, lies in this: that I read the 'Diary of Eve' all through, to her last night; in it Eve frequently mentions things she saw for the first time but, *instantly knew what they were* & named them—though she had never seen them before."

One of their fireside discussions while at Stormfield was about the discovery that a friend of John's, William Stone Booth, had made of an acrostic in the plays and sonnets usually attributed to Shakespeare that revealed the author to have really been Francis Bacon. Mark Twain was inclined to be skeptical and scoffing. They sent him Booth's book *Some Acrostic Signatures of Francis Bacon* and another book by G.G. Greenwood, *The Shakespeare Problem Restated.* It is difficult to tell who or what caused them to entangle themselves in the thickets of the "Did Bacon Write Shakespeare?" controversy and embrace the Bacon hypothesis. Another Baconian was John's classmate and fellow poet, Walter Conrad Arensberg, son of a Pittsburgh steel manufacturer and so staunch a convert to the Bacon hypothesis that he established a Francis Bacon Foundation.

There is no need here to examine the apparatus of hidden acrostics that Booth elicited from the Shakespeare canon to prove his thesis. Shakespearian scholars, even Helen's good friend, the genial William Allan Neilson, dismissed it. "No Shakespearian scholar was ever convinced by the Baconians," he later told Nella Braddy, "but those who started out with preconceived Bacon ideas had been." Helen was outraged that scholars and editors dismissed the Booth book without even reading it. "To think they should be so scornful at the idea that the most learned, the most travelled, the most versatile man of his time could have written the poems and plays of Shakespeare, while they go about hugging the belief that a common, uneducated, unknown rustic actor wrote them," she lamented to the book's author.

When John Macy inquired of Gilder whether *The Century* might be interested in an article by Helen on the subject, Gilder voiced dismay: "Frankly I am a good deal distressed that Helen should be taken up with this Bacon puzzle." He would look at the article, but he cautioned them to remember that " 'he who strikes at a king must strike to kill!' Unless the documentation in this case is perfect—you and yours will be censured and Helen will be injured." The suggestion that her foray into this controversy was at the instigation of Teacher and John angered her. She became stubborn. The article went to Gilder. He turned it down. "I suppose Mr. Macy has prepared your mind concerning my attitude toward this Booth-Baconian book, and I am sorry to say that your article does not change my feeling." It grieved Gilder "beyond words to think of you directing your beautiful mind to it. . . . You have read a great deal on the subject, but there is a great deal that you have not been able to take in at your age, and for you to come out with a partisan article on the subject will not be impressive to the public mind and only involves you in controversy which alienates you for the time being from a true literary career. . . . You must forgive me for feeling so deeply about this. The development of your mind has been one of the things in this life in which I have been most interested, and I am simply broken-hearted over your wasting your talents on the Baconian hypothesis."

After Richard Gilder died, she wrote in *Teacher* without naming him, "How could he dream that they [Teacher and John] would interfere with my right as a free woman to say whatever I liked! I mention this not on account of its importance but because it was the first time that I had let outsiders know I would think for myself." Her back was up, and she submitted the article to another magazine with a request to the editor that if he would not print it to send it on to *The North American Review:* "I suppose it is taking an unbusiness-like advantage for a woman to appeal to the chivalry of an editor. But several friends have tried to prevent me from publishing my views on this question. I am hoping that you may be the knight who will come to my aid and take my rash opinions out of the dungeon-keep of prejudice. I do not think there can be much prejudice in your office against the Baconian hypothesis. Mr. Clemens's brilliant book must have converted his publishers and their advisers to disbelief in William Shakespere [sic] of Stratford."

But no magazine would publish it. Mark Twain was their only ally. In fact, the canny Scotsman Neilson, discussing the Bacon adventure, suggested that Teacher and Mark Twain may have been the key to it, for both were irrational and impulsive. Macy had sent Helen's article to Mark Twain. He, too, gently tried to slow Helen down. "The reader's job should be made *easy,* not difficult," and Helen's directions for digging out the acrostics submerged in the Shakespearian text would simply weary him. "He *won't* do that hunting, anyway, for he is human, and the human being is an ass." Clemens thought the Booth book suffered from the same defect as Helen's article, but he considered Greenwood's book *The Shake-*

speare Problem Restated, another volume that the Wrenthamites had sent him, an "able" work. He had "emptied" some remarks about it into his autobiography "and then took a notion to slam them into *Harpers Monthly;* but that would put them off much too long; so I made a booklet of them, to be issued to-day."

"A perfectly negligible book," Neilson called the small volume *Is Shakespeare Dead?,* in which Clemens suggested that we knew as little about Shakespeare as we did about Satan. But Clemens quickly realized that although he was venerated, he had not killed the king, and wrote to his friends in Wrentham suggesting that, like him, they had better quit the field:

> In that booklet I courteously hinted at the long-ago well established fact that even the most gifted human being is merely an ass, and always an ass, when his forbears have furnished him an idol to worship. Reasonings cannot convert him, facts cannot influence him. I wrote the booklet for pleasure—*not* in the expectation of convincing anybody that Shakespeare did not write Shakespeare. And don't you write [with] any such expectation. Such labors are not worth the ink, and the paper, except when you do them for the pleasure of it. Shakespeare, the Stratford tradesman, will still be the divine Shakespeare to our posterity a thousand years hence.
>
> I am chained to Stormfield, by the doctor's orders; not to stir a rod from the premises until the cold weather comes.

A few months later this friend, too, was dead. "He entered into my limited world with enthusiasm just as he might have explored Mars," Helen later wrote. "Blindness was an adventure that kindled his curiosity. He treated me not as a freak but as a handicapped woman seeking a way to circumvent extraordinary difficulties."

XX

"I Must Speak"

"Let every man get off his fellow man's back. . . ."

The preface to *The World I Live In,* dated July 7, 1908, was a poignant, although humorously phrased, plea to editors that they ask her to write on subjects other than her blindness and deafness:

> Every book is in a sense autobiographical. But while other self-recording creatures are permitted at least to seem to change the subject, apparently nobody cares what I think of the tariff, the conservation of our natural resources, or the conflicts which revolve about the name of Dreyfus. If I offer to reform the educational system of the world, my editorial friends say, 'That is interesting. But will you please tell us what idea you had of goodness and beauty when you were six years old. . . . The editors are so kind that they are no doubt right in thinking that nothing I have to say about the affairs of the universe would be interesting. But until they give me an opportunity to write about matters that are not-me, the world must go uninstructed and unreformed, and I can only do my best with the one small subject upon which I am allowed to discourse.

It annoyed her always to have to write about herself, to have editors, even good friends like Gilder, warn her off matters not related to her personal experience. "I found myself utterly confined to one subject—

myself, and it was not long before I had exhausted it." Dr. Bell was among the few who perceived the ache, the anxiety, the ambition behind her plea in *The World I Live In;* and after he had read it, he assured her: "You must not put me among those who think that nothing you have to say about the affairs of the universe would be interesting. . . . The glimpse you give us into your own world is so fascinating and interesting that I would like to hear what you have to say about things outside."

Helen's sense that she had exhausted herself as a subject coincided with a growing awareness that private philanthropy as a way of helping the deaf and the blind, while it had an important role to play, had limitations, and that the state was the key to adequate help. The realization had been implicit in the help she gave to establish a Massachusetts Commission for the Blind and the emphasis that she had placed on work opportunities for the blind. Her colleague in that lobbying effort, Charles F.F. Campbell, had become superintendent of the industrial department of the commission, and the governor had asked her to become a member. She accepted hesitantly:

> I could have wished that you had appointed in my stead my teacher, Mrs. Macy, whose long experience gives her unique qualification in all the work for the blind. What reconciles me is the fact, which you doubtless took into account, that she must always be at my side to give me the benefit of her wisdom.

Although at first she was chiefly concerned with work opportunities for the blind, a census of the blind that the commission undertook shifted her focus. The census showed "that much blindness is unnecessary, that perhaps a third of it is the result of disease which can be averted by timely treatment." This was a reference to *ophthalmia neonatorm,* the blindness of newborn infants caused by mothers infected with venereal disease. The information not only shook her; it outraged her to learn that it was chiefly prudery that prevented a candid discussion of an affliction that could be prevented. Always ready to risk her prestige in the interests of what she considered right, she sailed into the problem with an article for the *Ladies' Home Journal* on "Preventable Blindness." *Ophthalmia neonatorum* was easily prevented by a solution of nitrate of silver dropped into each eye of the newborn child, she noted. Prudery, ignorance, negligence alone stood in the way of the use of this simple preventive measure. The "mothers in every state" must demand legislation mandating preventive treatment. "Prevention has come to be the all-important arm of medical science. . . . American women can accomplish almost anything that they set their hearts on, and the mothers of the land together with the physicians can abolish infantile ophthalmia, yes wipe it out of the civilized world."

A keynote address a few months later to the annual convention of the American Association of Workers for the Blind placed equal stress on the problems of preventable blindness and on work opportunities for the blind. She spoke to the meeting as the representative of the Massachusetts Commission. It took place at the Perkins Institution, and her willingness to appear there marked a truce in her relationship with that Institution. "The facts are not agreeable reading," she said of infantile blindness, "often they are revolting. But it is better that our sensibilities should be shocked than that we should be ignorant of facts upon which rest sight, hearing, intelligence, morals and the life of the children of men."

The more she thought about the problems of the prevention and the care of the blind and the deaf, the larger the number of culprits that drew her wrath. In "Vultures That Prey on My Kind," drafted in 1908, she savagely condemned not only quack medicines, but the businessmen purveyors who enriched themselves "preying on the credulity and superstition of suffering people," the newspapers that published their advertisements and even the politicians. "Before this article is printed Mr. Taft or Mr. Bryan will have been elected President of the United States. I am wondering how either of them is going to support, as Mr. Roosevelt has supported, the work of the American League of Health to which I belong, one of whose principal objects is to stamp out the patent medicine fraud. Mr. Bryan's *Commoner* contains patent medicine advertisements such as no reputable magazine will accept. Mr. Taft owes part of his political success to his brother's newspaper which is full of objectionable advertising." She ended the article with an unprecedently blunt treatment of the cause of infantile ophthalmia. "It may be objected that women cannot be entrusted with such a painful revelation. They must be. I cannot help it. . . . The time has come for plain speaking." She saw herself as a crusader for the right, leading a vast constituency: "To you, my people, I turn with the faith that you will face the problem of social regeneration and work out the salvation of your children."

The only part of this article that the *Ladies' Home Journal* printed was, in revised form, the final section on infantile blindness, which it published in its January 1909 issue under the title "I Must Speak." It was an effective piece of advocacy, and the *Journal*'s editor, Edward W. Bok, delightedly sent her a congratulatory letter that he had received from a Connecticut physician: "I should like to have every ninth grade (grammar) and every high school teacher in America read and study that plea of Miss Keller and instill its teaching into the minds of their pupils in such a manner as to fix it permanently. . . . You can well afford to ignore the protests and clamorings of the prudish and puritanical, if you continue to publish matter with so high a purpose and so well put as this fine plea of the talented blind girl."

Helen's work for the blind prepared her intellectually for the ideological earthquake that struck the Wrentham household in 1909. John Macy joined the Socialist party and soon was joined by Helen. The Socialists, under the charismatic leadership of Eugene V. Debs, were sinking their roots everywhere. "Socialism is coming," the Socialist weekly *The Appeal to Reason* had predicted in 1902. "It is coming like a prairie fire and nothing can stop it. . . . The next few years will give the nation to the Socialist Party." In 1909 the party was in the midst of its fastest growth. It appealed to immigrant worker, farmer, eastern intellectual, millionaire and pauper. The circulation of *The Appeal to Reason* reached almost a half million, chiefly among farmers. Jack London and Upton Sinclair were among its intellectual luminaries, and Charles Beard was one of the young lecturers holding forth at the newly established Rand School in New York. For the young man or woman who wished to protest a system that spawned trusts and millionaires side by side with slums and abject poverty, joining the Socialists seemed an effective and arresting step.

John Macy later told his biographer that he became a Socialist "largely through observing the asininities of the present system." On this matter he was in the lead at Wrentham, Helen following in his wake, and Annie —who by class feeling and social origin should have been in the forefront —holding out the longest. She was even against woman suffrage. Helen was an ardent advocate of votes for women. English suffragists considered her one of their major contacts in New England and in 1909 asked her to write "on *any subject* in which you yourself feel interested—sex problems or any other problem that will appeal to women. . . ." But Teacher was not much interested in the "woman" movement. She did not believe that giving women the vote would change society for the better. Unlike John and Helen she had no faith in human perfectibility, either female or male.

"She was not a woman suffragist, and I was," wrote Helen in *Teacher*. "She was very conservative at the time. She was never a standard-bearer. . . . The more we talked, the less we thought alike, except in our desire of good and our intense longing for intelligence as a universal attribute of mankind. . . . Like Mark Twain, she was very pessimistic with regard to progress. Even the work for the blind was no exception. . . . she was doubtful about the capacity of the average blind person to achieve a full life."

Helen and John were young, and administering a shock to the established and the respectable has its special attraction to the young. They enjoyed the dismay of sober-sided editors over their espousal of the Baconian hypothesis. Helen rather liked writing about *ophthalmia neonatorum,* just because it was "a subject forbidden in society."

But still she was a social reformer rather than the revolutionist that John proclaimed himself to be. That is clear from the letter that she wrote her mother in early 1910 that was decidedly pro-T.R. Prices were soaring that winter. "How hard it is to get hold of those conscienceless corporations! I hope the people will stand firm in refusing to put up with unlawful prices." She blamed the nation's economic woes on President Taft's conservatism. "From the first I didn't like Mr. Taft's messages. They had a dignified air, but didn't 'feel' right somehow for a man leading in a national struggle for large reforms. Now he doesn't seem to be acting up to the standard of the Roosevelt administration. I am glad the ex-President is coming back from the African jungles before long."

The Wrentham household fell on hard times financially. In April 1909 she resigned from the Massachusetts Commission for the Blind. The need to have everything translated to her in the manual language slowed up its meetings, she felt, especially when discussion and debate became most animated. But another reason for her resignation was a decision, later abandoned, to move to Maine, where they might live more cheaply. Lucy Fuller, back from a stay in France, came to see them and was so distressed by "the lack of certain advantages which she thinks we should have" that she decided to bring Helen's plight to the attention of Andrew Carnegie and ask him to place her on his pension list. The Carnegie pensions, designed to supplement the salaries of men and women in public life who were making outstanding contributions, were handsome—five thousand dollars a year during the recipient's lifetime.

Carnegie was only too happy to add Helen to the list, but Helen turned him down.

> Your sympathy is most precious, and it fills me with tender pride to know that I have your respect. . . . I realize that a large sum of money would broaden my work and increase my pleasures. But my kind

friends have given me the necessary equipment, education, books and a house to live in. I lack no essential comfort. There are many things which I should be happy to do for others if I had more money. But is this not true of most human beings, that they wish for what they have not? Are there not millions of deserving people who would like just a little more, so that they might increase the joy in the lives of their dear ones? But we millions cannot have this little more. I hope to enlarge my life and work by my own efforts, and you, sir, who have won prosperity from small beginnings, will uphold me in my decision to fight my battles without further help than I am now receiving from loyal friends and a generous world.

Carnegie was remarkably sensitive to the problems that proud and gifted people had with accepting his largesse. He replied gallantly to this rebuff. He quoted Helen's statement about fighting her battles "without further help than I am now receiving from loyal friends" and added, "Mrs. Carnegie and I gladly go on probation until you realize that they [sic] are 'loyal friends.'" Lucy Fuller was a little irked: "Does Helen know that Professor William James was on Mr. Carnegie's pension list?" she wrote Annie. "And a friend who is here tells me that President Eliot is also there and took it among the first."

But Helen's erstwhile determination to make it on her own, added to deepening socialist sympathies, made it difficult for her to accept subvention, even from so philanthropic a figure as Carnegie. "The trouble with the generation which is now happily passing," Macy would write in his book on *Socialism in America,* "is that it did little else than strive for individual fortune. Its heroism, its representative products, typical though grotesquely exaggerated, are Morgan, Rockefeller, and Carnegie." "As I journey on," Helen wrote after her thirtieth birthday, "I leave behind thoughts that once looked like reason. I gain new thoughts which serve me better because they are more equal to the rushing, swirling and sometimes inclement atmosphere of the world." To accept a Carnegie pension seemed inconsistent with her new convictions. "My joys and sorrows are bound up indissolubly with the joys and sorrows of my fellowmen, and I feel far more blessed to see them receiving new opportunities, better tools with which to do their work, than I could feel if I received more for myself when I already have a fair share, and millions have less than their rightful portion."

A careful observer might have sensed Helen's growing radicalization, and by the end of 1910 she was ready to declare herself publicly. A federal court had jailed Fred Warren, the editor of the socialist *Appeal to Reason,* for sending "scurrilous, defamatory and threatening" literature through the mails. She came to his defense, striking a blow for several causes at the same time: "For a mere woman, denied participation in government, must needs speak timidly of the mysterious mental processes of men, and especially eminent judges," she began. The denunciation of the federal courts (including the Supreme Court) that followed was scarcely timid. "One need not be a Socialist to realize the significance, the gravity, not of Mr. Warren's offence, but of the offence of the judges against the Constitution of the United States and against democratic rights. It is provided that 'Congress shall make no law. . . . abridging the freedom of speech or of the press.' Surely that means that we are free to print and mail any innocent matter. What Mr. Warren printed and mailed had been established as innocent. . . . I learn that our physicians are making great progress in the cure and prevention of blindness. What surgery of politics, what antiseptic of common sense and right thinking shall be applied to cure the blindness of our judges and to prevent the blindness of the people who are the court of last resort?"

Helen's letter sent a shiver of excitement through the American socialist movement. It was widely reprinted in the socialist press. But when a friend at the *Boston Transcript* wrote an article about it, the editor-in-chief cut it out. "The money power behind the newspapers is against Socialism," she wrote of this episode, "and the editors obedient to the hand that feeds them will go to any length to put down Socialism and undermine the influence of Socialists!" She turned a speech on "The Conservation of Eyesight" before the Massachusetts Association for Promoting the Interest of the Blind into an indictment of "our commercial society":

> This case of blindness, the physician says, resulted from ophthalmia. It was really caused by a dark, overcrowded room, by the indecent herding together of human beings in unsanitary tenements. . . . The trouble is that most of us do not understand the essential relation between poverty and disease. I do not believe there is any one in this City of Kind Hearts who would willingly receive dividends if he knew that they had been paid in part with blinded eyes and broken backs. If you doubt that there is any such connection between our prosperity and the sorrows of others, consult those bare but illuminating reports of industrial commissions and labor bureaus. . . . In them

you will find the fundamental causes of much blindness and crooked-
ness, of shrunken limbs and degraded minds. . . .

An editorial that she wrote at this time for *The Matilda Ziegler Magazine
for the Blind* on "The Unemployed Blind," she subcaptioned when she
reprinted it in *Out of the Dark* as "A Later View," to distinguish it from
earlier statements in which she had suggested the solution was an employment agency and the teaching of special vocational skills. *The Ziegler
Magazine,* named after Mrs. William Ziegler, who endowed it, had been
welcomed in 1906 by Helen: "I have waited many years for such a
magazine"; but she cautioned the editor that the sightless preferred a
periodical "as nearly as possible like those published for the seeing. We
are not children to be written down to, not specialists interested only in
blindness. We are human beings of varied intelligence and many interests
and aspirations." The editor, Walter G. Holmes, who became one of her
closest friends, said that that was his intention and that he wanted Helen
as a frequent contributor.

Her editorial in the April 1911 issue on the unemployed blind was a
tacit vindication of Anagnos. He had defended Perkins against Helen's
attacks on it for failing to teach the blind vocational skills by saying it was
not a want of training but a want of jobs caused by trustification that was
at the root of the lack of jobs for the blind. The unemployment of the
blind, Helen now wrote,

> is only part of a greater problem. There are, it is estimated, a million
> laborers out of work in the United States. Their inaction is not due
> to physical defects or lack of ability or of intelligence, or to ill health
> or vice. It is due to the fact that our present system of production
> necessitates a large margin of idle men. . . . The workman has nothing
> to sell but his labor. He is in strife, in rivalry with his fellows for a
> chance to sell his power. Naturally the weaker workman is thrust
> aside. . . . We can subsidize the work of the sightless; we can build
> special institutions and factories for them, and solicit the help of
> wealthy patrons. But the blind man cannot become an independent,
> self-supporting member of society, he can never do all that he is
> capable of, until all his seeing brothers have opportunity to work to
> the full extent of their ability. We know now that the welfare of the
> whole people is essential to the welfare of each.

This was subversive doctrine, and it was to Walter Holmes's credit that he printed it, especially as Helen went on to urge the sightless to study the economic problems of the seeing by reading two popular socialist primers, Robert Hunter's *Poverty* and Edmond Kelly's *Twentieth Century Socialism*—"not for 'theory,' as it is sometimes scornfully called, but for facts about the labor conditions of America."

Her new approach to suffrage for women showed how deeply committed she had become to the socialist analysis. The English suffragist movement asked her to comment on Israel Zangwill's plea, "not votes for Liberals, or votes for Labour, but votes for women." "It makes no difference whether the Tories or the Liberals in Great Britain, the Democrats or the Republicans in the United States, or any party of the old model in any other country, get the upper hand," Helen wrote in reply. "To ask any such party for women's rights is like asking the czar for democracy. . . . The enfranchisement of women is a part of the vast movement to enfranchise all mankind. You ask for votes for women. What good can votes do you when ten-elevenths of the land of Great Britain belongs to 200,000 and only one eleventh to the rest of the forty million? Have your men with their millions of votes freed themselves from this injustice?"

She was indignant at the treatment of the "brave" English suffragists. But she was equally indignant "when the women cloakmakers of Chicago are abused by the police. I am filled with anguish when I think of the degradation, the enslavement and the industrial tyranny which crushes millions and drags down women and children." Bravo! the secretary of Local Ottawa of the Canadian Socialist Party saluted her. He had entertained great hopes for her at the time he had read *The Story of My Life*, only to be disappointed by the shallowness of the book that followed it, *Optimism*. But in her article on unemployment for *The Ziegler Magazine*, he wrote her, "you have dealt so ably, so feelingly—might I say—with questions, which to Humanity as a whole, far transcend in importance those of blindness, deafness, or any individual physical or mental infirmity, that I am again filled with expectancy as to your realizing the vision I once had of you as a real Saviour of the race." Her friendships with the great and the powerful, and having "the whole world, or at least the reading portion of it," interested in what she wrote, in his view underscored both her power and her responsibility.

Helen responded to this letter warmly with a careful account of the evolution of her thinking on social questions. We have already quoted her frank acknowledgement that *Optimism* had been a product of inexperience and ignorance of "the extent of moral blindness" in the world. She could not write that way now:

> I have always been interested in all kinds of practical work to lessen human suffering. It happens that the first opportunity which came to me was to help the blind and the deaf. In my study of defectives I became conscious of the deeper problems which underlie their condition.

> It is difficult for me to get a hearing on any subject not connected with myself and my own experience. When I write seriously about the broader aspects of human life, people are apt to laugh and tell me that I know nothing about the practical world. They will listen to me when I tell them about heaven. But they turn away when I point out a verifiable fact about the earth under their feet. Besides, most editors of magazines and their readers too, I assume, prefer optimistic generalizations about progress and uplift which overlook all the unpleasant facts of our existence.

> I shall keep on trying, and letters like yours encourage me to do what I can towards the righting of social injustice.

Study economics! was her reply to young Quaker women in Alabama who advised her that they intended to study the work "of our greatest women." That might seem like "strange" advice from one who had "shunned" that "dismal science" while at college, she explained. "I thought it was a pathless wilderness of statistics and fruitless theories. But now I know that economics is life itself. . . . I think that the Quakers will derive much benefit from such books as Robert Hunter's *Poverty,* H.G. Wells's *New Worlds for Old* and Spargo's *Bitter Cry of the Children.*" They should seek out the facts and causes of poverty by studying the people "at their doors."

> Young women hitherto have been engaged in superficial charities— giving bread to the poor, but not understanding why poverty exists, consoling the sick, but not grasping the great causes of disease, raising fallen sisters, but ignorant of the great harm of necessity that struck them down. All this philanthropic endeavor is altruistic, most noble in motive, but it is not profound. It does not get to the bottom of

things. We see well-intentioned efforts thwarted and rendered all but useless because they seek cures, and not prevention.

The local elections of 1910 and 1911 brought the Socialist party impressive gains. In Milwaukee it took control of the municipal government and sent Victor Berger to Congress. Thirty-three cities and towns were ruled by the Socialists on the eve of the 1912 Presidential election. In Schenectady, New York, a Presbyterian minister with only a weak party organization behind him had won the mayoralty in November 1911. This was considered a striking portent of the way the tides of history were flowing. Young Walter Lippmann, recently out of Harvard, became Mayor Lunn's executive secretary.

As 1912 dawned, Helen herself was panting for action, eager for a chance to translate words into deeds. In her room she had hung a large red flag. John had introduced her to the writings of Karl Marx, and she subscribed to a German socialist bimonthly printed in Braille. The German Social-Democratic Party was the largest and most effective in the world. She read in German Braille Karl Kautsky's classic exposition of the Erfurt program of the German socialists, and she had a reader come in regularly to read her the articles in the *International Socialist Review* that seemed promising. Her letters breathed defiance and militancy. "I, too, am a Socialist," she wrote the bride-to-be of Richard Dana Longfellow, whom the newspapers described as a Socialist, "and needless to say, deeply interested in the movement which in a few years shall make the world a better place to live in." The marriage was to take place in Cambridge in the shadow of Harvard University, "which is perhaps the most imposing monument to dead ideas in the country where such monuments are numerous. Imagine it—one of the most primal, vital acts of your life to be enacted on the spot that in days to come shall be visited by sightseers eager to look upon the historic ruins of plutocracy!"

For Helen, participation in the socialist movement was another bridge to the external world, the "not-me" world, as she had put it. It was an escape from "the egocentric predicament" to which she in her deaf-blindness was more vulnerable than most. The struggle of the working class had the throb of life in it, a vividness and reality that her life usually lacked. She knew she was stirring up controversy; but that added to the movement's attractiveness, for controversy meant that the world was paying attention to her.

Absorbed as she was in the dream of a socialist commonwealth whose arrival she considered imminent, Theodore Roosevelt's challenge to President Taft seemed to her, and to John, of little moment. Nor were they interested in the candidacy of Woodrow Wilson. To choose between the Republicans and Democrats, was to choose "between Tweedledum and Tweedledee." Editors turned down the pieces that she submitted reflecting these new convictions; even *The Century* had returned her article "on women with thanks and kind regards." But she did not interpret the rejections as a sign that history might not be moving to her side.

John's immersion in socialist thought and Marxism coincided with a frantic effort to finish his *Spirit of American Literature,* which Walter Hines Page was eager to publish under the Doubleday imprint. Helen rejoiced in John's progress as a writer even as she lamented her own slowness. "Let us give three cheers for John," she wrote her mother. "He has finished his book on American Literature." And she added a revealing comment: "It must be a fine book from what I have heard about it." Revealing, because little that Helen wrote was not read (and edited) by John, but evidently he did not reciprocate. *The Spirit of American Literature* was a splendidly written book that attracted wide attention. It was destined to become a standard college text on the subject. Years later, John proudly sent his classmate and colleague in the Bacon caper, Walter Arensberg, an academician's appreciation of the book's part in the rise "of a new school in American criticism—a revolt against the classical cultural traditions of Paul Elmer More, George Edward Woodberry, Bliss Perry, et al. The revolt was inaugurated by John Macy who in 1912 analyzed *The Spirit of American Literature* and found it tepid and meager. Van Wyck Brooks, Randolph Bourne, and Waldo Frank have carried on the tradition begun by Macy."

Macy's book showed him to be an innovative force in America criticism. Without the dream of revolution perhaps he could not have written it, but that dream now pulled him onto paths that represented a detour from his basic interests. Walter Lippmann, finding the administrative duties of an executive secretary too alien to his concerns as a writer and thinker, and Schenectady too limiting and parochial, resigned as Mayor Lunn's aide and recommended John as his successor. "I am sure you will find him an asset to the city, a power to your administration and a delightful person to have as a friend," he advised the mayor.

The dream of revolution drew him to Schenectady, but an additional factor propelling him out of Wrentham was an increasing irritability in his relations with Annie. They had been married seven years. Annie no longer was the saucy colleen whom he had wooed but a woman of Falstaffian girth in her mid-forties, moody, ailing, often exhausted. It seemed like a good idea to be apart, although Annie as well as Helen said they would follow him to Schenectady in the fall. Whatever their intentions, Schenectady was less interested in John than it was in Helen, and the headline of the story in the Schenectady press that announced his appointment read NOTED BLIND GIRL COMING WITH MACY and a subhead declared that RETIREMENT OF WALTER LIPPMAN WILL BRING FAMOUS YOUNG WOMAN TO SCHENECTADY TO LIVE.

A few weeks later Mayor Lunn announced the establishment of a Board of Public Welfare to coordinate the work of the city departments that dealt with human resources and said he would appoint Helen Keller as a member if she carried out her plan to move to Schenectady in the fall. "The Board of Public Welfare cannot solve the central problems of poverty," the mayor said. "The nation, not the city, must do that. But this board can study the problem of poverty in Schenectady, can make known the facts and can show the remedy." In Wrentham Helen reacted cautiously to the appointment, but not to the board's scope. She knew that such a board was to be established, she told reporters, but as yet she had heard nothing from the mayor. But she had large ambitions: "One thing I would try to do would be to wipe out the slums, for it is there that sickness, disease and immorality are born."

The news of Helen's imminent appointment created a sensation second only to Schenectady's having elected a Socialist mayor. Statements and interviews with Helen on how she intended to make Schenectady a better place to live appeared in many places. Whatever Teacher may have felt about the move to Schenectady on behalf of a cause in which she did not believe, Helen's imagination and hopes ran away with her: "Helen Keller's life has, as a matter of fact only just begun," she told an interviewer for the *Omaha Daily News* speaking of herself in the third person. "All the rest that has gone before has been as nothing. Only the merest preparation— the getting ready to do really great things that shall, perhaps, help all mankind." It was a Press Association interview, widely reprinted. "John said he was much pleased with it," she informed her mother.

The *Knickerbocker Press* of Albany published a similar interview, with a box at the top of the column-long story that summarized her views and hopes:

BY HELEN KELLER

Should I be appointed to the board of public welfare in Schenectady I will first of all try in some way to improve conditions among the extremely poor.

I would try to wipe out the slums.

Poverty is the fundamental cause of almost every evil. Poverty drives people to vice. The only way to bring about any permanent improvement is to prevent rather than to alleviate.

Let every man get off his fellow man's back, so he can stand on his own feet and do his own work with his own hands and faculties.

No money belongs to us that is not earned.

Let us get rid of our money that is received from invested capital.

I am convinced that the world is growing better. There are more healthy, happy children today than ever before.

Her eagerness to plunge into the fray for a better world increased her determination to improve her speech. She met Charles A. White, a voice specialist at the Boston Conservatory of Music, and he persuaded her to let him help her. He and his wife became frequent visitors at Wrentham. By the beginning of the summer he and Helen were ready to show what they had accomplished. Together with Teacher they attended the ninth summer meeting of the American Association to Promote the Teaching of Speech to the Deaf which took place at the Rhode Island Institute for the Deaf in Providence. Helen spoke and recited a poem. White then lectured on his method of teaching Helen. "My friends seemed delighted with the results," Helen wrote her mother. "I was told that many people understood me, even those who weren't used to the speech of the deaf! It was the first time that I had ever spoken without being interpreted. It was the first time that Teacher has been able to sit and listen to me without feeling strained, anxious about my being understood. . . . Dr. Bell was there and his enthusiasm made me very happy."

What Dr. Bell said to the convention was more than enthusiastic: "I am perfectly astonished in the change in Helen's voice." Her progress, he added, was "great good news" to all teachers of the deaf.

Much of that summer Helen and Teacher and the Whites, with occasional visits by John, spent as guests at the summer home of Mrs. William Thaw, whose son had shot Stanford White. Mrs. Thaw was rarely there, preoccupied as she was with her son's fate, but her cottage in the Alleghenies near Pittsburgh was well staffed and relieved them all, especially the ailing Mrs. Macy, of household burdens. Solicitude for Teacher no doubt persuaded Helen to accept Mrs. Thaw's hospitality, but it did seem inconsistent to preach that "no money belongs to us that is not earned" and then take a holiday made possible by unearned income. But if the contradiction troubled Helen, she did not indicate it in her letters. When Nella Braddy asked Dr. Neilson about the ethics of a socialist's accepting such favors, their old friend thought they consoled themselves with the view that "taking the money is like spoiling the enemy." But then Neilson may have been seeking to justify his own reluctance to follow them down the socialist path. They seem not to have realized, he went on, "that the roots of the evil go far beyond any system into the roots of human nature."

In mid-August a speech before the International Otological Congress at the Harvard Medical School confirmed the progress in enunciation, voice quality and projection that had struck Dr. Bell so forcibly at Providence. She not only spoke but sang for the ear experts from all over the world: "I was able to make myself understood without an interpreter," she jubilantly informed her mother, "and that in a larger hall than the one where I spoke in Providence."

All summer the press had been querying her and the mayor and John whether and when she would come to Schenectady. But the rapid improvement in her speech under White's tutelage and the predictions of the otologists at Harvard that before long she would speak well in public turned her thoughts away from Schenectady. A straw in the wind was a story in the Albany press at the end of August. Based on an interview with

Macy, it reported that Helen Keller, who had recovered the partial use of her voice, "promises to become one of the greatest of Socialist lecturers within the next few months. Miss Keller's proposed removal to Schenectady is a part of a program through which she expects to become the most influential Socialist lecturer among the women of the United States, at the same time speaking in the interests of deaf, dumb and blind children." Helen was highly enthusiastic over the prospects of her lecture tour, Macy told the reporter. "Mr. Macy added that he considered it highly probable that she would prefer lecture travel to settling in a city, and conducting a more quiet campaign for Socialism."

Macy did not say that an additional reason for Helen's change of plans was his own growing restlessness with Schenectady. As Helen had informed her mother in mid-August, "Our plans for the fall are not at all settled yet. Perhaps you've read in the papers that Mayor Lunn appointed me to a position. That isn't true. The fact is, if we should go to Schenectady, he says he will appoint me a member of the Commission of Public Welfare, and he has kept a place open on the board for me with this idea in view. We don't think, however, that John wants to stay there much longer. He seems to want almost any kind of work rather than that of a secretary." He had also concluded that "A Socialist administration within a capitalist society cannot do anything essentially socialistic."

John's mind was made up for him by his wife's illness, which had been undermining her strength and which suddenly required hospitalization and an operation. On September 20 he submitted his resignation: "Mrs. Macy's illness makes it necessary for me to leave Schenectady. While she is in the hospital I ought to be constantly with Miss Keller, and for many months Mrs. Macy will need the rest and quiet of her country home. So I must return to Wrentham immediately. I cannot tell you how deeply I regret to leave Schenectady."

HELEN KELLER WILL NOT AID SOCIALISTS, read the headline on the story of John's resignation in the *Knickerbocker Press.*

Teacher underwent major surgery. Its nature is nowhere described, except that Nella Braddy underscored its seriousness: "It was by no means certain that Mrs. Macy would live." She was so weak afterwards that when Helen was allowed to visit her she could scarcely spell on her fingers. John read to Annie every afternoon for two hours when she was allowed to sit up, and for Helen it was an especially disturbed time. "O, how good it will be when we are all together again in our pretty little home!" she wrote her mother. But that home was beginning to disintegrate; and instead of setting out on a lecture tour with Teacher as she had expected, she found herself packed off to Washington to stay with the Phil Smiths.

XXI

The Red Flag

"... my new and larger work. ..."

Helen put on as pleasant a face as possible for her month-long stay in Washington with Lenore Smith. Lenore was a devoted friend; nevertheless, this was a form of exile for Helen. She sought to ease it by an almost daily letter to Wrentham, written on an ancient typewriter that she compared to a "one-horse shay" and that she had knocked off its swinging desk perch the first day she was in the unfamiliar surroundings of Lenore's home. Phil Smith, Lenore's husband, was off on a field trip for the Geological Survey and Lenore "keeps saying how glad she is that she brought me back with her—if only for company." She slept in "Phil's library ... so I ought to grow wiser every day." They stopped in at the Congressional Library to borrow some books in Braille. "To see the way I was greeted, you'd have thought I was the President of the United States." Only a final, impulsive postscript to her first letter betrayed her loneliness: "Do tell me promptly, both of you, ANYTHING that happens to you. I can't rest easy or come home well or live through another experience if you don't. Your own and John's 'Billy.'"

Among the books she borrowed from the Congressional Library was *Anne of Green Gables* by Lucy Maud Montgomery. Mark Twain had called Anne, although Canadian, "the most lovable character in American fiction," and Helen thought he was right in this as in so many other things. She could not praise Anne, because "I think she is my duplicate in many ways. I recognize in her nearly all my faults and deficiencies, most of my moods, impulses and secret thoughts. She is a great trial to others in the same way that I am, speaking in large terms. Like me she takes the joys and sorrows of life tremendously and like me she has a passion for everything which 'gives scope for imagination.' " Anne of Green Gables is indeed like Helen, now "wild with excitement," now overcome by the "tragicalness" of it all, a "dunce in geometry" and a whiz-bang in composition, tremulously responsive to the world about her, dazzlingly temperamental, able to show and give love, yet occasionally a nurser of longtime grudges and maddeningly obstinate; above all, as Helen notes, a romantic, lapsing into reverie at the slightest pretext, creating through imagination and fantasy a world more gorgeously hued than the real one, in which good and evil were splendidly arrayed against each other.

"No, no, no!" Helen protested to Teacher. "Don't you dare say again that you and John are 'dull people'! I've too many faults without thinking that. The trouble is, you're too vital, too full of pent-up genius, and that's a precious trouble, you know. . . . Even if you were dull, I could easily graft upon you the wit that I find here. It mayn't grow in my own garden; but then purchased stock may be just as good and superior. I'm having glorious fun hearing extracts from the Harper articles on Mark Twain. . . ."

Dr. and Mrs. Arthur L. Day—he was then the head of the physical laboratory of the Carnegie Institute—were close friends of the Smiths. The family was quite musical, and two of the children played for Helen, one on the violin, the other on the cello, while Mrs. Day accompanied them on the piano: "Think of it, I could feel the two instruments at once. I loved the cello, it was so rich, vibrant and thrilling! Afterwards Mrs. Day sang for me some songs in German which Lenore spelled into my hand. I almost cried when she sang 'Wiegenlied'. . . ." Vibrations coursed through her hand, some sense of the timbre of an instrument; but she was never able to identify a piece of music.

They visited Dr. Bell's daughter, Daisy Fairchild. Her husband was a naturalist, then engaged in the pioneer work of enlarging photographs of insects. He persuaded Helen to finger a queen bee that he had captured and placed in a net: "It seemed as if it were not an insect I touched, but vibration embodied." The Fairchilds gave her news of Dr. Bell, who was "working hard on his hydroplanes. So far he has attained a speed of fifty miles an hour."

But what was going on at Wrentham? her second letter went on. "Are you giving directions every minute of the day? Is John reading to you or running in and out like a will-o'-the-wisp, now pruning a tree, now writing poetry, now prowling from room to room to find work for a rainy day?'' A startling and revealing question—was Teacher "giving directions every minute of the day?" Suddenly Lenore Smith's comment to Nella Braddy years later that Teacher "mothered" John takes on a different hue. If Teacher was behaving like a general, there were no troops at Wrentham, especially now that Helen was not there—except for John, and that proud man did not take easily to another's commands. He had had enough of that with his "midget" mother. Helen lived in daily anxiety that she was a bother to Lenore. She turned down invitations to appear at meetings because "it is impossible for Lenore to go." The organizations that wanted her thereupon badgered Lenore, "and all her trouble is on my poor account."

Although Helen addressed her daily letter to Teacher, it was John who answered, but not until a week after Helen had arrived in Washington. "John's letter [lost] did me more good than anything else had done yet. I confess I was very homesick and inclined to discouragement. I really don't know why. But I'm better able to forget it now, we're so busy rushing around and having experiences which I shall long remember. Indeed it's difficult to get even a hurried letter to you these days. But writing to you helps me through the days and makes home seem a little nearer."

Lenore was no socialist, and that placed considerable constraint upon their conversation. She could not have been more devoted and attentive, "but, oh my, she is such a bigoted plutocrat! What do you think? I can't be tolerant and candid and say pleasant things about people like Washington (George) without her exclaiming, 'Oh, but he's a plutocrat.' . . . I feel somewhat like a prisoner at times. I don't feel free to talk about social questions obviously unwelcome in this atmosphere. . . ." She hesitated to ask Lenore to take her to some of the new government agencies such as the Bureau of Child Labor: "I am her guest, you see, and there might be some embarrassment for her in the questions I wished to ask, even though I should not express a single opinion."

Her socialist convictions made her feel quite superior, almost condescending, toward the government officials she met socially. "This neighborhood is giving me a splendid concrete illustration of the pitiful social blindness which it is so difficult yet so necessary to remove. There are many intellectuals living near here, some of them charming and clever, who confirm all that Paul La Fargue says about them. I don't argue with them of course; but Lenore tells me what they say about economics, and even I am amazed at their apparent stupidity and want of self-respect. They are honest, hardworking, shamefully treated by the Government and so forth; but I guess that most of them will be left far behind in any great movement to make this world a better and a pleasanter one."

"No, I am not planning an article about Washington as the wicked Capital of the United States," she assured Teacher and John. "I've no use for 'reform' work in that direction. It will always be hopeless until all the people unite and control the government for the benefit of all." But when "gradualism" came clad in the authority of the British labor movement, she embraced that, too, despite her scorn for efforts to bring about changes within the system.

"Dear, dear!" another letter ended. "Here is a lady to see me, a Miss [Margaret] Macmillan from England. She is on the Bradford Board for the Deaf, and has been active in the work for the deaf for nine years." Although she fussed over the prospect of having to entertain Miss Macmillan, the English visitor impressed her, as she wrote her mother:

> She works for the children of the very poor, and she has succeeded in putting some very important things through for their benefit. She told me how very serious the conditions are under which the great majority of the English people now live. They are so bad in fact that the average child of the workman is threatened with lifelong invalidism. Miss MacMillan has established some night-camps where sick children can sleep in the fresh air, receive proper medical treatment and physical training and thus gain a better chance to escape the horrible influence of the slums. Think of it, every summer eight thousand sick children are sent to the health center in Deptford where she works. Now her supreme effort is to induce the city authorities to establish similar night-camps all over the country.

Praise from certain people meant a great deal to her, and it delighted her to have Miss Macmillan say "I had been a help to her in her work, that it was my education which had inspired her with the idea of training these poor children in a new way." And to cap her pleasure in the interview, "before she left she told me she was a Socialist."

Helen's letter to her mother reporting this visit, written on the latter's birthday, was unusual in its lavish tribute to her mother's share in her education. She did not often do that, she was so focused on Teacher. Miss Macmillan's stress on the help and inspiration she had drawn from Helen's example should make Teacher feel "she is truly a benefactor of mankind. . . . And you, too, mother, you have a share in the beautiful work. For you have helped me all you could in my first years, you have kept me healthy and active, you strove to stimulate my mind, so that it would not be quenched in darkness and silence."

Phil Smith was returning in a couple of weeks, and Helen was anxious to get back to Wrentham. But Teacher still was a convalescent, and Kate Keller decided she was needed in Wrentham. Helen was delighted:

> It means that you will be there to see something of my new and larger work. Whatever success comes to me seems incomplete because you are so often not at my side to be glad with me. But now you will have a chance to realize more fully into what new worlds of thought, feeling and aspiration I am entering, and see what new and fascinating fields of knowledge and of action are opening before me. This visit in Washington is truly a flood of fresh experiences, impressions, observations, and it is only a foretaste of what I am likely to have in the near future.

Lenore might have seemed a "plutocrat" to Helen whose imagination tended to dramatize and simplify. Actually, Helen's friend was quite socially minded. "I'm going with Lenore this morning to visit some of the worst alleys in the city. She asked me herself, and I thought I might be interested, especially as she is planning to help the poor here this winter. There are some active workers who are trying to induce the authorities to have these alleys cleaned up [they were not until Eleanor Roosevelt's day] and give the people better dwellings." For Helen this was tepid reformism. Even the presidential campaign, which was roaring to a furious climax—and which in the confrontation between Theodore Roosevelt's progressivism and Woodrow Wilson's New Freedom was establishing the liberal agenda for decades to come—seemed to her of only marginal interest. "I am hungry for news that counts," she wrote Wrentham, "I hear nothing but newspaper gossip about Mr. Roosevelt and campaign fund disclosures. Is the Lawrence strike still on? What about the trial of Ettor and Giovannitti? Please, please don't throw me out of it all, it makes me too homesick. Can't you read between the lines?"

Teacher and Helen had sent money to the jailed leaders. In the eyes of the American Left the upsurge of militant unionism led by the Industrial Workers of the World (IWW) that attended the Lawrence strike overshadowed the election campaign. Precipitated by a cut in wages of the women and children in the mills, whose hours had been shortened by legislative mandate, the giant shutdown in the textile town of ninety thousand north of Boston was later described by Paul Brissenden as "a social revolution *in parvo.*" The IWW, with its tenets of direct action, "one big union," general strike and boycott—and a little sabotage if necessary—had moved in to give the strike direction. The strikers were predominantly Italian, and the IWW sent in Joseph Ettor, an experienced IWW organizer. He took with him his twenty-seven-year-old Italian-born friend, Arturo Giovannitti, a poet and editor of the Italian labor paper *Il Proletario.*

Other Wobbly leaders arrived to lend a hand—Elizabeth Gurley Flynn, whose fiery oratory had earned her the sobriquet "the red flame"; her "lover," as the newspapers described anarchist Carlo Tresca, himself an eloquent spellbinder; and most important of all, the already legendary William "Big Bill" Haywood. The latter was a member of the National Executive Committee of the Socialist Party, but in profound disagreement with Debs and the leaders of right wing of the Socialist party, who believed that socialism could be advanced by the ballot box and peaceful change. Haywood had a talent for pungent, provocative statement: "[N]o Socialist can be a law-abiding citizen," he had declared in a debate with Eugene Debs. "When we come together and are of a common mind, and the purpose of our minds is to overthrow the capitalist system, we become conspirators against the United States Government. . . . I again want to justify direct action and sabotage. . . ."

In Lawrence the IWW used militant, innovative tactics—mass demonstrations, boycotts, a dramatic exodus of strikers' children in the dead of winter from the city to the homes of sympathizers around the country. Police and militia sought to prevent the exodus and waded in with clubs. A woman striker was killed, and Ettor and Giovannitti were charged with being accomplices to the murder. Fifteen thousand workers came from industrial towns around Boston to a rally in the Common addressed by Elizabeth Gurley Flynn. The mill owners yielded. The pay cuts were restored. Months later Ettor and Giovannitti, who had spent his time in jail writing poetry, were acquitted. John Macy attended their trial.

On the crest of its triumph the IWW emerged with a national reputation for militancy and effectiveness. Unions sprang up in the mill towns all over

Massachusetts, and along with them came strikes, many of them led by the IWW. The syndicalist organization was at the height of its popularity, and one of those who joined was John Macy. The knitting mills of Little Falls, New York, not far from Schenectady, were struck by the IWW. Haywood arrived to direct it, and John Macy went to lend a hand. The IWW did not ordinarily admit middle-class people to membership, but the workers in Little Falls took him in, he later wrote, "in spite of my protest that the admission of a parasitic journalist is contrary to the spirit of the IWW. Since I am technically a wage-earner and not an employer of labor, I could be admitted under the rule. Probably there are not enough like me in the organization to do it serious harm."

A few days after John's arrival at Little Falls, Haywood was able to announce at an enthusiastic strike rally that he had received a check from Helen Keller. It was for $87.50, a sum that Helen had received for writing tender messages of Christmas goodwill to be used on Christmas cards. "Will you give it to the brave girls who are striking so courageously to bring about the emancipation of the workers of Little Falls," her letter said. "If they are denied a living wage, I also am defrauded. While they are industrial slaves I cannot be free. . . ." Helen's letter, however, eschewed the class warfare rhetoric of the Wobblies. "Until the spirit of love for our fellowmen, regardless of race, color or creed, should fill the world, making real in our lives and our deeds the actuality of human brotherhood—until the great mass of the people shall be filled with the sense of responsibility for each other's welfare, social justice can never be attained." Haywood read the letter to the hushed crowd.

In the presidential election Debs amassed 897,000 votes, 6 percent of the total vote cast, and "the largest percentage of a presidential vote ever polled by the Socialist Party." But Debs's success was flawed by the split within the Socialist party between the Haywood faction, which advocated "direct action"—meaning force and sabotage—and the majority Debs faction, which placed its reliance upon "political action." In mid-1912 the right wing had amended the constitution of the party to ban membership by advocates of sabotage and violence. The clause was aimed at Haywood and his followers. The election over, party conservatives initiated a referendum to recall Haywood from the National Executive Committee for his continued advocacy of sabotage. A group of Socialist intellectuals attacked the antisabotage clause and defended Haywood. They included Walter Lippmann, Max Eastman (editor of the newly established *Masses*), Margaret Sanger (who later pioneered birth control and at that time was chairman of the women's committee of the Socialist party and had been in charge of the children's exodus from Lawrence), Osmond K. Fraenkel, J.G. Phelps Stokes, William English Walling and Louis Boudin. Helen did not sign the statement. She did not favor sabotage and violence. But she was on Haywood's side and so wrote to *The Call.* She pleaded for "harmony" in the party. "It is with the deepest regret that I have read the attacks upon Comrade Haywood which have appeared in the *National Socialist.* It fills me with amazement to see such a narrow spirit, and such an ignoble strife between two factions which should be one, and that, too, at a most critical period in the struggle of the proletariat." She deplored the right wing's moves against Haywood. "What? Are we to put differences of party tactics before the desperate needs of the workers?"

The pleas of the intellectuals had little effect. With about 30 percent of the party's membership casting ballots, Haywood was recalled by a vote of 23,495 to 10,944. Haywood dropped out of the party, as did many of his followers. Of the antisabotage amendment and the subsequent expulsion, John Macy later wrote, "With this virtuous resolution the Socialist Party crossed its hands upon its heart, lifted its eyes piously to heaven, and rejoiced in the plaudits of the bourgeoisie." The Wobbly leaders became friends of the Wrentham household, especially Ettor and Giovannitti; and when the latter in 1914 published a collection of his poems, *Arrows in the Gale,* the introduction was written by Helen.

Socialism gave direction and excitement to Helen's life and provided a theme for her writing. "Something asleep in me waked when I read the radical literature," she later told Nella Braddy. Blindness and deafness kept her off the picket line, unlike that other "rebel girl" Elizabeth Gurley Flynn; but she lived in a state of high passion and constant advocacy that was a blessed relief from the sense of isolation that usually engulfed her and of which she rarely complained—"an inhuman silence which severs and estranges . . . a silence which isolates cruelly, completely." Her participation in the socialist movement gave her a sense of comradeship with millions throughout the world. Her article for *The Call* on "How I Became a Socialist" was picked up by the socialist press abroad. It included a paean to the red flag. *The New York Times* had published an editorial on "The Contemptible Red Flag," which it deplored as the symbol "of lawlessness and anarchy the world over." Helen's response was full of youthful ardor and defiance:

I am no worshipper of cloth of any color, but I love the red flag and what it symbolizes to me and other Socialists. I have a red flag hanging in my study, and if I could I should gladly march it past the offices of the *Times* and let all the reporters and photographers make the most of the spectacle. According to the inclusive condemnation of the *Times,* I have forfeited all right to respect and sympathy, and I am to be regarded with suspicion. Yet the editor of the *Times* wants me to write him an article! How can he trust me to write for him if I am a suspicious character?

Her nonradical friends did not know what to make of her socialist zealotry. It discomfited them to have the saintly Helen turn into socialist agitator; but most of them, like Lenore, teasingly eluded her taunts and anathemas and continued to treat her as the miracle of courtesy and intelligence that she also was. She could, when necessary, present that visage to the world rather than that of "the rebel girl," as she did at the dedication ceremonies of the "Lighthouse" of the New York Association for the Blind. The New York world of wealth and culture was there. The presiding officer was that witty pillar of the conservative establishment, Joseph H. Choate, the former ambassador to Britain. President Taft took time out from winding up his duties in Washington to attend. A bishop, a priest and a rabbi delivered suitable invocations. The president of the City College and of the Association for the Blind, John H. Finley, opened the ceremonies. Mr. Taft was delayed, and Choate put Helen in the thronelike oak chair that had been specially made for the President's capacious frame. "I am the first woman to be President of the United States," Helen quipped. Picking up the stout gavel that a blind cabinet-maker had carved, Choate rapped for order as the audience laughed: "I could govern a room full of London suffragettes with this." Choate was told that the President was at the door, and Helen arose to take her own seat. It was a false alarm. "This is a curious sort of President," said Choate. "Now he is here and now he isn't." Helen chimed in, "And I shall not abdicate again." The President arrived. He was escorted to the platform by a squad of blind Boy Scouts from the public schools. He spoke, Helen after him. "I have often wondered," Taft began, "when I read the Declaration of Independence of Jefferson, signed by all those people we like to think we are descended from, what the blind must think about the statement that all men are born free and equal. Behind those eyes that do not see there must be a good deal of question. We are not equal in opportunity or environment. What is meant is that it is the aspiration of a popular government to bring about as near equality as possible. That is why we are here. . . ."

It was Helen's turn. Whatever the audience of notables may have thought of her socialist preaching, they gave her an almost reverent hearing. She thanked the President for adding to his burdens the additional one of assistance to the blind. Her assignment was to make the appeal for contributions. "I ask you to help us still more. I am shameless in my begging. . . . I hope you will help us extend this work and establish a lighthouse in every city. I hope you will work with us, striving to hasten the day when there shall be no blind child untaught, no blind man or woman unaided. Then, indeed, shall God's face shine upon us, and we shall all be saved."

The suffrage struggle, as was evident from Choate's and Helen's sallies, was very much on people's minds. A few weeks later Helen went to Washington for a suffrage "pageant" that women's groups had organized for the day before Woodrow Wilson's inauguration. Helen was scheduled to speak, but her speech hailing the struggle of women to emancipate themselves as a part of a larger liberation movement was never delivered. The rally was disrupted. In a syndicated article the next day about Wilson's inauguration she paid her respects to the Capitol police:

The Woman Suffrage Pageant yesterday was in some ways more significant than the inauguration today. It symbolized the coming of the new, not the passing of the old. Owing to some misunderstanding I was caught in a jostling throng, and never took the part which was assigned to me in the demonstration. The stupid inefficiency of the Washington police allowed the people to block the streets, and the parade was broken, a failure as a spectacle. Today, of course, many of us women are indignant and disappointed. . . . Police and soldiers are very capable when it comes to protecting a factory against striking mill-girls. . . . Let us please have no more antisuffragette arguments based on the superior organizing faculty of men. Some of the women were trampled and hurt. If it were not for that, we should not take this little disaster seriously. For after all, our real parade is not a theatrical affair in the holiday streets of Washington. It is a determined, ceaseless march in the work-a-day world. Nothing can stop it. The idle, the thoughtless, the reactionary may get in the way, and our ranks may be apparently disordered. But the Women's Army is moving on in every nation. It will not be long before a president shall ride down these broad avenues elected by the people of America, women and men.

The American suffrage movement was split over tactics. In London Mrs. Carrie Chapman Catt, president of the International League of Woman Suffragettes, favored what she called the slow but sure methods of moderation, while Mrs. O.H.P. Belmont threatened to introduce Mrs. Pankhurst's militant methods into the American struggle on her return from London. "Your movement resembles a battle," Mrs. Catt told Mrs. Pankhurst, "ours is a process of evolution. Yours is picturesque and very tragic, ours is commonplace but sure."

Helen was on the side of the militants. She favored the smashing of windows, hunger strikes, anything that will bring publicity to the cause, reported *The New York Times.* "I believe the women of England are doing right," she told its reporter. "Mrs. Pankhurst is a great leader. The women of America should follow her example. They would get the ballot much faster if they did. They cannot hope to get anything unless they are willing to fight and suffer for it. The pangs of hunger during the hunger strike simply are a sample of the suffering they must expect.

"But I am a militant suffragette because I believe suffrage will lead to Socialism and to me Socialism is the ideal cause."

A press service had sent out only a few sentences of her account of the disruption of the women's parade at Wilson's inaugural, but her scathing assessment of Wilson it had sent out in full:

Dr. Woodrow Wilson, historian, student of government, has said: 'Nothing was settled in the election of 1908 but the name of the next President.' The same thing is true of the election of 1912. Mr. Wilson stands for no great idea. He has not been swept into power by an aroused people. The great capitalist party broke into two, and the other capitalist party, the Democratic, walked through the broken ranks of the enemy. Mr. Wilson is not a Tilden who has brought his party back to a declaration of honest tough principles. He is not even a Bryan. For Mr. Bryan's ideas were more advanced in relation to 1896 than are Mr. Wilson's ideas in relation to the year 1912. . . . Capitalism is still king. The great industrial empire, which is the reality behind our democratic institutions, is powerful as ever, and nothing that Mr. Wilson can do or will do, need give uneasiness to the sovereigns of industry or hope to the subjects. . . .

I met Mr. Wilson many years ago in Princeton. From his firm hand and the few sentences which he spoke to me, I judged that he was a man of sincere character and unusual moral force. No one doubts his integrity. But does he realize the facts he must face? He has been Governor of New Jersey. There have been great strikes in his state. Has he said one word or done one thing that indicates a perception on his part of the industrial struggle? Does he understand that it is not government which controls industry; but industry controls, shapes and determines government?

Mr. Wilson finds something hard, cold, unfeeling in the world of business and labor and has set himself the task of humanizing every process 'without impairing the good.' But the facts are hard, cold and unfeeling. The world is divided into owners and wageworkers. . . .

Mr. Wilson, then, represents the passing of an era, not the inauguration of a new age. Conditions proclaim the coming of the new age, and conditions are stronger than the President, stronger than the Constitution. Mr. Wilson is an old-fashioned Democrat and an admirable specimen of his class. For him as an individual I have the utmost respect. But the future belongs to a much greater class—the new-fashioned democrat. . . . When such a democrat is elected president of the United States, I shall feel not only the thrill of excitement which fills me today but a deep hopeful joy. . . .

With reason, the *Madison Daily State Journal* printed Helen's contribution with an editor's note calling it "the most remarkable article printed anywhere on the inauguration at Washington yesterday."

She and Teacher had begun to make paid appearances on the lecture platform. The first time in Montclair, New Jersey, had been an ordeal, the platform "a pillory where I stood cold, riveted, trembling, voiceless." Like Eleanor Roosevelt, who a decade later faced down the same terrors as the moment approached to go to the podium, she prayed, "O God, let me pour out my voice freely." She felt she had disgraced her tutor Mr. White: "I felt my voice soaring and I knew that meant falsetto; frantically I dragged it down till my words fell about me like loose bricks." She came off the stage in tears, sure that she had failed despite the kind and sympathetic words that were spoken to her; but it was the beginning of a fifty-year career on the lecture circuit.

They hired the Tremont Temple in Boston for their next appearance. John sent out letters to all their friends. Many came, including Edward Clement, the former editor of the *Transcript.* He wrote John afterwards: "I wanted to tell Mrs. Macy how perfectly delightful her address was— how well-judged and proportioned, how modest, genuine and altogether charming it was from beginning to end. It told us, at last, just what all want to know about the most wonderful feat in education on record. It is her due—simple justice—that she should have credit for working out the true principles of teaching, instinctively. . . . out of her heart and intuitions *before* Montessori!"

He had been seated two thirds of the way back from the stage and had found it difficult "to keep the thread of Helen's discourse. But the sentences I caught were thrillingly beautiful and freighted with significance. As James Mackenzie said, coming out, her stand for Socialism is a big asset for the cause. If it were true that as [the] poor *Transcript* used to say, you took advantage of your exclusive opportunity to poison her mind—you would have done a bit of work that must have immense consequences. But fancy anybody doing anything to that mind against that will!"

John was very helpful—not only in making lecture arrangements but in working up the text of what they said. In January 1913 he negotiated a contract with Walter Hines Page of Doubleday to publish a collection of Helen's sociological essays under the title *Out of the Dark.* As usual he drove a hard bargain, as Page's letter attests:

> The English publishers always pay five percent, or more, greater royalty than the American publishers can pay. I suppose that this is due to the cheapness of their labor, but whatever it is due to, it is a fact that the American publisher can't pay their royalties and live.
>
> It is impossible to hope for any large sale for a book of essays on different subjects. I go the utmost limit, therefore, in making this proposition to you on Miss Keller's 'Out of the Dark.' You will notice that this is somewhat better than the contract I proposed in my last letter.
>
> We will give you 15 percent on the first 5,000 copies, and 20 percent after that, and I hope this is satisfactory.

Out of the Dark created the least stir of all of Helen's books, perhaps because many of its essays had already appeared, or perhaps, as one sympathetic reviewer noted, because the writing lacked freshness and surprise. "It must be acknowledged," the reviewer for the *Ohio State Journal* commented, "that if she were not Helen Keller, the wonderful blind and deaf girl, her declarations of opinion might seem obvious and her judgments not original." But the fact that a deaf-blind woman could develop the social vision and grasp reflected in the book's essays seemed to reviewers "almost as much of a miracle as any of the wonderful physical achievements which are recorded of her." That was the view taken by reviewers who sympathized with her opinions. Her critics drew an opposite conclusion. The *Brooklyn Eagle* considered her views erroneous and questioned her right to have opinions on sociological subjects. Her mistakes, the paper said, "spring out of the manifest limitations of her development." The *Eagle* should fight fair, Helen protested. "Let it attack my ideas and oppose the aims and arguments of socialism. It is not fair fighting or good argument to remind me and others that I cannot see or hear." Another conservative paper, the *New York Sun,* thought it incongruous that one who had benefited so greatly from the capitalistic system should dispense "socialistic commonplaces."

But as Clement had suggested to John Macy after Helen's speech in Tremont Temple, the really insidious attack upon her was that which suggested she was John's puppet. "Mr. and Mrs. Macy are enthusiastic Marxist propagandists," one publication wrote, "and it is scarcely surprising that Miss Keller depending on this lifelong friend for her most intimate knowledge of life, should have imbibed such opinions." Teacher, as we have seen, was neither Marxist nor socialist. In fact the arguments between John and Teacher over socialism were carried on continuously, even on trains, where they went at it at the top of their voices. Helen for a time even called her a "weak sister." Teacher compared herself to Balfour, the urbane leader of British conservatism, "seeing both sides," she said, "and never getting anywhere." John had gone into socialism deeply, reading Karl Marx carefully. John did influence Helen, but only because his ideas appealed to her deeply emotional nature and to a commitment to the underdog that long preceded his appearance on the scene.

XXII

End of the Wrentham Triangle

"Her happiness is bound up with mine."—Helen about Teacher

Affairs were not going well in the Wrentham household. In May 1913 John sailed to Europe—alone, while Helen and Annie fulfilled lecture engagements. "We went to New York with John last Thrusday to see him off," she wrote her mother. "He said we had to go with him, and although the parting was hard, yet we felt better afterwards because we had seen him begin the first real holiday of his life. . . . I do hope that it will do all for him that we three want it to. The thought of it was the only thing that kept him up all these weary weeks."

John was tired, but tired of his marriage to Teacher, not because his work was so exhausting. None of the letters that they exchanged during the better than four months that he was in Europe have survived, but Helen later spoke of the anguished tears that Teacher shed as she transcribed her letters to him to the typewriter.

John was weary, but it was Helen and Teacher who were doing the work, keeping the household solvent by paid lectures throughout New England. As Helen wrote to her sister in 1933: "From the year 1905, when Teacher was married, until 1920, when I rose up in my wrath and said John should not have another penny of my earnings, we were constantly paying considerable sums for him—for his family, for his tailors, his books and a trip of four months and a half in Europe, and for any one he wished to assist. . . ."

The trip was in fact a last-ditch effort to save the Macy marriage, and Helen was able to finance it because she had finally capitulated and accepted a pension from Carnegie. In the spring, when she and Teacher had been in New York, they came to tea with the Carnegies at their invitation. Did she still refuse his annuity? the old philanthropist inquired. "Yes, I haven't been beaten yet." Well, he replied, it was hers whenever she would take it. Was it true she had become a socialist? When she said that she had, he launched into a criticism of socialism and threatened to take Helen across his knees and spank her if she did not come to her senses. "You believe in the brotherhood of man, in peace among nations, in education for everybody," Helen bravely replied. "All those are Socialist beliefs." She would send him *Out of the Dark*. What did she lecture about? he pressed her; and when she replied "happiness," he commented that that was "a good subject." How much did people have to pay to hear her? A dollar and a dollar and a half, she informed him. That was "too much, far too much," he advised. "You would make more money if you charged fifty cents—not more than seventy-five cents as a limit."

Shortly afterwards, she and Teacher were in Maine fulfilling a lecture engagement. Teacher collapsed with the flu, and Helen found herself alone, unable to telephone, unable to move about. "My helplessness terrified me." Finally Teacher was able to reach a doctor on the phone, and with the assistance of the manager of the hotel they boarded a train and went home. A week later she wrote Carnegie telling him what had happened and saying that she had been foolish not to let him assist her. The return mail brought a check and a handsome letter from Carnegie:

> The fates are kind to us indeed—I thought that text of mine* would reach your brain and penetrate your heart. 'There are a few great souls who can rise to the height of allowing others to do for them what they would like to do for others.' And so you have risen. I am happy indeed—one likes to have his words of wisdom appreciated. Remember, Mrs. Carnegie and I are the two to be thankful, for it is beyond question more blessed to give than receive.

With John away, the summer was spent at Wrentham, with occasional expeditions elsewhere. She and Teacher went down to the Cape to attend the "Sagamore Sociological Conference" of Bull Moosers, Socialists,

*See page 368.

Wobblies. The Whites went with them, for he was still giving her voice lessons. She was prevailed upon to speak, which she did briefly; a large part of what she said was a defense of her right to have views on social and economic issues. Even people at the conference seemed to think, she noted, "that one deaf and blind cannot know about the world of people, of ideas, of facts. Well, I plead guilty to the charge that I am deaf and blind, though I forget the fact most of the time. It is true that I cannot hear my neighbors discussing the questions of the day. But, judging from what is repeated to me of their discussions, I feel that I do not miss much. I can read. I can read the views of well informed people, of thinkers like Alfred Russell Wallace, Sir Oliver Lodge, Ruskin, H.G. Wells, Bernard Shaw, Karl Kautsky, Darwin and Karl Marx. I have magazines in raised print published in America, England, France, Germany and Austria."

Of course she did not see things firsthand when they happened, but neither did most of the people at the conference. She had never been a captain of industry or a soldier or strikebreaker, but she had studied those "professions." "At all events, I claim my right to discuss them. I have the advantage of a mind trained to think, and that is the difference between myself and most people, not my blindness and their sight." The really blind were those who did not see the "ill-paid, ill-fed, ill-clothed and ill-housed." The really deaf were those who did not hear the cries of the people against poverty and social injustice.

They met many figures in the progressive movement at the conference. George W. Perkins, the Morgan partner and steel magnate who had been the chief financial backer of the Progressive party, pleaded for understanding of the capitalists. They were not a bad lot when you got to know them, and they were concerned with the welfare of their workers, at least in the steel industry. That brought Arturo Giovannitti to his feet, open-shirted, hair flowing, "as beautiful," it seemed to Teacher, who spelled her impressions into Helen's hand, "as a young avenging God." He gave facts and figures on the "benevolence" of the steel companies. He was passion incarnate besides the sobersided Perkins. The latter was taken aback; "but it was hardly fair," said Teacher, "for Arturo was so beautiful, that if he had been the apostle of the devil himself he would have won the meeting over with him." Perkins sought out Helen afterwards, but she scarcely concealed her hostility. Arturo they took home with them to Wrentham.

Whatever letters were exchanged between John and Wrentham during his four and a half months in Europe have disappeared. But a letter has survived that Teacher wrote him on hotel stationery in New York on their return from the South. It was early morning. They had just come off a Pullman train and were waiting for their rooms to be made up. "Just in. Found your telegram and letter. The letter has comforted me a little but I still feel disappointed not to see you." They had found a letter from Arturo to Helen. "I'm glad you like Arturo. He needs your affection. Send him the check by all means and do whatever you think best about the poor chap in Little Falls jail. You probably are wondering why I haven't sent more money for deposits. I promised Mr. Glass [their lecture agent] to send him five hundred of the Knoxville fee which I did by draft and I have five hundred in cash in my bag."

The letter was signed "lovingly," but their return to Wrentham was attended by bitter quarrels. John was drinking heavily. Helen's books deal only in the vaguest terms with the breakup. "Mr. Macy was considering leaving us," she wrote of the period that followed her acceptance of the Carnegie pension. "He had wearied of the struggle. He had many reasons for wishing to go. I can write about that tense period of suffering only in large terms." They were on the road again in late October and early November; and by the time they returned to Boston, John had moved into an apartment there, "right on the Fenway." They stayed in the apartment when they were in Boston, but Teacher hated it, perhaps because she saw it as another step in John's separation. One night in a fit of anger and despair she stamped out of the apartment, announcing that she would not return. John seized upon the episode to charge her with the responsibility for wanting a separation and a divorce.

In January 1914 Helen and Teacher and Helen's mother set out on a transcontinental lecture tour, their hearts heavy with the disintegration of Teacher's marriage. Helen sought to hold it together. It was she who wrote to John, a cheery letter as if all were well and the earth were not collapsing under their feet: "While we were in Canada, every one said we were 'wonderful, fascinating, charming and beautiful women.' I was 'the great pupil,' Teacher was 'the great teacher,' and mother was 'the great mother.' "

But John, who had gone to work as literary editor of the *Boston Herald,* was in no mood to banter and replied with a letter full of his grievances against Teacher. This he carefully sent to Kate Keller to read to Helen. Helen replied on January 25 from Appleton, Wisconsin:

Mother has read your letter to her to me from beginning to end. It has amazed me and filled my heart with sorrow. If you ever loved

Teacher or me, I beseech you to be calm, fair, kind, to consider what you have said in that letter.

You are wrong, John, in thinking that Teacher has tried to influence me against you. She never has. She has always tried to make me see how very good and helpful you have been to us both. She has impressed it upon me that very few men would have endured my foolish tears, my fussy and exacting ways as you have all these years, and I love you for it. She never told me that she thought you pushed me out of my place at the table, one night at the apartment until mother read it in your letter! I know you put me in a seat away from you but I thought it natural that you should have Mrs. White beside you, as she was a guest, and I think so now. But it hurt Teacher to think that you should have any one else in my seat when I was to be at home only a few days.

As to my voice, you know, John, and every one else knows that for twenty years we worked hard together to make it better. She never claimed to know anything about the science of the voice. She simply tried, as you yourself used to try, in every way possible to help me speak better, and I love her for it. Mr. White has often expressed to me in glowing words the warmest enthusiasm for her work, and his indignation that some people did not give her the credit for it. She gives him full credit in every lecture as a fine voice teacher, and she loves to do it. No, there has not been an 'unintelligent nagging' or nagging of any kind about my voice. Please, please be fair, be just.

We do not have John's letter; but his accusations, as mirrored in Helen's reply, sound familiar. Anagnos and Gilman, and less clearly Wright, Humason, had all felt that Teacher had soured their relations with Helen. And Helen herself, in her last book, *Teacher,* would acknowledge in veiled terms what had been evident to Miss Fuller back in 1888—that Teacher resisted the effort to teach her to speak. The long letter to John went on:

You say you can 'never explain to me what your life with Teacher has been.' I remember that in spite of many hard trials in the past we have had happy days, many of them, when we three seemed to feel in each other's handclasp a bit of heaven. Have you forgotten it all that you say such bitter things about my teacher, about her who has

made my darkness beautiful and rent asunder the iron gates of silence? Have you forgotten all the sunshine, all the laughter, all the
long walks, drives and jolly adventures, all the splendid books we
read together? Have you forgotten how exultantly you used to say,
after you helped me with a difficult task: 'There! we are happy now
because we have a piece of faithful workmanship to show.' Have you
forgotten that at times, when we had all been impatient, you would
say to me: 'If we were not a trouble to each other, we could not love
as we do.'

I know how imperious, changeable and quick-tempered Teacher is.
I have suffered just as much from those failings as you have: but my
love for her has never wavered, never will. Perhaps she owes her
success to some of those very failings. You know—you have often
told me as much—that the education of a deaf blind child is a tremendous strain upon the faculties and the health of a teacher, and that
only a few can stay with such a child more than a year or two. Only
Teacher's splendid vigor has make it possible for her to stick to her
colossal task during twenty-six years. Think of it!

This was, of course, the essential point in Helen's relationship with
Teacher; and Helen, wise girl, always was aware of the strain upon
Teacher to serve as her "other self" twenty-four hours of the day. Others
who undertook the task only briefly found it too nervewracking a routine.
One of John's major grievances was Teacher's insistence on centering the
life of the household, including her own activities, around Helen. He
chafed under what he considered to be his wife's neglect of him; and
Teacher, recalling their marriage bargain in regard to Helen, fumed.
Helen continued:

You say that she 'has never been a wife to you, or done any of the
things that a woman might be expected to do.' You know, we have
shared everything we had with you. You have helped us in all our
literary work, and all that has come from it has belonged to you as
much as to us. You know, too, that you have dictated as freely as we
what ought to be done with any gains we had from our work, and
we have looked up to you in all our problems, all our difficulties, all
our undertakings. Do you remember that I refused to take lessons
from Mr. Devol years ago because you so evidently disapproved of

the plan. If you still think I am 'dominated' by Teacher, this proves that you yourself have done it, and I love you none the less for it.

Again: Teacher does not like the lecturing: but she was glad to do it last year when she thought some money would take you to Italy and give you the change you desired. I copied all the letters she wrote to you last summer, often with her tears running over my hand. She really felt that she was doing and saying things to make you happy and bring you back to us again well and strong. And now you say that 'she has played a game'—that she has been untrue to you!

Be careful, John, what you say. If you love me, as you tell mother you do, be careful. The world before which we three stand will certainly judge what we do and say, and I believe that the world will judge fairly of us, as it always has.

I know that in the past year Teacher has changed in some essential respects. By talking with her daily I have learned that you have helped her to see the world, the workers and economic, social and moral conditions as she never saw them before. Living so close to her as I do, I can prove, absolutely prove, that she has new aims, a new conviction, a new vision of life, a new ideal and a new inspiration to service, and you will know it too some day. Believe me, John, from this work the great jury of the world will pass its verdict upon her actions and sentiments, and upon yours. They will also say that this trouble is my affair; Teacher is my affair, just as all suffering humanity is my affair.

Now, dear, you have every one of Teacher's failings, as I can show you from my experience with you: and your letter has proved that you have more grievous ones than she has, and I still cherish you. When I first heard your letter, I thought you had destroyed my love for you. Once you said you were a sworn foe to all who brought such charges against Teacher, and I thought I was too. But now I know that you have not killed my love, and you never can. Does not love—true love —suffer all things, believe all things, hope all things, endure all things. Love suffers long and is patient. It gives without stint, without measure and asks for nothing in return. It expects only good from the dear one through all trials and disillusionments. With such a love I cling to you, as I cling to Teacher. You and I are comrades journeying hand in hand to the end. When the way is dark, and the shadows fall, we draw closer.

Of course I do not ask you to give Teacher what you cannot give. Why should I? Why should anyone? It is something over which you have no control. But you certainly did give us something better when you were in New York last December. You did more for us unexpectedly in little ways than ever before, and I knew then that you had a new, nobler feeling. Oh, John, recall that feeling, foster it more and more, give up everything for it, and believe me, undreamed sweetness and peace shall come into your life. It shall no longer seem to you 'a poor life.' I have lived to know that love which is love casts out the ghosts of dead affections, dead hopes, wasted years and disappointed ambitions. Let your heart speak for 'my Helen' as you so fondly call me, prompt you to exceed what you have thought you could do, match my love with your own for us both, as you once said you would. I have unfaltering faith in you. One day you asked me to trot in the same team with you, and now I ask you. Whether you choose to or not, I promise that you shall find me unchanged.

Affectionately,
'Billy'

John's response was an even harsher letter about Teacher than the first. This brought from Helen an equally passionate defense of Annie. His letter had made her wretched, she wrote from Milwaukee on February 8:

I confess, I had hoped for a gentler, more magnanimous answer. I have said little about it to Teacher. She is wretched too, and seems to think there is nothing to be gained by discussion. But I have had several talks with mother, and we both feel that your attitude towards Teacher is hard and unreasonable. Perhaps I ought not to write what I think. But you know it is my nature to speak my mind, and there are some things I want to say before we drop the subject.

I may perhaps never know all that you have suffered the past ten years. But what I do know is that all has not been suffering. I have a good memory, and I remember distinctly that we have had many, many bright days together. In spite of all that you may say to the contrary, the happy days outnumber the unhappy ones. Before now you have always acknowledged this, and you would still if you could only put those hard feelings out of your heart. Never, since I have known you, have you made such sweeping charges against Teacher. You say, 'she has not played fair.' I do not know what you mean. You do not explain, except that you say you cannot trust her. Practically you call her 'a living lie,' as Mr. Anagnos used to call me. You do not use those words but that is what you imply.

You, her husband, my brother, dare to say such things about your wife, my teacher! And further, you declare that you can 'abundantly prove' what you say. This you cannot do because it is a lie, and when you come to your senses, John, you will know this. I have lived with her twenty-six years. Mother has known her as long, and loves her and trusts her implicitly. No one can be 'a living lie' and keep the affection of her near friends during all that time. We realize how quick-tempered and changeable Teacher is. We know that when she gets angry she blurts out things which she does not mean in the very least. But we also know that she bears no malice, and is quick to ask forgiveness. You once said to me: 'When Teacher gets mad, she says wrong things blindly. But I go and say mean things to a man with my eyes wide open.'

Three selfish men [presumably Anagnos, Sanborn and Gilman], whom neither you nor I respect, brought charges against her similar to those which you now make, and you know how false they were because you had the facts before you, and you told me how flimsy and contemptible the charges were. You fought her battle then and I thought you had a knightly heart. What has happened to you John, to justify such cruel, suspicious language?

It is striking how those who turn against Teacher end up with charges that she was a humbug. Annie was as cunning and manipulative as a master politician, and her many stratagems that seemed only venial offenses when viewed from the inside became unforgivable in the eyes of the disenchanted.

Next, you write: 'It is Teacher's act which involves separation from me.' But she did not tell mother or me that she would not return to the apartment. In fact, mother did not know that she had asked you

to consult a lawyer until the lawyer's letter reached Teacher in Detroit. Of course we understand that a divorce involves separation. But
that is a very different matter from what you say. You tell me that 'she
left my house with the express and final decision never to return.' She
did not say so to mother or to me or to any other person that we know
of, unless she said it to you, and we do not know about that. But even
if she did say so to you, how could you believe that we would never
come back to the apartment? Where else could we go? The apartment
is full of our things, and we think of it as our home—not a happy
home, to be sure, but all the home we have in the world. Mother and
I both understand that Teacher and I are to return in May.

You say you have 'an absolute contempt for the law, its sanctions and
releases.' Yet you seem to think the law a good thing for Teacher.
You fling out legal terms about her acts as if they were words to
conjure with. You obey your attorney's orders and write to her only
with his permission. She has not consulted a lawyer, except through
you and she does not know the legal bearings of her acts, except as
you interpret them.

John's recriminations devastated Teacher. Not since she had walked out
into the night after Gilman had ordered her separated from Helen had she
felt it such a misery to continue to live. Thoughts that she was going insane
haunted her waking hours, and she escaped from them only by a frenzy
of work and activity. Sometimes after a sleepless night she laid her head
on Helen's shoulder and said, "How I shrink from this day." But then she
took hold of herself with the thought, "Our audiences have nothing to do
with what has happened to me." She had Helen's story to tell, and that
might encourage others to bear equally oppressive burdens.

Helen did not want to interfere, her letter of February 8 went on, but
she had a sister's right to speak her mind:

You say that my love for you and your love for me is not in question.
In one sense that is true: but in another sense it is not true. For I have
loved Teacher dearly through all the circumstances of our life together, and her happiness is bound up with mine.

Again, you say that 'the question of my voice is not essential to this
matter.' That is very true. What right, then, had you to write in your

letter to mother about Teacher's 'unintelligent nagging' having a bad effect upon my voice? Because you mentioned it, I referred to it in my letter to you. Come to think of it, had it not been for Teacher's 'unintelligent nagging' for twenty years, Mr. White would have had no voice to work upon! The fact of the whole matter is, your mind is so prejudiced that everything seems wrong to you now.

You tell me that our contracts with the Pond Bureau were signed before any of us dreamed of your going to Europe. Of course that is true. But what I said in my letter to you is perfectly true too. We were both glad and happy to do work which we hated when we thought that some money would take you to Italy and give you the change you desired. Your answer is a quibble.

As to the money question, mother knows, and every one of our friends knows, that Teacher is generous to a fault. You speak of her making 'a disgraceful row' on two occasions when you proposed to send some money to your mother. You say nothing about the many times that money was sent to your family when Teacher did not 'make a disgraceful row'! You know, John, and I know, that she helped your family even before she was married. You should remember that during the years which followed it was often very difficult for us to pay our own bills, and still we had your family to help. You should also remember, John, that when you were in Schenectady, and we were still in debt, you never sent us any money, though of course you may have paid some bills that I did not know of. Afterwards we paid your debt to Mrs. Hopkins, and we were glad to do it, and we have always been glad to do whatever we could to help you, even if Teacher sometimes made 'a disgraceful row.' I realize that she was very extravagant. But so were you and she herself got the money to pay most of our bills. You tell me she acknowledged in a letter to you 'that it never occurred to her until last year that you had any independent rights in our money.'

Money matters, once the initial passion that brought Teacher and John together had subsided, were bound to cause difficulties. They never had enough; and John felt that his contributions to the household's earning power—he edited Helen's letters and speeches as well as her books—entitled him to share and share alike and to do so without having to consult Teacher.

You ought to remember that, nevertheless, all these years ALL the money we had has gone to pay our expenses, yours as well as Teacher's and mine. Since we have had more money, there has really been no question about your right to send money to your family or to any one else, and you have availed yourself of that right, have you not? Teacher's talk about, and her attitude towards money has never been 'evil and sordid.' You will find it difficult, if not impossible to convince any of her friends of the truth of that statement. If it were in part true, she would be a rich woman today. She would have married riches, and she could have secured money from many sources if she had made the least concession to those who have it in abundance. You ought to be ashamed to use such words.

As to the checks you speak of, Teacher told mother that she destroyed them because she thought that if there was to be a separation, you would not be the one to attend to our business. But later, when you spoke to her about it, she thought that it would not make any difference one way or the other: so she made the checks out again. She told me some months ago that she was sorry she had not let you manage our financial affairs from the beginning. But neither mother nor I see why she should. She also said she was sorry she had made such expensive changes in our house.

But the talk about money was too painful and demeaning, and she turned to another charge in John's letter:

The idea of her changing her opinions, her attitude towards life 'to get the better of you' as you put it in your letter to mother, is preposterous. What do you mean by 'to get the better of me?' If it means live more peaceably with you, I consider it a wonderful piece of self-effacement. But I know that she is not made that way. She never in her life changed her opinions in order to get peace or happiness. It is past belief that you should think any such thing even for a moment. You say to me 'you cannot know what is in the mind of another person.' Yet in your letter to mother you accused Teacher of changing her opinions 'to get the better of you.' That is a little inconsistent, John, is it not?

Teacher's difficulty now is not that you no longer love her, but that your whole attitude towards her is one of distrust and suspicion. Yet her love for you has survived all this wreck and misery and confusion, and I must say I am surprised. She never talks unkindly to me, or, I believe, to any one else about you. And here are your two letters full of harsh things about her, which you reiterate over and over as if you enjoyed saying them! The trouble with you is, you have apparently conceived an antipathy for her. That is what makes it impossible for you to live and work and be decent.

To sum up, mother and I feel that Teacher has had something to bear on her side as you have on yours. The faults you have are such that they have made it difficult for her to live with you quite happily. You should not forget that some of the 'disgraceful rows' you talk about so much arose out of your inconsiderateness and self-indulgent habits. I know that those habits often upset our housekeeping, and that they would have tried the temper of any housewife. Perhaps they seem trivial to your masculine mind: but to a woman nothing is trivial that upsets the order of her household and brings confusion into the family life.

I love you both, I always shall, and I think that you both loved me well enough to hold my hands and support my weakness through all the years allotted to me. Every word of your two bitter letters about Teacher is cruelly stamped upon my mind, and will darken every day of my life as my physical blindness has never done. You, and you alone can lift this burden of sorrow from my heart. My love for you makes me confident that somehow, somewhere, sometime, you will again be the dear brother and generous friend that I have known for twelve years.

This letter she signed "affectionately your sister, Helen." She no longer felt comfortable using his nickname for her, "Billy"; his nickname for Annie was "Bill."

By March the lecture tour took them to Salt Lake City and then on to the West Coast. It was the same everywhere—rooms full of newspaper people, photographers, callers of all kinds with questions about the deaf, the blind, the feeble-minded; disagreeable arguments about their share of the gross receipts; letters, telegrams and telephones to be answered. And always as a recurrent theme the harrowing argument with John. "I have not written to you since I received your unkind and altogether unbrotherly note in St. Louis because my work was very hard, and I tried to keep unpleasant thoughts out of my mind all I could." They fought about the apartment in Boston. "You know, John, that you took that apartment in Boston because YOU wanted it, not because we did." They quarreled about the division of income. "I have always been willing, glad to share with you, evenly or any way that pleased you, all I had. But do you think it is fair or generous or consistent to say you 'hate our money,' and in the same letter to tell us that you deposited a thousand dollars of that 'hated' money for yourself?" They fought over who was responsible for the separation. "You say 'it was Annie, and not I, that wrecked us.' If it was she you DROVE her to it. Your first letter to mother showed that you did and when the facts are known everybody else will see it. You know also, I believe, that Teacher left the apartment that night because she had to in order to fulfill her [lecture] contract. You are not, then, playing fair to lay all the blame upon her and take advantage of the necessity which forced her to go away at that time. Apparently you are making circumstances fit in with your wishes. I imagine it is possible for a woman to tell her husband that she thinks they had better separate, without wishing to 'leave his domicile.' " This, she said, was her last letter on the subject, but how did he believe they could work together in the future, as he had evidently proposed, "when you keep saying that Teacher is dishonest, that you cannot be harassed by a woman whom you cannot trust, that she has lied and deceived you?"

She reproached him for not keeping her informed:

> I have not heard for many weeks about matters on which you always used to inform me so particularly—correspondence, opportunities to help in a good cause, Arturo's book and so forth. I understand that you have taken Mr. Fagan as secretary to attend to some of my correspondence. Well, if you do not want to write yourself, why not let him write the home news, and so help me straighten out the many details which always come up when I return home? I love to be of use to others, and I do not let any one spare me in my tasks and I never shall.

This is the first mention of Peter Fagan, a socialist colleague of John's on the *Herald.* He will reappear in our story. Helen's letter was signed "lovingly." She still had not given up hope.

If John was unmoved by Helen's pleas, others continued to find her irresistible, "the sweetest, finest, noblest spirit in the world," as the editor of the *Kansas City Star,* W. R. Nelson, called her. She had visited the office of the *Star* to urge the importance of plain speaking on the subject of preventable blindness in babies. When it was suggested that she write an article for publication, she sat down to her typewriter in her hotel room and wrote a column-length plea for action against *ophthalmia neonatorum.* "We felt it was the most interesting thing we had in the paper today and so we printed it on the first page," the managing editor informed her.

From Vancouver on April 4 she reported to John, "We have now killed over a hundred lectures and many other bugbears besides, and survived. I really wonder that Teacher is able to go on. I know you want me to tell you just how she is. She is very, very tired, though she will NOT admit it. At times she trembles so much that we marvel when she gets through the lecture, and nothing happens." In Vancouver they were "almost killed with kindness—receptions, teas, calls and motor drives." She tried to write him a "breezy letter" of the kind he liked but had to lay the letter aside because she was overcome with homesickness; "but now I have sense enough to remember that there is no home to miss now because you are not there. . . ." She described the vast vistas of wild flowers, of orchards and overhanging cliffs through which they had traveled. "Yes, I love the immense, sprawling, opulent West." Everywhere the Socialists greeted them warmly:

> I am now a member of the Los Angeles local of the Socialist Party. They also asked Teacher to join, and she at once said she would. But they have not yet sent her a red card as they promised to. . . . You see, I cannot rest, I am feverishly seeking for new channels of usefulness, and I need you more and more. No, dear, we cannot do our best work without you. We have tried, and it is just as if you had died. Do write to me about things that really interest us all, tell me what you can of Socialist news, and suggest how I can help the workers as you used to.

She enclosed a bit of redwood and a rockrose. "Even so do two aching hearts send out thoughts of you and a prayer for pity and for a home."

But hopes that the relationship between Annie and John might be repaired foundered on the realities of the clash of temperaments and the inability to transcend their respective frailties that became evident on Helen and Annie's return to Boston. In May the two women went to

Buffalo for a lecture. Teacher fell down the steps and was badly bruised. Helen wrote John to report on her condition. Her note ended sadly, "As to the furniture, you need not do anything about it until you hear about our plans."

The loss of John made Teacher lean on Helen more than ever. "She kept demanding my love in a way that was heartbreaking. For days she would shut herself up almost stunned, trying to think of a plan that would bring John back or weeping as only women who are no longer cherished weep." It tormented Helen's mother to see Teacher suffer. All Teacher's plans, which required John's varied abilities to realize, were now falling about her in ruins, Kate Keller told her daughter. "To no one, except myself in the silence of the night," wrote Helen in *Teacher,* "did she speak of her anguish or the terrible dreams that pursued her." Her sight had worsened; her body had thickened to the point of causing her great discomfort. Only her hopes for Helen sustained her.

part five

HELEN *and* TEACHER *and* POLLY

XXIII

Socialist Joan of Arc

"She is the creator of a soul, but you had the soul to be created."—Montessori to Helen.

Separations are rarely tidy and definitive. Despite the harsh letters of the spring, in the autumn John was back with them at Wrentham. He was propelled there as much, perhaps, by having to evacuate his Boston apartment (which had been gutted by a fire caused "by some carelessness of his—a cigarette left burning it was thought," ruining Helen's and Annie's belongings as well as his own) as he was by hopes of a reconciliation with Annie.

Their fees from lectures, together with an annual income from such sources as the Carnegie pension, the Rogers annuity and help from the ever loyal Mrs. Thaw, enabled them to live in some comfort. Helen began to refer to Wrentham as their "baronial estate." It had new "big granite posts" as a gateway and a garden of perennials and a privet hedge around it. Teacher and John decided that Helen should have a cozier study and tore it up to install a fireplace with a white marble mantel, red tiles and a glass door so that she could walk out into a fragrant copse directly. She had a sunshine-flooded bedroom, and they filled its window with begonias, chrysanthemums, ferns and heliotrope. New draperies were hung and several of the rooms were repapered, and a sewing room was established where all the mending, darning, pressing and manicuring—and the nursing of the maid's baby—could "be done comfortably."

John loved to work around the house. He thinned out the trees so that the large elms and maples might have more room to spread their thickening boughs. He moved spruces. He shifted the driveway. They even acquired a Great Dane, a four-month-old puppy, big and affectionate, which they named Thora. Another sign of relative affluence was their considerable household staff. They took on a Swiss maid, Lena, with a six-month-old baby who had been abandoned by the father; an auburn-haired Irish girl with blue eyes and a winning brogue, to cook; and a houseboy, a Russian-born waif, Ian Bittman, who washed windows, cleaned rugs and ran errands, and whom they vainly tried to teach to drive a motorcar, "but he doesn't seem to have the brains for that sort of thing."

They used their motorcar for frequent jaunts, among them a trip through the Green Mountains as far as Lake Champlain. John chauffeured them with the usual travails that attended motor travel over roads intended for the horse and buggy.

It was a relief to Helen to report to her mother the minutiae of Wrentham life, not only because of John's involvement in them but because her spirit was oppressed by the war in Europe, which had erupted in August and seemed "to fill the whole earth" with woe, strife and cruelty. She was, as President Wilson urged Americans to be, neutral in thought and deed, because she was a Socialist, a longtime advocate of peace and a foe of militarism, and also because of sympathy with the Germany of thought and culture.

> I haven't taken sides, as you know; but I get hot because almost everybody is down upon Germany. Not a word is said about the centuries in which 'perfidious Albion' has pushed her conquests to the ends of the earth, strewing her path with blood, tears and untold crimes. Now people prate of her fighting for peace, freedom, justice, and behold, she enters into an unnatural alliance against a kindred nation—with 'the Servian king-murderers,' as the Germans say, and with Russia—the most despotic power upon earth!

Professor William Stern, the head of the Laboratory of Applied Psychology in Berlin, who had visited her during his stay at Clark University and who had written about her for German scientific journals, asked that she examine the German position in the war: "The reason I send this letter to you, is that I know that your world-ramifying house has become a central point for widespread communion, and that from it many invisible bonds lead out to important personalities."

Her willingness to show Dr. Stern's letter to an interviewer from the *New Bedford Sunday Standard* showed that she did not reject its arguments. Later she requested her German publisher to turn over the proceeds of the German translation of *The Story of My Life* to blinded German soldiers. "I am neutral, yes," she replied to critics, "but I consider my second country the land of Beethoven, Goethe, Kant and Karl Marx."

Whatever pro-German sympathies Helen entertained were fiercely challenged by William English Walling, the intellectual leader of the Socialist party's left wing. He had bitterly attacked the German Social Democrats for voting war credits to the Kaiser. "We invited him down for Sunday," she wrote her mother. "He has just left and I am glad he came. For he is very interesting, and has had wide experience in his work for the Revolution. Of course we discussed the War, and we tried to think of some way to get hold of public opinion, so that another such war might never occur. Surely the world ought to take a day off and think. Surely all well-disposed people—philanthropists, pacifists, eugenists, friends of the people—should get together at once and make a supreme effort to check the appalling waste of human life, arrest the swift retrograde of whatever civilization we have attained."

In her lectures that autumn, chiefly in New England, she dreaded the questions about the war. "Are you a neutral?" she was invariably asked, and was glad to be able to say yes, "and I added that I liked the people of all nations, but not their armies and navies." A heckler asked, "Which part of the brain do you use?" "The whole of it," she promptly answered, and continued, "Which part do you use?" *Neutral* inadequately described her basic conviction about the war. She sympathized with the view of the Wobblies that the workers' answer to the "bosses'" war should be a general strike in all countries. That was hardly a proposition to be advanced from the lecture platform, yet Helen was always uncomfortable when concealing her beliefs. She, John and Annie thought that the general strike should be the recourse of the American workers in the event that the United States abandoned the neutrality that President Wilson had proclaimed. They spent the 1914 Thanksgiving holidays in New York with Arturo Giovannitti and his wife, Caroline, whose ardently voiced syndicalism strongly influenced their own. John's next book, *Socialism in America,* was partial to the IWW and was dedicated to the Giovannittis. "Tell mother," Teacher said to Helen, "John has begun his new book and he seems much better in some ways." Also while on that trip to New York they visited the top of the Woolworth Building, which Helen described

as one of "the countless wonders of that fascinating city. . . . From what
the others said, the view must have been the sight of a lifetime." They
traveled to the Giovannittis' by subway. "The noise was demoniac, and
the cars were crammed with humanity. I was surprised that the people
seemed so well behaved; I was not pushed or punched so hard as I have
been in less crowded places."

Fears that the war might interfere with their 1915 lecture tour, which
was to take them as far as the West Coast and was being arranged by the
Pond Lecture Bureau, proved unfounded: "Mr. Pond thinks he may book
me with the Schuberts [sic] for two weeks in San Francisco." In preparing
for this trip they took on an additional assistant—Polly Thomson, a young
Scotswoman who wanted to stay and settle in the United States. She was
sturdy, quick-witted and practical minded. "She seems to know just what
I want without my telling her," Helen wrote her sister, Mildred Tyson.
According to Nella Braddy, she quickly learned to balance a checkbook,
read a timetable, map out a cross-country schedule, even to manage the
household and (in a pinch) to cook. She acted as Helen's secretary, and
in crowds as her bodyguard. Although she had never heard of Helen
Keller before she came to Wrentham at the end of October 1914 and did
not know the manual language, she stayed with Helen until her death
forty-five years later. She was, said Nella, "as intolerant as John Knox,"
and "conservative in every field except politics," but her loyalty to Helen
and Teacher would be total.

"You ask how Polly looks. I cannot describe her," she wrote her
mother,

> but they say she is very good-looking. I know she is efficient and most
> helpful. She is taking lessons in hair-dressing and manicuring; so she
> will save us a good deal on the long tour.
>
> Of course, we think of you as going with us. Polly's being along
> won't make any difference. Polly will 'boss' me, and you will look
> after Teacher. As we understand the plan of the tour, we start for the
> middle West the second week in January, go through Ohio, Indiana,
> Iowa, Kansas, St. Louis down to Texas as far as El Paso, then to Lower
> California, and up to San Francisco and back home through Califor-
> nia. It will all be most interesting for you, I am sure; so do come. We
> shall both love to have you with us.

By the time they began their trip John had moved once again to the St.
Botolph Club in Boston. He wanted to get away. He had volunteered and

been accepted for an American volunteer ambulance unit; but "the armchair patriots," he later told Ernest Gruening, his biographer in the *Dictio-*
nary of American Biography, "were not able to find money for my passage
or expenses."

Their lectures at this time were well attended and lucrative. In Montclair, New Jersey, Dr. Bell had introduced them; in New Haven, former
President Taft. The great and illustrious were eager to meet them—
Thomas A. Edison, Henry Ford, Judge Ben Lindsey, Enrico Caruso.
Helen discovered a special bond with Edison. He was "very deaf, and he
couldn't understand me. He said my vowels were all right, but he couldn't
get my consonants. How I wish I could have someone like him to hear
me every day." She sat next to the inventor and read his lips. "He expects
soon to perfect a machine that will produce speaking pictures. . . . I asked
him if he thought something could be invented that would enable the
blind to read ink print books, and he said, 'Yes, I do.' He tried it once.
I begged him to keep on, and he said he would." He played his "marvellous phonograph" for her and invited them back to spend a day in his
laboratory. "A day at Mr. Edison's laboratory which I hear is guarded by
detectives—can you believe it?"

In Detroit Henry Ford personally conducted her around his mass-pro-
duction factory, which—because of its conveyor belt methods, he told her
—could produce a car farmers were able to afford. The high point of their
1915 tour was the Helen Keller Day at the Panama-Pacific Exposition in
San Francisco and their meeting with Dr. Maria Montessori. They had
already met the great Italian educator in New York. Miss Anne George,
who was head of the Montessori School in Washington and the translator
of Dr. Montessori's classic book, *The Montessori Method,* acted as interpreter. "We discussed the 'House of Childhood' schools, social problems
and the failure of the church to make Christianity a living reality upon the
earth," Helen wrote, but that scarcely conveyed the highly emotional
quality of the encounter:

"Say to her," said the "Dottoressa," as she was called in the *Boston*
Herald's account, "that I am too much moved to express what I feel."

Placing her hands on Dr. Montessori's shoulders, Helen enunciated
distinctly, "Blessed are the feet of her who comes across the seas with a
message of liberty to the children of America."

"How clearly she speaks," commented the Dottoressa, "and her face
is lighted with her soul." Helen went on to express her pleasure that Dr.
Montessori's meeting the night before had been crowded.

"Not all the thousands," she instantly rejoined, "mean one tenth as much to me as this meeting."

"I myself am a product of the Montessori method," Helen continued, as her hand sought Annie's lips.

"Does she know that I have written a dedication to her for my new book?" Dr. Montessori asked Teacher.

"She knows that you have dedicated the book to her, but she does not know what you have written."

"I have said that I have learned from you as pupil learns from master," Dr. Montessori said to Helen.

Quick to sense a lack of appreciation of Teacher, Helen, turning to Annie, remonstrated, "But you should have said that of her."

"Of both, for you are one. She is the creator of a soul, but you had the soul to be created."

They disagreed only over whether education or socialism should have priority. "I began as a sympathizer with revolutionists of all kinds," explained Dr. Montessori. "Then I came to feel that it is in the liberation of this, what we have in our hearts, that is the beginning and end of revolution."

Helen protested: "But surely we never can have the Montessori system or any other good system of education so long as the conditions of the home, of the parents, of the workers, are so intolerable."

"Certainly, certainly, that is true. But we must educate children so that they will know how to free themselves and others from bondage. And the first thing is to bring our children under the care of worthy teachers. You and Mrs. Macy symbolize such education, the education of the future, the development of a soul by the union of an inspiring teacher and the child whose soul has grown freely with such stimuli as it needs and without the stimuli that debase and hinder growth."

When they had said good-bye in New York, Dr. Montessori apologized for not having tried to express her feelings about Annie: "I feel as if her heart were in my own heart, and praising her would be like praising myself." At the San Francisco fair, where both she and Teacher received "Teacher's Medals," she reverted to the theme of Mrs. Macy as her mirror image. Asked repeatedly to comment on Teacher's work, she said, "I have been called a pioneer," and then, pointing to Teacher, added, "but there is your pioneer."

The fair was thronged with teachers and educators on Helen Keller

Day. Helen spoke before Teacher, delighting more strongly in the recognition given Teacher than in the honors she herself received:

> My teacher was irregularly instructed. There were gaps and deficiencies in her education that she had the rare wisdom herself to see. She brought to her work a freshness, a clear openmindedness that contributed much toward her success. She was fearless in her experiments. All the qualities of the teacher born were hers. She stimulated in her pupil a desire to know more than she had time or knowledge to teach. She aroused curiosity, aspiration and joyous effort.

Somewhere she must have recognized the justice in John's complaint that in marrying Teacher he had married an institution, for her speech emphasized:

> She could have lived her own life, and had a better chance of happiness than most women. Her power of diamond-clear, audacious thought and the splendor of her unselfish soul that have made her a teacher of teachers, might have made her a great leader in the emancipation of women. But she has closed these doors to herself and refused to consider anything that would take her from me or interfere with her labor of love. Even now when she has a household and new demands are always being made upon her time and strength, she never lets pass a chance to lighten the weight that burdens my activities and hampers my work. . . . She has given me the best years of her womanhood, and you see her still giving herself to me day by day. . . .

When Teacher was handed the fair's Teacher's Medal, she acknowledged that the education of one child constituted her whole achievement as an educator, but the medal suggested that her experience might have a larger meaning for education. In lucid and powerful sentences she held the audience spellbound with her philosophy of education:

> You see before you a teacher whose mature years have been passed wholly in the performance of one task, the training of one human being. For years I have known the teacher's one supreme reward, that of seeing the child she has taught grow into a living force in the

world. And today has brought me the happiness of knowing that my work is an inspiration to other teachers. . . .

Here is no dazzling personage [she said, pointing to Helen], no startling circumstance. A young woman, blind, deaf and dumb from infancy, has, through the kind of education that is the right of every child, won her way out of darkness and silence, has found speech and has brought a message of cheer to the world. Men and women have listened and have rejoiced, they have learned to love the brave girl. They love her for her sweetness and courage, and for the lesson she has taught.

What she has accomplished without sight and hearing suggests the forces that lie dormant in every human being. . . . If Helen Keller, lacking the two senses that are usually considered the most important, has become a writer of ability and a leader among women, why should we not expect the average child, possessed of all its faculties, to attain a far higher ability and knowledge than the schools of today develop? Many realize that there is something radically wrong with a system of education that obviously does not educate.

Every child begins life as an eager, active little creature, always doing something, always trying to get something that he wants very much. Even before he can utter a word, he succeeds in making known his desires by cries and grimaces. He invents and devises ways to get the things he wants. He is the star performer in his little world; he is the horse, the coachman, the policeman, the robber, the chauffeur, the automobile. He will be anything that requires initiative [and] action. The one thing he never voluntarily chooses to be is the grown up personage that sits in the car and does nothing.

Our educational system spoils this fine enthusiasm. . . . Our schools. . . . kill imagination in the bud. They uproot the creative ideals of childhood and plant in their place worthless ideals of ownership. The fine soul of the child is of far greater importance than high marks, yet the system causes pupils to prize high grades above knowledge, and he goes from the schools into his life work believing always that the score is more important than the game, possession more praiseworthy than achievements.

She went on to speak of Helen's education and the methods that she had followed to keep Helen's interest from flagging and to enable her to take the lead in the choice of the next lesson. She ended with a tribute to Maria Montessori.

> To that wonderful woman, Dr. Maria Montessori, belongs the honor and the everlasting gratitude of mankind for having systematized these ideals of education and recorded them in her book, a book that is at once a thrilling human document, a scientific textbook, a prophecy and a torch to all those whose work it is to teach little children. Dr. Montessori learned, as I learned, and as every teacher must learn, that only through freedom can individuals develop self-control, self-dependence, will power and initiative. There is no education except through self-education. There is no effective discipline except self-discipline. All that parents and teachers can do for the child is to surround him with right conditions. He will do the rest; and the things he will do for himself are the only things that really count in his education.

The organizers of the Exposition printed Helen Keller's little speech, which, though affecting, did not compare with Mrs. Macy's remarkable statement. That was relegated to the mimeograph machine. But both of them had become accustomed to that disparity in public response to their respective contributions.

When they returned from their long tour at the end of May, the house was full of guests, including Mildred and her baby daughter, Katherine, whom Helen dubbed "Merry Sunshine," and the Giovannittis. But John was not there, and despite the presence of family and friends Helen was depressed. Under protest they acceded to the pressures of the Pond Bureau to work the Chautauqua circuit in August in Indiana, Illinois and Iowa. She had finally realized that she had gone as far as she could in improving her voice and it was not good enough. For about twenty minutes her audiences by straining were able to follow her, and then Teacher had to take over to repeat what she was saying. "We still meet people on our tours who say that my voice is improving," she informed Charles White, "and I find it easier to talk with strangers even above the noise of a crowded hall or a train. But, I need hardly to tell you, my voice has not brought the happiness that I anticipated. It is true, it has brought money and some measure of freedom from financial worries but our hearts are as heavy as last year's nest. It is like a banquet with costly viands, wines, fruits, and—no guests." The house without John was empty. "Our home is as pretty as ever. The garden, they tell me, is a perfect blaze of color, and it is packed with fragrance. But oh, how everything speaks of the past!"

She missed John the more because there was so much she wanted to talk with him about politics and particularly the war. Germany's U-boat campaign, the sinking of the *Lusitania,* turned public feeling against Germany. Woodrow Wilson, yielding to the pressure of the pro-Allied group in his cabinet, became an advocate of preparedness. The mood of the country, nevertheless, was doggedly noninterventionist, and Wilson was preparing to run for reelection in 1916 on a platform of "He kept us out of the war." An international women's congress met at The Hague under the presidency of Jane Addams in 1915 and drew up a peace platform that was a forerunner of Wilson's Fourteen Points. There were forty-seven women in the United States delegation. But Helen was not among them. Undoubtedly her lecture commitments would have prevented her attendance, but she might have sent a message. It is more likely that ideological disagreement caused her to keep her distance. She was fiercely antipreparedness and antiwar; but like the members of the Zimmerwald Left faction in Europe that included such left-wing figures as Lenin, Rosa Luxemburg and Karl Liebknecht, she had no faith in bourgeois governments sitting together to make a compromise peace. "The Socialist should not lend himself to any of the bourgeois peace programs, to 'limitation of armament,' international arbitration enforced by a world police, the creation of a citizen army, or that silliest of pseudo-feminist ideas, a birth strike," John Macy wrote in *Socialism in America;* and though Helen saw little of John, their viewpoints remained strikingly alike—remarkably close to the syndicalist position of the IWW.

Her response to Henry Ford's telegram inviting a hundred leading Americans to sail on his peace ship, the *Oscar II,* to meet with leading Europeans to pave the way to a negotiated settlement, indicated her skepticism of a peace negotiated by bourgeois governments. Her new lecture agent, Mrs. Marcia Stevenson of Iowa City, who was setting up Helen's winter schedule, telegraphed in some agitation: PAPERS ANNOUNCE THAT YOU ARE GOING TO EUROPE ON FORD PEACE TRIP. CITIES HAVING JANUARY DATES GREATLY ALARMED. Teacher wired back, WE ARE NOT GOING ON FORD PEACE TRIP. In turning down Ford Helen was not wholly negative about his initiative. "I sincerely hope that

it may be possible to bring the war more speedily to a close." But in a note
to herself she commented:

> I am not altogether satisfied with the letter I have just mailed to Mr.
> Ford. As I think over his peace plan, many puzzling questions start
> in my mind. I wonder and wonder how he will reach the men in the
> trenches with his peace propaganda. Surely, the powers that made the
> War and that keep the men in the trenches will not permit Mr. Ford's
> interference; and even if they did, how would all the soldiers get
> together between the landing of the *Oscar* and Christmas? Still, I wish
> I were on board the Peace Ship, it would be a most interesting
> adventure. Anyway, my heart is too full of longing for peace to throw
> any word of obstruction in the way of its consummation. It is not for
> me to say that Mr. Ford's plan cannot succeed.

But a few weeks later she had changed her mind. "Nothing will come
of this plan," she wrote in the Socialist *Call,* "because he won't use the
only means to make it a success—get the soldiers themselves to quit
fighting." The same issue of the *Call* announced that she would speak
about the Ford project before the Labor Forum at the Washington Irving
High School in New York and would advocate a general strike as the
speediest way to bring about an end to the war.

This was too much for the *Sun,* which deplored the use of a school
auditorium for such advocacy. Two thousand enthusiastic partisans turned
out to hear Helen. The meeting was presided over by Rose Pastor Stokes,
herself a firebrand, married to the millionaire Socialist J.G. Phelps Stokes.
When a saint begins to scatter anathemas, the walls tremble. A scheme of
the capitalist class further to enslave the worker—that was Helen's characterization of the preparedness program. "And will you working men fight
for the flag? Does it symbolize anything to you but the country which
treats you with the clenched fist when you strike for higher wages?" she
asked amid the wild applause that attended Mrs. Macy's translation of the
staccato questions. "Let no working men join this army which Congress
is trying to build up," she pleaded. Only the munitions makers and bank-
ers like J.P. Morgan stood to gain from preparedness. "I look upon the
world as my fatherland, and every war has for me the horror of a family
feud. I hold true patriotism to be the brotherhood and mutual service of
all men." The only preparedness the United States needed was justice and
well-being at home. The worker had nothing to gain or fear from the war

except a change of masters. "Let the workers form one great world-wide union, and let there be a globe encircling revolt to gain for the workers true liberty and happiness." As the crowd surged toward the platform, Rose Pastor Stokes, in a powerful final flourish, moved that a copy of Helen's speech be sent to the President. A roar of approval came back and a flushed Helen, practically overwhelmed by the crowd, against which six policemen sought to protect her, was escorted to her waiting automobile.

> Nobody can have the heart to criticize poor little Helen Keller [said the *New York Herald* the following morning] for talking when opportunity offers. Talking is to her a newly discovered art, and it matters not if she does talk of things concerning which she knows nothing, could not possibly know anything.

> But why should the so-called Labor Forum be permitted to use the pathos of her personality to promote a propaganda of disloyalty and anarchy?

> And what right has the Board of Education to turn over one of this city's school buildings for the purposes of such propaganda?

Even *The Outlook,* a liberal publication that ordinarily approved of everything Helen said, was startled. Her sweeping claims that the movement for national defense was a Morgan plot, it considered wholly "unsubstantiated." Her assertion that American workers had nothing to defend showed an astonishing insensitivity to the U.S. institutions that differentiated America "from the military autocracies of Europe." Industrial liberty, it went on, would not be won by "indifference to those who fight here, or in other lands," to maintain the political liberties through which alone the worker could go on "to secure the extension of liberty to industrial vocations."

Antiwar sentiment was rampant in New York City, where the Socialists were strong, and Helen's speech reverberated everywhere. She was the toast of the left wing and of the feminists, who were proud of Helen as a woman as well as an opponent of preparedness. Hundreds had been turned away at Washington Irving High School, and the Labor Forum together with the Woman's Peace Party decided to hire Carnegie Hall for a second speech by Helen. She had left on a lecture trip through the West but, excited by the audience's passionate response, quickly agreed to return. She stipulated, however, that there should be no admission charge, so that the workers could hear her. HELEN KELLER TO DEFY JINGOES, the *Call* headline read.

Defiant the speech assuredly was. "The future of the world rests in the hands of America," she told the packed hall. "The future of America rests on the leaders of eighty million working men and women and their children." To end the war and capitalism "all you need to do . . . is to straighten up and fold your arms." She pitched into the arguments of the preparedness groups that America was in danger of attack from Germany and Japan. "With full control of the Atlantic Ocean and the Mediterranean Sea the Allies failed to land enough men to defeat the Turks at Gallipoli. . . . The conquest of America by water is a nightmare confined exclusively to ignorant persons and members of the Navy League." Adroitly she turned the very efficiency of the warmaking powers into an argument for staying out: Look what the Germans have accomplished by the welfare state measures that they had instituted in preparation for war, she urged her listeners. "For eighteen months it has kept itself free from invasion while carrying on an extended war of conquest. . . . It is your business to force these reforms on the Administration. . . . Let there be no more talk about what a government can or cannot do. All these things have been done by all the belligerent nations in the hurly-burly of war. Every fundamental industry has been managed better by the governments than by private corporations." This speech, too, ended with a plea for a strike against war and war preparations.

The poet Anna Strunsky Walling, who was in the audience, wrote of the impression Helen made:

> You walked forward as if you wanted to run:
> Eagerness was in your feet, in the lift of your head,
>   in your brilliant smile.
> You walked forward and took your place at the edge of
>   the platform, facing the great audience. . . .
> Oh, unforgettable experience of my soul when first the
>   effulgence of your courage and your youth laid its
>   spell upon me!

A few years later, after America's entry into the war had shattered the socialist movement—William English Walling among others having bolted the Socialists to support Wilson—and Versailles had shattered

Wilson's hopes of wringing a better world out of the cauldron of war, Mrs. Walling sent Helen a copy of her poem, which she labelled "unfinished"; and Helen's reply revealed how hungry her immured spirit was for a sense of comradeship:

> How your poem brings it all back—the meeting at Carnegie Hall, the enormous audience and the patience and the hearty applause with which they listened to my halting speech! How like a dream my part of it all seems! I can hardly realize that those hundreds upon hundreds of people whose presence I still feel came to hear me. But they did, and I have never again felt separated from my fellowmen by the silent dark! Any sense of isolation is impossible since the doors of my heart were thrown open, and all the world came in. It is good to have this passionate, complete sense of being part of all that lives and throbs, rejoices and suffers, strives and achieves.

She dreamed revolution and general strike. She gave a widely reprinted interview disclosing that she had become a member of the IWW. "I may be a dreamer, but dreamers are necessary to make facts." She had become an IWW "because I found out that the Socialist party was too slow. It is sinking in the political bog. It is almost, if not quite, impossible for the party to keep its revolutionary character so long as it occupies a place under the government and seeks office under it. . . . Nothing is to be gained by political action. That is why I became an IWW."

Her interviewer was taken aback by the violent, uncompromising views being uttered by this gentle woman. She wanted to protect her against herself and questioned the advisability of printing some of her replies. "I don't give a damn about semi-radicals," was Helen's response.

Teacher was present during the interview, as were some other friends of Helen, who are not identified. They, too, were startled and nervous: "It will make a sensation," one of them commented. "It will ruin her for further peace work. She will lose her following." Helen brushed the objectors aside.

She was not an absolute pacifist, she went on. "I am for peace because I think workers can gain their ends by putting their hands in their pockets. The world is theirs then." Teacher betrayed her skepticism by propounding on behalf of the interviewer the next question: "And with the world in their possession, wouldn't the people promptly proceed to build up institutions and situations almost identical with the ones you deplore?"

Helen was not fazed. The world could not be run any worse than it was by its present economic masters, and "at least the underdog would have a chance at the envied bone."

As the interview progressed and Helen's replies increased in pugnacity, her face, said the interviewer, took on a glow and exaltation:

> I feel like Joan of Arc at times. My whole being becomes uplifted. I, too, hear the voices that say 'come,' and I will follow no matter what the cost, no matter what the trials I am placed under. Jail, poverty, calumny—they matter not. Truly He has said, 'Woe unto you that permit the least of mine to suffer.'

She needed to see the world as a contest between Good and Evil. Her imagination—cut off by blindness and deafness from many of the signals that brute experience sends most of us counseling caution, compromise, grayness instead of black and white—lent itself to dichotomies between the party of the future and the party of the past. At Radcliffe, Horace's "golden mean" had appeared to her as a shabby escape from confronting the truth. "I tell you," she wrote in an unpublished statement defending her views at this time, "there is no peace between the teachings of Christ and any form of slavery. So when I stand up to speak for the enslaved, the injured, the oppressed of the earth, I speak not because I have aught to say, but because I should be a coward, a hypocrite if I did not say my word for what I think is just. . . ." If she kept some grip on reality, it was because of Teacher, a woman of practical common sense.

In Buffalo for a lecture the press pursued her. What had she meant at Carnegie Hall when she had jibed at "Roosevelt and other war mad persons?" Theodore Roosevelt had become the leading spokesman for intervention and preparedness, she replied:

> He is the most bloodthirsty man in the United States. When he is not dreaming of plunging this country into war and shedding the blood of men he is writing books about his own prowess in shedding the blood of animals.

And who was the most bloodthirsty man in Europe? the interviewer pressed on. "The Czar," Helen answered immediately, "and she smiled the sweet, quick smile that is so charged with life, so warm with womanliness. 'I know you expected me to say the Kaiser,' she added, 'but the

Kaiser has never turned cannon upon his own people as the Czar has done. The Kaiser never massacred the Jews.' " A moment later as an afterthought she bade her interviewer "put Rockefeller in with Roosevelt and the Czar." He had a "greater blood guilt if not greater bloodthirst" than Roosevelt.

This savage thrust at John D. Rockefeller was occasioned by the "Ludlow massacre," which had taken place in 1914 on Colorado coal properties belonging to the oil magnate. "I have followed, step by step, the developments in Colorado, where women and children have been ruthlessly slaughtered," she told the press at the time. "Mr. Rockefeller is the monster of capitalism. He gives charity and in the same breath he permits the helpless workmen, their wives and children to be shot down." She herself had once been helped by John D. Rockefeller, but that did not mute her criticism; perhaps it even sharpened it.

She seemed at this time to be seeking martyrdom. She had always felt that she was destined for some great purpose; and she welcomed the opportunity to lead, as Joan of Arc had led her people, even if it meant immolation on the stake. It gave her, as she wrote Anna Strunsky Walling, a sense of communion with humanity that freed her from her overwhelming sense of isolation. By curious coincidence she received a letter at just about that time from Lucy Randolph Mason, then a YWCA Industrial Secretary in Richmond, Virginia, and at the beginning of a brave career as a lonely advocate of unionism and liberalism in the South. It suggested that to American working girls Helen Keller was a more meaningful figure than Joan of Arc. There were eight thousand girls in the factories of Richmond, and Lucy Mason's problem was how to reach them. She found that telling them stories during their lunch period was a way of establishing communication. She managed to cover eight factories each week with stories about "Famous Women." Somebody at the YWCA suggested Helen Keller, and so she boned up on *The Story of My Life.* "I wish you could have stood in the center of the throng of girls crowding around me to hear what you achieved—Joan of Arc was 'not in it' with you for sheer human interest. . . . I loved their faces as they listened so eagerly, so understandingly to the way in which you and that marvelous teacher overcame obstacles. Not a girl did I find who did not respond to that story, the best in her rising to meet the courage with which you set out to conquer difficulty."

But there were others who attacked her—the newspapers, Theodore Roosevelt understandably—she now dubbed him "His Highness of Oyster Bay"—and *Life* magazine, at the time a humorous journal much read in barber shops. In a caustic paragraph it linked her with Henry Ford, whose peace ship had become a butt of derision:

> Perhaps as a blind leader of the blind Helen belonged with Henry's crew. Peace-making is a blind business; so is war-making. Helen and Henry are two very kind hearts, imperfectly equipped to see the whole of life. Henry called his expedition a crusade, and there was one crusade in which ten thousand virgins were enlisted, but they did not get to the Holy City.

The revolution-breathing speech in Carnegie Hall, the press interview in which she had revealed her membership in the IWW, distressed her mother. To reassure her Helen sent her an editorial from a Midwest paper "which may perhaps help you to understand why I am so deeply interested in social and industrial problems that seem so wholly outside the 'limits of my personal world.' I am grieved to think of all the uneasiness I may cause you, and I do long for you to see my heresies and heterodoxical 'nonsense' in the best possible light. . . . In La Crosse [Wisconsin] I was asked some straight questions on the platform about Socialism, preparedness and woman suffrage, so I had a better opportunity for propaganda than in Muscatine, and I made the most of it."

In an unpublished letter to the *Brooklyn Eagle* Helen sought to explain where she got her sense of mission and commitment to the working class, when "in fact everything has stood in the way of my having such feelings." She dealt first with her right to have unorthodox views. Her sources of information were "as reliable as anybody else's." She read widely. She had visited slums, shops, factories, traveled across the continent three times. She did not deny her limitations, but "the great editor Mr. Pulitzer was obliged to work under similar disadvantages." So did Fawcett, the blind English postmaster general. "Huber, the blind naturalist, needed constant assistance from others in his studies." Francis Parkman, the great American historian, "was terribly handicapped by imperfect vision," and the French historian Thierry was "quite blind. I must say, I do get quite tired of hearing young men, who cannot write a dozen sentences without maltreating their mother tongue, assume a pitying or supercilious tone when they write about me for their papers." She hardly knew how to account for her feelings

on subjects that seem to you out of my sphere. I suppose they are
mostly temperamental, as there exists no influence which could have
given rise to them. I come of a dominant race. In my veins runs the
blood of fighting ancestors. My family all belonged to the master
class, and were proud of their birth and social prestige, and they held
slaves. Now, even since childhood, my feelings have been with their
slaves. I am dispossessed with them. I am disenfranchised with them,
I feel all the bitterness of their humiliation when a white man may
take a job or a home he wants, while they are driven out of houses
and churches—nay, and are even terrorized and lynched if they compete in doing profitable work for the master class. And my sympathies
are with all the workers who struggle for justice. . . .

My family were also Presbyterians and Episcopalians, and some of
them were dyed-in-the-grain Calvinists. Now I am a Swedenborgian.
For many years I had only one friend of that faith near me [Hitz], and
he was always most anxious for me to be independent in my religious
views. Now there is no one near me who takes the slightest interest
in the New Church. Its spirituality and idealism appeal to me. It also
fosters all kinds of true freedom, places humanity above party, country, race, and it never loses sight of the essence of Jesus's gospel—
the supreme and equal worth of each individual soul. That doctrine
is the heart of Christianity. . . .

Again, I have departed from the traditions of my forbears, male and
female, in the espousal of woman suffrage. My mother has always
believed in equal suffrage, but so far as I know, the rest of the family
believe that they have all the rights they want. Most of my dear
friends are anti-suffragists. Even the one nearest to me in the world,
my teacher, is sometimes distressingly lukewarm. She still expects
men to look after her affairs and protect her. I do not believe that any
sex, class or race can safely trust its protection in any hands but its
own.

She wanted no quarter, asked no one's pity. She had weapons "as strong
as any one else's." She had drawn strength at the beginning of 1916 by
identification with Joan of Arc. Now she invoked the name of Jesus.

I shall fight with the strength won from ceaseless battling with silence
and darkness, with my faith, with my love, with the love of thousands

that love me. "Who is this but the carpenter's son?" said the doubters of Jesus two thousand years ago when, amazed, they beheld Him teaching with authority among the reputed wise and mighty of the land, nay, standing out alone against their oppressive theology and greed. Did not Wilberforce's critics tell him he should confine himself to his sermons as he had always done before he attempted to free Britain's slaves? Did not the doubters cry to Dr. Seguin, "What have we to do with thee," when he only wanted to free a mind imprisoned in idiot clay? Many of the great friends of humanity have been as far from the world's field of battle as I was, and their "limited information of life" has ever been urged as an evidence of their ineligibility. . . . I have chosen these champions, these lovers of mankind, and in their company I find peace. . . .

She did not inject her socialist views into her formal lecture. That had a set pattern. Teacher went onto the stage first and spoke in her musical voice about the education of Helen. She then led Helen onto the platform. To accustom the audience to the strangeness of Helen's voice, she had Helen repeat slowly sentences that Helen read with her fingers on Teacher's lips. Then Helen repeated the lines of "Abide With Me." The audience thus prepared, Helen launched into what she called her "Message of Happiness," a series of epigrams, mottolike statements counseling hope, cheeriness and good works. The audience followed the high-pitched, strangely inflected voice with difficulty, but there was always an ovation at the end because of admiration for the courage behind the effort.

It was in the question period that politics inevitably arose. In Pittsburgh, where they appeared under the patronage of their old friend Mrs. William Thaw, who stood by them despite Helen's militant radicalism, she was asked to predict the outcome of the war in Europe. "Miss Keller's face instantly assumed an aspect of comical dolefulness and she disavowed any ability as a psychic," wrote the reporter for the *Dispatch*. But she ventured the view that "some crowned gentlemen will be out of jobs." What should be done with them? another questioner followed up. They "might earn a living in the American moving pictures," she replied quickly.

In Helen's arsenal of causes she embraced the movements against child labor and capital punishment, Margaret Sanger's crusade for birth control and, most urgently of all, and with a priority equal to the antipreparedness struggle, woman suffrage. An amendment to the Constitution that would give women the right to vote had languished in Congress since 1869. But successive waves of progressivism had led to women's enfranchisement in ten Western states, and Illinois gave women the right to vote for President. Politicians thereupon began to pay attention to the women's vote; and suffragists, under the leadership of Dr. Alice Paul, who had worked with the Pankhursts in England, formed the National Woman's Party.

Despite Helen's reservations about the efficacy of political action, she made an exception with regard to woman suffrage and joined the new party. Socialist dogmas about the subordination of women's rights to the larger struggle of the working class for liberation also were discarded. "Political power shapes the affairs of state," she wrote in the *Call* in late 1915 in an article on "Why Men Need Woman Suffrage." "Rights are things that we get when we are strong enough to claim them." She noted ruefully the rebuff dealt to a women's group in Albany when it presented a petition signed by five thousand women on behalf of a welfare measure. Forced to cool their heels in an antechamber, they waited patiently; and when finally they inquired of the chairman what had happened to the bill, they were blandly told that he knew nothing about it. But they had handed him a petition signed by five thousand women, he was reminded. "Oh," he replied, "a petition signed by five thousand women is not worth the paper it is written on. Get five men to sign and we'll do something about it." Women were demanding the vote, wrote Helen, because they wanted "five thousand women to count for more than five men."

The suffragists swarmed all over the national nominating conventions in 1916. Helen, as a special correspondent, was at the Chicago convention of the Republican party in June, which nominated Charles Evans Hughes to oppose Wilson:

> For the first time in the history of America women have become a great factor in the selection of a presidential candidate, and the creation of a party's platform. They are seen everywhere here in Chicago in these convention discussions where a very few years ago their appearance would have caused untold comment. And their influence is affecting every "deal" that the politicians are making. Greatest of all, they have just formed a "woman's party," the birth of which I saw as it was started winging its way down the ages. . . .
>
> The time is ripe for us; there are now four million women voters in the United States [as a result of action by the states]. The party that turns them down is dead politically. Of course our victory is not won; we shall have to work long and endure much before our dreams are

realized. But the new woman's party will give the two old parties a jolt at the presidential election that will set them thinking and acting.

The women were not able to get the suffrage amendment into the Republican platform, but Hughes personally endorsed it, and ex-President Roosevelt, who supported Hughes, did likewise. Even Woodrow Wilson overcame his "instinctive repugnance" to the woman's movement and endorsed it in principle—asserting, however, that it should come by way of state action rather than federal amendment. The women, as Helen had predicted, still had to picket, to petition, to stage hunger strikes. But in September 1918, just before the congressional midterm elections, Wilson considered it politic to appear before a joint session of Congress to urge the amendment's passage as a measure "vital to winning the war."

A sense of the gathering momentum and power of the women's movement was about all that militants like Helen had to cheer them as the 1916 presidential campaign began. Debs's refusal to run on the Socialist ticket —saying it was time for a younger man—had sent the Socialists to a journalist, Allen Benson, who had been catapulted into prominence by his proposal that the issue of war and peace should be decided by national referendum. A large number of Socialists, fearful that otherwise Hughes might win, supported Wilson. The President was a conflicted man, preparing for war and trying to exert America's power for a negotiated peace. He met and impressed a group of *Masses* editors, including Max Eastman and John Reed; and even Allan Benson suggested that those who could not vote for him should vote for the Democratic candidate. And Helen, despite her scorn for compromisers, made friendly references to Wilson.

An antipreparedness Chautauqua tour that she and Teacher embarked upon in the summer of 1916 (Polly Thomson had gone to Scotland to visit her dying mother) was a fiasco. They needed the money. Their arrangement with their lecture agent, Mrs. Stevenson, was 20 percent to her, the remainder to them, but they had to pay their traveling expenses. Their fees ranged from $250 to $500. They worked hard, especially on the Chautauqua circuit. They had not wanted to do summer Chautauqua, but Mrs. Stevenson had assured them, "There is a tremendous demand for Helen Keller's lecture on Preparedness, and of course if you want to serve that cause you will have an opportunity to reach thousands of people in the very best towns in the west."

As the summer approached there was a war scare—war with Mexico. In case of war, Helen informed Mrs. Stevenson, she would cancel the

Chautauqua commitments. She would lecture only on antipreparedness, and such a speech would be "untimely." Teacher was more emphatic. If there were war, Helen's speech would be considered "an act of treason" and "the people [would] not listen." Helen evidently was not prepared to go as far as her Wobbly comrades and go against the law in the event of war. War with Mexico or not, the Chautauqua leaders told Mrs. Stevenson, there was need for "a lecture on Preparedness for Peace. . . . Jane Addams isn't well enough to help steady the ship and she and Helen Keller are the only women the country will listen to, so there is the situation as it appears to us out here."

The war scare abated, and Helen and Teacher set forth with Peter Fagan as their secretary. Their instinct had been sound. "Most of our audiences were indifferent to the question of war and peace," Helen later recalled. They returned to Wrentham dispirited. The Wobblies alone seemed to be holding the red flag bravely and defiantly aloft, at least on economic issues, though even they were divided on the issue of civil disobedience in the event of war. Thirty thousand iron ore miners in the Mesabi Range in Minnesota were on strike under IWW leadership. She sent them "all I can share of my earnings." She appealed for public support. "Will citizens who believe in justice remain silent while [Carlo] Tresca and the other leaders of the Mesabi Range strikers are being tried for their lives on an utterly groundless charge of murder?"

But urgent as were the calls upon her of the IWW, of the National Woman's Party and of the antipreparedness campaign, suddenly all was overshadowed by Teacher's frightening symptoms of consumption and by Helen's romance with her Socialist secretary, Peter Fagan.

XXIV

Helen in Love

"His love was a bright sun that shone upon
my helplessness and isolation."

Few people spoke the language of love more spontaneously than
Helen. Tenderness, solicitude, sensual responsiveness, suffused her being
and embraced all around her in their compass. She herself coined the word
vibrascope to describe her susceptibilities and ardors. Despite the deprivation of sight and hearing—themselves, of course, powerful stimuli to
arousal, especially the eye—she was made to love and be loved. In *The
Story of My Life* she recalls that soon after Teacher arrived in Tuscumbia
she had asked her the meaning of the word *love:*

> I had found a few early violets in the garden and brought them to
> my teacher. She tried to kiss me: but at that time I did not like to have
> anyone kiss me except my mother. Miss Sullivan put her arm gently
> around me and spelled into my hand, "I love Helen."
>
> "What is love?" I asked.
>
> She drew me closer to her and said, "It is here," pointing to my heart,
> whose beats I was conscious of for the first time. Her words puzzled
> me very much because I did not then understand anything unless I
> touched it.
>
> I smelt the violets in her hand and asked, half in words, half in signs,
> a question which meant, "Is love the sweetness of flowers?"

"No," said my teacher.

Again I thought. The warm sun was shining on us.

"Is this not love?" I asked, pointing in the direction from which the heat came. "Is this not love?"

Helen was disappointed in the reply. A few days later she was still puzzling about the meaning of the word *love,* when after clouds and showers the sun again broke forth:

Again I asked my teacher, "Is this not love?"

"Love is something like the clouds that were in the sky before the sun came out," she replied. Then in simpler words than these, which at the time I could not have understood, she explained: "You cannot touch the clouds you know; but you feel the rain and know how glad the flowers and the thirsty earth are to have it after a hot day. You cannot touch love either; but you feel the sweetness that it pours into everything. Without love you would not be happy or want to play."

The beautiful truth burst upon my mind—I felt that there were invisible lines stretched between my spirit and the spirit of others.

Helen's shyness about kissing and being kissed yielded to the newly discovered delights of communicating with her fellow human beings. Soon she was "hugging and kissing" everyone. And from Boston in 1888 she wrote her mother, "Clifton did not kiss me because he does not like to kiss little girls. He is shy. I am very glad that Frank and Clarence and Robbie and Eddie and Charles and George were not very shy."

The cuddly child of Perkins days whose ardent spirit had warmed the aging literary lions of Boston had in her thirties turned into a shapely woman whose words and actions glowed with affection and sympathy. Georgette Leblanc, a deliciously beautiful chanteuse, companion for many years of Maurice Maeterlinck and herself brimful of sentiment and sentimentality, visited Helen at Wrentham, and was quickly taken captive. She described her two meetings with Helen in *The Girl Who Found the Bluebird,* published in 1913. "You have but to observe the girl for a moment to feel in her an impetuous force, captive passions that at first knock impatiently at closed doors and then escape by unsuspected routes. . . . Very few people give so powerful an impression of vitality. . . ." Between the two women there were shivers of recognition, and Leblanc describes Helen responding to touch and gesture as though she had received "an electric shock."

She spent a whole day with Helen and the Macys and left regretful that she was scheduled to leave for France without having asked Helen what she thought about love. She postponed her sailing and wrote Annie asking that she be received again and begging that Helen not be told she was coming. As she entered the study, Helen was concentrated on her type-writer:

> I kiss her, I stoop over her cheek, passing my arm around her neck; but she draws herself up, panting as though an electric current had touched her. Her nervous hands seek mine; then they run along my arms, my neck, my cheeks, my hair and, for a second, they doubt: her quivering nostrils recognize some subtle odor, her lips move, she is just about to speak my name. . . . But it is impossible! She knows that I am gone: this very morning she was glad of the fine weather and hoping that the sea would be merciful to my pangs. She rejects the syllables that force themselves upon her and feverishly continues her examination. I am wearing quite different clothes; and that also disconcerts her. Nevertheless, she finds the game exciting. Her face lights up with pleasure, for the feast of hearts has already begun. She laughs, I laugh too; and my gaiety removes her last doubts. Then she kisses me, hugs me, shows me her affection with adorable smiles and gestures. . . .

Leblanc, a famous beauty, takes note that Helen cannot see herself in the mirror that is in her room: "The mirror tells me: it has not instructed her; it has never told her her charms and defects; it has never revealed her image to her. That image lives and dies in the mirror, whereas with us it is the revealer, teaching us, correcting us and becoming the eternal companion of a grace which it unceasingly abandons and directs by turn. . . . We shall never ourselves know how far that inseparable sister influences our gravest actions and deeds." And that leads Leblanc to another melancholy, uniquely feminine reflection on the significance of Helen's sightless eyes: "But, though we have need to see ourselves in order to find fulfillment, it is not in the glance of the docile and faithful mirror that we really know ourselves. It is by the look of others; for the eyes of others seem to pour out the beauty that fills them. There is here a mysterious interchange. Does not the woman who loves rise and grow to the height of the eyes that contemplate her?"

Finally Leblanc gets to the questions that had brought her back to Wrentham—how Helen got at reality and what love meant to her. "What others learn from life," replied Helen, "I have learnt from books that are my sphere." Here Annie, who had been listening and watching, chimed in:

'There is nothing that Helen does not know; I have never hidden anything from her; besides, she is too clear-sighted for it to have been possible.'

'Then I may safely ask her what she thinks of love and happiness?'

'Oh, certainly!' replied Mrs. Macy. 'She has thought a great deal of the love and happiness of women.'

And she at once communicates my question to Helen.

Helen remains impassive and says, slowly:

'All real love is precious.'

But I insist:

'I am not speaking of love in general, Helen.'

Then I see a soft light of resignation pass over her face; and, in a serious tone, she says:

'What woman has not longed for love? But . . . I think it is forbidden me, like music and light. . . .'

I look at the blind girl. She sighs and lowers her lids as though her eyes might betray her. I see her youth and the glow of health in her cheeks; a dull rebellion stirs me; and, with my natural inclination for sympathy, I feel a need to depreciate [sic] the too-delicious joys which a barbarous injustice seems to deny her:

'Ah, you could be loved, Helen, you could, I am sure of it; but I do not know that you ought to wish it. You would not have done what you have done, if you had known love. You do not know how dangerous it is. . . . No, do not regret love. It is the enemy of our intelligence, of our strength and even of our worth. You see, Helen, between two intelligent people, experience of love, though it be favourable to the man, may be fatal to the woman. Whereas the man becomes stronger by a love which his nature orders and measures, the woman is lost in a sentiment that submerges her. . . ."

Ideology and intellectualism tinged Helen's views on love and marriage when she was interviewed about them in Chicago in June 1915. Husband and wife should rule a household like a "bicameral government," she said, and that was an impossibility as long as man had the "money bags." Her ideal man "will be handsome for eugenic reasons. . . . He doesn't have to be rich. I am paying my own passage through the world and am proud of it." Men should be "tender, yet strong and full of humor," like Mark Twain—but not, she emphasized, pounding Teacher's palm, like Napoleon, "nor Bismarck, nor T.R. T.R. is a boisterous politician. . . . I should never marry a man like T.R." Marriage should be based on love, she went on, but "all women should marry if they can get any one to marry them. Yes, they should. It's essential for the race—and evolution in the world." The happiness of the children should be a primary consideration in the household. "The state should pay for the upkeep of each child for there is no greater service to the state than a woman's gift of a child—a greater service than the building of a warship."

These were not conventional views; but neither were they the emancipated views on sexuality and marriage that characterized the life-styles of some of Helen's friends among the radicals, especially the Wobblies and anarchists. The love affairs of Emma Goldman and Elizabeth Gurley Flynn, of Carlo Tresca, John Reed and Max Eastman, were well publicized. While high society and high politics had their quota of unconventional relationships, their practitioners did not make a political platform out of them. John Macy, who was a friend of John Reed and Max Eastman, certainly accepted the sexual revolution as part of his advocacy of a total transformation of society and its values. What Helen and Annie believed on this point they nowhere indicated, nor did they say whether and how they achieved sexual fulfillment.

For a time, of course, Annie had achieved such fulfillment through her relationship with John. A note that she scrawled, probably many years later, is haunting testimony to that fulfillment:

Last night you came to me, John. I do not know if it was a dream or your spirit presence. I felt your step so near and you were the very same—your manner and the smell of your clothes. I held your hand so tight and you called me Bill, but I felt the same glad thrill I always felt when you put my hand on your lips and said Hello Bill. Oh I was so happy because you had come back to me. Home isn't just the same when you are not there. We walked in the hill wood and we hunted toadstools and got a basket full that were good to eat. We walked home through the field and you said, "This is like the old times," and the way you said it brought peace to my heart. I can't tell if it was a dream or a vision. I only know I have been happier today because you called me Bill in the dear old way.

So far as Helen was concerned, Georgette Leblanc was probably right in suggesting, as she did, that Helen's sublimation of her sexual energies was the source of her energy, vitality and singlemindedness in overcoming the obstacles of deafness and blindness. The one love affair to which Helen admitted wrings the heart with its pathos. It showed that for all her independence and sturdy obstinacy, she was a prisoner—a prisoner of those who loved and cherished her.

They returned to Wrentham in September 1916 deeply discouraged by the indifferent reception they had been given on their summer Chautauqua tour. Teacher was seriously ill, her body wracked by a cough that the doctor thought might be consumption. She was warned that she might die of tuberculosis and that her best chance of survival was to go to Saranac. They decided that they would have to break up housekeeping at Wrentham. Polly, who had returned from Scotland, was to go with Teacher. Helen would go to Alabama with her mother. The sense of utter aloneness and vulnerability that had oppressed her in late 1912 when the Macys had packed her off to Washington to stay with Lenore again overcame her. She loved her mother and sister, but exile in Montgomery meant an end to her work:

What could I do? I could not imagine myself going on with my work alone. To do anything in my situation, it was essential to have about me friends who cared deeply for the things I did. My experience of the summer had brought home to me the fact that few people were interested in my aims and aspirations. Once more I was overwhelmed by a sense of my isolation.

In that mood she received a startling proposal:

> I was sitting alone in my study one evening, utterly despondent. The young man who was still acting as my secretary in the absence of Miss Thomson, came in and sat down beside me. For a long time he held my hand in silence, then he began talking to me tenderly. I was surprised that he cared so much about me. There was sweet comfort in his loving words. I listened all a-tremble. He was full of plans for my happiness. He said if I would marry him, he would always be near to help me in the difficulties of life. He would be there to read to me, look up material for my books and do as much as he could of the work my teacher had done for me.
>
> His love was a bright sun that shone upon my helplessness and isolation. The sweetness of being loved enchanted me, and I yielded to an imperious longing to be part of a man's life. . . .

The young man was Peter Fagan, twenty-nine years old—Helen was thirty-six. He had been John Macy's assistant, and when Polly Thomson had to visit her family in Scotland, John had suggested they take Peter as Helen's secretary on the Chautauqua tour. We know little about him. He left no records of his own and disappeared quietly and discreetly, making no effort to trade on his romance with Helen when it ended in fiasco. Their lecture agent, Mrs. Stevenson, liked him, writing at the end of the Chautauqua tour, "Mr. Fagan is certainly a first-class secretary"; and to judge by his next letter to Mrs. Stevenson, he also had a sense of humor. "Just at present everyone in the house is disgustingly industrious, and the weather gives promise of an early winter—beginning, I should say, day before yesterday." The little we know of Peter Fagan comes via Helen's severely edited account in *Midstream* and notes left by Nella Braddy of her talks in 1927 with Teacher, Polly and Helen. He was described to Nella as a "violent" socialist, but this was an inept form of disparagement in view of Helen's own militancy. But it reflected Kate Keller's disapproval. The latter disliked Peter Fagan, perhaps because she felt he abetted Helen's radicalism. Teacher, on the other hand, preoccupied with her ailments and her discouragement over John's abandonment of her, did not take Peter seriously. He seemed helpful, having learned the manual language and Braille, but insignificant. Fagan sensed the hostility or indifference to him of those closest to Helen and persuaded her to keep silent about their decision to get married. Helen wanted to tell her mother, and especially Teacher

> about the wonderful thing that had happened to me; but the young man said, 'Better wait a bit, we must tell them together. We must try to realize what their feelings will be. Certainly, they will disapprove at first. Your mother does not like me, but I shall win her approval by my devotion to you. Let us keep our love secret a little while. Your teacher is too ill to be excited just now, and we must tell her first.'

Only the need for deception marred Helen's happiness in her decision to get married, and she told Peter a few nights before Teacher was scheduled to leave for Saranac that she intended to tell Teacher the next morning. But the matter was taken out of her hands. Ian, the Russian boy whom Teacher had trained to cook and look after the house, came to say good-bye. He always called Teacher "my madam." "My madam," he said that morning, "my heart is sad." Teacher thought he was referring to the imminent breakup of the household. She was sad, too, she replied, "and if ever I start housekeeping again I'll send for you." "No," Ian said, "It isn't that. It's Miss Helen. Harry and I know." Harry Lamb was their chauffeur. Ian proceeded to tell her that Fagan had been making love to Miss Helen and that the two were planning to elope. Annie could not believe it, but she sent for Mrs. Keller and told her, especially as a story appeared in that morning's *Boston Globe* reporting that Peter Fagan had indeed applied for a license to wed Miss Keller. It emanated from the office of the City Registrar Edward McGlenen.

Mrs. Keller rushed into Helen's room, her hand shaking as she spelled to her daughter—who, it must be borne in mind, was thirty-six years old and a worldwide celebrity—"What have you been doing with that creature? The papers are full of a dreadful story about you and him. What does it all mean? Tell me!" Helen, frightened and anxious to shield her lover, denied everything. Whatever her private turmoil, she was, according to Nella Braddy's informants, "calm as a cucumber" in her denials, all the time coolly combing her hair by the window. But Mrs. Keller was not convinced. She told Teacher she thought Helen was lying. "Why, Helen can't deceive me," Annie retorted, and Helen was summoned to her bedside. She persisted in her denials, and Annie was persuaded that there was nothing to the story: "My mother ordered the young man out of the house that very day. She would not even let him speak to me, but he wrote me a note in Braille, telling me where he would be, and begging me to keep him informed."

The papers were filled with denials. Peter Fagan denied he had ever been to City Hall, not to mention applying for a license. He was engaged to another girl, he insisted, whom he refused to name. When Helen and Annie's lawyer, Mr. Robert L. Raymond, advised Annie that the story looked true and what was needed was a written denial from Helen, Helen promptly sat down and wrote one out. Annie in a formal statement to the press called the story "an abominable falsehood." But there was no denial from the city registrar, and the papers learned that the application for the wedding license had been made jointly by Miss Keller and Mr. Fagan. "One part of the document," reported the *Times,* "was filled in with a peculiar print-like writing, resembling that of a blind person. Mr. Fagan's name was signed to the paper."

After quoting all the denials, *The New York Times* account went on to repeat that "a close friend of the trio"—could it have been John Macy? —insisted that Mr. Fagan still expected to marry Miss Keller. "Fagan told me all his troubles," said the anonymous informant. "He told me that denials were necessary in order to soothe Mrs. Macy's feelings. Fagan told me he was going to marry Miss Keller, and I know that he consulted a lawyer about the marriage laws in the Southern States through which they were to travel."

Helen and her mother were booked to return to Alabama by way of a boat that stopped at Savannah, from where they would take the train to Montgomery. Mrs. Keller, getting wind of the news that Fagan might be a fellow passenger, abruptly changed plans, and she and Helen hastened home by train while Fagan sailed alone. The change in itinerary upset the scheme that he had hatched with Helen's consent, to abduct her on the way from the boat to the train and elope to Florida where a minister friend of his would marry them.

But Mrs. Keller was not rid of Fagan. One morning in Montgomery Helen's sister, Mildred, saw her talking to a strange man out on the porch. He was spelling into Helen's hand animatedly. Mildred rushed upstairs to alert her mother, who immediately suspected it was Peter. Mildred's husband, Warren Tyson, was told. He got his gun, and all went out on the porch. Fagan stood up to the gun and bravely said he loved Helen and wanted to marry her, but in the end they ran him off the premises.

Peter and Helen persisted. Some days afterward Mildred was awakened by the sound of someone on the porch. She awakened her husband. He did not share her fright. He guessed at once that it was Sister Helen. And it was. How she had been able to stay in touch with Peter the family was never able to figure out, but she had. She was expecting him that night, had packed her bag and gone down to wait for him on the porch. He never came; or if he did, he decided there was trouble in wait and departed.

"It is a terrible picture to me," wrote Nella Braddy at the end of her notes on the episode made in January 1927, "of the blind deaf-mute girl waiting on the porch all night for a lover who never came."

Of these later developments Annie, who was on the point of fleeing Lake Placid for Puerto Rico, was unaware. Mrs. Keller begged Helen not to write to her about it: "The shock would kill her, I am sure."

When, more than ten years later, Helen came to write about the episode, she found herself unable to account for her behavior:

> I seem to have acted exactly opposite to my nature. It can be explained only in the old way—that love makes us blind and leaves the mind confused and deprives it of the use of judgment. I corresponded with the young man for several months [these letters appear to have been destroyed]; but my love dream was shattered. It had flowered under an inauspicious star. The unhappiness I had caused my dear ones produced a state of mind unfavorable to the continuance of my relations with the young man. The love which had come unseen and unexpected departed with tempest on its wings.

She was a captive of those who believed they were protecting her interests. Her mother's reaction was predictable: "We have no models of a mother who encourages her daughter's sexuality," writes Nancy Friday. Helen was sure, however, that had Annie not been in Saranac, "she would have understood, and sympathized with us both." Was Helen correct? Teacher, too, was one of Helen's jailers. Would Peter Fagan have joined the long list of men—Anagnos, Wright, Humason, Gilman, perhaps even John Macy, whose relationship to Helen she destroyed when it appeared to threaten her primacy in Helen's life and affections?

"The brief love will remain in my life, a little island of joy surrounded by dark waters," wrote Helen. "I am glad that I have had the experience of being loved and desired." A sad poem about the episode stressed renunciation and sublimation:

What earthly consolation is there for one like me
Whom fate has denied a husband and the joy of motherhood?
At the moment my loneliness seems a void that will always
    be immense.
Fortunately I have much work to do.
More than ever before, in fact,
And while doing it, I shall have confidence as always,
That my unfilled longings will be gloriously satisfied
In a world where eyes never grow dim, nor ears dull.

When she had said good-bye to Teacher on November 21 it seemed to
her that "some grim destiny" was taking Teacher from her forever; and
this dreadful fear was shadowed by another—who would take care of her?
Teacher, too, worried over Helen's future. From Lake Placid she informed Helen that laboratory tests of her sputum showed "positive pul-
monary affection." As the doctors were advising her that she would have
to stay at Placid for a year, she addressed herself to Helen's question about
what was to become of her:

> You are never out of my thoughts. They keep me awake at night, and
> daylight brings no satisfactory answers to them. When I married John
> I thought I had solved the greatest of them. He promised me that in
> case of my death, which in the natural course would come before his,
> he would be a brother to you, look after your happiness, and take
> charge of your affairs. For years my mind was at rest on this—to you
> and me—most important of matters. Ever since he left us, I have
> worried. He seemed, and still seems, the only one to take care of you
> when I go. Perhaps, dear, it would be best all round to let him do
> what he can to make things a little easier for you when I am gone.
> He understands your business better than any one else. And would
> it not be better in every way to let the suffering, the unhappiness, that
> has come to all three of us die with me? You still love John. I am sure
> you do love him. Such love as we have felt for John never dies
> altogether. For my own part, I think of him constantly; and since I
> have been ill much of my bitterness has gone from my thoughts of
> him. I wish you could forgive and forget too. You would be much
> happier if you could, Helen. If that cannot be, why I suppose you will
> have to depend upon lawyers to advise you in business matters. Mr.
> Raymond is, I think, a good man and would always do all in his power

for you. I have often wished that you knew Phillips better. If you would write him oftener you would soon get to feel nearer to him. I think he is a very fine boy and if you give him a chance he may prove a good friend as well as kind brother. Of course, dear, life will never be just the same again for any of us—it never is after these great changes—we cannot expect it. We can only try to be brave and patient for the sake of those who will have to live with us and take care of us. I am trying very hard to get well for your sake, for the sake of the things you want to do. . . .

Teacher found Lake Placid unbearable, with its bad weather, its "elderly stodgy people" and medical tyrants, and with the loneliness that she felt away from Helen even though Polly was with her. Before Helen was able to reply to her letter about John, she decided impulsively, on the basis of a steamship company's advertisement, to decamp for Puerto Rico. Her first letter from San Juan, written about Christmas time, telling Helen what she had done, was a lyric to the island's beauty. She had found a little shack in the hills that cost them fifteen dollars a month and where she and Polly had set up housekeeping. She wanted Helen and "Mother" to come down and "rough it" along with them. She also asked that Harry, their chauffeur, come down with the car. Island communications, she discovered, were pretty primitive and they were helpless without a car.

Teacher luxuriated in Puerto Rico. Whether it was the escape from the wintry rigors of the Adirondacks, the immediate sense of convalescence that invaded her in the hot sun, the lush splendors of the tropical foliage or separation from Helen, the sensual part of her nature welled up and poured itself into her letters. "Something that has slept in me is awake and watchful," she announced in her first communication. She is glad she did not

inherit the New England conscience. If I did, I should be worrying about the state of sin I am now enjoying in Porto Rico. One can't help being happy here, Helen—happy and idle and aimless and pagan— all the sins we are warned against. I go to bed every night soaked with sunshine and orange blossoms, and fall to sleep to the soporific sound of oxen munching banana leaves.

We sit on the porch every evening and watch the sunset melt from one vivid colour to another—rose, asphodel (Do you know what colour that is? I thought it was blue, but I have learned that it is golden yellow, the colour of Scotch broom) to violet, then deep purple. Polly and I hold our breaths as the stars come out in the sky —they hang low in the heavens like lamps of many colours—and myriads of fireflies come out on the grass and twinkle in the dark trees!

Her images are voluptuous. "The feel of the sudden hot sun after a downpour excites me. . . . Isn't it queer? The bayonet plant makes me want to run, I'm sure I feel the sting of its long, sharp fingers in my flesh." Helen must come.

Yes, she would love to come down, Helen replied, but she feared that it would mean work for Teacher, for whom absolute rest was necessary; in the meantime there were practical details that had to be settled. Mr. Raymond had been pressing her for a decision on the custody of their investments: "I enclose a letter from Mr. Raymond and a paper he wants me to sign placing the bonds in trust. If you approve the arrangement, please return the paper to me, so that I can sign it. Of course, I want the income on the bonds paid to you during your life, and the principal over to you at my death, if I [don't] survive you. . . . He sent me a list of investments and told me to keep it. I am taking up all the small responsibilities I can. . . ."*

*The bonds Helen and Annie transferred to Robert L. Raymond were listed as follows:

1 Adirondack Elec. Pwr. 5%	994.44	
1 New England Pwr. 5%	989.44	
1 American Tel. & Tel. 4%	919.81	
1 Detroit Edison 5%	1036.11	
1 Central Maine Pwr. 5%	997.77	4937.57

In addition Helen and Annie were the beneficiaries of the $10,000 that remained in the Education Fund that Mrs. Hutton and others had set up in the 1890s. This was invested by Mr. Raymond as follows:

2 Consumers Pwr. 5%	1898.33	
2 Union Elec. L & Pwr. 5%	2031.67	
1 American Tel. & Tel. 5%	988.33	
1 Texas Electric Rwy. 5%	924.17	
2 Northern States Pwr. 5%	1896.11	
1 Buffalo Gen. Elec. 6%	1003.50	
1 Alabama Pwr. Co. 6%	1003.50	9745.61

Balance, cash on hand	254.39
Total Investments	14937.57

Helen also received an annual pension from Mr. Carnegie of $5,000, $600 annually from the trust set up by Mr. Rogers, and gifts from time to time from Mrs. Thaw.

But she soon reverted to the problem of who would take care of her if Teacher's illness were fatal:

> Speaking of checks, it reminds me, I have one or two plain questions to ask you. If anything should happen to you suddenly, to whom would you wish me to turn for help in business matters? How could I best protect myself against any one who might not be honest or reliable? Mother loves me with a deep, silent love; but in all probability she will not be with me constantly.
>
> Another thing, if you should be taken from me, or unable to attend to our affairs, what should I do with all our papers? Whom could I trust to go over them with me? I hate to worry you with these questions; but I know enough to realize my dependence upon others, and I try to think, plan and consult you so that I may find the right person or persons to depend upon. Oh, Teacher, how alone and unprepared I often feel, especially when I wake in the night! Please don't think, however, that I let this problem weigh upon my mind more than I can help. The wonder is, I don't worry more. Look at Madame Galeron, the deaf-blind poet. She has had her gifted father, her husband, her grown-up daughter, several able friends to help her in emergencies, and here you and I are with nothing settled! Won't you try to consider these problems calmly, while you listen to the wind rustling in the palms and breathe deeply the heavenly air you love, then write me what you think best. I need suggestions that you can make now while you are free and can think quietly.

Poor Helen! Was she hoping what she did not dare to say—that Teacher herself would see that she needed Peter Fagan? If that was her intent, Teacher did not address herself to the possibility. She did not even know of Helen's pathetic attempts at elopement, and as her spirit and health revived under the beneficent rays of the sun and the absence of responsibility, she became a little impatient with Helen's self-flagellation:

> Helen, you must not worry about the future. I am not going to die yet—I know that I am going to get well. I don't feel ill a bit. In fact, if it weren't for that horrid laboratory report, I shouldn't know there was anything wrong with me.

But even if I should die, there is no reason why you should not go on with life. Somebody would help you with the reading, I am sure of that. If you quietly observe the life about you, and your life in particular, you will see that the future cannot possibly be as hopeless as the beginning seemed before I came to you.

Besides, you believe in the loving watchfulness of a Heavenly Father. (I have not that consolation, but I am deeply glad that you have it.) There is always a way out of the most difficult situation if we really want to get out of it. The merciful Providence—or whatever power there is in the universe—has so ordained things that our little world will go on without us. Indeed, it will not miss us long.

It is a comfort to know that the waters close over us quickly. Only a few remember the splash and struggle, and fancy it was important really. Was it James Russell Lowell who said, 'I have lost the Atlantic (meaning the magazine) but my cow has calved, as if nothing had happened.'

I daresay we are making all this fuss for nothing. Cheer up, the worst is yet to come.

By the end of January, Teacher felt well enough to write: "My plan is to return home—alas! there is no home for us, but we shall find one, probably in New York—in April." Harry and the car had arrived. "Don't think I'm frightfully extravagant! They bring cars down for very little and the expense of keeping it isn't much." Then a confession and avowal. "Dear, I do want to get well for your sake. You do need me still. Your letters make me realize it more and more. This separation is teaching us both a number of things is it not?"

There was no mention of Peter Fagan. Indeed, there was no place for him. If he and Helen had married, he, too, would have discovered—as John had before him—that he had married an institution whose nucleus consisted of Teacher and Helen, and this was an atom not to be smashed.

XXV

Separation from Teacher

"I am so full of longing to serve."

Teacher repeatedly stressed the self-reliance that she encouraged in Helen, and Helen on her part just as often claimed that she asserted her independence to the point of wilfulness and obstinacy. It comes as a shock, therefore, to discover Teacher breaking up Helen's relationship with others, especially men, who might threaten her protégé's dependence upon her. The Peter Fagan episode has a special interest because it is the only case where Helen did not end up siding with Teacher—in fact disobeyed, lied and conspired in pursuit of her own yearnings. Perhaps Helen was correct in asserting in *Midstream* that had Teacher been well, had she not been compelled because of illness to remove herself from the scene, she would have abetted the romance. But Teacher in her talks with Nella Braddy never said so.

And perhaps Teacher's holding on to Helen, although tainted by a possessiveness that arose out of her own needs, was right. Some of the keenest observers of the human soul, such as Dr. Montessori and Mark Twain, saw them as one. "You are a wonderful creature," Mark Twain had written Helen, "you and your other half together—Miss Sullivan, I mean, for it took the pair of you to make a complete and perfect whole." The poet Richard Watson Gilder, reading Teacher's account of her first meeting with Helen in Tuscumbia, said it would take a Blake to paint the picture of those two souls rushing toward each other.

The letters the two exchanged during the five months when Teacher first went to Lake Placid, then to Puerto Rico, showed anew how dependent on Teacher Helen really was. A word of caution is necessary. The original letters have disappeared, probably consumed in the fire at Arcan Ridge, Westport, where Helen lived the final years of her life. They were originally written in Braille, presumably to shield their contents from prying eyes. It was Helen who transcribed them onto her typewriter for Nella ten years later. It is possible that she edited the contents in transcription. The letters, nevertheless, are revealing. They show that Helen, despite her sense of mission, found it difficult to write without Teacher to prod her; that Teacher's analyses of men and events reflected a much firmer grasp of what Freud called "the reality principle" than Helen's; that the latter's zeal and enthusiasm was balanced by Teacher's sense of prudence; and that Teacher by no means was the conservative that Helen, with Teacher's complicity, portrayed her to be.

Millenarian hopes sustained Helen. Teacher preferred to look at the realities. Teacher, in Puerto Rico, accepted that life never again would be the same for them, even if she did not die. Helen flung back the eternal cry of the rebel, "Don't you dare tell me it's too late." As Woodrow Wilson fulfilled Teacher's cynical prediction that he would take America into the war, Helen had a "wonderful dream" of the battlefield dead awakening, touched to life by the kisses of angels, as the cry resounded through the world, "Cease slaying," and "armies dispersed" as "enemies embraced weeping." And she must have written that even if Teacher should die, they would be reunited in eternity, for what else could have provoked Teacher to reply:

> It pains me deeply, Helen, not to be able to believe as you do. It hurts me not to share the religious part of your life. To me, as you well know, this life is the most important thing. What we do Now and Here matters much because our acts affect other human beings.
>
> I am fond of the Bible as poetry. I find beauty and delight in it, but I do not believe that it was any more inspired by God than all fine writing is,—inspired. The future is dark to me. I believe that love is eternal, and that it will eternally manifest itself in life. I use the word eternal in the sense that it is as far as my imagination can reach.
>
> With you the belief in a future where the crooked places will be made straight is instinctive. Faith in conscious immortality helps you to find life worth living despite your limitations and difficulties. The idea of

living forever in some place called Heaven does not appeal to me. I am content that death should be final, except as we live in the memory of others.

Helen's separation from Teacher coincided with America's approaching entry into the war. Although both—with Helen, however, in the lead—had resolutely opposed the moves toward war, the final act found them forlornly sidelined. "I know very little of what is going on," Teacher wrote from Puerto Rico in March. "We seldom see a paper; and when we do it's two weeks old. I don't know this minute whether we are at war with Germany or not. And, bless you, I don't seem to care greatly."

Helen did care. Even more she craved the sense of having an influence on events. But Montgomery was almost as remote from the centers of action and decision as San Juan. Nor did Helen's family live in the state of political and intellectual tension in which she flourished. Her family was loving, but it did not share her politics. Neither did Montgomery, although it outdid itself in warmth and hospitality. "Parties, dresses, babies, weddings—and obesity are the topics of conversation," she lamented to Teacher. There was little more than family gossip and society to report. She adored her two nieces: Katherine, who was "merry sunshine," and Patty, "another sunbeam." Katherine took her round the block every day, "and it is a joy to see her so full of sweet importance." Their mother, Mildred, "is doing all she can to give me pleasure. Friends old and new come to see me every day, and I go out walking and motoring."

On the eastern seaboard groups with which she was allied, like the Woman's Peace Party and the National Woman's Party, girded for final struggles against America's entry into the war and for passage of the suffrage amendment. They debated furiously whether the struggle for the vote was more important than the fight for peace. Those who considered votes for women the crucial issue had supported Hughes in the presidential election; the others had supported Wilson, Helen among them.* In London, Mrs. Pankhurst had come out in support of the Allied war effort, but her daughter Sylvia was "mobbed and jailed," Helen indignantly informed Teacher, for staging an antiwar demonstration in London's East End. "Think of it, Teacher—her country is against her, her brave, much

*Gertrude Gordon, who interviewed her for the *Pittsburgh Press* (the clipping is undated), wrote, "Miss Keller is strongly in favor of all peace movements. She also is a strong partisan of President Wilson and said she thought he would be reelected."

persecuted mother and sister are against her. The misguided sentiments
of women of the whole world are against her. Yet she stands unflinchingly
for a sane, humane civilization."

Helen had been asked to do an article on the suffrage issue, presumably
by the Woman's Peace Party, but she was unable to get it done. Teacher's
comment reveals how much Helen needed her as a goad:

> I am sorry, dear, that you find it so difficult to write the suffrage
> article. I should think it would be rather good fun. It is too bad that
> writing should come so hard with you, especially when it is your only
> medium of self-expression. I sympathize with you, writing is 'a lonely,
> dreary business' if you don't love to play with words. But is there any
> other way that you can reach the mind and the heart of the public?
> You are interested in the questions of the day and the handicapped.
> You desire to serve mankind. How can you do that, except by writ-
> ing? It would be wonderful if we could put forth thoughts as a tree
> puts forth buds, leaves and fruit, without effort, but it just doesn't
> happen that way.

She had abandoned the article, she informed Teacher in a letter dated
April 4, two days after Wilson had asked Congress to declare war. "I'm
not greatly interested in the ballot for women—or for men either for that
matter. There are many problems before the nation, and their solution
calls for many other weapons beside the ballot." But her invocation of the
syndicalist ideology may also have rationalized an escape from a literary
chore that she found difficult, perhaps because she was not clear as to what
she wanted to say, and because there was no one in Montgomery—neither
Teacher nor John—with whom she could talk the problems through.
Montgomery women were little interested in such matters. "Yes, it is true
that most people you meet in Montgomery lack individuality." Teacher
commiserated with her. "It is equally true of most places. Individuality is
not encouraged in the United States. I have read that the French delight
in it, even in eccentricity. But our people do not like to excite remark
because of their ideas. I remember that in school it was the commonplace,
docile girls who were favorites with the teachers."

"I know that you can't talk to your family as you really feel," another
letter said sympathetically. "Don't hesitate to write me all that is in your
mind."

One subject on which Helen did not talk with her family or their

Montgomery friends was the South's treatment of the Negro. Her family knew her views on the subject. In 1916 she had ventured into the explosive field of black human rights when she sent a check of one hundred dollars to Oswald Garrison Villard, the vice-president of the National Association for the Advancement of Colored People, along with a letter that declared her position:

> I warmly endorse your efforts to bring before the country the facts about the unfair treatment of the colored people in some parts of the United States. What a comment upon our social justice is the need of an association like yours! It should bring a blush of shame to the face of every true American to know that ten million of his countrymen are denied the equal protection of the laws. . . . The outrages against the colored people are a denial of Christ. The central fire of His teaching is equality. His gospel proclaims in unequivocal words that the souls of all men are alike before God. Yet there are persons calling themselves Christians who profit from the economic degradation of their colored fellow-countrymen. Ashamed in my very soul I behold in my own beloved south-land the tears of those who are oppressed, those who must bring up their sons and daughters in bondage to be servants, because others have their fields and vineyards, and on the side of the oppressor is power. . . .

Du Bois printed the letter in *The Crisis,* which he edited for the NAACP, and someone signing himself "Alabamian" paid to have the article reprinted in *The Selma Journal.* Many of Helen's relatives lived in Selma, including her cousin Mrs. J. A. Lassiter. "Alabamian" charged Helen with advocacy of social equality of whites and Negroes, of defamation of her own people, and charged her teacher with having indoctrinated her with such disloyal notions: "The people who did such wonderful work in training Miss Keller must have belonged to the old Abolition Gang for they seem to have thoroughly poisoned her mind against her own people." *The Selma Journal* sympathized with "Alabamian" editorially and described Helen's letter as "full of untruths, full of fawning and bootlicking phrases."

A storm blew up. Helen's mother implored her to explain and modify her position. Helen gave her a letter, which her mother gave to the *Selma Times,* in which she said that she did not find in her letter to Villard "a phrase that justifies the editors' assertion that I advocate the social equality of white people and Negroes, so repugnant to all. The equality I advocated in my letter is the equality of all men before the law. . . ." An Alabamian who signed himself "Justice" defended Helen in the *Selma Times* as an "Alabama woman honored all over the world" who was wrongfully being charged with "statements of disloyalty to the South and to the integrity of Southern institutions. . . . The junta who have sought to make capital against woman's suffrage by making an heroic stand for white supremacy, alleging that Miss Keller, or somebody else wants to break down racial differences, will not be able to get off with the 'goods.' "

Helen did not change her views, but out of deference to her family she muffled them. She kept her most important thoughts to herself. How would Montgomery have reacted if it had learned that its sweet Helen had asked the National Institute for the Blind in London to put into embossed print for her Mikhail Bakunin's *God and the State,* a book that preached atheism, destruction of the state and the rejection of political action? The Institute had offered to do transcriptions for Helen without charge, but its secretary general drew the line at Bakunin. "Well, it is just what you and I feared," Helen lamented to Teacher. The secretary general had returned the book, saying that "he cannot ask any of the volunteers to transcribe it. Never mind, I can keep it until I find someone to read it or copy it for me. The incident shows that I absolutely need an assistant who is likeminded if we are ever to take up any work, even for the blind, again. And where can I hope to find such a girl?"

One did come along, but evidently not someone with whom she felt she could read and discuss the views of the anarchist apostle of universal insurrection:

> What do you think? I've found a sort of self-appointed companion for a few weeks at least. You remember the Jewish girl, Rebecca Mack, in Cincinnati? Well, she is visiting her aunt, Mrs. Stern, who lives very near us, and she calls on me every day. She says she came here chiefly to see me and to help me in whatever way she could. She walks with me and reads as much as her poor sight will permit. I like her, she is only nineteen years old, and I am surprised she has taken such a fancy to a person my age. She has an active mind, and talks better than many older people. Besides, she is interested in work for the blind—nay, fascinated by it. They say she has musical talent, and her mother is most anxious for her to develop it. But Rebecca declares she would much rather devote herself to the welfare of the sightless,

and I've a strong feeling that she will. Oh no, I am not thinking of taking her as a companion. But her ungrudging, wide-armed friendship is most touching, and I know you will want to thank her sometime for being so lovely with me.

Rebecca has several scrapbooks that mother is looking over.* They contain everything she can find that I have spoken or written for papers and magazines, and mother says they are quite interesting. Rebecca has also collected many items about you and John and my family. I will send you a copy of a poem by John which we found in one of the scrapbooks. I never saw it, and I thought perhaps you hadn't seen it either.

Helen had not been in Montgomery very long when she reported that the Warren Tyson house in which she was staying had almost burned down with all of them in it. This was the third time that she had had a close brush with fire or smoke, unspoken testimony to how much she relied on the vigilant eyes of others, especially Teacher, to keep her out of danger. In Tuscumbia, before Teacher had arrived, the flames of the fireplace, to which little Helen had been drawn, had set fire to her frock and scorched the child before her nurse could suffocate the flames by throwing a blanket over her. And two decades later, Helen's first letter to the Macys on their honeymoon reported how she had been blackened by the soot of a kerosene lamp and did not even know it.

They had just been through a "terrible excitement," her letter of February 7 began,

> but thank God, every one is safe and well. So don't be worried by the news in this letter.
>
> A fire broke out in my room Monday night. Fortunately, I wasn't asleep. At first I noticed a strange odor; but it was exactly like the odor of steam in the kitchenpipe; so I paid no attention to it. Then came a light odor like smoke from out-of-doors. I had noticed it so frequently in our house and elsewhere, it didn't disturb me. But suddenly I smelt tar and burning wood. I sprang up, threw a window open and rushed to mother's room. She found a flame six feet high in my room and called Warren. . . .

*Miss Mack left these scrapbooks, numbering sixty-three volumes, to the American Foundation for the Blind. They are invaluable source material.

The fire department arrived quickly and ordered them all out of the house. Bundled up in blankets, they went down the street to Grandma Tyson's. The fire had been caused by a defective flue, the firemen discovered, and had started "right under my bed!" Mildred was the only cool head in the family. "She didn't try to put out the fire, she looked after the children and saw to it that we were all wrapped up. The fright affected mother more than any of us. She doesn't seem to be herself at all."

"You poor child!" Teacher wrote back. "It was awful, waiting in the dark and feeling those frantic sounds and not knowing what was going on." She understood Mrs. Keller's sense of shock. The separation was teaching them both how much Helen still needed her, she observed.

In early 1917 Germany declared unrestricted submarine warfare against shipping, including American vessels, bound for allied ports. The U-boat danger increased Mrs. Keller's reluctance to take a ship to Puerto Rico, as almost every letter from Teacher begged them to do. Helen worried over the danger to Teacher when she would be able to come home. "I hate to have you so far away while we're on the verge of war, and those dread submarines are scouring the oceans for whatever they can destroy." But she did not consider the German blockade a cause for war: "I can't see the difference between a German and a British blockade, except that one is under the sea and the other on top."

She clung tenaciously to neutrality as between the Entente and the Central Powers. On November 11, 1916, she wrote her German publisher, Robert Lutz, asking that her royalties from books translated into German be donated to aid German soldiers and sailors blinded in the war. Lutz, replying by *Tauchbootbrief* (U-boat letter) dated January 11, 1917, gave her a meticulous accounting of all the money that he owed her and intended to turn over to the war blind. "Please—for the record," he went on, "let me know your approval of the content of this letter. I am sending it by U-boat and would appreciate, if it were possible, if you sent your answer the same way, that is, by the same U-boat returning to Germany. Much luck!

"As you see from the enclosure, I shared your letter with the German press, and your warmhearted resolutions have found approval everywhere."

He added a postscript on March 3: "My letter was returned to me, because due to political differences between Germany and America the U-boat did not leave. I hope that the enemies of Germany will allow this letter to go through." Although Wilson had broken relations with Germany on February 3, the letter did reach Helen, quite speedily in fact, for on March 11 she wrote Teacher that she was waiting for Miss Schepke, "that fire-eating little German," to come and help her with the translation.

Publication of Helen's letter in the German press produced a violent reaction in France. The Paris press quoted her letter to French academician M. Brieux after he had called upon her in which she had said: "France still holds its place as the nation most gifted with the genius for promoting a humane humanity. Is it not from France that the world has learned how to give light to the blind, knowledge to the deaf, language to the dumb lip and mind to the idiot clay? For this all the world loves France, even the Germans when they are not fighting. . . ."

How then, inquired Professor Drouot of the Paris Institute for Deaf-Mutes, could she say—as the German press alleged she had said—"My admiration for the Germans has increased further as well as my surprise at their marvelous ability for organization, their marvelous courage, their power of resistance. I am neutral but I always think of the land of Goethe, of Kant and Karl Marx, that is to say, as my second homeland!" He hoped she had been misquoted, Drouot went on. If the French had failed, it was in the naive assumption "that our rightful position was sufficient to alter the position of those who called themselves neutral. . . . If your sympathies go only to the blind German soldiers, how are we to forget that those men who today are suffering, were the aggressors?"

Drouot's reproaches distressed Helen. It upset friends like Mrs. Thaw that Helen should appear to be pro-German. "I can only say that my compassion for the sufferers in all lands is unbounded," she explained to Teacher. "If any of my books were published in France, I should unhesitatingly give the royalties from them to the French blinded. I enclose my answer to Mr. Drouot. He is a fine worker for the deaf, and he is one of the few Fenchmen who have ever shown an interest in me." The original of Helen's letter has disappeared. A part is quoted by Nella Braddy. It is as good an exposition of Helen's attitude on the eve of America's entry into the war as there is:

> I am neutral, uncompromisingly neutral. I have never at any time espoused the cause of Germany or the cause of any of the belligerent nations. . . . I am opposed to all wars except those that are really fought for freedom. I do not object to war merely because it takes life. The French Revolution cost thousands of lives, and history has justified the French Revolution. I object to the kind of war Europe is fighting, and the kind of war America is getting ready to fight—

a war for trade, and a place in the sun. In one of the Braille papers for the blind from Paris, *La Revue Braille,* I read this: 'We are fighting for our morals, our faith, our civilization. We shall fight until we conquer, we shall never turn back until we are the first Military Nation in Europe. There is a consensus of opinion among the thinkers and literary men of France in this matter.' I read these words many times before I could believe my fingers. Not a word of defense could I find. It was an avowal of militarism, and militarism is Germany's unpardonable crime against humanity.

Teacher did not send on her letter to Mr. Drouot. "It is not always possible to know whether it is wise to explain one's position in such matters when the other person's point of view is the opposite of one's own, and when circumstances tend to make both parties extremely emotional. I can understand Professor Drouot's point of view, although I can't sympathize with it." Then Teacher offered Helen some advice. She did so tactfully and understandingly:

> You know, dear, you are an impassioned reformer [by] temperament. We both fight for peace like soldiers on a battlefield. How often have I said that we both make too much of a battlefield of life! Maybe there would be more peace in the world if we cultivated the gentler virtues. It is up to us who think we are in the right to try and be patient and tolerant towards everybody. God Himself cannot make this a kindlier world without us.

> It is conceivable that Professor Drouot has his part in the plan of the Lord. The Good Samaritan couldn't have helped the wounded man without the ass.

Helen accepted Teacher's advice, but reluctantly. "I agree with you that even the foolish Drouots may have their place in God's Plan of Good. I love what you say about the good Samaritan and the ass. I am glad of every laugh that helps keep me sane in this crazy world. At the same time I know you think with me that, as Emerson said, we must 'not omit the arming of the soul.' "

Helen's letter was dated April 9. America had been at war since April 6. "There is little to tell—little that is bright or good. All happiness has left us with the departure of peace from our land." There were angry debates among the Socialists over the course of action the Socialist party should follow in the event the United States declared war. Morris Hillquit, the party's most thoughtful spokesman, began to prepare the party's followers. Under all circumstances the party will oppose entry into the war, he said in a letter to the *Times.* But he opposed a general strike, as advocated by the party's left wing. No war had ever been prevented by a general strike, he argued, nor had the socialist movement ever attempted to organize a strike against war.

Helen was furious:

> Teacher, I am going to remain faithful unto the death, with God's help, in my social beliefs; but I am thoroughly angry with the American Socialist Party, and I am tempted to break with it. Its apostasy is grievous. It has turned traitor to the workers by saying it opposes the class war. And the motion to call for a strike against war has been voted down! Shame upon those who wear the mask of Socialism! But I must be brave and loving in my public as well as my private life; so I shall stick by the workers, no matter what they do.

Teacher was more realistic, more resigned to what seemed to her as inevitable, and very severe in her judgment of Wilson:

> Of course you can't shut out of your mind the horror of this awful war. There is nothing we can do about it but wait. I think we shall jump into it before many months. I don't see what good that will do, but we, as individuals, have done all we can to keep America out of the maelstrom. You can understand now why Bill Haywood derided the idea that any country is civilized. . . .

> You know I have never trusted President Wilson. He is an egotist, a tyrant at heart who wants to be Bismarck without Bismarck's intelligence. When the bankers get nervous about their loans, they will force him to enter the War. But you know, Helen, that in history we have found the worst things, the most dreadful disasters served as stepping-stones to a new epoch. The blight and ruin and horror of the French Revolution were necessary to awaken subject peoples to a sense of their human rights. Who knows? This War may topple to earth the brutal stupidities and uglinesses of this huge, materialized plutocracy. The waste of capital may be so prodigious that capitalism

will not be able to rise again. The sacrifice will be beyond calculation, but perhaps the benefits will also be enormous. Oh dear, what a dismal letter this is! and oh, how out of key with my surroundings!

Another letter (the sequence of these letters is a little unclear, as none of Teacher's were dated) returned to the theme of the Left's hopes in Wilson. Did it echo discussions she had had with Helen? Helen's letter that occasioned it has not survived:

> I am not influenced in the least by Upton Sinclair's faith in President Wilson. Sinclair is one of those parlor Socialists that Joe Ettor despises. He would be just the one to be caught by Wilson's verbiage. No, no! Wilson is not a great humanist. All his words and acts are controlled by a fixed idea. I am not clear as to just what the idea is, but it will be disclosed as events unfold. One thing is certain, everything he does will be for the world's supreme good. Exploitation is always benevolent—it is the Christian pose. I am afraid that nothing short of a revelation from above could open my mind and heart to see anything approaching altruism in President Wilson's deeds and many words.

After America's entry she wrote again. She trembled at the thought that she had to return to the North "with its turmoil, its hypocrisies, its silly fads and sillier conventions." She preferred to stay on her island Eden:

> Here I find freedom from the vexations of wars and politics and duties that have never interested me. . . . Didn't I tell you that entering the world war was one of the high purposes Providence had in store for America? The Socialists—the intellectual variety—have behaved in all countries like the proverbial sheep. A few, a very few —Debs, Liebknecht, Jaurès and Bertrand Russell (but they killed Jaurès, and they will kill Liebknecht when he becomes a menace) have kept their heads. Hatred of Germany will soon transform their idealism into a hundred percent patriotism. I don't believe any of them have read Karl Marx, and if they have, they haven't a glimmering of what it means. Well, so be it: I feel no urge to enlighten them.

The last, as Teacher's biographer noted, was "pure sauciness on her part, for she had not read Karl Marx either."

Although Teacher had known for some time that she planned to return north in April, there had been little discussion of future plans between herself and Helen. She was in fact quite discouraged about herself. "We all feel old and tired sometimes," Helen wrote sympathetically. "You know how I've struggled and struggled from the time I lost my sight and hearing, and I'm beginning to feel age creeping on. Blind people often age rapidly, and I've had the additional obstacle of deafness to tax my gray matter, my endurance and resources. We both have had unusual burdens laid upon us for reasons that I cannot yet fathom. Now I find myself different from those I love, in temperament and in my views—and thank God, you haven't so much of that hardship as I. But I must not complain, I firmly believe that all will come out right in the end."

It was an unanswerable argument: Who had a right to give up if Helen did not? They could live simply, Helen went on, and she was casting about for a "wise plan. . . . You're my precious trust now, and God and the world call upon me to act." She was sure of one thing: she did not want to go back to Wrentham. It had too many unhappy associations. Even more, she feared that a return to Wrentham would mean a reversion to the old patterns of overwork and strain. In part, she discounted Teacher's cheery bulletins about how much better she felt physically. These were subjective feelings, not a physician's diagnosis. Teacher would have to return to Lake Placid for more tests. So far as anyone knew, she still was infected with the germs of consumption. Undoubtedly reflecting the anxieties and pressures of her family, Helen begged her, "Please, please don't feel badly if you don't find me waiting at home. I really think it best to wait until I know what the doctor's report is."

Helen herself had benefited from the enforced leisure of Montgomery. The long walks with Mildred—six miles in an hour and a half—careful eating, the slow pace of life, had all contributed to an inner calm. "I'm quieter myself these days," were her final words to Teacher. "They say the tenseness in my vocal organs is less, and Mildred says 'Never say a word about nerves, you don't show a sign of them!' If I only, only can keep what this long bitter separation has helped me to get, you'll know that my storming tendency is weakening."

But love overcame prudence; and when Teacher and Polly docked at New York in late April, Helen and her mother were there to meet them. They reached one decision quickly—to sell Wrentham. They did so by June. The Jordan Marsh Company, a Boston department store, purchased the twenty-one acres and its two large houses as a rest home for its six hundred employees. Her own plans for the future were uncertain, Helen told reporters, even where they might live.

Teacher had written their lecture agent from Puerto Rico inquiring whether any lecturing might be possible that summer, but soon after their return to the mainland Polly advised Mrs. Stevenson that Annie found the change of climate difficult and that the doctor did not want her to undertake any Chautauqua work. "If Helen is well enough to go out this summer," Mrs. Stevenson suggested, "I would be willing to go and give your lecture just as at Georgetown, Texas." Helen "seems to shrink from doing it," Polly replied, "as she feels anything might come up and she would be lost without Mrs. Macy!" The meaning of the exclamation point is unclear: Did Polly consider it absurd for self-reliant, strongopinioned Helen to plead her dependence upon Teacher, or was it meant to indicate her surprise that Helen should be so dependent?

They spent the summer in a cottage on Lake St. Catherine in Vermont. At the end of the summer they went to Lake Placid. While Teacher underwent reexamination, Helen and Polly climbed Whiteface, reaching two thirds of the way to the crest. They were scolded on their return to the Lake Placid Club for having gone without a guide. "I shall always remember the pleasure you expressed in the smell and feel of the mountain trail," a college girl who waited on them at the club wrote her thirty-three years later. Then the great news came. The doctor informed Teacher that the diagnosis of consumption had been wrong. The test showing tuberculosis must have been that of someone else.

Three happy people went to New York to find a place to live. The headwaiter at the Prince George Hotel, where they stayed, told them of a roomy house for sale in Forest Hills, at that time a suburban, almost rural area, fourteen miles from Times Square. They moved in October. Helen, Teacher and Polly were sleeping in the midst of rolled-up rugs, she reported to her mother. For three days they had done nothing "but run up and down stairs lugging books, china, linen and clothes." Teacher, with the help of a friend from Cambridge days, Ned Holmes, an architect and inventor, had hung pictures, arranged books, set out china and silverware, while Polly, with a temporary maid to assist her, "cleaned, scrubbed, swept, mopped, dusted." Their Great Dane Sieglinde, offspring of Thora, who had remained at Wrentham, arrived and "leaped upon us and clawed us with delirious joy. . . . We are getting to know the stores, theaters and eating places of every nationality in New York, so that our life here can never be so monotonous as it used to be at times." But despite the city's gastronomic lures, she and Teacher were dieting, "going without break-fast for a while."

Ned, whom they had found on arrival in New York desperately ill at St. Luke's Hospital, later moved in with them. He became their standby and escort—unwilling, they discovered, for reasons that they did not at that time understand, to go home to his family, never complaining, "stead-fast, sympathetic and helpful." Ned was not a conversationalist. "We expect to have Ned and Captain Barbour [skipper of the boat that had taken Teacher and Polly to Puerto Rico] for dinner soon. I guess we shall have to work like Trojans to entertain them; they don't talk much." A brief reference to John Macy, who was in Boston, indicated that they were still in touch with him. "I suppose I ought to write to John soon and tell him about our new home. I haven't sent him a line since we left Lake St. Catherine, and he has certainly not been negligent about writing to me." His problems were money and alcohol, and he was constantly appealing to Helen and Teacher for help.

Helen was impatient to pitch into the political battle again. They enter-tained some officers stationed at a nearby camp, feeding them dinner and wine, although they had been warned against doing the latter. Afterwards they went down to the town square, and Helen spoke to a large gathering of soldiers: "I told them how glad I was to feel their presence so near to me, and then I said, 'A hundred years ago our fathers dedicated this flag to freedom. They declared that it should be a symbol of the equality of all men under the Constitution. I want you to live to make this declaration true and, if necessary, to die to uphold this principle.' " The three thou-sand people at the meeting seemed responsive. "They say I spoke very well." It was a careful statement, meant to persuade, not challenge, her audience. When Helen wanted to resort to them, few were better at using the arts of diplomacy to convince or to disarm.

She had hoped to have a chance to say a few things "mildly" to the newspapers "about the harshness, intolerance and mad folly of those who are persecuting, imprisoning and lynching Socialists, 'I.W.W.s' and other 'agitators.' " But only one reporter turned up at the house, and he was unable to get anything straight. "He poked in a sentence like this at the end, 'That flag stands for a nation that obeys the law and respects women. Then liberty shall not perish from the earth.' "

Before this speech she had written Emma Goldman about her eagerness to rejoin the struggle. The anarchist leader had appealed to her for support when she and her anarchist colleagues were convicted under the Espionage Act of conspiracy to sabotage the Draft Act. She had been away, Helen wrote, when she had heard of the arrest of Emma and her comrades:

> My heart was troubled and I wanted to do something and I was trying to make up my mind what to do when your letter came. Believe me, my very heart-pulse is in the revolution that is to inaugurate a freer, happier society. Can you imagine what it is to sit idling these days of fierce action, of revolution and daring possibilities? I am so full of longing to serve, to love and be loved, to help things along and to give happiness. It seems as if the very intensity of my desire must bring fulfillment, but, alas, nothing happens. Why have I this passionate desire to be a part of a noble struggle when fate has sentenced me to days of ineffectual waiting? There is no answer. It is tantalizing almost to the point of frenzy. But one thing is sure—you can always count upon my love and support. Those who are blinded in eye because they refuse to see tell us that in times like these wise men hold their tongues. But you are not holding your tongue, nor are the IWW comrades holding their tongues—blessings upon you and them. No, Comrade, you must not hold your tongue, your work must go on, although all the earthly powers combine against it. Never were courage and fortitude so terribly needed as now. . . .

Helen's omission of the Socialists in this letter showed the stubborness of her loyalties more than the keenness of her political perceptions. By one of history's ironies, the Socialist party, which she had damned so roundly in late January, in an action that the left wing considered its finest hour had stood firm against U.S. entry into the war. At its emergency convention in April it had called for demonstrations, mass actions and petitions to shorten the war and establish a lasting peace. The IWW ironically had taken the rather lordly view that "the present war between the capitalist nations [is] of small importance when compared to the great class struggle in which we are engaged," and never officially came out against American participation in the war or against conscription. "Yet it was the IWW," ruefully noted Elizabeth Gurley Flynn, one of its leaders, "that bore the full impact of wartime prosecution as soon as the war was declared."

On September 5, 1917, a national dragnet rounded up 166 members of the IWW, including Haywood, Ettor, Giovannitti and Flynn. This was indeed close to home. Arturo was a frequent visitor at Forest Hills, as was

Carlo Tresca, Elizabeth Gurley Flynn's friend. But the Socialists also were being harried, their offices raided, their officials jailed, their publications muzzled. Helen realized that she had been wrong to omit the Socialists from the list of those who were the target of government repression. She arrived in New York as Hillquit's campaign for mayor on an antiwar platform was reaching a tremendous climax because of the support it was attracting. She sent him a carefully drafted but eloquent message. The New York *Call* described it as "the great human document that this great municipal campaign has brought forth. Though physically blind, she sees with her soul's vision the true issues of this campaign."

> I have refrained from writing, or giving utterance to the fierce protest in my heart against the war madness that is sweeping away the reason and common sense of our people, because I believed that President Wilson would defend our liberties and stay with his strong hand the forces that are invading them. I have waited and waited for some word from the White House. . . .
>
> I do not know if your election would bring about a speedy peace. But I do know that it would encourage us to look forward to a people's peace—a peace without victory, a peace without conquests or indemnities. I would that a large vote cast for you would be a strong protest against the Prussian militarism that is taking possession of our government. . . .
>
> If I had the right to vote, I would vote for you, Mr. Hillquit, because a vote for you would be a blow at the militarism that is one of the chief bulwarks of capitalism, and the day that militarism is undermined, capitalism will fall.

Hillquit's spectacular antiwar campaign was surprisingly effective. He amassed 145,332 votes, only some 7,000 fewer than John Purroy Mitchell, who ran second. The Tammany candidate won. This was 22 percent of the vote as against the less than 5 percent the Socialist candidate for mayor had garnered four years before.

In spite of—or perhaps because of—the impressive Socialist vote, the Justice Department on November 20 indicted *The Masses* and seven of its staff on conspiracy charges, including Max Eastman, John Reed, Floyd Dell and Art Young. The magazine promptly staged a huge solidarity ball in support of itself. Helen was there, as was Emma Goldman. It was their first meeting. "The electric current of her vibrant fingers on my lips and her sensitized hand over mine," wrote Emma, "spoke more than mere tongue. It eliminated physical barriers and held one in the spell of her inner world."

Despite its inability to prevent America's entrance into the war, despite the furious wave of repression that swept the nation, the Left lost little of its apocalyptic sense that victory for the revolution was imminent. Extraordinary events in far-off Russian bolstered this feeling. Those events, beginning in March, had registered even in Montgomery. "There has been an almost bloodless revolution in Russia," Helen had excitedly reported to Teacher. She particularly noted that Catherine Breshkovskaya, "the Little Grandmother of the Revolution," who had toured the United States at the turn of the century under the auspices of the American Friends of Russian Freedom, had been released from a Czarist prison and was back in Petrograd, active again in politics on behalf of the Socialist Revolutionary party. By November 1917 the revolution had become more bloody; the Socialist Revolutionary Alexander Kerensky had been overthrown by the Bolsheviks on a program of immediate peace. And on November 8 the Bolshevik-led Congress of Soviets broadcast to the world a "Decree of Peace" that proposed immediate negotiations by all the belligerents to end the war.

This was an electrifying event to Helen, a fulfillment, it seemed, of her dream vision of the war ending, enemies embracing. A burst of lyricism marked the event in her notebook:

> The news has come that Russia has offered to the agonizing world a magnificent peace—a peace without indemnities, conquest or annexation. It is a miracle that makes me dizzy with joy, as if earth should burst into light and music all round me. To me it is a name spoken as with pentecostal tongues of fire—the divine peace of brotherhood. A little while ago it was a name borne across vast Gethsemanes of blood, and today it is everywhere a struggling beam of peace. It is another miracle how steadily this light beats up through an atmosphere murky with calumny and misrepresentation, and Russia in the deepest misery meanwhile, yet benign, triumphant! Verily it is a name at the sound whereof thrones shall [tumble], and the list of falling empires shall rise. It is a name which will be sneered at and reviled then revered. Surely as Russia moves forward, transfigured,

with healing for the anguish of mankind, her presence will be a flood of sweetness poured into the turbulent sea of cynicism and oppression. . . .

To Helen and many others the leather-jacketed Bolsheviks, with their readiness to use force, their contempt of bourgeois governments and bourgeois niceties and manners, seemed in spirit and life-style remarkably like the IWWs, one hundred of whose leaders were sitting in the Cook County Jail awaiting trial and to each of whom Helen had sent a Christmas gift—a tie, two pairs of socks, a handkerchief. She turned a speech before the New York Civic Club in January 1918 into an impassioned defense of the Wobblies: "I love them for their needs, their miseries, their endurance and their daring spirit." The IWW program would be achieved, she confidently predicted, "and at no distant date—as the revolutionary climax of our age."

Others were making the same identification between the Bolsheviks and the Wobblies. John Reed returned to the United States from Russia where he had watched what he would call the *Ten Days That Shook the World.* He came to Forest Hills to visit Helen and Teacher. He, too, saw the IWWs as America's Bolsheviks. He covered their trial for the *Liberator.* "As for the prisoners," he said of the men in the dock, "I doubt if ever in history there has been a sight just like them. One hundred and one lumberjacks, harvest hands, miners, editors . . . who believe the wealth of the world belongs to him who creates it . . . the outdoor men, hardrock blasters, tree-fellers, wheat binders, longshoremen, the boys who do the strong work of the world. . . .

"To me, fresh from Russia, the scene was strangely familiar. . . . The IWW trial . . . looked like a meeting of the Central Executive Committee of the All-Russian Soviet or Workers and Deputies in Petrograd!"

On a visit to Boston in April a reporter interviewed Helen. Was she for Wilson? She shook her head. New York State had just given women the right to vote. What would she do with her vote? the reporter asked.

"Can't tell yet," Helen answered cautiously.

"Would you vote for President Wilson again if you had the chance?"

"No!" very decidedly.

"Why not?"

"Because," with dignity, "he is not my party candidate."

"Are you a Republican, then?"

"No, indeed. I am a Socialist and a Bolshevik."

The flabbergasted reporter turned to Teacher, whose laugh she interpreted to mean that she should take Helen's pronouncement with a grain of salt.

Teacher was sympathetic with the Bolshevik Revolution, but she and Helen had a living to make. As it was, invitations to lecture had dwindled to a trickle. Teacher gave Helen's hand an admonitory slap. "Only red-handed workmen are admitted to the party of the Bolsheviki," Teacher reminded her companion. "You are poking your nose in where you are not wanted."

XXVI

Helen Goes to Hollywood

"Its possibilities far exceed the *Birth of a Nation.*"

While Teacher was in Puerto Rico, she and Helen in their letters occasionally had envisaged simplifying their lives in order to free themselves of the tensions of the lecture circuit. But this was the kind of dream most busy people, especially celebrities, entertain briefly, only to set aside as their constituencies renew their demands upon them and they find a reduced standard of living unattractive. Helen, Teacher and Polly—for Polly had now become an inseparable part of the menage—were by no means in straitened circumstances, as their newly refurbished house in Forest Hills attested; but they felt a need for more money and had been in touch with their lecture agent, Mrs. Stevenson, about autumn and winter engagements.

The lecture circuit, they discovered, had become a victim of the war. Mrs. Stevenson sent them an appeal for help that the president of the International Lyceum and Chautauqua Associations had addressed to the White House. It lamented that because of "stringency, economy and even patriotism, many communities feel they must not have their usual Chautauquas and lecture courses. Nothing less than the advice of the President to the Country to continue these institutions can save the situation for many of us." The appeal went unheeded, and Helen and Teacher concluded the Chautauqua business looked pretty hopeless.

The slump in the lecture business made them more receptive to a bid from that new El Dorado, Hollywood. And by February 1918—close to the time when Helen proclaimed herself a "Socialist and a Bolshevik"— they were deep in negotiations to make a movie out of Helen's life. In view of those talks it distressed Teacher to have Helen needlessly flaunt views that the vast majority of Americans despised. The story, fortunately, did not go beyond the Boston paper in which it had appeared. Helen, moreover, bore a charmed life. Criticism, hysteria and sanctions that destroyed the careers of many of Helen's comrades usually exempted her, and those who did attack her were largely ignored. Westbrook Pegler, the columnist who made a vocation out of slinging mud at Eleanor Roosevelt, complained toward the end of his life that he was not able to make it stick. Helen had a similar immunity. Nothing ever shook the public's conviction that here was someone who wished only to do good, and even more important, someone who had prevailed against the most extraordinary odds, whose joyousness and tenderness had survived some of the greatest trials in American history—an authentic American heroine.

Helen was always on the lookout for ways by which she might influence public opinion; and when the chance to make a motion picture out of her life appeared, she grasped at it eagerly. The motion picture industry was demonstrating its ability to reach millions. When D.W. Griffith's *Birth of a Nation* was shown at the White House, Woodrow Wilson commented, "It is like writing history with lightning." That it was distorted history, prejudicial to the black man, did not belie the effectiveness of the medium. The film was one of the greatest money-makers on the American screen. When it was suggested to Helen that her life story could be another *Birth of a Nation,* that it lent itself to cinematic dramatization by a Hollywood that was athirst for "story" material, Helen found the prospect exhilarating. She had an apostolic message for the world that she believed Hollywood would enable her to communicate far beyond the audiences she had been able to reach in the past. Nor did Hollywood's reputation for conferring riches upon those who had something it wanted dim its appeal to Helen. It might seem a little inconsistent with Helen's egalitarian convictions, but Teacher's needs reconciled her to the contradiction. "It was only the hope of providing for Teacher that had led me to Hollywood to have a film made of my life story," she wrote in *Teacher.*

The idea for a film based on Helen's life originated with a historian who had a flair for reaching a mass market. Francis Trevelyan Miller, who carefully appended *LL.D.* and *Litt.D.* to his title as editor-in-chief of the Search Light Library, was as effective a salesman as he was a historian. He had put together a *Photographic History of the American Civil War* in ten volumes and was in the process of issuing a twelve-volume *Photographic History of the Great War*. His literary plans were stated like communiqués. He was all set "to organize my new eighteen volume *History of the World*" when he had come upon Helen's *Story of My Life*. Its "creative power and imagination . . . soul power and insight" had so inspired him that his own contribution "of thirty-seven historical works to our literature seems insignificant. . . ." In Helen's work he had glimpsed the unfolding of a "soul-vision," an "undiscovered world" innate in every human being, which Helen's story could help make a reality:

> My suggestion is that we reach the whole seeing world through the medium of Motion Pictures. This is the greatest medium that we have for appealing to the hearts and sympathies of the people, with its 20,000 theaters in the United States alone, and a daily attendance of 15,000,000 people, according to government estimates. Moreover. the Motion Pictures speak a universal language—they can be seen and understood in every nation in every part of the world.

In mid-January 1918, Helen, Teacher and Polly met with Dr. Miller at his office. He was an astute fellow with a sixth sense for fathoming what he thought the other wanted to hear. He talked about Helen's intellectual attainments. They seemed almost "incredible," but then he quickly added, "I can explain it only from the fact that she must have been under the hand of a master, thus Mrs. Macy's achievement places them both in the ranks of genius." He was ready, he told them, to set aside all his other work "and begin immediately to study all the material relating to Miss Keller's life and arrange in its technical form for motion picture production." He thought that $100,000 would have to be raised to produce the picture, asserted that he and Helen should receive "a liberal salary," and suggested that Helen would make "from $50,000 to $100,000 through this production." On February 1, Teacher formally authorized him and his representatives "to proceed towards the realization of the project," including the preparation of "a plot synopsis," and to make a canvass of the possibilities of raising the finances needed.

An accompanying letter from Helen set forth the theme she expected the film to embody:

It will help me carry farther the message that has so long burned in my heart—a message of courage, a message of a brighter, happier future for all men. I dream of a day when all who go forth sorrowing and struggling shall bring their golden sheaves home with them in joy. I dream of a liberty that shall find its way to all who are bound by circumstances and poverty. As the dungeon of sense in which I once lay was broken by love and faith, so I desire to open wide all the prison-doors of the world. . . .

They decided that they needed the help of Elizabeth Marbury, a fabulously successful theatrical agent with a sure sense for what the public wanted in the way of entertainment. The project excited her, but she asked for a "plot synopsis." Dr. Miller, although new to this art form, undertook to prepare one in a few weeks. By the beginning of April, Miller's agent sent the draft to Miss Marbury with a little sales talk of his own. The dramatization of the Helen Keller story, he rhapsodized, "can only result in a record-breaking financial success as well as an artistic triumph." Miller's synopsis showed "a great human psychologist, a master of human emotions" at work. "Moreover, he has a large following: his thirty-seven books have sold more than $4,000,000 gross. The motion-picture market has been stagnating for new ideas—something original and vital." The enterprise would have Helen Keller's prestige and cooperation, and they, he pointed out, were worth "at least $500,000 in news publicity." His letter to Miss Marbury ended with a Hollywoodian flourish: "Its possibilities far exceed the *Birth of a Nation.*"

Miller's letter to Helen that accompanied his script was equally grandiloquent:

> The month of March has been the greatest month of my whole literary experience. I have spent years in analyzing the laws of cause and effect behind nations and epochs, and in psychological investigations into the characters and lives of the moulders of civilization. But never before have I delved so deeply into the Spiritual forces—into the real world of your existence.

He was satisfied that Helen's was "the real existence. . . . Your world *sees;* our world is spiritually blind." If his manuscript had not caught the essence of her experience, "remember that it is all subject to your guidance. . . ." The two of them must help lead the world to its *Deliverance,* the title he had, on Helen's suggestion, given the script.

Whatever the excesses of Dr. Miller's rhetoric, he had some conception of the technique of a plot synopsis and, what was more important, had caught Helen's image of herself. "I am delighted with your conception of the drama of my life as illustrating the struggles, hopes and aspirations of mankind," she wrote a week later. (This letter, dated April 10, 1918, may not have been sent, but it embodied her sentiments.) "It is poetic and stirs me to the deepest depths." She recapitulated her spiritual pilgrimage, and then in a few phrases again recited the faith of the idealist and romantic: "The world is what we think of it. It measures up to our idea of it. The soul shapes outward circumstances to its needs. What else is imagination given us for?" She praised Dr. Miller as one of "few" who had truly seen "the very sweetness and light that have gladdened me [and] have lifted me up in revolt against the powers of darkness" to challenge "the night of ignorance, oppression and poverty" that held the mass of mankind in its grip. Could Dr. Miller suggest "a good way of saying this acceptably, yet boldly"?

The cover page on Dr. Miller's synopsis read like a poster:

——Prospectus and Plot Synopsis——
for the
Greatest Human Drama of all Times
. . . . . .

H E L E N   K E L L E R

——*Deaf-Dumb-Blind*——
The Most Wonderful Girl in the World
in

*D E L I V E R A N C E
or
T H E   W O R L D   F O R   H U M A N I T Y

An Inspiring Revelation
which brings Hope and Courage
To the People of all Nations and Races
. . . . . .
Dramatized by

FRANCIS TREVELYAN MILLER (Litt.D., LL.D.)
(The American Historian)

*This name is tentative—the final title will be selected by Producers and Dramatist form a long list now being prepared.

. . . . . .

Five Powerful Acts—Eight Reels

I—THE WORLD I LIVE IN   III—KINGDOM OF THE BLIND
II—THE MIRACLE OF LIFE   IV—OUT OF THE DARK
V—VICTORY

With a Cast of *WORLD CELEBRITIES* who have never before
appeared on the screen

The hyperbole of Dr. Miller's introduction made the superlatives of the Anagnos reports seem by comparison like the soul of trenchancy, but that was what Hollywood wanted.

The purpose of this introduction is to establish the motif of the powerful drama, DELIVERANCE, in which we are to see a little child, blind, deaf, and dumb, as primitive and wild as the elements —first conquered by love; then conquering her own emotions; then conquering her own world of light and knowledge, until she accomplishes her own DELIVERANCE from all bondage, and sets out on an heroic crusade for the DELIVERANCE of humanity. . . .

We see her with her distinguished friends, the most eminent men and women of the times. . . . This gives us an opportunity to present in garden-party scenes, amid beautiful flowers and settings, the celebrities with whom she is constantly associated—her friend, Caruso, singing to her as in ecstasy she 'listens with her finger tips'; to Paderewski at the piano; to Ysaÿe with the violin. . . .

We see her with the great inventors; Dr. Bell, the inventor of the telephone; Edison, the genius of light and sound; Marconi, the inventor of the wireless—the men who have conquered worlds from which she is forever barred. We see her with the Wrights as she steps into an aeroplane. . . .

We see Helen as she stands before Kings as she pleads for humanity. We see her as she moves among the poor, the outcast, the unfortunate —as they extend their helpless hands to the modern Jeanne d'Arc who comes from the realm of darkness over which she has risen supreme, to help struggling Humanity.

Miss Marbury's reaction was "splendid material," "most promising." All that remained to be settled, Dr. Miller informed Helen, were "some slight alterations that Miss Marbury states will be absolutely necessary (according to her wide experience) in placing the whole proposition on a sound business basis and securing the largest degree of profits from the enterprise."

Miss Marbury had immediately spotted the weakness of the synopsis. It was a series of tableaux with captions, not a story. There was no conflict. The concept of two "deliverances," Helen's release from blindness and deafness and her later release from social and political blindness, was a worthy theme, but exhibitors already had a horror of what the trade called "the high-brow picture." Love would have to be introduced, romance, adventure—if necessary, invented—if the picture were to have mass appeal.

Helen and Teacher refused to countenance such falsification. They parted company with Miss Marbury and sought other ways of getting the picture produced. Despite Dr. Miller's optimism and conviction that they had a masterpiece in the making, the whole project began to seem unreal again. A long letter to her mother on May 7 made no mention of the film. It was full of news—of loyal Ned Holmes, "smiling and silent," who still was with them, but she did not mention that he was representing them in negotiations with Miller and others. She spoke of attending a reception of the American-British-French-Belgian Fund for the benefit of blinded soldiers. The not wholly successful appeal that two blinded officers had made to the audience to give until giving meant sacrifice, reminded Helen "how Teacher and I had worked ourselves almost crazy trying to help the New York Association for the Blind years ago—and then those millionaires wouldn't give anything—at least Miss Holt said that to us." She was going to lunch with some of her Wright-Humason schoolmates, and she was fixing up a speech for the summer "in case we should do Chautauqua work." She was also preparing a speech on Walt Whitman for a dinner in his honor that was being given by Whitman's friend and biographer, Marxist socialist Horace Traubel. "Then there is the Italian grammar and Dante, which I find pretty hard at times." It was not the letter of someone who was planning to spend the next few months in Hollywood.

But suddenly it all came together. The funding crisis was surmounted when Charles M. Schwab, the steel magnate, a neighbor and friend of Mrs. Thaw, was persuaded by intermediaries, primarily Dr. Edwin Liebfreed, to put up $250,000 to produce the picture. At the end of May a formal contract was signed between Helen and Annie on one side and Dr. Miller as president of the "Helen Keller Film Corporation" on the other, author-

izing the production, distribution and leasing of the film. Helen and
Teacher were paid $10,000 on signing. Another $10,000 would be paid
upon completion of the film. Other paragraphs spoke of royalties up to
$500,000 after deductions for overhead, expenses and repayment of
investors. The contract also provided that Helen and Teacher were to
come to Hollywood to be available for consultation, and in the case of
Helen, for a role in the film. It was, of course, the day of the silent films.
Director George Foster Platt was engaged, a studio in Hollywood leased.
Helen wrote Dr. Bell:

> When we saw you in New York several weeks ago, we told you that
> the story of my life was to be dramatized for a motion picture, and
> we asked you if you would be willing to appear in it. You laughed
> and said, 'Do you expect me to go to California to have my picture
> taken?' Well, it is not quite as bad as that—not quite. The present plan
> is to have several pictures made here and in Boston and vicinity
> before we start West where the main part of the picture will be made.
> . . . The producers are very desirous to have you appear with Caruso
> and my teacher and me in the opening scene of the drama. . . . You
> know that Gibbon has told us how, when he wrote the last lines of
> the last page of 'The Decline and Fall,' he went out into the garden
> and paced up and down in his acacia walk overlooking Lausanne and
> the mountains. . . . I conceive of the picture-drama as my walk under
> the acacias. I mean, in a sense, it will be the finish of my life story.
> . . . You can readily see, if the people who are taking part in the drama
> are not the real people who have walked with me under the acacias,
> this message will lose something of its force and genuineness. A
> number of the friends whose love and devotion have enriched my life
> are gone. Phillips Brooks, Oliver Wendell Holmes, Edward Everett
> Hale, Henry Rogers, Samuel Clemens and many others would have
> a place in the picture if they were living. You and Mrs. William Thaw
> are almost the only ones left who entered the acacia walk with me
> where it begins in the sweet dawn of childhood.

It was he who had heartened Teacher and herself for the struggle: "Again
and again you said to me, 'Helen, let no sense of limitations hold you back.
You can do anything you think you can. Remember that many will be
brave in your courage.' "
The letter reached Bell in Nova Scotia. He would do anything for her

sake that he could, but he could not get down to the States before Helen left for California:

> You must remember that when I met you first I wasn't seventy-one years old and didn't have white hair, and you were only a little girl of seven, so it is obvious that any historical picture will have to be made with substitutes for both of us. You will have to find someone with dark hair to impersonate the Alexander Graham Bell of your childhood, and then perhaps your appearance with me in a later scene when we both are as we are now may be interesting by contrast.

Dr. Bell did appear, and money matters were settled. However, a new crisis arose before they left for California—over Helen's radicalism. There were advance rumblings at the Walt Whitman dinner, to which Helen and Teacher took Dr. Miller. "Helen's speech was brilliant," he wrote Ned Holmes, but did "Mrs. Macy and Helen realize what a hot-bed of treason developed at the Whitman dinner?" Helen had to be protected. "I know you will be very careful that she does not allow spies and enemies of our Homeland to come into her presence and use her beautiful soul and mind for an endorsement of their nefarious schemes. . . ." Her great mission could be destroyed "by dangerous associations in these war times." A few weeks later he was more insistent. It is unclear whether another plea for the IWW or for Soviet Russia occasioned his letter. Helen had joined John Dewey, Thorstein Veblen, Carlton J. Hayes and others in a plea in *The New Republic* for a fair trial for the imprisoned IWWs. The Department of Justice was sufficiently upset to warn the magazine against reprinting the statement. Miller—a staunch Republican, historian general of the Sons and Daughters of the Pilgrims, whose advisory boards on his histories were studded with admirals and generals—was understandably horrified. Dr. Liebfreed, who controlled the purse strings, shared his alarm. "He is of German origin," Miller wrote Holmes, "but he is heart and soul against the despotism of the military caste that is ruling Germany." Theaters would be shut to them, he warned. If Helen persisted, the government could visit all sorts of harassments upon them. He requested "a letter of assurance that can be read to all our associates to establish their confidence. Otherwise our whole epoch-making project may collapse."

Helen must have agreed to be more discreet, for a few weeks later she, Teacher and Polly set out for Hollywood. Ned Holmes was left to watch

over Forest Hills and their Great Dane Sieglinde. The company had
leased the Brunton Studio, and the filming began. Platt was a director of
sensitivity, eager to realize what Helen and Teacher hoped the film would
be, with his own view that they should aim for movement, compactness
and continuity rather than lavishness. A child actress played the part of
Helen in her early years. Miller's script consisted not of dialogue but of
captions that preceded a series of frames. Thus Series 9 heralded Helen's
birth: "Soon comes an eventful hour at Ivy Green." Frame 37 dealt with
the arrival of Anne Sullivan: "I pray God that you can teach her." Then
a series of frames dealt with the episodes that playwright William Gibson
more than three decades later presented so tellingly in *The Miracle Worker.*
Dr. Miller sensed that here was drama. His script reflected the state of the
cinematographic art at the time:

43

THE BATTLE BEGINS
Within the Walls of Darkness and Silence, Patience and Love struggle
with Ignorance

44

"It is a tremendous task, Mrs. Keller. . . . Sometimes it seems almost
impossible."

45

A moment of discouragement

48

Through days of ceaseless struggle.

50

THE SUPREME MOMENT OF REVELATION
  The Walls Crumble . . .
    The Light Penetrates . . .
      A Soul Awakes . . .

51

"W-A-T-E-R!"

52

"That living word awakened my soul, gave it light, hope, joy, set it free . . . Everything had a name, and each name gave birth to a new thought."

From Helen Keller's
"The Story of My Life"

52A

"B-A-B-Y"

53

THE MIRACLE OF MIRACLES

"In a few hours she had added thirty new words to her vocabulary."

From Miss Sullivan's letter written that next day.

"We were too early," Miller wrote Helen in 1950 when he read that Robert Flaherty might direct a talking picture based on Helen's life. "The story requires conversation, dramatic action, and magnetic personalities in its leading roles."

In the later scenes Helen played herself. The director together with Annie devised a system of stamping on the floor to convey his instructions to her. First Polly Thomson or Annie spelled into her hand what she was supposed to do in the next series of "takes" and the effect they were trying for—walk toward the window on her right, hold up her hands to the sun, discover the bird's cage, express surprise, pleasure. A series of taps on the floor signaled each action. It was a difficult process. She often stood for half an hour before the camera began to grind. The studio lights grew hotter; the sweat rolled off her made-up face; her hands grew moist. But she was a born trooper and took the twice-a-day sessions in her stride. The director often was unable to hold back his tears as he tapped out "be natural" and Helen, who could not see the result, tried gamely to fulfill his wishes. Unlike the vacancy of expression that often attended the deaf-blind victim, her face was capable of great animation. Frequent flickers and starts of feeling seemed to be registering little inner electric shocks. Her gestures were equally expressive. But to synchronize gesture and feeling was a laborious process.

It was not Helen's acting ability, however, that caused the greatest difficulty, but the story line, or rather its absence. A series of tableaux did not make gripping film fare—as Miss Marbury had foreseen. For conflict, emotional impact, character development, they sought solutions in symbolism. A fierce battle was staged before the cave of Father Time between Knowledge and Ignorance for control of Helen's mind. Instead of an undergraduate love affair, and because of her passion for the Greek myths, she was given a love affair with the mythical Ulysses that included a realistic shipwreck on the Isle of Circe. In the final part of the picture, to show her triumph over physical limitations, she took her first flight in helmet and goggles in an aeroplane, over the protests of Teacher, as well as her mother and her brother Phillips Brooks, in uniform, who had arrived for roles in the last part of the picture.

A penultimate scene with hundreds of extras, the blind, the maimed, the halt—all of them fearing the flu, which was then raging everywhere—showed Helen as the Mother of Sorrows touching the kneeling petitioners with her torch of hope. The grand finale was to be a scene in which Helen was ushered into a meeting of the Big Four to urge them to bring the war to a close; and the final spectacle, so dearly beloved of Hollywood, presented Helen on a large white charger, blowing a trumpet and leading thousands of shipyard and factory workers, people of all nations, toward "deliverance."

They enjoyed their stay in Hollywood—indeed, found it exciting. Helen and Polly, joined occasionally by Teacher, regularly rode the trails of unsettled Beverly Hills, where a coyote might still be heard. They met Hollywood's glamorous stars—Lillian Gish, Constance Talmadge, Douglas Fairbanks, Mary Pickford and what Teacher described as a "roomful of others." Charlie Chaplin had them to dinner at a club along with Dr. Miller, Upton Sinclair and his wife. He confessed to Annie that just before their arrival he had debated whether to run away. He took to Teacher, however, and talked to no one else throughout dinner, telling her much about his life, complaining about his current marriage. He took great pride in *A Dog's Life,* a film that he had just made and that would be called "his first real masterpiece." Had she seen it? When Teacher said no, he asked her whether she thought he was disgusting. Yes, she replied. She had always thought of him as a custard-pie thrower. Would she come to his studio? Would Helen be interested? They did so, and he had *A Dog's Life* and *Man-At-Arms* screened for them as Annie interpreted and they alternately wept and laughed.

They themselves did not entertain. Teacher claimed it was too expensive. But it may also have been Hollywood's tendency (Chaplin was an exception) to lionize Helen and ignore Annie, an indignity to which Teacher never submitted easily. As usual in her book *Teacher* Helen mentions Teacher's resentment obliquely. "Everybody was friendly, but in their compliments to me I was unintentionally left with a defrauded feeling. Few, if any, spoke of Teacher as one who deserved special praise. . . . However, Teacher was her exuberant, charming self with Charles Chaplin. They had both endured poverty and the deformations it creates in body and soul."

At the end of October she took time off to lead a Liberty Bond rally in Los Angeles. She had kept her word to Dr. Miller and muted her social and political statements. She had gone further, telegraphing Secretary of the Treasury McAdoo on October 5, "I want to help you sell Liberty Bonds." He accepted with alacrity and gave it out to the press. Now she stood before a hushed crowd and urged it to "strike out for the dawn" by the purchase of a bond. It was twelve days before the Armistice. Many who were critical of the government's repressions under the Espionage Act had nevertheless rallied to Wilson's statement of war aims. "I am glad America stands before the world for man's holy dream of liberty. Buy a Liberty Bond and hasten the day when war shall be impossible between nations," she said in slow, high-pitched, painfully enunciated phrases that Teacher translated.

After her talk, telegrams received by Helen from Caruso, Mrs. Thaw, Charles Evans Hughes, Elihu Root, Adolph Lewisohn, William G. McAdoo—all subscribing to more bonds—were read to the crowd.

By the end of December the filming was finished. There was nothing yet to look at, but everyone was confident that when the film was cut and edited, it would be a success. They had to borrow money to get back to Forest Hills. Dr. Liebfreed refused to advance it to them, and in the end they had to borrow the funds from Ned Holmes. Their troubles with Liebfreed were only beginning. He had decided to take control of the film, discharging all the staff, including the director, Mr. Platt. "The people in Mr. Schwab's office refused to discuss the matter with anybody," Annie wrote Mildred. "Their lawyer was very nasty at first. They presumed that the picture was finished, and that they had the film locked up in the bank." Dr. Liebfreed then discovered that the titles had still to be written and that Dr. Miller's contract stipulated that he should write them. "Then I told them I should get out an injunction and stop procedure. Dr. Liebfreed caved in." Dr. Miller was reinstalled as writer, but they could not persuade Liebfreed to have Platt do the editing and cutting, and with the inimitable high-handedness of money men in show business, Platt was not even invited to the advance screening—"his own work. Think of it!" They were "tired and sick of the whole business. We only hope that after the picture is sold, we shall have little to do with our capitalist, and that the box office receipts will perfume our remembrance of the past year. . . ."

The screening produced a new confrontation over what should come out and what should go in. Teacher and Liebfreed were the primary antagonists. Purple with rage, he cited the mounting costs. Teacher in a fury charged him with breach of his word. Both were angry; both shouted. Occasionally Liebfreed remembered Helen and addressed a few honeyed words to her, and then returned to the attack. "He wanted a commercial 'thriller,'" wrote Helen, "and Teacher and I asked for an historical record, and these two points of views appeared irreconcilable." They refused to consent to its public exhibition or sale. They stated their objections in several letters to Dr. Miller and finally, in desperation, to Mrs. Thaw. That kindly woman forwarded Helen's letter to Mr. and Mrs. Schwab, her Pittsburgh neighbors, with the grieved observation that Helen's "two letters from California were so joyous and hopeful, that by contrast this from which I quote some paragraphs, is the more painful. I can see that to have her hopes shattered as to being able to provide, indirectly, an object lesson to other afflicted ones, is only less bitter than to have her whole attitude toward life and its duties misrepresented in so heartless a fashion as her letter indicates." Helen's letter in part read:

> We started out to make an honest picture of my life, my struggles, triumphs, aspirations. . . . Well, more than two-thirds of our conception of the picture has been realized. But towards the end we seem to have fallen down somehow. For instance, there is a scene called 'The Council-Chamber,' where all the great generals, kings and statesmen are assembled in a sort of peace conference. I enter in a queer medieval costume and proclaim the Rights of Man rather feebly. There is no foundation in fact for such a scene, and the symbolism is not apparent. We want it omitted.

> This scene is followed by a Pageant with me on horseback, leading all the peoples of the world to freedom—or something. It is altogether too hilarious to typify the struggles of mankind for liberty.

These are our two vital objections to the picture, but there are minor ones; for instance, our friends—those who are gone, such as Bishop Brooks and Mark Twain and others; and the ones we love who are still living, but not in the picture either—Dr. Bell, Mr. Edison and yourself. My Wrentham house, which is historic, does not appear in the picture. Then we think there should be a scene of Evergreen, showing what is being done to re-educate our blinded soldiers. It is a work very near to my heart, as you know, and we are sure it will be a helpful picture in many ways.

According to our contract, we have the right to reject the picture if it does not satisfy us. Of course we did not want to take this extreme step. We hoped that Dr. Liebfreed would live up to his agreement. But we have been sadly disappointed. . . .

A few changes were made. The council chamber scene was eliminated, but the spectacular ending, with hundreds of extras rushing pell-mell behind Helen on her white charger, remained. Wrentham was not filmed, nor was the scene they wanted with Dr. Bell. Despite Mrs. Thaw's letter and their threats of an injunction they were kept completely on the outside, an experience typical of Hollywood's dealing with the authors of books.

"We had very little definite information about the picture," Helen lamented to her mother in early July,

until two weeks ago when in desperation Ned called upon Mr. Shubert. You may not know it but it is more difficult to see Mr. Shubert than the President of the United States—or even the Mikado of Japan. Ned was permitted to talk with Mr. S. only two minutes and a half. He learned that the picture had been sold, and that it would open in Shubert's Broadway theatre next October. That means we shall not receive our payment until then. We have been frightfully 'hard up,' mother. I don't remember a time since college days when we were so much 'up against it.' But we shall manage all right. Our credit is good, and people understand. Every one believes in the success of the picture, and that keeps them quiet and contented because they know they will receive their money eventually.

The picture opened at the Lyric Theater in August. Helen was sent two boxes for her use, but she did not attend. Actors Equity was on strike, and she refused to cross its picket line. She felt that Shubert had rushed to present the picture in order to break the strike. "I am afraid that the actors and some of my friends may construe my presence as a lack of sympathy with the strikers. In order to avoid possible misunderstanding, I feel that it is better for me not to come to the Lyric Theater Monday night," she wrote.

The reviewers were enthusiastic. *The New York Times* called it "one of the triumphs of the motion picture," with the opening night audience several times breaking into spontaneous applause. In places it was "over-burdened with moralizing and its optimism is sometimes spread too thickly," but in the main it was "compelling. . . . And, let it be repeated, the story, as a story, grips and holds the interest as few photo stories do." The *New York Sun* credited the director, George Platt, whom Liebfreed would not let into the studio for the screening, for "a new technique . . . a method approximating that of the speaking stage. . . . It is one of the most compact photo plays ever screened, each flash upon the silver sheet being filled with action that has a meaning." Another paper could not praise *Deliverance* "too highly." It was an "educational picture in the highest sense."

Despite the fine reviews the Shuberts soon sold the distribution rights for $50,000 to a Chicago distributor, George Kleine, claiming later that they had never been able to make any profit out of it. The always hopeful Dr. Miller was elated that Mr. Kleine now had charge of the distribution. "He is one of the most successful in the business; he has made several million dollars as a distributor; among his productions was 'Quo Vadis.' He is enthusiastic over 'Deliverance' and declares that it will break all records. If half what he thinks comes true, then none of us need worry over the future."

But it was not a commercial success. As Kleine sadly reported to Helen in 1928: "It is a fact that a feature film which is produced with the usual heavy outlay cannot succeed financially unless it goes over well in moving picture theatres. 'Deliverance' has been appreciated by what may be called the more refined classes and thinking people, but it did not succeed in drawing crowds to the box office." It is doubtful that Helen and Teacher received more than the original ten thousand dollars at the signing. They were the kind of people, she commented ruefully, "who come out of an enterprise poorer than when we went into it."

They now had to face up to the realization that no magic wand would wave over their lives and bring them comfort and security forever. And *Deliverance* signaled another subtle shift, especially in Helen's point of view. Soon after she returned to the East, she was back in the political fray. She protested Allied intervention against the Bolshevik regime. She said yes to an appeal from Roger Baldwin, just out of jail as a conscientious objector, to set up an American Civil Liberties Union. She joined a group of American "intellectual workers" responding to an appeal by Henri Barbusse and Hugo von Hofmannsthal to put aside hatred and work for reconcilation of yesterday's enemies. She paid public homage to Debs, sitting in jail for violation of the Espionage Act, "one of the most beautiful tributes that has been paid to Debs":

> I write because my heart cries out, and will not be still. I write because I want you to know that I should be proud if the Supreme Court convicted me of abhorring war, and doing all in my power to oppose it. . . .

> Every trial of men like you, every sentence against them, tears away the veil that hides the face of the enemy. . . .

> We were driven into this war for liberty, democracy and humanity. Behold what is happening all over the world today! . . .

> You dear comrade! I have long loved you because you are an apostle of brotherhood and freedom. . . . I have followed in the trail of your footsteps. . . .

Debs would remain in prison until December 25, 1921, when he was released by President Harding.

But though Helen remained loyal to her socialist convictions, and revolution flared more brightly than ever in the consciousness of the Left, Helen's image of her own role in such events had begun to change. And *Deliverance* symbolized the change. The picture of herself as a latter-day Joan of Arc leading the workers in their emancipation struggle faded. "I was glad when it was all over," she wrote of her experience with *Deliverance* in *Midstream*, "and my quaint fancy of leading the people of the world to victory has never been so ardent since."

XXVII

On the Vaudeville Circuit

". . . till they loved you big and far."—Carl Sandburg

In the mid-1890s, a little before Captain Keller's death, that harassed man, overburdened with debts, had horrified his wife and Teacher with his pressure on Helen and Annie to go into vaudeville. On the train from New York to Boston Annie had met Mr. Keith, just at the beginning of assembling his great vaudeville empire. He had offered to present them on the stage at five hundred dollars a week, but Teacher turned him down. When Captain Keller heard what Annie had done, he was indignant, "but before he could force acceptance," Annie told Nella Braddy, "he died." In 1919, as their hopes dwindled of making themselves secure for life through *Deliverance,* and since their Chautauqua tours as well as Hollywood experience had inured them to exhibiting themselves to make a living, far from turning down a vaudeville contract, they sought it. With the postwar inflation eating up their income, they went into vaudeville, "which paid us much better than lecturing," explained Helen. "We did not have to work so hard either. . . ."

The proposal was made to them by a musician, George Lewis. Inspired by *Deliverance* he had written a song, "Star of Happiness," dedicated to Helen, for which Dr. Miller wrote the lyrics. It was published by the same company whose hit tune that season was the durable "Yes, We Have No Bananas." "Star of Happiness" would have a briefer career. Lewis had had some experience in vaudeville and, spurred by the enthusiastic reviews of

"Deliverance," suggested to Helen and Annie that they could make a financial killing on the vaudeville circuit, which was then still in its golden age. He persuaded Harry and Herman Weber, "Managers, Producers and Promoters of Vaudeville Attractions," to audition Helen and Teacher. The Webers doubted that a deaf-blind woman could interest a vaudeville audience, which was rowdier and more intent on entertainment than the education-bent, sober folk who formed the Chautauqua constituency. Impressed, however, by the reviews of *Deliverance,* they agreed to journey to Forest Hills to meet Helen and Mrs. Macy. The wit and gaiety of the Forest Hills household first disarmed, then enchanted them. It might work, they conceded. It was worth a try.

Curiosity about them there was. They opened in Mount Vernon in February to a standing-room-only audience. The original twenty-minute act was introduced by George Lewis, who presented Teacher. Later they dispensed with Lewis, and the curtain would rise on a drawing-room set with Teacher seated at a piano. She described briefly, in her splendid stage voice, how she came into Helen's life, the latter's educational achievements, her writings and what the great and illustrious thought of her:

> Mark Twain, her life-long friend, has said: 'The two greatest characters in the 19th century are Napoleon and Helen Keller. Napoleon tried to conquer the world by physical force and failed. Helen tried to conquer the world by power of mind—and succeeded.' Whittier and Oliver Wendell Holmes were her friends. Caruso has poured his golden notes into her hand. Godowsky has played to her by the hour. Maeterlinck, the poet, has called her 'The Living Bluebird.' . . . Today she is the Star of Happiness to all struggling humanity.

Here the orchestra played Lewis's theme song as Helen entered and went to the piano. Teacher took her by the hand and led her to the front of the stage. "Can you tell when the audience applauds?" Annie asked. "Oh, yes, I hear it with my feet." Annie then went through the essentials of what has come to be known as "the miracle," when, with water gushing out of the well, she spelled W-A-T-E-R into Helen's hand and Helen suddenly realized that Annie's finger motions in her hand were the names of things. She went on to describe how Helen had learned to speak, and then she and Helen demonstrated how the latter had learned the gutturals, labials, nasals, vowels and consonants, a demonstration that ended with Helen's saying to the audience, as she had said at the time, "I am not dumb now." Helen then took over and made a short speech, unlike any ever made before on a vaudeville stage. Every word was still a battle to enunciate, the tone and pitch still a little unearthly, but the transfixed audience struggled along with her:

> What I have to say to you is very simple. My Teacher has told you how a word from her hand touched the darkness of my mind and I awoke to the gladness of life. I was dumb; now I speak. I owe this to the hands and hearts of others. Through their love I found my soul and God and happiness. Don't you see what it means? We live by each other and for each other. Alone we can do so little. Together we can do so much. Only love can break down the walls that stand between us and our happiness. The greatest commandment is: 'Love ye one another.' I lift up my voice and thank the Lord for the love and joy and the promise of life to come.

A strong, ministerial voice offstage then intoned the refrain of "Star of Happiness":

> Wonderful star of light!
> Out from the darkness of night. . . .

At its end Helen raised her right hand and said, "This is my message of hope and inspiration to all mankind."

The Mount Vernon audience had sat spellbound, following each movement and gesture with a rare concentration and palpable sympathy. The tension was broken only after the audience was invited to ask questions, which were conveyed to Helen by Annie and answered with quick sallies. Mount Vernon was a triumph, but it was out-of-town. Could they repeat it in New York at the Palace Theater, the testing place and goal of all vaudeville acts? The Palace bill that week included trained seals, acrobats and tap dancers and was headed by a talented dancer, Bessie Clayton. The reviewers ignored all but Helen and Teacher. "Before she had been on the stage two minutes," wrote the *Tribune,* "Helen Keller had conquered again, and the Monday afternoon audience at the Palace, one of the most critical and cynical in the world, was hers." The *Times* spoke of her "enthusiastic reception," and the *World* called it a "success," adding, "everybody is happy." Some of the reviews even reported her answers to the questions to show her "pretty wit":

"What is Miss Keller's age?"

"There is no age on the vaudeville stage," was the instantaneous response.

"Does Miss Keller think of marriage?"

"Yes, are you proposing to me?"

"Does talking tire you, Miss Keller?"

"Did you ever hear of a woman who tired of talking?"

She and Teacher were held over a second week, a sure sign of success at the Palace. From New York they went to Baltimore and then to Pittsburgh. There the faithful Mrs. Thaw bought all the boxes and filled them with her friends, only to be appalled on arrival when she looked at the program and saw the acts that surrounded Helen and Teacher. She sent for the manager and demanded that the program be changed at once. A loyal friend, she refused to believe that Helen and Teacher knew anything about the sort of acts with which they were billed to appear.

Many criticized their going into vaudeville. Even Helen felt uncomfortable. "At first it seemed strange to find ourselves on a program with dancers, acrobats and trained animals. But the very differences between ourselves and the other actors gave novelty and interest to our work." "Why have you gone into vaudeville?" newspaper reporters invariably asked. "To make money," became her immediate and frank reply, adding, "I do not seem to hold onto it." The *World* reported that she received "as high a salary as anyone in vaudeville. The attitude of E.F. Albee and others in the Keith vaudeville firm on this point was that at various times persons of no worth had received large sums to enter vaudeville on the strength of mere notoriety and that Miss Keller was entitled to as much, whether her appearance was a success as vaudeville entertainment or not."

By May they were sufficiently seasoned to size up their audiences. They did not like those in Buffalo, but Providence was "just dear." They got rid of George Lewis: "He meant well, but was of no real assistance to us. The managers didn't like him, and somehow he irritated the electricians in the theatres. No one seemed to think his music added in any way to our act. Polly now makes the arrangements, and rather enjoys it." Instead of Lewis's "Star of Happiness" the orchestra played Mendelssohn's "Spring Song."

While they were in Providence, Ned Holmes turned up, still adrift from work and family. He drove them to Boston, and they visited South Boston, where the Perkins Institution used to be. The school had moved to

Watertown, Massachusetts, and where its buildings had once stood there were now factories. They did not visit Wrentham as they had the year before. That had been too wrenching an experience for Helen. At that time they had visited John Macy—in fact that had been the reason for their trip. He had been very ill. "He looked dreadfully, and seemed like a feeble old man," Helen had reported to her mother. This time they avoided him:

> We don't see John now. I was really disgusted with him, mother. He kept asking, dunning Teacher for money. Now, you know it is money I am trying to earn to provide for Teacher, not to waste on John. So I wrote him a letter repeating what I said last fall—that I didn't want to work with him, that if he persisted in coming to the house, I would go away. I begged him to go to work at anything and prove to his friends that the John Macy they once knew was not utterly given over to selfishness and alcohol. Well, he wrote that he would terminate his relations with us and trouble Teacher no more. So far he has kept his word. I hated to write such a letter, believe me. But what could I do, I couldn't bear to have Teacher treated thus, or to see his last spark of manhood quenched without an effort to save it. I don't know, though, what Teacher will do. She seems to feel terribly about the letter, and she says simply, she can't help it. She does try hard for my sake to let things take their course, but—. You know her warm heart and her constant remembrance of what John was to her once.

They returned to Forest Hills at the end of June 1920, with their agent, Harry Weber, hellbent on booking them for "a long tour" that would cover the country and keep them busy for almost a year. If they went on that tour, she advised her mother, and if all the ifs that might shipwreck them did not happen, "we shall be able to lay by a nice little sum." After their initial success at the Palace, Weber had proposed a fee of $1500 a week in the big houses and $1250 in the small ones. That was "not acceptable," Annie firmly told him. "I have been advised by competent authority that the act is worth more." The increase that they were unable to get in March they did obtain now, and more. Everything was set for the long tour, Weber advised them; "I am getting $2,000 in most of the houses and $1750 in the out [of] towns." He scheduled them to open at the Palace in Chicago on September 20.

Having obtained acceptable fees for his clients, Weber was bewildered suddenly to learn that they were pulling out of the whole project. "After careful consideration of all aspects of the matter," Helen notified him, "we have decided not to go on the tour, and furthermore to give up Vaudeville altogether." Helen's postscript puzzled Weber even more. "Please do not assume that we are dissatisfied with the terms of your offer. The question is not one of money at all." If not money, then what was it? the surprised man asked. Could he come to see them?

The problem was with Teacher, Helen confided to her mother. When they had received Weber's letter announcing that the financial arrangements were "o.k.," Teacher suddenly announced

"I can't do it! I don't want to make all that money at such a sacrifice of our peace when I don't know what good it would do in the end!" The truth is, mother, she was not happy in that sort of work. I didn't mind so much. I rather enjoyed the excitement, and besides, as you know, I was trying to provide something for her against the days when she could work no more. But I did feel as she did that we were out of key with vaudeville life. I'm afraid a great need of money blinded us at first to some undesirable aspects of the matter. But finally we made up our minds that we would rather earn a little and live our own lives according to our ideals than earn a great deal and lose our peace of mind. So there went another of our "big" chances, and—left us happy! Now, what will you do with us two? I'm sure Mildred will be down on us for "foolishness." But somehow I feel as if you would understand. I remember your saying when you first heard of the Vaudeville proposition, "I know neither of you will like making all that money, there are so many things to spoil the good work that you would try to do. It isn't like the old lecture tours where you had audiences who were really interested and worth talking to." So perhaps you will be glad with us that our affairs have taken this turn.

Nevertheless, the resistance to a new tour was not Helen's but Teacher's. She was fifty-four years old, increasingly burdened with bad health and general weariness. She had never liked the public platform. The glare of the stage lights were an ordeal for her eyes. The noise and confusion backstage distressed her. She did not like living cheek-to-jowl with acrobats, tap dancers, monkeys, horses. Even Helen was a problem for her: "It saddens me to remember how I troubled her with my propensity to answer awkward questions with little or no reserve," Helen wrote in *Teacher*. Helen, in fact, found "the world of vaudeville much more amusing than the world I had always lived in, and I liked it." But she yielded to Teacher.

After a visit to Forest Hills Weber—accustomed to dealing with temperamental clients—saw that Teacher, not Helen, was the problem; and his letter to them afterward suggested that he had sensed another reason for Teacher's recalcitrance. Perhaps it was only the typical reaction of the booking agent when a client balked—if it's not the money, it must be the billing. In any case he wrote Annie on September 24:

> After carefully considering the matter of your cancelling the route I offered, I have come to the conclusion that you, my dear Mrs. Macy are the one to be considered, first, last and always in the presentation of your offering. You are the 'divinity of patience' and after carefully considering what you have gone through I do really think you are the one real attraction in this offering and it is without question that you are the one to be considered—first and always in salary as well as billing.
>
> If you would reconsider and make a short tour as we originally planned—I would see that your name would be featured as big as Miss Keller's or bigger if you want—as I have said above, I believe you are *the attraction* of your offering, and it has been awkward of me not to have recognized this fact before. Couldn't I possibly induce you to make a short tour under these arrangements, or can I have the pleasure of talking to you some time in the very near future?

Whether that letter did it, or whether Teacher responded to Helen's unhappiness at the prospect of sitting idle, she agreed to go back on the road. The tour took them to the West Coast by way of Canada and back to the East by a more southerly route. "We have just sent off a Christmas box to you," she wrote her mother from San Francisco. "We had to send it early because after this we shall have no more time to go shopping. . . . O my, what a whirl we all are in—visitors who stay until I am almost in tears, pictures to be taken for the Bible Society, or a newspaper, and always letters, letters, letters! I hope it won't be quite such a siege in Los Angeles, where we stay for two weeks."

But the alternative to busyness was an isolation that would intensify if people lost interest, if they did not bother her, if there were not new sights to be explained, new people to encounter. Will Cressy, an old hand on the vaudeville circuits, sensed what isolation might mean as he watched her backstage. Cressy, a prolific writer and performer in vaudeville skits, was a keen observer. For a decade he did a column, "Three Minutes in One"—a forerunner of the Broadway gossip columns of Walter Winchell and Leonard Lyons—for the *New York Star,* a vaudeville industry weekly:

> Naturally in my long stage experience I have met many beautiful and many talented women. But I never met one who attracted me and fascinated me as does Helen Keller. I follow her around like a pet dog. Whatever she is doing I watch her. And someway I never get over the feeling of she sitting there in that steel cell, alone, in total silence and absolute darkness, stretching out her hands to get into touch with the world that must seem so far away to her.

> I have sat in her room and watched her waiting so patiently and yet so eagerly to be told what is going on; what is being said and done. Her hands are continually seeking Miss Sullivan's lips to know if she is speaking. Or her hands are flying to Miss Sullivan's hands to spell out some question.

He had watched her as she sat off at the side of the stage waiting for Annie to come for her to lead her onto the stage:

> There she sits, in that invisible steel cell of hers, alone in all the universe. And yet, is she as lonely as I think she is? A thousand different expressions are chasing each other over her face. Her head is perched to one side as if she was listening; and yet she cannot hear. Her great big wide-open beautiful eyes are continually shifting around as if she was looking for something; and yet she cannot see. But yet, in some mysterious way, she SENSES many things. Let anyone walk by that she has grown to know, and she learns them as quickly as she does everything else, and she will look up and smile. She recognizes the vibration of their footsteps. If there is dancing going on on the stage, or the music is playing she is beating time, smiling, and weaving back and forth and from side to side in time with the music. And always she is smiling.

And then Miss Sullivan comes and gets her and leads her on through the 'Center Door' onto the stage. There is generally a large bouquet of flowers sitting on the piano to the right. Helen will stop, lift her head, sniff, and with hands outstretched leave Miss Sullivan and go straight over to those flowers, gather them into her arms and bury her face in them, as she joyfully inhales their fragrance.

Cressy then described the act and Helen's arresting way of handling questions. "And there may be quicker-witted people somewhere in the world than this same Miss Helen Keller, but if there are I have never met them." He described a night performance when the lower floor of the theater was filled with Shriners. She sent for Cressy and wanted to know what a Shriner was. He showed her his Shriner's fez and explained the meaning of the emblems and insignia.

"Do you know what a Shriner is?" someone in the audience inevitably asked.

"Yes, a Shriner is a man in a round hat who makes a lot of noise in the theater."

"What do you think of this particular lot of Shriners?"

"I have never seen a finer appearing lot of men," she replied gravely. And then as the audience exploded in appreciative laughter, she herself, observed Cressy, "fairly doubled over with laughter." Cressy ended his piece with a little sermon:

> Now on the level, some of you fellows who have been feeling a little discouraged, who thought you were not getting a fair show in this world, who have felt that some other fellows were getting all the best of it, and that there was not much chance for you—don't you feel as if you would like to crawl into a hole somewhere—and pull the hole in after you? Every time I see, or even think of Helen Keller, and Miss Anne Sullivan, and the obstacles they have overcome, I feel ashamed of all the hands and feet and arms and legs and eyes and ears and tongues I have got, and the comparatively little I have accomplished with them compared to what these two women have done.
>
> Don't you?

The social pressures that attended the vaudeville tour Helen found to be lighter than those of the Chautauqua circuit. Not only was the pay much better, but they usually were booked for a whole week in a city, and that meant time for rest and preparation. Their act lasted only twenty minutes in the afternoon and evening. That compared well with the ninety minutes they spent on the lecture platform. Moreover, "we were not required, as formerly in the lectures, to accept the well-meant but wearisome hospitality of those who engaged us."

There were for Helen added dividends. In Cleveland they crossed paths with David Warfield, who was finishing a week's engagement in *The Return of Peter Grimes.* Hearing that Helen Keller was in town, he called on her. With Helen resting her fingers on his lips he told her that he was planning at last to realize a lifelong ambition to appear as Shylock in *The Merchant of Venice.* In Providence, the tenor John McCormack had come to see her. Helen wanted him to sing for her, but he was too flustered and almost ran away when Helen proposed to read his lips with her fingers. It was in Cleveland that her answer to one question brought down the house:

"Which is the greatest affliction, deafness, dumbness, blindness?" she was asked.

"None," she replied.

"What then is the greatest human affliction?" the questioner persisted.

"Boneheadedness," she replied.

Many of her quick sallies were not as spontaneous as they appeared. With businesslike foresight they began to list the questions usually asked, together with answers Helen might give. In the end the list ran to seventeen pages. The questions mirrored the times—prohibition, Harding "normalcy," the Ku Klux Klan. Helen's comments did not hide her convictions—indeed, she revealed them with an audacity that is still somewhat breathtaking.

Q. Do you think any government wants peace?
A. The policy of governments is to seek peace and pursue war.
Q. Can you feel moonshine?
A. No, but I can smell it.
Q. What do you think is the most important question before the country today?
A. How to get a drink.

But at other times when asked what she thought about prohibition, she shrugged and replied, "I'm tired of it as a universal subject of conversation."

Q. What is your definition of a Bolshevik?

A. Anyone whose opinions you particularly dislike.

Q. Who are the three greatest men of our time?

A. Lenin, Edison and Charlie Chaplin.

Q. What do you think of Soviet Russia?

A. Soviet Russia is the first organized attempt of the workers to establish an order of society in which human life and happiness shall be of the first importance, and not the conservation of property for a privileged class.

Q. Do you think any nation really wants peace?

A. I think all the other nations would like to see Russia disarm.

Q. Who are the most unhappy people?

A. People who have nothing to do.

Q. What brings the greatest satisfaction?

A. Work, accomplishment.

Q. What have you enjoyed most in life?

A. Overcoming difficulties.

Q. What do you think of Mr. Harding?

A. I have a fellow-feeling for him; he seems as blind as I am.

Q. Can you suggest any tax that people would willingly pay?

A. Yes, a tax on millionaires.

Q. What do you think of ex-President Wilson?

A. I think he is the greatest individual disappointment the world has ever known.

Q. What did America gain by the war?

A. The American Legion and a bunch of other troubles.

Q. Do you think America has been true to her ideals?

A. I'm afraid to answer that, the Ku Klux Klan might give me a ducking.

Q. What is your idea of happiness?

A. Helpfulness.

Q. What is your idea of unhappiness?

A. Having nothing to do.

Q. Who is your favorite hero in real life?

A. Eugene V. Debs. He dared to do what other men were afraid to do.

Q. Who is your favorite heroine in real life?

A. Kate O'Hare because she was willing to go to jail for her ideal of world peace and brotherhood.

Q. Do you think the voice of the people is heard at the polls?

A. No, I think money talks so loud that the voice of the people is drowned.

Q. What is the greatest obstacle to universal peace?

A. The human race.

Q. What is the slowest thing in the world?

A. Congress.

Q. Do you believe in college education for women?

A. Oh. God knows they need all the education they can get.

Q. What is the most discussed topic today?

A. Woman, of course.

Q. Do you think women are men's intellectual equals?

A. I think God made woman foolish so that she might be a suitable companion to man.

Q. Can you give a good reason for the open shop?

A. There is none.

Q. Do you think that all political prisoners should be released?

A. Certainly. They opposed the World War on the ground that it was a commercial war. Now every one with a grain of sense says it was. Their crime is they said it first.

Q. What is the matter with America?

A. Read *Babbitt* and you will find out.

Q. What is the outstanding deficiency of Americans?

A. Lack of originality. Everything is standardized, even our thoughts. The central motive of all our action is 'What will others think about us?'

Q. What do you think of war?

A. Read John Dos Passos's *The Three Soldiers,* and you will know what I think of war, the most atrocious of human follies.

Q. Do you desire your sight more than anything else in the world?

A. No! No! I would rather walk with a friend in the dark than walk alone in the light.

Q. Which quality do you admire most in your teacher?

A. Her sense of humor; her many-sided sympathy; her passion for service.

Q. Can you see any way out of our troubles?

A. Have you thought of divorce?

On October 5, 1921, Helen wrote a letter to reach her mother on her 64th birthday. They were in Seattle, having crossed the continent via

Canada, their second transcontinental journey, and Helen was full of the "splendors" of the Canadian Rockies and the autumn foliage, whose vivid hues were constantly reported to her by Teacher and Polly. "Canada has always been good to us, but especially so on this tour." She signed the letter "Your affectionate child."

Ever since her stay in Montgomery while Teacher was in Puerto Rico, Helen had grown closer to her mother. When Teacher and Polly had returned from Puerto Rico, Mrs. Keller went with them for the summer to Lake St. Catherine in Vermont. Christmas 1919 Helen had spent with her family in Montgomery while Teacher remained in New York. After that long visit Mrs. Keller had written a poignant farewell note filled with presentiments of death: "How many times since you went away I have waked suddenly with the feeling that your step across the hall had waked me! Who knows? Perhaps as one grows older, the curtain which separates one from those one loves grows thinner. Be very sure that if I go first, if it is possible, I shall let you know how, and where I am. Yes. I shall remember." Teacher had lamented her inability to share Helen's belief in a life after death. Was Kate Keller hoping that in such a life she might achieve the closeness to her daughter that Helen's need for Annie had prevented in this life? "My fire is out, and I am very cold, so goodnight and goodbye, dear," the letter ended. Mrs. Keller lived another year and a half. But not long after Helen's birthday letter, two hours before she went onto the stage in Los Angeles, a telegram from her sister informed her that their mother had died. "Dearest Sister," Helen wrote on November 20, 1921:

> This is the first chance I have had to sit down quietly for a few minutes, and even now my heart aches so that I can hardly write. But I want you to feel my arms around you and the wee ones while I am waiting to hear from you. It is so hard for me to be far away at this time! And this is a road full of memories of mother's journeyings with us in days gone by. As we go from city to city, I shall long and long for the touch of her hand, and I do not know how I shall bear the loneliness, or when I can get to you. We have signed all our contracts up to April, and that means we cannot leave our work now. But if Teacher's strength gives out by then, she will take a rest, and I will come to you. Be sure that I shall come when I can.

How strange it all is: It seems as if we were dreaming, and I should wake any minute to find a letter from mother, saying she was in Texas. Only last summer she was with us, and she told me how much she enjoyed the rest, the sunshine and the lovely country when she felt well enough to go motoring. I begged her to stay longer, but she simply would not. She insisted that she was better, and Teacher must rest a bit. As soon as she was able to use the Braille machine after her illness, she wrote a lovely letter about her visit to Hendersonville, and how cheerful she was! What a joy it was to have her own dear words in Braille! You know she never felt that she was writing to me as she wished to when she used her pen. . . .

I know that she would want us to feel near her, and look forward to seeing her again in a more beautiful world. Just as she was leaving me at the station in New York, she said suddenly, 'Helen, you will not see me again, but whatever happens, I shall wait for you.' Afterwards she wrote, 'Do not let your feelings spoil your work, always do the best you can, and think of mother watching until you come.'

Another blow fell on Helen in Des Moines in early January. Teacher was unable to go on with the act. She lost her voice because of bronchitis. For a week she had to be attended by a doctor and nurse. It had happened once before during the tour, in Toronto, when her ailments were diagnosed as influenza, and Polly had substituted for her. Fearful that it would happen again, Teacher had prepared Polly as a replacement:

Polly and I go on the stage twice a day. She tells how 'Miss Sullivan' taught me, and then I answer questions and give my message as usual. Of course I feel lost without Teacher. You know how imperfect my speech is at best, and how anxious I am to use all the wise counsel she gives to help me out. But they say Polly and I are managing well.

After engagements at Hot Springs, Tulsa and in several Texas cities, the "long tour" ended at the Palace in Chicago. The managers had all accepted Polly as a substitute for Teacher without complaint. "She has done wonderfully. She speaks well, she does not show any nervousness on the stage and people tell me she looks pretty." Carl Sandburg was in her audience one day at the Chicago Palace and wrote a letter to Helen that he did not send until six years later because he feared it was "a little high flown." He no longer felt that way about it, so he was sending it on:

I saw and heard you last night at the Palace and enjoyed it a thousand ways. It was interesting to watch that audience minute by minute come along till they loved you big and far. For myself, the surprise was to find you something of a dancer, shifting in easy postures like a good blooded race horse. I thrilled along with the audience to your saying you hear applause with your feet registering to vibration of the stage boards. Possibly the finest thing about your performance is that those who hear and see you feel that zest for living, the zest you radiate, is more important than any formula about how to live life.

The tour was a success, but it was a sad group that returned to Forest Hills. Helen soon afterward went to Montgomery, a journey that gave her the feeling that her mother had died a second time: "The only thought that upheld me was that in the Great Beyond where all truth shines revealed she would find in my limitations a satisfying sense of God's purpose of good which runs like a thread of gold through all things." She stayed in Montgomery through the middle of June. She liked it no more and no less than she had during her separation from Teacher in 1917, except that she felt even lonelier without her mother, more bored and more outraged.

"Smile as I will," she confided to Teacher from Montgomery, "I feel always an ocean rolling between my mind and the minds of people I meet here—the brackish ocean of ignorance, prejudice, caste and self-complacency." But she was devoted to her family and brought Mildred and her three daughters north with her to Forest Hills. The pleasures of the summer were shadowed by the shrinkage of vaudeville engagements. "No Vaudeville work in sight, not a 'peep' from Harry Weber's office!" she wrote her sister at the end of 1922. "Our funds are disappearing rapidly. . . . Already I have had to break into the trust I put into Mr. Raymond's hands for current expenses! He didn't like it at all. . . . But what can we do! We must live and pay the bills."

Nineteen twenty-three did nothing to improve their financial position. "No work in prospect," she wrote Mildred at its end. "We were never a real Vaudeville attraction, I guess. . . . It is possible that we may get work to do the first of the year for the 'American Foundation for the Blind.' A gentleman is coming to see us Thursday afternoon, and we hope he will make us some sort of proposition." A new phase was beginning in her life.

XXVIII

A Proposal of Marriage

"I have come to feel that it was intended for me to live and die unmated, and I have become reconciled to my fate."

In 1922 one of their oldest friends died, Alexander Graham Bell. Helen had last seen him in 1920, when he told her he was going to devote the rest of his life to work on the hydroplane and forecast transatlantic flights within a decade and other engineering and scientific marvels. They had not seen much of him in recent years, but they had the feeling that he was always there ready to help them out, as he did in agreeing to Helen's request that he appear in *Deliverance.* The world was an emptier place without him.

It had been Bell who at the time of Teacher's marriage to John had advised Helen, if she found the right man, to "build her own nest," and to whom she had replied that she had nothing to bring a man that would compensate for the burden she would be to him, quoting at the time Elizabeth Barrett Browning's lines:

> What can I give thee back, O liberal
> And princely giver. . . .

She now again had occasion to invoke those arguments.

In early September 1922 a letter arrived at Forest Hills for Helen from a gentleman in Kansas City, whom we will call "E," proposing marriage. Teacher acknowledged it. "I have read the letter with the deepest interest and sympathy," she replied, but she needed time to think about it "before communicating your proposal to Miss Keller." He would prefer to have an answer from Miss Keller herself, E replied with some vigor. But on second thought he decided to defer to Annie's judgment and said as much in a follow-up letter the next day.

Teacher sought to reassure him. "My attitude is sympathetic and sincere." She had asked friends in Kansas City about him. "I have not communicated your proposition to Miss Keller, and it seems advisable not to disturb her peace of mind until I am satisfied with the practicability of your plan." E responded agreeably. It was Mrs. Macy's duty to check on him and he did not consider her act unfriendly, but would she send her letters to his office—he was an insurance man—"as my family is not to be 'in' on this for some little time to come."

It is unclear what Teacher learned about E, but within two weeks she did communicate E's proposal of marriage to Helen. The latter took several weeks to reply. Her letter was carefully considered, and for that reason even more poignant in its candid recognition of her limitations. Suddenly the mechanisms that she had developed within her prisoner's cage by which to reach out to the world, shake it and demand that attention be paid to her, were laid aside—the optimism, the ready smile, the gaiety and quick sally, the rushes of love—and the letter permitted others to glimpse the vulnerable sensibility quivering at the core:

> Ever since the day when your letter was read to me three weeks ago, I have been turning and turning again in my mind what I should say to you. There have been many unavoidable distractions, for instance, the sudden illness of my secretary, Miss Thomson, which upset our household considerably, and necessitated daily visits to the hospital in the city. Then there was a Vaudeville engagement in Washington which lasted a week. Such a state of things is not favorable for the thinking out of a difficult problem.

> Frankly, I am at a loss how to write what is to be written. But I realize that you are waiting to hear from me, and that further delay would be extremely unkind. It would be so much easier to say things if I knew you! As it is, we are like two boats signalling each other in a dense fog. I try vainly to visualize you in my thoughts as a real man. In spite of your very self-revealing letter, you seem remote, almost mythical.

However, I will answer the general sense of your letter. And first let me thank you from the depths of my heart for your brave thought of me. Proud and full of pleasure I certainly am to know that a good man has had the courage to think of me as a possible wife. All the primitive instincts and desires of the heart, which neither physical disabilities or suppression can subdue, leap up within me to meet your wishes. Since my youth I have desired the love of a man. Sometimes I have wondered rebelliously why Fate had trifled with me so strangely, why I was tantalized with bodily capabilities I could not fulfil. But Time, the great discipliner, has done his work well, so that I have learned not to reach out for the moon, and not to cry aloud for the spilled treasures of womanhood. I have come to feel that it was intended for me to live and die unmated, and I have become reconciled to my fate.

I suppose if I were younger, I would snatch at the possibility of joy which your offer holds out to me. In youth we fly toward happiness, even when we know that we shall bruise our wings against the jagged edge of consequences. Beside gray hairs and wrinkles the years bring us caution. Experience dulls the splendid audacity of youth. We measure the chasm between us and the things we desire, and in due course of time we come to bear "the whips and arrows of outrageous fortune" with resolute equanimity.

You have knowledge of human nature. You understand the workings of the normal mind. But I wonder if you know the consequences of the triple affliction of blindness, deafness and imperfect speech. You have read my books. Perhaps you have received a wrong impression of me from them. One does not grumble in print, or hold up one's broken wings for the thoughtless and indifferent to gaze at. One hides as much as possible one's awkwardness and helplessness under a fine philosophy and a smiling face. What I have printed gives no knowledge of my actual life. You see and hear, therefore you cannot easily imagine how complicated life is when one has to be led everywhere and assisted to do the simplest things. Somehow your letter has made me acutely aware of my situation and the discomforts of it. I realize, as perhaps you cannot, the almost unthinkable difference between your life and mine.

You seem to have lived a full, normal man's life. I have lived inwardly. They say that all women partake of the nature of children.

I am absurdly childish in many ways. My nearest friends tell me I know nothing about the real world. In some respects my life has been a very lonely one. Books have been my most intimate companions. My part in domestic affairs is usually that of a wistful looker-on. My piled-up disabilities shut me out from the practical business of daily life. I stand, blind and deaf, at the outer gates of a hustling, bustling world. Do you not see that such limitations as mine disqualify me for marriage?

Your willingness to marry me under the circumstances fills me with amazement. I tremble to think what an inescapable burden I should be to a husband. It is a noble gift you offer me—the treasures of a richly stored mind, intellectual companionship and the prospect of growing old along with a generous, warm-hearted comrade. I feel a deep sense of chagrin that my own hands are so empty. Would that they held the riches every woman wishes to bestow upon the man who desires her—beauty, helpfulness and the bright roses of youth! Without the sense of power which comes to us when we know that we can give joy as well as receive it, life must ever be disappointing and humiliating.

Now, dear friend—for so I shall always think of you, you have wished to be so kind, you have singled me out for such special favor and consideration—I would not have you imagine that I am a disappointed or unhappy woman. I am not tragic or desponding by nature. Temperamentally I am buoyant and hopeful. Through the darkness I always see a light—a bright star that no misfortune ever quite hides from me. Sometimes I think that star of faith shines brighter in proportion to my deprivations. In my effort to make you understand the seriousness of my disadvantages, I may have given you a wrong impression of my attitude toward life. Happiness is a condition of the mind, and has very little to do with outward circumstances. Usually I am too occupied with the things I can do to be much troubled about the things I cannot do. But with your proposal before me, I felt constrained to ask myself many questions as to my practical fitness to become a wife, and, as I have frankly confessed to you, the answers are generally disconcerting. They set forth such an appalling array of "disqualifications" that my letter sounds very much like a Jeremiad—a wailing and sighing out of the dark, which is contrary to every fibre of my being!

With an embossed book on my knee, or seated at my typewriter, I am not conscious of any handicap. In spirit and mind I am untrammelled. Imagination rides Olympian horses. Once my foot is in the stirrup, I am off to the uttermost isles of thought. I ought to say also that I have received the most wonderful kindness from my fellow-creatures. Every one has given me of his best in proportion to the richness of his nature and the goodness of his heart.

I am writing this in my little study, which is like the deck of a ship, where the winds blow, and the sun comes first in the morning, and the scents from my evergreen walk drift up to me like happy memories. It is delightful to sit here and think of you as my friend—a friend who has reached out from afar, seeking to light a new torch in my darkness. If my heart's wishes take effect, we shall meet some day face to face. Perhaps that moment is not far distant. That rests with you.

E was touched but unpersuaded. She was too modest, too honest, he replied. He was conferring no favors upon her. Since psychology knew nothing of "souls," he would say only that she was to him "a marvelous and beautiful human personality. . . . It may, indeed, be true that your 'limitations disqualify you for marriage' to the conventional mortal, but I have all my life been reasonably free from conventional ruts." He well understood her desire to become better acquainted. He was a widower who had lived happily for twenty-eight years with his late wife. He enclosed a group photograph of his family, four girls and a boy of fifteen. He also enclosed some "Rhymes" written in 1916 as a protest against the Billy Sunday campaign in Kansas City.

He tended to wordiness. The next day he sent another single-spaced three-page letter. How could she be sure what Fate intended for her? he asked. He was offering his hand; why not take the chance? She was not the only woman in the world denied the love of a man, denied children, although she desired both. Too often such women were held back by convention and tradition. The axis of his own life was the belief that every human being had the natural, inborn right to realize his full potentialities, so long as he did no injustice to fellow human beings. He had some physical impairments of his own to match hers. At the age of eight a freight car had severed the toes of his right foot, and four of his left, but he was able to wear ordinary shoes, stuffing cork where the toes would have been. He never used a cane and he was sure he could outwalk her on a five-mile hike.

Helen's lengthy reply to these letters underscored the unthinkability of considering marriage with a man whom she had not even met. A marriage of convenience was equally unthinkable. She acknowledged that she was prey to powerful sex drives, but the answer to them, she had learned, was work and sympathy:

> Your two letters came, the first ten days ago, and the other last week. The photographs did not arrive until Thursday evening.
>
> I am sorry to have to begin another letter with explanations. In my first letter I spoke of the illness of my secretary Miss Thomson. We thought then she would come out of the hospital in a few days, but she returned only last Sunday. Much time has been consumed in going backward and forward to the city, and attending to matters which Miss Thomson usually looks after. Then I am constantly interrupted by people who want one thing or another.
>
> Yesterday it was a picture that had to be taken to advertise an automobile. Why any one should think my picture would help to sell a car I cannot imagine. But the agent of the "Marmon Company" did think so, and I gave up three precious hours to satisfy his whim.
>
> Today a lady physician from Poland wishes to interview me about the subconscious mind and autosuggestion. She is trying to raise money in this country to re-educate the world! If you ever pray, send up one prayer that I may get through the interview without revealing my "pet complex"!
>
> Tomorrow I have to have another picture taken to be used on the cover of a magazine. So the days go by, filled with the trivial, the absurd, the nothings, while the things I want to do are pushed aside and neglected. There is little time for reading or conversation with people really worth while. I only manage to snatch an hour here and there for my letters. They are seldom finished at one sitting, and very often they are disconnected and unsatisfactory. I might have sent you a little note of acknowledgement, but I had a real letter in my mind.

I felt there were many things to be said that could not be dashed off any old way. I wanted my answer to your two last letters to be clearly thought out, definite and final.

Mrs. Macy read them into my hand. She was very sweet and patient about it. But you know the manual alphabet is a slow affair at best and I confess, I felt a little vexed that I could not run away upstairs with your letters and read them quietly by myself. You see what an advantage you have over me even in this small matter. You can read my letters as often as you choose and quote from them ad libitum, while I must content myself with hearing yours only once, and I should not dare to risk quoting you at length!

But as I think back over what you said, I recall gratefully the generous vehemence with which you swept aside my limitations from your thoughts of me. I wish I had a store of fresh thanks to express my appreciation. We are alike in this respect. I am not conscious of my friends'—or of other people's physical deficiencies. My mind instinctively dwells upon their beautiful capabilities of mind and heart. It is sweet to have others see me as I love to be seen—not deaf or blind, but dwelling "in the light of things," with horizons boundless as faith and the myriad-toned chorus of life pulsing through me endlessly.

I find that few people seem to have a happy sense of the adequacy of the inner life. Because I cannot see or hear, the thoughtless suppose life must be a blank to me. They do not understand that things have other precious values beside color and sound. It never occurs to them to FEEL a flower, and they do not know what they miss— the exquisite shape of leaf and stem and bud. I do not suppose light suggests to them the radiating, life-giving warmth of the sun. True, I cannot see the stars scattered like gold-dust in the heavens, but other stars just as bright shine in my soul.—And by the way, my SOUL is very real and very important to me. The scientists may not have discovered the soul. Possibly there are a good many other things in the universe which they have not "established scientifically." But the Thoughts of God are long, long thoughts, and even the wisest can turn only a few pages in the Book of Knowledge. I gather from the tone of your letters more than from expressed opinions that you have an agnostic turn of mind. My own mind rebels against skepticism and denial, and responds with joy and eagerness only to indomitable faith and hope. For my part, I believe that the universe is made of the same stuff as I am. Surely there is no other key to unlock the meaning of existence. To me the soul is a Land of Promise splendid with immortal youth and hope and inexhaustible possibilities. This conception fills me with a sense of expansion—sunshine without and sunshine within.

"Who makes much of miracles?
As to me, I know of nothing else but miracles."

There! you see how Pegasus has run off with me. He's forever taking the bit between his teeth—and away we go without rhyme or reason, and only a vigorous prodding of the spur ever brings us back to the place we started from.

Well, as I was about to say before Pegasus fled with me "down the dusky aisles of the mind," I am deeply touched by the entire confidence which you would bestow upon me in the untried hazards and struggles of a unique life-enterprise. You would share every adventure, every hardship with me, you would lead me to shining heights and distances afar beyond the reach of my mind's surmise. Through your letters runs a comradely spirit which attracts me immensely.

Twenty years ago I might perhaps have found this attraction irresistible. In youth we follow the will-o'-the-wisp Desire joyously, while she leads us open-eyed through pleasant but impracticable dreams.

But, dear friend, there are numberless sane certainties which I know that put marriage out of the question for me. No, it is not that I am afraid or distrustful. I know your intentions are generous and honorable. As for myself, I have battled too long against a triple foe to be afraid of anything, and if I thought there was the smallest reason to expect happiness for us both in the plan you propose, I should risk everything, "taking the sunshine and the thunder with equal cheer." But I do not believe there is one chance in a thousand that we should suit each other. The idea of marrying a man whom I have never met even as an acquaintance is unthinkable. I shudder at the prospect of marriage without love. You write touchingly to me about our common intellectual interests. But my woman's intuition tells me that however triumphantly we may "compass the world of mind," we must remember our heart-life and its imperious demands.

Please recollect, we are strangers. I am still in a thick fog when I try to visualize you, and your two pleasant letters have not cleared the atmosphere greatly. Your letters—your proposal—your expectations are so many pebbles thrown into a little pool nestling placidly in the deep shade of a dark forest. I wonder if you can imagine what a disturbance you have created—how all the little wild sleeping creatures of the imagination have started awake, scurrying round the pool like so many rabbits, chipmunks and fieldmice! They are all wondering and guessing and conjecturing who the intruder is, what he is like, what his real motives are in seeking out the enchanted Princess of the Dark Forest. Hitherto only the expected and privileged traveller has ventured beyond the magic boundary of her domain, and it is asserted by all who have any knowledge of the Princess that only a romantic knight will be given the key to the wonder-world of her heart. But enough of this nonsense. I fear it will not get us anywhere, and it will not dispel the illusive fog of strangeness which hangs between you and me.

It is true, your photographs have been described to me. The impression I have received of you and your children is that of a charming, bright-minded family. As Mrs. Macy added touch after touch of sympathetic description, you and the children seemed to emerge from the cardboard frame, and for a moment stand before me, emanating a spirit of friendliness, geniality and nobility. But mind you, this vivid impression did not last long. In a moment the heavy fog enveloped you again. It will take more than letters, more than photographs to lift it permanently. One fair and sunny day in the beautiful sometime, perhaps, we shall meet and clasp hands. In that "hand-picture" we shall know each other face to face, and the fog will have vanished forever.

I had written thus far when your letter of November 22nd came with the obvious intention of correcting any wrong impressions which your other letters might have given me. It is an evidence of your tender conscience, and I am on all accounts obliged to you for it.

At the same time, I do not think you have written anything beyond a true exposition of your philosophy of life. You seem to attach a value to certain ideas and opinions beyond what I do. I take liberalism, radicalism, and unconventionality for granted. Already Socialism seems to me a feeble protest against the accumulated evils of the social order under which we live. I adore intelligent, candid argument on serious subjects. I find opposition exhilarating. It affects me much the same way that a great tempest does. Friends say that the complexion of my opinions is decidedly "red." I am sure they are. I am tired of mock radicalism and parlor reforms. And the hypocrisy of Christians so-called irritates me to the point of desperation! I believe in Soviet Russia. I believe that the heroes of the Russian Revolution are men of lofty purpose, and that they are leading the way to a truer, saner, nobler civilization. They seem to have yielded some important concessions to the old order, but in this present defeat I see future fulfillment. Anyway, the struggle going on in Russia inspires, yes, fills me with hope.

> "The torrent roar'd and we did buffet it
> With lusty sinews, throwing it aside
> And stemming it with heart of controversy!"

Here endeth the fortieth interruption.

I wonder what I was saying when your third letter came? I do believe I have lost the thread of my discourse, and this letter is in danger of limping to "a lame and impotent conclusion."

At this moment one thought is uppermost in my mind—"I must make it clear to Mr. E that the essential point of this letter is my determination NOT to marry. There are a number of practical reasons against it which I do not think I need give here because the emotional reason is the main one. The thought of marrying for specified reasons—as one builds a house to live in, or buys an interesting book as a companion for lonely hours—does not appeal to me.

In my first letter I told you that time had done its work well, and that I no longer cried for the spilled treasures of womanhood. I did not mean to imply by this observation a forced and melancholy resignation. Through the wise, loving ministrations of my teacher, Mrs. Macy, who since my earliest childhood has been a light to me in all dark places, I faced consciously the strong sex-urge of my nature and turned that life-energy into channels of satisfying sympathy and work. I never dreamed of suppressing that God-given creative impulse, I simply directed the whole force of my heart-energy to the accomplishment of difficult tasks and the service of others less fortunate than myself. Consequently I have led a happy and, I hope, a useful life. I have had the joy of feeling flowers of ministering affection bloom under my hands, as the shy arbutus sends forth its sweetness from leafy obscurity. A great, throbbing sympathy has knit me to my fellow-creatures with unbreakable bonds. Deafness and blindness have never made me unhappy because through them I have found special ways of helping others. I FEEL that my individual pain counts not a whit more than the outcry of one little child of humanity caught in the cruel trap of exploitation—there are millions of these little creatures in our own great country mortally wounded in spirit and body! By narrowing the sphere about me God has brought me closer to them and given me the desire to help restore them to their human heritage. My limitations have been a wall for me to stand up against and defy the forces of cruelty, selfishness and hypocrisy in the world.

Do you get my point of view, dear friend? I hope you do, and that you will be able to take my "No" philosophically. I shall always think of you as a special friend, and I wish you every good thing in the world. May you find a woman as true, kind and responsive as you are generous.

Please take my "No" as final. I shall be glad if you do not refer again to your proposal, but leave the matter where it now stands.

With kind regards from Mrs. Macy, I am,

Always your friend,
Helen Keller

P.S. I am sending the photographs and your letters. In your first letter I think you said if nothing came of it, you would like to have your correspondence returned. We can now take a new start on the firm ground of friendship.

H.K.

Although she had said no, she was not wholly uninterested in E's reaction, as her account of E's proposal to Mildred hinted:

Here's a news item that will make you open your eyes quite wide. But mind, you mustn't mention it on any account, or it will get into the papers. Well, I've received—a proposal of marriage from a very handsome widower in Kansas City. No, no joke about it. He has really proposed to me by correspondence. He has written to me three times and sent photographs of himself and his five beautiful children. Two of them are married, both graduates from western universities. The other three are all in school—a boy fifteen, and two girls, one ten and the other eighteen. He said he had been interested in me for a number of years, and he seemed to think we would enjoy each other's companionship and grow old together happily. I wrote him that I was sure he didn't realize what it would mean for him to marry a woman so handicapped and dependent upon the assistance of others as I am. He wrote back brushing all that aside, and saying that he thought we were 'on the way to a great new happiness.' I replied that there were numberless emotional and practical considerations which put marriage out of the question for me. I reminded him that we are strangers, and I asked him please to regard my 'no' as final. I returned his letters and the photographs. I said, however, that I was very grateful to him for his brave thought of me, and that I should always think of him as a special friend. What will happen next, I wonder? Don't you dare tell Warren [Mildred's husband] about this—he would tease the life out of me as he did after hearing about the 'cow-boy proposal.'

E declined to be discouraged by Helen's no. "We are citizens of the same realm," he protested. "We speak the same language; we thrive in the same atmosphere; Are there not to be heard between us the voices of like calling to like?" He would not consider her no final until after they had met. He expected to come East in June for a Princeton class reunion and hoped to see her then. Pushing aside Helen's age, he stressed the joy of having a child of her own. His first letter to Mrs. Macy, he recalled, had said, "For another thing it seems to me, and I do not hesitate to say it, that of all women in the world she ought to be the last to fail in the attainment of the experience of the joys of motherhood. And, whatever be her own inclination on the point, it seems reasonably clear to me that purely on the grounds of eugenics she owes the world a child or two— even though *Who's Who* tells us she is past forty-two." In his desperation he appended a postscript, appealing to Teacher. "To my dear, patient Mrs.

Macy: Many thanks. And, please, is there nothing, whether with or without HER knowledge you might feel a warrant in saying to me?"

Helen loved children. No letter from a child ever went unanswered, and usually she wrote at great length. Mildred's children, beginning with Katherine, "little merry sunshine," and her brother Phillips's, gave her great pleasure, and she constantly was sending them little gifts. Children meant so much to her that E's reference to her having a child was cruel and callous, although not meant to be so, for Helen was almost forty-three, and even if she had married, the probability of having a child was slight.

Helen decided to end the correspondence:

> There is a Syrian proverb which seems to me to introduce this letter quite diplomatically. "Silence," says the wise man of the East, "is the greatest ornament of woman. If she knew this, she would be a wellspring of joy unto her household." Although you are not of my household, yet I think I can fit the proverb to our situation. If you take this wisdom to heart, you will not feel like scolding me for my protracted silence. On the contrary, you will praise my virtue and admire my reticence. Moreover, it may occur to you that silence in man also is at times ornamental.

> Forgive me if I speak frankly. I feel that silence following my last letter to you would have been truly golden. An unusual and interesting episode would have ended in a dignified manner. Your letter, with the accompanying caricature of yourself, has, it seems to me, given a touch of grotesqueness to the whole affair.

> I do not wish to appear ungrateful. Indeed I appreciate all your generous intentions, especially your long letter in Braille, which I know it must have taken you hours and hours to punch out on the slate, and for which I thank you sincerely. I had thought we might continue to write to each other occasionally on the basis of friendship. But now it seems to me better not to attempt a correspondence which would inevitably lead to misunderstandings and futile expositions.

> I do not want to marry you, and even if I did, there are excellent reasons why I should not. Your reasons why I should marry somebody do not appeal to me particularly. I confess, I felt a sort of pleasure and interest in your first letters, also a curiosity as to the personality of the man who has the courage to make such a proposi-

tion under the circumstances, but never for a moment did I consider the possibility of marrying you.

I suppose I should have said this in the beginning without confusing my meaning with so many words, in which case this correspondence would not have continued so uselessly and been broken off so abruptly. No, please understand that I am content with my life as it is. To me it is full of wonders—absolute wonders, with God's Hand over all, even if I have missed some of the precious sweet fruits of life.

Now, dear Mr. E, this is my last word on the subject. I have cleared up all doubts in your mind, and that you will do me the kindness to consider the matter as closed—irrevocably.

With New Year's greetings, I am. . . .

So far as one can make out, Helen turned E down before having met him. Perhaps what she had seen of the marital relationship—her mother's difficulties as well as Teacher's breakup with John—caused her to recoil from entering such a relationship herself.

While Helen sought to terminate E's suit, Teacher was having her own difficulties with John, who wanted a divorce. At the time he was literary editor of *The Nation,* published by Oswald Garrison Villard. He was living with a sculptress, a lovely deaf-mute, and was the father of a little girl. Sometimes he brought the child to *The Nation* offices, and his assistant remembers Villard wandering in and out murmuring, "that poor illegitimate little baby." His associates on the magazine recall him as gentle and sensitive, still attractive with his shantung silk shirts and the flowing silk bow ties that were one of the hallmarks of Bohemia. His hair now was white, so black ties had superseded the white. Alcoholism had ravaged his face, which had the mottled, flushed appearance of the lush. Liquor was an expensive addiction during prohibition; and when he came to write *About Women,* one of his indictments of the "feminist" tribe was the responsibility of the Women's Christian Temperance Union for the Eighteenth Amendment. "Her motive in depriving men of liquor, and even of tobacco, seems to her righteous and noble . . . but unconsciously she is impelled by the desire to spoil a man's pleasure, whether it be evil or innocent."

John's mother, that five-foot veteran of the suffrage battle, came to New

York. She blamed John's alcoholism and his failure to write the books of which he was capable on Annie's refusal to give him a divorce. Since John was unwilling to talk to Annie directly about it, his strong-minded mother, accustomed to ruling the family roost, took it upon herself to visit Annie in Forest Hills.

Teacher seemed to agree to the divorce, but she always found a reason to delay the initiation of proceedings. Her lawyer had to go to Washington, then she was too busy. When another appointment with her lawyer was at last set up, the lawyer canceled because he had to be in court. Then Polly sailed for Scotland, and Teacher was again "too busy to think much about this matter. When Polly returns September the 8th, I will try again to find out how to proceed, and if a divorce can be had without unpleasant publicity."

E did call on Helen when he came East for his class reunion in June. But she said nothing that might rekindle hopes. A brailled letter in mid-September, Helen did not even answer. In November he informed Annie by registered mail, "I am now in a definite way withdrawing any and all proposals that I have made, or may be considered to have made, to her."

> What can I give thee back, O liberal
> And princely giver, who has bought the gold
> And purple of thine heart, unstained, untold,
> And laid them on the outside of the wall
> For such as I to take or leave withal,
> In unexpected largess? Am I cold,
> Ungrateful, that for these most manifold
> High gifts, I render nothing back at all?
> Not so; not cold—but very poor instead.

E quoted *Tristam Shandy* and Bertrand Russell, but he was no Robert Browning. If he had been, who knows but that this tale, too, might have ended:

> My own Beloved, who hast lifted me
> From this dear flat of earth where I was thrown,
> And, in betwixt the languid ringlets, blown
> A life-breath, till the forehead hopefully
> Shines out again, as all the angels see,
> Before thy saving kiss!

XXIX

Campaign for the Blind

"The message and demonstration which they alone can give never fails
to move the audience to great emotion, making a tremendous appeal
for the work of the Foundation."

"Of course, you are well acquainted with the fact that, when Miss
Keller was a little girl, Mr. Anagnos raised astonishing sums of money for
the Kindergarten for the Blind in Massachusetts, by letting Helen make
the appeal." So Charles F. F. Campbell, energetic and engaging, and a
longtime worker for the blind, wrote Major Migel, president of the
American Foundation for the Blind, who had consulted him about ways
of raising a three-year budget for the recently established national clearing
house for the blind. Campbell, a friend of Helen's and Teacher's from
Massachusetts days, when he had directed the first state commission for
the blind, continued his brief on the indispensability of Helen:

> The scenes enacted by Henry Ward Beecher, when people of wealth
> came forward and threw money and jewelry at his feet, were repeated
> to a certain extent, in the presence of Helen Keller when she made
> her plea for little blind children. Those of us intimately acquainted
> with Miss Keller scarcely realize the psychological effect of having
> such a person speak on behalf of her own people.

Campbell was currently head of the Detroit League for the Handicapped and familiar with the fund-raising problems of such enterprises.
From time to time he had talked with Helen and Teacher about helping

national work for the blind, and he knew that "nothing would please them more than to do their part." He raised the question about how they should be paid:

> At first thought it might be suggested that a fixed sum, plus a commission upon all over a certain amount raised should be given, but it would be infinitely more effective if some of the present donors to the Foundation would underwrite the Helen Keller campaign so that it could truthfully be said that her services had been contributed to the cause and that she received no portion whatever of the money raised during her tour. It goes without saying that Mrs. Macy and Miss Keller should receive a very handsome honorarium for their service. . . .

Campbell sent a copy of his correspondence with Migel to the "girls" at Forest Hills, as he called them. "Never let on that you knew Mr. M[igel] wrote to me or what I said to him. I am *sure* you will be 'approached' to help."

The Foundation had already approached Helen and her Teacher. Its primary interest in meeting with them was to obtain the use of portions of the film *Deliverance,* but at the meeting a suggestion had arisen (who floated it is not clear) that Helen and Teacher might be willing to participate themselves in a limited number of places. But nothing had come of Teacher's carefully hedged hints of a willingness to become involved in the Foundation's campaign. By the end of 1923, however, Helen and Teacher were keeping in touch with the new Foundation through its research director, Robert Irwin. He was turning out to be the most forceful and thoughtful member of the permanent staff. Bob Irwin's history would immediately commend him to Helen. Blinded at five, he had gone on to become the University of Washington's first blind graduate, afterward getting an M.A. at the Harvard Graduate School. He had specialized in education for the blind. He dealt in concepts rather than personalities and bolstered his positions with a careful mobilization of statistics—as he had done in Cleveland, where he had successfully argued for day school classes for blind children. He had become the American Foundation's research director after fifteen years of work with the Ohio school system and state legislature. He and his wife, Mary, formerly a social worker, who was sighted and a woman of charm and intelligence, were at Forest Hills for Christmas Eve turkey, as was Walter Holmes, the editor of *The Matilda*

Ziegler Magazine for the Blind, and Elizabeth Garrett of the Illinois Society for the Prevention of Blindness. They sang carols and talked about the Foundation.

"You will be interested to know," Irwin wrote Campbell shortly afterward, "that as a result of your suggestion to Mr. Migel some time ago, the Foundation is arranging for a series of meetings in and around New York . . . at which Helen Keller will be the star performer." "The plan is for Teacher and me," Helen informed Mildred, "to go from city to city, hold meetings and solicit funds. We understand that most of the meetings will take place afternoons in the private houses of society people." They would start in the suburbs of New York and see how the format worked. Their expenses would be covered. "But nothing has been settled definitely yet. I'm afraid the work is too strenuous for us, handicapped as we both are in many ways, and I shall certainly not decide in a hurry."

Their appearances at the initial meetings in Westchester and northern New Jersey were in some ways a reprise of their vaudeville act. Teacher told the story of Helen's education. She had told it hundreds of times, and when the time came for her to speak, it was with dismay that she thought of telling the same story again. "But after I get started, the spirit of those intense days when I began her education enters me, and then it seems as if I were telling it for the first time. The story has universal appeal." After Teacher set the stage, Helen answered questions and made the plea for money for the Foundation.

An advance woman—Ida Hirst-Gifford, a New Jersey native, trained as a musician but with a flair for organization that she had demonstrated in wartime supervision of fifty blind workers as armature winders—set up the meetings in northern New Jersey. She pulled together committees of sponsors, saw to it that proper meeting places were secured, the newspapers informed, and at the meetings themselves accompanied at the piano the blind violinist Edwin Grasse, who was also a part of the program. From the outset Helen showed her ability to draw the crowds. "I am very glad that such is the case," Campbell wrote them in March, "for it will make it much easier for you to talk terms when the time comes, as it undoubtedly will." The Foundation understandably would try to get their help at a minimum of cost, but he wanted to see them rewarded liberally. "Only too well do I realize how foolish I have been for the past sixteen years in struggling along with the 'Outlook' and never getting a nickel out of it."

Helen's name was magic. By the end of March she was sending out on personal stationery appeal letters for the Foundation. The Hackensack audience, Irwin informed Migel, was one of the most responsive in his experience, and Teacher had been deeply moved by Major Migel's sending her a bouquet of roses. A very serious infection in her better eye was a source of much distress. "In spite of the anxiety she went through the meeting like a wonderful soldier." Because of the crowds that wanted to hear Helen, they quickly abandoned meetings in private homes. In the Oranges the overflow had to be accommodated at the Brick Presbyterian Church, "and in Newark five hundred were turned away," confirmed Ida Hirst-Gifford. "When Mrs. Macy and Miss Keller appear, they are always received with marked reverence. The message and demonstration which they alone can give never fails to move the audience to great emotion, making a tremendous appeal for the work of the Foundation." Each meeting had yielded a substantial collection—not large gifts, but sufficient to net the Foundation a respectable sum.

Major Migel—an alert, perceptive man who had made a fortune partly because of his ability to make decisions quickly—realized immediately that the Foundation needed Helen and Teacher, that with them it could have a major national impact on ameliorating the conditions of the blind, while without them it would simply be one among many philanthropic organizations. "Immediately upon your return I hope to have the great pleasure of seeing you both—if possible we can have a little conference as to the approaching Fall campaign, with an endowment fund as our goal," he wrote Teacher. He sent a message of thanks to Campbell. Helen and Teacher had held "seven meetings, addressed about 10,000 people, and have had subscribed to our Foundation approximately $8,000—a most wonderful record. . . ." He knew how highly Helen and Annie regarded him—"possibly you might care to write them a little note and tell them how happy you undoubtedly feel about it." Campbell promptly forwarded Migel's note to Helen and Teacher, telling them that he had advised the Major that he hoped "a satisfactory arrangement could be worked out so that you would derive practical benefit from the undertaking."

Teacher did not need the advice. She had her own appreciation of their importance to the Foundation and was determined to drive a hard bargain. Between, on the one hand, her realization that her earning years were nearly over and her resolve, therefore, to provide for their futures and, on the other, the awareness of Major Migel, himself unsalaried, that the public looked askance at money-raising drives where the costs of the campaign ate up most of the contributions, the stage was set for Teacher's last confrontation.

In 1921 the American Association for the Instruction of the Blind (AAIB) and the American Association of Workers for the Blind (AAWB) at their respective conventions had called for the creation of an American Foundation for the Blind, with Bureaus of Information, Education and Research. It was Major Migel, one of those designated as a trustee of the new agency, who donated seven thousand of the ten thousand dollars the trustees agreed were a prerequisite to opening an office. Subsequently he agreed to become president, urged to do so by the younger men, who feared that otherwise the new foundation might become the captive of the old guard, meaning the superintendents of the established institutions for the blind.

"I can tell you very little about Mr. Migel's biography," Robert Irwin informed the AAWB twenty years later, when it was preparing to award the Major its Shotwell Medal, "except that he was formerly a silk manufacturer but retired many years ago. . . . Mr. Migel is very shy about publicity." His full name was Moses Charles Migel. He was born in 1866, which made him the same age as Teacher. He was born in Texas, to which his family had moved from Canal Street in New York because of his father's asthma. His father died, and by 1880 his mother, Hannah, with six children returned to New York, and Moses C. Migel as the eldest son became the family's principal breadwinner. He went into the silk business, and by the early 1900s he was the owner of plants and mills in New York, Long Island and Providence and did so well that at the age of forty he withdrew from managerial activities. This much Frances Koestler was able to establish when she wrote her lively book *The Unseen Minority,* but much about his early years and his family background he and his children kept shrouded in mystery. "Moses" suggests that the family was originally Jewish, and there are reports that it originally hailed from Eastern Europe. The Major avoided the use of his given name and asked his associates to refer to him as "Major Migel."

In his secretiveness about his origins he was very like Teacher, who still found it difficult to speak about her beginnings at the Tewksbury almshouse. Both were persons of considerable achievement, but thin-skinned, especially in matters involving their status. Teacher encouraged their friends to call her "Teacher," just as Migel insisted on "Major."

An energetic man, Migel looked around for other things to do after he had retired from business. What interested him in the blind is not clear, but he began to spend Monday evenings reading aloud to residents of a New York home for blind men and women. He soon ran up against the many systems of Braille in which books for the blind were printed. There was English Braille, American Braille, and New York Point, all with their passionate advocates. There were Braille readers in each system, and Walter Holmes was obliged to print *The Ziegler Magazine* in two editions, one in American Braille, the other in New York Point. "A plague on all these points," Helen had written in 1907. "Let us have one system, whether it is an ideal one or not. For my part I wish nothing had been invented except European Braille. There was already a considerable library in this system when the American fever for invention plunged us into the Babel of points which is typical of the many confusions from which the blind suffer throughout the United States."

When Migel heard that there was a movement among the workers for the blind to agree on a single finger-reading system, he contributed handsomely to the project. He became treasurer of the Uniform Type Commission that was established by the AAIB and the AAWB. His work on this commission led to his appointment by Governor Whitman of New York as chairman of the New York State Commission for the Blind. During the war he showed his administrative acumen in pulling together a consortium of silk manufacturers to provide the government with the silk it needed as an ingredient in packing ammunition. Under Migel's leadership the consortium used its monopoly to lower instead of raise prices to the government. After the Armistice the American Red Cross asked him to go to France to take charge of the repatriation of blinded servicemen. He accepted the assignment, and at his own expense he recruited a team of nurses trained to work with the blind to accompany him. He served seven months in France with the assimilated military rank of "Major."

In 1906 he had married a Chilean woman, a devout Roman Catholic from an aristocratic but not wealthy family. She was petite, dark haired and submissive, a woman who deferred to her husband at home and never inquired into what he did elsewhere. He was tall, carried himself erectly, affected a jaunty attitude and was a handsome dresser. He was, according to Mrs. Koestler, "a bon vivant . . . a master-mixer of giant-sized old fashioneds, a confirmed cigar and cigarette smoker . . . a man who played cards for high stakes, bet heavily on horses and even owned a few." His attitude toward women "was courtly but tinged with indulgent condescension. Intellectual brilliance or business competence on a woman's part never failed to amaze him." He was quick to anger and did not like to lose an argument. He was to meet his match in Teacher, and they would fight —to a draw.

In 1923, when the original executive director of the Foundation left, Migel himself took over the organization's direction, aided by Robert Irwin, who later became the director, and by Charles B. Hayes, who ran the Foundation's Bureau of Information and Publicity. A year earlier the Foundation had absorbed the Uniform Type Commission and the magazine *Outlook for the Blind*. The Foundation was "a big thing," Helen wrote her sister, and had many purposes, as many as the varied needs of the blind:

> I haven't given you any details about this work, have I? For instance, there is a question of embossing more and better literature for the sightless. There has been little progress in printing for the blind since the beginning because it is not commercially important enough to interest experts and inventors. Of course they give their attention where the reward is greatest. As you know, the Braille writers we must use are clumsy, and liable to get out of order. It is believed that all the apparatus for the blind could be greatly improved if only enough time and money were spent on it. Then it is desirable to increase opportunities of usefulness for the blind as far as possible, and enlist the interest of their fellow-citizens, so that they will give them a chance to become self-supporting. Again, no proper provision has been made for the care and education of the deaf-blind. Neither the schools for the deaf nor the schools for the sightless want them because they require much constant attention, and should have special teachers. One of the Foundation's objects is to seek out deaf-blind children, and see that the state where they live gives them opportunity to receive special instruction. The chief part of the enterprise is the prevention of blindness. You will be delighted to hear that the opthalmia of the new-born has been practically wiped out in Massachusetts. It can be eradicated everywhere. All these matters appeal to our common-sense when we understand them. But naturally, the general public can't grasp them so readily. A nation-wide campaign of publicity, legislation and money-raising must be carried on for some time to come.

With the constructive work of the Foundation firmly charted, Migel and his fellow trustees concluded that the time was propitious for an appeal to the public for financial help. That had led him to Helen and Teacher. The success of their pilot meetings in the vicinity of New York encouraged him to invite them to a meeting of the Foundation's executive committee to discuss a six-month campaign for the coming fall and winter. His letter outlined a proposal in connection with the campaign. They were to commit themselves to five meetings weekly, either in the afternoon or the evening, partly to raise an endowment fund of $2,000,000 and partly to solicit memberships. Twenty meetings a month, he anticipated, would together gross the Foundation $20,000, against which they envisaged expenses of $6,035, including $750 monthly for Teacher and Helen when working in the vicinity of New York. This would be increased to $1,000 to cover living expenses away from home. Should the two of them secure large gifts there would be extra compensation. He was opposed to a "commission" arrangement: "As you undoubtedly know, we ourselves are opposed—and the public at large are *very greatly opposed*—to any specific arrangement with a representative on a percentage basis, and we wish to keep entirely clear of such criticism."

Teacher was every bit as wily a negotiator as Migel. She replied to the Major proposing a flat $2,000 a month for the six months of the campaign, and four, not five, meetings a week. The Major, accustomed to having his own imperious way, suddenly found himself in a confrontation with an antagonist of "powerful temperament," as he later described Teacher. He began to retreat. He knew the Foundation needed the three women and he did not trust himself, so he sent Irwin and Hayes to negotiate with them. They became the women's advocates. Irwin's report urged Migel to place "the Helen Keller party on a $2,000 a month basis, regardless of where they are working." As for commissions on large gifts, Teacher was willing to leave that to him. "She realizes that no commission arrangement would be considered ethical. She thinks, however, it should be in the neighborhood of five percent on large amounts."

Concerned for public appearances, Migel undertook to finance the $2,000 a month out of his own pocket. It was a generous gesture, but Teacher and Helen preferred to be on the Foundation payroll rather than under obligation to Migel. They brought their lawyer, Judge William Ashley, into the negotiations, and that further riled the Major. He decided to let the women know that he had other options, namely the employment of a fund-raising firm. He proposed that all confer together at his offices on August 7, 1924.

Teacher promptly fired an answering salvo across the Major's bow:

THANK YOU FOR YOUR KIND LETTER. I AM STILL OCCUPIED WITH THE OCULIST. THE TROUBLE WITH MY EYES DOES NOT ABATE. I SHALL NOT BE AT THE CONFERENCE TOMORROW. IF YOU THINK OTHER AGENCIES CAN RAISE THE TWO MILLION DOLLARS WITHOUT HELEN KELLER, WE SHALL BE MOST WILLING TO WITHDRAW, AND FURTHER NEGOTIATIONS WILL NOT BE NECESSARY. I SHALL ADVISE MR. ASHLEY OF OUR ENTIRE WILLINGNESS TO BE RELEASED. WE REALIZE IT WOULD BE A CONSIDERABLE SAVING TO THE FOUNDATION IF THE FUND COULD BE RAISED THROUGH ONE OF THE PUBLICITY AGENCIES. THE BLIND MAKE A STRONG APPEAL UPON PUBLIC SYMPATHY.

The contract was finally signed in October—on Teacher's terms. It stipulated that they were to give their services to raise an endowment fund of two million dollars "to be known as the 'Helen Keller Endowment—American Foundation for the Blind.'" Migel and Hayes signed for the Foundation, Helen and Teacher for themselves. Polly Thomson, although she was to be in the Helen Keller party, was not a signatory, an indication of her secondary status in the Forest Hills household at the time.

Each side in the Foundation negotiations had taken the measure of the other. Migel knew that he needed Helen, but he realized that he could not have her without Teacher and that to cross that formidable lady meant to place all his plans at peril. He was able to bend. "That you and Helen will visit us for a few minutes at the Foundation offices on Wednesday, October 22nd, the day of our Board meeting," he wrote Teacher, "pleases me exceedingly, as I know all our Trustees will be very happy to see you both." When Teacher, with flirtatious audacity, asked that he contribute to the work of deaf-mutes in a New England organization that interested her, he promptly complied, eliciting a cordial letter of thanks from Helen.

One item the contract did not cover—the special compensation they were to receive for large gifts. There was, moreover, a problem of money to meet their current expenses. Scheduled to see the Major, Teacher, an old hand at extracting help from the wealthy, thought it prudent to outline their plight before her appointment:

The situation is very distressing to me. It would never have arisen if we had a little more money. The fact is, we are at the end of our resources, unless we encroach upon what we have invested, which of course we are very reluctant to do. Our little house is mortgaged already; and the work we are doing for the Foundation puts a Vaudeville engagement out of the question, and ready money with it. Our bills this month are unusually large, as they include doctors' and dentists' bills and expenses incidental to preparations for the tour, in addition to our usual household budget. To cut down expenses, I am selling our car, which is the only luxury we permit ourselves, and which in a real sense is not a luxury, as Helen and I find it very difficult to get about in the city on account of our combined limitations. Harry, the chauffeur and man-of-all-work, is going west to find a position for himself. I hope this plain statement of facts will prepare you for a clearer understanding of Mr. Ashley's call. . . .

Migel responded generously. Helen heard about his check for one thousand dollars as she was speaking over the radio—that "mysterious contrivance," as she called the microphone. "I told my invisible audience that I held in my hand a thousand dollars' worth of happiness for the blind."

Although the Foundation campaign was to be in the name of Helen Keller, its organizers, which now included a public relations firm, thought it prudent to have it headed by Dr. Henry Van Dyke as national chairman:

Teacher had to go to Princeton the other day to have a motion picture taken with Dr. Van Dyke, who is our national chairman. . . . We are using the first act of my picture [*Deliverance*], paying twenty dollars for each exhibition. We have added some new reels showing what the blind can do, and the picture will be shown at each public meeting.

Helen gave her sister to understand that she herself had chosen Dr. Van Dyke. He was the acme of respectability, a former clergyman whose sermons *The Gospel for an Age of Doubt* were widely read, as were his essays about the outdoor life, especially *Fisherman's Luck*. He had just retired as professor of English literature at Princeton, and also had among his attainments a tour as minister to the Netherlands. His collected works in seventeen volumes had just been published. He would help shield the Endowment drive against the zealous patriotic groups that had mushroomed in the country as a concomitant of the war and the Bolshevik Revolution and that already had Helen under surveillance.

"Is it not rather a pity," S. Stanwood Menken, president of the "National Security League," wrote Migel, whom he addressed as "Dear Mac,"

> that one for whom our system of education has done so much as it has for Miss Keller—notwithstanding her remarkable achievements under great affliction—should be induced to write as she does? The pity of it is that it does not reflect upon Miss Keller, but upon those responsible for her education, and for the contact she has had with persons who bear the taint of Communism. . . .

> We have known of Communists occasionally in the schools and colleges, but did not know that they sought out those without complete physical equipment for the purposes of deception.

Migel passed this letter on to Helen and Teacher, but evidently realized that he could not lay down the law to these proud women and suggest the wisdom of an apolitical stance. In reality, Helen's views on society and politics were mellowing. The social revolution no longer was the guiding star of her thought and action. Wartime repressions had destroyed the IWW. Some of its members had joined the Communists, but they were a group of quarrelsome sects, many of them underground. The Socialists were weaker than they had ever been; moreover, Helen had washed her hands of the international socialist movement because of the failure of most of the socialist parties to stand up against the war.

"We seldom see any of our 'radical' friends now," she wrote Iva and Joe Ettor, who were living in Los Angeles. "We haven't been in sympathy with their attitude since the war. We are heartily disgusted with the A.F. of L. and their blind leader. If only Jehovah in his infinite mercy would take Gompers to Heaven, there might be some hope of an American labor party worthy of the name. . . . As for the Socialist Party—if any such thing has survived the war—its influence is hopelessly reactionary. . . . Isn't it a pitiful spectacle to see France bullying, prodding and pricking poor Germany! . . . Russia seems to be the only light in the universal gloom. . . . I for one believe that the Russian way is the right way—the only possible route to the Promised Land."

"When I first heard the glorious words 'Soviet Republic of Russia,' " she had written in November 1921, "it was as if a new light shone through my darkness." Liberals as well as radicals supported recognition and relief for the infant regime. The implications of the new tyrannical rule in

Moscow were still too obscure, too confused, too subject to challenge, to have an effect upon the American Left. As a result of the civil wars, foreign intervention and—although this was perceived by only a handful—Bolshevik policies and practices, Russia, which had been the world's bread basket before the war, was now swept by famine. Unable to join a "Hunger Banquet for Russian War Relief," she wrote the Minneapolis organizers of the event, "Our people are too prone to accept without examination whatever they read in the newspapers. They are told that the famine in Russia is due to Bolshevism, and that the money they give to alleviate suffering will go to strengthen the hands of the fanatics who have brought about the ruin of their country. And the workers! How easily they have been deceived and befuddled by the powers that exploit them! They seem to have put into their master's keeping not only their tools, but also their heads and hearts."

In November 1923, just as she was beginning her exploratory talks with the Foundation, Major Pond, under whose auspices she had first lectured, wrote in the *New York Herald* that "Helen Keller, as long as she played her part correctly, was one of my biggest platform successes. She was an inspiration to the world. America went wild over her. Then, in Boston, she became interested in radicalism and in a short time that ended her career. As a social revolutionist it was different, especially since she owed a great part of her success to the very capitalists she condemned."

Migel, whose wartime work for the government had won the plaudits of the American Legion, no doubt was fully aware that Helen's politics might impair the Foundation's fund raising. To compound his anxieties, on the very eve of the six-month campaign, Helen pitched in to the 1924 presidential race with a rousing endorsement of Robert LaFollette, one of the "wilful men," as President Wilson had dubbed them, who had voted against U.S. entry into the war. He was now the third party candidate against Calvin Coolidge, the Republican incumbent, and John W. Davis, the conservative Democrat who had emerged from the deadlocked Democratic convention at Madison Square Garden as the compromise choice.

She apologized for the delay in writing him, she wrote the Progressive party candidate, "but if you know how my heart rejoiced when I heard of your nomination, my silence would not seem to you like indifference. . . ." She had hesitated to endorse him, because she knew that the opposition papers "will cry out at the 'pathetic exploitation of deaf and blind Helen Keller by the "motley elements" who support La Follette. . . .'"

So long as I confine my activities to social service and the blind, they compliment me extravagantly, calling me 'archpriestess of the sightless,' 'wonder woman' and 'a modern miracle.' But when it comes to a discussion of poverty, and I maintain that it is the result of wrong economics—that the industrial system under which we live is at the root of much of the physical deafness and blindness in the world—that is a different matter! It is laudable to give aid to the handicapped. Superficial charities make smooth the way of the prosperous, but to advocate that all human beings should have leisure and comfort, the decencies of life, is an Utopian dream, and one who seriously contemplates its realization must indeed be deaf, dumb and blind.

She rejoiced in his nomination. His support by a number of "thoughtful Democrats and Republicans" was a sure sign "of a new spirit in the nation. I believe we have heard the swan song of the old parties."

Her endorsement meant a great deal to the LaFollettes. "I wish I could tell you how deeply moved we were when our son read your letter aloud to us at the family table. I am especially grateful for such expressions of confidence and appreciation from those who are disinterested and seeking only the public good. . . . Your name is a message in itself and the stand you have taken is of great practical value and usefulness."

Although LaFollette's candidacy drew a respectable 16 percent of the vote to Davis's 24 percent, Coolidge won handily, and it was scarcely the "swan song" of the old parties that Helen had expected. But it did mark the end of Helen's participation in politics. She did not again make a public political endorsement until she supported Franklin D. Roosevelt for a fourth term in 1944.

She soft-pedaled her politics presumably at the request of the Foundation. There is no document to that effect, but many of the Foundation's trustees were conservative businessmen, as were the men who would have to give the green light in various communities to the Foundation's fund raising effort. Independently of the political convictions of the trustees, there was a cogent case against Helen, the Foundation's chief fund raiser, proclaiming views that were likely to give offense to many potential donors. And Helen quickly realized the logic of being in a position to appeal to men and women of all political persuasions. "The National Committee," Helen wrote Migel, "is a happy thought." It was headed by Professor Van Dyke and would also help soften criticism of Helen's politics.

Even so, not all communities welcomed the Foundation's campaign. Cincinnati protested the use of Helen, objecting to the "exploitation of her infirmity" and to the large fees she was being paid. The philanthropic agencies in Chicago also vetoed a campaign by the Foundation. The Helen Keller meetings would be "purely sentimental," the critics alleged. Apart from these few rebuffs the Foundation drive was welcomed. The campaign opened in Reading, Pennsylvania, and moved on to Philadelphia. A luncheon that was presided over by Public Service Commissioner J. Henry Scattergood, a leader of Philadelphia's influential and generous Quaker community, brought out Philadelphia society and the social work community. The commissioner was so taken with the three women that he invited them to attend Quaker meeting on Sunday before their big money-raising affair at the Academy of Music. Helen was moved to speak and expressed her deep affection and respect for the Society of Friends. That touched off a moving comment by Dr. Rufus Jones, the leader of the Friends. "Then our family had the treat of having the three ladies as our guests at dinner before the great meeting in the city," reported Henry Scattergood in the *Friends' Intelligencer.*

PURSES FLY OPEN TO HELEN KELLER was the headline over the story that described the meeting at the Academy. Their old friend Edward Bok presided. Dr. Van Dyke spoke first, describing the work of the Foundation: "We have a leader who knows the whole story of this affliction," he ended, adding, "and her teacher, Mrs. Macy, is a miracle worker." Two reels of film on Helen's education were shown while a blind organist played appropriately sympathetic music. Teacher followed with a brief explanation of how the miracle had been wrought. Then Edward Bok presented Helen: "We are often tempted to say, 'What can we do,' we're only one, and how can we do anything? And that with all our faculties! Then look at Helen Keller and see what she has done, blind and deaf as she is, and see if you can ever again ask such a question about yourself." Finally Helen made the appeal speech for the cause that she described as dearest to her heart.

At its end Bok asked all who intended to sign contribution pledge cards to wave them over their heads. "What does it look like?" Helen asked, and then answered her own question, "Like the fluttering of birds." Bok slipped his own pledge card into Teacher's hand. She tapped out the figure to Helen, who impulsively sprung to her feet, flung her arms around Bok and kissed him. "That's just for the chairman," he called over his shoulder to the audience. The contribution was for $5,000, and all in all they raised $21,000 that afternoon.

Another announcement at the meeting brought a special burst of applause. Mr. Bok read a letter accepting the honorary chairmanship of the American Foundation for the Blind. It was from President Coolidge.

XXX

Teacher's Last Confrontation

"A man of your imperious disposition is apt to regard a different point of
view as more or less unfriendly."

"Beggars," "housebreakers," "mendicants," were some of the
epithets invoked by Helen to describe their work for the American Foundation. Although they were quite skilled, almost artful, at money raising,
neither Helen nor Teacher enjoyed it. "Oh my, what a strenuous business
this beggar's life is!" She lamented to her sister at the end of 1924. "We
set out to raise that large sum [two million dollars] in six months, and now
it seems a thousand years ahead." It humiliated them to appear "as mendicants at the doors of plenty, even though we were laboring with all our
might to raise the blind from beggary." Teacher hated it more than did
Helen; her resistance to the work, said Helen, boiled over continually out
of "a volcano of resentment." Class feeling was part of it—the gut hatred
that the poor Irish had for the white Anglo-Saxon Protestants who controlled much of the nation's wealth. She was, moreover, sensitive to the
point of touchiness to philanthropists, who, despite high-sounding professions of sympathy and understanding, looked down, she and Helen felt,
upon the blind.

Her nature rebelled, too, because it was unable to realize its full powers.
"If Teacher had been left free to choose her destiny, she would never have
limited herself to the cause of the blind," Helen wrote in *Teacher*. "It was
only because she saw a chance of usefulness to them that she joined her
wealth of mind and heart to my endeavors." She herself was so con-

stituted, continued Helen, "that I would have worked with equal zest for the crippled or the poor or the oppressed."

Teacher, however, was not a crusader, at least not in the all-out sense that Helen was, committing herself to various causes, whether it was woman's suffrage, syndicalism, socialism, Bolshevism, or Francis Bacon as the author of the plays attributed to Shakespeare. Annie was a gifted teacher, the master teacher that Dr. Bell had long ago recognized and acclaimed. She secretly yearned to write a book, part autobiography, part pedagogical thesis, modeled perhaps on William James's *Talks to Teachers,* which John Macy once had read to her and which she was rereading. Helen sensed the restlessness in Teacher that flowed from a spirit that was denied its true bent. In a revealing passage in her book about her mentor, she described a camping trip that the two of them took up to Maine and Canada in the summer of 1924. Polly had gone to Scotland to visit her family. Harry Lamb chauffeured them, putting up tents, collecting firewood for campfires, in general performing the more arduous chores. In the Maine woods they completely escaped the endless flow of visitors, the continual ringing of the telephones, the daily sack of mail. In the quietude of the firs and pines, by the banks of the Kennebunk River, Helen felt Teacher to be at peace. Her own spirit responded to Teacher's, and they achieved a moment of complete communion: "I was released for a while from the remorseful thought (she never in her life suggested it) that perhaps her individuality was subordinated to my own."

It was no wonder then that Teacher more keenly than Helen chafed under the obligations of money raising, a work that she did as much because it helped keep Helen and her afloat financially as out of a desire to serve the blind. "For three years we covered the country from coast to coast," Helen wrote of their work for the Foundation that began in 1924. "We addressed 250,000 people at 249 meetings in 123 cities."

Like many crusaders Helen assumed that right had only to be proclaimed and the virtuous would flock to its banner. Major Migel had questioned whether setting a two million dollar target for the Endowment was realistic, but he yielded to Helen, supported by Teacher, on the matter. But by the end of 1924 it was clear that though the virtuous came to Helen's meetings, the contributions did not match the numbers. "The essential difficulty we encounter," Teacher wrote Migel, "is [that] the American Foundation had not an emotional appeal, and a good many people seem to believe that Helen Keller is being used to promote a project which is vague and futuristic. But if we keep our chins up, and square our shoulders, the world will ultimately take us at our own valuation."

Their most successful meeting after that in Philadelphia was in Detroit, a success to which Charlie Campbell substantially contributed. He helped set the stage conceptually by giving an interview in which he cautioned Detroiters that "pitying the poor blind" was "the bunk. . . . Help the blind to truly help themselves; that's much better than tears." He explained that the American Foundation, which was coming to solicit support from the city, was "the central research laboratory for all the agencies which are striving to help the blind. It gathers information from all over, sifts it, tries it out, and then in turn, passes the information back to us and every other agency for the blind."

At the same time he cautioned Helen, Annie and the Foundation not to expect too much from Detroit. The city's population had doubled in the last ten years. "That means that the great majority of the men here who are rich are young and still chiefly occupied with making and not giving money." Campbell, an old hand at the business, knew that the key to a successful Detroit campaign was to get the right man as chairman. He appealed to Charles B. Warren, who had been designated by President Coolidge as the new attorney general. He accepted on the condition that he would not have to ask for funds. "After he had met you," Campbell later wrote his "dear girls," "and became enthused, he was willing to do more and more of the appealing." He presided at the big meeting in Orchestra Hall. "Do you think that blindness is the greatest of afflictions?" he asked Helen, who read the question off his lips. "No, it is worse to have eyes and yet not see," Helen responded. It was a question she had been asked before, and her reply as usual brought a burst of applause.

Despite Campbell's pessimism about the younger men in the auto industry, the boxes in Orchestra Hall were filled. When Helen finished her speech, Warren presented her with a check for $10,000 as the first contribution. "I do not believe the donors would desire their names mentioned," he said, "but I shall tell you that this comes from Mr. and Mrs. Henry Ford." In all, the appeal brought in more than $40,000. Afterwards Helen held an impromptu reception backstage. One of those who came and embraced her was Madame Gabrilowitsch, whom Helen had known as little Clara Clemens in the days of her friendship with her father. Campbell wrote them after they moved on:

I talked with Mr. Warren this morning and he feels confident that we will be able to get quite a little more before the fund is closed here. As a matter of fact, he was so pepped up with the whole affair that, if he had been able to follow up his impulses, he would have tried to get more out of his audience last night. He says that practically all of the big givers in the hall were his personal friends and he would have felt justified in asking them to give more.

A few days later, still exultant, he reported another agreeable development as a result of their presence:

Whatever else has happened your trip has brought you in contact with the Fords. I rode downtown this afternoon with Mrs. Edsel Ford and she says her husband was delighted with your letter. I am convinced that you have interested him profoundly, not only in the work as a whole but in yourself and Teacher.

So impressed was the Foundation with Campbell's results that they tried once again—as they had in early 1924—to persuade him to ask for a leave of absence and work with the campaign. But his board turned him down. The Foundation should build its own campaign organization, he advised Migel:

Those who have worked with Miss Keller during a period of years realize the strange drawing power of her personality. There can be no question that, if your campaign can be put on a firm basis, Miss Keller will bring not only a good deal of money to the Foundation but she will sell the fact that such an organization exists, which, at the present time, is one of the difficulties that your campaign workers have to face.

As the Helen Keller caravan moved westward, Helen's "strange drawing power" manifested itself in a way that opened up to the Foundation a new road to usefulness. In Des Moines she spoke before a joint assembly of the Iowa Legislature and, wrote the governor to Migel afterwards, "convinced the Iowa Legislature of the importance of doing something for the blind that is permanent and lasting. I am enclosing under separate cover a copy of the message which I delivered to the Iowa Legislature and note what I said concerning our school for the Blind." Similarly, in Denver she addressed the Colorado Legislature and urged enactment of a bill for the state's blind. The legislators crowded the floor and packed the galleries to hear her plead that "the great need of the blind is not charity, but opportunity." The Foundation learned from these experiences that in Helen it had a formidable lobbyist. Before she left Denver she spoke at a luncheon of the Federation of Republican Women. Teacher sat to the right of the governor. He was, she told Nella Braddy, "a Ku Kluxer. She told him she was a Catholic, anti-Klan, a socialist" and looked at him with a mild defiance. A politician, he thrust out his hand and said "shake." "We came to understand what must be the exhaustion of campaigning political candidates," Helen wrote in *Midstream,* "but we had an advantage over the politicians: they met divided support while our cause appealed to all parties."

On reaching the West Coast they fell under the spell of its climate, and they decided to spend the summer in California. Teacher's sight was now almost down to 10 percent of a person's normal vision. She tired easily. A summer in California appealed to her, and she tried to get the Foundation to finance their working on the West Coast, but a foray into Hollywood brought little response except from Mary Pickford. And even the latter, although she invited them to spend a day on the set and spoke of producing "a picture depicting a blind girl" and giving part of the proceeds to Helen's work, sent only a small check in the end.

Despite Teacher's recommendation that they should be allowed to continue, Migel advised them that the executive board had decided to drop fund-raising activities until the autumn and directed Charles Hayes, the Foundation's director of information, who was managing their tour, to return to the office by June 15 at "the very latest."

To sweeten the rebuff he recalled their "little chat as to some extra compensation that might be given Helen on larger gifts that might be received through her instrumentality. This matter I shall arrange with you when I see you and same should amply cover any traveling expenses that you might incur in your return to the East."

Hauteur tinged Teacher's reply. The Lions Clubs had invited them to attend their convention in Cedar Point, Ohio, and were paying their railroad fares east. "I do remember your conversation with regard to extra compensation for larger gifts that might come directly through Helen. They have been very few and Helen is only too glad to contribute whatever she [sic] may think should come to her to the Endowment Fund." This gesture was relegated to a postscript of a four-page, single-spaced letter that on the whole was conciliatory and that analyzed the results of the campaign thus far. She acknowledged that their expectations—expectations, it will be recalled, that were mainly theirs, not Migel's—of raising a two-million-dollar fund "were naively childish" and unrealistic:

> You may recollect that when we first discussed methods of raising money, I thought we should get it from the people in small donations, and you, on the other hand, thought we should try to get large gifts from the rich. . . .
>
> The last few meetings, when we asked the people for pledges of twenty-five cents a month for a year, the response was spontaneous, and quite satisfactory. . . . When the people once get this idea, the Fund will grow rapidly, and then wealthy givers will see that our work has a just claim to be taken seriously. . . . An inexpensive little bank with Helen's name on it, and a few words of appeal, either on the bank or a slip of paper, would be sufficient.

If Migel needed additional proof of Helen's powerful appeal, her appearance before the International Convention of the Lions Clubs would have provided it. The Lions had already been exploring the possibilities of making assistance to the blind their special concern. Helen's appearance before their convention cemented the relationship. "I am your opportunity," she told the vast audience. "I am knocking at your door. I want to be adopted." She asked them to foster and sponsor the work of the Foundation. "I appeal to you, you who have your sight, your hearing, you who are brave and strong and kind. Will you not constitute yourselves Knights of the Blind in this crusade against darkness?"

The convention did so, and later, when Teacher was in one of her perennial rows with the Foundation over its treatment of the Helen Keller party, she was very punctilious about the details of how the relationship came about:

> While on the subject of 'Who's Who' in the Foundation, (yourself excepted, for I regard you as the moving spirit of the Foundation) Mr. Irwin has in my hearing taken to himself the credit of enlisting the cooperation of the Lions Clubs. To be sure, he is a member of that organization; but he certainly did not get the Lions as a body to support our work. Helen did that. We were in San Francisco in 1925

when letters began to come from secretaries and representatives of Lions Clubs begging us to attend the National Convention to be held at Cedar Point, Ohio that summer. At first we refused, as we were planning to spend the summer in California for my health; but the requests became so urgent that we decided to attend the Convention, whatever the personal inconvenience might be. We went and talked to five thousand Lions. After the meeting they unanimously elected Helen honorary member of the Lions, and pledged themselves to be her knights in the crusade against darkness. We returned to California at our own expense. The Lions paid only for the trip east, assuming that we were coming home. Since 1925 we have sent books and photographs and special letters to Lions Clubs at our own expense. If the truth were known that we have spent a considerable part of our munificent salary on postage and courtesies!

Even the new-comers to the Foundation are better paid than Helen is. And may I remind you that when the money-raising tour ended in June, 1926, fifteen months elapsed in which she received—not a penny!

While they were in California they visited the "magic garden" in Santa Rosa of the famed plant breeder Luther Burbank. The latter was then seventy-six, a mystic as well as a wizard at coaxing Nature's secrets out of her. He came down the path to greet them "with beautiful courtesy" and took them through the "rows and rows of plants." He guided Helen's hands over leaf and blossom, including the spineless cactus that he had developed. Helen found his personality—part seer, part naturalist—immensely sympathetic:

> He has the rarest of gifts, the receptive spirit of a child. When plants talk to him, he listens. That is why they tell him so many things about themselves. Only a wise child can understand the language of flowers and trees. Mr. Burbank feels the individuality, or genius of the plant—that something which invents, changes, urges and adds or drops characteristics as the plant advances. So he encourages the plant to put forth the best of which it is capable. In the same way, he says, every human being should be given a chance to grow in freedom and develop his powers according to the inner law of his nature.

He took them into his house, introduced them to his wife and daughter, even gave Helen a contribution to the Foundation. "Your work is so wonderful, so full of the creative energy of life," she wrote him afterwards. He confirmed her own outlook on life: "There is no room for pessimism or indifference in a philosophy like yours, so instinct with the joy of growth and the vigor of creation. O, what a different world this will be when men understand as you do the sweet law of growth, and express it in acts, in education, in their lives." Six months later he was dead. "I marvel at the deep sense of loneliness I experienced when I heard of his death," she wrote Mrs. Burbank. "I talked with him but twice, once for just a few minutes. This, and a few letters are all that gives me a right to call him 'friend.' Yet it was the sweetest friendship that one could wish. . . ."

After a summer in California Helen, Annie and Polly returned home via a leisurely trip by steamship through the Panama Canal. The latter was "a marvellous achievement, and it makes me very proud of my country," Helen wrote, and the city of Balboa was "clean and well planned, with splendid public buildings, hospitals and laboratories." They had a pleasant stopover in Havana, but on the whole the cruise was a disappointment:

> The heat was terrific, and in spite of the glorious blue ocean and the magnificent sunsets, we felt the monotony of the voyage keenly. We read, walked the deck, talked with a few people, ate almost incessantly and drank forbidden sunshine which was sold on the ship openly—and it was an American ship too! Strange, isn't it, that Americans at sea should be permitted to drink all they want to, and yet when they get in sight of land, they must not look on wine that is red or white, or whiskey that is old and good, or beer that is the only proper drink when you are dying of thirst.

Teacher must have practiced an unwonted abstinence, since Helen also reported to her sister that she had lost fifty pounds and as a result walked longer distances than before and no longer tired so quickly. They returned to a house full of plasterers. A ceiling upstairs had fallen in, and water had leaked through to the hall and living room. Beset by costly house repairs and their usual splurges at Fifth Avenue dress and hat shops, the need for money again asserted itself imperiously. Their sense of living a hand-to-mouth existence coincided with negotiations to renew their contract with the Foundation. "I never think about money until I haven't any," Teacher wrote in an autobiographical sketch at about this time.

> I dislike acquisitiveness, arrogance and authority. Yet there are times when I appear to condone them. John Macy used to say to me, 'You resemble the rich in the vulgarity of your tastes. You desire an extravagant house, the finest apparel, the fastest horse and automobile, expensive food, pedigreed dogs and more things than I can enumerate that are the blood of the poor.'

To Annie's chagrin the Major had not personally greeted them on their return home. But at last he was coming to Forest Hills for a talk. Annie alerted him to be ready for a tough bargaining session with a lengthy letter detailing their financial problems. "I realize that $2,000 per month seems a very liberal payment for soliciting funds," she began. It embarrassed her to have to talk about their needs, and if they were "financially independent, nothing would induce us to accept a salary for what we are doing." Out of Helen's annual income of $7,000 one person could live comfortably, "but she is peculiarly dependent on the services of others. Her limitations and my imperfect sight make the assistance of a third person absolutely necessary." Appearances at luncheons, receptions and public meetings necessitated "very nice clothes and a good many of them. . . . Obviously we have to go to the best hotels. . . . Another very considerable item of expense is taxicab and automobile hire." Their house in Forest Hills was not well built, and they would like to buy a sounder building that had just come on the market across the street. They could manage its purchase if they returned to vaudeville, and there had been overtures from the Orpheum circuit. She had "great confidence" in Migel's judgment, she asserted, and hoped that when he came "we shall be able to reach a sensible solution."

The negotiations were lengthy. Although the Major, sensitive to criticisms that the Foundation was spending too heavily on staff, especially on the "Helen Keller party," was determined on economy, the first discussion did not go too badly. Helen and Annie agreed to continue to work for the Foundation on the old basis of $2,000 a month, especially as he suggested that ways might be found to provide them with additional income outside of the budget. Teacher delighted Migel with a proposal that the 1926 campaign open in Washington, perhaps in the D.A.R.'s Constitution Hall, "where we could secure national recognition immediately—with President Coolidge presiding. . . ."

But having signed the contract, Teacher and Helen discovered that the emphasis of the 1926 campaign would be on securing memberships in the Foundation, not contributions to the Helen Keller Endowment Fund:

> When I learned last night that we were no longer to work for the Fund, but for memberships I felt as if I had been actually knocked down and stamped upon. When I told Helen Keller what was expected of her, she was indignant. She expressed astonishment that you had not mentioned the change of plans when you talked with us here or in your office. I signed the agreement you had drawn up with the impression that it was a continuation of last year's efforts, and there is nothing in the agreement to indicate a new objective. We cannot understand why you did not tell us of your decision to work for memberships. . . .

They discovered another misapprehension—there would not be additional financial help outside the contract. Teacher poured her anger into another letter to Migel, ". . . your way of disposing of our serious difficulties is a great strain of friendship." What she was not able to say to him face to face, she punched out on the typewriter:

> A man of your imperious disposition is apt to regard a different point of view as more or less unfriendly. Nevertheless, I am going to tell you that your treatment of Helen Keller and me does not confirm the high opinion I had formed of you. Your words and deeds do not harmonize. While expressing a profound appreciation of our endeavors to raise the Endowment Fund for the Foundation, you bargain with us like a railroad magnate employing stokers or road-menders. When talking business you apparently have little sense of the nature of the work we are doing for the Foundation, or of anything except securing our labor as cheaply as possible.
>
> Of the need of economy no one has a more realizing sense than I have; but it is a mistake to begin economizing on the driving power of the engine. The salary we have accepted, though large, I am aware in the abstract, is smaller than what you should offer for the services of three persons one of whom, probably is the only person in the world who could carry such an undertaking through. . . .
>
> The large gifts from Mr. Mather, Mr. Bok, the Fords, Mr. Doheny, Mrs. Alexander and many others were undoubtedly tributes to Helen

Keller. Yet not a word of greeting or expression of appreciation have we received from the Board of Directors, nor any official recognition of the three thousand dollars which she contributed to the Fund by not accepting a percentage on the Mather, Bok and Ford gifts. . . .

You expressed surprise that rich men have responded so feebly to our appeal. Your own attitude towards our personal problems illustrates and answers the question. It was natural for us to assume that you would be interested, and really desire to lighten our burden. Yet you turned us down quite as inexplicably as financiers have done with the Foundation. . . .

We deeply appreciate what you have done for the blind. We realize fully how generous you have been. We also understand fully that you are under no obligation whatever to assist us personally. We regret that we trespassed so far upon your patience as to trouble you with a recital of our affairs, and I assure you that we shall not annoy you in that way again.

Again Migel dumped the negotiations with the Forest Hills collective into Bob Irwin's capable hands. They had arrived at an agreement, the latter reported wearily, "after two very protracted conferences with Mrs. Macy." Memberships would be the primary objective, but those secured at the Helen Keller meetings would be known as "Helen Keller memberships" and the individual gifts obtained through the efforts of Helen and Teacher would be placed in the Helen Keller Endowment Fund. He had also agreed that "Mrs. Macy be given an opportunity from time to time to confer with those in control of the Foundation's activities regarding plans for the campaign."

The terms of this truce between Teacher and the Major suggest that money aside, she was as concerned with using Helen to assert her power and authority over the Foundation's policies as she was with the proper approach to funding assistance to the blind. Since she herself strongly advocated a drive for small gifts, including the distribution of Helen Keller penny banks, her objections to a membership drive seem inconsistent and self-contradictory.

While these matters were being ironed out, the reliable Ida Hirst-Gifford went to Washington to prepare the opening meeting of the 1926 campaign. The DAR was most cooperative, hailing Helen in a resolution as "truly a heroic figure," but Constitution Hall was not available. Dr. Gilbert Grosvenor, son-in-law of Dr. Bell, agreed to serve as chairman, and the list of patrons included Chief Justice and Mrs. Taft and four other justices, six members of the President's Cabinet, among them Andrew Mellon and Herbert Hoover, a glittering array of ambassadors, the speaker of the House, the Vice-President, and the president general of the DAR; and while President Coolidge found it impossible to attend, he did receive Helen and Teacher before the meeting, and Mrs. Coolidge—who had been a teacher of the deaf and dumb—received them the following day.

Helen's droll encounter with the taciturn President was caught by the press. Helen referred to the letters that the President had written as honorary president of the Foundation and commented: "Silence is golden, speech is silver. Your words on behalf of the blind are bright jewels in my dark casket." That was the purple prose. She hesitated, then plunged ahead: "They say you are cold, but you are not. You are a dear President."

Coolidge thawed. "You have a wonderful personality and I am glad to meet you," he replied, as Helen with her fingers to his lips reported his words. She and the President then posed for the photographers on the snow-covered lawn. From the White House Helen drove to Capitol Hill to call on Thomas D. Schall, the blind senator from Minnesota whom she already had met. As the reporters watched, the two conversed animatedly. He was still recovering from a campaign in which he had made two hundred eighty-seven speeches, he said.

"What did you find to say two hundred eighty-seven times?" Helen inquired.

"Oh, I just said the same things over," he replied.

"That's just what I'd do too," she laughingly rejoined.

She expressed a wish to see Senator Borah, a leading advocate of disarmament (though an opponent of the League of Nations), and Senator Schall immediately called him on the telephone. "I would come further than your office to meet Helen Keller," Borah replied gallantly. After being photographed with both the senators, Helen clasped their hands and exclaimed, "This is a league of friends against a league of force," and kissed Borah on both cheeks. At tea that day she was entertained by another Washington eminence, Mrs. James Wadsworth, Jr., the daughter of John Hay, who had been Lincoln's secretary and Theodore Roosevelt's secretary of state.

The days in Washington accomplished precisely what Teacher had hoped—the Foundation's 1926 campaign was launched with great éclat. They also demonstrated anew Helen's indispensability to the Foundation. Teacher did not permit Migel to overlook their success, and when the Foundation appeared to be taking credit for the publicity, she wrote him:

Miss Hill [in charge of publicity for the Foundation in Washington] did not arrange for the picture of Helen with the President. She has a letter from Mr. Sanders, the President's secretary, addressed to Mrs. Hicks, in which he said he would arrange the meeting, etc, etc. But when we reached the White House at twenty minutes of twelve, we found that nothing had been done about it. You should know that every day at noon the President receives the public. So there was no special compliment in meeting Miss Keller. Mr. Sanders was reluctant about troubling the President to pose for a photograph. Mr. Earl of the "A.A.P." went to Mr. Sanders and told him about the importance of the publicity, not from the Foundation point of view, but as news. Mr. Sanders told him to go out and get the photographers together. Mr. Earl got some of them, and the President unwillingly consented. Mr. Earl was the only one who got the picture of Helen with her arm around the President. Afterwards I talked to the press and gave verbatim what Helen had said to the President, and what he had said to her. The reporters flew to their various offices, and the news was all over the country, and the pictures too, when we returned to the hotel three o'clock. When we left the White House, Mr. Earl took us to call on Mr. Schall. This was Mr. Earl's suggestion, not Miss Hill's. While in Mr. Schall's office, Helen expressed a desire to meet Senator Borah, whom she had admired for years. This was arranged by Mr. Schall, and the pictures were taken by Mr. Earl.

The meeting with Mrs. Coolidge was also rather inadequately handled. It took all the experience at my command to have it go off as well as it did. Before our party—Miss Thomson, Helen and myself —had left the White House grounds, a *Times* reporter jumped on the running-board and got our account of the interview. It was in his office in New York before we reached the hotel and told Miss Hill about it. Miss Hill's follow-up stories were very nice; but the account most pleasing to the Coolidges was the one written by Miss Corinne Rich in one of the Hearst papers—I think the *Post*—I have not the time to look it up now. When the President of the United States and the first lady of the land meet an international character and converse, that makes front page news and nothing short of a national calamity could have stopped the Washington publicity. But Miss Hill will have other opportunities to show her ability—and I am sure she must have real ability to have pleased you.

A meeting with the President, the resolution of the DAR and the gala meeting presided over by Dr. Grosvenor might be thought to have discouraged the superpatriots. But in February, Fred. R. Marvin, "Editor-in-Chief" of a patriotic publication, circulated a letter to his correspondents around the country impugning Helen Keller's loyalty. He enclosed two affidavits from men who "stand high in Milwaukee both in business life and as officers of the Intelligence Department of the Reserve Corps." One affidavit noted that in the Fern Room of the Pfister Hotel in Milwaukee, Helen replied to a query about her position on communism that "she is actively interested in the doctrines and teachings of Communism, Socialism and Soviet Russia, and that the red flag is the true symbol of the welfare of mankind." The other affidavit asserted that when Miss Keller was asked whether she knew that the avowed purpose of the Communists was to overthrow the government "and to raise the red flag above the White House," she had answered "in effect that she favored the red flag because to her it meant 'Brotherhood.' "

Marvin added some charges of his own. Helen Keller was on the national committee of the American Civil Liberties Union, "a notoriously radical movement" whose "moving spirit," Roger N. Baldwin, just recently had been toastmaster at a banquet given for Elizabeth Gurley Flynn, a member of the IWW and the Communist party. Marvin reminded his correspondents that Major Pond had "dropped Helen Keller from his list of speakers because she was too radical. Miss Keller herself is probably not at fault. . . . Her popularity and her prominence are being clearly used by those who would destroy this Government." He urged his correspondents, particularly women, to think carefully before inviting "radical speakers" into their communities.

None of this affected the campaign. At the end of May, a successful if exhausting tour completed, Teacher received a placatory note from Migel:

Since attending the meeting in Washington, I have realized more than ever the tremendous task which the *modus operandi* of our campaign devolves upon you.

I appreciate fully how much you and Helen and Miss Thomson are giving of yourselves—mentally and physically,—and as I study the schedule of meetings from time to time, and follow you from place to place, meeting after meeting, I feel more and more keenly how indefatigably you are exerting your energies for the Cause, and how deeply we are indebted to you.

Although net figures are not available at present, your labors have produced most encouraging results,—but far more important than calculation in dollars and cents, is the educational value of your tour, in presenting to the public more forcefully and interestingly than anything else could possibly do, the tremendous opportunities open to the Blind.

Dr. Van Dyke and others have expressed the firm belief that this is truly the most important effect of our campaign, and the most permanent.

The campaign ended in Birmingham. From there Helen and Teacher went to spend several weeks with Mildred and her family in Montgomery. Polly returned to Forest Hills before sailing to Scotland. Teacher was very concerned about being inadequately dressed:

We have been terribly embarrassed over our clothes. Some friends of the Fulenwiders invited us to a barbecue, and we had nothing to wear, except the dresses we travelled in. We did look out of the picture, every one was so daintily dressed with pretty hats. It's strange, isn't it, that we never seem to have suitable apparel when the time comes, and I suppose we pay more for clothes than most people.

The barbecue was a gala affair. The governor of Alabama and the mayor of Montgomery were among the hundred guests. The garden was aglow with Japanese lanterns, and there were huge masses of calla lilies, red, pink and yellow. "I don't believe you have any idea how delicious barbecued meat is," Helen wrote in a letter to Polly, which was otherwise full of such instructions as to pay the life insurance premium and to "be sure and have the bank-book balanced when you send it, so that Teacher will know what is in the bank."

The chief note sounded in Teacher's letter to Polly was one of weariness and boredom:

I'm afraid this letter is as rocky and barren as my life looks to me at present. But don't think my feelings have anything to do with my environment. Every one here is very dear and kind, and they are trying to do everything in the world to make life pleasant for us. But somehow things have got a wrong twist in them—or perhaps it is truer to say I have got a wrong twist in me. For the first time in my life the game doesn't interest me—doesn't seem worth while. But enough of this.

Although they were in Montgomery, their next year's contract with the Foundation was already under discussion. Teacher and Helen let it be known that they could not afford to go on the road again for $2,000 a month and that they were receiving lucrative lecture offers. Bob Irwin proposed to the Foundation's treasurer, Herbert H. White, who with Migel away was in charge, that "Helen Keller be placed on the staff of the Foundation, at $5,000 a year, in addition to the amount paid when on the road." But Teacher and Helen did not know of this. And when White sent Helen a bonus check of $1,000 for her previous winter's work, Teacher fired off a characteristic salvo. The letter was ostensibly from Helen and flabbergasted White, a top executive of the Connecticut Mutual Life Insurance Company, whose work at the Foundation, like Migel's, was a labor of love. Her first impulse had been to pocket the check, she wrote him from Montgomery, "for I felt that Mrs. Macy and I had earned it." But she also agreed with him that it in no way compensated them for the extra meetings and the two large donations they had obtained. As they had explained before, "every cent of our salary went for expenses." Mrs. Macy received no separate compensation.

> Mr. Migel has always referred to her as if she were on the payroll of the Foundation; and when the Executive Board wished to express the appreciation of Mrs. Macy's and my services to the cause of the blind, it included Miss Thomson on equal terms with us in its vote of thanks. If the Board wished to honor Mr. Migel for his contributions to the Foundation, would it inscribe the name of his secretary on parchment in a similar manner?

The Foundation's attitude toward the two of them, Helen continued, "has always been that of an employer. It has assumed that we were for sale and has negotiated to buy us as cheaply as possible." But they were not for sale, and in fact were disinclined to work for the Foundation next year.

"Anyway I am returning the check because Mrs. Macy and I feel that it would in some subtle way hamper us, and curtail our freedom of decision when the time comes to discuss plans for the future." In a letter to Polly two days earlier, Teacher described the situation more matter-of-factly.

> Mr. White, the Treasurer, sent Helen a check for a thousand dollars, which we returned because we are not at all sure that we shall continue with the Foundation next year. If I can possibly see any way of staying at home and paying expenses, I shall do so.

A nonplussed Mr. White forwarded Helen's letter and the reply he proposed to make to Bob Irwin, who was in Missouri. He telegraphed back that White's reply handled Helen's letter admirably. WOULD OFFER CHECK AS YOU SUGGEST SEND LETTER TO KELLER IN BRAILLE STOP THIS LETTER FROM KELLER IS TEACHERS COMPOSITION DOUBT KELLERS KNOWING MUCH ABOUT IT.

White's letter was wholly conciliatory. He apologized for anything that he might have said that disturbed her "natural and rightful feelings of sensitivity and self-respect." The officers and directors of the Foundation appreciated her and Mrs. Macy's efforts:

> We are plain business men with the welfare of a struggling institution at heart and I fear we may have failed to understand clearly your point of view and the thoughts and impressions that would naturally come to you in your relation with the Foundation. . . . Speaking personally, it seems as if the Almighty Father has chosen you, set you apart as it were, to lead the people out of darkness, to give them hope and courage, to show them the way of release. The marvelous love and devotion of Mrs. Macy to which you so readily and intelligently responded have qualified you both for His beneficent purpose. . . .

There had been no "bargain and sale" approach to arranging the terms of their cooperation. At the time, he recalled, the terms seemed "fair and satisfactory to all. If the estimates have been found incorrect it is because of our inability to forecast clearly unforeseen contingencies." The check was still at her disposal, his letter ended. She should feel safe to use it without loss of self-respect. It would not commit her to the Foundation any further than she wished.

Teacher got scant sympathy from Charlie Campbell when she reported the new flare-up in their relations with the Foundation. Although Mr. Migel had been away and had not figured in these exchanges, she evidently held him responsible. "I realize that you do not feel comfortable toward Mr. Migel," Campbell wrote her. "I am sure you will not misunderstand me when I say I regret this. Whatever one may think of Mr. Migel's way of doing things one has to admit that he has been very much interested in the work for the blind and I cannot help feeling that that interest is genuinely unselfish. He has nothing personal to gain by doing anything at all for the Foundation or the blind in general."

The tempest abated. The executive board met in the fall and offered the Helen Keller party two thousand dollars a month for the six-month campaign in 1927 plus a salary of five thousand dollars for Helen for additional services. It was "a tremendous temptation," Helen replied, but her answer was no:

> I had already made up my mind when your letter came not to continue the campaign for the Foundation this year. After thinking the matter over all summer, I decided that I owed it to myself and to others beside the blind to lay off for a year and bring my autobiography up to date. Doubleday and Page have been imploring me to do this for a long time, and my friends everywhere urge me not to put it off any longer. Naturally, I am desirous to complete my life-story while I am in a mood for it. The only reason I have not done it before now is, I did not have sufficient income to stay at home and write. Mrs. Macy and I had to lecture, or appear in Vaudeville or work for the Foundation in order to live with the degree of comfort we have always enjoyed. I need not tell you that such various activities unfit one for writing a book. When I am on the road, I can do nothing outside of the daily routine, and when we stop work in June, I am too weary and nervous to think. I do not even feel like reading, not to mention sorting the material which has accumulated during twenty-five years!
>
> The money difficulty remains the same. Even now I hesitate to say no to the Foundation's splendid offer. However, it must be no this time; for it is now or never. But when I have finished my book, I shall be willing to take to the road again if by that time the Foundation has

not completed the Endowment Fund and wants me to continue the campaign.

The Foundation's executive board responded magnanimously. By a resolution it expressed its regret and acceptance of Helen's decision. It hoped that Helen and Teacher would continue their active interest in the Foundation's work and offered an honorarium of two thousand dollars for four articles by Helen to be used by the Foundation in furthering its work for the blind.

XXXI

"Six Hands"

"That you should bid my book live makes me feel as Esther must have felt when Ahasuerus held out his staff to her."—Helen to John Macy

As far back as 1921 Doubleday, now located in Garden City, impressed with the continuing sale of Helen's *The Story of My Life,* had urged Helen to go on with her story. The Doubledays—"Effendi," the founding father of the house, and his brother Russell—considered the publication of *The Story of My Life* one of the "high points" in their publishing experience. This was high praise from a house that published Rudyard Kipling and Joseph Conrad.

Helen wanted to continue, yet dreaded doing so. She advanced many reasons. How could she do so without interrupting her work for the blind, which she considered more important? And even if she did take a leave of absence from the Foundation, there would be constant interruptions; and a writer needed peace and solitude to concentrate on her thoughts. Such a book, moreover, would have to be about herself, and she "did not care to bring that subject up again." So Nella Braddy Henney, an editorial assistant at Doubleday whose regular services were placed at Helen's disposal at the end of 1926, explained Helen's resistance to the project.

There was, however, another reason—Helen's doubts about her competence as a writer. They had emerged briefly in 1917 when Teacher had reproached her for putting aside an article on suffrage.* Although she

*See page 453.

considered herself a writer, from the time that John Macy had left the Wrentham household she had published very little. It had been the three of them—Helen with her unique experience of coping with her limitations and her assurance of a large audience for whatever she wrote, Annie with her Celtic gift of lyricism and pungent phrasing, John with his sense of structure and style—who had produced the series of books, beginning with *The Story of My Life* and ending with *Out of the Dark,* that had established Helen's reputation as a writer. And without John's trenchant editorial blue pencil both women doubted that they could carry on Helen's autobiography. But they knew that they had a story to tell, a story almost as remarkable as the original one; and when Nella Braddy—young, clearly competent and sympathetic—appeared at Forest Hills ready to assist them while remaining on the Doubleday payroll, they put aside their fears and set to work.

But not, as it turned out, on the autobiography. Helen decided that she first had to do a book about Emanuel Swedenborg, the Swedish seer and mystic to whose doctrines she had long been a convert. "It was a chance for me to escape from a task that I dreaded," she wrote of this detour from the writing of *Midstream* to what was for her a labor of love—love for Swedenborg and for William Hitz, who had introduced her to his teachings and whom she would describe in *My Religion* as "the friend I loved best next to my Teacher."

The invitation to do the book came from the Reverend Paul Sperry, minister of the New Jerusalem congregation in Washington and secretary of the General Convention of the New Jerusalem. (The church founded by Swedenborg's followers is called the Church of the New Jerusalem or the New Church.) There had been an upsurge of interest in Swedenborg, he wrote her on August 13, 1926, and the New Church wanted to publish a book about him and his gospel "by a person well qualified and also well known to the general public." For six weeks Helen did not reply, and Sperry wrote again. To this new query she answered that she was indeed interested. She had been trying to decide whether she could do the book he wanted:

> I began trying to clarify in my own mind my impression of Swedenborg and his works. Had I a clear conception of his personality? How could I explain to an impatient and skeptical public his extraordinary claim of having been for twenty-seven years in daily communication with the spiritual world? . . . I read everything I have in raised print

on Swedenborg, and then, I confess, I felt overwhelmed by the subject. . . .

Yet I was reluctant to tell you I could not do it because it would be such a joy to me if I might be the instrument of bringing Swedenborg to a world that is spiritually deaf and blind. I put off from day to day writing to you with the hope that I might have something worthwhile to send you—a plan, at least, of a book. I have written about forty pages, approaching the subject from different angles; but I am not satisfied. I am still listening for the right word that shall dispel all darkness and confusion.

She was prepared to undertake the book, her letter went on, and thought she could finish it rather quickly. But she would need help, someone to look up the passages she wanted in her Braille books and copy them out for her, and could he "suggest ways of constructing the book[?] For construction is not one of my strong points."

A shiver of anticipation went through the officials of the New Church. They were more than ready to provide her with the assistance she wanted, and what would she desire as remuneration? An editorial secretary was found. It is not clear who provided her, and she was not very satisfactory. Nella Braddy helped while inventorying for *Midstream* what the Forest Hills files contained. She had little interest in the Swedenborg project. Neither did Teacher. She considered Swedenborg's teachings a kind of "gifted madness." Helen described her attitude in *Teacher*:

I did not expect help from her, as she had no faith in religion, and I could have cried when she put herself in my place, imagining what my faith must mean, and spelled into my hand long articles on the Swedish seer and the New Church, of which he did not wish to be regarded as the founder. She also read me how his writings had influenced Elizabeth Barrett Browning, William Dean Howells, and the elder James, father of William and Henry James. I had already read in Braille Emerson's *Representative Men,* which includes Swedenborg.

By the end of the year Helen had accumulated a manuscript of 110 pages. Sperry asked to see it, but Helen resisted turning it over to him. Sperry reassured her. "It is perfectly natural that you should be dissatisfied with what you have written out the first time. I think most of us ministers have that feeling every week." He was sure that what she had written was "spontaneous, unlabored and fresh. [It] is just what we want."

Although she declined to show the manuscript to Sperry, she did submit it to Doubleday. Sperry hastened to Forest Hills. "It was a great satisfaction to me to find that Miss Keller could read my lips and that we could therefore converse directly without troubling you," he wrote Teacher afterwards. He hoped that when the publishers were through with reading the manuscript either they or Teacher would send it to him at once. Doubleday found that the personal note prevailed over the theology. It was a moving human document, and they wanted to publish it. That pleased Helen. She preferred that it be issued by a regular publisher, and evidently she received no other remuneration than the regular royalty.

She finally sent the manuscript to Sperry, still filled with anxiety over what she conceived to be its inadequacies. "Now that the fabric is finished, I submit it to you for your inspection, not with a thought that you will find it a cloth of gold, but with the earnest hope that the love and reverence with which I cherish the image of Swedenborg in my heart may shine like a light in what I have written." Doubleday published *My Religion* in October 1927. She had not heard from either Effendi or Russell Doubleday, and such was her insecurity that she sent a telegram asking Russell whether he had read the manuscript. MY IMPRESSION GATHERED FROM A HURRIED GLANCE AT THE BOOK IS THAT YOU UNDERRATE IT, Russell Doubleday telegraphed back. And long before the book appeared, Effendi in a graceful gesture of approbation sent her a check "for comforts for yourself and your immediate household" and promised her a like amount each year. Russell sent her another check in January 1928, royalties on the sale of *The Story of My Life.* "I am very glad to see that *My Religion* is doing so well. I knew that was a good book and was sure that the public would appreciate it. Let me say again that we are so happy to be your publisher, and I am personally delighted to have been able to work with you." They were more eager than ever "to give the waiting public your new book."

In her little book, which became a standard text of the New Church, she emphasized the liberating aspects of Swedenborg's teachings (see Epilogue). They were a release from the harsh rigors of Calvinism with its bleak doctrine of predestination and of a stern rather than a loving Deity. Swedenborg's writings also were a blessed counterpoint to what she conceived to be the aridities of eighteenth-century rationalism. In its positive aspects Swedenborg's teaching and personal experience confirmed her own insights—that the reality of the world does not derive from the senses but from the spirit, that the world of sensible things, even the Bible, must be construed as symbolic emanations of God's wisdom, goodness and love. "The more I learn, the less I think I know, and the more I understand of my sense experience, the more I perceive its shortcomings and its inadequacy as a basis of life."

Swedenborg's "twenty-seven stout octavo volumes" were for her "crammed full of details of definite contacts with the spiritual universe" that lay on the other side of the veil of the senses. His reading of the Bible as metaphor, as a parabolic account "of the spiritual life of the race from the beginning down to the Jewish era," revolutionized her understanding of that book. "He did not make a new Bible but the Bible all new." She dealt with Swedenborg's claim to have been in constant intercourse with another world for more than a quarter of a century:

> That is nothing new to my experience. Daily I place implicit faith in my friends with eyes and ears, and they tell me how often their senses deceive and lead them astray. Yet out of their evidence I gather countless precious truths with which I build my world, and my soul is enabled to picture the beauty of the sky and listen to the song of birds. All about me may be silence and darkness, yet within me, in the spirit, is music and brightness, and colour flashes through all my thoughts. So out of Swedenborg's evidence from beyond earth's frontier I construct a world that shall measure up to the high claims of my spirit when I quit this wonderful but imprisoning house of clay.

She does not know whether she has the "mystic sense," but she does have a faculty

> that brings distant objects within the cognizance of the blind so that even the stars seem to be at our very door. This sense relates me to the spiritual world. It surveys the limited experience I gain from an imperfect touch world, and presents it to my mind for spiritualization. This sense reveals the Divine to the human in me, it forms a bond between earth and the Great Beyond, between now and eternity, between God and man. It is speculative, intuitive, reminiscent. There is not only an objective physical world, but also an objective spiritual world.

She had been particularly helped by a paragraph from Swedenborg's *Arcana Coelestia:*

> It is the interior man that sees and perceives what goes on without him, and from this interior source the sense-experience has its life; for from no other than this subjective source is there any faculty of feeling or sensation. But the fallacy that the sense comes from without is of such a nature and so common that the natural mind cannot rid itself of it, not even the rational mind, until it can think abstractly from sense.

Her final page was really the key to her whole adherence to Swedenborgianism. To her the natural world is vague and remote, while the spiritual word was open and intense:

> I cannot imagine myself without religion. I could as easily fancy a living body without a heart. To one who is deaf and blind, the spiritual world offers no difficulty. Nearly everything in the natural world is as vague, as remote from my senses as spiritual things seem to the minds of most people. I plunge my hands deep into my large Braille volumes containing Swedenborg's teachings, and withdraw them full of the secrets of the spiritual world. The inner, or 'mystic,' sense, if you like, gives me vision of the unseen. . . .

She prefaced her little book with a psalm of exaltation to Swedenborg, quoting first the line "Heaven unbarred to her her lofty gates":

> O light-bringer of my blindness,
> O spirit never far removed!
> Ever when the hour of travail deepens,
> Thou art near;
> Set in my soul like jewels bright
> Thy words of holy meaning,
> Till Death with gentle hand shall lead me
>   to the Presence I have loved—
> My torch in darkness here,
> My joy eternal there.

The Reverend John Haynes Holmes, a preacher of the social gospel who in the twenties had turned the Community Church into an ecumenical

John Albert Macy circa 1900. Photograph credit: Pach Brothers, Cambridge,
Massachusetts. Courtesy of the AFB.
He had a sense of humor as well as a seriousness of purpose.

Helen and Anne Sullivan
Macy circa 1914.
Courtesy of the PSB.

Helen and Anne Sullivan Macy,
circa 1915. Photograph credit:
Barlow Studio, Seymour, Indiana.
*"She was not a woman suffragist and
I was. She was very conservative
at the time."*

Helen, John Albert Macy, and Anne Sullivan Macy circa 1914.
Courtesy of the AFB.
"Think of my happiness! I am to have two teachers instead of one."

Helen, making up for a vaudeville act, circa 1920.
Courtesy of the AFB.

Helen, Anne Sullivan Macy, and
Polly Thomson, dressed for a vaudeville act.
Courtesy of the AFB.
She and Teacher made paid appearances.

Hollywood: (l. to r.) Anne Sullivan Macy, Helen, Mary Pickford,
Polly Thomson, Charles B. Hayes, Douglas Fairbanks, and an unknown man.
Courtesy of the AFB.

Hollywood, 1918: Polly Thomson, Anne Sullivan Macy,
Helen, and Charlie Chaplin. Photograph credit: Culver.
Courtesy of the AFB.

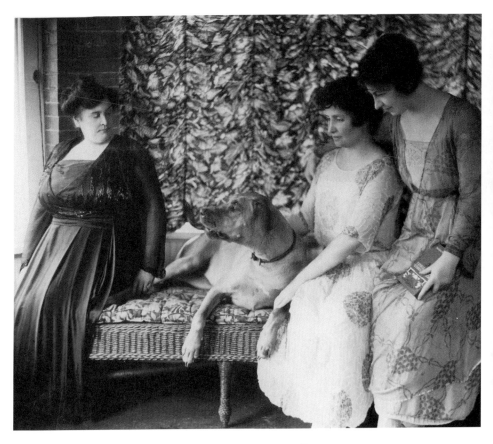

Anne, Helen, and Polly at Forest Hills, circa 1920.
Courtesy of the AFB.

Helen on board ship near the Orkney
Islands, 1932. Courtesy of the AFB.
*The captain manipulated the
smoke from his funnel so that it traced
a large K in the sky.*

Helen, George Bernard Shaw, and Lady Astor, 1932.
Photograph credit: International News Photo. Courtesy of the AFB.
". . . he was not particularly gracious to me that afternoon."

ABOVE: Helen, blinded veteran, and Polly Thomson, November 25, 1946.
Photograph credit: War Ministry of Italy. Courtesy of the AFB.
"The crowning experience of my life."

BELOW: Helen visiting wounded soldiers, circa 1946. Courtesy of the PSB
and Keith Henney. *"They do not want to be treated as heroes.*
They want to be able to live naturally, and to be treated as human beings."

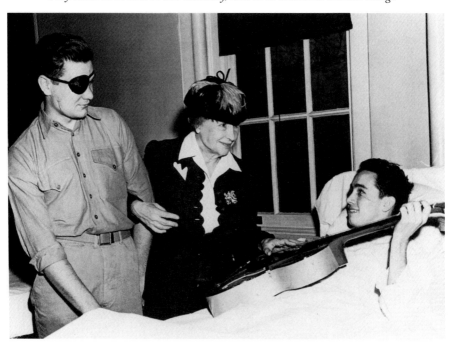

Helen at dedication of Anne
Sullivan Macy Foundation,
Radcliffe College, June 1960.
Courtesy of the AFB.

RIGHT: Helen touching statue of
Kanjinwaje, Nara, Japan, 1948.
Courtesy of the AFB.
". . .the Great Buddha which
I was the first woman
in the world to touch. . . ."

BELOW: Helen, Martha Graham,
and dancers at Martha Graham's
studio, circa 1954. Scene from film
Helen Keller in *Her Story*,
produced by Nancy Hamilton.
Courtesy of the AFB.

Helen reading braille, 1950.
Photograph credit: Erich Kastan, N.Y. Courtesy of the AFB.

LEFT: Helen and Calvin Coolidge,
January 1926.
Courtesy of the AFB.
*"They say you are cold, but you are
not. You are a dear President."*

BELOW: Helen and Henry Wallace
at Madison Square Garden,
September 21, 1944. International
News Photo. Courtesy of the AFB.
*She regarded him as the authentic
legatee of Roosevelt's policies.*

BELOW: Helen, Polly Thomson,
and Prime Minister Nehru,
1955. Punjab Photo
Service, New Delhi.
Courtesy of the AFB.
*"Proudly I shall cherish in
memory the quiet evening
we spent with you and your
daughter, Indira, just as if we
were members of your family."*

At "Chip-Chop," home of Katharine Cornell, on Martha's Vineyard: (l. to r.)
Joseph P. Lash, Trude Lash, Eleanor Roosevelt, Helen, Katharine Cornell,
circa 1954. Photograph credit: Nancy Hamilton. Courtesy of the AFB.

Eleanor Roosevelt and Helen, February 1955.
Courtesy of the New York Public Library and the AFB.

Helen, shortly before her 80th birthday, 1960.
Photograph credit: Wide World Photos. Courtesy of the AFB.

center, wrote that Helen's book clarified Swedenborg's teaching "as does no other book that I have ever read. It commends with a sweet persuasion and, at times, a passionate conviction."

The New Church people were delighted with the book, but Helen was unhappy about it. When she read it in embossed form, her disappointment intensified: "I am particularly chagrined over the construction, which seems to me dismally chaotic." She hoped, however, that the book could be recommended to the sightless so that they could "derive some of the happiness I have from Swedenborg's interpretation of the Bible. I think no other writer ever had so profound an understanding of the realities of the spirit and the inner faculties which take the place of sight and hearing."

My Religion has often been reprinted. Cassettes and large-print editions have been made for the blind and visually handicapped. New Church scholars found inaccuracies and exaggerations in regard to Swedenborg's life and achievements, but Helen declined to make the changes they suggested. William James once spoke of his Swedenborgian father as having found in the Swedish scientist-seer a "bundle of truths" that sufficed him for the remainder of his life. Helen's book was an exposition of why that "bundle" suited her personally; and in that regard it is, as Doubleday perceived it to be, a moving document. The book's half-century career (a paperback edition with an introduction by Dr. Norman Vincent Peale was published for the Swedenborg Foundation in 1974) showed both its ecumenical appeal and its helpfulness to many.

The Reverend Paul Sperry, whose idea the book had been, had only one moment of unhappiness. At the end of 1929 the *New York World* wrote that Helen was a convert to the Persian religious cult of Baha Ullah, more popularly known as Baha'i. She was deeply upset, she wrote hurriedly to Sperry, and asked that he help her correct the misunderstanding: "It is most important to me that I should not be misinterpreted in my religion. As you know, since I was sixteen years old I have been a strong believer in the doctrines of Emanuel Swedenborg. Why should I change my faith, since it opens my spiritual eyes to all that is beautiful and noble in the thought and beliefs of men, and makes my dark, silent world sweet and livable? . . . I have a profound respect for the teachings of Baha Ullah, just as I have for the noble thoughts of all great prophets and seers. But it never occurred to me that any one would think that I had 'adopted the Persian religion' because I was speaking to Bahai followers."

Early in 1927, while Helen was in the middle of her Swedenborg labors, the American Foundation had inquired about her availability for the fall campaign. She was unable to answer them: "The truth is, my autobiography is not progressing as fast as I at first thought it would." Polly Thomson was off on a round-the-world cruise with her uncle. They had not been able to find anyone sufficiently adept in the manual language to be of real service. "Mrs. Macy has gone through the material with the assistance of one of Doubleday and Page's [sic] readers, but that is the merest beginning. The material must be gone over many times and read to me besides. We were getting along nicely until Mrs. Macy's eyes gave out the middle of January."

"Yesterday (Jan. 21, 1927)," Nella Braddy wrote in her notes, "in the afternoon I read to Miss Keller for the first time. I went very slowly, though as fast as I could and how she was able to keep up with me was more than I know, for by the time I was spelling the end of a sentence I had forgotten what the beginning was, but she seemed to have no trouble." Despite a retentive memory, Helen's inability to review what she had written unless it had been brailled or was read to her imposed formidable barriers. To remind her what was on a typewritten page she would with a hairpin prick an identifying phrase in Braille on the top margin. There were many such pages dating back to her sophomore year in Radcliffe as well as full sheets of Braille, for she had always known that someday she would go on with her autobiography. But the process of recovery and review was laborious. "Hammering out ideas without being able to see what one is doing," she lamented to the Doubledays, "is one of the most exasperating trials of blindness."

In the preliminary stages, fortunately, Nella with Teacher's help was able to pull out of the cabinets full of material the notes, letters and clippings that seemed to them to be the raw material of chapters. But Nella was a newcomer to the household, and Teacher had to go through many of the files beforehand and decide what could be turned over to her. As Teacher needed heavy double-lensed glasses to read at all, this, too, made slow going. There were serious emotional obstacles. "The years had been rich, but they had been painful," Nella wrote with understatement. "Sometimes it seemed as if they could not bring themselves to live through them again."

Armed with her gleanings from the files and her talks with Teacher and Helen, Nella returned to the Doubleday offices in Garden City, not far from Forest Hills, and worked up first drafts. Helen disliked that procedure and in protest cited the way John Macy had worked with her:

I realized from your reaction to the changes I made in the first chapters that we did not have the same thing in mind. Apparently, you thought I would read the manuscript, only changing a word or phrase here and there, and perhaps make suggestions. My idea was that I could do anything I liked with it. I can easily see that what I did might not improve it, and we might have to talk it over, as Mr. Macy and I used to. It is impossible for me to have any idea of a chapter as a whole from reading the end of a paragraph and the beginning of another.

My deafness prevents me from getting as quickly as my teacher does what the connection is. I confess that most of the time I am utterly confused. We are reversing the procedure that I used to follow in the making of my other books. I wrote the book as well as I could. Then Mr. Macy read it, made suggestions and advised me about the construction. If I liked his idea, I agreed, and he recast the page. All the material was there, and we selected what seemed best.

Now the material is in Garden City, and you bring at intervals several days apart chapters which are hurriedly read to me in parts. It is utterly impossible for me to keep the matter or sequence in mind.

Please do not think, Nella, that in stating these facts I intend the slightest criticism of you. But I do feel the book is more yours than mine, although I may have written every word. . . . It is almost the same way that captains of industry make books. . . .

"Helen had reason to write this letter," Nella wrote on its margin. "The upshot was that I spent longer hours in Forest Hills, 10 or 12 hours instead of 6 or 8."

"The book is progressing fairly well," Teacher wrote Major Migel at the end of April. "It simply bristles with difficulties. Fortunately Helen is well and of good courage. As for me, I am all right, except for the pain in my eyes which is terribly intrusive at times, and interferes with work." But in September Helen informed Migel that she would not resume work for the Foundation either in 1927 or (probably) in 1928: "I regret to say my autobiography is still far from completion. . . . There have been many interruptions, and some more serious difficulties which have greatly hindered me. I feel that it would not be wise to lay the book aside now. I simply must go on with it. This means I shall not find it possible to take up the work for the Foundation for some time."

Migel, who had spent the last three months in Europe, discovered anew that dealing with the Forest Hills women was like handling a charged wire. Helen protested the Foundation's sending out appeal letters in her name without her having read them—"letters that I should never have permitted under my signature." She did not wish to be a front—either for Nella or for the Foundation. Self-respect and intellectual integrity demanded that her status as a celebrity be used for the purposes that she stipulated. She was no one's puppet.

By the end of 1927 the early chapters—dealing with her final years at Radcliffe, her first years in Wrentham, their friendship with Mark Twain, their early work for the blind—had been drafted. Helen typed away in the attic on the third floor. As she brought down the yellow sheets to Teacher and Nella, they went to work with scissors and paste. The edited chapters had then to be read to Helen, a triangular process where Nella read to Teacher who translated the pages into manual language to Helen. The first chapters were shown to Doubleday. Its editors were enthusiastic and wanted the completed book for fall publication. But work was slowed again when Helen caught her heel on the attic stairs and was badly bruised in the resulting fall. "The greatest inconvenience I experienced was not being able to use the typewriter," she wrote Effendi. Her correspondence had gone "utterly to pieces, and the autobiography too. My courage almost collapses at the thought of starting things again." But she was pleased enough with the Mark Twain chapter to ask Effendi whether he did not want it for the new magazine *Personality* that he was publishing under his personal supervision. He replied:

> About Mark Twain—I was crazy to print the article in *Personality* as I regarded it as very remarkable and very beautiful, but I could not afford to pay more than $250 for it and I figured it was worth at least $1,000. I discussed it with Mrs. Henney and advised that she should send it to the *Ladies Home Journal.* I think the whole autobiography should bring a large sum of money, but this is easier said than done. Of course if our concern can help you with it, especially Russell who is a good salesman, we shall be delighted.

By March 1928 she was hard at work again, and chapters took shape —on Dr. Bell, her acceptance of the Carnegie pension, her beginnings as a lecturer, her socialist views—the latter in subdued form. It was difficult to deal with John Macy and his importance to her, and even more difficult to describe her romance with Peter Fagan. But the most difficult section related to Teacher. The latter did not want Helen to deal with her life, except as a "record of the work we have done together the past twenty years—not a record of ourselves except as instruments in the ultimate deliverance of the blind." And Teacher, Helen wrote, grew "less reasonable as I approached the end of *Midstream*. She compelled me to use an unnatural constraint in the chapter I called 'My Guardian Angel.' She did not permit any reference to her humble birth or the almshouse, her sufferings and disappointments. Actually I felt humiliated, as if I had lied to God Himself, and I never spoke of *Midstream* to her after an experience that caused aversion to myself. For I loved Teacher and not myself in her."

Helen did not say what this "experience" was. The clearest explanation of why Teacher tried to keep Helen from writing about her life is given in Nella's journals. In 1960 Dr. David M. Levy, a psychiatrist who together with his wife had become close friends of Helen and Polly, was inquiring about Helen's religious views: David asked Helen how it was when she herself had such deep faith Teacher was an unbeliever. Helen hesitated, clasped her hands, lowered her head, then spoke slowly. Well, deep down in her heart she did believe. This means that Helen believes [commented Nella] what she wants to believe, for it is not true, and this is one of the reasons why Teacher wanted me to write the story of her life. She knew Helen would sentimentalize it.

Another reason was Teacher's desire to write her own book. For the same files that turned up Helen's jottings and memoranda over the years produced much of an autobiographical nature that Teacher had written. Mention has already been made of Teacher's rereading of William James's *Talks to Teachers:* "One day I discovered her rereading William James's *Talks to Teachers,* which she had enjoyed through John Macy's expressive voice," wrote Helen. "Although I was stabbed to the soul by the thought of her failing sight, I appreciated the lovefilled associations she had with the book, and I did not remonstrate as was my habit at other times."

Helen finally had learned the full truth about Annie's grim childhood in Feeding Hill and Tewksbury in a trip all of them took to Teacher's birthplace in mid-1927. Major Migel had financed the trip, and considering the bristling character of Teacher's dealings with the Major, her letter has to be quoted:

Helen and I very much want to take a little trip about the middle of May, and it has occurred to me that you might like to finance it. I have often thought of the exceeding friendliness of your visit at Christmas-time, and your generous offer to help us financially. We have managed to get through the winter without availing ourselves of the fund you said you would place at our service. The trip we are contemplating is not exactly a pleasure excursion, though we expect to enjoy it, and we both need a little outing desperately. The trip is in connection with Helen's autobiography. We think it would refresh our memories, and bring back incidents and events which have faded from our minds to revisit the scenes of our earlier years in Massachusetts. The idea is to motor to the various points of interest Helen is writing about. For instance, we should visit my birthplace near Springfield, Massachusetts, and call on Professor Neilson, who was one of Helen's few friends in Cambridge. Then we would go to Boston and visit the old Perkins Institution and the new one at Watertown, where we would be Mr. Allen's guests. Obviously the pleasantest way to do this would be by automobile. It would be extremely awkward getting about by public conveyances. I think it would take a week to carry out the plan we have in mind. One of the staff of Doubleday and Page [sic], Mrs. Henney, would accompany us and take photographs. Doubleday and Page want us to make the trip, and no doubt if they knew our circumstances, they would advance us the necessary money. But the thought came to me that it would be lovely if you would like to help us in such a pleasant way. You can readily see that the trip would involve a good deal of expense. There would be five of us, Helen, Miss Thomson, Mrs. Henney and myself and the driver. I believe the Packard Company would give us a special rate on a car, and provide the chauffeur.

She estimated the cost at $500. Having screwed up enough courage to ask him to underwrite their trip, she now felt, she wrote him a few weeks later, that she had better report that "our finances are very low. . . . May I have a thousand dollars in addition to the five hundred, please?" The day before Migel sailed for Europe, he sent her the $1,500. But the check was drawn on the account of the American Foundation for the Blind. Although he had assured her "more than once that no one need know anything about such a transaction," she wrote him returning the check, he should try to imagine her feelings "when I learned that everyone in the office knew I had asked you for money."

The trip to Feeding Hills was more in the interests of jogging Teacher's memories than Helen's. She was preparing to let Nella do for her what she was doing for Helen. She did not want a book about herself, she maintained; "she had hoped it would never be written, but long before I [Nella] knew, friends of hers had told her that, with or without her consent, the story would be told some day, perhaps after her death. . . . Once one who had loved her threatened to write it, and while he never did, and perhaps never intended to, the threat bothered her a little." This last was undoubtedly a reference to John Macy.

Nella, sensing a story that in its way was every bit as interesting as Helen's, had begun to pull it out of Teacher. They were thrown together for hours in the little office on the second floor at Forest Hills, and while they waited for Helen to bring down from the attic what she had banged out on the typewriter, they talked about everything: "On the days when I was adroit, we talked of Mrs. Macy, and it was on one of those that she told for the first time the story of her years in Tewksbury. Even Helen had not known of it."

Helen does not appear to have known what was brewing, for in the final pages of *Midstream* in her tribute to Teacher she wrote, "She delights in the silence that wraps her life in mine, and says that the story of her teaching is the story of her life, her work is her biography." Perhaps that explains the sense of humiliation with which she wrote in *Teacher* about her mentor's refusal to allow her to deal with the facts of Annie's life. Nella would later discover that Helen seemed to have blocked out from her mind Teacher's story of her early years. "For one thing she learned about it too late," was Nella's explanation. "For another an old unhappy personal problem which was already solved insofar as it could be would never disturb Helen very much." That is not the impression one gets from reading *Teacher*. If Helen resisted speaking about Tewksbury and Feeding Hills, it reflected her resentment, her "humiliation" over Teacher's unwillingness to take her into her confidence in regard to her early years. In the summer of 1928 they corrected the final galleys, and Helen repeated the lines that she had written at the end of the book: "I have written the last line of the last autobiography I shall write. . . . I lift my tired hands from the typewriter. I am free."

Writing books no longer gave her the joy that it had given her when

John was her collaborator. She described the ordeal of writing *Midstream* in some remarks that she turned over to Nella.

> Alas, I am not an easy, prolific writer. I turn and turn a sentence about, as one turns a ball in one's hand. I am never carried off my feet on the wings of a colorful inspiration. I take on the hue of an Irish landscape when an author friend tells me how much pleasure he gets out of writing his books! I wonder why he accepts money for giving himself so much joy! A friend tells me she goes to the typewriter with gladness when she is writing a story. I shamefacedly confess that I go to my desk with lagging feet and heartquakes. I often droop over my spiritless, inactive hands, my mind utterly devoid of writeable thoughts, and when I go back to a page I wrote a few days ago, my mind is full of childish terror and rage, it so obviously must be rewritten. When I remember the books I have written it is with pain, not joy; for I cannot forget the stern labor that went into them, the countless times I read them, the exasperating stupidities I discovered on the twentieth perusal, the trivialities that I thought brilliant epigrams, the unaccountable lapses of memory that had to be rectified by recourse to histories and encyclopedias. Then there is the problem of presenting unpleasant opinions so that people will lap them up like treacle. Then there are the pet paragraphs that the 'perfectly frank' critic insists must be deleted. . . .

Poor Helen, she does not seem to have known that most of her colleagues in the writing domain would confess to the same qualms and agonies. The first reactions to the finished manuscript at Doubleday should have comforted her. The copy editor did his work and then uncharacteristically sent her a letter: "It is a monument in the field of autobiography, as well as a great moral triumph. . . . My opinion means nothing, and my congratulating you is an impertinence in itself, but may I do so, most heartily and sincerely?" "I finished it last night," Russell Doubleday wrote her, "and I hasten to write you to say that I am delighted with it. It is a noble book." Nella Braddy had given him "an inkling of the terrific struggle it has been to produce it."

The chief editor, Lyman Beecher Stowe, on the point of retirement, wrote her out of his long experience in the publishing business: "Every once in a while in our interesting business an obligation becomes a delight and an inspiration." That was the case with her autobiography. He found some of her descriptions of nature among "the most pictorially effective that I ever remember to have read. . . . Should an omnipotent power offer to restore to you your lost physical senses in exchange for your artistic sensibilities I wonder if you would not lose more than you would gain by accepting the offer? Certainly your public would in any case."

Stowe had touched upon a sensitive point. The book was a success commercially and critically, but in both *The New York Times* and the *Herald-Tribune* there was imbedded in otherwise enthusiastic reviews a question mark. Alice Beal Parsons started out her review in *Books* with arresting praise for the significance of Helen's accomplishment: "When the score or so of great achieving personalities of our century are weeded out of the too garrulous pages of a hundred annual Who's Whos I suspect that Helen Keller will be among them." But the enthusiasm for Helen did not carry over to the book:

> One does not learn from this book what the world seems like to one who cannot see or hear. Miss Keller like all the rest of the world, describes by analogy. 'The shoulder of the moon turned pink as she threw a scarlet scarf over her head.' But Miss Keller has never seen the moon and never seen a scarf. She doesn't know what pink is. She explains that her description of things is like that of a man who might write about London after reading many books about it and without having seen it. But the supposititious [sic] man has seen other cities and all the thousand component elements that go to make them. I am not questioning Miss Keller's intense and living conceptions, and probably her life could best serve its many generous and useful ends by emphasizing the ways in which she resembles other people instead of the way in which she differs from them. But an exact description of the actual images in her mind would be immensely interesting.

A similar note crept into *The New York Times*'s review. It is a subject that will be dealt with in the next chapter. What *did* register in her mind when she spoke of her senses reporting the blueness of the sky, "the sweet voice of the violin," the "muted hoof of wild deer in the woods," to mention a few of the images that she invoked? Her answer was what it had always been, as she said at a Book and Authors luncheon shortly after the appearance of *Midstream*. "When eyes are blind, the mind seeks new ways of seeing. My fingers look not with two eyes but with ten eyes, and the whole body is alert to perceive and hears the voice of life."

When *The Nation* at the time of the publication of *The Story of My Life* had questioned the validity of images rooted in sight and hearing, John Macy had defended her, calling her critics "sense arrogant." She used the same epithet at the Book and Authors luncheon.

She sent a copy of *Midstream* to John with some fear and trepidation. Although he was in the hospital, he was prompt to write approvingly. She answered:

> I am pleased that you like *Midstream.* You will never know how constantly you were in my thoughts during the writing of the book. Sometimes you seemed so close, I fancied that you touched my hand to correct an error or make a suggestion, and sometimes you seemed so distant, you were like one whose personality I had dreamed; but always you were in my mind, and how I longed for your reassuring approval! I imagine you reading *Midstream* with varied emotions—following me through the pages with a ghost of your old self in every footfall. The fancy haunts me quite unspeakably.
>
> I accept gratefully your praise of the book. May I let out just one wee sigh amid the chorus of rejoicing at the memory of the stern labor that went into *Midstream,* the heartquakes that I had when I discovered in each revision commissions whose name was legion, and omissions of incidents which seemed essential to my story. Occasionally I fought to bring them back into the stream; but usually the current was too strong in the opposite direction. Some of the deleted paragraphs are still thorns in the author's mind. The pain is lessened somewhat, though, since you haven't missed them—at least haven't felt the structure wobble dangerously. You were ever a conscientious critic, and that you should bid my book live makes me feel as Esther must have felt when Ahasuerus held out his staff to her.
>
> Our life is still rather confused at times. There is always more to do than six hands can manage—meetings for the blind off and on, letters that stare me in the face reproachfully day after day, and an interminable stream of appeals for all kinds of causes. One would think I was appointed of God official guide to mortals through the mazes of life to mansions in the sky! *Midstream* is giving me more trouble than a Chinese funeral, what with a new host of letters, a torrent of books

to be autographed and interviews to be given. Getting out a book is worse than any kind of funeral when I come to think of it—at least we don't know how much trouble we are to others when we are dead.

Hoping that Hamlet will soon be himself again, I am, with affectionate thoughts that never fail to turn theewards.

XXXII

The Dupe of Words

"I am one of those who see and yet believe."

Nella's first effort to read to Helen consisted of an article in *The Atlantic Monthly* by Charles Magee Adams. He had been blind for nineteen years, and his contention—like Helen's and Annie's—was that the psychology of the blind person in no way differs from that of the sighted individual. The perusal of the article precipitated a discussion of Helen's thought processes that so fascinated Nella that she recorded it almost verbatim in her notes.

It was early in Nella's relationship with the Forest Hills household, and, significantly, Teacher took the lead in the interrogation. What crossed Helen's mind, Teacher asked her, when the word *horse* was said? For Teacher and Nella it conjured up visual images, Teacher of a fine bay, Nella of a dappled gray. Helen's response to the word was muscular, tactile, kinetic. "His long face," she said, and showed what she meant with her hands, "his big form," and again she gestured with her hands, and "his short hair, his mane and tail, if he has a tail." "What color?" Teacher asked. "That depends upon what I am told," replied Helen; but his temperament she could assay for herself by the "twitching of his ears," his tail switching back and forth and other manifestations of spiritedness.

Teacher and Nella turned to the word *city*—not a particular city, but the concept. "Long streets," Helen replied instantly, "houses, tramping feet, smells from windows, tobacco, pipes, gas, fruits, aromas, tiers upon tiers of odor. Automobiles. A whirr that makes me shiver. A rumble. It seems to have no shape but to be a concentrated mass of vibrations coming down upon me." New York left her with a dense, imprisoning sensation. "She feels the gloom of the narrow streets," observed Nella. "Traffic is wearisome and depressing. She is weighed down with vibrations."

Teacher and Nella switched to Helen's mental picture of a *house.* "Some houses are friendly," Helen commented, abandoning sensory impressions for judgmental ones, "and hold out their arms to me." Teacher asked for an example. "Gretchen's little house," Helen answered. That house, Teacher explained to Nella, was five times the size of theirs. If it seemed small to Helen, Teacher suggested that that was because it contained many objects Helen could touch, and that made her happy. Questions that related to space within houses and the placement of objects in them received indistinct and uncertain replies. Although she had stayed for weeks at a time in Mrs. Thaw's Pittsburgh house, she was unable to remember which side of the hall the stairway was on, and she hesitated a considerable time before answering Teacher's follow-up query about the position of the stairway at Wrentham, even the location of her study there.

It seemed to Nella that Teacher was as much interested in the discussion as she was herself. But surely after four decades with Helen Teacher must have known the answers. Was she trying perhaps to show Nella Helen's limitations? If Nella was to help with Helen's book, not to mention her own, she should know them.

The two of them asked Helen what her friends meant to her. "A touch of the hand," Helen began, "the footstep, the feel of the face, of the skin." In her notes Nella commented that Helen seemed to be particularly sensitive to the way people spelled into her hand, their way of reacting to conversations with her, whether they were pleasant and receptive or disagreeable—a blind persons's fear that sighted people shrink back from contact with her. She was interested in talk that revealed the minds of her associates, their odors and gestures. She was, reported Nella, "very conscious of irritability."

That interested Teacher, who remarked to Nella that she herself was very irritable. Who was the most irritable person she knew? Teacher asked Helen. "Let me think," Helen hesitated, and when she did not respond, Teacher goaded her on: "What about me?" She was irritable, Helen acknowledged, but added quickly, "Faults are not as much faults in some people as they are in others." Her mother had been irritable, she went on. Teacher changed the subject. What about Mr.

Hitz? "A gentle, quiet figure, walking along softly with his hand lightly on my arm, his slow, quaint spelling, his long beard, which I knew was white, his soft hair, his bald spot"—here she giggled—"his loose clothes, his oddity of gait." She had never seen a more charming picture, Teacher broke in, than of the two of them walking around Wrentham, "the young blind girl and the old man spelling into her hand, neither of them paying the slightest attention to where they were going and sitting down on everything they could find to sit on."

How and where Helen obtained her knowledge, what it consisted of, were questions that intrigued Nella. She quickly came to know of the skepticism, occasionally cynicism, that had dogged the careers of the two women. From the time of the "Frost King" episode there had always been a question of how much of what Helen said and wrote and thought was her own and how much Annie's. In the introduction that Nella wrote to *Midstream*—and it was a measure of the extent to which Helen, Teacher and Polly had come to trust this competent, owlish-eyed figure that they had asked her to write it—she brought up the problem of how Helen could describe scenes and impressions "she obviously can't know through direct sensation." She built up her ideas of color, wrote Nella, "through association and analogy. Pink is 'like a baby's cheek or a soft Southern breeze.' . . . All that Miss Keller claims for her world is that there is a workable correspondence between it and ours, since she finds no incongruity in living both at the same time. . . . Philosophers . . . see only too clearly how much of what we all know and feel has come to us not through personal knowledge, but through the accumulated experiences of our ancestors and contemporaries as it is handed down and given to us in words." Nella also insisted in her introduction that "no attack that has ever been made has been withheld from her."

Helen made much of her enjoyment of music. She accomplished the latter by placing her fingers upon a vibrant instrument or a singer's lips. In the twenties she made the additional discovery that her fingers placed upon the vibrating disc of a radio receiver conveyed the rhythmic pulse of the music, to which she responded in face and bodily movement as if transported to Elysium. Heifetz played for her, as did the Zuller Quartet. Enrico Caruso sang for her the aria of the blinded, chained Samson from *Samson et Dalila* as both—indeed all in the room—wept. She was able to distinguish between instruments and rhythms. After listening to Beethoven's Ninth Symphony, she wrote the New York Symphony Orchestra that she had spent "a glorious hour last night listening over the radio.

. . . I could actually distinguish the cornets, the rolls of the drums, deep-toned viols and violins singing in lovely unison."

But she could not distinguish one composition from another. Nella cautioned against exaggerating her appreciation of music. It was entirely tactile, external stimuli that filtered through her superbly sensitive nature to become the occasion for vivid fantasy. The art historian and critic Professor Meyer Schapiro gave an example of this in Helen's response to "geometric shapes . . . as metaphors of the divine . . ." and quoted some words written by Helen before abstract art arose:

> How does the straight line feel? It feels, as I suppose it looks, straight
> —a dull thought drawn out endlessly. It is unstraight lines, or many
> straight and uncurved lines together, that are eloquent to the touch.
> They appear and disappear, are now deep, now shallow, now broken
> off or lengthened or swelling. They rise and sink beneath my fingers,
> they are full of sudden starts and pauses, and their variety is inexhaust-
> ible and wonderful.

"From the reference to touch," Professor Schapiro went on, "some of you have guessed I'm sure, the source of these words. The author is a blind woman, Helen Keller. Her sensitiveness shames us whose open eyes fail to grasp these qualities of form."

One of the critical appraisals of Helen's knowledge of the external world was made by a distinguished French savant, Pierre Villey-Desmeserets, who, blind himself from the age of four and a half, was a professor of literature at the University of Caen in France. Nella bravely quoted Villey-Desmeserets observations on Helen from *The World of the Blind,* including the wounding judgment that she was a "dupe of words, and her aesthetic enjoyment of most of the arts is a matter of auto-suggestion rather than perception." Nella sought to mitigate the professor's comment by interpreting it: "He is right but this is true of all of us."

Villey-Desmeserets was far from a hostile critic. He admired Helen. Without hearing or sight, he wrote—by means only of the manual alphabet, Braille and lip reading—she had been "able to take her place in that intellectual aristocracy formed by very cultivated people of whom there are so few." Moreover, he believed—and this was a view that Helen and Annie shared—that cognition or understanding is as much a matter of what the heart and mind bring to the data of the senses as it is of the richness and variety of the data. There are very few ideas, he maintained, "which come to us uniquely by means of the eyes," and nearly all elements of a visual sensation "are to be found in the tactile sensation." Not color, but nearly everything else, can be learned through touch. Villey-Desmeserets spoke of a "veritable tactile sight." Its images "are less real, certainly less complex, and considerably less extensive than visual images, but, like them, one and many at the same time, perceived in their entirety and also in detail, by the inner eye of consciousness."

He viewed intelligence as Leibnitz did, not as did Locke:

> Our study has given us something definite with regard to the question so long debated between the senses and the intelligence. *Nihil est in intellectu quod non fuerit in sensu,* said Locke. Leibnitz corrected this formula by adding: *nisi intellectu ipse.* We see how right Leibnitz was in making this reserve and how great this inner power of intellect is in individuals like Helen Keller and Marie Heurtin who although deprived of nine-tenths of our sensations, arrived, notwithstanding, at a complete development.

It is within this context of overall admiration and approval that Villey-Desmeserets asserted Helen to be a "dupe of words" who exaggerated to herself her own aesthetic enjoyments. He asks what the reader is to think of descriptive passages in which trees emerged in a snowfall "like so many white phantoms," and the hues of leaves and grapes are described to evoke autumn. He dwelled on this, he explained, not only because he wanted to get at Helen's mental processes but because it pointed to "the weak point of this wonderful education of a fine intelligence." Helen did not distinguish between sentiments suggested by words and sentiments prompted by sensations:

> We must remember that, for Helen Keller, words have often been not only what they are for a normal individual, the sign of sensation, always associated with it and evoking it by sheer habit, but literally the substitute for sensations. Words have taken the place of the absent, and unknown, sensation. This is the case, in a certain measure, for the blind person who hears, but very much more for the deaf-blind. Then Helen Keller's verbal memory was strangely exact. This was an excellent thing, certainly, as the verbal memory helped in her development enormously where words had to play a considerable part.

There was, however, a great risk with this advantage. Helen Keller did not allow her mind the time, necessarily long for an individual who had only the sense of touch at her command, to obtain all the direct impressions that she might have had for these words that she had too easily assimilated. As a result of this we have all that wordiness, which was from henceforth difficult to restrain. Whole phrases, either read in Braille or from the hand of her teacher, kept coming frequently both in her conversation and in her writings, and these phrases, which she did not recognize as borrowed ones, she believed were her own. She did not distinguish what she drew from the stores of her memory and what she owed to her individual impressions.

A *New Yorker* interviewer, Robert M. Coates, was taken aback by an almost rococo derivative quality in Helen's discourse:

She talks bookishly. Never having heard a voice, she has never learned the easy vocabulary of ordinary discourse. To express her ideas, she falls back on the phrases she has learned from books, and uses words that sound stilted, poetical metaphors. 'Mine is a reasonably happy life. I have the immeasurable fires of the mind for light,' she will say, as one would remark, 'I have a good time on the whole.' It is perhaps because of this habit of phraseology that many people attribute to her a sentimentality of outlook which neither [her] life nor her writings would justify.

In this regard Coates noted her stress on self-reliance. She was "gay, spirited, sturdy" and detested most being pitied or patronized. "My whole desire has been to have my own door key," she told him, "and go and come like people who can see."

Privately, judgments such as Villey-Desmeserets were blows to Helen's self-regard; and yet she had rarely stood higher in the world's esteem. H.G. Wells, who met her in 1931 during a lecture trip to the United States, called her "the most wonderful being in America," perhaps because she had urged Americans to follow "the advice of men like Wells." *Good Housekeeping* included her among the nation's twelve greatest women, and *The Pictorial Review* gave her its annual $5,000 award for a noteworthy contribution by a woman. "Just imagine receiving $5,000 during this depression," she commented. Such accolades helped her accept the blows from men like Villey-Desmeserets with greater equanimity than might otherwise have been the case.

Another blow came from an outstanding American neurologist, Dr. Frederick Tilney. Effendi Doubleday persuaded her to submit to tests that his friend Tilney had devised to show whether the acute development of senses such as touch and smell enabled her to compensate for the senses she did not have. Tilney was a professor of neurology at Columbia University. He assumed when he began that Helen's sensory apparatus in the areas of touch, taste and smell were far superior to the average. His tests, however, which were carried on during the winter of 1927–1928 with Helen's cooperation, showed that in these respects she was normal, not above average. The results astonished Helen, particularly in regard to smell. She had always been both proud and uneasy over her power of smell, uneasy because a highly developed sense of smell distinguished animals. She wrote Tilney a long letter about the importance of the sense of smell to her:

> The sense of smell is the esthetic sense, I think, even more than sight. I know that odors give me a vivid conception of my surroundings. I can smell my landscape because, when I walk or drive through the country, so many odors tell me of fields, streams, honey-sweet valleys and hillsides covered with pines. If, as we are told, the ten thousand Greeks 'shouted for joy when they saw the sea,' I can imagine there must have been still more rejoicing when its bracing breath filled their nostrils. . . . I am very sensitive to unpleasant odors. They have a depressing influence upon me; for they suggest all manner of dread things—disease, accidents, coming evil and unhappy lives. . . .

Tilney's comment on this letter was laconic. "When tested objectively, Miss Keller's olfactory sense shows nothing above the normal average."

Helen's sense of smell may not have been more acute than the average. It certainly was more developed and better trained, and consequently, more discriminating. Professor Loye Miller, a noted paleontologist and ornithologist, recalled Helen's visit in 1914 to his home on the Arroyo Seco in Los Angeles: "I stopped under a California maple that was just about to leaf out and drew a small branch down for Miss Keller to feel. Her sensitive fingers went lightly over the branch and she spoke the one word 'buds,' then placed it to her nose and exclaimed 'O Maple!' Now Miss Keller had never before been West. This was a California maple not yet in leaf. Half the people visiting us when the tree was in active growth didn't recognize it as a maple and were loath to believe me when I told them its name, yet this alert girl recognized it instantly. Now I have long used my sense of smell in the study of plants and animals. In fact as Miss Keller left, she said to me, 'I am glad to meet someone who uses his nose.'" Louise Duffus, the widow of Robert L. Duffus, the writer and *New York Times* editorialist (both were good friends of Helen's in Westport after World War II), described Helen walking out-of-doors. "She would rub her face on the bark of the trees and pat them and get down to smell the flowers and run her hands over them. Of course you know that with one whiff she could distinguish the different fragrance of purple and white lilac, and a red, white, or pink rose."

Tilney found the same to be true about her senses of touch and taste, her response to pressure, temperature and vibration. "It thus appears," Dr. Tilney wrote, "that her sensory organization for the primary conductions of afferent impulses is not above the average." But there was consolation for Helen in his next remark: "Her sensory supremacy is entirely in the realm of intellect. She has developed a richness of association far surpassing the average. Indeed, hers is an exceptional capacity even in the class rated as intellectual." The cases of Laura Bridgman as well as Helen Keller

> illustrate how one area of the brain may be expanded to counteract deficiencies in other areas. Helen Keller shows the resultant expansion in understanding and knowledge when the brain is properly importuned to develop them. Many brains could be made more efficient by pursuing proper methods of development. The difficulty is not in the brain's potential power to respond, but rather in the general lack of desire to demand the improvement.

His findings disappointed Helen, and she felt that he, for his part, must be disappointed in her. She wrote Effendi:

> . . . I hardly expect to see him [Tilney] any more. I'm afraid the tests showed me up badly; for I haven't heard from him since he found out that there was nothing extraordinary about me. When you see him, please tell him that I have forgotten everything, except his not taking me fishing last summer. I suppose the tests showed that I couldn't tell a fish from a thumb-screw. That's a stab at my vanity—something a woman can't forgive.

Tilney, as we have seen, had drawn a different conclusion—how much the human brain is capable of when pushed hard as Helen did—but Helen's attention focused on the less complimentary observations, in respect to which she was like most writers. Effendi sought to assuage her feelings and to reassure her of Tilney's regard. The doctor had been reading *Midstream* in his office when a patient came in, Effendi reported: "He said to the patient: 'I can do you more good by reading some paragraphs from this book than I can by examining your pulse and heart. Sit down there and I will read you a lot of it'—which he did and he said that it helped her much more than if he had examined her heart and lungs."

Effendi also sent Helen 228 shares of Doubleday stock with the hope that it "may add to your income in a substantial way." But Helen was not to be consoled. Her normal self-confidence had been shaken. Another letter to Effendi apologized for its length and earnestness and expressed surprise that her letters gave him pleasure:

> Of course, that is my wish, and a cause of wonder too. For, although I am in the visible world with you, yet I miss the thousand colorful impressions and the actual talk that entertain you. I am not much good at reporting the lighter aspects of life, they flit by me like butterflies, and only now and then I get the flick of a wing, therefore please be indulgent. Mrs. Macy says I am as ponderous as Dr. Johnson without his wit. I'd give anything in the world if I could have some of Madame de Sévigné's inventiveness and sparkle. I am interested up to my eyes in everything, but I am not clever enough to imitate her charming animation.

Tilney's articles on his tests of Helen had not scanted Teacher's contribution to Helen's achievement. Helen's "genius," he wrote in Effendi's magazine *Personality,* "will live in the dark world of those who do not see. It will live, too, for those who, though gifted with all their senses, would make the most of their endowments." And Helen's "glorious mind," he continued, "is the fruit and product of the indefatigable efforts of another great woman, Miss Keller's incomparable teacher."

But among those who considered Helen "a dupe of words" there were some who did not think so highly of Teacher's methods. That was particularly true of Dr. Thomas D. Cutsforth, a plainspoken clinical psychologist, himself blind since the age of eleven, who at the beginning of 1933 published *The Blind in School and Society,* a book that was revolutionary in its approach and destined to become a classic. Cutsforth argued that blindness was not just the absence or impairment of a single sense that can be compensated by the other senses—notably touch—but that it "changes and utterly reorganizes the entire mental life of the individual. . . . The sensory equipment and processes of observing are organized quite differently in the blind from the normal seeing child." In his view Helen had been better adjusted to her real world prior to the arrival of Annie Sullivan:

> The child Helen appears, from all accounts, to have had the situation well in hand from the paternal Captain down to the family dog. She was markedly egocentric in her social behavior. The adult Helen is still so, but along lines which are more in accord with the practices of the majority. With all her education in visual verbal concepts, there is far less experiential reality and situational insight in the adult Helen than there was in the untutored child.

Helen, he contended, had been taught the way the seeing world experiences and employs such visual concepts as form, size, color, brightness, movement, spatial distance. Through verbal mastery of these concepts she had achieved "a workable parity" with the seeing, but the price she had had to pay was "word-mindedness." Verbalism was not an exclusive attribute of the blind. "It exists in any situation that demands the use of abstract concepts not verified by concrete experience." It was to be found in every college community, particularly among students "who have never come into contact with social reality outside their highly protected home and college environments." Helen Keller particularly illustrated a facility "to express and socialize that which she herself cannot possibly experience," as, for example, when she writes of "a mist of green," of "soft clouds tumbling over each other in the sky" and of "blue pools of dog violets and the cascades of golden primroses." The average reader, said Cutsforth, construes these expressions in their usual sense, but that is a sense

> from which the writer is excluded. It must not be supposed, however, that the passage is meaningless to the writer. The visual words connote emotion or attitude rather than objective experience. To the writer the paragraph represents a set of ideas entirely different from the objective reality expressed in the sentences, which represent as

nearly as possible what the experience would be to those who both see and hear. The implied chicanery in this unfortunate situation does not reflect upon the writer personally, but rather upon her teacher and the aims of the educational system in which she has been confined during her whole life. Literary expression has been the goal of her formal education. Fine writing, regardless of its meaningful content, has been the end toward which both she and her teacher have striven. Her own experience and her own world were neglected whenever possible, or, when this could not be done, they were metamorphosed into auditory and visual respectability. Her own experiential life was rapidly made secondary, and it was regarded as such by the victim.

In order for one to comprehend this situation, in which one personality capitulated completely to a system of education or another person's values, it is necessary to understand the entire life history of the process. In this case the process was a lifetime, and the capitulation took place on an infantile level, when the personal affection and confidence of the child Helen were given completely to her teacher. From that time on, Helen's world contracted by expanding into that of her teacher. Her teacher's ideals became her ideals, her teacher's likes became her likes, and whatever emotional activity her teacher experienced she experienced.

Cutsforth's criticism of Teacher's methods had merit. Helen's education, because of Teacher's own limitations as well as Helen's handicaps—which would have kept her out of the laboratory at Radcliffe even if she had been minded to enroll in the courses in science—had been excessively literary. Given Helen's mental powers, it is interesting to speculate whether she might not have made reports from the world of darkness of even greater help to scientist, philosopher and educator, and to the deaf-blind, if she had had a teacher who, like William James, stressed the importance of thinking *things,* not words.

Neither Helen nor Teacher ever replied directly to Dr. Cutsforth's book. Among some who were on the staff of the American Foundation at the time, there was doubt that they even knew of the book. A friend of Cutsforth recalls his saying that he thought that at least he would have hit a nerve, have stirred them up; but he never had any reaction. Even when Helen wrote *Teacher* in the fifties, after the American Foundation for the Blind had reprinted Cutsforth's book because of demands for it from the field, she was silent about it. Some AFB staff scientists believed that the book had been withheld from Helen by Teacher and Polly.

Nella, however, records conversations with Helen that indicate that Helen did know of the book. Another AFB psychologist, Dr. Berthold Lowenfeld, who entertained Helen and Polly at his home in Berkeley when later he became superintendent of the California School for the Blind, and who was a good friend and an admirer of Cutsforth, was sure that both Helen and Teacher had been aware of the book. "No question but that they knew about it, but they had their own way of coping with such challenges. After all, what answer could Helen give?" In the late 1950s, without explanation, Helen vetoed the nomination of Dr. Cutsforth for the Migel Medal, which was awarded annually by the American Foundation for the Blind for "outstanding service to the blind." The nomination had been made by the Foundation's professional staff and was supported by the two other trustees who had a vote in the matter. Criticism of her teacher was intolerable to Helen, and if it could not be argued with, she kept her own counsel and when the opportunity arose paid the critic back. Cutsforth was only another in a list that began with Anagnos and Sanborn.

Foundation records show that Helen and Teacher were apprised of the book by Bob Irwin at the time of its publication. Irwin's neighbor, a publisher to whom the manuscript had been submitted, had asked him for his views. "I went over it," Irwin wrote Helen in March 1933, "and decided it was poor in many respects, and that it would do much more harm than good. . . . I headed it off from being published by the Crowell people, but Appleton and Company have now issued it and are advertising it widely." He had asked Dr. Samuel Hayes, a psychologist who worked closely with the Foundation, to review the book for him, and he sent Helen a copy of Hayes's paper, which he subsequently published in the Foundation's magazine, *The Outlook*. It was a hostile review that questioned the wisdom of publishing a book for the general reader that dealt with the fantasy life and sex behavior of the blind. Irwin also published a companion review by a leader of the Canadian blind, S. C. Swift, himself blind, who was somewhat more favorable: "There are some books so brutally frank as to be positively attractive—at least at first sight," but on closer reading proved the author to be mainly a bull in a china shop.

None of the three—Irwin, Hayes or Swift—mentioned Cutsforth's criticisms of Teacher's methods with Helen. Irwin was well aware that the

Foundation was so identified with Helen and Teacher that whatever damaged them would injure the Foundation. And in the interests of his own relations with the two he wanted it on the record that he had done his best to head the book off. Irwin's opposite number in England, the general secretary of the National Institute for the Blind, W. Mac Eagar—whom all his friends, including Helen and Teacher, called "Mac"—had a different view: "We are all very much interested here in Cutsforth's book. . . . I regret on personal reasons his attack on the Helen Keller type of culture, but I don't suppose Cutsforth's ideas will percolate into the public mind until many years after Miss Keller's death." Cutsforth, he felt, had raised the fundamental question concerning the education of the blind: Was its objective to make the blind child "as much like a sighted person as possible, or was it to develop his full potentialities as a blind person?" When Irwin informed him that he had advised against publication, Mac Eagar expressed regret. Cutsforth's criticisms of institutional life and of teaching the blind applied as much to England as to the United States, he said.

Conciliatory and fair-minded, Irwin retreated somewhat: "Please get me right about Cutsforth. What I objected to principally in his book was two or three chapters on the blind themselves from which the casual reader might gather the impression that they were a morbid, perverted lot." "Aren't we all morbid and perverted?" countered Eagar. "Certainly Cutsforth did not give me the impression that he thought the blind more morbid or perverted than other folks." Irwin retreated further: "I am urging all the teachers in our schools to read Cutsforth for I think the book will do them good, but I am also discouraging my seeing laymen friends who know blind people only as ordinary human beings without sight, from wasting their time with the volume."

Helen and Teacher knew that to reply directly and publicly would only draw attention to the book. They looked around for a champion, as Dr. Bell, Hitz and John Macy had been at the turn of the century. They found him in Dr. James Kerr Love, a famous Scottish aurist who had known them since early Wrentham days:

> Dr. Love is preparing an article about me which he calls 'The Mind of Helen Keller.' It is by way of reply to current criticisms of Teacher's educational method and my presumptuous use of color terms in my descriptions of the visible world. He wants to bring out some fresh facts which he has elicited from Teacher and me. We both

feel that he is most competent to give a definitive answer to our critics
for he has a lifelong knowledge of the deaf and their problems.*

"Certainly send it to me," Dr. Love wrote Helen about the Cutsforth
book, "and tell me where my reply should be sent. On the face of it I
should say: not having met you or your teacher he has entered where most
of us would fear to tread. Mrs. Macy's work with you has no parallel and
so any critic must be careful." Love undertook to answer the question that
no one had asked before: "What had become of the impressions gathered
into Helen's mind, and stored away somewhere during the nineteen
months of seeing and hearing? Were they lost or had they merely for the
time lost their labels?"

"I look forward to further talks with you on your early work with
Helen," he wrote Teacher, indicating the thrust of his thinking. "The
early words you taught her were such as she must have [heard] in her first
two years. Did you create them or resurrect them?"

On the basis of his experience with sudden deafness that occurred in the
first three years of life, he stated in his article that "unless means are at
once taken to perpetuate the speech, the names of objects get wiped out
or the labels are lost. Such lost speech may be resurrected by the teacher.
It is easier to recover speech in such a child than to create speech in a
deaf-born child." The same was true, he contended, of a deaf-blind child,
particularly one with the intellectual powers that Helen had demonstrated
and that Dr. Tilney among others had confirmed. With the aid of Annie
Sullivan Helen had resurrected "the once vivid impressions of early childhood—those of colour and sound. Those impressions for a time lost their
names, but the percepts were not lost." He quoted William Wordsworth's
lines from his ode, "Intimations of Immortality from Recollections of
Early Childhood":

> There was a time when meadow, grove and stream,
> The earth and every common sight
>> To me did seem
>> Apparell'd in celestial light
> The glory and freshness of a dream.

*The "fresh facts" that he elicited were indeed interesting and were published in the English
magazine *The Teacher of the Deaf*. I have incorporated the "fresh" material in my account of
Helen's early years.

He had intentionally left Wordsworth's verse incomplete, Love continued, for the poet finished thus: "The things which I have seen I now can see no more." But Wordsworth had an unbroken series of subsequent impressions that obscured his earlier ones. Helen had none of this except through the senses of touch and smell, "therefore, her perceptions were recoverable."

Such in essence was Love's refutation of Cutsforth's charge of "chicanery" in Helen's use of the language of sound and visual perception. What of the additional charge that Helen described to Nella as follows: "You know, Dr. Cutsforth declares that Teacher's method destroyed the real Helen and substituted one of her own design." Love did not deal with this directly. The American Foundation's National Consultant on Education, Dr. Susan Jay Spungin, often deals with deaf-blind children. Their impairments are usually a direct result of the rubella epidemic of the 1960s. Such children often behave very much like children diagnosed as autistic. ". . . [T]he marvellous thing was that Helen Keller was able to communicate with the outside world at all," comments Dr. Spungin. "Many of these rubella children don't even know there is a world out there." Annie Sullivan's methods went beyond Dr. Howe's work with Laura Bridgman, in the unusual education that she gave Helen once she had reestablished her communications with the outside world. Little similarity existed between the intellectually pinched, strait-laced and reclusive Laura who feared to venture beyond the confines of Perkins and Helen, a spirited woman of charm, whose inquisitive mind ranged widely over literature, history, current events and religion. Madame Montessori had recognized a kindred spirit in Teacher precisely because her methods of teaching Helen had so much in common with her own concept of education flowing from interest and motivation, and from learning by doing. Although Helen's later education was "excessively literary," a not uncommon fault even among the sighted, Teacher's letters from Tuscumbia still arrest one by their lucid exposition of the relationship of experience to verbalization,* and by her encouragement of the child Helen to handle everything—furry animal, coarse bark, fragile petal—in order to irradiate a word with its correlatives in the senses, limited though the latter were.

Dr. Lowenfeld, friend of both Helen and Cutsforth, qualified his endorsement of Cutsforth's observations on Helen and Teacher by his praise

*See pages 55–56 and 201–203.

of Helen's use of language, a use that he felt was rather customary among writers: "We ought to recognize that Helen Keller had an unusual facility with words and was extremely good at expressing her impressions, even if the impressions were stimulated. This is an art and writers are capable of doing it. Writers often write without rst-hand knowledge of the scenes or events they are describing."

Helen was reading deeply in Joseph Conrad at the end of the twenties. She was much struck by *The End of the Tether*. "I wonder," she remarked to Nella, "where he got his knowledge of the blind." Conrad's tale, set in the Malacca Straits, is of a ship's captain who is going blind. He describes the process "as if the light were ebbing out of the world." Because of a dependent daughter the captain was afraid to acknowledge that "the game was up." Helen of course did not consciously remember "going blind," but she was acutely living through its agonies with Teacher. Conrad's captain "had not dared to consult a doctor." Helen lived with Teacher's dread in that regard, and it seemed extraordinary to her that Conrad should be so knowing of the psychology of someone in the grip of this terrifying loss. Yet Conrad in particular among writers of the early twentieth century, in whose tales seas, ships, jungles are made palpable presences, was a vivid proof of the indispensability to the writer of ears and eyes.

Helen sought bravely to demonstrate what a gifted blind writer, even a deaf-blind writer, can achieve through empathy, intuition, insight. That was the attraction to her in later life of the concept of extrasensory perception. In Helen's later years she wrote Robert Duffus, after a discussion of Dr. Rhine's experiments in ESP:

> It has always been a strong belief with me that there are powers in many animals which can be developed beyond the physical senses, and it is a gratification to note that orthodox scientists are beginning to seek other causes than mechanical ones to explain telepathy and the incredible travels of migratory birds flying from the North to tropical countries and seeking out their old nests, eels finding their way swimming thousands of miles to the Sargasso Sea and back to the waters of Scandinavia. Surely, if creatures without the reasoning faculty can perform such wonders, Man endowed with spiritual and intellectual powers can achieve phenomena not to be explained by mechanism but by laws still waiting to be discovered.

Helen did not need to seek justification in extrasensory perception for the reality that she had constructed out of her experience. Attesting to her ability to construct a world of meanings are the distinguished German philosopher Ernst Cassirer and, in his philosophical essays, the novelist Walker Percy. Cassirer had discovered with delight that Helen's and Teacher's accounts of the water episode illustrated with astonishing clarity the crucial difference between the physical world of signs and the world of meanings, which he considered to be the distinctively human one (*An Essay on Man*, 1944). Until the episode at the water pump, he wrote, Helen had learned to associate certain things and events with tappings in her hand. But such associations did "not imply any understanding of what human speech is and means." The child had to make a "much more significant discovery. It has to understand that *everything has a name*—that the symbolic function is not restricted to particular cases but is a principle of *universal* applicability which encompasses the whole field of human thought. In the case of Helen Keller this discovery came as a sudden shock. . . . It works an intellectual revolution. The child begins to see the world in a new light. It has learned the use of words not merely as mechanical signs or symbols but as an entirely new instrument of thought. A new horizon is opened up, and henceforth the child will roam at will in this incomparably wider and free area."

To understand words as symbols, not just as signals, was Helen's "open sesame" to that wider world of human culture. The case of Helen Keller, Cassirer went on, proves that this was the key that unlocked almost all doors despite the deprivation of some of the senses:

> The case of Helen Keller, who reached a very high degree of mental development and intellectual culture, shows us clearly and irrefutably that a human being in the construction of his human world is not dependent upon the quality of his sense material. If the theories of sensationalism were right, if every idea were nothing but a faint copy of an original sense impression, then the condition of a blind, deaf, and dumb child would indeed be desperate. For it would be deprived of the very sources of human knowledge; it would be, as it were, an exile from reality. . . . If the child has succeeded in grasping the meaning of human language, it does not matter in which particular material this meaning is accessible to it. As the case of Helen Keller proves, man can construct his symbolic world out of the poorest and scantiest of materials. . . .

For Walker Percy, Helen Keller was the key to the discovery of the "Delta Factor," his term for man's breakthrough into the daylight of language and consciousness and knowing—or, as he states it dramatically at the beginning of *The Message in the Bottle* (1975), *"How I Discovered the Delta Factor Sitting at My Desk One Summer Day in Louisiana in the 1950's Thinking about an Event in the Life of Helen Keller on Another Summer Day in Alabama in 1887."* Before the shock at the water pump, "Helen had behaved like a good responding organism. Afterward she acted like a rejoicing symbol-mongering human. Before, she was little more than an animal. Afterward, she became wholly human. Within the few hours of the breakthrough and the several hours of exploiting it Helen had concentrated the months of the naming phase that most children go through somewhere around their second birthday."

Late in 1931 Helen, accompanied by Polly, visited the newly opened observation tower atop the Empire State Building, then the tallest building in the world. "I wrote her asking her what she really 'saw' from that height," reported Dr. John H. Finley, the scholarly and cultivated associate editor of *The New York Times* and president of the New York Association for the Blind. Dr. Finley had first met Helen as a young girl at the Huttons' in Princeton. They had become friends. Introducing her to a meeting, Dr. Finley said of Helen of the middle years, "She writes and speaks such beautiful English—I have often said that there are some advantages in being deaf and blind, for she has never heard an ungrammatical or an ignoble word, nor seen an ugly thing in her beautiful earth."

Dr. Finley, in presenting the letter, quoted a passage from Cicero's "Tusculan Disputations":

> When Democritus lost his sight he could not, to be sure, distinguish black from white; but all the same he could distinguish good from bad, just from unjust, honorable from disgraceful, expedient from inexpedient, great from small, and it was permitted him to live happily without seeing changes of color; it was not permissible to do so without true ideas.

The *Times* published her answer to Finley's query, and the president of the Empire State Corporation, former governor Alfred E. Smith, considered it so remarkable that he republished it as a pamphlet.

Here is what Helen's "extrasensory" insights made of the scene before her:

Frankly, I was so entranced 'seeing,' that I did not think about the sight. If there was a subconscious thought of it, it was in the nature of gratitude to God for having given the blind seeing minds. . . .

I will concede that my guides saw a thousand things that escaped me from the top of the Empire Building, but I am not envious. For imagination creates distances that reach to the end of the world. It is as easy for the imagination to think in stars as in cobble-stones. . . .

There was the Hudson—more like the flash of a swordblade than a noble river. The little island of Manhattan, set like a jewel in its nest of rainbow waters, stared up into my face, and the solar system circled about my head! Why, I thought, the sun and the stars are suburbs of New York, and I never knew it! I had a sort of wild desire to invest in a bit of real estate on one of the planets. . . .

Let cynics and supersensitive souls say what they will about American materialism and machine civilization. Beneath the surface are poetry, mysticism and inspiration that the Empire Building somehow symbolizes. In that giant shaft I see a groping toward beauty and spiritual vision. I am one of those who see and yet believe. . . .

She saw the mysticism and inspiration of things below their surfaces and in this sense was one of Emerson's "meritocracy"—those who "see general effects and are not too learned to love the imagination and power and the spirits of solitude."

XXXIII

Teacher's Descent into Darkness

"In youth I would have gone round the world for a compliment. Now
I am indifferent."—Teacher.

Teacher's flawed and failing eyesight had shadowed her whole
adult existence, from the time it had been restored to her while she was
a student at Perkins. In 1929 she had finally had her right eye removed
by Dr. Conrad Berens. He had to do it, Dr. Berens, one of the nation's
leading ophthalmologists explained, to relieve her of the pain. "She is
never free from pain," Helen wrote Effendi shortly before the operation,
and added that he could well imagine her (Helen's) dread of anything
happening to Annie if she considered how "necessary she is to my happiness, how all these years she has helped me with her counsel and encouragement." When Teacher finally was persuaded to go to Dr. Berens, he
was shocked by her account of the long series of operations on her eyes,
some almost amateurish. He put off operating on her remaining eye, as
he knew he would have to do. A cataract was growing over it, but the
cornea was paper thin from previous operations, and he was determined
not to operate on her remaining eye until she was practically blind, especially as there was little chance that she would come out of it with any sight
at all. He had developed a lively admiration for his patient, traveled almost
daily out to Forest Hills in bad times and refused to charge her a cent.

"I thoroughly agree with you," their old friend Charlie Campbell wrote
them from Detroit. "It is much harder for a person who has had the use
of sight to lose it in adult life than for those who have never known its

use at all." She had less than one-tenth vision, she informed Major Migel.

Teacher was sixty-four in 1930 and saw nothing in old age to recommend it. She had given up the struggle with her cumbersome body. She left it to Polly to pilot Helen around, a task that the sturdy Scotswoman with brown eyes and soft brown hair performed willingly and faithfully. But when it came to Helen Teacher fully trusted no one. Helga Lende, the young librarian of the Foundation, was sent out to Forest Hills to help her and Helen during one of Polly's absences. Miss Lende was made acutely uncomfortable by Teacher's asking her to help her go through Polly's files to see what was there. In some illuminating autobiographical notes that Teacher dictated to Helen and that the latter withheld from Nella—whimsically called "Foolish Remarks of a Foolish Woman"—she ascribed her less agreeable character traits to the years in Feeding Hills and Tewksbury. "I doubt if life or eternity for that matter is long enough to erase the errors and ugly blots scored upon my brain by those dismal years."

More and more, as darkness set in, Helen took charge, planning and scheming how to keep Teacher from yielding to despair. *Midstream* completed, she had returned to work for the Foundation, addressing meetings, making timely appearances in aid of legislation, writing letters of appeal to key donors. Only Helen could write a half-column letter appealing for contributions that the *Times* not only published but supported editorially, saying that pleader as well as plea caused "a slow tightening around the heart . . . [and] satisfaction will be the sure reward of those who can associate themselves through their gifts with her gallant spirit."

Yet miserable as Teacher felt, she was not so far gone as to forego a battle, especially for Helen and more money: "You know, Mr. Migel, that it is Helen who has interested the public in the Foundation—put it on the map, so to speak," she wrote the Major at the beginning of 1930. "Mr. Rockefeller and his father have been interested in Helen most of her life, and if Dr. Harry Emerson Fosdick had not on several occasions mentioned her in his sermon and talked about her over the radio, Mr. Irwin would have found it most difficult to reach the ears even of Mr. Rockefeller's secretary. . . . Now, Mr. Migel, when you compare what Mr. Irwin and Mr. Hayes receive in salary with Helen's $200 a month, you cannot but see the incongruity. . . ."

Even though Teacher exempted Mr. Migel from these complaints and directed them against the trustees, the letter made Helen uneasy; and the

same day that Teacher dispatched her bill of grievances, Helen wrote him
half in apology:

> There is no disguising the fact that things are going very badly with
> my teacher these days. She has not been able to read even the head-
> lines of a newspaper for more than a week. She is very nervous and
> naturally discouraged. I can take no interest in my work just now, my
> heart is so heavy. All my life I have lived in a dark and silent world,
> and I seldom think of my limitations, and they never make me sad;
> but to see the light failing in another's eyes is terrible, especially when
> one is unable to do anything to avert the tragedy.
>
> Please, dear Mr. Migel, try to be patient with our complaints and
> difficulties. It is not our habit to cry out against the bludgeonings of
> chance; but these days we are living at high tension, and all round us
> is uncertainty and the dark. And what are friends for, if not to worry
> them a little?

He could never be impatient with her, the Major replied. "You know
how I feel towards you all, although occasionally Teacher does try me a
little." He went out to Forest Hills and proposed that her monthly stip-
ened be increased to $500, plus $100 for clerical expenses. Dr. Berens
had suggested that Teacher needed quiet and rest, and the Major amiably
helped them plan a trip to Europe. The problem was to persuade Teacher
to move. When he informed them that the Foundation's trustees had
concurred in the financial arrangements, Helen rewarded him with a
"You are wonderful!" encomium, "so sympathetic and gentle with the
three female Jeremiahs. . . . Your proposition is entirely satisfactory to all
of us. We are rather appalled that our large salary should come at a time
when we feel less able to earn it. You know how far from well my teacher
is. . . . I intend to leave everything and devote myself to her the next three
months. . . ."

But not, as it turned out, before she and Polly made a trip to Washington to testify on behalf of a bill to appropriate $75,000 to reprint books
in Braille for the blind. It had been drafted under the leadership of Bob
Irwin, and Migel had persuaded Republican Congresswoman Ruth Baker
Pratt to introduce the measure, which in fact was an unprecedented step
in government aid for the blind. Migel, Irwin and Helen all went down
to testify. Afterward Helen wrote Migel, "I think the Foundation 'did

itself proud.' Mr. Irwin was full of information, and our President's remarks were simple, direct and moving, and Polly spelled into my hand, 'He looks so distinguished!' Charlie Campbell said just the right thing—he always does, he is a born actor. . . . One of the New York papers carried the picture of Mrs. Pratt and me." As for Helen's testimony, her impact, wrote the Foundation's official historian, was "memorable."

Having done what Migel had asked, she had news for him: "We are sailing on the *President Roosevelt* next week for Plymouth—Please don't laugh! We are really going this time, unless Teacher gets into a contrary mood. Mr. Macy used to say if she was drowned, they must look upstream for her body. . . . Dr. Berens is determined that Teacher must go away. . . . I am hoping that the change will put new life and courage into Teacher's heart."

The crossing on the *President Roosevelt* was rough. A two-day gale tossed them about their stateroom. Toilet articles bounced. Apples and oranges leaped into the air and rolled all over the cabin floor. While Teacher wailed from her berth and Polly scrambled, Helen was beside herself with glee. Always starved for strong experiences, she loved the wildness, even persuaded Polly to take her up to the deck; and though the biting spray and mountainous waves quickly drove them below, Helen was impatient to go out again. Teacher, however, "wept and moaned and wished she had never left her happy, comfortable home." When the sea quieted, the captain invited Helen up to the bridge, where she "inhaled great draughts of eternal space" and in the pilot house hungrily accepted his offer to "feel the gyro, the magnetic compass and the radio direction-finder. I thought of all these devices as arms of the master of the ship controlled by his mind."

A week later they were in a Cornwall cottage in Hannafore, West Looe, that had been rented for them by a friend of Polly's sister, a journalist, Augustus Muir. It was on the edge of the Cornish cliffs amid "banks and banks" of primroses, violets and forget-me-nots. Helen walked daily with Polly along the cliffs that rose sheerly out of the sea. Although Teacher refused to accompany them, in the Cornish setting of fragrance and beauty her spirits began to improve. They stayed in touch with the Foundation through Migel's secretary, Mrs. Amelia Gladu Bond, who reported the large contributions for which Helen should send thank-you notes, as well as other news. Their own letters, filled with descriptions of the countryside, repeatedly asked about John Macy's book *About Women*. It was scheduled for spring publication, and Teacher feared that she might figure in it. She did not. Amelia sent it to them, commenting, "I was disappointed; it is clever in some parts, but on the whole—oh well—." "Teacher has read snatches of it and thinks pretty much as you do about it," Polly reported back. On Macy's title page he inscribed these words from Nietzsche: "Of man there is little here; therefore do their women masculinize themselves, for only he who is man enough will save the woman in woman." His essay, Macy insisted, was "not an attack on women, except on certain kinds of women, especially assertive feminists, and women who pay men the doubtful compliment of imitating them and interfering women who try to run the whole show and reform the male actors. The discerning reader will perceive that this book is addressed to men. It is a slight prod to American men to bestir themselves and not allow the country, especially in its cultural and intellectual aspects, to be enfeebled by feminization."

Teacher did not wholly disagree. She spoke about the relationship of the sexes in her "Foolish Remarks": "All that is pleasuring you find in women—and all that is humiliating too. They feed you with honey and smiles—and pluck out your heart while you sleep and fling it to the swine. No wonder Amiel wrote: 'Woman is certainly our angel and our demon, the best and the worst of this base world, that which gives us life and death, happiness and despair. From her comes peace and trouble, virtue and vice, ecstasy and remorse, hell and Heaven for man on this earth. . . .' " But perhaps she also had John in mind when she wrote, "I wish Americans could grasp the simple fact that a man of the world—a gentleman in the European sense—carries an atmosphere, an outlook, a power which all their [American men's] smartness, snappiness and boasting cannot convey. I get so suffocated with their smug ways and cocksuredness about everything founded on nothing but emptiness of thought." She could see woman as Lilith; she could also see her as victim. Her thoughts on marriage were astonishingly prescient of the feminist consciousness of the sixties and seventies:

> It may well be, or I think so, that the mere idea of marriage as a strong possibility, likely to weaken the will by distracting its direct aim in the life of practically every young girl, is the simple secret of her confessed inferiority in men's pursuits and professions today. If, instead of looking for some nonexistent feminine inferiority of brain-power, educationalists would cast a look at the effect during the training and learning years of such an under-thought—'But after all I may get

married,' and at the fiercely desperate corners where a young man passes in a spirit of life or death, they might count that in. And, in consequence, when they draw up their comparative tables, set their statistics of women's work, not against the mass of thus unhand-icapped men, but against some restricted group of those only who have a weakening third responsibility before their eyes in a crisis other than straight success or failure; such as, for example, rich men's sons, who cannot be absolutely in earnest. The vast mass of men, then, have to depend on themselves alone; the vast mass of women hope or expect to get their life given to them. It is the first condition of a woman adventurer to do as Isadora and bar from the beginning any such dependence.

They planned to return to the United States at the end of May but found themselves pushing the date further and further off. "We both, I feel," Teacher wrote in her autobiographical notes, "have earned the right to live for the remainder of our lives where we please. We have spent our days, as it were, in a railroad station, meeting many, but knowing few." Helen felt prey to "a growing wanderlust. . . . I am eager to see the world before I am gone from it." So she wrote Nella. Her most candid letter from abroad was written to Teacher's biographer. Both Teacher and Helen had come to feel very close to Nella. "[We] have no better friend in the world than yourself," Helen had written her earlier. To Nella she confided that it had been a relief to be abroad on her fiftieth birthday. "It was good not to have to wear a company smile and make a silly speech about feeling fifty years young. Anniversary speeches are nearly always pathetic in their insistence that experience is a satisfactory substitute for the dreams of youth. No matter how rich the experiences life brings us, there is always the touch of melancholy in the vanishing of the bright flowers of spring." The "spell of Britain" was upon them, "and I thought we might as well wear our garments of enchantment as long as possible and forget the straight jacket of routine and publicity which Teacher and I have worn the best part of our lives."

They had to vacate the Looe cottage in mid-June. The Muirs found them a four-hundred-year-old country house, Trout Hall, in Essex, near Cambridge. It was not available before early July, so they decided it was a good time to go to Ireland, partly in an effort to find out something about Teacher's family. Helen hastened to report her impressions of Ireland to Nella, but "Teacher says I'm not to include hers." Teacher's own notes to Nella explain why: "I feel sensitive about everything I hear Polly and Helen discuss. I hate its poverty and melancholy, its heroes and martyrs, and, above all, I hate their comments. I find myself raging inwardly while outwardly pretending that they have discovered the real Ireland. All the time a fierce ache gnaws at my heart. I experience a similar emotional ache when I hear the sea at night, and its moan keeps me from sleep." Helen found Ireland "baffling . . . lovable, detestable and intensely tragic."

For their two-week tour they had rented a chauffeur-driven Daimler. "That is the King's car, I would have you know," Helen preened a little in a letter to Lenore Smith. But the luxury car also made Teacher acutely uncomfortable. The drive from Waterford, where they had landed, to Killarney depressed them. "Most of the cottages were poor, and the small towns drab and silent, and the women in their black shawls made the scene still more gloomy, but Killarney. . . . You must see Killarney, Nella. I have never in my life had so many adjectives of color, of grandeur and of romance poured into my hand in an effort to give me some idea of the indescribable beauty that is Killarney." The journey to County Kerry and Limerick in search of Teacher's forebears proved fruitless, but the visit affected them all strongly: "I wonder if there is any other place in this world where superlative beauty and grandeur are so startlingly contrasted with bleak poverty and hopelessness as in County Kerry."

Helen's descriptions were labored compared to Teacher's notes: "For hours we drove through desolate bog-lands, rocky wastes," reported Helen, which once were "superb forests" until Queen Elizabeth ordered them to be felled because the rebellious Irish took refuge in them, and "not a single tree or bush survived." Teacher's note about the bogs has a haunting dirgelike quality:

> The bogs influence me strangely. The weird rocks on the hillside watch me, and their expression is intense. I find myself waiting for them to speak to me, and deep down in my soul I know their message will break my heart. The long violet shadows call to me to follow them over the rocks and cliffs down, down, to the sea, whose cruel white hands will drag me from the light and the warm sun forever.

In Ireland she found a sadness to match her own temperament:

> When one stops talking in Ireland, one hears the murmur of grieving and death. One feels that death and the sweetbreathing earth are one.

Her forests and streams, her shores and mountain crags always left me melancholy. I missed the settled and ordered life of humanity.

The scent of Ireland is the smoke of peat fires. . . .

Hearing plays an important part in the perceptions of the Irish—the herons call to each other over the dark waters. It is easy to hear in Ireland. A banshee wails from every bush, and wild sea-birds beat their wings against the shore.

At last we came, with a great jump in my heart, to the River Shannon, in the busiest part of Limerick—the Shannon I had seen in my night- and daydreams since my childhood. Why does one not say or do something unusual at such moments? When one comes to an utmost emotion, one sits quiet in one's seat and says inanely, 'So this is the Shannon.' Nothing more original or significant came to my tongue.

I stood in the little white chapel at Cratloe in the County Clare, and wondered if my parents had been christened and married there. The countryside is very poor and nearly deserted. The river Shannon flows like a blue ribbon through the green fields, and the old castle stands grim and threatening 'on the threshold of quiet.'

Here I am in Limerick. All day we have been seeing the country, the Shannon and the old castle. Helen and Polly climbed the broken, moss-covered steps almost to the turret. The keeper would not let them go farther because there were missing steps and a treacherous crevice. I have not enjoyed myself. The thought of visiting these scenes in a handsome automobile driven by a man in livery made me very uncomfortable. In imagination I saw my forbears working in these fields or trudging bare-foot to their comfortless thatched cot- tages or, driven by extreme poverty, trekking toward a port from which they would sail to distant lands never to look upon their beloved green isle again. There is always the ghost of an emigrant ship in the Irish mind.

Their two-week stay in Ireland ended in Dublin, where they took ship for Southampton. The Daimler met them there. Ireland had dampened their spirits, and they were happy to "caravan" through southern England along a road originally built by the Romans. "There are ancient landmarks at every turn," Helen delightedly wrote Migel, "Saxon dykes, Roman walls, Norman castles and abbeys and place names which indicate the successive conquerors of the land. As we journeyed Londonwards, I felt as if I were part of a royal progress." They ran out of money and cabled the Major. He immediately sent them $1,000. The Foundation was glad that they had decided to stay on, Amelia informed them, "but even at the risk of seeming too selfish, I'll admit that we hope you will start on your return trip no later than September 25th—and we are focussing our attention on the S.S. *President Roosevelt* due here the first week in October."

"I am writing this letter in a spacious room" Helen wrote Migel from Trout Hall. "The ceiling is low. The floor undulates like the deck of a ship. There is a great fire-place and a large French window which lets in every ray of sunshine there is. I like to sit in the broad window-seat and read, while the fragrance of many flowers and box hedges in the garden floats up to me. . . . you said we should see England in the month of roses and that is just what we have done."

They did not try to see London; "we were overwhelmed by it. Comparing it with New York, Teacher said, 'It looks like a vast, crouching beast.' To placate it, we pretended to like it." They did visit Cambridge, but usually they were content to stay in Trout Hall, reading—Helen obtained books in Braille from the National Lending Library for the Blind in London—writing, talking with the handful of visitors who knew they were in England, for they had somehow managed to keep their visit "a dark secret," and playing cards—Helen solitaire, Teacher bridge. If Helen sometimes felt restless to be back in the thick of activity, the beneficial effects upon Teacher reconciled her to the prolongation of their stay. Teacher "is glad now that we carried her off to England. She still has bad days when she worries about her eye; but her general health is improving, and most of the time she is in good spirits. . . . Occasionally we get her to walk with us, but she prefers to read. She declares that she gets all the exercise she needs going from book-case to book-case."

They reached New York harbor at the beginning of October, and Helen hurried out to Detroit to fulfill a promise to Charlie Campbell to dedicate his training cottage for blind children. She visited the huge River Rouge plant in the company of the Edsel Fords. They also took her to the Edison Laboratory. Father and son were generous contributors to the Foundation. The old routine of appearances, speeches and appeal letters resumed. She should not feel embarrassed trying to raise money, Charlie Campbell consoled her: "Dear girl, never allow yourself to be disturbed over anything of the kind. . . . You never need to feel sensitive or apologetic because you go forth as beggars on behalf of those who have lost their sight." "It's terribly hard to raise money just now," Helen explained to Lenore Smith, "Many people are afraid to give. We must take strenuous measures. In fact, we are breaking into the houses of the rich with the demand, 'Your money or your peace of mind!' So far we have got away with the booty—thirty thousand dollars in one week!!!"

A new kind of recognition awaited her and Teacher. President Charles E. Beury of Temple University offered them both the honorary degree of Doctor of Humane Letters. Helen accepted, but Teacher despite all Helen's pleading declined: "It is a valuation to which I do not consider my education commensurate. All my life I have suffered in connection with my work from a sense of deficiency of equipment," she explained to Beury. Whatever honor she deserved would be adequately paid in honoring Helen. The University tried unsuccessfully to get her to reconsider. She hoped, however, that she would be allowed to accompany Helen and Polly, she wrote Dr. Edward Newton, famous bibliophile and chairman of the board of trustees. "I should indeed be grieved if declining the degree lost me the pleasure and benefit I should derive from being your guest on that occasion."

The more Teacher sought to remain in the background, the more she was precipitated to stage center at the ceremonies. She tried to remain out of sight, one in an audience of thirty-five hundred at the joint commencement–Founders Day exercises in the Grace Baptist Temple. But Dr. Beury, in introducing Dr. Newton, who was to present the degree to Helen, read Teacher's letter refusing to accept an honorary degree because, as he interpreted her letter, she felt she "was unworthy of the honor." Dr. Newton picked up that theme, and Helen ended her little speech with a tribute to Teacher. "Together we went through Radcliffe College. Day after day during four years she sat beside me in the lecture halls and spelled into my hand word by word what the professors said; and nearly all the books she read to me in the same way. Yet when I received my degree from Radcliffe not a word of recognition was given her! The pain caused me by that indifference or thoughtlessness is still a thorn in my memory."

That was enough to bring the governor of Pennsylvania, Gifford Pinchot, there to receive an honorary doctorate of laws, to his feet, to propose with Dr. Newton's agreement that the audience by a rising vote direct that the degree be conferred on Mrs. Macy. It was ordered by acclamation. One figure remained seated—Teacher. "It was quite like you," Beury wrote her afterwards, "to quietly and modestly come into our exercises by a side door and under the circumstances I am glad that you did it that way. . . . The statements and demonstrations made should be conclusive of your worthiness to receive an honorary degree." The University would not insist, but its leaders felt that she was entitled to the recognition.

Teacher was quite contrite. She had meant to speak to him afterwards, "but the kind references to me moved me so deeply, speech deserted me, and I fled in a panic." She realized that civility and good manners required that she yield. Perhaps some day when he and Mrs. Beury came to New York they might dine together and he could deliver the piece of parchment. In the end, the degree was conferred upon her the following year, at the 1932 Founders Day exercises. In her "Foolish Remarks of a Foolish Woman" she noted that "honors which would have transported us with joy if they had come earlier have no thrill in them, especially when they are forty years overdue. . . . In youth I would have gone round the world for a compliment. Now I am indifferent.

"Why, Oh curious ones, do you stop at my door today and peer into my face wonderingly? You have passed me with miserly glances sixty years and longer."

Not only did the recognition and acclaim come too late, but she was driven by a deep-rooted sense of failure. "I lack real application. If I had it, I should by now be a well educated woman. But I do not like to grind at tasks which do not interest me. My energy is almost inexhaustible when I am interested, but I have no vitality for things I do not care about. . . . Only in Helen have I kept the fire of a purpose alive. Every other dream flame has been blown out by some interfering fool." But her spirits rose when she thought of Helen: "As on some morning height abides a bloom no change can blight, so on my heart, too deep for change, glows a bright thought of Helen."

But these were sentiments too private to expose in her Founders Day speech. It was as remarkable as her Commencement Day performance at Perkins forty-six years earlier, especially from one who in her private notes reaffirmed, "I have never been a standard-bearer, I am too self-indulgent and changeable."

It was 1932. The nation was in the grip of a devastating economic crisis. She intended to speak about education, she said, "in the light of present-day knowledge and need."

Certain periods in history suddenly lift humanity to an observation point where a clear light falls upon a world previously dark. Everything seems strangely different. Familiar ideas put on new garments and parade before us. Scholars and thinkers scrutinize events with a new intensity to learn their meaning, and the people look for a sign, a miracle.

I believe we are living in the beginning of such a renaissance. The creative achievement of three men, Lenin, Gandhi and Einstein, proclaim it.

Every renaissance comes to the world with a cry, the cry of the human spirit to be free.

This aspiration is basic in present-day thought. It is manifesting itself in many ways and many places against great opposition.

The Russian Revolution is the most disturbing manifestation of the new spirit that has come into the world, and by far the most hopeful; for, no matter how mistaken Communist ideas may be, the experience and knowledge gained by trying them out have given a tremendous impetus to thought and imagination. And, whatever the outcome of the experiment, it is inspiring to see the youth of Russia working together to raise themselves from the level of beasts of burden into an atmosphere of investigation and discovery. Surely, the greatest social experiment in history should arouse the profoundest interest in every one who is trying to understand economics, industry and politics.

The Great War proved how confused the world is on these vital questions, and depression is proving it again. We have no firm hold on any knowledge or philosophy that can lift us out of our difficulties. And, what is more discouraging, we fail to recognize the gravity of the situation. We are afraid of ideas, of experimenting, of change. We shrink from thinking a problem through to a logical conclusion. We imagine that we want to escape our selfish and commonplace existence, but we cling desperately to our chains. Our material eye cannot see that a stupid chauvinism is driving us from one noisy, destructive, futile agitation to another.

The one hope was in education, she went on, and quoted Sir Norman Angell on the need for an education that dealt with the realities of war and depression, of armaments and isolation:

Education in the light of present-day knowledge and need calls for some spirited and creative innovations both in the substance and the purpose of current pedagogy. A strenuous effort must be made to train young people to think for themselves and take independent charge of their lives. Only when we have worked purposefully and long on a problem that interests us, and in hope and in despair wrestled with it in silence and alone, relying on our own unshaken will—only then have we achieved education.

Many of the nation's leaders of the blind were in the audience. "It was the best speech of the kind I ever heard Teacher make," Bob Irwin, not usually given to flattery, wrote Helen. "One of the Temple professors told me after the meeting that it was the best speech he ever heard made at a college graduation."

In the Foundation's successful campaign for the Pratt bill to provide federally funded reading services for the blind, Migel, Bob Irwin and Helen had constituted an effective lobbying team on Capitol Hill. That was in 1930. Now, two years later, the same trio went into action to convoke an international conference of workers for the blind. The last such conference had taken place in England before the war. A renewed exchange of experiences seemed imperative in light of all that had happened since 1914, but the costs of such a conference, particularly travel expenses for the blind and their sighted companions, seemed prohibitive.

But Bob Irwin, supported by the American Association of Workers for the Blind, pressed insistently to have the United States take the lead and had persuaded the Major, who in turn enlisted the help of Republican leader Senator George H. Moses of the Foreign Relations Committee to introduce a joint Congressional resolution that authorized President Hoover to call a world conference of the blind. Migel also made a substantial contribution to the United States share of the conference costs, as did John D. Rockefeller, Jr., and other Foundation friends. President Hoover made a personal contribution as well as issuing the invitations. Thirty-two nations sent delegates in response to the President's invitation.

A high point of the conference was a reception at the White House. Would the First Lady receive the delegates? Helen inquired of Mrs. Hoover. "I so earnestly desire that the delegates carry back to their countries a pleasant memory of America's interest in the blind." Both the President and Mrs. Hoover would receive them, she was informed. A few days later Mrs. Hoover's secretary wrote Teacher:

The President and Mrs. Hoover would like to have the pleasure of seeing more of Miss Keller than is possible from the few minutes when she brings her group to meet them on the twenty-second. Accordingly they wish to invite her to luncheon or to spend the night at the White House within the next week or two, if her program permits and if she enjoys making such visits.

Helen wrote the First Lady afterwards:

It was wonderful! The kindness with which the President and you received the delegates to the world congress of workers for the blind last Wednesday, and the President not only spoke words of encouragement, but shook hands with them all! Then the delightful hospitality you bestowed upon Mrs. Macy, Miss Thomson and myself! We are all still talking about that happy visit, your sweet thoughtfulness and the President's interesting talk, your friendly guests, the flowers breathing sweet welcome and the White House we saw in such a new way through your eyes. . . .

Helen not only arranged the White House reception for the conference delegates, but helped raise the conference budget, welcomed the delegates, gave a reception of her own for them and was in and out of many of the sessions. Teacher, except for the White House visit, appeared only once, to speak at a dinner given by Major Migel in honor of Dr. Edward E. Allen, who after forty years of service to Perkins had just been retired as its director. The timing had outraged Charlie Campbell: "You know of poor Mr. Allen's retirement from Perkins," he signaled the Forest Hills trio. "Not only that, but they went behind his back and selected a minister, who probably has only seen blind beggars on the street, for his successor." Teacher's graceful tribute to Dr. Allen as an "educator" was fully understood by the workers of the blind. "I never saw an embarrassing situation handled with such generous courtesy," she wrote Migel. "You were regal."

The liveliest issue at the conference arose over the role of the state in relation to the blind. This was primarily a debate between the British and French delegations. The latter, led by Paul Guinot, the secretary general of the French National Federation of Civilian Blind, insisted that private philanthropy had failed and that only the blind "can claim the right to organize the new work which will lead them to ultimate victory." He was right in principle, but his abrasive manner aroused resistance. Helen took no part in this significant debate, perhaps out of deference to the large contribution private philanthropy was making to the blind in the United States through the American Foundation for the Blind. And her approach to change was now much more gradual. She no longer believed, she told an interviewer, "as I did when I was young, in sudden reform." She preferred the stress of Captain Ian Fraser, the head of St. Dunstan's in London, on a pragmatic mixture of private philanthropy with government programs, of national and local financing.

Whatever the reason for her reticence, she also may have felt that she should remain above all factions. She was at the time cultivating a husband-and-wife team that would, before the thirties were over, bring about a revolution in America's approach to the disadvantaged, including the blind. In 1929 Helen sent the newly elected governor of New York, Franklin D. Roosevelt, a fund raising letter, asking him to become a member of the American Foundation for the Blind. Roosevelt declined, but forgot to sign his name to the letter. Helen returned it with a message hand lettered on the back:

PLEASE, DEAR MR. ROOSEVELT SIGN YOUR FULL NAME. SOMETHING TELLS ME YOU ARE GOING TO BE THE NEXT PRESIDENT OF THE 'LAND OF THE FREE AND THE HOME OF THE BRAVE,' AND THIS SEEMS A GOOD TIME TO GET YOUR AUTOGRAPH. IT MAY INTEREST YOU TO KNOW I HAVE NEVER ASKED FOR ANY ONE'S AUTOGRAPH BEFORE. WITH ALL GOOD WISHES

> I AM, CORDIALLY YOURS,
> HELEN KELLER

A charmed Roosevelt returned the letter signed as requested. They were both professionals in the art of making use of people. To remind him of her existence a few months later she sent him an inscribed copy of *Midstream*. He intended to read it in Warm Springs, he thanked her. "Some day I want your advice on the problem of the state's care of the blind, and if you come to Albany this winter I hope you will come to visit us at the Mansion." When Roosevelt was reelected in 1930 in a landslide victory that immediately made him front runner in the race for the Democratic nomination for the Presidency in 1932, she wrote him a handsome note of congratulation: "I cannot recall a public servant who has gone into office with a more magnificent backing of intelligent people since I have taken an interest in better government." She had not meant to write at length, "but something generous and compelling in your personality offers a temptation stronger than I can resist." She asked to be remembered to Mrs. Roosevelt. "I have a sweet memory of meeting her at the sale for the blind last year." Roosevelt responded in kind. Hers was "about the nicest letter I have had since Election Day. I appreciate all that you say and I hope some day this winter that I may tell you so in person."

But when Helen took him up and asked him in February to open up the international conference, he declined—"either the Legislature will still be in session or I shall be in the midst of what we call the thirty-day bill period, during which I cannot get away from my work."

She sat out the 1932 campaign. Whether Roosevelt's rebuff together with Hoover's solicitude played any part in her decision is not clear. She was still a socialist, she told the press, but she did not intend to vote. She was too busy with her own campaign for the Endowment, she explained impishly. "I have a good job, and I'm not bothered with politics."

An added consequence of the World Conference had been a quantum leap in Teacher's trust in Migel's leadership. It would have important results for Helen's future after Teacher was gone:

> It has been a strenuous month for everybody, hasn't it? But I think much has been accomplished. There will be no trouble about the position of the Foundation. From now on it will have an international influence. It is widely known in America today. Prominent people like the President and several members of his cabinet have expressed a deep interest in our work. I wish you could have heard the President's splendid little speech to the delegates. No one seems to have taken it down, but Helen has written to Mrs. Hoover asking her to have one of the secretaries get the speech, if possible. Two presidents of colleges, Mr. [Glenn] Frank of Wisconsin and Dr. [Robert Maynard] Hutchins of Chicago, were also guests, and heard the President's warm words of commendation. I imagine it was the first time work for the blind had been discussed in the White House since Helen talked to President [Theodore] Roosevelt about Miss [Winifred] Holt's activities. Our respect for President Hoover deepened

as he talked with us. He may not be a great statesman, but he is a man of much charm, modesty and understanding. . . .

I feel that the future of the Foundation will be glorious and fruitful in exactly the proportion that you are its moving spirit. Of course there is abundant work for every one, but if all is to go well, you must keep the leading role.

XXXIV

Death of Teacher

"My admiration for you—one in two, two in one—has increased, if that is possible."—Russell Doubleday

It seemed to the "Three Musketeers," as Major Migel affectionately dubbed the Forest Hills trio, that they had entertained almost every delegate to the World Conference, keeping open house and lunching or dining as many of the foreign visitors as possible. So when officials of the United States Lines said that they could cross the ocean as guests of the line if they could be ready within a week to sail on the *Leviathan* for France, the weary women, including Teacher, decided that they didn't care where they went so long as they were able to get away.

By the day of sailing they had managed to pack two trunks, a hatbox, a shoebag, four large suitcases, three small suitcases, three rugs and three extra coats and dispatched them to the boat by truck, while they—plus Teacher's black Scottie, from which she would not be separated and which was an added reason why they made their destination France rather than England—set out by car. They were held up by a traffic jam at the Queens Bridge, causing United States Lines officials to wonder whether Teacher had again changed her mind, as she had done the year before. Finally they reached the pier at ten thirty to join their twenty breakfast guests, who had assembled as directed at nine thirty. But it was a gay party and did not end until the ship was pulling up anchor.

The crossing was uneventful, their arrival at Cherbourg a marvel of efficient management. A ship line representative met them in Cherbourg;

a porter for each piece of luggage saw that it was stowed on the boat train for Paris while the women motored through Normandy. Even Teacher enjoyed the trip, and at its end she delighted in Paris, despite its outdoor cafes, which seemed an invasion of her privacy, as did the pissoirs. Unlike London, which she still thought of as "dark and crouching," Paris seemed "open and bright." Again the United States Lines came to their rescue and through a tourist office located a small villa for them in Concarneau, Brittany, only eighty feet from the ocean. It belonged to a Viennese artist, and they were able to retain "Madame's servant," an excellent cook who also did all the housework and marketing and who became their friend. The house was small, and the bathtub, Teacher commented wryly, was of "the oddest shape, tall and narrow, extremely hazardous for one of my bulk." Even though the weather would be foul—*"déluge en permanence,"* Teacher called it—there they stayed through September, except for a trip to Yugoslavia.

Reporting their arrival to Nella, Teacher began her letter with an account of an extraordinary dream:

> I dreamed about you last night. We seemed to be in the little office upstairs at Forest Hills, and, as usual, you had a pile of manuscripts in front of you. You began to read aloud, and the thought came to me, I have given her the Porto Rico letters by mistake! Helen will never forgive me. You said 'At last' in such a natural voice that I woke up, still feeling troubled. I told Helen my dream this morning and she said, 'Why, that's just what you would do if I let you have the letters.'

The Puerto Rico letters had been written in American Braille, and Helen was resisting copying them. Nella does not explain why; but, as suggested earlier, Helen always had in mind doing her own book about Teacher, and that may have been the reason she delayed, just as she did not turn over to Nella Teacher's "Foolish Remarks of a Foolish Woman."

"Teacher keeps pretty well," Polly reported to Major Migel's secretary, Mrs. Bond, "though some days she might be better. I trust she will get through the summer without any trouble. Helen as usual is very well, and writing a lot of letters." Teacher's health did not survive the summer. Her spirits sank so low that she made out her will and, thinking of Helen's future, left the little trust fund that she shared with Helen from the days of Mrs. Hutton to Polly on the assumption that Polly would stay with

Helen. The making of the will brought Helen face to face again with the question she had asked Teacher at the time of the Puerto Rican separation: What was to become of her if Teacher should die? As she wrote Mildred and Phillips in January 1932:

> Last summer while we were in France, Teacher was very ill several times with a sinus trouble that affects her general health as well as her sight, and I became alarmed.

> The thought that when she was gone I might be subjected to one person who would manage everything filled me with apprehension, and I felt utterly unprepared for the vicissitudes of existence. When Teacher was a little better, I talked with her about my future. I told her how afraid I was of complications and impositions in one form or another. She agreed with me that I could not very well take charge of my practical affairs alone, and that I could not carry on my work for the American Foundation from Montgomery or Dallas [where her brother lived].

They were awaiting Migel's arrival in France. He had won their confidence and affection, and he in turn had come to love Helen and admire Teacher, whom he saw as a difficult woman of rare quality. They decided to discuss their anxieties with him. He would make a characteristically bold and farsighted decision: Helen was a national asset for which the Foundation should henceforth assume responsibility.

Otherwise the summer was uneventful, except for the trip to Yugoslavia. Its delegate to the World Conference had been with them on the *Leviathan* and had begged them to come to Yugoslavia. Such a visit would be of great help to the blind of that Balkan kingdom. When he made it clear their expenses would be paid, they indicated an interest. One day the postman arrived at their door with a large envelope, "which he wouldn't deliver until we produced our passports, and in which was an invitation from the Yugoslav Government to visit that country as its guests to stimulate public interest in the work for the blind."

From the moment the train crossed the border, they learned what it was to be an official guest of a country. "For once in our lives, [we] were sumptuously entertained wherever we went," Teacher wrote their old friend Lenore Smith. They were tendered a banquet on a riverboat, and they floated down the Danube "to the accompaniment of gypsy music, dancing and laughter." They called on King Alexander at his summer palace. "He is very good-looking . . . friendly and easy to talk with." He spoke French and had been well briefed. He assured them that Helen's visit was indeed stimulating wide public interest in the blind. Earlier that day Helen had addressed an audience of two thousand at the University. The King wanted to know just how Teacher had taught Helen, and as Teacher went through the old vaudeville routine, he exclaimed repeatedly, *"C'est merveilleux!"* At the end he decorated all three with the Order of Saint Sava. Helen, always ready with a graceful tribute, said of him afterward: "It is said that there is in every country an empty throne waiting for a bold man to seize it. There is no empty throne in Yugoslavia. King Alexander I fills his throne completely by the force of his personality, his decision, his courage, his vision. He is a great individual in a position to do great things. And this is the great task of achieving unity and harmony among the three major races of his kingdom—the Serbs, Croats, and Slovenes."

From Belgrade they went to Zagreb and Ljubljana and were met at each station by great crowds "with flags and flowers and bands playing 'The Star-Spangled Banner,' school children singing it and speeches of welcome." They ended their week-long visit at Bled in the mountains, a watering place for the diplomatic colony during the summer. There they were entertained by the American ambassador.

Teacher hated it all. "To Helen and Polly it was an adventure, to me it was a nightmare of the deepest dye. Of course that's because I'm old and infinitely sickened of many things. . . . Polly and I decided that Helen's insides must be made of cast iron fastened down with hoops of steel, she wasn't affected a bit by the food or drink or heat."

Although Helen protested her dislike of public life and its attendant claims upon her energies and privacy, she quickly missed it when it was absent. When a letter came from Migel announcing his imminent arrival, she quickly replied that her heart had given "a happy bound. . . . How dear you are to say that you missed us! We, too, have done some missing. Ours has been a rather dull summer. . . ."

They returned to the United States at the end of September, and soon afterward she was interviewed at Forest Hills. She sounded a foreboding note when a reporter asked her what she had seen in Europe. Without hesitation she replied, "Preparation for war and international hostility everywhere. If the present state of things keeps up in Europe, there will be war again within five years." She also conceded to a reporter's question that she was plumper than when she had left in May: "Yes, I'm told I'm heavier, but that's not my wish or fault! In Yugoslavia an ordinary meal will consist of beer, pork, goose and cheese cake served all at once. And if one does not eat all, the host is offended. So I must be plumper."

She showed the reporters her St. Sava decoration; but, haunted by the fear of an approaching war, she flashed another decoration, the "Two Percent Club" button of the movement founded by Albert Einstein. He had said that if 2 percent of mankind should resist war, there could be no war. She had called on Einstein during his visit to New York earlier in the year. Running her hands lightly over his face and hair, she had said, "You have always inspired me." "I have been a great admirer of you always," he had replied.

The most urgent business that autumn was the arrangement of a "guardianship" for Helen in the event of Teacher's death. Migel suggested that she appoint a committee of three to look after her finances, and a subcommittee of advisers "who would be more intimate, and discuss private problems with me as they arose." She had thought of Mildred and her husband, Warren Tyson, and her brother Phillips Brooks for the committees, but tactfully she explained to them that they were too far away:

> It did not seem practicable to put you on the committees. Teacher and I did not know what to do. After much earnest consideration, we asked Mr. Migel if he would be kind enough to become one of the committee, and to suggest two others who would be responsible for the business end. He asked Mr. Harvey Gibson, the banker, and Mr. William Ziegler, the son of the lady who gave the blind the 'Ziegler Magazine,' to advise with him. This committee would pay the salary of whoever lives with me and check up all our expenditures annually, and in this way protect me. As you know, the greater part of my income is in trust funds which cease with my death. The property I own is this house and its furnishings and the money I make from my books and the articles I sell.
>
> The sub-committee would include Mrs. Thomas Bond, Mr. Migel's secretary and a very good friend of ours, Mr. O. J. Anderson, whom I have mentioned in my letters to you, and Mrs. Keith Henney, who edited 'Midstream' and wrote the preface. She is now working on Teacher's life, and I could always advise with her about my writings.

As long as I am physically fit, I shall want to be engaged in some useful occupation. Idleness is the worst enemy of the blind.

The lawyer drafting the documents said he needed the concurrence of her sister and brother. "I told him I would write to you at once to find out if you approved the plan. I am quite sure you will. It has nothing at all to do with my independent action in making a will or disposing in any manner I wish of the house or any other property I may acquire. . . . During her life Teacher would serve on both committees." Both did approve—Phillips enthusiastically, grateful that the "folks" in New York were dealing so generously and solicitously with his sister; Mildred hesitantly, concerned that Helen's family would have no way of stepping in and protecting her interests.

The investment committee was set up as Migel advised; the advisory committee had some changes: Phillips and Polly were named to it, Nella was left off. Helen's income at this time, apart from what she received from the Foundation and her writings, included the $5,000 annual pension from Carnegie, $800 a year from the Eleanor Hutton Trust and $600 from the trust set up by H.H. Rogers and administered by the Unitarian Association. She also turned over to the newly established Helen Keller Trust Custody Account a small portfolio of stocks:

228 shares Doubleday Doran & Company
50 shares L. Bamberger & Co. 6-1/2% Preferred
30 shares Standard Oil of California
4 shares Standard Oil of Indiana.

By the spring of 1932 the lawyer had done his work and the legal forms were signed. In a memorandum that Migel drafted about the "Helen Keller Trust," he described the arrangements as follows:

As long as Mrs. Macy is here, the Trustees will delegate all their powers to Mrs. Macy so that the relationship which has existed between Helen Keller and Mrs. Macy for practically a lifetime will remain undisturbed—Mrs. Macy acting for Helen in every capacity as heretofore—with the added opportunity, however, of consulting the Trustees on any matter on which Mrs. Macy might desire counsel.

For Teacher and Helen it meant security and peace of mind. "For the first time my Teacher and I," Helen wrote Migel, "feel that our life-ship is being steered by wise, trusty hands, and we can live out our days without anxiety, except that which is inseparable from existence here below." She began to share with Migel some of the very personal letters she received and to solicit his views. That pleased Migel enormously, "as I believe you have arrived fully at the conclusion that my interest in, and my love for you are founded on a rock." Helen's reply to this was a love letter:

> Your warm interest in everything good that befalls me is like a kind hand caressing me. For many years I thought it was your goodness to the blind—your kindness to everybody, the happy grace of your deeds. I thought it was your wise counsel I loved—the generous color and sunlight you brought into sad hearts and somber tasks. I thought it was your sympathy I loved—the cheer and the flowers you scattered along my path. I thought it was all these things that I loved, but all the time it was you I loved.

Helen's anxieties were now totally focused on Teacher. "I am almost blind now," Teacher wrote Lenore, explaining why she might not accompany Helen and Polly to Boston, where Helen was to speak at Symphony Hall. "The only way I can see anything is by using a powerful drug to expand the clear field of the pupil a tiny bit. I feel old and helpless. . . . Perhaps, if I ever make up my mind to have the cataract removed, and the operation is a success, I may feel different. At present I only long to die out of my difficulties, but even this is not permitted."

In early May they sailed on the *President Roosevelt.* "A lot of people came to see us off," Helen wrote Nella from shipboard. "One of our staterooms was a veritable conservatory. Max Schling sent me American Beauty roses four feet high!" They had sunshine every day and stars every night. This time their visit was not to be a "dark secret." Glasgow University was to give her an honorary degree. "Already requests are coming in by radio. The *London Daily Express* wants an article, and the National Institute for the Blind wants me to open its new massage school. On the 22nd of June I am to speak for the New Church of Scotland. Oh dear! How I wish I might be invisible for five months!"

They went back to Looe, the fishing village on the Cornish coast, which Helen described ecstatically to Dr. Finley as divided by a river with "precipitous cliffs" on both sides, to which the "houses cling, while gulls, thousands of them, soared and swooped in and out of the harbor." Interviewers and photographers descended upon them "like an Alpine torrent." She described a visit to Thomas Hardy country to the cottage of Egdon Heath where he was born and the churchyard where he was buried. Her letter so charmed Dr. Finley that he had it printed in *The New York Times Magazine.*

Migel and Bob Irwin sent them the important Foundation news. It had obtained grants to develop a "talking book" that through the use of phonograph records would enable the blind with fairly normal hearing to dispense with the cumbersome volumes in Braille. "Both the Victor people and the Bell Telephone Laboratories have cooperated with us splendidly. A few days ago the Victor Company made us another test record. The copy was taken from the chapter on Mark Twain in your *Midstream.*" Helen objected to the Foundation's concern with the talking book. Because of the depression and widespread unemployment, the blind were worse off than ever. It seemed to her almost frivolous for the Foundation to become involved with talking books. She may also unconsciously have been indifferent to an invention that could not benefit the deaf-blind.

But for Braillists like herself there was also good news in the Migel-Irwin letters. After two decades of negotiations British and American representatives had reached agreement on a uniform Braille system. "Should you happen to be in the vicinity [London] on July 18th and 19th, perhaps you would be able to drop into the National Institute for the Blind to give us all your blessing. I am sure it would help to limber up some of those stiff-necked old Braillists."

Migel added some political news. He knew Helen's passion for politics, one that she shared with Teacher: "Only an Irish love of politics," the latter wrote, "has kept alive my interest in world affairs." It looked as if the Democrats would nominate Franklin D. Roosevelt, Migel wrote, "but I am hoping this may not eventuate and that a man like Newton D. Baker, much stronger in every way, mentally and intellectually, might be the nominee."

They broke camp at Looe for Glasgow, where Helen was to be honored. Dr. James Kerr Love was among their hosts. The Loves, Helen wrote, "were among the few who perceived the interwoven quality of our lives." Such a perception was the key to the hearts of Teacher and herself. The awarding of the degree was preceded by a "robing ceremony" at which Helen was presented with her academic robe. Scottish teachers of the deaf and the blind, honored by having Helen honored, had collected the funds for the robe. The ceremony of robing was performed by Mrs. James Kerr Love; and, decked out in the scarlet robe with purple trimmings, Helen responded: "As I stand before you in these glorious garments, I feel like Judith, who, before presenting herself at the tent of Holofernes, arrayed herself in her richest attire. . . . So you have decked me out in splendour for the ceremony at the University of Glasgow."

Her little speech finished, Dr. Love put a question to her: "If you could gratify the dearest wish of your heart what would it be?" Her answer was simple, "I would wish for world peace—that all wars should cease." On the day the degree was awarded the *Glasgow Herald* wrote, "The University honours itself in laureating such indomitable souls as Miss Keller. Through such individual lives there is mirrored something of the majesty and determination of humanity."

From Glasgow they went to Canterbury, Kent, where they had rented a cottage not far from London. Life became truly hectic. Both she and Teacher addressed the British Medical Association. Helen opened the massage school at the National Institute for the Blind. Its director, W. Mac Eagar, endeared himself to her by his admiration for Teacher. She spent some time at St. Dunstan's. It was headed now by Captain Ian Fraser, who had headed the British delegation at the World Conference and had succeeded Sir Arthur Pearson. He was a Conservative M.P. and blind. He took them to the House of Commons to dine. They attended a Royal Garden Party at Buckingham Palace, where they met King George and Queen Mary. She did not find the latter "stiff and distant" at all. "She gave me a warm handshake and listened with such interest to what I had to say. I told her how much I loved the gardens at Buckingham Palace and she wanted to know how I could enjoy flowers I could not see. I explained to her that I could smell their fragrance and feel their beauty."

Also in London they gave a tea for the Uniform Braille Committee. And they met George Bernard Shaw at Lady Astor's. Shaw had been one of her and Teacher's heroes ever since they had attended *Pygmalion* and *Saint Joan,* and they arrived at Lady Astor's tense with expectation, only to be told he was having a nap. They settled down to wait, on tenterhooks, anxious, too, that they might be late for their next engagement. Finally he appeared. It turned out to be a chilling encounter. Helen later told the story in a syndicated article for the North American Newspaper Alliance:

> I held out my hand. He took it indifferently. I could scarcely believe my sensations. Here was a hand bristling with egotism as a Scotch

thistle with thorns. It was not the sort of hand that one would associate with the compassionate interpreter of Joan of Arc.

'I'm so happy to meet you,' I said inanely. 'I've wanted to know you for ever so long.'

'Why do all you Americans say the same thing?' he taunted.

'Why do you hate us Americans so?' I murmured.

'I don't hate you,' he answered. Mrs. Macy's hand gave me the inflection of his voice, which implied that Americans could never rise to the level of his contempt.

'Then why don't you come to America?' I asked.

'Why should I? All America comes to see me.'

Lady Astor laid her hand on his arm and shook it a little, as if he were a child behaving badly before company. 'Shaw,' she said, 'don't you realize that this is Helen Keller? She is deaf and blind.'

His answer must have shocked everybody, but a few moments passed before I knew what it was. A quiver ran through Mrs. Macy's hand —I was shut off from the scene, and I stood wondering and waiting. Then slowly Mrs. Macy spelled to me what Mr. Shaw had said:

'Why, of course! All Americans are deaf and blind—and dumb.'

Publication of the story caused a small international scandal. Shaw insisted he must have been misinterpreted to Miss Keller:

My compliment to her on seeing and hearing so much better than most of her countrymen could not have been misunderstood as an insult by even the stupidest observer (such a brutality would have banished me from decent English society); but I cannot answer for the manner in which it was conveyed to her.

It is possible that Miss Keller may not have fully understood the English social point of honor, which was to avoid any air of sympathizing with Miss Keller as an unfortunate person, and make her feel as much as possible that she was a highly distinguished visitor at no disadvantage whatsoever with us.

Lady Astor was "horrified that you should have misunderstood him so seriously. . . . He is one of the kindest men that ever lived—and would not willingly hurt anyone. I remember just how he said—'All Americans are deaf and blind' but I thought more to comfort you than be rude. I feel responsible for his having met you and really sad that you should have done him such harm." Helen stood her ground. "I am glad to believe as you do that Mr. Shaw 'is one of the kindest men that ever lived.' I know he is one of the greatest, but in all fairness I think you will grant that he was not particularly gracious to me that afternoon."

London, except for the episode with Shaw, had treated them magnificently, but they decided that they had to get away. "What a hectic and unsettled summer we have had," Polly wrote home. They fled to the north of Scotland where Polly hoped "the high dry air" would cure Teacher's cold and sinus trouble. Her brother, the Reverend Robert Thomson, a pastor at Bothwell, near Edinburgh, found them a 150-year-old farmhouse at South Arcan in Ross-shire. It was on a high hill, a mile from the road, with a commanding view of the heather-clad hills.

As they drove up in front of the house on August 23, Teacher recorded in "Foolish Remarks,"

> we saw a gull close to the door. It lifted wide wings and flew away over the corn-fields. As I entered a telegram was put into my hand telling of John's death. Now my heart is full of withered emotions. My eyes are blinded with unshed tears. Today only the dead seem to be travelling. I wish I was going his way. The House of Life is shattered with the wounds he inflicted, the broken walls are of his forgetting.
>
> Three thousand miles away his body, once so dear, lies cold and still. The dreadful drama is finished, the fierce struggle that won only despair is ended.
>
> The essence of him was old. I will not retail the things he did. I am not his historian. Much will be hid of what was deeply, intimately mine. Some may tell how we did thus and so, but who can know what we refrained from doing, the paths [we] did not take, the secret separate ways down which we looked and longed for, but took another journey after bright, strange things we dreamed? Deep in the grave our dust will stir at what is written in our biographies.

How many little things death dredges up after the storm!—moments of rapture shared, books we read together, walks hand in hand, drives through pine woods, people met and flickering interest in the things they did and said.

I have been homesick many a year for his arms. Perhaps it was wrong to look too deep within. Now he is dead.

How often he read immortal verse and taught me to understand the shining soul of it! Love is ever in flight, it gleams and goes, it is the irised wing of a fugitive dream, but imagination once kindled is the life of the spirit, and lives forever.

What dreams! What tremulous expectations! What clouds of suspicion, of jealousy! What amazing cruelties of looks and tones and sudden denials! There is more pain than joy in the most passionate love—pain and waste for a brief ecstasy. One but glances away, and all is gone—all that golden abundance of beauty and joy, of hope, of excitement and adventure.

O the witchery of youth—youth that laughs and sings and dares to believe all things possible! And how vivid the memories of our youth are! As I write them down years and years afterward, my heart leaps to the whisper of a name, a touch, the first kiss that lives in every kiss. Those vanished golden hours, those warm, loving hands and lips murmuring shy words which are the sweet blossoms of life's springtime are gone past recall. Gone? No! they flash before me more real than the realities of mature years.

Now I wait for death—not sad, not heroically but just a bit tired. To love and succeed is a fine thing, to love and fail is the next best, and the best of all is to fail and yet keep on loving.

John had died of a stroke, she subsequently learned, while lecturing on American literature at Unity House, the summer camp that the International Ladies' Garment Workers' Union maintained, and still maintains, in the Poconos for its members. Macy was a familiar name to the Jewish waistmakers as a frequent contributor of leading articles to the English section of the *Jewish Daily Forward.* According to family sources his views in his final years were Trotskyist, but like Teacher and Helen he seems to have dropped all political activity.

It might have comforted Teacher that in his way John, too, had still loved her. Perhaps she did know. Nella Henney did, and thereby hangs a mystery. In Nella's journals there are several letters and journal entries that suggest that she was in touch with John, perhaps in connection with her biography of Teacher. A letter to Nella from Dr. Blanche Colton Williams, the head of the Hunter College English department, who was abroad at the time of John's death, thanked Nella for letting her know:

> Somehow, it was fitting that I should learn from you; he so valued *that* work of yours, and you and he and I made one of the triangles that helped to form the pattern of his later years, shadowy and fragile though the triangle was. . . .
>
> It will always be a source of some dismal comfort to me that I was able to give John a small post in the Hunter Summer Session. Only ten days before I left from London, I had from him a letter telling me how much he appreciated the work he was doing. . . .
>
> I have thought of writing Mrs. Macy; but I do not know whether she would care to have me do so. It seems so sad that, after all, any woman —even in a business relation—should have known more of her husband in late years than she herself knew! Not that I should hint that idea to her, however. I feel pretty sure that he loved her at the bottom of his heart, all the time. He never spoke of her without a kind of proud stiffening of the neck: 'Mrs. Macy.'

On their return to New York Helen and Polly went campaigning for the Foundation. Teacher, on whose eyes the drops were ceasing to have any effect, remained at home. A new crisis arose in Helen's relations with the Foundation. It was an old argument or, as some people at the Foundation viewed it, Helen's old obsession—that her fund raising efforts should be devoted exclusively to raising the Endowment Fund, and not applied toward the current expenses of the Foundation. Considering that the Foundation was in a way now her guardian and protector, her protests showed an independence of spirit, a strength of will that bordered on the reckless. It gave her sleepless nights, but she decided that she had to stand by her convictions: "The truth is, Mr. Migel, I am not happy in this campaign." The Endowment was being ignored, and "there is nothing for me to do but resign," the resignation to take effect

January 1 "as we have booked the meetings up to the end of December." Helen had the unrealistic idea that the Foundation should restrict its expenditures to what could be paid out of Endowment income and memberships and donations given specifically for expenses. Otherwise, she saw herself "begging for the blind the rest of my days—a prospect which does not appeal to me."

The letter greeted Migel on his return from Washington. It shocked him, he wrote her, not so much because of the threat of resignation "but because you write me this way at all." It was always possible to talk matters over. Her request gave him no problems. "We have agreed at the Foundation that all net income from your meetings shall be applied absolutely and entirely to the Endowment.

"Please be prepared for a scolding."

Instead of a scolding, the Foundation elected her to its board of trustees; and a tribute that Migel offered to Helen at a *Pictorial Review* luncheon at this time showed how much thought he had given to her contribution, not only to the blind but to all those with whom she worked. The *Pictorial Review* award of $5,000 was no small prize. In 1931 the prize had gone to Jane Addams, and the year before that to Carrie Chapman Catt. Although some of Helen's friends begged her to keep the money for personal use, she turned it over to the Foundation to be used for the deaf-blind as she directed. Migel was ill on the day of the award luncheon, and his tribute was read for him by Mrs. Migel. He called Helen in his message "the Guardian Angel of the Blind," and he spoke of his surprised delight in her "freshness of mind," her "sympathetic understanding," her "indomitable will," her "sense of humor" and her "loving desire to serve all humanity and particularly the unfortunate." He described her labors for the Endowment Fund and her readiness to cross a continent if need be to persuade a legislature or a public official. He recalled sitting next to Congresswoman Ruth Baker Pratt during Helen's testimony on her bill. "I asked her, 'Why are you weeping?' 'I don't know,' she replied. 'Why are YOU weeping?!'

"I have often tried to analyze what it is in Helen Keller that so awakens the better part of our natures—the desire to be up and doing for any cause that she has espoused. It is not pity—not emotion—it must be the great soul within her. . . ."

Helen was accustomed to public praise, but Migel's tribute moved her. It had given her, she wrote him, "as exquisite a kind of pleasure as anything that has ever been spelled into my hand about myself, it was so understanding, so sincere, so tender, so everything one loves to have a friend say about one!''

There were other polls that testified to her deep hold on the public conscience. *Good Housekeeping* listed her among the nation's twelve greatest women, and a poll taken by the National Council of Women to name the twelve outstanding women of the last one hundred years selected Harriet Beecher Stowe, Julia Ward Howe, Frances E. Willard, Susan B. Anthony, Carrie Chapman Catt, Mary E. Woolley, Mary Baker Eddy, Clara Barton, Helen Keller, Amelia Earhart Putnam, Jane Addams and Mary Lyon.

During the 1932–1933 Endowment campaign, she and Polly held about eighty meetings and "raised only twenty-thousand dollars"; but as she pointed out to Robert L. Raymond, the Boston lawyer who had handled the Eleanor Hutton Trust Fund, "Knowing as you do the lean and hungry conditions of most people's pocketbooks these days, you can imagine what a trying time it has been." Their own fund had "come out pretty well through this horrible mess," Raymond comforted her, and added, "we must all, I feel sure, give Roosevelt great credit for his quite miraculous power of influencing people."

An article in the January 1933 *Atlantic Monthly*, "Three Days to See," attracted wide comment because it pulled people out of their own misfortunes and caused them to think how well off they were. The first day, Helen wrote, "I should want to see the people whose kindness, gentleness and companionship have made my life worth living." The second day she would arise in time to see the dawn and spend her day in the museums, which housed "the condensed history of the earth and its inhabitants," and see with her eyes the many objects that she had explored with her hands. The third day she would make the rounds of the city to get a sense of "the workaday world of the present," beginning with the quiet little suburb of Forest Hills in which she lived. "I who am blind can give one hint to those who see—one admonition to those who would make full use of the gift of sight: Use your eyes as if tomorrow you would be stricken blind."

The article appeared as the American economy was grinding to a standstill. It "has opened my eyes to the innumerable things that I enjoy," Russell Doubleday wrote her, "and it has helped to make me put aside some of the things that worry me." He wanted to publish a collection of her articles, with this one as the leadoff piece. Helen doubted that she had enough articles of real value to make a book. Constant traveling and speaking made writing difficult. "I hope you won't wear yourself out raising all this money," Effendi counseled her. "I wish I had the power to endow all your schemes but this crisis in business has prevented my carrying out a lot of plans I had."

It was the bleak and fear-stricken month before Roosevelt took office. Helen addressed herself to the incoming First Lady: "We have met only twice for a moment, but I have been drawn to you by your earnest, constructive efforts on behalf of the underprivileged, and since Election Day I have felt the bond of sympathy grow stronger and stronger between us. I cannot tell you with what pride and satisfaction I have followed your courageous activities. Your talks over the radio have in them the ring of conscience and vision." She would send Mrs. Roosevelt a corsage made up of blossoms of her favorite colors and hoped Mrs. Roosevelt would wear it at some point during the inaugural ceremonies as a token of her sensitivity to the needs of the blind. Mrs. Roosevelt thanked her, and soon there were other requests of the White House. Migel asked the new President to permit the blind to run newsstands in federal buildings. He agreed, but the Treasury resisted. Would Helen write the President? She hated to bother him at such a time, her letter began, but he had given some thought to the problem, and it was "so rare to find a man of world responsibilities who has room in his consideration for small groups of handicapped people." Roosevelt reaffirmed his order. "I have no thanks warm enough or eloquent enough to express my appreciation," she wrote him back, and appended another request, this one personal in nature: Would he expedite the issuance of a reentry permit to Polly Thomson? She was not an American citizen and was reluctant to leave the country without assurance of reentry.

"This is the situation. My Teacher has been far from well and now her sight has almost completely failed. Her physician says that if she is to gain strength for the hard days to come, she must go away quietly for a long rest, and that is why we have decided to go to Scotland far from all sight and sound of work." They needed Miss Thomson. "Without her we should be utterly lost and unhappy." Roosevelt passed the word to the immigration authorities, and on June 14 they boarded the *President Harding* bound again for Arcan Ridge in the Highlands. Migel was at the boat to see them off. That astute man had weathered the hard times sufficiently well to permit him to give the Foundation $100,000 with which to build a headquarters. He wanted her approval. "I was happy to begin the voyage with your dear words of greeting and the proud thought of your splendid gift to the Foundation." A few weeks later he informed her that

John Markle, the philanthropist, "was good enough to leave us a legacy of $100,000. . . . We have been jumping around with joy." It was she who had written Markle, Helen noted. It was a brief paragraph in a seven-page letter, but nevertheless it kept the record clear.

The Highlands were giving them the peace they sought, she reported to Migel, but she was involved in an auction sale of a bullock to interest the people of Scotland in the deaf-blind. "I shall appear in the ring with all the bullocks and offer for sale the one which has been selected as the best of the lot." Would he make a donation? He cabled fifty dollars. Her letter was full of news. They had chartered a little boat that took them to the Orkneys and the Shetlands, and in leaving Scapa Flow the captain manipulated "the smoke from the funnel so that it traced a huge K in the heavens."

Before they left Scotland, they spent a week with the Loves and several days with Lord and Lady Aberdeen. Lord Aberdeen was one of the grandees of the Highlands and a friend from 1928, when he had spoken over the radio about Helen. He and his wife were devoted to the three women and had given them a Shetland collie named Dileas. They were passionately fond of animals and always had two or three dogs around. Her letter to Migel went on about their social activities. "The Duke and Duchess of Montrose have invited us to visit them at Buchanan Castle. . . . The Marchioness of Tweeddale has asked us to tea tomorrow at Brahan (?) Castle. This invitation is regarded as the highwater mark of our social triumphs." Had she detected a note of the "blues" in Migel's letter?

> I hope not. I read that things are on the upgrade in America. The papers here are full of President Roosevelt's efforts to bring back prosperity. He is a very courageous and able man, his intelligence is above the average given presidents. I hope, though, he won't work his dictatorial powers to the bone. Some of his acts seem autocratic from this distance. One wonders if there is a shred of democracy left in the United States.

What were the Foundation's plans? They were tempted to stay on at Arcan Ridge. This inclination hardened into decision when Dr. Berens arrived and found Teacher's eye still inflamed, and since he could not operate while there was any inflammation, he advised them to remain where they were. When Helen heard the Foundation's plans, she became more adamant about not returning:

IF EXECUTIVE COMMITTEE DECIDES CONTINUING ENDOWMENT
CAMPAIGN WILL RETURN AT ONCE. TALKING BOOKS A LUXURY
THE BLIND CAN DO WITHOUT FOR THE PRESENT. WITH TEN MIL-
LION PEOPLE OUT OF WORK AM UNWILLING TO SOLICIT MONEY
FOR PHONOGRAPHS. AFFECTIONATELY HELEN.

The Foundation bristled, so she wrote stating the medical facts and
asked for a leave of absence. "As for our salaries you will do what you
think best." Migel talked with Berens and then recommended to the
board that it grant them a "sabbatical" with pay. Wall Street's elation over
Roosevelt's decisiveness, he added in a footnote, was beginning to wane.
"The President seems surrounded by a corps of advisers who are presumably very theoretical and everyone here, who has any financial standing
whatsoever, is worried and anxious."

Nella's book about Teacher came out in the autumn. Helen had tried
to persuade *The New York Times* to serialize it "as it did General Pershing's
life," but had been turned down. Despite this setback the book was a great
success, both with the reviewers and with such old friends as Lenore
Smith, Charlie Campbell, Ed Chamberlin, John Wright, Nina Rhoades
and Mabel Brown Spencer. The latter had roomed with Teacher at Perkins. "It seemed very much like the old girl of fifty years ago who used
to keep me laughing most of the time," she wrote Nella. "It's a magnificent book," Russell Doubleday wrote Helen, "and fortunately the critics
have appreciated it." Earlier, when he had read the manuscript, he had
exclaimed, "My admiration for you two—one in two, two in one—has
increased, if that is possible."

Helen's letter to Nella was generous with its praise. "You can imagine
how the fire burned out as we talked far into the night." The book should
finish the gossip and criticism "which began with Mr. Anagnos's first
report and has continued ever since."

Teacher did not write: "I do not think you are likely to hear from
Teacher. She is far from being in a writing mood. She is almost totally
blind now, and it exasperates her that she can't see a word. I have never
known her to be so impatient and rebellious before."

Helen refused to give up hope that Teacher might recover some vision,
but Teacher reproached Fate for its fickleness, and her last penciled note
(in "Foolish Remarks") as her sight failed reflected a somber and elegiac
mood:

Why did you not ask your questions before my heart was cold, my hair gray? What does it matter now who my father was? Or my mother? How my childhood was nurtured? Your words of praise or blame or sympathy or scorn cannot touch me. I am as indifferent as a stone. Love has betrayed me; friendship is a broken reed; life has pierced me in a thousand ways, but the wounds are all dry. I think I have forgotten how they used to bleed. You have kept aloof, proud world, too long. The time for confidence is passed. The most safe abode for my secret is where the darkness shelters all.

Nella met the press, presumably with the authorization of Teacher, and reported that Helen was in seclusion in Scotland so that she could nurse her friend who was going blind and coach her in the Braille system. Nella also told the reporters that on Teacher's last birthday Helen's gift had been a book about George Bernard Shaw. She had written on the flyleaf: "To my beloved Teacher. They tell me George Bernard Shaw has tired the sun with talking. That may be so, but we know he was the mocking bird who waked up the world from little aims and from sordid hopes and futile fame."

The *Times* story also implied that they were staying in Scotland because they were destitute. That upset Migel. "From all my letters to Helen," he wrote Polly, "I am certain you will gather that no matter what your needs might be, I am always at your disposal, so that this particular article has been a source of distress to me." He suspected that Teacher might have had something to do with the story. If he was wrong, his letter should not be shown to her. "We cannot account for their [the Press's] wild statements," Polly wrote back, "other than Miss Braddy's inexperience." Polly's letter ended on a note that seemed to reflect exasperation with Nella. People thought that Teacher was benefiting financially from Nella's book. That was not the case. Nella had offered to share the profits with her, but only during Teacher's lifetime. That seemed unfair to Teacher, and she had refused to sign the contract, saying that the book in a legal sense was undoubtedly Nella's. "Teacher will never speak of this but I thought you should know." Helen, too, ascribed the misstatements in the interview to Nella's inexperience. "She must have uttered some half joking remarks about our retirement to the bleak hills of Scotland, and the reporters were only too glad to make a sensational story out of them."

Teacher now was visited by "a ghastly siege of carbuncles" that kept her in bed and at times required the care of a trained nurse. They tried the waters and sulphur baths at nearby Strathpeffer, "but alas, she had only one bath, she was too weak to continue them."

Helen almost broke down as she told reporters on their return to the United States in the autumn of Teacher's approaching blindness. Forest Hills was undergoing repairs and painting. Migel advised them against staying there, but Teacher refused. As he had predicted, the fumes soon drove them out. "I sometimes wish Teacher would listen to me a little more seriously, and be guided a trifle by me." Within a week she had to check into Doctors Hospital. Even Helen was allowed only an occasional visit. Helen brought her a talking book, P.G. Wodehouse's *Very Good, Jeeves,* to cheer her up a little. Later Alexander Woollcott was one of those who came in to read to her. Wit, raconteur, drama critic and popular broadcaster under the rubric of "The Town Crier," he had read Nella's biography and was so impressed by Teacher that he had asked to visit her.

Helen conscripted him for service to the blind. She asked him to appeal for funds over one of his broadcasts to provide the blind with the "phonographs" that a few years earlier she had so haughtily dismissed. She also enlisted Will Rogers, Edwin C. Hill, and other broadcasters.

ANYTHING YOU WANT OK, Will Rogers replied. "I succeeded in persuading Will Rogers, John McCormack, Edwin C. Hill, Lowell Thomas to broadcast about the talking books," she wrote Lenore, "and Alexander Woollcott to read from *While Rome Burns* for the records. I hope you heard Will Rogers and the splendid message President Roosevelt, without being solicited, sent through him encouraging me in my efforts for the blind." Her letter to Lenore explained why Teacher had refused to let her come to New York and be with her while Helen and Polly were in Boston. In addition to her other ailments she was in agony from neuritis. "You know her sudden changes of old, and will understand, I am sure." The ordeal of another operation on her eyes hung over her, but Dr. Berens was still holding off. To Lenore, Helen confided an opinion of Nella's biography that was somewhat different from her public attitude: "As for me, I am naturally the reader most concerned and the hardest to please. The book does not present Teacher to me as I know her, and my fingers ache to write something about her more to my liking."

As much as taking care of Teacher permitted it, she worked for the Foundation. On a lobbying trip to North Carolina she persuaded the legislature to set up a commission for the blind, and she went to Washington to berate it for failure to require preventive measures against *ophthalmia neonatorum,* an old crusade.

One plea for help electrified her. Takeo Iwahashi, "a blind Japanese gentleman" whose autobiography, *Light Out of Darkness,* she had read, called on her and invited her to visit Japan on behalf of the Japanese blind. It was "a unique opportunity" and she should not miss it, Teacher urged. "But I simply can't go without you," she replied. They spent the summer in the Catskills, but after only a brief time in New York in the autumn, took off for Jamaica, Teacher hoping to recapture there the idyllic Puerto Rican experience. "The island is beautiful!" Helen wrote Migel, who as a substantial stockholder in the United Fruit Company had opened many doors to them on the island. "Nature has created a masterpiece, but it seems man has done his best to mar its splendor. The utter poverty and ignorance of most of the natives are distressing beyond words." When she had expressed such feelings to some white visitors to the island, they had said, "Oh, they are used to their burdens, they don't mind them as white people would." "Oh, the pity of custom-blinded minds," she exclaimed.

The trips south, the trips north, to tropical islands, to mountains, were intended to help Teacher, at least to divert her. But usually when they reached their destination she had to take to her bed. Finally in April 1936 Dr. Berens operated on her. It meant running the risk of "losing the little sight she had, but she was willing to take the risk." She seemed more resigned than a year ago, Polly informed Lenore. Afterwards she was afraid to ask Dr. Berens his prognosis. For a moment her vision seemed to improve, "the eye looks very good," and the doctor was very pleased, but back home she was "weak, very shaky." Then the eye began to pain her, the sort of pain that had obliged Dr. Berens to remove her other eye. Also she began to suffer gastric pains. "What is really the matter with Teacher," their Forest Hills physician told Polly, "is senility." She was seventy. They found a place in Canada, La Corniche, a village in the Laurentians; and Herbert Haas, a Forest Hills neighbor who had quietly and unobtrusively begun to help with Teacher as butler and chauffeur when they were away, drove them there. Helen loved it. There were fine walks "following a rope that winds in and out among the great firs and silver birches," and bathing in the lake. She was reading Clarence Day's *Life with Father* and Lincoln Steffen's *Autobiography*—"ten big Braille volumes." But Teacher was miserable, and Polly took her to New York to consult the doctor, leaving Helen with Herbert. "My only news is loneliness," she wrote Teacher in the first of almost daily letters, "but I can bear anything that is a step on the road to your recovery." The Bob Irwins were coming up to be with her. "I stayed in the water about three-quarters of an hour this afternoon. I lengthened my rope so that I could get into deeper water. . . . how strange everything seems without you." She played checkers and dominos with Herbert in the evening. He was relaxed, friendly and humorous and had learned the manual language. He took her for a walk through the dense woods. "I was glad of a chance to touch great rocks covered with moss and ferns. . . . I got some idea of what a 'hike' through the Canadian forests must be like,—heavy underbrush, crumbly hummocks like the Adirondacks and almost impenetrable tangles of vines and evergreens." Bob Irwin, although blind, rowed them around the lake at evening calm. "Birds were singing on both sides of the water—Wilson thrushes, Bob thought." Russell Doubleday wrote that he was retiring; "I cannot imagine the firm without him, can you?" Effendi had died two years earlier.

She had much to say about the Steffens autobiography, and when she reached the last Braille volume she stated a conclusion that showed there was an awareness of the old Adam in her, even if she rarely permitted its verbal expression: "Steffens is right, it seems to me, in putting intelligence before 'righteousness' in the Pharisaic sense, and that only sinners—those who discover in themselves the crook or the thief or some other pernicious ego—can be saved." She was looking forward to the return home as she finished the book. "Every time I know you are better, I sleep more peacefully." Polly left Teacher with a nurse and went up to Lac Archambault to drive down with Helen and Herbert, the dogs and the luggage.

But the heat soon drove them away from Forest Hills, especially as the doctors wanted Teacher to take a little exercise and get some sun. They rented a beach cottage in Peconic Bay on Eastern Long Island. One day Teacher surprised them by walking down to the water and wading in, only to become dizzy and collapse. The two women half carried and half led her back to bed. "I am trying so hard to live for you," Teacher sobbed. By the next day she had to be taken to the hospital in an ambulance. She had suffered a coronary thrombosis. "She [Helen] has taken Teacher's illness wonderfully, Lenore, she is very calm and philosophical," Polly informed their oldest friend, whom Helen wanted kept posted as if she were a member of the family.

Helen's calmness surprised Polly. In *Teacher,* which Helen finished writing when she herself was in her seventies, older than Teacher at the time of her final illness, she observed that growing old had not been

Teacher's "real tragedy." "The tragedy was the fact that as a child she had not received the training or acquired that mental outlook that would have enabled her to enjoy far more independence, to listen to the counsels of reason, and to use her sight prudently."

"I wonder whether Teacher will ever be able to come down again," Polly observed when she had been brought from the hospital to Forest Hills in an ambulance. She was not. TEACHER SINKING RAPIDLY, Polly telegraphed Lenore on October 15. The Theodore Roosevelt Memorial Association announced that it was awarding two gold medals for 1936— to Helen and to Mrs. Macy, "for a cooperative achievement of heroic character. . . . The achievement has been in the truest sense a collaboration." The Association noted that it was the first time that it had awarded two medals for one deed, a deed that had "been possible only because the devotion and native genius of Mrs. Macy were matched in Miss Keller by intelligence, courage and indomitable determination."

But when Helen sought to interest Teacher in such news, her reply was that the Angel of Death was coming for her soon and that they should have everything in order at his arrival. Polly jotted down the farewell messages that she uttered in moments of lucidity on October 15:

Good-bye John Macy, I'll soon be with you, good-bye, I loved you.

I wanted to be loved. I was lonesome—then Helen came into my life. I wanted her to love me and I loved her. Then later Polly came and I loved Polly and we were always so happy together—my Polly, my Helen. Dear children, may we all meet together in harmony.

My Jimmy, I'll lay these flowers by your face—don't take him away from me. I loved him so, he's all I've got. She took the bed clothes and threw(?) (the) bucket of flowers out of there.

Teacher was complimenting nurse and nurse said, Oh, you are playing to the gallery. Teacher threw her head back smiling and said, 'I've play-acted all my life and I shall play up till I die!'

Polly will take care of Helen. As the years go on her speeches won't be so brilliant as what people will think [sic] but my guiding hand won't be there to take out what should be taken out.

Thank God I gave up my life that Helen might live. God help her to live without me when I go.

She died on October 20. In "Foolish Remarks of a Foolish Woman," the final entry was captioned by Helen, "Teacher sets sail with this message." Clearly it had been written before the final days:

> Helen Keller's development suggests to me that the loss of one or more faculties may, by way of discipline, drive the handicapped person to deeper levels of will-power than is required of normally equipped human beings. I have no doubt whatever that most people live in a very restricted sphere of their potential capacities. They make use of only a small portion of their possible powers and of the resources of their minds. It is as if, out of all their physical furnishings, they should use only a fraction of each sense. When the complete destruction of one or more senses creates an emergency, we see how much greater our resources are than we supposed. May not deafness and blindness be a way of getting at latent functional possibilities?

And Helen, in the same collection of notes, wrote, "Petulant, capricious, humorous as she was, she always had an uncanny ability to slip the halo from her own head to mine." But the world had recognized, as Russell Doubleday put it, that they were two in one, one in two, and never more so than in the final tributes. The funeral services were at the Marble Collegiate Church. The pastor, Reverend Edmund E. Wylie, read from the scriptures, a quartet sang "Going Home" and the Reverend Dr. Harry Emerson Fosdick delivered the eulogy. He spoke of Teacher's "sheer artistry. . . . Through her remarkable work her friend became a world figure, bringing new confidence in the capacity of the human being to overcome his obstacles. Yet all the while the teacher remained in the background, quiet and truly great."

The honorary pallbearers were selected and personally invited by Helen. They were Mr. Migel, Dr. Berens, Harvey D. Gibson, Russell Doubleday, Dr. Finley, Louis Bamberger, Dr. Allen, Dr. Neilson, Robert Irwin, Dr. Philip S. Smith, William Ziegler, Jr. and Dr. William F. Saybelt. Alexander Woollcott, who declined to be a pallbearer because of a sense of personal unworthiness, wrote:

> I think everyone at the funeral felt immeasurably impoverished, but one and all were stricken most by the tragedy of Helen parted from Teacher after fifty years. All of us [were] heart-sick at the mere thought of that unimaginable separation. Surely all eyes in the church

were riveted on the sight of Polly Thomson and Helen Keller following the coffin together, the tears pouring down Miss Thomson's
cheeks. And just as the two of them passed the pew where I sat, I saw
the swift, bird-like fluttering of Helen's hands—saw and with a quickened heartbeat knew what I had seen—Helen—think of it—Helen
comforting her companion.

Canon Anson Phelps Stokes of the National Cathedral in Washington
had telephoned the church to say that the bishop and chapter of the
cathedral "will consider it a privilege to offer the right of sepulchre in the
Cathedral for Mrs. Anne Sullivan Macy . . . and the Bishop has authorized
me to inform you that he will recommend to the Chapter at its next
meeting that the privilege of sepulchre at the Cathedral should also be
offered to Miss Keller."

Teacher was the first woman offered this honor on her own merits. The
committal service, presided over by Bishop James E. Freeman, was on
November 2. "Among the great teachers of all time," said the bishop,
"she occupies a commanding and conspicuous place." The urn containing
Teacher's ashes was placed in the columbarium adjoining the chapel
where the services were held. Helen spoke a few words that were recorded by Lenore: "Blessings upon the receptacle of the precious dust
which my heaven-sent Teacher wore as a garment as she wrought her
miracle of liberation thru Him who is the Lord of Life and Love."

part six

HELEN *and* POLLY

XXXV

Helen Without Teacher

". . . to stand on my own feet socially and economically."

In Nella's notes she recorded one of Teacher's last utterances as reported by her nurse:

> One night towards the end when Annie Sullivan lay in the bed upstairs the nurse said, 'Dear Teacher, you must not worry about Helen. She will be taken care of.' 'I know that,' Teacher answered. 'It is my dear Polly that I am worried about. I know how many people will fight not to stand back of Helen but beside her. I don't know if Polly will be strong enough.'

Many of Helen's friends, according to Nella, thought that "Polly would not do. Helen must give up public life, go home to Alabama and live quietly with her sister."

Teacher knew both the assets and the limitations of this reserved Scotswoman who had joined them in 1914. She had secretly gone to meetings to watch how Polly managed on the platform with Helen, and she had left satisfied. Polly liked pretty things, indeed had her own weakness for living expensively. She would see that Helen was well dressed and attractively groomed. But as Teacher foresaw on her deathbed, she lacked the literary sparkle that Teacher had often introduced into Helen's writings and replies and that made the difference between the arresting statement and the conventional. "As the years go on, her speeches won't be so brilliant." Nor did Polly have the flair for politics and public relations by which Teacher had kept Helen in the forefront of the work for the blind.

Polly herself had doubts. No one was able to take Teacher's place, yet Teacher was the standard by which most people would judge her. Teacher had pushed hard, often stormily, but then dissolved tension with a sally and laughter. Polly was dour and matter-of-fact and already was disliked "in certain quarters," recorded Nella; but there were friends of Helen's who believed in her. "One whose support was absolute was Lenore Smith and it was largely because of Lenore that objections subsided."

But of course Lenore was persuasive in dispelling doubts about Polly, because she better than almost anyone, except possibly Nella, knew the wishes of Teacher and Helen. Those wishes were made evident in Teacher's will, written in Concarneau in 1931 and never revised, in which, with Helen's consent, she bequeathed to Polly the Eleanor Hutton Educational Trust Fund. Its appraised value when Robert L. Raymond delivered it to her in November 1936 was $22,814.05. Teacher's will also stipulated that all her letters, manuscripts and the like be given to Nella, "in trust with the understanding that she is willing to assist Helen Keller in her literary work" and that after Nella was finished with them they be turned over to the American Foundation for the Blind.

So although Polly, as we have seen, never was admitted fully into the unity that made Teacher and Helen "two in one, one in two," it was the judgment of both Teacher and Helen that she would be loyal—to the point, as Nella put it, that the rest of the world might die so that Helen would live.

Polly was five years younger than Helen. She had been born in Glasgow of middle-class parents. Her father, a draftsman in an engineering firm, had died when she was twelve and left her mother with four children to bring up. Her two brothers graduated from the University, David becoming an eye, ear and nose specialist and Robert an ordained minister of the Church of Scotland. The two sisters, Polly and Margaret, did not marry and devoted themselves to their brothers. Polly never went beyond public school and came out of this experience with "a sense of inferiority from which she never recovered," and which sent her to the United States in 1913 to look for a career, as a governess or preferably a companion, the quest that finally brought her to Wrentham as secretary-housekeeper to Teacher and Helen.

She was always busy, a willing and tireless worker, quiet, self-possessed "and withal deferential." This last pleased Teacher, as did her Scottish burr. When Nella first met her in the 1920s, "already her face was a mask for her thoughts and feelings," and when uncertain she often retreated into silence. From her photographs she seems neither beautiful nor elegant, but plain and sober. However, Dr. Berens for one thought her "extremely attractive," so the photographs may not do her justice.

It was to Polly's brother the minister that she and Helen fled to repair their devastated lives. They had made the decision to get away immediately after their return to Forest Hills from the funeral. Its familiar surroundings only made Teacher's absence the more unbearable. The Bob Irwins realized this and urged Helen, Polly and Herbert to spend the night with them. "You know that you and Polly can let down at our house, and be perfectly at home." Afterward Helen thanked him for his thoughtfulness. "Our hands met as those of comrades in a strange new darkness. Never have I trodden the stones and thorns of personal disaster as I am doing now."

In the same vein she wrote Migel from the *Deutschland,* on which they had taken passage when the United States Lines were struck: "For a while I feel as if I had lost the eyes and ears within my limitations. It is as if all objects dear to my touch and paths familiar to my feet had vanished, but I try to believe that, as you say, 'time is a great healer,' and to wait until my blinding sorrow breaks to let in the radiance of the Life Beyond." She was grateful for "the thoughtful interest with which you took charge of my small affairs."

By then the *Deutschland* was off Land's End. Her shipboard diary vividly chronicled her ascent out of numbness. "Most of the time I appear to myself to be a somnambulist, impelled only by an intense faith," was her description of her feeling on going abroad. The first day out was "a day dreadful beyond words. I am beginning to come out of the stupor of grief, and every nerve is a-quiver." Two days later she reports, "Gradually I am regaining my habit of 'looking around.' " But the next day despair again overwhelms her: "What earthly consolation is there for one like me whom fate has denied a husband and the joy of motherhood? At the moment my loneliness seems a void that will always be immense. Fortunately I have much work to do. . . ." One day out of Southampton she writes, "Today I had a lunch of frankfurters and sauerkraut—the first meal I have eaten with any relish in many weeks." The next day, "My first consciousness of time. . . ."

They stayed in London at the Park Lane, as always, and the first morning walked along the Mall and Piccadilly. Helen had none of Teacher's dislike for that city. To Teacher it seemed, in contrast to New York's skyscrapers and the light and openness of Paris, "to crouch." Helen, by contrast, found it a "gentle city," endlessly fascinating. Among their first visitors at the Park Lane were the Augustus Muirs. He was the writer who had found them the cottage in Looe in Cornwall in 1930. That summer he had tried to persuade Teacher and Helen to keep a diary, which he said would be an invaluable record in time to come. Now he pushed Helen to undertake the project on her own. She was evidently waiting to be prodded and became so fired with the idea that she began immediately to make notes on her shipboard feelings. "It will not be as laborious as writing a book," Polly explained to Lenore. "This must be brief—simple, the day's doings, concealing nothing, giving the absolute truth. This of course will not interfere with the little book on Teacher."

Mac Eagar, the director of the National Institute for the Blind, came for them in his car. "Polly's flying fingers could scarcely keep pace with Mac's pithy comments." At the National Institute for the Blind Helen was shown and acquired a new Braille writer and taught how to manipulate it. "I shall be sorry to say good-bye to my little old 'Stainsby Wayne' which has traveled with me for years." Braille machine and typewriter were indispensable to her, almost as much so as eyes to the sighted. "Often my hands feel cramped or limp," she wrote in the journal that she had begun to keep, "which does not surprise me, as they have never been still, except in sleep, since I was two years old. They mean the world I live in—they are eyes, ears, channels of thought and good will. Sooner would I lose my health and even the ability to walk (and walking is among the few cherished bits of personal liberty I possess) than the use of these two hands." She did not usually speak of her limitations. But Teacher's death made her aware anew how fragile her ties were with the world.

There was, of course, Polly. Eleanor Roosevelt once said of her Miss Thomson, Malvina, "She makes life possible for me." Polly did the same for Helen; but just as Malvina was no Louis Howe, so Polly was no Annie Sullivan. With Teacher's death "it was as if the fire of Teacher's mind through which I had so vividly experienced the light, the music, and the glory of life had been withdrawn."

They were leaving for Glasgow on a nonstop train, *The Flying Scot:* "As always, I shall pack my own bags, so that I may know where everything is, and be as independent as I may under the circumstances." After a few days with Polly's brother Robert at The Manse they planned to take rooms in some quiet Scottish inn; but Robert and his wife made things so comfortable for them, giving them their drawing room as a study, that she decided to stay, especially as the family's three children would brighten her life. "I need soul-sunshine for downcast moods and a correspondence that seems interminable."

She and Polly went to work on a mass of American mail. For three hours Polly read letters of condolence into her hand. Helen became conscious of how much Teacher had spared her by knowing what to include and what to put aside. "Absent-mindedly I made a stupid remark, Polly got nervous, and sharp words flew between us. For several minutes we sat mute with stinging tears in our eyes and a sense of frustration: then we broke down, remembering Teacher's prayer that we might be reunited." No new outbursts at Polly were recorded, but a few days later she wrote in her journal, "Every hour I long for the thousand bright signals from her vital beautiful hand. That was life!"

She sent a difficult letter to Nella telling her of Muir's proposal and her talk with a young London publisher whom Muir had brought to see her, Michael Joseph, "who wants a book of between eighty and ninety or a hundred thousand words." She thought that she would do it, and if Nella had any comments, "I should be glad to have them at your earliest convenience. Really I am interested in this new adventure, it will help divert my thoughts from a grief that will be long in healing." Then a new note. She wanted to be on her own:

> Teacher often expressed a regret that she did not employ a literary agent who could push our fortunes untrammeled by other duties. Now I have made up my mind to find a reliable agent and try out alone whatever powers I possess. If I succeed it will be another tribute to her who most believed in me. People will see that I have a personality, not gifted but my own, and that I can stand on my feet socially and economically. . . . Who knows—the time may be ripe for me to shape my life anew and confirm further my message to the handicapped.

She had been faithful so far, she wrote home on December 7, to the journal project, "and it has proved a godsend, helping me to discipline my mind back to steady work and renewed interest in what goes on about me." Both Muir and Polly's brother, whom she allowed to read parts, were well pleased. "If I succeed, it will be another way of showing people that Teacher's work not only has brightened my dark silence, but also rendered me strong and mentally independent. I have written Nella about the Diary and my desire to stand on my own feet socially and economically."

While in Glasgow they went to West Kilbride to spend a few days with the Loves. "He had his 79th birthday not long ago, and he performed forty-three operations in one week." But that did not convert her to his custom of a nap after lunch, which he said prolonged life. "Longevity does not matter much to me personally, since I have eternity to live in and earth time seems too long waiting to rejoin my loved ones who have gone first."

Her letters and journal were full of comments on the abdication crisis precipitated by King Edward's announcement that he intended to marry the divorced Mrs. Simpson. Last night, she noted, all sat around the fire in The Manse, "stunned" by the King's contemplated marriage. His decision to abdicate distressed her: "Many persons have a wrong idea of what constitutes true happiness. It is not attained through self-gratification but through fidelity to a worthy purpose. . . ."

Twice while in Glasgow they went to the cinema: "People sometimes express surprise that a deaf-blind person can get any pleasure in the cinema. Polly reads me the titles, spells the dialogue, and describes the facial expressions and the costumes, which is pretty rapid work." How much pleasure, one wonders, did she really get? How much relaxation? Or was the need it really fulfilled the passion to feel herself a part of the everyday world? Among the movies that she saw were *If I Had a Million* and *Fury,* a blazing indictment of lynching. The latter stirred her morally and politically. "Since childhood, my heart has been hot against lynching; whether the victim is white or black," she commented.

Two developments buoyed Helen's spirits during the stay in Glasgow. Takeo Iwahashi, who had been urging her since 1935 to come to Japan in aid of the blind and to promote Japanese-American goodwill, renewed his invitation. "Of course Polly and I said 'yes' to ourselves, but wired a cautious reply." They asked for details—length, purpose, auspices, expenses, who would accompany them around Japan. "Nevertheless, we are determined to start as soon as possible. I have sent Mr. Migel a letter expressing my earnest wish to go and asking for his counsel." She felt certain of his consent; he had just proposed to the trustees of the Foundation that her title be changed from "trustee" to "Counsellor of the Bureau of National and International Relations." "This pleases me very much, it seems to convey a larger idea of my attitude towards movements for the blind in all lands." The "international" function dovetailed with her almost compulsive need to travel. Hitherto she had defended it in her mind as rest and therapy for Teacher, but the itch to get away from familiar surroundings was lodged powerfully within her being, sometimes assuming an almost feverish importunity. Behind it was her ever-lurking fear that it was easy for the world to overlook the deaf-blind Helen Keller. Travel, both at home and abroad, appealed to her just because it meant tight schedules, endless meetings, receptions, newspaper interviews, speeches, people eager to describe to her their country's institutions for the blind and its scenic wonders. And at the moment it helped take her mind away from the loneliness that she felt because of Teacher's absence. Gradually "we are rallying our powers to the standard Teacher carried so long," she reported to Dr. Finley, thanking him for the lovely words the *Times* had carried editorially about Teacher, but "I still feel lost in an immense loneliness. . . ."

They returned to London at the end of January, enroute to Paris for the unveiling of Gutzon Borglum's statue of Thomas Paine, at which she had agreed to speak; but in London they learned that the unveiling had been postponed. They decided to go to Paris anyway and arrived in time to attend a reception in the sculptor's honor at the George V Hotel. She was introduced to the sculptor and demonstrated that she had lost none of her ability to ensnare the mighty. She liked the firmness and vitality of his hand, told him she admired him because he "thought greatly" through his sculptures. "When skill and daring imagination meet, a masterpiece is born." Borglum liked that. "That is my struggle," he said, "to embody in art the elemental forces that have moulded men's minds."

Back at the Hotel Lancaster Nelson Cromwell called. One of the founding partners of Sullivan and Cromwell in 1870, he had retired from the firm having, among other accomplishments, shaped the corporate structure of United States Steel and drafted the legal instruments that made it possible for the United States to control the Panama Canal. He was an ardent admirer of France and spent much of his time in that country. He was also a trustee of the Foundation and had been, along with Helen, on the founding board of the "Permanent Blind Relief War Fund for Soldiers and Sailors of the Allies" established after the war. He was a large, courtly man with a handsome moustache and, old though he was, thick curly locks. He enfolded Helen in his arms. They talked for hours, and he urged Helen to identify herself with the blind of every religion, race and tongue. He approved of her trip to Japan and encouraged her to include China.

Would she make a record expressing gratitude to the French government for setting up a talking book program that he had promoted? She quickly agreed, and she and Polly hurried to get ready for a dinner for Gutzon Borglum. She was seated next to the sculptor, and again their spirits seemed to be attuned to each other. Borglum endeared himself to her by saying that Teacher had been a sort of sculptor—"your Praxiteles, breathing life into your sense-shut faculties."

On a sudden impulse she told the sculptor she had long cherished the wish to touch Rodin's sculptures. "Would you like to see them tomorrow if it can be arranged?" He had known Rodin; "I will go to the museum to show the masterpieces to you." The next day he came for her. The museum was ready. For an hour the public was excluded, the silk cords were dropped, and under Borglum's guidance she explored Rodin's world with her sense of touch. Borglum led her first to the famed bust of Victor Hugo. Both hands freed from her sleeves, with fingers spread, she reached up and felt his massive forehead, then down over the face, the eyes, the beard, then back to the forehead, "where she found and spoke of the trouble in his brow." Then Borglum led her to "The Thinker." "In every limb I felt the throes of emerging mind. . . . Rodin might have named it "Trying to Think." It reminded her of "the force that shook me when Teacher spelled 'Water.' " "Few people have understood the elemental meaning of Rodin's symbol as you do," commented Borglum. She had sensed in the statue "the struggle for existence in which the body goes as far as it can and conscious thinking begins." They went on to "The Burghers of Calais," a group of six figures larger than life, six men who gave themselves up to the English in order that their city might be spared. "It is a work sadder to touch than a grave, because it is a conquered city typified," commented Helen. It caused her heart to contract. Borglum said afterward, "I shall never forget that hour with Helen Keller. . . . From it I learned that the soul, over and above the body, *has* eyes." When they invited him to lunch with them at the Hotel Lancaster before their departure, he agreed willingly.

Her other Paris gallant, Nelson Cromwell, made their stay in Paris very agreeable, placing his limousine at their disposal. "Ever we move in a show," she noted as the usual cortege of photographers, reporters, couturiers with hats and dresses to show them, fell in behind. They drove out to Versailles, where they had been in 1931 with Teacher. The latter had always insisted that she did not like to travel; but once on the way, recalled Helen sadly, "she made things hum and our hearts glow with her appreciative outbursts, quick sallies, instructive glances at history and literature. No matter how others' love surrounds me, a glory is gone from my wanderings." The day before departure they lunched with Cromwell at his princely mansion, "and he entertained us like princesses." George Raverat, who had attended the World Conference of the Blind and had directed the work of the Permanent Blind Relief War Fund, was there with his wife. There was a gold service for the luncheon in a dining room bedecked with gorgeous wall tapestries, which the host asked her to finger. Afterward all went to the recording studio and made the disc. Later she listened to the disc with her fingers and picked a discordant vibration —her own muffled voice. She was unhappy, but there was nothing to be done. Elsewhere she noted how a cage of lovebirds were frightened "when they heard my odd voice."

They sailed on the *Champlain* from Le Havre. When the *Europa* bound for New York passed them in mid-ocean, one of its passengers sent her a cable—it was from Borglum. Later he would send Helen a valentine. Such was the impression she had made.

Back in Forest Hills they were conscious of the changes taking place around them. The nearby marsh was being transformed into a parkway in preparation for the World's Fair. The subway had been extended to Forest Hills, and she and Polly promptly traveled to midtown on it. "I like any mode of transit, subway, elevated or the bus that brings me into closer contact with the people." Psychologically, however, they were preparing themselves to leave Forest Hills. "I can never, never get used to this house without Teacher," Helen burst out at Polly at breakfast. "Nor can I," the latter answered, "not once in all the twenty-four hours does it seem like our home without her." At the same time Forest Hills did not seem to Helen to have been part of Teacher's life. Her strong sense of the separateness of body and soul was reflected in her attitude: "Teacher's real self is alive with us, yet it was never in this house. The home of her personality was in Wrentham, and something I cannot control turns my thoughts to her there. Only her poor tortured body sojourned in this place. No! not even in my loneliest moments do I wish her back here."

The days went swiftly. Iwahashi's reply on the arrangements had been more than satisfactory. Major Migel suggested to the Japanese that Helen should be the guest of the government, and they agreed with alacrity. A long letter from Iwahashi alarmed her: "It sounds as if we were expected to make six speeches in each city. This is a physical impossibility. I shall consult Mr. Migel and see what can be done." Two Japanese reporters came to see her. Would she speak on peace as well as the education of the blind and the deaf? they asked. She feared "the militarists would repent allowing me to enter Japan if I did." "But if you pray for world peace as a part of your goodwill message," they assured her, "it will be an influence for higher things." Her governmental sponsors in Japan, she learned, would be the Ministries of Foreign Affairs, Education and Home Affairs. Migel said that he would inquire of the White House whether President Roosevelt wished to send a message to the Japanese people via Helen.

The Foundation was in a good humor. It had been left $100,000 by a woman who, they thought, had heard Helen speak for the Foundation in 1926. "Now I dare hope again that I may raise the second million." was Helen's reaction. Migel journeyed out to Forest Hills to discuss with her and Polly the Foundation's plans for them the next October. As she had said she would do, she investigated literary agents. Nella came for dinner and subsequently spent a day with them helping with materials for the lectures in Japan. Helen no longer felt close to Doubleday, and Nella set out to repair that. She and Keith invited her and Polly to dinner. Later the chief editor of Doubleday, Mr. Maule, came in. They were bringing out a new edition of *Midstream*. They would be happy to handle the correspondence with her German publisher, Otto Schramm, who had asked her to delete the favorable references to Lenin in *Midstream*. She had refused and directed him to cease publication of the book. He wrote endless letters defending his standpoint on Lenin, Bolshevism and the like, and Helen was happy to have Doubleday take on the burden of answering them. Maule also indicated Doubleday's interest in publishing the American edition of her journal.

She had a row with Polly over what she would wear to town. It was mid-March, still very cold, but she did not like to wear her fur coat. She preferred her less cumbersome "Glasgow coat," as she called it, having bought it there. "I lost my temper because Polly said it looked shabby and I could not wear it to town." She also lost her temper at what she construed to be an effort to run her life for her. Who and what occasioned the effort she did not say:

> A gust of irritability is blowing through me just now because there has been a recurrence of a tendency in some people to try to run my affairs. This seems all the stranger to me because since I was seventeen I have arranged my own life. At the age of twenty-two I began working very hard for whatever money I have earned during the past

thirty-four years. Of my own accord I have undertaken public responsibilities in America and other lands. After Teacher's health broke down I worked very much alone with Polly's hand to furnish information and her voice to reinforce my halting speech. Yet there are still those who appear to think it is incumbent upon them to alter my life course according to their own ideas! There was some excuse when I was young and bewildered in the search of something worth doing. But mother and Teacher knew me better than anyone else ever did, and they never dictated the course of action I should follow. There have always been other friends with power to advance the work for the blind, and they respect my desire as a human being to be free. It is beautiful to consider how their cooperation has increased my happiness and rendered possible whatever I have accomplished. However, unless I keep on my guard against uncalled-for though well-meant interference, they cannot help me any more than they can help any other person who weakly surrenders his will to another.

Helen's sturdy sense of independence was closely bound up with her feminism—how closely, she indicated in a letter to Eleanor Roosevelt after having read *This Is My Story:*

> . . . It is a superb document of womanhood freeing itself from the countless social inhibitions, timidities, family paternalism and pleasant inertia so vividly portrayed in Edith Wharton's *The Age of Innocence.*
>
> Tenderly I sympathize with your girlhood aspirations to independence and the tremulous self-consciousness you overcame.—Oh, how that limitation still pursues me in my speech and public appearances! What unusual spirit you must have had to shape alone a life not out of dominating conventionalities but out of your concepts of women as human beings! The two lessons you took to heart we cannot learn too early—that power cannot last or preserve its beneficence without love for the people, that without serious acceptance of individual responsibility and cosmic righteousness wealth brings chaos 'and weaves karma.'
>
> Because you have so bravely struck out on a self-chosen trail, you inspire other women with confidence in themselves and in life. You

show them how through rightly directed intelligence and will power they can evolve higher capabilities and raise the average of human accomplishment. . . .

May I commit the indiscretion of sending you my *Out of the Dark?* It contains several chapters on the modern woman I wrote when I was making discoveries somewhat similar to your own. Some of the things I said at the time are now out of date, but the spirit of revolt which animated us both remains.

"Words of praise," Eleanor Roosevelt wrote back, "from one who stands for the embodiment of courage to all of us means more than I can say."

Before Helen and Polly left for Japan, they spent endless hours at Bendel's ordering dresses for their journey. They went down to the Customs House at the Battery to fill out long forms for Polly's passport, and mostly Helen worked on her speeches for Japan, sometimes from five in the morning to ten at night. The speeches had to be written, memorized and practiced. There was a breathless day of final packing, and at last the moment of departure arrived. Migel and Amelia were at Grand Central Station to see them off on the Twentieth Century Limited. So were some of their other friends as well as a large delegation of Japanese. In Chicago, where they changed trains, the reporters wanted to know what she thought of President Roosevelt's Supreme Court Plan. She hoped that "the President's changes in the Supreme Court might prove beneficent," she replied, a little evasively but on the whole affirmatively. In San Francisco at the St. Francis Hotel a message was put into her hands. It was from the President and was sent from Warm Springs, Georgia:

I have learned that in response to an invitation from a Reception Committee representing various Japanese associations, and sponsored by the Japanese Government, you are to visit Japan this spring to give a series of lectures there. I feel confident that your presence will prove a lasting inspiration to those Japanese laboring under physical handicap, and that your association, brief as it may be, with Japanese individuals and groups interested in humanitarian endeavor will contribute to promoting that spirit of friendship and good-will between our people and the people of Japan upon which good international relations must rest. As you are so well qualified to convey to the Japanese people the cordial greetings of the American people, I take this opportunity to express my hope for the success of your mission. . . .

On April 1 they boarded the *Asama-Maru.* "Why, oh why," she wailed in her journal, "did I start this diary, knowing how crowded my life has been for many years?" But having gone so far she was reluctant to throw it all away. A week later she was in Honolulu. "I noted that two extra meetings had been put in between that of the Legislature and the Lions' Luncheon." It was a hectic day, a foretaste of their schedule when they would arrive in Japan. Back on board the *Asama-Maru,* she worked on her speeches, going up on deck at five in the morning to practice them aloud. As they approached Japan messages began to pour in. "The Committee, the nation and the cherry-blossoms await you," cabled the chairman of the reception committee, Prince Iyesato Tokugawa, president of the House of Peers and sixteenth descendant of the first Tokugawa Shogun. As she prepared to land, Helen wrote, "And as I stood on deck this morning in the midst of dawn, looking westward to the land where a Great Adventure awaits me, I thought I could feel her [Teacher] by my side."

Helen's story had long been known to the Japanese, an article about her having appeared as early as 1897. Yet it is difficult to ascribe the tumultuous character of her reception and her "spectacular tour," as the *Japan Times* described her circuit of thirty-nine cities and ninety-seven lectures, simply to admiration for Helen's achievement in overcoming enormous obstacles. "No foreign visitor had ever been accorded such an enthusiastic reception," wrote Nicholas C. Rhoden and Jami Hooper in their splendidly researched article for the *Akita Journal,* "not a prince or president, kaiser or king.' Over and above respect for Helen as a person, her visit gave the forces of moderation within Japan a chance to demonstrate against the militarists. Prince Tokugawa himself was a living symbol of Japanese-American friendship, heading the society by that name as well as having led the Japanese delegation to the Washington disarmament conference in 1921.

Beginning with the ebullient scenes at the Yokohama dock, where thousands of children waving Japanese and American flags greeted her, and continuing through the round of official receptions in Tokyo, her visit acquired a political as well as humanitarian character.

Ambassador Grew accompanied her to the banquet given by the government in her honor. The turnout astounded him. On the platform, he noted, were the prime minister, the foreign minister, the home minister, the governor of the Prefecture, the mayor of Tokyo, Prince Tokugawa and Marquis Okubo, president of the Foundation for the Blind. He particularly noticed in the audience Baron Shidehara "and many of the highest people in the country." It was a moment in Japanese prewar history when a moderate cabinet was in power and was seeking to bring the younger officers and military under control. Grew's previous entry in his own diary noted that "for the moment it might almost appear that there was a tendency to revert to the 'Shidehara diplomacy' and that the moderate influences in the country are becoming more articulate and possibly more influential than they have been for a long time." The reception for Helen was, in effect, a demonstration by the moderates against the military extremists. But no one made a point of this. It was dangerous to challenge the young officers openly. Her visit, wrote *Asahi,* "has been the occasion for the awakening of the people to the condition of private institutions devoted to the promotion of the welfare of the blind, deaf, and dumb. . . . Let us hope that the Government will fix a definite policy and carry it out."

The Keller party as it set out from Tokyo consisted of Helen and Polly and the Takeo Iwahashis. He was the leading champion of the blind in Japan and had translated Helen's *Story of My Life* into Japanese; he doubled as their interpreter. In addition there were two maids and a man assigned to handle their baggage. Everywhere there were crowds of newspapermen and photographers.

She made numerous speeches in and around Tokyo. Her themes were sight conservation, ways in which the blind might help themselves, messages of encouragement. The biggest obstacle, she quickly discovered, was a cultural one—the semireligious belief that physical handicaps were visitations of the gods, to be lived with patiently. She had only to cite her own development as an answer to such fatalism, and she thought by the end of her tour that the national attitude was indeed changing. In Tokyo, also, she was a guest at the annual Imperial Cherry Blossom Viewing Party in the imperial gardens. The guest list was headed by the princes and princesses of the realm, the cabinet, the diplomatic corps. She was received by the emperor and empress, a rare privilege for a foreign visitor.

In the middle of May they were permitted a short rest in Nara, the ancient capital of the Empire. "Helen is making history here," Polly wrote Amelia. "Her influence is going to be tremendous in the cause of women, and the work for the handicapped is now put on its feet and recognized by the Government right down the line." She went on to talk about Nara. "Helen and I touched the famous bronze Buddha seated on lotus leaves, the only two women ever to touch and get near that sacred figure. It was a dusty, tiresome business. Oh, Oh, the things a celebrity has to do. Poor Helen!" But that was not how Helen felt about touching the Buddha at all. She described Nara's enchantment, with its thousands of shrines and lanterns, the giant cryptomerias, the tame deer that took rice cakes from their hands and "the Great Buddha which I was the first woman in the world to touch, (how kind and understanding the high priest was). . . ."

In Nara Helen worked on her journal. "I have been frightfully troubled over it," Polly confided to Amelia. "Helen has simply had no time to devote to it, not even on the ship, as she was busy with speeches. She is now at April 3rd, and we want to conclude April 14th, Teacher's birthday. I pray it can be finished during these few quiet days. But even then it has to be copied into Braille and revised." Two weeks more of strenuous touring and another few days of rest as guests of Baron Sumitomo, "the Rockefeller of Japan," at his villa near Kobe, which commanded a dazzling view of the Inland Sea and the mountains, of pine woods and restful green lawns. The baron was in Washington, but he had left orders to have a cook sent from the Oriental Hotel in Kobe, "so we have the most delicious food you ever tasted." "I was sorry not to meet Baron Sumitomo," Helen wrote Migel. "I think we might have won him as a knight of the blind." The third leg of their tour took them to the Northeast as far as Hokkaido, with a stop in the Akita Prefecture, home of the Akita dog—a large, powerful, alert animal, responsive and dignified, with a massive head and a large curled tail. Helen had been told about the Akita in Tokyo and immediately had said she wanted one. "But you already have four large ones at home," Polly protested. "I want to have a pure Japanese dog," she insisted, and when they reached Akita she was provided with a puppy by a member of the police force, who promised to have it at the boat when she sailed for home.

Their tour ended in Osaka. Migel and others at the Foundation worried lest Helen in her enthusiasm should overdo it. Migel cabled her to that effect. She should end the tour in Japan, not go on to Korea and Manchukuo. Helen was not to be swayed. "I am resolved not to return to America until the work I set out to do for the handicapped in Nippon is finished. It is the only weapon against the most desolating and life-wrecking sorrow I have ever endured." She had had good news about the journal, reported Polly. "Had a fine long letter from Nella. She is quite impressed with the Journal. All it needs is a little brushing up in spots, but of course, Helen has to revise it and that will take a long time."

They returned to Tokyo before leaving for Korea and Manchuria. Helen was at Ambassador Grew's Fourth of July reception at the embassy and to his assembled guests the ambassador said:

> Never before has an American created so great an atmosphere of friendship in Japan. She is a second Admiral Perry, but whereas he opened the door with fear and suspicion, she has done it with love and affection. Thus her trip has borne two-fold fruit. Not only has she immensely aided the cause of the blind and disabled in this country but also has tremendously furthered friendly relations between Japan and the United States.

It is not clear why Helen insisted on going to Korea and Manchuria (then the puppet state of Manchukuo,) since it constituted a form of acceptance of Japanese sovereignty, unless perhaps she saw her mission to help the blind as one that transcended boundaries of race, color, religion and nation. As it happened, she arrived in those countries just as Japan launched full-scale war against China. "Wherever we go we hear the crowds shouting 'Banzai! Banzai!' as the troops march northward," she wrote Dr. Finley from Korea. The Japanese gave the usual justification of imperialism—the improvements that Japan had brought to impoverished and backward lands in the form of reforestation, flood control, education —arguments that Helen was willing to entertain.

As they traveled toward Mukden and Dairen in Manchuria, trains were darkened at night, as were cities. Their meetings had to be held in the afternoon. "Polly and I held our last meeting for the blind at Dairen, Manchuria, July 24th," she wrote Migel on her return to the United States.

> By that time we were tired, and taking the hot consequences of midsummer in an excessively humid climate. But Manchuria fascinated me as a land being reclaimed from the desert, the agelong terror of brigands and ignorance. No, I do not forget that Japan demeaned itself as a world bandit seizing that country, but while hating imperialism, I can see that Manchuria must somehow be developed and disciplined if it is to become a vigorous, self-governing nation.

Back in Japan, they had to wait for ten days before their ship sailed. Although the war preempted Japanese attention, they received a touching sendoff, with crowds at dockside to wish them well, their stateroom deluged with flowers, gifts and telegrams. "There were exquisite orchids on a daintily carved sampan with crickets to sing good wishes from Prince and Princess Takamatsu." Their Akita puppy was there waiting for them, the first purebred Akita to be imported into the United States. She named it Kamikaze, "Golden Wind," underscoring the irony, in light of the significance *Kamikaze* later acquired for Americans, of this goodwill mission. She was relieved to escape the war atmosphere. "I do not know whom I feel more sorry for—the long enduring shamefully insulted Chinese dying by the thousands for freedom they are beginning to understand, or the Japanese millions staggering under the heaviest taxation in their history." Her heart ached as she bade good-bye to Takeo Iwahashi and his wife, who had accompanied them for five months and who would remain friends and collaborators from then on.

Polly had one major worry on their return, apart from what the Foundation expected of them—the completion of Helen's journal. She appealed to Nella:

> So, so pleased you found the journal interesting. When oh when is Helen going to work on it. She is of course tired now but she seems to be putting off and off doing anything about it. Alas, Nella, I fear as Teacher and I knew so well in past years Helen has to have someone behind her just to make her sit right down and do the job. But I may say frankly, Helen just *can't* do certain kinds of writing. Helen has little or no humor and she can't say things in the clever modern way. Helen has not got that particular gift. You will have to give her some help, I'm afraid Nella. If only we had a space of time I know it would not be difficult. But we are *still* waiting to find out what our duties are this coming autumn. . . .

Nella was a skillful and resourceful editor. Though humor was not a strong point, she went to work with a will that no doubt was whetted by her recollection of Helen's having kept her at arms length in the early stages of this literary venture. Instead of returning to Forest Hills, as Helen and Polly had planned, they checked into the Mayo Clinic at Rochester, Minnesota. Although Helen had insisted throughout the Japanese tour that "my health continues splendid," her tests disclosed "a diseased gall-bladder which has caused me severe pain off and on for years.

The doctors advise me to have it removed, and I am determined to do it while I am strong."

The operation went well. The doctors at the clinic, from the famed Dr. Charles Mayo on, were fascinated with Helen, and they permitted Polly to be present at the operation. "A wonderful experience," that strong woman wrote Nella. But as strong as Polly was, there were many duties that she found herself unable to handle, and she passed them on to Nella. There were letters to be answered, an article to be written. "You know the situation so well—you have all the understanding and tenderness required. I may tell you now Nella, publicity so far as I am concerned will always be distasteful to me." And if there was any communication needed with the press, Nella should do it; the very thought that she should do it terrified her. She thanked Nella for her "wonderful kindness in wanting to help me. I most certainly lean upon you and shall be forever grateful to you for helping me out of my difficulties."

Herbert, who had taken care of the house while they were gone, had driven out in their new Buick to drive them back; but the doctors thought a car trip inadvisable, so he left with Kamikaze his only passenger. "What a dear, dear laddie he is," Polly said of him as he left. Dr. Dixon, who had performed the operation, was pleased with Helen's progress but told her she could not do any work for the Foundation until January. "So Nella perhaps we could get at the Journal during that quiet period."

The "quiet" interlude also was the occasion of a ceremony of considerable symbolic significance in Helen's life. She appeared in court as a character witness in the grant of United States citizenship to Polly. Afterward she held Polly's hand and commented: "Now that Miss Thomson is a citizen I have a new feeling of safety; safe because I shall know that she will always be with me."

The *Journal* was published in spring 1938 by Doubleday, Doran in the United States and by Michael Joseph in England. "This book answers effectually the question, 'What will Helen Keller do without Teacher?' " wrote *The Volta Review. The New York Times Book Review* and the *Herald Tribune Books* sounded the same theme. All agreed that the *Journal* was a book that brought the reader nearer to the real Helen Keller than any of her other books had done, and that it showed an informed woman who kept up a lively interest in current affairs and books, formed her own, often arresting, opinions, a woman who was self-willed, positive and determined to run her own life—a course in which she was loyally assisted by Polly Thomson. While the *Journal* stopped with Helen's arrival at

Yokohama, the tour of Japan, as we have seen, confirmed Helen's ability and will to carry on her work without Teacher. The *Journal* is a story of an intense grief and tragedy, but also of Helen's ability to surmount tragedy and to carry on alone. She had been trained to do so by Teacher, asserted Nella, but there had been an ambivalence in Teacher's encouragement of Helen's independence. It had been Helen who kept pressing her to make plans for the event of their separation.

XXXVI

"Anything Helen Keller Is For, I Am For" — F.D.R.

The Social Security Act enacted in 1935 not only undergirded the vagaries of American capitalism with a system of unemployment insurance and old age pensions, but it granted federal assistance to categories that were uninsurable—dependent children, the aged and the incapacitated, including the blind. The statute as approved in 1935 would be considerably amended, but within less than a decade it significantly enhanced the status and well-being of the blind. It also transformed the work of the Foundation, which had in fact been instrumental in seeing to it that the blind were included in the original bill. In this operation the guiding spirit was Bob Irwin, the Foundation's blind director; his helpers were Migel and Helen. It was the same trio that had worked effectively in behalf of that innovative measure of federal aid to the blind in the final years of the Hoover administration, the Pratt Bill for federal funding of books in Braille for the blind. By 1935 this measure had been broadened to help fund the production of talking book records, another brainchild of Bob Irwin.

Under the talking book program, the Foundation undertook to raise the funds to manufacture and supply the blind with machines—a modified form of phonograph—on which to play back the recorded books. As has been noted, Helen took violent exception to participating in the Foundation's money-raising campaign for this purpose, relenting only to the extent of writing Will Rogers, Alexander Woollcott and other popular radio commentators to ask them to help the Foundation promote the talking books effort. That was at the end of 1934. The resulting publicity was so enormous, the talking books so obviously a boon to the blind, that the Foundation decided to give the program priority in its activities. For this it needed Helen. Her special hold on public feeling had been demonstrated anew when Will Rogers as toastmaster at a Democratic dinner attended by the President early in 1935 mentioned his forthcoming broadcast on behalf of the talking books. Whereupon Roosevelt passed a slip to Rogers on which he had jotted: "Anything Helen Keller is for, I am for."

Helen's support, therefore, was critical to the Foundation's campaign; and Helen was being obstinate, refusing to head up the Foundation's Talking Book Committee. Amelia Bond, Migel's secretary and also in many matters his deputy, who considered herself a good friend of the Forest Hills trio, thought she might be able to persuade Helen to change her mind. Her visit only produced an angry scene. Although Amelia had been a guest in her house, Helen wrote furiously,

> . . . you took advantage of a friendly visit to insult me. You treated me like an imbecile because I happened to differ from Mr. Migel on a matter of procedure. . . . Your interpretation of my motives in declining to be Chairman of the talking-book committee or even to become a member of it was in the extreme insulting to my mentality and sense of honor. . . .
>
> I have not forgotten that you descended upon me like an avalanche of bricks twice at the Doctors' Hospital while I was full of anxiety about my Teacher. In the role of an inquisitor, not a sympathetic friend, you fired one impertinent question after another at me—'Why don't you do your own work?' 'Why do you spend so much time writing form letters and get your teacher to work on them?' 'You are timid, you should act for yourself.' Again, you said you had known for some time that my teacher did my work. And on Sunday you capped the climax by calling me 'an empty shell.'

She was prepared to accept criticism from Mr. Migel, Helen went on, but not from her, and she resented her characterization of Migel's feelings:

Finally, Amelia, you said that I refused to have anything more to do with the talking book because I hate Robert Irwin. How could you dare to say such a thing? I DO NOT HATE ROBERT. He is a gentleman, he is my friend, and I am very fond of him. I often differ with him as to his methods of procedure and campaigning, but never for personal reasons. His attitude in discussing the talking-book question with me was in striking contrast with your own.

She added a postscript to this somewhat adolescent outburst: "I wish you to know, Amelia, that THIS letter is mine, and has not been dictated or advised or approved by my teacher or any one else." Amelia's answer was affectionate, restrained and dignified. "If I loved you less, I would resent your letter and its groundless accusations. However, I am aware, from my own harrowing experience, how difficult it is to be reasonable and calm when one's heart is torn with anguish over the well-being of one's best beloved."

Helen sent a copy of her letter to Bob Irwin. He wrote her a propitiatory note, thanking her for what she had said about him, adding, "I hope that you may always count me as a friend even though we may not exactly see eye to eye as to the way to achieve the great objectives we are both striving for." As a result of her missionary work with Will Rogers and Woollcott and the President's endorsement, the talking book project "will have great weight with the public."

But Helen was not appeased. When Walter Holmes, "Uncle Walter," editor of *The Matilda Ziegler Magazine for the Blind*—which he had begun in 1907 with a sendoff letter from Helen and to which Helen often contributed—asked her to write an appeal letter for talking books that William Ziegler, a Foundation trustee, might use, she responded with a lengthy irate letter "to make it clear why I am so determined not to yield to my friends in the matter of the talking book." The latter was only the latest in a series of Foundation projects of which she did not approve. Her bill of grievances was surprising: The Foundation had spent too much money on the World Conference for the Blind, too much time on a campaign to give radios to the blind, too much effort on devising a new Braille writer. It had done nothing comparable to the talking books on behalf of the "deaf-blind . . . the loneliest human beings on earth." She had wanted the Foundation to sponsor the production of a "Helen Keller doll" that would give work to the blind and help increase the Endowment Fund. The Foundation had rejected the proposal as impracticable, and when she considered doing it as "a private enterprise . . . objected to it as an undignified way of 'commercializing my name' and my limitations." She listed other complaints, all of which she said should serve to explain her "obstinacy" in regard to the talking books.

During all this furor Migel had been in Palm Beach, although it is doubtful whether Amelia would have undertaken to press Helen as she did if she had not known how Migel felt about her recalcitrance. But he had long ago learned that to get anywhere with the Forest Hills women, he had to avoid direct confrontation. He returned to New York at the end of February, sending ahead of him a warm considerate letter and a large basket of Florida conserves. Helen prepared him, apologizing somewhat for the letter she had written Walter Holmes: "I was irritated that such a request should be made through Mr. Holmes instead of directly to me, and also because it seemed unlikely that Mr. Ziegler did not know my attitude towards the talking-book campaign. . . . It is more distressing to me than you will ever know that I should so often find myself in opposition to what seems desirable to you for the welfare of the blind. . . . What troubles me most is the grief I cause you who are so genuinely kind and thoughtful of your 'Three Musketeers.' I wish intensely that we might reach some permanent understanding which would enable us to work together harmoniously."

Suddenly her opposition to Foundation policies subsided. The reason is not wholly clear. Teacher's illness, the possibility of her death, made a break with the Foundation unthinkable. The invitation to visit Japan had arrived, something she very much wanted to accept, and it was a result of Takeo Iwahashi's attendance at the World Conference, the funding of which she had just protested. She was encountering increasing difficulty raising money for the Endowment at the same time that the talking books were spectacularly successful. Migel's persuasiveness combined with his unfailing helpfulness played a part, as did her realization that the precedent of federal funding was useful in the Foundation's efforts to get other types of federal aid for the blind—especially work and educational opportunities, for which she had fought since her appearance before the Massachusetts Commission for the Blind in 1905. Whatever the explanation, she surrendered, gracefully and unconditionally, to Migel:

> Since I saw you last I have been thinking very, very earnestly about my recent attitude towards the Foundation, and I have come to the conclusion that I have been too stubborn. I seem to have overempha-

sized the differences between us. As I see matters now, I have criti-cized my colleagues too harshly. After all, I have no monopoly of wisdom or wordly *savoir faire*. My motto is 'Suaviter in modo, fortiter in re,' but at times I get confused and forget one or the other half of it.

I was wholly sincere in my opposition to the talking-book campaign because it appeared to me untimely when people both blind and seeing were crying out for Practical help in the problems of daily life. I realize now, however, that I should not desert the ship just because the captain chooses a different course from the one I have contem-plated. I should have more quickly recognized that the captain is master of his ship. The trouble is I have always regarded the raising of the Endowment Fund as my one objective and I have been on edge, as it were, because I have not finished this task. I have some-times felt that the Foundation was frustrating me unnecessarily. Now it has become clear to me that Service is our chief aim, and I would rather make mistakes than do nothing for others. I know I shall be much happier to go on working with you than to continue in a state of opposition which helps no one.

Therefore I say to you very definitely that I do not wish to bring any complaints before the board of trustees when it meets. Since I have accepted the fact that the completion of the Endowment is not our principal concern, all other difficulties will come in as part of the day's work. It would be embarrassing for me to lay my personal complaints before the board. I prefer to put everything into your hands and abide by the outcome, even though we agree to disagree.

Irwin sent her a handsome letter. Migel had told him that she would praise the talking books on a radio program. "I am delighted to hear this as it has been a source of the keenest regret to all of us that we did not have the weight of your great personality and your genius for interpreting to the public the needs of the blind. Now that you are with us I am sure we are going to succeed in this great undertaking."

Hitherto the aim of the Foundation in Washington had been to increase the Library of Congress appropriation for books for the blind so as to include talking books as well as books in Braille, while it raised privately the funds to produce the "phonographs." Now the Foundation wrote

Roosevelt to ask whether Helen and Major Migel could not see him about having the government manufacture the "phonographs" under the work relief program. They did see the President a few weeks later, and at the end of the meeting he called Frank C. Walker of the National Emergency Council and directed him to expedite the project. He also told Harry Hopkins, the head of the Works Progress Administration, and Frances Perkins, the secretary of labor, of his personal interest.

Administrative difficulties had to be ironed out; but by the autumn of 1935 the President had signed an executive order transferring from the Treasury to the Library of Congress $211,500 for the construction of five thousand talking book machines, and the Library of Congress appointed the Foundation as its agent to supervise their manufacture. That will be "a nice messy job," Irwin wrote Helen, but "what a job it would be to raise the money from private sources!"

While the negotiations were proceeding for the federal funding of the "phonographs," Helen asked Roosevelt to sign H.R. 6371, which authorized an appropriation of $175,000, of which $75,000 was to be used for talking book records. Roosevelt signed and wrote Helen cordially: "A few days ago when I signed H.R. 6371 I derived a great deal of pleasure at the thought that in lending my approval to this Bill, I was contributing my mite to the cause of which your name is symbolical and to which you have lent your untiring energy." He signed it "your friend." The "phonograph" production became a WPA project under the supervision of the Foundation. "What a wonderful thing this W.P.A. has been to the blind," Irwin wrote Helen enthusiastically at the end of 1936.*

The Foundation, in the meantime, had gone after larger objectives. Again with Irwin, Migel and Helen in the lead, it had secured the inclusion of the blind in the provisions of the Social Security Act. The Wagner-Lewis bill, when it was introduced in January 1935, contained no reference to the blind. But Bob Irwin noted that it did provide for matching grants to the states for aid to crippled children. Why not the blind? he asked, and he promptly went to work to get the bill so amended. "The principal provision," he informed Helen, "is an appropriation of $1,500,000 annually to be used in assisting state commissions for the blind on what would work out to be practically a 50-50 matching of Federal and State funds." It was worth fighting for, and the leaders of the other organizations of the blind concurred; but he was not hopeful, he cautioned

*By 1942, when the WPA went out of existence, it had produced 23,000 machines.

Helen. The bill's sponsors want "us to wait until next year. . . . The proposed amendment is so important that I have had a Braille copy made of it so that you can study it at your leisure." Migel, meanwhile, having returned from Palm Beach, went to see Senator Wagner, a friend, and when the bill was reported out of the Finance Committee it had incorporated a new Title X that established the blind as a category to receive grant assistance from the federal government. But Irwin and his associates hoped for more: They wanted Title X expanded to include funds for diagnostic and rehabilitative services for the blind.

Helen undertook to go to Washington to persuade the key Senators—Wagner, the chairman of the Finance Committee; Pat Harrison; and Hugo Black from Helen's home state of Alabama—to try to amend the bill on the floor. "With this help from the Government," Irwin counseled, her, "we could probably clean up our job during the next three or four years, and have the satisfaction of seeing something like adequate provision for the blind in every State in the Union. Without some such Federal help, it will probably take us a generation to obtain this end."

Migel went with her to Washington. "I knew you understood," she wrote Wagner afterward, "that the benefit derived from the federal grant of three million dollars would be vastly enhanced if a more concrete statement was made of what should be done for them." To Black she wrote as "a fellow-Alabamian." She was particularly glad "to feel my dear birthstate holding out a hand to me when you said you would do all you could for the blind of America. What I tried to say to you with halting speech was this: We desire a definition of aid to the blind that conforms with the dignity of their manhood and their capacity to help themselves and their families."

The bill was amended as she and Migel had urged, and in amended form it passed the Senate. A jubilant Migel telegraphed her: I CANNOT ALLOW THE DAY TO PASS WITHOUT TELLING YOU THAT THE WONDERFUL RESULT IN THE SENATE IS DUE TO YOUR PLEA LAST WEEK. YOU HAVE BROUGHT ABOUT NOT ONLY A BOON TO THE BLIND OF THIS COUNTRY BUT A CONSTRUCTIVE PLAN TO ASSIST IN THEIR REHABILITATION. AM CERTAIN YOU FEEL AS HAPPY AS I DO. . . .

The celebration was premature. "I understand that Mr. Migel has told you," Bob Irwin informed her, "that the Conference Committee [to reconcile Senate and House versions] struck out those beautiful clauses that you persuaded Senator Wagner and Pat Harrison to put through the Senate. It still has the provision for matching 50-50 the amounts appropriated for the blind in the various states. Most of the states are writing to us for suggestions as to how to amend their pension laws so that they might benefit from the Federal grant. It is giving us an opportunity to propose a clause making double allowance for the deaf-blind."

In spite of these setbacks, Helen's regard for Roosevelt, who had made passage of the Social Security Act "must" legislation, turned to adulation. "The blind of America have cause to bless him," she wrote Migel. "He has done more for their well-being than any other President of the United States. . . . Some people criticize President Roosevelt severely, but when all is said, he has made a nation's concern the problem of the un-privileged." Migel agreed. "What you say as to the President being tre-mendously concerned in ameliorating the condition of the unprivileged is perfectly true." She should convey her feelings to him, he advised. They were having trouble with the director of the budget, then called the auditor general, and they might have to appeal to the President again.

Helen did not vote in the 1936 elections. Election Day came just after Teacher's death, and she was on the high seas bound for Scotland in the hopes of recovering from her state of psychic numbness. Would she have voted for him otherwise? She had not supported a presidential candidate since the elder La Follette's race in 1924. Political nonpartisanship fitted the necessities of her work for the blind, and that might have kept her away from the ballot box in any case. But Roosevelt had made a convert of her. Together with Polly's brother the minister, she listened over the radio at The Manse in Bothwell to Roosevelt's inaugural on January 20. She thought with a pang how she and Teacher had listened to his first inaugural speech in 1933. This one stirred her more deeply:

> Since I was twenty-one I have read every speech of a newly-elected president; and none except Woodrow Wilson's, has given me reason-able hope of achievement as this one has. . . . More than any other president, I believe, since Lincoln has he stressed the need to find in Government a means to promote the economic security and well-being of all the people. For the world to hear he has condemned the injustice under which millions live in ignorance and one-third of the nation face hardship, ill-housed, ill-clad, ill-nourished. If only Con-gress and the people would stand solidly behind Roosevelt. . . .

Another important advance in federal help to the blind was taken in 1938, and again Helen's help was indispensable. The Wagner-O'Day Act of 1938 began with a letter to Migel from Peter Salmon, the engaging blind Irishman who headed the Industrial Home for the Blind: "I don't think that the Foundation could possibly do anything that would result in more jobs for the blind in a shorter period of time than to pursue this proposition of getting the Federal and State Governments to purchase brooms and possibly mops from the blind." After Bob Irwin cleared the proposal with other blind agencies, particularly the legislative committees of the American Association of Workers for the Blind and the American Association of Instructors of the Blind, Senator Wagner and Congresswoman O'Day introduced the bill, which was broadened in the Senate from "brooms and mops" to include "other suitable commodities." The bill went through the Senate easily, but it languished in the House committee and would have died there but for a last-resort parliamentary device under which a representative on the last day of a Congressional session could request a suspension of the rules from the floor in order to take up a particular bill. But passage under such a suspension had to be unanimous.

House Speaker William N. Bankhead of Alabama, whose support for the bill had been gained as a result of Helen's solicitation, suggested the parliamentary maneuver after Helen had appealed to him. "I am delighted as well as grateful that it did pass," Helen wired the speaker, "and I realize the extreme pressure of important work under which you and the House of Representatives gave my handicapped fellows a vital advantage that will go far towards solving their problem of productive self-support."

Under the bill the President appointed a "Committee of Purchases of Blind-Made Products" that consisted of six representatives of government departments and one private citizen "conversant with the problems incident to the employment of the blind." He asked Helen to be that seventh member. She promptly accepted; but when apprised of how much work it would involve, she begged off in favor of Migel. A National Industries for the Blind was established by the Foundation. By the end of 1940 it was producing through its associated "workshops for the blind"—whose agent the Foundation in effect became—cocoa mats, mattresses, pillow cases, whisk brooms and several different types of mobs and swabs. "Your letter to Speaker Bankhead of the House was of tremendous help in getting the Wagner-O'Day bill passed," Bob Irwin wrote Helen later. "The interest you aroused in Bankhead saved the day for the bill at the most critical hour."

Helen's enthusiasm for Roosevelt's New Deal went hand in hand with support for his policy of aid to the democracies. As was true for so many other liberals toward the end of the thirties, her staunch hatred of war found itself in conflict with her even more powerful hatred of fascism. She had never been an absolute pacifist, not even during the World War. She felt that there were "just" wars; but that war had not been one of them. At its end she had been among the signatories of Henri Barbusse's manifesto signed by intellectuals on both sides pleading for a peace of reconciliation. In the twenties she had urged the cancellation of war debts and universal disarmament, but the rise of the fascist dictatorships filled her with horror. At the end of her "sabbatical" in Scotland she gave a widely quoted interview sharply condemnatory of Hitler and Mussolini. "What terrible deeds that man has committed," she said of the German chancellor, adding with uncharacteristic pugnacity, "I do hope there will be some way of ridding the world of this Hitler thing." She rebuked Mussolini for an edict drafting eight-year-old Italians for compulsory military instruction, turning Italy, she said, "into a vast military gymnasium. It is too shocking for words to think that little Italian children are being thrown into military life and taught hate and conquest. Mussolini must not forget that he who lives by the sword shall perish by the sword."

She had her own personal quarrel with the Nazis. At least one of her books had been thrown into the infamous bonfire in Berlin, the "burning of the books" that had attended Hitler's coming to power. Her German publisher denied that any of her books had been burned, but Helen stood her ground, saying that *Out of the Dark,* which had an essay on "Why I Became a Socialist," was among those burned. In 1936 Otto Schramm, her German publisher, advised her that German laws prohibited the printing of passages that expressed a friendly feeling toward the Russian experiment, and that he "must cut out of the German edition of *Midstream* the part about Lenin." Would she let him know, please, whether she had revised her views about Russian Bolshevism? Schramm's letter "excited a turmoil of insurrection in me," Helen noted in her journal. "As if I would change my mind at his dictation! I shall ask him to discontinue the publication of my books." She did so a few weeks later, and in the course of her letter rejected the Nazi view that Bolshevism threatened the destruction of Europe.

Her views on Soviet Russia were strongly influenced at the time by Walter Duranty, the *New York Times* correspondent in Moscow. She had spent an afternoon with him in the spring of 1935, imbibing his optimistic view of Soviet developments. The Soviet government, Duranty asserted, was striving sincerely for the people's welfare. The working people of Germany might overturn Nazism and join Russia in a peace front. She thought Duranty remarkably free from anti-Soviet bias and at the end of 1936 sent his book *I Write As I Please* as a Christmas gift to friends. But two months later the Soviet government announced the first of its purge trials. They sickened Helen. "These trials are utterly incomprehensible to me in a country as progressive as modern Russia. They read exactly like a repetition with different names of the hysterical witchcraft trials once held in Puritan New England. Apparently there is the same frenzied fear among the Soviet leaders and the same determination to force the prisoners to admit to crimes they have never committed." Asked by shipboard reporters in early 1937 whom she considered the greatest man in the world, she mentioned Einstein and Roosevelt, but declined to include Stalin: "I do not think he has the imagination or breadth of judgment or generous humanity which were among Lenin's most conspicuous characteristics."

Her German publisher's letter had also attacked the Spanish Republic. This had outraged her: "How dare you stigmatize as a 'reign of terror' the Spanish people's superhuman heroism in efforts to win their rightful freedom?" The civil war in Spain most sharply pointed up the conflict in her heart between hatred of war and resistance to fascism. Civil war horrified her; nevertheless, "my heart bleeds for the defenders of Madrid, but it is proud tears I shed for the masses who are giving their lives to create a more enlightened and civilized nation. I shall not believe until the last that their superhuman heroism is to end in defeat." So she wrote at the end of 1936. And three years later when Franco was victorious and the few hundred survivors of the Abraham Lincoln Brigade gathered at a memorial meeting in Manhattan Center, she sat on the platform next to Lieutenant Colonel John Gates, youthful former commander of the brigade, and said that the brigade in its fight for democracy furnished a "shining light in a world of darkness."

After her return from Japan and the publication of her *Journal* she resumed her work for the Foundation. There were appearances before legislatures, appeal letters to potential donors, speeches at fund raising meetings. The Foundation organized a Helen Keller Day on March 3, 1938, the fiftieth (actually it was the fifty-first) anniversary of her meeting with Teacher, the day she regarded as her "spiritual birthday." Roosevelt obligingly sent her a letter for the occasion; but as a fund raising device the Helen Keller Day proved disappointing, with the contributions scarcely matching the expenses, and the drive was discontinued in April. She now spoke of the million-dollar Endowment Fund as a finished campaign.

Apart from Foundation duties, her greatest preoccupation was her book about Teacher. The chief obstacle to progress, she felt, was a lack of time and quiet in which to write. She had a form card printed:

> At present Miss Keller is wholly taken up with literary work she has neglected many years. To her regret she cannot sponsor the countless causes that appeal to her. Nor can she comply with the multitude of requests she receives daily. She needs all her strength for the tasks now incumbent upon her.

Her life was further disturbed by her decision to sell her Forest Hills home. "The house in Forest Hills has been sold—$9,000 cash," Polly informed Lenore in mid-1938, "and we are to vacate at the end of September." The transaction was handled by her trustees, but a decision as to where she would live hung over her.

But first she decided to flee the country. No mail would be forwarded. Nella and the Foundation would handle it. Her name would not be on the passenger list. Only Polly and Herbert would accompany her, since she could not work without them. Herbert, having learned Braille, was almost as indispensable as Polly.

In the early thirties, while they were still living in Forest Hills, a youthful Herbert Haas had attached himself to the three women. He was quiet, considerate and good-humored, and so helpful that the women made little effort to check his antecedents, especially as he was willing to take care of an ailing Teacher during Helen's and Polly's absences on Foundation business. Teacher grew so fond of him that before she died she said to him, "I leave Helen and Polly in your hands." He was a conscientious manager of the household, could repair Helen's typewriter and Braille machine as well as the car, tended their roses lovingly and was always ready for a game of checkers with Helen.

Friends unwittingly added to the pressure that she felt to finish the book about Teacher. "I am so glad you are to do your own book on Annie Sullivan," Woollcott wrote her from his own retreat in Bomoseen, Vermont. "No one in the world has such a story to tell and no one in the world but you can tell it." Perhaps what hindered and delayed her was not lack of time and solitude, but how to walk the fine line of presenting Teacher the way she was, flawed and all too human, without seeming disloyal.

Writing would be easier in France, Helen decided. He hoped to see them before they sailed, Woollcott wrote, "if the powder magazine doesn't blow up ahead of schedule and keep you from sailing at all." It was the middle of the Munich crisis. Woollcott postscripted: "It delights me that on all great matters you are always on the same side I'm on. To hell with Hitler and his like the world around."

Then she abandoned her plan to go to France. "It is extremely difficult to put my mind on matters which seem of small moment beside the tragic sinister world situation," she explained to Dr. Finley. "The perfidy of France and Britain to Czechoslovakia" haunted her. An assistant at the Israelitische institute for the blind in Vienna had written her that the Nazis had closed the institute and driven out the students to beg or starve. Such wanton cruelty toward the afflicted and powerless did not happen, she thought, "among savage tribes—there are even cannibals with a code of gentlemen—it has happened in a country known during centuries for its civilization, art and learning." Could not something be done for the Jewish blind—and the deaf, too—in Austria and Germany? She turned to Rabbi Stephen Wise, an ally in many good fights, "knowing what an undiscourageable tower of strength he is to the hunted and the impoverished."

As a longtime student of the Bible, the resettlement of Palestine by the Jews gripped her imagination. "I have long felt that their problem can be solved only if they have a homeland where they can develop unmolested their peculiar genius in religion, art and social justice," she had noted in her journal in January 1937. She read regularly the *Jewish Braille Review for the Blind* and regretted that the argument was seldom advanced that seemed so compelling to her to whom the Bible was history—"that the Jews held the land long before an Arab invader appeared. . . . What have the Arabs done to develop Palestine?"

The Braille volumes of the Old and New Testament were among the books in her library that were worn down with reading. When Upton Sinclair replied to her appeal to help the Chinese blind with a copy of his book *Our Lady* about Mary, she thanked him and described her own feminist-colored ideas concerning the mother of Jesus:

> I have never thought of Mary simply as a mother. I imagine her as a silent, unrecognized genius, enslaved, burdened with drudgery, yet breaking away from deep-set traditions with the courage of Deborah,

thinking universal thoughts which she uttered with difficulty in few words, but which were a potent stimulus to the Seer she bore. The very fact that, though as a child He broke through restraints in an unheard-of manner, she substituted wise-hearted observation for authority points to a woman of marvellous intelligence.

With France after Munich no longer a refuge from the world's distractions, she became more impatient to move into a home of her own. It was being built for her by the Foundation just outside of Westport, on land donated to the Foundation for the purpose by Gustavus A. Pfeiffer. He had turned over four and a half acres, part of his large holdings in the area. He lived there with his wife and kinfolk. A nephew, Robert M. Pfeiffer, a Harvard professor of Hebrew and other Oriental languages, had a home there that the Pfeiffers dubbed "Harvard House."

"Uncle Gus," as everyone in the family called Helen's benefactor, was an Iowan who after graduation from pharmacy school had joined his brother in opening a drugstore in 1894. This launched him on a spectacular career in pharmaceuticals, in which he picked up companies along the route and combined them finally into the huge Warner-Hudnut concern with plants and agents all over the world. In 1929 an appeal letter from Helen for the Foundation had moved him to send her $500, which was followed by other cash contributions and, after a visit by Helen in 1931, by a gift of 150 shares of preferred stock.

His gift had given her "a new impulse and fresh enthusiasm to go on with difficult tasks," Helen wrote back. The Pfeiffers invited her to dinner: "I think you know that I have a collection of chess sets. With your wonderful gift to see and understand intuitively, I believe you would enjoy being in our chess room. One of the chess sets is said to have been made before Columbus discovered America."

Her thank-you letter afterward was a paean to his chess collection. It ended with the suggestion that a book should be written about it. "Why do you not write it yourself, Mr. Pfeiffer? You would certainly not have a more interested reader than myself if you did." She had an imagination that was easily stirred and the rare gift of wanting to convey to those around her how she had been moved. "Whatever you are," William James had said of her, "you are a blessing." Her presence still made men and women feel nobler and wish to protect her. Uncle Gus was not the last in a long line of conquests that included titans of literature, philosophy, science and business.

Encouraged by his successive gifts to the Foundation, Migel in 1932 invited him to serve on the Foundation's board of trustees. He accepted and soon became one of the board's stalwarts, serving on the executive and budget committees. In August 1938 her personal trustees—Migel, Harvey Gibson and William Ziegler—had disposed of her Forest Hills house. Tell them, she bade Migel, that "I am touched that they should still bestow attention upon my little concerns, and I feel strong for all vicissitudes guided with the staff of their counselling good-will." A few months later construction began on their house in Westport. Uncle Gus, in addition to providing the land, also contributed generously to the building costs, as did Major Migel. And while they waited for the house to be built, they lived at Harvard House, since Professor Pfeiffer was away.

"Tell me," she asked an interviewer from the *New York Post,* Maureen McKernan, "do you know a Gaelic word meaning 'teacher' which I can call my new home? . . . She was Irish, so the word must be Gaelic. If you can find out the word let me know." In the end the house was named Arcan Ridge, after the farm on a hill in the Scottish Highlands that was indelibly associated with Teacher. The Pfeiffers turned the key over to her:

> How wonderful it all is! You, Mr. and Mrs. Pfeiffer, have so taken me by surprise with your delightful plotting and planning, I can hardly speak. . . . There is no counting the treasures to which the key symbolically opens the door. It means a home in New England to which affection and memory have ever bound me, a place nearer Heaven where Teacher is, a sanctuary where rural solitude will again sweeten my days. . . . I look upon Arcan Ridge as a spiritual trust. . . .

"We have never loved a place more than Arcan Ridge," she wrote Lenore. "It is a Colonial house surrounded by meadows, woods, brooks and the old New England stone walls you will remember. I am especially delighted with my study which has spacious bookshelves, thirty-five cubbyholes and windows hospitable to the sun. Above all, there is seclusion essential to literary endeavor. The landscaping will be started in the spring, we came here too late to do anything about it. If only all goes well with Polly and Herbert, I shall be content."

By the following year the shrubs and flowers were in, chosen for their fragrance so that she might see them through their perfumes. The house had a huge living room that was furnished in rose and yellow curtains. The dining room was furnished in eighteenth-century style. Polly's quarters adjoined her bedroom, and also nearby was her study, at the center of which stood a capacious desk piled high with manuscript material, chiefly in Braille. The house was white and rambling, with green shutters, and stood on a hill at the end of a birch-lined road. She would stay at Arcan Ridge for the rest of her life. It meant a new group of friends, Westport neighbors, beginning with the Pfeiffer family, which adopted her as one of their own.

The move to Arcan Ridge coincided with the beginning of another meaningful friendship. On a train from Boston to New York, Helen and Polly went into the dining car for dinner. At another table Katharine Cornell sat with Anne Gugler, an actress and the wife of Eric Gugler, a well-known architect who had designed houses for Miss Cornell and her husband, the producer Guthrie McClintic, at Martha's Vineyard and Snedens Landing. Anne Gugler had met Helen through Dorothy Eustis of The Seeing Eye, Inc., a dog-guide and training foundation, who had brought Helen to her house in the Murray Hill section of Manhattan. Helen, even before she was through the front door, had begun to run her hands over the woodwork and was so eager to talk with her hostess that she disregarded Polly and "grabbed me by the throat," said Anne Gugler, referring to Helen's way of reading lips. The train had lurched as Helen and Polly came in, and Miss Cornell, looking up, expressed an interest in meeting Helen, so Anne took her over. They hit it off well. Shortly afterward "Kit" and her husband invited her to dinner and to the theatre, to a performance of *Mamba's Daughters* by DuBose Heyward. She was excited at the prospect, she told the reporter for the *Post*. "What could be more wonderful for me than to know Miss Cornell?" she exclaimed, thrusting Polly's hand aside to speak for herself. "She has done such great things, carrying the drama to the people from one end of the country to the other." "The play is a terrific upheaval of emotion in a great, primitive, child-loving soul," she wrote Migel after the evening, "and Ethel Waters's Hagar is a monumental revelation I shall always remember with tremendous awe."

Kit invited her to Martha's Vineyard, where her lovely cluster of houses sat right on the beach. Helen may have been keyed up and tense at going to the theater with Kit; the latter was equally tense at having Helen as her house guest. When Helen and Polly arrived, she insisted that Nancy Hamilton, her manager and close friend, stay with her because she was somewhat intimidated by the prospect of being alone with Helen. Nancy herself was somewhat intimidated; and when Kit took herself off to show Polly the house, leaving Nancy alone with Helen, she sat silent and abashed. But only for a moment. In her bluff, outgoing way Nancy was equal to any situation, and soon the two were trying to communicate. Kit returned and a swim was proposed. Nancy said that she swam in the nude. Helen replied that since she could not have the pleasure of seeing, she would wear a bathing suit.

That was the way the friendship between Katharine Cornell and her entourage, and Helen and hers, began, and although Helen was sixty, it sank deep roots and enriched her final years. To a reporter from *The New York Times* who came to interview her in connection with her sixtieth birthday, she said, "I find life an exciting business."

XXXVII

"The Crowning Experience of My Life"

"In the first World War I was a convinced pacifist. . . ."

In Memorial Day thoughts that Helen jotted down some time in the thirties, she declared what seemed to her truisms: "When we consider honestly the history of each successive war it becomes evident that the ideals for which they were fought have not been realized." The radicalism of her youth still shaped her thinking, especially when she thought that there might be another war: "Governments are not the guardians of peace, but rather the instruments of force and violence. Unless their militarism is checked by the people, another world war will be upon us before we know it." She had kind words, however, for Roosevelt, whom she quoted as having said, "The common people . . . must have a say in the making of peace and war."

But hatred of war yielded before an even greater abomination—fascism. Munich shattered her. "I can see no light in this great darkness at present. I am an optimist but I can see only the faintest hope." That hope rested in a coalition of the democracies and a boycotting of "the brutal empires of Germany, Italy and Japan." She included Stalin's Russia in the roster of the peace coalition "because it is a peace-loving country," and she preached the boycott to all and sundry: "The boycott is a powerful weapon if enough of the people employ it. I myself will buy nothing that is made in Japan, or Germany, or Italy." But her advocacy of a boycott of aggressors did not keep her from acceptance of a second Akita dog, a gift from the Japanese Foreign Office after her first one died of distemper. "I express my sincere gratitude to the Japanese people for this splendid dog," she said on picking up Kenzan Go at the pier in June 1939. Kenzan Go, with a reddish-golden coat like that of a chow, had been especially trained for her. "To me he will be a symbol of the general good-will that the Japanese people extended to me during my tour of Japan two years ago." Helen did not explain how she reconciled this exemption with her advocacy of the boycott, except that she chose to interpret it as a gesture from the "people" rather than the government of Japan.

When war broke out in Europe in September 1939, her first response, like that of most Americans, was to urge the United States to stay out of it. "All that is beauty, wisdom and progress must, I fear, retreat before the insanities loosed upon Europe and Asia. Whole-heartedly I pray that America may stay out of the maelstrom and preserve democracy, its most vital gift to betrayed, spiritually deaf-blind people." She had spent the summer far away from the headlines at the Eden Valley Ranch in the Canadian Rockies, hard at work on her book about Teacher. "I stuck to my desk, except for a walk before breakfast. To my joy the manuscript grew until I had an amount in Braille equivalent to a hundred and fifty pages on the typewriter." But then Polly came down "with an atrocious attack of herpes," and they ended up at the Mayo Clinic. And after that "our precious Herbert" had to be operated on for a peptic ulcer. She had agreed to do four meetings a month for the Foundation, but now she wrote the indefatigable Ida Hirst-Gifford, who prepared the meetings for her, that she would not consent to any engagements after November: "I have accomplished much on the book, but you will understand, I am sure, that a book worthy of the name means slow attention and ruthless revision, and if it is ever to be finished, I must return to it as soon as possible after the November meetings." The doctors at Mayo, moreover, had advised her to give up public meetings for the time being, Polly even more so. "That is why I need quiet to finish a book which I know is a sacred duty and to lay in fresh resources for whatever work is left me on earth."

The sense of mission, of having been placed upon earth to accomplish an important purpose—the "Joan of Arc" characteristic—still was strong with her, still shaped her formidable energies into a powerful instrument. And as the war, particularly after Hitler's invasion of the Low Countries and the collapse of France, made concentration upon her book impossible, she yearned to find a role for herself. An interviewer in *The New York Times* on her sixtieth birthday had described her as "a convinced pacifist," and a neighbor of Kit Cornell's at Snedens Landing asked her guidance. Much as she wanted to follow "the Christian way," she was unable to reconcile herself to passivity in the face of the fascist conquests. Had Helen any advice for her? "Perhaps God will help me through you." Helen found the letter "noble" and moving and responded at length:

> In the first World War I was a convinced pacifist, and I continued to hold that attitude until some months ago. Then the atrocious happenings in Europe, the life-and-death quality of Nazi aggression and the uniqueness of this conflict as I saw it—a duel between humane ideologies and a brutality deadly with a false philosophy—tore me away, not from my ideal but from the joy of embodying it in the letter. For I realize that 'the letter killeth, but the Spirit giveth life.'

> With you I feel that permanent peace is Christ's Way, but I am certain He forbids us to let our country fall a victim to the foes both of spiritual and civil liberty as emphatically as He forbids us to use the Sabbath as an excuse for laxity in beneficent activity. . . .

> The last twenty-five years have been so abominable with intolerance, the enslavement of 'non-Aryan' peoples, beliefs worshipping a golden image of a modern Babylon, the casting out of reluctant populations upon a hard-pressed, alien world that when this war broke out, I was almost relieved. I had hoped for a time that America might stay above the battle because then it would be better able to rehabilitate a broken humanity, but now I have come to a decision. It is better for all of us who uphold freedom, though often sinned against, to be improverished by war, yes, and physical death than to submit to politico-social doctrines which place Baal in the form of dictatorship over us, murder the soul and destroy human rights, liberty, happiness, independent thinking as 'the concepts of chaos.'

> Frankly, the phrase 'defense' strikes me as nugatory, not to say hypocritical. You know the old British axiom, 'The best way to defend is to attack.'

Helen supported Roosevelt in his bid for a third term as President. Because of her position with the Foundation, she did not shout it from the rooftops, and the only reference to it is a note that Polly scrawled on a letter from Dr. S.C.F. Dixon of the Mayo Clinic. Dixon had operated on

Helen in 1937, and they had become good friends. In 1938, when they went out to the clinic for a checkup, he had taken Helen and Polly to a Minnesota-Purdue football game.* Dixon wrote her after the 1940 election: "We voted for F.D.R. Did you? I think Hitler is afraid of Roosevelt." Helen's reply noted down by Polly was on the margin of Dr. Dixon's letter: "This surely I believe [namely that Hitler was afraid of Roosevelt] and was one of the reasons I was for *F.D.R.* I still believe Willkie was backed by appeasers and isolationists, and after meeting representatives of big business who seemed willing to give up a lot for immense advantages Fascism would give them, I am content to stick to Roosevelt. But perhaps I am all cock-eyed. I don't understand politics anyway."

She had not been involved in the campaign. She made it a rule to avoid organizational obligations except to the blind. That may have been why she escaped entanglement with the myriad of Popular Front organizations that enlisted the sympathies of men and women of goodwill in the late thirties. She had made one exception—Spain, appearing, as was noted, at a memorial meeting of the Friends of the Abraham Lincoln Brigade, signing an appeal circulated by the American Friends of Spanish Democracy for "Lifting of the Arms Embargo on the Spanish Government" and writing letters of encouragement to Robert Raven, a Lincoln Brigade volunteer blinded in front of Madrid. "It makes me proud to have as a friend such a true soldier in the cause of Loyalist Spain," she wrote him.

It is not clear who asked her to serve as honorary chairman of the American Rescue Ship Mission, but in November 1940 she was writing on her own letterhead to people like Van Wyck Brooks, President Mac-Cracken of Vassar and Dr. John Haynes Holmes of the Community Church, asking them to join her in sponsoring a project to transport refugees in French concentration camps from France to Mexico. "The Vichy Government has agreed to allow them to leave France if Mexico will admit them. Mexico has agreed. . . . Lynn Fontanne, Rockwell Kent, Dorothy Parker and Herman Shumlin are among those associated with the initiating group, the United American Spanish Aid Committee, which will administer the funds." She also wrote Eleanor Roosevelt, who scrawled at the bottom of the letter, "Tell Helen Keller I will do what I can." "She has mentioned it in her column," her secretary, Mrs. Thompson, wrote back.

---

*"It seemed to me a hurricane of youth and energy and courage," she wrote in the newspapers afterwards.

But the United American Spanish Aid Committee, Mrs. Roosevelt soon learned, was a communist-controlled group that had been ousted from the Spanish Refugee Relief Campaign. As Harold Ickes and Bishop Francis J. McConnell informed the press, the ousted group had sabotaged efforts to get refugees to safety without regard to politics. The executive secretary of the ousted group had been Fred Biedenkapp, a Communist wheelhorse. Apprised of these facts, Mrs. Roosevelt resigned on December 17, 1940, writing Helen:

> I have just discovered that the group sponsoring the American Rescue Ship Mission is the group which left the Spanish Committee, and, much as I regret it, I feel there are other groups serving the same purpose with which I would be happier to be affiliated. Therefore I am now resigning and hope you will not use my name any further. I feel sure you did not know this, and therefore I am writing to you personally to express why I feel I must withdraw my name.

Helen did not yield easily. To her the attack on the Rescue Ship Mission was reminiscent of the savage campaigns against the IWWs in the days of her and John Macy's association with that militant group. A letter from Art Young, the roly-poly Socialist cartoonist whose pointed drawings had enlivened the pages of the old *Masses* and who had been a comrade in the struggle to keep America out of the first war, confirmed her in her resolve. The attack on communism, he wrote her, was only the latest onslaught against the people in a long line that during his lifetime had included "populism, pacifism, anarchism, I.W.W.'s. . . . Dear Helen we all know that what you want is a better world for mankind."

It was the period of the Nazi-Soviet pact and the Soviet invasion of Finland, when Molotov was declaring that the difference between democratic capitalism and fascism was a mere matter of taste. Liberals were not inclined to help causes that ostensibly were for objectives they supported, but in reality were controlled by the communists for wholly different purposes. "Alas, Nella," Polly wrote as the resignations from the committee and the newspaper attacks showed no signs of abatement, "I'll never forgive myself, I should have known better. Yes, I did have all the data put into Braille for Helen so she would know what she was doing—I am still to blame. The list of sponsors certainly helped to fool us."

Essentially the Rescue Ship Mission was controlled by the Communists, although Biedenkapp had been replaced after Mrs. Roosevelt's resignation by a more ambiguous figure, Helen Bryan. As Dean Mildred Thompson of Vassar, a staunch liberal, explained to Helen when asked why she had withdrawn:

> It was clearly stated to me both in personal letter and in advertising sheet that the ship was ready to go subject only to our gift of money, $200 per person. Now it appears that no ship is ready and never has been ready. In fact the financial statement shows that an option has been secured on a ship but other reports make it appear quite dubious whether the ship is suitable for the purpose proposed. Clearly I misunderstood the status of the American Rescue Ship Mission, and while I remain friendly and sympathetic with the essential purpose of trying to help the Spanish refugees in France, I feel it necessary to work through some other organization. . . .

Helen and Polly set about frantically to try to get the facts. "If only Nella and I could have some one find out direct from the Rescue Ship Mission all that has been done under Helen's name and to get at the true state of affairs. Helen is behind the cause wholeheartedly as you know but there may be elements there we are ignorant of. . . . You know we have no business sense, Helen and I. That is why I have always been wary about Helen giving her name no matter how worthy the cause seemed to be. I wonder how we can obtain the information we need."

The next day Polly wrote Nella again. They had to get at the root of the problem "and that soon. It hovers over Helen and me like an ugly dream. We can't think straight and it's affecting Helen's work."

The new secretary of the Ship Mission, Helen Bryan, informed her that a board of directors was being created and listed the names. Several of them were well-known for their Communist ties. Polly forwarded a copy of her letter to Nella:

> Don't you think Nella, Helen could resign by saying the work connected with the American Rescue Ship Mission is taking too much of her time, that when she gave her name she understood it would not involve any work—that her literary work is suffering from the constant interruptions and also she expects to leave on a lecture trip in connection with the blind (to raise money) and she simply cannot continue with the A.R.S.M. . . .

"I am as anxious as anyone else for Helen to get out of the Rescue Ship Mission," Nella replied, "but I feel that she must have awfully solid ground under her feet when she does it." She suggested questions that Helen should put to Miss Bryan when they talked with her. How were the refugees to be selected? What did Helen Bryan have to say about the accusations of communism? Who would see to it that the funds raised were spent in ways the contributors intended? Who was carrying on the negotiations with Vichy? Helen as chairman had no right to resign on grounds of having too much else to do or for reasons of health. "Be ruthless in asking the questions. Make her give full answers and satisfactory answers and have the stenographer on hand again to take down what is said. I feel that this is really the crucial interview."

On February 3 Helen and Polly again interviewed Helen Bryan. The first session had been a runaround. "They never told us anything," said Polly. "It may be that we were too simple about it—we simply followed our hearts." In the interim a friend had checked on Miss Bryan and learned that she had done some work for the Quakers, as she claimed, but the Friends had suspected her of communist leanings. "Heretofore she has been executive secretary for the New York Chapter of the League for Peace and Democracy and has also been very active in the American Student Union."

At this second interview Helen asked the questions, Polly served as communicator and a stenographer recorded the exchanges. A few days later Helen resigned. As Polly told the press afterward, Helen had found the answers vague, evasive and contradictory. "Miss Keller trusted her heart." Helen's dignified letter of resignation avoided charges of communist affiliation against individuals and expressed no views on communism as a philosophy.

> The past few weeks I have made many careful inquiries about the American Rescue Ship Mission because I have been troubled by newspaper charges and private accusations connected with its activities. As a result of this investigation I conclude that I am not equal to keeping track of the endless happenings, complications and rivalries which surround the mission.
>
> On account of my handicap I am a slow worker. It was because my heart was pierced by the plight of the Spanish refugees that I tried to help them. But now I find the extra effort for the mission too heavy

a burden in addition to my life's work under the American Foundation for the Blind. Therefore I am resigning from the American
Rescue Ship Mission altogether.

My affectionate interest in the refugees remains. It grieves me deeply
that circumstances did not leave me free to do what I should like to
for them, but I shall rejoice at whatever is accomplished in the rescue
and rehabilitation of those heroic champions of Spanish freedom.

The letter showed, wrote Nella, that "Helen can handle her own affairs,
publicity included, better than anyone can handle them for her." Dr. John
Haynes Holmes, the venerable pastor of the Community Church, who
also had resigned, wrote, "I feel that you have done the right thing, and
certainly in the right spirit. The pity [is] that you had to undergo so trying
and painful an experience." Even Art Young was reconciled to her resignation: "I knew that you would not have done so except for reasons that
in no way reversed your principles and devotion to this merciful undertaking." "I'm so glad Art Young took it the way he did," Nella commented,
"and I think most of the sincere ones in that group feel exactly as he does.
One thing to remember about the *New Masses* is that it is not under the
same editorship as during the last war." Helen in the future should take
a firm stand against sponsorship of campaigns, dinners or anything else,
even the President's "March of Dimes" drive. "She may not want to make
any such statement as that she is never going to sponsor anything else, but
that she is never going to sponsor anything else except when she can take
an active part in the proceedings."

Renunciation of the Rescue Ship campaign renewed her yearning for
a mission connected with the war effort. She felt that she had made real
progress on her book about Teacher, and in the absence of other proposals
she informed the Foundation that she was ready to give it some time in
the spring. It sent her on a tour that took her to New Mexico and Utah
and, on the return trip, to Texas and Missouri, and a few weeks later to
Florida. The major purpose was to persuade the states to increase their
appropriations and services to the blind. In New Mexico she stirred "wild
enthusiasm," according to the press, by speaking a few words in Spanish.
In Houston she put in a word for the Lend-Lease Bill: "I believe in giving
aid to the democracies, but I hope the United States doesn't enter more
actively in the conflict. Britain is no longer an empire in the old sense of
the word. It now stands for democracy." In Tallahassee, the capital of

Florida, there was the usual standing-room-only crowd to hear her address the joint session to urge the establishment of a state council for the blind. The bill sailed through the lower house, but it took a special plea from Helen in late May to get the Senate to act, as it did, before adjournment. She was equally effective before a joint session of the Utah Legislature, and the president of the Mormon Church later presented her with seven volumes constituting the Book of Mormon printed in Braille. Ida Hirst-Gifford reported to Foundation headquarters the benefits to the blind that had flowed from her appearance in Salt Lake City. In many of the capitals her faithful "knights," the Lions Clubs, sponsored public meetings for her. The public still was fascinated, still was moved by her.

She spent her sixty-first birthday at Arcan Ridge, she wrote her new friends, the Heinemans of Chicago. Clare Heineman was Migel's cousin and almost as generous as he in the gifts she lavished on Helen. Helen loved Arcan Ridge. She had begun the day "with an hour in the dewy stillness of my communion walk," she wrote Clare. The walk was through trees and shrubs with the aid of cedar railings and ropes that Herbert had put out so that she could guide herself. Then she worked on Teacher's biography. "The next surprise was a box of beautiful salmon all the way from Mr. Migel up in Brunswick, Canada—two, each weighing twenty pounds!" Her other news was about Japan. She had many Japanese friends in the United States as a result of her 1937 trip, and two of them took her and Polly to a Japanese restaurant. The dishes "called up countless heart-warming memories of Nippon and its inimitable artistic hospitality." Then they visited the Japanese Institute with its ten thousand volumes in Japanese and English; "long may they serve as messengers of understanding and beneficent cooperation between the two countries." Arcan Ridge was filled with souvenirs of Japan—five Gifu lanterns on the porch, a large Koto and a Japanese "good luck hammer."

Helen's affection for the Japanese people and culture was undiminished despite Japan's prolonged war and occupation of China and despite the intensifying confrontation between Japan and the United States. Symbolically, her Akita, Kenzan Go, chose late October 1941—just as the Japanese fleet was secretly assembling for its attack upon Pearl Harbor—to disappear. Helen appealed to the police to help her locate the dog. The wire services carried the story. Twenty-four hours later, after a night of wandering around the countryside, Kenzan Go returned home on his own.

Pearl Harbor extinguished, at least temporarily, whatever sentiments of friendship for the Japanese still lingered in her heart. Her response to the attack was the outrage that almost all Americans felt. She praised the President's leadership in the crisis. Roosevelt after Pearl Harbor was a busy man, but he took time to acknowledge her letter. "You always, and rightly, interpret events in spiritual terms." Churchill was in Washington to concert Anglo-American strategy in the new situation, and his address to Congress appealed to her: "It is not only a great message to the English-speaking peoples but also, I think, a fateful document which future historians will look upon as one of the corner-stones of a new society."

Her enthusiasm for Churchill and Anglo-American unity did not keep her from urging collaboration with Russia, which was then handing the Nazi Panzers their first major setback. Russian resistance seemed to vindicate her old hope, never fully relinquished, in communism's promises. "The renewal of official amity between the United States and Soviet Russia," she wrote the Women's Anti-Nazi Conference in Moscow, "is a cause for thankfulness. Of course it is only a seal to us who have read the throbbing sympathy between groups in the two countries that understood each other's ideals and experiments to create a genuine democracy, but it is undeniable proof that ignorance and prejudice cannot separate forever peoples into whom freedom has breathed a soul. I am on the way with you, and therefore I love you."

She went down to Washington to spend a weekend with the Phil Smiths. They arranged for her to meet Archibald MacLeish, "who embodies to me a new spirit in the Library of Congress as well as in American literature"; and her adventures among the Washington great "culminated when I stood before President Roosevelt—'the foremost man of the world'—who makes fateful decisions for America and humanity." Otherwise she traveled very little at this time. "The 'Teacher' biography is progressing better than usual, thanks to the restrictions of rubber and gasoline which conspire to keep us at home."

A new satisfaction in her life was a friendship with the sculptor Jo Davidson. She had always been highly responsive to sculpture, an art responsive to her sense of touch. The sculpted head, like the live one, yielded its many secrets to her appreciative fingers. Roosevelt had allowed her to touch his face when he had received her briefly, "and how at home I felt with him!" When Ruth Gordon was invited to tea with Alexander Woollcott to meet Helen, the alert actress was struck by the way Helen patted Alec's face: "Then she patted it again and made sounds. 'Helen says she thinks your moustache has gotten smaller, Alec.' " Woollcott patted

Helen's face. "Tell her hers hasn't," Polly tapped, and Helen's laugh led all the rest.

Davidson, like Woollcott, made Helen laugh. With his bushy black beard and natural conviviality he was a joy to everyone around him. It seemed as if everyone famous were his friend, having become so in the course of sitting for him, for he talked, wittily and perceptively, as his fingers nimbly sketched and worked. He immediately endeared himself to Helen because as an art student he had learned the deaf-mute alphabet and found he still could spell into Helen's hand. "A spontaneous sympathy sprang up between us," and he asked her to sit for him. She and Polly came to his studio on his farm in Bucks County, and as soon as they "stepped across our threshold, the house was flooded with sunshine." He placed her hand on one of the bronze portrait busts in the studio.

"This is President Roosevelt," she said.

"Yes, it is," the sculptor told her.

Helen continued to run her fingers over the bust. "This was made," she said, "while he was much younger than when I last visited him."

"It was made in 1933," said Davidson.

"Oh, I visited him a few weeks ago, so that accounts for it."

Davidson at the time was the outstanding portraitist in sculpture, and while his style was not innovative, he sought in his likenesses to get at his sitter's essential character. He was not wholly satisfied with the bronze bust he did of Helen and persuaded her to return "to make another in terra cotta. . . . Polly was delighted with the result," Helen wrote Clare. "She said the terra cotta is warm, soft, and colorful, bringing out the light around my face to which she is accustomed."

Apart from personal friendships, correspondence and writing, there was little for her to do, and her unhappiness with her forced inactivity was reflected in her delight in her appointment by the Connecticut State Defense Council as an honorary member of its Air Raid Protective Division. An invitation to inspect the "report centers" from which warnings and orders would be conveyed in the event of an alert exhilarated her. They had started a vegetable garden at Arcan Ridge, and Herbert built a chicken house down by the kennel "so that we can have hens to lay eggs and sometimes enjoy a satisfying dinner."

Russia's decisive victory at Stalingrad sent progressive hopes, including Helen's, soaring again that with the Nazi incubus lifted Soviet power would at last be used to fulfill human aspirations rather than repress them. Her FBI file noted her congratulatory telegram to an American-Soviet

Friendship dinner celebrating the twenty-fifth anniversary of the Red Army.*

She was not disposed, therefore, to listen to critics of the Soviet Union.

> The end of March, while we were in the city we lunched with Katharine Cornell, and who do you think was with her? Countess Alexandra Tolstoy! She reminded me of Teacher in her dynamic vitality, impulsive moods and generous nature. She has not Teacher's large view of world events, and I had all I could do to curb my argumentative tongue when the Countess spoke of Russia as if it was hopelessly lost to Christianity and civilization.

She did not curb her tongue the next time she met the Countess and some of her White Russian friends, and found herself in a heated wrangle not only with them but with Guthrie McClintic, at whose house the encounter took place. He was a man of conservative views and explosive temperament who was not able to abide Helen's acclaim of Russia at the expense of American achievements. She felt obliged to explain herself more fully afterwards:

> In a frank, intimate talk one does not watch one's words too closely, and I fear I did not express myself well. Soviet Russia is truly a gigantic, complex, thought-testing phenomenon in human nature, and I suppose the opinions concerning its development are as countless as the varieties of religious dogma.
>
> You were right, Guthrie, in saying there can really be no comparison in standards of achievement between two basically different race geniuses like Russia and America. I did not intend that at all.—It seems to me the height of presumption to compare our own revolution covering a small area, fought only a hundred and fifty years after the Pilgrims landed at Plymouth, with Russia's sevenfold revolution that was fed by innumerable sources of oppression, ignorance and serfdom during twelve centuries. . . . Possibly you may know that Gleb Botkin's father was Czar Nicholas's physician, and very close to

---

*The FBI report on Helen Keller states, "The FBI has not conducted an investigation with regard to Helen Adams Keller. The files of this Bureau, however, do reflect the following pertinent information concerning this individual. . . ." The first item listed her as a signatory, according to *The Daily Worker* on April 9, 1938, of an appeal by the American Friends of Spanish Democracy to lift the arms embargo against Spain.

the royal family. His son also is very bitter against the Soviet regime, yet he told me he rejoiced that the miserable social futility and boredom he witnessed in his country had been swept away by the holocaust.

Also I agreed with you in what you said about America's magnificent progress in many directions. But that does not change the miracle of Russia acquiring ninety percent literacy in twenty-five years, does it? Nor does it prevent me from blushing over the horrible stains upon our own history—chattel slavery, the savageries of brutal industrialism and child labor. . . .

She had an inexhaustible capacity for enthusiasm and hope. She had no feeling of getting older, she announced on her sixty-third birthday when she and Polly lunched with Kit Cornell. "In fact I am younger today than I was at twenty-five. Of course the furrows of suffering have been dug deeper, but so have those of understanding and sympathy and inner happiness. Whatever age may do to my earthly shell, I shall never grow cynical or indifferent—and one cannot measure the reserve power locked up in that assurance." She was sure that the world, despite "the tremendous darkness" of the war, was "stumbling . . . towards a new earth and Heaven."

Suddenly her longing for a war-connected job was fulfilled. American military hospitals were filling up with wounded servicemen; and Nella, who had "perceived how the war had coiled itself about my mind with burning anguish," suggested to her, "Why not go to the wounded soldiers and find out for yourself what you can do for them. . . . Remember, they have adjustments just as you had when you were a child. . . . You owe a debt to the soldiers. We all do. Perhaps you can pay yours." Nella's challenge emboldened Helen to put aside scruples about broken speech, clumsiness and slowness and ask the Foundation to arrange some visits to the war wounded. She began with the Walter Reed and Bethesda Hospitals in Washington. Lenore Smith, who was slightly older than Helen but still active in Washington's civic life, accompanied her and Polly. Lenore must have had the same sense of Helen's yearning to be of use that Nella did, for afterward she wrote Major Migel, which she did not often do, telling him what a "tremendous success" Helen's visit had been. That did not surprise him, Migel commented to Helen; and though the hospital tour was "strenuous and taxing," he was sure it gratified her to be making a contribution. Helen thanked Lenore for the "beautiful letter" she had written Migel:

> It seemed natural to have you with me at the hospitals as you often have been in events which try my fortitude or tax my powers to help others whose limitations differ from my own. Just think, Lenore, you were present when Teacher and I started our work in public at the Massachusetts State House for the Blind. Since then I have grown familiar with every movement for the blind and done what I could for my deaf fellows, but never have I felt as diffident as I did before I spoke at the Walter Reed Hospital and Bethesda Naval Hospital. What message did I have, I wondered, for men who had borne the cruelest war ordeal on record and who must lie still in bed day after day! That you, so unsparing in your standards, should have thought I did some good means more to me than I can ever express.

A doctor told Eleanor Roosevelt of the impact of Helen's visit on some blind soldiers, and she reported what he said in "My Day": "Just to know of her presence seemed to encourage the boys." Henri Bendel, of the famous and expensive Fifth Avenue shop of which Helen and Polly were steady patrons, wrote that he had gone into the army and was at Officers' Candidate School. "Your name was mentioned by our Colonel, a Colonel Rice, in a talk he was giving us. It was used as an example of a person with an objective." After the Washington tours she visited the Military Hospital in Atlantic City, "addressing six different groups and talking with the sick and wounded individually. The warm appreciative way my message was received gave me the needed self-confidence." From Atlantic City they went to the Naval Hospital in Philadelphia. The ever-jovial Jo Davidson accompanied them. "I spoke to the physicians and nurses, and had an informal, happy visit with the blinded and deafened servicemen who are being rehabilitated according to the most advanced methods." The American Foundation for the Blind decided to plan a tour of military hospitals for her.

She saw much of Jo and his wife Florence. The talk and company were always stimulating at their home. One evening she met Van Wyck Brooks there. She discovered that he lived not too far from her in Connecticut and was engaged on his monumental history of American literature focusing on New England. Lin Yutang and the film producer Bob Flaherty also were there, and "sparks flew on every subject—China, books, Roosevelt and Dewey, philosophy and post-war reconstruction. The only element lacking to make my satisfaction complete was Teacher's presence. She delighted in inspiring discussions, sallies of wit and large views of world affairs."

It was Jo Davidson who involved Helen in the establishment of an "Independent Voters Committee of the Arts and Sciences for Roosevelt." Disregarding her 1940 trouble with the Spanish Refugee Rescue Ship, she joined Jo, Ethel Barrymore, Van Wyck Brooks, Tom Benton, Bob Flaherty, Norman Cousins and Tallulah Bankhead in the circulation of a letter to artistic, literary, scientific and stage folk inviting them to set up a committee to reelect Roosevelt.

Helen's active involvement in politics startled Nella, who always was on the alert to protect Helen's interests. They met at the Harvard Club, and she argued with Helen; afterward she felt that the obligations of friendship required her to state her feelings in writing. Helen in return explained her attitude on politics in some detail, and the letter revealed how radical she remained:

> Your letter was another evidence of the loyal friendship and conscientious care with which you lead me to weigh my public acts and utterances before I commit them irrevocably. Just to make sure that my 'wild, strong will' does not run away with me and overturn the chariot of the American Foundation for the Blind, which drives it anyhow out of harm's path, I have again examined the possible consequences of casting my vote for F.D. Roosevelt, and I shall march up to the cannon's mouth just the same.

> Seriously, Nella, my voting for Roosevelt seems to me no worse than taking part in this War after I had been a pacifist from my youth up. I still feel like a deserter, and I know that the conflict began as a rankly imperialistic one, but what could I do when it developed into a peoples' war of liberation?

> Oh no! I do not mean to imply that I look upon Roosevelt as a leader of the masses. As I told you that day at the Harvard Club, I do not think America has had a genuine people's president since Lincoln's day, and the people's party does not yet exist which would command my allegiance. Also I realize that it is impossible for even the greatest statesman or one nation to steer a frenzied world beating itself against

destitution, rabid nationalism and ignorance. I am voting for Roosevelt because I believe he is sincere in advocating comprehensive policies for international cooperation out of which alone a stable progressive world can arise. Reading his own words, 'World collaboration must be the people's doing,' I feel that he recognizes his limits and America's, surely it does take a kind of greatness to make such an admission in a cruelly slanderous campaign.

Besides, despite apparent glaring inconsistencies in his attitude towards the people, I am sure if Roosevelt is re-elected, his administration will continue at least tolerant of the labor movement whose steady growth is essential to America's higher democracy and closer union with other countries. . . . A bucketful of water is small, and so is a vote, yet how mighty the aggregate of votes may be to check appalling fascist influences in this country, carry the War to complete victory and extend the international agreements we must have for post-war reconstruction. My conscience will not let me off from voting so long as I see an added chance of world betterment in Roosevelt's leadership during the next four years.

It is perfectly true that my work for the blind is a trust, and in order to fulfill its duties justly I must keep it as the centre of my external activities. But it has never occupied a centre in my personality or inner relations with mankind. That is because I regard philanthropy as a tragic apology for wrong conditions under which human beings live, losing their sight or hearing or becoming impoverished, and I do not conceal this awkward position from anybody. One can, and does dishonor one's trust through suave compliance quite as much as through lack of considerate caution. There is an even higher trust— to keep my essential freedom so that wherever possible I may release fettered minds and imprisoned lives among the blind, let alone those who see. . . .

Bob Irwin was getting in touch with military hospitals around the country about her tour, and the Teacher book hung over her head "like Damocles's sword," but she not only supported Roosevelt, she campaigned actively. She spoke at a luncheon of the Women's Division of the Independent Citizens' Committee for Political Action and was one of a galaxy of speakers at the Madison Square Garden Rally organized by Jo

Davidson's committee. He had telephoned Wallace to ask him to speak. Wallace had agreed even though he had been dropped from the ticket, replaced by Harry S Truman. There were cries of "Wallace in 'forty-eight" when he rose to speak. Other speakers were Helen, Dr. Harlow Shapley, Serge Koussevitzky, Fredric March, Orson Welles, Sinclair Lewis, Dr. Channing Tobias, Quentin Reynolds and others. Roosevelt later told Davidson that Bob Hannegan, the Democratic national chairman, had said to him, "That artist friend of yours is crazy, selling tickets for a political meeting in Madison Square Garden." Hannegan, Davidson wrote in his memoirs, "had offered to fill the house, but our committee turned him down. We were novices, but we sold our tickets. Madison Square Garden overflowed its capacity."

Her political sensitivities heightened by her involvement in the campaign, she made a dramatic appeal on behalf of the Negro blind in early October. A subcommittee of the House Committee on Labor was holding hearings around the country on aid to the physically handicapped. Helen used an appearance before the subcommittee at the Federal Court House in New York City to plead for a "handicap allowance" for two subgroups, "the hardest pressed and the least cared-for among my blind fellows," the Negro blind and the deaf-blind. Of the former she said:

> In my travels up and down the continent I have visited their shabby school buildings and witnessed their pathetic struggle against want. I have been shocked by the meagerness of their education, lack of proper medical care, and the discrimination which limits their employment chances. I feel it a disgrace that in this great wealthy land such injustice should exist to men and women of a different race—and blind at that! It is imperative that colored people without sight be granted financial aid worthy of their human dignity and courage in the face of fearful obstacles.

Shortly after the election, whose victorious outcome she celebrated with Jo and his cohorts, she and Polly set off on a coast-to-coast tour of military hospitals organized by the Foundation. Often the wounded men were astonished to have her enter their wards. She was a legend of whom they had read in school or heard about from their parents. "If she were alive she'd be one hundred," one skeptical GI commented. "Next to the doctors'," Eleanor Roosevelt said, Helen's visits "are probably the most healing that can come to them." Her cheerfulness and serenity of spirit buoyed not only the wounded but their doctors and nurses as well. "What gives you the courage to go on?" a wounded man asked her. "The Bible and poetry and philosophy," she answered. And when he went on to ask, "How do you feel when God seems to desert you?" she had to answer, she said, "I never had that feeling."

Her curiosity about new methods of treatment was relentless. Dr. George W. Corner, then head of the department of embryology of the Carnegie Institution of Washington, was chairman of a government committee that was studying the possibilities of new devices to enable reading by war-blinded soldiers. The committee did not want to raise false hopes, so the project was secret. Somehow Helen got wind of it and asked to come to see him: "She wanted to know about my committee's plans and to encourage us." He was impressed by her "considerable understanding" of the pertinent scientific questions. Suspecting that she had never had a chance to study a scientific model by touch, he asked her whether she would like to examine a model of a human embryo:

> I brought a plaster model of an embryo of about five weeks, magnified to a height of about fifteen inches from its original length of a quarter inch. Miss Keller's eager fingers went over the model systematically, beginning at the head. She was surprised by the large proportional size of the head and heart. She felt the branchial bars (which she knew about already). She found the emerging arm and leg buds and smiled when she felt the caudal appendage. She then went back to the head and asked, 'Where are the eyes?' I explained that the rudiments of the eyes were present but were still buried under the skin of the face. Not until a few days later would the eyelids break apart and reveal the eyes. After a little silence, Miss Keller said, 'How long the little creature has to wait for light!'

After her tour ended, she spoke to the press and emphasized the "veritable miracles in surgical and medical skill" that she had witnessed. A reporter asked what she thought a wounded man expected of his country. Helen leaned forward as Polly tapped the question into her hand. "They do not want to be treated as a class apart," she exclaimed. "They do not want to be treated as heroes. They want to be able to live naturally, and to be treated as human beings." She gave touching examples of what she meant in an article that she wrote for *The New York Times Magazine:*

Often it was not verbal encouragement that was asked of me but a kiss or the laying of my hand on a weary head. This always made me feel as if I were partaking of a sacrament. A patient, appealingly young, came up to rest his head on my shoulder and was silent for a moment, evidently bracing himself for a new try at life. A drop of sweetness stole into my grief over the paralyzed as they tried to put their wasted arms around me, not always successfully, but their wish was a benediction I shall treasure forever.

A boy of 18 on his way to the operating table said he knew he would come through all right after I had embraced him. Another to whom I wished speedy recovery after an operation said, 'I don't want your wishes but your love,' and seemed cheered by my assurance that he had it. Another soldier, obviously dying, held my hand as if I had been his mother. One said, 'My, I have not had a kiss like that in years. My mother used to kiss me that way.'

Her visit with the war wounded, she said, was "the crowning experience of my life." To Migel she wrote of "the happiness that has attended upon my way since Polly and I began our tour of Government hospitals."

She had interrupted her tour to attend Roosevelt's inaugural in response to a special invitation from the inaugural committee. In Washington she joined up with Jo and Florence Davidson. Lincoln's inaugural, she wrote Clare Heineman, must have been something like this "austere ceremony." "The severe simplicity of the ceremonies, F.D.R.'s brief yet momentous address as we stood on the snow-mantled ground under the magnolia trees, the informality of the reception at the White House," all seemed appropriate to someone fresh from visits to the wounded. Inside the White House she and Polly and the Davidsons joined the receiving line and were greeted by Mrs. Roosevelt and Mrs. Truman. As they moved away, the President's daughter, Mrs. John Boettiger, with whom they had spent an afternoon in Seattle, took them to greet the President "in a room with just his family about him. . . . Upon his worn face shines the heroic ambitions of Hercules to subdue the beasts of greed and deliver the earth from robber states. . . . He trusts the progressive tendencies converging toward a nobler goal," she wrote Van Wyck Brooks.

The evening of the inaugural the Davidsons took her and Polly to the Lowell Melletts for dinner. Other guests included Justice Hugo Black and Thurman Arnold, who started a discussion of "the different roads by which Soviet Russia and the United States must reach genuine democracy, conscious responsibility versus economic determinism."

David E. Lilienthal, the head of the Tennessee Valley Authority, had attended the inaugural and was checking out of the Willard Hotel when Jo Davidson rushed at him to embrace him. "I have the greatest treat in the world for you; you have got to take a few minutes to come upstairs," he insisted. Lilienthal demurred; he was headed for Union Station. "I want you to meet Helen Keller; she is upstairs; she is talking about you to everyone, you and your achievement and your book. You must take a moment to go up and see her." Lilienthal yielded; and soon Polly was spelling his name, "beating out the syllables," it seemed to Lilienthal, into Helen's hands. "Her head jerked back and a lovely but strange series of sounds came forth—a cry—such wonderful motions of the head, of pleasure and incredulity. . . . Very wonderful things she was saying, too, as the companion reported them: 'No one in the United States has done so magnificent and beautiful a thing as David Lilienthal.' " When the TVA chairman mentioned Tuscumbia's closeness to Muscle Shoals, she was pleased, and she ended the conversation as Lilienthal took his leave, "And now there are to be many more TVAs—fifteen perhaps."

That was what she felt Roosevelt's reelection and the war's end meant. She believed in Roosevelt's "forward-looking courage," she wrote Van Wyck late in March. Because of it "his name will remain forever luminous in the acts of the conferences in Cairo, Teheran, Dumbarton Oaks, Yalta —and soon it will be the shaping of the World Security Organization at San Francisco! That is a mind stretching spectacle for us just emerging from pigmy chauvinism, is it not?"

A few weeks later Roosevelt was dead. She heard the news in Charleston at a naval hospital. "The company went mute and limp. . . . What a sombre prospect this must open up of unfulfilled projects, constructive policies endangered, momentous issues trembling in the balance at the San Francisco Conference! It is an irreplaceable void we workers for the handicapped feel now that the tangible tokens of his sympathy and counsel are withdrawn. My hospital visits have lost an indefinable something which buoyed me up while he was among us." But he had left an inspiring heritage. "The vision he had to see Soviet Russia's greatness still leads us on. The genius of Britain with which he collaborated continues mighty on earth. The United Nations . . ."

Roosevelt, like other Presidents before him, had been honorary chairman of the American Foundation for the Blind, and the Foundation passed an engrossed resolution commemorating his service to the handicapped. Helen presented it to Mrs. Roosevelt at a brief ceremony in the Foundation's headquarters. The late President, Helen said, had shown "the same heroic quality in the setting free of his higher faculties despite a cruel handicap" that he later used in "cleaving channels through tradition for world statesmanship and international brotherhood." In accepting the tribute Mrs. Roosevelt noted that "the last twelve or fifteen years have been a period of great growth in the rights of human beings . . . and in the belief that every human being has a contribution to make to society." This development she attributed in part to the fact that "my husband knew what it was to face a handicap and conquer it."

"As I stood and listened to Miss Keller speak," she wrote in her column afterwards, "I thought how wonderfully both Miss Keller and my husband typified the triumph over physical handicap."

XXXVIII

A Mind of Her Own

"I cannot lend my name to the campaign for Henry Wallace."

As the war in Europe ended, Helen and the Foundation planned a new mission to make use of Helen's talents and desire to serve the handicapped. She continued to visit military hospitals and would do so for another year; but on June 27, 1945, she celebrated her sixty-fifth birthday at Peter Salmon's Brooklyn Industrial Home for the Blind and with considerable satisfaction announced the Foundation's establishment of an industrial and training program for the deaf-blind—the fulfillment, she said, "of a life-long dream." She made the announcement at Peter Salmon's Brooklyn Home because its factory, which included thirteen deaf-blind, had won the Army-Navy "E" for its production of brooms and mops, thus vindicating Helen's conviction that the deaf-blind, appropriately trained, were able to attain a self-supporting status. The deaf-blind, she declared proudly, "did eighty percent of the operations the blind do. They are fully self-supporting."

Her constant emphasis with the deaf-blind as well as the blind was on self-reliance and independence, and she applied this injunction to more than the blind and the deaf-blind. "Blindness with a big B has never interested me," she wrote in a *New York Times Magazine* article that described her visits to the military hospitals. "I have always looked upon the blind as a part of the whole of society, and my desire has been to help them regain their human rights so as to enable them to keep a place of usefulness and dignity in the world economy. What I say of the blind applies equally to all hindered groups—the deaf, the lame, the impoverished, the mentally disturbed."

But there was another center to her life, a personal life not connected with her work for the handicapped and the Foundation. It focused on Arcan Ridge and three circles of friends—her Westport neighbors, especially the Pfeiffers and Eddie Clarks; Kit Cornell and her entourage; and Jo Davidson and his politically oriented companions. Arcan Ridge was where she rose with the sun to weed and dig her hands into the soil, to trim the borders, even to cut the grass. The roses and honeysuckle, ivy and rock plants, that they had put in during the first years had taken root and flourished. She knew each tree by touch. Often she ran down the ramp to "Helen's walk," as Polly called the handrail that Herbert had built. At Arcan Ridge in the summer she luxuriated "in freedom from the tyranny of clothes (I wear a sun dress all day), travel, hotel and war's bruising realities."

"Dinner with Helen and Gaetano Salvemini at Professor Robert Pfeiffer's," Van Wyck Brooks noted in his journal. Salvemini was the Lauro de Bosis Lecturer on Italian Civilization at Harvard. He had been a professor of history at the University of Florence and was the author of an outstanding history of the French Revolution. Bernard Berenson had described Salvemini as "a prophet and defender of every good cause." He had been challenged to a duel by the Duce before he escaped from an Italian prison. Robert Pfeiffer's wife Matilde was a fellow Florentine, and the Salveminis often were at Harvard House in Westport. This particular evening, described by Brooks, Mrs. Pfeiffer played an Italian song. "Helen stood by with her left hand on the piano top, waving gently with her right hand, keeping perfect time. She feels the vibrations through the piano and the floor. In this way she recognizes many compositions."

Often Helen and Polly went to New York, likely as not for a visit with Kit Cornell or dinner with the Jo Davidsons or lunch with Nella at the Harvard Club. She and Polly went to Laurence Olivier's portrayal of Henry IV in house seats procured for them by Kit and Guthrie. "We felt as if a king and a queen had honored us," she wrote her "Dearest of Katharines," thanking her and Guthrie for "those hard-won tickets," and accepting her invitation to visit them on Martha's Vineyard. A week later they traveled to New York again to visit Eleanor Brooks at Doctors' Hospital. "From there we rushed to Jo Davidson's to bid him and Florence goodbye before they left by plane for Paris at midnight. The studio was crowded as usual with a variegated throng of friends."

Davidson had kept the Independent Citizens' Committee for the Arts and Sciences alive after the 1944 campaign as a form of left-wing pressure on the administration, and Helen wholly approved—particularly after Roosevelt's death. She spoke at its Madison Square Garden rally on December 4, 1945. She attended the November 1945 reception at the Soviet Consulate in New York, declaring as she entered the building, according to her FBI file, "Finally I am on Soviet soil." She sent greetings to a February 1946 meeting of the Veterans of the Abraham Lincoln Brigade, and she needed no urging from Davidson to support the Independent Citizens' Committee.

Nella tried to dampen the rekindling of Helen's left-wing enthusiasm, which expressed itself particularly in her support of Henry Wallace. Helen had met him at the 1944 rally for Roosevelt and had been so taken with his speech and person that afterward she had sent him a fan letter. The letter had been rewritten at Nella's suggestion, eliminating a section about "conspiracies to encircle the Soviet Union," but it approved Wallace's "understanding appreciation of the Soviet Union." Her final draft, she informed Nella, "is in the spirit of all I have written about and for Soviet Russia since 1917. You would despise me, I know, if I, even to avoid dogmatism, adopted an attitude like Max Eastman, who, I happen to be aware from personal data, is a renegade without courage." Wallace had replied to her letter, calling it "one of the most inspiring letters which I have ever received." What particularly impressed Wallace was not so much her endorsement of his stand on the Soviet Union as her approval of his emphasis on the "three-fourths of mankind" submerged in poverty and illiteracy that should be helped through the United Nations. "The forgotten masses which populate three-fourths of the world," Wallace agreed, "unlettered as they are, undernourished as they are, and uninspired as they are, nevertheless are turning over in their sleep."

Like many other progressives, including Eleanor Roosevelt, she had looked to Wallace for leadership after Roosevelt's death. His sharpening criticism of the overmilitarization of American foreign policy in 1946 appealed to her own deep-seated antimilitarism, as did his insistence that the United States shared some of the blame for the breakup of the wartime Grand Alliance. When he was forced out of Truman's Cabinet in September 1946 she was wholly on his side. Wallace's forced resignation followed a speech at Madison Square Garden in which he criticized Russia

as well as America and Great Britain. Truman had approved the speech
in advance, but after Secretary of State Byrnes, who was negotiating with
Molotov in Paris, protested, Truman withdrew his approval:

> Friday night [she wrote Nella] I was stunned by the radio announce-
> ment of Henry Wallace's forced resignation after the President had
> publicly approved the Madison Square Garden speech, and professed
> respect for the right of the Secretary of State to express his views. The
> indignant remarks of various commentators bore out my feelings with
> regard to the Administration, which has never given me the slightest
> cause to renounce my extreme left-wing views. I have long suspected
> that both the Democratic and the Republican parties, backed by high
> financiers and other powerful vested interests, are working towards
> imperialism, and now the proof glares me in the face. You know what
> potential explosions that trend contains. The American people includ-
> ing myself have, I think, been ignominiously slow about supporting
> Wallace in his struggle to check the disgraceful squabbles between
> the supposed Allies and restore F.D. Roosevelt's magnanimous for-
> eign policy as a counsellor and friend of mankind.

But she put politics aside in the interests of a tour of Europe on behalf
of the American Foundation for the Overseas Blind, a sister organization
of the American Foundation for the Blind. "It will be necessary for us to
raise as much money as possible," she announced in a signed syndicated
article, "in order to help the blind of Europe even a little bit." As she
explained to Nella:

> Now for the flight to Britain. I cannot say the prospect elates me.
>
> It will mean heartache as I sense over there gusts from the world's
> distress, famine, hope of peace deferred and international discord.
> But I feel a deep necessity of going. The American Foundation began
> early this year a drive through the Foundation for the Overseas Blind
> to aid the destitute sightless of Europe and I am expected to make
> further appeals on their behalf. I receive constantly piteous letters
> from the European Blind begging help, and by going to England and
> Paris, where the headquarters of the Foundation for the Overseas
> Blind are, I think I can gather firsthand information which I must
> have in order to lay their desperate needs before the American public
> effectively and raise funds for their relief.

Almost as an afterthought she exclaimed, "Oh dear! the 'Teacher' book will be at a standstill again. However, as Iphigenia says, 'Any road to any end may run,' and in some way past hoping I may regain undisturbed leisure for the biography." But just as her visits to American military hospitals had given her conscience the alibi it needed not to confront the difficulties presented by the Teacher book, so she would continue to give other demands on her time priority over the book.

She and Polly flew to Europe, their first transatlantic flight, in October for a two-month stay. Tell Helen she will be welcome at St. Dunstan's, Ian Fraser cautioned Migel, but there will be many changes. His own house had been bombed out, and he was living in cramped quarters, but she should visit the St. Dunstan's rehabilitation center at Brighton, and the National Institute for the Blind in London will receive her happily. The visits to the war-blinded in England and later on the continent were little different from touring the military hospitals in the United States, and Helen's appearance was as much a tonic there as in America.

From London she went to Paris, where her inspection tours of the hospitals and the war-ravaged facilities for the blind were guided by Georges Raverat, an old friend who would head up the European work of the American Foundation for the Overseas Blind. Raverat helped persuade her to visit Athens and Rome. She accepted with alacrity. It meant a chance to visit the Parthenon and the Coliseum. Herbert, who also had come to Europe, was left behind in Paris. As they descended from the plane in Athens, they were met by Eric Boulter, the blind director of foreign-sponsored services for the blind in Greece. Polly handed him a heavy bag. "Would you mind looking after it? It's got four bottles of whisky in it." Oho, said Eric to himself. Here are real people with dislikes, preferences, humor and passion.

One of Helen's abominations, he soon discovered, was King George of the Hellenses, whom British bayonets had put back on the throne. Eric argued with her, for he hoped that Helen would help him obtain royal patronage for his work. Helen was not persuaded, but in the interests of the blind she went to the palace with Eric to be presented to the king. While waiting in the anteroom they found themselves with Princess Katharine, the king's youngest sister. Through Eric and Polly the princess talked with Helen and quickly fell under her spell. She decided impulsively that here was a woman she could trust.

"Do you mind if I talk about a personal matter?" she asked. Her family wanted her to marry a member of the Spanish royal family, but she had fallen in love with a young British military attaché.

"What shall I do?" Helen responded to the young woman's openness. "As a member of the royal family you have obligations. But that isn't the only factor. In the end you should make your own decision."

"I tried to put him out of my mind," the princess replied, "but I still love him."

"Well, then, you should marry him!"

She did. After that encounter, the session with the king was anticlimactic, but the king did assure Eric of his help. That did not obviate the need for help from America, and Eric handed Helen a long list of materials and equipment that he needed from the AFOB.

The visit to Greece was "a superlatively moving event," as much because of her visit to the Parthenon as to the installations for the blind. From the time she had studied the Greek classics, the Parthenon had occupied a vivid place in her imagination. To prepare her for the visit the head of the American School in Athens first took her to his office, where he showed her with the use of a small model what she was about to see. They went to the Parthenon at dawn. She felt the fluted columns and her comment astonished her companions. "How interesting, they are meant to see out from, not to be looked at." As she moved along Pausanias' Walk she went on, "It is to use, this temple, not to look out from."

In Rome, in addition to viewing the Coliseum, she had an interview with Pope Pius XII arranged by Myron Taylor, the President's special envoy to His Holiness. Polly, staunch Scotch Presbyterian, tried to avoid the audience, telling the ambassador that their plane was leaving for Paris and they did not have the time. "That is all right," he said. "I will send you in my plane." Polly bowed to the inevitable. The audience started out lamely. His Holiness had not been well briefed. Thinking he was passing his hands over the celebrated blind woman, he selected Polly for his attention. The mistake was corrected, and there was some exchange of sentiments that no one seems to have recorded, except that Helen responded by asking him to care for the blind. "He has not taken advantage of his opportunity," Helen later told Nella.

While in Rome they heard that disaster had struck at home. Arcan Ridge had burned to the ground, the result evidently of a malfunctioning furnace. Bob Irwin, unable to get hold of Helen and Polly, telephoned Raverat, who gave the news to Herbert, and that hapless man walked the streets of Paris in black despair awaiting Helen's return. Finally, Migel's secretary, Amelia, after getting assurances that the house would be rebuilt, reached Polly. "Over transatlantic phone to Paris she confirmed the news," wrote Nella. "It was bad, completely bad. The voice at the Paris end disappeared and for two or three minutes Amelia was afraid of what she and I and a few others have dreaded above all else—she was afraid that Polly was overcome. She and I knew that Polly's high blood pressure was an ever-present danger. . . . Then the voice returned. A few days later we all had cables. Their world was gone; the girls would build a new one. Against the background of suffering and horror they had seen in Europe this task did not seem impossible."

"To lose all your possessions at my age is hard," Helen told the press, and then dismissed the subject to speak of her tour.

But her friends—Lenore, Nella, the Davidsons, Kit, the Pfeiffers, Migel —were considerably wrought up, and there was much conferring over what might be done. The Stuart Grummonses, Westport neighbors, proposed that a public subscription be started to raise $50,000 for Helen and Polly. "NBH was perfectly horrified," Nella recorded in her diary.

> Long ago Teacher had said that if Helen went before the public to collect for herself she would get a fantastic amount of money. But Helen never had asked anything for herself, only for the blind and the deaf-blind. She had always found it humiliating to beg even for them, but for them and them alone (and the deaf) she had always been willing to stand by the wayside with her cup in her hand. If now she asked that it be filled for her, the public having emptied its pockets, would find that the job was done. Never afterwards would it be possible for Helen Keller to beg for anyone else. NBH voted an emphatic No. The Davidsons agreed and so, when NBH explained to Sandra, did the Grummons.

Again the Pfeiffers and Migel came to the rescue. Louise and Gustavus Pfeiffer cabled her:

ALL MEMBERS OF COLONY DEEPLY SYMPATHIZE WITH YOU AND MISS POLLY IN LOSS OF ARCAN RIDGE. ROBERT AND MATILDE JOIN US IN OFFERING HOSPITALITY OF HARVARD HOUSE UNTIL JUNE FIRST. ON YOUR RETURN WE SHALL WISH TO DISCUSS PERMANENT HOME PLANS WITH YOU. PLEASE CABLE PFEIFFER QUICKPILL NEW YORK YOUR RETURN DATE. HOMESTEAD CREW MAKING CAREFUL

SEARCH AT ARCAN RIDGE AND VALUABLES RECOVERED WILL BE
STORED FOR YOU. AFFECTIONATE REGARDS.

Migel cabled similarly: GRIEVED ABOUT ARCAN RIDGE SHALL EN-
DEAVOR ASSIST AS FAR AS POSSIBLE IN SAD SITUATION. MR. PFEIFFER
HAS ALREADY ARRANGED FOR YOUR OCCUPANCY OF HARVARD HOUSE
TEMPORARILY UNTIL NEW HOME IS READY. THANK HEAVEN YOU
WERE NOT HOME TIME OF CATASTROPHE. AMELIA JOINS ME IN SEND-
ING HEARTS BEST LOVE.

Among the first thoughts that gripped Helen when she heard the news
was the loss of her books. Blind Bob Irwin understood that: PLANNING
TO ARRANGE FOR BRAILLE TRANSCRIBING SOME OF YOUR MOST PRE-
CIOUS BOOKS CABLE LIST OF TITLES YOU WISH MOST REPLACED IN
YOUR LIBRARY. And what Bob was unable to do, the officials at the
National Institute for the Blind in London and the Library of Congress
said that they would try to make up.

Pfeiffer's men were still working in the charred ruins when Nella and
Amelia braced themselves to travel to Westport and take a look. "It is an
awful thing to see a black hole where once a house has stood," wrote
Nella. "Priceless Oriental vases were twisted bits of metal, fragments of
drapery and upholstery had not quite burned. Books—*Out of the Dark,* etc.
lay so charred that they could never be redeemed. Pages of manuscript
were flying around. NBH succored the beginning of the Japanese diary
and certain paragraphs from the epic poem which John Macy had wanted
Helen to write. 'Dry these out,' she said to David Gillies. 'Save them and
everything that looks like a typewritten page, no matter if it only has a
paragraph on it. Save everything that is in Braille. Miss Keller will know
what it means.' "

Nella noted that a steel door between house and garage had saved some
of Herbert's things, "but the irretrievable and irreplaceable, Helen's
manuscripts were gone." Helen would have to begin her book about
Teacher anew.

While all this was going on at home Helen and Polly kept on with their
tour. On November 29 they went to Buckingham Palace to call on Queen
Elizabeth. Afterwards she wrote:

Almost before I knew it, we were going up to another room and there
was Her Majesty alone, coming forward to greet us with a warm,
most winning simplicity. . . . I thanked her for her motherly interest

in all work for the blind and the deaf and she touched me deeply by saying that my conquest of difficulties had given her courage. I went on to tell her how I loved her for the fidelity with which she had stayed in London despite its horrible bombings. 'The people and I upheld each other,' was her quick reply. . . . I was surprised to count all the precious moments she had granted us and lingered only to ask if I might send my greetings to Their Highnesses the Princesses. Her Majesty said she would give them my message, and rising, she took from a bowl nearby fragrant sprigs of rosemary, lavender and sweet citronella and put them into my hand with a smiling goodbye.

They spent a few weeks in Scotland with Polly's family, then flew home. Reaching an overcast La Guardia Airport after a harrowing trip, they were informed they might have to fly on to Washington. But the pilot found an opening, and ten hours later they landed, to be met by Amelia and Ida Hirst-Gifford and Uncle Gus. "Then there you were," she wrote the latter at Christmastime, "waiting long for us at the airport after driving all the way from Westport and smiling as we had our picture taken together, and there was the watchful care with which you had David drive us home. No, we can never be homeless where friends raise up walls of good will about us."

By nine that evening they were installed at Harvard House. Matilde Pfeiffer had come over from Cambridge, Massachusetts, to see that everything was ready for them. Polly telephoned Nella. "How are you?" the latter asked. "Pretty low," Polly replied in a voice so somber it stabbed Nella's heart.

They agreed to meet at the Harvard Club after the weekend. Nella rounded up the Jo Davidsons and Kit Cornell, who had herself just returned from Europe. Helen, Polly and Nella met Kit on the steps of the club "and we all cried a little when we came together." So did Florence Davidson when she and Jo arrived a little later. Wrote Nella in her journal: "Katharine Cornell was never more beautiful and she had never liked Jo and Florence so much. The Davidsons, for their part, had never seen her intimately before, where they could feel her warmth. Everyone of us thought much more highly of everyone else because we had Helen and Polly with us again."

But there was an undercurrent of tension. Kit Cornell had been to England to speak with Kate O'Brien about the dramatization of a new play for her. She agreed with Helen and Polly that the British were dealing with postwar shortages and privations magnificently, especially in comparison with the French. "This subject was soft-pedalled after the arrival of the Davidsons," commented Nella, "for they are known Francophiles." Helen was eager for news about Wallace, but her talk with Davidson was peppered with digs at the former Vice-President. He was allowing his mind to lie fallow, Helen complained, evidently disappointed that he had not mounted a white charger and stormed the Truman White House after his resignation from the Cabinet. The Davidsons, a little more mildly, indicated that they, too, were disappointed in him. He had become publisher of a magazine, they told her; and Nella added in brackets, making it unclear whether the exclamation point was hers or the company's, "[but what a magazine, the New Republic!]." Florence Davidson chimed in that at Joe's studio a few days earlier Wallace had said, "I am not a Communist," and the poor man's protest was considered by the Davidsons as a concession to the witch hunters.

Discord intruded into the gathering again when the subject of the Catholic Church came up. Kit, too, had had an audience with the Pope when she was in Italy and "loved it," reported Nella. "The drama alone would have appealed to her—the long walk with Swiss guards, the riot of color, the stately figure in his robes at the end. Aside from that she admires Pacelli—spoke of the beauty of his face and especially of his hands." The Davidsons, Nella went on, hated the Church as a bulwark of reaction. "Polly and Helen are not far behind them." They jarred Kit with a mocking account of their own audience. Kit said good-bye, and the rest went on to Jo's studio to inspect a new plaster bust of the sculptor, which Helen recognized by touch, as well as the bronze bust of herself. Everyone wanted to do something to help repair the damage from the fire. Nella undertook to put together a new address book for them. The Davidsons were to send two rough, serviceable coats for country wear. All were relieved by Helen's serenity. To Nella she seemed "perfectly tranquil. The undercurrent of distress and worry, kept under tight control, belonged to Polly. The whole business has struck her much harder than anyone else." There seemed to be only one comfort, Nella wrote afterward, the "destruction of letters and papers Teacher herself had not been equal to. We make a new start."

Kit, it turned out, had left the Harvard Club uneasy and troubled. She unburdened herself to Nella at lunch alone a few days later:

> We talked at some length about Jo Davidson. Katharine Cornell has known him and seen him around for many years. Thinks he is superfi-

cial. I spoke of his gift for photographic accuracy in his sculptures. 'That's just it,' she said. 'He gives you that and nothing more.'

Helen's redness troubles her and apparently sets Guthrie McClintic wild. She fears the Jo Davidson influence but I told her not to worry —that their radicalism was much older than their acquaintance with him, that it was deep and fundamental and that it was not increasing by leaps and bounds as she had thought.

Helen and Polly's jocular description of their audience with the Pope offended her—she hated to have them say things that would make the Pope a figure of fun to Jo. She herself admires him and thinks he is doing the best he can. 'What else can a poor Pope do?'

But Katharine adores Helen and Polly and is sensitive enough to realize that Polly needs building up—simply for the sake of her own ego and the job she is doing. The job is magnificent and Katharine thinks that in a way it is more remarkable than Teacher's, for Polly has none of the excitement and exhilaration of creating, hers is just the day in and day out work. Katharine thinks Teacher's about the greatest job that has been done—perfectly wonderful and unprece-dented—still hopes to act it some day. . . .

Helen poured out her discontent with politics in America in a letter to Eric Boulter. She had become deeply attached to him in Athens and already had urged Bob Irwin to employ him for the American Foundation for the Overseas Blind. She wrote him:

Here in America we are living through a bitter period of retrograde. Since F.D.R.'s death an uninspired, inefficient administration has made havoc of the far-seeing, beneficent policies for which he gave his life. Isolationism threatens to disrupt international friendship. Race discrimination is rampant. As in Greece every effort is put forth to stifle radicalism. Liberals are not allowed the use of any broadcast-ing stations. The manufacture of bombs continues, and it dismays me to see how little the people are doing individually to prevent atomic warfare. How it will all end it is impossible to predict. I only hope that the people may be aroused to a sense of their danger before it is too late to assert their human dignity and put into office men who grasp the supreme issue—'One world or none.'

Whether or not it was a result of Kit Cornell's admonition about Helen's "redness"—which Nella immediately would have conveyed to Helen, adding to it her own general view that she was a "trustee" of the blind, and now of the overseas blind as well, and must not allow anything to jeopardize her work for them—when Jo asked her to speak at the Madison Square Garden rally that was part of the Wallace buildup, she declined. She did so gracefully. Unable to join Davidson and his friends at his studio on his birthday, she sent him an affectionate message of congratulations "as an artist, a thinker and a lofty free spirit in one . . . one who unites in himself simple, childlike happinesses and the strong man's triumphs." But then she added:

> Now I find it harder than ever not to accept your invitation to say my word on the U.S. foreign policy at Madison Square Garden Monday night. I grieve to be absent at such a crucial moment in what has developed into a literally day-to-day struggle of humanity towards world civilization. But alas! My own tasks are multiplying and I must race to keep abreast with them if I am to fulfill an equally urgent trust in bringing prompt, effective aid to the economically beleaguered blind of Europe.

But the "tasks" did not keep her from attendance at the rally, to which she, Polly and Nella went squired by Ethel and Eddie Clark. They were part of the Westport colony; he had been on General Eisenhower's staff in Europe. "Harvard man, Social Register," wrote Nella, "and though in the beginning he came from Iowa . . . he can now order in French and command the waiters' respect when he asks for wine." The Garden was packed as they went in. Polly spotted the Russian consul in difficulties about admission. "But you must get in," Polly cried grandly. "Come with me." And Nella added that Polly also took it upon herself "to ask the Russian to stick by her and go afterwards to a party."

Davidson opened the meeting, then turned it over to Professor Harlow Shapley of Harvard. "The two main protests of the evening," reported Nella, "were against Truman's project for lending money to support the present regimes in Greece and Turkey, and the 'witch-hunt' for Communists in the Government Service, the latter so drastic a measure that some of the mildest people have been moved to speak against it, Mrs. Roosevelt for one." The main speaker was Wallace. "He stood in the center of the Garden, under the lights, waving his arms in the politicians' manner, a grey, middle-aged man without personal magnetism. He is no orator. His speech was not subversive, but it was not inspiring. . . . We were all ready for a great climax. It did not come. Wallace was adequate and that was all." But when he came off the platform, Helen rushed forward and threw her arms around him to the popping of the flashbulbs of the photographers.

Meanwhile, much planning and discussion had gone on at the Foundation about how to initiate the appeal for funds for the American Foundation for the Overseas Blind. Helen's first meeting was scheduled to take place in early April. "I am glad indeed that a tea to launch the campaign for the overseas blind is to take place April 17th at the Cosmopolitan Club," she wrote Uncle Gus. "I hope you and Mrs. P. can look in. I need all the courage I can muster to launch an enterprise competing with many other good causes that besiege those who are both able and willing to give." Myron Taylor, who had arranged their reluctant audience with the Pope, introduced her. It was a good beginning. Bob Irwin asked Eric Boulter to come over to the United States for an interview. But Migel, now in his eighties, still was the directing force in the Foundation. "When you joined the staff of either of the two Foundations," Boulter recalled, although William Ziegler, Jr., a shy and soft-spoken man was now president, "the key was the final interview with the Major." After he had satisfied Irwin, the latter told him, "Okay, now comes the cruncher. You have to go to see the Major. If he likes you I can confirm the appointment." Irwin bade him good luck. "You will know whether you're in or not. If you're in he'll offer you a glass of bourbon."

The interview took place. At its end Migel said, "It's nice to have met you. I'll be in touch with you." No bourbon. But as Boulter reached the door, Migel stopped him. "Before you go, why don't we have a glass of bourbon?" His control was almost absolute, and he rather enjoyed demonstrating it. Grateful as Helen was to Migel for all his help to her personally, she thought he wielded too much power—that he was, in effect, a one-man jury on what the Foundation should do. Or at least that was how some Foundation people interpreted her attitude. The same sources, who preferred not to be identified, also ascribed to Helen the belief that Migel followed his own set ideas on what needed to be done for the blind, rather than allowing the blind themselves to evolve a program on what was good for them.

No doubt there were such feelings among some of the blind. Whether their ascription to Helen is correct is less clear. Differences she indeed had with Migel, yet he always favored her personally and leaned over backward to accommodate her views. Bob Irwin, the blind director of the Foundation, fathered most of the ideas that were the stuff and substance of the Foundation's work. Some of his partisans criticized Migel for allowing Helen to overshadow Irwin's contribution to the Foundation and to the blind. In any case, in mid-1947 when the Australian Institution for the Blind invited Helen to tour that continent, it was to Migel that she went for advice and approval, both of which he gave, and for a leave of absence, which he said he would recommend to the trustees. And when a little later a letter arrived from Takeo Iwahashi, her prewar host in Japan, inviting her to make a return visit, she explored with a sympathetic Migel the possibilities of a round-the-world tour that would begin in the Pacific and Orient and end in the Near East.

At the end of May she and Polly vacated Harvard House and went to spend the summer with Clare Heineman, now widowed and living alone in her handsome mansion in Chicago. They ended their stay with Clare in August, she informed Migel, "and here we are in a small Pennsylvania mountain village waiting for word to move into Arcan Ridge 2nd." Ten months after the fatal fire, at the end of September, they moved into the new twelve-room house. It was almost a replica of the first, except that a sun porch with a special heat-collecting glass had been added off the dining room; its balcony was designed to give Helen a place to walk. The house was filled with books in Braille, including the Bible and a set of Shakespeare that had been sent her by the National Institute for the Blind in London. There was a Braille writer as well, and a piece of the Parthenon from Greece. To Kit Cornell Helen reported that "the Library of Congress is sending me 144 volumes and among them is "Antony and Cleopatra" [in which Miss Cornell was currently appearing], the first time it has been embossed for the blind in this country."

The house still was sparsely furnished, but by the end of November they gave their first party. Nella went up for it and was met at the station by the Eddie Clarks. "Jo and Florence had already arrived and both were on fire for they had just had lunch with Henry Wallace and Wallace had agreed quietly to run for the presidency, if asked, knowing that he would fail. Hannah Dorner and the Rosens had driven the Davidsons to the Wallaces and had dropped them off at Arcan Ridge on the way back to New York. The Davidsons believe that Wallace is Christlike and that he is ready to be crucified for the people." The only dissent at the party was sounded by Mrs. Van Wyck Brooks, a pretty, white-haired woman whom the writer had married after the death of the first Mrs. Brooks a year earlier. Before Davidson could finish his first sentence, Gladys Brooks, in her high-pitched voice, interrupted, "But, Jo, do you think it is practical?" Jo "hit the ceiling" at the interruption, Nella reported, but Van Wyck said, "Now Jo, this is not a public meeting, and there is no one here you have to convert." Davidson calmed down, but a few sentences further Gladys broke in again, "But with my feminine practicality. . . ."

"It was hard going," Nella went on, "but we did finally learn that two pieces of business had been discussed at Wallace's, first his candidacy on a third party, only that they will not (yet) call it that. They want it to be an upsurge of liberal-progressive thought and though they are all ready for failure, Jo says, 'And by God we may win.' . . . Jo says, and I felt it very acute of him, that Wallace is more like Wilson than any of our other great political figures. Helen says Wallace is her man." The other plan discussed with Wallace was to launch a protest against the Committee on Un-American Activities (the Dies Committee). "They want a thousand big names. . . ."

Helen's involvement with the Wallace movement under the auspices of the Independent Citizens' Committee of Arts, Sciences and Professions, her appearance under the latter's auspices at a rally in favor of civilian control of atomic energy, her sponsorship of the Committee of One Thousand's drive against the House Un-American Activities Committee, worried the Foundation. "Dear Helen," Irwin wrote her in November 1947, "Enclosed is a clipping from the *Daily Worker.* There is a rumor going about that Congressman Thomas is going to investigate the Foundation very soon." The clipping probably referred to greetings that Helen sent, in the company of many leading American Communists, to Mother Ella Reeve Bloor, eighty-seven years old and a legendary figure in the American labor movement, whom Helen had known in her Wrentham days. Representative J. Parnell Thomas, a Republican from New Jersey, was one of the most demagogic of the witch-hunting tribe until he was indicted and jailed for payroll padding.

Foundation fears of a witch-hunting smear were not eased when Westbrook Pegler began to attack Helen in his column. Pegler quoted Ed Sullivan, a rival columnist: "At the Larry Adler opening, at Cafe Society, famous Helen Keller was able to follow the harmonica rhythms this way: A friend finger-coded the tempo into the palm of Miss Keller's hand. Sitting at the same table, Jo Davidson alternately cried 'Bravo!' and caricatured Larry on a napkin." Pegler's chief target was Larry Adler, whom the witch hunters finally drove into exile in London. But the columnist also paid his respects to Helen: "She knowingly chose her political company a long time ago. No news here," and he added that she had been cited "eleven times down to 1943 by the Dies Committee on Un-American Activities."

His treatment of Helen was gentle for Pegler, but it was an added sign that Helen and her work for the blind might be engulfed in the rising anticommunist hysteria that was taking hold of the country and would come to a head a few years later in McCarthyism. The Pegler column was affecting contributions, Irwin wrote William Ziegler, the president of the Foundation. He submitted a letter to be sent to offended contributors. It stressed the patriotism of the men and women associated with the Foundation, including John Foster Dulles, explained Helen's lifelong attachment to ideas of "universal brotherhood," and said that "naturally some of the Socialistic and Communistic leaders have taken advantage of her interest in the humanitarian side of their professings." That was the formulation Irwin proposed to use in a form letter of reply, but his cover letter to Ziegler expressed his own views more bluntly: "Helen Keller's habit of playing around with Communists or near-Communists has long been a source of embarrassment to her conservative friends. Please advise me."

A tug of war ensued over Helen's politics, with the Foundation, Lenore Smith, Nella and Kit on one side, Jo Davidson and his friends on the other. Nella recorded the struggle:

> The pressure against Helen to take active part in the presidential selection in behalf of Wallace is tremendous. Harlow Shapley has written to say that in Chicago on January 16 she was elected honorary chairman of the Arts, Sciences and Professions Council of the Progressive Citizens of America. Einstein and Jo Davidson have also been invited to be honorary chairmen. Jo will of course accept (probably has already) and Einstein probably will. Jo spent nearly half an hour on the telephone yesterday (March 1) urging Helen to accept. He is very persuasive, very seductive, and left Polly feeling like a coward but still holding out. A telegram came from Dorothy Parker asking her, Helen, that is, to join the national sponsoring reception committee for the impending visit to this country of Mme. Joliot-Curie who is coming under the auspices of the joint Anti-Fascist Refugee Committee. Einstein and Shapley are among the members. It is hard for Helen to refuse such requests. Florence Davidson wants Helen to give her name to the Women for Wallace group and she

and Jo are both so insistent that I am afraid a chilliness is about to develop on their friendship which has meant so much on both sides. Jo accuses Polly of not presenting the situation to Helen fairly. Accuses Polly, of all people!

Neither pressure of friends nor personal fears for her reputation would have kept Helen from supporting the Wallace candidacy. But the memory of having been duped by the Communists in the Spanish refugee ship affair was ever-present. An even greater factor for caution was the need of official support for her impending round-the-world trip. General MacArthur had approved her visit to Japan. She hoped that President Truman would give her the same sort of letter that Roosevelt had given her on her first visit. This was her life's work. She did not wish to place it in jeopardy. Finally but unmistakably she said no to Davidson:

> Now I am starting on my long world tour, and before correspondence becomes almost an impossibility, I want to say some things to you, most affectionately but with a firm will and mind of my own.
>
> All my adult life I have held unswervingly to one principle, not excepting the blind or the deaf or any group--never give my name to a cause, be it ever so noble, unless I read and consider carefully the basic facts upon which it rests. A 'name' does not command my respect if it does not spring out of the integrity of one's purpose and thought. Often I have refused to assist movements for the handicapped when I was doubtful of their wisdom or beneficence. I still ache at the memory of disappointments I have brought upon good people who tried to overrule me. Every decisive act, I believe, must be clearly thought out as well as good-intentioned. Want of intelligent thinking is as harmful as lack of heart, and this brings me to the point of this letter. I cannot lend my name to the campaign for Henry Wallace.
>
> For a year, owing to the extremely pressing work for the blind of Europe, I have not been able to keep in touch connectedly with public questions, not even those which touch me most as a citizen, and now I have no time at all to read the ever-changing statements, editorials and comments upon Wallace. He has my warmest admiration and esteem, but that is emotional, wholly separate from opportunity to

reflect calmly on the right things to say of his statesmanship. Lovingly I envy you the gift of carrying on two or more diverse kinds of work at once. . . . With our arms around you in thought and a long goodbye, I am,

Devotedly your friend . . .

XXXIX

True and False Fears

"The fact is, I have fought for every increase in pay we have, and I am proud to earn a salary to which I am entitled."

Helen was almost sixty-eight when she and Polly departed for Australia and the Orient. "How do you approach old age?" a high school student inquired: "You are the first person who has asked me pointblank that question," Helen replied. "I cannot help smiling—I who have declared these many years that there is no age to the spirit. Age seems to me only another physical handicap, and it excites no dread in my mind— I who have lived so triumphantly with my limitations." Never count how many years you have, she went on, but how many interests:

> All my life I have tried to avoid ruts, such as doing things my ancestors did before me, or leaning on the crutches of other people's opinion, or losing my childhood sense of wonderment. I am glad to say I still have a vivid curiosity about the world I live in. . . . It is as natural for me to believe that the richest harvest of happiness comes with age as to believe that true sight and hearing are within, not without. . . .

But Helen's closest friends saw that age was taking its toll. "Polly realizes keenly as I do and have and as Ethel is beginning to," recorded Nella, "that Helen is slowing down. She is not nearly so quick on the uptake as she used to be and when one is spelling to her it is easy to see often that she is not getting it. The expression of a deaf person pretending to hear comes over her face. It is cleverly contrived and would fool any but the initiates. Polly and I both cover for her, but Ethel sees and the time is not far off when everyone will see." Polly explained to Nella that one of the reasons she kept the thermostat low at Arcan Ridge was Helen's tendency when it was warmer to doze off in the middle of work at her desk. "Herbert feels," Nella went on, "that this trip to Australia must be their last and I think they must begin slowly to retire from public view."

Evidently Helen's friends at the Foundation saw the same signs. Although they approved the trip to Australia, they had opposed Helen's determination to stretch it into a round-the-world journey. "Why don't you make her stay at home?" Harvey Gibson, head of the Manufacturer's Trust Company and one of Helen's personal trustees, asked Migel. "I've done all I can," Migel replied; and the Major seemed to think, commented Nella, that "the reason for their going was that Polly wanted to travel." But of course Helen was the insatiable one.

People at the Foundation always blamed Polly, as in the past Migel had blamed Teacher, when Helen did something they did not like. "That woman!" was the way the senior Pfeiffers often referred to her. When a friend who had had Thanksgiving dinner with them reported to William Ziegler, the president of the Foundation and also a personal trustee of Helen's, that Polly had complained that they were starving, the trustees were outraged, and Migel bluntly told Polly so when they visited the Foundation offices. Polly later reported his words to Helen:

> As soon as we got a moment's quiet on the train, Polly told me how shockingly she had been accused of giving the impression that we were starving. Think how we felt—it seemed a violation of our gratitude, a blow in our faces. We reviewed the past year so full of the heart-warm, painstaking thoughtfulness with which you had undertaken to rebuild our house, and indeed all the years during which your uniform kindness had upheld us, and we were bewildered at the falseness and crudeness of the allegation. What hurt Polly so deeply was your thinking her capable of such a slander.

Perhaps Polly had not meant to convey a sense of physical privation, certainly not of hunger; but Helen's letter went on to say that "surprise has repeatedly been expressed by people who entered our house that there were no servants to run so large an establishment." And in fact the

Foundation's trustees recognized that the two women were running into financial difficulties, because at the same session at which Migel rebuked Polly he had handed Helen a check for $10,000 for household furnishings, also informing her that her salary was to be increased.

While the Foundation worried over whether Helen was equal to the exigencies of a Pacific tour and even enlisted her brother Phillips's help, their most intimate friends worried about Polly—the shock to her self-esteem from the Migel accusation and the possible effects of a strenuous world tour on her blood pressure. The "girls," as Nella called them, went to Washington for appearances in the public schools, arranged by Lenore, where Helen appealed for funds to supply Braille slates to overseas blind children. The Smiths sensed that Migel's charge had shaken Polly and that she needed building up. They knew her health was more fragile than Helen's. After their visit Philip Smith wrote Polly: "Perhaps you are too close . . . to evaluate correctly the enormous part you personally have had in making those dreams [of Helen's] realities. . . . Both you and Teacher stand on your separate pedestals. . . . You have especially heavy responsibilities because you must act almost entirely on your own judgment and intuition. It therefore behooves you to take especially good care not to be swamped and broken down by the load."

"All I ask," Nella wrote Polly, "is that you don't kill yourselves, either one of you. Polly, it took more than anyone else in the world had to go on with Helen when the sails were set and the winds were fair. Now with storms ahead you are asked to rise to the heights that Teacher scaled. This is not fair, but I know you will do it. She gave us a measure by which to judge women. . . . Helen is one of our saints. It hurts to be a saint. Just now it hurts more than ever and what hurts us who are on the sidelines is that there is nothing we can do. All we can say is that we are with you and God help you!" Helen gave Nella power of attorney and Polly gave her the combination of the house safe.

The first leg of their journey, to Australia and New Zealand, went without a hitch. From the moment that Helen walked down the ramp alone, as Polly always had her do once her hand was set firmly on the rail, moving freely and lightly, smiling radiantly, she seemed a veritable goddess to the Australian notables on hand to greet her. From Sydney to Perth she toured installations for the blind, made notes on their needs, and at the end, at their request, sent in a list of suggestions to Prime Minister J.B. Chifley, whom she had met in Canberra. She dwelt on the need for a greater effort to prevent blindness and deafness. She had worried lest the prime minister consider her an interfering Yank, but he received the recommendations cordially and promised to discuss them with the minister of health and social services.

From Australia they went to New Zealand, then back to Australia; and all in all, when they set out by plane for Japan in August, they had put in five months of constant lecturing. They were flown from Sydney to Japan by the Australian Royal Air Force in a converted bomber and landed at Iwakuni Airport in southern Honshu, which was in the British zone of occupation. They were met by various military dignitaries of SCAP (Supreme Commander for the Allied Powers), for it was at General MacArthur's invitation that she had come. MacArthur's domination of the islands was so absolute that President Truman had declined to give Helen a message for the Japanese people, as Roosevelt had done, saying that he made it a rule to do so only through official diplomatic and military channels.

Nelson Neff of MacArthur's health and welfare section had been placed in charge of the Helen Keller visit and traveled with her and Polly, as did WAC Captain Lane Carlson. As the bomber taxied down the runway and the ramp was being wheeled out, those two asked themselves, What are we to expect? Of one thing they were certain—the travelers would be exhausted from the long trip. Captain Carlson had even prepared an ambulance. But instead the women appeared "fresh as two daisies, impeccably dressed and cheerful," and greeted with large smiles the British colonel who sprinted up the ramp to escort them down. After introductions he took everyone to his residence for a "high" tea that included sandwiches and cakes. The formalities over, the colonel turned to Helen and Polly—someone had briefed him well—and said, "Girls, I think it is time for a more proper libation." He motioned to his aide. "John, bring out the Scotch and ice." That was Neff's and Carlson's recollection of the arrival. Helen's account emphasized the friendliness of the Japanese people, the schoolchildren who crowded the railroad station at Iwakuni and would not let her hands go as they boarded the *Palestine,* a veteran Pullman car that had been refurbished by SCAP for Helen's six-week tour. The journey to Tokyo was long, with rain showers on the way, and Neff feared that the famous view of Mount Fuji would be obscured, but suddenly the clouds parted, "and behold, we had a most fantastic view of Fuji in all its glory." That called for a celebration, Neff declared, and a bottle of chilled champagne was broken out. Neff, a sensitive man, raised a toast to Teacher's memory.

The size of the turnout in Tokyo eclipsed her first visit. SCAP officials, led by General Crawford Sams, chief of SCAP's health and welfare section, representatives of the government and of the metropolis, editors of the "Mainichi" newspapers, pressed flowers into their hands and overwhelmed them with their warmth. "Finally Polly and I managed to reach our beloved friends Takeo and Kyo Iwahashi who were waiting for us. After we had embraced each other, we walked together in the blaze of Klieg lights along a scarlet carpet which had formerly been kept exclusively for the Emperor." The crowd, Neff thought, might have gotten out of hand but for a large force of MPs. They were quartered at the old Imperial Hotel. The next day they paid an official call on General Sams, then visited the Supreme Commander, who tendered a lunch for them in his residence. General MacArthur did all the talking—about himself and what he was doing in Japan. Helen and Polly found it difficult to get in as much as a question. Afterward Helen addressed an open meeting in the vast courtyard outside the walls of the Imperial Palace. Neff estimated the crowd at three hundred thousand. Others placed the figure at fifty thousand. They called on "their Majesties" in a visit that was kept "as simple as Japanese etiquette would permit." Between the imperial household's attention to detail in connection with such a visit, and SCAP's, nothing was overlooked. A nobleman of the household had called Neff and over a cup of tea had delicately indicated that one item the ladies might require still was unobtainable even by the court—toilet tissue. "We were able to supply the Marquis's requirements," wrote Neff later.

From Tokyo they set off in the *Palestine* for a tour of Japanese cities, speaking everywhere, to government officials concerned with the blind, to U.S. Army agencies, to private groups, to the press and at public meetings. But then they encountered a scene of sheer horror. They arrived for their usual appeal meeting at Hiroshima, "but no sooner had we arrived there than the bitter irony of it all gripped us overwhelmingly, and it cost me a supreme effort to speak." How did one solicit funds from people who carried the stigmata of "desolation, irreplaceable loss and mourning?" The face of a welfare officer who became part of their group was seared by atomic burns—"a shocking sight. He let me touch his face, and the rest is silence—the people struggle on and say nothing about their lifelong hurts. . . . And it was to these people that I made the appeal!" she exclaimed in her letter to Nella. They went on to Nagasaki, "and it too has scorched a deep scar in my soul. . . . Polly says there never has been such revolt in her soul before, and life will not be the same to her after

Hiroshima and Nagasaki." Helen sternly renewed her resolve "to do what lies in my power to fight against the demons of atomic warfare and for the constructive uses of atomic energy."

The constant travel, the speeches, the appeals, were to culminate in a nationwide Bluebird Day in Helen's honor when funds were to be raised for the Japanese blind. Helen took the unrelenting pressures of the tour in her stride, but Polly began to wilt. In Osaka she looked so bad that Neff cancelled a tea prepared by the local U.S. commander. The latter was angered, but at Neff's request had Polly examined by his doctor. Her blood pressure had shot up alarmingly. Neff called General Sams and had the physician discuss the findings with him. "Cancel the rest of the trip," the general ordered. "Polly is in no condition to carry on; bring both of the ladies back to Tokyo immediately." At headquarters Polly was given a thorough checkup, and General Sams informed Helen and Polly that he was calling a halt to the rest of the trip. That also ended their plans to go on to Korea, China and India.

The tour of Japan, although stopped in mid-career, was a success. The Bluebird Day drive, backed as it was by the "Mainichi" papers and the occupation forces as well as by Japanese officialdom, produced over one hundred million yen for the blind of Japan. Accustomed though Helen was to adulation, the "aura of homage, adoring and enthusiastic," that surrounded her everywhere was "embarrassing as well as exciting." At the end of October, after a sixty-one-day stay, they boarded the Army transport *Shanks* at Yokohama. She left, said Helen in a message to the Japanese people, "with a sweet sadness in my heart." She thanked the people for their affectionate reception and the gifts that had poured in upon them, but she could not forget Hiroshima and Nagasaki, "so frightfully shattered" yet still having the will to give. "What can I say to such invincible spirit of generosity?"

The army met them at Seattle with a car and a doctor, saw them settled in a hotel and drove them to the night train to Minneapolis, where they went to the Mayo Clinic. "We were both checked over," Polly reported to Takeo, "and the reports were, Helen very well. I would require to give up the old hectic life, live quietly and normally which means no more lecture tours." Herbert drove out to the Mayo Clinic. He knew the true situation. So did Nella, but the Foundation, including Migel, had been kept in ignorance. In desperation Migel's alter ego, Amelia, called Nella to ask what the latter had heard from Rochester (where the Mayo Clinic was located). Nothing as yet, Nella replied, and went on with a report to Herbert on her conversation:

> Then she asked why the girls were coming home. I said it was because Polly was tired, worn out. Polly, she said, would never come home for that reason and Mr. Migel had decided (which means of course that Amelia had also decided) that Helen, not Polly, was sick and Polly was covering for her by giving out that she was tired. Amelia, I said, Polly is exhausted, she is at the breaking point, the danger point, her public life is over, she has to live quietly or she won't live at all, at any minute now she is apt to pop off with a heart attack or a cerebral hemorrhage, that is, *if she does not live quietly.* If she does live quietly, the chances are that she will stay alive for many years.

Amelia wanted to know Nella's authority for her statement. She had been informed, she said, by General Eddie Clark, Helen's Westport neighbor, who had received messages from his close friend General Sams, chief medical officer of the U.S. armed forces in Japan. Nella also talked about money with Amelia, who protested that Nella did not quite understand the situation, "that Helen had always been able to get whatever she needed for any purpose." That remark betrayed "twinges of conscience" at the Foundation, Nella thought. But Amelia was really their friend, Nella's letter to Herbert went on. She had immediately talked with Migel, and they had concluded that "something really has to be done to ease Polly's burden." Their first thought was that Nella and Keith should give up their house in Garden City "and share the house in Westport." Nella quickly put a stop to that line of reasoning, telling Amelia that "there were a thousand reasons in the way," but the important point, she went on in her letter to Herbert, was that "Mr. Migel is ready to do something. Let's see what. The fundamental thing is that when a person is given a rich man's house she should be given a rich man's income to go with it. Let's see if this ever occurs to him. Let's see in short, what occurs to him and Amelia without any help from us."

But that, Nella realized, would get them nowhere, and after Helen and Polly returned to Arcan Ridge, she spent a week there surveying their needs and drafting a memorandum addressed to Helen's trustees. "Because I am closer to Miss Keller and Miss Thomson than anyone else and because I am able to use the techniques required to be of service to Miss Keller, I am the only visitor now allowed," the memorandum to Helen's trustees began. "I do not count as a visitor," she added in an effort to assuage injured feelings at the Foundation, but Migel and Amelia might well have felt that they, too, deserved to come under that exception. They had been unable to reach Arcan Ridge. Forbidden to visit, they were unable even to phone, for the telephone had been disconnected, ostensibly to protect Polly, but also because Polly was in a state of jitters, fearful that she might not be able to serve Helen any longer and in a panic over how little money she had on which to fall back in her old age.

"Stop worrying! . . . Don't bother your head with finances," Lenore, who knew the situation at Arcan Ridge, admonished her. "Keep in your mind the fact that you have been taken care of so far, and it is going to be a continuing privilege for the 'powers that be' [meaning the Foundation] to take care of you." She and Phil stood ready to help, but did not want to appear to the "powers that be" to be "butting in":

> I don't know how much you have kept in touch with Amelia and Mr. Migel while you have been on the trip, or how much you have told them about your reason for returning and your present condition. If they have not heard details from you personally, they may be upset and possibly annoyed, for after all, they have stood back of you for a good many years. They may not understand the situation and may resent the fact that they cannot see you, not realizing how bad conversation or excitement may be for you. I suppose at the present time anything you do may react unfavorably on you, but it might not be any harder for you to have a talk with Amelia than for you to lie abed and think! . . . You are lucky to have Nella so capable and devoted. . . .
>
> > Don't be discouraged!
> > Put up a good Scotch fight!
> > No one will ever let you down!

The two women still had a useful career ahead of them, Nella's memorandum had continued, but "the old barnstorming days are over." From what she had observed at Arcan Ridge, Helen needed an annual income of $20,000 to keep her house and office going. That would enable her to employ a maid-cook-housekeeper who was urgently needed as such and, equally imperative, as an understudy for Polly.

This last was much on Nella's mind, and on Lenore's, with whom Nella was in touch. Herbert had said something of which she and Lenore were keenly mindful: "When Teacher went Helen knew that she still had Polly. If Polly were to go she would have nothing." In Japan, Nella heard to her horror, when Helen saw Polly failing, "she asked Polly, if the time came when she saw that she was going, that she, Polly, would give her, Helen, certain tablets that would make it possible for her to follow." During a stopover in Manila in June, Polly had informed Lenore that she had written her niece Miss Effie Thomson in Glasgow to come over to be trained to take her place. Lenore immediately talked with the State Department's Mrs. Ruth Shipley, who said that there would be no problem of an immigration visa. Effie had begun to learn the manual language and should arrive soon, Nella wrote; she should be given a secretarial course and be made a part of the household at $2,000 a year. She also recommended that Herbert's salary be raised to $3,500 and Polly's to $5,000. All these salaries would be paid out of Helen's $20,000, as would $5,000 to cover household expenses, and $1,000 for copying into Braille material that Helen required.

Migel's reaction to Nella's memorandum began with an "I told you so." Harvey Gibson was abroad, but to William Ziegler, Helen's third trustee, Migel recalled that he had tried to dissuade Helen from going to the Orient. "But after having agreed to abandon the greater part of the undertaking, Helen visited me again and informed me that she had a 'call' and that she was unable to sleep at night because of abandoning this so-called 'crusade,' and naturally, there was nothing to be done and a leave of absence was finally arranged for by the Foundation upon Helen's urgent request. The unfortunate results now present a serious situation."

They should meet and discuss Mrs. Henney's memorandum. He himself was motoring up to Westport to talk with Helen and hoped to arrive "at some understanding as to their actual needs, etc." He did not like Nella's reference to Arcan Ridge as a "rich man's home." Helen's committee had favored a smaller house, he recalled. It was Helen and Polly who had insisted on a replica of the one that had burnt down.

After his visit Migel reported to Ziegler again. He had found the condition there "rather lamentable," largely because there was no substitute for Polly, and the latter was under strict orders to remain quiet. "We have frequently stressed the thought that there should be an understudy for Polly, but this suggestion for some reason or other has never met with favor either by Helen or Polly." As a stopgap measure he proposed an immediate grant of $5,000 to Helen. When Gibson returned, the trustees took up the matter and voted to increase the gift to Helen to $6,000 and to increase her permanent salary commensurately, so that she would be assured of the annual income of $20,000 that Nella had recommended. This of course included the Carnegie pension and other trusts. Helen thanked Migel. He had come to Westport to tell her the news and to bring some Christmas gifts. "I realize how it fatigues you to drive such long distances." But her letter to her brother Phillips, who tended to see the Foundation's point of view, showed that she felt little gratitude.

> I finally secured sixty-three hundred dollars a year and an allowance of twelve hundred for clerical assistance. . . . Last February a friend who saw into our situation went to see one of my trustees, Mr. Ziegler, and told him how difficultly we were living. (We did not discover until long afterwards who that friend was.) Mr. Migel was very angry when he heard of this, and accused Polly and me of circulating the tale that we were starving. We had nothing whatever to do with our friend's calling on Mr. Ziegler, as we never talked about our finances with any one.

> When we returned from Japan, Polly had broken down, and the outlook was discouraging. We had tried to save something for our old age, for illness, doctors' bills and hospitals if necessary, but the margin was a narrow one. It was then that Nella and her husband Keith, Lenore and Phil Smith got together to see what could be done because they realized that our finances should be more adequate. After much careful consultation, Nella submitted a letter she had written to my trustees and telling them of our needs and the upkeep which a house like ours requires. As a result, we are to receive about twelve thousand dollars from the Foundation for one year. And remember, Phillips, how our taxes are rising higher and higher.

> All along the way I have suffered exasperation, pettiness and humiliating implications and what I want to impress upon you is, Mr. Migel and Mrs. Bond are evidently desirous to spread the idea of how 'generous' and 'wonderful' they and the Foundation are to us. The fact is, I have fought for every increase in pay we have, and I am proud to earn a salary to which I am entitled. Polly has worked until she is no longer able to bear the tumult of public life and I resent any one's implying that the salary is a bounty conferred upon us both. It

is Nella Henney, who, by writing to my trustees, has brought them to a consciousness of our true situation and secured justice for us both.

Her letter ended with the news that Effie had arrived. "What a blessing it is to have her bright, young presence in our home! She is intelligent and not aggressive. She can spell, and she reads letters to me, she types, she drives the car, and is a real help to Herbert."

Herbert had become indispensable to Helen and Polly, and they had made him a part of the household. Polly even sought to teach him some of the finer points of social etiquette; he sat at the dinner table in a dinner jacket. Herbert bothered the Pfeiffers, especially Mrs. Pfeiffer—"a servant treated like a member of the family—and she blamed Polly," recorded Nella. Herbert was one of the reasons why the Pfeiffers had cooled toward Helen and done so little toward the rebuilding of the house. Helen had discovered that there was a price attached to their goodwill. As Nella wrote, "A certain stated night, at least once a month, was called Colony night and everybody got together. Helen and Polly could not join in this and they soon made it clear that they were not, socially speaking, at the Pfeiffer's beck and call to be shown off." And even more important, there was irritation in Helen's support of Wallace, which angered Mrs. Pfeiffer in particular.

Herbert made others besides the Pfeiffers uneasy. Migel and Amelia disliked him—partly, thought Nella, because he is "much closer to the girls than they are, much deeper into the secrets of their lives." The Clarks declined to invite him to dinner, Kit Cornell did not include him in her invitations, even the Phil Smiths balked, and Nella reported that her own children resented his calling them as well as Nella by their first names. "The measure of the ridiculousness of this entire situation is the difficulty that any one of us would have in explaining it to Helen. These small social distinctions have no meaning for her. She loves Herbert, loves him specifically and not merely as she loves all mankind. She does love all mankind, which makes it hard for her to love individuals."

Herbert was very closemouthed about himself and his past, and Nella advised Polly that she ought to try to find out more than she had been told. They learned that he had spent his youth in an orphan asylum, had been married and had a daughter, but that his wife had divorced him to marry his brother. The daughter was grown up; but, wrote Nella, Polly "has not received her; wonders what to do."

Their feeling for Herbert was quite understandable. There were few people who were ready to give up their personal lives in order to serve Helen. Even Nella, loyal and devoted as she was, drew a line; for Polly, picking up on the thought that had occurred to Migel and Amelia, had suggested to Nella that she and Keith move to Arcan Ridge:

> Polly, it would never be possible for Keith and me to share a house with Helen. Never. Keith is much too frail—no one but me knows how frail and I probably don't know the half of it. The summers in New Hampshire keep him alive. We could not give them up and we could not take Helen with us. The house in Westport is much too far away from New York and is much too small to accommodate us. We are so terribly cramped for space in the seven rooms we have here that we are adding a workroom as soon as building conditions permit. And even with outside help I am not strong enough to look after Helen, even if I were capable of doing it, which I am not. Don't think that I have not given a great deal of thought to this—I had already before you spoke of it the other day. I know that it is out of the question. Absolutely. We can only pray that Helen will go first and in the meantime rack our brains for someone to come in and begin to help you—a sort of lady's maid who could be chauffeur would be good if we could find such a person. And in the meantime, of course, your biggest job is to take care of yourself.

In June 1948 Bob Irwin reached sixty-five, which under rules that he himself had established meant mandatory retirement. The trustees began the search for a successor. How much Helen was consulted is unclear. "The Foundation," wrote Frances A. Koestler, was "now a complex enterprise with assets in cash, securities, and real estate in excess of two million dollars, a staff of over a hundred to be directed, a budget close to $350,000, and a far-flung program that stood on the threshold of sizeable expansion." The trustees felt that they needed a young man, one accustomed to handling large sums of money, able to cope with the network of state and federal laws that had come to govern services for the blind, with professional prestige among workers for the blind. Would a blind man be able to handle the job? some of the trustees asked. Had not the time come "to seek a sighted executive from the wider world of commerce"?

As word of this filtered down to the professional staff, the senior members addressed a joint letter to the Foundation's president, urging the selection of a blind man, asserting that blindness was "an indispensable link" between the Foundation executive and those whom he would serve. The American Association of Workers for the Blind was also alerted and began to mobilize on behalf of a blind successor to Bob Irwin. Their alarm was unnecessary, according to Jansen Noyes, Jr., a member of the search committee and later the Foundation's president. The committee never seriously considered the selection of a sighted person. The staff protest was nevertheless a significant development, an advance tremor heralding the earthquake that shook the nation two decades later of insistence by minorities, including the handicapped, upon their rights as human beings.

Helen took little part in the selection of a successor to Irwin, but her lifelong themes as a deaf-blind person—self-reliance; work, not charity; respect for individual rights, not pity—certainly played their part in this revolution.

The Foundation chose M. Robert Barnett, thirty-two years old and head of the Florida State Council for the Blind, as its new director. He was personable and handsome, with wavy dark hair, and wrote and spoke well. "He combined the pleasant manners and social ease of a Southerner with a ready sense of humor and the confident air of a man who, mainly through his own efforts, had surmounted both a difficult boyhood and the trauma of sudden blindness," wrote Foundation historian Koestler.

Nella liked him from the moment she saw him and in this reflected the attitude of Helen and Polly. "He is blind, but does not look blind. Later in the afternoon when he stood at the fireplace [in Arcan Ridge] with his back to the flames he made a noble figure. He is a man you instinctively trust. . . . Mr. Barnett talked with Helen about the use of her name: he does not want to cheapen it; will not send out the dunning letters over her signature, will use it only in the first appeal letters and then only once a year probably." He asked Helen to write President Truman to urge that government work for the blind not be transferred to the Labor Department. Helen readily agreed. Barnett furnished her the necessary information, and Helen wrote the letter the next day.

"The whole talk with Mr. B.," Nella went on, "showed the difference between the relation of Helen Keller to the AFB under Irwin and under the new regime. Irwin was secretive and jealous; Barnett talked frankly about everything, including finances. . . . We all have perfect confidence in Barnett and we all like Whittington." C.H. "Dick" Whittington was close to Barnett, who had brought him north and appointed him an assistant director in charge of technical and production services.

Helen now had a pattern of life that she and Polly found agreeable. Speeches were limited; a good deal of time she spent writing—messages, articles for magazines. These as well as the speeches were submitted to Nella, who commented with her customary crispness. "I don't like these speeches you are making," she said on one occasion; on another she urged Helen to "try again." Nella and Keith were spending more and more of their time on Foss Mountain in Snowville, New Hampshire, but she was the soul of promptitude and conscientiousness. When Helen sent her the draft of an article for a house magazine published by Richard Hudnut, she immediately wrote back that Helen had three articles in the piece and should separate them—one on the sense of smell, the second a travelogue, the third about Jo Davidson. Helen pulled together the material about her sense of smell to the satisfaction of both Nella and the Richard Hudnut Company.

She and Polly saw a good deal of Katharine Cornell and Nancy Hamilton. Sponsored by Kit Cornell, she became a member of the Cosmopolitan Club. "Helen is now a member of the conservative or 'posh' Cosmopolitan Club," Polly wrote the Davidsons. "K. Cornell was the one who got her in. We'll want to show you off within those stuffy walls." Helen loved to take friends to the Club for lunch, although Nella remained ready to use her right to have them to lunch at the Ladies' Annex of the Harvard Club. When Helen proposed to have Takeo Iwahashi and his wife, who were touring blind installations in the United States under the auspices of Helen and General MacArthur, to dinner at the Cosmopolitan Club, that select establishment said that it accepted no party larger than eight even if the hostess was Helen Keller and her guests were to include Dr. Hideki Yukawa, Nobel Prize winner in 1949 for his discovery of the meson. "Sam at the Harvard Club seemed very happy to take care of us," wrote Nella. The latter was enchanted with Takeo:

> One might have thought that Helen or Yukawa would be the center of our group, but it was Takeo. Love flowed towards him from us all. I have never seen Keith so immediately taken with a man. Not that Takeo monopolized the talk; he talked because we wanted him to, because we kept begging him to. His gaiety and sense of humor coupled with his spiritual beauty made us realize that we were in the presence of a great man—a truly religious man, one of the saints of our time.

Nella, ordering the dinner in advance, had suggested broiled chicken. Polly vetoed it—"too difficult for the blind"—she said, so they had roast beef.

Takeo had established a "Helen Keller Foundation for the Blind" in Japan. That may have prompted the move, initiated by Barnett, to change the name of the AFB to the Helen Keller Foundation. To his surprise he ran into difficulties. "Mr. Migel said he would not object if the others wanted it, but that some of the other trustees are strong against it." Whittington thought that they were afraid of Pegler. Nella doubted that. Although Migel often had objected to Helen's association with liberals and radicals and had recently said to Barnett that he wished Helen would have nothing to do with Jo Davidson, Nella thought that Migel's vanity was involved: "So long as it is the AFB it is *his* Foundation." When Barnett saw that he was getting nowhere, he quietly desisted. There is no record that Helen opposed the move to rename the Foundation.

In the spring of 1950 she and Polly were back in Europe. Much of the time there they spent with the Davidsons. The sculptor had a comfortable apartment and studio in Paris and a large manor, named Bêcheron. They first went to Portofino in Italy to stay with Countess Margot Keller de Besozzi, whom Jo described as a "newly discovered" cousin. At the end of the visit there the Davidsons motored down to pick them up and drive them to Bêcheron, but first they visited Florence and that stalwart spirit Professor Salvemini, who was back in Italy.

He had arranged for Helen to visit the Bargello and Medici tombs. Davidson was eager to see these sculptures through Helen's fingers:

> A movable scaffold was set up so that Helen could pass her hand over the sculptures of Donatello and Michelangelo. I have seen these sculptures before but never so intimately as when I watched her hands wandering over the forms, peering into the slightest crevices, into the most subtle undulations. She exclaimed with delight as she divined the slightly opened mouth of the singing young 'St. John the Baptist.'

> We who were below were transfixed as Helen contemplated Michelangelo's 'Night' and 'Dawn.' And when she came upon the 'Madonna and Child' and discovered the 'Suckling Babe,' she threw her arms around the group and murmured: 'Innocent greed.'

"She felt form," he later told his friend Julian Huxley, and he had "learnt something new from the manner in which she caressed Michelangelo's great figures."

Dissatisfied with his first portrait bust of Helen, Davidson persuaded her to sit for another portrait, which he felt should bring out "her wonderful hands." At "Bêcheron," while he talked, she posed eating fruit from the great cherry tree that stood in his courtyard. He had been to Yugoslavia and had become a great admirer of Tito, whose bust he made, much to the distress of his Stalinist friends back in New York. He wanted Helen to go with him and Florence to Israel, and she was willing. They talked about the witch-hunt in the United States. It was the time of Senator Joseph McCarthy—this "dreadful McCarthy business," Nella wrote Polly. It kept Davidson from returning to the United States. Did Helen remember that two of the figures of her youth, the brave Dr. Samuel Gridley Howe and Dr. Frank B. Sanborn, to escape a Senate investigating committee controlled by Southerners, set up to discredit the Abolitionists because of their support of John Brown, had taken temporary refuge in Canada? "What a world we live in," Davidson wrote her after her return. "Everybody writes me to stay where I am."

Difficult as Helen found the witch-hunt atmosphere of 1950, everything else was overshadowed for her in September by the unexpected death of Herbert. Although their closest friends had balked at Helen's and Polly's insistence on treating Herbert as a member of the family, they all realized his importance to them:

> On Sept. 12, 1950 [recorded Nella] Polly telephoned me and without the usual preliminaries spoke three paralyzing words: 'Herbert is dead.' She had gone to his room to take him some shaving cream. There was no response to her knock and since it was mid-morning she concluded that he was in the workshop making shelves that Helen had asked for at breakfast. She went in. He lay on the floor. He had been dead for some little time—cerebral hemorrhage—but was not yet cold.

> The forlorn women were alone in the house when I reached Arcan Ridge the next afternoon, their grief shadowed over with special hurt because they had just learned that Herbert had been reconciled with his wife for two years and had not told them. His wife and daughter had come that morning. 'The trouble is, Miss Thomson,' his wife said,

'that Herbert loved all of us.' He had tried to reconcile his loyalties and had not reached a conclusion when he died.

We were trying to eat supper when we heard a knock at the door. Katharine Cornell had taken the first boat from Martha's Vineyard and had hitchhiked the rest of the way. 'Oh, I did hope it would be like this, just the four of us!' she cried. And when Polly protested at her tiresome journey she said 'What are friends for if not to be with you at a time like this!'

She gave comfort in many ways, first by simply being there, then by saying, 'It was a sparing thing, not a deceiving thing that he had not told Helen and Polly about his wife,' then by placing herself at their disposal to be useful in any way in the reorganization of the household.

After the funeral which was conducted under the auspices of the New Apostolic Church of which Herbert's twenty-three year old daughter was a devoted member, a small group of us gathered in 'Uncle Gus's Barn,' where General Eddie Clark and his wife were our hosts. Everyone present had loved Herbert—the Robert Pfeiffers, the Grummons, Helen, Polly, Katharine Cornell and I—and we spent a long evening recalling his manifold acts of kindness and love. It was characteristic that the top paper on his desk was a note from some neighbors who were off on vacation giving directions about feeding their cat, Herbert's friend, the Chief of Police, took over the commission. Katharine Cornell left for Martha's Vineyard the next morning without quite knowing how she would get there.

Herbert had died, and Polly's niece Effie had not worked out. When they had realized the latter, Nella wrote, "We'll have to start a new search." Their friends worried about the two women living alone. They worried, too, about Helen's temptation to say yes to an invitation from South Africa to tour that commonwealth as she had Australia and New Zealand. "I hope that when the UN speech is over," Nella wrote Helen at the end of 1950, "she [Polly] will be able to rest, rest, rest for a while. . . . Think long and hard before you make any decision about South Africa."

XL

Tempest in a Teapot

"Homvuselelo"—Zulu for "You have aroused the consciousness of many."

In mid-February 1951 Helen and Polly boarded ship for Cape Town in South Africa. Helen's chief concern had become the blind and deaf of the world; and when the Reverend Arthur Blaxall of the South African National Council for the Blind, whom she had met at the 1931 World Conference, bade her come to spur support for the blind and the deaf, she experienced the same "call" that had sent her to the Far East. And Bob Barnett, unlike his predecessor Bob Irwin, did everything in the AFB's power to expedite the arrangements.

Travel was strenuous, and for Polly it was dangerous, but it was an escape from the housekeeping at Arcan Ridge and from beginning again, as Nella urged her, her book about Teacher. On a foreign tour they lived like visiting royalty. Everything was done for them, and the benefits for the deaf and blind that flowed from the magic of Helen's presence were indisputable. The State Department, moreover, recognized that along with Eleanor Roosevelt she was among America's best ambassadors. The years of activity that remained to Helen would be essentially years of travel.

Hazards that worried her friends, she rather enjoyed. The Union of South Africa was moving towards apartheid. She read Alan Paton's *Cry, the Beloved Country* and Gandhi's *Autobiography* in preparation for her trip. She sent a copy of the speech she intended to make to Arthur Blaxall, whom she described as a champion of the human rights of all men, for which he later would be jailed by Dr. Vorster. She wanted Blaxall's reaction to what she intended to say. "One requires skill and tact as well as enthusiasm to obtain the right help for the colored blind," she explained, "who, owing to their handicap are more subject to the arbitrary will of white society than their seeing fellows."

He approved the line she proposed to take. An AFB staffer, a South African by birth, Alfred Allen, accompanied them. In London enroute she met with John Wilson, secretary of the newly created Empire Society for the Blind, himself without sight. Most Africans were illiterate, he advised her. "Nearly all the village crafts of Africa are suitable to the blind— weaving, basketry, leatherwork, mat-making, pottery—and the obvious thing is to train in those occupations, even if that means not teaching Braille. The need is for craft teachers, not for literary school-teachers." She incorporated the thought in her speeches.

From the moment she and Polly were ushered into the Jan Christiaan Smuts suite at the Mount Nelson Hotel in Cape Town, there was the usual frenzy—reception committees, welcoming crowds, press interviews, visits to the institutions of the deaf and blind. As she wrote Barnett: "I had to remonstrate strongly with Mr. Blaxall before we could obtain a minimum of rest. We have eliminated a few luncheons and other minor social affairs, but the pace at which we are going is very tiring. We still have two meetings a day except Sundays and sometimes three, besides press interviews and visits to schools and colleges for the blind and the deaf."

Her itinerary included twenty-eight schools and institutions; she addressed forty-eight meetings and receptions; she visited every important urban center in the Union and ended her visit with an excursion to the Kruger National Park and a five-day visit to Victoria Falls and to Salisbury in Southern Rhodesia. Segregation was enforced everywhere, with the notable exception of the University of Witwatersrand, which awarded her an honorary degree. She accepted gladly because of the university's independence and liberalism—though these, too, were later brought into line.

She rebelled against the color line but conformed to it in the interests of those whom she was trying to help. "Again and again I have witnessed the failure of society to redeem the blind and the deaf simply because of racial prejudice—an offense against humanitarianism which life never forgives," she wrote in her account of the visit that was published in Cape Town. One valiant schoolteacher wrote her that he would have attended her special meetings for school children, "but he changed his mind when he found out that they had been arranged for the whites first and the non-whites second. He believed that this had been done without consulting me. . . . I wrote how all my sentiments cried out against discrimination and how fervently I prayed for the time when the various races of Africa would take an equal share in promoting the welfare and happiness of their handicapped." Segregation was a fact of life in Helen's native South, and institutions for the deaf and blind conformed there with the law and custom. The racial revolution was only beginning in the United States, and Helen, while protesting the fact of segregation in South Africa, complied in order to improve the treatment of the Africans. The blacks recognized her contribution. The Zulus gave her the name *Homvuselelo,* meaning "You have aroused the consciences of many."

They returned to Arcan Ridge and a flood of minor irritations connected mainly with their inability to find and hold on to domestic help. They had tried a woman whom Kit and Nancy had recommended. "No initiative," Nella wrote of her attitude. "Not clear what she thought her position was beyond sitting like a lady to telephone someone in case disaster overtook Polly and Helen." Before leaving for South Africa Polly had sent her away. "So ends an unfortunate chapter," commented Nella, "the worst part of which is that after this and Effie, Polly is determined not to try again for that kind of help."

The problem no longer stemmed from lack of money. Clare Heineman had died and left each of them $25,000. Helen had received $10,000 and Polly $5,000 in Nelson Cromwell's will. Part of the difficulty was Polly's attitude. She gave herself airs, liked to hobnob with the famous, but was curt with those she considered her inferiors. She infuriated workers at the Foundation, walking around its corridors and offices—the "lady bountiful," Barnett described her—bestowing her approvals like some princess royal. She mistreated domestic help, was haughty and overbearing toward servants; and they put up with it, when they did, said Barnett, "only because they loved Helen."

One of Helen's trustees, Harvey Gibson, had died, and Migel wrote James S. Adams, a general partner in Lazard Frères, generous supporter of medical research into cancer as well as blindness and a longtime benefactor of Helen, asking him to take Gibson's place. Migel's letter angered Helen and Polly:

They drew from the letter that Mr. M. was thinking of Helen as a ward, I think [recorded Nella] not altogether with justification, for it was of finances only that he wrote and H&P no more than Teacher have any judgment about finances. I pointed out that Mr. M. pays part of H's salary *out of his own pocket* and that he and Amelia had been admirable custodians of their property since even during the depression they had not lost a penny. Helen wanted to write Mr. M. a rather nasty letter, but I persuaded her out of it, at least for the moment. . . . One difficulty is that the girls for four months have been treated like royalty and they are having to come down to earth. . . .

Migel was eighty-five. He had served Helen and the blind faithfully and well. Helen's annoyance with him reflected her need for a sense of independence; it also bordered on ingratitude. But she welcomed James Adams to her group of trustees: "Indeed I am proud that a man with so many far-reaching interests and responsibilities should think it worth while to watch over my small affairs. Knowing you as I do personally, I shall feel an endearing human touch in our new relations. It will be a precious comfort to me that I can always turn to you for understanding and wise counsel. Polly too is happy in the thought of you as a counsellor." Her relationship with Adams and his wife Marvelle and son Peter would be a happy one.

They made a rare trip to Montgomery. Again we must rely on Nella for the realities: "The visit to Mildred was not happy. Mildred and her family are rock-bound, old-fashioned Southerners, not interested in the things Helen cares for, not interested in trying to catch a glimpse of the horizons that Helen has seen. Their comment on the *Ladies' Home Journal* was that Helen looked so old in the pictures and they had not thought enough of the article even to keep it." Later she wrote Polly, "It saddens me to think of Helen and her family and absolutely terrifies me when I reflect upon the possibility that she may have to spend her last years with them."

Their friends fretted over the unprotected life Helen and Polly led at Arcan Ridge. In the back of their minds was the ever-present fear that Polly might be felled by a stroke and there Helen would be, almost helpless. With Barnett's encouragement they experimented with having Dick Whittington make his home with them and commute to New York. But Lenore took a dislike to him when on a trip to Washington she heard him regale a friend with reports on the Arcan Ridge household. Polly turned on him, and that was the end of that approach. Their friends rarely met without the talk sooner or later getting around to what needed to be done at Arcan Ridge: "Ethel [Clark] and Katharine both felt," recorded Nella, "that Polly ought to leave Helen at home and have more of a life of her own, but this Polly would never do. What happens is that at parties in Fairfield, as the evening wears on and Helen grows tired Polly seems to neglect her. The hosts feel guilty (for Helen's sake). . . ."

Household help did not last long—primarily because of Polly. She was a "perfectionist" about the house, and their friends agreed that anyone but a dedicated soul like Polly "would find it hard to work for them." Barnett began to look more critically at the expense chits Polly sent in. Every trip seemed to involve a jaunt to Bendel's and other expensive shops. "Bob Barnett," she said to him once, "I am sick and tired of *Helen* being driven around in that old Buick. She's got to have a Cadillac." Barnett added, "I honestly think Helen didn't give a damn."

Polly was lonely at Arcan Ridge, but Helen had learned to cope with loneliness. Nella, who always hoped to write a book about Helen—the years with Polly—described a typical scene at Arcan Ridge: "She [Helen] sits on the floor a great deal, by Polly's side if Polly is at the desk. One day when I took Ethel Clark in to see her we found her sitting on the floor in the corner with her back to the room, a Braille book on her lap. She had on a blue sweater and her head was bent over the book. She looked like a little girl who had been sent to the corner for punishment and was not minding it very much." Helen and Polly took Nancy Hamilton to Gloucester House, famous for its fish dishes:

> Polly in a quite emotional way began talking about her and Helen's friends—said they could count them on their fingers. I came first and Lenore was mentioned, probably second. She included Amelia, of whom Nancy had never heard, an interesting point to me, for it shows that deep down Polly does recognize that Amelia is a friend. Helen gave very grudging assent. What surprised Nancy was to find herself included—saddened her a bit, too, for it brought poignant realization of how very lonely the girls are. It was right that Nancy should be on the list, along with Kit, for they are among the very few that have never asked anything of Helen and Polly, but on the contrary have extended themselves to think of ways to enrich their lives.

Jo Davidson had died a few months earlier, in December 1951; otherwise the list would surely have included him. He and Florence had hoped to take them around Israel. "Polly and I still dream of visiting that country," Helen had written him earlier in 1951. "My travels through the world would indeed be incomplete unless I breathed the air of that land tiny in bulk but spiritually mighty." The trip to Israel made Nella uneasy: "Helen has always been much interested in the Zionists and has never seen that there is an Arab side to the question. Jo and Florence are now in Israel and, as before, ecstatic about all they see." "Dear Helen and Polly," Florence wrote, "you will love it here and they will love you."

Jo helped them get the trip funded. He talked to the Israelis about picking up the bill for their expenses in Israel. "Be sure to cable me when Helen Keller is in Paris," the prime minister, David Ben-Gurion, had said to him, "and I myself will invite them." And Davidson also put them in touch with Bartley Crum, who arranged with Hadassah for a contribution to their travel expenses. Baruch sent a check for $1,000. Eric Boulter and Dr. Stauffer, formerly of the John Milton Society for the Blind, went to Washington to discuss the trip with the State Department, which suggested that it be broadened to include Egypt, Lebanon, Syria and Jordan. "Helen wrote Mr. Dean Acheson about the tour," Polly informed Florence, "and he wrote her a beautiful letter in reply saying the State Department would do everything possible to make the tour a success."

They left in April. "Both girls were *very* tired when they left," Nella wrote Lenore, "partly because of too much high-voltage social life on the eve of departure. . . . Polly was beset with apprehension—kept speaking of the strange feeling she had about this trip in contrast with the others they have made. I think it is because deep in her heart she knows how dangerous a chance she is taking in going so far alone with Helen."

Their stay in Egypt was a success, as indeed the whole trip turned out to be. Karl Meyer, head of the Swiss School for the Blind in Beirut, accompanied them on the Arab leg of the trip. They arrived in Cairo after midnight and went to the Semiramis Hotel along deserted streets, for the city was under martial law. The next day the press interviewed her on a balcony that overlooked the Nile. "The blind and the deaf," she said, "have minds that can be developed, hands that can be trained, and ambition which it is right for them to realize, and the public must aid them generously if they are to make the best of themselves and earn a living."

She visited institutions of the blind and the deaf. "From now henceforth," said the blind head of the Noor Society (Light for the Blind), Sheikh Sawy Shaalem, "the blind do not need to grieve; for our merciful God gave us Louis Braille for one eye, and Helen Keller for the other." She had tea at the Feminist Union, visited the pyramid of Cheops and spent a night in a friend's house, where she "felt the silence of the desert." An unfriendly *kamseen*—the hot wind from the desert—detained them in Alexandria, but on April 27 they reached Beirut—"a sweet, clean town on one of the most beautiful harbors in the world." They motored to Damascus, then to Amman and finally to Jerusalem, passing several camps of refugees, whose "dreadful poverty made me ache all over." On May 19 they entered Israel via the "Mandelbaum Gate Frontier" in Jerusalem. Helen had prepared some opening sentences for her speeches in Israel which she had had translated into Hebrew. They read:

CHA-VEH-REEM RAHV LEE HAH-DAH-VAHR LE-HEE-YOUGHT BEH CHEVRAHT-CHEM BAHM-DEE-NAH HAT-ZEE-RAH HAH-ZOUGHT, HAH-VEEL VEE-YESH HAH-CHEHM EH-MOON-AH HAH-ZAH-KAH, VE-HEE HEE EYN HAHN-SHAH-MATT.

In English this read, "Dear Friends: It is marvelous to be among you in this young Commonwealth because you have faith which is the sight of the soul." Eric's note with this translation said, "The only advice about pronunciation given by Mr. Crum is that the *CH* is to be pronounced gutturally."

They dined that evening, after having toured Jerusalem, with Golda Myerson (Golda Meir), then the minister of labor. "Met Golda Myerson," Polly had written Florence before their departure for the Middle East, "a beautiful woman indeed—Helen said 'Esther must have looked like her.'" They had tea with Ben-Gurion; he asked her to call him "BG." They talked about the Bible and Plato. She visited Kibbutzim and of course institutions for the blind. The latter had an unexpected sequel. The Israelis were very proud of a village for the blind that they had established to which in the influx of immigrants after the war they had sent any family that was headed by a blind person or included a blind person. Helen heard about the place called "Village for the Blind" and exploded. The blind must not be segregated, she insisted. "They should be trained for membership of normal society and not as a society of handicapped persons. You must break up that village." The Israelis did so. Its name was changed to Kfar Uriel, the Light of God. "That is why the 'pros' in my field," said Barnett, "respected her. She had a philosophy about the treatment of the blind and fought for it."

She visited the Israeli parliament, the Knesset; and its Speaker, Josef

Spinzrak, in welcoming this "very precious guest," as he called her, sounded a theme to which she could not but be responsive:

> And if you ask me whence the source of this strength which preserved our nation from annihilation and brought it to the renewal of its life as an independent State in the Holy Land—I would reply that it can be expressed in one word—and this word is the title of a book which you yourself wrote—OPTIMISM. By the faith of man in the power of his will, we came, after generations of exile to the restoration of our national life in our own land.

> And you, who are the very symbol of faith and the victory of noble human will—your coming is a blessed and encouraging sign to us in our life and in the faith we are treading.

Their escort during their almost two-week stay in Israel was Ruth Klüger, herself a legendary figure in Israel because of her exploits in getting endangered Jews out of the charnel house of Europe through the blockade set up by Great Britain, the mandatory power in Palestine, at the end of the war. Helen wrote Ruth from France,

> As you went with us to and from meetings, introduced us to the creators and leaders of Israel, or made us happy with your loving hospitality, it was amazing the way the book of your heroic life lay open before us. To think that we should have talked with a woman who endured such incredible hardships and dangers to bring 'illegal immigrants' safely to Israel. It must be an unspeakable satisfaction to you that you have not only enabled men, women and children to settle there, but also rescued great personalities whose genius and service to the people will be among the incalculable forces of Israel's future. It was a privilege to us to celebrate the Feast of First-fruits with you. . . .

From Israel they flew to Paris to stay with Florence and to celebrate the centenary of the death of Louis Braille, whom Helen called "the Gutenberg of the blind." She stood with members of Braille's family in the Pantheon when his ashes were deposited there with other French immortals. Before the solemn ceremony she had paid tribute to Braille at the Sorbonne, congratulating the French government for recognizing "the spirit and efforts of all who refuse to succumb to their limitations." She was made a Chevalier of the Legion of Honor. "She spoke in heavily accented but faultlessly grammatical French," Florence wrote Van Wyck Brooks. "Standing before the audience, she was radiant and the applause was tremendous."

They returned to the United States—to many of the old cares. "Most of the time," Nella noted in her journal, "Helen and Polly are alone which should not be." Every day they took their little walk in the morning and at dusk they walked from the house to the gate. Polly likened herself and Helen to two old maids. "The melancholy of their return, which was partly caused by the let-down from having been treated like princesses when they were abroad, has been to a large extent dissipated since they have been caught up in a new and heavy schedule of speeches and letters."

Parties and political talk—it was a presidential election year—helped dispel the tedium. Helen and Polly had the Clarks, who were deeply involved in the Eisenhower campaign, for dinner along with Robert and Louise Duffus. "After the Clarks left," recorded Nella, "Robert (a Democrat) lingered behind to tell them how disappointed the *Times* was in Eisenhower's failure to denounce McCarthy, the *Times* having announced itself in support of the general. Mr. Sulzberger had written an editorial and when Helen read it on Sunday she was so wrought up that she wrote Mr. Sulzberger a letter in praise of his stand. Mr. S. asked permission to publish it and it came out in the *Times* on Thursday."

They made their regular visit to the Mayo Clinic to be checked over. Polly was complaining of dizziness and feeling "funny" in the head. Their old friend Dr. Dixon said that Helen's health continued to be very good, but in regard to Polly he let it be known that he felt "that others should begin to learn the manual alphabet."

One project that fully engaged their interest was a documentary film about Helen that Nancy Hamilton was putting together. She had picked up the idea of such a film when Robert Flaherty, the producer of *Man of Aran,* after a brief flurry of interest, had abandoned it. She spent much time with Nella on the script. By 1952 there was always a camera on hand to record significant moments in Helen's life, such as the Louis Braille centenary celebration in Paris. "Had lunch with Nancy and Jimmy Shute at Harvard Club re documentary," recorded Nella at the end of 1952. "Shute thought my memo of last spring gave proper feeling; outlined what they planned; afterwards to Preview Theater to see Paris films and what has been done at Arcan Ridge. . . . Tomorrow Helen and Polly will be photographed going into Bendels, then inside with fabrics and hats, in afternoon at AFB in conference."

They had the power "to do immense harm" through the films, she cautioned Nancy. In that case, replied the filmmaker, "we might as well go out and cut our throats." The fakery of some scenes troubled Nella— scenes that might show Helen as "too perfect," that overrated her ability to enjoy music, that misconstrued what religion meant to her; scenes that showed her with society and celebrities rather than with "the humble people" who were her real constituency. "Main point (or a main point)," Nella went on, "Documentary thus far shows the triumphant end, not the continuing struggle—the long, long hours spent over the mail, the long, long hours composing speeches, memorizing them (H & P both have to memorize them), practicing them."

Such anxieties were superseded suddenly by a greater one, a prospect that paralyzed them with horror and for months would always be on their minds even when they were speaking of other things. "Alfred Knopf had telephoned Ken McCormick [chief editor at Doubleday and a friend of Helen and Polly] a few days before to say that they had this book about a deaf-blind girl and they did not want anyone to identify her with Helen Keller." The book was *The Story of Esther Costello* by Nicholas Monsarrat, a powerful writer, as he had demonstrated in *The Cruel Sea* and other works of fiction. Knopf sent Nella the manuscript that night.

The manuscript appalled Nella and she felt she had to alert Helen and Polly. She prepared a synopsis of the book: "Four children playing in a basement in Ireland dig up a bomb. . . . The explosion that follows kills three of them and renders the fourth deaf and blind and unable to talk. This is our heroine Esther Costello." The deaf-blind Esther lives in conditions of squalor and neglect until she is rescued by a rich American woman who out of compassion takes her to America. When doctors are unable to help her, Mrs. Manisty learns the manual language and teaches it to her. By accident Esther becomes a world celebrity. The pair take to the platform.

> The superemotionalism of the meeting discharges itself in rivers of money that pour in from audiences for the blind. From the beginning there is some degree of shoddiness and trickery in the handling of Esther, but the great corruption does not get under way until Mrs. Manisty's husband returns to take control. The Esther Costello Foundation for the Blind is established, high-pressure salesmanship and

advertising are employed. . . . Money is indeed given to the blind, but Manisty's idea is that charity begins at home. Much of it is kept and Esther's entourage lives at a pitch of extravagance which endangers their reputation. The racket is so profitable that they cannot bear to give it up after Esther regains her sight and hearing. . . . We are asked to believe that the shock of being raped by Mrs. Manisty's husband is enough to restore her sight and hearing. . . . They persuade her that for the sake of the blind she must let no one know that she is cured. They call in a disreputable physician who makes her look blind (they even consider making her blind in truth) and the show goes on.

A Boston reporter discovers the fraud and decides to abduct the girl with whom he is now in love and make the whole thing public. . . .

◦ Nella's shocked memorandum ended: "I have no doubt that Helen Keller was the starting point. Mr. Monsarrat was in Johannesburg when she was there and probably saw her. All I can say for him is that I think he has no real comprehension of what he has done. All I can hope is that whatever harm may come from the book will be to him and not to Helen Keller and not to the blind."

Nella was too genteel to describe Mrs. Manisty's husband in the lurid light in which Monsarrat painted him. As Eric Boulter later wrote describing the book's slur on the memories of Annie and Mr. John Macy:

Of even greater significance, on this same train of thought, is the fact that Mr. Bannister (Mr. Manacey [sic] in the original text) is portrayed as something of a sex-maniac in at least as far as Esther is concerned. He is discovered peeping through her window as she prepares for bed, scouting behind the shower curtain as she takes a bath and finally commits rape upon her, thus causing the return of sight and hearing. Here again we fear the effect on public thought insofar as Mr. Macy's relationship toward Helen were [sic] concerned.

Nella found it difficult to tell Helen and Polly. She called them about it six weeks later: "Seldom have I hated to make a telephone call more than the one yesterday morning," she wrote Polly afterward. "The book when it first appears will attract a great deal of attention because of Monsarrat's enormous success with *The Cruel Sea.* . . . The general public cannot fail to connect it with Helen because she is the one deaf-blind person that most people know, but they may not realize that she is the only one of whom it might be written.''

The book was scheduled to be published first in England by Cassells, preceded by serialization in the *Sunday Chronicle.* Helen's friends thought seriously about a libel suit, but from the beginning Helen firmly said no; it would only call attention to the book. Helen would not sue, Nella informed Knopf, nor would she; ''beyond that could not promise. The Foundation might. If the thing seemed harmful would use every weapon. . . .''

In the middle of the anguish caused by worry over the Monsarrat book, Helen and Polly embarked on a tour of Latin America. It had been organized for them by Nelson Neff, the man who had handled their second tour of Japan. He was now regional director of CARE's Latin American operations and accompanied them on a journey that took them to Brazil, Chile, Peru, Panama and Mexico. Helen left with Nella a statement on the Monsarrat book that the latter was authorized to release in the event that it became necessary. ''I have just heard the summary of a manuscript over which I am most indignant and sick at heart,'' it began. The book was a hoax that would do much damage to the blind and the deaf, it went on. The references to Teacher, she said, assuming that Mrs. Manisty was meant to represent Mrs. Macy, were insulting. ''There was nothing of the showman about her. Nor did money 'pour in' at our lectures. . . . There was nothing organized about our lives.'' The last paragraph of the statement showed her distress:

> After fifty years of toil, prayer and anxiety which I have given to the blind and the deaf, I confess that I do not want to appear in public again. Of course this would be cowardly in me, especially as God sustains me, and our friends everywhere who know Polly and me intimately and have seen our work will be loyal to us, but when the light and beauty of my life—service to others—seem threatened, I find it hard indeed not to be discouraged and weep.

Nella lunched with Eric Boulter and Van Wyck Brooks, who brought a lawyer friend along to discuss a counterattack. Van Wyck and his friend wanted Helen to sue. ''I knew that Helen did not want to sue.'' Nella

defended Knopf's decision to publish, since the book was already scheduled for publication in England. Van Wyck, who was planning to write
something about Helen, said that he would do it while keeping Monsarrat's accusations in the background of his thinking—"as we have," Nella
added, "in making the film." She informed them that she was trying to
get Helen to work again on the book about Teacher. The three fourths
that she had written had been destroyed in the fire. "I will myself write
the story of the years since Teacher's death if Helen doesn't."

They began to mobilize their immense network of friends abroad. As
Eric Boulter, who was a main mover in this campaign, later wrote:

> Nicholas Monsarrat was employed as an official of the British Infor-
> mation Services in Johannesburg at the time of Helen Keller's South
> African tour in 1951. When some of Helen's friends learned of the
> proposed publication of the book and noted similarities they took
> steps to trace the origin of the idea, and, through friends in South
> Africa, located Monsarrat's Secretary. She stated that Monsarrat had
> attended one or more of Helen's public meetings, had then instructed
> her to obtain comprehensive material on Helen's life and subse-
> quently began to write the book.

Troubled by the protests of Helen's friends, Knopf had written to
Monsarrat, who replied "in great annoyance," recorded Nella. "He professed the deepest admiration for Helen Keller and went so far as to say
that he wanted to dedicate the book to her. (Needless to say Helen
rejected this indignantly.)"

At the request of Bob Barnett and Helen, Eric wrote to the British
leaders of the blind, urging them to intercede with the British publishers
to delay publication and with Monsarrat to withdraw his manuscript. The
book, Boulter asserted, would not only damage Helen's personal and
professional reputation but would "undermine public confidence in established fund-raising procedures for the physically handicapped, particularly
such activities as are conducted by the handicapped themselves." Monsarrat became aware of the campaign against his book. He forbade his American publishers to show the manuscript to anyone without his permission.
Nella records that he felt she had had raised "a tempest in a teapot
. . . that he is on the side of the angels. . . . M knows that we have been
making inquiries about him in South Africa and England and feels that he
is being pursued. As he is. . . ." At Polly's suggestion Nella wrote Mac

Eagar, the retired head of the National Institute for the Blind: "Helen's and Polly's friends here are willing to do *anything,*" she advised him. "Our difficulty is to act wisely."

Colligan, the present director of the National Institute, undertook to get in touch with Cassells. "I can't disguise the fact that it is going to be difficult to stop publication in this country but we'll have a very good try at it armed with the ammunition which you have sent me." He talked with a director of Cassells:

> He was very much inclined to play the whole matter down and to blame Knopf for having precipitated a storm in a tea-cup by sending a copy of the book to Nella Braddy Henney. Cassells stoutly maintains that the book cannot conceivably be held to bear any relationship whatever to the life of Helen Keller and in fact Nicholas Monsarrat has never read The Life of Helen Keller and was unaware that such a book was in existence. At Monsarrat's request, Cassells have made one or two alterations in the script. It no longer refers to the Manistys; they have become the Bannisters and the husband is known as Captain Bannister, an ex-army officer.

Ian Fraser, MP and chairman of St. Dunstan's, was strongly opposed to efforts to stop its publication. He doubted that the British general public would identify Esther Costello with Helen; the latter was not that well-known in England. The British tradition of freedom of the press and the arts, moreover, was so strong that any attempt "to stop publication, whether by banning or action for libel or persuasion, often has the opposite effect by stimulating publicity where it would not otherwise occur." Another opinion came from John Wilson of the British Empire Society for the Blind. He had shown the materials to a barrister who thought that there was "a prima facie case of libel against Helen Keller."

Soon, however, everyone agreed with Sir Ian Fraser that any legal action would only encourage publicity. That had been Helen's view all along. Van Wyck Brooks now opposed legal recourse: "I have an idea that the book when it comes out will be innocuous or fizzle." He had alerted Bob Duffus of the *Times.* "He will be active warning the editor of the Book Review, etc." Mac Eagar advised them that unless Helen sued, her British friends on their own could not do anything. "His dirt can't stain Helen permanently but the distress it inflicts on her is dreadful to think of."

Nella thought that Monsarrat was in retreat. "There is no continent, no city where he can escape from Helen's friends," she wrote Van Wyck:

> His defense that the book is an imaginative effort ties him in a knot. If the monstrous charges that he makes against the workers for the blind and the deaf-blind are imaginative there can be no forgiveness for him. Of course he claims that the corruption in philanthropy is real and that his heroine is the creature of the brain. The two go together and he cannot separate them. . . .
>
> There have been times when I have felt terribly alone in all this. I am still the only one in Helen's group that has read the manuscript, but Eric will be a rock of Gibraltar for us all.

The first installments had begun to appear in the *Sunday Chronicle*. Eric forwarded them to Nella, noting that Monsarrat had changed the name "Esther Costello Foundation for the Blind" to "Esther Costello Fund for the Blind." He added that he, too, was "impressed by the puerile quality of Monsarrat's work and am rapidly forming the conclusion that very few people will take it seriously." The *Reader's Digest* and the two book clubs, Nella learned from Knopf, had turned the book down "and had expressed some horror at its quality and general content." That would be the general reaction, Nella thought, "and I am awfully glad that we had nothing to do with it. As things stand now I think the less we do the better, since it looks as if the book is going to take care of itself." But it was Nella who had set the alarm bells ringing in the first place.

Just before the book appeared, Lenore Smith and her son Sidney came over from Wolfeboro in New Hampshire to visit the Henneys on Foss Mountain. Nella told them about the Monsarrat book. "They all refused to take the Monsarrat book very seriously," Nella recorded afterward. " 'If Helen isn't strong enough for that,' Sidney said, 'it is just too bad.' We all agreed that Helen could outride it."

The book was a failure. *The New York Times* Sunday reviewer, John Barkham, called it a "painful, repellent novel that leaves a bitter taste in the mouth," although he had grudging admiration for what he called Monsarrat's "bag of tricks." Orville Prescott in the daily *Times* felt similarly: "The book is short, lurid and morbidly readable; but . . . also . . . revolting." Taliaferro Boatright in the *Herald Tribune*'s *Books* felt that

"Esther's story is more a case history than novel. Mr. Monsarrat has a valid theme—the abuse of generosity—and a plot line. But he does not have a novel."

"No paper has given a good review," Nella exulted in a letter to Polly. No reviewer had mentioned Helen Keller or Anne Sullivan Macy.

part seven
HELEN

XLI

"Helen's Aloneness Does Not Bear Thinking About"

"I want to read more of Plato and Kant and Swedenborg."

Toward the end of their tour of Latin America, Nelson Neff had cautioned friends like Nella and Eric Boulter, "The girls will finish this one all right, but please urge the powers that be—no more country-to-country hops. It is just expecting too much!" But that was not the way Helen and Polly saw it. There were a few places they had not visited—India, Red China, the Soviet Union, Scandinavia—and they were eager to get to all of them. Barnett and Boulter, commented Nella pessimistically, would oppose the trips, "but the girls will win out." Nella wanted Helen to return to the book about Teacher, but she doubted whether they were able "to settle down happily to lonely days of writing."

Helen had begun to age. Her fingers were less sensitive. "She says she has to warm them now before she can read with them," recorded Nella. "I am inclined also to think that her other senses may be less keen, including smell, for when I was last at Arcan Ridge she identified a spike of stock as hyacinth." In the past Helen had used all her wiles to ensure the world's attention. Now she cared less. The deafness and blindness that hitherto had walled her off from mankind was turning into a shell into which she could withdraw. Still, when Nella brought them together with Ken McCormick, Doubleday's editor-in-chief, he felt that it was like running into "charge of electricity. You felt that if she had five senses she would explode, there was so much vitality." And David Lilienthal, who in the mid-fifties was living at Redding Ridge, Connecticut, was bewitched by her "almost girlish excitement and her laughter and her intense interest in everything." "Such animation," he wrote a little later. "When a particularly funny remark is made and handed on to her, she clicks on the floor in delight, slaps her thigh, and puts her hand over her mouth, depending on how exuberant she feels." Lilienthal thought it was "all part of the great joy she feels."

Helen's slowing down was apparent only to her intimates, but Polly was ailing visibly. High blood pressure, hardening of the arteries, loss of memory and facial disfiguration reminded their friends that a disabling stroke might hit her at any moment. They wanted her to train a substitute, a "Polly's Polly." She not only resisted that, but made it difficult even for Helen's oldest friends, like Lenore and Nella, to talk with her alone. The less she was able to serve Helen, the more tightly she clung to her. The jealousy and possessiveness that she had been able to conceal to all but close friends now became painfully obvious to many.

Lenore and Nella discussed the situation during Lenore's visit to Foss Mountain in the autumn of 1953. Lenore had spelled for Helen as far back as Gilman School days, and Teacher had wanted to take her on permanently. Her late husband, Phil, had stopped that by marrying her and saving her from a job that exhausted and drained her—"just as Keith did in my life," interpolated Nella. "Teacher had always pushed Helen away from her," Lenore went on, "while Polly has taken an exactly opposite course. Lenore said that even at a dinner party Polly would not allow her to do the spelling and that she did not think Polly would consent to Helen's paying a visit to her alone as she used to do when Teacher was alive. (I don't think so either.)" Ironically, it had been Lenore, Nella noted, who had saved Polly from being pushed out when Teacher died: "Polly entered the house as an upper servant. Teacher knew before her death that Polly and Helen had to stay together but all that last week when Lenore was there in Forest Hills she spent the time when she took Helen out for a daily walk persuading Helen to try it with Polly—at least for a while."

These were private anxieties, however, which neither Lenore nor Nella, so far as is known, communicated to Helen at that time, except in the indirect sense of continually stressing the need to bolster Polly with an understudy.

An event that increasingly absorbed Helen's interest was the progress of the documentary film based on her life that Nancy Hamilton was producing. In October 1953 she went down to the White House to be filmed with President Eisenhower for the documentary. "Polly and Helen both dread it," recorded Nella, but the session went smoothly. Nella copied a transcript into her journal:

> The President was at his desk signing something when Miss Keller and Miss Thomson entered. He came forward smiling.
>
> PRES.   So nice to see you again Miss Keller. It is wonderful of you to come down here.
>
> H.K.   I am proud to meet you, Mr. President, who did the enormous work of one of the Titans who won the world for democracy.
>
> (The President was very moved. Miss Thomson said she saw a tear in his eye. To smooth over the moment she spoke.)
>
> P.T. to H.K.   How many times have you been in Washington?
>
> H.K.   Nearly every year since I was a child and I love this beautiful city, especially on a sunny day like this.
>
> H.K.   Mr. President, may I touch your face? I want to put my hand on your face and see your celebrated smile.
>
> H.K.   (after going over his face carefully) You have a beautiful smile.
>
> PRES.   But not much hair. (Laughter) I am deeply touched at your coming to see me, Miss Keller.
>
> H.K.   This is a day I shall never forget.
>
> PRES.   I shall not forget it either.
>   Exeunt.

Old friends were disappearing. During the summer G.A. Pfeiffer had died. His wife had died earlier. She had not liked Polly, a hostility that Polly reciprocated; but after her death "they came to know Mr. Pfeiffer better and like the rest of the Colony called him 'Uncle Gus.' " Migel, in his late eighties, in dark glasses and always with a cane, appeared old and feeble, but his mind was still alert, and with the loyal Amelia in the background he kept in touch with Helen's affairs and everything that went on at the Foundation.

It was to Migel that Helen appealed in the festering dispute between Bob Barnett and Eric Boulter over the respective roles of the AFB and the AFOB. She had turned against Barnett. During the "Esther Costello" alarm, he had shocked Nella by saying to her, "I wish she [Helen] would resign." His impatience may have been quickened by Helen's embarrassing support of a Communist-sponsored peace congress in Vienna. "I am with you in your wonderful movement with all my heart," she had cabled, disregarding that the invitation had come from Prague. When this was pointed out to her and she realized it was a Communist-manipulated affair, she had sent a second cable repudiating the Congress on the grounds that it was not a true peace movement. Thereupon the Congress announced that Helen really was with them but the American police state had shut her up. Helen refused the Voice of America's request for a rousing repudiation of communism in all its forms because, she said, the blind were free in Yugoslavia to communicate with the rest of the world. The farthest she would go was to declare "I do not believe in dictatorial Communism. I never have. . . . I do not believe in deception in any form." More effective from the Voice of America's point of view was Barnett's broadcast over its many-languaged network: "Miss Keller had already repudiated the Vienna Congress on the grounds that it is not a true peace movement, but a mask for Stalinist propaganda. Miss Keller also wishes me to say for her that the use made of the already repudiated statement by the editors of *Rude Pravo* is only further proof that the Congress in Vienna is a screen for purposes other than peace."

The episode did not have any serious repercussions, but it added to Barnett's uneasiness and impatience with the women at Arcan Ridge. "At first I was happy under the new Executive Director," Helen complained to Migel, "who was most communicative with me. . . . But for months the attitude of the Executive Director towards me has been different. He seems to have ignored me as a Counsellor of the AFB on International Relations,—an honor which I owe to you, Mr. Migel. I wonder what has caused this change." Polly even began to praise Bob Irwin. At least he had a clear mind and expressed himself concisely. "Why Robert did not know even how to dress properly." She had not noticed anything wrong with Barnett's dress, Nella commented, "whereupon Polly said, 'You wouldn't.' "

The nub of Helen's complaint to Migel, and to Ziegler, was Barnett's lack of interest in the international work carried out through the AFOB. Boulter suspected that Barnett was an isolationist who if a depression came would not hesitate to cut down on the activities of the AFOB. The latter had originally been an independent organization, Helen's letter to her trustees went on. "I feel strongly that the time has come for it to regain its independence." The trustees, Helen and Polly learned, were "101 percent for Robert," but Migel and Ziegler did urge him to have lunch with them and clear the air. "Polly told me that she found out that she was considered an S.O.B. to get along with; said she didn't care, but of course she does." Nella postscripted that "none of the trustees like Eric very much—feel that he talks too much and think that he is after Robert's job."

By the end of 1953 Nancy had assembled the various tracks of the documentary into a cohesive statement with Katharine Cornell as the narrator. She gave it a first showing to a few friends, including Adele Levy, Kit's neighbor at the Vineyard, who had put up much of the $60,000 that it had cost to produce the film:

> We [wrote Nella] were all deeply moved. One man said he wept all the way through, but he was not sad. Keith said the emotion was like weeping at a wedding. Brenda [Forbes], I think it was who said we all felt the way we ought to feel. Mrs. Levy said she was undone and was very proud to have had a part in it. We went in with the feeling of being about to attend a First Night in which we were all deeply concerned; came out feeling that it was a great success.

Helen and Polly were present, Helen joining the laughter at "the many little spots of gaiety" and commenting afterward, "It was a very human document." Polly invited everyone to Sardi's for a drink. Unfortunately she had engaged a table only for four and there were ten, so it was all a little hectic and confused. Two weeks later Nancy showed the picture to the Foundation people, including the Migels, Amelia, Barnett, Boulter and Evelyn Seide. "The whole Foundation group seemed greatly pleased," recorded Nella. A week later an audience of four hundred saw it. Ken McCormick found it a powerful experience, the more so because of the complete lack of sentimentality and the use of understatement throughout. Buoyed by its apparent universal appeal, hopes soared for a great commercial success, and Helen even drafted a statement turning over her profits from *The Unconquered,* as it was now called, to a "Special Helen Keller Fund for the Deaf-Blind." Although it did win an Academy Award, it was not a commercial success. James Adams with his banker's connections asked the moguls of Hollywood about its prospects. They told him that "it was a dead duck" in terms of a mass audience.

Spurred on, however, by the approval the film gained from the people whom Helen respected, she turned again to her own book about Teacher.

She was seeking the right approach, she said, and one day she came down from her study and handed Polly the opening pages. It began in Athens, and Polly thought it was going to be as much about their travels as about Teacher and she liked that. "Helen was on fire with her book," Nella noted, "and working very hard indeed." She went to her desk at seven-thirty and except for lunch and a little walk stayed there until five. "She was very tired in the evening," but that was natural; she was, after all, almost seventy-four. The documentary film and her own book made her more than usually mindful of Teacher. She even permitted herself a mildly deprecatory remark about Polly: "Much as I appreciate all that Polly is doing to enable me to follow Teacher's beam," she told Nella, "it is Teacher who is with me all the time."

The book drained her emotionally. Nella came to Arcan Ridge to work with her. "She looked deaf-blind and seemed tired. Of her own initiative she talked very little and I did not urge her." Suddenly Helen left them and went upstairs to work and spent most of the day there while Nella and Polly watched the Army-McCarthy hearings on television.

When Helen finally did come down, she began to talk of Teacher's eyes and the suffering that they had caused her. "She spoke of Teacher's grief when she knew John Macy was leaving her. 'I thought she would go out of her mind.' Then suddenly Helen's face crumpled and she began to weep." Nella had seen her shed tears before "in tenderness and sorrow, but this was the first time I had ever seen her break down in anguish."

"How can I bear the burden of this sacrifice?" she said, and Nella in recording it commented in her journal, "Her suffering is intense in recalling the past." Her loneliness saddened Nella: " 'I never thought I would have to do a job like this alone. Polly can't help because she can't write. I need a collaborator. I don't know how to put Katharine and Van Wyck and Jo down on paper.' I assured her that I would be as much of a collaborator as I could. . . ."

A few weeks later Helen and Polly went to Foss Mountain to stay with Nella and Keith for a fortnight. Evelyn Seide and her husband drove them up. Partly it was to get away from the seventy-fourth birthday celebrations, but mostly it was to write, and Nella gave her her Smith-Corona portable. "Then with her Braille notes she went to work." They made "a line of chairs from the bathroom to her work table," but she also guided herself by the edge of the rug, and Nella warned her housekeeper not to help her. Helen needed to feel herself as independent as possible. Before her departure she packed her papers herself, including her Braille slate, and when she was done she set out for the dining room alone.

She was very apprehensive about the book before she came here. She had given Polly about fifty pages shortly before they left Arcan Ridge. This was the first that Polly had seen. Her reaction and mine when I read them gave Helen great confidence and this confidence increased as we kept talking. . . . She is now glad that the original manuscript was burned for she says it was not good, she had not the right perspective. . . . She spoke of being 'unworlded' by Teacher's death and said she was like Meleager. . . . Her life was quenched when Teacher died, she said, like Meleager's when his mother threw into the fire the brand upon which his life depended, but unlike Meleager she has arisen again and with greater power.

And indeed she has. She has dug into herself and has learned many things that no one could have taught her, not even Teacher. I have been greatly impressed by the profundity of this manuscript. Up to the time of reading it I myself had not much confidence in Helen's ability to write about Teacher, but I have now. . . .

Often I felt that she was working too hard—many times she went back to the typewriter after tea and the afternoon walk, but she is so full of what she wants to get down that it would be cruel to interrupt her. Besides, she is not easy to interrupt when she doesn't want to be.

Another batch of manuscript arrived at Nella's at the end of August. "I thought the first of it excellent, but this is even better. I think it is going to be the best thing she has ever written." Helen took time off to visit Kit at Martha's Vineyard. Mrs. Roosevelt was visiting friends, and Kit Cornell invited everyone for tea. Helen eagerly explored Eleanor Roosevelt's face with her fingers and read her lips. "I wish we might all have been together longer," Helen wrote her "dearest of Katharines" afterward, "and nothing could have meant more to me than a real talk with Mrs. Roosevelt. . . ." Nancy sent Nella prints of snapshots she made. "Helen looks *so* much younger than Mrs. Roosevelt," the loyal Nella wrote Polly (Helen was in fact four years older).

A few weeks later they were out at the Mayo Clinic in Rochester. Polly's face was operated on for removal of a tumor. "As soon as I knew there was no malignancy I was sure we could meet the rest of it," Nella wrote her reassuringly. "Dr. Dixon told Katharine that there will be only a slight change." But the psychological effect was profound:

Lunch with Helen and Polly at the Club Nov. 9. Much relieved to see that Polly's face is as little distorted as it is. It is noticeable, but harder on her than on those who look at her. She was in a highly emotional state when she first came in, partly because of this, partly because she was giving me another batch of pages from Helen's book. She always turns them over with great trepidation, feeling deeply her own inadequacies in this area as compared with Teacher. (I read the pages on the way home, finished shortly after dinner, and hastened to telephone to reassure her.)

We talked of the forthcoming visit to India and Pakistan, then probably to the Philippines, maybe Japan, though Japan without Takeo who died late in Oct. or very early in Nov., will not be the same. Polly began to say that this would be their last trip but I cut her off, for as long as they are able to travel they will be going forth like this. Then Polly admitted that she thought they could do a great deal of good in Red China and confessed that she wanted to go to Russia. Helen is no longer starry-eyed about Russia, but she would go.

Polly had tried to keep the Pacific trip a secret from Nella, "afraid," Nella told Van Wyck, "that I would forbid it." That was ridiculous, she added, "as if I would forbid them to do anything. . . . This was a projection of her own conscience." By the end of 1954 the *Teacher* manuscript was completed. "I was able to tell her as soon as we sat down at the Club on Wednesday that I had finished reading her manuscript . . . that I thought she had written with passion and insight, that a living woman came out of the pages and that altogether it was a magnificent piece of work. I spoke truly. When we were in the club car on the way to Westport she said, 'This has been one of the happiest days of my life. I kept thinking of what you told me at the Club.' God send that I told her right!" Nella added, but her journal shows that she told her only the partial truth of what she felt. The manuscript went to Ken McCormick, who said "he liked it very much."

Completion of the manuscript, the imminence of her departure for India, which was to be celebrated by a banquet tendered by the AFB, and the announcement by Harvard that she would receive an honorary degree on her return—the first ever given to a woman—all served to buoy her spirits. What did she want to do, Nella asked her, now that *Teacher* was finished—not another book? "Study foreign languages," she answered. "I want to read more of Plato and Kant and Swedenborg. I wonder if I shall have the courage to learn Russian." The big farewell dinner at the Waldorf on February 1 went off in fine style. "Mrs. Roosevelt spoke with great warmth." The ambassadors from the countries on their itinerary spoke well, "the one from India a little too long." Amelia and Dr. Berens thought they had never seen Helen look more tired, but the local doctor gave both Helen and Polly a clean bill of health. "We shall be gone four months," she informed Mrs. Adams.

India with their warm reception by Prime Minister Nehru was the high point of their trip. In New Delhi she saw him several times, at the minister of education's "at home" dinner and in public:

> Proudly I shall cherish in memory the quiet evening we spent with you and your daughter Indira, just as if we were members of your family. I cannot thank you for such a beautiful compliment in words, I can only remember its sincerity and your kindly permitting me to touch your face. It was a face whose real nobility and high-domed brow one needs the gift of a Poet to describe. It looked what I had always seen in my mind, a personality that elevates human ideals and goals and shoves the world nearer to true Civilization. How I longed to have among my treasures a book that vibrates with your soul, 'Nehru's Letters to His Daughter.'

> Miss Thomson and I will be in Delhi again from the 6th to the 9th of April, and we hope to see you again. I wonder if there will be any chance of our visiting the Taj Mahal.

Before she left India Nehru addressed the Lok Sabha, India's parliament, and gave a wide-ranging commentary on world affairs. Helen thought enough of his views to have them transcribed into Braille for her use.

They covered the country's length and breadth, visited Gandhi's tomb and the Taj Mahal. She took time off to go over the Braille page proofs of *Teacher,* which Nella air-expressed at a cost of ninety dollars. "I can't remember if I told you," Nella wrote her a little later, "that Ken and in fact everybody who read your manuscript felt that it needed a kind of foreword or preamble giving a sketch of the factual background and Ken asked me to write it." She had it brailled and sent it "with a transcript for Polly." She also reported that Houghton-Mifflin was so impressed by the publicity her tour was receiving in the American press that if she was planning a book about the trip they wanted to see it. "I told them no, of course, and said that in any case Doubleday was your regular publisher." She had other good news. The State Department wanted to purchase *The Unconquered* for use overseas.

Helen and Polly returned at the beginning of June, having circumnavigated the globe. Seventy-fifth birthday greetings were already beginning to pour in. There was an affectionate note from Eleanor Roosevelt:

> From all sides I have been hearing of the wonderful job you have done on your goodwill tour, and I have felt proud that you were representing our country. All of us when we go abroad are ambassadors in our own right but I think your unselfishness and deep devotion to the cause of humanity everywhere has a very special appeal. There can be no doubt that you left a spark of your spirit everywhere you went and that your efforts will produce good results for many years to come.
>
> I feel sure that notes of praise and gratitude are pouring in to you but I think your greatest reward must lie in your own knowledge that you have left no stone unturned in trying to share your own inner happiness with all mankind.

These two stalwart champions of equal rights for women came closer in their final years. In September 1954 Mrs. Roosevelt had permitted the American Association for the United Nations to organize a large public dinner to celebrate her seventieth birthday. Helen had written: "Not only am I proud of Mrs. Roosevelt because she represents the noblest traditions of American womanhood and citizenship, I honor her even more because in word, deed and constant endeavor she champions the cause of mankind."

A week before Helen's birthday she went up to Cambridge to receive her honorary degree at the Harvard commencement exercises. "When Helen's name was called the entire audience rose for standing ovation. Later they rose for ex-Pres. Conant, then for [Konrad] Adenauer, but not for any of the other honorees. . . . She never looked more beautiful—all in white with a white dress with tiny green flowers on it. She wore a corsage of white gardenias which the Swedenborg Church sent her." C.C. Burlingham, distinguished lawyer and member of the Harvard Corporation, had sought for years to persuade the university to give an honorary degree to a woman. He concluded that Eleanor Roosevelt was too radical for Harvard and urged that Helen be considered.

On her birthday she was inundated with telegrams from all over the world, including one from Vice-President Nixon, and with flowers. Thomas Watson of IBM sent her seventy-five American Beauty roses; the Burmese government sent her a somewhat smaller bouquet of the same flower. Ethel Clark brought a big bowl of bright red lilies; Lillian Svanda, Helen and Polly's cook, gave her a "Colonial bouquet"—a yellow rose set in white flowers. Kit and Nancy sent two small pottery birds, and Adele Levy gave the AFB a contribution of $1,000. There were boxes of edibles from her family and fruit from former President Truman.

But behind the scenes of honor and achievement, there were increasing difficulties, and they centered on Polly. She complained often of Helen's slowness in comprehending the things that were spelled into her hand. "I had no trouble," Nella noted, "but having been warned, I was careful and slow. I don't know whether there is a mental block in Helen or not against Polly's spelling." She developed this theme further in a comment on the presidential campaign:

> Helen is not well informed on the current situation . . . not in any way. This has been true for a long time and Polly has been on the defensive about it. For instance, Helen knows nothing about the terrible recent developments in her own state of Alabama. Ken [McCormick at the Brussels] asked for her opinion and Polly said she didn't know anything about it, that she had been so busy that she, Polly, had not wanted to bother her, Helen, with it. This may not be anything to worry about, but could be disastrous if Helen steps out with a dogmatic statement which reveals her ignorance.
>
> She and Polly are still strong for Adlai Stevenson. Ken has lost the intense and gratifying enthusiasm he had during the last campaign. Admires Truman. Feels that he was always right on the big issues. . . .

There was the usual trouble with household help. Polly dismissed another maid; "I think there is no human being who can live in the house with Polly in a subordinate position or perhaps in any position—no one but Helen, and Polly is subordinate to Helen," commented Nella. Nella herself was not a "cosy person" to know, "a New England type," commented Ken McCormick; and even if she was not—she hailed from Georgia—"she wore the uniform and knew the drill."

Teacher came out in time for the Christmas sale. Ken told Nella that it had been "a strong seller—1,000 copies the first two weeks in December —but not sensational." She had never expected it to be a best-seller, Nella replied; it was really a mood piece, "more like a book of poetry than a biography." He had met people, Ken added cautiously, "who find the intensity of the emotion just too much." Nella's reservations about *Teacher* were even stronger than she indicated to Ken. Despite the fact that the *Reader's Digest* bought two thousand dollars worth, by the end of 1956 the book had quietly sunk beneath the waves, and Nella wrote in her Journal:

> Helen's style, even in *Teacher,* is rather ornate and dated. In his Christmas letter Lawrence Lee wrote [to Nella]: 'I liked Helen's book, but not so well as your Times Book Review article—it was *Magazine* rather.* It is understandable but her work seemed inconclusive, lacking in the sharpness and hardness worthy of Teacher. How could she, however, write objectively and deeply where such tenderness is felt?' With this I do not altogether agree. I think Helen was wonderfully objective, but I do think her style, quite properly in view of her mysticism, lacks sharpness of definition.

Was it really a matter of style and mysticism, or was it Helen's inability ever to cut free of Teacher, a dependency that is reflected in her book, where critical observations are started only to be quickly suffused in apologetics? But this raises the old problem: Was Helen's dependency on Teacher on balance a strengthening relationship? (This author believes it was.) Of course the unmystical Nella's own standards of what should go into a biography represented a kind of prudishness that muted problems and characteristics in the name of loyalty and good taste. Louise Hall Tharp's book about the Howes, *Three Saints and a Sinner,* had just appeared, and Nella wrote Polly:

> There is no privacy any more for the living or the dead. I don't see any particular point at this late hour in revealing that Dr. Howe wanted to divorce his wife—it was important to them, but not espe-

*"Helen Keller at Seventy-Five" by Nella Braddy Henney, *New York Times Magazine,* June 1955.

cially so to anyone else. . . . Up to now the Howes have done most of the writing about the family, but apparently from here on out other people are to rake over the coals. It is gruesome to think that this time will come for Helen also, but fortunately she has told everything and there will be no licking of the lips over revelations.

At about this time Nella obtained Helen's agreement to leave her papers and manuscripts to the Library of Congress. Nella distrusted the use the Foundation might make of Helen's papers. The decision caused considerable distress at the American Foundation for the Blind, which had been the custodian of those of Helen's papers that she had turned over and had assumed that the rest would follow upon the deaths of Helen and Polly. An article on the deaf-blind by Don Murray in the *Saturday Evening Post* once again raised the most troublesome question about the Teacher-Helen relationship when it stated that Teacher had made Helen "frighteningly dependent on one person." That challenged a part of the Sullivan-Keller canon that Nella guarded as zealously as anyone else. She wrote the editors of the *Post:*

It was always the aim of her teacher Anne Sullivan Macy to make Helen independent of her. How well she succeeded can be understood by anyone who has kept up with Miss Keller's writings during the last two decades and has followed her travels in virtually every part of the world as she has continued the great humanitarian work for the handicapped which she and her teacher began many years ago. . . . Even without Miss Thomson, Helen Keller would carry on, for at seventy-seven she still has tremendous energy and strength and, above all, the inspiration of 'Teacher.' She is dependent to be sure (aren't we all?) but not on any one person.

Although Nella leaped to Teacher's defense, she used the article to good effect with Polly, on whom she felt Helen was indeed "frighteningly dependent." Murray's article, she thought, had made Polly realize Helen's situation. "I think Polly will make an earnest attempt really to find someone to live with them."

The memory of Annie Sullivan had become a complicating factor in Nella's relationship with Polly, and perhaps even with Helen, for sometimes what Polly blurted out Helen thought but would not say. The issue arose acutely when the script of William Gibson's *The Miracle Worker* was sent to Nella to read. "I became very excited about it. Here at last, I thought, is something of great literary merit and dramatic power." She saw Gibson when he came down to New York on business. "Almost the first thing he said was, 'You can see that I am enamored of Annie Sullivan.'" He had based his script on Annie's letters in *The Story of My Life.* Of his own accord he had written into his contract with CBS that 10 percent of what he made would go to whatever charity Helen designated. But Nella saw breakers ahead and sent the script to Polly.

"Polly did not like *The Miracle Worker,*" she wrote Ken McCormick. "For one thing I think any treatment of the early years of Teacher's life makes her uncomfortable and she 'cringed' at some of the words put into Teacher's mouth. I had a few misgivings on this myself, but I felt that Teacher *was* crude when she first went to Alabama and that Mr. Gibson's deviations from the canon were justified for dramatic emphasis." She had the script brailled so that Helen might read it herself. "I am out on a limb," Nella entered in her journal, "because I liked the script very much more than Helen and Polly did and I shall be nervous until after it is all over." It was to be shown on *Playhouse 90.* "The responsibility was mine, for I had overriden Helen and Polly's objections." Everyone thought it was "magnificent," including, Nella thought, Polly. She arranged for Helen and Polly to meet Gibson and his wife, a psychiatrist at the Austen Riggs Clinic, at lunch at the Harvard Club. "They are prepared to like him and did, spending most of the time reminiscing about Teacher and the period when Polly began to take over under Teacher's watchful eye."

"Polly began 1957 in a state of nervous exhaustion," Nella wrote, adding, "I have never known Polly so close to the absolute breaking point." That lent urgency to the search for a substitute. Helen's friends set great store in her niece Katherine Tyson, a newspaperwoman in Montgomery who lived there with her mother. The results were recorded by Nella:

One of the pipe dreams about Helen had gone a-glimmering. Polly has been saying since last summer that Katherine Tyson would come up to take over, that she was fully prepared and very willing. I told Polly that she ought to be introduced to the people with whom they deal in shopping and Polly wrote her to suggest that she spend a week with them this summer and get acquainted with them. It now appears that Katherine has no intention of uprooting herself, she likes her job, is doing well in it, and besides feels that she must be with her mother.

She will come to tide over and she and Mildred and Brooks and Ravia are more than ready to supply a home to Helen or Polly, but it would have to be in Alabama or Texas and Polly said Helen wouldn't like that. This is *very* disturbing.

Despite the signs of an approaching breakdown, in May Polly escorted Helen to Iceland—at the request of the State Department—and to Scandinavia.

Disasters struck upon their return. First Helen checked into the hospital for a foot operation, to have a callus removed from the bottom of her foot, as Polly put it. But the callus was a bone tumor, which turned out not to be malignant but did require the removal of a toe. The operation was performed at Memorial Hospital by a surgeon who had been recommended by Jimmy Adams. The surgeon had just performed an operation on Mrs. Adams's stomach, and the banker had financed some of the research upon which he was engaged. The episode divided Helen's friends—Adams and the trustees on one side, Kit Cornell and Nella on the other. There were the usual controversies about the skill of the surgeon, whom one doctor consulted by Kit called a butcher and a charlatan. He was, in fact—as Nella subsequently acknowledged—"a great surgeon"; but Kit's and Nella's actions deeply offended Jimmy Adams, who considered himself as solicitous of Helen's interests as they were. "Very shocked," Nella recorded a few weeks later, "to learn in the evening from Nancy that Jimmy Adams has turned violently against us or at least some of us: Kit, Nancy, Lillian and me."

Helen was scarcely back home when the catastrophe all had long feared, happened. Polly was felled by a cerebral hemorrhage while she and Helen were alone at Arcan Ridge. "In all my imaginings," recorded Nella, who herself was in the hospital for an operation on her left eyelid, "I had never thought Polly and I might both be struck at once, leaving Helen, at least temporarily, terribly alone." As soon as Nella was out of the hospital she hurried to Arcan Ridge. She went with considerable trepidation. "I had been told how Polly always broke down and cried when anyone came in and I knew of the relapse that followed Robert Barnett's visit." Just because of the closeness of Nella's relationship to Helen and Polly, she feared that "jealousy or resentment" might flare up; but when she put her arms around Polly and said in her deep voice, "We are not licked yet," Polly did not resist.

She and Helen lunched on trays at Polly's bedside. Afterward Helen led her into the study and asked her to close the door for privacy. Then Helen described in meticulous detail the circumstances of Polly's collapse. They had gone down to the kitchen to fix some lunch when Polly began to sway and have trouble breathing. She managed to tell Helen that she wanted to go out on the terrace for air. It was cold, and Helen persuaded Polly to come in, but Polly was intent on preparing lunch. As fast as she turned on the burners of the electric stove, Helen turned them off. Polly's legs began to buckle, and Helen led her to the bathroom. Polly gave up trying to fix lunch but would not lie down, insisting on going back to the stove. Her legs buckled again, and Helen got her to her feet. She persuaded her to sit down, but Polly struggled to her feet again and fell to the floor. Helen felt Polly's pounding temples. Finally the postman, seeing the open terrace door, came in—this was two and a half hours after Polly was stricken—and help was summoned. But it had been a dreadful ordeal for Helen.

Two nurses, Mrs. Miller and Mrs. Winifred Corbally, now spelled each other. Mrs. Seide, "a little saint" according to Nella, was in and out to handle the mail. A Finnish couple who had worked for Baruch was tried out. As Polly saw the reign of the household slip from her hands, her depression deepened. "How long, O Lord?" became her constant refrain. But Nella was concerned for Helen:

> Ever since Teacher's death Polly has been urged with reason, with prayer, with love, with terror, to provide a substitute for herself for Helen. All in vain. 'When the time comes,' she has said to me, 'I will train somebody.' The time is here and nothing is farther from her mind. She is so immersed in herself and why-did-this-have-to-happen-to-me that she gives small thought to Helen. The old pitiful jealousy is still there.

Evelyn Seide knew the manual language but did not dare to use it in Polly's presence. Mrs. Corbally and Mrs. Miller, quickly sensing the distress it caused Polly to have anyone else do anything for Helen, had refrained from learning the alphabet. Even Nella's presence caused her anxiety. "I do have things I must talk with Helen about," Nella recorded, "and I am now the only one who can keep her generally informed." In one talk they had in private Helen told her, " 'It is a pity that I have never been able to feel towards Polly as I did towards Teacher.' And I told her that no one feels towards anyone else as we felt towards Teacher. We spoke of Polly's possessiveness (I am the only one Polly will allow to spell to Helen) and Mrs. Corbally and Nell [Mrs. Miller] both say that what she resents most is having anyone else do anything for Helen, even moving a chair for her. 'Too much so,' Helen said, 'but I have always had my work and have been able to manage.' "

William Ziegler died. The group around Kit Cornell—and Helen herself—wanted Dr. David Levy, an outstanding psychiatrist, to succeed him as one of Helen's trustees; but the Foundation trustees selected Jansen Noyes, Jr., of Hemphill, Noyes as president of the Foundation and as one of Helen's trustees.

During the summer Helen contracted a virus with nausea and vomiting. The doctor was summoned by Mrs. Seide, and Polly was told about it; but full of her own ailments, she was completely unconcerned with Helen's. When Nella heard this, she wrote, "Helen's aloneness hardly bears thinking about." She went up to Arcan Ridge and snatched a moment's talk with Helen alone:

N. Polly doesn't like to have anyone but herself do things for you.
H. Isn't it pathetic!
N. Polly grows tired of people.
H. Alas!
N. I fear she is now growing tired of Mrs. Corbally.
H. I am afraid she is. I am sorry, she is a sweet girl.
N. If Mrs. Corbally goes you will have to have someone else in her place.

Helen's cautious unresponsiveness to Nella's probings and leading questions suggested that she understood quite well not only Polly's limitations, but also her own handicaps that made Polly's loyal service irreplaceable. Occasionally Helen betrayed her almost heartbreakingly realistic perception of her total dependence on others. She could never allow herself to forget that devoted friends like Nella and Lenore Smith, or her own kin, when confronted with the possibility of giving up their private lives in order to marry their fortunes to hers, always drew back from becoming that "other self" that Teacher had once said every blind person needs to enable him to transcend his handicap. In *The Open Door,* a selection of excerpts from Helen's writings that Doubleday published in 1957 with an introduction by Katharine Cornell, Helen wrote:

No one knows—no one can know—the bitter denials of limitation better than I do. I am not deceived about my situation. It is not true that I am not sad or rebellious; but long ago I determined not to complain. The mortally wounded must strive to live out their days cheerfully for the sake of the others. That is what religion is for—to keep the heart brave to fight out to the end with a smiling face. This may not be a very lofty ambition, but it is a far cry from surrendering to fate. But to get the better of fate even to this extent one must have work and the solace of friendship and an unwavering faith in God's Plan of Good.

Nella described the situation with Polly to Lenore Smith, who drove over from Wolfeboro to Foss Mountain in September:

As far as I know Lenore is the last person alive who called Teacher Annie; it was a younger generation that began calling her Teacher. I asked her if Teacher had died of cancer and she said she really didn't know, rather thought so, but had never heard the word pronounced and she was in the house that last week. . . . Teacher's great fascination, to women as well as men; it was she rather than Helen who attracted John Macy, Phil Smith, Dr. Neilson, and Ned Holmes, all of whom learned the manual alphabet so as to talk with Helen. Teacher *never* left Helen out, never allowed anyone else to leave her out; as long as she lived she kept encouraging other people to use the alphabet and she was always ready to turn Helen over to anyone capable of spelling to her.

Another of Helen's links with the past was severed in October when Major Migel, in his early nineties, died. Nella hoped that either Dr. Levy or Amelia would replace him as one of Helen's trustees:

It was Amelia who kept him from turning against Polly to a degree that might have ousted Polly. He never liked Polly, nor she him. One of Polly's special resentments was that while Teacher was alive Mr. Migel was lavish with his gifts. Those stopped abruptly after Teacher's death. One of Mr. Migel's special resentments against Polly was her total lack of appreciation for what Amelia did to get the house at Arcan Ridge rebuilt. . . . Amelia would quiet him by saying, 'Remember that Polly has kept Helen active for 20 years.'

The Major was replaced by his son Richard, a good man, but not the commanding figure his father had been. Amelia had been his principal advocate. The person chosen had to be someone of wealth from the AFB board, she explained to Nella. That would leave Jimmy Adams in his position as "financial dictator," Nella wrote gloomily. "Kit and I agreed last night over the telephone that we (meaning her and Nancy and the Levys and me) cannot work with him. He has a rabid hate for us all." But later when Polly had convulsions and had to be rushed to Bridgeport Hospital, "Jimmy proved to be a bulwark as he has in the past—got around-the-clock nurses for Polly and in general took charge."

Peter Adams, the son of James Adams, has described his parents' relationship with Helen. Peter had learned the manual language in order to be able to talk with Helen directly and as an undergraduate had written her biography. "I think of my dad and my mother as her neighbors rather than trustees. What they did for her in her last thirty years was the neighborly act of helping her to do what she wanted to do." Far from trying to shape Helen in his own image, Jim Adams—whose basic interest was in medical research rather than health care—found himself helping a woman who was constantly on the go to raise money for treatment rather than research. "But who was he to tell Helen Keller how to spend her time? Within two years after Helen died, my father was out of the business of being a neighbor and became leader of an organization—Research to Prevent Blindness—something he had never been able to persuade Helen to take a moment's interest in. If as a trustee he had thought to shape her, this would surely be the documentary record of a failure, and my father was a very persuasive man."

With Polly in the hospital, communication with Helen was easier. It was she, not Polly, Nella learned, who had floated the idea that they should move into a smaller, cozier house. That surprised Nella. She and Evelyn had thought the idea was Polly's—to get a place where there would be no room for anyone but herself and Helen.

Certain issues still aroused Helen's interest. "Peace is very much on Helen's mind," Nella wrote, "She has spoken of it every time I have seen her during the past couple of years. She feels that she betrayed a sacred thing when she laid aside her pacifism during the last war and is determined not to do it again. She says that Polly will stand by her on this and I tell her that I hope I shall have the strength to do it."

The pullings and haulings between the Cornell group on one side and her trustees on the other, and the pressure to find a "Polly's Polly," caused

Helen to withdraw further into her shell. "I am old and I am tired," she said one day to Mrs. Corbally. "I want to be left alone to lead my life the way I want to." Mrs. Corbally told Nella that Miss Helen was especially happy when she was with her books and had spoken of how much there was to read before the end came.

Nella did not go to Arcan Ridge for Helen's seventy-ninth birthday; she feared that her presence might upset Polly. Friends who did visit Arcan Ridge found the place gloomy. If they arrived without warning, Polly refused to see them, and Helen refused to come down without Polly. They had to content themselves with Mrs. Seide and Mrs. Corbally and went away feeling that Helen was a prisoner—but that, commented Nella, "is by Helen's choice." Helen no longer went for drives in the car, which she once had enjoyed doing. "I am old and tired," she protested, "and I want to be left alone."

One of the few developments that stirred her interest was the progress of *The Miracle Worker*. "Bill [Gibson] wrote her about the developments and she read the letter to the household." The play—perhaps just because it was so extraordinarily good—precipitated a break between Nella and Helen's trustees and finally between Helen and Nella. After the *Playhouse 90* telecast plans took shape to bring it to Broadway and perhaps to make a movie of it. Nella had scrupulously kept Helen and Polly informed about every stage of the negotiations and dealings with Gibson. But after Polly's stroke communication became more difficult. "Bill Gibson telephoned me the other day," she wrote Helen in August 1958. His *Two for the Seesaw* was having a "fabulous success," and he proposed to pour a large part of his profits into putting *The Miracle Worker* on the stage. They were all very fortunate, she added, in having Bill Gibson do it. In October she again wrote Helen: "With definite plans to bring *TMW* to the Broadway stage I want to recapitulate. We have already granted Bill Gibson the dramatic rights to the play—we did this before it appeared on television. Now we must sign a supplementary contract which is primarily concerned with the percentage of the money that we are to receive." *TMW* might bring in "a great deal of money, especially if the play is afterwards made into a movie." Under the supplementary contract "we shall get 20 per cent of all that Bill gets—that is, 20 per cent of his share of the gross proceeds. This will be divided equally between us, half to you because of *The Story of My Life*, half to me because of *Anne Sullivan Macy*." Seven copies of the contract had to be signed, each page initialed by the signatories. "I shall of course relieve you of this chore by using my Power of

Attorney, but I do want to keep you and Polly fully abreast of what is going on and to have your approval at every stage."

Helen's trustees, Jimmy Adams particularly, had gotten wind of the agreement with Gibson and understandably were vexed that Nella had not consulted them. Her first reaction was impatient irritation. "Mr. Adams never did call me and I am not going to call him," she informed Evelyn Seide, "but if he bothers you again simply refer him to me again and I will answer any questions he wants to ask. . . . There has been no secret about the possibility of a play and a movie for *TMW* since the first agreement was signed in 1956." A few days later the trustees formally demanded that Nella send them copies of the contract with Gibson as well as her power of attorney. Polly was in no condition to review proposals submitted to Helen, they explained, so they had "now assumed the duty of considering and advising upon any important steps taken in Helen Keller's behalf." Nella underestimated the strength of Adams's as well as the Foundation's annoyance with her. She felt sure, moreover, of Helen's support. "Some anxieties can be kept from Helen—this long drawn out hassle about the power of attorney she gave me for instance," she recorded at the end of June.

At the request of Jansen Noyes, Sullivan and Cromwell had examined the various documents connected with Helen's granting Nella the power of attorney and concluded that Helen had every right to make such a grant and that it would be "in force and effect until Miss Keller decides to revoke it." Adams had gone to Europe, and Noyes, whom Nella found more sympathetic and kindly, met with her; she described to him how she had exercised her powers under the grant:

> I felt better after talking with you—I have really been sick with worry about this whole thing—in fact, more than once since 1928 when Mrs. Macy asked me to keep an eye on Helen's writings, I have been sick with worry. I have always felt that if I made a wrong decision I could never face myself afterwards—and I have had to go out on many a shaky limb. I don't mean to bother you, but it is good to know I have someone I can turn to if need be.

Noyes, in a friendly letter, advised Nella that it would be in her best interest "to submit any further contracts to the Trustees for review by their counsel. I rather feel that this will give you considerable peace of mind

and would allow the Trustees to assure themselves of having done everything which they possibly can in Helen's behalf.''

From the moment of its tryout in Boston the stage version of *The Miracle
Worker* was a smash hit. A troubled Anne Bancroft, who played the part
of Annie Sullivan, came to see Nella in Boston. The reaction of the
audience during the curtain calls had distressed her. The first round of
applause was as strong for her as it was for Patty Duke, who played Helen.
After that, there was barely a polite trickle of applause for Miss Bancroft.
''I told her it had always been like that with Teacher, the people would
trample her so as to get at Helen.''

On December 18 Helen left an uncharacteristic and disturbing message
for Nella:

> Fri. Dec. 18 as Helen left for the hospital with Mrs. Corbally she said
> to Nell. If Mrs. Henney telephones, tell her not to come up. I am too
> disturbed to see anybody. This hurt, but I knew then that she had
> reached the stage that she occupied during Teacher's last days. She
> is totally inaccessible to anybody her whole mind concentrated upon
> Polly. . . .

But Nella misread what was brewing. Helen had turned against her. On
January 15, 1960, she sent Nella a cold note signed by witnesses:

> Dear Nella:
>
> Due to Polly's illness I have decided that all of my business affairs
> should be handled by my personal trustees, James S. Adams, Richard
> H. Migel, and Jansen Noyes, Jr.
>
> I therefore desire to cancel the power of attorney granted by me to
> you on March 5, 1948.
>
> I am deeply grateful to you for all you have done to help me with
> my books and articles.
>
> > Sincerely yours,
> > Helen Keller

The abrupt lawyer's note—and Helen's unwillingness to communicate
with a friend whose whole existence in recent years had been devoted to

serving her—paralyzed Nella, the more so since she did not know what had happened. She sought comfort from Nancy Hamilton and recorded afterward, "Helen is now without an intimate friend, within her family or on the outside, though her family is devoted and she has many friends who are as devoted as they have been allowed to be."

Nella's suspicions centered on Polly. As she wrote Lenore:

> I don't think anyone could quite realize what a blockbuster it was for me on the morning of January 16 when I read (special delivery) Helen's letter repudiating me, but you more than most.
>
> During the summer I became aware that Polly was developing an increasing hostility to *The Miracle Worker*. I sympathized with her because I knew that it was unbearable to her to have anything important connected with Helen going on without her. In her half-mad mind she began to feed Helen with just what sort of half-mad lies I do not know. At any rate, her final gift to me was the destruction of Helen's confidence in me. Helen has refused to see me and so I am cloudy in details. . . .
>
> Helen's trustees have taken over in all departments. One of them at least is a very good man, but Helen is left without an intimate friend and I see breakers and shoals ahead. So do the trustees and now they want to patch up things between Helen and me. It may be too late, but I will of course always do all I can for her.

"The long suspense continues," Nella recorded on March 11, "and I remain in darkness trying to imagine what the worst possible outcome can be so as to brace myself for it. No word from anyone for about a month. Mrs. Corbally still insists that everything is going to be all right, that truth and right must prevail, and Mr. Noyes was still hopeful when I last talked with him. . . . Dread receiving the mail every morning."

Nancy Hamilton commiserated with her. "Nancy thinks he [Jim Adams] more than Polly is responsible for Helen's flare-up over *The Miracle Worker*. I think he had his part in it and that he played it with glee, but I still think Polly's jealousy was the primary cause."

Was it Polly? Helen never explained. When Mildred came north she tried to reconcile the two. "She's on my side, but Helen simply takes her hand away when my name is mentioned. I think Helen must know that she has done wrong—at least in not seeing me. I still have no idea what terrible thought was planted in her mind." Even the trustees were distressed. They were very firm about taking away Nella's power of attorney and ensuring that Helen's papers and the profits from the movie based on *The Miracle Worker* came to the Foundation. But they were aware that the break with Nella left an emptiness in Helen's life that none of them could fill.

What, then, might have occasioned Helen's turning her back on her old friend? Back in 1934 when the contract for *Anne Sullivan Macy* was negotiated, Teacher had resented Nella's offer to split the profits from the book with her only during Teacher's lifetime and had refused to sign the contract, saying that the book was Nella's. At the time Polly had written Migel, "Teacher will never speak of this but I thought you should know." Undoubtedly Helen knew of this, but if she did not, Polly would have reminded her when the trustees raised the issue of whether any of the profits from the movie should go to Nella. Where an injury to Teacher was concerned Helen was unforgiving. Peter Salmon, the genial Irishman to whom she would leave a considerable sum of money in her will out of gratitude for his work in showing that the deaf-blind could do almost everything the blind could, learned that the deaf-blind have "a way of dropping people." Once they become persuaded that they are being exploited or taken advantage of, they will turn their back on the offending person or group with an implacable finality. "When Helen Keller dropped someone, she dropped him." Conceivably, too, in the halcyon days of Nella's friendship with Polly, she might have spoken very freely about Teacher's unwillingness to have Helen write her story for fear that she would sentimentalize it. Teacher's attitude had been a sore point with Helen at the time, and that memory would have been rendered more painful in light of the failure of her own book about Teacher—a book that Nella had praised extravagantly. This is the writer's hunch; Helen left no explanation.

"I had always intended to write something about Polly and Helen since 1936 and Polly expected me to do it," Nella sadly recorded. "But I am not sure that I can now. And I would not in any case offer anything for publication until after Helen's death."

"The doctor does not think she will live much longer," Helen advised Kit after spending Christmas and New Year's with Polly in the hospital. "It has been heartbreaking for me to realize how she has been sacrificed to help my efforts in behalf of the blind, she was always so brave and eager to push the work for which Teacher had fitted us both. I can only pray that she may soon be among the friends awaiting me in Heaven, strong and full of joy in the beautiful work they have done on earth."

On March 21, 1960, Polly died. "Helen took it quietly," Nella recorded, "and sent beautiful cables (so Evelyn told me later) to Bert and Margaret [Thomson]." "Our sweet Polly has left me," she telegraphed Polly's brother the minister. "I saw her yesterday and I thank God that the years of anguish are over." Later she wrote him at greater length: "Now I sit by her empty chair thinking of the fidelity with which she helped me in my difficult work and the tireless cheer with which she took part in our amazing adventures. I am sure that now they have met in Heaven, Teacher is prouder of Polly than ever. It will be most lonely for me, but I shall rejoice in Polly's beautiful new life."

In Polly's will she left everything except for some personal objects to her family in Scotland. Her holdings in securities, according to figures penciled in by Amelia in 1959, totaled $80,457. She had savings accounts in four different banks amounting to another $36,504. Her furs, including a mink coat, were valued for insurance purposes at $8,000, and her jewelry at $14,925.

The funeral services were in Bridgeport. Phillips Keller and Mildred Tyson were present. Nella joined Nancy and other friends at Grand Central Station for the trip up. "Problems," she wrote afterward. "Who will dress Helen now? Not E . . . she hasn't the taste and the dress-makers at Bendel's and Saks cannot be trusted. . . . Mildred? Nancy? Who will rehearse her speeches with her and stand beside her on the platform as interpreter? I think there will probably be no more major speeches. . . . Who to watch her letters to make sure she is not tricked into support of Communism or some other ism?"

The trustees had arranged for the urn containing Polly's ashes to be deposited next to Teacher's at the National Cathedral. Helen tried to stop that. "Helen balky. Says Polly has already had a service in Bridgeport and that's enough." She declined to attend the committal service in Washington when Noyes took Polly's ashes down. Mr. Noyes, a Washington friend wrote Lenore Smith, "was most friendly and spoke of Helen's very positive belief that all that mattered was that she would meet Polly in Heaven."

But so far as the world was concerned, Helen wanted it to realize that she and Teacher were bound to each other in a way that admitted no others.

XLII

"As Long as I Have Breath"

". . . to awake from a troubled dream . . ."

On Helen's eightieth birthday there were the usual tributes and interviews. Robert Duffus did the piece for *The New York Times Magazine* —not Nella this time—and the *Herald-Tribune* printed a question-and-answer interview in its *This Week* section. Asked in the latter about her plans for the immediate future, Helen replied with her usual zest, "I will always—as long as I have breath—work for the handicapped." And when the same interviewer asked her for a statement of her basic philosophy, her indomitable spirit rose above the Verduns, Hiroshimas, Auschwitzes and Gulags that had happened in the years since she had written *Optimism* as she affirmed: "God gave us life for happiness not misery. And I believe that happiness, attained, should be shared." Who knows, Robert Duffus speculated, "what Helen Keller would have achieved if she had not been handicapped." Perhaps, he added, the conquest of her limitations was necessary to the realization of her "high intelligence and purity of soul." She agreed; "I have made my limitations tools of learning and true joy," she told the interviewer.

She continued to do the things she had always done, as much as the energies of an eighty-year-old woman permitted; and the information that was communicated to her by those relative tyros in the manual language, Mrs. Seide and Mrs. Corbally, enabled her to stay abreast of events. Both had learned to use the manual language, despite Polly's resistance; both were loyal and conscientious. But neither had Polly's sixth-sense understanding of what Helen wanted and needed to know of Polly, not to mention Teacher. But they carried on as best they could. At Helen's eightieth birthday luncheon at the Gotham Hotel, where Helen presented the first Helen Keller International Award to blind Colonel Edwin A. Baker, the head of the Canadian Institute for the Blind, Evelyn spelled the words of the ceremony into Helen's hand and repeated to the audience what she said. Mildred was in the audience (she had stayed on at Arcan Ridge after Polly's funeral) and later went with Helen, as did Mrs. Corbally, to the Radcliffe commencement. There Helen was to dedicate the Anne Sullivan Macy Memorial Fountain. The Radcliffe alumnae had written her a year earlier asking for a list of flowers in her garden. When the time came for her to speak she suddenly said, "I haven't seen the garden and until I do I shall not speak." Slightly startled herself, Mrs. Corbally explained the situation to the president of the alumnae and, while the audience waited, they went to the fountain which overlooked the Helen Keller Garden. Helen knelt down and smelled the flowers and all that she chose to say was "Water!" But back on the platform she exclaimed: "What a marvelous symbol this garden is of the life my Teacher wrought for me. . . . I am thrilled more than ever by the miracle that turned me from a dumb wild creature into a joyous child and enlarged my mind—until lo! it received the gifts of Radcliffe College and the opportunity to build up a brighter world for the unfortunate."

From Cambridge they went to visit Katharine Cornell at the Vineyard. The weather was foul and Kit came to fetch them in a private boat. She passed out yellow slickers and Helen clambered over the other boats to board Kit's with the spryness of a youngster. The next day it was fine and she went for a swim in the surf. Mildred was frightened for her. "She swims," Mrs. Corbally assured her, "and I definitely swim." The Leonard Bernsteins came for dinner. Afterward he played and Nancy Hamilton steered Helen over to the piano so that she could catch its vibrations. He began with "a funeral-like dirge and she kept time to that," recalled Mrs. Corbally.

Abruptly he shifted to a light medley of his own and she immediately shifted her beat. "He jumped up overcome and left the room." "I hope you will never leave her," Dr. Levy said to Winnie [Corbally] as he bade them good-night.

Another guest at Kit's was Francis Robinson, her company manager. He was tall and courtly and hailed from the same part of Alabama as the

Kellers. In the weekly letter that he wrote his mother, he told of his
meeting:

> I am still under the spell of Helen Keller. She said she liked my laugh.
> Her sister was there, a lovely lady from Montgomery, Alabama.
> . . . I asked when she learned the manual speech and she said, 'Oh,
> Helen taught it to us before we could spell!' God looks after his own.
> When Polly Thomson went in the hospital for what they knew was
> the last time the sweet nurse, a little Connecticut lady, took up manual
> and has mastered it—since December. Not as fast as Polly of course
> but Helen has lost no contact with the outside world. Her silences
> stab you. She can't be in on everything all the time and I watch and
> marvel at the patience, her manners at the table, never spills a drop
> of anything.

The eightieth birthday was difficult for Nella. She had been invited to
the luncheon at the Gotham. Eric Boulter had asked Helen whether Nella
should be included and she had said yes, but Nancy Hamilton had told
Eric that that was not good enough, and Nella agreed: "I think I might
easily have run the risk of public repudiation." Evelyn Seide later described the telegrams that had poured in, including one from the presidential candidate Vice-President Richard Nixon. "Helen jerked her hand
away as soon as she realized from whom it came."

A letter from Nella to Nancy Hamilton informed her of a significant
change in Helen's will:

> Helen's papers will not go to the Library of Congress as planned, but
> to the American Foundation for the Blind and that in turn means I
> think that no scholar of the future will ever be able to study unexpur-
> gated records. My papers will go to the Library of Congress, but they
> are so full of indiscretions that they will have to bear a legend 'Not
> to be opened until——.' I think we should all get together on this and
> maybe gather up photostats of revealing letters that the owners want
> to keep. No hurry on this score, but a bland inhuman picture of
> Helen ought not to stand. David said Helen was captive. I add in
> chains.

Nella later changed her mind and left her papers to Perkins rather than
the Library of Congress—the one place she was determined to keep them

from was the Foundation. Neither institution has expurgated the records that were made available to them.

Nella and the group around Katharine Cornell considered Helen "a captive" of the Foundation, but that was true only in the sense that with Polly's death and Nella's banishment she had to rely on assistants chosen by the Foundation. Jimmy Adams, whose Greenwich estate was not too far from Arcan Ridge, kept a solicitous eye out for Helen's needs. To staff the household adequately in the final days of Polly's illness he had put together a special fund, to which his own family foundation and the Pfeiffer Foundation each pledged $5,000 a year and Elmer Bobst $2,500 a year for five years, over and above Helen's other income.

" 'Isn't Helen wonderful?' Jimmy Adams said to Nancy on Helen's birthday. 'Isn't she beautiful? Perfectly free now and happier than she has ever been, making her own decisions, etc., etc.' All but said, 'Isn't it marvellous that Polly isn't around any more?' "

"Those were the fun years," insisted Winnie Corbally. "It was a time of her life when she could have fun. Miss Helen was a rogue. . . . We had oodles of fun. We would go to a hot-dog stand. Polly Thomson would turn in her grave. She would never allow hot dogs in the house. But Miss Helen loved them. 'Don't forget the mustard,' she would say." Winnie accompanied her to Montgomery to Mildred's—"a charming Southern lady"—and they went to Dallas to visit Phillips and his wife, Ravia—"I know she would have loved to have lived near them." Winnie went to great pains to keep Helen's family informed of her doings. That was different from Polly, who, knowing how Helen felt, had discouraged too much closeness.

In early September as Nella and Keith sat after dinner in their Foss Mountain retreat, the telephone rang. A man's voice that Nella did not recognize came over the telephone:

'This is one of your boyfriends!' I said I was always glad to hear from a boyfriend and then he said 'I have some of your girl friends here who want to talk with you!' I did not know that it was Eddie [Clark] until Ethel came on and said Helen wanted to speak to me. My name had come up naturally in the course of the evening's talk and they began reminiscing about the wonderful times we have all had together in the past, like that marvellous evening with the Marches after *Long Day's Journey into Night.* Presently Eddie said, 'Why don't we call Nella?' This too was natural, every now and then when the girls were having a good time at the Clarks Eddie and Ethel used to call to say wish you were here. When Helen came on she asked what Keith was doing and sent him her love; she asked about the coons and said she might come up some time. Mrs. Corbally spelled to her what I said. I was too shook up to say much. I asked Mrs. Corbally if any pressure had been put on Helen and she said No. Eddie signed off and said Helen was beaming. After he had driven Helen and Mrs. C. home Ethel called me back to assure me again that there was no pressure on Helen, that she seemed happy, that it had been a very happy evening and they would all sleep better because of it. She said the last thing Mrs. Corbally said as they were leaving was I am so glad it happened. Ethel thinks Mrs. C. adequate as interpreter for Helen, that she seems to be a good woman, nothing vicious about her (this no doubt a side reference to one who we do think is vicious). I am so glad that this renewal of contact came about in a way that was easy for Helen, I think she has wanted an opening. I have much to be grateful to the Clarks for.

Some correspondence ensued, but the old intimacy was finished. They did not see each other again. Nella had been hurt too badly to make overtures that might be rejected, and Helen's vital energies were not up to the task of seeking Nella out. And what had caused the breach remained unexplained. Checks began to arrive from the film of *The Miracle Worker*. "I became slightly nauseated as I endorsed it," Nella recorded, "thinking what it had cost me and Helen." Nella decided to donate $10,000 to the American Foundation for the Blind for a Polly Thomson Memorial Room. Didn't she want the money to be used for a joint memorial to Polly and Teacher? Noyes inquired. "I said No, it should be for Polly alone."

Helen did not agree with Nella's decision:

I appreciate your kindness in wishing to remember Polly in your will. There is one sentence in your letter which causes me to feel that you are mistaken with regard to Teacher. So far as I know, nothing has been done concretely in her memory. You know it was she who guided me through the difficulties and complications I met when I decided to cast my life with the American Foundation for the Blind. It was from her wisdom and understanding of the sightless that Polly gained her ability to carry on our activities. We who knew and loved Polly for her splendid and tireless efforts will always honor her, but

I cannot help feeling that Teacher's share in my Foundation enterprise was the most important part.

So many engagements are turning up before I go south. I do not know if I can see you until I come back sometimes in the winter. With affectionate greetings to you and Keith.

But why Polly alone? What was in Nella's mind? Had she overcome her original belief that Polly was responsible for Helen's turning her back on her? Was she now inclined to blame Helen?

She left her own papers, including many of Annie's, as well as her notes for her biography of Teacher, to the Perkins Institution. She did so on the flimsy ground that Teacher had been a product of Perkins. The decision implicitly underscored her own special relationship to Teacher who, in her eyes, was the more remarkable of the two.

A routine of sorts had been established at Arcan Ridge. The house was fully staffed, managed by Mrs. Seide, who was there almost every day. She and her husband had declined Bob Barnett's suggestion that they move to Arcan Ridge. She had pleaded the need to take care of an aging and ailing mother. For the trustees Jimmy Adams made Helen his special responsibility. They swam in his pool, spent Christmas eve with his family. Helen's old charm still worked. "Everyone," said Barnett, "wanted to adopt Helen Keller." But she was a frail woman, whose age was partly concealed by the wig she constantly wore. She spent much of the winter in Dallas with Phillips: "I am sure Sister Helen and Mrs. Corbally are enjoying their stay here in Texas. . . . I do not think we will have any trouble keeping them here until the weather gets much better at Arcan Ridge," Phillips wrote Adams. "We think Mrs. Corbally is really a Godsend and represents the perfect companion for Sister Helen." Mrs. Corbally was a sweet, helpful woman, Nella noted. Both she and Evelyn Seide knew the manual language, but neither was competent to fill in the larger picture for Helen. Anne Bancroft came to see Nella again. "Who does [Helen] have to talk to?" the actress asked Nella. "No one about the big things," Nella replied. "Mrs. Corbally has more taste and sensitivity than Evelyn, but no more education."

Then in October 1961 Helen suffered a slight stroke. She had gone to Greenwich to discuss some revisions in her will with Adams. She had a cocktail and then as they proceeded toward the dining room suddenly complained, "I feel funny." Mrs. Corbally made her sit down. She seemed to recover and went on to enjoy a hearty lunch. But back at Arcan Ridge, Mrs. Corbally summoned her doctor, who immediately diagnosed a stroke and sent her to the hospital in Bridgeport for tests. Adams looked in on her a few weeks later. She had "aged greatly during the past month. From time to time she seemed to feel that she is living back in the period with Teacher and John Macy, but other than this I thought her mind seemed quite clear and normal, although certainly slower than usual."

Adams sent a copy of this letter to Helen's third trustee, Richard Migel, and also enclosed Dr. Morris B. Chick's report:

> I had Drs. Paget and Bayliss see her and they both concur with my feelings that she had suffered a mild stroke approximately one month ago. This has left her with a slight mental confusion at times but no outward evidence of paralysis.
>
> It is my opinion that Miss Keller has reached a stage in her life where she will have to completely retire from public appearances and from here on in will have to be cared for with round-the-clock nursing service. She is not now, and probably never will be, capable of taking long trips or attending benefits. I suppose we must all realize that Miss Helen is 81 years of age and old age comes to all of us. We all realize what a great service she has done in the past and now I believe it is time that she be retired. Her condition is static and I cannot offer much hope for further improvement. I think we can be glad that she seems content and is in no obvious distress.

There were periods of alertness, but Helen's ability and interest in communicating with the outside world diminished markedly. Mrs. Corbally took over handling her correspondence, especially with her family. "Miss Helen is beside me," she wrote Mildred and Phillips at the end of 1963, "and when I told her I was writing to you she said, 'My affectionate love to all.'"

She suffered a series of slight strokes—"a break in one of the smaller blood vessels," the doctor described one to Mrs. Corbally. "There was nothing alarming at any time—just a general breaking down that cannot be prevented." She had not improved, Winnie's next letter informed the family. "She is certainly getting older and is very very bent over and walks very poorly—one needs to use great care when taking her from one place to another."

For the first time since she and Annie had set up house together, Helen's self reliance left her. Polly's death, the rejection of Nella, her strokes, made her totally dependent on her trustees, her family and Mrs. Corbally. She had lost control of her life. Almost unconsciously, because of who and what they were, those around her tried to turn her into something other than she had been. Her brother Phillips tried to eliminate the participation of a Swedenborgian minister from her funeral service "when the time comes." He and Mildred would prefer a prominent Presbyterian minister, he wrote Winnie. "I understand that at one time Sister Helen was more or less interested in the Swedenborgian faith with which none of us are very familiar, but I am sure also that she has had little connection with or interest in Swedenborgism."

Jansen Noyes stopped that. He sent Phillips a copy of a statement Helen had drafted outlining clearly her own desires. Noyes, Adams and Richard Migel felt "an obligation to follow Helen's own expressed wishes, and that we should stick with the plans which had been made earlier." Phillips retreated: "Naturally Sister Helen's wishes in this matter are of first consideration to us all and if she said Mr. Priestnal (a Swedenborgian) was her choice it is entirely satisfactory to me."

It was the time of Martin Luther King, of racial boycott and protests in Alabama, of the marches on Selma. The reactions of Phillips and Mildred were typically those of the white South and Mrs. Corbally sympathized with them: "Mr. FBI Hoover surely did tell M.L. King what he thought of him and he is not backing down one bit," she wrote Phillips, unaware evidently that Helen had, fifty years earlier, stirred up a row in Selma by a contribution to the NAACP, and that she loathed the witch-hunters. "The best thing the old U.S. can do is make mighty sure they hang on to the FBI and Hoover," her letter continued. Mike Wallace in a series called *Biography* did what he called a "valentine" to Helen Keller. But at the very end of the segment he portrayed Helen in the years since Polly's death as "alone" except for an inner radiance. He did not mention Mrs. Corbally. She wrote Phillips a little resentful. "In my book he is a first class 'Parlor Pink' and that's all," the sympathetic Phillips replied.

Helen said nothing. How much she was aware of is unclear. "My poor darling is walking that last mile so very slowly," Mrs. Corbally wrote Phillips in September 1967. Helen's trustees had a change of heart about arrangements for her funeral. It seemed unnecessary to have a service in Connecticut as well as at the National Cathedral, so they eliminated the former, and Adams asked Barnett to write a nice note to the Swedenborgian minister, the Reverend Mr. Priestnal, explaining why there would be no need for him. "Dear Jim," Phillips wrote Adams from Dallas. "Just a note to express to you again the appreciation of the Keller family for the change you are making in the funeral arrangements when and as required. We never went for the Swedenborgian stuff at all and it was hanging regretfully over our heads."

Mrs. Carolyn Lyon Remington of Rochester, a daughter of the Edmund Lyon who had taken Helen and Teacher to Niagara Falls in 1893, on an impulse while driving home from Florida decided to call on Helen in Westport. Mrs. Corbally knew how long-standing were the ties that bound Helen to this distinguished Rochester family. She had Helen seated in a pink negligée, the bedroom was flooded with sun, a braille book rested on the table beside her. "Shall I take my hair down so that Miss Helen can stroke it as she stroked my curls many long years ago?" Mrs. Remington asked Winnie. Mrs. Corbally approved, the hair came down, and the fingers that once had beaten out messages with the swiftness of a bird's wings slowly caressed Mrs. Remington's head. Shortly afterward she received a note from Mrs. Corbally, "When you took down your hair, you dropped some hair pins. Miss Helen is wearing them in her hair."

A few weeks later Helen was dead. Helen's ashes were taken in a burial urn to Washington for the services at the Cathedral. They were presided over by the Cathedral's dean, the Very Reverend Francis B. Sayre, Jr.. She would have liked that, for he was a man of progressive spirit. The choir of the Perkins Institute flew down to sing at the service, and Senator Lister Hill of Alabama, a former classmate of Helen's brother, delivered a tribute. The veiled urn containing her ashes rested on the high altar, and afterward there was a private committal service in the columbarium, where her urn was placed next to Teacher's and Polly's.

Two days later Marguerite Levine, the Foundation's archivist, was passing by the offices of the Swedenborg Foundation and noted that there was to be a memorial service for Helen Keller at the New Church (Swedenborgian) on East Thirty-fifth Street at which the Reverend Clayton S. Priestnal would officiate. She went, and on Monday she reported to the Foundation's executives that she had gone. "The service was simple, warm and the music program was beautifully executed."

In Senator Lister Hill's tribute to Helen Keller at the National Cathedral he closed with a quotation from *My Religion* expressive of Helen's radiant faith:

What is so sweet as to awake from a troubled dream and behold a beloved face smiling upon you? I have to believe that such shall be our awakening from earth to heaven. My faith never wavers that each dear friend I have 'lost' is a new link between this world and the happier land beyond the morn. My soul is for the moment bowed down with grief when I cease to feel the touch of their hands or hear a tender word from them; but the light of faith never fades from my sky.

XLIII

Epilogue: Helen's Religion

Helen's father and his family were Presbyterians. He was a deacon and took an active part in church affairs. Her mother and her people were Episcopalians. Unable, however, to communicate with Helen after she became deaf and blind, the Kellers had made no effort to give her religious instruction. Annie on her arrival in Tuscumbia was in no hurry to repair the omission. An indifferent Catholic herself, she felt that she had no right to impose her skeptical and alienated views on the child. This fitted in with Anagnos's pedagogical view that Helen's religious ideas should be allowed to develop from within instead of her taking them from without. Helen's native brilliance, her "natural religious inclination," he thought, provided a rare opportunity to test the origin of religious ideas: Were they innate? What shape might they take when freed of the supernaturalism and superstitions of established creeds?

The Kellers did not object, and Anagnos thought that Annie agreed. She did, but found Anagnos's wishes difficult to fulfill. "It is impossible to isolate a child in the midst of society," she later wrote, "so that he should not be influenced by the beliefs of those with whom he associates." When Helen was nine, a "zealous aunt," as Helen described her later, "decided that it was time I should learn the catechism." The aunt did not agree with Annie that Helen would not understand a word of it and that she was not ready for religious instruction. Annie kept Anagnos informed:

A short time ago A. undertook to give Helen an idea of deity. She began by telling her that 'God is everywhere.' The child instantly asked to be shown him. A. found herself in a difficult position, but she proceeded to add to Helen's perplexity by telling her that 'God made her and all the people in the world out of dust.' This bit of information amused the little woman greatly. In speaking of it to her mother afterwards she said: 'A. told me many funny things. She says Mr. God is everywhere, but has not a body like that of my father and does not live in a house!' Then the poor, puzzled child added: 'A. says God made me out of dust! I think she is a great joker! I am made of flesh and blood and bones, and I was born nearly nine years ago. A. must not make too many mistakes!'

Helen's artless inquiries did not disturb Anagnos. They showed her religious ideas unfolding naturally. Annie, moreover, tried to comply with his advice not to instruct the child herself. "When you are older," she sought to stay Helen's questions, "and can understand what your aunt told you, you will read and learn much about God and His World."

But Helen persisted in her questions after they came to Boston, and Annie decided that her awakening curiosity about the creation and meaning of the universe deserved a fuller and more adequate response than she was able to give. She did not consult Anagnos, who was then in Europe on a leave of absence; but Fanny Marrett, the teacher at Perkins to whom she felt closest, told her of the remarkable sermons being preached by Phillips Brooks at the Trinity Church in Boston. With Fanny she attended several of his services. Here was a man of large wisdom, true piety, witty and handsome to boot. He was the one to answer Helen's questions.

She wrote Anagnos what she had done:

You will see from her [Helen's] letter that she knows about God. It was impossible to keep the knowledge from [her] any longer. She had met with so many references to religious things in books that her curiosity was awakened. What could I do but satisfy her thirst for this new knowledge in as broad and Christian a way as I could? I went to Mr. Brooks for advice. I found him very willing to help both Helen and myself. I shall guard Helen very carefully against those notions and opinions which made Laura's religion so repulsive to all but the most narrow of Christians.

Anagnos's indignation over this disregard of his advice flowed over into his annual report, which he wrote upon his return: "Unfortunately, Miss Sullivan took a different view of the matter" from his own. "She could not rise above the sway of popular notions and common prejudices. . . . She deemed it her duty to . . . [turn] the current of Helen's thoughts into the ordinary channels of theology." Anagnos vented his feelings after a quarrel over what should be said in the report on Helen's religious education. As Annie wrote him:

> Of course it is your privilege to write whatever you please about Helen's religious instruction, but at the same time, I claim for myself the same right. I trust you will not omit from my report anything which explains my position in the matter. It is an important subject, at least some people think it is, and as the responsibility rests wholly with me, I do not wish to be misunderstood. I say this because you gave me to understand last winter that you considered what I said on this subject the merest nonsense.

In her section of the report Annie published extracts from the exchange of letters between Helen and the Rt. Rev. Phillips Brooks:

> Why does the great Father in heaven think it is best for us to have very great sorrow and pain sometimes? I am always happy, and so was Little Lord Fauntleroy; but dear little Jakey's life was full of sadness, and God did not put the light in his eyes, and he was blind, and his father was not gentle and loving. Do you think Jakey loved his Father in heaven more because his other father was unkind to him? How did God tell people that his home was in heaven? When people do very wrong and hurt animals and treat children unkindly, God is grieved; but what will he do to them to teach them to be pitiful and loving? Please tell me something that you know about God. I like so much to hear about my loving Father who is so good and wise.

To this appeal Dr. Brooks replied that God is love:

> Let me tell you how it seems that we come to know about the heavenly Father. It is from the power of love which is in our own hearts. Love is at the soul of everything. Whatever has not the power of loving must have a very dreary life indeed. . . . All the love that is

in our hearts comes from him, as all the light which is in the flowers comes from the sun; and the more we love the more near we are to God and his love. . . .

But God does not only want us to be *happy*. He wants us to be *good*. He wants that most of all. He knows that we can be really happy only when we are good. A great deal of the trouble that is in the world is medicine which is very bad to take, but which is good to take because it makes us better. We see how good people may be in great trouble when we think of Jesus, who was the greatest sufferer that ever lived, and yet was the best Being, and so, I am sure, the happiest Being, that the world has ever seen. . . .

And so love is everything: and if anybody asks you, or if you ask yourself what God is, answer, 'God is love!' That is the beautiful answer which the Bible gives.

As Dr. Brooks had anticipated, his letter only released a flood of additional questions:

It fills my heart with joy to know that God loves me so much that he wishes me to live always, and that he gives me everything that makes me happy,—loving friends, a precious little sister, sweet flowers, and, best of all, a heart that can love and sympathize and a mind that can think and enjoy. I am thankful to my heavenly Father for giving me all these precious things. But I have many questions to ask you,— some things that I cannot understand, because I am quite ignorant; but when I am older I shall not be so much puzzled.

What is a spirit? Did Jesus go to school when he was a child? Teacher cannot find anything about it in the Bible. How does God *deliver people from evil?* Why do the people say that the Jews were very wicked, when they did not know any better?

Where is heaven? My teacher says it does not matter where it is, so long as we know that it is a beautiful place, and that we shall see God there and be always happy. But I should like to know where it is and what it is like. What is conscience? Once I wished very much to read my new book about Heidi when Teacher told me to study. Something whispered to me that it would be wrong to disobey dear teacher. Was it *conscience* that whispered to me it would be wrong to disobey?

Dr. Brooks replied:

I think that it is God's care for us all that makes us care for one another. It is because we are in the Father's house that we know that all people are our brothers and sisters. God is very anxious that we should know that he is our Father. We can imagine something of how any father must feel whose children do not know that he is their father. He must be very anxious to tell them, and so God tries in every way to tell us. I think he writes it even upon the beautiful walls of the great house of nature which we live in, that he is our Father; as a child who found herself living in a lovely house might guess that he who built that house and put her there loved her dearly.

And then again, God tells us in our hearts that he is our Father. That is what we call conscience,—God's voice in our hearts. You say that you try to do what is right in order to please your teacher, and you ask whether that is conscience. But what is it that makes you want to please your teacher? Why do you want to show her that you love her? It is God in your heart that makes you grateful and makes you want to make other people happy. . . .

I suppose that Jesus went to school when he was a little boy. Indeed, we have one story of his going up to the temple and asking the wise doctors the questions which had come up in his mind, and that was really going to school. At any rate, we know that he lived in his mother's house and was very obedient. And so we know that even in the simplest things, in obedience and faithfulness to those who love us, we may be like God.

Helen also told of a visit to Bishop Brooks, for he had been elevated to the episcopacy, and how he had taken her on his knees and told her in the simplest language "the wonderful story of Jesus Christ, and my eyes filled with tears, and my heart beat with love for the gentle Nazarene who restored sight to the blind and speech to the mute, healed the sick, fed the hungry and turned sorrow into joy." Dr. Brooks affected her powerfully. When a new baby was born to the Kellers, Helen persuaded them to name him Phillips Brooks. And the bishop, who refused to go to a doctor because "he will feel my pulse and I hate to be pawed over" welcomed Helen's embraces and her delighted explorations of his face and head with her sensitive hands and fingers. He helped me grasp, she later wrote, "the central truth that God is Love and that His Love is the 'Light of all men.' "

The bishop, however, had never fully answered her queries about "What is a spirit?' and what the relationship was between divine love and the material world. That moment of discovery and intuition was her own:

> I had been sitting quietly in the library for half an hour. I turned to my teacher and said, 'Such a strange thing had happened! I have been far away all this time and I haven't left the room.' 'What do you mean, Helen?' she asked surprised. 'Why,' I cried, 'I have been in Athens.' Scarcely were the words out of my mouth when a bright amazing realization seemed to catch my mind and set it ablaze. I perceived the realness of my soul and its sheer independence of all conditions of place and body. It was clear to me that it was because I was a spirit that I had so vividly 'seen' and felt a place thousands of miles away. Space was nothing to spirit! In that new consciousness shone the presence of God, Himself a Spirit everywhere at once, the Creator dwelling in all the universe simultaneously.

But spiritual puzzles still persisted. Many of the stories in the Bible, which her aunt had held up as a divine book, seemed little different from the Greek and Roman myths that she was reading, scarcely a reflection of "the Being whose face shone so benign, beautiful and radiant in my heart." The mentor who came to fill this void was the gentle John Hitz, "the bearded Secretary," as Anagnos called the head of Bell's Volta Bureau. He put into her hands a copy in raised letters of Swedenborg's *Heaven and Hell:*

> I opened the big book, and lo, my fingers lighted upon a paragraph in the preface about a blind woman whose darkness was illumined with beautiful truths from Swedenborg's writings. She believed that they imparted a light to her mind which more than compensated for the loss of earthly light. She never doubted that there was a spiritual body within the material one with perfect senses, and that after a few dark years the eyes within her eyes would open to a world infinitely more wonderful, complete, and satisfying than this. My heart gave a joyous bound. Here was a faith that I felt so keenly—the separateness between soul and body, between a realm I could picture as a whole and the chaos of fragmentary things and irrational contingencies

which my limited physical senses met at every turn. I let myself go, as healthy, happy youth will, and tried to puzzle out the long words and the weighty thoughts of the Swedish seer.

There was something else in Swedenborg that appealed to her strongly. It related to the condemnation of Jews and others who were not Christians —a question that Bishop Brooks had not answered:

> I had been told by narrow people that all who were not Christians would be punished, and naturally my soul revolted, since I knew of wonderful men who lived and died for truth as they saw it in the pagan lands. But in *Heaven and Hell* I found that 'Jesus' stands for Divine Good, Good wrought into deeds, and 'Christ' divine Truth, sending forth new thought, new life and joy into the minds of men; therefore no one who believes in God and lives right is ever condemned.

Deeply moved by her interest, Hitz began to devote a part of each day —usually "the quiet morning hours before breakfast"—to transcribing Swedenborg's writings into Braille. She was indebted to Swedenborg, she later wrote, "for a richer interpretation of the Bible, a deeper understanding of the meaning of Christianity and a precious sense of the Divine Presence in the world. . . . His central doctrine is simple. It consists of three main ideas: God as Divine Love, God as Divine Wisdom and God as Power for use." But there was also the promise of rebirth after death into a life where she would see again.

From the age of sixteen she considered herself a Swedenborgian, but her interpretation of his teachings was genial, tolerant and liberal, consistent with what she had learned from Bishop Brooks and the impulses of her own overflowing heart. "I was not conscious of any difference between what Mr. Brooks taught me and what I read in Swedenborg," she wrote in 1927 to a leader of the Swedenborgian Church, a sentiment that she omitted from her little volume on *My Religion.* Not, until the early thirties did she become a member of any church, including the New Church; and Uncle Ed Chamberlin, who saw a good deal of her at the turn of the century, thought her religious views at the time closer to those of Unitarianism—"the Boston Religion," as it was dubbed—than to those of any other denomination.

It was at about this time—1899–1900—that Sister Mary Joseph of the

Incarnation of the order of St. Dominic entered into correspondence with Helen. The Sister received special dispensation from the Pope to do Braille work for Helen and had sent her some selections from the Breviary. Helen was grateful: "The 'Pater Noster' I was glad to have, as I had often wondered how the beautiful 'Lord's Prayer' was said in Latin. I enjoyed 'O Gloriosa' too, and thought how sweet it must be as it rises heavenward from lips and hearts warm with love for the gentle Virgin." Each of Helen's letters was commented on by Sister Mary Joseph, and she found these remarks of Helen's "consoling." "I thought the incipient devotion the child here manifests to the Blessed Virgin was so consoling that in giving the original letter away—to Bishop Wigger—I had it duplicated. I have shown them to a great many persons, but have been very careful that they should not find their way into print, lest it should cause Helen to cease writing freely to me."

On Helen's twentieth birthday, Sister Mary Joseph sent her several booklets of poems and devotions by Catholic authors. Helen thanked her, saying that as she reached her twentieth birthday she had been reluctant to turn her back on the years of childhood, but that when the "Palma Ascendenti" by Father Rockford was put into her hand "the kind words filled me with fresh courage and resolution." Letters were exchanged more frequently, and Helen reported in some detail on her thoughts and activities. Sister Mary sent her lives of St. Thomas and St. Francis Xavier. Again Helen thanked her, but a note of demurral sounded in her letter. She admired St. Francis Xavier's courage and perserverance, "but it seems to me that he could and should have spared his frail body the cruel scourgings mentioned in the 'Latin lessons.' He needed all the strength he had and by self-torment exhausted it before his time. Such things distress and perplex me." The saints she liked best, she went on, were Francis of Assisi and Jeanne d'Arc. "Indeed I love them and think of them as two of the noblest, most self-sacrificing persons that ever lived. But I already know a good deal about them from what I have read in History; so you need not take the trouble to copy their biographies. However, I would like to know something about St. Teresa; only her name is known to me at present."

St. Teresa's style and the sweetness of spirit in her words attracted her. It inspired her to read the lives of the saints, she informed Sister Mary, but again there was a note of hesitation: "Sometimes their faith and manner of life are not quite the same as those to which I am accustomed." Helen's qualms did not restrain Sister Mary's missionary zeal. She sent

Helen the Catholic Breviary in Braille. That alarmed Helen, who wrote her from Nova Scotia:

> I will read the Prayer-Book you sent me when I return to the States, but really, dear Sister Mary, I do not see how I can change my creed. Why, I should be obliged to change my very nature and wrench myself from the convictions and life-deep sentiments which are woven in the warp and woof of my life. I have sympathy in real measure, and I can easily put myself in your place and see the things that give you joy or pain; but I must keep my own place, if I am to think honestly and live as I think our Father desires me to. . . .

That did not discourage Sister Mary. She summarized Helen's letter and her own response: "She defines her theological position in this letter—She has three articles in her creed—she believes in the paternity of God, the brotherhood of man and the spiritual life. I asked her what Bishop Brooks would say to her about leaving out the cross—*spes unica.* I asked the Bishop at the visitation to let my sister send me 'The Letters of an Innocent Man,' that I might copy for Helen all those in which he speaks of his Calvary, his dolorous via crucis, etc.—and *he a Jew*—and I called the book, 'The Shadow of the Cross in the Prison of Dreyfus.' "

Helen was grateful for that letter, she replied, for she took "a watchful interest in everything that concerned the Dreyfus case, and my friends told me that those letters were themselves a splendid refutation of the charges" brought against him.

> Speaking of St. Helen, I know the Creed, but the Crucifixion is really a fact too cruel for me to rehearse in my prayers or thoughts. We all turn with horror from instruments of torture. How much more must I shrink from the cross on which the greatest of God's children died! So I take my creed from Jesus's own beautiful words and think of the Cross only to love him all the more for the sacrifice He made that the world might live a brighter, better life.

Sister Mary found a few crumbs of comfort in this reply: "She says 'I know the Creed,' and she also speaks of the Catholic Church as 'the Church,' but she speaks of our Divine Lord as if she were a Unitarian. I must now show her that the cross is far more than 'an instrument of torture,' that it has a divine power to transform weakness into invincible strength."

Helen's remarks about the crucifixion were revealing. She fitted into William James's category of those who practiced "the religion of healthy-mindedness." Despite her blindness and deafness her soul was of "sky-blue" radiance, with little patience for the tragic character of life. Contrast Helen's attitude toward the crucifixion with Simone Weil's: "Every time I think of the crucifixion of Christ I commit the sin of envy."

Helen's *The Story of My Life* had begun to appear in the *Ladies' Home Journal,* and Sister Mary offered several suggestions, especially in regard to her treatment of the Bible. Helen accepted most of them, but was undecided "what I shall write or not write about the Bible; but whatever I say, I shall try to show people that I love the Bible as I love no other book. No, dear Sister Mary, I do not want to hurt the feelings of any one, and I am trying not to let my opinions run away with the little prudence I have."

She should not have pressed Helen on this, Sister Mary wrote in her next commentary: "Had I been wiser I would have ended the matter there, but I very imprudently sent her the 8th Chapter of 'Faith of our Fathers' on the 'Church and the Bible,' as well as 'What Christ Revealed' and it was more than she could stand. This is the only one of her letters in which she shows temper, but it was my fault."

> You were very kind to send me what Cardinal Gibbons said about the Church and the Bible. I understand better than I did before why all Catholics are not provided with Bibles. I found the very facts he has set forth about the way the Bible came to be what it is in the course, English 35, I took last year. But, since you spoke of it, I think I had better tell you that in the revision of my story I did not take back all I had said about the Bible. I softened it down, however, as much as I could. You see there are many things I cannot admit, and so long as I do not admit them, I must say what I really think when I am asked.
>
> I thank you for offering to make it possible for me to meet someone who might be able to satisfy me with regard to the objectionable passages of the Bible. But I do not feel like entering into argument. Certain fundamental questions would come up to which I can find no satisfactory answer, except in experience. One of the themes—the vital one, is whether people must suffer eternally for refusing to accept what the Church gives. I find this treated in "What Christ Revealed." Dr. Jouin is very clear and strong in his explanation. Still

I have an unconquerable faith in the sincerity and goodness of many friends who hold opinions quite different from mine or yours, and if they are found to be wicked, as Cardinal Gibbons declares people to be who will not listen to the Chruch, let me share their fate rather than be false and unloving. I beg and beseech you, let us drop this subject on which all else depends.

Sister Mary desisted. The two continued to exchange letters until 1907, Sister Mary undertaking to braille books other than exclusively religious ones. There were no further clashes over creed. Each respected the other's standpoint. It is interesting to speculate what might have happened had Helen become a convert to the Roman Catholic Church. An angellike figure with a powerful sense that her afflictions had been visited upon her for some purpose that she did not yet fully understand, she inspired strong men and women to reverence, awe, pity and wonder. When even that caustic ironist Mark Twain considered her "a miracle," she seemed destined for a saint's career, which, harnessed to the vast institutional powers of the Church, would have made her a mighty force for winning others to that faith.

But while Helen read with sympathy the books and tracts that Sister Mary brailled for her, she responded to the nun's solicitude for her spiritual salvation with gratitude, not commitment. That she reserved for John Hitz, who during the same period, after she had expressed a wish to know more of Swedenborg's writings, had "laboriously compiled books of explanations and extracts" to facilitate the religious study of his *innigste geliebte Tochter Helene.*

When in 1908 he collapsed and died of a heart attack at the Washington railroad terminal where he had gone to meet Helen, she wrote that she "could not have borne the loss of such an intimate and tender friend if I had thought he was indeed dead. But his noble philosophy and certainty of the life to come braced me with an unwavering faith that we should meet again in a world happier and more beautiful than anything of my dreaming."

Swedenborgianism freed her of the fear of death. "I cannot understand why anyone should fear death. Life here is more cruel than death—life divides and estranges, while death, which at heart is life eternal, reunites and reconciles. I believe that when the eyes within my physical eyes shall open upon the world to come, I shall simply be consciously living in the country of my heart."

bibliography

BOOKS BY HELEN KELLER

Helen Keller: Her Socialist Years. Ed. Philip S. Foner. New York: International, 1967.

Helen Keller in Scotland. London: 1933.

Helen Keller's Journal. New York: 1938.

Let Us Have Faith. New York: 1941.

Midstream: My Later Life. New York: Greenwood, 1968.

My Religion. New York: Pyramid, 1974.

The Open Door. New York: 1957.

Optimism, an Essay. New York: 1903.

Out of the Dark. New York: 1913.

Peace at Eventide. London: 1932.

The Song of the Stone Wall. New York: 1910.

The Story of My Life. New York: Andor, 1976.

Teacher: Anne Sullivan Macy. New York: 1955.

The World I Live In. New York: 1908.

BOOKS RELATING TO HELEN KELLER

Allen, Katherine G. *Edward E. Allen,* privately printed. 1940.

Bell, Daniel. *Marxian Socialism in the United States.* Princeton: Princeton University Press, 1952.

Braddy, Nella (Henney). *Anne Sullivan Macy.* New York: 1933.

Brooks, Van Wyck. *Helen Keller: Sketch for A Portrait.* New York: 1956.

Bruce, Robert V. *Bell: Alexander Graham Bell and the Conquest of Solitude.* Boston: Little, Brown, 1973.

Cassirer, Ernst. *Essay on Man: An Introduction to a Philosophy of Human Culture.* New Haven: Yale University Press, 1944.

Chapman, John Jay. *Selected Writings.* Ed. Jacques Barzun. New York: 1957.

Cutsforth, Thomas D. *The Blind in School and Society: A Psychological Study.* New York: American Foundation for the Blind, 1951.

Davidson, Jo. *Between Sittings.* New York: 1951.

Elliott, Maud Howe. *Three Generations.* Boston: 1923.

Elliott, Maud Howe and Florence Howe Hall. *Laura Bridgman.* Boston: 1903.

Flynn, Elizabeth Gurley. *The Rebel Girl, an Autobiography: My First Life.* New York: International, 1973.

Fraiberg, Selma. *Insights from the Blind: Developmental Studies of Blind Children.* New York: Basic Books, 1977.

Gibson, William. *The Miracle Worker: A Play for Television.* New York: Knopf, 1957.

Goldman, Emma. *Living My Life.* Ed. Richard and Anna M. Drinnon. New York: New American Library, 1977.

Grew, Joseph C. *Ten Years in Japan.* Connecticut: Greenwood, 1973.

Gruening, Ernest. *Many Battles: The Autobiography of Ernest Gruening.* New York: Liveright, 1973.

Harrity, Richard and Ralph G. Martin. *The Three Lives of Helen Keller.* New York: 1962.

Howe, Helen. *The Gentle Americans.* New York: Queens House, 1977.

Howe, Julia Ward. *Reminiscences.* Boston: 1899.

Hutton, Laurence. *Talks in A Library with Laurence Hutton.* Darby, Pennsylvania: Folcroft, 1973.

Jastrow, Joseph. *The Subconscious.* Cambridge, Mass.: 1906.

Koestler, Frances A. *The Unseen Minority: A Social History of Blindness in the United States.* New York: McKay, 1976.

Lawrence, William. *Life of Phillips Brooks.* New York: 1930.

Leblanc, Georgette. *The Girl Who Found the Bluebird.* New York: 1913.

Lowenfeld, Berthold. *The Changing Status of the Blind.* Springfield, Illinois: Thomas, 1975.

Lyde, Elsie L. *Trustable & Preshus Friends.* Ed. Jane Douglass. New York: Harcourt Brace, 1977.

Macy, John. *Edgar Allen Poe.* New York: Haskell House, 1975.

——. *The Spirit of American Literature.* Chicago: Johnson, 1969.

——. *Socialism in America.* New York: 1916.

——. "Massachusetts," *These United States.* Ed. Ernest H. Gruening. New York, Arno, 1924.

——. *About Women.* New York: 1930.

Mitchell, Arthur. *About Dreaming, Laughing and Blushing.* London: 1905.

Monsarrat, Nicholas. *The Story of Esther Costello.* New York: 1953.

Percy, Walker. *The Message in the Bottle.* New York: Farrar, Straus & Giroux, 1975.

Putnam, Peter. *Cast Off the Darkness.* New York: 1957.

Renshaw, Patrick. *The Wobblies.* New York: 1967.

Repplier, Agnes. *Agnes Irwin.* New York: 1934.

Richards, Laura E. *The Life of Dr. Samuel Gridley Howe.* 2 vols.

Shannon, David A. *The Socialist Party of America.* New York: 1955.

Tharp, Louise Hall. *Three Saints and a Sinner.* New York: 1956.

Villey-Desmeserets, Pierre. *The World of the Blind.* New York: 1930.

MAGAZINES AND OTHER MATERIALS RELATING TO HELEN KELLER

American Annals of the Deaf, published by the American Association to Promote the Teaching of Speech to the Deaf, Washington, D.C. Later known as *The Association Review.*

Annual Report of the Perkins Institution, 1887 through 1896. Boston.

Helen Keller Scrapbooks at the Perkins Institution.

Outlook for the Blind, published by the American Foundation for the Blind, New York.

Rebecca Mack Scrapbooks at the American Foundation for the Blind.

Souvenir of Helen Keller. 2nd ed. Vol. I. Washington, D.C.: Volta Bureau. 1892.

Souvenir of Helen Keller. Vol. II. Washington, D.C.: Volta Bureau. 1899.

St. Nicholas Magazine.

"Years of Triumph," published by the American Foundation for the Blind. New York: 1969.

Youth's Companion.

index

Bridgman, Laura (*Cont.*)
  49, 63, 199, 294, 575; Howe and,
  15–18, 22; religion of, 777
Briggs, LeBaron R., 313
Brissenden, Paul, 385
British Empire Society for the Blind,
  736
British Medical Association, 612
Brohman, Rudolph, 320
Brooklyn Eagle, 393, 429
Brooks, Eleanor, 689
Brooks, Gladys, 701–2
Brooks, Phillips, 128, 151, 153, 170,
  481, 608, 777–82
Brooks, Van Wyck, 670, 680, 681,
  685, 689, 701–702, 734–38
Brown, John, 20, 21
Browning, Elizabeth Barrett, 553
Browning, Robert, 271
Bryan, Helen, 671–74
Bryan, William Jennings, 204, 365
Burbank, Luther, 538–39
Burlingham, C. C., 750
Burns, Jimmy, 11
Burroughs, John, 194
Butler, Benjamin, 26–28, 34
Byron, George Gordon, 15

C

Call, the (Socialist periodical), 387,
  423, 425, 432, 466
Cambridge, ASM-HK home in,
  262–63
Cambridge School for Young Ladies,
  198, 200, 207–29
Campbell, Charles F. F., 309, 364,
  517–20, 587–88, 590, 595; AFB
  contributions, 534–35, 549; Henney book and, 621; on Perkins, 600
Campbell, Francis J., 340
Canby, Margaret T., 133, 141–42,
  148–49, 160, 288
capital punishment, HK view on,
  431

Carlson, Lane, 709
Carlyle, Thomas, 19
Carnegie, Andrew, 367–68, 395; HK
  pension from, 413, 434, 715
Carney Catholic Hospital, 30
Caruso, Enrico, 417, 482, 488, 570
Cassirer, Ernst, 584
Caswell, A. O., 134n, 337
Catholic Church, 8, 9
Catt, Carrie Chapman, 390, 617
Century, The, 188, 207, 211, 217, 287,
  342, 350, 360–61
Century Company, 340–42
Chamberlin, Ida, 255–58, 265–66
Chamberlin, Joseph Edgar ("Uncle
  Ed"), 162, 164, 204, 236, 245–46,
  263, 303, 310–11, 621; on HK reli-
  gion, 782
"Chant of Darkness, The" (HK poem),
  341–43, 350
"Chant of the Stone Wall, A" (HK
  poem), 343
Chaplin, Charlie, 481–82
Chapman, John Jay, 15, 32
Chapman, Jonathan, 17, 21
Chicago Post, 285
Chicago World's Fair (1893), 174–77
Chick, Morris B., 772
Chifley, J. B., 708–9
Choate, Joseph H., 388–89
Choate, Rufus, 16
Christian Register, The, 37
Churchill, Winston, 676
Churchman, The, 287
Clark, Ethel and Eddie, 699, 701, 716,
  722, 731, 751, 769–70
Clarke, Francis D., 185n
Clarke School for the Deaf, 20, 154,
  172
Clayton, Bessie, 489
Clemens, Samuel Langhorne (Mark
  Twain): Bacon-Shakespeare contro-
  versy and, 360–62; on HM-ASM re-
  lationship, 289–90, 450; HK educa-
  tion fund and, 209–10; HK
  friendship with, 193–94, 304–6,
  357–62, 380–81, 439, 488; *Innocents*

G

Gabrilowitsch, Clara Clemens, 534
Gallaudet, E. M., 313n
Gallaudet, Thomas, 48
Gates, John, 660
Gentle Americans, The (Howe), 14, 333
George V of England, 612
George II of Greece, 692–93
George, Anne, 417–18
Gibson, Harvey D., 608, 627, 664, 707, 714–15, 725
Gibson, William, 479, 753–54, 760–61
Gilded Age, The (Clemens-Warner), 194
Gilder, Richard Watson, 188, 211–14, 287, 305–6, 307, 327; as HK publisher, 340–43, 351, 360–61, 450
Gillette, William, 194
Gillies, David, 695
Gilman, Arthur, 207–29, 233, 253, 288, 295
Giovannitti, Arturo, 384–87, 396–97, 415–16, 421, 465
Giovannitti, Caroline, 415–16, 421
Girl Who Found the Bluebird, The (Leblanc), 436–40
Gish, Lillian, 481
Glasgow University, HK honorary degree from, 610–12
Glocke, Die (Schiller), 268
God and the State (Bakunin), 455
"God in Nature" (Martineau), 342
Goethe, Johann Wolfgang von, 265–66
Goldman, Emma, 439, 464–65, 467
Gompers, Samuel, 527
Good Housekeeping list of great women, 573, 618
Goodson Gazette, The, 133
Gordon, Gertrude, 452n
Gordon, Ruth, 676
Grasse, Edwin, 519
Greenfield, Josh, 297
Greenwood, G. G., 360–62
Greer, David H., 209, 257–58
Grew, Joseph C., 643–46
Grosvenor, Gilbert, 543, 545

Gruening, Ernest, 344, 417
Grummons, Stuart, 694, 722
Gugler, Anne, 665
Gugler, Eric, 665
Guinot, Paul, 600

H

Haas, Herbert, 624–25, 661, 668, 692–94, 711–14, 716–17, 721–22
Hadassah, 728
Hadley School for the Blind, 43
Hale, Edward Everett: ASM friendship with, 323, 327, 330–32; HK friendship with, 45, 82–83, 123–24, 151–53, 169, 183, 245, 248, 311, 354; on HK writing, 285, 307
Hall, David Prescott, 134n, 337
Hall, Florence Howe, 123–24, 177
Hall, G. Stanley, 272–73
Hamilton, Nancy, 665–66, 719, 727, 751, 767, 768; Katharine Cornell and, 665–66; Nella Henney and, 755, 759, 763, 765; *Unconquered* (documentary on HK), 731–32, 742–45
handicapped people: government aid for, 364, 644–45; HK concern for, 20, 306, 688–89, 766
Hannegan, Robert E., 683
Harding, Warren G., 486
Harrison, Pat, 656–57
Hartford Institution for Deaf Mutes, 113
Harvard University, HK honorary degree from, 748, 750–51
Haüy, Valentin, 15
Hay, John, 305
Hayes, Charles B., 523–25, 536, 588
Hayes, Lydia, 141
Hayes, Samuel, 579
Haywood, William "Big Bill," 385–87, 460, 465
Heady, Morrison, 86
Hearst, Mrs. William Randolph, 209
Heaven and Hell (Swedenborg), 781–82

Keller, Helen Adams (*Cont.*)

L

JOSEPH P. LASH (1909–1987) is best known for his biography *Eleanor and Franklin,* which won the Pulitzer Prize, the National Book Award and the Francis Parkman Prize as well as establishing itself as an international best-seller. A leader in the militant youth movement of the 1930s, Joseph Lash served in the United States Army Air Forces from 1942 to 1945, receiving a decoration for work in the South Pacific. After helping to found Americans for Democratic Action, he joined the *New York Post,* as a United Nations correspondent and specialist in foreign affairs from 1950 until 1961, and as an editorial writer for 1961 until 1966.

Among Joseph Lash's other distinguished writings are a biography of Dag Hammarskjöld; *Eleanor Roosevelt: A Friend's Memoir; Eleanor: The Years Alone; From the Diaries of Felix Frankfurter;* and *Roosevelt and Churchill,* which won the Samuel Eliot Morrison Prize.

Book Three of The Malloreon

DEMON LORD OF
KARANDA

By David Eddings
Published by Ballantine Books

THE BELGARIAD
Book One: *Pawn of Prophecy*
Book Two: *Queen of Sorcery*
Book Three: *Magician's Gambit*
Book Four: *Castle of Wizardry*
Book Five: *Enchanters' End Game*

THE MALLOREON
Book One: *Guardians of the West*
Book Two: *King of the Murgos*
Book Three: *Demon Lord of Karanda*
Book Four: *Sorceress of Darshiva**
Book Five: *The Seeress of Kell**

HIGH HUNT

* *Forthcoming*

Book Three of The Malloreon

DEMON LORD OF
KARANDA

DAVID EDDINGS

A Del Rey Book

Ballantine Books · New York

A Del Rey Book
Published by Ballantine Books

Copyright © 1988 by David Eddings

Maps by Shelly Shapiro

Library of Congress Cataloging-in-Publication Data

Eddings, David.
  Demon lord of Karanda.

  (The Malloreon : bk. 3)
  "A Del Rey book."
  I. Title. II. Series: Eddings, David.
Malloreon ; bk. 3.
PS3555.D38D46   1988   813'.54   88-47804
ISBN 0-345-33004-8

Design by Holly Johnson

Manufactured in the United States of America

10 9 8 7 6 5 4

For Patrick Janson-Smith,
a very special friend,
from writer, wife, and Fatso.

At this time I would again like to express my indebtedness to my wife, Leigh Eddings, for her support, her contributions, and her wholehearted collaboration in this ongoing story. Without her help, none of this would have been possible.

I would also like to take this opportunity to thank my editor, Lester del Rey, for his patience and forbearance, as well as for contributions too numerous to mention.

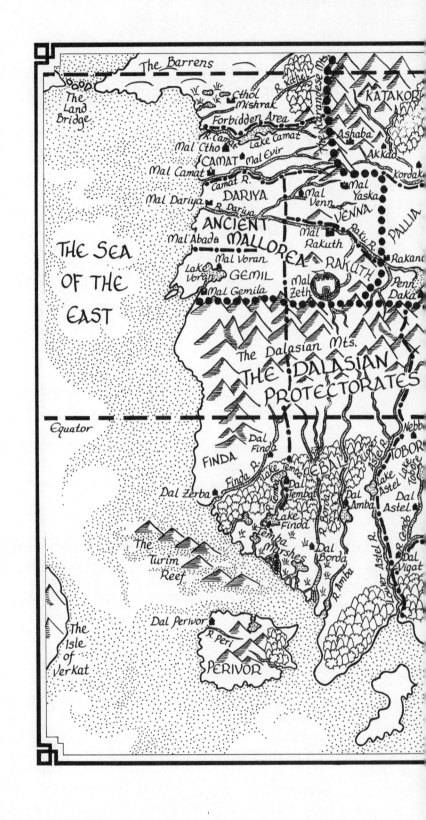

Prologue

Being a brief history of Mallorea and the races that dwell there.
—Digested from *The Chronicles of Angarak*
University of Melcene Press

Tradition places the ancestral home of the Angaraks somewhere off the south coast of present-day Dalasia. Then Torak, Dragon God of Angarak, used the power of the Stone, Cthrag Yaska, in what has come to be called "the cracking of the world." The crust of the earth split, releasing liquid magma from below and letting the waters of the southern ocean in to form the Sea of the East. This cataclysmic process

1

continued for decades before the world gradually assumed its present form.

As a result of this upheaval, the Alorns and their allies were forced to retreat into the unexplored reaches of the western continent, while the Angaraks fled into the wilderness of Mallorea.

Torak had been maimed and disfigured by the Stone, which rebelled at the use to which the God put it, and the Grolim priests were demoralized. Thus leadership fell by default to the military; by the time the Grolims recovered, the military had established *de facto* rule of all Angarak. Lacking their former preeminence, the priests set up an opposing center of power at Mal Yaska, near the tip of the Karandese mountain Range.

At this point, Torak roused himself to prevent the imminent civil war between priesthood and military rule. But he made no move against the military headquarters at Mal Zeth; instead, he marched to the extreme northwest of Malorea Antiqua with a quarter of the Angarak people to build the Holy City of Cthol Mishrak. There he remained, so absorbed by efforts to gain control of Cthrag Yaska that he was oblivious to the fact that the people had largely turned from their previous preoccupation with theological matters. Those with him in Cthol Mishrak were mostly a hysterical fringe of fanatics under the rigid control of Torak's three disciples, Zedar, Ctuchik, and Urvon. These three maintained the old forms in the society of Cthol Mishrak while the rest of Angarak changed.

When the continuing friction between the Church and military finally came to Torak's attention, he summoned the military High Command and the Grolim Hierarchy to Cthol Mishrak and delivered his commands in terms that brooked no demur. Exempting only Mal Yaska and Mal Zeth, all towns and districts were to be ruled jointly by the military and priesthood. The subdued Hierarchy and High Command immediately settled their differences and returned to their separate enclaves. This enforced truce freed the generals to turn their attention to the other peoples living in Mallorea.

The origins of these people are lost in myth, but three races had predated the Angaraks on the continent: the Dalasians of the southwest; the Karands of the north; and the Melcenes of the East. It was to the Karands the military turned its efforts.

The Karands were a warlike race with little patience for cultural niceties. They lived in crude cities where hogs roamed freely in the muddy streets. Traditionally, they were related to the Morindim of the far north of Gar og Nadrak. Both races were given to the practice of demon worship.

At the beginning of the second millenium, roving bands of Karandese brigands had become a serious problem along the eastern frontier, and the Angarak army now moved out of Mal Zeth to the western fringes of the Karandese Kingdom of Pallia. The city of Rakand in southwestern Pallia was sacked and burned, and the inhabitants were taken captives.

At this point, one of the greatest decisions of Angarak history was made. While the Grolims prepared for an orgy of human sacrifice, the generals paused. They had no desire to occupy Pallia, and the difficulties of long-distance communication made the notion unattractive. To the generals, it seemed far better to keep Pallia as a subject kingdom and exact tribute, rather than to occupy a depopulated territory. The Grolims were outraged, but the generals were adamant. Ultimately, both sides agreed to take the matter before Torak for his decision.

Not surprisingly, Torak agreed with the High Command; if the Karands could be converted, he would nearly double the congregation of his Church as well as the size of his army for any future confrontation with the Kings of the West. "Any man who liveth in boundless Mallorea shall bow down and worship me," he told his reluctant missionaries. And to insure their zeal, he sent Urvon to Mal Yaska to oversee the conversion of the Karands. There Urvon established himself as temporal head of the Mallorean Church in pomp and luxury hitherto unknown to the ascetic Grolims.

The army moved against Katakor, Jenno, and Delchin, as well as Pallia. But the missionaries fared poorly as the Karandese magicians conjured up hordes of demons to defend their society. Urvon finally journeyed to Cthol Mishrak to consult with Torak. It is not clear what Torak did, but the Karandese magicians soon discovered that the spells previously used to control the demons were no longer effective. Any magician could now reach into the realms of darkness only at the peril of life and soul.

The conquest of the Karands absorbed the attention of both military and priesthood for the next several centuries, but ultimately the resistance collapsed and Karanda became a subject nation, its peoples generally looked upon as inferiors.

When the army advanced down the Great River Magan against the Melcene Empire, however, it met a sophisticated and technologically superior people. In several disastrous battles, in which Melcene war chariots and elephant cavalry destroyed whole battalions, the Angaraks abandoned their efforts. The Angarak generals made overtures of peace. To their astonishment, the Melcenes quickly agreed to normalize relations and offered to trade horses, which the Angaraks previously lacked. They refused, however, even to discuss the sale of elephants.

The army then turned to Dalasia, which proved to be an easy conquest. The Dalasians were simple farmers and herdsmen with little skill for war. The Angaraks moved into Dalasia and established military protectorates during the next ten years. The priesthood seemed at first equally successful. The Dalasians meekly accepted the forms of Angarak worship. But they were a mystical people, and the Grolims soon discovered that the power of the witches, seers, and prophets remained unbroken. Moreover, copies of the infamous *Mallorean Gospels* still circulated in secret among the Dalasians.

In time, the Grolims might have succeeded in stamping out

the secret Dalasian religion. But then a disaster occurred that was to change forever the complexion of Angarak life. Somehow, the legendary sorcerer Belgarath, accompanied by three Alorns, succeeded in evading all the security measures and came unobserved at night to steal Cthrag Yaska from the iron tower of Torak in the center of Cthol Mishrak. Although pursued, they managed to escape with the stolen Stone to the West.

In furious rage, Torak destroyed his city. Then he ordered that the Murgos, Thulls, and Nadraks be sent to the western borders of the Sea of the East. More than a million lives were lost in the crossing of the northern land bridge, and the society and culture of the Angaraks took long to recover.

Following the dispersal and the destruction of Cthol Mishrak, Torak became almost inaccessible, concentrating totally on various schemes to thwart the growing power of the Kingdoms of the West. The God's neglect gave the military time to exploit fully its now virtually total control of Mallorea and the subject kingdoms.

For many centuries, the uneasy peace between Angaraks and Melcenes continued, broken occasionally only by little wars in which both sides avoided committing their full forces. The two nations eventually established the practice of each sending children of the leaders to be raised by leaders of the other side. This led to a fuller understanding by both, as well as to the growth of a body of cosmopolitan youths that eventually became the norm for the ruling class of the Mallorean Empire.

One such youth was Kallath, the son of a high-ranking Angarak general. Brought up in Melcene, he returned to Mal Zeth to become the youngest man ever to be elevated to the General Staff. Returning to Melcene, he married the daughter of the Melcene Emperor and managed to have himself declared Emperor following the old man's death in 3830. Then, using the Melcene army as a threat, he managed to get himself declared hereditary Commander in Chief of the Angaraks.

The integration of Melcene and Angarak was turbulent. But in time, the Melcene patience won out over Angarak brutality. Unlike other peoples, the Melcenes were ruled by a bureaucracy. And in the end, that bureaucracy proved far more efficient than the Angarak military administration. By 4400, the ascendancy of the bureaucracy was complete. By that time, also, the title of Commander in Chief had been forgotten and the ruler of both peoples was simply the Emperor of Mallorea.

To the sophisticated Melcenes, the worship of Torak remained largely superficial. They accepted the forms out of expediency, but the Grolims were never able to command the abject submission to the Dragon God that had characterized the Angaraks.

Then in 4850, Torak suddenly emerged from his eons of seclusion to appear before the gates of Mal Zeth. Wearing a steel mask to conceal his maimed face, he set aside the Emperor and declared himself Kal Torak, King and God. He immediately began mustering an enormous force to crush the Kingdoms of the West and bring all the world under his domination.

The mobilization that followed virtually stripped Mallorea of able-bodied males. The Angaraks and Karands were marched north to the land bridge, crossing to northermost Gar og Nadrak, and the Dalasians and Melcenes moved to where fleets had been constructed to ferry them across the Sea of the East to southern Cthol Murgos. The northern Malloreans joined with the Nadraks, Thulls, and northern Murgos to strike toward the Kingdoms of Drasnia and Algaria. The second group of Malloreans joined with the southern Murgos and were to march northwesterly. Torak meant to crush the West between the two huge armies.

The southern forces, however, were caught in a freak storm that swept off the Western Sea in the spring of 4875 and that buried them alive in the worst blizzard of recorded history. When it finally abated, the column was mired in fourteen-foot snowdrifts that persisted until early summer. No theory

6

has yet been able to explain this storm, which was clearly not of natural origin. Whatever the cause, the southern army perished. The few survivors who struggled back to the east told tales of horror that were truly unthinkable.

The northern force was also beset by various disasters, but eventually laid siege to Vo Mimbre, where they were completely routed by the combined armies of the West. And there Torak was struck down by the power of Cthrag Yaska (there called the Orb of Aldur) and lay in a coma that was to last centuries, though his body was rescued and taken to a secret hiding place by his disciple Zedar.

In the years following these catastrophes, Mallorean society began to fracture back into its original components of Melcene, Karanda, Dalasia, and the lands of the Angaraks. The Empire was saved only by the emergence of Korzeth as Emperor.

Korzeth was only fourteen when he seized the throne from his aged father. Deceived by his youth, the separatist regions began to declare independence of the imperial throne. Korzeth moved decisively to stem the revolution. He spent the rest of his life on horseback in one of the greatest bloodbaths of history, but when he was done, he delivered a strong and united Mallorea to his successors. Henceforth, the descendants of Korzeth ruled in total and unquestioned power from Mal Zeth.

This continued until the present Emperor, Zakath, ascended the throne. For a time, he gave promise of being an enlightened ruler of Mallorea and the western kingdoms of the Angaraks. But soon there were signs of trouble.

The Murgos were ruled by Taur Urgas, and it was evident that he was both mad and unscrupulously ambitious. He instigated some plot against the young Emperor. It has never been established clearly what form his scheming took. But Zakath discovered that Taur Urgas was behind it and vowed vengeance. This took the form of a bitter war in which Zakath began a campaign to destroy the mad ruler utterly.

It was in the middle of this struggle that the West struck. While the Kings of the West sent an army against the East, Belgarion, the young Overlord of the West and descendant of Belgarath the Sorcerer, advanced on foot across the north and across the land bridge into Mallorea. He was accompanied by Belgarath and a Drasnian and he bore the ancient Sword of Riva, on the pommel of which was Cthrag Yaska, the Orb of Aldur. His purpose was to slay Torak, apparently in response to some prophecy known in the West.

Torak had been emerging from his long coma in the ruins of his ancient city of Cthol Mishrak. Now he roused himself to meet the challenger. But in the confrontation, Belgarion overcame the God and slew him with the Sword, leaving the priesthood of Mallorea in chaos and confusion.

Part One

RAK HAGGA

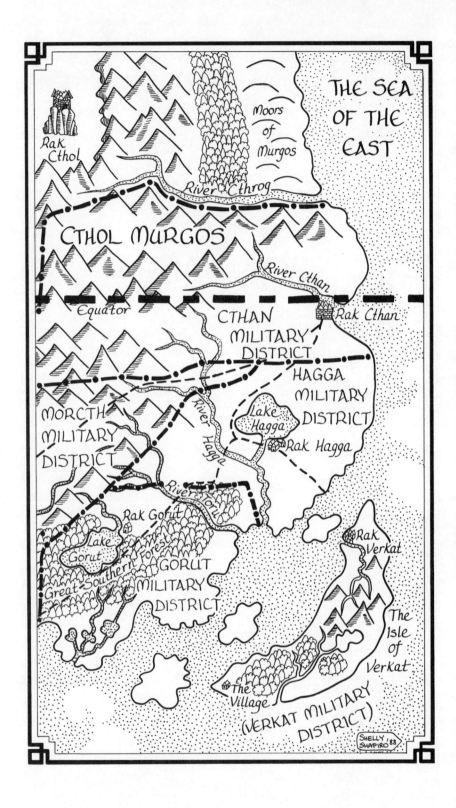

CHAPTER ONE

The first snow of the season settled white and quiet through the breathless air onto the decks of their ship. It was a wet snow with large, heavy flakes that piled up on the lines and rigging, turning the tarred ropes into thick, white cables. The sea was black, and the swells rose and fell without sound. From the stern came the slow, measured beat of a muffled drum that set the stroke for the Mallorean oarsmen. The sifting flakes settled on the shoulders of the sailors and in the folds of their scarlet cloaks as they pulled steadily through the snowy morning. Their breath steamed in the chill dampness as they bent and straightened in unison to the beat of the drum.

Garion and Silk stood at the rail with their cloaks pulled tightly around them, staring somberly out through the filmy snowfall.

"Miserable morning," the rat-faced little Drasnian noted, distastefully brushing snow from his shoulders.

Garion grunted sourly.

"You're in a cheerful humor today."

"I don't really have all that much to smile about, Silk," Garion went back to glowering out at the gloomy black-and-white morning.

Belgarath the Sorcerer came out of the aft cabin, squinted up into the thickly settling snow, and raised the hood of his stout old cloak. Then he came forward along the slippery deck to join them at the rail.

Silk glanced at the red-cloaked Mallorean soldier who had unobstrusively come up on deck behind the old man and who now stood leaning with some show of idleness on the rail several yards aft. "I see that General Atesca is still concerned about your well-being," he said, pointing at the man who had dogged Belgarath's steps since they had sailed out of the harbor at Rak Verkat.

Belgarath threw a quick disgusted glance in the soldier's direction. "Stupidity," he said shortly. "Where does he think I'm going?"

A sudden thought came to Garion. He leaned forward and spoke very quietly. "You know," he said, "we *could* go someplace, at that. We've got a ship here, and a ship goes wherever you point it—Mallorea just as easily as the coast of Hagga."

"It's an interesting notion, Belgarath," Silk agreed.

"There are four of us, Grandfather," Garion pointed out. "You, me, Aunt Pol, and Durnik. I'm sure we wouldn't have much difficulty in taking over this ship. Then we could change course and be halfway to Mallorea before Kal Zakath realized that we weren't coming to Rak Hagga after all." The more he thought about it, the more the idea excited him. "Then we could sail north along the Mallorean coast and anchor in a cove or inlet someplace on the shore of Camat. We'd only be a week or so from Ashaba. We might even be able to get there before Zandramas does." A bleak smile touched his lips. "I'd sort of like to be waiting for her when she gets there."

"It's got some definite possibilities, Belgarath," Silk said. "Could you do it?"

Belgarath scratched thoughtfully at his beard, squinting out into the sifting snow. "It's possible," he admitted. He looked at Garion. "But what do you think we ought to do with all these Mallorean soldiers and the ship's crew, once we get to the coast of Camat? You weren't planning to sink the ship and drown them all, were you, the way Zandramas does when she's finished using people?"

"Of course not!"

"I'm glad to hear that—but then how did you plan to keep them from running to the nearest garrison just as soon as we leave them behind? I don't know about you, but the idea of having a regiment or so of Mallorean troops hot on our heels doesn't excite me all that much."

Garion frowned. "I guess I hadn't thought about that," he admitted.

"I didn't think you had. It's usually best to work your way completely through an idea before you put it into action. It avoids a great deal of spur-of-the-moment patching later on."

"All right," Garion said, feeling slightly embarrassed.

"I know you're impatient, Garion, but impatience is a poor substitute for a well-considered plan."

"Do you mind, Grandfather?" Garion said acidly.

"Besides, it might just be that we're *supposed* to go to Rak Hagga and meet with Kal Zakath. Why would Cyradis turn us over to the Malloreans, after she went to all the trouble of putting *The Book of Ages* into my hands? There's something else going on here, and I'm not sure we want to disrupt things until we find out a little more about them."

The cabin door opened, and General Atesca, the commander of the Mallorean forces occupying the Isle of Verkat, emerged. From the moment they had been turned over to him, Atesca had been polite and strictly correct in all his dealings with them. He had also been very firm about his intention to deliver them personally to Kal Zakath in Rak Hagga. He was a tall, lean man, and his uniform was bright scarlet, adorned with numerous medals and decorations. He carried himself with erect dignity, though the fact that his nose had been broken at some time in the past made him look more like a street brawler than a general in an imperial army. He came up the slush-covered deck, heedless of his highly polished boots. "Good morning, gentlemen," he greeted them with a stiff, military bow. "I trust you slept well?"

"Tolerably," Silk replied.

"It seems to be snowing," the general said, looking about and speaking in the tone of one making small talk for the sake of courtesy.

"I noticed that," Silk said. "How long is it likely to take us to reach Rak Hagga?"

"A few more hours to reach the coast, your Highness, and then a two-day ride to the city."

Silk nodded. "Have you any idea why your Emperor wants to see us?" he asked.

"He didn't say," Atesca answered shortly, "and I didn't think it appropriate to ask. He merely told me to apprehend you and to bring you to him at Rak Hagga. You are all to be treated with utmost courtesy as long as you don't try to escape. If you do that, his Imperial Majesty instructed me to be more firm." His tone as he spoke was neutral, and his face remained expressionless. "I hope you gentlemen will excuse me now," he said. "I have some matters that need my attention." He bowed curtly, turned, and left them.

"He's a gold mine of information, isn't he?" Silk noted dryly. "Most Melcenes love to gossip, but you've got to pry every word out of this one."

"Melcene?" Garion said. "I didn't know that."

Silk nodded. "Atesca's a Melcene name. Kal Zakath has

some peculiar ideas about the aristocracy of talent. Angarak officers don't like the idea, but there's not too much they can do about it—if they want to keep their heads."

Garion was not really that curious about the intricacies of Mallorean politics, so he let the matter drop, to return to the subject they had been discussing previously. "I'm not quite clear about what you were saying, Grandfather," he said, "about our going to Rak Hagga, I mean."

"Cyradis believes that she has a choice to make," the old man replied, "and there are certain conditions that have to be met before she can make it. I've got a suspicion that your meeting with Zakath might be one of those conditions."

"You don't actually believe her, do you?"

"I've seen stranger things happen and I always walk very softly around the Seers of Kell."

"I haven't seen anything about a meeting of that kind in the Mrin Codex."

"Neither have I, but there are more things in the world than the Mrin Codex. You've got to keep in mind the fact that Cyradis is drawing on the prophecies of *both* sides, and if the prophecies are equal, they have equal truth. Not only that, Cyradis is probably drawing on some prophecies that only the Seers know about. Wherever this list of preconditions came from, though, I'm fairly certain that she won't let us get to this 'place which is no more' until every item's been crossed off her list."

"Won't *let* us?" Silk said.

"Don't underestimate Cyradis, Silk," Belgarath cautioned. "She's the receptacle of all the power the Dals possess. That means that she can probably do things that the rest of us couldn't even begin to dream of. Let's look at things from a practical point of view, though. When we started out, we were a half a year behind Zandramas and we were planning a very tedious and time-consuming trek across Cthol Murgos—but we kept getting interrupted."

"Tell me about it," Silk said sardonically.

15

"Isn't it curious that after all these interruptions, we've reached the eastern side of the continent ahead of schedule and cut Zandramas' lead down to a few weeks?"

Silk blinked, and then his eyes narrowed.

"Gives you something to think about, doesn't it?" The old man pulled his cloak more tightly about him and looked around at the settling snow. "Let's go inside," he suggested. "It's really unpleasant out here."

The coast of Hagga was backed by low hills, filmy-looking and white in the thick snowfall. There were extensive salt marshes at the water's edge, and the brown reeds bent under their burden of wet, clinging snow. A black-looking wooden pier extended out across the marshes to deeper water, and they disembarked from the Mallorean ship without incident. At the landward end of the pier a wagon track ran up into the hills, its twin ruts buried in snow.

Sadi the eunuch looked upward with a slightly bemused expression as they rode off the pier and onto the road. He lightly brushed one long-fingered hand across his shaved scalp. "They feel like fairy wings," he smiled.

"What's that?" Silk asked him.

"The snowflakes. I've almost never seen snow before— only when I was visiting a northern kingdom—and I actually believe that this is the first time I've ever been out of doors when it was snowing. It's not too bad, is it?"

Silk gave him a sour look. "The first chance I get, I'll buy you a sled," he said.

Sadi looked puzzled. "Excuse me, Kheldar, but what's a sled?" he asked.

Silk sighed. "Never mind, Sadi. I was only trying to be funny."

At the top of the first hill a dozen or so crosses leaned at various angles beside the road. Hanging from each cross was a skeleton with a few tattered rags clinging to its bleached bones and a clump of snow crowning its vacant-eyed skull.

"One is curious to know the reason for that, General Atesca," Sadi said mildly, pointing at the grim display at the roadside.

"Policy, your Excellency," Atesca replied curtly. "His Imperial Majesty seeks to alienate the Murgos from their king. He hopes to make them realize that Urgit is the cause of their misfortunes."

Sadi shook his head dubiously. "I'd question the reasoning behind that particular policy," he disagreed. "Atrocities seldom endear one to the victims. I've always preferred bribery myself."

"Murgos are accustomed to being treated atrociously." Atesca shrugged. "It's all they understand."

"Why haven't you taken them down and buried them?" Durnik demanded, his face pale and his voice thick with outrage.

Atesca gave him a long, steady look. "Economy, Goodman," he replied. "An empty cross really doesn't prove very much. If we took them down, we'd just have to replace them with fresh Murgos. That gets to be tedious after a while, and sooner or later one starts to run out of people to crucify. Leaving the skeletons there proves our point—and it saves time."

Garion did his best to keep his body between Ce'Nedra and the gruesome object lesson at the side of the road, trying to shield her from that hideous sight. She rode on obliviously, however, her face strangely numb and her eyes blank and unseeing. He threw a quick, questioning glance at Polgara and saw a slight frown on her face. He dropped back and pulled his horse in beside hers. "What's wrong with her?" he asked in a tense whisper.

"I'm not entirely sure, Garion," she whispered back.

"Is it the melancholia again?" There was a sick, sinking feeling in the pit of his stomach.

"I don't think so." Her eyes were narrowed in thought, and she absently pulled the hood of her blue robe forward to

17

cover the white lock in the midnight of her hair. "I'll keep an eye on her."

"What can I do?"

"Stay with her. Try to get her to talk. She might say something to give us some clues."

Ce'Nedra, however, made few responses to Garion's efforts to engage her in conversation, and her answers for the remainder of that snowy day quite frequently had little relevance to either his questions or his observations.

As evening began to settle over the war-ravaged countryside of Hagga, General Atesca called a halt, and his soldiers began to erect several scarlet pavilions in the lee of a fire-blackened stone wall, all that remained of a burned-out village. "We should reach Rak Hagga by late tomorrow afternoon," he advised them. "That large pavilion in the center of the encampment will be yours for the night. My men will bring you your evening meal in a little while. Now, if you'll all excuse me—" He inclined his head briefly, then turned his horse around to supervise his men.

When the soldiers had completed the erection of the pavilions, Garion and his friends dismounted in front of the one Atesca had indicated. Silk looked around at the guard detachment moving into position around the large red tent. "I wish he'd make up his mind," he said irritably.

"I don't quite follow you, Prince Kheldar," Velvet said to him. "Just who should make up his mind?"

"Atesca. He's the very soul of courtesy, but he surrounds us with armed guards."

"The troops might just be there to protect us, Kheldar," she pointed out. "This *is* a war zone, after all."

"Of course," he said dryly, "and cows might fly, too—if they had wings."

"What a fascinating observation," she marveled.

"I wish you wouldn't do that all the time."

"Do what?" Her brown eyes were wide and innocent.

"Forget it."

The supper Atesca's cooks prepared for them was plain, consisting of soldiers' rations and served on tin plates, but it was hot and filling. The interior of the pavilion was heated by charcoal braziers and filled with the golden glow of hanging oil lamps. The furnishings were of a military nature, the kinds of tables and beds and chairs that could be assembled and disassembled rapidly, and the floors and walls were covered with Mallorean carpets dyed a solid red color.

Eriond looked around curiosuly after he had pushed his plate back. "They seem awfully partial to red, don't they?" he noted.

"I think it reminds them of blood," Durnik declared bleakly. "They like blood." He turned to look coldly at the mute Toth. "If you've finished eating, I think we'd prefer it if you left the table," he said in a flat tone.

"That's hardly polite, Durnik," Polgara said reprovingly.

"I wasn't trying to be polite, Pol. I don't see why he has to be with us in the first place. He's a traitor. Why doesn't he go stay with his friends?"

The giant mute rose from the table, his face melancholy. He lifted one hand as if he were about to make one of those obscure gestures with which he and the smith communicated, but Durnik deliberately turned his back on him. Toth sighed and went over to sit unobstrusively in one corner.

"Garion," Ce'Nedra said suddenly, looking around with a worried little frown, "where's my baby?"

He stared at her.

"Where's Geran?" she demanded, her voice shrill.

"Ce'Nedra—" he started.

"I hear him crying. What have you done with him?" She suddenly sprang to her feet and began to dash about the tent, flinging back the curtains that partitioned off the sleeping quarters and yanking back the blankets on each bed. "Help me!" she cried to them. "Help me find my baby!"

19

Garion crossed the tent quickly to take her by the arm. "Ce'Nedra—"

"No!" she shouted at him. "You've hidden him somewhere! Let me go!" She wrenched herself free of his grasp and began overturning the furniture in her desperate search, sobbing and moaning unintelligibly.

Again Garion tried to restrain her, but she suddenly hissed at him and extended her fingers like talons to claw at his eyes.

"Ce'Nedra! Stop that!"

But she darted around him and bolted out of the pavilion into the snowy night.

As Garion burst through the tent flap in pursuit, he found his way barred by a red-cloaked Mallorean soldier. "You! Get back inside!" the man barked, blocking Garion with the shaft of his spear. Over the guard's shoulder, Garion saw Ce'Nedra struggling with another soldier; without even thinking, he smashed his fist into the face in front of him. The guard reeled backward and fell. Garion leaped over him, but found himself suddenly seized from behind by a half-dozen more men. "Leave her alone!" he shouted at the guard who was cruelly one of the little Queen's arms behind her.

"Get back inside the tent!" a rough voice barked, and Garion found himself being dragged backward step by step toward the tent flap. The soldier holding Ce'Nedra was half lifting, half pushing her back toward the same place. With a tremendous effort, Garion got control of himself and coldly began to draw in his will.

"That will be enough!" Polgara's voice cracked from the doorway to the tent.

The soldiers stopped, looking uncertainly at each other and somewhat fearfully at the commanding presence in the doorway.

"Durnik!" she said then. "Help Garion bring Ce'Nedra back inside."

Garion shook himself free of the restraining hands and he

and Durnik took the violently struggling little Queen from the soldier and pulled her back toward the pavilion.

"Sadi," Polgara said as Durnik and Garion entered the tent with Ce'Nedra between them, "do you have any oret in that case of yours?"

"Certainly, Lady Polgara," the eunuch replied, "but are you sure that oret is appropriate here? I'd be more inclined toward naladium, personally."

"I think we've got more than a case of simple hysteria on our hands, Sadi. I want something strong enough to insure that she doesn't wake up the minute my back's turned."

"Whatever you think best, Lady Polgara." He crossed the carpeted floor, opened his red leather case, and took out a vial of dark blue liquid. Then he went to the table and picked up a cup of water. He looked at her inquiringly.

She frowned. "Make it three drops," she decided.

He gave her a slightly startled look, then gravely measured out the dosage.

It took several moments of combined effort to get Ce'Nedra to drink the contents of the cup. She continued to sob and struggle for several moments, but then her struggles grew gradually weaker, and her sobbing lessened. Finally she closed her eyes with a deep sigh, and her breathing became regular.

"Let's get her to bed," Polgara said, leading the way to one of the curtained-off sleeping chambers.

Garion picked up the tiny form of his sleeping wife and followed. "What's wrong with her, Aunt Pol?" he demanded as he laid her gently on the bed.

"I'm not positive," Polgara replied, covering Ce'Nedra with a rough soldier's blanket. "I'll need more time to pin it down."

"What can we do?"

"Not very much while we're on the road," she admitted candidly. "We'll keep her asleep until we get to Rak Hagga. Once I get her into a more stable situation, I'll be able to work

21

on it. Stay with her. I want to talk with Sadi for a few moments."

Garion sat worriedly by the bed, gently holding his wife's limp little hand while Polgara went back out to consult with the eunuch concerning the various drugs in his case. Then she returned, drawing the drape shut behind her. "He has most of what I need," she reported quietly. "I'll be able to improvise the rest." She touched Garion's shoulder and bent forward. "General Atesca just came in," she whispered to him. "He wants to see you. I wouldn't be too specific about the cause of Ce'Nedra's attack. We can't be sure just how much Zakath knows about our reasons for being here, and Atesca's certain to report everything that hapapens, so watch what you say."

He started to protest.

"You can't do anything here, Garion, and they need you out there. I'll watch her."

"Is she subject to these seizures often?" Atesca was asking as Garion came through the draped doorway.

"She's very high-strung," Silk replied. "Sometimes circumstances get the best of her. Polgara knows what to do."

Atesca turned to face Garion. "Your Majesty," he said in a chilly tone, "I don't appreciate your attacking my soldiers."

"He got in my way, General," Garion replied. "I don't think I hurt him all that much."

"There's a principle involved, your Majesty."

"Yes," Garion agreed, "there is. Give the man my apologies, but advise him not to interfere with me again—particularly when it concerns my wife. I don't really like hurting people, but I can make exceptions when I have to."

Atesca's look grew steely, and the gaze Garion returned was just as bleak. They stared at each other for a long moment. "With all due respect, your Majesty," Atesca said finally, "don't abuse my hospitality again."

"Only if the situation requires it, General."

"I'll instruct my men to prepare a litter for your wife,"

Atesca said then, "and let's plan to get an early start tomorrow. If the Queen is ill, we want to get her to Rak Hagga as soon as possible."

"Thank you, General," Garion replied.

Atesca bowed coldly, then turned and left.

"Wouldn't you say that was a trifle blunt, Belgarion?" Sadi murmured. "We *are* in Atesca's power at the moment."

Garion grunted. "I didn't like his attitude." He looked at Belgarath, whose expression was faintly disapproving. "Well?" he asked.

"I didn't say anything."

"You didn't have to. I could hear you thinking all the way over here."

"Then I don't have to say it, do I?"

The next day dawned cold and raw, but the snow had stopped. Garion rode at the side of Ce'Nedra's horse-borne litter with his face mirroring his concern. The road they followed ran northwesterly past more burned-out villages and shattered towns. The ruins were covered with a thick coating of the clinging wet snow that had fallen the previous day, and each of them was encircled by a ring of those grim, occupied crosses and stakes.

It was about midafternoon when they crested a hill and saw the lead-gray expanse of Lake Hagga stretching far to the north and east; on the near shore was a large, walled city.

"Rak Hagga," Atesca said with a certain relief.

They rode on down the hill toward the city. A brisk wind was blowing in off the lake, whipping their cloaks about them and tossing the manes of their horses.

"All right, gentlemen," Atesca said over his shoulder to his troops, "let's form up and try to look like soldiers." The red-cloaked Malloreans pulled their horses into a double file and straightened in their saddles.

The walls of Rak Hagga had been breached in several places, and the tops of the battlements were chipped and pitted from the storms of steel-tipped arrows that had swept

23

over them. The heavy gates had been burst asunder during the final assault on the city and hung in splinters from their rusty iron hinges.

The guards at the gate drew themselves up and saluted smartly as Atesca led the way into the city. The battered condition of the stone houses within the walls attested to the savagery of the fighting which had ensued when Rak Hagga had fallen. Many of them stood unroofed to the sky, their gaping, soot-blackened windows staring out at the rubble-choked streets. A work gang of sullen Murgos, dragging clanking chains behind them, labored to clear the fallen building stones out of the slushy streets under the watchful eyes of a detachment of Mallorean soldiers.

"You know," Silk said, "that's the first time I've ever seen a Murgo actually work. I didn't think they even knew how."

The headquarters of the Mallorean army in Cthol Murgos was in a large, imposing yellow-brick house near the center of the city. It faced a broad, snowy square, and a marble staircase led up to the main door with a file of red-cloaked Mallorean soldiers lining each side.

"The former residence of the Murgo Military Governor of Hagga," Sadi noted as they drew near the house.

"You've been here before, then?" Silk asked.

"In my youth," Sadi replied. "Rak Hagga has always been the center of the slave trade."

Atesca dismounted and turned to one of his officers. "Captain," he said, "have your men bring the Queen's litter. Tell them to be very careful."

As the rest of them swung down from their mounts, the captain's men unfastened the litter from the saddles of the two horses that had carried it and started up the marble stairs in General Atesca's wake.

Just inside the broad doors stood a polished table, and seated behind it was an arrogant-looking man with angular eyes and an expensive-looking scarlet uniform. Against the far wall stood a row of chairs occupied by bored-looking officials.

"State your business," the officer behind the table said brusquely.

Atesca's face did not change expression as he silently stared at the officer.

"I said to state your business."

"Have the rules changed, Colonel?" Atesca asked in a deceptively mild voice. "Do we no longer rise in the presence of a superior?"

"I'm too busy to jump to my feet for every petty Melcene official from the outlying districts," the colonel declared.

"Captain," Atesca said flatly to his officer, "if the colonel is not on his feet in the space of two heartbeats, would you be so good as to cut his head off for me?"

"Yes, sir," the captain replied, drawing his sword even as the startled colonel jumped to his feet.

"Much better," Atesca told him. "Now, let's begin over again. Do you by chance remember how to salute?"

The colonel saluted smartly, though his face was pale.

"Splendid. We'll make a soldier of you yet. Now, one of the people I was escorting—a lady of high station—fell ill during our journey. I want a warm, comfortable room prepared for her immediately."

"Sir," the colonel protested, "I'm not authorized to do that."

"Don't put your sword away just yet, Captain."

"But, General, the members of his Majesty's household staff make all those decisions. They'll be infuriated if I overstep my bounds."

"I'll explain it to his Majesty, Colonel," Atesca told him. "The circumstances are a trifle unusual, but I'm sure he'll approve."

The colonel faltered, his eyes filled with indecison.

"Do it, colonel! Now!"

"I'll see to it at once, General," the colonel replied, snapping to attention. "You men," he said to the soldiers holding Ce'Nedra's litter, "follow me."

Garion automatically started to follow the litter, but Polgara took his arm firmly. "No, Garion. I'll go with her. There's nothing you can do right now, and I think Zakath's going to want to talk to you. Just be careful of what you say." And she went off down the hallway behind the litter.

"I see that Mallorean society still has its little frictions," Silk said blandly to General Atesca.

"Angaraks," Atesca grunted. "Sometimes they have a little difficulty coping with the modern world. Excuse me, Prince Kheldar. I want to let his Majesty know that we're here." He went to a polished door at the other end of the room and spoke briefly with one of the guards. Then he came back. "The Emperor is being advised of our arrival," he said to them. "I expect that he'll see us in a few moments."

A rather chubby, bald-headed man in a plain, though obviously costly, brown robe and with a heavy gold chain about his neck approached them. "Atesca, my dear fellow," he greeted the general, "they told me that you were stationed at Rak Verkat."

"I have some business with the Emperor, Brador. What are you doing in Cthol Murgos?"

"Cooling my heels," the chubby man replied. "I've been waiting for two days to see Kal Zakath."

"Who's minding the shop at home?"

"I've arranged it so that it more or less runs itself," Brador replied. "The report I have for his Majesty is so vital that I decided to carry it myself."

"What could be so earth-shaking that it would drag the Chief of the Bureau of Internal Affairs away from the comforts of Mal Zeth?"

"I believe that it's time for his Imperial Exaltedness to tear himself away from his amusements here in Cthol Murgos and come back to the capital."

26

"Careful, Brador," Atesca said with a brief smile. "Your fine-tuned Melcene prejudices are showing."

"Things are getting grim at home, Atesca," Brador said seriously. "I've *got* to talk with the Emperor. Can you help me to get in to see him?"

"I'll see what I can do."

"Thank you, my friend," Brador said, clasping the general's arm. "The whole fate of the empire may depend on my persuading Kal Zakath to come back to Mal Zeth."

"General Atesca," one of the spear-armed guards at the polished door said in a loud voice, "his Imperial Majesty will see you and your prisoners now."

"Very good," Atesca replied ignoring the ominous word "prisoners." He looked at Garion. "The Emperor must be very eager to see you, your Majesty," he noted. "It often takes weeks to gain an audience with him. Shall we go inside?"

CHAPTER TWO

Kal Zakath, the Emperor of boundless Mallorea, lounged in a red-cushioned chair at the far end of a large plain room. The Emperor wore a simple white linen robe, severe and unadorned. Though Garion knew that he was at least in his forties, his hair was untouched by gray and his face was unlined. His eyes, however, betrayed a kind of dead weariness, devoid of any joy or even any interest in life. Curled in his lap lay a common mackerel-striped alley cat, her eyes closed and her forepaws alternately kneading his thigh. Although the Emperor himself wore the simplest of clothes, the guards lining the walls all wore steel breastplates deeply inlaid with gold.

"My Emperor," General Atesca said with a deep bow, "I have the honor to present his Royal Majesty, King Belgarion of Riva."

Garion nodded briefly, and Zakath inclined his head in response. "Our meeting is long overdue, Belgarion," he said in a voice as dead as his eyes. "Your exploits have shaken the world."

"Yours have also made a certain impression, Zakath." Garion had decided even before he had left Rak Verkat that he would not perpetuate the absurdity of the Mallorean's self-bestowed "Kal."

A faint smile touched Zakath's lips. "Ah," he said in a tone which indicated that he saw through Garion's attempt to be subtle. He nodded briefly to the others, and his attention finally fixed itself upon the rumpled untidy form of Garion's grandfather. "And of course you, sir, would be Belgarath," he noted. "I'm a bit surprised to find you so ordinary looking. The Grolims of Mallorea all agree that you're a hundred feet tall—possible two hundred—and that you have horns and a forked tail."

"I'm in disguise," Belgarath replied with aplomb.

Zakath chuckled, though there was little amusement in that almost mechanical sound. Then he looked around with a faint frown. "I seem to note some absences," he said.

"Queen Ce'Nedra fell ill during our journey, your Majesty," Atesca advised him. "Lady Polgara is attending her."

"Ill? Is it serious?"

"It's difficult to say at this point, your Imperial Majesty," Sadi replied unctuously, "but we have given her certain medications, and I have every confidence in Lady Polgara's skill."

Zakath looked at Garion. "You should have sent word on ahead, Belgarion. I have a healer on my personal staff—a Dalasian woman with remarkable gifts. I'll send her to the Queen's chambers at once. Our first concern must be your wife's health."

"Thank you," Garion replied with genuine gratitude.

Zakath touched a bellpull and spoke briefly with the servant who responded immediately to his summons.

"Please," the Emperor said then, "seat yourselves. I have no particular interest in ceremony."

As the guards hastily brought chairs for them, the cat sleeping in Zakath's lap half opened her golden eyes and looked around at them. She rose to her paws, arched her back, and yawned. Then she jumped heavily to the floor with an audible grunt and waddled over to sniff at Eriond's fingers. With a faintly amused look, Zakath watched his obviously pregnant cat make her matronly way across the carpet. "You'll note that my cat has been unfaithful to me—again." He sighed in mock resignation. "It happens fairly frequently, I'm afraid, and she never seems to feel the slightest guilt about it."

The cat jumped up into Eriond's lap, nestled down, and began to purr contentedly.

"You've grown, boy," Zakath said to the young man. "Have they taught you how to talk as yet?"

"I've picked up a few words, Zakath," Eriond said in his clear voice.

"I know the rest of you—by reputation at least," Zakath said then. "Goodman Durnik and I met on the plains of Mishrak ac Thull, and of course I've heard of the Margravine Liselle of Drasnian Intelligence and of Prince Kheldar, who strives to become the richest man in the world."

Velvet's graceful curtsy of acknowledgement was not quite so florid as Silk's grandiose bow.

"And here, of course," the Emperor continued, "is Sadi, Chief Eunuch in the palace of Queen Salmissra."

Sadi bowed with fluid grace. "I must say that your Majesty is remarkable well informed," he said in his contralto voice. "You have read us all like an open book."

"My chief of intelligence tries to keep me informed, Sadi. He may not be as gifted as the inestimable Javelin of Boktor, but he knows about *most* of what's going on in this part of the world. He's mentioned that huge fellow over in the corner, but so far he hasn't been able to discover his name."

"He's called Toth," Eriond supplied. "He's a mute, so we have to do his talking for him."

"And a Dalasian besides," Zakath noted. "A very curious circumstance."

Garion had been closely watching this man. Beneath the polished, urbane exterior, he sensed a kind of subtle probing. The idle greetings, which seemed to be no more than a polite means of putting them at their ease, had a deeper motive behind them. In some obscure way he sensed that Zakath was somehow testing each of them.

The emperor straightened then. "You have an oddly assorted company with you, Belgarion," he said, "and you're a long way from home. I'm curious about your reasons for being here in Cthol Murgos."

"I'm afraid that's a private matter, Zakath."

One of the Emperor's eyebrows rose slightly. "Under the circumstances, that's hardly a satisfactory answer, Belgarion. I can't really take the chance that you're allied with Urgit."

"Would you accept my word that I'm not?"

"Not until I know a bit more about your visit to Rak Urga. Urgit left there quite suddenly—apparently in your company—and reappeared just as suddenly on the plains of Morcth, where he and a young woman led his troops out of an ambush I'd gone to a great deal of trouble to arrange. You'll have to admit that's a peculiar set of circumstances."

"Not when you look at it from a practical standpoint," Belgarath said. "The decision to take Urgit with us was mine. He'd found out who we are, and I didn't want an army of Murgos on our heels. Murgos aren't too bright, but they can be an inconvenience at times.

Zakath looked surprised. "He was your prisoner?"

Belgarath shrugged. "In a manner of speaking."

The Emperor laughed rather wryly. "You could have wrung

31

almost any concession from me if you had just delivered him into my hands, you know. Why did you let him go?"

"We didn't need him anymore," Garion replied. "We'd reached shores of Lake Cthaka, so he really wasn't any kind of threat to us."

Zakath's expression narrowed slightly. "A few other things happened as well, I think," he observed. "Urgit has always been a notorious coward, wholly under the domination of the Grolim Agachak and of his father's generals. But he didn't seem very timid while he was extricating his troops from the trap I'd laid for them, and all the reports filtering out of Rak Urga seem to suggest that he's actually behaving like a king. Did you by any chance have anything to do with that?"

"It's possible, I suppose," Garion answered. "Urgit and I talked a few times, and I told him what he was doing wrong."

Zakath tapped one forefinger against his chin, and his eyes were shrewd. "You may not have made a lion of him, Belgarion," he said, "but at least he's no longer a rabbit." A chill smile touched the Mallorean's lips. "In a way, I'm rather glad about that. I've never taken much satisfaction in hunting rabbits." He shaded his eyes with one hand, although the light in the room was not particularly bright. "But what I can't understand is how you managed to spirit him out of the Drojim Palace and away from the city. He has whole regiments of bodyguards."

"You're overlooking something, Zakath," Belgarath said to him. "We have certain advantages that aren't available to others."

"Sorcery, you mean? Is it really all that reliable?"

"I've had some luck with it from time to time."

Zakath's eyes had become suddenly intent. "They tell me that you're five thousand years old, Belgarath. Is that true?"

"Seven, actually—or a little more. Why do you ask?"

"In all those years, hasn't it ever occurred to you simply to seize power? You could have made yourself king of the world, you know."

Belgarath looked amused. "Why would I want to?" he asked.

"All men want power. It's human nature."

"Has all your power really made you happy?"

"It has certain satisfactions."

"Enough to make up for all the petty distractions that go with it?"

"I can endure those. At least I'm in a position where no one tells me what to do."

"No one tells me what to do either, and I'm not saddled with all those tedious responsibilities." Belgarath straightened. "All right, Zakath, shall we get to the point? What are your intentions concerning us?"

"I haven't really decided that yet." The Emperor looked around at them. "I presume that we can all be civilized about the present situation?"

"How do you mean, civilized?" Garion asked him.

"I'll accept your word that none of you will try to escape or do anything rash. I'm aware that you and a number of your friends have certain specialized talents. I don't want to be forced to take steps to counteract them."

"We have some rather pressing business," Garion replied carefully, "so we can only delay for just so long. For the time being, however, I think we can agree to be reasonable about things."

"Good. We'll have to talk later, you and I, and come to know one another. I've had comfortable quarters prepared for you and your friends, and I know that you're anxious about your wife. Now, I hope you'll excuse me, but I have some of those tedious responsibilities Belgarath mentioned to attend to."

Although the house was very large, it was not, strictly speaking, a palace. It appeared that the Murgo governors-general of Hagga who had ordered it built had not shared the grandiose delusions which afflicted the rulers of Urga, and so the building was more functional than ornate.

33

"I hope you'll excuse me," General Atesca said to them when they had emerged from the audience chamber. "I'm obliged to deliver a full report to his Majesty—about various matters—and then I must return immediately to Rak Verkat." He looked at Garion. "The circumstances under which we met were not the happiest, your Majesty," he said, "but I hope you won't think too unkindly of me." He bowed rather stiffly and then left them in the care of a member of the Emperor's staff.

The man who led them down a long, dark-paneled hallway toward the center of the house was obviously not an Angarak. He had not the angular eyes nor the stiff, bleak-faced arrogance that marked the men of that race. His cheerful, round face seemed to hint at a Melcene heritage, and Garion remembered that the bureaucracy which controlled most aspects of Mallorean life was made up almost excusively of Melcenes. "His Majesty asked me to assure you that your quarters are not intended to be a prison," the official told them as they approached a heavily barred iron door blocking off one portion of the hallway. "This was a Murgo house before we took the city, and it has certain structural peculiarities. Your rooms are in what once were the women's quarters, and Murgos are fanatically protective of their women. It has to do with their concept of racial purity, I think."

At the moment, Garion had little interest in sleeping arrangements. All his concern was for Ce'Nedra. "Do you happen to know where I might find my wife?" he asked the moon-faced bureaucrat.

"There at the end of this corridor, your Majesty," the Melcene replied, pointing toward a blue-painted door at the far end of the hall.

"Thank you." Garion glanced at the others. "I'll be back in a little while," he told them and strode on ahead.

The room he entered was warm and the lighting subdued. Deep, ornately woven Mallorean carpets covered the floor and soft green velvet drapes covered the tall, narrow windows.

Ce'Nedra lay in a high-posted bed against the wall opposite the door, and Polgara was seated at the bedside, her expression grave.

"Has there been any change?" Garion asked her, softly closing the door behind him.

"Nothing as yet," she replied.

Ce'Nedra's face was pale as she slept with her crimson curls tumbled on her pillow.

"She *is* going to be all right, isn't she?" Garion asked.

"I'm sure of it, Garion."

Another woman sat near the bed. She wore a light green, cowled robe; despite the fact that she was indoors, she had the hood pulled up, partially concealing her face. Ce'Nedra muttered something in a strangely harsh tone and tossed her head restlessly on her pillow. The cowled woman frowned. "Is this her customary voice, Lady Polgara?" she asked.

Polgara looked at her sharply. "No," she replied. "As a matter of fact, it's not."

"Would the drug you gave her in some way affect the sound of her speech?"

"No, it wouldn't. Actually, she shouldn't be making any sounds at all."

"Ah," the woman said. "I think perhaps I understand now." She leaned forward and very gently laid the fingertips of one hand on Ce'Nedra's lips. She nodded then and withdrew her hand. "As I suspected," she murmured.

Polgara also reached out to touch Ce'Nedra's face. Garion heard the faint whisper of her will, and the candle at the bedside flared up slightly, then sank back until its flame was scarcely more than a pinpoint. "I should have guessed," Polgara accused herself.

"What is it?" Garion asked in alarm.

"Another mind is seeking to dominate your wife and to subdue her will, your Majesty," the cowled woman told him. "It's an art sometimes practiced by the Grolims. They discovered it quite by accident during the third age."

35

"This is Andel, Garion," Polgara told him. "Zakath sent her here to help care for Ce'Nedra."

Garion nodded briefly to the hooded woman. "Exactly what do we mean by the word 'dominate'?" he asked.

"You should be more familiar with that than most people, Garion," Polgara said. "I'm sure you remember Asharak the Murgo."

Garion felt a sudden chill, remembering the force of the mind that had from his earliest childhood sought that same control over his awareness. "Drive it out," he pleaded. "Get whomever it is out of her mind."

"Perhaps not quite yet, Garion," Polgara said coldly. "We have an opportunity here. Let's not waste it."

"I don't understand."

"You will, dear," she told him. Then she rose, sat on the edge of the bed and lightly laid one hand on each of Ce'Nedra's temples. The faint whisper came again, stronger this time, and once again the candles all flared and then sank back as if suffocating. "I know you're in there," she said then. "You might as well speak."

Ce'Nedra's expression grew contorted, and she tossed her head back and forth as if trying to escape the hands touching her temples. Polgara's face grew stern, and she implacably kept her hands in place. The pale lock in her hair began to glow, and a strange chill came into the room, seeming to emanate from the bed itself.

Ce'Nedra suddenly screamed.

"Speak!" Polgara commanded. "You cannot flee until I release you, and I will not release you until you speak."

Ce'Nedra's eyes suddenly opened. They were filled with hate. "I do not fear thee, Polgara," she said in a harsh, rasping voice delivered in a peculiar accent.

"And I fear you even less. Now, who are you?"

"Thou knowest me, Polgara."

"Perhaps, but I will have your name from you." There was a long pause, and the surge of Polgara's will grew stronger.

36

Ce'Nedra screamed again—a scream filled with an agony that made Garion flinch. "Stop!" the harsh voice cried. "I will speak!"

"Say your name," Polgara insisted implacably.

"I am Zandramas."

"So. What do you hope to gain by this?"

An evil chuckle escaped Ce'Nedra's pale lips. "I have already stolen her heart, Polgara—her child. Now I will steal her mind as well. I could easily kill her if I chose, but a dead Queen may be buried and her grave left behind. A mad one, on the other hand, will give thee much to distract thee from thy search for the Sardion."

"I can banish you with a snap of my fingers, Zandramas."

"And I can return just as quickly."

A frosty smile touched Polgara's lips. "You're not nearly as clever as I thought," she said. "Did you actually believe that I twisted your name out of you for my own amusement? Were you ignorant of the power over you that you gave me when you spoke your own name? The power of the name is the most elementary of all. I can keep you out of Ce'Nedra's mind now. There's much more, though. For example, I know now that you're at Ashaba, haunting the bat-infested ruins of the House of Torak like a poor ragged ghost."

A startled gasp echoed through the room.

"I could tell you more, Zandramas, but this is all beginning to bore me." She straightened, her hands still locked to the sides of Ce'Nedra's head. The white lock at her brow flared into incandescence, and the faint whisper became a deafening roar. "Now, begone!" she commanded.

Ce'Nedra moaned, and her face suddenly contorted into an expression of agony. An icy, stinking wind seemed to howl through the room, and the candles and glowing braziers sank even lower until the room was scarcely lit.

"Begone!" Polgara repeated.

An agonized wail escaped Ce'Nedra's lips, and then that wail became disembodied, coming it seemed from the empty

37

air above the bed. The candles went out, and all light ceased to glow out of the braziers. The wailing voice began to fade, moving swiftly until it came to them as no more than a murmur echoing from an unimaginable distance.

"Is Zandramas gone?" Garion asked in a shaking voice.

"Yes," Polgara replied calmly out of the sudden darkness.

"What are we going to say to Ce'Nedra? When she wakes up, I mean."

"She won't remember any of this. Just tell her something vague. Make some light, dear."

Garion fumbled for one of the candles, brushed his sleeve against it, and then deftly caught it before it hit the floor. He was sort of proud of that.

"Don't play with it, Garion. Just light it."

Her tone was so familiar and so commonplace that he began to laugh, and the little surge of his will that he directed at the candle was a stuttering sort of thing. The flame that appeared bobbled and hiccuped at the end of the wick in a soundless golden chortle.

Polgara looked steadily at the giggling candle, then closed her eyes. "Oh, Garion," she sighed in resignation.

He moved about the room relighting the other candles and fanning the braziers back into life. The flames were all quite sedate—except for the original one, which continued to dance and laugh in blithe glee.

Polgara turned to the hooded Dalasian healer. "You're most perceptive, Andel," she said. "That sort of thing is difficult to recognize unless you know precisely what you're looking for."

"The perception was not mine, Lady Polgara," Andel replied. "I was advised by another of the cause of her Majesty's illness."

"Cyradis?"

Andel nodded. "The minds of all our race are joined with hers, for we are but the instruments of the task which lies upon her. Her concern for the Queen's well-being prompted

38

her to intervene." The hooded woman hesitated. "The Holy Seeress also asked me to beg you to intercede with your husband in the matter of Toth. The Goodman's anger is causing that gentle guide extreme anguish, and his pain is also hers. What happened at Verkat had to happen—otherwise the meeting between the Child of Light and the Child of Dark could not come to pass for ages hence."

Polgara nodded gravely. "I thought it might have been something like that. Tell her that I'll speak with Durnik in Toth's behalf."

Andel inclined her head gratefully.

"Garion," Ce'Nedra murmured drowsily, "where are we?"

He turned to her quickly. "Are you all right?" he asked, taking her hand in his.

"Mmmm," she said. "I'm just so very sleepy. What happened—and where are we?"

"We're at Rak Hagga." He threw a quick glance at Polgara, then turned back to the bed. "You just had a little fainting spell is all," he said with a slightly exaggerated casualness. "How are you feeling?"

"I'm fine, dear, but I think I'd like to sleep now." And her eyes went closed. Then she opened them again with a sleepy little frown. "Garion," she murmured, "why is that candle acting like that?"

He kissed her lightly on the cheek. "Don't worry about it, dear," he told her, but she had already fallen fast asleep.

It was well past midnight when Garion was awakened by a light tapping on the door of the room in which he slept. "Who is it?" he asked, half rising in his bed.

"A messenger from the Emperor, your Majesty," a voice replied from the other side of the door. "He instructed me to ask if you would be so good as to join him in his private study."

"Now? In the middle of the night?"

"Such was the Emperor's instruction, your Majesty."

"All right," Garion said, throwing off his blankets and swinging around to put his feet on the cold floor. "Give me a minute or so to get dressed."

"Of course, your Majesty."

Muttering to himself, Garion began to pull on his clothes by the faint light coming from the brazier in the corner. When he was dressed, he splashed cold water on his face and raked his fingers through his sandy hair, trying to push it into some semblance of order. Almost as an afterthought he ducked his head and arm through the strap attached to the sheath of Iron-grip's sword and shrugged it into place across his back. Then he opened the door. "All right," he said to the messenger, "let's go."

Kal Zakath's study was a book-lined room with several leather-upholstered chairs, a large polished table and a crackling fire on the hearth. The Emperor, still clad in plain white linen, sat in a chair at the table, shuffling through a stack of parchment sheets by the light of a single oil lamp.

"You wanted to see me, Zakath?" Garion asked as he entered the room.

"Ah, yes, Belgarion," Zakath said, pushing aside the parchments. "So good of you to come. I understand that your wife is recovering."

Garion nodded. "Thank you again for sending Andel. Her aid was very helpful."

"My pleasure, Belgarion." Zakath reached out and lowered the wick in the lamp until the corners of the room filled with shadows. "I thought we might talk a little," he said.

"Isn't it sort of late?"

"I don't sleep very much, Belgarion. A man can lose a third of his life in sleep. The day is filled with bright lights and distractions; the night is dim and quiet and allows much greater concentration. Please, sit down."

Garion unbuckled his sword and leaned it against a bookcase.

"I'm not really all *that* dangerous, you know," the Emperor said, looking pointedly at the great weapon.

Garion smiled slightly, settling into a chair by the fire. "I didn't bring it because of you, Zakath. It's just a habit. It's not the kind of sword you want to leave lying around."

"I don't think anyone would steal it, Belgarion."

"It *can't* be stolen. I just don't want anybody getting hurt by accidentally touching it."

"Do you mean to say that it's *that* sword?"

Garion nodded. "I'm sort of obliged to take care of it. It's a nuisance most of the time, but there've been a few occasions when I was glad I had it with me."

"What *really* happened at Cthol Mishrak?" Zakath asked suddenly. "I've heard all sorts of stories."

Garion nodded wryly. "So have I. Most of them get the names right, but not very much else. Neither Torak nor I had very much control over what happened. We fought, and I stuck that sword into his chest."

"And he died" Zakath's face was intent.

"Eventually, yes."

"Eventually?"

"He vomited fire first and wept flames. Then he cried out."

"What did he say?"

"'Mother,'" Garion replied shortly. He didn't really want to talk about it.

"What an extraordinary thing for him to do. Whatever happened to his body? I had the entire ruin of Cthol Mishrak searched for him."

"The other Gods came and took it. Do you suppose we could talk about something else? Those particular memories are painful."

"He *was* your enemy."

Garion sighed. "He was also a God, Zakath—and killing a God is a terrible thing to have to do."

"You're a strangely gentle man, Belgarion. I think I respect you more for that than I do for your invincible courage."

41

"I'd hardly say invincible. I was terrified the whole time—
and so was Torak, I think. Was there something you really
wanted to talk about?"

Zakath leaned back in his chair, tapping thoughtfully at his
pursed lips. "You know that eventually you and I will have
to confront each other, don't you?"

"No," Garion disagreed. "That's not absolutely certain."

"There can only be one King of the World."

Garion's look grew pained. "I've got enough trouble trying
to rule one small island. I've never wanted to be King of the
World."

"But I have—and do."

Garion sighed. "Then we probably will fight at that—
sooner or later. I don't think the world was intended to be
ruled by one man. If you try to do that, I'll have to stop you."

"I am unstoppable, Belgarion."

"So was Torak—or at least he thought so."

"That's blunt enough."

"It helps to avoid a lot of misunderstandings later on. I'd
say that you've got enough trouble at home without trying to
invade my kingdom—or those of my friends. That's not to
mention the stalemate here in Cthol Murgos."

"You're well informed."

"Queen Porenn is a close personal friend. She keeps me
advised, and Silk picks up a great deal of information during
the course of his busisness dealings."

"Silk?"

"Excuse me. Prince Kheldar, I mean. Silk's a nickname of
sorts."

Zakath looked at him steadily. "In some ways we're very
much alike, Belgarion, and in other ways very different, but
we still do what necessity compels us to do. Frequently, we're
at the mercy of events over which we have no control."

"I suppose you're talking about the two Prophecies?"

Zakath laughed shortly. "I don't believe in prophecy. I only
believe in power. It's curious, though, that we've both been

faced with similar problems of late. You recently had to put down an uprising in Aloria—a group of religious fanatics, I believe. I have something of much the same nature going on in Darshiva. Religion is a constant thorn in the side of any ruler, wouldn't you say?"

"I've been able to work around it—most of the time."

"You've been very lucky then. Torak was neither a good nor kindly God, and his Grolim priesthood is vile. If I weren't busy here in Cthol Murgos, I think I might endear myself to the next thousand or so generations by obliterating every Grolim on the face of the earth."

Garion grinned at him. "What would you say to an alliance with that in mind?" he suggested.

Zakath laughed briefly, and then his face grew somber again. "Does the name Zandramas mean anything to you?" he asked.

Garion edged around that cautiously, not knowing how much information Zakath had about their real reason for being in Cthol Murgos. "I've heard some rumors," he said.

"How about Cthrag Sardius?"

"I've heard of it."

"You're being evasive, Belgarion." Zakath gave him a steady look, then passed his hand wearily across his eyes.

"I think you need some sleep," Garion told him.

"Time for that soon enough—when my work is done."

"That's up to you, I guess."

"How much do you know about Mallorea, Belgarion?"

"I get reports—a little disjointed sometimes, but fairly current."

"No. I mean our past."

"Not too much, I'm afraid. Western historians tried very hard to ignore the fact that Mallorea was even there."

Zakath smiled wryly. "The University of Melcena has the same shortsightedness regarding the West," he noted. "Anyway, over the past several centuries—since the disaster at Vo Mimbre—Mallorean society has become almost completely

43

secular. Torak was bound in sleep, Ctuchik was practicing his perversions here in Cthol Murgos, and Zedar was wandering around the world like a rootless vagabond—what ever happened to him, by the way? I thought he was at Cthol Mishrak."

"He was."

"We didn't find his body."

"He isn't dead."

"He's not?" Zakath looked stunned. "Where is he, then?"

"Beneath the city. Belgarath opened the earth and sealed him up in solid rock under the ruin."

"Alive?" Zakath's exclamation came out in a choked gasp.

"There was a certain amount of justification for it. Go on with your story."

Zakath shuddered and then recovered. "With the rest of them out of the way, the only religious figure left in Mallorea was Urvon, and he devoted himself almost exclusively to trying to make his palace at Mal Yaska more opulent than the imperial one at Mal Zeth. Every so often he'd preach a sermon filled with mumbo jumbo and nonsense, but most of the time he seemed to have forgotten Torak entirely. With the Dragon God and his disciples no longer around, the real power of the Grolim Church was gone—oh, the priests babbled about the return of Torak and they all paid lip service to the notion that one day the sleeping God would awaken, but the memory of him grew dimmer and dimmer. The power of the Church grew less and less, while that of the army—which is to say the imperial throne—grew more and more."

"Mallorean politics seem to be very murky," Garion observed.

Zakath nodded. "It's part of our nature, I suppose. At any rate, our society was functioning and moving out of the dark ages—slowly, perhaps, but moving. Then you suddenly appeared out of nowhere and awakend Torak—and just as suddenly put him permanently back to sleep again. That's when all our problems started."

44

"Shouldn't it have ended them? That's sort of what I had in mind."

"I don't think you grasp the nature of the religious mind, Belgarion. So long as Torak was there—even though he slept—the Grolims and the other hysterics in the empire were fairly placid, secure and comfortable in the belief that one day he would awaken, punish all their enemies, and reassert the absolute authority of the unwashed and stinking priesthood. But when you killed Torak, you destroyed their comfortable sense of security. They were forced to face the fact that without Torak they were nothing. Some of them were so chagrined that they went mad. Others fell into absolute despair. A few, however, began to hammer together a new mythology—something to replace what you had destroyed with a single stroke of that sword over there."

"It wasn't entirely my idea," Garion told him.

"It's results that matter, Belgarion, not intentions. Anyway, Urvon was forced to tear himself away from his quest for opulence and his wallowing in the adoration of the sycophants who surrounded him and get back to business. For a time he was in an absolute frenzy of activity. He resurrected all the moth-eaten old prophecies and twisted and wrenched at them until they seemed to say what he wanted them to say."

"And what was that?"

"He's trying to convince people that a new God will come to rule over Angarak—either a resurrection of Torak himself or some new deity infused with Torak's spirit. He's even got a candidate in mind for this new God of Angarak."

"Oh? Who's that?"

Zakath's expression became amused. "He sees his new God every time he looks in a mirror."

"You're not serious!"

"Oh, yes. Urvon's been trying to convince himself that he's at least a demigod for several centuries now. He'd probably have himself paraded all over Mallorea in a golden chariot—except that he's afraid to leave Mal Yaska. As I understand it, there's a very nasty hunchback who's been hungering to kill him for eons—one of Aldur's disciples, I believe."

Garion nodded. "Beldin," he said. "I've met him."

"Is he really as bad as the stories make him out to be?"

"Probably even worse. I don't think you'd want to be around to watch what he does, if he ever catches up with Urvon."

"I wish him good hunting, but Urvon's not my only problem, I'm afraid. Not long after the death of Torak, certain rumors started coming out of Darshiva. A Grolim priestess—Zandramas by name—also began to predict the coming of a new God."

"I didn't know that she was a Grolim," Garion said with some surprise.

Zakath nodded gravely. "She formerly had a very unsavory reputation in Darshiva. Then the so-called ecstacy of prophecy fell on her, and she was suddenly transformed by it. Now when she speaks, no one can resist her words. She preaches to multitudes and fires them with invincible zeal. Her message of the coming of a new God ran through Darshiva like wildfire and spread into Regel, Voresebo, and Zamad as well. Virtually the entire northeast coast of Mallorea is hers."

"What's the Sardion got to do with all this?" Garion asked.

"I think it's the key to the whole business," Zakath replied. "Both Zandramas and Urvon seem to believe that whoever finds and possesses it is going to win out."

"Agachak—the Hierarch of Rak Urga—believes the same thing," Garion told him.

Zakath nodded moodily. "I suppose I should have realized that. A Grolim is a Grolim—whether he comes from Mallorea or Cthol Murgos."

"It seems to me that maybe you should go back to Mallorea and put things in order."

"No, Belgarion, I won't abandon my campaign here in Cthol Murgos."

"Is personal revenge worth it?"

Zakath looked startled.

"I know why you hated Taur Urgas, but he's dead, and Urgit's not at all like him. I can't really believe that you'd sacrifice your whole empire just for the sake of revenging yourself on a man who can't feel it."

"You know?" Zakath's face looked stricken. "Who told you?"

"Urgit did. He told me the whole story."

"With pride, I expect." Zakath's teeth were clenched, and his face pale.

"No, not really. It was with regret—and with contempt for Taur Urgas. He hated him even more than you do."

"That's hardly possible, Belgarion. To answer your question, yes, I *will* sacrifice my empire—the whole world if need be—to spill out the last drop of the blood of Taur Urgas. I will neither sleep nor rest nor be turned aside from my vengeance, and I will crush whomever stands in my path."

"Tell him," the dry voice in Garion's mind said suddenly.

"What?"

"Tell him the truth about Urgit."

"But—"

"Do it, Garion. He needs to know. There are things he has to do, and he won't do them until he puts this obsession behind him."

Zakath was looking at him curiously.

"Sorry, just receiving instructions," Garion explained lamely.

"Instructions? From whom?"

"You wouldn't believe it. I was told to give you some information." He drew in a deep breath. "Urgit isn't a Murgo," he said flatly.

"What are you talking about?"

"I said that Urgit isn't a Murgo—at least not entirely. His mother was, of course, but his father was not Taur Urgas."

"You're lying!"

"No, I'm not. We found out about it while we were at the Drojim Palace in Rak Urga. Urgit didn't know about it either."

47

"I don't believe you, Belgarion!" Zakath's face was livid, and he was nearly shouting.

"Taur Urgas is dead," Garion said wearily. "Urgit made sure of that by cutting his throat and burying him head down in his grave. He also claims that he had every one of his brothers—the *real* sons of Taur Urgas—killed to make himself secure on the throne. I don't think there's one drop of Urga blood left in the world."

Zakath's eyes narrowed. "It's a trick. You've allied yourself with Urgit and brought me this absurd lie to save his life."

"Use the Orb, Garion," the voice instructed.

"How?"

"Take it off the pommel of the sword and hold it in your right hand. It'll show Zakath the truths that he needs to know."

Garion rose to his feet. "If I can show you the truth, will you look?" he asked the agitated Mallorean Emperor.

"Look? Look at what?"

Garion walked over to his sword and peeled off the soft leather sleeve covering the hilt. He put his hand on the Orb, and it came free with an audible click. Then he turned back to the man at the table. "I'm not exactly sure how this works," he said. "I'm told that Aldur was able to do it, but I've never tried it for myself. I think you're supposed to look into this." He extended his right arm until the Orb was in front of Zakath's face.

"What is that?"

"You people call it Cthrag Yaska," Garion replied.

Zakath recoiled, his face blanching.

"It won't hurt you—as long as you don't touch it."

The Orb, which for the past months had rather sullenly obeyed Garion's continued instruction to restrain itself, slowly began to pulsate and glow in his hand, bathing Zakath's face in its blue radiance. The Emperor half lifted his hand as if to push the glowing stone aside.

"Don't touch it," Garion warned again. "Just look."

But Zakath's eyes were already locked on the stone as its

blue light grew stronger and stronger. His hands gripped the edge of the table in front of him so tightly that his knuckles grew white. For a long moment he stared into that blue incandescence. Then, slowly, his fingers lost their grip on the table edge and fell back onto the arms of his chair. An expression of agony crossed his face. "They have escaped me," he groaned with tears welling out of his closed eyes, "and I have slaughtered tens of thousands for nothing." The tears began to stream down his contorted face.

"I'm sorry, Zakath," Garion said quietly, lowering his hand. "I can't change what's already happened, but you had to know the truth."

"I cannot thank you for this truth," Zakath said, his shoulders shaking in the storm of his weeping. "Leave me, Belgarion. Take that accursed stone from my sight."

Garion nodded with a great feeling of compassion and shared sorrow. Then he replaced the Orb on the pommel of his sword, re-covered the hilt, and picked up the great weapon. "I'm very sorry, Zakath," he said again, and then he quietly went out of the room, leaving the Emperor of boundless Mallorea alone with his grief.

CHAPTER THREE

"Really, Garion, I'm perfectly fine," Ce'Nedra objected again.

"I'm glad to hear that."

"Then you'll let me get out of bed?"

"No."

"That's not fair," she pouted.

"Would you like a little more tea?" he asked, going to the fireplace, taking up a poker, and swinging out the iron arm from which a kettle was suspended.

"No, I don't," she replied in a sulky little voice. "It smells, and it tastes awful."

"Aunt Pol says that it's very good for you. Maybe if you

drink some more of it, she'll let you get out of bed and sit in a chair for a while." He spooned some of the dried, aromatic leaves from an earthenware pot into a cup, tipped the kettle carefully with the poker, and filled the cup with steaming water.

Ce'Nedra's eyes had momentarily come alight, but narrowed again almost immediately. "Oh, *very* clever, Garion," she said in a voice heavy with sarcasm. "Don't patronize me."

"Of course not," he agreed blandly, setting the cup on the stand beside the bed. "You probably ought to let that steep for a while," he suggested.

"It can steep all year if it wants to. I'm not going to drink it."

He sighed with resignation. "I'm sorry, Ce'Nedra," he said with genuine regret, "but you're wrong. Aunt Pol says that you're supposed to drink a cup of this every other hour. Until she tells me otherwise, that's exactly what you're going to do."

"What if I refuse?" Her tone was belligerent.

"I'm bigger than you are," he reminded her.

Her eyes went wide with shock. "You wouldn't actually *force* me to drink it, would you?"

His expression grew mournful. "I'd really hate to do something like that," he told her.

"But you'd do it, wouldn't you?" she accused.

He tought about it a moment, then nodded. "Probably," he admitted, "if Aunt Pol told me to."

She glared at him. "All right," she said finally. "Give me the stinking tea."

"It doesn't smell all *that* bad, Ce'Nedra."

"Why don't *you* drink it, then?"

"I'm not the one who's been sick."

She proceeded then to tell him—at some length—exactly what she thought of the tea and him and her bed and the room and of the whole world in general. Many of the terms she used were very colorful—even lurid—and some of them were in languages that he didn't recognize.

"What on earth is all the shouting about?" Polgara asked, coming into the room.

"I absolutely *hate* this stuff!" Ce'Nedra declared at the top of her lungs, waving the cup about and spilling most of the contents.

"I wouldn't drink it then," Aunt Pol advised calmly.

"Garion says that if I don't drink it, he'll pour it down my throat."

"Oh. Those were *yesterday's* instructions." Polgara looked at Garion. "Didn't I tell you that they change today?"

"No," he replied. "As a matter of fact, you didn't." He said it in a very level tone. He was fairly proud of that.

"I'm sorry, dear. I must have forgotten."

"When can I get out of bed?" Ce'Nedra demanded.

Polgara gave her a surprised look. "Any time you want, dear," she said. "As a matter of fact, I just came by to ask if you planned to join us for breakfast."

Ce'Nedra sat up in bed, her eyes like hard little stones. She slowly turned an icy gaze upon Garion and then quite deliberately stuck her tongue out at him.

Garion turned to Polgara. "Thanks awfully," he said to her.

"Don't be snide, dear," she murmured. She looked at the fuming little Queen. "Ce'Nedra, weren't you told as a child that sticking out one's tongue is the worst possible form of bad manners?"

Ce'Nedra smiled sweetly. "Why, yes, Lady Polgara, as a matter of fact I was. That's why I only do it on special occasions."

"I think I'll take a walk," Garion said to no one in particular. He went to the door, opened it, and left.

Some days later he lounged in one of the sitting rooms that had been built in the former women's quarters where he and the others were lodged. The room was peculiarly feminine. The furniture was softly cushioned in mauve, and the broad widows had filmy curtains of pale lavender. Beyond the windows lay a snowy garden, totally embraced by the tall wings of this bleak Murgo house. A cheery fire crackled in the half-moon arch of a broad fireplace, and at the far corner of the room an artfully contrived grotto, thick with green fern and moss, flourished about a trickling fountain. Garion sat brooding out at a sunless noon—at an ash-colored sky spitting white pellets that were neither snow nor hail, but something in between—and realized all of a sudden that he was homesick for Riva. It was a peculiar thing to come to grips with here on the opposite end of the world. Always before, the word "homesick" had been associated with Faldor's farm—the kitchen, the broad central courtyard, Durnik's smithy, and all the other dear, treasured memories. Now, suddenly, he missed that storm-lashed coast, the security of that grim fortress hovering above the bleak city lying below, and the mountains, heavy with snow, rising stark white against a black and stormy sky.

There was a faint knock at the door.

"Yes?" Garion said absently, not looking around.

The door opened almost timidly. "Your Majesty?" a vaguely familiar voice said.

Garion turned, looking back over his shoulder. The man was chubby and bald and he wore brown, a plain serviceable color, though his robe was obviously costly, and the heavy gold chain about his neck loudly proclaimed that this was no minor official. Garion frowned slightly. "Haven't we met before?" he asked. "Aren't you General Atesca's friend—uh—"

"Brador, your Majesty," the brown-robed man supplied. "Chief of the Bureau of Internal Affairs."

"Oh, yes. Now I remember. Come in, your Excellency, come in."

"Thank you, your Majesty." Brador came into the room and moved toward the fireplace, extending his hands to its warmth. "Miserable climate." He shuddered.

"You should try a winter in Riva," Garion said, "although it's summer there right now."

Brador looked out the window at the snowy garden. "Strange place, Cthol Murgos," he said. "One's tempted to believe that all of Murgodom is deliberately ugly, and then one comes across a room like this."

"I suspect that the ugliness was to satisfy Ctuchik—and Taur Urgas," Garion replied. "Underneath, Murgos probably aren't much different from the rest of us."

Brador laughed. "That sort of thinking is considered heresy in Mal Zeth," he said.

"The people in Val Alorn feel much the same way." Garion looked at the bureaucrat. "I expect that this isn't just a social call, Brador," he said. "What's on your mind?"

"Your Majesty," Brador said soberly, "I absolutely *have* to speak with the Emperor. Atesca tried to arrange it before he went back to Rak Verkat, but—" He spread his hands helplessly. "Could you possibly speak to him about it? The matter is of the utmost urgency."

"I really don't think there's very much I can do for you, Brador," Garion told him. "Right now I'm probably the last person he'd want to talk to."

"Oh?"

"I told him something that he didn't want to hear."

Brador's shoulders slumped in defeat. "You were my last hope, your Majesty," he said.

"What's the problem?"

Brador hesitated, looking around nervously as if to assure himself that they were alone. "Belgarion," he said then in a very quiet voice, "have you ever seen a demon?"

"A couple of times, yes. It's not the sort of experience I'd care to repeat."

"How much do you know about the Karands?"

"Not a great deal. I've heard that they're related to the Morindim in northern Gar og Nadrak."

"You know more about them than most people, then. Do

you know very much about the religious practices of the Morindim?"

Garion nodded. "They're demon worshippers. It's not a particularly safe form of religion, I've noticed."

Brador's face was bleak. "The Karands share the beliefs and practices of their cousins on the arctic plains of the West," he said. "After they were converted to the worship of Torak, the Grolims tried to stamp out those practices, but they persisted in the mountains and forests." He stopped and looked fearfully around again. "Belgarion," he said, almost in a whisper, "does the name Mengha mean anything to you?"

"No. I don't think so. Who's Mengha?"

"We don't know—at least not for certain. He seems to have come out of the forest to the north of Lake Karanda about six months ago."

"And?"

"He marched—alone—to the gates of Calida in Jenno and called for the surrender of the city. They laughed at him, of course, but then he marked some symbols on the ground. They didn't laugh any more after that." The Melcene bureaucrat's face was gray. "Belgarion, he unloosed a horror on Calida such as man has never seen before. Those symbols he drew on the ground summoned up a host of demons—not one, or a dozen, but a whole army of them. I've talked with survivors of that attack. They're mostly mad—mercifully so, I think—and what happened at Calida was utterly unspeakable."

"An *army* of them?" Garion exclaimed.

Brador nodded. "That's what makes Mengha so dreadfully dangerous. As I'm sure you know, usually when someone summons a demon, sooner or later it gets away from him and kills him, but Mengha appears to have absolute control of all the fiends he raises and he can call them up by the hundreds. Urvon is terrified and he's even begun to experiment with magic himself, hoping to defend Mal Yaska against Mengha. We don't know where Zandramas is, but her apostate Grolim cohorts are desperately striving also to summon up these fiends. Great Gods, Belgarion, help me! This unholy infection will spread out of Mallorea and sweep the world. We'll all be engulfed by howling fiends, and no place, no matter how remote, will provide a haven for the pitiful remnants of mankind. Help me to persuade Kal Zakath that his petty little war here in Cthol Murgos has no real meaning in the face of the horror that's emerging in Mallorea."

Garion gave him a long, steady look, then rose to his feet. "You'd better come with me, Brador," he said quietly. "I think we need to talk with Belgarath."

They found the old sorcerer in the book-lined library of the house, poring over an ancient volume bound in green leather. He set his book aside and listened as Brador repeated what he had told Garion. "Urvon and Zandramas are also engaging in this insanity?" he asked when the Melcene had finished.

Brador nodded. "According to our best information, Ancient One," he replied.

Belgarath slammed his fist down and began to swear. "What are they thinking of?" he burst out, pacing up and down. "Don't they know that UL himself had forbidden this?"

"They're afraid of Mengha," Brador said helplessly. "They feel that they must have some way to protect themselves from his horde of fiends."

"You don't protect yourself from demons by raising more demons," the old man fumed. "If even one of them breaks free, they'll all get loose. Urvon or Zandramas might be able to handle them, but sooner or later some underling is going to make a mistake. Let's go see Zakath."

"I don't think we can get in to see him just now, Grandfather," Garion said dubiously. "He didn't like what I told him about Urgit."

"That's too bad. This is something that won't wait for him to regain his composure. Let's go."

The three of them went quickly through the corridors of

the house to the large antechamber they had entered with General Atesca upon their arrival from Rak Verkat.

"Absolutely impossible," the colonel at the desk beside the main door declared when Belgarath demanded to see the Emperor immediately.

"As you grow older, Colonel," the old man said ominously, "you'll discover just how meaningless the word 'impossible' really is." He raised one hand, gestured somewhat theatrically, and Garion heard and felt the surge of his will.

A number of battle flags mounted on stout poles projected out from the opposite wall perhaps fifteen feet from the floor. The officious colonel vanished from his chair and reappeared precariously astride one of those poles with his eyes bulging and his hands desperately clinging to his slippery perch.

"Where would you like to go next, Colonel?" Belgarath asked him. "As I recall, there's a very tall flagpole out front. I could set you on top of it if you wish."

The colonel stared at him in horror.

"Now, as soon as I bring you down from there, you're going to persuade your Emperor to see us at once. You're going to be very convincing, Colonel—that's unless you want to be a permanent flagpole ornament, of course."

The colonel's face was still pasty white when he emerged from the guarded door leading to the audience chamber, and he flinched violently every time Belgarath moved his hand. "His Majesty consents to see you," he stammered.

Belgarath grunted. "I was almost sure that he would."

Kal Zakath had undergone a noticeable transformation since Garion had last seen him. His white linen robe was wrinkled and stained, and there were dark circles under his eyes. His face was deathly pale, his hair was unkempt, and he was unshaven. Spasmlike tremors ran through his body, and he looked almost too weak to stand. "What do you want?" he demanded in a barely audible voice.

"Are you sick?" Belgarath asked him.

"A touch of fever, I think." Zakath shrugged. "What's so

important that you felt you had to force your way in here to tell me about it?"

"Your empire's collapsing, Zakath," Belgarath told him flatly. "It's time you went home to mend your fences."

Zakath smiled faintly. "Wouldn't that be so very convenient for you?" he said.

"What's going on in Mallorea isn't convenient for anybody. Tell him, Brador."

Nervously, the Melcene bureaucrat delivered his report.

"Demons?" Zakath retorted sceptically. "Oh, come now, Belgarath. Surely you don't expect me to believe that, do you? Do you honestly think that I'll run back to Mallorea to chase shadows and leave you behind to raise an army here in the West to confront me when I return?" The palsylike shaking Garion had noted when they had entered the room seemed to be growing more severe. Zakath's head bobbed and jerked on his neck, and a stream of spittle ran unnoticed from one corner of his mouth.

"You won't be leaving us behind, Zakath," Belgarath replied. "We're going with you. If even a tenth of what Brador says is true, I'm going to have to go to Karanda and stop this Mengha. If he's raising demons, we're *all* going to have to put everything else aside to stop him."

"Absurd!" Zakath declared agitatedly. His eyes were unfocused now, and his weaving and trembling had become so severe that he was unable to control his limbs. "I'm not going to be tricked by a clever old man into—" He suddenly started up from his chair with an animallike cry, clutching at the sides of his head. Then he toppled forward to the floor, twitching and jerking.

Belgarath jumped forward and took hold of the convulsing man's arms. "Quick!" he snapped. "Get something between his teeth before he bites off his tongue!"

Brador grabbed up a sheaf of reports from a nearby table, wadded them up, and jammed them into the frothing Emperor's mouth.

"Garion!" Belgarath barked. "Get Pol—fast!"

Garion started toward the door at a run.

"Wait!" Belgarath said, sniffing suspiciously at the air above the face of the man he was holding down. "Bring Sadi, too. There's a peculiar smell here. Hurry!"

Garion bolted. He ran through the hallways past startled officials and servants and finally burst into the room where Polgara was quietly talking with Ce'Nedra and Velvet. "Aunt Pol!" he shouted, "Come quickly! Zakath just collapsed!" Then he spun, ran a few more steps down the hall, and shouldered open the door to Sadi's room. "We need you," he barked at the startled eunuch. "Come with me."

It took only a few moments for the three of them to return to the polished door in the anteroom.

"What's going on?" the Angarak colonel demanded in a frightened voice, barring their way.

"Your Emperor is sick," Garion told him. "Get out of the way." Roughly he pushed the protesting officer to one side and yanked the door open.

Zakath's convulsions had at least partially subsided, but Belgarath still held him down.

"What is it, father?" Polgara asked, kneeling beside the stricken man.

"He threw a fit."

"The falling sickness?"

"I don't think so. It wasn't quite the same. Sadi, come over here and smell his breath. I'm getting a peculiar odor from him."

Sadi approached cautiously, leaned forward, and sniffed several times. Then he straightened, his face pale. "Thalot," he announced.

"A poison?" Polgara asked him.

Sadi nodded. "It's quite rare."

"Do you have an antidote?"

"No, my lady," he replied. "There isn't an antidote for

59

thalot. It's always been universally fatal. It's seldom used be-cause it acts very slowly, but no one ever recovers from it."

"Then he's dying?" Garion asked with a sick feeling.

"In a manner of speaking, yes. The convulsions will sub-side, but they'll recur with increasing frequency. Finally . . ." Sadi shrugged.

"There's no hope at all?" Polgara asked.

"None whatsoever, my lady. About all we can do is make his last few days more comfortable."

Belgarath started to swear. "Quiet him down, Pol," he said. "We need to get him into bed and we can't move him while he's jerking around that way."

She nodded and put one hand on Zakath's forehead. Garion felt the faint surge, and the struggling Emperor grew quiet.

Brador, his face very pale, looked at them. "I don't think we should announce this just yet," he cautioned. "Let's just call it a slight illness for the moment until we can decide what to do. I'll send for a litter."

The room to which the unconscious Zakath was taken was plain to the point of severity. The Emperor's bed was a narrow cot. The only other furniture was a single plain chair and a low chest. The walls were white and unadorned, and a char-coal brazier glowed in one corner. Sadi went back to their chambers and returned with his red case and the canvas sack in which Polgara kept her collection of herbs and remedies. The two of them consulted in low tones while Garion and Brador pushed the litter bearers and curious soldiers from the room. Then they mixed a steaming cup of a pungent-smelling liquid. Sadi raised Zakath's head and held it while Polgara spooned the medicine into his slack-lipped mouth.

The door opened quietly, and the green-robed Dalasian healer, Andel, entered. "I came as soon as I heard," she said. "Is the Emperor's illness serious?"

Polgara looked at her gravely. "Close the door, Andel," she said quietly.

The healer gave her a strange look, then pushed the door shut. "Is it that grave, my lady?"

Polgara nodded. "He's been poisoned," she said. "We don't want word of it to get out just yet."

Andel gasped. "What can I do to help?" she asked coming quickly to the bed.

"Not very much, I'm afraid," Sadi told her.

"Have you given him the antidote yet?"

"There is no antidote."

"There must be. Lady Polgara—"

Polgara sadly shook her head.

"I have failed, then," the hooded woman said in a voice filled with tears. She turned from the bed, her head bowed, and Garion heard a faint murmur that somehow seemed to come from the air above her—a murmur that curiously was not that of a single voice. There was a long silence, and then a shimmering appeared at the foot of the bed. When it cleared, the blindfolded form of Cyradis stood there, one hand slightly extended. "This must not be," she said in her clear, ringing voice. "Use thine art, Lady Polgara. Restore him. Should he die, all our tasks will fail. Bring thy power to bear."

"It won't work, Cyradis," Polgara replied, setting the cup down. "If a poison affects only the blood, I can usually manage to purge it, and Sadi has a whole case full of antidotes. This poison, however, sinks into every particle of the body. It's killing his bones and organs as well as his blood, and there's no way to leech it out."

The shimmering form at the foot of the bed wrung its hands in anguish. "It cannot be so," Cyradis wailed. "Hast thou even applied the sovereign specific?"

Polgara looked up quickly. "Sovereign specific? A universal remedy? I know of no such agent."

"But it doth exist, Lady Polgara. I know not its origins nor its composition, but I have felt its gentle power abroad in the world for some years now."

Polgara looked at Andel, but the healer shook her head helplessly. "I do not know of such a potion, my lady."

"Think, Cyradis," Polgara said urgently. "Anything you can tell us might give us a clue."

The blindfolded Seeress touched the fingertips of one hand lightly to her temple. "Its origins are recent," she said, half to herself. "It came into being less than a score of years ago— some obscure flower, or so it seemeth to me."

"It's hopeless, then," Sadi said. "There are millions of kinds of flowers." He rose and crossed the room to Belgarath. "I think we might want to leave here—almost immediately," he murmured. "At the first suggestion of the word 'poison,' people start looking for the nearest Nyissan—and those associated with him. I think we're in a great deal of danger right now."

"Can you think of *anything* else, Cyradis?" Polgara pressed. "No matter how remote?"

The Seeress struggled with it, her face strained as she reached deeper into her strange vision. Her shoulders finally sagged in defeat. "Nothing," she said. "Only a woman's face."

"Describe it."

"She is tall," the Seeress replied. "Her hair is very dark, but her skin is like marble. Her husband is much involved with horses."

"Adara!" Garion exclaimed, the beautiful face of his cousin suddenly coming before his eyes.

Polgara snapped her fingers. "And Adara's rose!" Then she frowned. "I examined that flower very closely some years back, Cyradis," she said. "Are you absolutely sure? There are some unusual substances in it, but I didn't find any particular medicinal qualities in any of them—either in any distillation or powder."

Cyradis concentrated. "Can healing be accomplished by means of a fragrance, Lady Polgara?"

Polgara's eyes narrowed in thought. "There are some minor remedies that are inhaled," she said doubtfully, "but—"

"There are poisons that can be administered in that fashion, Lady Polgara," Sadi supplied. "The fumes are drawn into the lungs and from there into the heart. Then the blood carries them to every part of the body. It could very well be the only way to neutralize the effects of thalot."

Belgarath's expression had grown intent. "Well, Pol?" he asked.

"It's worth a try, father," she replied. "I've got a few of the flowers. They're dried, but they *might* work."

"Any seeds?"

"A few, yes."

"Seeds?" Andel exclaimed. "Kal Zakath would be months in his grave before any bush could grow and bloom."

The old man chuckled slyly. "Not quite," he said, winking at Polgara. "I have quite a way with plants sometimes. I'm going to need some dirt—and some boxes or tubs to put it in."

Sadi went to the door and spoke briefly with the guards outside. They looked baffled, but a short command from Andel sent them scurrying.

"What is the origin of this strange flower, Lady Polgara?" Cyradis asked curiously, "How is it that thou art so well acquainted with it?"

"Garion made it." Polgara shrugged, looking thoughtfully at Zakath's narrow cot. "I think we'll want the bed out from the wall, father," she said. "I want it surrounded by flowers."

"Made?" the Seeress exclaimed.

Polgara nodded. "Created, actually," she said absently. "Do you think it's warm enough in here, father? We're going to want big, healthy blooms, and even at best the flower's a bit puny."

"I did my best," Garion protested.

"Created?" Cyradis' voice was awed. Then she bowed to Garion with profound respect.

63

When the tubs of half-frozen dirt had been placed about the stricken Emperor's bed, smoothed, and dampened with water, Polgara took a small leather pouch from her green canvas sack, removed a pinch of miniscule seeds, and carefully sowed them in the soil.

"All right," Belgarath said, rolling up his sleeves in a workmanlike fashion, "stand back." He bent and touched the dirt in one of the tubs. "You were right, Pol," he muttered. "Just a little too cold." He frowned slightly, and Garion saw his lips move. The surge was not a large one, and the sound of it was little more than a whisper. The damp earth in the tubs began to steam. "That's better," he said. Then he extended his hands out over the narrow cot and the steaming tubs. Again Garion felt the surge and the whisper.

At first nothing seemed to happen, but then tiny specks of green appeared on the top of the dampened dirt. Even as Garion watched those little leaves grow and expand, he remembered where he had seen Belgarath perform this same feat before. As clearly as if he were there, he saw the courtyard before King Korodullin's palace at Vo Mimbre and he saw the apple twig the old man had thrust down between two flagstones expand and reach up toward the old sorcerer's hand as proof to the skeptical Sir Andorig that he was indeed who he said he was.

The pale green leaves had grown darker, and the spindly twigs and tendrils that had at first appeared had already expanded into low bushes.

"Make them vine up across the bed, father," Polgara said critically. "Vines produce more blossoms, and I want a lot of blossoms."

He let out his breath explosively and gave her a look that spoke volumes. "All right," he said finally. "You want vines? Vines it is."

"Is it too much for you, father?" she asked solicitously.

He set his jaw, but did not answer. He did, however, start to sweat. Longer tendrils began to writhe upward like green snakes winding up around the legs of the Emperor's cot and reaching upward to catch the bedframe. Once they had gained that foothold, they seemed to pause while Belgarath caught his breath. "This is harder than it looks," he puffed. Then he concentrated again, and the vines quickly overspread the cot and Kal Zakath's inert body until only his ashen face remained uncovered by them.

"All right," Belgarath said to the plants, "that's far enough. You can bloom now." There was another surge and a peculiar ringing sound.

The tips of all the myriad twiglets swelled, and then those buds began to split, revealing their pale lavender interiors. Almost shyly the lopsided little flowers opened, filling the room with a gentle-seeming fragrance. Garion straightened as he breathed in that delicate odor. For some reason, he suddenly felt very good, and the cares and worries which had beset him for the past several months seemed to fall away.

The slack-faced Zakath stirred slightly, took a breath, and sighed deeply. Polgara laid her fingertips to the side of his neck. "I think it's working, father," she said. "His heart's not laboring so hard now, and his breathing's easier."

"Good," Belgarath replied. "I hate to go through something like that for nothing."

Then the Emperor opened his eyes. The shimmering form of Cyradis hovered anxiously at the foot of his bed. Strangely, he smiled when he saw her, and her shy, answering smile lighted her pale face. Then Zakath sighed once more and closed his eyes again. Garion leaned forward to make sure that the sick man was still breathing. When he looked back toward the foot of the bed, the Seeress of Kell was gone.

CHAPTER FOUR

A warm wind came in off the lake that night, and the wet snow that had blanketed Rak Hagga and the surrounding countryside turned to a dreary slush that sagged and fell from the limbs of the trees in the little garden at the center of the house and slid in sodden clumps from the gray slate roof. Garion and Silk sat near the fire in the mauve-cushioned room, looking out at the garden and talking quietly.

"We'd know a great deal more, if I could get in touch with Yarblek," Silk was saying. The little man was dressed again in the pearl-gray doublet and black hose which he had favored during those years before they had begun this search, although he wore only a few of the costly rings and ornaments which had made him appear so ostentatiously wealthy at that time.

"Isn't he in Gar og Nadrak?" Garion asked. Garion had also discarded his serviceable travel clothing and reverted to his customary silver-trimmed blue.

"It's hard to say exactly where Yarblek is at any given time, Garion. He moves around a great deal; but no matter where he goes, the reports from our people in Mal Zeth, Melcene, and Maga Renn are all forwarded to him. Whatever this Mengha is up to is almost certain to have disrupted trade. I'm sure that our agents have gathered everything they could find out about him and sent it along to Yarblek. Right now my scruffy-looking partner probably knows more about Mengha than Brador's secret police do."

"I don't want to get sidetracked, Silk. Our business is with Zandramas, not Mengha."

"Demons are everybody's business," Silk replied soberly, "but no matter what we decide to do, we have to get to Mallorea first—and that means persuading Zakath that this is serious. Was he listening at all when you told him about Mengha?"

Garion shook his head. "I'm not sure if he even understood what we were telling him. He wasn't altogether rational."

Silk grunted. "When he wakes up, we'll have to try again." A sly grin crossed the little man's face. "I've had a certain amount of luck negotiating with sick people," he said.

"Isn't that sort of contemptible?"

"Of course it is—but it gets results."

Later that morning, Garion and his rat-faced friend stopped by the Emperor's room, ostensibly to inquire about his health. Polgara and Sadi were seated on either side of the bed, and Andel sat quietly in the corner. The vines that had enveloped the narrow cot had been pulled aside, but the air in the room was still heavy with the fragrance of the small, lavender flowers. The sick man was propped into a half-sitting position by pillows, but his eyes were closed as Silk and Garion entered. His cat lay contentedly purring at the foot of the bed.

"How is he?" Garion asked quietly.

"He's been awake a few times," Sadi replied. "There are still some traces of thalot in his extremities, but they seem to be dissipating." The eunuch was picking curiously at one of the small flowers. "I wonder if these would work if they were distilled down to an essence," he mused, "or perhaps an attar. It might be very interesting to wear a perfume that would ward off any poison." He frowned slightly. "And I wonder if they'd be effective against snake venom."

"Have Zith bite someone," Silk suggested. "Then you can test it."

"Would you like to volunteer, Prince Kheldar?"

"Ah, no, Sadi," Silk declined. "Thanks all the same." He looked at the red case lying open on the floor in the corner. "Is she confined, by the way?" he asked nervously.

"She's sleeping," Sadi replied. "She always takes a little nap after breakfast."

Garion looked at the dozing Emperor. "Is he coherent at all—when he's awake, I mean?"

"His mind seems to be clearing," Polgara told him.

"Hysteria and delirium are some of the symptoms brought on by thalot," Sadi said. "Growing rationality is an almost certain sign of recovery."

"Is that you, Belgarion?" Zakath asked almost in a whisper and without opening his eyes.

"Yes," Garion replied. "How are you feeling?"

"Weak. Light-headed—and every muscle in my body screams like an abscessed tooth. Aside from that, I'm fine." He opened his eyes with a wry smile. "What happened? I seem to have lost track of things."

Garion glanced briefly at Polgara, and she nodded. "You were poisoned," he told the sick man.

Zakath looked a bit surprised. "It must not have been a very good one then," he said.

"Actually, it's one of the very best, your Imperial Majesty," Sadi disagreed mildly. "It's always been universally lethal."

"I'm dying then?" Zakath said it with a peculiar kind of satisfaction, almost as if he welcomed the idea. "Ah, well," he sighed. "That should solve many problems."

"I'm very sorry, your Majesty," Silk said with mock regret, "but I think you'll live. Belgarath tampers with the normal course of events from time to time. It's a bad habit he picked up in his youth, but a man needs *some* vices, I suppose."

Zakath smiled weakly. "You're a droll little fellow, Prince Kheldar."

"If you're really keen on dying, though," Silk added outrageously, "we could always wake Zith. One nip from her almost guarantees perpetual slumber."

"Zith?"

"Sadi's pet—a little green snake. She could even curl up at your ear after she bites you and purr you into eternity."

Zakath sighed, and his eyes drooped shut again.

"I think we should let him sleep," Polgara said quietly.

"Not just yet, Lady Polgara," the Emperor said. "I've shunned sleep and the dreams which infest it for so long that it comes unnaturally now."

"You *must* sleep, Kal Zakath," Andel told him. "There are ways to banish evil dreams, and sleep is the greatest healer."

Zakath sighed and shook his head. "I'm afraid you won't be able to banish *these* dreams, Andel." Then he drowned slightly. "Sadi, is hallucination one of the symptoms of the poison I was given?"

"It's possible," the enunuch admitted. "What horrors have you seen?"

"Not a horror," Zakath replied. "I seem to see the face of a young woman. Her eyes are bound with a strip of cloth. A peculiar peace comes over me when I see her face."

"Then it was not an hallucination, Kal Zakath," Andel told him.

"Who is this strange blind child, then?"

69

"My mistress," Andel said proudly. "The face which came to you in your direst hour was the face of Cyradis, the Seeress of Kell, upon whose decision rests the fate of all the world—and of all other worlds as well."

"So great a responsibility to lie upon such slender shoulders," Zakath said.

"It is her task," Andel said simply.

The sick man seemed to fall again into a doze, his lips lightly touched with a peculiar smile. Then his eyes opened again, seemingly more alert now. "Am I healed, Sadi?" he asked the shaved-headed eunuch. "Has your excellent Nyissan poison quite run its course?"

"Oh," Sadi replied speculatively, "I wouldn't say that you're entirely well yet, your Majesty, but I'd guess that you're out of any immediate danger."

"Good," Zakath said crisply, trying to shoulder his way up into a sitting position. Garion reached out to help him. "And has the knave who poisoned me been apprehended yet?"

Sadi shook his head. "Not as far as I know," he answered.

"I think that might be the first order of business, then. I'm starting to feel a little hungry and I'd rather not go through this again. Is the poison common in Cthol Murgos?"

Sadi frowned. "Murgo law forbids poisons and drugs, your Majesty," he replied. "They're a backward sort of people. The Dagashi assassins probably have access to thalot, though."

"You think my poisoner might have been a Dagashi, then?"

Sadi shrugged. "Most assassinations in Cthol Murgos are carried out by the Dagashi. They're efficient and discreet."

Zakath's eyes narrowed in thought. "That would seem to point a finger directly at Urgit, then. The Dagashi are expensive, and Urgit has access to the royal treasury."

Silk grimaced. "No," he declared. "Urgit wouldn't do that. A knife between your shoulder blades maybe, but not poison."

"How can you be so sure, Kheldar?"

"I know him," Silk replied a bit lamely. "He's weak and a little timid, but he wouldn't be a party to a poisoning. It's a contemptible way to resolve political differences."

"Prince Kheldar!" Sadi protested.

"Except in Nyissa, of course," Silk conceded. "One always needs to take quaint local customs into account." He pulled at his long, pointed nose. "I'll admit that Urgit wouldn't grieve too much if you woke up dead some morning," he said to the Mallorean Emperor, "but it's all just a little too pat. If your generals believed that it was Urgit who arranged to have you killed, they'd stay here for the next ten generations trying to obliterate all of Murgodom, wouldn't they?"

"I'd assume so," Zakath said.

"Who would benefit the most by disposing of you and rather effectively making sure that the bulk of your army doesn't return to Mallorea in the foreseeable future? Not Urgit, certainly. More likely it would be somebody in Mallorea who wants a free hand there." Silk squared his shoulders. "Why don't you let Liselle and me do a little snooping around before you lock your mind in stone on this? Obvious things always make me suspicious."

"That's all very well, Kheldar," Zakath said rather testily, "but how can I be sure that my next meal won't have another dose of exotic spices in it?"

"You have at your bedside the finest cook in the world," the rat-faced man said, pointing grandly at Polgara, "and I can absolutely guarantee that she won't poison you. She might turn you into a radish if you offend her, but she'd never poison you."

"All right, Silk, that will do," Polgara told him.

"I'm only paying tribute to your extraordinary gifts, Polgara."

Her eyes grew hard.

"I think that perhaps it might be time for me to be on my way," Silk said to Garion.

"Wise decision," Garion murmured.

71

The little man turned and quickly left the room.

"Is he really as good as he pretends to be?" Zakath asked curiously.

Polgara nodded. "Between them, Kheldar and Liselle can probably ferret out any secret in the world. Silk doesn't always like it, but they're almost a perfect team. And now, your Majesty, what would you like for breakfast?"

A curious exchange was taking place in the corner. Throughout the previous conversation, Garion had heard a faint, drowsy purr coming from Zith's earthenware bottle. Either the little snake was expressing a general sense of contentment, or it may have been one of the peculiarities of her species to purr while sleeping. Zakath's pregnant, mackerel-striped cat, attracted by that sound, jumped down from the bed and curiously waddled toward Zith's little home. Absently, probably without even thinking about it, she responded to the purr coming from the bottle with one of her own. She sniffed at the bottle, then tentatively touched it with one soft paw. The peculiar duet of purring continued.

Then, perhaps because Sadi had not stoppered the bottle tightly enough or because she had long since devised this simple means of opening her front door, the little snake nudged the cork out of the bottle with her blunt nose. Both creatures continued to purr, although the cat was now obviously afire with curiosity. For a time Zith did not reveal herself, but lurked shyly in her bottle, still purring. Then, cautiously, she poked out her head, her forked tongue flickering as she tested the air.

The cat jumped straight up to a height of about three feet, giving vent to a startled yowl. Zith retreated immediately back into the safety of her house, though she continued to purr.

Warily, but still burning with curiosity, the cat approached the bottle again, moving one foot at a time.

"Sadi," Zakath said, his voice filled with concern.

"There's no immediate danger, your Majesty," the eunuch assured him. "Zith never bites while she's purring."

Again the little green snake slid her head out of the bottle. This time the cat recoiled only slightly. Then, curiosity overcoming her natural aversion to reptiles, she continued her slow advance, her nose reaching out toward this remarkable creature. Zith, still purring, also extended her blunt nose. Their noses touched, and both flinched back slightly. Then they cautiously sniffed at each other, the cat with her nose, the snake with her tongue. Both were purring loudly now.

"Astonishing," Sadi murmured. "I think they actually like each other."

"Sadi, please," Zakath said plaintively. "I don't know how you feel about your snake, but I'm rather fond of my cat, and she *is* about to become a mother."

"I'll speak with them, your Majesty," Sadi assured him. "I'm not sure that they'll listen, but I'll definitely speak with them."

Belgarath had once again retired to the library, and Garion found him later that day poring over a large map of northern Mallorea. "Ah," he said, looking up as Garion entered, "there you are. I was just about to send for you. Come over here and look at this."

Garion went to the table.

"The appearance of this Mengha fellow might just work to our advantage, you know."

"I don't quite follow that, Grandfather."

"Zandramas is here at Ashaba, right?" Belgarath stabbed his finger at a spot in the representation of the Karandese mountains.

"Yes," Garion said.

"And Mengha's moving west and south out of Calida, over here." The old man poked at the map again.

"That's what Brador says."

"He's got her blocked off from most of the continent, Garion. She's been very careful here in Cthol Murgos to avoid populated areas. There's no reason to believe that she's going

73

to change once she gets to Mallorea. Urvon's going to be to the south of her at Mal Yaska, and the wastes to the north are virtually impassable—even though it's nearly summer."

"Summer?"

"In the northern half of the world it is."

"Oh. I keep forgetting." Garion peered at the map. "Grandfather, we don't have any idea of where 'the place which is no more' might be. When Zandramas leaves Ashaba, she could go in any direction."

Belgarath squinted at the map. "I don't think so, Garion. In the light of all that's happened in Mallorea—coupled with the fact that by now she knows that we're on her trail—I think she almost *has* to be trying to get back to her power base in Darshiva. Everybody in the world is after her, and she needs help."

"*We* certainly aren't threatening her all that much," Garion said moodily. "We can't even get out of Cthol Murgos."

"That's what I wanted to talk to you about. You've got to persuade Zakath that it's vital for us to leave here and get to Mallorea as quickly as possible."

"Persuade?"

"Just do whatever you have to, Garion. There's a great deal at stake."

"Why me?" Garion said it without thinking.

Belgarath gave him a long, steady look.

"Sorry," Garion muttered. "Forget that I said it."

"All right. I'll do that."

Late that evening, Zakath's cat gave birth to seven healthy kittens while Zith hovered in anxious attendance, warning off all other observers with ominous hisses. Peculiarly, the only person the protective little reptile would allow near the newborn kittens was Velvet.

Garion had little success during the next couple of days in his efforts to steer his conversations with the convalescing Zakath around to the subject of the necessity for returning to Mallorea. The Emperor usually pleaded a lingering weakness as a result of his poisoning, though Garion privately suspected subterfuge on that score, since the man appeared to have more than enough energy for his usual activities and only protested exhaustion when Garion wanted to talk about a voyage.

On the evening of the fourth day, however, he decided to try negotiation one last time before turning to more direct alternatives. He found Zakath seated in the chair near his bed with a book in his hands. The dark circles beneath his eyes had vanished, the trembling had disappeared entirely, and he seemed totally alert. "Ah, Belgarion," he said almost cheerfully, "so good of you to stop by."

"I thought I'd come in and put you to sleep again," Garion replied with slightly exaggerated sarcasm.

"Have I been that obvious?" Zakath asked.

"Yes, as a matter of fact you have. Every time I mention the words 'ship' and 'Mallorea' in the same sentence, your eyes snap shut. Zakath, we've got to talk about this, and time is starting to run out."

Zakath passed one hand across his eyes with some show of weariness.

"Let me put it this way," Garion pressed on. "Belgarath's starting to get impatient. I'm trying to keep our discussions civil, but if he steps in, I can almost guarantee that they're going to turn unpleasant—very quickly."

Zakath lowered his hand, and his eyes narrowed. "That sounds vaguely like a threat, Belgarion."

"No," Garion disagreed. "As a matter of fact, it's in the nature of friendly advice. If you want to stay here in Cthol Murgos, that's up to you, but *we* have to get to Mallorea—and soon."

"And if I choose not to permit you to go?"

"Permit?" Garion laughed. "Zakath, did you grow up in the same world with the rest of us? Have you got even the remotest idea of what you're talking about?"

"I think that concludes this interview, Belgarion," the Emperor said coldly. He rose stiffly to his feet and turned to his bed. As usual, his cat had deposited her mewling little brood in the center of his coverlet and then gone off to nap alone in her wool-lined box in the corner. The irritated Emperor looked with some exasperation at the furry little puddle on his bed. "You have my permission to withdraw, Belgarion," he said over his shoulder. Then he reached down with both hands to scoop up the cluster of kittens.

Zith reared up out of the very center of the furry heap, fixed him with a cold eye, and hissed warningly.

"Torak's teeth!" Zakath swore, jerking his hands away. "This is going too far! Go tell Sadi that I want his accursed snake out of my room immediately!"

"He's taken her out four times already, Zakath," Garion said mildly. "She just keeps crawling back." He suppressed a grin. "Maybe she likes you."

"Are you trying to be funny?"

"Me?"

"Get the snake out of here."

Garion put his hands behind his back. "Not me, Zakath. I'll go get Sadi."

In the hallway outside, however, he encountered Velvet, who was coming toward the Emperor's room with a mysterious smile on her face.

"Do you think you could move Zith?" Garion asked her. "She's in the middle of Zakath's bed with those kittens."

"*You* can move her, Belgarion," the blond girl said, smiling the dimples into her cheeks. "She trusts you."

"I think I'd rather not try that."

The two of them went back into the Emperor's bedchamber.

"Margravine," Zakath greeted her courteously, inclining his head.

She curtsied. "Your Majesty."

"Can you deal with this?" he asked, pointing at the furry pile on his bed with the snake still half-reared out of the center, her eyes alert.

"Of course, your Majesty." She approached the bed, and the snake flickered her tongue nervously. "Oh, *do* stop that, Zith," the blond girl chided. Then she lifted the front of her skirt to form a kind of pouch and began picking up kittens and depositing them in her improvised basket. Last of all she lifted Zith and laid her in the middle. She crossed the room and casually put them all into the box with the mother cat, who opened one golden eye, made room for her kittens and their bright green nursemaid, and promptly went back to sleep.

"Isn't that sweet?" Velvet murmured softly. Then she turned back to Zakath. "Oh, by the way, your Majesty, Kheldar and I managed to find out who it was who poisoned you."

"What?"

She nodded, frowning slightly. "It came as something of a surprise, actually."

The Emperor's eyes had become intent. "You're sure?"

"As sure as one can be in these cases. You seldom find an eyewitness to a poisoning; but he was in the kitchen at the right time, he left right after you fell ill, and we know him by reputation." She smiled at Garion. "Have you noticed how people always tend to remember a man with white eyes?"

"*Naradas?*" Garion exclaimed.

"Surprising, isn't it?"

"Who's Naradas?" Zakath demanded.

"He works for Zandramas," Garion replied. He frowned. "That doesn't make any sense, Velvet. Why would Zandramas want to kill him? Wouldn't she want to keep him alive?"

She spread her hands. "I don't know, Belgarion—not yet, anyway."

"Velvet?" Zakath asked in puzzlement.

She smiled the dimples into her cheeks again. "Isn't it silly?" She laughed. "I suppose these little nicknames are a form of affection, though. Belgarion's question is to the point, however. Can you think of any reason why Zandramas might want to kill you?"

"Not immediately, but we can wring that answer out of her when I catch her—and I'll make a point of doing that, even if I have to take Cthol Murgos apart stone by stone."

"She isn't here," Garion said absently, still struggling with the whole idea. "She's at Ashaba—in the House of Torak."

Zakath's eyes narrowed suspiciously. "Isn't this convenient, Belgarion?" he said. "I *happen* to get poisoned right after your arrival. Belgarath *happens* to cure me. Kheldar and Liselle *happen* to discover the identity of the poisoner, who *happens* to work for Zandramas, who *happens* to be at Ashaba, which *happens* to be in Mallorea—a place which just *happens* to be where you so desperately want to go. The coincidence staggers the imagination, wouldn't you say?"

"Zakath, you're starting to make me tired," Garion said irritably. "If I decide that I need a boat to get to Mallorea, I'll *take* one. All that's kept me from doing that so far are the manners Lady Polgara drilled into me when I was a boy."

"And how do you propose to leave this house?" Zakath snapped, his temper also starting to rise.

That did it. The rage that came over Garion was totally irrational. It was the result of a hundred delays and stumbling blocks and petty interruptions that had dogged him for almost a year now. He reached over his shoulder, ripped Iron-grip's sword from its sheath, and peeled the concealing leather sleeve from its hilt. He held the great blade before him and literally threw his will at the Orb. The sword exploded into blue flame. "How do I propose to leave this house?" he half shouted at the stunned Emperor. "I'll use *this* for a key. It works sort of like this." He straightened his arm, leveling the blazing sword at the door. "Burst!" he commanded.

Garion's anger was not only irrational, it was also somewhat excessive. He had intended no more than the door—and possibly a part of the doorframe—simply to illustrate to Zakath the intensity of his feeling about the matter. The Orb, however, startled into wakefulness by the sudden jolt of his angry will, had overreacted. The door, certainly, disappeared, dissolving into splinters that blasted out into the hallway. The doorframe also vanished. What Garion had *not* intended, however, was what happened to the wall.

White-faced and shaking, Zakath stumbled back, staring at the hallway outside that had suddenly been revealed and at the rubble that filled it—rubble that had a moment before been the solid, two-foot-thick stone wall of his bedroom.

"My goodness," Velvet murmured mildly.

Knowing that it was silly and melodramatic, but still caught up in that towering, irrational anger, Garion caught the stunned Zakath by the arm with his left hand and gestured with the sword he held in his right. "Now, we're going to go talk with Belgarath," he announced. "We'll go through the hallways *if* you'll give me your word not to call soldiers every time we go around a corner. Otherwise, we'll just cut straight through the house. The library's sort of in that direction, isn't it?" he pointed at one of the still-standing walls with his sword.

"Belgarion," Velvet chided him gently, "now really, that's no way to behave. Kal Zakath has been a very courteous host. I'm sure that now that he understands the situation, he'll be more than happy to cooperate, won't you, your Imperial Majesty?" She smiled winsomely at the Emperor. "We wouldn't want the Rivan King to get *really* angry, now would we? There are so many breakable things about—windows, walls, houses, the city of Rak Hagga—that sort of thing."

They found Belgarath in the library again. He was reading a small scroll, and there was a large tankard at his elbow.

"Something's come up," Garion said shortly as he entered.

"Oh?"

"Velvet tells us that she and Silk found out that it was Naradas who poisoned Zakath."

"Naradas?" the old man blinked. "That's a surprise, isn't it?"

"What's she up to, Grandfather? Zandramas, I mean."

"I'm not sure." Belgarath looked at Zakath. "Who's likely to succeed you if somebody manages to put you to sleep?"

Zakath shrugged. "There are a few distant cousins scattered about—mostly in the Melcene Islands and Celanta. The line of the succession is a little murky."

"Perhaps that's what she has in mind, Belgarath," Velvet said seriously. "If there's any truth in that Grolim Prophecy you found in Rak Hagga, she's got to have an Angarak king with her at the time of the final meeting. A tame king would suit her purposes much better than someone like his Majesty here—some third or fourth cousin she could crown and anoint and proclaim king. Then she could have her Grolims keep an eye on him and deliver him to her at the proper time."

"It's possible, I suppose," he agreed. "I think there may be a bit more to it than that, though. Zandramas has never been that straightforward about anything before."

"I hope you all realize that I haven't the faintest notion of what you're talking about," Zakath said irritably.

"Just how much does he know?" Belgarath asked Garion.

"Not very much, Grandfather."

"All right. Maybe if he does know what's going on, he won't be quite so difficult." He turned to the Mallorean Emperor. "Have you ever heard of the Mrin Codex?" he asked.

"I've heard that it was written by a madman—like most of the other so-called prophecies."

"How about the Child of Light and the Child of Dark?"

"That's part of the standard gibberish used by religious hysterics."

"Zakath, you're going to have to believe in *something*. This is going to be very difficult for you to grasp if you don't."

"Would you settle for a temporary suspension of skepticism?" the Emperor countered.

"Fair enough, I suppose. All right, now, this gets complicated, so you're going to have to pay attention, listen carefully, and stop me if there's anything you don't understand."

The old man then proceeded to sketch in the ancient story of the "accident" that had occurred before the world had begun and the divergence of the two possible courses of the future and of the two consciousnesses which had somehow infused those courses.

"All right," Zakath said. "That's fairly standard theology so far. I've had Grolims preaching to the same nonsense since I was a boy."

Belgarath nodded. "I just wanted to start us off from common ground." He went on then, telling Zakath of the events spanning the eons between the cracking of the world and the Battle of Vo Mimbre.

"Our point of view is somewhat different," Zakath murmured.

"It would be," Belgarath agreed. "All right, there were five hundred years between Vo Mimbre and the theft of the Orb by Zedar the Apostate."

"Recovery," Zakath corrected. "The Orb was stolen from Cthol Mishrak by Iron-grip the thief and by—" He stopped, and his eyes suddenly widened as he stared at the seedy-looking old man.

"Yes," Belgarath said, "I really *was* there, Zakath—and I was there two thousand years before, when Torak originally stole the Orb from my Master."

"I've been sick, Belgarath," the Emperor said weakly, sinking into a chair. "My nerves aren't really up for too many of these shocks."

Belgarath looked at him, puzzled.

"Their Majesties were having a little discussion," Velvet explained brightly. "King Belgarion gave the Emperor a little demonstration of some of the more flamboyant capabilities of the Sword of the Rivan King. The Emperor was quite impressed. So was most everybody else who happened to be in that part of the house."

Belgarath gave Garion a chill look. "Playing again?" he asked.

Garion tried to reply, but there was nothing he could really say.

"All right, let's get on with this," Belgarath continued

briskly. "What happened after the emergence of Garion here is all recent history, so I'm sure you're familiar with it."

"Garion?" Zakath asked.

"A more common—and familiar—form. 'Belgarion' is a bit ostentatious, wouldn't you say?"

"No more so than 'Belgarath.'"

"I've worn 'Belgarath' for almost seven thousand years, Zakath, and I've sort of rubbed off the rough edges and corners. Garion's only been wearing his 'Bel' for a dozen years, and it still squeaks when he turns around too quickly."

Garion felt slightly offended by that.

"Anyway," the old man continued, "after Torak was dead, Garion and Ce'Nedra got married. About a year or so ago, she gave birth to a son. Garion's attention at that time was on the Bear-cult. Someone had tried to kill Ce'Nedra and had succeeded in killing the Rivan Warder."

"I'd heard about that," Zakath said.

"Anyway, he was in the process of stamping out the cult— he stamps quite well once he puts his mind to it—when someone crept into the Citadel at Riva and abducted his infant son—my great-grandson."

"No!" Zakath exclaimed.

"Oh, yes," Belgarath continued grimly. "We thought that it was the cult and marched to Rheon in Drasnia, their headquarters, but it was all a clever ruse. Zandramas had abducted Prince Geran and misdirected us to Rheon. The leader of the cult turned out to be Harakan, one of the henchmen of Urvon—is this coming too fast for you?"

Zakath's face was startled, and his eyes had gone wide again. "No," he said, swallowing hard. "I think I can keep up."

"There isn't too much more. After we discovered our mistakes, we took up the abductor's trail. We know that she's going to Mallorea—to a 'place which is no more.' That's where the Sardion is. We have to stop her, or at least arrive there at the same time. Cyradis believes that when we all arrive at this 'place which is no more,' there's going to be one of those confrontations between the Child of Light and the Child of Dark which have been happening since before the beginning of time—except that this is going to be the last one. She'll choose between them, and that's supposed to be the end of it."

"I'm afraid that it's at that point that my skepticism reasserts itself, Belgarath," Zakath said. "You don't acutally expect me to believe that these two shadowy figures that predate the world are going to arrive at this mysterious place to grapple once more, do you?"

"What makes you think they're shadowy? The spirits that are at the core of the two possible destinies infuse real people to act as their instruments during these meetings. Right now, for example, Zandramas is the Child of Dark. It used to be Torak—until Garion killed him."

"And who's the Child of Light?"

"I thought that would be obvious."

Zakath turned to stare incredulously into Garion's blue eyes. "You?" he gasped.

"That's what they tell me," Garion replied.

CHAPTER FIVE

Kal Zakath, dread Emperor of boundless Mallo-rea, looked first at Belgarath, then again at Garion, and finally at Velvet. "Why do I feel that I'm losing control of things here?" he asked. "When you people came here, you were more or less my prisoners. Now somehow I'm yours."

"We told you some things you didn't know before, that's all," Belgarath told him.

"Or some things that you've cleverly made up."

"Why would we do that?"

"I can think of any number of reasons. For the sake of argument I'll accept your story about the abduction of Bel-garion's son, but don't you see how that makes all your motives completely obvious? You need my aid in your search. All this mystical nonsense, *and* your wild story about Urgit's parentage, could have been designed to divert me from my campaign here in Cthol Murgos and to trick me into returning with you to Mallorea. Everything you've done or said since you've come here could have been directed toward that end."

"Do you really think we'd do that?" Garion asked him.

"Belgarion, if *I* had a son and someone had abducted him, I'd do *anything* to get him back. I sympathize with your situation, but I have my own concerns, and they're here, not in Mallorea. I'm sorry, but the more I think about this, the less of it I believe. I could not have misjudged the world so much. Demons? Prophecies? Magic? Immortal old men? It's all been very entertaining, but I don't believe one word of it."

"Not even what the orb showed you about Urgit?" Garion asked.

"Please, Belgarion, don't treat me like a child." Zakath's lips were twisted into an ironic smile. "Isn't it altogether possible that the poison had already crept into my mind? And isn't it also possible that you, like any other of the charlatans who infest village fairs, used a show of mysterious lights and suggestions to make me see what you wanted me to see?"

"What *do* you believe, Kal Zakath?" Velvet asked him.

"What I can see and touch—and precious little else."

"So great a skepticism," she murmured. "Then you do not accept one single out-of-the-ordinary thing?"

"Not that I can think of, no."

"Not even the peculiar gift of the Seers at Kell? It's been fairly well documented, you know."

He frowned slightly. "Yes," he admitted, "as a matter of fact, it has."

"How can you document a vision?" Garion asked curiously.

"The Grolims were seeking to discredit the Seers," Zakath replied. "They felt that the easiest way to do that was to have these pronouncements about the future written down and then wait to see what happened. The bureaucracy was instructed to keep records. So far, not one of the predictions of the Seers has proven false."

"Then you *do* believe that the Seers have the ability to know things about the past and the present and the future in ways that the rest of us might not completely understand?" Velvet pressed.

Zakath pursed his lips. "All right, Margravine," he said reluctantly, "I'll concede that the Seers have certain abilities that haven't been explained as yet."

"Do you believe that a Seer could lie to you?"

"Good girl," Belgarath murmured approvingly.

"No," Zakath replied after a moment's thought. "A Seer is incapable of lying. Their truthfulness is proverbial."

"Well, then," she said with a dimpled smile, "all you need to do to find out if what we've told you is the truth is to send for a Seer, isn't it?"

"Liselle," Garion protested, "that could take weeks. We don't have that much time."

"Oh," she said, "I don't think it would take all that long, If I remember correctly, Lady Polgara said that Andel summoned Cyradis when his Majesty here lay dying. I'm fairly sure we could persuade her to do it for us again."

"Well, Zakath," Belgarath said. "Will you agree to accept what Cyradis tells you as the truth?"

The Emperor squinted at him suspiciously, searching for some kind of subterfuge. "You've manipulated me into a corner," he accused. He thought about it. "All right, Belgarath," he said finally. "I'll accept whatever Cyradis says as the truth—if you'll agree to do the same."

"Done then," Belgarath said. "Let's send for Andel and get on with this."

As Velvet stepped out into the hall to speak with one of the guards who trailed along behind the Emperor wherever he went, Zakath leaned back in his chair. "I can't believe that I'm even considering all the wild impossibilities you've been telling me," he said.

Garion exchanged a quick look with his grandfather, and then they both laughed.

"Something funny, gentlemen?"

"Just a family joke, Zakath," Belgarath told him. "Garion and I have been discussing the possible and the impossible since he was about nine years old. He was even more stubborn about it than you are."

"It gets easier to accept after the first shock wears off," Garion added. "It's sort of like swimming in very cold water. Once you get numb, it doesn't hurt quite so much."

It was not long until Velvet reentered the room with the hooded Andel at her side.

"I believe you said that the Seeress of Kell is your mistress, Andel," Zakath said to her.

"Yes, she is, your Majesty."

"Can you summon her?"

"Her semblance, your Majesty, if there is need and if she will consent to come."

"I believe there's a need, Andel. Belgarath has told me certain things that I have to have confirmed. I know that Cyradis speaks only the truth. Belgarath, on the other hand, has a more dubious reputation." He threw a rather sly, sidelong glance at the old man.

Belgarath grinned at him and winked.

"I will speak with my mistress, your Majesty," Andel said, "and entreat her to send her semblance here. Should she consent, I beg of you to ask your questions quickly. The effort of reaching half around the world exhausts her, and she is not robust." Then the Dalasian woman knelt reverently and lowered her head, and Garion once again heard that peculiar murmur as of many voices, followed by a long moment of silence. Again there was that same shimmer in the air; when it had cleared, the hooded and blindfolded form of Cyradis stood there.

"We thank you for coming, Holy Seeress," Zakath said to her in an oddly respectful tone of voice. "My guests here have told me certain things that I am loath to believe, but I have agreed to accept whatever you can confirm."

"I will tell thee what I can, Zakath," she replied. "Some things are hidden from me, and some others may not yet be revealed."

"I understand the limitations, Cyradis. Belgarion tells me that Urgit, the King of the Murgos, is not of the blood of Taur Urgas. Is this true?"

"It is," she replied simply. "King Urgit's father was an Alorn."

"Are any of the sons of Taur Urgas still alive?"

"Nay, Zakath. The line of Taur Urgas became extinct some twelve years ago when his last son was strangled in a cellar in Rak Goska upon the command of Oskatat, King Urgit's Seneschal."

Zakath sighed and shook his head sadly. "And so it has ended," he said. "My enemy's line passed unnoticed from this world in a dark cellar—passed so quietly that I could not even rejoice that they were gone, nor curse the ones who stole them from my grasp."

"Revenge is a hollow thing, Zakath."

"It's the only thing I've had for almost thirty years now." He sighed again, then straightened his shoulders. "Did Zandramas really steal Belgarion's son?"

"She did, and now she carries him to the Place Which Is No More."

"And where's that?"

Her face grew very still. "I may not reveal that," she replied finally, "but the Sardion is there."

"Can you tell me what the Sardion is?"

"It is one half of the stone which was divided."

"Is it really all *that* important?"

"In all of Angarak there is no thing of greater worth. The Grolims all know this. Urvon would give all his wealth for it. Zandramas would abandon the adoration of multitudes for it. Mengha would give his soul for it—indeed, he hath done so already in his enlistment of demons to aid him. Even Agachak, Hierarch of Rak Urga, would abandon his ascendancy in Cthol Murgos to possess it."

"How is it that a thing of such value has escaped my notice?"

"Thine eyes are on worldly matters, Zakath. The Sardion is not of this world—no more than the other half of the divided stone is of this world."

"The other half?"

"That which the Angaraks call Cthrag Yaska and the men of the West call the Orb of Aldur. Cthrag Sardius and Cthrag Yaska were sundered in the moment which saw the birth of the opposing necessities."

Zakath's face had grown quite pale, and he clasped his hands tightly in front of him to control their trembling. "It's all true, then?" he asked in a hoarse voice.

"All, Kal Zakath. All."

"Even that Belgarion and Zandramas are the Child of Light and the Child of Dark?"

"Yes, they are." He started to ask her another question, but she raised her hand. "My time is short, Zakath, and I must now reveal something of greater import unto thee. Know that thy life doth approach a momentous crossroads. Put aside thy lust for power and thy hunger for revenge, as they are but childish toys. Return thou even to Mal Zeth to prepare thyself for *thy* part in the meeting which is to come."

"*My* part?" He sounded startled.

"Thy name and thy task are written in the stars."

"And what is this task?"

"I will instruct thee when thou art ready to understand what it is that thou must do. First thou must cleanse thy heart of that grief and remorse which hath haunted thee."

His face grew still, and he sighed. "I'm afraid not, Cyradis," he said. "What you ask is quite impossible."

"Then thou wilt surely die before the seasons turn again. Consider what I have told thee, and consider it well, Emperor

89

of Mallorea. I will speak with thee anon." And then she shimmered and vanished.

Zakath stared at the empty spot where she had stood. His face was pale, and his jaws were set.

"Well, Zakath?" Belgarath said. "Are you convinced?"

The Emperor rose from his chair and began to pace up and down. "This is an absolute absurdity!" he burst out suddenly in an agitated voice.

"I know," Belgarath replied calmly, "but a willingness to believe the absurd is an indication of faith. It might just be that faith is the first step in the preparation Cyradis mentioned."

"It's not that I don't *want* to believe, Belgarath," Zakath said, in a strangely humble tone. "It's just—"

"Nobody said that it was going to be easy," the old man told him. "But you've done things before that weren't easy, haven't you?"

Zakath dropped into his chair again, his eyes lost in thought. "Why me?" he said plaintively. "Why do *I* have to get involved in this?"

Garion suddenly laughed.

Zakath gave him a cold stare.

"Sorry," Garion apologized, "but *I've* been saying 'why me?' since I was about fourteen. Nobody's ever given me a satisfactory answer, but you get used to the injustice of it after a while."

"It's not that I'm trying to avoid any kind of responsibility, Belgarion. It's just that I can't see what possible help I could be. You people are going to track down Zandramas, retrieve your son, and destroy the Sardion. Isn't that about it?"

"It's a little more complicated than that," Belgarath told him. "Destroying the Sardion is going to involve something rather cataclysmic."

"I don't quite follow that. Can't you just wave your hand and make it cease to exist? You *are* a sorcerer, after all—or so they say."

"That's forbidden," Garion said automatically. "You can't unmake things. That's what Ctuchik tried to do, and he destroyed himself."

Zakath frowned and looked at Belgarath. "I thought *you* killed him."

"Most people do." The old man shrugged. "It adds to my reputation, so I don't argue with them." He tugged at one earlobe. "No," he said, "I think we're going to have to see this all the way through to the end. I'm fairly sure that the only way the Sardion can be destroyed is as a result of the final confrontation between the Child of Light and the Child of Dark." He paused, then sat up suddenly, his face intent. "I think Cyradis slipped and gave us something she hadn't intended, though. She said that the Grolim priesthood all desperately wanted the Sardion, and she included Mengha in her list. Wouldn't that seem to indicate that Mengha's also a Grolim?" He looked at Andel. "Is your young mistress subject to these little lapses?"

"Cyradis cannot misspeak herself, Holy Belgarath," the healer replied. "A Seeress does not speak in her own voice, but in the voice of her vision."

"Then she *wanted* us to know that Mengha is—or was—a Grolim, and that the reason he's raising demons is to help him in his search for the Sardion." He thought about it. "There's another rather bleak possibility, too," he added. "It might just be that his demons are using him to get the Sardion for themselves. Maybe that's why they're so docile where he's concerned. Demons by themselves are bad enough, but if the Sardion has the same power as the Orb, we *definitely* don't want it to fall into their hands." He turned to Zakath. "Well?" he said.

"Well what?"

"Are you with us or against us?"

"Isn't that a little blunt?"

"Yes, it is—but it saves time, and time's starting to be a factor."

Zakath sank lower in his chair, his expression unreadable. "I find very little benefit for *me* in this proposed arrangement," he said.

"You get to keep living," Garion reminded him. "Cyradis said that you'll die before spring if you don't take up the task she's going to lay in front of you."

Zakath's faint smile was melancholy, and the dead indifference returned to his eyes. "My life hasn't really been so enjoyable that I'd consider going out of my way to prolong it, Belgarion," he replied.

"Don't you think you're being just a little childish, Zakath?" Garion snapped, his temper starting to heat up again. "You're not accomplishing a single thing here in Cthol Murgos. There's not one solitary drop of Urga blood left for you to spill, and you've got a situation at home that verges on disaster. Are you a King—or an Emperor, or whatever you want to call it—or are you a spoiled child? You refuse to go back to Mal Zeth just because somebody told you that you ought to. You even dig in your heels when someone assures you that you'll die if you don't go back. That's not only childish, it's irrational, and I don't have the time to try to reason with somebody whose wits have deserted him. Well, you can huddle here in Rak Hagga and nurse all your tired old griefs and disappointments until Cyradis' predictions catch up with you, for all I care, but Geran is my son, and I'm going to Mallorea. I've got work to do, and I don't have time to coddle you." He had saved something up for last. "Besides," he added in an insulting, offhand tone, "I don't need you anyway."

Zakath came to his feet, his eyes ablaze. "You go too far!" he roared, slamming his fist down on the table.

"Amazing," Garion said sarcastically. "You *are* alive after all. I thought I might have to step on your foot to get any kind of response out of you. All right, now that you're awake, let's fight."

"What do you mean, fight?" Zakath demanded, his face still flushed with anger. "Fight about what?"

"About whether or not you're going with us to Mallorea."

"Don't be stupid. Of course I'm going with you. What we *are* going to fight about is your incredible lack of common courtesy."

Garion stared at him for a moment and then suddenly doubled over in a gale of helpless laughter.

Zakath's face was still red, and his fists were clenching and unclenching. Then a slightly sheepish expression came over his face, and he, too, began to laugh.

Belgarath let out an explosive breath. "Garion," he said irritably, "let me know when you're going to do something like that. My veins aren't what they used to be."

Zakath wiped at his eyes, though he was still laughing. "How long do you think it might take for you and your friends to get packed?" he asked them.

"Not too long," Garion replied. "Why?"

"I'm suddenly homesick for Mal Zeth. It's spring there now, and the cherry trees are in bloom. You and Ce'Nedra will love Mal Zeth, Garion."

Garion was not entirely sure if the omission of the "Bel" was inadvertent or an overture of friendship. He *was*, however, quite sure that the Emperor of Mallorea was a man of even greater complexity than he had imagined.

"I hope you'll all excuse me now," Zakath said, "but I want to talk with Brador and get a few more details about what's been going on in Karanda. This Mengha he told me about seems to be mounting an open insurrection against the crown, and I've always had a violent prejudice against that sort of thing."

"I can relate to that," Garion agreed blandly.

For the next few days the road between Rak Hagga and the port city of Rak Cthan was thick with imperial messengers. Finally, on a frosty morning when the sun was bright and the sky dark blue and when misty steam rose from the dark waters of Lake Hagga, they set out, riding across a winter-browned plain toward the coast. Garion, his gray Rivan cloak drawn about him, rode at the head of the column with Zakath, who seemed for some reason to be in better spirits than he had been at any time since the two had met. The column which followed them stretched back for miles.

"Vulgar, isn't it?" the Mallorean said wryly, looking back over his shoulder. "I'm absolutely surrounded by parasites and toadies, and they proliferate like maggots in rotten meat."

"If they bother you so much, then why not dismiss them?" Garion suggested.

"I can't. They all have powerful relatives. I have to balance them very carefully—one from this tribe to match the one from that clan. As long as no one family has too many high offices, they spend all their time plotting against each other. That way they don't have the time to plot against me."

"I suppose that's one way to keep things under control."

As the sun moved up through the bright blue winter sky at this nether end of the world, the frost gently dissolved from the long stems of dead grass or fell lightly from the fern and bracken to leave ghostly white imprints of those drooping brown fronds on the short green moss spread beneath.

They paused for a noon meal that was every bit as sumptuous as one that might have been prepared back in Rak Hagga and was served on snowy damask beneath a wide-spread canvas roof. "Adequate, I suppose," Zakath said critically after they had eaten.

"You're overpampered, my lord," Polgara told him. "A hard ride in wet weather and a day or so on short rations would probably do wonders for your appetite."

Zakath gave Garion an amused look. "I thought it was just you," he said, "but this blunt outspokenness seems to be a characteristic of your whole family."

Garion shrugged. "It saves time."

"Forgive my saying this, Belgarion," Sadi interjected, "but what possible interest can an immortal have in time?" He sighed rather mournfully. "Immortality must give one a great deal of satisfaction—watching all one's enemies grow old and die."

"It's much overrated," Belgarath said, leaning back in his chair with a brimming silver tankard. "Sometimes whole centuries go by when one doesn't *have* any enemies and there's nothing to do but watch the years roll by."

Zakath suddenly smiled broadly. "Do you know something?" he said to them all. "I feel better right now than I've felt in over twenty-five years. It's as if a great weight has been lifted from me."

"Probably an aftereffect of the poison," Velvet suggested archly. "Get plenty of rest, and it should pass in a month or so."

"Is the Margravine always like this?" Zakath asked.

"Sometimes she's even worse," Silk replied morosely.

As they emerged from beneath the wide-spread canvas, Garion looked around for his horse, a serviceable roan with a long, hooked nose, but he could not seem to see the animal. Then he suddenly noticed that his saddle and packs were on a different horse, a very large dark gray stallion. Puzzled, he looked at Zakath, who was watching him intently. "What's this?" he asked.

"Just a little token of my unbounded respect, Garion," Zakath said, his eyes alight. "Your roan was an adequate mount, I suppose, but he was hardly a regal animal. A King needs a kingly horse, and I think you'll find that Chretienne can lend himself to any occasion that requires ceremony."

"Chretienne?"

"That's his name. He's been the pride of my stable here in Cthol Murgos. Don't you have a stable at Riva?"

Garion laughed. "My kingdom's an island, Zakath. We're more interested in boats than in horses." He looked at the proud gray standing with his neck arched and with one hoof lightly pawing the earth and was suddenly overcome with gratitude. He clasped the Mallorean Emperor's hand warmly. "This is a magnificent gift, Zakath," he said.

"Of course it is. I'm a magnificent fellow—or hadn't you noticed? Ride him, Garion. Feel the wind in your face and let the thunder of his hooves fill your blood."

"Well," Garion said, trying to control his eagerness, "maybe he and I really ought to get to know each other."

Zakath laughed with delight. "Of course," he said.

Garion approached the big gray horse, who watched him quite calmly.

"I guess we'll be sharing a saddle for a while," he said to the animal. Chretienne nickered and nudged at Garion with his nose.

"He wants to run," Eriond said. "I'll ride with you, if you don't mind. Horse wants to run, too."

"All right," Garion agreed. "Let's go then." He gathered the reins, set his foot in the stirrup, and swung up into the saddle. The gray was running almost before Garion was in place.

It was a new experience. Garion had spent many hours riding—sometimes for weeks on end. He had always taken care of his mounts, as any good Sendar would, but there had never really been any personal attachment before. For him, a horse had simply been a means of conveyance, a way to get from one place to another, and riding had never been a particular source of pleasure. With this great stallion, Chretienne, however, it was altogether different. There was a kind of electric thrill to the feel of the big horse's muscles bunching and flowing beneath him as they ran out across the winter-brown grass toward a rounded hill a mile or so distant, with Eriond and his chestnut stallion racing alongside.

When they reached the hilltop, Garion was breathless and laughing with sheer delight. He reined in, and Chretienne reared, pawing at the air with his hooves, wanting to be off again.

"Now you know, don't you?" Eriond asked with a broad smile.

"Yes," Garion admitted, still laughing, "I guess I do. I wonder how I missed it all these years."

"You have to have the right horse," Eriond told him wisely. He gave Garion a sidelong glance. "You know that you'll never be the same again, don't you?"

"That's all right," Garion replied. "I was getting tired of the old way anyhow." He pointed at a low string of hills out-lined against the crisp blue sky a league or so on ahead. "Why don't we go over there and see what's on the other side?" he suggested.

"Why not?" Eriond laughed.

And so they did.

The Emperor's household staff was well organized, and a goodly number of them rode on ahead to prepare their night's encampment at a spot almost precisely halfway to the coast. The column started early the following morning, riding again along a frosty track beneath a deep blue sky. It was late af-ternoon when they crested a hill to look out over the expanse of the Sea of the East, rolling a dark blue under the winter sun and with smoky-looking cloud banks the color of rust blurring the far horizon. Two dozen ships with their red sails furled stood at anchor in the indented curve of a shallow bay far below, and Garion looked with some puzzlement at Zakath.

"Another symptom of the vulgar ostentation I mentioned." The Emperor shrugged. "I ordered this fleet down here from the port at Cthan. A dozen or so of those ships are here to transport all my hangers-on and toadies—as well as the hum-bler people who actually do the work. The other dozen are here to escort our royal personages with suitable pomp. You have to have pomp, Garion. Otherwise people might mistake a King or an Emperor for an honest man."

"You're in a whimsical humor this afternoon."

"Maybe it's another of those lingering symptoms Liselle

mentioned. We'll sleep on board ship tonight and sail at first light tomorrow.''

Garion nodded, touching Chretienne's bowed neck with an odd kind of regret as he handed his reins to a waiting groom.

The vessel to which they were ferried from the sandy beach was opulent. Unlike the cramped cabins on most of the other ships Garion had sailed aboard, the chambers on this one were nearly as large as the rooms in a fair-sized house. It took him a little while to pin down the reason for the difference. The other ships had devoted so little room to cabins because the bulk of the space on board had been devoted to cargo. The only cargo *this* ship customarily carried, however, was the Emperor of Mallorea.

They dined that evening on lobster, served in the low-beamed dining room aboard Zakath's floating palace. So much of Garion's attention for the past week or more had been fixed on the unpredictable Emperor that he had not had much opportunity to talk with his friends. Thus, when they took their places at the table, he rather deliberately sat at the opposite end from the Mallorean. It was with a great deal of relief that he took his seat between Polgara and Durnik, while Ce'Nedra and Velvet diverted the Emperor with sparkling feminine chatter.

"You look tired, Garion," Polgara noted.

"I've been under a certain strain," he replied. "I wish that man wouldn't keep changing every other minute. Every time I think I've got him figured out, he turns into somebody else."

"It's not a good idea to categorize people, dear," she advised placidly, touching his arm. "That's the first sign of fuzzy thinking."

"Are we actually supposed to eat these things?" Durnik asked in a disgusted sort of voice, pointing his knife at the bright red lobster staring up at him from his plate with its claws seemingly at the ready.

"That's what the pliers are for, Durnik," Polgara explained in a peculiarly mild tone. "You have to crack it out of its shell."

He pushed his plate away. "I'm not going to eat something that looks like a big red bug," he declared with uncharacteristic heat. "I draw the line at some things."

"Lobster is a delicacy, Durnik," she said.

He grunted. "Some people eat snails, too."

Her eyes flashed, but then she gained control of her anger and continued to speak to him in that same mild tone. "I'm sure we can have them take it away and bring you something else," she said.

He glared at her.

Garion looked back and forth between the two of them. Then he decided that they had all known each other for far too long to step delicately around any problems. "What's the matter, Durnik?" he asked bluntly. "You're as cross as a badger with a sore nose."

"Nothing," Durnik almost snapped at him.

Garion began to put a few things together. He remembered the plea Andel had made to Aunt Pol concerning Toth. He looked down the table to where the big mute, his eyes lowered to his plate, seemed almost to be trying to make himself invisible. Then he looked back at Durnik, who kept his face stiffly turned away from his former friend. "Oh," he said, "now I think I understand. Aunt Pol told you something you didn't want to hear. Someone you liked very much did something that made you angry. You said some things to him that you wish now you hadn't said. Then you found out that he didn't really have any choice in the matter and that what he did was really right after all. Now you'd like to make friends with him again, but you don't know how. Is that sort of why you're behaving this way—and being so impolite to Aunt Pol?"

Durnik's look was at first stricken. Then his face grew red—then pale. "I don't have to listen to this," he burst out, coming to his feet.

"Oh, sit down, Durnik," Garion told him. "We all love each other too much to behave this way. Instead of being embarrassed and bad-tempered about it, why don't we see what we can do to fix it?"

Durnik tried to meet Garion's eyes, but finally lowered his head, his face flaming. "I treated him badly, Garion," he mumbled, sinking back into his chair again.

"Yes," Garion agreed, "you did. But it was because you didn't understand what he was doing—and why. I didn't understand myself until the day before yesterday—when Zakath finally changed his mind and decided to take us all to Mal Zeth. Cyradis knew that he was going to do that, and that's why she made Toth turn us over to Atesca's men. She *wants* us to get to the Sardion and meet Zandramas, and so she's going to arrange it. Toth will be the one who does what she thinks has to be done to accomplish that. Under the present circumstances, we couldn't find a better friend."

"How can I possibly—I mean, after the way I treated him?"

"Be honest. Admit that you were wrong and apologize."

Durnik's face grew stiff.

"It doesn't have to be in words, Durnik," Garion told his friend patiently. "You and Toth have been talking together without words for months." He looked speculatively up at the low-beamed ceiling. "This is a ship," he noted, "and we're going out onto an ocean. Do you imagine that there might be a few fish out there in all that water?"

Durnik's smile was immediate.

Polgara's sigh, however, was pensive.

The smith looked almost shyly across the table. "How did you say that I'm supposed to get this bug out of its shell, Pol?" he asked, pointing at the angry-looking lobster on his plate.

They sailed northeasterly from the coast of Hagga and soon left winter behind. At some point during the voyage they crossed that imaginary line equidistant from the poles and once again entered the northern half of the world. Durnik and Toth, shyly at first, but then with growing confidence, resumed their friendship and spent their days at the ship's stern, probing the sea with lines, bright-colored lures, and various baits gleaned from the galley.

Zakath's humor continued to remain uncharacteristically sunny, though his discussions with Belgarath and Polgara centered on the nature of demons, a subject about which there was very little to smile. Finally, one day when they had been at sea for about a week, a servant came up to Garion, who stood at the portside rail watching the dance of the wind atop the sparkling waves, and advised him that the Emperor would like to see him. Garion nodded and made his way aft to the cabin where Zakath customarily held audience. Like most of the cabins aboard the floating palace, this one was quite large and ostentatiously decorated. Owing to the broad windows stretching across the ship's stern, the room was bright and airy. The drapes at the sides of the windows were of crimson velvet, and the fine Mallorean carpet was a deep blue. Zakath, dressed as always in plain white linen, sat on a low, leather-upholstered divan at the far end of the cabin, looking out at the whitecaps and the flock of snowy gulls trailing the ship. His cat lay purring in his lap as he absently stroked her ears.

"You wanted to see me, Zakath?" Garion asked as he entered.

"Yes. Come in, Garion," the Mallorean replied. "I haven't seen much of you for the past few days. Are you cross with me?"

"No," Garion said. "You've been busy learning about demons. I don't know that much about them, so I couldn't have added all that much to the discussions." He crossed the cabin, pausing at one point to stoop and unwrap a ferociously playful kitten from around his left ankle.

"They love to pounce." Zakath smiled.

A thought came to Garion, and he looked around warily. "Zith isn't in here, is she?"

Zakath laughed. "No. Sadi's devised a means of keeping her at home." He looked whimsically at Garion. "Is she really as deadly as he says?"

101

Garion nodded. "She bit a Grolim at Rak Urga," he said. "He was dead in about a half a minute."

Zakath shuddered. "You don't have to tell Sadi about this," he said, "but snakes make my flesh creep."

"Talk to Silk. He could give you a whole dissertation about how much he dislikes them."

"He's a complicated little fellow, isn't he?"

Garion smiled. "Oh, yes. His life is filled with danger and excitement, and so his nerves are as tightly wound as lute strings. He's erratic sometimes, but you get used to that after a while." He looked at the other man critically. "You're looking particularly fit," he noted, sitting down on the other end of the leather couch. "Sea air must agree with you."

"I don't think it's really the air, Garion. I think it has to do with the fact that I've been sleeping eight to ten hours a night."

"Sleep? You?"

"Astonishing, isn't it?" Zakath's face went suddenly quite somber. "I'd rather that this didn't go any further, Garion," he said.

"Of course."

"Urgit told you what happened when I was young?"

Garion nodded. "Yes."

"My habit of not sleeping very much dates from then. A face that had been particularly dear to me haunted my dreams, and sleep became an agony to me."

"That didn't diminish? Not even after some thirty years?"

"Not one bit. I lived in continual grief and guilt and remorse. I lived only to revenge myself on Taur Urgas. Cho-Hag's saber robbed me of that. I had planned a dozen different deaths for the madman—each more horrible than the one before—but he cheated me by dying cleanly in battle."

"No," Garion disagreed. "His death was worse than anything you could possibly have devised. I've talked with Cho-Hag about it. Taur Urgas went totally mad before Cho-Hag killed him, but he lived long enough to realize that he had

102

finally been beaten. He died biting and clawing at the earth in frustration. Being beaten was more than he could bear."

Zakath thought about it. "Yes," he said finally. "That would have been quite dreadful for him, wouldn't it? I think that maybe I'm less disappointed now."

"And was it your discovery that the Urga line is now extinct that finally laid the ghost that's haunted your sleep all these years?"

"No, Garion. I don't think that had anything to do with it. It's just that instead of the face that had always been there before, now I see a different face."

"Oh?"

"A blindfolded face."

"Cyradis? I don't know that I'd recommend thinking about her in that fashion."

"You misunderstand, Garion. She's hardly more than a child, but somehow she's touched my life with more peace and comfort than I've ever known. I sleep like a baby and I walk around all day with this silly euphoria bubbling up in me." He shook his head. "Frankly, I can't stand myself like this, but I can't help it for some reason."

Garion stared out the window, not even seeing the play of sunlight on the waves nor the hovering gulls. Then it came to him so clearly that he knew that it was undeniably true. "It's because you've come to that crossroads in your life that Cyradis mentioned," he said. "You're being rewarded because you've chosen the right fork."

"Rewarded? By whom?"

Garion looked at him and suddenly laughed. "I don't think you're quite ready to accept that information yet," he said. "Could you bring yourself to believe that it's Cyradis who's making you feel good right now?"

"In some vague way, yes."

"It goes a little deeper, but that's a start." Garion looked at the slightly perplexed man before him. "You and I are caught up together in something over which we have absolutely no control," he said seriously. "I've been through it before, so I'll try to cushion the shocks that are in store for you as much as I can. Just try to keep an open mind about a peculiar way of looking at the world." He thought about it some more. "I think that we're going to be working together—at least up to a point—so we might as well be friends." He held out his right hand.

Zakath laughed. "Why not?" he said, taking Garion's hand in a firm grip. "I think we're both as crazy as Taur Urgas, but why not? We're the two most powerful men in the world. We should be deadly enemies, and you propose friendship. Well, why not?" He laughed again delightedly.

"We have much more deadly enemies, Zakath," Garion said gravely, "and all of your armies—and all of mine—won't mean a thing when we get to where we're going."

"And where's that, my young friend?"

"I think it's called 'the place which is no more.'"

"I've been meaning to ask you about that. The whole phrase is a contradiction in terms. How can you go someplace which doesn't exist any more?"

"I don't really know," Garion told him. "I'll tell you when we get there."

Two days later, they arrived at Mal Gemila, a port in southern Mallorea Antiqua, and took to horse. They rode eastward at a canter on a well-maintained highway that crossed a pleasant plain, green with spring. A regiment of red-tunicked cavalrymen cleared the road ahead of them, and their pace left the entourage which usually accompanied the Emperor far behind. There were way stations along the highway—not unlike the Tolnedran hostels dotting the roads in the west—and the imperial guard rather brusquely ejected other guests at these roadside stops to make way for the Emperor and his party.

As they pressed onward, day after day, Garion began slowly to comprehend the true significance of the word "boundless" as it was applied to Mallorea. The plains of Algaria, which had always before seemed incredibly vast, shrank into insignificance. The snowy peaks of the Dalasian mountains, lying to the south of the road they traveled, raked their white talons at the sky. Garion drew in on himself, feeling smaller and smaller the deeper they rode into this vast domain.

Peculiarly, Ce'Nedra seemed to be suffering a similar shrinkage, and she quite obviously did not like it very much. Her comments became increasingly waspish; her observations more acid. She found the loose-fitting garments of the peasantry uncouth. She found fault with the construction of the gangplows that opened whole acres at a time behind patiently plodding herds of oxen. She didn't like the food. Even the water—as clear as crystal, and as cold and sweet as might have sprung from any crevice in the Tolnedran mountains—offended her taste.

Silk, his eyes alight with mischief, rode at her side on the sunny midmorning of the last day of their journey from Mal Gemila. "Beware, your Majesty," he warned her slyly as they neared the crest of a hillside sheathed in pale spring grass so verdant that it almost looked like a filmy green mist. "The first sight of Mal Zeth has sometimes struck the unwary traveler blind. To be safe, why don't you cover one eye with your hand? That way you can preserve at least partial sight."

Her face grew frosty, and she drew herself to her full height in her saddle—a move that might have come off better had she been only slightly taller—and said to him in her most imperious tone, "*We* are not amused, Prince Kheldar, and *we* do not expect to find a barbarian city at the far end of the world a rival to the splendors of Tol Honeth, the only truly imperial city in the—"

And then she stopped—as they all did.

The valley beyond the crest stretched not for miles, but for leagues, and it was filled to overflowing with the city of Mal Zeth. The streets were as straight as tautly stretched strings, and the buildings gleamed—not with marble, for there was not marble enough in all the world to sheath the buildings of this enormous city—but rather with an intensly gleaming, thick white mortar that seemed somehow to shoot light at the eye. It was stupendous.

"It's not much," Zakath said in an exaggeratedly deprecating tone. "Just a friendly little place we like to call home." He looked at Ce'Nedra's stiff, pale little face with an artful expression. "We really should press on, your Majesty," he told her. "It's a half-day's ride to the imperial palace from here."

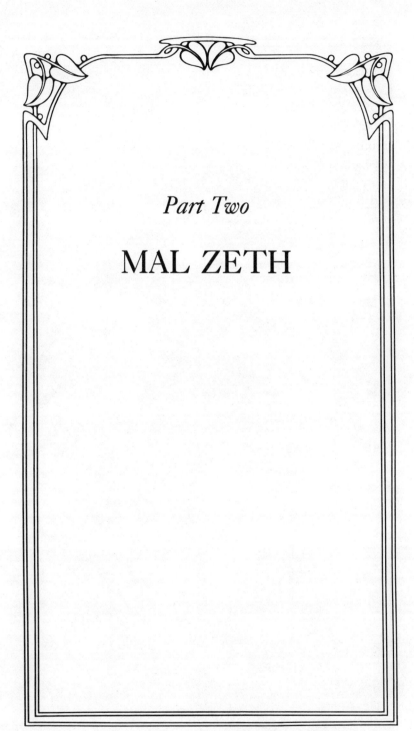

Part Two

MAL ZETH

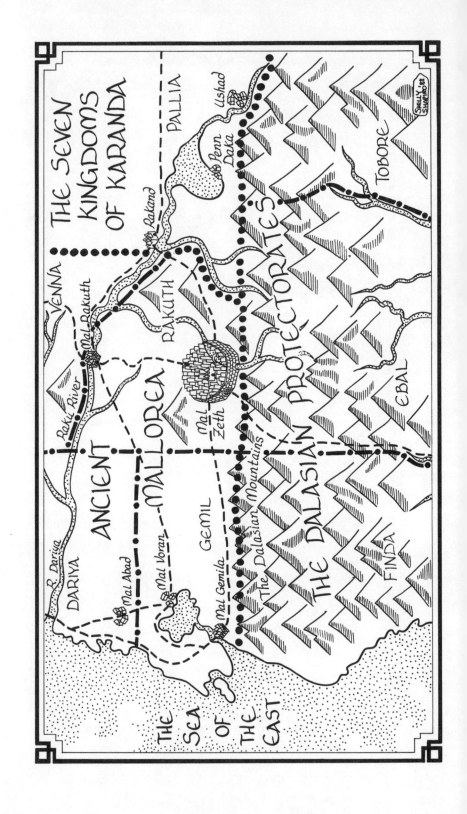

CHAPTER SIX

The gates of Mal Zeth, like those of Tol Honeth, were of bronze, broad and burnished. The city lying within those gates, however, was significantly different from the capital of the Tolnedran Empire. There was a peculiar sameness about the structures, and they were built so tightly against each other that the broad avenues of the city were lined on either side by solid, mortar-covered walls, pierced only by deeply inset, arched doorways with narrow white stairways leading up to the flat rooftops. Here and there, the mortar had crumbled away, revealing the fact that the buildings beneath that coating were constructed of squared-off timbers.

109

Durnik, who believed that all buildings should be made of stone, noted that fact with a look of disapproval.

As they moved deeper into the city, Garion noticed the almost total lack of windows. "I don't want to seem critical," he said to Zakath, "but isn't your city just a little monotonous?"

Zakath looked at him curiously.

"All the houses are the same, and there aren't very many windows."

"Oh," Zakath smiled, "that's one of the drawbacks of leaving architecture up to the military. They're great believers in uniformity, and windows have no place in military fortifications. Each house has its own little garden, though, and the windows face that. In the summertime, the people spend most of their time in the gardens—or on the rooftops."

"Is the whole city like this?" Durnik asked, looking at the cramped little houses all packed together.

"No, Goodman," the Emperor replied. "This quarter of the city was built for corporals. The streets reserved for officers are a bit more ornate, and those where the privates and workmen live are much shabbier. Military people tend to be very conscious of rank and the appearances that go with it."

A few doors down a side street branching off from the one they followed, a stout, red-faced woman was shrilly berating a scrawny-looking fellow with a hangdog expression as a group of soldiers removed furniture from a house and piled it in a rickety cart. "You had to go and do it, didn't you, Actas?" she demanded. "You had to get drunk and insult your captain. Now what's to become of us? I spent all those years living in those pigsty privates' quarters waiting for you to get promoted, and just when I think things are taking a turn for the better, you have to destroy it all by getting drunk and being reduced to private again."

He mumbled something.

"What was that?"

"Nothing, dear."

110

"I'm not going to let you forget this, Actas, let me tell you."

"Life does have its little ups and downs, doesn't it?" Sadi murmured as they rode on out of earshot.

"I don't think it's anything to laugh about," Ce'Nedra said with surprising heat. "They're being thrown out of their home over a moment's foolishness. Can't someone do something?"

Zakath gave her an appraising look, then beckoned to one of the red-cloaked officers riding respectfully along behind them. "Find out which unit that man's in," he instructed. "Then go to his captain and tell him that I'd take it as a personal favor if Actas were reinstated in his former rank—on the condition that he stays sober."

"At once, your Majesty." The officer saluted and rode off.

"Why, thank you, Zakath," Ce'Nedra said, sounding a little startled.

"My pleasure, Ce'Nedra." He bowed to her from his saddle. Then he laughed shortly. "I suspect that Actas' wife will see to it that he suffers sufficiently for his misdeeds anyway."

"Aren't you afraid that such acts of compassion might damage your reputation, your Majesty?" Sadi asked him.

"No," Zakath replied. "A ruler must always strive to be unpredictable, Sadi. It keeps the underlings off balance. Besides, an occasional act of charity toward the lower ranks helps to strengthen their loyalty."

"Don't you ever do anything that isn't motivated by politics?" Garion asked him. For some reason, Zakath's flippant explanation of his act irritated him.

"Not that I can think of," Zakath said. "Politics is the greatest game in the world, Garion, but you have to play it all the time to keep your edge."

Silk laughed. "I've said the exact same thing about commerce," he said. "About the only difference I can see is that in commerce you have money as a way of keeping score. How do you keep score in politics?"

Zakath's expression was peculiarly mixed—half amused and half deadly serious. "It's very simple, Kheldar," he said.

"If you're still on the throne at the end of the day, you've won. If you're dead, you've lost—and each day is a complete new game."

Silk gave him a long, speculative look, then looked over at Garion, his fingers moving slightly. —*I need to talk to you— at once—*

Garion nodded briefly, then leaned over in his saddle. He reined in.

"Something wrong?" Zakath asked him.

"I think my cinch is loose," Garion replied, dismounting. "Go on ahead. I'll catch up."

"Here, I'll help you, Garion," Silk offered, also swinging down from his saddle.

"What's this all about?" Garion asked when the Emperor, chatting with Ce'Nedra and Velvet, had ridden out of earshot.

"Be very careful with him, Garion," the little man replied quietly, pretending to check the straps on Garion's saddle. "He let something slip there. He's all smiles and courtesy on the surface, but underneath it all he hasn't really changed all that much."

"Wasn't he just joking?"

"Not even a little. He was deadly serious. He's brought us all to Mal Zeth for reasons that have nothing to do with Mengha or our search for Zandramas. Be on your guard with him. That friendly smile of his can fall off his face without any warning at all." He spoke a little more loudly then. "There," he said, tugging at a strap, "that ought to hold it. Let's catch up with the others."

They rode into a broad square surrounded on all sides by canvas booths dyed in various hues of red, green, blue, and yellow. The square teemed with merchants and citizens, all dressed in varicolored, loose-fitting robes that hung to their heels.

"Where do the common citizens live if the whole city's divided up into sections based on military rank?" Durnik asked.

Brador, the bald, chubby Chief of the Bureau of Internal Affairs, who happened to be riding beside the smith, looked around with a smile. "They all have their ranks, Goodman," he replied, "each according to his individual accomplishments. It's all very rigidly controlled by the Bureau of Promotions. Housing, places of business, suitable marriages— they're all determined by rank."

"Isn't that sort of overregimented?" Durnik asked pointedly.

"Malloreans love to be regimented, Goodman Durnik." Brador laughed. "Angaraks bow automatically to authority; Melcenes have a deep inner need to compartmentalize things; Karands are too stupid to take control of their own destinies; and the Dals—well, nobody knows what the Dals want."

"We aren't really all that different from the people in the West, Durnik," Zakath said back over his shoulder. "In Tolnedra and Sendaria, such matters are determined by economics. People gravitate to the houses and shops and marriages they can afford. We've just formalized it, that's all."

"Tell me, your Majesty," Sadi said, "how is it that your people are so undemonstrative?"

"I don't quite follow you."

"Shouldn't they at least salute as you ride by? You *are* the Emperor, after all."

"They don't recognize me." Zakath shrugged. "The Emperor is a man in crimson robes who rides in a golden carriage, wears a terribly heavy jeweled crown, and is accompanied by at least a regiment of imperial guards all blowing trumpets. I'm just a man in white linen riding through town with a few friends."

Garion thought about that, still mindful of Silk's half-whispered warning. The almost total lack of any kind of self-aggrandizement implicit in Zakath's statement revealed yet another facet of the man's complex personality. He was quite sure that not even King Fulrach of Sendaria, the most modest of all the monarchs of the West, could be quite so self-effacing.

113

The streets beyond the square were lined with somewhat larger houses than those they had passed near the city gates, and there had been some attempt at ornamentation here. It appeared, however, that Mallorean sculptors had limited talent, and the mortar-cast filigree surmounting the front of each house was heavy and graceless.

"The sergeant's district," Zakath said laconically.

The city seemed to go on forever. At regular intervals there were squares and market places and bazaars, all filled with people wearing the bright, loose-fitting robes that appeared to be the standard Mallorean garb. When they passed the last of the rigidly similar houses of the sergeants and of those civilians of equal rank, they entered a broad belt of trees and lawns where fountains splashed and sparkled in the sunlight and where broad promenades were lined with carefully sculptured green hedges interspersed with cherry trees laden with pink blossoms shimmering in the light breeze.

"How lovely," Ce'Nedra exclaimed.

"We do have some beauty here in Mal Zeth," Zakath told her. "No one—not even an army architect—could make a city this big uniformly ugly."

"The officers' districts aren't quite so severe," Silk told the little Queen.

"You're familiar with Mal Zeth, then, your Highness?" Brador asked.

Silk nodded. "My partner and I have a facility here," he replied. "It's more in the nature of a centralized collection point than an actual business. It's cumbersome doing business in Mal Zeth—too many regulations."

"Might one inquire as to the rank you were assigned?" the moon-faced bureaucrat asked delicately.

"We're generals," Silk said in a rather grandly offhand manner. "Yarblek wanted to be a field marshal, but I didn't think the expense of buying that much rank was really justified."

"Is rank for sale?" Sadi asked.

114

"In Mal Zeth, everything's for sale," Silk replied. "In most respects it's almost exactly like Tol Honeth."

"Not entirely, Silk," Ce'Nedra said primly.

"Only in the broadest terms, your Imperial Highness," he agreed quickly. "Mal Zeth has never been graced by the presence of a divinely beautiful Imperial Princess, glowing like a precious jewel and shooting beams of her fire back at the sun."

She gave him a hard look, then turned her back on him.

"What did I say?" the little man asked Garion in an injured tone.

"People always suspect you, Silk," Garion told him. "They can never quite be sure that you're not making fun of them. I thought you knew that."

Silk sighed tragically. "Nobody understands me," he complained.

"Oh, I think they do."

The plazas and boulevards beyond the belt of parks and gardens were more grand, and the houses larger and set apart from each other. There was still, however, a stiff similarity about them, a kind of stern sameness that insured that men of equal rank would be assigned to rigidly equal quarters.

Another broad strip of lawns and trees lay beyond the mansions of the generals and their mercantile equivalents, and within that encircling green there arose a fair-sized marble city with its own walls and burnished gates.

"The imperial palace," Zakath said indifferently. He frowned. "What have you done over there?" he asked Brador, pointing at a long row of tall buildings rising near the south wall of the enclosed compound.

Brador coughed delicately. "Those are the bureaucratic offices, your Majesty," he replied in a neutral tone. "You'll recall that you authorized their construction just before the battle of Thull Mardu."

Zakath pursed his lips. "I hadn't expected something on quite such a grand scale," he said.

"There are quite a lot of us, your Majesty," Brador explained, "and we felt that things might be more harmonious if each bureau had its own building." He looked a bit apologetic. "We really *did* need the space," he explained defensively to Sadi. "We were all jumbled together with the military, and very often men from different bureaus had to share the same office. It's really much more efficient this way, wouldn't you say?"

"I think I'd prefer it if you didn't involve me in this discussion, your Excellency," Sadi answered.

"I was merely attempting to draw upon your Excellency's expertise in managing affairs of state."

"Salmissra's palace is somewhat unique," Sadi told him. "We *like* being jumbled together. It gives us greater opportunities for spying and murder and intrigue and the other normal functions of government."

As they approached the gates to the imperial complex, Garion noticed with some surprise that the thick bronze gates had been overlaid with beaten gold, and his thrifty Sendarian heritage recoiled from the thought of such wanton lavishness. Ce'Nedra, however, looked at the priceless gates with undisguised aquisitiveness.

"You wouldn't be able to move them," Silk advised her.

"What?" she said inattentatively.

"The gates. They're much to heavy to steal."

"Shut up, Silk," she said absently, her eyes still appraising the gates.

He began to laugh uproariously, and she looked at him, her green eyes narrowing dangerously.

"I think I'll ride back to see what's keeping Belgarath," the little man said.

"Do," she said. Then she looked at Garion, who was trying to conceal a broad grin. "Something funny?" she asked him.

"No, dear," he replied quickly. "Just enjoying the scenery is all."

The detachment of guards at the gates was not as burnished nor plumed as the ceremonial guards at the gates of Tol Honeth. They wore polished shirts of chain mail over the customary red tunic, baggy breeches tucked into the tops of knee-high boots, red cloaks, and pointed conical helmets. They nonetheless looked very much like soldiers. They greeted Kal Zakath with crisp military salutes, and, as the Emperor passed through the gilded gates, trumpeteers announced his entrance into the imperial compound with a brazen fanfare.

"I've always hated that," the Mallorean ruler said confidentially to Garion. "The sound grates on my ears."

"What irritated me were the people who used to follow me around hoping that I might need something," Garion told him.

"That's convenient sometimes."

Garion nodded. "Sometimes," he agreed, "but it stopped being convenient when one of them threw a knife at my back."

"Really? I thought your people universally adored you."

"It was a misunderstanding. The young man and I had a talk about it, and he promised not to do it any more."

"That's all?" Zakath exclaimed in astonishment. "You didn't have him executed?"

"Of course not. Once he and I understood each other, he turned out to be extraordinarily loyal." Garion sighed sadly. "He was killed at Thull Mardu."

"I'm sorry, Garion," Zakath said. "We all lost friends at Thull Mardu."

The marble-clad buildings inside the imperial complex were a jumble of conflicting architectural styles, ranging from the severely utilitarian to the elaborately ornate. For some reason Garion was reminded of the vast rabbit warren of King Anheg's palace at Val Alorn. Although Zakath's palace did not consist of one single building, the structures were all linked to each other by column-lined promenades and galleries which passed through parklike grounds studded with statues and marble pavilions.

Zakath led them through the confusing maze toward the

middle of the complex, where a single palace stood in splendid isolation, announcing by its expanse and height that it was the center of all power in boundless Mallorea. "The residence of Kallath the Unifier," the Emperor announced with grand irony, "my revered ancestor."

"Isn't it just a bit overdone?" Ce'Nedra asked tartly, still obviously unwilling to concede the fact that Mal Zeth far out-stripped her girlhood home.

"Of course it is," the Mallorean replied, "but the osten-tation was necessary. Kallath had to demonstrate to the other generals that he outranked them, and in Mal Zeth one's rank is reflected by the size of one's residence. Kallath was an undisguised knave, a usurper and a man of little personal charm, so he had to assert himself in other ways."

"Don't you just love politics?" Velvet said to Ce'Nedra. "It's the only field where the ego is allowed unrestricted play—as long as the treasury holds out."

Zakath laughed. "I should offer you a position in the gov-ernment, Margravine Liselle," he said. "I think we need an imperial deflator—someone to puncture all our puffed-up self-importance."

"Why, thank you, your Majesty," she said with a dimpled smile. "If it weren't for my commitments to the family busi-ness, I might even consider accepting such a post. It sounds like so much fun."

He sighed with mock regret. "Where were you when I needed a wife?"

"Probably in my cradle, your Majesty," she replied innocently.

He winced. "That was unkind," he accused.

"Yes," she agreed. "True, though," she added clinically.

He laughed again and looked at Polgara. "I'm going to steal her from you, my lady," he declared.

"To be your court jester, Kal Zakath?" Liselle asked, her face no longer lightly amused. "To entertain you with clever insults and banter? Ah, no. I don't think so. There's another side to me that I don't think you'd like very much. They call me 'Velvet' and think of me as a soft-winged butterfly, but this particular butterfly has a poisoned sting—as several people have discovered after it was too late."

"Behave, dear," Polgara murmured to her. "And don't give away trade secrets in a moment of pique."

Velvet lowered her eyes. "Yes, Lady Polgara," she replied meekly.

Zakath looked at her, but did not say anything. He swung down from his saddle, and three grooms dashed to his side to take the reins from his hand. "Come along, then," he said to Garion and the others. "I'd like to show you around." He threw a sly glance at Velvet. "I hope that the Margravine will forgive me if I share every home owner's simple pride in his domicile—no matter how modest."

She laughed a golden little laugh.

Garion dismounted and laid an affectionate hand on Chretienne's proud neck. It was with a pang of almost tangible regret that he handed the reins to a waiting groom.

They entered the palace through broad, gilded doors and found themselves in a vaulted rotunda, quite similar in design to the one in the Emperor's palace in Tol Honeth, though this one lacked the marble busts that made Varana's entryway appear vaguely like a mausoleum. A crowd of officials, military and civilian, awaited their Emperor, each with a sheaf of important-looking documents in his hand.

Zakath sighed as he looked at them. "I'm afraid we'll have to postpone the grand tour," he said. "I'm certain that you'll all want to bathe and change anyway—and perhaps rest a bit before we start the customary formalities. Brador, would you be good enough to show our guests to their rooms and arrange to have a light lunch prepared for them?"

"Of course, your Majesty."

"I think the east wing might be pleasant. It's away from all the scurrying through the halls in this part of the palace."

"My very thought, your Majesty."

119

Zakath smiled at them all. "We'll dine together this evening," he promised. Then he smiled ironically. "An intimate little supper with no more than two or three hundred guests." He looked at the nervous officials clustered nearby and made a wry face. "Until this evening, then."

Brador led them through the echoing marble corridors teeming with servants and minor functionaries.

"Big place," Belgarath observed after they had been walking for perhaps ten minutes. The old man had said very little since they had entered the city, but had ridden in his customary half doze, although Garion was quite sure that very little escaped his grandfather's half-closed eyes.

"Yes," Brador agreed with him. "The first Emperor, Kallath, had grandiose notions at times."

Belgarath grunted. "It's a common affliction among rulers. I think it has something to do with insecurity."

"Tell me, Brador," Silk said, "didn't I hear somewhere that the state secret police are under the jurisdiction of your bureau?"

Brador nodded with a deprecating little smile. "It's one of my many responsibilities, Prince Kheldar," he replied. "I need to know what's going on in the empire in order to stay on top of things, so I had to organize a modest little intelligence service—nothing on nearly the scale of Queen Porenn's, however."

"It will grow with time," Velvet assured him. "Those things always do, for some reason."

The east wing of the palace was set somewhat apart from the rest of the buildings in the complex and it embraced a kind of enclosed courtyard or atrium that was green with exotic flowering plants growing about a mirrorlike pool at its center. Jewellike hummingbirds darted from blossom to blossom, adding splashes of vibrant, moving color.

Polgara's eyes came alight when Brador opened the door to the suite of rooms she was to share with Durnik. Just beyond an arched doorway leading from the main sitting room was a large marble tub sunk into the floor with little tendrils of steam rising from it. "Oh, my," she sighed. "Civilization—at last."

"Just try not to get waterlogged, Pol," Belgarath said.

"Of course not, father," she agreed absently, still eyeing the steaming tub with undisguised longing.

"Is it really all that important, Pol?" he asked her.

"Yes, father," she replied. "It really is."

"It's an irrational prejudice against dirt." He grinned at the rest of them. "I've always been sort of fond of dirt myself."

"Quite obviously," she said. Then she stopped. "Incidentally, Old Wolf," she said critically as they all began to file out, "if your room happens to be similarly equipped, you should make use of the facilities yourself."

"Me?"

"You smell, father."

"No, Pol," he corrected. "I stink. *You* smell."

"Whatever. Go wash, father." She was already absently removing her shoes.

"I've gone as much as ten years at a time without a bath," he declared.

"Yes, father," she said. "I know—only the Gods know how well I know. Now," she said in a very businesslike tone, "if you'll all excuse me . . ." She very deliberately began to unbotton the front of her dress.

The suite of rooms to which Garion and Ce'Nedra were led was, if anything, even more opulent than that shared by Durnik and Polgara. As Garion moved about the several large chambers, examining the furnishings, Ce'Nedra went directly toward the bath, her eyes dreamy and her clothes falling to the floor behind her as she went. His wife's tendency toward casual nudity had occasionally shocked Garion in the past. He did not *personally* object to Ce'Nedra's skin. What disturbed him had been that she had seemed oblivious to the fact that sometimes her unclad state was highly inappropriate. He recalled with a shudder the time when he and the Sendarian ambassador had entered the royal apartment at Riva just as Ce'Nedra was in the process of trying on several new undergarments she had received from her dressmaker that very morning. Quite calmly, she had asked the ambassador's opinion of various of the frilly little things, modeling each in turn for him. The ambassador, a staid and proper Sendarian gentleman in his seventies, received more shocks in that ten minutes than he had encountered in the previous half century, and his next dispatch to King Fulrach had plaintively requested that he be relieved of his post.

"Ce'Nedra, aren't you at least going to close the door?" Garion asked her as she tested the water's temperature with a tentative toe.

"That makes it very hard for us to talk, Garion," she replied reasonably as she stepped down into the tub. "I hate to have to shout."

"Oh?" he said. "I hadn't noticed that."

"Be nice," she told him, sinking into the water with a contented sigh. Curiously she began to unstopper and sniff the crystal decanters lined along one side of the tub which contained, Garion assumed, the assorted condiments with which ladies seasoned their bath water. Some of these she restoppered disapprovingly. Others she liberaly sprinkled into her bath. One or two of them she rubbed on herself in various places.

"What if somebody comes in?" Garion asked her pointedly. "Some official or messenger or servant or something?"

"Well, what if they do?"

He stared at her.

"Garion, darling," she said in that same infuriatingly reasonable tone, "if they hadn't intended for the bath to be used, they wouldn't have prepared it, would they?"

Try as he might, he could not find an answer to that question.

She laid her head back in the water, letting her hair fan out around her face. Then she sat up. "Would you like to wash my back for me?" she asked him.

An hour or so later, after an excellent lunch served by efficient servants, Silk stopped by. The little thief had also bathed and changed clothes once again. His pearl-gray doublet was formally elegant, and he once again dripped jewels. His short, scraggly beard had been neatly crimmed, and there was a faint air of exotic perfume lingering about him. "Appearances," he responded to Garion's quizzical look. "One always wants to put one's best foot forward in a new situation."

"Of course," Garion said dryly.

"Belgarath asked me to stop by," the little man continued. "There's a large room upstairs. We're gathering there for a council of war."

"War?"

"Metaphorically speaking, of course."

"Oh. Of course."

The room at the top of a flight of marble stairs to which Silk led Garion and Ce'Nedra was quite large, and there was a thronelike chair on a dais against the back wall. Garion looked about at the lush furnishings and heavy crimson drapes. "This isn't the throne room, is it?" he asked.

"No," Silk replied. "At least not Kal Zakath's official one. It's here to make visiting royalty feel at home. Some kings get nervous when they don't have official-looking surroundings to play in."

"Oh."

Belgarath sat with his mismatched boots up on a polished table. His hair and beard were slightly damp, evidence that, despite his pretended indifference to bathing, he had in fact followed Polgara's instructions. Polgara and Durnik were talking quietly at one side, and Eriond and Toth were nearby. Velvet and Sadi stood looking out the window at the formal garden lying to the east of Zakath's sprawling palace.

"All right," the old sorcerer said, "I guess we're all here now. I think we need to talk."

123

—I wouldn't say anything too specific— Silk's fingers said in the gestures of the Drasnian secret language. *—It's almost certain that there are a few spies about—*

Belgarath looked at the far wall, his eyes narrowed as he searched it inch by inch for hidden peepholes. He grunted and looked at Polgara.

"I'll look into it, father," she murmured. Her eyes grew distant, and Garion felt the familiar surge. After a moment she nodded and held up three fingers. She concentrated for a moment, and the quality of the surge changed, seeming somehow languorous. Then she straightened and relaxed her will. "It's all right now," she told them calmly. "They fell asleep."

"That was very smooth, Pol," Durnik said admiringly.

"Why, thank you, dear," she smiled, laying her hand on his.

Belgarath put his feet on the floor and leaned forward. "That's one more thing for us all to keep in mind," he said seriously. "We're likely to be watched all the time that we're here in Mal Zeth, so be careful. Zakath's a sceptic, so we can't really be sure just how much of what we've told him he believes. It's altogether possible that he has other things in mind for us. Right now he needs our help in dealing with Mengha, but he still hasn't entirely abandoned his campaign in Cthol Murgos, and he might want to use us to bring the Alorns and the others into that war on his side. He's also got problems with Urvon and Zandramas. We don't have the time to get caught up in internal Mallorean politics. At the moment, though, we're more or less in his power, so let's be careful."

"We can leave any time we need to, Belgarath," Durnik said confidently.

"I'd rather not do it that way unless we have absolutely no other choice," the old man replied. "Zakath's the kind of man who's very likely to grow testy if he's thwarted, and I don't want to have to creep around dodging his soldiers. It takes too much time and it's dangerous. I'll be a lot happier if we can leave Mal Zeth with his blessing—or at least with his consent."

"I want to get to Ashaba before Zandramas has time to escape again," Garion insisted.

"So do I, Garion," his grandfather said, "but we don't know what she's doing there, so we don't know how long she's likely to stay."

"She's been looking for something, father," Polgara told the old man. "I saw that in her mind when I trapped her back in Rak Hagga."

He looked at her thoughtfully. "Could you get any idea of what it was, Pol?"

She shook her head. "Not specifically," she replied. "I think it's information of some kind. She can't go any further until she finds it. I was able to pick that much out of her thoughts."

"Whatever it is has to be well hidden," he said. "Beldin and I took Ashaba apart after the Battle of Vo Mimbre and we didn't find anything out of the ordinary—if you can accept the idea that Torak's house was in any way ordinary."

"Can we be sure that she's still there with my baby?" Ce'Nedra asked intently.

"No, dear," Polgara told her. "She's taken steps to hide her mind from me. She's rather good, actually."

"Even if she's left Ashaba, the Orb can pick up her trail again," Belgarath said. "The chances are pretty good that she hasn't found what she's looking for, and that effectively nails her down at Ashaba. If she has found it, she won't be hard to follow."

"We're going on to Ashaba, then?" Sadi asked. "What I'm getting at is that our concern about Mengha was just a ruse to get us to Mallorea, wasn't it?"

"I think I'm going to need more information before I make any decisions about that. The situation in northern Karanda is serious, certainly, but let's not lose sight of the fact that our primary goal is Zandramas, and she's at Ashaba. Before I can decide anything, though, I need to know more about what's going on here in Mallorea."

"My department," Silk volunteered.

"And mine," Velvet added.

"I might be able to help a bit as well," Sadi noted with a faint smile. He frowned then. "Seriously though, Belgarath," he continued, "you and your family here represent power. I don't think we're going to have much luck at persuading Kal Zakath to let you go willingly—no matter how cordial he may appear on the surface."

The old man nodded glumly. "It might turn out that way after all," he agreed. Then he looked at Silk, Velvet, and Sadi. "Be careful," he cautioned them. "Don't let your instincts run away with you. I need information, but don't stir up any hornets' nests getting it for me." He looked pointedly at Silk. "I hope I've made myself clear about this," he said. "Don't complicate things just for the fun of it."

"Trust me, Belgarath," Silk replied with a bland smile.

"Of course he trusts you, Kheldar," Velvet assured the little man.

Belgarath looked at his impromptu spy network and shook his head. "Why do I get the feeling that I'm going to regret this?" he muttered.

"I'll keep an eye on them, Belgarath," Sadi promised.

"Of course, but who's going to keep an eye on you?"

CHAPTER SEVEN

That evening they were escorted with some ceremony through the echoing halls of Zakath's palace to a banquet hall that appeared to be only slightly smaller than a parade ground. The hall was approached by way of a broad, curved stairway lined on either side with branched candelabra and liveried trumpeteers. The stairway was obviously designed to facilitate grand entrances. Each new arrival was announced by a stirring fanfare and the booming voice of a gray-haired herald so thin that it almost appeared that a lifetime of shouting had worn him down to a shadow.

Garion and his friends waited in a small antechamber while the last of the local dignitaries were announced. The fussy

127

chief of protocol, a small Melcene with an elaborately trimmed brown beard, wanted them to line up in ascending order of rank, but the difficulties involved in assigning precise rank to the members of this strange group baffled him. He struggled with it, manfully trying to decide if Sorcerer outranked King or Imperial Princess until Garion solved his problem for him by leading Ce'Nedra out onto the landing at the top of the stairs.

"Their Royal Majesties, King Belgarion and Queen Ce'Nedra of Riva," the herald declaimed grandly, and the trumpets blared.

Garion, dressed all in blue and with his ivory-gowned Queen on his arm, paused on the marble landing at the top of the stairs to allow the brightly clad throng below the time to gawk at him. The somewhat dramatic pause was not entirely his idea. Ce'Nedra had dug her fingernails into his arm with a grip of steel and hissed, "Stand still!"

It appeared that Zakath also had some leaning toward the theatrical, since the stunned silence which followed the herald's announcement clearly indicated that the Emperor had given orders that the identity of his guests remain strictly confidential until this very moment. Garion was honest enough with himself to admit that the startled buzz which ran through the crowd below was moderately gratifying.

He began down the stairway, but found himself reined in like a restive horse. "Don't run!" Ce'Nedra commanded under her breath.

"Run?" he objected. "I'm barely moving."

"Do it slower, Garion."

He discovered then that his wife had a truly amazing talent. She could speak without moving her lips! Her smile was gracious, though somewhat lofty, but a steady stream of low-voiced commands issued from that smile.

The buzzing murmur that had filled the banquet hall when they had been announced died into a respectful silence when they reached the foot of the stair, and a vast wave of bows and curtsies rippled through the crowd as they moved along the carpeted promenade leading to the slightly elevated platform upon which sat the table reserved for the Emperor and his special guests, domestic and foreign.

Zakath himself, still in his customary white, but wearing a gold circlet artfully hammered into the form of a wreath woven of leaves as a concession to the formality of the occasion, rose from his seat and came to meet them, thereby avoiding that awkward moment when two men of equal rank meet in public. "So good of you to come, my dear," he said, taking Ce'Nedra's hand and kissing it. He sounded for all the world like a country squire or minor nobleman greeting friends from the neighborhood.

"So good of you to invite us," she replied with a whimsical smile.

"You're looking well, Garion," the Mallorean said, extending his hand and still speaking in that offhand and informal manner.

"Tolerable, Zakath," Garion responded, taking his cue from his host. If Zakath wanted to play, Garion felt that he should show him that he could play, too.

"Would you care to join me at the table?" Zakath asked. "We can chat while we wait for the others to arrive."

"Of course," Garion agreed in a deliberately commonplace tone of voice.

When they reached their chairs, however, his curiosity finally got the better of him. "Why are we playing 'just plain folks'?" he asked Zakath as he held Ce'Nedra's chair for her. "This affair's a trifle formal for talking about the weather and asking after each other's health, wouldn't you say?"

"It's baffling the nobility," Zakath replied with aplomb. "Never do the expected, Garion. The hint that we're old, old friends will set them afire with curiosity and make people who thought that they knew everything just a little less sure of themselves." He smiled at Ce'Nedra. "You're positively ravishing tonight, my dear," he told her.

129

Ce'Nedra glowed then looked archly at Garion. "Why don't you take a few notes, dear?" she suggested. "You could learn a great deal from his Majesty here." She turned back to Zakath. "You're so very kind to say it," she told him, "but my hair is an absolute disaster." Her expression was faintly tragic as she lightly touched her curls with her fingertips. Actually, her hair was stupendous, with a coronet of braids interwoven with strings of pearls and with a cascade of coppery ringlets spilling down across the front of her left shoulder.

During this polite exchange, the others in their party were being introduced. Silk and Velvet caused quite a stir, he in his jewel-encrusted doublet and she in a gown of lavender brocade.

Ce'Nedra sighed enviously. "I wish I could wear that color," she murmured.

"You can wear any color you want to, Ce'Nedra," Garion told her.

"Are you color-blind, Garion?" she retorted. "A girl with red hair can *not* wear lavender."

"If that's all that's bothering you, I can change the color of your hair anytime you want."

"Don't you dare!" she gasped, her hands going protectively to the cascade of auburn curls at her shoulder.

"Just a suggestion, dear."

The herald at the top of the stairs announced Sadi, Eriond, and Toth as a group, obviously having some difficulty with the fact that the boy and the giant had no rank that he could discern. The next presentation, however, filled his voice with awe and his bony limbs with trembling. "Her Grace, the Duchess of Erat," he declaimed, "Lady Polgara the Sorceress." The silence following that announcement was stunned. "And Goodman Durnik of Sendaria," the herald added, "the man with two lives."

Polgara and the smith descended the stairs to the accompaniment of a profound silence.

The bows and curtsies which acknowledged the legendary

couple were so deep as to resemble genuflections before an altar. Polgara, dressed in her customary silver-trimmed blue, swept through the hall with all the regal bearing of an Empress. She wore a mysterious smile, and the fabled white lock at her brow glowed in the candlelight as she and Durnik approached the platform.

Meanwhile, at the top of the stairs, the herald had shrunk back from the next guest, his eyes wide and his face gone quite pale.

"Just say it," Garion heard his grandfather tell the frightened man. "I'm fairly sure that they'll all recognize the name."

The herald stepped to the marble railing at the front of the landing. "Your Majesty," he said falteringly, "My lords and ladies, I have the unexpected honor to present Belgarath the Sorcerer."

A gasp ran through the hall as the old man, dressed in a cowled robe of soft gray wool, stumped down the stairs with no attempt at grace or dignity. The assembled Mallorean notables pulled back from him as he walked toward the table where the others had already joined Zakath.

About halfway to the imperial platform, however, a blond Melcene girl in a low-cut gown caught his eye. She stood stricken with awe, unable to curtsy or even to move as the most famous man in all the world approached her. Belgarath stopped and looked her up and down quite slowly and deliberately, noting with appreciation just how revealing her gown was. A slow, insinuating smile crept across his face, and his blue eyes twinkled outrageously.

"Nice dress," he told her.

She blushed furiously.

He laughed, reached out, and patted her cheek. "There's a good girl," he said.

"Father," Polgara said firmly.

"Coming, Pol." He chuckled and moved along the carpet toward the table. The pretty Melcene girl looked after him, her eyes wide and her hand pressed to the cheek he had touched.

"Isn't he disgusting?" Ce'Nedra muttered.

"It's just the way he is, dear," Garion disagreed. "He doesn't pretend to be anything else. He doesn't have to."

The banquet featured a number of exotic dishes that Garion could not put a name to and several which he did not even know how to eat. A deceptively innocent-looking rice dish was laced with such fiery seasonings that it brought tears to his eyes and sent his hand clutching for his water goblet.

"Belar, Mara, and Nedra!" Durnik choked as he also groped about in search of water. So far as he could remember, it was the first time Garion had ever heard Durnik swear. He did it surprisingly well.

"Piquant," Sadi commented as he calmly continued to eat the dreadful concoction.

"How can you eat that?" Garion demanded in amazement.

Sadi smiled. "You forget that I'm used to being poisoned, Belgarion. Poison tends to toughen the tongue and fireproof the throat."

Zakath had watched their reactions with some amusement. "I should have warned you," he apologized. "The dish comes from Gandahar, and the natives of that region entertain themselves during the rainy season by trying to build bonfires in each other's stomachs. They're elephant trappers, for the most part, and they pride themselves on their courage."

After the extended banquet, the brown-robed Brador approached Garion. "If your Majesty wouldn't mind," he said, leaning forward so that Garion could hear him over the sounds of laughter and sprightly conversation from nearby tables, "there are a number of people who are most eager to meet you."

Garion nodded politely even though he inwardly winced. He had been through this sort of thing before and knew how tedious it usually became. The Chief of the Bureau of Internal Affairs led him down from the platform into the swirl of brightly clad celebrants, pausing occasionally to exchange greetings with various fellow officials and to introduce Garion. Garion braced himself for an hour or two of total boredom. The plump, bald-headed Brador, however, proved to be an entertaining escort. Though he seemed to be engaging Garion in light conversation, he was in fact providing a succinct and often pointed briefing even as they went.

"We'll be talking with the kinglet of Pallia," he murmured as they approached a group of men in tall, conical felt caps who wore leather which had been dyed an unhealthy-looking green color. "He's a fawning bootlicker, a liar, a coward, and absolutely not to be trusted."

"Ah, there you are, Brador," one of the felt-capped men greeted the Melcene with a forced heartiness.

"Your Highness," Brador replied with a florid bow. "I have the honor to present his Royal Majesty, Belgarion of Riva." He turned to Garion. "Your Majesty, this is his Highness, King Warasin of Pallia."

"Your Majesty," Warasin gushed, bowing awkwardly. He was a man with a narrow, pockmarked face, close-set eyes, and a slack-lipped mouth. His hands, Garion noticed, were not particularly clean.

"Your Highness," Garion replied with a slightly distant note.

"I was just telling the members of my court here that I'd have sooner believed that the sun would rise in the north tomorrow than that the Overlord of the West would appear at Mal Zeth."

"The world is full of surprises."

"By the beard of Torak, you're right, Belgarion—you don't mind if I call you Belgarion, do you, your Majesty?"

"Torak didn't have a beard," Garion corrected shortly.

"What?"

"Torak—he didn't have a beard. At least he didn't when I met him."

"When you—" Warasin's eyes suddenly widened. "Are

you telling me that all those stories about what happened at Cthol Mishrak are actually *true?*" he gasped.

"I'm not sure, your Highness," Garion told him. "I haven't heard all the stories yet. It's been an absolute delight meeting you, old boy," he said, clapping the stunned-looking kinglet on the shoulder with exaggerated camaraderie. "It's a shame that we don't have more time to talk. Coming, Brador?" He nodded to the petty king of Pallia, turned, and led the Melcene away.

"You're very skilled, Belgarion," Brador murmured. "Much more so than I would have imagined, considering—" He hesitated.

"Considering the fact that I look like an unlettered country oaf?" Garion supplied.

"I don't know that I'd put it exactly that way."

"Why not?" Garion shrugged. "It's the truth, isn't it? What was pigeyes back there trying to maneuver the conversation around to? It was pretty obvious that he was leading up to something."

"It's fairly simple," Brador replied. "He recognizes your current proximity to Kal Zakath. All power in Mallorea derives from the throne, and the man who has the Emperor's ear is in a unique position. Warasin is currently having a border dispute with the Prince Regent of Delchin and he probably wants you to put in a good word for him." Brador gave him an amused look. "You're in a position right now to make millions, you know."

Garion laughed. "I couldn't carry it, Brador," he said. "I visited the royal treasury at Riva once, and I know how much a million weighs. Who's next?"

"The Chief of the Bureau of Commerce—an unmitigated, unprincipled ass. Like most Bureau Chiefs."

Garion smiled. "And what does *he* want?"

Brador tugged thoughtfully at one earlobe. "I'm not entirely certain. I've been out of the country. Vasca's a devious one, though, so I'd be careful of him."

"I'm always careful, Brador."

The Baron Vasca, Chief of the Bureau of Commerce, was wrinkled and bald. He wore the brown robe that seemed to be almost the uniform of the bureaucracy, and the gold chain of his office seemed almost too heavy for his thin neck. Though at first glance he appeared to be old and frail, his eyes were as alert and shrewd as those of a vulture. "Ah, your Majesty," he said after they had been introduced, "I'm so pleased to meet you at last."

"My pleasure, Baron Vasca," Garion said politely.

They chatted together for some time, and Garion could not detect anything in the baron's conversation that seemed in the least bit out of the ordinary.

"I note that Prince Kheldar of Drasnia is a member of your party," the baron said finally.

"We're old friends. You're acquainted with Kheldar then, Baron?"

"We've had a few dealings together—the customary permits and gratuities, you understand. For the most part, though, he tends to avoid contact with the authorities."

"I've noticed that from time to time," Garion said.

"I was certain that you would have. I won't keep your Majesty. Many others here are eager to meet you, and I wouldn't want to be accused of monopolizing your time. We must talk again soon." The baron turned to the Chief of the Bureau of Internal Affairs. "So good of you to introduce us, my dear Brador," he said.

"It's nothing, my dear Baron," Brador replied. He took Garion by the arm, and they moved away from Vasca.

"What was that all about?" Garion asked.

"I'm not altogether sure," Brador replied, "but whatever he wanted, he seems to have gotten."

"We didn't really say anything."

"I know. That's what worries me. I think I'll have my old friend Vasca watched. He's managed to arouse my curiosity."

During the next couple of hours Garion met two more gaudily dressed petty kings, a fair number of more soberly garbed bureaucrats, and a sprinkling of semi-important nobles and their ladies. Many of them, of course, wanted nothing more than to be seen talking to him so that later they could say in a casual, offhand fashion, "I was talking with Belgarion the other day, and he said—" Others made some point of suggesting that a private conversation might be desirable at some later date. A few even tried to set up specific appointments.

It was rather late when Velvet finally came to his rescue. She approached the place where Garion was trapped by the royal family of Peldane, a stodgy little kinglet in a mustard yellow turban, his simpering, scrawny wife in a pink gown that clashed horribly with her orange hair, and three spoiled royal brats who spent their time whining and hitting each other. "Your Majesty," the blond girl said with a curtsy, "Your wife asks your permission to retire."

"Asks?"

"She's feeling slightly unwell."

Garion gave her a grateful look. "I must go to her at once, then," he said quickly. He turned to the Peldane royalty. "I hope you'll all excuse me," he said to them.

"Of course, Belgarion," the kinglet replied graciously.

"And please convey our regards to your lovely wife," the queenlet added.

The royal brood continued to howl and kick each other.

"You looked a bit harried," Velvet murmured as she led Garion away.

"I could kiss you."

"Now that's an interesting suggestion."

Garion glanced sourly back over his shoulder. "They should drown those three little monsters and raise a litter of puppies instead," he muttered.

"Piglets," she corrected.

He looked at her.

"At least they could sell the bacon," she explained. "That way the effort wouldn't be a total loss."

"Is Ce'Nedra really ill?"

"Of course not. She's made as many conquests as she wants to this evening, that's all. She wants to save a few for future occasions. Now it's time for the grand withdrawal, leaving a horde of disappointed admirers, who were all panting to meet her, crushed with despair."

"That's a peculiar way to look at it."

She laughed affectionately, linking her arm in his. "Not if you're a woman, it's not."

The following morning shortly after breakfast, Garion and Belgarath were summoned to meet with Zakath and Brador in the Emperor's private study. The room was large and comfortable, lined with books and maps and with deeply upholstered chairs clustered about low tables. It was a warm day outside, and the windows stood open, allowing a blossom-scented spring breeze to ruffle the curtains.

"Good morning, gentlemen," Zakath greeted them as they were escorted into the room. "I hope you slept well."

"Once I managed to get Ce'Nedra out of the tub." Garion laughed. "It's just a bit too convenient, I think. Would you believe that she bathed three times yesterday?"

"Mal Zeth is very hot and dusty in the summertime," Zakath said. "The baths make it bearable."

"How does the hot water get to them?" Garion asked curiously. "I haven't seen anyone carrying pails up and down the halls."

"It's piped in under the floors," the Emperor replied. "The artisan who devised the system was rewarded with a baronetcy."

"I hope you don't mind if we steal the idea. Durnik's already making sketches."

"I think it's unhealthy myself," Belgarath said. "Bathing should be done out of doors—in cold water. All this pampering softens people." He looked at Zakath. "I'm sure you didn't

137

ask us here to discuss the philosophical ramifications of bathing, though."

"Not unless you really want to, Belgarath," Zakath replied. He straightened in his chair. "Now that we've all had a chance to rest from our journey, I thought that maybe it was time for us to get to work. Brador's people have made their reports to him, and he's ready to give us his assessment of the current situation in Karanda. Go ahead, Brador."

"Yes, your Majesty." The plump, bald Melcene rose from his chair and crossed to a very large map of the Mallorean continent hanging on the wall. The map was exquisitely colored with blue lakes and rivers, green prairies, darker green forests and brown, white-topped mountains. Instead of simply being dots on the map, the cities were represented by pictures of buildings and fortifications. The Mallorean highway system, Garion noted, was very nearly as extensive as the Tolnedran network in the west.

Brador cleared his throat, fought for a moment with one of Zakath's ferocious kittens for the long pointer he wanted to use, and began. "As I reported to you in Rak Hagga," he said, "a man named Mengha came out of this immense forest to the north of Lake Karanda some six months ago." He tapped the representation of a large belt of trees stretching from the Karandese range to the Mountains of Zamad. "We know very, very little about his background."

"That's not entirely true, Brador," Belgarath disagreed. "Cyradis told us that he's a Grolim priest—or he used to be. That puts us in a position to deduce quite a bit."

"I'd be interested to hear whatever you can come up with," Zakath said.

Belgarath squinted around the room, and his eyes fixed on several full crystal decanters and some polished glasses sitting on a sideboard across the room. "Do you mind?" he asked, pointing at the decanters. "I think better with a glass in my hand."

"Help yourself," Zakath replied.

The old man rose, crossed to the sideboard, and poured himself a glass of ruby-red wine. "Garion?" he asked, holding out the decanter.

"No, thanks all the same, Grandfather."

Belgarath replaced the crystal stopper with a clink and began to pace up and down on the blue carpet. "All right," he said. "We know that demon worship persists in the back country of Karanda, even though the Grolim priests tried to stamp out the practice when the Karands were converted to the worship of Torak in the second millennium. We also know that Mengha was a priest himself. Now, if the Grolims here in Mallorea reacted in the same way that the ones in Cthol Murgos did when they heard about the death of Torak, then we know that they were thoroughly demoralized. The fact that Urvon spent several years scrambling around trying to find prophecies that would hint at the possibility of a justi- fication for keeping the Church intact is fairly good evidence that he was faced with almost universal despair in the ranks of the Grolims." He paused to sip at his wine. "Not bad," he said to Zakath approvingly. "Not bad at all."

"Thank you."

"Now," the old man continued, "there are many possible reactions to religious despair. Some men go mad, some men try to lose themselves in various forms of dissipation, some men refuse to admit the truth and try to keep the old forms alive. A few men, however, go in search of some new kind of religion—usually something the exact opposite of what they believed before. Since the Grolim Church in Karanda had concentrated for eons on eradicating demon worship, it's only logical that a few of the despairing priests would seek out demon-masters in the hope of learning their secrets. Remem- ber, if you can actually control a demon, it gives you a great deal of power, and the hunger for power has always been at the core of the Grolim mentality."

"It does fit together, Ancient One," Brador admitted.

"I thought so myself. All right, Torak is dead, and Mengha

139

suddenly finds that his theological ground has been cut out from under him. He probably goes through a period of doing all the things that he wasn't allowed to do as a priest—drinking, wenching, that sort of thing. But if you do things to excess, eventually they become empty and unsatisfying. Even debauchery can get boring after a while."

"Aunt Pol will be amazed to hear that you said that," Garion said.

"You just keep it to yourself," Belgarath told him. "Our arguments about my bad habits are the cornerstone of our relationship." He took another sip of his wine. "This is really excellent," he said, holding up the glass to admire the color of the wine in the sunlight. "Now then, here we have Mengha waking up some morning with a screaming headache, a mouth that tastes like a chicken coop, and a fire in his stomach that no amount of water will put out. He has no real reason to go on living. He might even take out his sacrificial gutting knife and set the point against his chest."

"Isn't your speculation going a bit far afield?" Zakath asked.

Belgarath laughed. "I used to be a professional storyteller," he apologized. "I can't stand to let a good story slip by without a few artistic touches. All right, maybe he did or maybe he didn't think about killing himself. The point is that he had reached the absolute rock bottom. That's when the idea of demons came to him. Raising demons is almost as dangerous as being the first man up the scaling ladder during an assault on a fortified city, but Mengha has nothing to lose. So, he journeys into the forest up there, finds a Karandese magician, and somehow persuades him to teach him the art—if that's what you want to call it. It takes him about a dozen years to learn all the secrets."

"How did you arrive at that number?" Brador asked.

Belgarath shrugged. "It's been fourteen years since the death of Torak—or thereabouts. No normal man can seriously mistreat himself for more than a couple of years before he starts to fall apart, so it was probably about twelve years ago that Mengha went in search of a magician to give him instruction. Then, once he's learned all the secrets, he kills his teacher, and—"

"Wait a minute," Zakath objected. "Why would he do that?"

"His teacher knew too much about him, and *he* could also raise demons to send after our defrocked Grolim. Then there's the fact that the arrangement between teacher and pupil in these affairs involves lifetime servitude enforced with a curse. Mengha could not leave his master until the old man was dead."

"How do you know so much about this, Belgarath?" Zakath asked.

"I went through it all among the Morindim a few thousand years ago. I wasn't doing anything very important and I was curious about magic."

"Did you kill your master?"

"No—well, not exactly. When I left him, he sent his familiar demon after me. I took control of it and sent it back to him."

"And it killed him?"

"I assume so. They usually do. Anyway, getting back to Mengha. He arrives at the gates of Calida about six months ago and raises a whole army of demons. Nobody in his right mind raises more than one at a time because they're too difficult to control." He frowned, pacing up and down staring at the floor. "The only thing I can think of is that somehow he's managed to raise a Demon Lord and get it under control."

"Demon Lord?" Garion asked.

"They have rank, too—just as humans do. If Mengha has a grip on a Demon Lord, then it's that creature that's calling up the army of lesser demons." He refilled his glass, looking faintly satisfied with himself. "That's probably fairly close to Mengha's life story," he said, sitting down again.

"A virtuoso performance, Belgarath," Zakath congratulated him.

"Thank you," the old man replied. "I thought so myself." He looked at Brador. "Now that we know him, why don't you tell us what he's been up to?"

Brador once again took his place beside the map, fending off the same kitten with his pointer. "After Mengha took Calida, word of his exploits ran all through Karanda," he began. "It appears that the worship of Torak was never really very firmly ingrained in the Karands to begin with, and about the only thing that kept them in line was their fear of the sacrificial knives of the Grolims."

"Like the Thulls?" Garion suggested.

"Very much so, your Majesty. Once Torak was dead, however, and his Church in disarray, the Karands began to revert. The old shrines began to reappear, and the old rituals came back into practice." Brador shuddered. "Hideous rites," he said. "Obscene."

"Even worse than the Grolim rite of sacrifice?" Garion asked mildly.

"There was some justification for that, Garion," Zakath objected. "It was an honor to be chosen, and the victims went under the knife willingly."

"Not any of them that I ever saw," Garion disagreed.

"We can discuss comparative theology some other time," Belgarath told them. "Go on, Brador."

"Once the Karands heard about Mengha," the Melcene official continued, "they began to flock to Calida to support him and to enlist themselves on the side of the demons. There's always been a subterranean independence movement in the seven kingdoms of Karanda, and many hotheads there believe that the demons offer the best hope of throwing off the yoke of Angarak oppression." He looked at the Emperor. "No offense intended, your Majesty," he murmured.

"None taken, Brador," Zakath assured him.

"Naturally, the little kinglets in Karanda tried to keep their people from joining Mengha. The loss of subjects is always painful to a ruler. The army—our army—was also alarmed by the hordes of Karands flocking to Mengha's banner, and they tried to block off borders and the like. But, since a large portion of the army was in Cthol Murgos with his Majesty here, the troops in Karanda just didn't have the numbers. The Karands either slipped around them or simply overwhelmed them. Mengha's army numbers almost a million by now—ill-equipped and poorly trained, perhaps, but a million is a significant number, even if they're armed with sticks. Not only Jenno but also Ganesia are totally under Mengha's domination, and he's on the verge of overwhelming Katakor. Once he succeeds there, he'll inevitably move on Pallia and Delchin. If he isn't stopped, he'll be knocking on the gates of Mal Zeth by Erastide."

"Is he unleashing his demons in these campaigns?" Belgarath asked intently.

"Not really," Brador replied. "After what happened at Calida, there's no real need for that. The sight of them alone is usually enough to spring open the gates of any city he's taken so far. He's succeeded with remarkably little actual fighting."

The old man nodded. "I sort of thought that might have been the case. A demon is very hard to get back under control once it's tasted blood."

"It's not really the demons that are causing the problems," Brador continued. "Mengha's flooded all the rest of Karanda with his agents, and the stories that they're circulating are whipping previously uncommitted people into a frenzy." He looked at the Emperor. "Would you believe that we actually caught one of his missionaries in the Karandese barracks right here in Mal Zeth?" he said.

Zakath looked up sharply. "How did he get in?" he demanded.

"He disguised himself as a corporal returning from convalescent leave at home," Brador replied. "He'd even gone

143

so far as to give himself a wound to make his story look authentic. It was very believable the way he cursed Murgos."

"What did you do to him?"

"Unfortunately, he didn't survive the questioning," Brador said, frowning. He bent to remove the kitten from around his ankle.

"Unfortunately?"

"I had some interesting plans for him. I take it rather personally when someone manages to circumvent my secret police. It's a matter of professional pride."

"What do you advise, then?" Zakath asked.

Brador began to pace. "I'm afraid that you're going to have to bring the army back from Cthol Murgos, your Majesty," he said. "You can't fight a war on two fronts."

"Absolutely out of the question." Zakath's tone was adamant.

"I don't think we have much choice," Brador told him. "Almost half of the forces left here in Mallorea are of Karandese origin, and it's my considered opinion that to rely upon them in any kind of confrontation with Mengha would be sheer folly."

Zakath's face grew bleak.

"Put it this way, your Majesty," Brador said smoothly. "If you weaken your forces in Cthol Murgos, it's quite possible that you'll lose Rak Cthaka and maybe Rak Gorut, but if you don't bring the army home, you're going to lose Mal Zeth."

Zakath glared at him.

"There's still time to consider the matter, Sire," Brador added in a reasonable tone of voice. "This is only *my* assessment of the situation. I'm sure you'll want confirmation of what I've said from military intelligence, and you'll need to consult with the High Command."

"No," Zakath said bluntly. "The decision is mine." He scowled at the floor. "All right, Brador, we'll bring the army home. Go tell the High Command that I want to see them all at once."

"Yes, your Majesty."

Garion had risen to his feet. "How long will it take to ship your troops back from Cthol Murgos?" he asked with a sinking feeling.

"About three months," Zakath replied.

"I can't wait that long, Zakath."

"I'm very sorry, Garion, but none of us has any choice. Neither you nor I will leave Mal Zeth until the army gets here."

CHAPTER EIGHT

The following morning, Silk came early to the rooms Garion shared with Ce'Nedra. The little man once again wore his doublet and hose, though he had removed most of his jewelry. Over his arm he carried a pair of Mallorean robes, the lightweight, varicolored garments worn by most of the citizens of Mal Zeth. "Would you like to go into the city?" he asked Garion.

"I don't think they'll let us out of the palace."

"I've already taken care of that. Brador gave his permission—provided that we don't try to get away from the people who are going to be following us."

"That's a depressing thought. I hate being followed."

"You get used to it."

"Have you got anything specific in mind, or is this just a sight-seeing tour?"

"I want to stop by our offices here and have a talk with our factor."

Garion gave him a puzzled look.

"The agent who handles things for us here in Mal Zeth."

"Oh. I hadn't heard the word before."

"That's because you aren't in business. Our man here is named Dolmar. He's a Melcene—very efficient, and he doesn't steal too much."

"I'm not sure that I'd enjoy listening to you talk business," Garion said.

Silk looked around furtively. "You might learn all kinds of things, Garion," he said, but his fingers were already moving rapidly.—*Dolmar can give us a report on what's really happening in Karanda*— he gestured.—*I think you'd better come along*—

"Well," Garion said with slightly exaggerated acquiescence, "maybe you're right. Besides, the walls here are beginning to close in on me."

"Here," Silk said, holding out one of the robes, "wear this."

"It's not really cold, Silk."

"The robe isn't to keep you warm. People in western clothing attract a lot of attention on the streets of Mal Zeth, and I don't like being stared at." Silk grinned quickly. "It's very hard to pick pockets when everybody in the street is watching you. Shall we go?"

The robe Garion put on was open at the front and hung straight from his shoulders to his heels. It was a serviceable outer garment with deep pockets at the sides. The material of which it was made was quite thin, and it flowed out behind him as he moved around. He went to the door of the adjoining room. Ce'Nedra was combing her hair, still damp from her morning bath.

147

"I'm going into the city with Silk," he told her. "Do you need anything?"

She thought about that. "See if you can find me a comb," she said, holding up the one she had been using. "Mine's starting to look a little toothless."

"All right." He turned to leave.

"As long as you're going anyway," she added, "why don't you pick me up a bolt of silk cloth—teal green, if you can find it. I'm told that there's a dressmaker here in the palace with a great deal of skill."

"I'll see what I can do." He turned again.

"And perhaps a few yards of lace—not too ornate, mind. Tasteful."

"Anything else?"

She smiled at him. "Buy me a surprise of some kind. I love surprises."

"A comb, a bolt of teal green silk, a few yards of tasteful lace, and a surprise." He ticked them off on his fingers.

"Get me one of those robes like you're wearing, too."

He waited.

She pursed her lips thoughtfully. "That's all I can think of, Garion, but you and Silk might ask Liselle and Lady Polgara if they need anything."

He sighed.

"It's only polite, Garion."

"Yes, dear. Maybe I'd better make out a list."

Silk's face was blandly expressionless as Garion came back out.

"Well?" Garion asked him.

"I didn't say anything."

"Good."

They started out the door.

"Garion," Ce'Nedra called after him.

"Yes, dear?"

"See if you can find some sweetmeats, too."

Garion went out into the hall behind Silk and firmly closed the door behind him.

"You handle that sort of thing very well," Silk said.

"Practice."

Velvet added several items to Garion's growing list, and Polgara several more. Silk looked at the list as they walked down the long, echoing hallway toward the main part of the palace. "I wonder if Brador would lend us a pack mule," he murmured.

"Quit trying to be funny."

"Would I do that?"

"Why were we talking with our fingers back there?"

"Spies."

"In our private quarters?" Garion was shocked, remembering Ce'Nedra's sometimes aggressive indifference to the way she was dressed—or not dressed—when they were alone.

"Private places are where the most interesting secrets are to be found. No spy ever passes up the opportunity to peek into a bedroom."

"That's disgusting!" Garion exclaimed, his cheeks burning.

"Of course it is. Fairly common practice, though."

They passed through the vaulted rotunda just inside the gold-plated main door of the palace and walked out into a bright spring morning touched with a fragrant breeze.

"You know," Silk said, "I like Mal Zeth. It always smells so good. Our office here is upstairs over a bakery, and some mornings the smells from downstairs almost make me swoon."

There was only the briefest of pauses at the gates of the imperial complex. A curt gesture from one of the pair of unobtrusive men who were following them advised the gate guards that Silk and Garion were to be allowed to pass into the city.

"Policemen do have their uses sometimes," Silk said as they started down a broad boulevard leading away from the palace.

The streets of Mal Zeth teemed with people from all over the empire and not a few from the West was well. Garion was a bit surprised to see a sprinkling of Tolnedran mantles among the varicolored robes of the local populace, and here and there were Sendars, Drasnians, and a fair number of Nadraks. There were, however, no Murgos. "Busy place," he noted to Silk.

"Oh, yes. Mal Zeth makes Tol Honeth look like a country fair and Camaar like a village market."

"It's the biggest commercial center in the world, then?"

"No. That's Melcene—of course Melcene concentrates on money instead of goods. You can't even buy a tin pot in Melcene. All you can buy there is money."

"Silk, how can you make any kind of profit buying money with money?"

"It's a little complicated." Silk's eyes narrowed. "Do you know something?" he said. "If you could put your hands on the royal treasury of Riva, I could show you how to double it in six months on Basa Street in Melcene—with a nice commission for the both of us thrown in for good measure."

"You want me to speculate with the royal treasury? I'd have an open insurrection on my hands if anybody ever found out about it."

"That's the secret, Garion. You don't let anybody find out."

"Have you ever had an honest thought in your entire life?"

The little man thought about it. "Not that I recall, no," he replied candidly. "But then, I've got a well-trained mind."

The offices of the commercial empire of Silk and Yarblek here in Mal Zeth were, as the little man had indicated, rather modest and were situated above a busy bakeshop. Access to that second floor was by way of an outside stairway rising out of a narrow side street. As Silk started up those stairs, a certain tension that Garion had not even been aware of seemed to flow out of his friend. "I *hate* not being able to talk freely," he said. "There are so many spies in Mal Zeth that every word you say here is delivered to Brador in triplicate before you get your mouth shut."

"There are bound to be spies around your office, too."

"Of course, but they can't hear anything. Yarblek and I had a solid foot of cork built into the floors, ceilings, and walls."

"Cork?"

"It muffles all sounds."

"Didn't that cost a great deal?"

Silk nodded. "But we made it all back during the first week we were here by managing to keep certain negotiations secret." He reached into an inside pocket and took out a large brass key. "Let's see if I can catch Dolmar with his hands in the cash box," he half whispered.

"Why? You already know that he's stealing from you."

"Certainly I do, but if I can catch him, I can reduce his year-end bonus."

"Why not just pick his pocket?"

Silk tapped the brass key against his cheek as he thought about it. "No," he decided finally. "That's not really good business. A relationship like this is founded on trust."

Garion began to laugh.

"You have to draw the line *somewhere*, Garion." Silk quietly slipped his brass key into the lock and slowly turned it. Then he abruptly shoved the door open and jumped into the room.

"Good morning, Prince Kheldar," the man seated behind a plain table said quite calmly. "I've been expecting you."

Silk looked a bit crestfallen.

The man sitting at the table was a thin Melcene with crafty, close-set eyes, thin lips, and scraggly, mud-brown hair. He had the kind of face that one instantly distrusts.

Silk straightened. "Good morning, Dolmar," he said. "This is Belgarion of Riva."

"Your Majesty." Dolmar rose and bowed.

"Dolmar."

Silk closed the door and pulled a pair of chairs out from the brown, cork-sheathed wall. Although the floor was of ordinary boards, the way that all sounds of walking or moving pieces of furniture were muted testified to the thickness of the cork lying beneath.

"How's business?" Silk asked, seating himself and pushing the other chair to Garion with his foot.

"We're paying the rent," Dolmar replied cautiously.

"I'm sure that the baker downstairs is overjoyed. Specifics, Dolmar. I've been away from Mal Zeth for quite a while. Stun me with how well my investments here are doing."

"We're up fifteen percent from last year."

"That's all?" Silk sounded disappointed.

"We've just made quite a large investment in inventory. If you take the current value of that into account, the number would be much closer to forty percent."

"That's more like it. Why are we accumulating inventory?"

"Yarblek's instructions. He's at Mal Camat right now arranging for ships to take the goods to the west. I expect that he'll be here in a week or so—he and that foulmouthed wench of his." Dolmar stood up, carefully gathered the documents from the table, and crossed to an iron stove sitting in the corner. He bent, opened the stove door, and calmly laid the parchment sheets on the small fire inside.

To Garion's amazement, Silk made no objection to his factor's blatant incendiarism. "We've been looking into the wool market," the Melcene reported as he returned to his now-empty table. "With the growing mobilization, the Bureau of Military Procurement is certain to need wool for uniforms, cloaks, and blankets. If we can buy up options from all the major sheep producers, we'll control the market and perhaps break the stranglehold that the Melcene consortium has on military purchases. If we can just get our foot in the door of the Bureau, I'm sure that we can get a chance to bid on all sorts of contracts."

Silk was pulling at his long, pointed nose, his eyes narrowed in thought. "Beans," he said shortly.

"I beg your pardon?"

"Look into the possibility of tying up this year's bean crop. A soldier can live in a worn-out uniform, but he has to eat. If we control the bean crop—and maybe coarse flour as well— the Bureau of Military Procurement won't have any choice. They'll *have* to come to us."

"Very shrewd, Prince Kheldar."

"I've been around for a while," Silk replied.

"The consortium is meeting this week in Melcene," the factor reported. "They'll be setting the prices of common items. We really want to get our hands on that price list if we can."

"I'm in the palace," Silk said. "Maybe I can pry it out of somebody."

"There's something else you should know, Prince Kheldar. Word has leaked out that the consortium is also going to propose certain regulations to Baron Vasca of the Bureau of Commerce. They'll present them under the guise of protecting the economy, but the fact of the matter is that they're aimed at you and Yarblek. They want to restrict western merchants who gross more than ten million a year to two or three enclaves on the west coast. That wouldn't inconvenience smaller merchants, but it would probably put us out of business."

"Can we bribe someone to put a stop to it?"

"We're already paying Vasca a fortune to leave us alone, but the consortium is throwing money around like water. It's possible that the baron won't stay bribed."

"Let me nose around inside the palace a bit," Silk said, "before you double Vasca's bribe or anything."

"Bribery's the standard procedure, Prince Kheldar."

"I know, but sometimes blackmail works even better." Silk looked over at Garion, then back at his factor. "What do you know about what's happening in Karanda?" he asked.

"Enough to know that it's disastrous for business. All sorts of perfectly respectable and otherwise sensible merchants are closing up their shops and flocking off to Calida to enlist in Mengha's army. Then they march around in circles singing

'Death to the Angaraks' while they wave rusty swords in the air.''

"Any chance of selling them weapons?" Silk asked quickly.

"Probably not. There's not enough real money in northern Karanda to make it worthwhile to try to deal with them, and the political unrest has closed down all the mines. The market in gem stones has just about dried up."

Silk nodded glumly. "What's really going on up there, Dolmar?" he asked. "The reports Brador passed on to us were sort of sketchy."

"Mengha arrived at the gates of Calida with demons." The factor shrugged. "The Karands went into hysterics and then fell down in the throes of religious ecstasy."

"Brador told us about certain atrocities," Garion said.

"I expect that the reports he received were a trifle exaggerated, your Majesty," Dolmar replied. "Even the most well trained observer is likely to multiply mutilated corpses lying in the streets by ten. In point of fact, the vast majority of the casualties were either Melcene or Angarak. Mengha's demons rather scrupulously avoided killing Karands—except by accident. The same has held true in every city that he's taken so far." He scratched at his head, his close-set eyes narrowing. "It's really very shrewd, you know. The Karands see Mengha as a liberator and his demons as an invincible spearhead of their army. I can't swear to his *real* motives, but those barbarians up there believe that he's a savior come to sweep Karanda clean of Angaraks and the Melcene bureaucracy. Give him another six months or so, and he'll accomplish what no one has ever been able to do before."

"What's that?" Silk asked.

"Unify all of Karanda."

"Does he use his demons in the assault on every city he takes?" Garion asked, wanting to confirm what Brador had told them.

Dolmar shook his head. "Not any more, your Majesty. After what happened at Calida and several other towns he took early in his campaign, he doesn't really have to. All he's been doing lately is march up to the city. The demons are with him, of course, but they don't have to do anything but stand there looking awful. The Karands butcher all the Angaraks and Melcenes in town, throw open their gates, and welcome him with open arms. Then his demons vanish." He thought a moment. "He always has one particular one of them with him, though— a shadowy sort of creature that doesn't seem to be gigantic the way they're supposed to be. He stands directly behind Mengha's left shoulder at any public appearance."

A sudden thought occurred to Garion. "Are they desecrating Grolim temples?" he asked.

Dolmar blinked. "No," he replied with some surprise, "as a matter of fact, they're not—and they don't seem to be any Grolims among the dead, either. Of course it's possible that Urvon pulled all his Grolims out of Karanda when the trouble started."

"That's unlikely," Garion disagreed. "Mengha's arrival at Calida came without any kind of warning. The Grolims wouldn't have had time to escape." He stared up at the ceiling, thinking hard.

"What is it, Garion?" Silk asked.

"I just had a chilling sort of notion. We know that Mengha's a Grolim, right?"

"I didn't know that," Dolmar said with some surprise.

"We got a bit of inside information," Silk told him. "Go ahead, Garion."

"Urvon spends all of his time in Mal Yaska, doesn't he?"

Silk nodded. "So I've heard. He doesn't want Beldin to catch him out in the open."

"Wouldn't that make him a fairly ineffective leader? All right, then. Let's suppose that Mengha went through his period of despair after the death of Torak and then found a magician to teach him how to raise demons. When he comes back, he offers his former Grolim brethren an alternative to Urvon—along with access to a kind of power they'd never experienced before. A demon in the hands of an illiterate and fairly stupid Karandese magician is one thing, but a demon controlled by a Grolim sorcerer would be much worse, I think. If Mengha is gathering disaffected Grolims around him and training them in the use of magic, we have a *big* problem. I don't think I'd care to face a legion of Chabats, would you?"

Silk shuddered. "Not hardly," he replied fervently.

"He has to be uprooted then," Dolmar said, "and soon."

Garion made a sour face. "Zakath won't move until he gets his army back from Cthol Murgos—about three months from now."

"In three months, Mengha's going to be invincible," the factor told him.

"Then we'll have to move now," Garion said, "with Zakath or without him."

"How do you plan to get out of the city?" Silk asked.

"We'll let Belgarath work that out." Garion looked at Silk's agent. "Can you tell us anything else?" he asked.

Dolmar tugged at his nose in a curious imitation of Silk's habitual gesture. "It's only a rumor," he said.

"Go ahead."

"I've been getting some hints out of Karanda that Mengha's familiar demon is named Nahaz."

"Is that significant?"

"I can't be altogether sure, your Majesty. When the Grolims went into Karanda in the second millennium, they destroyed all traces of Karandese mythology, and no one has ever tried to record what few bits and pieces remained. All that's left is a hazy oral tradition, but the rumors I've heard say that Nahaz was the tribal demon of the original Karands who migrated into the region before the Angaraks came to Mallorea. The Karands follow Mengha not only because he's a political leader, but also because he's resurrected the closest thing they've ever had to a God of their own."

"A Demon Lord?" Garion asked him.

"That's a very good way to describe him, your Majesty. If

the rumors are true, the demon Nahaz has almost unlimited power."

"I was afraid you were going to say that."

Later, when they were back out in the street, Garion looked curiously at Silk. "Why didn't you object when he burned those documents?" he asked.

"It's standard practice." the rat-faced man shrugged. "We never keep anything in writing. Dolmar has everything committed to memory."

"Doesn't that make it fairly easy for him to steal from you?"

"Of course, but he keeps his thievery within reasonable limits. If the Bureau of Taxation got its hands on written records, though, it could be a disaster. Do you want to go back to the palace now?"

Garion took out his list. "No," he said. "We've got to take care of this first." He looked glumly at the sheet. "I wonder how we're going to carry it all."

Silk glanced back over his shoulder at the two unobtrusive spies trailing along behind them. "Help is only a few paces away." He laughed. "As I said before, there are many uses for policemen."

During the next several days, Garion discovered that the imperial palace at Mal Zeth was unlike any court in the West. Since all power rested in Zakath's hands, the bureaucrats and palace functionaries contested with each other for the Emperor's favor and strove with oftentimes wildly complicated plots to discredit their enemies. The introduction of Silk, Velvet, and Sadi into this murky environment added whole new dimensions to palace intrigue. The trio rather casually pointed out the friendship between Garion and Zakath and let it be generally known that they had the Rivan King's complete trust. Then they sat back to await developments.

The officials and courtiers in the imperial palace were quick to grasp the significance and the opportunities implicit in this new route to the Emperor's ear. Perhaps even without formally discussing it, the trio of westerners neatly divided up the possible spheres of activity. Silk concentrated his attention on commercial matters, Velvet dabbled in politics, and Sadi delicately dipped his long-fingered hands into the world of high-level crime. Though all of them subtly let it be known that they were susceptible to bribery, they also expressed a willingness to pass along various requests in exchange for information. Thus, almost by accident, Garion found that he had a very efficient espionage apparatus at his disposal. Silk and Velvet manipulated the fears, ambitions, and open greed of those who contacted them with a musicianlike skill, delicately playing the increasingly nervous officials like well-tuned instruments. Sadi's methods, derived from his extensive experience in Salmissra's court, were in some instances even more subtle, but in others, painfully direct. The contents of his red leather case brought premium prices, and several high-ranking criminals, men who literally owned whole platoons of bureaucrats and even generals, quite suddenly died under suspicious circumstances—one of them even toppling over with a blackened face and bulging eyes in the presence of the Emperor himself.

Zakath, who had watched the activities of the three with a certain veiled amusement, drew the line at that point. He spoke quite firmly with Garion about the matter during their customary evening meeting on the following day.

"I don't really mind what they're doing, Garion," he said, idly stroking the head of an orange kitten who lay purring in his lap. "They're confusing all the insects who scurry around in the dark corners of the palace, and a confused bug can't consolidate his position. I like to keep all these petty bootlickers frightened and off balance, since it makes it easier to control them. I really must object to poison, however. It's far too easy for an unskilled poisoner to make mistakes."

"Sadi could poison one specific person at a banquet with a hundred guests," Garion assured him.

"I have every confidence in his ability," Zakath agreed, "but the trouble is that he's not doing the actual poisoning himself. He's selling his concoctions to rank amateurs. There are *some* people here in the palace that I need. Their identities are general knowledge, and that keeps the daggers out of their entrails. A mistake with some poison, however, could wipe out whole branches of my government. Could you ask him not to sell any more of it here in the palace? I'd speak to him personally, but I don't want it to seem like an official reprimand."

"I'll have a talk with him," Garion promised.

"I'd appreciate it, Garion." The Emperor's eyes grew sly. "Just the poisons, though. I find the effects of some of his other compounds rather amusing. Just yesterday, I saw an eighty-five-year-old general in hot pursuit of a young chambermaid. The old fool hasn't had that kind of thought for a quarter of a century. And the day before that, the Chief of the Bureau of Public Works—a pompus ass who makes me sick just to look at him—tried for a solid half hour in front of dozens of witnesses to walk up the side of a building. I haven't laughed so hard in years."

"Nyissan elixirs do strange things to people." Garion smiled. "I'll ask Sadi to confine his dealings to recreational drugs."

"Recreational drugs," Zakath laughed. "I like that description."

"I've always had a way with words," Garion replied modestly.

The orange kitten rose, yawned, and jumped down from the Emperor's lap. The mackerel-tabby mother cat promptly caught a black and white kitten by the scruff of the neck and deposited it exactly where the orange one had been lying. Then she looked at Zakath's face and meowed questioningly.

"Thank you," Zakath murmured to her.

Satisfied, the cat jumped down, caught the orange kitten, and began to bathe it, holding it down with one paw.

"Does she do that all the time?" Garion asked.

Zakath nodded. "She's busy being a mother, but she doesn't want me to get lonely."

"That's considerate of her."

Zakath looked at the black and white kitten in his lap, who had all four paws wrapped around his hand and was gnawing on one of his knuckles in mock ferocity. "I think I could learn to survive without it," he said, wincing.

CHAPTER NINE

The simplest way to avoid the omnipresent spies infesting the imperial palace was to conduct any significant conversations out in the open, and so Garion frequently found himself strolling around the palace grounds with one or more of his companions. On a beautiful spring morning a few days later he walked with Belgarath and Polgara through the dappled shade of a cherry orchard, listening to Velvet's latest report on the political intrigues which seethed through the corridors of Zakath's palace.

"The surprising thing is that Brador is probably aware of most of what's going on," the blond girl told them. "He doesn't *look* all that efficient, but his secret police are everywhere." Velvet was holding a spray of cherry blossoms in front of her face, rather ostentatiously inhaling their fragrance.

"At least they can't hear us out here," Garion said.

"No, but they can *see* us. If I were you, Belgarion, I still wouldn't talk too openly—even out of doors. I happened to come across one industrious fellow yesterday who was busily writing down every word of a conversation being conducted in whispers some fifty yards away."

"That's a neat trick," Belgarath said. "How did he manage it?"

"He's stone-deaf," she replied. "Over the years, he's learned to understand what people are saying by reading the shape of the words from their lips."

"Clever," the old man murmured. "Is that why you're so busily sniffing cherry blossoms?"

She nodded with a dimpled smile. "That and the fact that they have such a lovely fragrance."

He scratched at his beard, his hand covering him mouth. "All right," he said. "What I need is some sort of disruption— something to draw Brador's police off so that we can slip out of Mal Zeth without being followed. Zakath is rock hard on the point of not doing anything until his army gets back from Cthol Murgos, so it's obvious that we're going to have to move without him. Is there anything afoot that might distract all the spies around here?"

"Not really, Ancient One. The petty kinglet of Pallia and the Prince Regent of Delchin are scheming against each other, but that's been going on for years. The old King of Voresebo is trying to get imperial aid in wresting his throne back from his son, who deposed him a year or so ago. Baron Vasca, the Chief of the Bureau of Commerce, is trying to assimilate the Bureau of Military Procurement, but the generals have him stalemated. Those are the major things in the air right now. There are a number of minor plots going on as well, but nothing earthshaking enough to divert the spies who are watching us."

"Can you stir anything up?" Polgara asked, her lips scarcely moving.

"I can try, Lady Polgara," Velvet replied, "but Brador is right on top of everything that's happening here in the palace. I'll talk with Kheldar and Sadi. It's remotely possible that the three of us can engineer something unexpected enough to give us a chance to slip out of the city."

"It's getting fairly urgent, Liselle," Polgara said. "If Zandramas finds what she's looking for at Ashaba, she'll be off again, and we'll wind up trailing along behind her in the same way that we were back in Cthol Murgos."

"I'll see what we can come up with, my lady," Velvet promised.

"Are you going back inside?" Belgarath asked her.

She nodded.

"I'll go with you." He looked around distastefully. "All this fresh air and exercise is a little too wholesome for my taste."

"Walk a bit farther with me, Garion," Polgara said.

"All right."

As Velvet and Belgarath turned back toward the east wing of the palace, Garion and his aunt strolled on along the neatly trimmed green lawn lying beneath the blossom-covered trees. A wren, standing on the topmost twig of a gnarled, ancient tree, sang as if his heart would burst.

"What's he singing about?" Garion asked, suddenly remembering his aunt's unusual affinity for birds.

"He's trying to attract the attention of a female," she replied, smiling gently. "It's that time of year again. He's being very eloquent and making all sorts of promises—most of which he'll break before the summer's over."

He smiled and affectionately put his arm about her shoulders.

She sighed happily. "This is pleasant," she said. "For some reason when we're apart, I still think of you as a little boy. It always sort of surprises me to find that you've grown so tall."

There wasn't too much that he could say to that. "How's Durnik?" he asked. "I almost never see him these days."

"He and Toth and Eriond managed to find a well-stocked trout pond on the southern end of the imperial grounds," she replied with a slightly comical upward roll of her eyes. "They're catching large numbers of fish, but the kitchen staff is beginning to get a bit surly about the whole thing."

"Trust Durnik to find water." Garion laughed. "Is Eriond actually fishing too? That seems a little out of character for him."

"I don't think he's very serious about it. He goes along mostly for Durnik's company, I think—and because he likes to be outside." She paused and then looked directly at him. As so many times in the past, he was suddenly struck to the heart by her luminous beauty. "How has Ce'Nedra been lately?" she asked him.

"She's managed to locate a number of young ladies to keep her company," he replied. "No matter where we go, she's always able to surround herself with companions."

"Ladies like to have other ladies about them, dear," she said. "Men are nice enough, I suppose, but a woman needs other women to talk to. There are so many important things that men just don't understand." Her face grew serious. "There hasn't been any recurrence of what happened in Cthol Murgos, then?" she asked.

"Not so far as I can tell. She seems fairly normal to me. About the only unusual thing I've noticed is that she never talks about Geran any more."

"That could just be her way of protecting herself, Garion. She might not be able to put it into words exactly, but she's aware of the melancholia that came over her at Prolgu, and I'm sure that she realizes that if she gives in to it, she'll be incapacitated. She still thinks about Geran, I'm sure—probably most of the time—but she just won't talk about him." She paused again. "What about the physical side of your marriage?" she asked him directly.

Garion blushed furiously and coughed. "Uh—there really hasn't been much opportunity for that sort of thing, Aunt Pol—and I think she has too many other things on her mind."

She pursed her lips thoughtfully. "It's not a good idea just to ignore that, Garion," she told him. "After a while, people grow apart if they don't periodically renew their intimacy."

He coughed again, still blushing. "She doesn't really seem very interested, Aunt Pol."

"That's your fault, dear. All it takes is a little bit of planning and attention to detail."

"You make it sound awfully calculated and cold-blooded."

"Spontaneity is very nice, dear, but there's a great deal of charm to a well-planned seduction, too."

"Aunt Pol!" he gasped, shocked to the core.

"You're an adult, Garion dear," she reminded him, "and that's one of an adult man's responsibilities. Think about it. You can be quite resourceful at times. I'm sure you'll come up with something." She looked out over the sun-washed lawns. "Shall we go back inside now?" she suggested. "I think it's almost lunch time."

That afternoon, Garion once again found himself strolling about the palace grounds, this time accompanied by Silk and Sadi the eunuch. "Belgarath needs a diversion," he told them seriously. "I think he has a plan to get us out of the city, but we've got to shake off all the spies who are watching us for long enough for him to put it into motion." He was busily scratching at his nose as he spoke, his hand covering his mouth.

"Hay fever?" Silk asked him.

"No. Velvet told us that some of Brador's spies are deaf, but that they can tell what you're saying by watching your lips."

"What an extraordinary gift," Sadi murmured. "I wonder if an undeaf man could learn it."

"I can think of some times myself when it might have been useful," Silk agreed, covering his mouth as he feigned a cough. He looked at Sadi. "Can I get an honest answer out of you?" he asked.

"That depends on the question, Kheldar."

"You're aware of the secret language?"

"Of course."

"Do you understand it?"

"I'm afraid not. I've never met a Drasnian who trusted me enough to teach me."

"I wonder why."

Sadi flashed him a quick grin.

"I think we can manage if we cover our mouths when we speak," Garion said.

"Won't that become a little obvious after a while?" Sadi objected.

"What are they going to do? Tell us to stop?"

"Probably not, but we might want to pass on some disinformation sometimes, and if they know that we know about this way of listening, we won't be able to do that." The eunuch sighed about the lost opportunity, then shrugged. "Oh, well," he said.

Garion looked at Silk. "Do you know of anything that's going on that we could use to pull the police off our trail?"

"No, not really," the little man replied. "At the moment the Melcene consortium seems to be concentrating on keeping this year's price list a secret and trying to persuade Baron Vasca that Yarblek and I should be restrained to those enclaves on the west coast. We've got Vasca pretty much in our pockets, though—as long as he stays bribed. There's a great deal of secret maneuvering going on, but I don't think anything is close to coming to a head right now. Even if it did, it probably wouldn't cause a big enough stink to make the secret police abandon their assignment to watch us."

"Why not go right to the top?" Sadi suggested. "I could talk to Brador and see if he's susceptible to bribery."

"I don't think so," Garion said. "He's having us watched

on specific orders from Zakath. I doubt that any amount of money would make him consider risking his head."

"There are other ways to bribe people, Belgarion." Sadi smiled slyly. "I have some things in my case that make people feel *very* good. The only trouble with them is that after you've used them a few times, you have to keep on using them. The pain of stopping is really quite unbearable. I could *own* Brador within the space of a week and make him do anything I told him to do."

Garion felt a sudden surge of profound distaste for the entire notion. "I'd really rather not do that," he said, "or only as a last resort."

"You Alorns have a peculiar notion of morality," the eunuch said, rubbing at his shaved scalp. "You chop people in two without turning a hair, but you get queasy at the idea of poisons or drugs."

"It's a cultural thing, Sadi," Silk told him.

"Have you found anything else that might work to our advantage?" Garion asked.

Sadi considered it. "Not by itself, no," he replied. "A bureaucracy lends itself to endemic corruption, though. There are a number of people in Mallorea who take advantage of that. Caravans have a habit of getting waylaid in the Dalasian Mountains or on the road from Maga Renn. A caravan needs a permit from the Bureau of Commerce, and Vasca has been known on occasion to sell information about departure times and routes to certain robber chiefs. Or, if the price is right, he sells his silence to the merchant barons in Melcene." The eunuch chuckled. "Once he sold information about one single caravan to three separate robber bands. There was a pitched battle on the plains of Delchin, or so I'm told."

Garion's eyes narrowed in thought. "I'm beginning to get the feeling that we might want to concentrate our attention on this Baron Vasca," he said. "Velvet told us that he's *also* trying to take the Bureau of Military Procurement away from the army."

"I didn't know that," Silk said with some surprise. "Little Liselle is developing quite rapidly, isn't she?"

"It's the dimples, Prince Kheldar," Sadi said. "I'm almost totally immune to any kind of feminine blandishment, but I have to admit that when she smiles at me, my knees turn to butter. She's absolutely adorable—and totally unscrupulous, of course."

Silk nodded. "Yes," he said. "We're moderately proud of her.

"Why don't you two go look her up?" Garion suggested. "Pool your information about this highly corruptible Baron Vasca. Maybe we can stir something up—something noisy. Open fighting in the halls of the palace might just be the sort of thing we need to cover our escape."

"You have a genuine flair for politics, Belgarion," Sadi said admiringly.

"I'm a quick learner," Garion admitted, "and, of course, I keep company with some very disreputable men."

"Thank you, your Majesty," the eunuch replied with mock appreciation.

Shortly after supper, Garion walked through the halls of the palace for his customary evening conversation with Zakath. As always, a soft-footed secret policeman trailed along some distance behind.

Zakath's mood that evening was pensive—almost approaching the bleak, icy melancholy that had marked him back in Rak Hagga.

"Bad day?" Garion asked him, removing a sleeping kitten from the carpet-covered footstool in front of his chair. Then he leaned back and set his feet on the stool.

Zakath made a sour face. "I've been whittling away at all the work that piled up while I was in Cthol Murgos," he said. "The problem is that now that I'm back, the pile just keeps getting higher."

"I know the feeling," Garion agreed. "When I get back to

Riva, it's probably going to take me a year to clear my desk. Are you open to a suggestion?"

"Suggest away, Garion. Right now, I'll listen to anything." He looked reprovingly at the black and white kitten who was biting his knuckles again. "Not so hard," he murmured, tapping the ferocious little beast on the nose with his forefinger.

The kitten laid back its ears and growled a squeaky little growl at him.

"I'm not trying to be offensive or anything," Garion began cautiously, "but I think you're making the same mistake that Urgit made."

"That's an interesting observation. Go on."

"It seems to me that you need to reorganize your government."

Zakath blinked. "Now, that *is* a major proposal," he said. "I don't get the connection, though. Urgit was a hopeless incompetent—at least he was before you came along and taught him the fundamentals of ruling. What is this mistake that he and I have in common?"

"Urgit's a coward," Garion said, "and probably always will be. You're not a coward—sometimes a bit crazy, maybe, but never a coward. The problem is that you're both making the same mistake. You're trying to make all the decisions yourselves—even the little ones. Even if you stop sleeping altogether, you won't find enough hours in the day to do that."

"So I've noticed. What's the solution?"

"Delegate responsibility. Your Bureau Chiefs and generals are competent—corrupt, I'll grant you, but they know their jobs. Tell them to take care of things and only bring you the major decisions. And tell them that if anything goes wrong, you'll replace them."

"That's not the Angarak way, Garion. The ruler—or Emperor, in this case—has always made all decisions. It's been that way since before the cracking of the world. Torak made every decision in antiquity, and the Emperors of Mallorea have followed that example—no matter what we may have felt about him personally."

"Urgit made the exact same mistake," Garion told him. "What you're both forgetting is that Torak was a God, and his mind and will were unlimited. Human beings can't possibly hope to imitate that sort of thing."

"None of my Bureau Chiefs or generals could be trusted with that kind of authority," Zakath said, shaking his head. "They're almost out of control as it is."

"They'll learn the limits," Garion assured him. "After a few of them have been demoted or dismissed, the rest will get the idea."

Zakath smiled bleakly. "That is also not the Angarak way, Garion. When I make an example of someone, it usually involves the headsman's block."

"That's an internal matter, of course," Garion admitted. "You know your people better than I do, but if a man has talent, you can't really call on him again if you've removed his head, can you? Don't waste talent, Zakath. It's too hard to come by."

"You know something?" Zakath said with a slightly amused look. "They call me the man of ice, but in spite of your mild-seeming behavior, you're even more cold-blooded than I am. You're the most practical man I've ever met."

"I was raised in Sendaria, Zakath," Garion reminded him. "Practicality is a religion there. I learned to run a kingdom from a man named Faldor. A kingdom is very much like a farm, really. Seriously, though, the major goal of any ruler is to keep things from flying apart, and gifted subordinates are too valuable a resourse to waste. I've had to reprimand a few people, but that's as far as it ever went. That way they were still around in case I needed them. You might want to think about that a little bit."

"I'll consider it." Zakath straightened. "By the way," he said, "speaking of corruption in government—"

"Oh? Were we speaking about that?"

"We're about to. My Bureau Chiefs are all more or less dishonest, but your three friends are adding levels of sophistication to the petty scheming and deceit here in the palace that we're not really prepared to cope with."

"Oh?"

"The lovely Margravine Liselle has actually managed to persuade the King of Pallia *and* the Prince Regent of Delchin that she's going to intercede with you in their behalf. Each of them is absolutely convinced that their long-term squabble is about to come out into the open. I don't want them to declare war on each other. I've got trouble in Karanda already."

"I'll have a word with her," Garion promised.

"And Prince Kheldar virtually owns whole floors of the Bureau of Commerce. He's getting more information out of there than I am. The merchants in Melcene gather every year to set prices for just about everything that's sold in Mallorea. It's the most closely guarded secret in the empire, and Kheldar just bought it. He's deliberately undercutting those prices, and he's disrupting our whole economy."

Garion frowned. "He didn't mention that."

"I don't mind his making a reasonable profit—as long as he pays his taxes—but I can't really have him gaining absolute control over all commerce in Mallorea, can I? He *is* an Alorn, after all, and his political loyalties are a little obscure."

"I'll suggest that he moderate his practices a bit. You have to understand Silk, though. I don't believe he even cares about the money. All he's interested in is the game."

"It's still Sadi who concerns me the most, though."

"Oh?"

"He's become rather intensely involved in agriculture."

"Sadi?"

"There's a certain plant that grows wild in the marshes of Camat. Sadi's paying a great deal for it, and one of our prominent bandit chiefs has put all of his men to work harvesting it—and protecting the crop, of course. There have already been some pitched battles up there, I understand."

"A bandit who's harvesting crops is too busy to be robbing travelers on the highways, though," Garion pointed out.

"That's not exactly the point, Garion. I didn't mind so much when Sadi was making a few officials feel good and act foolish, but he's importing this plant into the city by the wagon load and spreading it around through the work force—and the army. I don't care for the idea at all."

"I'll see what I can do to get him to suspend operations," Garion agreed. Then he looked at the Mallorean Emperor through narrowed eyes. "You do realize, though, that if I rein the three of them in, they'll just switch over to something new—and probably just as disruptive. Wouldn't it be better if I just took them out of Mal Zeth entirely?"

Zakath smiled. "Nice try, Garion," he said, "but I don't think so. I think we'll just wait until my army gets back from Cthol Murgos. Then we can all ride out of Mal Zeth together."

"You are the most stubborn man I've ever met," Garion said with some heat. "Can't you get it through your head that time is slipping away from us? This delay could be disastrous—not only for you and me, but for the whole world."

"The fabled meeting between the Child of Light and the Child of Dark again? I'm sorry, Garion, but Zandramas is just going to have to wait for you. I don't want you and Belgarath roaming at will through my empire. I *like* you, Garion, but I don't altogether trust you."

Garion's temper began to heat up. He thrust his jaw out pugnaciously as he rose to his feet. "My patience is starting to wear a little thin, Zakath. I've tried to keep things between us more or less civil, but there *is* a limit, and we're getting rather close to it. I am *not* going to lie around your palace for three months."

"That's where you're wrong," Zakath snapped, also rising to his feet and unceremoniously dumping the surprised kitten to the floor.

172

Garion ground his teeth together, trying to get his temper under control. "Up to now, I've been polite, but I'd like to remind you about what happened back at Rak Hagga. We can leave here any time we want to, you know."

"And the minute you do, you're going to have three of my regiments right on your heels." Zakath was shouting now.

"Not for very long," Garion replied ominously.

"What are you going to do?" Zakath demanded scornfully. "Turn all my troops into toads or something? No, Garion, I know you well enough to know that you wouldn't do that."

Garion straightened. "You're right," he said, "I wouldn't, but I was thinking of something a bit more elemental. Torak used the Orb to crack the world, remember? I know how it was done and I could do it myself if I had to. Your troops are going to have a great deal of trouble following us if they suddenly run into a trench—ten miles deep and fifty miles wide—stretching all the way across the middle of Mallorea."

"You wouldn't!" Zakath gasped.

"Try me." With a tremendous effort, Garion brought his anger under control. "I think perhaps it's time for us to break this off," he said. "We're starting to shout threats at each other like a pair of schoolboys. Why don't we continue this conversation some other time, after we've both had a chance to cool off a bit?"

He could see a hot retort hovering on Zakath's lips, but then the Emperor also drew himself up and regained his composure, though his face was still pale with anger. "I think perhaps you're right," he said.

Garion nodded curtly and started toward the door.

"Garion," Zakath said then.

"Yes?"

"Sleep well."

"You too." Garion left the room.

Her Imperial Highness, the Princess Ce'Nedra, Queen of Riva and beloved of Belgarion, Overlord of the

173

West, was feeling pecky. "Pecky" was not a word that her Imperial Highness would normally have used to describe her mood. "Disconsolate" or "out of sorts" might have had a more aristocratic ring, but Ce'Nedra was honest enough with herself privately to admit that "pecky" probably came closer to the mark. She moved irritably from room to room in the luxurious apartment Zakath had provided for her and Garion with the hem of her favorite teal green dressing gown trailing along behind her bare feet. She suddenly wished that breaking a few dishes wouldn't appear quite so unladylike.

A chair got in her way. She almost kicked it, but remembered at the last instant that she was not wearing shoes. Instead she deliberately took the cushion from the chair and set it on the floor. She plumped it a few times, then straightened. She lifted the hem of her dressing gown to her knees, squinted, swung her leg a few times for practice, and then kicked the cushion completely across the room. "There!" She said. "Take that!" For some reason it made her feel a little better.

Garion was away from their rooms at the moment, engaged in his customary evening conversation with Emperor Zakath. Ce'Nedra wished that he were here so that she could pick a fight with him. A nice little fight right now might modify her mood.

She went through a door and looked at the steaming tub sunk in the floor. Perhaps a bath might help. She even went so far as to dip an exploratory toe in the water, then decided against it. She sighed and moved on. She paused for a few moments at the window of the unlighted sitting room that overlooked the verdant atrium at the center of the east wing of the palace. The full moon had risen early that day and stood high in the sky, filling the atrium with its pale, colorless light, and the pool at the center of the private little court reflected back the perfect white circle of the queen of the night. Ce'Nedra stood for quite some time, looking out the window, lost in thought.

The she heard the door open and then slam shut. "Ce'Nedra, where are you?" Garion's voice sounded a trifle testy.

"I'm in here, dear."

"Why are you standing around in the dark?" he asked, coming into the room.

"I was just looking at the moon. Do you realize that it's the same moon that shines down on Tol Honeth—and Riva, too, for that matter?"

"I hadn't really thought about it," he replied shortly.

"Why are you being so grumpy with me?"

"It's not you, Ce'Nedra," he answered apologetically. "I had another fight with Zakath, is all."

"That's getting to be a habit."

"Why is he so unreasonably stubborn?" Garion demanded.

"That's part of the nature of Kings and Emperors, dear."

"What's that supposed to mean?"

"Nothing."

"Do you want something to drink? I think we've still got some of that wine left."

"I don't think so. Not right now."

"Well I do. After my little chat with his pigheaded imperialness, I need something to calm my nerves." He went back out, and she heard the clink of a decanter against the rim of a goblet.

Out in the moon-bright atrium something moved out from the shadows of the tall, broad-leafed trees. It was Silk. He was wearing only his shirt and hose, he had a bath sheet over his shoulder, and he was whistling. He bent at the edge of the pool and dipped his fingers into the water. Then he stood up and began to unbutton his shirt.

Ce'Nedra smiled, drew back behind the drape, and watched as the little man disrobed. Then he stepped down into the pool, shattering the reflected moon into a thousand sparkling fragments. Ce'Nedra continued to watch as he lazily swam back and forth in the moon-dappled water.

Then there was another shadow under the trees, and Liselle came out into the moonlight. She wore a loose-fitting robe, and there was a flower in her hair. The flower was undoubtedly red, but the wan light of the full spring moon leeched away the color, making it appear black against the blond girl's pale hair. "How's the water?" she asked quite calmly. Her voice seemed very close, almost as if she were in the same room with the watching Ce'Nedra.

Silk gave a startled exclamation, then coughed as his mouth and nose filled with water. He spluttered, then recovered his composure. "Not bad," he replied in an unruffled tone.

"Good," Liselle said. She moved to the edge of the pool. "Kheldar, I think it's time that we had a talk."

"Oh? About what?"

"About this." Quite calmly she unbelted her robe and let it fall to the ground about her feet.

She wasn't wearing anything under the robe.

"You seem to have a little difficulty grasping the idea that things change with the passage of time," she continued, dipping one foot into the water. Quite deliberately, she pointed at herself. "This is one of those things."

"I noticed that," he said admiringly.

"I'm so glad. I was beginning to be afraid that your eyes might be failing." She stepped down into the pool and stood waist-deep in the water. "Well?" she said then.

"Well what?"

"What do you plan to do about it?" She reached up and took the flower from her hair and carefully laid it on the surface of the pool.

Ce'Nedra darted to the door on silent, bare feet. "Garion!" she called in an urgent whisper. "Come here!"

"Why?"

"Keep your voice down and come here."

He grumbled slightly and came into the darkened room. "What is it?"

She pointed at the window with a muffled giggle. "Look!" she commanded in a delighted little whisper.

Garion went to the window and looked out. After a single glance, he quickly averted his eyes. "Oh, my," he said in a strangled whisper.

Ce'Nedra giggled again, came to his side, and burrowed her way under his arm. "Isn't that sweet?" she said softly.

"I'm sure it is," he whispered back, "but I don't think we ought to watch."

"Why not?"

The flower Liselle had laid on the water had floated across the intervening space, and Silk, his expression bemused, picked it up and smelled it. "Yours, I believe," he said, holding it out to the pale-skinned girl sharing the pool with him.

"Why, yes, I believe it is," she replied. "But you haven't answered my question."

"Which question?"

"What are you going to do about this?"

"I'll think of something."

"Good. I'll help you."

Garion firmly reached out and pulled the drape shut.

"Spoilsport," Ce'Nedra pouted.

"Never mind," he told her. "Now come away from the window." He drew her out of the room. "I can't understand what she's up to," he said.

"I thought that was fairly obvious."

"Ce'Nedra!"

"She's seducing him, Garion. She's been in love with him since she was a little girl and she's finally decided to take steps. I'm so happy for her that I could just burst."

He shook his head. "I will *never* understand women," he said. "Just when I think I've got everything worked out, you all get together and change the rules. You wouldn't believe what Aunt Pol said to me just this morning."

"Oh? What was that?"

"She said that I ought to—" He stopped abruptly, his face

177

suddenly going beet red. "Ah—never mind," he added lamely.

"What was it?"

"I'll tell you some other time." He gave her a peculiar look then. It was a look she thought she recognized. "Have you taken your evening bath yet?" he asked with exaggerated casualness.

"Not yet. Why?"

"I thought I might join you—if you don't mind."

Ce'Nedra artfully lowered her lashes. "If you really want to," she said in a girlish voice.

"I'll light some candles in there," he said. "The lamp's a bit bright, don't you think?"

"Whatever you prefer, dear."

"And I think I'll bring in the wine, too. It might help us to relax."

Ce'Nedra felt an exultant little surge of triumph. For some reason her irritability had entirely disappeared. "I think that would be just lovely, dear."

"Well," he said, extending a slightly trembling hand to her, "shall we go in, then?"

"Why don't we?"

CHAPTER TEN

The following morning when they gathered for breakfast, Silk's expression was faintly abstracted as if he had just realized that someone had somehow outbargained him. The little man steadfastly refused to look at Velvet, who kept her eyes demurely on the bowl of strawberries and cream she was eating.

"You seem a trifle out of sorts this morning, Prince Kheldar," Ce'Nedra said to him in an offhand manner, though her eyes sparkled with suppressed mirth. "Whatever is the matter?"

He threw her a quick, suspicious look.

179

"There, there," she said, fondly patting his hand. "I'm sure that you'll feel much better after breakfast."

"I'm not very hungry," he replied. His voice was just a little sullen. He stood up abruptly. "I think I'll go for a walk," he said.

"But my dear fellow," she protested, "you haven't eaten your strawberries. They're absolutely delicious, aren't they, Liselle?"

"Marvelous," the blond girl agreed with only the faintest hint of her dimples showing.

Silk's scowl deepened, and he marched resolutely toward the door.

"May I have yours, Kheldar?" Velvet called after him. "If you're not going to eat them, that is?"

He slammed the door as he went out, and Ce'Nedra and Velvet exploded into gales of silvery laughter.

"What's this?" Polgara asked them.

"Oh, nothing," Ce'Nedra said, still laughing. "Nothing at all, Lady Polgara. Our Prince Kheldar had a little adventure last night that didn't turn out exactly the way he expected it to."

Velvet gave Ce'Nedra a quick look and flushed slightly. Then she laughed again.

Polgara looked at the giggling pair, and then one of her eyebrows went up. "Oh. I see," she said.

The flush on Velvet's cheeks grew rosier, although she continued to laugh.

"Oh, dear." Polgara sighed.

"Is something wrong, Pol?" Durnik asked her.

She looked at the good, honest man, assessing his strict Sedarian principles. "Just a small complication, Durnik," she replied, "Nothing that can't be managed."

"That's good." He pushed back his bowl. "Do you need me for anything this morning?"

"No, dear," she replied, kissing him.

He returned her kiss and then stood up, looking across the

table at Toth and Eriond, who sat waiting expectantly. "Shall we go then?" he asked them.

The three of them trooped out, their faces alight with anticipation.

"I wonder how long it's going to take them to empty all the fish out of that pond," Polgara mused

"Forever, I'm afraid, Lady Polgara," Sadi told her, popping a strawberry into his mouth. "The grounds keepers restock it every night."

She sighed. "I was afraid of that," she said.

About midmorning, Garion was pacing up and down one of the long, echoing halls. He felt irritable, and a sort of frustrated impatience seemed to weigh him down. The urgent need to get to Ashaba before Zandramas escaped him again was so constantly on his mind now that he could think of almost nothing else. Although they had come up with several possible schemes, Silk, Velvet, and Sadi were still searching for a suitable diversion—something startling enough to draw off Brador's secret policemen so that they could all make good their escape. There was obviously little chance of changing Zakath's mind, and it began to look increasingly as if Garion and his friends were going to have to "do it the other way," as Belgarath sometimes put it. Despite his occasional threats to Zakath, Garion didn't really want to do that. He was quite sure that to do so would permanently end his growing friendship with the strange man who ruled Mallorea. He was honest enough to admit that it was not only the friendship he would regret losing but the political possibilities implicit in the situation as well.

He was about to return to his rooms when a scarlet-liveried servant came up to him. "Your Majesty," the servant said with a deep bow, "Prince Kheldar asked me to find you for him. He'd like to have a word with you."

"Where is he?" Garion asked.

"In the formal garden near the north wall of the complex, your Majesty. There's a half-drunk Nadrak with him—and a

181

woman with a remarkably foul mouth. You wouldn't believe some of the things she said to me."

"I think I know her," Garion replied with a faint smile. "I'd believe it." He turned then and walked briskly through the hallways and out into the palace grounds.

Yarblek had not changed. Though it was pleasantly warm in the neatly manicured formal garden, he nonetheless still wore his shabby felt overcoat and his shaggy fur hat. He was sprawled on a marble bench under a leafy arbor with a broached ale keg conveniently at hand. Vella, as lush as ever, wandered idly among the flower beds, dressed in her tight-fitting Nadrak vest and leather trousers. Her silver-hilted daggers protruded from the tops of her boots and from her belt, and her walk was still that same challenging, sensual strut, a mannerism she had practiced for so long that it was by now automatic and probably even unconscious. Silk sat on the grass near Yarblek's bench, and he, too, held an ale cup.

"I was just about to come looking for you," he said as Garion approached.

The rangy Yarblek squinted at Garion. "Well, well," he said, blinking owlishly, "if it isn't the boy-King of Riva. I see that you're still wearing that big sword of yours."

"It's a habit," Garion shrugged. "You're looking well, Yarblek—aside from being a little drunk, that is."

"I've been cutting down," Yarblek said rather piously. "My stomach isn't what it used to be."

"Did you happen to see Belgarath on your way here?" Silk asked Garion.

"No. Should I have?"

"I sent for him, too. Yarblek's got some information for us, and I want the old man to get it first hand."

Garion looked at Silk's coarse-faced partner. "How long have you been in Mal Zeth?" he asked.

"We got in last night," Yarblek replied, dipping his cup into the ale keg again. "Dolmar told me that you were all here in the palace, so I came by this morning to look you up."

"How long are you going to stay in town?" Silk asked him.

Yarblek tugged at his scraggly beard and squinted up at the arbor. "That's kind of hard to say," he said. "Dolmar picked up *most* of what I need, but I want to nose around the markets a bit. There's a Tolnedran in Boktor who said that he's interested in uncut gem stones. I could pick up a quick fortune on that transaction—particularly if I could sneak the stones past Drasnian customs."

"Don't Queen Porenn's customs agents search your packs pretty thoroughly?" Garion asked him.

"From top to bottom," Yarblek laughed, "And they pat me down as well. They *don't*, however, lay one finger on Vella. They've all learned how quick she is with her daggers. I've made back what I paid for her a dozen times over by hiding little packages here and there in her clothes." He laughed coarsely. "And of course the hiding is sort of fun, too." He belched thunderously. "Par'me," he said.

Belgarath came across the lawn. The old man had resisted all of Zakath's tactful offers of less disreputable raiment, and still wore, defiantly, Garion thought, his stained tunic, patched hose, and mismatched boots. "Well, I see that you finally got here," he said to Yarblek without any preamble.

"I got tied up in Mal Camat," the Nadrak replied. "Kal Zakath is commandeering ships all up and down the west coast to bring his army back from stinking Cthol Murgos. I had to hire boats and hide them in the marshes north of the ruins of Cthol Mishrak." He pointed at the ale keg. "You want some of this?" he asked.

"Naturally. Have you got another cup?"

Yarblek patted here and there at his voluminous coat, reached into an inside pocket, and drew out a squat, dented tankard.

"I like a man who comes prepared."

"A proper host is always ready. Help yourself. Just try not to spill too much." The Nadrak looked at Garion. "How about you?" he asked. "I think I could find another cup."

"No. Thanks anyway, Yarblek. It's a little early for me."

Then a short, gaudily dressed man came around the arbor. His clothes were a riot of frequently conflicting colors. One sleeve was green, the other red. One leg of his hose was striped in pink and yellow and the other covered with large blue polka dots. He wore a tall, pointed cap with a bell attached to the peak. It was not his outrageous clothing that was so surprising, however. What caught Garion's eye first was the fact that the man was quite casually walking on his hands with both feet extended into the air. "Did I hear somebody offer somebody a little drap of somethin' to drink" he asked in a strange, lilting brogue that Garion did not quite recognize.

Yarblek gave the colorful little fellow a sour look and reached inside his coat again.

The acrobat flexed his shoulders, thrusting himself into the air, flipped over in midair, and landed on his feet. He briskly brushed off his hands and came toward Yarblek with an ingratiating smile. His face was nondescript, the kind of face that would be forgotten almost as soon as it was seen, but for some reason, it seemed to Garion to be naggingly familiar.

"Ah, good master Yarblek," the man said to Silk's partner, "I'm sure that yer the kindest man alive. I was near to perishin' of thirst, don't y' know?" He took the cup, dipped into the ale keg, and drank noisily. Then he let out his breath with a gusty sound of appreciation. "'Tis a good brew ye have there, Master Yarblek," he said, dipping again into the keg.

Belgarath had a peculiar expression on his face, partly puzzled but at the same time partially amused.

"He came tagging along when we left Mal Camat," Yarblek told them. "Vella finds him amusing, so I haven't chased him off yet. She turns a little shrill when she doesn't get her own way."

"The name is Feldegast, fine gentlemen," the gaudy little fellow introduce himself with an exaggerated bow. "Feldegast the juggler. I be also an acrobat—as ye've seen fer yerselves—

184

a comedian of no mean ability, and an accomplished magician. I can baffle yer eyes with me unearthly skill at prestidigitation, don't y' know. I kin also play rousin' tunes on a little wooden whistle—or, if yer mood be melancholy, I kin play ye sad songs on the lute to bring a lump to yer throat and fill yer eyes with sweet, gentle tears. Would ye be wantin' to witness some of me unspeakable talent?"

"Maybe a little later," Belgarath told him, his eyes still a little bemused. "Right now we have some business to discuss."

"Take another cup of ale and go entertain Vella, comedian," Yarblek said to him. "Tell her some more off-color stories."

"'Twill be me eternal delight, good Master Yarblek," the outrageous fellow said grandly. "She's a good strappin' wench with a lusty sense of humor and a fine appreciation fer bawdy stories." He dipped out more ale and then capered across the lawn toward the dark-haired Nadrak girl.

"Disgusting," Yarblek growled, looking after him. "Some of the stories he tells her make *my* ears burn, but the nastier they are, the harder she laughs." He shook his head moodily.

"Let's get down to business," Belgarath said. "We need to know what's going on in Karanda right now."

"That's simple," Yarblek told him. "Mengha, that's what's going on. Mengha and his cursed demons."

"Dolmar filled us in," Silk said. "We know about what happened at Calida and about the way that Karands are flocking in to join his army from all over the seven kingdoms. Is he making any moves toward the south yet?"

"Not that I've heard," Yarblek replied. "He seems to be consolidating things through the north right now. He's whipping all of the Karands into hysteria, though. If Zakath doesn't do something quickly, he's going to have a full-scale revolution on his hands. I can tell you, though, that it's not safe to travel in northern Karanda right now. Mengha's shrieking Karands control everything to the coast of Zamad."

"We have to go to Ashaba," Garion told him.

"I wouldn't advise it," Yarblek said bluntly. "The Karands are picking up some very unsavory habits."

"Oh?" Silk said.

"I'm an Angarak," Yarblek said, "and I've been watching Grolims cut out human hearts to offer to Torak since I was a boy, but what's happening in Karanda turns even *my* stomach. The Karands stake captives out on the ground and then call up their demons. The demons are all getting fat."

"Would you care to be a little more specific?"

"Not really. Use your imagination, Silk. You've been in Morindland. You know what demons eat."

"You're not serious!"

"Oh, yes—and the Karands eat the scraps. As I said—some very unsavory habits. There are also some rumors about the demons breeding with human females."

"That's abominable!" Garion gasped.

"It is indeed," Yarblek agreed with him. "The women usually don't survive their pregnancies, but I've heard of a few live births."

"We have to put a stop to that," Belgarath said bleakly.

"Good luck," Yarblek said. "Me, I'm going back to Gar og Nadrak just as soon as I can get my caravan put together. I'm not going anywhere near Mengha—or the tame demon he keeps on a leash."

"Nahaz?" Garion asked.

"You've heard the name then?"

"Dolmar told us."

"We should probably start with him," Belgarath said. "If we can drive Nahaz back to where he came from, it's likely that the rest of the demons will follow their lord."

"Neat trick," Yarblek grunted.

"I have certain resources," the old man told him. "Once the demons are gone, Mengha won't have anything left but a rag tag army of Karandese fanatics. We'll be able to go on about our business and leave the mopping up to Zakath." He smiled briefly. "That might occupy his mind enough to keep him from breathing down our necks."

Vella was laughing raucously as she and Feldegast the juggler approached the arbor. The little comedian was walking on his hands again—erratically and with his feet waving ludicrously in the air.

"He tells a good story," the lush-bodied Nadrak girl said, still laughing, "but he can't hold his liquor."

"I didn't think he drank all that much," Silk said.

"It wasn't the ale that fuddled him so bad," she replied. She drew a silver flask from under her belt. "I gave him a pull or two at this." Her eyes suddenly sparkled with mischief. "Care to try some, Silk?" she offered, holding out the flask.

"What's in it?" he asked suspiciously.

"Just a little drink we brew in Gar og Nadrak," she said innocently. "It's as mild as mothers' milk." She demonstrated by taking a long drink from the flask.

"Othlass?"

She nodded.

"No thanks." He shuddered. "The last time I drank that, I lost track of a whole week."

"Don't be so chicken-livered, Silk," she told him scornfully. She took another drink. "See? It doesn't hurt a bit." She looked at Garion. "My lord," she said to him. "How's your pretty little wife?"

"She's well, Vella."

"I'm glad to hear that. Have you got her pregnant again yet?"

Garion flushed. "No," he replied.

"You're wasting time, my lord. Why don't you run back to the palace and chase her around the bedroom a time or two?" Then she turned to Belgarath. "Well?" she said to him.

"Well what?"

She smoothly drew one of her knives from her belt. "Would you like to try again?" she asked, turning deliberately so that her well-rounded posterior was available to him.

187

"Ah, thanks all the same, Vella," he said with a kind of massive dignity, "But it's a bit early."

"That's all right, old man," she said. "I'm ready for you this time. Any time you're in a patting frame of mind, feel free. I sharpened all my knives before we came—especially for you."

"You're too kind."

The drunken Feldegast lurched, tried to regain his balance, and toppled over in an unceremonious heap. When he stumbled to his feet, his plain face was splotched and distorted, and he stood hunched over with his back bowed to the point where he almost looked deformed.

"I think the girl got the best of you, my friend," Belgarath said jovially as he moved quickly to help the inebriated juggler to right himself. "You really ought to straighten up, though. If you stand around bent over like that, you'll tie your insides in knots." Garion saw his grandfather's lips moving slightly as he whispered something to the tipsy entertainer. Then, so faint that it was barely discernible, he felt the surge of the old man's will.

Feldegast straightened, his face buried in his hands. "Oh dear, oh dear, oh dear," he said. "Have y' poisoned me, me girl?" he demanded of Vella. "I can't remember ever bein' taken by the drink so fast." He took his hands away. The splotches and distortion were gone from his face, and he looked as he had before.

"Don't ever try to drink with a Nadrak woman," Belgarath advised him, "particularly when she's the one who brewed the liquor."

"It seems that I heard a snatch of conversation whilst I was entertainin' the wench here. Is it Karanda ye be talkin' about—and the woeful things happenin' there?"

"We were," Belgarath admitted.

"I display me talents betimes in wayside inns and taverns—for pennies and a drink or two, don't y' know—and a great deal of information comes into places like that. Sometimes if ye make a man laugh and be merry, ye kin draw more out of him than ye can with silver or strong drink. As it happened, I was in such a place not long ago—dazzlin' the onlookers with the brilliance of me performance—and happens that whilst I was there, a wayfarer came in from the east. A great brute of a man he was, and he told us the distressful news from Karanda. And after he had eaten and finished more pots of good strong ale than was good for him, I sought him out and questioned him further. A man in me profession can't never know too much about the places where he might be called upon to display his art, don't y' know. This great brute of a man, who should not have feared anythin' that walks, was shakin' and tremblin' like a frightened babe, and he tells me that I should stay out of Karanda as I valued me life. And then he tells me a very strange thing, which I have not yet put the meanin' to. He tells me that the road between Calida and Mal Yaska is thick with messengers goin' to and fro, hither and yon. Isn't that an amazin' thing? How could a man account fer it? But there be strange things goin' on in the world, good masters, and wonders to behold that no man at all could ever begin to imagine."

The juggler's lilting brogue was almost hypnotic in its charm and liquidity, and Garion found himself somehow caught up in the really quite commonplace narrative. He felt a peculiar disappointment as the gaudy little man broke off his story.

"I hope that me tale has brought ye some small entertainment an' enlightenment, good masters," Feldegast said ingratiatingly, his grass-stained hand held out suggestively. "I make me way in the world with me wits and me talents, givin' of them as free as the birds, but I'm always grateful fer little tokens of appreciation, don't y' know."

"Pay him," Belgarath said shortly to Garion.

"What?"

"Give him some money."

Garion sighed and reached for the leather purse at his belt.

189

"May the Gods all smile down on ye, young master," Feldegast thanked Garion effusively for the few small coins which changed hands. Then he looked slyly at Vella. "Tell me, me girl," he said, "have ye ever heard the story of the milkmaid and the peddler? I must give ye fair warnin' that it's a naughty little story, and I'd be covered with shame to bring a blush to yer fair cheeks."

"I haven't blushed since I was fourteen," Vella said to him.

"Well then, why don't we go apart a ways, an' I'll see if I can't remedy that? I'm told that blushin' is good fer the complexion."

Vella laughed and followed him back out onto the lawn.

"Silk," Belgarath said brusquely, "I need that diversion—now."

"We don't really have anything put together yet," Silk objected.

"Make something up, then." The old man turned to Yarblek. "And I don't want you to leave Mal Zeth until I give you the word. I might need you here."

"What's the matter, Grandfather?" Garion asked.

"We have to leave here as quickly as possible."

Out on the lawn, Vella stood wide-eyed and with the palms of her hands pressed to her flaming cheeks.

"Ye'll have to admit that I warned ye, me girl," Feldegast chortled triumphantly. "Which is more than I can say about the deceitful way ye slipped yer dreadful brew into me craw." He looked at her admiringly. "I must say, though, that ye bloom like a red, red rose when ye blush like that, and yer a joy to behold in yer maidenlike confusion. Tell me, have ye by chance heard the one about the shepherdess and the knight-errant?"

Vella fled.

That afternoon, Silk, who normally avoided anything remotely resembling physical exertion, spent several hours in the leafy atrium in the center of the east wing, busily piling stones across the mouth of the tiny rivulent of fresh, sparkling water which fed the pool at the center of the little garden. Garion watched curiously from the window of his sitting room until he could stand it no longer. He went out into the atrium to confront the sweating little Drasnian. "Are you taking up landscaping as a hobby?" he asked.

"No," Silk replied, mopping his forehead, "just taking a little precaution, is all."

"Precaution against what?"

Silk held up one finger. "Wait," he said gauging the level of the water rising behind his improvised dam. After a moment, the water began to spill over into the pool with a loud gurgling and splashing. "Noisy, isn't it?" he said proudly.

"Won't that make sleep in these surrounding rooms a little hard?" Garion asked.

"It's also going to make listening almost impossible," the little man said smugly. "As soon as it gets dark, why don't you and I and Sadi and Liselle gather here. We need to talk, and my cheerful little waterfall should cover what we say to each other."

"Why after dark?"

Silk slyly laid one finger alongside his long, pointed nose. "So that the night will hide our lips from those police who don't use their ears to listen with."

"That's clever," Garion said.

"Why, yes. I thought so myself." Then Silk made a sour face. "Actually, it was Liselle's idea," he confessed.

Garion smiled. "But she let you do the work."

Silk grunted. "She claimed that she didn't want to break any of her fingernails. I was going to refuse, but she threw her dimples at me, and I gave in."

"She uses those very well, doesn't she? They're more dangerous than your knives."

"Are you trying to be funny, Garion?"

"Would I do that, old friend?"

As the soft spring evening descended over Mal

Zeth, Garion joined his three friends in the dim atrium beside Silk's splashing waterfall.

"Very nice work, Kheldar," Velvet complimented the little man.

"Oh, shut up."

"Why, Kheldar!"

"All right," Garion said, by way of calling the meeting to order, "what have we got that we can work with? Belgarath wants us out of Mal Zeth almost immediately."

"I've been following your advice, Belgarion," Sadi murmured, "and I've been concentrating my attention on Baron Vasca. He's a man of eminent corruption and he has his fingers in so many pies that he sometimes loses track of just who's bribing him at any given moment."

"Exactly what's he up to right now?" Garion asked.

"He's still trying to take over the Bureau of Military Procurement," Velvet reported. "That bureau is controlled by the General Staff, however. It's mostly composed of colonels, but there's a General Bregar serving as Bureau Chief. The colonels aren't *too* greedy, but Bregar has a large payroll. He has to spread quite a bit of money around among his fellow generals to keep Vasca in check."

Garion thought about that. "Aren't you bribing Vasca as well?" he asked Silk.

Silk nodded glumly. "The price is going up, though. The consortium of Melcene merchant barons is laying a lot of money in his path, trying to get him to restrict Yarblek and me to the west coast."

"Can he raise any sort of force? Fighting men, I mean?"

"He has contacts with a fair number of robber chiefs," Sadi replied, "and they have some pretty rough and ready fellows working for them."

"Is there any band operating out of Mal Zeth right now?"

Sadi coughed rather delicately. "I just brought a string of wagons down from Camat," he admitted. "Agricultural products for the most part."

Garion gave him a hard look. "I thought I asked you not to do that any more."

"The crop had already been harvested, Belgarion," the eunuch protested. "It doesn't make sense to just let it rot in the fields, does it?"

"That's sound business thinking, Garion," Silk interceded.

"Anyway," Sadi hurried on, "the band that's handling the harvesting and transport for me is one of the largest in this part of Mallorea—two or three hundred anyway, and I have a goodly number of stout fellows involved in local distribution."

"You did all this in just a few weeks?" Garion was incredulous.

"One makes very little profit by allowing the grass to grow under one's feet," Sadi stated piously.

"Well put," Silk approved.

"Thank you, Prince Kheldar."

Garion shook his head in defeat. "Is there any way you can get your bandits into the palace grounds?"

"Bandits?" Sadi sounded injured.

"Isn't that what they are?"

"I prefer to think of them as entrepreneurs."

"Whatever. Can you get them in?"

"I sort of doubt it, Belgarion. What did you have in mind?"

"I thought we might offer their services to Baron Vasca to help in his forthcoming confrontation with the General Staff."

"Is there going to be a confrontation?" Sadi looked surprised. "I hadn't heard about that."

"That's because we haven't arranged it yet. Vasca's going to find out—probably tomorrow—that his activities have irritated the General Staff, and that they're going to send troops into his offices to arrest him and to dig through his records to find enough incriminating evidence to take to the Emperor."

"That's brilliant," Silk said.

"I liked it—but it won't work unless Vasca's got enough men to hold off a fair number of troops."

"It can still work," Sadi said. "At about the same time that Vasca finds out about his impending arrest, I'll offer him the use of my men. He can bring them into the palace complex under the guise of workmen. All the Bureau Chiefs are continually renovating their offices. It has to do with status, I think."

"What's the plan here, Garion?" Silk asked.

"I want open fighting right here in the halls of the palace. *That* should attract the attention of Brador's policemen."

"He was born to be a King, wasn't he?" Velvet approved. "Only royalty has the ability to devise a deception of that scale."

"Thanks," Garion said dryly. "It's not going to work, though, if Vasca just takes up defensive positions in his bureau offices. We also have to persuade him to strike first. The soldiers won't really be coming after him, so we're going to have to make him start the fight himself. What kind of man is Vasca?"

"Deceitful, greedy, and not really all that bright," Silk replied.

"Can he be pressured into any kind of rashness?"

"Probably not. Bureaucrats tend to be cowardly. I don't think he'd make a move until he sees the soldiers coming."

"I believe I can make him bolder," Sadi said. "I have something very nice in a green vial that would make a mouse attack a lion."

Garion made a face. "I don't much care for that way," he said.

"It's the results that count, Belgarion," Sadi pointed out. "If things are that urgent right now, delicate feelings might be a luxury we can't afford."

"All right," Garion decided. "Do whatever you have to."

"Once things are in motion, I might be able to throw in just a bit of additional confusion," Velvet said. "The King of Pallia and the Prince Regent of Delchin both have sizable retinues, and they're on the verge of open war anyway.

There's also the King of Veresebo, who's so senile that he distrusts everybody. I could probably persuade each of them that any turmoil in the halls is directed at *them* personally. They'd put their men-at-arms into the corridors at the first sound of fighting."

"Now that's got some interesting possibilities," Silk said, rubbing his hands together gleefully. "A five-way brawl in the palace ought to give us all the opportunity we need to leave town."

"And it wouldn't necessarily have to be confined to the palace," Sadi added thoughtfully. "A bit of judicious misdirection could probably spread it out into the city itself. A general riot in the streets would attract quite a bit of attention, wouldn't you say?"

"How long would it take to set it up?" Garion asked.

Silk looked at his partners in crime. "Three days?" he asked them, "Maybe four?"

The both considered it, then nodded.

"That's it then, Garion," Silk said. "Three or four days."

"All right. Do it."

They all turned and started back toward the entrance to the atrium. "Margravine Liselle," Sadi said firmly.

"Yes, Sadi?"

"I'll take my snake back now, if you don't mind."

"Oh, of course, Sadi." She reached into her bodice for Zith.

Silk's face blanched, and he stepped back quickly.

"Something wrong, Kheldar?" she asked innocently.

"Never mind." The little man turned on his heel and went on through the green-smelling evening gesticulating and talking to himself.

CHAPTER ELEVEN

His name was Balsca. He was a rheumy-eyed sea-faring man with bad habits and mediocre skills who hailed from Kaduz, a fish-reeking town on one of the northern Melcene Islands. He had signed on as a common deck hand for the past six years aboard a leaky merchantman grandiosely named *The Star of Jarot*, commanded by an irascible peg-leg captain from Celanta who called himself "Woodfoot," a colorful name which Balsca privately suspected was designed to conceal the captain's true identify from the maritime authorities.

Balsca did not like Captain Woodfoot. Balsca had not liked any ships' officers since he had been summarily flogged ten years back for pilfering grog from ship's stores aboard a ship of the line in the Mallorean navy. Balsca had nursed his grievance from that incident until he had found an opportunity to jump ship, and then he had gone in search of kindlier masters and more understanding officers in the merchant marine.

He had not found them aboard *The Star of Jarot*.

His most recent disillusionment had come about as the result of a difference of views with the ship's bosun, a heavy-fisted rascal from Pannor in Rengel. That altercation had left Balsca without his front teeth, and his vigorous protest to the captain had evoked jeering laughter followed by his being unceremoniously kicked off the quarterdeck by a nail-studded leg constructed of solid oak. The humiliation and the bruises were bad enough, but the splinters which festered for weeks in Balsca's behind made it almost impossible for him to sit down, and sitting down was Balsca's favorite position.

He brooded about it, leaning on the starboard rail well out of Captain Woodfoot's view and staring out at the lead-gray swells surging through the straits of Perivor as *The Star of Jarot* beat her way northwesterly past the swampy coast of the southwestern Dalasian Protectorates and on around the savage breakers engulfing the Turim Reef. By the time they had cleared the reef and turned due north along the desolate coast of Finda, Balsca had concluded that life was going out of its way to treat him unfairly, and that he might be far better off seeking his fortune ashore.

He spent several nights prowling through the cargo hold with a well-shielded lantern until he found the concealed compartment where Woodfoot had hidden a number of small, valuable items that he didn't want to trouble the customs people with. Balsca's patched canvas sea bag picked up a fair amount of weight rather quickly that night.

When *The Star of Jarot* dropped anchor in the harbor of Mal Gemila, Balsca feigned illness and refused his shipmates' suggestion that he go ashore with them for the customary end-of-voyage carouse. He lay instead in his hammock, moaning

197

theatrically. Late during the dog watch, he pulled on his tarred canvas sea coat, the only thing of any value that he owned, picked up his sea bag and went on silent feet up on deck. The solitary watch, as Balsca had anticipated, lay snoring in the scuppers, snuggled up to an earthenware jug; there were no lights in the aft cabins, where Woodfoot and his officers lived in idle luxury; and the moon had already set. A small ship's boat swung on a painter on the starboard side, and Balsca deftly dropped his sea bag into it, swung over the rail, and silently left *The Star of Jarot* forever. He felt no particular regret about that. He did not even pause to mutter a curse at the vessel which had been his home for the past six years. Balsca was a philosophical sort of fellow. Once he had escaped from an unpleasant situation, he no longer held any grudges.

When he reached the docks, he sold the small ship's boat to a beady-eyed man with a missing right hand. Balsca feigned drunkenness during the transaction, and the maimed man—who had undoubtedly had his hand chopped off as punishment for theft—paid him quite a bit more for the boat than would have been the case had the sale taken place in broad daylight. Balsca immediately knew what that meant. He shouldered his sea bag, staggered up the wharf, and began to climb the steep cobblestone street from the harbor. At the first corner, he made a sudden turn to the left and ran like a deer, leaving the surprised press gang the beady-eyed man had sent after him floundering far behind. Balsca was stupid, certainly, but he was no fool.

He ran until he was out of breath and quite some distance from the harbor with all its dangers. He passed a number of alehouses along the way, regretfully perhaps, but there was still business to attend to, and he needed his wits about him.

In a dim little establishment, well hidden up a dank, smelly alleyway, he sold Captain Woodfoot's smuggled treasures, bargaining down to the last copper with the grossly fat woman who ran the place. He even traded his sea coat for a landsman's tunic, and emerged from the alley with all trace of the sea

198

removed from him, except for the rolling gait of a man whose feet have not touched dry land for several months.

He avoided the harbor with its press gangs and cheap grog shops and chose instead a quiet street that meandered past boarded-up warehouses. He followed that until he found a sedate workman's alehouse where a buxom barmaid rather sullenly served him. Her mood, he surmised, was the result of the fact that he was her only customer, and that she had quite obviously intended to close the doors and seek her bed—or someone else's, for all he knew. He jollied her into some semblance of good humor for an hour or so, left a few pennies on the table, and squeezed her ample bottom by way of farewell. Then he lurched into the empty street in search of further adventure.

He found true love under a smoky torch on the corner. Her name, she said, was Elowanda. Balsca suspected that she was not being entirely honest about that, but it was not her name he was interested in. She was quite young and quite obviously sick. She had a racking cough, a hoarse, croaking voice, and her reddened nose ran constantly. She was not particularly clean and she exuded the rank smell of a week or more of dried sweat. Balsca, however, had a sailor's strong stomach and an appetite whetted by six months' enforced abstinence at sea. Elowanda was not very pretty, but she was cheap. After a brief haggle, she led him to a rickety crib in an alley that reeked of moldy sewage. Although he was quite drunk, Balsca grappled with her on a lumpy pallet until dawn was staining the eastern sky.

It was noon when he awoke with a throbbing head. He might have slept longer, but the cry of a baby coming from a wooden box in the corner drove into his ears like a sharp knife. He nudged the pale woman lying beside him, hoping that she would rise and quiet her squalling brat. She moved limply under his hand, her limbs flaccid.

He nudged her again, harder this time. Then he rose up and looked at her. Her stiff face was locked in a dreadful rictus—a hideous grin that made his blood run cold. He suddenly realized that her skin was like clammy ice. He jerked his hand away, swearing under his breath. He reached out gingerly and peeled back one of her eyelids. He swore again.

The woman who had called herself Elowanda was as dead as last week's mackerel.

Balsca rose and quickly pulled on his clothes. He searched the room thoroughly, but found nothing worth stealing except for the few coins he had given the dead woman the previous night. He took those, then glared at the naked corpse lying on the pallet. "Rotten whore!" he said and kicked her once in the side. She rolled limply off the pallet and lay face down on the floor.

Balsca slammed out into the stinking alley, ignoring the wailing baby he had left behind him.

He had a few moments' concern about the possibility of certain social diseases. *Something* had killed Elowanda, and he had not really been all that rough with her. As a precaution, he muttered an old sailors' incantation which was said to be particularly efficacious in warding off the pox; reassured, he went looking for something to drink.

By midafternoon, he was pleasantly drunk and he lurched out of a congenial little wine shop and stopped, swaying slightly, to consider his options. By now Woodfoot would certainly have discovered that his hidden cabinet was empty and that Balsca had jumped ship. Since Woodfoot was a man of limited imagination, he and his officers would certainly be concentrating their search along the waterfront. It would take them some time to realize that their quarry had moved somewhat beyond the sight, if not the smell, of salt water. Balsca prudently decided that if he were to maintain his lead on his vengeful former captain, it was probably time for him to head inland. It occurred to him, moreover, that someone might have seen him with Elowanda, and that her body probably had been found by now. Balsca felt no particular responsibility for her death, but he was by nature slightly shy about talking with policemen. All in all, he decided, it might just be time to leave Mal Gemila.

He started out confidently, striding toward the east gate of the city; but after several blocks, his feet began to hurt. He loitered outside a warehouse where several workmen were loading a large wagon. He carefully stayed out of sight until the work was nearly done, then heartily offered to lend a hand. He put two boxes on the wagon, then sought out the teamster, a shaggy-bearded man smelling strongly of mules.

"Where be ye bound, friend?" Balsca asked him as if out of idle curiosity.

"Mal Zeth," the teamster replied shortly.

"What an amazing coincidence," Balsca exclaimed. "I have business there myself." In point of fact, Balsca had cared very little where the teamster and his wagon had been bound. All he wanted to do was to go inland to avoid Woodfoot or the police. "What say I ride along with you—for company?"

"I don't get all that lonesome," the teamster said churlishly.

Balsca signed. It was going to be one of *those* days. "I'd be willing to pay," he offered sadly.

"How much?"

"I don't really have very much."

"Ten coppers," the teamster said flatly.

"Ten? I haven't got that much."

"You'd better start walking then. It's that way."

Balsca sighed and gave in. "All right," he said. "Ten."

"In advance."

"Half now and half when we get to Mal Zeth."

"In advance."

"That's hard."

"So's walking."

Balsca stepped around a corner, reached into an inside pocket, and carefully counted out the ten copper coins. The horde he had accumulated as a result of his pilferage aboard *The Star of Jarot* had dwindled alarmingly. A number of possibilities occurred to him. He shifted his sheath knife around until it was at his back. If the teamster slept soundly enough and if they stopped for the night in some secluded place, Balsca was quite certain that he could ride into Mal Zeth the proud owner of a wagon and a team of mules—not to mention whatever was in the boxes. Balsca had killed a few men in his time—when it had been safe to do so—and he was not particularly squeamish about cutting throats, if it was worth his while.

The wagon clattered and creaked as it rumbled along the cobbled street in the slanting afternoon sunlight.

"Let's get a few things clear before we start," the teamster said. "I don't like to talk and I don't like having people jabber at me."

"All right."

The teamster reached back and picked up a wicked-looking hatchet out of the wagon bed. "Now," he said, "give me your knife."

"I don't have a knife."

The teamster reined in his mules. "Get out," he said curtly.

"But I paid you?"

"Not enough for me to take any chances with you. Come up with a knife or get out of my wagon."

Balsca glared at him, then at the hatchet. Slowly he drew out his dagger and handed it over.

"Good. I'll give it back to you when we get to Mal Zeth. Oh, by the way, I sleep with one eye open and with this in my fist." He held the hatchet in front of Balsca's face. "If you even come near me while we're on the road, I'll brain you."

Balsca shrank back.

"I'm glad that we understand each other." The teamster shook his reins, and they rumbled out of Mal Gemila.

Balsca was not feeling too well when they reached Mal Zeth. He assumed at first that it was a result of the peculiar swaying motion of the wagon. Though he had never been seasick in all his years as a sailor, he was frequently land-sick.

This time, however, was somewhat different. His stomach, to be sure, churned and heaved, but, unlike his previous bouts of malaise, this time he also found that he was sweating profusely, and his throat was so sore that he could barely swallow. He had alternating bouts of chills and fever, and a foul taste in his mouth.

The surly teamster dropped him off at the main gates of Mal Zeth, idly tossed his dagger at his feet and then squinted at his former passenger. "You don't look so good," he observed. "You ought to go see a physician or something."

Balsca made an indelicate sound. "People die in the hands of physicians," he said, "or if they do manage to get well, they go away with empty purses."

"Suit yourself." The teamster shrugged and drove his wagon into the city without looking back.

Balsca directed a number of muttered curses after him, bent, picked up his knife, and walked into Mal Zeth. He wandered about for a time, trying to get his bearings, then finally accosted a man in a sea coat.

"Excuse me, mate," he said, his voice raspy as a result of his sore throat, "but where's a place where a man can get a good cup of grog at a reasonable price?"

"Try the Red Dog Tavern," the sailor replied. "It's two streets over on the corner."

"Thanks, mate," Balsca said.

"You don't look like you're feeling too good."

"A little touch of a cold, I think." Balsca flashed him a toothless grin. "Nothing that a few cups of grog won't fix."

"That's the honest truth." The sailor laughed his agreement. "It's the finest medicine in the world."

The Red Dog Tavern was a dark grogshop that faintly resembled the forecastle of a ship. It had a low, beamed ceiling of dark wood and portholes instead of windows. The proprietor was a bluff, red-faced man with tattoos on both arms and an exaggerated touch of salt water in his speech. His 'Ahoys' and 'Mateys' began to get on Balsca's nerves after a while, but after three cups of grog, he didn't mind so much. His sore throat eased, his stomach settled down, and the trembling in his hands ceased. He still, however, had a splitting headache. He had two more cups of grog and then fell asleep with his head cradled on his crossed arms.

"Ahoy, mate. Closing time," the Red Dog's proprietor said some time later, shaking his shoulder.

Balsca sat up, blinking. "Must have dropped off for a few minutes," he mumbled hoarsely.

"More like a few hours, matey." The man frowned, then laid his hand on Balsca's forehead. "You're burning up, matey," he said. "You'd better get you to bed."

"Where's a good place to get a cheap room?" Balsca asked, rising unsteadily. His throat hurt worse now than it had before, and his stomach was in knots again.

"Try the third door up the street. Tell them that I sent you."

Balsca nodded, bought a bottle to take with him and surreptitiously filched a rope-scarred marlinespike from the rack beside the door on his way out. "Good tavern," he croaked to the proprietor as he left. "I like the way you've got it fixed up."

The tattooed man nodded proudly. "My own idea," he said. "I thought to myself that a seafaring man might like a homelike sort of place to do his drinking in—even when he's this far from deep water. Come back again."

"I'll do that," Balsca promised.

It took him about a half an hour to find a solitary passerby hurrying home with his head down and his hands jammed into his tunic pockets. Balsca stalked him for a block or so, his rope-soled shoes making no sound on the cobblestones. Then, as the passerby went by the dark mouth of an alleyway, Balsca stepped up behind him and rapped him smartly across the base of the skull with his marlinespike. The man dropped like a poleaxed ox. Balsca had been in enough shipboard fights and tavern brawls to know exactly where and how hard to hit his man. He rolled the fellow over, hit him alongside the head once again just to be on the safe side, and then methodically began to go through the unconscious man's pockets. He found several coins and a stout knife. He put the coins in his pocket, tucked the knife under his broad leather belt, and pulled his victim into the alley out of the light. Then he went on down the street, whistling an old sea song.

He felt much worse the following day. His head throbbed, and his throat was so swollen that he could barely talk. His fever, he was sure, was higher, and his nose ran constantly. It took three pulls on his bottle to quiet his stomach. He knew that he should go out and get something to eat, but the thought of food sickened him. He took another long drink from his bottle, lay back on the dirty bed in the room he had rented, and fell back into a fitful doze.

When he awoke again, it was dark outside, and he was shivering violently. He finished his bottle without gaining any particular relief, then shakily pulled on his clothing, which he absently noted exuded a rank odor, and stumbled down to the street and three doors up to the inviting entrance to the Red Dog.

"By the Gods, matey," the tattooed man said, "ye look positively awful."

"Grog," Balsca croaked. "Grog."

It took nine cups of grog to stem the terrible shaking which had seized him.

Balsca was not counting.

When his money ran out, he staggered into the street and beat a man to death with his marlinespike for six pennies. He lurched on, encountered a fat merchant, and knifed him for his purse. The purse even had some gold in it. He reeled back to the Red Dog and drank until closing time.

"Have a care, matey," the proprietor cautioned him as he thrust him out the door. "There be murdering footpads about, or so I've been told—and the police are as thick as fleas on a mangy dog in the streets and alleys in the neighborhood."

Balsca took the jug of grog he had bought back to his shabby room and drank himself into unconsciousness.

He was delirious the following morning and he raved for hours, alternating between drinking from his jug of grog and vomiting on his bed.

It took him until sunset to die. His last words were, "Mother, help me."

When they found him, some days later, he was arched rigidly backward, and his face was fixed in a hideous grin.

Three days later, a pair of wayfarers found the body of a bearded teamster lying in a ditch beside his wagon on the road to Mal Gemila. His body was arched stiffly backward, and his face was locked in a grotesque semblance of a grin. The wayfarers concluded that he had no further need of his team and wagon, and so they stole it. As an afterthought, they also stole his clothes and covered the body with dead leaves. Then they turned the wagon around and rode on back to Mal Zeth.

Perhaps a week after Balsca's largely unnoticed death, a man in a tarred sea coat came staggering into a run-down street in broad daylight. He was raving and clutching at his throat. He lurched along the cobblestone street for perhaps a hundred feet before he collapsed and died. The dreadful grin fixed on his foam-flecked lips gave several onlookers nightmares that night.

The tatooed proprietor of the Red Dog Tavern was found dead in his establishment the following morning. He lay amidst the wreckage of the several tables and chairs he had smashed during his final delirium. His face was twisted into a stiff, hideous grin.

During the course of that day, a dozen more men in that part of the city, all regular patrons of the Red Dog Tavern, also died.

The next day, three dozen more succumbed. The authorities began to take note of the matter.

But by then it was too late. The curious intermingling of classes characteristic of a great city made the confining of the infection to any one district impossible. Servants who lived in that shabby part of town carried the disease into the houses of the rich and powerful. Workmen carried it to construction sites, and their fellow workmen carried it home to other parts of the city. Customers gave it to merchants, who in turn gave it to other customers. The most casual contact was usually sufficient to cause infection.

The dead had at first been numbered in the dozens, but by the end of the week hundreds had fallen ill. The houses of the sick were boarded up despite the weak cries of the inhabitants from within. Grim carts rumbled through the streets, and workmen with camphor-soaked cloths about their lower faces picked up the dead with long hooks. The bodies were stacked in the carts like logs of wood, conveyed to cemeteries, and buried without rites in vast common graves. The streets of Mal Zeth became deserted as the frightened citizens barricaded themselves inside their houses.

There was some concern inside the palace, naturally, but the palace, walled as it was, was remote from the rest of the city. As a further precaution, however, the Emperor ordered that no one be allowed in or out of the compound. Among those locked inside were several hundred workmen who had been hired by Baron Vasca, the Chief of the Bureau of Commerce, to begin the renovations of the bureau offices.

It was about noon on the day after the locking of the palace gates that Garion, Polgara, and Belgarath were summoned to an audience with Zakath. They entered his study to find him gaunt and hollow-eyed, poring over a map of the imperial city. "Come in. Come in," he said when they arrived. They entered and sat down in the chairs he indicated with an absent wave of his hand.

"You look tired," Polgara noted.

"I haven't slept for the past four days," Zakath admitted.

He looked wearily at Belgarath. "You say that you're seven thousand years old."

"Approximately, yes."

"You've lived through pestilence before?"

"Several times."

"How long does it usually last?"

"It depends on which disease it is. Some of then run their course in a few months. Others persist until everybody in the region is dead. Pol would know more about that than I would. She's the one with all the medical experience."

"Lady Polgara?" the Emperor appealed to her.

"I'll need to know the symptoms before I can identify the disease," she replied.

Zakath burrowed through the litter of documents on the table in front of him. "Here it is." He picked up a scrap of parchment and read from it. "High fever, nausea, vomiting. Chills, profuse sweating, sore throat, and headache. Finally delirium, followed shortly by death."

She looked at him gravely. "That doesn't sound too good," she said. "Is there anything peculiar about the bodies after they've died?"

"They all have an awful grin on their faces," he told her, consulting his parchment.

She shook her head. "I was afraid of that."

"What is it?"

"A form of plague."

"*Plague?*" His face had gone suddenly pale. "I thought there were swellings on the body with that. This doesn't mention that." He held up the scrap of parchment.

"There are several different varieties of the disease, Zakath. The most common involves the swellings you mentioned. Another attacks the lungs. The one you have here is quite rare, and dreadfully virulent."

"Can it be cured?"

"Not cured, no. Some people manage to survive it, but that's probably the result of mild cases or their body's natural

208

resistance to disease. Some people seem to be immune. They don't catch it no matter how many times they've been exposed."

"What can I do?"

She gave him a steady look. "You won't like this," she told him.

"I like the plague even less."

"Seal up Mal Zeth. Seal the city in the same way that you've sealed the palace."

"You can't be serious!"

"Deadly serious. You have to keep the infection confined to Mal Zeth, and the only way to do that is to prevent people from carrying the disease out of the city to other places." Her face was bleak. "And when I say to seal the city, Zakath, I mean totally. *Nobody* leaves."

"I've got an empire to run, Polgara. I can't seal myself up here and just let it run itself. I have to get messengers in and send orders out."

"Then, inevitably, you will rule an empire of the dead. The symptoms of the disease don't begin to show up until a week or two after the initial infection, but during the last several days of that period, the carrier is already dreadfully contagious. You can catch it from somebody who looks and feels perfectly healthy. If you send out messengers, sooner or later one of them will be infected, and the disease will spread throughout all of Mallorea."

His shoulders slumped in defeat as the full horror of what she was describing struck him. "How many?" he asked quietly.

"I don't quite understand the question."

"How many will die here in Mal Zeth, Polgara?"

She considered it. "Half," she replied, "if you're lucky."

"*Half?*" he gasped. "Polgara, this is the largest city in the world. You're talking about the greatest disaster in the history of mankind."

209

"I know—and that's only if you're lucky. The death rate could go as high as four-fifths of the population."

He sank his face into his trembling hands. "Is there anything at all that can be done?" he asked in a muffled voice.

"You must burn the dead," she told him. "The best way is just to burn their houses without removing them. That reduces the spread of the disease."

"You'd better have the streets patrolled, too," Belgarath added grimly. "There's bound to be looting, and the looters are going to catch the disease. Send out archers with orders to shoot looters on sight. Then their bodies should be pushed back into the infected houses with long poles and burned along with the bodies already in the houses."

"You're talking about the destruction of Mal Zeth!" Zakath protested violently, starting to his feet.

"No," Polgara disagreed. "We're talking about saving as many of your citizens as possible. You have to steel your heart about this, Zakath. You may eventually have to drive all the heathly citizens out into the fields, surround them with guards to keep them from getting away, and then burn Mal Zeth to the ground."

"That's unthinkable!"

"Perhaps you ought to start thinking about it," she told him. "The alternative could be much, much worse."

CHAPTER TWELVE

"Silk," Garion said urgently, "you've got to stop it."

"I'm sorry, Garion," the little man replied, looking cautiously around the moonlit atrium for hidden spies, "but it's already in motion. Sadi's bandits are inside the palace grounds and they're taking their orders from Vasca. Vasca's so brave now that he's almost ready to confront Zakath himself. General Bregar of the Bureau of Military Procurement knows that something's afoot, so he's surrounded himself with troops. The King of Pallia, the Prince Regent of Delchin, and the old King of Voresebo have armed every one of their retainers. The palace is sealed, and nobody can bring in any outside

211

help—not even Zakath himself. The way things stand right now, one word could set it off."

Garion started to swear, walking around the shadowy atrium and kicking at the short-cropped turf.

"You *did* tell us to go ahead," Silk reminded him.

"Silk, we can't even get out of the palace right now—much less the city. We've stirred up a fight, and now we're going to be caught right in the middle of it."

Silk nodded glumly. "I know," he said.

"I'll have to go to Zakath," Garion said. "Tell him the whole story. He can have his imperial guards disarm everybody."

"If you thought it was hard to come up with a way to get out of the palace, start thinking about how we're going to get out of the imperial dungeon. Zakath's been polite so far, but I don't think his patience—or his hospitality—would extend to this."

Garion grunted.

"I'm afraid that we've outsmarted ourselves," Silk said. He scratched at his head. "I do that sometimes," he added.

"Can you think of *any* way to head it off?"

"I'm afraid not. The whole situation is just too inflammable. Maybe we'd better tell Belgarath."

Garion winced. "He won't be happy."

"He'll be a lot less happy if we don't tell him."

Garion sighed. "I suppose you're right. All right, let's go get it over with."

It took quite some time to locate Belgarath. They finally found him standing at a window in a room high up in the east wing. The window looked out over the palace wall. Beyond that wall fires ranged unchecked in the stricken city. Sheets of sooty flame belched from whole blocks of houses, and a pall of thick smoke blotted out the starry sky. "It's getting out of hand," the old man said. "They should be pulling down houses to make firebreaks, but I think the soldiers are afraid to leave their barracks." He swore. "I hate fires," he said.

"Something's sort of come up," Silk said cautiously, looking around to see if he could locate the spy holes in the walls of the room.

"What is it?"

"Oh, nothing all that much," Silk replied with exaggerated casualness. "We just thought that we'd bring it to your attention, is all." His fingers, however, were twitching and flickering. Even as he spoke quite calmly, improvising some minor problem with the horses for the edification of the spies they all knew were watching and listening, his dancing fingers laid out the entire situation for the old man.

"You *what?*" Belgarath exclaimed, then covered the outburst with a cough.

—*You told us to devise a diversion, Grandfather*— Garion's hands said as Silk continued to ramble on about the horses.

—*A diversion, yes*— Belgarath's fingers replied, —*but not pitched battles inside the palace. What were you thinking of?*—

—*It was the best we could come up with*— Garion replied lamely.

"Let me think about this for a minute," the old man said aloud. He paced back and forth for a while, his hands clasped behind his back and his face furrowed with concentration. "Let's go talk with Durnik," he said finally. "He's more or less in charge of the horses, so we'll need his advice." Just before he turned to lead them from the room, however, his fingers flickered one last time. —*Try not to walk too softly on the way downstairs*— he told them. —*I need to give you some instructions, and wiggling our fingers takes too long*—

As they left the room, Garion and Silk scuffed their feet and brought the heels of their boots down hard on the marble floor to cover Belgarath's whispering voice.

"All right," the old man breathed, scarcely moving his lips as they moved along the corridor toward the stairs leading down. "The situation isn't really irretrievable. Since we can't stop this little brawl you've arranged anyway, let it go ahead and happen. We *will* need the horses, though, so, Garion, I

213

want you to go to Zakath and tell him that we'd like to isolate our mounts from the rest of the stables. Tell him that it's to avoid having them catch the plague."

"Can horses catch the plague?" Garion whispered in some surprise.

"How should I know? But if *I* don't, you can be sure that Zakath won't either. Silk, you sort of ease around and let everybody know—quietly—that we're just about to leave and to get ready without being too obvious about it."

"Leave?" Garion's whisper was startled. "Grandfather, do you know a way to get out of the palace—and the city?"

"No, but I know someone who does. Get to Zakath with your request about the horses as quickly as you can. He's got his mind on so many other things right now that he probably won't give you any argument about it." He looked at Silk. "Can you give me any kind of idea as to when your little explosion is going to take place?"

"Not really," Silk whispered back, still scuffing his feet on the stairs as they went down. "It could happen at any minute, I suppose."

Belgarath shook his head in disgust. "I think you need to go back to school," he breathed irritably. "*How* to do something is important, yes, but *when* is sometimes even more important."

"I'll try to remember that."

"Do. We'd all better hurry, then. We want to be ready when this unscheduled little eruption takes place."

There were a dozen high-ranking officers with Zakath when Garion was admitted to the large, red-draped room where the Emperor was conferring with his men. "I'll be with you in a bit, Garion," the haggard-looking man said. Then he turned back to his generals. "We *have* to get orders to the troops," he told them. "I need a volunteer to go out into the city."

The generals looked at each other, scuffing their feet on the thick blue carpet.

"Am I going to have to order someone to go?" Zakath demanded in exasperation.

"Uh—excuse me," Garion interjected mildly, "but why does anybody have to go at all?"

"Because the troops are all sitting on their hands in their barracks while Mal Zeth burns," Zakath snapped. "They have to start tearing down houses to make fire breaks, or we'll lose the whole city. Someone has to order them out."

"Have you got troops posted outside the palace walls?" Garion asked.

"Yes. They have orders to keep the populace away."

"Why not just shout at them from the top of the wall?" Garion suggested. "Tell one of them to go get a colonel or somebody, then yell your orders down to him. Tell him to put the troops to work. Nobody can catch the plague from a hundred yards away—I don't think."

Zakath stared at him and then suddenly began to laugh ruefully. "Why didn't I think of that?" he asked.

"Probably because you weren't raised on a farm," Garion replied. "If you're plowing a different field from the man you want to talk to, you shout back and forth. Otherwise, you do an awful lot of unnecessary walking."

"All right," Zakath said briskly, looking at his generals, "which one of you has the biggest mouth?"

A red-faced officer with a big paunch and snowy white hair grinned suddenly. "In my youth, I could be heard all the way across a parade ground, your Majesty," he said.

"Good. Go see if you can still do it. Get hold of some colonel with a glimmer of intelligence. Tell him to abandon any district that's already burning and to tear down enough houses around the perimeter to keep the fire from spreading. Tell him that there's a generalcy in it for him if he saves at least half of Mal Zeth."

"Provided that he doesn't get the plague and die," one of the other generals muttered.

"That's what soldiers get paid for, gentlemen—taking

215

risks. When the trumpet blows, you're supposed to attack, and I'm blowing the trumpet—right now."

"Yes, your Majesty," they all replied in unison, turned smartly, and marched out.

"That was a clever idea, Garion," Zakath said gratefully. "Thank you." He sprawled wearily in a chair.

"Just common sense." Garion shrugged, also sitting down.

"Kings and Emperors aren't supposed to have common sense. It's too common."

"You're going to have to get some sleep, Zakath," Garion told him seriously. "You look like a man on his last legs."

"Gods," Zakath replied, "I'd give half of Karanda right now for a few hours' sleep—of course, I don't *have* half of Karanda any more."

"Go to bed, then."

"I can't. There's too much to do."

"How much can you do if you collapse from exhaustion? Your generals can take care of things until you wake up. That's what generals are for, isn't it?"

"Maybe." Zakath slumped lower in his chair. He looked across at Garion. "Was there something on your mind?" he asked. "I'm sure this isn't just a social visit."

"Well," Garion said, trying to make it sound only incidental, "Durnik's worried about our horses," he said. "We've talked with Aunt Pol—Lady Polgara—and she's not really sure whether horses can catch plague or not. Durnik wanted me to ask you if it would be all right if we took our animals out of the main stables and picketed them someplace near the east wing where he can keep an eye on them."

"Horses?" Zakath said incredulously. "He's worried about horses at a time like this?"

"You sort of have to understand Durnik," Garion replied. "He's a man who takes his responsibilities very seriously. He looks on it as a duty, and I think we can both appreciate that."

Zakath laughed a tried laugh. "The legendary Sendarian virtues," he said, "duty, rectitude and practicality." He

216

shrugged. "Why not?" he said. "If it makes Goodman Durnik happy, he can stable your horses in the corridors of the east wing if he wants."

"Oh, I don't think he'd want to do that," Garion replied after a moment's thought. "One of the Sendarian virtues you neglected to mention was propriety. Horses don't belong inside the house. Besides," he added, "the marble floors might bruise their hooves."

Zakath smiled weakly. "You're a delight, Garion," he said. "Sometimes you're so serious about the littlest things."

"Big things are made up of little things, Zakath," Garion replied sententiously. He looked at the exhausted man across the table, feeling a peculiar regret at being forced to deceive somebody he genuinely liked. "Are you going to be all right?" he asked.

"I'll survive, I expect," Zakath said. "You see, Garion, one of the big secrets about this world is that the people who desperately cling to life are usually the ones who die. Since I don't really care one way or the other, I'll probably live to be a hundred."

"I wouldn't base any plans on that kind of superstition," Garion told him. Then a thought came to him. "Would it upset you if we locked the doors of the east wing from the inside until this all blows over?" he asked. "I'm not particularly timid about getting sick myself, but I'm sort of concerned about Ce'Nedra and Liselle and Eriond. None of them are really terribly robust, and Aunt Pol said that stamina was one of the things that help people survive the plague."

Zakath nodded. "That's a reasonable request," he agreed, "and really a very good idea. Let's protect the ladies and the boy, if at all possible."

Garion stood up. "You've got to get some sleep," he said.

"I don't think I *can* sleep. There are so many things on my mind just now."

"I'll have someone send Andel to you," Garion suggested. "If she's half as good as Aunt Pol thinks she is, she should be able to give you something that would put a regiment to sleep." He looked at the exhausted man he cautiously considered to be his friend. "I won't be seeing you for a while," he said. "Good luck, and try to take care of yourself, all right?"

"I'll try, Garion. I'll try."

Gravely they shook hands, and Garion turned and quietly left the room.

They were busy for the next several hours. Despite Garion's subterfuges, Brador's secret police dogged their every step. Durnik and Toth and Eriond went to the stables and came back with the horses, trailed closely by the ubiquitous policemen.

"What's holding things up?" Belgarath demanded when they had all gathered once again in the large room at the top of the stairs with its dais and the thronelike chair at one end.

"I'm not sure," Silk replied carefully, looking around. "It's just a matter of time, though."

Then, out on the palace grounds beyond the bolted doors of the east wing, there was the sound of shouting and the thud of running feet, followed by the ring of steel on steel.

"Something seems to be happening," Velvet said clinically.

"It's about time," Belgarath grunted.

"Be nice, Ancient One."

Within their locked-off building there also came the rapid staccato sound of running. The doors leading out into the rest of the palace and to the grounds began to bang open and then slam shut.

"Are they all leaving, Pol?" Belgarath asked.

Her eyes grew distant for a moment. "Yes, father," she said.

The running and slamming continued for several minutes.

"My," Sadi said mildly, "weren't there a lot of them?"

"Will you three stop congratulating yourselves and go bolt those doors again?" Belgarath said.

Silk grinned and slipped out the door. He came back a few minutes later, frowning. "We've got a bit of a problem," he said, "The guards at the main door seem to have a strong sense of duty. They haven't left their posts."

"Great diversion, Silk," Belgarath said sarcastically.

"Toth and I can deal with them," Durnik said confidently. He went to the box beside the fireplace and picked up a stout chunk of oak firewood.

"That might be just a bit direct, dear," Polgara murmured. "I'm sure you don't want to kill them, and sooner or later they'll wake up and run straight to Zakath. I think we'll need to come up with something a little more sneaky."

"I don't care much for that word, Pol," he said stiffly.

"Would 'diplomatic' put a better light on it?"

He thought about it. "No," he said, "not really. It means the same thing, doesn't it?"

"Well," she conceded, "yes, probably. But it sounds nicer, doesn't it?"

"Polgara," the smith said firmly. It was the first time Garion had ever heard him use her full name. "I'm not trying to be unreasonable, but how can we face the world if we lie and cheat and sneak every time we go around a corner? I mean— really, Pol."

She looked at him. "Oh, my Durnik," she said, "I love you." She threw her arms about her husband's neck with a sort of girlish exuberance. "You're too good for this world, do you know that?"

"Well," he said, slightly abashed by a show of affection that he obviously believed should be kept very private, "it's a matter of decency, isn't it?"

"Of course, Durnik," she agreed in an oddly submissive tone. "Whatever you say."

"What are we going to do about the guards?" Garion asked.

"I can manage them, dear." Polgara smiled. "I can arrange it so that they won't see or hear a thing. We'll be able to leave with no one the wiser—assuming that father knows what he's talking about."

219

Belgarath looked at her, then suddenly winked. "Trust me," he said. "Durnik, bring the horses inside."

"Inside?" the smith looked startled.

Belgarath nodded. "We have to take them down into the cellar."

"I didn't know that this wing had a cellar," Silk said.

"Neither does Zakath," Belgarath smirked. "Or Brador."

"Garion," Ce'Nedra said sharply.

Garion turned to see a shimmering in the center of the room. Then the blindfolded form of Cyradis appeared.

"Make haste," she urged them. "Ye must reach Ashaba 'ere the week is out."

"Ashaba?" Silk exclaimed. "We have to go to Calida. A man named Mengha is raising demons there."

"That is of no moment, Prince Kheldar. The demons are thy least concern. Know, however, that the one called Mengha also journeys toward Ashaba. He will be caught up in one of the tasks which must be completed 'ere the meeting of the Child of Light and the Child of Dark can come to pass in the Place Which Is No More." She turned her blindfolded face toward Garion. "The time to complete this task is at hand, Belgarion of Riva, and shouldst those of thy companions upon whom the task hath been laid fail in its accomplishment, the world is lost. I pray thee, therefore, go to Ashaba." And then she vanished.

There was a long silence as they all stared at the spot where she had stood.

"That's it, then," Belgarath said flatly. "We go to Ashaba."

"*If* we can get out of the palace," Sadi murmured.

"We'll get out. Leave that to me."

"Of course, Ancient One."

The old man led them out into the hallway, down the stairs, and along the main corridor toward the stout door leading to the rest of the palace.

"Just a moment, father," Polgara said. She concentrated for a moment, the white lock at her brow glowing. Then Garion felt the surge of her will. "All right," she said. "The guards are asleep now."

The old man continued on down the corridor. "Here we are," he said, stopping before a large tapestry hanging on the marble wall. He reached behind the tapestry, took hold of an age-blackened iron ring, and pulled. There was a squeal of protesting metal and then a solid-sounding clank. "Push on that side," he said, gesturing toward the far end of the tapestry.

Garion went on down a few steps and set his shoulder to the tapestry. There was a metallic shriek as the covered marble slab turned slowly on rusty iron pivots set top and bottom in its precise center.

"Clever," Silk said, peering into the dark, cobweb-choked opening beyond the slab. "Who put it here?"

"A long time ago one of the Emperors of Mallorea was a bit nervous about his position," the old man replied. "He wanted to have a quick way out of the palace in case things started to go wrong. The passageway's been forgotten, so nobody's likely to follow us. Let's go bring out our packs and other belongings. We won't be coming back."

It took about five minutes for them to pile their things in front of the tapestry-covered panel, and by then Durnik, Toth, and Eriond were leading the horses along the marble corridor with a great clatter of hooves.

Garion stepped to the corner and peered around it at the main door. The two guards were standing rigidly, their faces blank and their eyes glassy and staring. Then he walked back to join the others. "Someday you'll have to show me how to do that," he said to Polgara, jerking his thumb back over his shoulder toward the two comatose soldiers.

"It's very simple, Garion," she told him.

"For you, maybe," he said. Then a thought suddenly came to him. "Grandfather," he said with a worried frown, "if this passage of yours comes out in the city, won't we be worse off than we were here in the palace? There's plague out there, you know, and all the gates are locked."

"It doesn't come out inside Mal Zeth," the old man replied. "Or so I've been told."

Out on the palace grounds the sounds of fighting intensified.

"They seem very enthusiastic, don't they?" Sadi murmured in a self-congratulatory way.

"Well, now," a familiar lilting voice came up out of the cellar beyond the panel. "Will ye stand there for hours pattin' yerselves on the backs an' allowin' the night to fly by with nothin' more accomplished at all? We've miles and miles to go, don't y' know? An' we won't get out of Mal Zeth this month unless we make a start, now will we?"

"Let's go," Belgarath said shortly.

The horses were reluctant to enter the dark, musty place behind the marble panel, but Eriond and Horse confidently went through with Garion's big gray, Chretienne, close behind; and the other animals somewhat skittishly followed.

It was not really a cellar, Garion realized. A flight of shallow stairs led down to what could be more properly described as a rough stone passageway. The horses had some difficulty negotiating the stairs, but eventually, following Eriond, Horse, and Chretienne, they reached the bottom.

At the top of the stairs the giant Toth pushed the hidden panel shut again, and the latch made an omniously heavy clank as it closed.

"One moment, father," Polgara said. In the close and musty-smelling darkness, Garion felt the faint surge of her will. "There," she said. "The soldiers are awake again, and they don't even know that we've been here."

At the bottom of the stairs the comic juggler, Feldegast, stood holding a well-shielded lantern. "'Tis a fine night fer a little stroll," he observed. "Shall we be off, then?"

"I hope you know what you're doing," Belgarath said to him.

"How could ye possibly doubt me, old man?" the comedian said with an exaggerated expression of injury. "I'm the very

soul of circumspection, don't y' know." He made a faint gri-
mace. "There's only one teensy-weensy little problem. It
seems that a certain portion of this passageway collapsed in
on itself a while back, so we'll be forced to go through the
steets up above for a triflin' bit of a way."

"Just *how* triflin—trifling?" Belgarath demanded. He
glared at the impudent comedian. "I wish you'd stop that,"
he said irritably. "What possessed you to resurrect a dialect
that died out two thousand years ago?"

"'Tis a part of me charm, Ancient Belgarath. Any man at
all kin throw balls in the air an' catch 'em again, but it's the
way a performer talks that sets the tone of his act."

"You two have met before, I take it?" Polgara said with
one raised eyebrow.

"Yer honored father an' me are old, old friends, me dear
Lady Polgara," Feldegast said with a sweeping bow. "I know
ye all by his description. I must admit, however, that I'm
overcome altogether by yer unearthly beauty."

"This is a rare rogue you've found, father," she said with
a peculiar smile on her face. "I think I could grow to like
him."

"I don't really advise it, Pol. He's a liar and a sneak and
he has uncleanly habits. You're evading the question, Feldegast—if that's what you want to call yourself. How far do we
have to go through the streets?"

"Not far at all, me decrepit old friend—a half a mile perhaps until the roof of the passage is stout enough again to
keep the pavin' stones where they belong instead of on the
top of our heads. Let's press on, then. 'Tis a long, long way
to the north wall of Mal Zeth, an' the night is wearin' on."

"Decrepit?" Belgarath objected mildly.

"Merely me way of puttin' things, Ancient One," Feldegast
apologized. "Be sure that I meant no offense." He turned to
Polgara. "Will ye walk with me, me girl? Ye've got an absolutely ravishin' fragrance about ye that quite takes me breath

away. I'll walk along beside ye, inhalin' and perishin' with sheer delight."

Polgara laughed helplessly and linked her arm with that of the outrageous little man.

"I *like* him," Ce'Nedra murmured to Garion as they followed along through the cobwebby passageway.

"Yer supposed to, me girl," Garion said in a not altogether perfect imitation of the juggler's brogue. "'Tis a part of his charm, don't y' know?"

"Oh, Garion," she laughed, "I love you."

"Yes," he said. "I know."

She gave him an exasperated look and then punched him in the shoulder with her little fist.

"Ouch."

"Did I hurt you?" she asked, taking his arm in sudden concern.

"I think I can stand it, dear," he replied. "We noble heroes can bear all sorts of things."

They followed Feldegast's lantern for a mile or more with the horses clattering along behind them through the cobweb-draped passageway. Occasionally they heard the rumble of the dead-carts bearing their mournful freight through the streets above. Here in the musty darkness, however, there was only the sound of the furtive skittering of an occasional errant mouse and the whisperlike tred of watchful spiders moving cautiously across the vaulted ceiling.

"I hate this," Silk said to no one in particular. "I absolutely hate it."

"That's all right, Kheldar," Velvet replied, taking the little man's hand. "I won't let anything hurt you."

"Thanks awfully," he said, though he did not remove his hand from hers.

"Who's there?" The voice came from somewhere ahead.

"'Tis only me, good Master Yarblek," Feldegast replied. "Me an' a few lost, strayed souls tryin' to find their way on this dark, dark night."

"Do you really enjoy him all that much?" Yarblek said sourly to someone else.

"He's the delight of my life," Vella's voice came through the darkness. "At least with him I don't have to look to my daggers every minute to defend my virtue."

Yarblek sighed gustily. "I had a feeling that you were going to say something like that," he said.

"My lady," Vella said, making an infinitely graceful curtsy to Polgara as the sorceress and the juggler, arm in arm, moved up to the place where a moss-grown rockfall blocked the passageway.

"Vella," Polgara responded in an oddly Nadrak accent. "May your knives always be bright and keen." There was a strange formality in her greeting, and Garion knew that he was hearing an ancient ritual form of address.

"And may you always have the means at hand to defend your person from unwanted attentions," the Nadrak dancing girl responded automatically, completing the ritual.

"What's happening up above?" Belgarath asked the felt-coated Yarblek.

"They're dying," Yarblek answered shortly, "whole streets at a time."

"Have you been avoiding the city?" Silk asked his partner.

Yarblek nodded. "We're camped outside the gates," he said. "We got out just before they chained them shut. Dolmar died, though. When he realized that he had the plague, he got out an old sword and fell on it."

Silk sighed. "He was a good man—a little dishonest, maybe, but a good man all the same."

Yarblek nodded sadly. "At least he died clean," he said. Then he shook his head. "The stairs up to the street are over here," he said, pointing off into the darkness. "It's late enough so that there's nobody much abroad—except for the dead-carts and the few delirious ones stumbling about and looking for a warm gutter to die in." He squared his shoulders. "Let's go," he said. "The quicker we can get through those streets up there, the quicker we can get back underground where it's safe."

"Does the passage go all the way to the city wall?" Garion asked him.

Yarblek nodded. "And a mile or so beyond," he said. "It comes out in an old stone quarry." He looked at Feldegast. "You never did tell me how you found out about it," he said.

"'Tis one of me secrets, good Master Yarblek," the juggler replied. "No matter how honest a man might be, it's always good to know a quick way out of town, don't y' know."

"Makes sense," Silk said.

"You ought to know," Yarblek replied. "Let's get out of here."

They led the horses to a flight of stone stairs reaching up into the darkness beyond the circle of light from Feldegast's lantern and then laboriously hauled the reluctant animals up the stairway, one step at a time. The stairway emerged in a rickety shed with a straw-littered floor. After the last horse had been hauled up, Feldegast carefully lowered the long trap door again and scuffed enough straw over it to conceal it. "'Tis a useful sort of thing," he said, pointing downward toward the hidden passage, "but a secret's no good at all if just anybody kin stumble over it."

Yarblek stood at the door peering out into the narrow alleyway outside.

"Anybody out there?" Silk asked him.

"A few bodies," the Nadrak replied laconically. "For some reason they always seem to want to die in alleys." He drew in a deep breath. "All right, let's go, then."

They moved out into the alley, and Garion kept his eyes averted from the contorted bodies of the plague victims huddled in corners or sprawled in the gutters.

The night air was filled with smoke from the burning city, the reek of burning flesh, and the dreadful smell of decay.

Yarblek also sniffed, then grimaced. "From the odor, I'd say that the dead-carts have missed a few," he said. He led the way to the mouth of the alley and peered out into the street. "It's clear enough," he grunted. "Just a few looters picking over the dead. Come on."

They went out of the alley and moved along a street illuminated by a burning house. Garion saw a furtive movement beside the wall of another house and then made out the shape of a raggedly dressed man crouched over a sprawled body. The man was roughly rifling through the plague victim's clothes. "Won't he catch it?" he asked Yarblek, pointing at the looter.

"Probably." Yarblek shrugged. "I don't think the world's going to miss him very much if he does, though."

They rounded a corner and entered a street where fully half the houses were on fire. A dead-cart had stopped before one of the burning houses, and two rough-looking men were tossing bodies into the fire with casual brutality.

"Stay back!" one of the men shouted to them. "There's plague here!"

"There's plague everywhere in this mournful city, don't y' know," Feldegast replied. "But we thank ye fer yer warnin' anyway. We'll just go on by on the other side of the street, if ye don't mind." He looked curiously at the pair. "How is it that yer not afraid of the contagion yerselves?" he asked.

"We've already had it," one replied with a short laugh. "I've never been so sick in my life, but at least I didn't die from it—and they say you can only catch it once."

"'Tis a fortunate man y' are, then," Feldegast congratulated him.

They moved on past the rough pair and on down to the next corner.

"We go this way," Feldegast told them.

"How much farther is it?" Belgarath asked him.

"Not far, an' then we'll be back underground where it's safe."

"*You* might feel safe underground," Silk said sourly, "but *I* certainly don't."

Halfway along the street Garion saw a sudden movement in one of the deeply inset doorways, and then he heard a feeble wail. He peered at the doorway. Then, one street over, a burning house fell in on itself, shooting flame and sparks high into the air. By that fitful light he was able to see what was in the shadows. The crumpled figure of a woman lay huddled in the doorway, and seated beside the body was a crying child, not much more than a year old. His stomach twisted as he started at the horror before his eyes.

Then, with a low cry, Ce'Nedra darted toward the child with her arms extended.

"Ce'Nedra!" he shouted, trying to shake his hand free of Chretienne's reins. "No!"

But before he could move in pursuit, Vella was already there. She caught Ce'Nedra by the shoulder and spun her around roughly. "Ce'Nedra!" she snapped. "Stay away!"

"Let me go!" Ce'Nedra almost screamed. "Can't you see that it's a baby?" She struggled to free herself.

Very coolly, Vella measured the little Queen, then slapped her sharply across the face. So far as Garion knew, it was the first time anyone had ever hit Ce'Nedra. "The baby's dead, Ce'Nedra," Vella told her with brutal directness, "and if you go near it, you'll die, too." She began to drag her captive back toward the others. Ce'Nedra stared back over her shoulder at the sickly wailing child, her hand outstretched toward it.

Then Velvet moved to her side, put an arm about her shoulders, and gently turned her so that she could no longer see the child. "Ce'Nedra," she said, "you must think first of your own baby. Would you want to carry this dreadful disease to him?"

Ce'Nedra stared at her.

"Or do you want to die before you ever see him again?"

With a sudden wail, Ce'Nedra fell into Velvet's arms, sobbing bitterly.

"I hope she won't hold any grudges," Vella murmured.

"You're very quick, Vella," Polgara said, "and you think very fast when you have to."

Vella shrugged. "I've found that a smart slap across the mouth is the best cure for hysterics."

Polgara nodded. "It usually works," she agreed approvingly.

They went on down the street until Feldegast led them into another smelly alley. He fumbled with the latch to the wide door of a boarded-up warehouse, then swung it open. "Here we are, then," he said, and they all followed him inside. A long ramp led down into a cavernous cellar, where Yarblek and the little juggler moved aside a stack of crates to reveal the opening of another passageway.

They led their horses into the dark opening, and Feldegast remained outside to hide the passage again. When he was satisfied that the opening was no longer visible, he wormed his way through the loosely stacked crates to rejoin them. "An' there we are," he said, brushing his hands together in a self-congratulatory way. "No man at all kin possibly know that we've come this way, don't y' know, so let's be off."

Garion's thoughts were dark as he trudged along the passageway, following Feldegast's winking lantern. He had slipped away from a man for whom he had begun to develop a careful friendship and had left him behind in a plague-stricken and burning city. There was probably very little that he could have done to aid Zakath, but his desertion of the man did not make him feel very proud. He knew, however, that he had no real choice. Cyradis had been too adamant in her instructions. Compelled by necessity, he turned his back on Mal Zeth and resolutely set his face toward Ashaba.

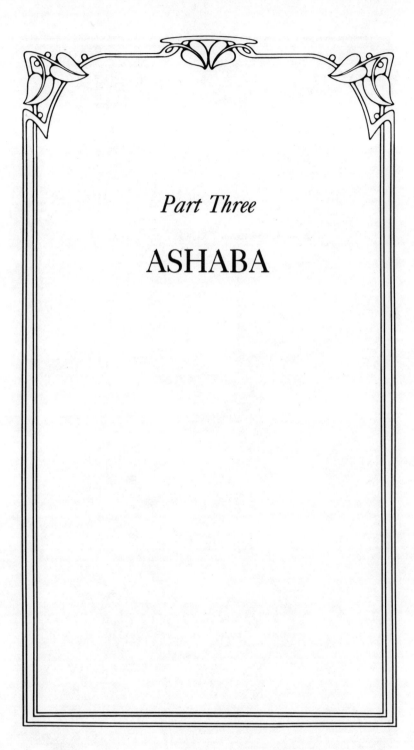

Part Three

ASHABA

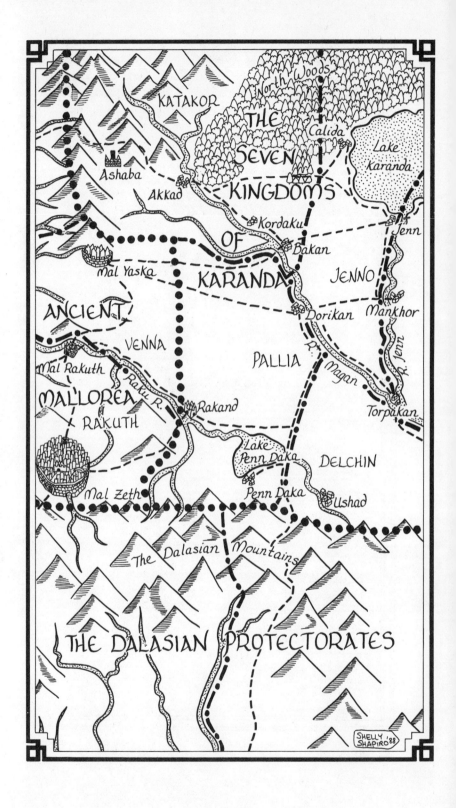

CHAPTER THIRTEEN

The road leading north from Mal Zeth passed through a fair, fertile plain where new-sprouted grain covered the damp soil like a low, bright green mist and the warm spring air was filled with the urgent scent of growth. In many ways, the landscape resembled the verdant plains of Arendia or the tidy fields of Sendaria. There were villages, of course, with white buildings, thatched roofs, and dogs that came out to stand at the roadside and bark. The spring sky was an intense blue dotted with puffy white clouds grazing like sheep in their azure pastures.

The road was a dusty brown ribbon laid straight where the

surrounding green fields were flat, and folded and curved where the land rose in gentle, rounded hills.

They rode out that morning in glistening sunshine with the sound of the bells fastened about the necks of Yarblek's mules providing a tinkling accompaniment to the morning song of flights of birds caroling to greet the sun. Behind them there rose a great column of dense black smoke, marking the huge valley where Mal Zeth lay burning.

Garion could not bring himself to look back as they rode away.

There were others on the road as well, for Garion and his friends were not the only ones fleeing the plague-stricken city. Singly or in small groups, wary travelers moved north, fearfully avoiding any contact with each other, leaving the road and angling far out into the fields whenever they overtook other refugees, and returning to the brown, dusty ribbon only when they were safely past. Each solitary traveler or each group thus rode in cautious isolation, putting as much empty air about itself as possible.

The lanes branching off from the road and leading across the bright green fields were all blocked with barricades of fresh-cut brush, and bleak-faced peasants stood guard at those barricades, awkwardly handling staffs and heavy, graceless crossbows and shouting warnings at any and all who passed to stay away.

"Peasants," Yarblek said sourly as the caravan plodded past one such barricade. "They're the same the world over. They're glad to see you when you've got something they want, but they spend all the rest of their time trying to chase you away. Do you think they actually believe that anybody would really *want* to go into their stinking little villages?" Irritably he crammed his fur cap down lower over his ears.

"They're afraid," Polgara told him. "They know that their village isn't very luxurious, but it's all they have, and they want to keep if safe."

"Do those barricades and threats really do any good?" he asked. "To keep out the plague, I mean?"

"Some," she said, "if they put them up early enough."

Yarblek grunted, then looked over at Silk. "Are you open to a suggestion?" he asked.

"Depends," Silk replied. The little man had returned to his customary travel clothing—dark, unadorned, and nondescript.

"Between the plague and the demons, the climate here is starting to turn unpleasant. What say we liquidate all our holdings here in Mallorea and sit tight until things settle down?"

"You're not thinking, Yarblek," Silk told him. "Turmoil and war are good for business."

Yarblek scowled at him. "Somehow I thought you might look at it that way."

About a half mile ahead, there was another barricade, this one across the main road itself.

"What's this?" Yarblek demanded angrily, reining in.

"I'll go find out," Silk said, thumping his heels against his horse's flanks. On an impulse, Garion followed his friend.

When they were about fifty yards from the barricade, a dozen mud-spattered peasants dressed in smocks made of brown sackcloth rose from behind it with leveled crossbows. "Stop right there!" one of them commanded threateningly. He was a burly fellow with a coarse beard and eyes that looked off in different directions.

"We're just passing through, friend," Silk told him.

"Not without paying toll, you're not."

"*Toll?*" Silk exclaimed. "This is an imperial highway. There's no toll."

"There is now. You city people have cheated and swindled us for generations and now you want to bring your diseases to us. Well, from now on, you're going to pay. How much gold have you got?"

"Keep him talking," Garion muttered, looking around.

235

"Well," Silk said to the wall-eyed peasant in the tone of voice he usually saved for serious negotiations, "why don't we talk about that?"

The village stood about a quarter of a mile away, rising dirty and cluttered-looking atop a grassy knoll. Garion concentrated, drawing in his will, then he made a slight gesture in the direction of the village. "Smoke," he muttered, half under his breath.

Silk was still haggling with the armed peasants, taking up as much time as he could.

"Uh—excuse me." Garion interrupted mildly, "but is that something burning over there?" He pointed.

The peasants turned to stare in horror at the column of dense smoke rising from their village. With startled cries, most of them threw down their crossbows and ran out across the fields in the direction of the apparent catastrophe. The wall-eyed man ran after them, shouting at them to return to their posts. Then he ran back, waving his crossbow threateningly. A look of anguish crossed his face as he hopped about in an agony of indecision, torn between his desire for money that could be extorted from these travelers and the horrid vision of a fire raging unchecked through his house and outbuildings. Finally, no longer able to stand it, he also threw down his weapon and ran after his neighbors.

"Did you really set their village on fire?" Silk sounded a little shocked.

"Of course not," Garion said.

"Where's the smoke coming from then?"

"Lots of places." Garion winked. "Out of the thatch on their roofs, up from between the stones in the streets, boiling up out of their cellars and granaries—lots of places. But it's only smoke." He swung down from Chretienne's back and gathered up the discarded crossbows. He lined them up, nose down, in a neat row along the brushy barricade. "How long does it take to restring a crossbow?" he asked.

"Hours." Silk suddenly grinned. "Two men to bend the

limbs with a windlass and another two to hook the cable in place."

"That's what I thought," Garion agreed. He drew his old belt knife and went down the line of weapons, cutting each twisted rope cable. Each bow responded with a heavy twang. "Shall we go, then?" he asked.

"What about this?" Silk pointed at the brushy barricade.

Garion shrugged. "I think we can ride around it."

"What were they trying to do?" Durnik asked when they returned.

"An enterprising group of local peasants decided that the highway needed a tollgate about there." Silk shrugged. "They didn't really have the temperament for business affairs, though. At the first little distraction, they ran off and left the shop untended."

They rode on past the now-deserted barricade with Yarblek's laden mules plodding along behind them, their bells clanging mournfully.

"I think we're going to have to leave you soon," Belgarath said to the fur-capped Nadrak. "We have to get to Ashaba within the week, and your mules are holding us back."

Yarblek nodded. "Nobody ever accused a pack mule of being fast on his feet," he agreed. "I'll be turning toward the west before long anyway. You can go into Karanda if you want to, but I want to get to the coast as quickly as possible."

"Garion," Polgara said. She looked meaningfully at the column of smoke rising from the village behind them.

"Oh," he replied. "I guess I forgot." He raised his hand, trying to make it look impressive. "Enough," he said, releasing his will. The smoke thinned at its base, and the column continued to rise as a cloud, cut off from its source.

"Don't overdramatize, dear," Polgara advised. "It's ostentatious."

"You do it all the time," he accused.

"Yes, dear, but I know how."

It was perhaps noon when they rode up a long hill, crested

237

it in the bright sunshine, and found themselves suddenly surrounded by mailed, red-tunicked Mallorean soldiers, who rose
up out of ditches and shallow gullies with evil-looking javelins
in their hands.

"You! Halt!" the officer in charge of the detachment of
soldiers commanded brusquely. He was a short man, shorter
even than Silk, though he strutted about as if he were ten
feet tall.

"Of course, Captain," Yarblek replied, reining in his horse.

"What do we do?" Garion hissed to Silk.

"Let Yarblek handle it," Silk murmured. "He knows what
he's doing."

"Where are you bound?" the officer asked when the rangy
Nadrak had dismounted.

"Mal Dariya," Yarblek answered, "or Mal Camat—wherever I can hire ships to get my goods to Yar Marak."

The captain grunted as if trying to find something wrong
with that. "What's more to the point is where you've come
from." His eyes were narrowed.

"Maga Renn." Yarblek shrugged.

"Not Mal Zeth?" The little captain's eyes grew even harder
and more suspicious.

"I don't do business in Mal Zeth very often, Captain. It
costs too much—all those bribes and fees and permits, you
know."

"I assume that you can prove what you say?" The captain's
tone was belligerent.

"I suppose I could—if there's a need for it."

"There's a need, Nadrak, because, unless you can prove
that you haven't come from Mal Zeth, I'm going to turn you
back." He sounded smug about that.

"Turn back? That's impossible. I have to be in Boktor by
midsummer."

"That's *your* problem, merchant." The little soldier
seemed rather pleased at having upset the larger man.
"There's plague in Mal Zeth, and *I'm* here to make sure that

it doesn't spread." He tapped himself importantly on the chest.

"Plague!" Yarblek's eyes went wide, and his face actually paled. "Torak's teeth! And I almost stopped there!" He suddenly snapped his fingers. "So *that's* why all the villages hereabouts are barricaded."

"Can you prove that you came from Maga Renn?" the captain insisted.

"Well—" Yarblek unbuckled a well-worn saddlebag hanging under his right stirrup and began to rummage around in it. "I've got a permit here issued by the Bureau of Commerce," he said rather dubiously. "It authorizes me to move my goods from Maga Renn to Mal Dariya. If I can't find ships there, I'll have to get another permit to go on to Mal Camat, I guess. Would that satisfy you?"

"Let's see it." The captain held out his hand, snapping his fingers impatiently.

Yarblek handed it over.

"It's a little smeared," the captain accused suspiciously.

"I spilled some beer on it in a tavern in Penn Daka." Yarblek shrugged. "Weak, watery stuff it was. Take my advice, Captain. Don't ever plan to do any serious drinking in Penn Daka. It's a waste of time and money."

"Is drinking all you Nadraks ever think about?"

"It's the climate. There's nothing else to do in Gar og Nadrak in the wintertime."

"Have you got anything else?"

Yarblek pawed through his saddlebag some more. "Here's a bill of sale from a carpet merchant on Yorba Street in Maga Renn—pockmarked fellow with bad teeth. Do you by any chance know him?"

"Why would I know a carpet merchant in Maga Renn? I'm an officer in the imperial army. I don't associate with riffraff. Is the date on this accurate?"

"How should I know? We use a different calendar in Gar og Nadrak. It was about two weeks ago, if that's any help."

The captain thought it over, obviously trying very hard to find some excuse to exert his authority. Finally his expression became faintly disappointed. "All right," he said grudgingly, handing back the documents. "Be on your way. But don't make any side trips, and make sure that none of your people leave your caravan."

"They'd better not leave—not if they want to get paid. Thank you, Captain." Yarblek swung back up into his saddle.

The officer grunted and waved them on.

"Little people should never be given any kind of authority," the Nadrak said sourly when they were out of earshot. "It lies too heavily on their brains."

"*Yarblek!*" Silk objected.

"Present company excepted, of course."

"Oh. That's different, then."

"Ye lie like ye were born to it, good Master Yarblek," Feldegast the juggler said admiringly.

"I've been associating with a certain Drasnian for too long."

"How did you come by the permit and the bill of sale?" Silk asked him.

Yarblek winked and tapped his forehead slyly. "Official types are always overwhelmed by official-looking documents—and the more petty the official, the more he's impressed. I could have proved to that obnoxious little captain back there that we came from any place at all— Melcene, Aduma in the Mountains of Zamad, even Crol Tibu on the coast of Gandahar—except that all you can buy in Crol Tibu are elephants, and I don't have any of those with me, so that might have made even him a little suspicious."

Silk looked around with a broad grin. "Now you see why I went into partnership with him," he said to them all.

"You seem well suited to each other," Velvet agreed.

Belgarath was tugging at one ear. "I think we'll leave you after dark tonight," he said to Yarblek. "I don't want some

240

other officious soldier to stop us and count noses—or decide that we need a military escort."

Yarblek nodded. "Are you going to need anything?"

"Just some food is all." Belgarath glanced back at their laden pack horses plodding along beside the mules. "We've been on the road for quite some time now and we've managed to gather up what we really need and discard what we don't."

"I'll see to it that you've got enough food," Vella promised from where she was riding between Ce'Nedra and Velvet. "Yarblek sometimes forgets that full ale kegs are not the *only* things you need on a journey."

"An' will ye be ridin' north, then?" Feldegast asked Belgarath. The little comic had changed out of his bright-colored clothes and was now dressed in plain brown.

"Unless they've moved it, that's where Ashaba is," Belgarath replied.

"If it be all the same to ye, I'll ride along with ye fer a bit of a ways."

"Oh?"

"There was a little difficulty with the authorities the last time I was in Mal Dariya, an' I'd like to give 'em time t' regain their composure before I go back fer me triumphant return engagement. Authorities tend t' be a stodgy an' unfergivin' lot, don't y' know—always dredgin' up old pranks an' bits of mischief perpetrated in the spirit of fun an' throwin' 'em in yer face."

Belgarath gave him a long, steady look, then shrugged. "Why not?" he said.

Garion looked sharply at the old man. His sudden acquiescence seemed wildly out of character, given his angry protests at the additions of Velvet and Sadi to their party. Garion then looked over at Polgara, but she showed no signs of concern either. A peculiar suspicion began to creep over him.

As evening settled over the plains of Mallorea, they drew off the road to set up their night's encampment in a parklike grove of beech trees. Yarblek's muleteers sat about one campfire, passing an earthenware jug around and becoming increasingly rowdy. At the upper end of the grove, Garion and his friends sat around another fire, eating supper and talking quietly with Yarblek and Vella.

"Be careful when you cross into Venna," Yarblek cautioned his rat-faced partner. "Some of the stories coming out of there are more ominous than the ones coming out of Karanda."

"Oh?"

"It's as if a kind of madness has seized them all. Of course, Grolims were never very sane to begin with."

"Grolims?" Sadi looked up sharply.

"Venna's a Church-controlled state," Silk explained. "All authority there derives from Urvon and his court at Mal Yaska."

"It *used* to," Yarblek corrected. "Nobody seems to know *who's* got the authority now. The Grolims gather in groups to talk. The talk keeps getting louder until they're sceaming at each other, and then they all reach for their knives. I haven't been able to get the straight of it. Even the Temple Guardsmen are taking sides."

"The idea of Grolims cutting each other to pieces is one I can live with," Silk said.

"Truly," Yarblek agreed. "Just try not to get caught in the middle."

Feldegast had been softly strumming his lute and he struck a note so sour that even Garion noticed it.

"That string's out of tune," Durnik advised him.

"I know," the juggler replied. "The peg keeps slippin'."

"Let me see it," Durnik offered. "Maybe I can fix it."

"'Tis too worn, I fear, friend Durnik. 'Tis a grand instrument, but it's old."

"Those are the ones that are worth saving." Durnik took the lute and twisted the loose peg, tentatively testing the pitch of the string with his thumb. Then he took his knife and cut several small slivers of wood. He carefully inserted them around the peg, tapping them into place with the hilt of his knife. Then he twisted the peg, retuning the string. "That should do it," he said. He took up the lute and strummed it a few times. Then, to a slow measure, he picked out an ancient air, the single notes quivering resonantly. He played the air through once, his fingers seeming to grow more confident as he went along. Then he returned to the beginning again, but this time, to Garion's amazement, he accompanied the simple melody with a rippling counterpoint so complex that it seemed impossible that it could come from a single instrument. "It has a nice tone," he observed to Feldegast.

"'Tis a marvel that ye are, master smith. First ye repair me lute, an' then ye turn around an' put me t' shame by playin' it far better than I could ever hope to."

Polgara's eyes were very wide and luminous. "Why haven't you told me about this, Durnik?" she asked.

"Actually, it's been so long that I almost forgot about it." He smiled, his fingers still dancing on the strings and bringing forth that rich-toned cascade of sound. "When I was young, I worked for a time with a lute maker. He was old, and his fingers were stiff, but he needed to hear the tone of the instruments he made, so he taught me how to play them for him."

He looked across the fire at his giant friend, and something seemed to pass between them. Toth nodded, reached inside the rough blanket he wore across one shoulder, and produced a curious-looking set of pipes, a series of hollow reeds, each longer than the one preceding it, all bound tightly together. Quietly, the mute lifted the pipes to his lips as Durnik returned again to the beginning of the air. The sound he produced from his simple pipes had an aching poignancy about it that pierced Garion to the heart, soaring through the intricate complexity of the lute song.

"I'm beginnin' t' feel altogether unnecessary," Feldegast said in wonder. "Me own playin' of lute or pipe be good enough fer taverns an' the like, but I be no virtuoso like these two." He looked at the huge Toth. "How is it possible fer a man so big t' produce so delicate a sound?"

"He's very good," Eriond told him. "He plays for Durnik and me sometimes—when the fish aren't biting."

"Ah, 'tis a grand sound," Feldegast said, "an' far to good t' be wasted." He looked across the fire at Vella. "Would ye be willin' t' give us a bit of a dance, me girl, t' sort of round out the evenin'?"

"Why not?" She laughed with a toss of her head. She rose to her feet and moved to the opposite side of the fire. "Follow this beat," she instructed, raising her rounded arms above her head and snapping her fingers to set the tempo. Feldegast picked up the beat, clapping his hands rhythmically.

Garion had seen Vella dance before—long ago in a forest travern in Gar og Nadrak—so he knew more or less what to expect. He was sure, however, that Eriond certainly—and Ce'Nedra probably—should not watch a performance of such blatant sensuality. Vella's dance began innocuously enough, though, and he began to think that perhaps he had been unduly sensitive the last time he had watched her.

When the sharp staccato of her snapping fingers and Feldegast's clapping increased the tempo, however, and she began to dance with greater abondon, he realized that his first assessment had been correct. Eriond should really not be watching this dance, and Ce'Nedra should be sent away almost immediately. For the life of him, however, he could not think of any way to do it.

When the tempo slowed again and Durnik and Toth returned to a simple restatement of the original air, the Nadrak girl concluded her dance with that proud, aggressive strut that challenged every man about the fire.

To Garion's absolute astonishment, Eriond warmly applauded with no trace of embarrassment showing on his young face. He knew that his own neck was burning and that his breath was coming faster.

Ce'Nedra's reaction was about what he had expected. Her

cheeks were flaming and her eyes were wide. Then she suddenly laughed with delight. "Wonderful!" she exclaimed, and
her eyes were full of mischief as she cast a sidelong glance at
Garion. He coughed nervously.

Feldegast wiped a tear from his eye and blew his nose gustily. Then he rose to his feet. "Ah, me fine, lusty wench,"
he said fulsomely to Vella, hanging a regretful embrace about
her neck and—endangering life and limb just a little in view
of her ever-ready daggers—bussing her noisily on the lips,
"it's destroyed altogether I am that we must part. I'll miss
ye, me girl, an' make no mistake about that. But I make ye
me promise that we'll meet again, an' I'll delight ye with a
few of me naughty little stories, an' ye'll fuddle me brains
with yer wicked brew, an' we'll laugh an' sing together an'
enjoy spring after spring in the sheer delight of each others'
company." Then he slapped her rather familiarly on the bottom and moved quickly out of range before she could find
the hilt of one of her daggers.

"Does she dance for you often, Yarblek?" Silk asked his
partner, his eyes very bright.

"*Too* often," Yarblek replied mournfully, "and every time
she does, I find myself starting to think that her daggers aren't
really all *that* sharp and that a little cut or two wouldn't really
hurt too much."

"Feel free to try at any time, Yarblek," Vella offered, her
hand suggestively on the hilt of one of her daggers. Then she
looked at Ce'Nedra with a broad wink.

"Why do you dance like that?" Ce'Nedra asked, still blushing slightly. "You *know* what it does to every man who
watches."

"That's part of the fun, Ce'Nedra. First you drive them
crazy, and then you hold them off with your daggers. It makes
them absolutely wild. Next time we meet, I'll show you how
it's done." She looked at Garion and laughed a wicked laugh.

Belgarath returned to the fire. He had left at some time
during Vella's dance, though Garion's eyes had been too busy

to notice. "It's dark enough," he told them all. "I think we can leave now without attracting any notice."

They all rose from where they had been sitting.

"You know what to do?" Silk asked his partner.

Yarblek nodded.

"All right. Do whatever you have to to keep me out of the soup."

"Why do you persist in playing around in politics, Silk?"

"Because it gives me access to greater opportunities to steal."

"Oh," Yarblek said. "That's all right then." He extended his hand. "Take care, Silk," he said.

"You, too, Yarblek. Try to keep us solvent if you can, and I'll see you in a year or so."

"If you live."

"There's that, too."

"I enjoyed your dance, Vella," Polgara said, embracing the Nadrak girl.

"I'm honored, Lady," Vella replied a bit shyly. "And we'll meet again, I'm sure."

"I'm certain that we will."

"Are ye sure that ye won't reconsider yer outrageous askin' price, Master Yarblek?" Feldegast asked.

"Talk to *her* about it," Yarblek replied, jerking his head in Vella's direction. "She's the one who set it."

"'Tis a hardhearted woman ye are, me girl," the juggler accused her.

She shrugged. "If you buy something cheap, you don't value it."

"Now that's the truth, surely. I'll see what I kin do t' put me hands on some money, fer make no mistake, me fine wench, I mean t' own ye."

"We'll see," she replied with a slight smile.

They went out of the circle of firelight to their picketed horses—and the juggler's mule—and mounted quietly. The moon had set, and the stars lay like bright jewels across the warm, velvet throat of night as they rode out of Yarblek's camp and moved at a cautious walk toward the north. When the sun rose several hours later, they were miles away, moving north-ward along a well-maintained highway toward Mal Rukuth, the Angarak city lying on the south bank of the Raku River, the stream that marked the southern border of Venna. The morning was warm, the sky was clear, and they made good time.

Once again there were refugees on the road, but unlike yesterday, significant numbers of them were fleeing toward the south.

"Is it possible that the plague has broken out in the north as well?" Sadi asked.

Polgara frowned. "It's possible, I suppose," she told him.

"I think it's more likely that those people are fleeing from Mengha," Belgarath disagreed.

"It's going to get a bit chaotic hereabouts," Silk noted. "If you've got people fleeing in one direction from the plague and people fleeing in the other from the demons, about all they'll be able to do is mill around out here on these plains."

"That could work to our advantage, Kheldar," Velvet pointed out. "Sooner or later, Zakath is going to discover that we left Mal Zeth without saying good-bye and he's likely to send troops out looking for us. A bit of chaos in this region should help to confuse their search, wouldn't you say?"

"You've got a point there," he admitted.

Garion rode on in a half doze, a trick he had learned from Belgarath. Though he had occasionally missed a night's sleep in the past, he had never really gotten used to it. He rode along with his head down, only faintly aware of what was happening around him.

He heard a persistent sound that seemed to nag at the edge of his consciousness. He frowned, his eyes still closed, trying to identify the sound. And then he remembered. It was a faint, despairing wail, and the full horror of the sight of the dying child in the shabby street in Mal Zeth struck him. Try though he might, he could not wrench himself back into wakefulness, and the continuing cry tore at his heart.

Then he felt a large hand on his shoulder, shaking him gently. Struggling, he raised his head to look full into the sad face of the giant Toth.

"Did you hear it, too?" he asked.

Toth nodded, his face filled with sympathy.

"It was only a dream, wasn't it?"

Toth spread his hands, and his look was uncertain.

Garion squared his shoulders and sat up in his saddle, determined not to drift off again.

They rode some distance away from the road and took a cold lunch of bread, cheese, and smoked sausage in the shade of a large elm tree standing quite alone in the middle of a field of oats. There was a small spring surrounded by a mossy rock wall not far away, where they were able to water the horses and fill their water bags.

Belgarath stood looking out over the fields toward a distant village and the barricaded lane which approached it. "How much food do we have with us, Pol?" he asked. "If every village we come to is closed up the way the ones we've passed so far have been, it's going to be difficult to replenish our stores."

"I think we'll be all right, father," she replied. "Vella was very generous."

"I like her." Ce'Nedra smiled. "Even though she does swear all the time."

Polgara returned the smile. "It's the Nadrak way, dear," she said. "When I was in Gar og Nadrak, I had to draw on my memories of the more colorful parts of my father's vocabulary to get by."

"Hallooo!" someone hailed them.

"He's over there." Silk pointed toward the road.

A man who was wearing one of the brown robes that identified him as a Melcene bureaucrat sat looking at them longingly from the back of a bay horse.

"What do you want?" Durnik called to him.

"Can you spare a bit of food?" the Melcene shouted. "I can't get near any of these villages and I haven't eaten in three days. I can pay."

Durnik looked questioningly at Polgara.

She nodded. "We have enough," she said.

"Which way was he coming?" Belgarath asked.

"South, I think," Silk replied.

"Tell him that it's all right, Durnik," the old man said. "He can probably give us some recent news from the north."

"Come on in," Durnik shouted to the hungry man.

The bureaucrat rode up until he was about twenty yards away. Then he stopped warily. "Are you from Mal Zeth?" he demanded.

"We left before the plague broke out," Silk lied.

The official hesitated. "I'll put the money on this rock here," he offered, pointing at a white boulder. "Then I'll move back a ways. You can take the money and leave some food. That way neither one of us will endanger the other."

"Makes sense," Silk replied pleasantly.

Polgara took a loaf of brown bread and a generous slab of cheese from her stores and gave them to the sharp-faced Drasnian.

The Melcene dismounted, laid a few coins on the rock, and then led his horse back some distance.

"Where have you come from, friend?" Silk asked as he approached the rock.

"I was in Akkad in Katakor," the hungry man answered, eyeing the loaf and the cheese. "I was senior administrator there for the Bureau of Public Works—you know, walls, aqueducts, streets, that sort of thing. The bribes weren't spectacular, but I managed to get by. Anyway, I got out just a few hours before Mengha and his demons got there."

Silk laid the food on the rock and picked up the money. Then he backed away. "We heard that Akkad fell quite some time ago."

The Melcene almost ran to the rock and snatched up and bread and cheese. He took a large bite of cheese and tore a chunk off the loaf. "I hid out in the mountains," he replied around the mouthful.

"Isn't that where Ashaba is?" Silk asked, sounding very casual.

The Melcene swallowed hard and nodded. "That's why I finally left," he said, stuffing bread in his mouth. "The area's infested with huge wild dogs—ugly brutes as big as horses— and there are roving bands of Karands killing everyone they come across. I could have avoided all that, but there's something terrible going on at Ashaba. There are dreadful sounds coming from the castle and strange lights in the sky over it at night. I don't hold with the supernatural, my friend, so I bolted." He sighed happily, tearing off another chunk of bread. "A month ago I'd have turned my nose up at brown bread and cheese. Now it tastes like a banquet."

"Hunger's the best sauce," Silk quoted the old adage.

"That's the honest truth."

"Why didn't you stay up in Venna? Didn't you know that there's plague in Mal Zeth?"

The Melcene shuddered. "What's going on in Venna's even worse than what's going on in Katakor or Mal Zeth," he replied. "My nerves are absolutely destroyed by all this. I'm an engineer. What do I know about demons and new Gods and magic? Give me paving stones and timbers and mortar and a few modest bribes and don't even mention any of that other nonsense to me."

"New Gods?" Silk asked. "Who's been talking about new Gods?"

"The Chandim. You've heard of them?"

"Don't they belong to Urvon the Disciple?"

"I don't think they belong to anybody right now. They've gone on a rampage in Venna. Nobody's seen Urvon for more than a month now—not even the people in Mal Yaska. The Chandim are completely out of control. They're erecting altars

out in the fields and holding double sacrifices—the first heart
to Torak and the second to this new God of Angarak—and
anybody up there that doesn't bow to *both* altars gets his heart
cut out right on the spot."

"That seems like a very good reason to stay out of Venna,"
Silk said wryly. "Have they put a name to this new God of
theirs?"

"Not that I ever heard. They just call him 'The new God
of Angarak, come to replace Torak and to take dreadful vengeance on the Godslayer.'"

"That's you," Velvet murmured to Garion.

"Do you mind?"

"I just thought you ought to know, that's all."

"There's an open war going on in Venna, my friend," the
Melcene continued, "and I'd advise you to give the place a
wide berth."

"War?"

"Within the Church itself. The Chandim are slaughtering
all the old Grolims—the ones who are still faithful to Torak.
The Temple Guardsmen are taking sides and they're having
pitched battles on the plains up there—that's when they're
not marauding through the countryside, burning farmsteads,
and massacring whole villages. You'd think that the whole of
Venna's gone crazy. It's as much as a man's life is worth to
go through there just now. They stop you and ask you which
God you worship, and a wrong answer is fatal." He paused,
still eating. "Have you heard about any place that's quiet—
and safe?" he asked plaintively.

"Try the coast," Silk suggested. "Mal Abad, maybe—or
Mal Camat."

"Which way are you going?"

"We're going north to the river and see if we can find a
boat to take us down to Lake Penn Daka."

"It won't be safe there for very long, friend. If the plague
doesn't get there first, Mengha's demons will—or the crazed
Grolims and their Guardsmen out of Venna."

251

"We don't plan to stop," Silk told him. "We're going to cut on across Delchin to Maga Renn and then on down the Magan."

"That's a long journey."

"Friend, I'll go to Gandahar if necessary to get away from demons and plague and mad Grolims. If worse comes to worst, we'll hide out among the elephant herders. Elephants aren't all that bad."

The Melcene smiled briefly. "Thanks for the food," he said, tucking his loaf and his cheese inside his robe and looking around for his grazing horse. "Good luck when you get to Gandahar."

"The same to you on the coast," Silk replied.

They watched the Melcene ride off.

"Why did you take his money, Kheldar?" Eriond asked curiously. "I thought we were just going to give him the food."

"Unexpected and unexplained acts of charity linger in people's minds, Eriond, and curiosity overcomes gratitude. I took his money to make sure that by tomorrow he won't be able to describe us to any curious soldiers."

"Oh," the boy said a bit sadly. "It's too bad that things are like that, isn't it?"

"As Sadi says, I didn't make the world; I only try to live in it."

"Well, what do you think?" Belgarath said to the juggler.

Feldegast squinted off toward the horizon. "Yer dead set on goin' right straight up through the middle of Venna—past Mal Yaska an' all?"

"We don't have any choice. We've got just so much time to get to Ashaba."

"Somehow I thought y' might feel that way about it."

"Do you know a way to get us through?"

Feldegast scratched his head. "'Twill be dangerous, Ancient One," he said dubiously, "what with Grolims and Chandim and Temple Guardsmen an' all."

"It won't be nearly as dangerous as missing our appointment at Ashaba would be."

"Well, if yer dead set on it, I suppose I kin get ye through."

"All right," Belgarath said. "Let's get started then."

The peculiar suspicion which had come over Garion the day before grew stronger. Why would his grandfather ask these questions of a man they scarcely knew? The more he thought about it, the more he became convinced that there was a great deal more going on here than met the eye.

CHAPTER FOURTEEN

It was late afternoon when they reached Mal Ra-kuth, a grim fortress city crouched on the banks of a muddy river. The walls were high, and black towers rose within those walls. A large crowd of people was gathered outside, imploring the citizens to let them enter, but the city gates were locked, and archers with half-drawn bows lined the battlements, threatening the refugees below.

"That sort of answers that question, doesn't it?" Garion said as he and his companions reined in on a hilltop some distance from the frightened city.

Belgarath grunted. "It's more or less what I expected," he

254

said. "There's nothing we really need in Mal Rakuth anyway, so there's not much point in pressing the issue."

"How are we going to get across the river, though?"

"If I remember correctly, there be a ferry crossin' but a few miles upstream," Feldegast told him.

"Won't the ferryman be just as frightened of the plague as the people in that city are?" Durnik asked him.

"'Tis an ox-drawn ferry, Goodman—with teams on each side an' cables an' pulleys an' all. The ferryman kin take our money an' put us on the far bank an' never come within fifty yards of us. I fear the crossin' will be dreadful expensive, though."

The ferry proved to be a leaky old barge attached to a heavy cable stretched across the yellow-brown river.

"Stay back!" the mud-covered man holding the rope hitched about the neck of the lead ox on the near side commanded as they approached. "I don't want any of your filthy diseases."

"How much to go across?" Silk called to him.

The muddy fellow squinted greedily at them, assessing their clothing and horses. "One gold piece," he said flatly.

"That's outrageous!"

"Try swimming."

"Pay him," Belgarath said.

"Not likely," Silk replied. "I refuse to be cheated—even here. Let me think a minute." His narrow face became intent as he stared hard at the rapacious ferryman. "Durnik," he said thoughtfully, "do you have your axe handy?"

The smith nodded, patting the axe which hung from a loop at the back of his saddle.

"Do you suppose you could reconsider just a bit, friend?" the little Drasnian called plaintively to the ferryman.

"One gold piece," the ferryman repeated stubbornly.

Silk sighed. "Do you mind if we look at your boat first? It doesn't look all that safe to me."

"Help yourself—but I won't move it until I get paid."

Silk looked at Durnik. "Bring the axe," he said.

Durnik dismounted and lifted his broad-bladed axe from its loop. Then the two of them climbed down the slippery bank to the barge. They went up the sloping ramp and onto the deck. Silk stamped his feet tentatively on the planking. "Nice boat," he said to the ferryman, who stood cautiously some distance away. "Are you sure you won't reconsider the price?"

"One gold piece. Take it or leave it."

Silk sighed. "I was afraid you might take that position." He scuffed one foot at the muddy deck. "You know more about boats than I do, friend," he observed. "How long do you think it would take this tub to sink if my friend here chopped a hole in the bottom?"

The ferryman gaped at him.

"Pull up the decking in the bow, Durnik," Silk suggested pleasantly. "Give yourself plenty of room for a good swing."

The desperate ferryman grabbed up a club and ran down the bank.

"Careful, friend," Silk said to him. "We left Mal Zeth only yesterday, and I'm already starting to feel a little feverish—something I ate, no doubt."

The ferryman froze in his tracks.

Durnik was grinning as he began to pry up the decking at the frong of the barge.

"My friend here is an expert woodsman," Silk continued in a conversational tone, "and his axe is terribly sharp. I'll wager that he can have this scow lying on the bottom inside of ten minutes."

"I can see into the hold now," Durnik reported, suggestively testing the edge of his axe with his thumb. "Just how big a hole would you like?"

"Oh," Silk replied, "I don't know, Durnik—a yard or so square, maybe. Would that sink it?"

"I'm not sure. Why don't we try it and find out?" Durnik

pushed up the sleeves of his short jacket and hefted his axe a couple of times.

The ferryman was making strangled noises and hopping up and down.

"What's your feeling about negotiation at this point, friend?" Silk asked him. "I'm almost positive that we can reach an accommodation—now that you fully understand the situation."

When they were partway across the river and the barge was wallowing heavily in the current, Durnik walked forward to the bow and stood looking into the opening he had made by prying up the deck. "I wonder how big a hole it *would* take to sink this thing," he mused.

"What was that, dear?" Polgara asked him.

"Just thinking out loud, Pol," he said. "But do you know something? I just realized that I've never sunk a boat before."

She rolled her eyes heavenward. "Men," she sighed.

"I suppose I'd better put the planks back so that we can lead the horses off on the other side," Durnik said almost regretfully.

They erected their tents in the shelter of a grove of cedar trees near the river that evening. The sky, which had been serene and blue since they had arrived in Mallorea, had turned threatening as the sun sank, and there were rumbles of thunder and brief flickers of lightning among the clouds off to the west.

After supper, Durnik and Toth went out of the grove for a look around and returned with sober faces. "I'm afraid that we're in for a spell of bad weather," the smith reported. "You can smell it coming."

"I hate riding in the rain," Silk complained.

"Most people do, Prince Kheldar," Feldegast told him. "But bad weather usually keeps others in as well, don't y' know; an' if what that hungry traveler told us this afternoon be true, we'll not be wantin' t' meet the sort of folk that be abroad in Venna when the weather's fine."

"He mentioned the Chandim," Sadi said, frowning. "Just exactly who are they?"

"The Chandim are an order within the Grolim Church," Belgarath told him. "When Torak built Cthol Mishrak, he converted certain Grolims into Hounds to patrol the region. After Vo Mimbre, when Torak was bound in sleep, Urvon converted about half of them back. The ones who reassumed human form are all sorcerers of greater or lesser talent, and they can communicate with the ones who are still Hounds. They're very close-knit—like a pack of wild dogs—and they're all fanatically loyal to Urvon."

"An' that be much of the source of Urvon's power," Feldegast added. "Ordinary Grolims be always schemin' against each other an' against their superiors, but Urvon's Chamdim have kept the Mallorean Grolims in line fer five hundred years now."

"And the Temple Guardsmen?" Sadi added. "Are they Chandim, or Grolims, too?"

"Not usually," Belgarath replied. "There are Grolims among them, of course, but most of them are Mallorean Angaraks. They were recruited before Vo Mimbre to serve as Torak's personal bodyguard."

"Why would a God need a bodyguard?"

"I never entirely understood that myself," the old man admitted. "Anyway, after Vo Mimbre, there are still a few of them left—new recruits, veterans who'd been wounded in earlier battles and sent home, that sort of thing. Urvon persuaded them that *he* spoke for Torak, and now their allegiance is to him. After that, they recruited more young Angaraks to fill up the holes in their ranks. They do more than just guard the Temple now, though. When Urvon started having difficulties with the Emperors at Mal Zeth, he decided that he needed a fighting force, so he expanded them into an army."

"'Tis a practical arrangement," Feldegast pointed out. "The Chandim provide Urvon with the sorcery he needs t' keep the other Grolims toein' the mark, an' the Temple

Guardsmen provide the muscle t' keep the ordinary folk from protestin' their lot."

"These Guardsmen, they're just ordinary soldiers, then?" Durnik asked.

"Not really. They're closer to being knights," Belgarath replied.

"Like Mandorallen, you mean—all dressed in steel plate and with shields and lances and war horses and all that?"

"No, Goodman," Feldegast answered. "They're not nearly so grand. Lances an' helmets and shields they have, certainly, but fer the rest, they rely on chain mail. They be most nearly as stupid as Arends, however. Somethin' about wearin' all that steel empties the mind of every knight the world around."

Belgarath was looking speculatively at Garion. "How muscular are you feeling?" he asked.

"Not very—why?"

"We've got a bit of a problem here. We're far more likely to encounter Guardsmen than we are Chandim, but if we start unhorsing all these tin men with our minds, the noise is going to attract the Chandim like a beacon."

Garion stared at him. "You're not serious! I'm not Mandorallen, Grandfather."

"No. You've got better sense than he has."

"I will *not* stand by and hear my knight insulted!" Ce'Nedra declared hotly.

"Ce'Nedra," Belgarath said almost absently, "hush."

"Hush?"

"You heard me." He scowled at her so blackly that she faltered and drew back behind Polgara for protection. "The point, Garion," the old man continued, "is that you've received a certain amount of training from Mandorallen in this sort of thing and you've had a bit of experience. None of the rest of us have."

"I don't have any armor."

"You've got a mail shirt."

"I don't have a helmet—or a shield."

"I could probably manage those, Garion," Durnik offered.

Garion looked at his old friend. "I'm terribly disappointed in you, Durnik," he said.

"You aren't afraid, are you, Garion?" Ce'Nedra asked in a small voice.

"Well, no. Not really. It's just that it's so stupid—and it *looks* so ridiculous."

"Have you got an old pot I could borrow, Pol?" Durnik asked.

"How big a pot?"

"Big enough to fit Garion's head."

"Now that's going too far!" Garion exclaimed. "I'm not going to wear a kitchen pot on my head for a helmet. I haven't done that since I was a boy."

"I'll modify it a bit," Durnik assured him. "And then I'll take the lid and make you a shield."

Garion walked away swearing to himself.

Velvet's eyes had narrowed. She looked at Feldegast with no hint of her dimples showing. "Tell me, master juggler," she said, "how is it that an itinerant entertainer, who plays for pennies in wayside taverns, knows so very much about the inner working of Grolim society here in Mallorea?"

"I be not nearly so foolish as I look, me lady," he replied, "an' I do have eyes an' ears, an' know how t' use 'em."

"You avoided that question rather well," Belgarath complimented him.

The juggler smirked. "I thought so meself. Now," he continued seriously, "as me ancient friend here says, 'tis not too likely that we'll be encounterin' the Chandim if it rains, fer a dog has usually the good sense t' take t' his kennel when the weather be foul—unless there be pressin' need fer him t' be out an' about. 'Tis far more probable fer us t' meet Temple Guardsmen, fer a knight, be he Arendish or Mallorean, seems deaf t' the gentle patter of rain on his armor. I shouldn't wonder that our young warrior King over there be of sufficient might t' be a match fer any Guardsman we might meet alone, but there always be the possibility of comin' across 'em in groups. Should there be such encounters, keep yer wits about ye an' remember that once a knight has started his charge, 'tis very hard fer him t' swerve or change direction very much at all. A sidestep an' a smart rap across the back of the head be usually enough t' roll 'em out of the saddle, an' a man in armor—once he's off his horse—be like a turtle on his back, don't y' know."

"You've done it a few times yourself, I take it?" Sadi murmured.

"I've had me share of misunderstandin's with Temple Guardsmen," Feldegast admitted, "an' ye'll note that I still be here t' talk about 'em."

Durnik took the cast iron pot Polgara had given him and set it in the center of their fire. After a time, he pulled it glowing out of the coals with a stout stick, placed the blade of a broken knife on a rounded rock, and then set the pot over it. He took up his axe, reversed it, and held the blunt end over the pot.

"You'll break it," Silk predicted. "Cast iron's too brittle to take any pounding."

"Trust me, Silk," the smith said with a wink. He took a deep breath and began to tap lightly on the pot. The sound of his hammering was not the dull clack of cast iron, but the clear ring of steel, a sound that Garion remembered from his earliest boyhood. Deftly the smith reshaped the pot into a flat-topped helmet with a fierce nose guard and heavy cheek pieces. Garion knew that his old friend was cheating just a bit by the faint whisper and surge he was directing at the emerging helmet.

Then Durnik dropped the helmet into a pail of water, and it hissed savagely, sending off a cloud of steam. The pot lid that the smith intended to convert into a shield, however, challenged even *his* ingenuity. It became quite obvious that, should he hammer it out to give it sufficient size to offer protection, it would be so thin that it would not even fend

261

off a dagger stroke, much less a blow from a lance or sword. He considered that, even as he pounded on the ringing lid. He shifted his axe and made an obscure gesture at Toth. The giant nodded, went to the river bank, returned with a pail full of clay, and dumped the bucket out in the center of the glowing shield. It gave off an evil hiss, and Durnik continued to pound.

"Un—Durnik," Garion said, trying not to be impolite, "a ceramic shield was not exactly what I had in mind, you know."

Durnik gave him a grin filled with surpressed mirth. "Look at it, Garion," he suggested, not changing the tempo of his hammering.

Garion stared at the shield, his eyes suddenly wide. The glowing circle upon which Durnik was pounding was solid, cherry-red steel. "How did you do that?"

"Transmutation!" Polgara gasped. "Changing one thing into something else! Durnik, where on earth did you ever learn to do that?"

"It's just something I picked up, Pol." He laughed. "As long as you've got a bit of steel to begin with—like that old knife blade—you can make as much more as you want, out of anything that's handy: cast iron, clay, just about anything."

Ce'Nedra's eyes had suddenly gone very wide. "Durnik," she said in an almost reverent whisper, "could you have made it out of gold?"

Durnik thought about it, still hammering. "I suppose I could have," he addmitted, "but gold's too heavy and soft to make a good shield, wouldn't you say?"

"Could you make another one?" she wheedled. "For me? It wouldn't have to be so big—at least not quite. Please, Durnik."

Durnik finished the rim of the shield with a shower of crimson sparks and the musical ring of steel on steel. "I don't think that would be a good idea, Ce'Nedra," he told her. "Gold is valuable because it's so scarce. If I started making it out of clay, it wouldn't be long before it wasn't worth anything at all. I'm sure you can see that."

"But—"

"No, Ce'Nedra," he said firmly.

"Garion—" she appealed, her voice anguished.

"He's right, dear."

"But—"

"Never mind, Ce'Nedra."

The fire had burned down to a bed of glowing coals. Garion awoke with a start, sitting up suddenly. He was covered with sweat and trembling violently. Once again he had heard the wailing cry that he had heard the previous day, and the sound of it wrenched at his heart. He sat for a long time staring at the fire. In time, the sweat dried and his trembling subsided.

Ce'Nedra's breathing was regular as she lay beside him, and there was no other sound in their well-shielded encampment. He rolled carefully out of his blankets and walked to the edge of the grove of cedars to stare bleakly out across the fields lying dark and empty under an inky sky. Then, because there was nothing he could do about it, he returned to his bed and slept fitfully until dawn.

It was drizzling rain when he awoke. He got up quietly and went out of the tent to join Durnik, who was building up the fire. "Can I borrow your axe?" he asked his friend.

Durnik looked up at him.

"I guess I'm going to need a lance to go with all that." He looked rather distastefully at the helmet and shield lying atop his mail shirt near the packs and saddles.

"Oh," the smith said. "I almost forgot about that. Is one going to be enough? They break sometimes, you know—at least Mandorallen's always did."

"I'm certainly not going to carry more than one." Garion jabbed his thumb back over his shoulder at the hilt of his

263

sword. "Anyway, I've always got this big knife to fall back on."

The chill drizzle that had begun shortly before dawn was the kind of rain that made the nearby fields hazy and indistinct. After breakfast, they took heavy cloaks out of their packs and prepared to face a fairly unpleasant day. Garion had already put on his mail shirt, and he padded the inside of his helmet with an old tunic and jammed it down on his head. He felt very foolish as he clinked over to saddle Chretienne. The mail already smelled bad and it seemed, for some reason, to attract the chill of the soggy morning. He looked at his new-cut lance and his round shield. "This is going to be awkward," he said.

"Hang the shield from the saddle bow, Garion," Durnik suggested, "and set the butt of your lance in the stirrup beside your foot. That's the way Mandorallen does it."

"I'll try it," Garion said. He hauled himself up into his saddle, already sweating under the weight of his mail. Durnik handed him the shield, and he hooked the strap of it over the saddle bow. Then he took his lance and jammed its butt into his stirrup, pinching his toes in the process.

"You'll have to hold it," the smith told him. "It won't stay upright by itself."

Garion grunted and took the shaft of his lance in his right hand.

"You look very impressive, dear," Ce'Nedra assured him.

"Wonderful," he replied dryly.

They rode out of the cedar grove into the wet, miserable morning with Garion in the lead, feeling more than a little absurd in his warlike garb.

The lance, he discovered almost immediately, had a stubborn tendency to dip its point toward the ground. He shifted his grip on it, sliding his hand up until he found its center of balance. The rain collected on the shaft of the lance, ran down across his clammy hand, and trickled into his sleeve. After a short while, a steady stream of water dribbled from his elbow. "I feel like a downspout," he grumbled.

"Let's pick up the pace," Belgarath said to him. "It's a long way to Ashaba, and we don't have too much time."

Garion nudged Chretienne with his heels, and the big gray moved out, at first at a trot and then in a rolling canter. For some reason that made Garion feel a bit less foolish.

The road which Feldegast had pointed out to them the previous evening was little traveled and this morning it was deserted. It ran past abandoned farmsteads, sad, bramble-choked shells with the moldy remains of their thatched roofs all tumbled in. A few of the farmsteads had been burned, some only recently.

The road began to turn muddy as the earth soaked up the steady rain. The cantering hooves of their horses splashed the mud up to coat their legs and bellies and to spatter the boots and cloaks of the riders.

Silk rode beside Garion, his sharp face alert, and just before they reached the crest of each hill, he galloped on ahead to have a quick look at the shallow valley lying beyond.

By midmorning, Garion was soaked through, and he rode on bleakly, enduring the discomfort and the smell of new rust, wishing fervently that the rain would stop.

Silk came back down the next hill after scouting on ahead. His face was tight with a sudden excitement, and he motioned them all to stop.

"There are some Grolims up ahead," he reported tersely.

"How many?" Belgarath asked.

"About two dozen. They're holding some kind of religious ceremony."

The old man grunted. "Let's take a look." He looked at Garion. "Leave your lance with Durnik," he said. "It sticks up too high into the air, and I'd rather not attract attention."

Garion nodded and passed his lance over to the smith, then followed Silk, Belgarath, and Feldegast up the hill. They dismounted just before they reached the crest and moved carefully to the top, where a brushy thicket offered some concealment.

The black-robed Grolims were kneeling on the wet grass before a pair of grim altars some distance down the hill. A limp, unmoving form lay sprawled across each of them, and there was a great deal of blood. Sputtering braziers stood at the end of each altar, sending twin columns of black smoke up into the drizzle. The Grolims were chanting in the rumbling groan Garion had heard too many times before. He could not make out what they were saying.

"Chandim?" Belgarath softly asked the juggler.

"'Tis hard t' say fer certain, Ancient One," Feldegast replied. "The twin altars would suggest it, but the practice might have spread. Grolims be very quick t' pick up changes in Church policy. But Chandim or not, 'twould be wise of us t' avoid 'em. There be not much point in engagin' ourselves in casual skirmishes with Grolims."

"There are trees over on the east side of the valley," Silk said, pointing. "If we stay in among them, we'll be out of sight."

Belgarath nodded.

"How much longer are they likely to be praying?" Garion asked.

"Another half hour at least," Feldegast replied.

Garion looked at the pair of altars, feeling an icy rage building up in him. "I'd like to cap their ceremony with a little personal visit," he said.

"Forget it," Belgarath told him. "You're not here to ride around the countryside righting wrongs. Let's go back and get the others. I'd like to get around those Grolims before they finish with their prayers."

They picked their way carefully through the belt of dripping trees that wound along the eastern rim of the shallow valley where the Grolims were conducting their grim rites and returned to the muddy road about a mile beyond. Again they set out at the same distance-eating canter, with Garion once more in the lead.

Some miles past the valley where the Grolims had sacrificed the two unfortunates, they passed a burning village that was spewing out a cloud of black smoke. There seemed to be no one about, though there were some signs of fighting near the burning houses.

They rode on without stopping.

The rain let up by midafternoon, though the sky remained overcast. Then, as they crested yet another hilltop in the rolling countryside, they saw another rider on the far side of the valley. The distance was too great to make out details, but Garion *could* see that the rider was armed with a lance.

"What do we do?" he called back over his shoulder at the rest of them.

"That's why you're wearing armor and carrying a lance, Garion," Belgarath replied.

"Shouldn't I at least give him the chance to stand aside?"

"To what purpose?" Feldegast asked. "He'll not do it. Yer very presence here with yer lance an' yer shield be a challenge, an' he'll not be refusin' it. Ride him down, young Master. The day wears on, don't y' know."

"All right," Garion said unhappily. He buckled his shield to his left arm, settled his helmet more firmly in place, and lifted the butt of his lance out of his stirrup. Chretienne was already pawing at the earth and snorting defiantly.

"Enthusiast," Garion muttered to him. "All right, let's go, then."

The big gray's charge was thunderous. It was not a gallop, exactly, nor a dead run, but rather was a deliberately implacable gait that could only be called a charge.

The armored man across the valley seemed a bit startled by the unprovoked attack, there having been none of the customary challenges, threats, or insults. After a bit of fumbling with his equipment, he managed to get his shield in place and his lance properly advanced. He seemed to be quite bulky, though that might have been his armor. He wore a sort of chain-mail coat reaching to his knees. His helmet was round and fitted with a visor, and he had a large sword sheathed at his waist. He clanged down his visor, then sank his spurs into his horse's flanks and also charged.

The wet fields at the side of the road seemed to blur as Garion crouched behind his shield with his lance lowered and aimed directly at his opponent. He had seen Mandorallen do this often enough to understand the basics. The distance between him and the stranger was narrowing rapidly, and Garion could clearly see the mud spraying out from beneath the hooves of his opponent's horse. At the last moment, just before they came together, Garion raised up in his stirrups as Mandorallen had instructed him, leaned forward so that his entire body was braced for the shock, and took careful aim with his lance at the exact center of the other man's shield.

There was a dreadful crashing impact, and he was suddenly surrounded by flying splinters as his opponent's lance shattered. His own lance, however, though it was as stout as that of the Guardsman, was a freshly cut cedar pole and it was quite springy. It bent into a tight arch like a drawn bow, then snapped straight again. The startled stranger was suddenly lifted out of his saddle. His body described a high, graceful arc through the air, which ended abruptly as he came down on his head in the middle of the road.

Garion thundered on past and finally managed to rein in his big gray horse. He wheeled and stopped. The other man lay on his back in the mud of the road. He was not moving. Carefully, his lance at the ready, Garion walked Chretienne back to the splinter-littered place where the impact had occurred.

"Are you all right?" he asked the Temple Guardsman lying in the mud.

There was no answer.

Cautiously, Garion dismounted, dropped his lance, and drew Iron-grip's sword. "I say, man, are you all right?" he asked again. He reached out with his foot and nudged the fellow.

The Guardsman's visor was closed, and Garion put the tip of his sword under the bottom of it and lifted. The man's eyes were rolled back in his head until only the whites showed, and there was blood gushing freely from his nose.

The others came galloping up, and Ce'Nedra flung herself out of the saddle almost before her horse and stopped and hurled herself into her husband's arms. "You were magnificent, Garion! Absolutely magnificent!"

"It did go rather well, didn't it?" he replied modestly, trying to juggle sword, shield, and wife all at the same time. He looked at Polgara, who was also dismounting. "Do you think he's going to be all right, Aunt Pol?" he asked. "I hope I didn't hurt him too much."

She checked the limp man lying in the road. "He'll be fine, dear," she assured him. "He's just been knocked senseless, is all."

"Nice job," Silk said.

Garion suddenly grinned broadly. "You know something," he said. "I think I'm starting to understand why Mandorallen enjoys this so much. It *is* sort of exhilarating."

"I think it has t' do with the weight of the armor," Feldegast observed sadly to Belgarath. "It bears down on 'em so much that it pulls all the juice out of their brains, or some such."

"Let's move on," Belgarath suggested.

By midmorning the following day, they had moved into the broad valley which was the location of Mal Yaska, the ecclesiastical capital of Mallorea and the site of the Disciple Urvon's palace. Though the sky remained overcast, the rain had blown on through, and a stiff breeze had begun to dry the grass and the mud which had clogged the roads. There were encampments dotting the valley, little clusters of people who had fled from the demons to the north and the plague to the south. Each group was fearfully isolated from its neighbors, and all of them kept their weapons close at hand.

Unlike those of Mal Rakuth, the gates of Mal Yaska stood open, though they were patrolled by detachments of mail-armored Temple Guardsmen.

"Why don't they go into the city?" Durnik asked, looking at the clusters of refugees.

"Mal Yaska's not the sort of place ye visit willin'ly, Goodman," Feldegast replied. "When the Grolims be lookin' fer people t' sacrifice on their altars, 'tis unwise t' make yerself too handy." He looked at Belgarath. "Would ye be willin' t' accept a suggestion, me ancient friend?" he asked.

"Suggest away."

"We'll be needin' information about what's happenin' up there." He pointed at the snow-capped mountains looming across the northern horizon. "Since I know me way about Mal Yaska an' know how t' avoid the Grolims, wouldn't ye say that it might be worth the investment of an hour or so t' have me nose about the central market place an' see what news I kin pick up?"

"He's got a point, Belgarath," Silk agreed seriously. "I don't like riding into a situation blind."

Belgarath considered it. "All right," he said to the juggler, "but be careful—and stay out of the alehouses."

Feldegast sighed. "There be no such havens in Mal Yaska, Belgarath. The Grolims there be fearful strict in their disapproval of simple pleasures." He shook the reins of his mule and rode on across the plain toward the black walls of Urvon's capital.

"Isn't he contradicting himself?" Sadi asked. "First he says it's too dangerous to go into the city and then he rides on in anyway."

"He knows what he's doing," Belgarath said. "He's in no danger."

"We might as well have some lunch while we're waiting, father," Polgara suggested.

He nodded, and they rode some distance into an open field and dismounted.

Garion laid aside his lance, pulled his helmet from his sweaty head, and stood looking across the intervening open space at the center of Church power in Mallorea. The city was large, certainly, though not nearly so large as Mal Zeth. The walls were high and thick, surmounted by heavy battlements, and the towers rising inside were square and blocky. There was a kind of unrelieved ugliness about it, and it seemed to exude a brooding menace as if the eons of cruelty and blood lust had sunk into its very stones. From somewhere near the center of the city, the telltale black column of smoke rose into the air, and faintly, echoing across the plain with its huddled encampments of frightened refugees, he thought he could hear the sullen iron clang of the gong coming from the Temple of Torak. Finally, he sighed and turned his head away.

"It will not last forever," Eriond, who had come up beside him, said firmly. "We're almost to the end of it now. All the altars will be torn down, and the Grolims will put their knives away to rust."

"Are you sure, Eriond?"

"Yes, Belgarion. I'm very sure."

They ate a cold lunch, and, not long after, Feldegast returned, his face somber. "'Tis perhaps a bit more serious than we had expected, Ancient One," he reported, swinging down from his mule. "The Chandim be in total control of the city, an' the Temple Guardsmen be takin' their orders directly from them. The Grolims who hold t' the old ways have all gone into hidin', but packs of Torak's Hounds be sniffin' out the places where they've hidden an' they be tearin' 'em t' pieces wherever they find 'em."

"I find it very hard to sympathize with Grolims," Sadi murmured.

"I kin bear their discomfort meself," Feldegast agreed, "but 'tis rumored about the market place that the Chandim an' their dogs an' their Guardsmen *also* be movin' about across the border in Katakor."

"In spite of the Karands and Mengha's demons?" Silk asked with some surprise.

"Now that's somethin' I could not get the straight of," the juggler replied. "No one could tell me why or how, but the Chandim an' the Guardsmen seem not t' be concerned about Mengha nor his army nor his demons."

"That begins to smell of some kind of accommodation," Silk said.

"There were hints of that previously," Feldegast reminded him.

"An alliance?" Belgarath frowned.

"'Tis hard t' say fer sure, Ancient One, but Urvon be a schemer, an' he's always had this dispute with the imperial throne at Mal Zeth. If he's managed t' put Mengha in his pocket, Kal Zakath had better look t' his defenses."

"Is Urvon in the city?" Belgarath asked.

"No. No one knows where he's gone fer sure, but he's not in his palace there."

"That's very strange," Belgarath said.

"Indeed," the juggler replied, "but whatever he's doin' or plannin' t' do, I think we'd better be walkin' softly once we cross the border into Katakor. When ye add the Hounds an' the Temple Guardsmen t' the demons an' Karands already there, 'tis goin' t' be fearful perilous t' approach the House of Torak at Ashaba."

"That's a chance we'll have to take," the old man said grimly. "We're going to Ashaba, and if anything—Hound, human, or demon—gets in our way, we'll just have to deal with it as it comes."

CHAPTER FIFTEEN

The sky continued to lower as they rode past the brooding city of the Grolim Church under the suspicious gaze of the armored Guardsmen at the gate and the hooded Grolims on the walls.

"Is it likely that they'll follow us?" Durnik asked.

"It's not very probable, Goodman," Sadi replied. "Look around you. There are thousands encamped here, and I doubt that either Guardsmen or Grolims would take the trouble to follow them all when they leave."

"I suppose you're right," the smith agreed.

By late afternoon they were well past Mal Yaska, and the snow-topped peaks in Katakor loomed higher ahead of them, starkly outlined against the dirty gray clouds scudding in from the west.

"Will ye be wantin' t' stop fer the night before we cross the border?" Feldegast asked Belgarath.

"How far is it to there from here?"

"Not far at all, Ancient One."

"Is it guarded?"

"Usually, yes."

"Silk," the old man said, "ride on ahead and have a look."

The little man nodded and nudged his horse into a gallop.

"All right," Belgarath said, signaling for a halt so that they could all hear him. "Everybody we've seen this afternoon was going south. Nobody's fleeing *toward* Katakor. Now, a man who's running away from someplace doesn't stop when the border's in sight. He keeps on going. That means that there's a fair chance that there's not going to be anybody within miles of the border on the Katakor side. If the border's not guarded, we can just go on across and take shelter for the night on the other side."

"And if the border *is* guarded?" Sadi asked.

Belgarath's eyes grew flat. "We're still going to go through," he replied.

"That's likely to involve fighting."

"That's right. Let's move along, shall we?"

About fifteen minutes later, Silk returned. "There are about ten Guardsmen at the crossing," he reported.

"Any chance of taking them by surprise?" Belgarath asked him.

"A little, but the road leading to the border is straight and flat for a half mile on either side of the guard post."

The old man muttered a curse under his breath. "All right then," he said. "They'll at least have time to get to their horses. We don't want to give them the leisure to get themselves set. Remember what Feldegast said about keeping your wits. Don't take any chances, but I want all of those Guardsmen on their backs after our first charge. Pol, you stay back with the ladies—and Eriond."

"But—" Velvet began to protest.

"Don't argue with me, Liselle—just this once."

"Couldn't Lady Polgara just put them to sleep?" Sadi asked. "The way she did with the spies back in Mal Zeth?"

Belgarath shook his head. "There are a few Grolims among the Guardsmen, and that particular technique doesn't work on Grolims. This time we're going to have to do it by main strength—just to be on the safe side."

Sadi nodded glumly, dismounted, and picked up a stout tree limb from the side of the road. He thumped it experimentally on the turf. "I want you all to know that this is not my preferred way of doing things," he said.

The rest of them also dismounted and armed themselves with cudgels and staffs. Then they moved on.

The border was marked by a stone shed painted white and by a gate consisting of a single white pole resting on posts on either side of the road. A dozen horses were tethered just outside the shed, and lances leaned against the wall. A single, mail-coated Guardsman paced back and forth across the road on the near side of the gate, his sword leaning back over his shoulder.

"All right," Belgarath said. "Let's move as fast as we can. Wait here, Pol."

Garion sighed. "I guess I'd better go first."

"We were hoping that you'd volunteer." Silk's grin was tight.

Garion ignored that. He buckled on his shield, settled his helmet in place, and once again lifted the butt of his lance out of his stirrup. "Is everybody ready?" he asked, looking around. Then he advanced his lance and spurred his horse into a charge with the others close on his heels.

The Guardsman at the gate took one startled look at the warlike party bearing down on him, ran to the door of the shed, and shouted at his comrades inside. Then he struggled into the saddle of his tethered horse, leaned over to pick up his lance, and moved out into the road. Other Guardsmen came boiling out of the shed, struggling with their equipment and stumbling over each other.

Garion had covered half the distance to the gate before more than two or three of the armored men were in their saddles, and so it was that the man who had been standing watch was forced to meet his charge alone.

The results were relatively predictable.

As Garion thundered past his unhorsed opponent, another Guardsman came out into the road at a half gallop, but Garion gave him no time to set himself or to turn his horse. The crashing impact against the unprepared man's shield hurled his horse from its feet. The Guardsman came down before the horse did, and the animal rolled over him, squealing and kicking in fright.

Garion tried to rein in, but Chretienne had the bit in his teeth. He cleared the pole gate in a long, graceful leap and charged on. Garion swore and gave up on the reins. He leaned forward and seized the big gray by one ear and hauled back. Startled, Chretienne stopped so quickly that his rump skidded on the road.

"The fight's back that way," Garion told his horse, "or did you forget already?"

Chretienne gave him a reproachful look, turned, and charged back toward the gate again.

Because of the speed of their attack, Garion's friends were on top of the Guardsmen before the armored men could bring their lances into play, and the fight had quickly turned ugly. Using the blunt side of his axe, Durnik smashed in one Guardsman's visor, denting it so severely that the man could no longer see. He rode in circles helplessly, both hands clutching at his helmet until he rode under a low-hanging limb, which smoothly knocked him off his horse.

Silk ducked under a wide, backhand sword stroke, reached down with his dagger, and neatly cut his attacker's girth strap.

The fellow's horse leaped forward, jumping out from under his rider. Saddle and all, the Guardsman tumbled into the road. He struggled to his feet, sword in hand, but Feldegast came up behind him and methodically clubbed him to earth again with an ugly lead mace.

It was Toth, however, who was the hardest pressed. Three Guardsmen closed on the giant. Even as Chretienne leaped the gate again, Garion saw the huge man awkwardly flailing with his staff for all the world like someone who had never held one in his hands before. When the three men came within range however, Toth's skill miraculously reemerged. His heavy staff whirled in a blurring circle. One Guardsman fell wheezing to earth, clutching at his broken ribs. Another doubled over sharply as Toth deftly poked him in the pit of the stomach with the butt of his staff. The third desperately raised his sword, but the giant casually swiped it out of his hand, then reached out and took the surprised man by the front of his mail coat. Garion clearly heard the crunch of crushed steel as Toth's fist closed. Then the giant looked about and almost casually threw the armored man against a roadside tree so hard that it shook the spring leaves from the highest twig.

The three remaining Guardsmen began to fall back, trying to give themselves room to use their lances, but they seemed unaware that Garion was returning to the fray—from behind them.

As Chretienne thundered toward the unsuspecting trio, a sudden idea came to Garion. Quickly he turned his lance sideways so that its center rested just in front of his saddlebow and crashed into the backs of the Guardsmen. The springy cedar pole swept all three of them out of their saddles and over the heads of their horses. Before they could stumble to their feet, Sadi, Feldegast, and Durnik were on them, and the fight ended as quickly as it had begun.

"I don't think I've ever seen anybody use a lance that way before," Silk said gaily to Garion.

"I just made it up," Garion replied with an excited grin.

"I'm sure that there are at least a half-dozen rules against it."

"We probably shouldn't mention it, then."

"I won't tell anybody if you don't."

Durnik was looking around critically. The ground was littered with Guardsmen who were either unconscious or groaning over assorted broken bones. Only the man Toth had poked in the stomach was still in his saddle, though he was doubled over, gasping for breath. Durnik rode up to him. "Excuse me," he said politely, removed the poor fellow's helmet, and then rapped him smartly on top of the head with the butt of his axe. The Guardsman's eyes glazed, and he toppled limply out of the saddle.

Belgarath suddenly doubled over, howling with laughter. *"Excuse me?"* he demanded of the smith.

"There's no need to be uncivil to people, Belgarath," Durnik replied stiffly.

Polgara came riding sedately down the hill, followed by Ce'Nedra, Velvet, and Eriond. "Very nice, gentlemen," she complimented them all, looking around at the fallen Guardsmen. Then she rode up to the pole gate. "Garion, dear," she said pleasantly, reining in her mount, "would you mind?"

He laughed, rode Chretienne over to the gate, and kicked it out of her way.

"Why on earth were you jumping fences in the very middle of the fight?" she asked him curiously.

"It wasn't altogether my idea," he replied.

"Oh," she said, looking critically at the big horse. "I think I understand."

Chretienne managed somehow to look slightly ashamed of himself.

They rode on past the border as evening began imperceptibly to darken an already gloomy sky. Feldegast pulled in beside Belgarath. "Would yer morals be at all offended if I was t' suggest shelterin' fer the night in a snug little smugglers' cave I know of a few miles or so farther on?" he asked.

Belgarath grinned and shook his head. "Not in the slightest," he replied. "When I need a cave, I never concern myself about the previous occupants." Then he laughed. "I shared quarters for a week once with a sleeping bear—nice enough bear, actually, once I got used to his snoring."

"'Tis a fascinatin' story, I'm sure, an' I'd be delighted t' hear it—but the night's comin' on, an' ye kin tell me about it over supper. Shall we be off, then?" The juggler thumped his heels into his mule's flanks and led them on up the rutted road in the rapidly descending twilight at a jolting gallop.

As they moved into the first of the foothills, they found the poorly maintained road lined on either side by mournful-looking evergreens. The road, however, was empty, though it showed signs of recent heavy traffic—all headed south.

"How much farther to this cave of yours?" Belgarath called to the juggler.

"'Tis not far, Ancient One," Feldegast assured him. "There be a dry ravine that crosses the road up ahead, an' we go up that a bit of a ways, an' there we are."

"I hope you know what you're doing."

"Trust me."

Somewhat surprisingly, Belgarath let that pass.

They pounded on up the road as a sullen dusk settled into the surrounding foothills and deep shadows began to gather about the trunks of the evergreens.

"Ah, an' there it is," Feldegast said, pointing at the rocky bed of a dried-up stream. "The footin' be treacherous here, so we'd best lead the mounts." He swung down from his mule and cautiously began to lead the way up the ravine. It grew steadily darker, the light fading quickly from the overcast sky. As the ravine narrowed and rounded a sharp bend, the juggler rummaged through the canvas pack strapped to the back of his mule. He lifted out the stub of a candle and looked at Durnik. "Kin ye be makin' me a bit of a flame, Goodman?" he asked. "I'd do it meself, but I seem t' have misplaced me tinder."

279

Durnik opened his pouch, took out his flint and steel and his wad of tinder, and, after several tries, blew a lighted spark into a tiny finger of fire. He held it out, shielded between his hands, and Feldegast lit his bit of candle.

"An' here we are now," the juggler said grandly, holding up his candle to illuminate the steep banks of the ravine.

"Where?" Silk asked, looking about in puzzlement.

"Well now, Prince Kheldar, it wouldn't be much of a hidden cave if the openin' was out in plain sight fer just anybody t' stumble across, now would it?" Feldegast went over to the steep side of the ravine to where a huge slab of water-scoured granite leaned against the bank. He lowered his candle, shielding it with his hand, ducked slightly, and disappeared behind it with his mule trailing along behind him.

The interior of the cave was floored with clean white sand, and the walls had been worn smooth by centuries of swirling water. Feldegast stood in the center of the cave holding his candle aloft. There were crude log bunks along the walls, a table and some benches in the center of the cave, and a rough fireplace near the far wall with a fire already laid. Feldegast crossed to the fireplace, bent, and lit the kindling lying under the split logs resting on a rough stone grate with his candle. "Well now, that's better," he said, holding his hands out to the crackling flames. "Isn't this a cozy little haven?"

Just beyond the fireplace was an archway, in part natural and in part the work of human hands. The front of the archway was closed off with several horizontal poles. Feldegast pointed at it. "There be the stable fer the horses, an' also a small spring at the back of it. 'Tis altogether the finest smugglers' cave in this part of Mallorea."

"A cunning sort of place," Belgarath agreed, looking around.

"What do they smuggle through here?" Silk asked with a certain professional curiosity.

"Gem stones fer the most part. There be rich deposits in the cliffs of Katakor, an' quite often whole gravel bars of the shiny little darlin's lyin' in the streams t' be had fer the trouble it takes t' pick 'em up. The local taxes be notorious cruel, though, so the bold lads in this part of these mountains have come up with various ways t' take their goods across the border without disturbin' the sleep of the hardworkin' tax collectors."

Polgara was inspecting the fireplace. There were several iron pothooks protruding from its inside walls and a large iron grill sitting on stout legs to one side. "Very nice," she murmured approvingly. "Is there adequate firewood?"

"More than enough, me dear lady," the juggler replied. "'Tis stacked in the stable, along with fodder fer the horses."

"Well, then," she said, removing her blue cloak and laying it across one of the bunks, "I think I might be able to expand the menu I'd planned for this evening's meal. As long as we have such complete facilities here, it seems a shame to waste them. I'll need more firewood stacked here—and water, of course." She went to the pack horse that carried her cooking utensils and her stores, humming softly to herself.

Durnik, Toth, and Eriond led the horses into the stable and began to unsaddle them. Garion, who had left his lance outside, went to one of the bunks, removed his helmet and laid it, along with his shield, under the bunk, and then he began to struggle out of his mail shirt. Ce'Nedra came over to assist him.

"You were magnificent today, dear," she told him warmly.

He grunted noncommittally, leaning forward and extending his arms over his head so that she could pull the shirt off.

She tugged hard, and the mail shirt came free all at once. Thrown off balance by the weight, she sat down heavily on the sandy floor with the shirt in her lap.

Garion laughed and quickly went to her. "Oh, Ce'Nedra," he said, still laughing, "I do love you." He kissed her and then helped her to her feet.

"This is terribly heavy, isn't it?" she said, straining to lift the steel-link shirt.

"You noticed," he said, rubbing at one aching shoulder. "And here you thought I was just having fun."

"Be nice, dear. Do you want me to hang it up for you?"

He shrugged. "Just kick it under the bunk."

Her look was disapproving.

"I don't think it's going to wrinkle, Ce'Nedra."

"But it's untidy to do it that way, dear." She made some effort to fold the thing, then gave up, rolled it in a ball, and pushed it far back under the bunk with her foot.

Supper that evening consisted of thick steaks cut from a ham Vella had provided them, a rich soup so thick that it hovered on the very edge of stew, large slabs of bread that had been warmed before the fire, and baked apples with honey and cinnamon.

After they had eaten, Polgara rose and looked around the cave again. "The ladies and I are going to need a bit of privacy now," she said, "and several basins of hot water."

Belgarath sighed. "Again, Pol?" he said.

"Yes, father. It's time to clean up and change clothes—for all of us." She pointedly sniffed at the air in the small cave. "It's definitely time," she added.

They curtained off a portion of the cave to give Polgara, Ce'Nedra, and Velvet the privacy they required and began heating water over the fire.

Though at first reluctant even to move, Garion had to admit that after he had washed up and changed into clean, dry clothes, he did feel much better. He sat back on one of the bunks beside Ce'Nedra, not even particularly objecting to the damp smell of her hair. He had that comfortable sense of being clean, well fed, and warm after a day spent out of doors in bad weather. He was, in fact, right on the edge of dozing off when there echoed up the narrow ravine outside a vast bellow that seemed to be part animal and part human, a cry so dreadful that it chilled his blood and made the hair rise on the back of his neck.

"What's that?" Ce'Nedra exclaimed in fright.

"Hush now, girl," Feldegast warned softly. He jumped to his feet and quickly secured a piece of canvas across the opening of the fireplace, plunging the cave into near-darkness.

Another soulless bellow echoed up the ravine. The sound seemed filled with a dreadful malevolence.

"Can we put a name to whatever it is?" Sadi asked in a quiet voice.

"It's nothing I've ever heard before," Durnik assured him.

"I think I have," Belgarath said bleakly. "When I was in Morindland, there was a magician up there who thought it was amusing to turn his demon out at night to hunt. It made a sound like that."

"What an unsavory practice," the eunuch murmured. "What do demons eat?"

"You really wouldn't want to know," Silk replied. He turned to Belgarath. "Would you care to hazard a guess at just how big that thing might be?"

"It varies. From the amount of noise it's making, though, I'd say that it's fairly large."

"Then it wouldn't be able to get into this cave, would it?"

"That's a gamble I think I'd rather not take."

"It can sniff out our tracks, I assume?"

The old man nodded.

"Things are definitely going to pieces here, Belgarath. Can you do anything at all to drive it off?" The little man turned to Polgara. "Or perhaps you, Polgara. You dealt with the demon Chabat raised back in the harbor at Rak Urga."

"I had help, Silk," she reminded him. "Aldur came to my aid."

Belgarath began to pace up and down, scowling at the floor.

"Well?" Silk pressed.

"Don't rush me," the old man growled. "I *might* be able to do something," he said grudgingly, "but if I *do*, it's going to make so much noise that every Grolim in Katakor is going to hear it—and probably Zandramas as well. We'll have the

283

Chandim or her Grolims hot on our heels all the way to Ashaba."

"Why not use the Orb?" Eriond suggested, looking up from the bridle he was repairing.

"Because the Orb makes even more noise than I do. If Garion uses the Orb to chase off a demon, they're going to hear it in Gandahar all the way on the other side of the continent."

"But it *would* work, wouldn't it?"

Belgarath looked at Polgara.

"I think he's right, father," she said. "A demon *would* flee from the Orb—even if it were fettered by its master. An unfettered demon would flee even faster."

"Can you think of anything else?" he asked her.

"A God," she shrugged. "All demons—no matter how powerful—flee from the Gods. Do you happen to know any Gods?"

"A few," he replied, "but they're busy right now."

Another shattering bellow resounded through the mountains. It seemed to come from right outside the cave.

"It's time for some kind of decision, old man," Silk said urgently.

"It's the noise the Orb makes that bothers you?" Eriond asked.

"That and the light. That blue beacon that lights up every time Garion draws the sword attracts a lot of attention, you know."

"You aren't all suggesting that I fight a demon, are you?" Garion demanded indignantly.

"Of course not," Belgarath snorted. "Nobody fights a demon—nobody *can*. All we're discussing is the possibility of driving it off." He began to pace up and down again, scuffing his feet in the sand. "I hate to announce our presence here," he muttered.

Outside, the demon bellowed again, and the huge granite slab partially covering the cave mouth began to grate back and forth as if some huge force were rocking it to try to move it aside.

"Our options are running out, Belgarath," Silk told him. "And so is our time. If you don't do something quickly, that thing's going to be in here with us."

"Try not to pinpoint our location to the Grolims," Belgarath said to Garion.

"You really want me to go out there and do it?"

"Of course I do. Silk was right. Time's run out on us."

Garion went to his bunk and fished his mail shirt out from under it.

"You won't need that. It wouldn't do any good anyway."

Garion reached over his shoulder and drew his great sword. He set its point in the sand and peeled the soft leather sheath from its hilt. "I think this is a mistake," he declared. Then he reached out and put his hand on the Orb.

"Let me, Garion," Eriond said. He rose, came over, and covered Garion's hand with his own.

Garion gave him a startled look.

"It knows me, remember?" the young man explained, "and I've got a sort of an idea."

A peculiar tingling sensation ran through Garion's hand and arm, and he became aware that Eriond was communing with the Orb in a manner even more direct than he himself was capable of. It was is if during the months that the boy had been the bearer of the Orb, the stone had in some peculiar way taught him its own language.

There was a dreadful scratching coming from the mouth of the cave, as if huge talons were clawing at the stone slab.

"Be careful out there," Belgarath cautioned. "Don't take any chances. Just hold up the sword so that it can see it. The Orb should do the rest."

Garion sighed. "All right," he said, moving toward the cave mouth with Eriond directly behind him.

"Where are you going?" Polgara asked the blond young man.

"With Belgarion," Eriond replied. "We both need to talk with the Orb to get this right. I'll explain it later, Polgara."

The slab at the cave mouth was rocking back and forth again. Garion ducked quickly out from behind it and ran several yards up the ravine with Eriond on his heels. Then he turned and held up the sword.

"Not yet," Eriond warned. "It hasn't seen us."

There was an overpoweringly foul odor in the ravine, and then, as Garion's eyes slowly adjusted to the darkness, he saw the demon outlined against the clouds rolling overhead. It was enormous, its shoulders blotting out half the sky. It had long, pointed ears like those of a vast cat, and its dreadful eyes burned with a green fire that cast a fitful glow across the floor of the ravine.

It bellowed and reached toward Garion and Eriond with a great, scaly claw.

"Now, Belgarion," Eriond said quite calmly.

Garion lifted his arms, holding his sword directly in front of him with its point aimed at the sky, and then he released the curbs he had placed on the Orb.

He was not in the least prepared for what happened. A huge noise shook the earth and echoed off nearby mountains, causing giant trees miles away to tremble. Not only did the great blade take fire, but the entire sky suddenly shimmered an intense sapphire blue as if it had been ignited. Blue flame shot from horizon to horizon, and the vast sound continued to shake the earth.

The demon froze, its vast, tooth-studded muzzle turned upward to the blazing blue sky in terror. Grimly, Garion advanced on the thing, still holding his burning sword before him. The beast flinched back from him, trying to shield its face from the intense blue light. It screamed as if suddenly gripped by an intolerable agony. It stumbled back, falling and scrambling to its feet again. Then it took one more look at the blazing sky, turned, and fled howling back down the ravine with a peculiar loping motion as all four of its claws tore at the earth.

"*That* is your idea of quiet?" Belgarath thundered from the cave mouth. "And what's all that?" He pointed a trembling finger at the still-illuminated sky.

"It's really all right, Belgarath," Eriond told the infuriated old man. "You didn't want the sound to lead the Grolims to us, so we just made it general through the whole region. Nobody could have pinpointed its source."

Belgarath blinked. Then he frowned for a moment. "What about all the light?" he asked in a more mollified tone of voice.

"It's more or less the same with that," Eriond explained calmly. "If you've got a single blue fire in the mountains on a dark night, everybody can see it. If the whole sky catches on fire, though, nobody can really tell where it's coming from."

"It does sort of make sense, Grandfather," Garion said.

"Are they all right, father?" Polgara asked from behind the old man.

"What could possibly have hurt them? Garion can level mountains with that sword of his. He very nearly did, as a matter of fact. The whole Karandese range rang like a bell." He looked up at the still-flickering sky. "Can you turn that off?" he asked.

"Oh," Garion said. He reversed his sword and resheathed it in the scabbard strapped across his back. The fire in the sky died.

"We really had to do it that way, Belgarath," Eriond continued. "We needed the light and the sound to frighten off the demon and we had to do it in such a way that the Grolims couldn't follow it, so—" He spread both hands and shrugged.

"Did you know about this?" Belgarath asked Garion.

"Of course, Grandfather," Garion lied.

Belgarath grunted. "All right. Come back inside," he said.

Garion bent slightly toward Eriond's ear. "Why didn't you tell me what we were going to do?" he whispered.

287

"There wasn't really time, Belgarion."

"The next time we do something like that, *take* time. I almost dropped the sword when the ground started shaking under me."

"That wouldn't have been a good idea at all."

"I know."

A fair number of rocks had been shaken from the ceiling of the cave and lay on the sandy floor. Dust hung thickly in the air.

"What happened out there?" Silk demanded in a shaky voice.

"Oh, not much," Garion replied in a deliberately casual voice. "We just chased it away, that's all."

"There wasn't really any help for it, I guess," Belgarath said, "but just about everybody in Katakor knows that *something's* moving around in these mountains, so we're going to have to start being very careful."

"How much farther is it to Ashaba?" Sadi asked him.

"About a day's ride."

"Will we make it in time?"

"Only just. Let's all get some sleep."

Garion had the same dream again that night. He was not really sure that it was a dream, since dreaming usually involved sight as well as sound, but all there was to this one was that persistent, despairing wail and the sense of horror with which it filled him. He sat up on his bunk, trembling and sweat-covered. After a time, he drew his blanket about his shoulders, clasped his arms about his knees, and stared at the ruddy coals in the fireplace until he dozed off again.

It was still cloudy the following morning, and they rode cautiously back down the ravine to the rutted track leading up into the foothills of the mountains. Silk and Feldegast ranged out in front of them as scouts to give them warning should any dangers arise.

After they had ridden a league or so, the pair came back

down the narrow road. Their faces were sober, and they motioned for silence.

"There's a group of Karands camped around the road up ahead," Silk reported in a voice scarcely louder than a whisper.

"An ambush?" Sadi asked him.

"No," Feldegast replied in a low voice. "They're asleep fer the most part. From the look of things, I'd say that they spent the night in some sort of religious observance, an' so they're probably exhausted—or still drunk."

"Can we get around them?" Belgarath asked.

"It shouldn't be too much trouble," Silk replied. "We can just go off into the trees and circle around until we're past the spot where they're sleeping."

The old man nodded. "Lead the way," he said.

They left the road and angled off into the timber, moving at a cautious walk.

"What sort of ceremony were they holding?" Durnik asked quietly.

Silk shrugged. "It looked pretty obscure," Silk told him. "They've got an altar set up with skulls on posts along the back of it. There seems to have been quite a bit of drinking going on—as well as some other things."

"What sort of things?"

Silk's face grew slightly pained. "They have women with them," he answered disgustedly. "There's some evidence that things got a bit indiscriminate."

Durnik's cheeks suddenly turned bright red.

"Aren't you exaggerating a bit, Kheldar?" Velvet asked him.

"No, not really. Some of them were still celebrating."

"A bit more important than quaint local religious customs, though," Feldegast added, still speaking quietly, "be the peculiar pets the Karands was keepin'."

"Pets?" Belgarath asked.

"Perhaps 'tis not the right word, Ancient One, but sittin'

289

round the edges of the camp was a fair number of the Hounds—
an' they was makin' no move t' devour the celebrants."

Belgarath looked at him sharply. "Are you sure?"

"I've seen enough of the Hounds of Torak t' recognize
'em when I see 'em."

"So there *is* some kind of an alliance between Mengha and
Urvon," the old man said.

"Yer wisdom is altogether a marvel, old man. It must be a
delight beyond human imagination t' have the benefit of ten
thousand years experience t' guide ye in comin' t' such
conclusions."

"*Seven* thousand," Belgarath corrected.

"Seven—ten—what matter?"

"*Seven* thousand," Belgarath repeated with a slightly offended expression.

CHAPTER SIXTEEN

They rode that afternoon into a dead wasteland, a region foul and reeking, where white snags poked the skeltonlike fingers of their limbs imploringly at a dark, roiling sky and where dank ponds of oily, stagnant water exuded the reek of decay. Clots of fungus lay in gross profusion about the trunks of long-dead trees and matted-down weeds struggled up through ashy soil toward a sunless sky.

"It looks almost like Cthol Mishrak, doesn't it?" Silk asked, looking about distastefully.

"We're getting very close to Ashaba," Belgarath told him. "Something about Torak did this to the ground."

"Didn't he know?" Velvet said sadly.

"Know what?" Ce'Nedra asked her.

"That his very presence befouled the earth?"

"No," Ce'Nedra replied, "I don't think he did. His mind was so twisted that he couldn't even see it. The sun hid from him, and he saw that only as a mark of his power and not as a sign of its repugnance for him."

It was a peculiarly astute observation, which to some degree surprised Garion. His wife oftentimes seemed to have a wide streak of giddiness in her nature which made it far too easy to think of her as a child, a misconception reinforced by her diminutive size. But he had frequently found it necessary to reassess this tiny, often willful little woman who shared his life. Ce'Nedra might sometimes behave foolishly, but she was never stupid. She looked out at the world with a clear, unwavering vision that saw much more than gowns and jewels and costly perfumes. Quite suddenly he was so proud of her that he thought his heart would burst.

"How much farther is it to Ashaba?" Sadi asked in a subdued tone. "I hate to admit it, but this particular swamp depresses me."

"You?" Durnik said. "I thought you liked swamps."

"A swamp should be green and rich with life, Goodman," the eunuch replied. "There's nothing here but death." He looked at Velvet. "Have you got Zith, Margravine?" he asked rather plaintively. "I'm feeling a bit lonesome just now."

"She's sleeping at the moment, Sadi," she told him, her hand going to the front of her bodice in an oddly protective fashion. "She's safe and warm and very content. She's even purring."

"Resting in her perfumed little bower." He sighed. "There are times when I envy her."

"Why, Sadi," she said, blushing slightly, lowering her eyes, and then flashing her dimples at him.

"Merely a clinical observation, my dear Liselle," he said to her rather sadly. "There are times when I wish it could be otherwise, but . . ." He sighed again.

"Do you really have to carry that snake there?" Silk asked the blond girl.

"Yes, Kheldar," she replied, "as a matter of fact, I do."

"You didn't answer my question, Ancient One," Sadi said to Belgarath. "How much farther is it to Ashaba?"

"It's up there," the old sorcerer replied shortly, pointing toward a ravine angling sharply up from the reeking wasteland. "We should make it by dark."

"A particularly unpleasant time to visit a haunted house," Feldegast added.

As they started up the ravine, there came a sudden hideous growling from the dense undergrowth to one side of the weedy track, and a huge black Hound burst out of the bushes, its eyes aflame and with foam dripping from its cruel fangs. "Now you are mine!" it snarled, its jaws biting off the words.

Ce'Nedra screamed, and Garion's hand flashed back over his shoulder; but quick as he was, Sadi was even quicker. The eunuch spurred his terrified horse directly at the hulking dog. The beast rose, its jaws agape, but Sadi hurled a strangely colored powder of about the consistency of coarse flour directly into its face.

The Hound shook its head, still growling horribly. Then it suddenly screamed, a shockingly human sound. Its eyes grew wide in terror. Then it began desperately to snap at the empty air around it, whimpering and trying to cringe back. As suddenly as it had attacked, it turned and fled howling back into the undergrowth.

"What did you do?" Silk demanded.

A faint smile touch Sadi's slender features. "When ancient Belgarath told me about Torak's Hounds, I took certain precautions," he replied, his head slightly cocked as he listened to the terrified yelps of the huge dog receding off into the distance.

"Poison?"

"No. It's really rather contemptible to poison a dog if you don't have to. The Hound simply inhaled some of that powder

293

I threw in its face. Then it began to see some very distracting things—*very* distracting." He smiled again. "Once I saw a cow accidentally sniff the flower that's the main ingredient of the powder. The last time I saw her, she was trying to climb a tree." He looked over at Belgarath. "I hope you didn't mind my taking action without consulting you, Ancient One, but as you've pointed out, your sorcery might alert others in the region, and I had to move quickly to deal with the situation before you felt compelled to unleash it anyway."

"That's quite all right, Sadi," Belgarath replied. "I may have said it before, but you're a very versatile fellow."

"Merely a student of pharmacology, Belgarath. I've found that there are chemicals suitable for almost every situation."

"Won't the Hound report back to its pack that we're here?" Durnik asked, looking around worriedly.

"Not for several days." Sadi chuckled, brushing off his hands, holding them as far away from his face as possible.

They rode slowly up the weed-grown track along the bottom of the ravine where mournful, blackened trees spread their branches, filling the deep cut with a pervading gloom. Off in the distance they could hear the baying of Torak's Hounds as they coursed through the forest. Above them, sooty ravens flapped from limb to limb, croaking hungrily.

"Disquieting sort of place," Velvet murmured.

"And *that* adds the perfect touch," Silk noted, pointing at a large vulture perched on the limb of a dead snag at the head of the ravine.

"Are we close enough to Ashaba yet for you to be able to tell if Zandramas is still there?" Garion asked Polgara.

"Possibly," she replied. "But even that faint a sound could be heard."

"We're close enough now that we can wait," Belgarath said. "I'll tell you one thing, though," he added. "If my great-grandson *is* at Ashaba, I'll take the place apart stone by stone until I find him and I don't care *how* much noise it makes."

Impulsively, Ce'Nedra pulled her horse in beside his,

leaned over, and locked her arms about his waist. "Oh, Belgarath," she said, "I love you." And she burrowed her face into his shoulder.

"What's this?" His voice was slightly surprised.

She pulled back, her eyes misty. She wiped at them with the back of her hand, then gave him an arch look. "You're the dearest man in all the world," she told him. "I might even consider throwing Garion over for you," she added, "if it weren't for the fact that you're twelve thousand years old, that is."

"Seven," he corrected automatically.

She gave him a sadly whimsical smile, a melancholy sign of her final victory in an on-going contest that no longer had any meaning for her. "Whatever," she sighed.

And then in a peculiarly uncharacteristic gesture, he enfolded her in his arms and gently kissed her. "My dear child," he said with brimming eyes. Then he looked back over his shoulder at Polgara. "How did we ever get along without her?" he asked.

Polgara's eyes were a mystery. "I don't know, father," she replied. "I really don't."

At the head of the ravine, Sadi dismounted and dusted the leaves of a low bush growing in the middle of the track they were following with some more of his powder. "Just to be on the safe side," he explained, pulling himself back into his saddle.

The region they entered under a lowering sky was a wooded plateau, and they rode on along the scarcely visible track in a generally northerly direction with the rising wind whipping at their cloaks. The baying of Torak's Hounds still sounded from some distance off, but seemed to be coming no closer.

As before, Silk and Feldegast raged out ahead, scouting for possible dangers. Garion again rode at the head of their column, his helmet in place and the butt of his lance riding in his stirrup. As he rounded a sharp bend in the track, he saw Silk and the juggler ahead. They had dismounted and were crouched behind some bushes. Silk turned quickly and motioned Garion back. Garion quickly passed on that signal and, step by step, backed his gray stallion around the bend again. He dismounted, leaned his lance against a tree, and took off his helmet.

"What is it?" Belgarath asked, also swinging down from his horse.

"I don't know," Garion replied. "Silk motioned us to stay out of sight."

"Let's go have a look," the old man said.

"Right."

The two of them crouched over and moved forward on silent feet to join the rat-faced man and the juggler. Silk put his finger to his lips as they approached. When Garion reached the brush, he carefully parted the leaves and looked out.

There was a road there, a road that intersected the track they had been following. Riding along that road were half-a-hundred men dressed mostly in furs, with rusty helmets on their heads and bent and dented swords in their hands. The men at the head of the column, however, wore mail coats. Their helmets were polished, and they carried lances and shields.

Tensely, without speaking, Garion and his friends watched the loosely organized mob ride past.

When the strangers were out of sight, Feldegast turned to Belgarath. "It sort of confirms yer suspicion, old friend," he said.

"Who were they?" Garion asked in a low voice.

"The ones in fur be Karands," Feldegast replied, "an' the ones in steel be Temple Guardsmen. 'Tis more evidence of an alliance between Urvon and Mengha, y' see."

"Can we be sure that the Karands were Mengha's men?"

"He's overcome Katakor altogether, an' the only armed Karands in the area be his. Urvon an' his Chandim control the Guardsmen—an' the Hounds. When ye see Karands an' Hounds together the way we did yesterday, it's fair proof of an alliance, but when ye see Karandese fanatics escorted by armed Guardsmen, it doesn't leave hardly any doubt at all."

"What *is* that fool up to?" Belgarath muttered.

"Who?" Silk asked.

"Urvon. He's done some fairly filthy things in his life, but he's never consorted with demons before."

"Perhaps 'twas because Torak had forbid it," Feldegast suggested. "Now that Torak's dead, though, maybe he's throwin' off all restraints. The demons would be a powerful factor if the final confrontation between the Church an' the imperial throne that's been brewin' all these years should finally come."

"Well," Belgarath grunted, "we don't have time to sort it out now. Let's get the others and move on."

They quickly crossed the road that the Karands and the Guardsmen had been following and continued along the narrow track. After a few more miles, they crested a low knoll that at some time in the past had been denuded by fire. At the far end of the plateau, just before a series of stark cliffs rose sharply up into the mountains, there stood a huge black building, rearing up almost like a mountain itself. It was surmounted by bleak towers and surrounded by a battlement-topped wall, half-smothered in vegetation.

"Ashaba," Belgarath said shortly, his eyes flinty.

"I thought it was a ruin," Silk said with some surprise.

"Parts of it are, I've been told," the old man replied. "The upper floors aren't habitable any more, but the ground floor's still more or less intact—at least it's supposed to be. It takes a very long time for wind and weather to tear down a house that big." The old man nudged his horse and led them down off the knoll and back into the wind-tossed forest.

It was nearly dark by the time they reached the edge of the clearing surrounding the House of Torak. Garion noted that the vegetation half-covering the walls of the black castle consisted of brambles and thick-stemmed ivy. The glazing in the windows had long since succumbed to wind and weather, and the vacant casements seemed to stare out at the clearing like the eye sockets of a dark skull.

"Well, father?" Polgara said.

He scratched at his beard, listening to the baying of the Hounds back in the forest.

"If yer open t' a bit of advice, me ancient friend," Feldegast said, "wouldn't it be wiser t' wait until dark before we go in? Should there be watchers in the house, the night will conceal us from their eyes. An' then, too, once it grows dark, there'll undoubtedly be lights inside if the house be occupied. 'Twill give us some idea of what t' expect."

"It makes sense, Belgarath," Silk agreed. "Walking openly up to an unfriendly house in broad daylight disturbs my sense of propriety."

"That's because you've got the soul of a burglar. But it's probably the best plan anyhow. Let's pull back into the woods a ways and wait for dark."

Though the weather had been warm and springlike on the plains of Rakuth and Venna, here in the foothills of the Karandese mountains there was still a pervading chill, for winter only reluctantly released its grip on these highlands. The wind was raw, and there were some places back under the trees where dirty windrows of last winter's snow lay deep and unyielding.

"Is that wall around the house going to cause us any problems?" Garion asked.

"Not unless someone's repaired the gates," Belgarath replied. "When Beldin and I came in here after Vo Mimbre, they were all locked, so we had to break them down to get in."

"Walkin' openly up to them gates might not be the best idea in the world, Belgarath," Feldegast said, "fer if the house do be occupied by Chandim or Karands or Guardsmen, 'tis certain that the gates are goin' t' be watched, an' there be a certain amount of light even on the darkest night. There be a sally port on the east side of the house though, an' it gives entry into an inner court that's sure t' be filled with deep shadows as soon as the night comes on."

"Won't it be barred off?" Silk asked him.

"T' be sure, Prince Kheldar, it was indeed. The lock, however, was not difficult fer a man with fingers as nimble as mine."

"You've been inside, then?"

"I like t' poke around in abandoned houses from time t' time. One never knows what the former inhabitants might have left behind, an' findin' is often times as good as earnin' or stealin'."

"I can accept that," Silk agreed.

Durnik came back from the edge of the woods where he had been watching the house. He had a slightly worried look on his face. "I'm not entirely positive," he said, "but it looks as if there are clouds of smoke coming out of the towers of that place."

"I'll just go along with ye an' have a bit of a look," the juggler said, and he and the smith went back through the deepening shadows beneath the trees. After a few minutes they came back. Durnik's expression was faintly disgusted.

"Smoke?" Belgarath asked.

Feldegast shook his head. "Bats," he replied. "Thousands of the little beasties. They be comin' out of the towers in great black clouds."

"Bats?" Ce'Nedra exclaimed, her hands going instinctively to her hair.

"It's not uncommon," Polgara told her. "Bats need protected places to nest in, and a ruin or an abandoned place is almost ideal for them."

"But they're so *ugly*!" Ce'Nedra declared with a shudder.

"'Tis only a flyin' mouse, me little darlin'," Feldegast told her.

"I'm not fond of mice, either."

"'Tis a very unforgivin' woman ye've married, young Master," Feldegast said to Garion, "brim-full of prejudices an' unreasonable dislikes."

"More important, did you see any lights coming from inside?" Belgarath asked.

"Not so much as a glimmer, Ancient One, but the house be large, an' there be chambers inside which have no windows. Torak was unfond of the sun, as ye'll recall."

"Let's move around through the woods until we're closer to this sally port of yours," the old man suggested, "before the light goes entirely."

They stayed back from the edge of the trees as they circled around the clearing with the great black house in its center. The last light was beginning to fade from the cloud-covered sky as they cautiously peered out from the edge of the woods.

"I can't quite make out the sally port," Silk murmured, peering toward the house.

"'Tis partially concealed," Feldegast told him. "If ye give ivy the least bit of a toe hold, it can engulf a whole buildin' in a few hundred years. Quiet yer fears, Prince Kheldar. I know me way, an' I kin find the entrance t' the House of Torak on the blackest of nights."

"The Hounds are likely to be patrolling the area around here after dark, aren't they?" Garion said. He looked at Sadi. "I hope you didn't use up all of your powder back there."

"There's more than enough left, Belgarion." The eunuch smiled, patting his pouch. "A light dusting at the entrance to Master Feldegast's sally port should insure that we won't be disturbed once we're inside."

"What do you think?" Durnik asked, squinting up at the dark sky.

"It's close enough," Belgarath grunted. "I want to get inside."

They led their horses across the weed-choked clearing until they reached the looming wall.

"'Tis this way just a bit," Feldegast said in a low voice as he began to feel his way along the rough black stones of the wall.

They followed him for several minutes, guided more by the faint rustling sound of his feet among the weeds than by sight.

"An' here we are, now," Feldegast said with some satisfaction. It was a low, arched entrance in the wall, almost totally smothered in ivy and brambles. Durnik and the giant Toth, moving slowly to avoid making too much noise, pulled the obstructing vines aside to allow the rest of them and the horses to enter. Then they followed, pulling the vines back in place once again to conceal the entrance.

Once they were inside, it was totally dark, and there was the musty smell of mildew and fungus. "May I borrow yer flint an' steel an' tinder again, Goodman Durnik?" Feldegast whispered. Then there was a small clinking sound, followed by a rapid clicking accompanied by showers of glowing sparks as Feldegast, kneeling so that his body concealed even those faint glimmers, worked with Durnik's flint and steel. After a moment, he blew on the tinder, stirring a tiny flame to life. There was another clink as he opened the front of a square lantern he had taken from a small niche in the wall.

"Is that altogether wise?" Durnik asked doubtfully as the juggler lighted the candle stub inside the lantern and returned the flint and steel.

"'Tis a well-shielded little bit of a light, Goodman," Feldegast told him, "an' it be darker than the inside of yer boots in this place. Trust me in this, fer I kin keep it so well concealed that not the tiniest bit of a glow will escape me control."

"Isn't that what they call a burglar's lantern?" Silk asked curiously.

"Well, now." Feldegast's whisper sounded slightly injured. "I don't know that I'd call it that, exactly. 'Tis a word that has an unsavory ring t' it."

"Belgarath," Silk chuckled softly. "I think your friend here has a more checkered past than we've been led to believe. I wondered why I liked him so much."

Feldegast had closed down the tin sides of his little lantern, allowing only a single, small spot of light feebly to illuminate the floor directly in front of his feet. "Come along, then," he told them. "The sally port goes back a way under the wall here, an' then we come t' the grate that used t' close it off. Then it makes a turn t' the right an' a little farther on, another t' the left, an' then it comes out in the courtyard of the house."

"Why so many twists and turns?" Garion asked him.

"Torak was a crooked sort, don't y' know. I think he hated straight lines almost as much as he hated the sun."

They followed the faint spot of light the lantern cast. Leaves had blown in through the entrance over the centuries to lie in a thick, damp mat on the floor, effectively muffling the sounds of their horses' hooves.

The grate that barred the passageway was a massively constructed criss cross of rusty iron. Feldegast fumbled for a moment with the huge latch, then swung it clear. "An' now, me large friend," he said to Toth, "we'll be havin' need of yer great strength here. The gate is cruel heavy, let me warn ye, an' the hinges be so choked with rust that they'll not likely yield easily." He paused a moment. "An' that reminds me— ah, where have me brains gone? We'll be needin' somethin' t' mask the dreadful squeakin' when ye swing the grate open." He looked back at the others. "Take a firm grip on the reins of yer horses," he warned them, "fer this is likely t' give 'em a bit of a turn."

Toth place his huge hands on the heavy grate, then looked at the juggler.

"Go!" Feldegast said sharply, then he lifted his face and bayed, his voice almost perfectly imitating the sound of one of the great Hounds prowling outside, even as the giant slowly swung the grate open on shrieking hinges.

302

Chretienne snorted and shied back from the dreadful howl, but Garion held his reins tightly.

"Oh, that was clever," Silk said in quiet admiration.

"I have me moments from time to time," Feldegast admitted. "With all the dogs outside raisin' their awful caterwallin', 'tis certain that one more little yelp won't attract no notice, but the squealin' of them hinges could have been an altogether different matter."

He led then on through the now-open grate and on along the dank passageway to a sharp right-hand turn. Somewhat farther along, the passage bent again to the left. Before he rounded that corner, the juggler closed down his lantern entirely, plunging them into total darkness. "We be approachin' the main court now," he whispered to them. "'Tis the time for silence an' caution, fer if there be others in the house, they'll be payin' a certain amount of attention t' be sure that no one creeps up on 'em. There be a handrail along the wall there, an' I think it might be wise t' tie the horses here. Their hooves would make a fearful clatter on the stones of the court, an' we'll not be wantin' t' ride them up an' down the corridors of this accursed place."

Silently they tied the reins of their mounts to the rusty iron railing and then crept on quiet feet to the turn in the passageway. There was a lessening of the darkness beyond the turn—not light, certainly, but a perceptible moderation of the oppressive gloom. And then they reached the inside entrance to the sally port and looked out across the broad courtyard toward the looming black house beyond. There was no discernible grace to the construction of that house. It rose in blocky ugliness almost as if the builders had possessed no understanding of the meaning of the word beauty, but had striven instead for a massive kind of arrogance to reflect the towering pride of its owner.

"Well," Belgarath whispered grimly, "that's Ashaba."

Garion looked at the dark house before him, half in apprehension and half with a kind of dreadful eagerness.

Something caught his eye then, and he thrust his head out to look along the front of the house across the court. At the far end, in a window on a lower floor, a dim light glowed, looking for all the world like a watchful eye.

CHAPTER SEVENTEEN

"Now what?" Silk breathed, looking at the dimly lighted window. "We've got to cross that courtyard to get to the house, but we can't be sure if there's somebody watching from that window or not."

"You've been out of the academy for too long, Kheldar," Velvet murmured. "You've forgotten your lessons. If stealth is impossible, then you try boldness."

"You're suggesting that we just walk up to the door and knock?"

"Well, I hadn't planned to knock, exactly."

"What have you got in mind, Liselle?" Polgara asked quietly.

"If there are people in the house, they're probably Grolims, right?"

"It's more than likely," Belgarath said. "Most other people avoid this place."

"Grolims pay little attention to other Grolims, I've noticed," she continued.

"You're forgetting that we don't have any Grolim robes with us," Silk pointed out.

"It's very dark in that courtyard, Kheldar, and in shadows that deep, any dark color would appear black, wouldn't it?"

"I suppose so," he admitted.

"And we still have those green silk slavers' robes in our packs, don't we?"

He squinted at her in the darkness, then looked at Belgarath. "It goes against all my instincts," he said, "but it might just work, at that."

"One way or another, we've got to get into the house. We have to find out who's in there—and why—before we can decide anything."

"Would Zandramas have Grolims with her?" Ce'Nedra asked. "If she's alone in that house and she sees a line of Grolims walking across the courtyard, wouldn't that frighten her into running away with my baby?"

Belgarath shook his head. "Even if she does run, we're close enough to catch her—particularly since the Orb can follow her no matter how much she twists and dodges. Besides, if she's here, she's probably got some of her own Grolims with her. It's not really so far from here to Darshiva that she couldn't have summoned them."

"What about him?" Durnik whispered the question and pointed at Feldegast. "He hasn't got a slavers' robe."

"We'll improvise something," Velvet murmured. She smiled at the juggler. "I've got a nice dark blue dressing gown that should set off his eyes marvelously. We can add a kerchief to resemble a hood and we can slip him by—if he stays in the middle of the group."

"'Twould be beneath me dignity," he objected.

"Would you prefer to stay behind and watch the horses?" she asked pleasantly.

"'Tis a hard woman y' are, me lady," he complained.

"Sometimes, yes."

"Let's do it," Belgarath decided. "I've got to get inside that house."

It took only a few moments to retrace their steps to the place where the horses were tied and to pull the neatly folded slavers' robes from their packs by the dim light of Feldegast's lantern.

"Isn't this ridiculous, now?" the juggler grumbled indignantly, pointing down at the blue satin gown Velvet had draped about him.

"I think it looks just darling," Ce'Nedra said.

"If there are people in there, aren't they likely to be patrolling the corridors?" Durnik asked.

"Only on the main floor, Goodman," Feldegast replied. "The upper stories of the house be almost totally uninhabitable—on account of all the broken windows an' the weather blowin' around in the corridors fer all the world like they was part of the great outdoors. There be a grand staircase just opposite the main door, an' with just a bit of luck we kin nip up the stairs an' be out of sight with no one the wiser. Once we're up there, we're not likely t' encounter a livin' soul—unless ye be countin' the bats an' mice an' an occasional adventuresome rat."

"You absolutely had to say that, didn't you?" Ce'Nedra said caustically.

"Ah, me poor little darlin'." He grinned at her. "But quiet yer fears. I'll be beside ye an' I've yet t' meet the bat or mouse or rat I couldn't best in a fair fight."

"It makes sense, Belgarath," Silk said. "If we all go trooping through the lower halls, sooner or later someone's bound to notice us. Once we're upstairs and out of sight, though,

I'll be able to reconnoiter and find out exactly what we're up against."

"All right," the old man agreed, "but the first thing is to get inside."

"Let's be off, then," Feldegast said, swirling his dressing gown about him with a flourish.

"Hide that light," Belgarath told him.

They filed out through the entrance to the sally port and marched into the shadowy courtyard, moving in the measured, swaying pace Grolim priests assumed on ceremonial occasions. The lighted window at the end of the house seemed somehow like a burning eye that followed their every move.

The courtyard was really not all that large, but it seemed to Garion that crossing it took hours. Eventually, however, they reached the main door. It was large, black, and nail-studded, like the door of every Grolim temple Garion had ever seen. The steel mask mounted over it, however, was no longer polished. In the faint light coming from the window at the other end of the house, Garion could see that over the centuries it had rusted, making the coldly beautiful face look scabrous and diseased. What made it look perhaps even more hideous were the twin gobbets of lumpy, semiliquid rust running from the eye sockets down the cheeks. Garion remembered with a shudder the fiery tears that had run down the stricken God's face before he had fallen.

They mounted the three steps to that bleak door, and Toth slowly pushed it open.

The corridor inside was dimly illuminated by a single flickering torch at the far end. Opposite the door, as Feldegast had told them, was a broad staircase reaching up into the darkness. The treads were littered with fallen stones, and cobwebs hung in long festoons from a ceiling lost in shadows. Still moving at that stately Grolim pace, Belgarath led them across the corridor and started up the stairs. Garion followed close behind him with measured tread, though every nerve screamed at him to run. They had gone perhaps halfway up the staircase when they heard a clinking sound behind them, and there was a sudden light at the foot of the stairs. "What are you doing?" a rough voice demanded. "Who are you?"

Garion's heart sank, and he turned. The man at the foot of the stairs wore a long, coatlike shirt of mail. He was helmeted and had a shield strapped to his left arm. With his right he held aloft a sputtering torch.

"Come back down here," the mailed man commanded them.

The giant Toth turned obediently, his hood pulled far over his face with his arms crossed so that his hands were inside his sleeves. With an air of meekness he started down the stairs again.

"I mean all of you," the Temple Guardsman insisted. "I order you in the name of the God of Angarak."

As Toth reached the foot of the stairs, the Guardsman's eyes widened as he realized that the robe the huge man wore was not Grolim black. "What's this?" he exclaimed. "You're not Chandim! You're—" He broke off suddenly as one of Toth's huge hands seized him by the throat and lifted him off the floor. He dropped his torch, kicking and struggling. Then, almost casually, Toth removed his helmet with his other hand and banged his head several times against the stone wall of the corridor. With a shudder, the mail-coated man went limp. Toth draped the unconscious form across his shoulder and started back up the stairs.

Silk bounded back down to the corridor, picked up the steel helmet and extinguished torch, and came back up again. "Always clean up the evidence," he murmured to Toth. "No crime is complete until you've tidied up."

Toth grinned at him.

As they neared the top of the stairs, they found the treads covered with leaves that had blown in from the outside, and the cobwebs hung in tatters like rotted curtains, swaying in the wind that came moaning in from the outside through the shattered windows.

The hall at the top of the stairs was littered. Dry leaves lay in ankle-deep windrows on the floor, skittering before the wind. A large, empty casement at the end of the corridor behind them was half covered with thick ivy that shook and rustled in the chill night wind blowing down off the slopes of the mountains. Doors had partially rotted away and hung in chunks from their hinges. The rooms beyond those doors were choked with leaves and dust, and the furniture and bedding had long since surrendered every scrap of cloth or padding to thousands of generations of industrious mice in search of nesting materials. Toth carried his unconscious captive into one of those rooms, bound him hand and foot, and then gagged him to muffle any outcry, should he awaken before dawn.

"That light was at the other end of the house, wasn't it?" Garion asked. "What's at that end?"

"'Twas the livin' quarters of Torak himself," Feldegast replied, adjusting his little lantern so that it emitted a faint beam of light. "His throne room be there, an' his private chapel. I could even show ye t' his personal bedroom, an' ye could bounce up an' down on his great bed—or what's left of it—just fer fun, if yer of a mind."

"I think I could live without doing that."

Belgarath had been tugging at one earlobe. "Have you been here lately?" he asked the juggler.

"Perhaps six months ago."

"Was anybody here?" Ce'Nedra demanded.

"I'm afraid not, me darlin'. 'Twas as empty as a tomb."

"That was before Zandramas got here, Ce'Nedra," Polgara reminded her gently.

"Why do ye ask, Belgarath?" Feldegast said.

"I haven't been here since just after Vo Mimbre," Belgarath said as they continued down the littered hall. "The house was fairly sound then, but Angaraks aren't really notorious for the permanence of their construction. How's the mortar holding out?"

"'Tis as crumbly as year-old bread."

310

Belgarath nodded. "I thought it might be," he said. "Now, what we're after here is information, not open warfare in the corridors."

"Unless the one who's here happens to be Zandramas," Garion corrected. "If she's still here with my son, I'll start a war that's going to make Vo Mimbre look like a country fair."

"And I'll clean up anything he misses," Ce'Nedra added fiercely.

"Can't you control them?" Belgarath asked his daughter.

"Not under the circumstances, no," she replied. "I might even decide to join in myself."

"I thought that we'd more or less erased the Alorn side of your nature, Pol," he said to her.

"That's not the side that was just talking, father."

"My point," Belgarath said, "at least the point I was trying to make before everybody started flexing his—or her—muscles, is that it's altogether possible that we'll be able to hear and maybe even see what's going on in the main part of the house from up here. If the mortar's as rotten as Feldegast says it is, it shouldn't be too hard to find—or make—some little crevices in the floor of one of these rooms and find out what we need to know. If Zandramas is here, that's one thing, and we'll deal with her in whatever way seems appropriate. But if the only people down there are some of Urvon's Chandim and Guardsmen or a roving band of Mengha's Karandese fanatics, we'll pick up Zandramas' trail and go on about our business without announcing our presence."

"That sounds reasonable," Durnik agreed. "It doesn't make much sense to get involved in unnecessary fights."

"I'm glad that *someone* in this belligerent little group has some common sense," the old man said.

"Of course, if it *is* Zandramas down there," the smith added, "I'll have to take steps myself."

"You, too?" Belgarath groaned.

"Naturally. After all, Belgarath, right is right."

They moved on along the leaf-strewn corridor where the

cobwebs hung from the ceiling in tatters and where there were skittering sounds in the corners.

As they passed a large double door so thick that it was still intact, Belgarath seemed to remember something. "I want to look in here," he muttered. As he opened those doors, the sword strapped across Garion's back gave a violent tug that very nearly jerked him off his feet. "Grandfather!" he gasped. He reached back, instructing the Orb to restrain itself, and drew the great blade. The point dipped to the floor, and then he was very nearly dragged into the room. "She's been here," he exulted.

"What?" Durnik asked.

"Zandramas. She's been in this room with Geran."

Feldegast opened the front of his lantern wider to throw more light into the room. It was a library, large and vaulted, with shelves reaching from the floor to the ceiling and filled with dusty, moldering books and scrolls.

"So *that* was what she was looking for," Belgarath said.

"For what?" Silk asked.

"A book. A prophecy, most likely." His face grew grim. "She's following the same trail that I am, and this would probably be just about the only place where she could find an uncorrupted copy of the Ashabine Oracles."

"Oh!" Ce'Nedra's little cry was stricken. She pointed a trembling hand at the dust-covered floor. There were footprints there. Some of them had obviously been made by a woman's shoes, but there were others as well—quite tiny. "My baby's been here," Ce'Nedra said in a voice near tears, and then she gave a little wail and began to weep. "H-he's walking," she sobbed, "and I'll never be able to see his first steps."

Polgara moved to her and took her into a comforting embrace.

Garion's eyes also filled with tears, and his grip on the hilt of his sword grew so tight that his knuckles turned white. He felt an almost overpowering need to smash things.

Belgarath was swearing under his breath.

"What's the matter?" Silk asked him.

"That was the main reason I had to come here," the old man grated. "I need a clean copy of the Ashabine Oracles, and Zandramas has beaten me to it."

"Maybe there's another."

"Not a chance. She's been running ahead of me burning books at every turn. If there was more than one copy here, she'd have made sure that I couldn't get my hands on it. That's why she stayed here so long—ransacking this place to make sure that she had the only copy." He started to swear again.

"Is this in any way significant?" Eriond said, going to a table that, unlike the others in the room, had been dusted and even polished. In the precise center of that table lay a book bound in black leather and flanked on each side by a candlestick. Eriond picked it up, and as he did so, a neatly folded sheet of parchment fell out from between its leaves. The young man bent, picked it up, and glanced at it.

"What's that?" Belgarath demanded.

"It's a note," Eriond replied. "It's for you." He handed the parchment and the book to the old man.

Belgarath read the note. His face went suddenly pale and then beet red. He ground his teeth together with the veins swelling in his face and neck. Garion felt the sudden building up of the old sorcerer's will.

"Father!" Polgara snapped, "No! Remember that we aren't alone here!"

He controlled himself with a tremendous effort, then crumpled the parchment into a ball and hurled it at the floor so hard that it bounced high into the air and rolled across the room. He swung back the hand holding the book as if he were about to send it after the ball of parchment, but then seemed to think better of it. He opened the book at random, turned a few pages, and then began to swear sulfurously. He shoved the book at Garion. "Here," he said, "hold on to this." Then he began to pace up and down, his face as black as a thundercloud, muttering curses and waving his hands in the air.

Garion opened the book, tilting it to catch the light. He saw at once the reason for Belgarath's anger. Whole passages had been neatly excised—not merely blotted out, but cut entirely from the page with a razor or a very sharp knife. Garion also started to swear.

Silk curiously went over, picked up the parchment, and looked at it. He swallowed hard and looked apprehensively at the swearing Belgarath. "Oh, my," he said.

"What is it?" Garion asked.

"I think we'd all better stay out of your grandfather's way for a while," the rat-faced man replied. "It might take him a little bit to get hold of himself."

"Just read it, Silk," Polgara said. "Don't editorialize."

Silk looked again at Belgarath, who was now at the far end of the room pounding on the stone wall with his fist. "'Belgarath,'" he read. "'I have beaten thee, old man. Now I go to the Place Which Is No More for the final meeting. Follow me if thou canst. Perhaps this book will help thee.'"

"Is it signed?" Velvet asked him.

"Zandramas," he replied. "Who else?"

"That is a truly offensive letter," Sadi murmured. He looked at Belgarath, who continued to pound his fist on the wall in impotent fury. "I'm surprised that he's taking it so well—all things considered."

"It answers a lot of questions, though," Velvet said thoughtfully.

"Such as what?" Silk asked.

"We were wondering if Zandramas was still here. Quite obviously, she's not. Not even an idiot would leave that kind of message for Belgarath and then stay around where he could get his hands on her."

"That's true," he agreed. "There's no real point in our staying here, then, is there? The Orb has picked up the trail

314

again, so why don't we just slip out of the house again and go after Zandramas?"

"Without findin' out who's here?" Feldegast objected. "Me curiosity has been aroused, an' I'd hate t' go off with it unsatisfied." He glanced across the room at the fuming Belgarath. "Besides, it's goin' t' be a little while before our ancient friend there regains his composure. I think I'll go along t' the far end of the hall an' see if I kin find a place where I kin look down into the lower part of the house—just t' answer some burnin' questions which have been naggin' at me." He went to the table and lighted one of the candles from his little lantern. "Would ye be wantin' t' come along with me, Prince Kheldar?" he invited.

Silk shrugged. "Why not?"

"I'll go, too," Garion said. He handed the book to Polgara and then pointedly looked at the raging Belgarath. "Is he going to get over that eventually?"

"I'll talk with him, dear. Don't be too long."

He nodded, and then he, Silk, and the juggler quietly left the library.

There was a room at the far end of the hall. It was not particularly large, and there were shelves along the walls. Garion surmised that it had at one time been a storeroom or a linen closet. Feldegast squinted appraisingly at the leaf-strewn floor, then closed his lantern.

The leaves had piled deep in the corners and along the walls, but in the sudden darkness a faint glow shone up through them, and there came the murmur of voices from below.

"Me vile-tempered old friend seems t' have been right," Feldegast whispered. "'Twould appear that the mortar has quite crumbled away along that wall. 'Twill be but a simple matter t' brush the leaves out of the way an' give ourselves some convenient spy holes. Let's be havin' a look an' find out who's taken up residence in the House of Torak."

Garion suddenly had that strange sense of reexperiencing

315

something that had happened a long time ago. It had been in King Anheg's palace at Val Alorn, and he had followed the man in the green cloak through the deserted upper halls until they had come to a place where crumbling mortar had permitted the sound of voices to come up from below. Then he remembered something else. When they had been at Tol Honeth, hadn't Belgarath said that most of the things that had happened while they were pursuing Zedar and the Orb were likely to happen again, since everything was leading up to another meeting between the Child of Light and the Child of Dark? He tried to shake off the feeling, but without much success.

They removed the leaves from the crack running along the far wall of the storeroom carefully, trying to avoid sifting any of them down into the room below. Then each of them selected a vantage point from which to watch and listen.

The room into which they peered was very large. Ragged drapes hung at the windows, and the corners were thick with cobwebs. Smoky torches hung in iron rings along the walls, and the floor was thick with dust and the litter of ages. The room was filled with black-robed Grolims, a sprinkling of roughly clad Karands, and a large number of gleaming Temple Guardsmen. Near the front, drawn up like a platoon of soldiers, a group of the huge black Hounds of Torak sat on their haunches expectantly. In front of the Hounds stood a black altar, showing signs of recent use, flanked on either side by a glowing brazier. Against the wall on a high dais was a golden throne, backed by thick, tattered black drapes and by a huge replica of the face of Torak.

"'Twas Burnt-face's throne room, don't y' know," Feldegast whispered.

"Those are Chandim, aren't they?" Garion whispered back.

"The very same—both human an' beast—along with their mail-shirted bully boys. I'm a bit surprised that Urvon has chosen t' occupy the place with his dogs—though the best use fer Ashaba has probably always been as a kennel."

316

It was obvious that the men in the throne room were expecting something by the nervous way they kept looking at the throne.

Then a great gong sounded from below, shimmering in the smoky air.

"On your knees!" a huge voice commanded the throng in the large room. "Pay obeisance and homage to the new God of Angarak!"

"*What?*" Silk exclaimed in a choked whisper.

"Watch an' be still!" Feldegast snapped.

From below there came a great roll of drums, followed by a brazen fanfare. The rotten drapes near the golden throne parted, and a double file of robed Grolims entered, chanting fervently, even as the assembled Chandim and Guardsmen fell to their knees and the Hounds and the Karands groveled and whined.

The booming of the drums continued, and then a figure garbed in cloth of gold and wearing a crown strode imperiously out from between the drapes. A glowing nimbus surrounded the figure, though Garion could clearly sense that the will that maintained the glow emanated from the gold-clad man himself. Then the figure lifted its head in a move of overweening arrogance. The man's face was splotched—some patches showing the color of healthy skin and others a hideous dead white. What chilled Garion's blood the most, however, was the fact that the man's eyes were totally mad.

"Urvon!" Feldegast said with a sudden intake of his breath. "You piebald son of a mangy dog!" All trace of his lilting accent had disappeared.

Directly behind the patch-faced madman came a shadowy figure, cowled so deeply that its face was completely obscured. The black that covered it was not that of a simple Grolim robe, but seemed to grow out of the figure itself, and Garion felt a cold dread as a kind of absolute evil permeated the air about that black shape.

Urvon mounted the dais and seated himself on the throne,

317

his insane eyes bulging and his face frozen in that expression of imperious pride. The shadow-covered figure took its place behind his left shoulder and bent forward toward his ear, whispering, whispering.

The Chandim, Guardsmen, and Karands in the throne room continued to grovel, fawning and whining, even as did the Hounds, while the last disciple of Torak preened himself in the glow of their adulation. A dozen or so of the black-robed Chandim crept forward on their knees, bearing gilded chests and reverently placing them on the altar before the dais. When they opened the chests, Garion saw that they were all filled to the brim with red Angarak gold and with jewels.

"These offerings are pleasing to mine eyes," the enthroned Disciple declared in a shrill voice. "Let others come forth to make also their offerings unto the new God of Angarak."

There was a certain amount of consternation among the Chandim and a few hasty consultations.

The next group of offerings were in plain wooden boxes; when they were opened, they revealed only pebbles and twigs. Each of the Chandim who bore those boxes to the alter surreptitiously removed one of the gilded chests after depositing his burden on the black stone.

Urvon gloated over the chests and boxes, apparently unable to distinguish between gold and gravel, as the line continued to move toward the altar, each priest laying one offering on the altar and removing another before returning to the end of the line.

"I am well pleased with ye, my priests," Urvon said in his shrill voice when the charade had been played out. "Truly, ye have brought before me the wealth of nations."

As the Chandim, Karands, and Guardsmen rose to their feet, the shadowy figure at Urvon's shoulder continued to whisper.

"And now will I receive Lord Mengha" the madman announced, "most favored of all who serve me, for he has delivered unto me this familiar spirit who revealed my high divinity unto me." He indicated the shadow behind him.

"Summon the Lord Mengha that he may pay homage to the God Urvon and be graciously received by the new God of Angarak." The voice that boomed that command was as hollow as a voice issuing from a tomb.

From the door at the back of the hall came another fanfare of trumpets, and another hollow voice responded. "All hail Urvon, new God of Angarak," it intoned. "Lord Mengha approacheth to make his obeisance and to seek counsel with the living God."

Again there came the booming of drums, and a man robed in Grolim black paced down the broad aisle toward the altar and the dais. As he reached the altar, he genuflected to the madman seated on Torak's throne.

"Look now upon the awesome face of Lord Mengha, most favored servant of the God Urvon and soon to become First Disciple," the hollow voice boomed.

The figure before the altar turned and pushed back his hood to reveal his face to the throng.

Garion stared, supressing a gasp of surprise. The man standing before the altar was Harakan.

CHAPTER EIGHTEEN

"Belar!" Silk swore under his breath.

"All bow down to the First Disciple of your God!" Urvon declaimed in his shrill voice. "It is my command that ye honor him."

There was a murmur of amazement among the assembled Chandim, and Garion, peering down from above, thought that he could detect a certain reluctance on the faces of some of them.

"Bow to him!" Urvon shrieked, starting to his feet. "He is my Disciple!"

The Chandim looked first at the frothing madman on the

dais and then at the cruel face of Harakan. Fearfully they sank to their knees.

"I am pleased to see such willing obedience to the commands of our God," Harakan observed sardonically. "I shall remember it always." There was a scarcely veiled threat in his voice.

"Know ye all that my Disciple speaks with my voice," Urvon announced, resuming his seat upon the throne. "His words are my words, and ye will obey him even as ye obey me."

"Hear the words of our God," Harakan intoned in that same sardonic voice, "for mighty is the God of Angarak, and swift to anger should any fail to heed him. Know further that I, Mengha, am now the sword of Urvon as well as his voice, and that the chastisement of the disobedient is in *my* hands." The threat was no longer veiled, and Harakan swept his eyes slowly across the faces of the assembled priests as if challenging each of them to protest his elevation.

"Hail Mengha, Disciple of the living God!" one of the mailed Guardsmen shouted.

"Hail Mengha!" the other Guardsmen responded, smashing their fists against their shields in salute.

"Hail Mengha!" the Karands shrieked.

"Hail Mengha!" the kneeling Chandim said at last, cowed finally into submission. And then the great Hounds crept forward on their bellies to fawn about Harakan's feet and to lick his hands.

"It is well," the enthroned madman declared in his shrill voice. "Know that the God of Angarak is pleased with ye."

And then another figure appeared in the throne room below, coming through the same rotted drapes which had admitted Urvon. The figure was slender and dressed in a robe of clinging black satin. Its head was partially covered by a black hood, and it was carrying something concealed beneath its robe. When it reached the altar, it tipped back its head in a derisive laugh, revealing a face with at once an unearthly beauty and an unearthly cruelty all cast in marble white. "You poor fools," the figure rasped in a harsh voice. "Think you to raise a new God over Angarak without my permission?"

"I have not summoned thee, Zandramas!" Urvon shouted at her.

"I feel no constraint to heed thy summons, Urvon," she replied in a voice filled with contempt, "nor its lack. I am not thy creature, as are these dogs. I serve the God of Angarak, in whose coming shalt thou be cast down."

"*I* am the God of Angarak!" he shrieked.

Harakan had begun to come around the altar toward her.

"And wilt thou pit thy puny will against the Will of the Child of Dark, Harakan?" she asked coolly. "Thou mayest change thy name, but thy power is no greater." Her voice was like ice.

Harakan stopped in his tracks, his eyes suddenly wary.

She turned back to Urvon. "I am dismayed that I was not notified of thy deification, Urvon," she continued, "for should I have known, I would have come before thee to pay thee homage and seek thy blessing." Then her lip curled in a sneer that distorted her face. "Thou?" she said. "*Thou*, a God? Thou mayest sit upon the throne of Torak for all eternity whilst this shabby ruin crumbles about thee, and thou wilt never become a God. Thou mayest fondle dross and call it gold, and thou wilt never become a God. Thou mayest bask in the canine adulation of thy cringing dogs, who even now befoul thy throne room with their droppings, and thou wilt never become a God. Thou mayest hearken greedily to the words of thy tame demon, Nahaz, who even now whispers the counsels of madness in thine ear, and thou wilt never become a God."

"I *am* a God!" Urvon shrieked, starting to his feet again.

"So? It may be even as thou sayest, Urvon," she almost purred. "But if thou *art* a God, I must tell thee to enjoy thy Godhood whilst thou may, then, for even as maimed Torak, thou art doomed."

322

"Who hath the might to slay a God?" he foamed at her.

Her laugh was dreadful. "Who hath the might? Even he who reft Torak of *his* life. Prepare thyself to receive the mortal thrust of the burning sword of Iron-grip, which spilled out the life of thy master, for *thus* I summon the Godslayer!"

And then she reached forward and placed the cloth-wrapped bundle which she had been concealing beneath her robe on the black altar. She raised her face and looked directly at the crack through which Garion was staring in frozen disbelief. "Behold thy son, Belgarion," she called up to him, "and hear his crying!" She turned back the cloth to reveal the infant Geran. The baby's face was contorted with fear, and he began to wail, a hopeless, lost sound.

All thought vanished from Garion's mind. The wailing was the sound he had been hearing over and over again since he had left Mal Zeth. It was *not* the wail of that doomed child in those plague-stricken streets that had haunted his dreams. It was the voice of his own son! Powerless to resist that wailing call, he leaped to his feet. It was as if there were suddenly sheets of flame before his eyes, flames that erased everything from his mind but the desperate need to go to the child wailing on the altar below.

He realized dimly that he was running through the shadowy, leaf-strewn halls, roaring insanely even as he ripped Iron-grip's sword from its sheath.

The moldering doors of long-empty rooms flashed by as he ran full tilt along the deserted corridor. Dimly behind him, he heard Silk's startled cry. "Garion! No!" Heedless, his brain afire, he ran on with the great Sword of Riva blazing in his hand before him as he went.

Even years later, he did not remember the stairs. Vaguely, he remembered emerging in the lower hall, raging.

There were Temple Guardsmen and Karands there, flinching before him and trying feebly to face him, but he seized the hilt of his sword in both hands and moved through them like a man reaping grain. They fell in showers of blood as he sheared his way through their ranks.

The great door to the dead God's throne room was closed and bolted, but Garion did not even resort to sorcery. He simply destroyed the door—and those who were trying desperately to hold it closed—with his burning sword.

The fire of madness filled his eyes as he burst into the throne room, and he roared at the terrified men there, who gaped at the dreadful form of the Godslayer, advancing on them, enclosed in a nimbus of blue light. His lips were peeled back from his teeth in a snarl, and his terrible sword, all ablaze, flickered back and forth before him like the shears of fate.

A Grolim jumped in front of him with one arm upraised as Garion gathered his will with an inrushing sound he scarcely heard. Garion did not stop, and the other Grolims in the throne room recoiled in horror as the point of his flaming sword came sliding out from between the rash priest's shoulder blades. The mortally wounded Grolim stared at the sizzling blade sunk into his chest. He tried with shaking hands to clutch at the blade, but Garion kicked him off the sword and continued his grim advance.

A Karand with a skull-surmounted staff stood in his path, desperately muttering an incantation. His words cut off abruptly, however, as Garion's sword passed through his throat.

"Behold the Godslayer, Urvon!" Zandramas exulted. "Thy life is at an end, God of Angarak, for Belgarion hath come to spill it out, even as he spilled out the life of Torak!" Then she turned her back on the cringing madman. "All hail the Child of Light!" she announced in ringing tones. She smiled her cruel smile at him. "Hail, Belgarion," she taunted him. "Slay once again the God of Angarak, for that hath ever been thy task. I shall await thy coming in the Place Which Is No More." And then she took up the wailing babe in her arms, covered it with her cloak again, shimmered, and vanished.

Garion was suddenly filled with chagrin as he realized that

he had been cruelly duped. Zandramas had not actually been here with his son, and all his overpowering rage had been directed at an empty projection. Worse than that, he had been manipulated by the haunting nightmare of the wailing child which he now realized *she* had put into his mind to force him to respond to her taunting commands. He faltered then, his blade lowering and its fire waning.

"Kill him!" Harakan shouted. "Kill the one who slew Torak!"

"Kill him!" Urvon echoed in his insane shriek. "Kill him and offer his heart up to me in sacrifice!"

A half-dozen Temple Guardsmen began a cautious, clearly reluctant, advance. Garion raised his sword again; its light flared anew, and the Guardsmen jumped back.

Harakan sneered as he looked at the armored men. "Behold the reward for cowardice," he snapped. He extended one hand, muttered a single word, and one of the Guardsmen shrieked and fell writhing to the floor as his mail coat and helmet turned instantly white-hot, roasting him alive.

"Now obey me!" Harakan roared. "Kill him!"

The terrified Guardsmen attacked more fervently then, forcing Garion back step by step. Then he heard the sound of running feet in the corridor outside. He glanced quickly over his shoulder and saw the others come bursting into the throne room.

"Have you lost your mind?" Belgarath demanded angrily.

"I'll explain later," Garion told him, still half-sick with frustration and disappointment. He returned his attention to the armored men before him and began swinging his great sword in wide sweeps, driving them back again.

Belgarath faced the Chandim on one side of the central aisle, concentrated for an instant, then gestured shortly. Suddenly a raging fire erupted from the stones of the floor all along the aisle.

Something seemed to pass between the old man and Pol-

325

gara. She nodded, and quite suddenly the other side of the aisle was also walled off by flame.

Two of the Guardsmen had fallen beneath Garion's sword, but others, accompanied by wild-eyed Karands, were rushing to the aid of their comrades, though they flinched visibly from the flames on either side of the aisle up which they were forced to attack.

"Combine your wills!" Harakan was shouting to the Chandim. "Smother the flames!"

Even as he closed with the Guardsmen and the Karands, beating down their upraised swords and hacking at them with Iron-grip's blade, Garion felt the rush and surge of combined will. Despite the efforts of Belgarath and Polgara, the fires on either side of the aisle flickered and grew low.

One of the huge Hounds came loping through the ranks of the Guardsmen facing Garion. Its eyes were ablaze, and its tooth-studded muzzle agape. It leaped directly at his face, snapping and growling horribly, but fell twitching and biting at the floor as he split its head with his sword.

And then Harakan thrust his way through the Guardsmen and Karands to confront Garion. "And so we meet again, Belgarion," he snarled in an almost doglike voice. "Drop your sword, or I will slay your friends—and your wife. I have a hundred Chandim with me, and not even you are a match for so many." And he began to draw in his will.

Then, to Garion's amazement, Velvet ran forward past him, her arms stretched toward the dread Grolim. "Please!" she wailed. "Please don't kill me!" And she threw herself at Harakan's feet, clutching at his black robe imploringly as she cringed and groveled before him.

Thrown off balance by this sudden and unexpected display of submissiveness, Harakan let his will dissipate and he backed away, trying to shake her hand from his robe and kicking at her to free himself. But she clung to him, weeping and begging for her life.

"Get her off me!" he snapped at his men, turning his head

slightly. And that briefest instant of inattention proved fatal. Velvet's hand moved so quickly that it seemed to blur in the air. She dipped swiftly into her bodice; when her hand emerged, she held a small, bright-green snake.

"A present for you, Harakan!" she shouted triumphantly. "A present for the leader of the Bear-cult from Hunter!" And she threw Zith full into his face.

He screamed once the first time Zith bit him, and his hands came up to claw her away from his face, but the scream ended with a horrid gurgle, and his hands convulsed helplessly in the air in front of him. Squealing and jerking, he reeled backward as the irritated little reptile struck again and again. He stiffened and arched back across the altar, his feet scuffing and scrabbling on the floor and his arms flopping uselessly. He banged his head on the black stone, his eyes bulging and his swollen tongue protruding from his mouth. Then a dark froth came from his lips, he jerked several more times, and his body slid limply off the altar.

"And *that* was for Bethra," Velvet said to the crumpled form of the dead man lying on the floor before the altar.

The Chandim and their cohorts again drew back in fear as they stared at the body of their fallen pack leader.

"They are few!" Urvon shrieked at them. "We are many! Destroy them all! Your God commands it!"

The Chandim gaped first at Harakan's contorted body, then at the crowned madman on the throne, then at the terrible little snake who had coiled herself atop the altar with her head raised threateningly as she gave vent to a series of angry hisses.

"That's about enough of this," Belgarath snapped. He let the last of the flames die and began to refocus his will. Garion also straightened, pulling in his own will even as he felt the frightened Chandim start to focus their power for a final, dreadful confrontation.

"What is all this now?" Feldegast laughed, suddenly coming forward until he stood between Garion and his foes. "Surely, good masters, we can put aside all this hatred and

327

strife. I'll tell ye what I'll do. Let me give ye a demonstration of me skill, an' we'll laugh together an' make peace between us once an' fer all. No man at all kin keep so great a hatred in his heart while he's bubblin' with laughter, don't y' know."

Then he began to juggle, seeming to pull brightly colored balls out of the air. The Grolims gaped at him, stunned by this unexpected interruption, and Garion stared incredulously at the performer, who seemed deliberately bent on self-destruction. Still juggling, Feldegast flipped his body onto the back of a heavy bench, holding himself upside down over it with one hand while he continued to juggle with his free hand and his feet. Faster and faster the balls whirled, more and more of them coming, it seemed out of thin air. The more the balls whirled, the brighter they became until at last they were incandescent, and the inverted little man was juggling balls of pure fire.

Then he flexed the arm that was holding him in place, tossing himself high over the bench. When his feet touched the floor, however, it was no longer Feldegast the juggler who stood there. In place of the roguish entertainer stood the gnarled, hunchbacked shape of the sorcerer Beldin. With a sudden evil laugh, he began to hurl his fireballs at the startled Grolims and their warriors.

His aim was unerring, and the deadly fireballs pierced Grolim robes, Guardsmen's mail coats, and Karandese fur vests with equal facility. Smoking holes appeared in the chests of his victims, and he felled them by the dozen. The throne room filled with smoke and the reek of burning flesh as the grinning, ugly little sorcerer continued his deadly barrage.

"*You!*" Urvon shrieked in terror, the sudden appearance of the man he had feared for so many thousands of years shocking him into some semblance of sanity, even as the terrified Chandim and their cohorts broke and fled, howling in fright.

"So good to see you again, Urvon," the hunchback said to him pleasantly. "Our conversation was interrupted the last time we were talking, but as I recall, I'd just promised to sink

a white-hot hook into your belly and yank out all your guts."
He held out his gnarled right hand, snapped his fingers, and
there was a sudden flash. A cruel hook, smoking and glowing,
appeared in his fist. "Why don't we continue with that line
of thought?" he suggested, advancing on the splotchy-faced
man cowering on the throne.

Then the shadow which had lurked behind the madman's
shoulder came out from behind the throne. "Stop," it said in
a voice that was no more than a crackling whisper. No human
throat could have produced that sound. "I need this thing,"
it said, pointing a shadowy hand in the direction of the gib-
bering Disciple of Torak. "It serves my purposes, and I will
not let you kill it."

"You would be Nahaz, then," Beldin said in an ominous
voice.

"I am," the figure whispered. "Nahaz, Lord of Demons
and Master of Darkness."

"Go find yourself another plaything, Demon Lord," The
hunchback grated. "This one is mine."

"Will you pit your will against mine, sorcerer?"

"If need be."

"Look upon my face, then, and prepare for death." The
demon pushed back its hood of darkness, and Garion recoiled
with a sharp intake of his breath. The face of Nahaz was
hideous, but it was not the misshapen features alone which
were so terrifying. There emanated from its burning eyes a
malevolent evil so gross that it froze the blood. Brighter and
brighter those eyes burned with evil green fire until their
beams shot forth toward Beldin. The gnarled sorcerer
clenched himself and raised one hand. The hand suddenly
glowed an intense blue, a light that seemed to cascade down
over his body to form a shield against the demon's power.

"Your will is strong," Nahaz hissed. "But mine is stronger."

Then Polgara came down the littered aisle, the white lock
at her brow gleaming. On one side of her strode Belgarath
and on the other Durnik. As they reached him, Garion joined

them. They advanced slowly to take up positions flanking Beldin, and Garion became aware that Eriond had also joined them, standing slightly off to one side.

"Well, Demon," Polgara said in a deadly voice, "will you face us all?"

Garion raised his sword and unleashed its fire. "And *this* as well?" he added, releasing all restraints on the Orb.

The Demon flinched momentarily, then drew itself erect again, its horrid face bathed in that awful green fire. From beneath its robe of shadow, it took what appeared to be a scepter or a wand of some kind that blazed an intense green. As it raised that wand, however, it seemed to see something that had previously escaped its notice. An expression of sudden fear crossed its hideous face, and the fire of the wand died, even as the intense green light bathing its face flickered and grew wan and weak. Then it raised its face toward the vaulted ceiling and howled—a dreadful, shocking sound. It spun quickly, moving toward the terrified Urvon. It reached out with shadowy hands, seized the gold-robed madman, and lifted him easily from the throne. Then it fled, its fire pushing out before it like a great battering ram, blasting out the walls of the House of Torak as it went.

The crown which had surmounted Urvon's brow fell from his head as Nahaz carried him from the crumbling house, and it clanked when it hit the floor with the tinny sound of brass.

Part Four

THE MOUNTAINS
OF ZAMAD

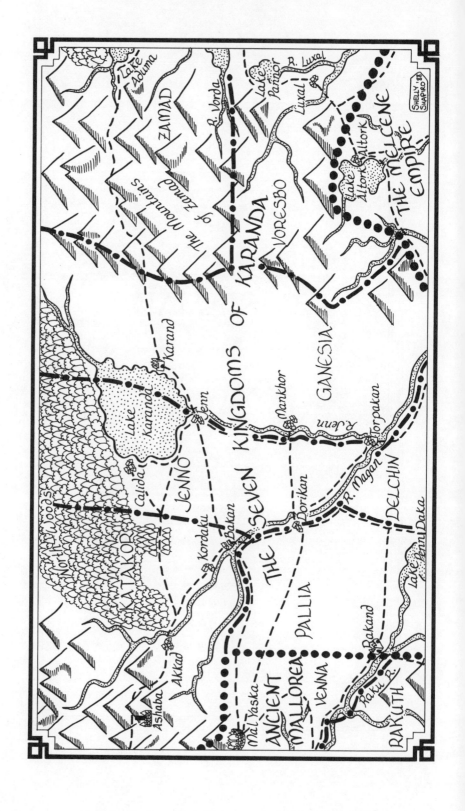

CHAPTER NINETEEN

Beldin spat out a rancid oath and hurled his glowing hook at the throne. Then he started toward the smoking
hole the fleeing demon had blasted out through the wall of
the throne room.

Belgarath, however, managed to place himself in front of
the angry hunchback. "No, Beldin," he said firmly.

"Get out of my way, Belgarath."

"I'm not going to let you chase after a demon who could
turn on you at any minute."

"I can take of myself. Now stand aside."

"You're not thinking, Beldin. There'll be time enough to

deal with Urvon later. Right now we need to make some decisions."

"What's to decide? You go after Zandramas and I go after Urvon. It's all pretty much cut and dried, isn't it?"

"Not entirely. In any event, I'm not going to let you chase after Nahaz in the dark. You know as well as I do that the darkness multiplies his power—and I haven't got so many brothers left that I can afford to lose one just because he's irritated."

Their eyes locked, and the ugly hunchback finally turned away. He stumped back toward the dais, pausing long enough to kick a chair to pieces on his way, muttering curses all the while.

"Is everyone all right?" Silk asked, looking around as he resheathed his knife.

"So it would seem," Polgara replied, pushing back the hood of her blue cloak.

"It was a bit tight there for a while, wasn't it?" The little man's eyes were very bright.

"Also unnecessary," she said, giving Garion a hard look. "You'd better take a quick look through the rest of the house, Kheldar. Let's make sure that it's really empty. Durnik, you and Toth go with him."

Silk nodded and started back up the blood-splashed aisle, stepping over bodies as he went, with Durnik and Toth close behind him.

"I don't understand," Ce'Nedra said, staring in bafflement at the gnarled Beldin, who was once again dressed in rags and had the usual twigs and bits of straw clinging to him. "How did you change places with Feldegast—and where is he?"

A roguish smile crossed Beldin's face. "Ah, me little darlin'," he said to her in the juggler's lilting brogue, "I'm right here, don't y' know. An' if yer of a mind, I kin still charm ye with me wit an' me unearthly skill."

"But I *liked* Feldegast," she almost wailed.

"All ye have t' do is transfer yer affection t' me, darlin'."

334

"It's not the same," she objected.

Belgarath was looking steadily at the twisted sorcerer. "Have you got any idea of how much that particular dialect irritates me?" he said.

"Why, yes, brother." Beldin grinned. "As a matter of fact I do. That's one of the reasons I selected it."

"I don't entirely understand the need for so elaborate a disguise," Sadi said as he put away his small poisoned dagger.

"Too many people know me by sight in this part of Mallore," Beldin told him. "Urvon's had my description posted on every tree and fence post within a hundred leagues of Mal Yaska for the last two thousand years, and let's be honest about it, it wouldn't be too hard to recognize me from even the roughest description."

"You are a unique sort of person, Uncle," Polgara said to him, smiling fondly.

"Ah, yer too kind t' say it, me girl," he replied with an extravagant bow.

"*Will* you stop that?" Belgarath said. Then he turned to Garion. "As I remember, you said that you were going to explain something later. All right—it's later."

"I was tricked," Garion admitted glumly.

"By whom?"

"Zandramas."

"She's still here?" Ce'Nedra exclaimed.

Garion shook his head. "No. She sent a projection here— a projection of herself and of Geran."

"Couldn't you tell the difference between a projection and the real thing?" Belgarath demanded.

"I wasn't in any condition to tell the difference when it happened."

"I suppose you can explain that."

Garion took a deep breath and sat down on one of the benches. He noticed that his bloodstained hands were shaking. "She's very clever," he said. "Ever since we left Mal Zeth, I've been having the same dream over and over again."

335

"Dream?" Polgara asked sharply. "What kind of dream?"

"Maybe dream isn't the right word," he replied, "but over and over again, I kept hearing the cry of a baby. At first I thought that I was remembering the cry of that sick child we saw in the streets back in Mal Zeth, but that wasn't it at all. When Silk and Beldin and I were in that room just above this one, we could see down into the throne room here and we saw Urvon come in with Nahaz right behind him. He's completely insane now. He think's he's a God. Anyway, he summoned Mengha—only Mengha turned out to be Harakan, and then—"

"Wait a minute," Belgarath interrupted him. "*Harakan* is Mengha?"

Garion glanced over at the limp form sprawled in front of the altar. Zith was still coiled atop the black stone, muttering and hissing to herself. "Well, he *was*," he said.

"Urvon made the announcement before all this broke out," Beldin added. "We didn't have the time to fill you in."

"That explains a great many things, doesn't it?" Belgarath mused. He looked at Velvet. "Did you know about this?" he asked her.

"No, Ancient One," she replied, "as a matter of fact, I didn't. I just seized the opportunity when it arose."

Silk, Durnik, and Toth came back into the body-strewn throne room. "The house is empty," the little man reported. "We've got it all to ourselves."

"Good," Belgarath said. "Garion was just telling us why he saw fit to start his own private war."

"Zandramas told him to." Silk shrugged. "I'm not sure why he started taking orders from her, but that's what happened."

"I was just getting to that," Garion said. "Urvon was down here telling all the Chandim that Harakan—Mengha—was going to be his first disciple. That's when Zandramas came in—or at least she seemed to. She had a bundle under her cloak. I didn't know it at first, but it was Geran. She and Urvon shouted at each other for a while, and Urvon finally insisted that he was a God. She said something like, 'All right. Then I will summon the Godslayer to deal with you.' That's when she put the bundle on the altar. She opened it, and it was Geran. He started to cry, and I realized all at once that it was *his* cry I'd been hearing all along. I just totally stopped thinking at that point."

"Obviously," Belgarath said.

"Well, anyway, you know all the rest." Garion looked around at the corpse-littered throne room and shuddered. "I hadn't altogether realized just how far things went," he said. "I guess I was sort of crazy."

"The word is berserk, Garion," Belgarath told him. "It's fairly common among Alorns. I'd sort of thought you might be immune, but I guess I was wrong."

"There was some justification for it, father," Polgara said.

"There's never a justification for losing your wits, Pol," he growled.

"He was provoked." She pursed her lips thoughtfully, then came over and lightly placed her hands on Garion's temples. "It's gone now," she said.

"What is?" Ce'Nedra sounded concerned.

"The possession."

"Possession?"

Polgara nodded. "Yes. That's how Zandramas tricked him. She filled his mind with the sound of a crying child. Then, when she laid the bundle that *seemed* to be Geran on the altar and Garion heard that same crying, he had no choice but to do what she wanted him to do." She looked at Belgarath. "This is very serious, father. She's already tampered with Ce'Nedra, and now it's Garion. She may try the same thing with others as well."

"What would be the point?" he asked. "You can catch her at it, can't you?"

"Usually, yes—*if* I know what's going on. But Zandramas is very skilled at this and she's very subtle. In many ways she's even better at it than Asharak the Murgo was." She looked around at them. "Now listen carefully, all of you," she told them. "If anything unusual begins to happen to you—dreams, notions, peculiar ideas, strange feelings—anything at all, I want you to tell me about it at once. Zandramas knows that we're after her and she's using this to delay us. She tried it with Ce'Nedra while we were on our way to Rak Hagga, and now—"

"Me?" Ce'Nedra said in amazement. "I didn't know that."

"Remember your illness on the road from Rak Verkat?" Polgara said. "It wasn't exactly an illness. It was Zandramas putting her hand on your mind."

"But nobody told me."

"Once Andel and I drove Zandramas away, there was no need to worry you about it. Anyway, Zandramas tried it first with Ce'Nedra and now with Garion. She could try it on any one of the rest of us as well, so let me know if you start feeling in the least bit peculiar."

"Brass," Durnik said.

"What was that, dear?" Polgara asked him.

He held up Urvon's crown. "This thing is brass," he said. "So's that throne. I didn't really think there'd be any gold left here. The house has been abandoned and wide open for looters for too many centuries."

"That's usually the way it is with the gifts of demons," Beldin told him. "They're very good at creating illusions." He looked around. "Urvon probably saw all this as unearthly splendor. He couldn't see the rotten drapes, or cobwebs, or all the trash on the floor. All he could see was the glory that Nahaz wanted him to see." The dirty, twisted man chuckled. "I sort of enjoy the idea of Urvon spending his last days as a raving lunatic," he added, "right up until the moment when I sink a hook into his guts."

Silk had been looking narrowly at Velvet. "Do you suppose you could explain something for me?" he asked.

"I'll try," she said.

338

"You said something rather strange when you threw Zith into Harakan's face."

"Did I say something?"

"You said, 'A present for the leader of the Bear-cult from Hunter.'"

"Oh, that." She smiled her dimples into life. "I just wanted him to know who was killing him, that's all."

He stared at her.

"You *are* getting rusty, my dear Kheldar," she chided him. "I was certain that you'd have guessed by now. I've done everything but hit you over the head with it."

"Hunter?" he said incredulously. *"You?"*

"I've been Hunter for quite some time now. That's why I hurried to catch up with you at Tol Honeth." She smoothed the front of her plain gray traveling gown.

"At Tol Honeth you told us that *Bethra* was Hunter."

"She *had* been, Kheldar, but her job was finished. She was supposed to make sure that we'd get a reasonable man as a successor to Ran Borune. First she had to eliminate a few members of the Honeth family before they could consolidate their positions, and then she made a few suggestions about Varana to Ran Borune while the two of them were—" She hesitated, glancing at Ce'Nedra, and then she coughed. "—ah—shall we say, entertaining each other?" she concluded.

Ce'Nedra blushed furiously.

"Oh, dear," the blond girl said, putting one hand to her cheek. "That didn't come out at all well, did it? Anyway," she hurried on, "Javelin decided that Bethra's task was complete and that it was time for there to be a new Hunter with a new mission. Queen Porenn was *very* cross about what Harakan did in the west—the attempt on Ce'Nedra's life, the murder of Brand, and everything that went on at Rheon—so she instructed Javelin to administer some chastisement. He selected me to deliver it. I was fairly sure that Harakan would come back to Mallorea. I knew that you were all coming here, too—eventually—so that's why I joined you." She looked

339

over at the sprawled form of Harakan. "I was absolutely amazed when I saw him standing in front of the altar," she admitted, "but I couldn't allow an opportunity like that to slip by." She smiled. "Actually, it worked out rather well. I was just on the verge of leaving you and going back to Mal Yaska to look for him. The fact that he turned out to be Mengha, too, was just sort of a bonus."

"I thought you were tagging along to keep an eye on *me*."

"I'm very sorry, Prince Kheldar. I just made that up. I needed some reason to join you, and sometimes Belgarath can be very stubborn." She smiled winsomely at the old sorcerer, then turned back to the baffled-looking Silk. "Actually," she continued, "my uncle isn't really upset with you at all."

"But you said—" He stared at her. "You *lied*!" he accused.

"'Lie' is such an ugly word, Kheldar," she replied, patting his cheek fondly. "Couldn't we just say that I exaggerated a trifle? I wanted to keep an eye on you, certainly, but it was for reasons of my own—which had nothing whatsoever to do with Drasnian state policy."

A slow flush crept up his cheeks.

"Why, Kheldar," she exclaimed delightedly, "you're actually blushing—almost like a simple village girl who's just been seduced."

Garion had been struggling with something. "What was the point of it, Aunt Pol?" he asked. "What Zandramas did to me, I mean?"

"Delay," she replied, "but more importantly, there was the possibility of defeating us before we ever get to the final meeting."

"I don't follow that."

She sighed. "We know that one of us is going to die," she said. "Cyradis told us that at Rheon. But there's always a chance that in one of these random skirmishes, someone *else* could be killed—entirely by accident. If the Child of Light— you—meets with the Child of Dark and he's lost someone whose task hasn't been completed, he won't have any chance

340

of winning. Zandramas could win by default. The whole point of that cruel game she played was to lure you into a fight with the Chandim and Nahaz. The rest of us, quite obviously, would come to your aid. In that kind of fight, it's always possible for accidents to happen."

"Accident? How can there be accidents when we're all under the control of a prophecy?"

"You're forgetting something, Belgarion," Beldin said. "This whole business started with an accident. That's what divided the Prophecies in the first place. You can read prophecies until your hair turns gray, but there's always room for random chance to step in and disrupt things."

"You'll note that my brother is a philosopher," Belgarath said, "always ready to look on the dark side of things."

"Are you two really brothers?" Ce'Nedra asked curiously.

"Yes," Beldin told her, "but in a way that you could never begin to understand. It was something that our Master impressed upon us."

"And Zedar was *also* one of your brothers?" She suddenly stared in horror at Belgarath.

The old man set his jaw. "Yes," he admitted.

"But you—"

"Go ahead and say it, Ce'Nedra," he said. "There's nothing you can possibly say to me that I haven't already said to myself."

"Someday," she said in a very small voice, "someday when this is all over, will you let him out?"

Belgarath's eyes were stony. "I don't think so, no."

"And if he *does* let him out, I'll go find him and stuff him right back in again," Beldin added.

"There's not much point in chewing over ancient history," Belgarath said. He thought a moment, then said, "I think it's time for us to have another talk with the young lady from Kell." He turned to Toth. "Will you summon your mistress?" he asked.

341

The giant's face was not happy. When he finally nodded, it was obviously with some reluctance.

"I'm sorry, my friend," Belgarath said to him, "but it's really necessary."

Toth sighed and then he sank to one knee and closed his eyes in an oddly prayerful fashion. Once again, as it had happened back on the Isle of Verkat and again at Rak Hagga, Garion heard a murmur as of many voices. Then there came that peculiar, multicolored shimmering in the air not far from Urvon's shoddy throne. The air cleared, and the unwavering form of the Seeress of Kell appeared on the dais. For the first time, Garion looked closely at her. She was slender and somehow looked very vulnerable, a helplessness accentuated by her white robe and her blindfolded eyes. There was, however, a serenity in her face—the serenity of someone who has looked full in the face of Destiny and has accepted it without question or reservation. For some reason, he felt almost overcome with awe in her radiant presence.

"Thank you for coming, Cyradis," Belgarath said simply. "I'm sorry to have troubled you. I know how difficult it is for you to do this, but there are some answers I need before we can go any further."

"I will tell thee as much as I am permitted to say, Ancient One," she replied. Her voice was light and musical, but there was, nonetheless, a firmness in it that spoke of an unearthly resolve. "I must say unto thee, however, that thou must make haste. The time for the final meeting draws nigh."

"That's one of the things I wanted to talk about. Can you be any more specific about this appointed time?"

She seemed to consider it as if consulting with some power so immense that Garion's imagination shuddered back from the very thought of it. "I know not time in thy terms, Holy Belgarath," she said simply, "but only for so long as a babe lieth beneath his mother's heart remains ere the Child of Light and the Child of Dark must face each other in the Place Which Is No More, and my task must be completed."

"All right," he said. "That's clear enough, I guess. Now, when you came to us at Mal Zeth, you said that there was a task here at Ashaba that needed to be accomplished before we could move on. A great deal has happened here, so I can't pinpoint exactly what that task was. Can you be a bit more specific?"

"The task is completed, Eternal One, for the Book of the Heavens sayeth that the Huntress must find her prey and bring him low in the House of Darkness in the sixteenth moon. And lo, even as the stars have proclaimed, it hath come to pass."

The old man's face took on a slightly puzzled expression.

"Ask further, Disciple of Aldur," she told him. "My time with you grows short."

"I'm supposed to follow the trail of the Mysteries," he said, "but Zandramas cut certain key passages out of the copy of the Ashabine Oracles she left here for me to find."

"Nay, Ancient One. It was not the hand of Zandramas which mutilated thy book, but rather the hand of its author."

"*Torak?*" he sounded startled.

"Even so. For know thou that the words of prophecy come unbidden, and ofttimes their import is not pleasing unto the prophet. So it was with the master of this house."

"But Zandramas managed to put her hands on a copy that hadn't been mutilated?" he asked.

The seeress nodded.

"Are there any other copies that Burnt-face didn't tamper with?" Beldin asked intently.

"Only two," she replied. "One is in the house of Urvon the Disciple, but that one lieth under the hand of Nahaz, the accursed. Seek not to wrest it from him, lest ye die."

"And the other?" the hunchback demanded.

"Seek out the clubfooted one, for he will aid thee in thy search."

"That's not too helpful, you know."

"I speak to thee in the words that stand in the Book of the

Heavens and were written ere the world began. These words have no language but speak instead directly to the soul."

"Naturally," he said. "All right. You spoke of Nahaz. Is he going to line our path with demons all the way across Karanda?"

"Nay, gentle Beldin. Nahaz hath no further interest in Karanda, and his legions of darkness abide no longer there and respond to no summons, however powerful. They infest instead the plains of Darshiva where they do war upon the minions of Zandramas."

"Where is Zandramas now?" Belgarath asked her.

"She doth journey unto the place where the Sardion lay hidden for unnumbered centuries. Though it is no longer there, she hopes to find traces of it sunk into the very rocks and to follow those traces to the Place Which Is No More."

"Is that possible?"

Her face grew very still. "That I may not tell thee," she replied. Then she straightened. "I may say no more unto thee in this place, Belgarath. Seek instead the mystery which will guide thee. Make haste, however, for Time will not stay nor falter in its measured pace." And then she turned toward the black altar standing before the dais where Zith was coiled, still muttering and hissing in irritation. "Be tranquil, little sister," she said, "for the purpose of all thy days is now accomplished, and that which was delayed may now come to pass." She then seemed, even though blindfolded, to turn her serene face toward each of them, pausing briefly only to bow her head to Polgara in a gesture of profound respect. At last she turned to Toth. Her face was filled with anguish, but she said nothing. And then she sighed and vanished.

Beldin was scowling. "That was fairly standard," he said. "I *hate* riddles. They're the entertainment of the preliterate."

"Stop trying to show off your education and let's see if we can sort this out," Belgarath told him. "We know that this is all going to be decided one way or the other in nine more months. That was the number I needed."

Sadi was frowning in perplexity. "How did we arrive at that number?" he asked. "To be perfectly frank, I didn't understand very much of what she said."

"She said that we have only as much time as a baby lies in its mother's womb," Polgara explained. "That's nine months."

"Oh," he said. Then he smiled a bit sadly. "That's the sort of thing I don't pay too much attention to, I guess."

"What was that business about the sixteenth moon?" Silk asked. "I didn't follow that at all."

"This whole thing began with the birth of Belgarion's son," Beldin told him. "We found a reference to that in the Mrin Codex. Your friend with the snake had to be here at Ashaba sixteen moons later."

Silk frowned, counting on his fingers. "It hasn't been sixteen months yet," he objected.

"Moons, Kheldar," the hunchback said. "Moons, not months. There's a difference, you know."

"Oh. That explains it, I guess."

"Who's this clubfoot who's supposed to have the third uncorrupted copy of the Oracles?" Belgarath said.

"It rings a bell somehow," Beldin replied. "Let me think about it."

"What's Nahaz doing in Darshiva?" Garion asked.

"Apparently attacking the Grolims there," Belgarath replied. "We know that Darshiva is where Zandramas originally came from and that the church in that region belongs to her. If Nahaz wants to put the Sardion in Urvon's hands, he's going to have to stop her. Otherwise, she'll get to it first."

Ce'Nedra seemed to suddenly remember something. She looked at Garion, her eyes hungry. "You said that you saw Geran—when Zandramas tricked you."

"A projection of him, yes."

"How did he look?"

"The same. He hadn't changed a bit since the last time I saw him."

"Garion, dear," Polgara said gently. "That's not really reasonable, you know. Geran's almost a year older now. He wouldn't look the same at all. Babies grow and change a great deal during their first few years."

He nodded glumly. "I realize that now," he replied. "At the time, I wasn't really in any condition to think my way through it." Then he stopped. "Why didn't she project an image of him the way he looks now?"

"Because she wanted to show you something she was sure you'd recognize."

"Now you stop that?" Sadi exclaimed. He was standing near the altar and he had just jerked his hand back out of Zith's range. The little green snake was growling ominously at him. The eunuch turned toward Velvet. "Do you see what you've done?" he accused. "You've made her terribly angry."

"Me?" she asked innocently.

"How would *you* like to be pulled out of a warm bed and thrown into somebody's face?"

"I suppose I hadn't thought about that. I'll apologize to her, Sadi—just as soon as she regains her composure a bit. Will she crawl into her bottle by herself?"

"Usually, yes."

"That might be the safest course, then. Lay the bottle on the altar and let her crawl inside and sulk a bit."

"You're probably right," he agreed.

"Are any of the other rooms in the house habitable?" Polgara asked Silk.

He nodded. "More or less. The Chandim and the Guardsmen were staying in them."

She looked around at the corpse-littered throne room. "Why don't we move out of here, then?" she suggested to Belgarath. "This place looks like a battlefield, and the smell of blood isn't that pleasant."

"Why bother?" Ce'Nedra said. "We're leaving to follow Zandramas, aren't we?"

"Not until morning, dear," Polgara replied. "It's dark and cold outside, and we're all tired and hungry."

"But—"

"The Chandim and the Guardsmen ran away, Ce'Nedra—but we can't be at all sure how far they went. And, of course, there are the Hounds as well. Let's not make the mistake of blundering out into a forest at night when we can't see what might be hiding behind the first tree we come to."

"It makes sense, Ce'Nedra," Velvet told her. "Let's try to get some sleep and start out early in the morning."

The little Queen sighed. "I suppose you're right," she admitted. "It's just that—"

"Zandramas can't get away from me, Ce'Nedra," Garion assured her. "The Orb knows which way she went."

They followed Silk out of the throne room and along the blood-spattered corridor outside. Garion tried as best he could to shield Ce'Nedra from the sight of the crumpled forms of the Guardsmen and Karands he had killed in his raging dash to the throne room of Torak. About halfway down the corridor Silk pushed open a door and held up the guttering torch he had taken from one of the iron rings sticking out of the wall. "This is about the best I can do," he told Polgara. "At least someone made an effort to clean it up."

She looked around. The room had the look of a barracks. Bunks protruded from the walls and there was a long table with benches in the center. There was a fireplace at the far end with the last embers of a fire glowing inside. "Adequate," she said.

"I'd better go look after the horses," Durnik said. "Is there a stable anywhere on the grounds?"

"It's down at the far end of the courtyard," Beldin told him, "and the Guardsmen who were here probably put in a supply of fodder and water for their own mounts."

"Good," Durnik said.

"Would you bring in the packs with my utensils and the stores, dear?" Polgara asked him.

"Of course." Then he went out, followed by Toth and Eriond.

"Suddenly I'm so tired that I can barely stand," Garion said, sinking onto a bench.

"I wouldn't be at all surprised." Beldin grunted. "You've had a busy evening."

"Are you coming along with us?" Belgarath asked him.

"No, I don't think so," Beldin replied, sprawling on the bench. "I want to find out where Nahaz took Urvon."

"Will you be able to follow him?"

"Oh, yes." Beldin tapped his nose. "I can smell a demon six days after he passes. I'll trail Nahaz just like a bloodhound. I won't be gone too long. You go ahead and follow Zandramas, and I'll catch up with you somewhere along the way." The hunchback rubbed at his jaw thoughtfully. "I think we can be fairly sure that Nahaz isn't going to let Urvon out of his sight. Urvon is—or was—a Disciple of Torak, after all. Even as much as I detest him, I still have to admit that he's got a very strong mind. Nahaz is going to have to talk to him almost constantly to keep his sanity from returning, so if our Demon Lord went to Darshiva to oversee his creatures there, he's almost certain to have taken Urvon along."

"You *will* be careful, won't you?"

"Don't get sentimental on me, Belgarath. Just leave me some kind of trail I can follow. I don't want to have to look all over Mallorea for you."

Sadi came from the throne room with his red leather case in one hand and Zith's little bottle in the other. "She's still very irritated," he said to Velvet. "She doesn't appreciate being used as a weapon."

"I told you that I'd apologize to her, Sadi," she replied. "I'll explain things to her. I'm sure she'll understand."

Silk was looking at the blond girl with an odd expression.

"Tell me," he said. "Didn't it bother you at all the first time you put her down the front of your dress?"

She laughed. "To be perfectly honest with you, Prince Kheldar, the first time it was all I could do to keep from screaming."

CHAPTER TWENTY

At first light the following morning, a light that was little more than a lessening of the darkness of a sky where dense cloud scudded before the chill wind blowing down off the mountains, Silk returned to the room in which they had spent the night. "The house is being watched," he told them.

"How many are there?" Belgarath asked.

"I saw one. I'm sure there are others."

"Where is he? The one that you saw?"

Silk's quick grin was vicious. "He's watching the sky. At least he looks like he's watching. His eyes are open and he's lying on his back." He slid his hand down into his boot, pulled out one of his daggers, and looked sorrowfully at its once-keen edge. "Do you have any idea of how hard it is to push a knife through a chain-mail shirt?"

"I think that's why people wear them, Kheldar," Velvet said to him. "You should use one of these." From somewhere amongst her soft, feminine clothing she drew out a long-bladed poniard with a needlelike point.

"I thought you were partial to snakes."

"Always use the appropriate weapon, Kheldar. I certainly wouldn't want Zith to break her teeth on a steel shirt."

"Could you two talk business some other time?" Belgarath said to them. "Can you put a name to this fellow who's suddenly so interested in the sky?"

"We didn't really have time to introduce ourselves," Silk replied, sliding his jagged-edged knife back into his boot.

"I meant what—not who."

"Oh. He was a Temple Guardsman."

"Not one of the Chandim?"

"All I had to go by was his clothing."

The old man grunted.

"It's going to be slow going if we have to look behind every tree and bush as we ride along," Sadi said.

"I realize that," Begarath answered, tugging at one earlobe. "Let me think my way through this."

"And while you're deciding, I'll fix us some breakfast," Polgara said, laying aside her hairbrush. "What would you all like?"

"Porridge?" Eriond asked hopefully.

Silk sighed. "The word is gruel, Eriond. Gruel." Then he looked quickly at Polgara, whose eyes had suddenly turned frosty. "Sorry, Polgara," he apologized, "but it's our duty to educate the young, don't you think?"

"What I think is that I need more firewood," she replied.

"I'll see to it at once."

"You're too kind."

Silk rather quickly left the room.

"Any ideas?" the hunchbacked Beldin asked Belgarath.

351

"Several. But they all have certain flaws in them."

"Why not let me handle it for you?" The gnarled sorcerer asked, sprawling on a bench near the fire and scratching absently at his belly. "You've had a hard night, and a ten-thousand-year-old man needs to conserve his strength."

"You really find that amusing, don't you? Why not say twenty—or fifty? Push absurdity to its ultimate edge."

"My," Beldin said. "Aren't we testy this morning? Pol, have you got any beer handy?"

"Before breakfast, Uncle?" she said from beside the fireplace where she was stirring a large pot.

"Just as a buffer for the gruel," he said.

She gave him a very steady look.

He grinned at her, then turned back toward Belgarath. "Seriously, though," he went on, "why not let me deal with all the lurkers in the bushes around the house? Kheldar could dull every knife he's carrying, and Liselle could wear that poor little snake's fangs down to the gums, and you still wouldn't be sure if you'd cleaned out the woods hereabouts. I'm going off in a different direction anyway, so why not let me do something flamboyant to frighten off the Guardsmen and the Kanrands and then leave a nice, wide trail for the Chandim and the Hounds? They'll follow me, and that should leave you an empty forest to ride through."

Belgarath gave him a speculative look. "Exactly what have you got in mind?" he asked.

"I'm still working on it." The dwarf leaned back reflectively. "Let's face it, Belgarath, the Chandim and Zandramas already know that we're here, so there's not much point in tiptoeing around any more. A little noise isn't going to hurt anything."

"That's true, I suppose," Belgarath agreed. He looked at Garion. "Are you getting any hints from the Orb about the direction Zandramas took when she left here?"

"A sort of a steady pull toward the east is all."

Beldin grunted. "Makes sense. Since Urvon's people were

352

wandering all over Katakor, she probably wanted to get to the nearest unguarded border as quickly as possible. That would be Jenno."

"Is the border between Jenno and Katakor unguarded?" Velvet asked.

"They don't even know for sure where the border is." He snorted. "At least not up in the forest. There's nothing up there but trees anyway, so they don't bother with it." He turned back to Belgarath. "Don't get your mind set in stone on some of these things," he advised. "We did a lot of speculating back at Mal Zeth, and the theories we came up with were related to the truth only by implication. There's a great deal of intrigue going on here in Mallorea, so it's a good idea to expect things to turn out not quite the way you thought they would."

"Garion," Polgara said from the fireplace, "would you see if you can find Silk? Breakfast is almost ready."

"Yes, Aunt Pol," he replied automatically.

After they had eaten, they repacked their belongings and carried the packs out to the stable.

"Go out through the sally port," Beldin said as they crossed the courtyard again. "Give me about an hour before you start."

"You're leaving now?" Belgarath asked him.

"I might as well. We're not accomplishing very much by sitting around talking. Don't forget to leave me a trail to follow."

"I'll take care of it. I wish you'd tell me what you're going to do here."

"Trust me." The gnarled sorcerer winked. "Take cover someplace and don't come out again until all the noise subsides." He grinned wickedly and rubbed his dirty hands together in anticipation. Then he shimmered and swooped away as a blue-banded hawk.

"I think we'd better go back inside the house," Belgarath suggested. "Whatever he's going to do out here is likely to involve a great deal of flying debris."

They reentered the house and went back to the room where they had spent the night. "Durnik," Belgarath said, "can you get those shutters closed? I don't think we want broken glass sheeting across the room."

"But then we won't be able to see," Silk objected.

"I'm sure you can live without seeing it. As a matter of fact, you probably *wouldn't* want to watch, anyway."

Durnik went to the window, opened it slightly, and pulled the shutters closed.

Then, from high overhead where the blue-banded hawk had been circling, there came a huge roar almost like a continuous peal of swirling thunder, accompanied by a rushing surge. The House of Torak shook as if a great wind were tearing at it, and the faint light coming from between the slats of the shutters Durnik had closed vanished, to be replaced by inky darkness. Then there came a vast bellow from high in the air above the house.

"A demon?" Ce'Nedra gasped. "Is it a demon?"

"A *semblance* of a demon," Polgara corrected.

"How can anybody see it when it's so dark outside?" Sadi asked.

"It's dark around the house because the house is *inside* the image. The people hiding in the forest should be able to see it very well—too well, in fact."

"It's *that* big?" Sadi looked stunned. "But this house is enormous."

Belgarath grinned. "Beldin was never satisfied with halfway measures," he said.

There came another of those huge bellows from high above, followed by faint shrieks and cries of agony.

"Now what's he doing?" Ce'Nedra asked.

"Some kind of visual display, I'd imagine." Belgarath shrugged. "Probably fairly graphic. My guess is that everyone in the vicinity is being entertained by the spectacle of an illusory demon eating imaginary people alive."

"Will it frighten them off?" Silk asked.

"Wouldn't it frighten you?"

From high overhead, a dreadful booming voice roared. "Hungry!" it said. "Hungry! Want food! More food!" There came a ponderous, earthshaking crash, the sound of a titanic foot crushing an acre of forest. Then there was another and yet another as Beldin's enormous image stalked away. The light returned, and Silk hurried toward the window.

"I wouldn't," Belgarath warned him.

"But—"

"You don't want to see it, Silk. Take my word for it. You don't want to see it."

The gigantic footsteps continued to crash through the nearby woods.

"How much longer?" Sadi asked in a shaken voice.

"He said about an hour." Belgarath replied. "He'll probably make use of all of it. He wants to make a lasting impression on everybody in the area."

There were screams of terror coming from the woods now, and the crashing continued. Then there was another sound— a great roaring that receded off into the distance toward the southwest, accompanied by the fading surge of Beldin's will.

"He's leading the Chandim off now," Belgarath said. "That means he's already chased off the Guardsmen and the Karands. Let's get ready to leave."

It took them a while to calm the wild-eyed horses, but they were finally able to mount and ride into the courtyard. Garion had once again donned his mail shirt and helmet, and his heavy shield hung from the bow of Chretienne's saddle. "Do I still need to carry the lance?" he asked.

"Probably not," Belgarath replied. "We're not likely to meet anybody out there now."

They went through the sally port and into the brushy woods. They circled the black house until they reached the east side, then Garion drew Iron-grip's sword. He held it lightly and swept it back and forth until he felt it pull at his

355

hand. "The trail's over there," he said, pointing toward a scarcely visible path leading off into the woods.

"Good," Belgarath said. "At least we won't have to beat our way through the brush."

They crossed the weed-grown clearing that surrounded the House of Torak and entered the forest. The path they followed showed little sign of recent use, and it was at times difficult to see.

"It looks as if some people left here in a hurry." Silk grinned, pointing at various bits and pieces of equipment lying scattered along the path.

They they came up over the top of a hill and saw a wide strip of devastation stretching through the forest toward the southwest.

"A tornado?" Sadi asked.

"No," Belgarath replied. "Beldin. The Chandim won't have much trouble finding his trail."

The sword in Garion's hand was still pointed unerringly toward the path they were following. He led the way confidently, and they increased their pace to a trot and pushed on through the forest. After a league or so, the path began to run downhill, moving out of the foothills toward the heavily forested plains lying to the east of the Karandese range.

"Are there any towns out there?" Sadi asked, looking out over the forest.

"Akkad is the only one of any size between here and the border," Silk told him.

"I don't think I've ever heard of it. What's it like?"

"It's a pigpen of a place," Silk replied. "Most Karandese towns are. They seem to have a great affinity for mud."

"Wasn't Akkad the place where the Melcene bureaucrat was from?" Velvet asked.

"That's what he said," Silk answered.

"And didn't he say that there are demons there?"

"There *were*," Belgarath corrected. "Cyradis told us that Nahaz has pulled all of his demons out of Karanda and sent them off to Darshiva to fight the Grolims there." He scratched at his beard. "I think we'll avoid Akkad anyway. The demons may have left, but there are still going to be Karandese fanatics there, and I don't think that the news of Mengha's death has reached them yet. In any event, there's going to be a fair amount of chaos here in Karanda until Zakath's army gets back from Cthol Murgos and he moves in to restore order."

They rode on, pausing only briefly for lunch.

By midafternoon, the clouds that had obscured the skies over Ashaba had dissipated, and the sun came back out again. The path they had been following grew wider and more well traveled, and it finally expanded into a road. They picked up the pace and made better time.

As evening drew on, they rode some distance back from the road and made their night's encampment in a small hollow where the light from their fire would be well concealed. They ate, and, immediately after supper, Garion sought his bed. For some reason he felt bone weary.

After half an hour, Ce'Nedra joined him in their tent. She settled down into the blankets and nestled her head against his back. Then she sighed disconsolately. "It was all a waste of time, wasn't it?" she said. "Going to Ashaba, I mean."

"No, Ce'Nedra, not really," he replied, still on the verge of sleep. "We had to go there so that Velvet could kill Harakan. That was one of the tasks that have to be completed before we get to the Place Which Is No More."

"Does all that really have any meaning, Garion?" she asked. "Half the time you act as if you believe it, and the other half you don't. If Zandramas had been there with our son, you wouldn't have just let her walk away because all the conditions hadn't been met, would you?"

"Not by so much as one step," he said grimly.

"The you *don't* really believe it, do you?"

"I'm not an absolute fatalist, if that's what you mean, but I've seen things come out exactly the way the Prophecy said

357

they were going to far too many times for me to ignore it altogether."

"Sometimes I think that I'll never see my baby again," she said in a weary little voice.

"You mustn't ever think that," he told her. "We *will* catch up with Zandramas, and we *will* take Geran home with us again."

"Home," she sighed. "We've been gone for so long that I can barely remember what it looks like."

He took her into his arms, buried his face in her hair, and held her close. After a time she sighed and fell asleep. In spite of his own deep weariness, however, it was quite late before he himself drifted off.

The next day dawned clear and warm. They made their way back to the road again and continued eastward with Iron-grip's sword pointing the way.

About midmorning, Polgara called ahead to Belgarath. "Father, there's someone hiding off to the side of the road just ahead."

He slowed his horse to a walk. "Chandim?" he asked tersely.

"No. It's a Mallorean Angarak. He's very much afraid— and not altogether rational."

"Is he planning any mischief?"

"He's not actually planning anything, father. His thoughts aren't coherent enough for that."

"Why don't you go flush him out, Silk?" the old man suggested. "I don't like having people lurking behind me—sane or not."

"About where is he?" the little man asked Polgara.

"Some distance back in the woods from that dead tree," she replied.

He nodded. "I'll go talk with him," he said. He loped his horse on ahead and reined in beside the dead tree. "We know you're back there, friend," he called pleasantly. "We don't mean you any harm, but why don't you come out in the open where we can see you?"

There was a long pause.

"Come along now," Silk called. "Don't be shy."

"Have you got any demons with you?" The voice sounded fearful.

"Do I look like the sort of fellow who'd be consorting with demons?"

"You won't kill me, will you?"

"Of course not. We only want to talk with you, that's all."

There was another long, fearful pause. "Have you got anything to eat?" The voice was filled with a desperate need.

"I think we can spare a bit."

The hidden man thought about that. "All right," he said finally. "I'm coming out. Remember that you promised not to kill me." Then there was a crashing in the bushes, and a Mallorean soldier came stumbling out into the road. His red tunic was in shreds, he had lost his helmet, and the remains of his boots were tied to his legs with leather thongs. He had quite obviously neither shaved nor bathed for at least a month. His eyes were wild and his head twitched on his neck uncontrollably. He stared at Silk with a terrified expression.

"You don't look to be in very good shape, friend," Silk said to him. "Where's your unit?"

"Dead, all dead, and eaten by the demons." The soldier's eyes were haunted. "Were you at Akkad?" he asked in a terrified voice. "Were you there when the demons came?"

"No, friend. We just came up from Venna."

"You said that you had something for me to eat."

"Durnik," Silk called, "could you bring some food for this poor fellow?"

Durnik rode to the pack horse carrying their stores and took out some bread and dried meat. Then he rode on ahead to join Silk and the fear-crazed soldier.

"Were *you* at Akkad when the demons came?" the fellow asked him.

359

Durnik shook his head. "No," he replied, "I'm with him." He pointed at Silk. Then he handed the fellow the bread and meat.

The soldier snatched them and began to wolf them down in huge bites.

"What happened at Akkad?" Silk asked.

"The demons came," the soldier replied, still cramming food into his mouth. Then he stopped, his eyes fixed on Durnik with an expression of fright. "Are you going to kill me?" he demanded.

Durnik stared at him. "No, man," he replied in a sick voice.

"Thank you." The soldier sat down at the roadside and continued to eat.

Garion and the others slowly drew closer, not wanting to frighten the skittish fellow off.

"What *did* happen at Akkad?" Silk pressed. "We're going in that direction, and we'd sort of like to know what to expect."

"Don't go there," the soldier said, shuddering. "It's horrible—horrible. The demons came through the gates with howling Karands all around them. The Karands started hacking people to pieces and then they fed the pieces to the demons. They cut off both of my captain's arms and then his legs as well, and then a demon picked up what was left of him and ate his head. He was screaming the whole time." He lowered his chunk of bread and fearfully stared at Ce'Nedra. "Lady, are you going to kill me?" he demanded.

"Certainly not!" she replied in a shocked voice.

"If you are, please don't let me see it when you do. And pleasy bury me someplace where the demons won't dig me up and eat me."

"She's not going to kill you," Polgara told him firmly.

The man's wild eyes filled with a kind of desperate longing. "Would *you* do it then, Lady?" he pleaded. "I can't stand the horror any more. Please kill me gently—the way my mother

360

would—and then hide me so that the demons won't get me."
He put his face into his shaking hands and began to cry.

"Give him some more food, Durnik," Belgarath said, his
eyes suddenly filled with compassion. "He's completely mad,
and there's nothing else we can do for him."

"I think I might be able to do something, Ancient One,"
Sadi said. He opened his case and took out a vial of amber
liquid. "Sprinkle a few drops of this on the bread you give
him, Goodman," he said to Durnik. "It will calm him and
give him a few hours of peace."

"Compassion seems out of character for you, Sadi," Silk
said.

"Perhaps," the eunuch murmured, "but then, perhaps you
don't fully understand me, Prince Kheldar."

Durnik took some more bread and meat from the pack for
the hysterical Mallorean soldier, sprinkling them liberally with
Sadi's potion. Then he gave them to the poor man, and they
all rode slowly past and on down the road. After they had gone
a ways, Garion heard him calling after them. "Come back!
Come back! Somebody—anybody—please come back and
kill me. Mother, please kill me!"

Garion's stomach wrenched with an almost overpowering
sense of pity. He set his teeth and rode on, trying not to listen
to the desperate pleas coming from behind.

They circled to the north of Akkad that afternoon, by-
passing the city and returning to the road some two leagues
beyond. The pull of the sword Garion held on the pommel
of his saddle confirmed the fact that Zandramas had indeed
passed this way and had continued on along this road toward
the northeast and the relative safety of the border between
Katakor and Jenno.

They camped in the forest a few miles north of the road
that night and started out once more early the following morning. The road for a time stretched across open fields. It was
deeply rutted and still quite soft at the shoulders.

"Karands don't take road maintenance very seriously," Silk observed, squinting into the morning sun.

"I noticed that," Durnik replied.

"I thought you might have."

Some leagues farther on, the road they were following reentered the forest, and they rode along through a cool, damp shade beneath towering evergreens.

Then, from somewhere ahead they heard a hollow, booming sound.

"I think we might want to go rather carefully until we're past that," Silk said quietly.

"What is that sound?" Sadi asked.

"Drums. There's a temple ahead."

"Out here in the forest?" The eunuch sounded surprised. "I thought that the Grolims were largely confined to the cities."

"This isn't a Grolim Temple, Sadi. It was nothing to do with the worship of Torak. As a matter of fact, the Grolims used to burn these places whenever they came across them. They were a part of the old religion of the area."

"Demon worship, you mean?"

Silk nodded. "Most of them have been long abandoned, but every so often you come across one that's still in use. The drums are a fair indication that the one just ahead is still open for business."

"Will we be able to go around them?" Durnik asked.

"It shouldn't be much trouble," the little man replied. "The Karands burn a certain fungus in their ceremonial fires. The fumes have a peculiar effect on one's senses."

"Oh?" Sadi said with a certain interest.

"Never mind," Belgarath told him. "That red case of yours has quite enough in it already."

"Just scientific curiosity, Belgarath."

"Of course."

"What are they worshiping?" Velvet asked. "I thought that the demons had all left Karanda."

Silk was frowning. "The beat isn't right," he said.

"Have you suddenly become a music critic, Kheldar?" she asked him.

He shook his head. "I've come across these places before, and the drumming's usually pretty frenzied when they're holding their rites. That beat up ahead is too measured. It's almost as if they're waiting for something."

Sadi shrugged. "Let them wait," he said. "It's no concern of ours, is it?"

"We don't know that for sure, Sadi," Polgara told him. She looked at Belgarath. "Wait here, father," she suggested. "I'll go on ahead and take a look."

"It's too dangerous, Pol," Durnik objected.

She smiled. "They won't even pay any attention to me, Durnik." She dismounted and walked a short way up the path. Then, momentarily, she was surrounded with a kind of glowing nimbus, a hazy patch of light that had not been there before. When the light cleared, a great snowy owl hovered among the trees and then ghosted away on soft, silent wings.

"For some reason that always makes my blood run cold," Sadi murmured.

They waited while the measured drumming continued. Garion dismounted and checked his cinch strap. Then he walked about a bit, stretching his legs.

It was perhaps ten minutes later when Polgara returned, drifting on white wings under the low-hanging branches. When she resumed her normal shape, her face was pale and her eyes were filled with loathing. "Hideous!" she said. "Hideous!"

"What is it, Pol?" Durnik's voice was concerned.

"There's a woman in labor in that temple."

"I don't know that a temple is the right sort of place for that, but if she needed shelter—" The smith shrugged.

"The temple was chosen quite deliberately," she replied. "The infant that's about to be born isn't human."

"But—"

"It's a demon."

Ce'Nedra gasped.

Polgara looked at Belgarath. "We have to intervene, father," she told him. "This *must* be stopped."

"How can it be stopped?" Velvet asked in perplexity. "I mean, if the woman's already in labor . . ." She spread her hands.

"We may have to kill her," Polgara said bleakly. "Even that may not prevent this monstrous birth. We may have to deliver the demon child and then smother it."

"No!" Ce'Nedra cried. "It's just a baby! You can't kill it."

"It's not that kind of baby, Ce'Nedra. It's half human and half demon. It's a creature of *this* world and a spawn of the other. If it's allowed to live, it won't be possible to banish it. It will be a perpetual horror."

"Garion!" Ce'Nedra cried. "You can't let her."

"Polgara's right, Ce'Nedra," Belgarath told her. "The creature can't be allowed to live."

"How many Karands are gathered up there?" Silk asked.

"There are a half dozen outside the temple," Polgara replied. "There may be more inside."

"However many they are, we're going to have to dispose of them," he said. "They're waiting for the birth of what they believe is a God, and they'll defend the newborn demon to the death."

"All right, then," Garion said bleakly, "let's go oblige them."

"You're not condoning this?" Ce'Nedra exclaimed.

"I don't like it," he admitted, "but I don't see that we've got much choice." He looked at Polgara. "There's absolutely no way it could be sent back to the place where demons originate?" he asked her.

"None whatsoever," she said flatly. "*This* world will be it's home. It wasn't summoned and it has no master. Within two years, it will be a horror such as this world has never seen. It *must* be destroyed."

"Can you do it, Pol?" Belgarath asked her.

"I don't have any choice, father," she replied. "I *have* to do it."

"All right, then," the old man said to the rest of them. "We have to get Pol inside that temple—and that means dealing with the Karands."

Silk reached inside his boot and pulled out his dagger. "I should have sharpened this," he muttered, looking ruefully at his jagged blade.

"Would you like to borrow one of mine?" Velvet asked him.

"No, that's all right, Liselle," he replied. "I've got a couple of spares." He returned the knife to his boot and drew another from its place of concealment at the small of his back and yet a third from its sheath down the back of his neck.

Durnik lifted his axe from its loop at the back of his saddle. His face was unhappy. "Do we really have to do this, Pol?" he asked.

"Yes, Durnik. I'm afraid we do."

He sighed. "All right, then," he said. "Let's go get it over with."

They started forward, riding at a slow walk to avoid alerting the fanatics ahead.

The Karands were sitting around a large, hollowed-out section of log, pounding on it with clubs in rhythmic unison. It gave forth a dull booming sound. They were dressed in roughly tanned fur vests and cross-tied leggings of dirty sackcloth. They were raggedly bearded, and their hair was matted and greasy. Their faces were hideously painted, but their eyes seemed glazed and their expressions slack-lipped.

"I'll go first," Garion muttered to the others.

"Shouting a challenge, I suppose," Silk whispered.

"I'm not an assassin, Silk," Garion replied quietly. "One or two of them might be rational enough to run, and that means a few less we'll have to kill."

"Suit yourself, but expecting rationality from Karands is irrational all by itself."

365

Garion quickly surveyed the clearing. The wooden temple was constructed of half-rotten logs, sagging badly at one end and surmounted along its ridgepole by a line of mossy skulls staring out vacantly. The ground before the building was hard-packed dirt, and there was a smoky firepit not far from the drummers.

"Try not to get into that smoke," Silk cautioned in a whisper. "You might start to see all sorts of peculiar things if you inhale too much of it."

Garion nodded and looked around. "Are we all ready?" he asked in a low voice.

They nodded.

"All right then." He spurred Chretienne into the clearing. "Throw down your weapons!" he shouted at the startled Karands.

Instead of obeying, they dropped their clubs and seized up a variety of axes, spears, and swords, shrieking their defiance.

"You see?" Silk said.

Garion clenched his teeth and charged, brandishing his sword. Even as he thundered toward the fur-clad men, he saw four others come bursting out of the temple.

Even with these reinforcements, however, the men on foot were no match for Garion and his mounted companions. Two of the howling Karands fell beneath Iron-grip's sword on Garion's first charge, and the one who tried to thrust at his back with a broad-bladed spear fell in a heap as Durnik brained him with his axe. Sadi caught a sword thrust with a flick of his cloak and then, with an almost delicate motion, dipped his poisoned dagger into the swordsman's throat. Using his heavy staff like a club, Toth battered two men to the ground, the sound of his blows punctuated by the snapping of bones. Their howls of frenzy turned to groans of pain as they fell. Silk launched himself from his saddle, rolled with the skill of an acrobat, and neatly ripped open one fanatic with one of his daggers while simultaneously plunging the other into the chest of a fat man who was clumsily trying to wield an axe. Chretienne whirled so quickly that Garion was almost thrown from his saddle as the big stallion trampled a Karand into the earth with his steel-shod hooves.

The lone remaining fanatic stood in the doorway of the crude temple. He was much older than his companions, and his face had been tattooed into a grotesque mask. His only weapon was a skull-surmounted staff, and he was brandishing it at them even as he shrieked an incantation. His words broke off suddenly, however, as Velvet hurled one of her knives at him with a smooth underhand cast. The wizard gaped down in amazement at the hilt of her knife protruding from his chest. Then he slowly toppled over backward.

There was a brief silence, punctuated only by the groans of the two men Toth had crippled. And then a harsh scream came from the temple—a woman's scream.

Garion jumped from his saddle, stepped over the body in the doorway, and looked into the large, smoky room.

A half-naked woman lay on the crude altar against the far wall. She had been bound to it in a spread-eagle position and she was partially covered by a filthy blanket. Her features were distorted, and her belly grossly, impossibly distended. She screamed again and then spoke in gasps.

"Nahaz! Magrash Klat Grichak! Nahaz!"

"I'll deal with this, Garion," Polgara said firmly from behind him. "Wait outside with the others."

"Were they any others in there?" Silk asked him as he came out.

"Just the woman. Aunt Pol's with her." Garion suddenly realized that he was shaking violently.

"What was that language she was speaking?" Sadi asked, carefully cleaning his poisoned dagger.

"The language of the demons," Belgarath replied. "She was calling out to the father of her baby."

"Nahaz?" Garion asked, his voice startled.

"She *thinks* it was Nahaz," the old man said. "She could be wrong—or maybe not."

367

From inside the temple the woman screamed again.

"Is anybody hurt?" Durnik asked.

"They are," Silk replied, pointing at the fallen Karands. Then he squatted and repeatedly plunged his daggers into the dirt to cleanse the blood off them.

"Kheldar," Velvet said in a strangely weak voice, "would you get my knife for me?" Garion looked at her and saw that her face was pale and that her hands were trembling slightly. He realized then that this self-possessed young woman was perhaps not quite so ruthless as he had thought.

"Of course, Liselle," Silk replied in a neutral tone. The little man quite obviously also understood the cause of her distress. He rose, went to the doorway, and pulled the knife out of the wizard's chest. He wiped it carefully and returned it to her. "Why don't you go back and stay with Ce'Nedra?" he suggested. "We can clean up here."

"Thank you, Kheldar," she said, turned her horse, and rode out of the clearing.

"She's only a girl," Silk said to Garion in a defensive tone. "She *is* good, though," he added with a certain pride.

"Yes," Garion agreed. "Very good." He looked around at the twisted shapes lying in heaps in the clearing. "Why don't we drag all these bodies over behind the temple?" he suggested. "This place is bad enough without all of this."

There was another scream from the temple.

Noon came and went unnoticed as Garion and the others endured the cries of the laboring woman. By midafternoon, the screams had grown much weaker, and as the sun was just going down, there came one dreadful last shriek that seemed to dwindle off into silence. No other sound came from inside, and after several minutes, Polgara came out. Her face was pale, and her hands and clothing were drenched with blood.

"Well, Pol?" Belgarath asked her.

"She died."

"And the demon?"

"Stillborn. Neither one of them survived the birth." She

looked down at her clothing. "Durnik, please bring me a blanket and water to wash in."

"Of course, Pol."

With her husband shielding her by holding up the blanket, Polgara deliberately removed all of her clothing, throwing each article through the temple doorway. Then she drew the blanket about her. "Now burn it," she said to them. "Burn it to the ground."

CHAPTER TWENTY-ONE

They crossed the border into Jenno about noon the following day, still following the trail of Zandramas. The experiences of the previous afternoon and evening had left them all subdued, and they rode on in silence. A league or so past the rather indeterminate border, they pulled off to the side of the road to eat. The spring sunlight was very bright and the day pleasantly warm. Garion walked a little ways away from the others and reflectively watched a cloud of yellow-striped bees industriously working at a patch of wild flowers.

"Garion," Ce'Nedra said in a small voice, coming up behind him.

"Yes, Ce'Nedra?" He put his arm around her.

"What really happened back there?"

"You saw about as much of it as I did."

"That's not what I mean. What happened inside the temple? Did that poor woman and her baby *really* just die—or did Polgara kill them?"

"*Ce'Nedra!*"

"I have to know, Garion. She was so grim about it before she went inside that place. She was going to kill the baby. Then she came out and told us that the mother and baby had both died in the birth. Wasn't that very convenient?"

He drew in a deep breath. "Ce'Nedra, think back. You've known Aunt Pol for a long time now. Has she ever told you a lie—ever?"

"Well—sometimes she hasn't told me the whole truth. She's told me part of it and kept the rest a secret."

"That's not the same as lying, Ce'Nedra, and you know it."

"Well—"

"You're angry because she said we might have to kill that thing."

"Baby," she corrected firmly.

He took her by the shoulders and looked directly into her face. "No, Ce'Nedra. It was a thing—half human, half demon, and all monster."

"But it was so little—so helpless."

"How do you know that?"

"All babies are little when they're born."

"I don't think that one was. I saw the woman for just a minute before Aunt Pol told me to leave the temple. Do you remember how big you were just before Geran was born? Well, that woman's stomach was at least five times as big as yours was—and she wasn't a great deal taller than you are."

"You aren't serious!"

"Oh, yes, I am. There was no way that the demon could have been born without killing its mother. For all I know, it might just simply have clawed its way out."

"It's own mother?" she gasped.

"Did you think it would love its mother? Demons don't know how to love, Ce'Nedra. That's why they're demons. Fortunately the demon died. It's too bad that the woman had to die, too, but it was much too late to do anything for her by the time we got there."

"You're a cold, hard person, Garion."

"Oh, Ce'Nedra, you know better than that. What happened back there was unpleasant, certainly, but none of us had any choice but to do exactly what we did."

She turned her back on him and started to stalk away.

"Ce'Nedra," he said, hurrying to catch her.

"What?" She tried to free her arm from his grasp.

"We didn't have any choice," he repeated. "Would you want Geran to grow up in a world filled with demons?"

She stared at him. "No," she firmly admitted. "It's just that . . ." She left it hanging.

"I know." He put his arms about her.

"Oh, Garion." She suddenly clung to him, and everything was all right again.

After they had eaten, they rode on through the forest, passing occasional villages huddled deep among the trees. The villages were rude, most of them consisting of a dozen or so rough log houses and surrounded by crude log palisades. There were usually a rather surprising number of hogs rooting among the stumps that surrounded each village.

"There don't seem to be very many dogs," Durnik observed.

"These people prefer pigs as house pets," Silk told him. "As a race, Karands have a strong affinity for dirt, and pigs satisfy certain deep inner needs among them."

"Do you know something, Silk," the smith said then. "You'd be a much more pleasant companion if you didn't try to turn everything into a joke."

"It's a failing I have. I've looked at the world for quite a

few years now and I've found that if I don't laugh, I'll probably
end up crying."

"You're really serious, aren't you?"

"Would I do that to an old friend?"

About midafternoon, the road they were following curved
slightly, and they soon reached the edge of the forest and a
fork in the rutted track.

"All right. Which way?" Belgarath asked.

Garion lifted his sword from the pommel of his saddle and
swept it slowly back and forth until he felt the familiar tug.
"The right fork," he replied.

"I'm *so* glad you said that," Silk told him. "The left fork
leads to Calida. I'd expect that news of Harakan's death has
reached there by now. Even without the demons, a town full
of hysterics doesn't strike me as a very nice place to visit. The
followers of Lord Mengha might be just a bit upset when they
hear that he's gone off and left them."

"Where does the right fork go?" Belgarath asked him.

"Down to the lake," Silk replied. "Lake Karanda. It's the
biggest lake in the world. When you stand on the shore, it's
like looking at an ocean."

Garion frowned. "Grandfather," he said, starting to worry,
"Do you think that Zandramas knows that the Orb can follow
her?"

"It's possible, yes."

"And would she know that it can't follow her over water?"

"I couldn't say for sure."

"But if she *does*, isn't it possible that she went to the lake
in order to hide her trail from us? She could have sailed out
a ways, doubled back, and come ashore just about anyplace.
Then she could have struck out in a new direction, and we'd
never pick up her trail again."

Belgarath scratched at his beard, squinting in the sunlight.
"Pol," he said. "Are there any Gromlins about?"

She concentrated a bit. "Not in the immediate vicinity,
father," she replied.

"Good. When Zandramas was trying to tamper with Ce'Nedra back at Rak Hagga, weren't you able to lock your thought with hers for a while?"

"Yes, briefly."

"She was at Ashaba then, right?"

She nodded.

"Did you get any kind of notion about which direction she was planning to go when she left?"

She frowned. "Nothing very specific, father—just a vague hint about wanting to go home.

"Darshiva," Silk said, snapping his fingers. "We know that Zandramas is a Darshivan name, and Zakath told Garion that it was in Darshiva that she started stirring up trouble."

Belgarath grunted. "It's a little thin," he said. "I'd feel a great deal more comfortable with some confirmation." He looked at Polgara. "Do you think you could reestablish contact with her—even for just a moment. All I need is a direction."

"I don't think so, father. I'll try, but . . ." she shrugged. Then her face grew very calm, and Garion could feel her mind reaching out with a subtle probing. After a few minutes, she relaxed her will. "She's shielding, father," she told the old man. "I can't pick up anything at all."

He muttered a curse under his breath. "We'll just have to go on down to the lake and ask a few questions. Maybe somebody saw her."

"I'm sure they did," Silk said, "but Zandramas likes to drown sailors, remember? Anyone who saw where she landed is probably sleeping under thirty feet of water."

"Can you think of an alternative plan?"

"Not offhand, no."

"Then we go on to the lake."

As the sun began to sink slowly behind them, they passed a fair-sized town set perhaps a quarter of a mile back from the road. The inhabitants were gathered outside the palisade surrounding it. They had a huge bonfire going, and just in front of the fire stood a crude, skull-surmounted altar of logs. A

374

skinny man wearing several feathers in his hair and with lurid designs painted on his face and body was before the altar, intoning an incantation at the top of his lungs. His arms were stretched imploringly at the sky, and there was a note of desperation in his voice.

"What's he doing?" Ce'Nedra asked.

"He's trying to raise a demon so that the townspeople can worship it," Eriond told her calmly.

"Garion!" She said in alarm. "Shouldn't we run?"

"He won't succeed," Eriond assured her. "The demon won't come to him any more. Nahaz has told them all not to."

The wizard broke off his incantation. Even from this distance, Garion could see that there was a look of panic on his face.

An angry mutter came from the townspeople.

"That crowd is starting to turn ugly," Silk observed. "The wizard had better raise his demon on the next try, or he might be in trouble."

The gaudily painted man with feathers in his hair began the incantation again, virtually shrieking and ranting at the sky. He completed it and stood waiting expectantly.

Nothing happened.

After a moment, the crowd gave an angry roar and surged forward. They seized the cringing wizard and tore his log altar apart. Then, laughing raucously, they nailed his hands and feet to one of the logs with long spikes and, with a great shout, they hurled the log up onto the bonfire.

"Let's get out of here," Belgarath said. "Mobs tend to go wild once they've tasted bloood." He led them away at a gallop.

They made camp that night in a willow thicket on the banks of a small stream, concealing their fire as best they could.

It was foggy the following morning, and they rode warily with their hands close to their weapons.

"How much farther to the lake?" Belgarath asked as the sun began to burn off the fog.

Silk looked around into the thinning mist. "It's kind of hard to say. I'd guess a couple more leagues at least."

Let's pick up the pace, then. We're going to have to find a boat when we get there, and that might take a while."

They urged their horses into a canter and continued on. The road had taken on a noticeable downhill grade.

"It's a bit closer than I thought," Silk called to them. "I remember this stretch of road. We should reach the lake in an hour or so."

They passed occasional Karands, clad in brown fur for the most part and heavily armed. The eyes of these local people were suspicious, even hostile, but Garion's mail shirt, helmet, and sword were sufficient to gain the party passage without incident.

By midmorning the gray fog had completely burned off. As they crested a knoll, Garion reined in. Before him there lay an enormous body of water, blue and sparkling in the midmorning sun. It looked for all the world like a vast inland sea, with no hint of a far shore, but it did not have that salt tang of the sea.

"Big, isn't it?" Silk said, pulling his horse in beside Chretienne. He pointed toward a thatch and log village standing a mile or so up the lake shore. A number of fair-sized boats were moored to a floating dock jutting out into the water. "That's where I've usually hired boats when I wanted to cross the lake."

"You've done business around here, then?"

"Oh, yes. There are gold mines in the mountains of Zamad, and deposits of gem stones up in the forest."

"How big are those boats?"

"Big enough. We'll be a little crowded, but the weather's calm enough for a safe crossing, even if the boat might be a bit overloaded." Then he frowned. "What are *they* doing?"

Garion looked at the slope leading down to the village and saw a crowd of people moving slowly down toward the lake shore. There seemed to be a great deal of fur involved in their

clothing in varying shades of red and brown, though many
of them wore cloaks all dyed in hues of rust and faded blue.
More and more of them came over the hilltop, and other people came out of the village to meet them.

"Belgarath," the little Drasnian called. "I think we've got
a problem."

Belgarath came jolting up to the crest of the knoll at a trot.
He looked at the large crowd gathering in front of the village.

"We need to get into that village to hire a boat," Silk told
him. "We're well enough armed to intimidate a few dozen
villagers, but there are two or three hundred people down
there now. That could require some fairly serious
intimidation."

"A country fair, perhaps?" the old man asked.

Silk shook his head. "I wouldn't think so. It's the wrong
time of year for it, and those people don't have any carts with
them." He swung down from his saddle and went back to the
pack horses. A moment or so later, he came back with a poorly
tanned red fur vest and a baggy fur hat. He pulled them on,
bent over, and wrapped a pair of sack cloth leggings about his
calves, tying them in place with lengths of cord. "How do I
look?" he asked.

"Shabby," Garion told him.

"That's the idea. Shab's in fashion here in Karanda." He
remounted.

"Where did you get the clothes?" Belgarath asked
curiously.

"I pillaged one of the bodies back at the temple." The
little man shrugged. "I like to keep a few disguises handy.
I'll go find out what's happening down there." He dug his
heels into his horse's flanks and galloped down toward the
throng gathering near the lakeside village.

"Let's pull back out of sight," Belgarath suggested. "I'd
rather not attract too much attention."

They walked their horses down the back side of the knoll
and then some distance away from the road to a shallow gully

that offered concealment and dismounted there. Garion climbed back up out of the gully on foot and lay down in the tall grass to keep watch.

About a half-hour later, Silk came loping back over the top of the knoll. Garion rose from the grass and signaled to him.

When the little man reached the gully and dismounted, his expression was disgusted. "Religion," he snorted. "I wonder what the world would be like without it. That gathering down there is for the purpose of witnessing the performance of a powerful wizard, who absolutely guarantees that he can raise a demon—despite the notable lack of success of others lately. He's even hinting that he might be able to persuade the Demon Lord Nahaz himself to put in an appearance. That crowd's likely to be there all day."

"Now what?" Sadi asked.

Belgarath walked down the gully a ways, looking thoughtfully up at the sky. When he came back, his look was determined. "We're going to need a couple more of those," he said, pointing at Silk's disguise.

"Nothing simpler," Silk replied. "There are still enough latecomers going down that hill for me to be able to waylay a few. What's the plan?"

"You, Garion, and I are going down there."

"Interesting notion, but I don't get the point."

"The wizard, whoever he is, is promising to raise Nahaz, but Nahaz is with Urvon and isn't very likely to show up. After what we saw happen at that village yesterday, it's fairly obvious that failing to produce a demon is a serious mistake for a wizard to make. If our friend down there is so confident, it probably means that he's going to create an illusion—since nobody's been able to produce the real thing lately. I'm good at illusions myself, so I'll just go down and challenge him."

"Won't they just fall down and worship *your* illusion?" Velvet asked him.

His smile was chilling. "I don't really think so, Liselle," he replied. "You see, there are demons, and then there are

378

demons. If I do it right, there won't be a Karand within five leagues of this place by sunset—depending on how fast they can run, of course." He looked at Silk. "Haven't you left yet?" he asked pointedly.

While Silk went off in search of more disguises, the old sorcerer made a few other preparations. He found a long, slightly crooked branch to use as a staff and a couple of feathers to stick in his hair. Then he sat down and laid his head back against one of their packs. "All right, Pol," he instructed his daughter, "make me hideous."

She smiled faintly and started to raise one hand.

"Not *that* way. Just take some ink and draw some designs on my face. They don't have to be too authentic-looking. The Karands have corrupted their religion so badly that they wouldn't recognize authenticity if they stepped in it."

She laughed and went to one of the packs, returning a moment later with an inkpot and a quill pen.

"Why on earth are you carrying ink, Lady Polgara?" Ce'Nedra asked.

"I like to be prepared for eventualities as they arise. I went on a long journey once and had to leave a note for someone along the way. I didn't have ink with me, so I ended up opening a vein to get something to write with. I seldom make the same mistake twice. Close your eyes, father. I always like to start with the eyelids and work my way out."

Belgarath closed his eyes. "Durnik," he said as Polgara started drawing designs on his face with her quill, "you and the others will stay back here. See if you can find some place a little better hidden than this gully."

"All right, Belgarath," the smith agreed. "How will we know when it's safe to come down to the lake shore?"

"When the screaming dies out."

"Don't move your lips, father," Polgara told him, frowning in concentration as she continued her drawing. "Did you want me to blacken your beard, too?"

"Leave it the way it is. Superstitious people are always

379

impressed by venerablility, and I look older than just about anybody."

She nodded her agreement. "Actually, father, you look older than dirt."

"Very funny, Pol," he said acidly. "Are you just about done?"

"Did you want the death symbol on your forehead?" she asked.

"Might as well," he grunted. "Those cretins down there won't recognize it, but it looks impressive."

By the time Polgara had finished with her art work, Silk returned with assorted garments.

"Any problems?" Durnik asked him.

"Simplicity itself." Silk shrugged. "A man whose eyes are fixed on heaven is fairly easy to approach from behind, and a quick rap across the back of the head will usually put him to sleep."

"Leave your mail shirt and helmet, Garion," Belgarath said. "Karands don't wear them. Bring your sword, though."

"I'd planned to." Garion began to struggle out of his mail shirt. After a moment, Ce'Nedra came over to help him.

"You're getting rusty," she told him after they had hauled off the heavy thing. She pointed at a number of reddish-brown stains on the padded linen tunic he wore under the shirt.

"It's one of the drawbacks to wearing armor," he replied.

"That and the smell," she added, wrinkling her nose. "You *definitely* need a bath, Garion."

"I'll see if I can get around to it one of these days," he said. He pulled on one of the fur vests Silk had stolen. Then he tied on the crude leggings and crammed on a rancid-smelling fur cap. "How do I look?" he asked her.

"Like a barbarian," she replied.

"That was sort of the whole idea."

"I didn't steal you a hat," Silk was saying to Belgarath. "I thought you might prefer to wear feathers."

Belgarath nodded. "All of us mighty wizards wear feathers," he agreed. "It's a passing fad, I'm sure, but I always like to dress fashionably." He looked over at the horses. "I think we'll walk," he decided. "When the noise starts, the horses might get a bit skittish." He looked at Polgara and the others who were staying behind. "This shouldn't take us too long," he told them confidently and strode off down the gully with Garion and Silk close behind him.

They emerged from the mouth of the gully at the south end of the knoll and walked down the hill toward the crowd gathering on the lake shore.

"I don't see any sign of their wizard yet," Garion said, peering ahead.

"They always like to keep their audiences waiting for a bit," Belgarath said. "It's supposed to heighten the anticipation or something."

The day was quite warm as they walked down the hill, and the rancid smell coming from their clothing grew stronger. Although they did not really look that much like Karands, the people in the crowd they quietly joined paid them scant attention. Every eye seemed to be fixed on a platform and one of those log altars backed by a line of skulls on stakes.

"Where do they get all the skulls?" Garion whispered to Silk.

"They used to be head-hunters," Silk replied. "The Angaraks discouraged that practice, so now they creep around at night robbing graves. I doubt if you could find a whole skeleton in any graveyard in all of Karanda."

"Let's get closer to the altar," Belgarath muttered. "I don't want to have to shove my way through this mob when things start happening." They pushed through the crowd. A few of the greasy-haired fanatics started to object to being thrust aside, but one look at Belgarath's face with the hideous designs Polgara had drawn on it convinced them that here was a wizard of awesome power and that it perhaps might be wiser not to interfere with him.

Just as they reached the front near the altar, a man in a

381

black Grolim robe strode out through the gate of the lakeside village, coming directly toward the altar.

"I think that's our wizard," Belgarath said quietly.

"A Grolim?" Silk sounded slightly surprised.

"Let's see what he's up to."

The black-robed man reached the platform and stepped up to stand in front of the altar. He raised both hands and spoke harshly in a language Garion did not understand. His words could have been either a benediction or a curse. The crowd fell immediately silent. Slowly the Grolim pushed back his hood and let his robe fall to the platform. He wore only a loincloth, and his head had been shaved. His body was covered from crown to toe with elaborate tattoos.

Silk winced. "That must have *really* hurt," he muttered.

"Prepare ye all to look upon the face of your God," the Grolim announced in a large voice, then bent to inscribe the designs on the platform before the altar.

"That's what I thought," Belgarath whispered. "That circle he drew isn't complete. If he were *really* going to raise a demon, he wouldn't have made that mistake."

The Grolim straightened and began declaiming the words of the incantation in a rolling, oratorical style.

"He's being very cautious," Belgarath told them. "He's leaving out certain key phrases. He doesn't want to raise a *real* demon accidentally. Wait." The old man smiled bleakly. "Here he goes."

Garion also felt the surge as the Grolim's will focused and then he heard the familiar rushing sound.

"Behold the Demon Lord Nahaz," the tattooed Grolim shouted, and a shadow-encased form appeared before the altar with a flash of fire, a peal of thunder, and a cloud of sulfur-stinking smoke. Although the figure was no larger than an ordinary man, it looked very substantial for some reason.

"Not too bad, really," Belgarath admitted grudgingly.

"It looks awfully solid to me, Belgarath," Silk said nervously.

"It's only an illusion, Silk," the old man quietly reassured him. "A good one, but still only an illusion."

The shadowy form on the platform before the altar rose to its full height and then pulled back its hood of darkness to reveal the hideous face Garion had seen in Torak's throne room at Ashaba.

As the crowd fell to its knees with a great moan, Belgarath drew in his breath sharply. "When this crowd starts to disperse, don't let the Grolim escape," he instructed. "He's actually seen the real Nahaz, and that means that he was one of Harakan's cohorts. I want some answers out of him." Then the old man drew himself up. "Well, I guess I might as well get started with this," he said. He stepped up in front of the platform. "Fraud!" he shouted in a great voice. "Fraud and fakery!"

The Grolim stared at him, his eyes narrowing as he saw the designs drawn on his face. "On your knees before the Demon Lord," he blustered.

"Fraud!" Belgarath denounced him again. He stepped up onto the platform and faced the stunned crowd. "This is no wizard, but only a Grolim trickster," he declared.

"The Demon Lord will tear all your flesh from your bones," the Grolim shrieked.

"All right," Belgarath replied with calm contempt. "Let's see him do it. Here. I'll even help him." He pulled back his sleeve, approached the shadowy illusion hovering threateningly before the altar and quite deliberately ran his bare arm into the shadow's gaping maw. A moment later, his hand emerged, coming, or so it appeared, out of the back of the Demon Lord's head. He pushed his arm further until his entire wrist and forearm were sticking out of the back of the illusion. Then, quite deliberately, he wiggled his fingers at the people gathered before the altar.

A nervous titter ran through the crowd.

"I think you missed a shred or two of flesh, Nahaz," the old man said to the shadowy form standing before him.

"There still seems to be quite a bit of meat clinging to my fingers and arm." He pulled his arm back out of the shadow and then passed both hands back and forth through the Grolim's illusion. "It appears to lack a bit of substance, friend," he said to the tattooed man. "Why don't we send it back where you found it? Then I'll show you and your parishoners here a *real* demon."

He put his hands derisively on his hips, leaned forward slightly from the waist, and blew at the shadow. The illusion vanished, and the tattooed Grolim stepped back fearfully.

"He's getting ready to run," Silk whispered to Garion. "You get on that side of the platform, and I'll get on this. Thump his head for him if he comes your way."

Garion nodded and edged around toward the far side of the platform.

Belgarath raised his voice again to the crowd. "You fall upon your knees before the reflection of the Demon Lord," he roared at them. "What will you do when I bring before you the King of Hell?" He bent and quickly traced the circle and pentagram about his feet. The tattooed priest edged further away from him.

"Stay, Grolim," Belgarath said with a cruel laugh. "The King of Hell is always hungry, and I think he might like to devour you when he arrives." He made a hooking gesture with one hand, and the Grolim began to struggle as if he had been seized by a powerful, invisible hand.

Then Belgarath began to intone an incantation quite different from the one the Grolim had spoken, and his words reverberated from the vault of heaven as he subtly amplified them into enormity. Seething sheets of varicolored flame shot through the air from horizon to horizon.

"Behold the Gates of Hell!" he roared, pointing.

Far out on the lake, two vast columns seemed to appear; between them were great billowing clouds of smoke and flame. From behind that burning gate came the sound of a multitude of hideous voices shrieking some awful hymn of praise.

"And now I call upon the King of Hell to reveal himself!" the old man shouted, raising his crooked staff. The surging force of his will was vast, and the great sheets of flame flickering in the sky actually seemed to blot out the sun and to replace its light with a dreadful light of its own.

From beyond the gate of fire came a huge whistling sound that descended into a roar. The flames parted, and the shape of a mighty tornado swept between the two pillars. Faster and faster the tornado whirled, turning from inky black to pale, frozen white. Ponderously, that towering white cloud advanced across the lake, congealing as it came. At first it appeared to be some vast snow wraith with hollow eyes and gaping mouth. It was quite literally hundreds of feet tall, and its breath swept across the now-terrified crowd before the altar like a blizzard.

"Ye have tasted ice," Belgarath told them. "Now taste fire! Your worship of the false Demon Lord hath offended the King of Hell, and now will ye roast in perpetual flames!" He made another sweeping gesture with his staff, and a deep red glow appeared in the center of the seething white shape that even now approached the shore of the lake. The sooty red glow grew more and more rapidly, expanding until it filled the encasing white entirely. Then the wraithlike figure of flame and swirling ice raised its hundred-foot-long arms and roared with a deafening sound. The ice seemed to shatter, and the wraith stood as a creature of fire. Flames shot from its mouth and nostrils, and steam rose from the surface of the lake as it moved across the last few yards of water before reaching the shore.

It reached down one enormous hand, placing it atop the altar, palm turned up. Belgarath calmly stepped up onto that burning hand, and the illusion raised him high into the air.

"Infidels!" he roared at them in an enormous voice. "Prepare ye all to suffer the wrath of the King of Hell for your foul apostasy!''

There was a dreadful moan from the Karands, followed by terrified screams as the fire-wraith reached out toward the crowd with its other huge, burning hand. Then, as one man, they turned and fled, shrieking in terror.

Somehow, perhaps because Belgarath was concentrating so much of his attention on the vast form he had created and was struggling to maintain, the Grolim broke free and jumped down off the platform.

Garion, however, was waiting for him. He reached out and stopped the fleeing man with one hand placed flat against his chest, even as he swept the other back and then around in a wide swing that ended with a jolting impact against the side of the tattooed man's head.

The Grolim collapsed in a heap. For some reason, Garion found that very satisfying.

CHAPTER TWENTY-TWO

"Which boat did you want to steal?" Silk asked as Garion dropped the unconscious Grolim on the floating dock that stuck out into the lake.

"Why ask me?" Garion replied, feeling just a bit uncomfortable with Silk's choice of words.

"Because you and Durnik are the ones who are going to have to sail it. I don't know the first thing about getting a boat to move through the water without tipping over."

"Capsizing," Garion corrected absently, looking at the various craft moored to the dock.

"What?"

"The word is 'capsize,' Silk. You tip over a wagon. You capsize a boat."

"It means the same thing, doesn't it?"

"Approximately, yes."

"Why make an issue of it, then? How about this one?" The little man pointed at a broad-beamed vessel with a pair of eyes painted on the bow.

"Not enough freeboard," Garion told him. "The horses are heavy, so any boat we take is going to settle quite a bit."

Silk shrugged. "You're the expert. You're starting to sound as professional as Barak or Greldik." He grinned suddenly. "You know, Garion, I've never stolen anything as big as a boat before. It's really very challenging."

"I wish you'd stop using the word 'steal.' Couldn't we just say that we're borrowing a boat?"

"Did you plan to sail it back and return it when we're finished with it?"

"No. Not really."

"Then the proper word is 'steal.' You're the expert on ships and sailing; I'm the expert on theft."

They walked farther out on the dock.

"Let's go on board this one and have a look around," Garion said, pointing at an ungainly-looking scow painted an unwholesome green color.

"It looks like a washtub."

"I'm not planning to win any races with it." Garion leaped aboard the scow. "It's big enough for the horses and the sides are high enough to keep the weight from swamping it." He inspected the spars and rigging. "A little crude," he noted, "but Durnik and I should be able to manage."

"Check the bottom for leaks," Silk suggested. "Nobody would paint a boat that color if it didn't leak."

Garion went below and checked the hold and the bilges. When he came back up on deck, he had already made up his mind. "I think we'll borrow this one," he said, jumping back to the pier.

"The term is still 'steal,' Garion."

Garion sighed. "All right, steal—if it makes you happy."

"Just trying to be precise, that's all."

"Let's go get that Grolim and drag him up here," Garion suggested. "We'll throw him in the boat and tie him up. I don't *think* he'll wake up for a while, but there's no point in taking chances."

"How hard did you hit him?"

"Quite hard, actually. For some reason he irritated me." They started back to where the Grolim lay.

"You're getting to be more like Belgarath every day," Silk told him. "You do more damage out of simple irritation than most men can do in a towering rage."

Garion shrugged and rolled the tattooed Grolim over with his foot. He took hold of one of the unconscious man's ankles. "Get his other leg," he said.

The two of them walked back toward the scow with the Grolim dragging limply along behind them, his shaved head bouncing up and down on the logs of the dock. When they reached the scow, Garion took the man's arms while Silk took his ankles. They swung him back and forth a few times, then lobbed him across the rail like a sack of grain. Garion jumped across again and bound him hand and foot.

"Here comes Belgarath with the others," Silk said from the dock.

"Good. Here—catch the other end of this gangplank." Garion swung the ungainly thing around and pushed it out toward the waiting little Drasnian. Silk caught hold of it, pulled it out farther, and set the end down on the dock.

"Did you find anything?" he asked the others as they approached.

"We did quite well, actually," Durnik replied. "One of those buildings is a storehouse. It was crammed to the rafters with food."

"Good. I wasn't looking forward to making the rest of this trip on short rations."

Belgarath was looking at the scow. "It isn't much of a boat, Garion," he objected. "If you were going to steal one, why didn't you steal something a little fancier?"

"You see?" Silk said to Garion. "I told you that it was the right word."

"I'm not stealing it for its looks, Grandfather," Garion said. "I don't plan to keep it. It's big enough to hold the horses, and the sails are simple enough so that Durnik and I can manage them. If you don't like it, go steal one of your own."

"Grumpy today, aren't we?" the old man said mildly. "What did you do with my Grolim?"

"He's lying up here in the scuppers."

"Is he awake yet?"

"Not for some time, I don't think. I hit him fairly hard. Are you coming on board, or would you rather go steal a different boat?"

"Be polite, dear," Polgara chided.

"No, Garion," Belgarath said. "If you've got your heart set on this one, then we'll take this one."

It took awhile to get the horses aboard, and then they all fell to the task of raising the boat's square-rigged sails. When they were raised and set to Garion's satisfaction, he took hold of the tiller. "All right," he said. "Cast off the lines."

"You sound like a real sailor, dear," Ce'Nedra said in admiration.

"I'm glad you approve." He raised his voice slightly. "Toth, would you take that boat hook and push us out from the pier, please? I don't want to have to crash through all these other boats to get to open water."

The giant nodded, picked up the long boat hook, and shoved against the dock with it. The bow swung slowly out from the dock with the sails flapping in the fitful breeze.

"Isn't the word 'ship,' Garion?" Ce'Nedra asked.

"What?"

"You called them boats. Aren't they called ships?"

He gave her a long, steady look.

390

"I was only asking," she said defensively.

"Don't. Please."

"What did you hit this man with, Garion?" Belgarath asked peevishly. He was kneeling beside the Grolim.

"My fist," Garion replied.

"Next time, use an axe or a club. You almost killed him."

"Would anyone else like to register any complaints?" Garion asked in a loud voice. "Let's pile them all up in a heap right now."

They all stared at him, looking a bit shocked.

He gave up. "Just forget that I said it." He squinted up at the sails, trying to swing the bow to the exact angle which would allow the sails to catch the offshore breeze. Then, quite suddenly, they bellied out and boomed, and the scow began to pick up speed, plowing out past the end of the pier and into open water.

"Pol," Belgarath said. "Why don't you come over here and see what you can do with this man? I can't get a twitch out of him, and I want to question him."

"All right, father." She went to the Grolim, knelt beside him, and put her hands on his temples. She concentrated for a moment, and Garion felt the surge of her will.

The Grolim groaned.

"Sadi," she said thoughtfully, "Do you have any nephara in that case of yours?"

The eunuch nodded. "I was just going to suggest it myself, Lady Polgara." He knelt and opened his red case.

Belgarath looked at his daughter quizzically.

"It's a drug, father," she explained. "It induces truthfulness."

"Why not do it the regular way?" he asked.

"The man's a Grolim. His mind is likely to be very strong. I could probably overcome him, but it would take time—and it would be very tiring. Nephara works just as well and it doesn't take any effort."

He shurgged. "Suit yourself, Pol."

391

Sadi had taken a vial of a thick green liquid from his case. He unstoppered it and then took hold of the Grolim's nose, holding it until the half-conscious man was forced to open his mouth in order to breathe. Then the eunuch delicately tilted three drops of the green syrup onto the man's tongue. "I'd suggest giving him a few moments before you wake him, Lady Polgara," he said, squinting clinically at the Grolim's face. "Give the drug time to take effect first." He restoppered the vial and put it back in his case.

"Will the drug hurt him in any way?" Durnik asked.

Sadi shook his head. "It simply relaxes the will," he replied. "He'll be rational and coherent, but very tractable."

"He *also* won't be able to focus his mind sufficiently to use any talent he may have," Polgara added. "We won't have to worry about his translocating himself away from us the moment he wakes up." She critically watched the Grolim's face, occasionally lifting one of his eyelids to note the drug's progress. "I think it's taken hold now," she said finally. She untied the prisoner's hands and feet. Then she put her hands on the man's temples and gently brought him back to consciousness. "How are you feeling?" she asked him.

"My head hurts," the Grolim said plaintively.

"That will pass," she assured him. She rose and looked at Belgarath. "Speak to him calmly, father," she said, "and start out with simple questions. With nephara it's best to lead them rather gently up to the important things."

Belgarath nodded. He picked up a wooden pail, inverted it, put it on the deck beside the Grolim, and sat on it. "Good morning, friend," he said pleasantly, "or is it afternoon?" He squinted up at the sky.

"You're not really a Karand, are you?" the Grolim asked. His voice sounded dreamy. "I thought you were one of their wizards, but now that I look at you more closely, I can see that you're not."

"You're very astute, friend," Belgarath congratulated him. "What's your name?"

"Arshag," the Grolim replied.

"And where are you from?"

"I am of the Temple at Calida."

"I thought you might be. Do you happen to know a Chandim named Harakan, by any chance?"

"He now prefers to be known as Lord Mengha."

"Ah, yes, I'd heard about that. That illusion of Nahaz you raised this morning was very accurate. You must have seen him several times in order to get everything right."

"I have frequently been in close contact with Nahaz," the Grolim admitted. "It was I who delivered him to Lord Mengha."

"Why don't you tell me about that? I'm sure it's a fascinating story and I'd really like to hear it. Take your time, Arshag. Tell me the whole story, and don't leave out any of the details."

The Grolim smiled almost happily. "I've been wanting to tell someone the story for a long time now," he said. "Do you really want to hear it?"

"I'm absolutely dying to hear it," Belgarath assured him.

The Grolim smiled again. "Well," he began, "It all started quite a number of years ago—not too long after the death of Torak. I was serving in the Temple at Calida. Though we were all in deepest despair, we tried to keep the faith alive. Then one day Harakan came to our temple and sought me out privately. I had journeyed at times to Mal Yaska on Church business and I knew Harakan to be of high rank among the Chandim and very close to the Holy Disciple Urvon. When we were alone, he told me that Urvon had consulted the Oracles and Prophecies concerning the direction the Church must take in her blackest hour. The Disciple had discovered that a new God was destined to rise over Angarak, and that he will hold Cthrag Sardius in his right hand and Cthrag Yaska in his left. And he will be the almighty Child of Dark, and the Lord of Demons shall do his bidding."

"That's a direct quotation, I take it?"

Arshag nodded. "From the eighth antistrophe of the Ashabine Oracles," he confirmed.

"It's a little obscure, but prophecies usually are. Go on."

Arshag shifted his position and continued. "The Disciple Urvon interpreted the passage to mean that our new God would have the aid of the demons in quelling his enemies."

"Did Harakan identify these enemies for you?"

Arshag nodded again. "He mentioned Zandramas—of whom I have heard—and one named Agachak, whose name is strange to me. He also warned me that the Child of Light would probably attempt to interfere."

"That's a reasonable assumption," Silk murmured to Garion.

"Harakan, who is the Disciple's closest advisor, had selected *me* to perform a great task," Arshag continued proudly. "He charged me to seek out the wizards of Karanda and to study their arts so that I might summon up the Demon Lord Nahaz and beseech him to aid the Disciple Urvon in his struggles with his enemies."

"Did he tell you how dangerous that task would be?" Belgarath asked him.

"I understood the perils," Arshag said, "but I accepted them willingly, for my rewards were to be great."

"I'm sure," Belgarath murmured. "Why didn't Harakan do it himself?"

"The Disciple Urvon had placed another task upon Harakan—somewhere in the West, I understand—having to do with a child."

Belgarath nodded blandly. "I think I've heard about it."

"Anyway," Arshag went on, "I journeyed into the forest of the north, seeking out the wizards who still practiced their rites in places hidden from the eyes of the Church. In time, I found such a one." His lip curled in a sneer. "He was an ignorant savage of small skill, at best only able to raise an imp or two, but he agreed to accept me as his pupil—and slave. It was he who saw fit to put these marks upon my body." He

394

glanced with distaste at his tattoos. "He kept me in a kennel and made me serve him and listen to his ravings. I learned what little he could teach me and then I strangled him and went in search of a more powerful teacher."

"Note how deep the gratitude of Grolims goes," Silk observed quietly to Garion, who was concentrating half on the story and half on the business of steering the scow.

"The years that followed were difficult," Arshag continued. "I went from teacher to teacher, suffering enslavement and abuse." A bleak smile crossed his face. "Occasionally, they used to sell me to other wizards—as one might sell a cow or a pig. After I learned the arts, I retraced my steps and repaid each one for his impertinences. At length, in a place near the barrens of the north, I was able to apprentice myself to an ancient man reputed to be the most powerful wizard in Karanda. He was very old, and his eyes were failing, so he took me for a young Karand seeking wisdom. He accepted me as his appentice, and my training began in earnest. The raising of minor demons is no great chore, but summoning a Demon Lord is much more difficult and much more perilous. The wizard claimed to have done it twice in his life, but he may have been lying. He did, however, show me how to raise the *image* of the Demon Lord Nahaz and also how to communicate with him. No spell or incantation is powerful enough to *compel* a Demon Lord to come when he is called. He will come only if he *consents* to come—and usually for reasons of his own.

"Once I had learned all that the old wizard could teach me, I killed him and journeyed south toward Calida again." He sighed a bit regretfully. "The old man was a kindly master, and I was sorry that I had to kill him." Then he shrugged. "But he was old," he added, "and I sent him off with a single knife stroke to the heart."

"Steady, Durnik," Silk said, putting his hand on the angry smith's arm.

"At Calida, I found the Temple in total disarray," Arshag went on. "My brothers had finally succumbed to absolute despair, and the Temple had become a vile sink of corruption and degeneracy. I suppressed my outrage, however, and kept to myself. I dispatched word to Mal Yaska, advising Harakan that I had been successful in my mission and that I awaited his commands in the Temple at Calida. In time, I received a reply from one of the Chandim, who told me that Harakan had not yet returned from the West." He paused. "Do you suppose that I could have a drink of water?" he asked. "I have a very foul taste in my mouth for some reason."

Sadi went to the water cask in the stern and dipped out a tin cup of water. "No drug is *completely* perfect," he murmured defensively to Garion in passing.

Arshag gratefully took the cup from Sadi and drank.

"Go on with your story," Belgarath told him when he had finished.

Arshag nodded. "It was a bit less than a year ago that Harakan returned from the West," he said. "He came up to Calida, and he and I met in secret. I told him what I had accomplished and advised him of the limitations involved in any attempts to raise a Demon Lord. Then we went to a secluded place, and I instructed him in the incantations and spells which would raise an image of Nahaz and permit us to speak through the gate that lies between the worlds and communicate directly with Nahaz. Once I had established contact with the Demon Lord, Harakan began to speak with him. He mentioned Cthrag Sardius, but Nahaz already knew of it. And then Harakan told Nahaz that during the long years that Torak slept, and Disciple Urvon had become more and more obsessed with wealth and power and had at last convinced himself that he was in fact a demigod, and but one step removed from divinity. Harakan proposed an alliance between himself and Nahaz. He suggested that the Demon Lord nudge Urvon over the edge into madness and then aid him in defeating all the others who were seeking the hiding place of Cthrag Sardius. Unopposed, Urvon would easily gain the stone."

"I gather that you chose to go along with them—instead

of warning Urvon what was afoot? What did *you* get out of the arrangement?"

"They let me live." Arshag shrugged. "I think Harakan wanted to kill me—just to be safe—but Nahaz told him that I could still be useful. He promised me kindgoms of my own to rule—and demon children to do my bidding. Harakan was won over by the Demon Lord and he treated me courteously."

"I don't exactly see that there's much advantage to Nahaz in giving the Sardion to Urvon," Belgarath confessed.

"Nahaz wants Cthrag Sardius for himself," Arshag told him. "If Urvon has been driven mad, Nahaz will simply take Cthrag Sardius from him and replace it with a piece of worthless rock. Then the Demon Lord and Harakan will put Urvon in a house somewhere—Ashaba perhaps, or some other isolated castle— and they'll surround him with imps and lesser demons to blind him with illusions. There he will play at being God in blissful insanity while Nahaz and Harakan rule the world between them."

"Until the *real* new God of Angarak arises," Polgara added.

"There will *be* no new God of Angarak," Arshag disagreed. "Once Nahaz puts his hand on Cthrag Sardius—the Sardion—*both* Prophecies will cease to exist. The Child of Light and the Child of Dark will vanish forever. The Elder Gods will be banished, and Nahaz will be Lord of the Universe and Master of the destinies of all mankind."

"And what does Harakan get out of this?" Belgarath asked.

"Dominion of the Church—and the secular throne of all the world."

"I hope he got that in writing," Belgarath said dryly. "Demons are notorious for not keeping their promises. Then what happened?"

"A messenger arrived at Calida with instructions for Harakan from Urvon. The Disciple told him that there must be a disruption in Karanda so violent that Kal Zakath would have no choice but to return from Cthol Murgos. Once the Emperor was back in Mallorea, it would be a simple matter to have him killed, and once he is dead, Urvon believes that he can manipulate the succession to place a tractable man on the throne—one he can take with him when he goes to the place where the Sardion lies hidden. Apparently, this is one of the conditions which must be met before the new God arises."

Belgarath nodded. "A great many things are starting to fall into place." he said. "What happened then?"

"Harakan and I journeyed again in secret to that secluded place, and I once again opened the gate and brought forth the image of Nahaz. Harakan and the Demon Lord spoke together for a time, and suddenly the image was made flesh, and Nahaz himself stood before us.

"Harakan instructed me that I should henceforth call him by the name Mangha, since the name Harakan is widely known in Mallorea, and then we went again to Calida, and Nahaz went with us. The Demon Lord summoned his hordes, and Calida fell. Nahaz demanded a certain repayment for his aid, and Lord Mengha instructed me to provide it. It was then that I discovered why Nahaz had let me live. We spoke together, and he told me what he wanted. I did not care for the notion, but the people involved were only Karands, so—" He shrugged. "The Karands regard Nahaz as their God, and so it was not difficult for me to persuade young Karandese women that receiving the attentions of the Demon Lord would be a supreme honor. They went to him willingly, each one of them hoping in her heart to bear his offspring—not knowing, of course, that such a birth would rip them apart like fresh-gutted pigs." He smirked contemptuously. "The rest I think you know."

"Oh, yes, we do indeed." Belgarath's voice was like a nail scraping across a flat stone. "When did they leave? Harakan and Nahaz, I mean? We know that they're no longer in this part of Karanda."

"It was about a month ago. We were preparing to lay siege to Torpakan on the border of Delchin, and I awoke one morning to discover that Lord Mengha and the Demon Nahaz were gone and that none of their familiar demons were any longer with the army. Everyone looked to me, but none of my spells or incantations could raise even the least of demons. The army grew enraged, and I barely escaped with my life. I journeyed north again toward Calida, but found things there in total chaos. Without the demons to hold them in line, the Karands had quickly become unmanageable. I found that I *could*, however, still call up the *image* of Nahaz. It seemed likely to me that with Mengha and Nahaz gone, I could sway Karandese loyalty to me, if I used the image cleverly enough, and thus come to rule all of Karanda myself. I was attempting a beginning of that plan this morning when you interrupted."

"I see," Belgarath said bleakly.

"How long have you been in this vicinity?" Polgara asked the captive suddenly.

"Several weeks," the Grolim replied.

"Good," she said. "Some few weeks ago, a woman came from the west carrying a child."

"I pay little attention to women."

"This one might have been a bit different. We know that she came to that village back on the lake shore and that she would have hired a boat. Did any word of that reach you?"

"There are few travelers in Karanda right now," he told her. "There's too much turmoil and upheavel. There's only one boat that left that village in the past month. I'll tell you this, though. If the woman you seek was a friend of yours, and if she *was* on board that boat, prepare to mourn her."

"Oh?"

"The boat sank in a sudden storm just off the city of Karand on the east side of the lake in Ganesia."

"The nice thing about Zandramas is her predictability," Silk murmured to Garion. "I don't think we're going to have much trouble picking up her trail again, do you?"

Arshag's eyelids were drooping now, and he seemed barely able to hold his head erect.

"If you have any more questions for him, Ancient One, you

should ask them quickly," Sadi advised. "The drug is starting to wear off, and he's very close to sleep again."

"I think I have all the answers I need," the old man replied.

"And I have what I need as well," Polgara added grimly.

Because of the size of the lake, there was no possibility of reaching the eastern shore before nightfall, and so they lowered the sails and set a sea anchor to minimize the nighttime drift of their scow. They set sail again at first light and shortly after noon saw a low, dark smudge along the eastern horizon.

"That would be the east coast of the lake," Silk said to Garion. "I'll go up to the bow and see if I can pick out some landmarks. I don't think we'll want to run right up to the wharves of Karand, do you?"

"No. Not really."

"I'll see if I can find us a quiet cove someplace, and then we can have a look around without attracting attention."

They beached the scow in a quiet bay surrounded by high sand dunes and scrubby brush about midafternoon.

"What do you think, Grandfather?" Garion asked after they had unloaded the horses.

"About what?"

"The boat. What should we do with it?"

"Set it adrift. Let's not announce that we came ashore here."

"I suppose you're right." Garion sighed a bit regretfully. "It wasn't a bad boat, though, was it?"

"It didn't tip over."

"Capsize," Garion corrected.

Polgara came over to where they were standing. "Do you have any further need for Arshag?" she asked the old man.

"No, and I've been trying to decide what to do with him."

"I'll take care of it, father," she said. She turned and went back to where Arshag still lay, once more bound and half asleep on the beach. She stood over him for a moment, then raised one hand. The Grolim flinched wildly even as Garion felt the sudden powerful surge of her will.

"Listen carefully, Arshag," she said. "You provided the Demon Lord with women so that he could unloose an abomination upon the world. That act must not go unrewarded. This, then, is your reward. You are now invincible. No one can kill you—no man, no demon—not even you yourself. *But*, no one will ever again believe a single word that you say. You will be faced with constant ridicule and derision all the days of your life and you will be driven out wherever you go, to wander the world as a rootless vagabond. Thus are you repaid for aiding Mengha and helping him to unleash Nahaz and for sacrificing foolish women to the Demon Lord's unspeakable lust." She turned to Durnik. "Untie him," she commanded.

When his arms and legs were free, Arshag stumbled to his feet, his tattooed face ashen. "Who are you, woman?" he demanded in a shaking voice, "and what power do you have to pronounce so terrible a curse?"

"I am Polgara," she replied. "You may have heard of me. Now go!" She pointed up the beach with an imperious finger.

As if suddenly seized by an irresistible compulsion, Arshag turned, his face filled with horror. He stumbled up one of the sandy dunes and disappeared on the far side.

"Do you think it was wise to reveal your identity, my lady?" Sadi asked dubiously.

"There's no danger, Sadi." She smiled. "He can shout my name from every rooftop, but no one will believe him."

"How long will he live?" Ce'Nedra's voice was very small.

"Indefinitely, I'd imagine. Long enough, certainly, to give him time to appreciate fully the enormity of what it was that he did."

Ce'Nedra stared at her. "Lady Polgara!" she said in a sick voice. "How could you do it? It's horrible."

"Yes," Polgara replied, "it is—but so was what happened back at that temple we burned."

CHAPTER TWENTY-THREE

The street, if it could be called that, was narrow and crooked. An attempt had been made at some time in the past to surface it with logs, but they had long since rotted and been trodden into the mud. Decaying garbage lay in heaps against the walls of crudely constructed log houses, and herds of scrawny pigs rooted dispiritedly through those heaps in search of food.

As Silk and Garion, once again wearing their Karandese vests and caps and their cross-tied sackcloth leggings, approached the docks jutting out into the lake, they were nearly overcome by the overpowering odor of long-dead fish.

402

"Fragrant sort of place, isn't it?" Silk noted, holding a handkerchief to his face.

"How can they stand it?" Garion asked, trying to keep from gagging.

"Their sense of smell has probably atrophied over the centuries," Silk replied. "The city of Karand is the ancestral home of all the Karands in all the seven kingdoms. It's been here for eons, so the debris—and the smell—has had a long time to build up."

A huge sow, trailed by a litter of squealing piglets, waddled out into the very center of the street and flopped over on her side with a loud grunt. The piglets immediately attacked, pushing and scrambling to nurse.

"Any hints at all? Silk asked.

Garion shook his head. The sword strapped across his back had neither twitched nor tugged since the two of them had entered the city early that morning on foot by way of the north gate. "Zandramas might not have even entered the city at all," he said. "She's avoided populated places before, you know."

"That's true, I suppose," Silk admitted, "but I don't think we should go any farther until we locate the place where she landed. She could have gone in any direction once she got to this side of the lake—Darshiva, Zamad, Voresebo—even down into Delchin and then on down the Magan into Rengel or Peldane."

"I know," Garion said, "but all this delay is very frustrating. We're getting closer to her. I can feel it, and every minute we waste gives her that much more time to escape again with Geran."

"It can't be helped." Silk shrugged. "About all we can do here is follow the inside of the wall and walk along the waterfront. If she came through the city at all, we're certain to cross her path."

They turned a corner and looked down another muddy

403

street toward the lake shore where fishnets hung over long poles. They slogged through the mud until they reached the street that ran along the shoreline where floating docks reached out into the lake and then followed it along the waterfront.

There was a certain amount of activity here. A number of sailors dressed in faded blue tunics were hauling a large boat half-full of water up onto the shore with a great deal of shouting and contradictory orders. Here and there on the docks, groups of fishermen in rusty brown sat mending nets, and farther on along the street several loiterers in fur vests and leggings sat on the log stoop in front of a sour-smelling tavern, drinking from cheap tin cups. A blowzy young woman with frizzy orange hair and a pockmarked face leaned out of a second-storey window, calling to passersby in a voice she tried to make seductive, but which Garion found to be merely coarse.

"Busy place," Silk murmured.

Garion grunted, and they moved on along the littered street.

Coming from the other direction, they saw a group of armed men. Though they all wore helmets of one kind or another, the rest of their clothing was of mismatched colors and could by no stretch of the imagination be called uniforms. Their self-important swagger, however, clearly indicated that they were either soldiers or some kind of police.

"You two! Halt!" one of them barked as they came abreast of Garion and Silk.

"Is there some problem, sir?" Silk asked ingratiatingly.

"I haven't seen you here before," the man said, his hand on his sword hilt. He was a tall fellow with lank red hair poking out from under his helmet. "Identify yourselves."

"My name is Saldas," Silk lied. "This is Kvasta." He pointed at Garion. "We're strangers here in Karand."

"What's your business here—and where do you come from?"

"We're from Dorikan in Jenno," Silk told him, "and we're here looking for my older brother. He sailed out from the village of Dashun on the other side of the lake awhile back and hasn't returned."

The redheaded man looked suspicious.

"We talked with a fellow near the north gate," Silk continued, "and he told us that there was a boat that sank in a storm just off the docks here." His face took on a melancholy expression. "The time would have been just about right, I think, and the description he gave us of the boat matched the one my brother was sailing. Have you by any chance heard about it, sir?" The little man sounded very sincere.

Some of the suspicion faded from the red-haired man's face. "It seems to me that I heard some mention of it," he conceded.

"The fellow we talked with said that he thought there might have been some survivors," Silk added, "one that he knew of, anyway. He said that a woman in a dark cloak and carrying a baby managed to get away in a small boat. Do *you* by chance happen to know anything about that?"

The Karand's face hardened. "Oh, yes," he said. "We know about *her*, all right."

"Could you by any chance tell me where she went?" Silk asked him. "I'd really like to talk with her and find out if she knows anything about my brother." He leaned toward the other man confidentially. "To be perfectly honest with you, good sir, I can't stand my brother. We've hated each other since we were children, but I promised my old father that I'd find out what happened to him." Then he winked outrageously. "There's an inheritance involved, you understand. If I can take definite word back to father that my brother's dead, I stand to come into a nice piece of property."

The red-haired man grinned. "I can understand your situation, Saldas." he said. "I had a dispute with my *own* brothers about our patrimony." His eyes narrowed. "You say you're from Dorikan?" he asked.

405

"Yes. On the banks of the northern River Magan. Do you know our city?"

"Does Dorikan follow the teachings of Lord Mengha?"

"The Liberator? Of course. Doesn't all of Karanda?"

"Have you seen any of the Dark Lords in the last month or so?"

"The minions of the Lord Nahaz? No, I can't say that I have—but then Kvasta and I haven't attended any worship services for some time. I'm sure that the wizards are still raising them though."

"I wouldn't be all that sure, Saldas. We haven't seen one here in Karand for over five weeks. Our wizards have tried to summon them, but they refuse to come. Even the Grolims who now worship Lord Nahaz haven't been successful and they're all powerful magicians, you know."

"Truly," Silk agreed.

"Have you heard anything at all about Lord Mengha's whereabouts?"

Silk shrugged. "The last I heard, he was in Katakor someplace. In Dorikan we're just waiting for his return so that we can sweep the Angaraks out of all Karanda."

The answer seemed to satisfy the tall fellow. "All right, Saldas," he said. "I'd say that you've got a legitimate reason to be in Karand after all. I don't think you're going to have much luck in finding the woman you want to talk to, though. From what I've heard, she *was* on your brother's boat and she *did* get away before the storm hit. She had a small boat, and she landed to the south of the city. She came to the south gate with her brat in her arms and went straight to the Temple. She talked with the Grolims inside for about an hour. When she left, they were all following her."

"Which way did they go?" Silk asked him.

"Out the east gate."

"How long ago was it?"

"Late last week. I'll tell you something, Saldas. Lord Mengha had better stop whatever he's doing in Katakor and

406

come back to central Karanda where he belongs. The whole movement is starting to falter. The Dark Lords have deserted us, and the Grolims are trailing after this woman with the baby. All we have left are the wizards, and they're mostly mad, anyway."

"They always have been, haven't they?" Silk grinned. "Tampering with the supernatural tends to unsettle a man's brains, I've noticed."

"You seem like a sensible man, Saldas," the redhead said, clapping him on the shoulder. "I'd like to stay and talk with you further, but my men and I have to finish our patrol. I hope you find your brother." He winked slyly. "Or *don't* find him, I should say."

Silk grinned back. "I thank you for your wishes about my brother's growing ill health," he replied.

The soldiers moved off along the street.

"You tell better stories that Belgarath does," Garion said to his little friend.

"It's a gift. That was a very profitable encounter, wasn't it? Now I understand why the Orb hasn't picked up the trail yet. We came into the city by way of the north gate, and Zandramas came up from the south. If we go straight to the Temple, the Orb's likely to jerk you off your feet."

Garion nodded. "The important thing is that we're only a few days behind her." He paused, frowning. "Why is she gathering Grolims, though?"

"Who knows? Reinforcements maybe. She knows that we're right behind her. Or, maybe she thinks she's going to need Grolims who have training in Karandese magic when she gets home to Darshiva. If Nahaz has sent his demons down there, she's going to need all the help she can get. We'll let Belgarath sort it out. Let's go to the Temple and see if we can pick up the trail."

As they approached the Temple in the center of the city, the Orb began to pull at Garion again, and he felt a surge of exultation. "I've got it," he said to Silk.

"Good." The little man looked up at the Temple. "I see that they've made some modifications," he observed.

The polished steel mask of the face of Torak which normally occupied the place directly over the nail-studded door had been removed, Garion saw, and in its place was a red-painted skull with a pair of horns screwed down into its brow.

"I don't know that the skull is all that big an improvement," Silk said, "but then, it's no great change for the worse either. I was getting a little tired of that mask staring at me every time I turned around."

"Let's follow the trail," Garion suggested, "and made certain that Zandramas left the city before we go get the others."

"Right," Silk agreed.

The trail led from the door of the Temple through the littered streets to the east gate of the city. Garion and Silk followed it out of Karand and perhaps a half mile along the highway leading eastward across the plains of Ganesia.

"Is she veering at all?" Silk asked.

"Not yet. She's following the road."

"Good. Let's go get the others—and our horses. We won't make very good time on foot."

They moved away from the road, walking through knee-high grass.

"Looks like good, fertile soil here," Garion noted. "Have you and Yarblek ever considered buying farmland? It might be a good investment."

"No, Garion." Silk laughed. "There's a major drawback to owning land. If you have to leave a place in a hurry, there's no way that you can pick it up and carry it along with you."

"That's true, I guess."

The others waited in a grove of large old willows a mile or so north of the city, and their faces were expectant as Garion and Silk ducked in under the branches.

"Did you find it?" Belgarath asked.

Garion nodded. "She went east," he replied.

"And apparently she took all the Grolims from the Temple along with her," Silk added.

Belgarath looked puzzled. "Why would she do that?"

"I haven't got a clue. I suppose we could ask her when we catch up with her."

"Could you get any idea of how far ahead of us she is?" Ce'Nedra asked.

"Just a few days," Garion said. "With any luck we'll catch her before she gets across the Mountains of Zamad."

"Not if we don't get started," Belgarath said.

They rode on back across the wide, open field to the highway leading across the plains toward the up-thrusting peaks lying to the east. The Orb picked up the trail again, and they followed it at a canter.

"What kind of a city was it?" Velvet asked Silk as they rode along.

"Nice place to visit," he replied, "but you wouldn't want to live there. The pigs are clean enough, but the people are awfully dirty."

"Cleverly put, Kheldar."

"I've always had a way with words," he conceded modestly.

"Father," Polgara called to the old man, "a large number of Grolims have passed this way."

He looked around and nodded. "Silk was right, then," he said. "For some reason she's subverting Mengha's people. Let's be alert for any possible ambushes."

They rode on for the rest of the day and camped that night some distance away from the road, starting out again at first light in the morning. About midday they saw a roadside village some distance ahead. Coming from that direction was a solitary man in a rickety cart being pulled by a bony white horse.

"Do you by any change have a flagon of ale, Lady Polgara?" Sadi asked as they slowed to a walk.

"Are you thirsty?"

"Oh, it's not for me. I detest ale personally. It's for that carter just ahead. I thought we might want some information."

409

He looked over at Silk. "Are you feeling at all sociable today, Kheldar?"

"No more than usual. Why?"

"Take a drink or two of this," the eunuch said, offering the little man the flagon Polgara had taken from one of the packs. "Not too much, mind. I only want you to *smell* drunk."

"Why not?" Silk shrugged, taking a long drink.

"That should do it," Sadi approved. "Now give it back."

"I thought you didn't want any."

"I don't. I'm just going to add a bit of flavoring." He opened his red case. "Don't drink any more from this flagon," he warned Silk as he tapped four drops of a gleaming red liquid into the mouth of the flagon. "If you do, we'll all have to listen to you talk for days on end." He handed the flagon back to the little man. "Why don't you go offer that poor fellow up there a drink," he suggested. "He looks like he could use one."

"You didn't poison it, did you?"

"Of course not. It's very hard to get information out of somebody who's squirming on the ground clutching at his belly. One or two good drinks from that flagon, though, and the carter will be seized by an uncontrollable urge to talk— about anything at all and to anybody who asks him a question in a friendly fashion. Go be friendly to the poor man, Kheldar. He looks dreadfully lonesome."

Silk grinned, then turned and trotted his horse toward the oncoming cart, swaying in his saddle and singing loudly and very much off-key.

"He's very good," Velvet murmured to Ce'Nedra, "but he always overacts his part. When we get back to Boktor, I think I'll send him to a good drama coach."

Ce'Nedra laughed.

By the time they reached the cart, the seedy-looking man in a rust-red smock had pulled his vehicle off to the side of the road, and he and Silk had joined in song—a rather bawdy one.

410

"Ah, there you are," Silk said, squinting owlishly at Sadi. "I wondered how long it was going to take you to catch up. Here—" He thrust the flagon at the eunuch. "Have a drink."

Sadi feigned taking a long drink from the flagon. Then he sighed lustily, wiped his mouth on his sleeve, and handed the flagon back.

Silk passed it to the carter. "Your turn, friend."

The carter took a drink and then grinned foolishly. "I haven't felt this good in weeks," he said.

"We're riding toward the east," Sadi told him.

"I saw that right off," the carter said. "That's unless you've taught your horses to run backward." He laughed uproariously at that, slapping his knee in glee.

"How droll," the eunuch murmured. "Do you come from that village just up ahead?"

"Lived there all my life," the carter replied, "and my father before me—and his father before him—and his father's father before that and—"

"Have you seen a dark-cloaked woman with a babe in her arms go past here within the last week?" Sadi interrupted him. "She probably would have been in the company of a fairly large party of Grolims."

The carter made the sign to ward off the evil eye at the mention of the word "Grolim." "Oh, yes. She came by all right," he said, "and she went into the local Temple here— if you can really call it a Temple. It's no bigger than my own house and it's only got three Grolims in it—two young ones and an old one. Anyway, this woman with the babe in her arms, she goes into the Temple, and we can hear her talking, and pretty soon she comes out with our three Grolims—only the old one was trying to talk the two young ones into staying, and then she says something to the young ones and they pull out their knives and start stabbing the old one, and he yells and falls down on the ground dead as mutton, and the woman takes our two young Grolims back out to the road, and they

411

join in with the others and they all go off, leaving us only that old dead one lying on his face in the mud and—"

"How many Grolims would you say she had with her?" Sadi asked.

"Counting our two, I'd say maybe thirty or forty—or it could be as many as fifty. I've never been very good at quick guesses like that. I can tell the difference between three and four, but after that I get confused, and—"

"Could you give us any idea of exactly how long ago all that was?"

"Let's see." The carter squinted at the sky, counting on his fingers. "It couldn't have been yesterday, because yesterday I took that load of barrels over to Toad-face's farm. Do you know Toad-face? Ugliest man I ever saw, but his daughter's a real beauty. I could tell you stories about *her*, let me tell you."

"So it wasn't yesterday?"

"No. It definitely wasn't yesterday. I spent most of yesterday under a haystack with Toad-face's daughter. And I know it wasn't the day before, because I got drunk that day and I don't remember a thing that happened after midmorning." He took another drink from the flagon.

"How about the day before that?"

"It could have been," the carter said, "or the day before that."

"Or even before?"

The carter shook his head. "No, that was the day our pig farrowed, and I know that the woman came by after that. It had to have been the day before the day before yesterday or the day before that."

"Three or four days ago, then?"

"If that's the way it works out," the carter shrugged, drinking again.

"Thanks for the information, friend," Sadi said. He looked at Silk. "We should be moving on, I suppose," he said.

"Did you want your jar back?" the carter asked.

"Go ahead and keep it, friend," Silk said. "I think I've had enough anyway."

"Thanks for the ale—and the talk," the carter called after them as they rode away. Garion glanced back and saw that the fellow had climbed down from his cart and was engaging in an animated conversation with his horse.

"Three days!" Ce'Nedra exlaimed happily.

"Or, at the most, four," Sadi said.

"We're gaining on her!" Ce'Nedra said, suddenly leaning over and throwing her arms about the eunuch's neck.

"So it appears, your majesty," Sadi agreed, looking slightly embarrassed.

They camped off the road again that night and started out again early the following morning. The sun was just coming up when the large, blue-banded hawk came spiraling in, flared, and shimmered into the form of Beldin at the instant its talons touched the road. "You've got company waiting for you just ahead," he told them, pointing at the first line of foothills of the Mountains of Zamad lying perhaps a mile in front of them.

"Oh?" Belgarath said, reining in his horse.

"About a dozen Grolims," Beldin said. They're hiding in the bushes on either side of the road."

Belgarath swore.

"Have you been doing things to annoy the Grolims?" the hunchback asked.

Belgarath shook his head. "Zamadramas has been gathering them as she goes along. She's got quite a few of them with her now. She probably left that group behind to head off pursuit. She knows that we're right behind her."

"What are we going to do, Belgarath?" Ce'Nedra asked. "We're so *close*. We can't stop now."

The old man looked at his brother sorcerer. "Well?" he said.

Beldin scowled at him. "All right," he said. "I'll do it, but don't forget that you owe me, Belgarath."

"Write it down with all the other things. We'll settle up when this is all over."

"Don't think I won't."

"Did you find out where Nahaz took Urvon?"

"Would you believe they went back to Mal Yaska?" Beldin sounded disgusted.

"They'll come out eventually," Belgarath assured him. "Are you going to need any help with the Grolims? I could send Pol along if you like."

"Are you trying to be funny?"

"No. I was just asking. Don't make too much noise."

Beldin made a vulgar sound, changed again, and swooped away.

"Where's he going?" Silk asked.

"He's going to draw off the Grolims."

"Oh? How?"

"I didn't ask him," Belgarath shrugged. "We'll give him a little while and then we should be able to ride straight on through."

"He's very good, isn't he?"

"Beldin? Oh, yes, very, very good. There he goes now."

Silk looked around. "Where?"

"I didn't see him—I heard him. He's flying low a mile or so to the north of where the Grolims are hiding, and he's kicking up just enough noise to make it sound as if the whole group of us are trying to slip around them without being seen." He glanced at his daughter. "Pol, would you take a look and see if it's working?"

"All right, father." She concentrated, and Garion could feel her mind reaching out, probing. "They've taken the bait," she reported. "They all ran off after Beldin."

"That was accommodating of them, wasn't it? Let's move on."

They pushed their horses into a gallop and covered the distance to the first foothills of the Mountains of Zamad in a short period of time. They followed the road up a steep slope

414

and through a shallow notch. Beyond that the terrain grew more rugged, and the dark green forest rose steeply up the flanks of the peaks.

Garion began to sense conflicting signals from the Orb as he rode. At first he had only felt its eagerness to follow the trail of Zandramas and Geran, but now he began to feel a sullen undertone, a sound of ageless, implacable hatred, and at his back where the sword was sheathed, he began to feel an increasing heat.

"Why is it burning red?" Ce'Nedra asked from behind him.

"What's burning red?"

"The Orb, I think. I can see it glowing right through the leather covering you have over it."

"Let's stop awhile," Belgarath told them, reining in his horse.

"What is it, Grandfather?"

"I'm not sure. Take the sword out and slip off the sleeve. Let's see what's happening."

Garion drew the sword from its sheath. It seemed heavier than usual for some reason, and when he peeled off the soft leather covering, they were all able to see that instead of its usual azure blue, the Orb of Aldur was glowing a dark, sooty red.

"What is it, father?" Polgara asked.

"It feels the Sardion." Eriond said in a calm voice.

"Are we that close?" Garion demanded. "Is this the Place Which Is No More?"

"I don't think so, Belgarion," the young man replied. "It's something else."

"What is it, then?"

"I'm not sure, but the Orb is responding to the other stone in some way. They talk to each other in a fashion I can't understand."

They rode on, and some time later the blue-banded hawk came swirling in, blurred into Beldin's shape, and stood in

415

front of them. The gnarled dwarf had a slightly self-satisfied look on his face.

"You look like a cat that just got into the cream," Belgarath said.

"Naturally. I just sent a dozen or so Grolims off in the general direction of the polar icecap. They'll have a wonderful time when the pan ice starts to break up and they get to float around up there for the rest of the summer."

"Are you going to scout on ahead?" Belgarath asked him.

"I suppose so," Beldin replied. He held out his arms, blurred into feathers, and drove himself into the air.

They rode more cautiously now, climbing deeper and deeper into the Mountains of Zamad. The surrounding country grew more broken. The reddish-hued peaks were jagged, and their lower flanks were covered with dark firs and pines. Rushing streams boiled over rocks and dropped in frothy waterfalls over steep cliffs. The road, which had been straight and flat on the plains of Ganesia, began to twist and turn as it crawled up the steep slopes.

It was nearly noon when Beldin returned again. "The main party of Grolims turned south," he reported. "There are about forty of them."

"Was Zandramas with them?" Garion asked quickly.

"No. I don't think so—at least I didn't pick up the sense of anyone unusual in the group."

"We haven't lost her, have we?" Ce'Nedra asked in alarm.

"No," Garion replied. "The Orb still has her trail." He glanced over his shoulder. The stone on the hilt of his sword was still burning a sullen red.

"About all we can do is follow her," Belgarath said. "It's Zandramas we're interested in, not a party of stray Grolims. Can you pinpoint exactly where we are?" he asked Beldin.

"Mallorea."

"Very funny."

"We've crossed into Zamad. This road goes on down into Voresebo, though. Where's my mule?"

"Back with the pack horses," Durnik told him.

As they moved on, Garion could feel Polgara probing on ahead with her mind.

"Are you getting anything, Pol?" Belgarath asked her.

"Nothing specific, father," she replied. "I can sense the fact that Zandramas is close, but she's shielding, so I can't pinpoint her."

They rode on, moving at a cautious walk now. Then, as the road passed through a narrow gap and descended on the far side, they saw a figure in a gleaming white robe standing in the road ahead. As they drew closer, Garion saw that it was Cyradis.

"Move with great care in this place," she cautioned, and there was a note of anger in her voice. "The Child of Dark seeks to circumvent the ordered course of events and hath laid a trap for ye."

"There's nothing new or surprising about that," Beldin growled. "What does she hope to accomplish?"

"It is her thought to slay one of the companions of the Child of Light and thereby prevent the completion of one of the tasks which must be accomplished ere the final meeting. Should she succeed, all that hath gone before shall come to naught. Follow me, and I will guide you safely to the next task."

Toth stepped down from his horse and quickly led it to the side of his slender mistress. She smiled at him, her face radiant, and laid a slim hand on his huge arm. With no apparent effort, the huge man lifted her into the saddle of his horse and then took the reins in his hand.

"Aunt Pol," Garion whispered, "is it my imagination, or is she really there this time?"

Polgara looked intently at the blindfolded Seeress. "It's not a projection," she said. "It's much more substantial. I couldn't begin to guess how she got here, but I think you're right, Garion. She's really here."

They followed the Seeress and her mute guide down the

steeply descending road into a grassy basin surrounded on all sides by towering firs. In the center of the basin was a small mountain lake sparkling in the sunlight.

Polgara suddenly drew in her breath sharply. "We're being watched," she said.

"Who is it, Pol?" Belgarath asked.

"The mind is hidden, father. All I can get is the sense of watching—and anger." A smile touched her lips. "I'm sure it's Zandramas. She's shielding, so I can't reach her mind, but she can't shield out my sense of being watched, and she can't control her anger enough to keep me from picking up the edges of it."

"Who's she so angry with?"

"Cyradis, I think. She went to a great deal of trouble to lay a trap for us, and Cyradis came along and spoiled it. She still might try something, so I think we'd all better be on our guard."

He nodded bleakly. "Right," he agreed.

Toth led the horse his mistress was riding out into the basin and stopped at the edge of the lake. When the rest of them reached her, she pointed down through the crystal water. "The task lies there," she said. "Below lies a submerged grot. One of ye must enter that grot and then return. Much shall be revealed there."

Belgarath looked hopefully at Beldin.

"Not this time, old man," the drawf said, shaking his head. "I'm a hawk, not a fish, and I don't like cold water any more than you do."

"Pol?" Belgarath said rather plaintively.

"I don't think so, father," she replied. "I think it's your turn this time. Besides, I need to concentrate on Zandramas."

He bent over and dipped his hand into the sparkling water. Then he shuddered. "This is cruel," he said.

Silk was grinning at him.

"Don't say it, Prince Kheldar." Belgarath scowled, starting to remove his clothing. "Just keep your mouth shut."

They were perhaps all a bit surprised at how sleekly muscular the old man was. Despite his fondness for rich food and good brown ale, his stomach was as flat as a board; although he was as lean as a rail, his shoulders and chest rippled when he moved.

"My, my," Velvet murmured appreciatively, eyeing the loincloth-clad old man.

He suddenly grinned at her impishly. "Would you care for another frolic in a pool, Liselle?" he invited with a wicked look in his bright blue eyes.

She suddenly blushed a rosy red, glancing guiltily at Silk.

Belgarath laughed, arched himself forward, and split the water of the lake as cleanly as the blade of a knife. Several yards out, he broached, leaping high into the air with the sun gleaming on his silvery scales and his broad, forked tail flapping and shaking droplets like jewels across the sparkling surface of the lake. Then his dark, heavy body drove down and down into the depths of the crystal lake.

"Oh, my," Durnik breathed, his hands twitching.

"Never mind, dear." Polgara laughed. "He wouldn't like it at all if you stuck a fishhook in his jaw."

The great, silver-sided salmon swirled down and disappeared into an irregularly shaped opening near the bottom of the lake.

They waited, and Garion found himself unconsciously holding his breath.

After what seemed an eternity, the great fish shot from the mouth of the submerged cave, drove himself far out into the lake, and then returned, skipping across the surface of the water on his tail, shaking his head and almost seeming to balance himself with his fins. Then he plunged forward into the water near the shore, and Belgarath emerged dripping and shivering. "Invigorating," he observed, climbing back up onto the bank. "Have you got a blanket handy, Pol?" he asked, stripping the water from his arms and legs with his hands.

"Show-off," Beldin grunted.

419

"What was down there?" Garion asked.

"It looks like an old temple of some kind," the old man answered, vigorously drying himself with the blanket Polgara had handed him. "Somebody took a natural cave and walled up the sides to give it some kind of shape. There was an altar there with a special kind of niche in it—empty, naturally— but the place was filled with an overpowering presence, and all the rocks glowed red."

"The Sardion?" Beldin demanded intently.

"Not any more," Belgarath replied, drying his hair. "It *was* there, though, for a long, long time—and it had built a barrier of some kind to keep anybody from finding it. It's gone now, but I'll recognize the signs of it the next time I get close."

"Garion!" Ce'Nedra cried. "Look!" With a trembling hand she was pointing at a nearby crag. High atop that rocky promontory stood a figure wrapped in shiny black satin. Even before the figure tossed back its hood with a gesture of supreme arrogance, he knew who it was. Without thinking, he reached for Iron-grip's sword, his mind suddenly aflame.

But then Cyradis spoke in a clear, firm voice. "I am wroth with thee, Zandramas," she declared. "Seek not to interfere with that which must come to pass, lest I make my choice here and now."

"And if thou dost, sightless, creeping worm, then all will turn to chaos, and thy task will be incomplete, and blind chance will supplant prophecy. Behold, I am the Child of Dark, and I fear not the hand of chance, for chance is *my* servant even more than it is the servant of the Child of Light."

Then Garion heard a low snarl, a dreadful sound—more dreadful yet because it came from his wife's throat. Moving faster than he thought was possible, Ce'Nedra dashed to Durnik's horse and ripped the smith's axe from the rope sling which held it. With a scream of rage, she ran around the edge of the tiny mountain lake brandishing the axe.

"Ce'Nedra!" he shouted, lunging after her. "No!"

Zandramas laughed with cruel glee. "Choose, Cyradis!"

she shouted. "Make thine empty choice, for in the death of the Rivan Queen, I triumph!" and she raised both hands over her head.

Though he was running as fast as he could, Garion saw that he had no hope of catching Ce'Nedra before she moved fatally close to the satin-robed sorceress atop the crag. Even now, his wife had begun scrambling up the rocks, screeching curses and hacking at the boulders that got in her way with Durnik's axe.

Then the form of a glowing blue wolf suddenly appeared between Ce'Nedra and the object of her fury. Ce'Nedra stopped as if frozen, and Zandramas recoiled from the snarling wolf. The light around the wolf flickered briefly, and there, still standing between Ce'Nedra and Zandramas stood the form of Garion's ultimate grandmother, Belgarath's wife and Polgara's mother. Her tawny hair was aflame with blue light, and her golden eyes blazed with unearthly fire.

"You!" Zandramas gasped, shrinking back even further.

Poledra reached back, took Ce'Nedra to her side, and protectively put one arm about her tiny shoulders. With her other hand she gently removed the axe from the little Queen's suddenly nerveless fingers. Ce'Nedra's eyes were wide and unseeing, and she stood immobilized as if in a trance.

"She is under my protection, Zandramas." Poledra said, "and you may not harm her."

The sorceress atop the crag howled in sudden, frustrated rage. Her eyes ablaze, she once again drew herself erect.

"Will it be now, Zandramas?" Poledra asked in a deadly voice. "Is this the time you have chosen for our meeting? You know even as I that should we meet at the wrong time and in the wrong place, we will *both* be destroyed."

"I do not fear thee, Poledra!" the sorceress shrieked.

"Nor I you. Come then, Zandramas, let us destroy each other here and now—for should the Child of Light go on to the Place Which Is No More unopposed and find no Child of Dark awaiting him there, then *I* triumph! If this be the time and place of your choosing, bring forth your power and let it happen—for I grow weary of you."

The face of Zandramas was twisted with rage, and Garion could feel the force of her will building up. He tried to reach over his shoulder for his sword, thinking to unleash its fire and blast the hated sorceress from atop her crag, but even as Ce'Nedra's apparently were, he found that his muscles were all locked in stasis. From behind him he could feel the others also struggling to shake free of the force which seemed to hold them in place as well.

"No," Poledra's voice sounded firmly in the vaults of his mind. "This is between Zandramas and me. Don't interfere."

"Well, Zandramas," she said aloud then, "what is your decision? Will you cling to life a while longer, or will you die now?"

The sorceress struggled to regain her composure, even as the glowing nimbus about Poledra grew more intense. Then Zandramas howled with enraged disappointment and disappeared in a flash of orange fire.

"I thought she might see it my way," Poledra said calmly. She turned to face Garion and the others. There was a twinkle in her golden eyes. "What took you all so long?" she asked. "I've been waiting for you here for months." She looked rather critically at the half-naked Belgarath, who was staring at her with a look of undisguised adoration. "You're as thin as a bone, Old Wolf," she told him. "You really ought to eat more, you know." She smiled fondly at him. "Would you like to have me go catch you a nice fat rabbit?" she asked. Then she laughed, shimmered back into the form of the blue wolf, and loped away, her paws seeming scarcely to touch the earth.

Here ends Book III of *The Malloreon*.
Book IV, *Sorceress of Darsheva*,
continues the search for Zandramas and for the Sardion,
which has been at many sites, but is now to be found
at the "Place Which Is No More"—whatever that means!

About the Author

David Eddings was born in Spokane, Washington, in 1931 and was raised in the Puget Sound area north of Seattle. He received a Bachelor of Arts degree from Reed College in Portland, Oregon, in 1954 and a Master of Arts degree from the University of Washington in 1961. He has served in the United States Army, worked as a buyer for the Boeing Company, has been a grocery clerk, and has taught English. He has lived in many parts of the United States.

His first novel, *High Hunt* (published by Putnam in 1973), was a contemporary adventure story. The field of fantasy has always been of interest to him, however, and he turned to *The Belgariad* in an effort to develop certain technical and philosophical ideas concerning that genre.

Eddings currently resides with his wife, Leigh, in the southwest.